THE PROFESSIONAL DIVER'S HANDBOOK

THE PROFESSIONAL DIVER'S HANDBOOK

John Bevan
Editor

SUBMEX

THE PROFESSIONAL DIVER'S HANDBOOK is published by Submex Limited
5 Nepean Close, Alverstoke, Gosport, PO12 2BH. E-mail: submex@submex.co.uk
Submex Limited is an underwater consultancy company serving the diving industry.

SECOND EDITION, 2005
Reprinted 2006

British Library Cataloguing in Publication Data.
A catalogue record for this book is available from the British Library.

ISBN: 0 9508242 3 2

Design: Ann Bevan.
Printed and bound in Scotland by Highland Printers Ltd.

Foreword to the second edition

The aim of *The Professional Diver's Handbook* is to provide an introduction to operational tasks, procedures, equipment and instrumentation together with associated technical information. It is not a diving manual and does not teach you how to dive.

This, the second edition, builds on the outstanding success of the first. *The Professional Diver's Handbook* has become the standard reference book, not only for working divers but also for underwater engineers.

Included in the second edition are many new subjects especially for the inland/inshore 'civils' diver.

I have maintained the emphasis on two of the most useful features of the Handbook: safety and illustration.

Where possible, the figure of a diver is included in drawings to provide an indication of scale.

Information on safety factors is provided throughout the Handbook in grey-shaded panels. This information is not exhaustive but it provides a basis on which to develop safe diving practices and risk assessments. A risk assessment is an essential part of planning any diving operation. So the very first chapter of this Handbook explains how to produce a risk assessment.

This Handbook is designed to give only an introduction to the various subjects. The reader should refer to detailed proprietary documentation to obtain more comprehensive information necessary to undertake any specific task.

John Bevan, PhD

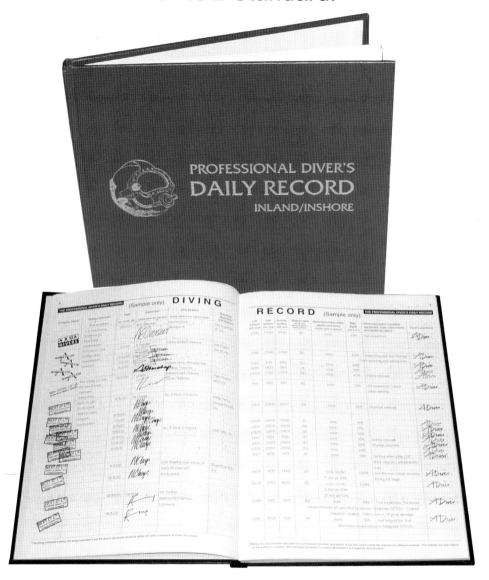

Acknowledgements

We are indebted to a large number of people for generously providing their time and expertise in suggesting topics, compiling information and proof-reading the final copy for this, the second edition of *The Professional Diver's Handbook*. Without their valuable advice, this book could not have been written. To every one, we offer our grateful thanks.

Gavin Anthony

David Beatty, Divemex
Keith Bentley
Richard Bird, Divex Ltd
Neil Brogden
David Brookes, Cooper Cameron UK Ltd
Andy Buchan, Buchan Technical Services
Keith Butterfield, Sub-Tech Systems Ltd

Ian Campbell
Kevin Casey
Jim Cattanach, Cooper Cameron UK Ltd
Graeme Clark, Divex Ltd

Bryan Dillon, Research and Salvage Ltd
Leslie Dolejal, Plugging Specialists International, SA

Gareth Evans, Sub-Surface Engineering
Sophia Exelby, Receiver of Wreck, Maritime and Coastguard Agency

Ian Gallett, Society for Underwater Technology
Jim Gill

Jim Hutchison, Medway Diving Contractors Ltd

Kevin Jaques, Divex Ltd
Chris Jenkins, Oceaneering International
Tim Jessop, TWI Ltd

Kevin Leadbetter, Port of London Authority

Ran Macdonald, Trident Underwater Engineering (Systems) Ltd
Howard McArthur, Qatar Subsea Services
Frances Meinert, Association of Scuba Service Engineers and Technicians
Robin Middleton, Maritime and Coastguard Agency

Trevor Nicholls, Environmental Agency

Roger O'Kane, MGD Consultancy Ltd
Mike O'Meara, Subsea 7

Michael Pett, Hydroweld
Andy Pettitt
Surgeon Vice-Admiral, Sir John Rawlins
Steve Roue, Falmouth Divers Ltd

Andrew Sadleir, Sadleir Technical Consultancy Ltd
Jim Sheppard, TWI (The Welding Institute)
Chris Sherman, Health and Safety Executive, UK
Don Shiers, BCD Marine Ltd
Sven Simpson

Martin Tarrant, Sub-Tech Systems Ltd

Gary Wallace-Potter
Neil Watkins
Pablo Welch
Steve Welsh
David Wilke, Smith Services, Red Baron Group

Contents

Diving Operations

1.1 PROJECT AND SAFETY MANAGEMENT

Diving Project Plan

A Diving Project Plan is produced by the diving contractor prior to the commencement of operations. In practice, the diving superintendent and diving supervisor contribute to its production. It can include:

a) The diving contractor's standard operating rules including:
   - General principles of the diving techniques to be used.
   - Any special needs for the particular diving operation.
   - Emergency contingency procedures including those required for the recovery of an unconscious diver.

b) Generic risk assessment.

c) Site specific risk assessments.

d) Details of every diving operation that makes up the project. (A diving operation is one which can be safely supervised by one person).

Each diving supervisor must be given a copy of that part of the Diving Project Plan which relates to his part of the project. It should be updated as necessary throughout the course of the diving project.

Risk Assessment

A risk assessment represents a simple and effective way of reducing accidents. It is the responsibility of the diving contractor to produce them. Several people normally contribute to producing Risk Assessments including project managers, superintendents, offshore managers, and supervisors.

TYPES OF RISK ASSESSMENT

Every type of diving operation should be covered by a risk assessment. There are two main types:

1. *Generic risk assessment*
   For convenience, where certain operations are repetitive, a Generic Risk Assessment is produced which will apply to all such operations. It needs to be up-dated whenever a change in the operation occurs.
2. *Site-specific risk assessment*
   When the location of a diving operation changes, then another Site-Specific Risk Assessment is produced to reflect the nature of any risks peculiar to the new site.

7 STEPS TO PRODUCING A RISK ASSESSMENT

It takes only seven simple steps to produce a Risk Assessment:

1. *Look for hazards*, ie, anything that can cause harm.
2. *Decide who might be harmed and how*, eg, the diver; limb entrapment.
3. *Evaluate the initial risk*. This is the risk *before* any special control measures have been taken into consideration. It is a combination of three things:
   a) The level of likelihood (high, medium, low) that somebody might be harmed by the hazard.
   b) The potential seriousness of the harm that may be caused.
   c) The number of people who may be harmed.
   See Fig. 1 to help evaluate the risk.
4. *Describe the control measures*. Describe the existing control measures and any additional ones that may be needed.
5. *Write down the findings*. See Fig. 2 for a suggested format.
6. *Evaluate the residual risk*. Use the Risk Evaluation Matrix (Fig. 1) again to re-evaluate the risk after taking the control measures. The aim is to reduce all risks to 'low' wherever possible.
7. *Review and revise* the Assessment as necessary.

For any one task a list of such hazards can be identified, both topside and underwater. Equally, additional hazards can be identified when using particular plant and equipment such as water-jetting tools, cranes or diving equipment. In these examples it might be expected that the procedures will be used many times. In such cases, the same Risk Assessment may be re-used (providing it is revised as necessary). This would therefore be an example of a *Generic Risk Assessment*.
Site-Specific Risk Assessments can also apply to topside as well as underwater. The procedure for producing one is exactly the same as for a generic risk assessment. Examples of topside risks are crane operations and the storage and handling of fuel, oxygen, compressed air, etc. Under water, different sites may have different hazards such as tides, bad visibility, cold water, sluices etc.

RISK EVALUATION MATRIX

This is a convenient way of assessing whether a risk is low, medium or high. It depends on a combination of the severity of the injury and the probability of it happening (see Fig. 1). For example, if a situation presented a risk that was *possible* and the resultant injury would be *slight*, then the risk would be *low*.

TIPS FOR PRODUCING A RISK ASSESSMENT

1. *Looking for hazards*
   a) Walk around the worksite and look afresh for possible risks.
   b) Ask employees (eg, divers, riggers, crane operators) if they are aware of any possible hazards.
   c) Encourage all personnel to report potential hazards, incidents and near-misses to the Diving Supervisor.
   d) Include unusual or infrequent events.
   e) Gather information from:
      - Operating instructions for plant and equipment.
      - Operational safety sections in this Handbook.
      - Previous accident/incident data.
      - Regulations and Codes of Practice.

Fig. 1 Risk Evaluation Matrix

Probability	Hazard severity*				
	Negligible	Slight	Moderate	High	Very high
Very unlikely Incident results from freak combination of factors	Low	Low	Low	Low	Low
Unlikely Incident results from rare combination of factors	Low	Low	Low	Medium	Medium
Possible Incident unlikely but could occur if additional factors occur	Low	Low	Medium	Medium	High
Likely Incident not certain but may occur if additional factors occur	Low	Medium	Medium	High	High
Very likely Incident almost inevitable	Medium	Medium	High	High	High

Low	Risk may be acceptable, nevertheless review the task to see if the risk can be reduced further.
Medium	Only proceed with appropriate management authorisation after consulting specialist and assessment personnel. Where possible redefine task in view of the anticipated hazards, or review to reduce risk.
High	Task must not proceed. Redefine or add further control measures to reduce risk. Reassess controls before commencing to ensure they are adequate.

* Hazard severity definitions:

Definition	Personnel	Task	Equipment	Environment
Negligible	Negligible injury or health implications. No absence from work.	Negligible loss of function/production.	None.	None.
Slight	Minor injury - first aid needed. Or non-DCI headache, nausea, dizziness, mild rashes.	Minor loss of function/production.	Minor remedial repairs required.	Minor.
Moderate	DCI, persistent dermatitis, acne or asthma.	Lost time incident. Significant loss of function/production.	Localised damage. Extensive repairs	Moderate pollution. Some restitution costs.
High	Single death or serious DCI, severe injury, poisoning, sensitisation or dangerous infection.	System shutdown.	Extensive damage	Severe pollution. Short-term localised damage. Significant restitution costs.
Very high	Multiple deaths, lung diseases or permanent debility.	System shutdown.	Extensive damage	Major pollution. Long-term damage. Very high restitution costs.

f) Concentrate on significant hazards which could cause injury or affect several people.

g) Ignore trivial items – use common sense.

2. *Decide who might be harmed and how*, include:
   a) Divers, attendants, standby divers.
   b) Life-support technicians.
   c) Riggers, welders, other workers on site.
   d) Trainees.
   e) Visitors.
   f) Members of the public.

3. *Evaluate the risk*
   This is the risk remaining *before* special control measures have been taken into consideration. Use the Risk Evaluation Matrix at Fig. 1 to designate *High*, *Medium* or *Low* level of risk.

4. *Describe the control measures*
   a) Identify control measures (see Fig. 2)
   b) Use recommendations from the operating procedures for plant and equipment.
   c) Check that the Regulations and ACoPs have been complied with.
   d) Add extra precautions as necessary. The aim is to reduce all risks to LOW wherever possible.
   e) When controls are in place they must be continuously monitored.
   f) Controls should be reviewed regularly and up-dated on the basis of feed-back.

5. *Write down the findings*
   This is conveniently done in the form of a table such as in the example in Fig. 3.

Fig. 2 Steps in identifying control measures

1. *Elimination.* Does the task need to be done at all?
2. *Substitution.* Can something else be used to reduce the risk?
   - Can a pulling machine be used instead of a lift bag?
   - Can a cold-cutting technique be used instead of a hot-cutting technique?
   - Can a mechanical device/ROV do the job instead of manual handling?
3. *Engineering controls.* Can equipment be used to reduce the risk?
   - Can a lift bag be used to reduce the weight of a heavy item?
   - Can light sticks help to locate items being lowered?
   - Can a safety interlock be installed to prevent accidental compression/decompression?
4. *Segregation.*
   - Can distance/barriers/guards be used to protect personnel?
   - Can the diver umbilical be restricted in length?
5. *Reduction in personnel/time exposure.* Limit the number of personnel exposed to the risk and control the time they are exposed.
   - Can the job be done with a two-man bell run rather than three-man?
6. *Personal protective equipment (PPE).* Is the PPE being used suitable, sufficient and appropriate?
   - Should a helmet be used instead of a band mask?
   - Should disposable overalls be used on top of diving suits in a pollution risk situation?
7. *Procedures.* Can procedures be used to specify the safe system of work to reduce risks?
   - Permit to work?
   - Checklists?
   - Work packs?
   - Risk assessments/job safety analyses?

Permit to Work

This is a formal written procedure used to control certain types of work, such as diving, which involve significant risk.

A Permit to Work certificate is issued to the diving supervisor by the organisation which has the operational authority over the work site. The purpose is to ensure that the operational authority:

a) is aware of and allows the diving operation to take place
b) keeps under strict control any other operations or factors which could affect the diving work, eg vessel movements, crane operations, etc.

Matters that may be recorded on a Permit to Work certificate for a diving operations can include:

The issuing authority name and address

Date

Work: Location
Description
Duration
Start time
Finish time
Plant and equipment to be used.
Measures to be made safe.

Issue of Permit: (on behalf of the operational authority)
Signature and job title of issuing person.
Time and date.

Receipt of permit: (on behalf of the diving contractor)
Signature, job title of receiving person (normally the diving supervisor).
Name of the diving contractor.
Time and date.

Completion of works: (on behalf of the diving contractor)
Signature, job title of receiving person (normally the diving supervisor).
Name of the diving contractor.
Time and date.

Cancellation of permit: (on behalf of the operational authority)
Signature, job title of issuing person.
Time and date.

Additional Permits to Work may be required before certain procedures are to be used including:

- hot-cutting.
- welding.
- explosive work.
- work in confined space.
- boat operations.
- crane operations.

An issuing operational authority (for example, the client of the diving contractor) may require the completion of a Diving Permit Conditions form prior to the issuing of the Permit to Work certificate. This form can include the following requirements and checks to be confirmed by the diving supervisor (where applicable):

- Diving contractor's name and address.
- Evidence of Employer's Liability Insurance cover.
- Minimum team strength of four.
- Diving supervisor's letter of appointment.
- Divers' (minimum of two) log books.
- Divers' (minimum of two) medical certificates.
- Divers' (minimum of two) competence certificates.
- Divers' (minimum of two) First Aid at Work certificates.
- Risk assessment.
- Project plan/Method statement.

Fig. 3 Example of a Risk Assessment record sheet

TASK RISK ASSESSMENT FORM

TRA number 25
Job Description *Removing redundant attachments*

JOB STEPS	HAZARD		INITIAL RISK			CONTROLS	RESIDUAL RISK		
	Hazard description and Effect	**Population at risk**	**Severity of hazard**	**Likelihood of occurrence**	**Risk rating**	**List all controls required**	**Severity of hazard**	**Likelihood of occurrence**	**Risk rating**
Separate the job into individual tasks and record them in sequence.	Describe all identified hazards and their effect for each task. Use hazard ID checklist, observation and experience. Note: additional hazards may be caused by interaction with other work.	Name all the types of personnel at risk. Note: include people outside the work group who may affected.	From matrix, identify severity with no controls in place for each hazard.	From matrix, identify likelihood with no controls in place for each hazard.	From matrix, classify risk rating for each hazard	Fully describe all controls applicable for each hazard, eg if PPE is used as a control it must be specifically described. If control can only be verified by documentation, then it must be available. All controls must be valid in that they reduce severity, likelihood or both.	From matrix, identify severity with controls in place for each hazard	From matrix, identify likelihood with controls in place for each hazard	From matrix, classify risk for each hazard
Cut off pad eye using oxy-arc	Ultraviolet light eye burn	Diver	Slight	Very likely	Medium	Use shaded eye shield	Negligible	Very unlikely	Low
	Electric shock	Diver	High	Possible	Medium	1. Attach ground cable near work. 2. Avoid getting between electrode and ground. 3. Do not change electrodes when torch is live. 4. Shut off torch when not in use. 5. Wear adequate rubber gloves.	Negligible	Possible	Low
	Explosion	Diver	High	Possible	Medium	1. Ensure no gas pocket is present or could form. 2. Use full helmet. 3. Offset head position from job.	Negligible	Possible	Low

Assessor's signature *A. Super* Date 1 Aug 2004

- Company's diving rules, including contingency procedures.
- Diving contractor's diving operations log.
- Method of communication with operational authority.
- Diving flag Alpha.
- Notification of any other operations which might affect the diving operation (eg, operators of vessels, dock gates, sluices, cranes, scaffolding, etc.
- Confirmation of full compliance with appropriate governmental regulations.
- Signature of the diving supervisor and date.

Method Statement

This lists each step or activity involved in a diving operation. Each item will refer, as necessary, to any drawings or procedures relevant to that specific activity and the person to whom it relates. In effect, it is the agenda and itinerary for any single diving operation.

Job Pack

The divers should have sight of the Diving Project Plan as well as any related Method Statement, Permits to Work, drawings, sketches, work procedures, etc that relate to their specific diving operation. This package is sometimes called the 'Job Pack', although different contractors may use their own terminology.

Tool Box meeting

The divers, supervisor(s) and any other relevant persons should hold a meeting prior to a diving operation to discuss all aspects of the operation. The Job Pack can provide the supporting material for the Tool Box meeting.

Safety meetings

It is good practice for diving contractors to hold regular safety meetings or briefings. These can vary from informal briefings at the start of a shift to weekly or monthly meetings. The matters discussed should be minuted and the minutes put on display.

1.2 EXPLORATION DRILLING PLATFORMS

Fig. 1 Operating profiles of some offshore exploration drilling rigs

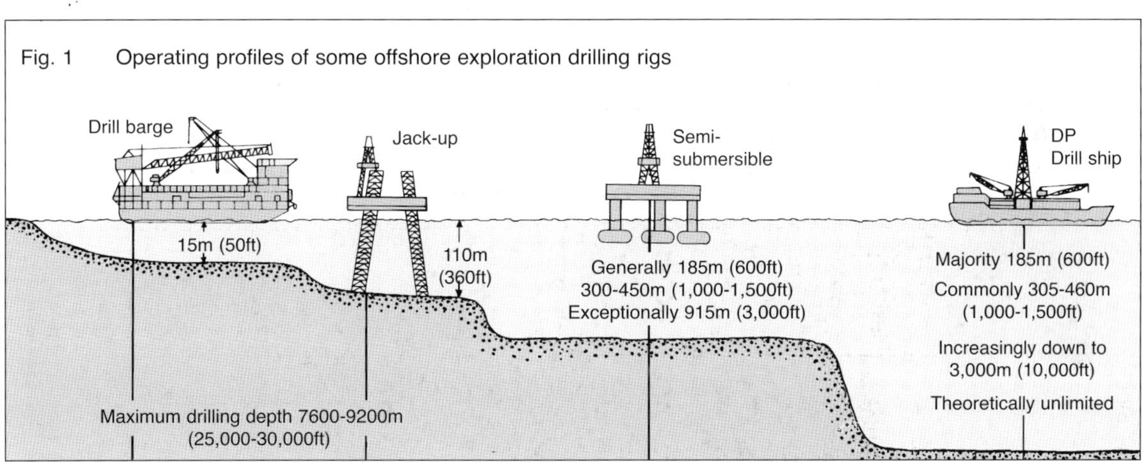
Drill barge
Jack-up
Semi-
submersible
DP
Drill ship
15m (50ft)
110m
(360ft)
Generally 185m (600ft)
300-450m (1,000-1,500ft)
Exceptionally 915m (3,000ft)
Majority 185m (600ft)
Commonly 305-460m
(1,000-1,500ft)
Increasingly down to
3,000m (10,000ft)
Theoretically unlimited
Maximum drilling depth 7600-9200m
(25,000-30,000ft)

Offshore drilling rigs are marine versions of conventional land drilling rigs. The main differences are due to two things: the increased distance between the drilling floor and the solid ground beneath, and the design considerations for being at sea.

The results have been the development of the marine riser and a seabed blow-out preventer stack with its guide base. Both provide work for divers within their depth range. Details of typical diver tasks concerned with the drilling equipment at the seabed are given in the section entitled, 'Drilling Rig Support'.

Offshore exploration drilling rigs may be supported on barges, jack-up barges, displacement ships or semi-submersible vessels. The diving tasks related specifically to the operation of these vessels are described in this section.

1. Jack-up drilling rigs

Jack-up rigs are essentially barges fitted with extendable legs. They can operate only in water as deep as their legs will allow. For this reason jack-up rigs are most suitable for the shallower water sites, usually down to 60m (200ft) although some have been used in depths of over 90m (300ft).

The barge is towed or self-propelled from site to site with its legs jacked up. As this is a rather unstable configuration, the jack-up requires relatively calm weather conditions for transportation. At the drill site the legs are lowered to the seabed. The barge then jacks itself up until it is sufficiently clear of the water to be able to withstand the anticipated sea states. Drilling may then start. After the drilling operations are complete the barge jacks up its legs and moves on to the next site.

DIVER TASKS ON JACK-UP RIGS

Usually only air diving is required on jack-up rigs due to the relatively shallow depths of the drilling sites.

1. Before a jack up reaches location buoys are normally dropped off to mark the centre and leg positions. Divers may be required to do a circular search of these positions to ensure that the legs will be clear of debris.
2. Divers may be required to measure the depth of penetration of the legs using an air probe.
3. In areas of strong currents divers will have to check for scour around the legs and, if necessary, fill scour holes with sandbags and build a protective wall of sandbags around the base of the legs.
4. Inspecting and repairing the hull.
5. Checking anchor racks and fairleads.

Fig. 2 Typical jack-up drilling production rig

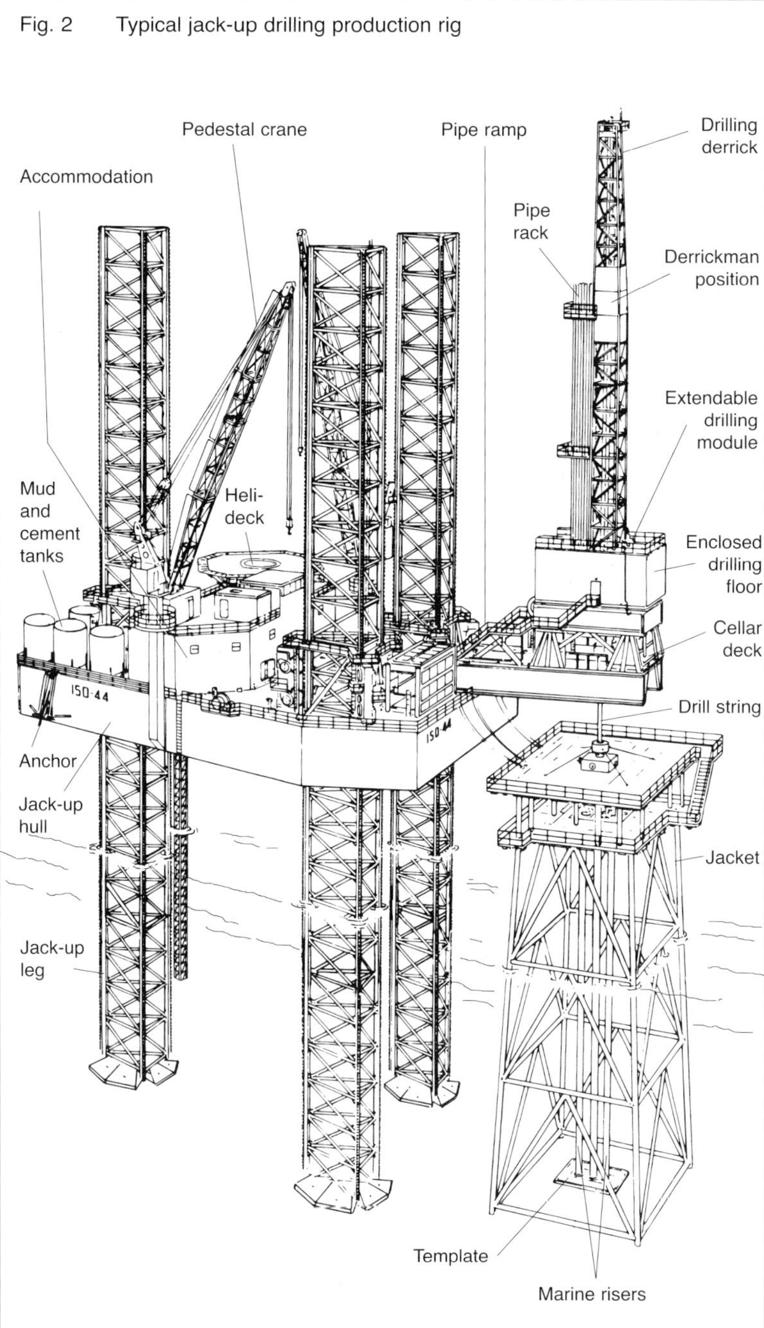
Pedestal crane
Pipe ramp
Drilling derrick
Accommodation
Pipe rack
Derrickman position
Extendable drilling module
Mud and cement tanks
Heli-deck
Enclosed drilling floor
Cellar deck
Drill string
Anchor
Jack-up hull
Jacket
Jack-up leg
Template
Marine risers

2. Semi-submersibles

Semi-submersibles are mobile working installations designed for use in water depths beyond the reach of jack-up rigs, ie depths greater than 90m (300ft). They are more stable than jack-up rigs and are often self-propelled. They consist of a drilling installation supported on submerged buoyant pontoons that can be ballasted to adjust their draft (see Fig. 3). Generally, the lower the platform the more stable it is. Many can operate all year round in most sea states.

Once the semi-submersible is on the drill site it maintains location by means of up to eight large anchors or by using computer-controlled dynamic positioning.

After the required number of wells has been drilled the well heads are sealed off and the semi-submersible moves off to operate in the next location.

DIVER TASKS ON A SEMI-SUBMERSIBLE

Air diving is used for work around the hull of the semi-submersible while bounce and saturation, mixed gas diving is used for drilling support on the sea bed. Air diving work includes:

1. Checking for debris and penetration of the pontoons (if resting on the seabed) when in shallow water
2. Infilling scour holes or building protective walls with sandbags if scour is prevalent.
3. Inspecting thrusters, pontoons and all under-water parts of the structure.
4. Assisting with the rigging of anchor pendant wires.
5. Assisting with the recovery of any lost or damaged equipment.
6. Inspecting and repairing the hull.
7. Checking anchor racks and fairleads.

Fig. 3 Typical semi-submersible drilling platform

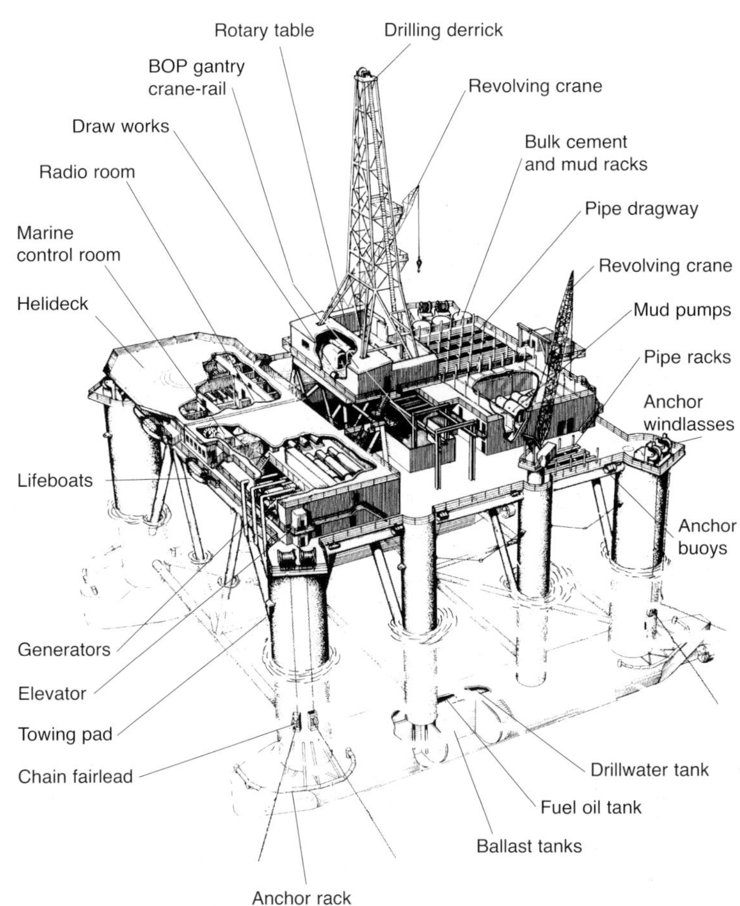
Rotary table
Drilling derrick
BOP gantry crane-rail
Revolving crane
Draw works
Bulk cement and mud racks
Radio room
Pipe dragway
Marine control room
Revolving crane
Helideck
Mud pumps
Pipe racks
Anchor windlasses
Lifeboats
Anchor buoys
Generators
Elevator
Towing pad
Chain fairlead
Drillwater tank
Fuel oil tank
Ballast tanks
Anchor rack

3. Drillships (see Fig. 4)

Drillships may be either conventional vessels converted for drilling or may be custom-built. Most have a derrick constructed over a central moonpool through which the drill is run. Drillships can drill in depths of over 1,500m (5,000ft) and use dynamic positioning to maintain location. Anchors may be used when working in shallow water. Because these vessels tend to pitch and roll more than semi-submersibles there is greater wear and tear on the drilling equipment and this means more inspection and repair work for divers.

DIVER TASKS ON DRILLSHIPS

1. Inspect, maintain and repair ship's accessory structures such as moonpool doors.
2. Inspect all the ship's thrusters and keep them clear of fouling.
3. Assist with the recovery of any lost or damaged equipment.
4. Inspecting and repairing the hull.
5. Checking anchor racks and fairleads.

Fig. 4 Typical drillship

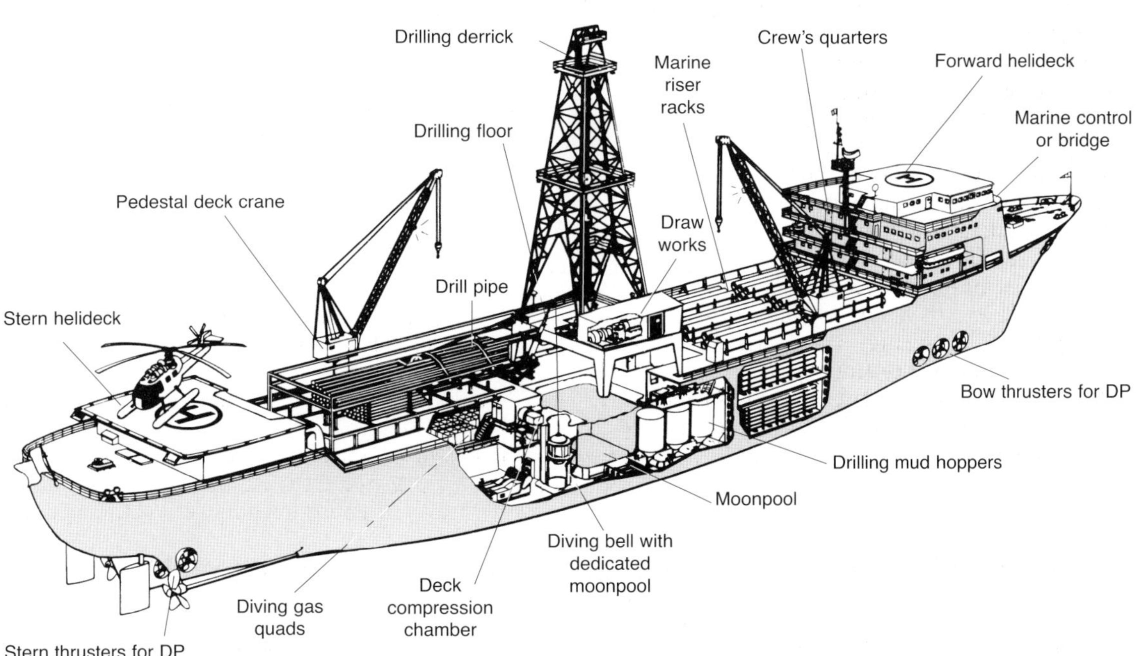
Drilling derrick
Crew's quarters
Marine riser racks
Forward helideck
Drilling floor
Marine control or bridge
Pedestal deck crane
Draw works
Drill pipe
Stern helideck
Bow thrusters for DP
Drilling mud hoppers
Moonpool
Diving bell with dedicated moonpool
Deck compression chamber
Diving gas quads
Stern thrusters for DP

1.3 DRILLING RIG SUPPORT

Most of the seabed diving work involves the inspection, maintenance and repair of the blow-out preventer and its connection to the permanent guidebase.

Blow-out Preventer (BOP)

A blow-out preventer is an assembly of hydraulically-operated rams which is lowered onto a permanent guide base on the seabed (see Fig. 1). The drill string enters the seabed through the BOP stack.

FUNCTIONS OF THE BOP

A blow-out is what can happen when the drill bit penetrates an area of pressure which is higher than the hydraulic head of pressure exerted by the drilling mud inside the drill hole. The result is the uncontrolled blow-out of this mud followed by the oil or gas.

The BOP is responsible for preventing this disastrous outcome and for bringing the well back under control by allowing heavier mud to be pumped down the drill shaft.

The blow-out must first be prevented by the closing of one or more pairs of rams in the BOP. Rams are hydraulically-operated pistons made of steel or tough rubber and are usually placed one on top of the other.

There are two kinds of ram:

1. Shear (or kill) rams which cut through the drill pipe when they close thus sealing off the BOP stack bore.
2. Pipe (or choke) rams which close and seal around the outside only of drill pipe.

Both types of ram have locks which keep them hydraulically closed once they have been activated. Once the rams have locked closed, heavier mud is pumped down two pipes called the kill and choke lines.

These lines are connected to the drill below the rams and can circulate the heavier mud while drilling operations and the BOP are shut down. Once the heavier mud pressure exceeds the down-hole pressure the BOP rams can be re-opened and drilling operations recommenced.

DIVER TASKS (see Figs. 2 – 8)

The main tasks include:

- Assistance with the guiding/lowering of the BOP onto the guidebase
- BOP stack inspection
- Checking of connections
- Trouble-shooting any electrical, hydraulic or mechanical malfunctions.

Fig. 1 Location of Blow-out Preventer

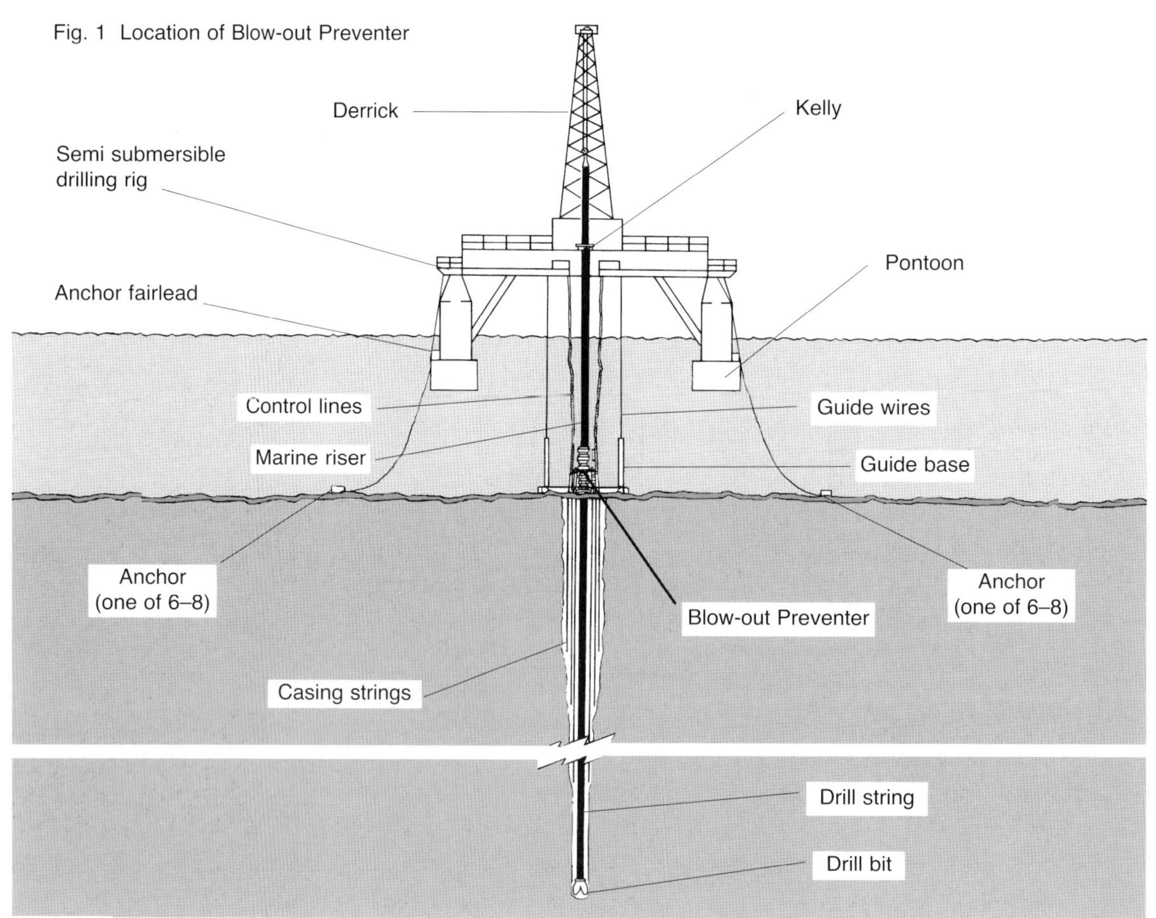
Derrick
Kelly
Semi submersible drilling rig
Pontoon
Anchor fairlead
Control lines
Guide wires
Marine riser
Guide base
Anchor (one of 6–8)
Anchor (one of 6–8)
Blow-out Preventer
Casing strings
Drill string
Drill bit

Fig. 2 Typical tasks on a Blow-out Preventer and Guidebase

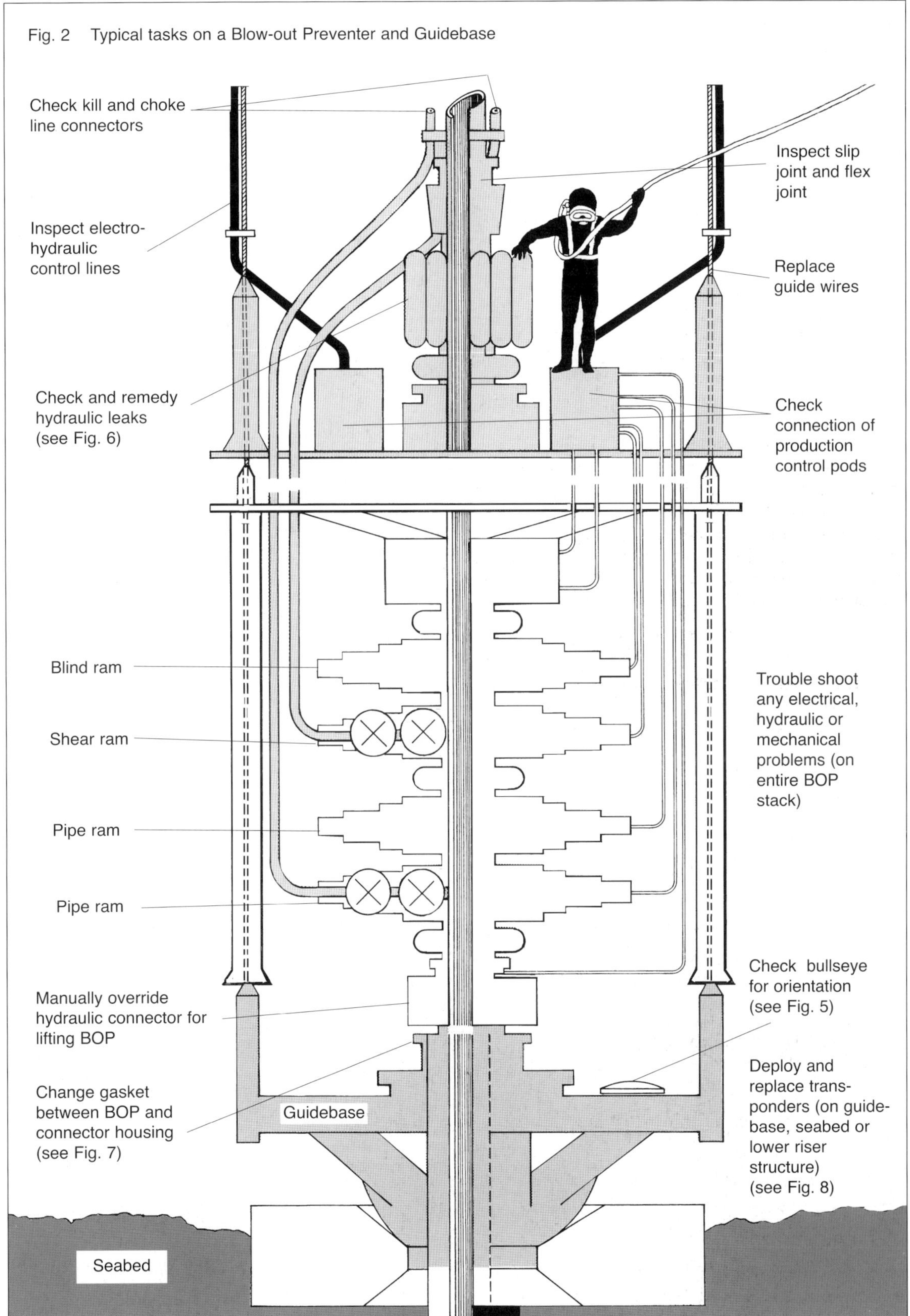
Check kill and choke line connectors
Inspect slip joint and flex joint
Inspect electro-hydraulic control lines
Replace guide wires
Check and remedy hydraulic leaks (see Fig. 6)
Check connection of production control pods
Blind ram
Shear ram
Trouble shoot any electrical, hydraulic or mechanical problems (on entire BOP stack)
Pipe ram
Pipe ram
Check bullseye for orientation (see Fig. 5)
Manually override hydraulic connector for lifting BOP
Deploy and replace transponders (on guidebase, seabed or lower riser structure) (see Fig. 8)
Change gasket between BOP and connector housing (see Fig. 7)
Guidebase
Seabed

Figs 2–8: It is important to note that all installations vary and before going underwater the diver should familiarise himself with photographs and drawings of the equipment on which he will be required to work.

Fig. 3 Guiding BOP into place on the wellhead

Diver clears debris from wellhead casing on the permanent guide base.

Fig. 4 Guidewire replacement

3/4" cables attached to the top of the guideposts run up to the drilling platform where they are spooled onto tuggers and maintained at constant tension. They frequently break and need to be replaced. There are many types but the usual method is a spelter on the end of the cable which fits into a slot on the guideposts.

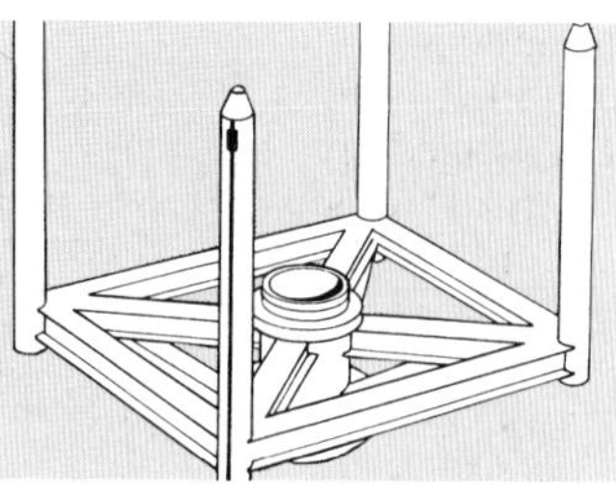

a) A permanent guidebase with four guideposts to which the guidelines have to be attached.

b) Diver manually removing the top of the guidepost assembly.

Fig. 5 Checking orientation of the guidebase

The diver observes the bubble in a bullseye mounted on the permanent guidebase and reports to the supervisor via the intercom.

Fig. 6 Checking and remedying hydraulic leaks

Diver locates hydraulic leaks by visual inspection and tightens up or replaces faulty hydraulic fittings. Leaks show up as cloudy, white liquid.

Fig. 7 Changing gasket between BOP and casing

The gasket may need to be replaced if a leak is discovered when pressure-testing the conductor housing by pumping fluid through the drill pipe. The gasket shown here is being fitted onto the wellhead casing. Depending on the size, these metal gaskets can be very heavy. If the hydraulic connector does not release when the BOP has to be lifted off the guidebase the diver will need to attach a tugger line to a key on the collet to release it.

Fig. 8 Deployment or replacement of transponders

Transponders are often attached to the guideposts on the permanent guidebase, on the corners of the lower riser package or even on the seabed around the wellhead.

1.4 PIPELAY BARGES

A pipelay barge, sometimes called a lay barge, handles pipeline of single or double sections which are welded together on board. The finished weld is radiographed and the joints coated with bitumen. Finally, the pipe is lowered down the stinger to the seabed as the barge pulls itself forward on its anchors. Pipelay barges are also used for construction tasks such as tie-ins and subsea pile installations.

Most barges are fitted with an articulated arm called a stinger or pontoon which is hinged onto the stern. The completed pipeline is fed through the stinger over a series of rollers and lowered under tension to the seabed.

There are three generations of pipelay barge:

1. The first generation are modified flat bottom barges which have the pipeline passed down a sloping deck into the sea (see Fig. 1).
2. The second generation are improved ship shaped hulls.
3. The third and most recent are semi-submersibles (see Fig. 2). Third generation semi-submersible barges have the advantage of being able to trim to suit the sea state and are more stable in rough weather.

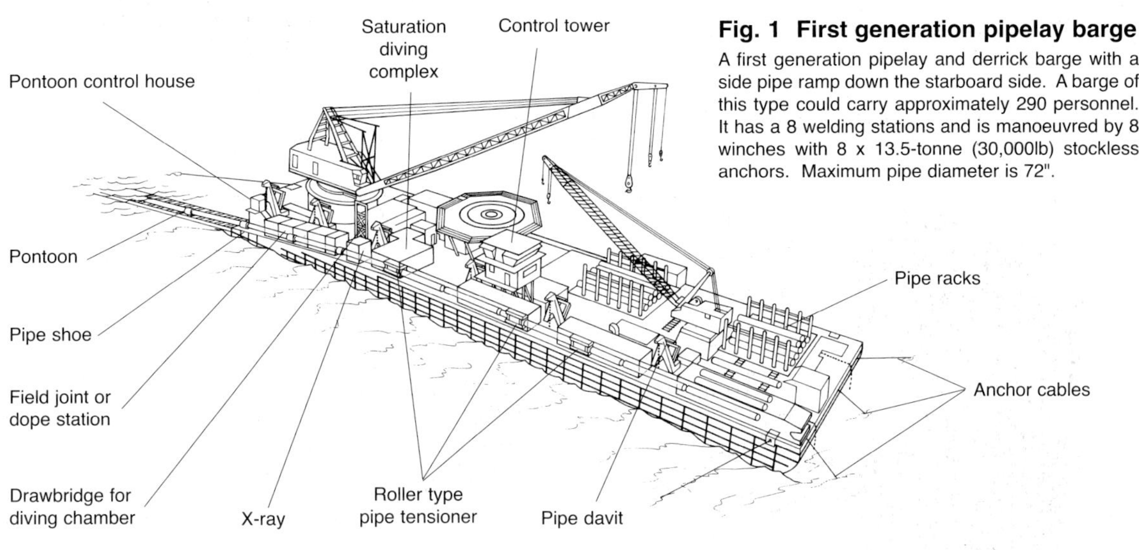
Saturation diving complex
Control tower
Pontoon control house
Pontoon
Pipe shoe
Field joint or dope station
Drawbridge for diving chamber
X-ray
Roller type pipe tensioner
Pipe davit
Pipe racks
Anchor cables

Fig. 1 First generation pipelay barge

A first generation pipelay and derrick barge with a side pipe ramp down the starboard side. A barge of this type could carry approximately 290 personnel. It has a 8 welding stations and is manoeuvred by 8 winches with 8 x 13.5-tonne (30,000lb) stockless anchors. Maximum pipe diameter is 72".

Fig. 2 Third generation pipelay barge

A semi-submersible third generation mobile offshore construction platform capable of operating in all weathers. The pipe assembly and stinger are run down the centre of the barge providing better access to the line up station from both sides, better stability and a balanced mooring system. This barge can accommodate approximately 350 personnel and is manoeuvred by 12 winches with 12 x 18-tonne (40,000lb) stockless anchors. Stern truss length is 40m (130ft) and the stinger length is 50m (170ft). Maximum pipe diameter 84".

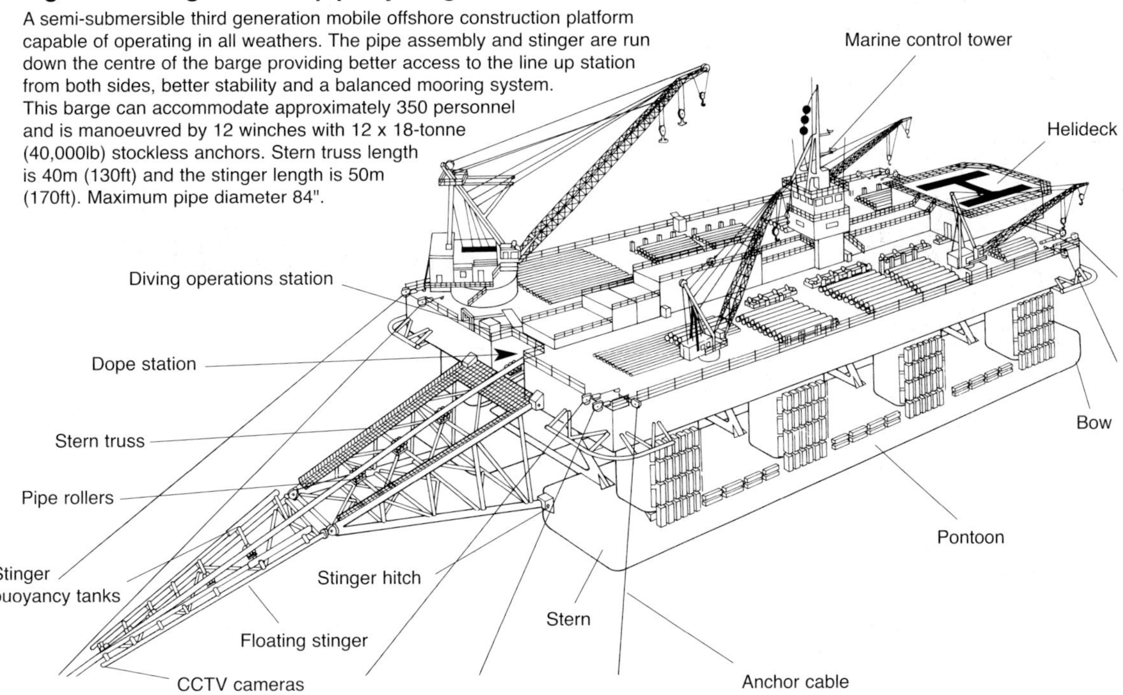
Marine control tower
Helideck
Diving operations station
Dope station
Stern truss
Pipe rollers
Stinger buoyancy tanks
Stinger hitch
Floating stinger
CCTV cameras
Stern
Anchor cable
Pontoon
Bow

TASKS IN LAYBARGE OPERATIONS

Diving from a laybarge requires the diver to be familiar with many different diving skills from diving on the stinger to installing a riser which is to be welded or flanged to the pipeline. It helps to have a good construction background and familiarity with all the necessary installation tools required to make tie-ins, such as bolt tensioning equipment, etc.

The work is of two kinds:

1. Shallow, surface-oriented air diving tasks on the stinger to check and maintain its efficient operation (see Fig. 3). When diving on stingers divers should have a means of indicating their position day and night and, where possible, have two methods of communication with the surface. Good weather is particularly important when diving on stingers since stinger movements in rough weather can make the job considerably more hazardous. Independent surface cover for the diver is essential at all times. Generally, this is provided from an inflatable or from the anchor handling vessel carrying suitable communications, standby diver and attendant. Diving operations are supervised from an air station set up just above the stinger hitch.
2. Deeper, possibly mixed gas work on the seabed associated with the pipe and work on the lay-down head and pipeline connections (see Fig. 4).

Fig. 3 Shallow Air Diving Tasks

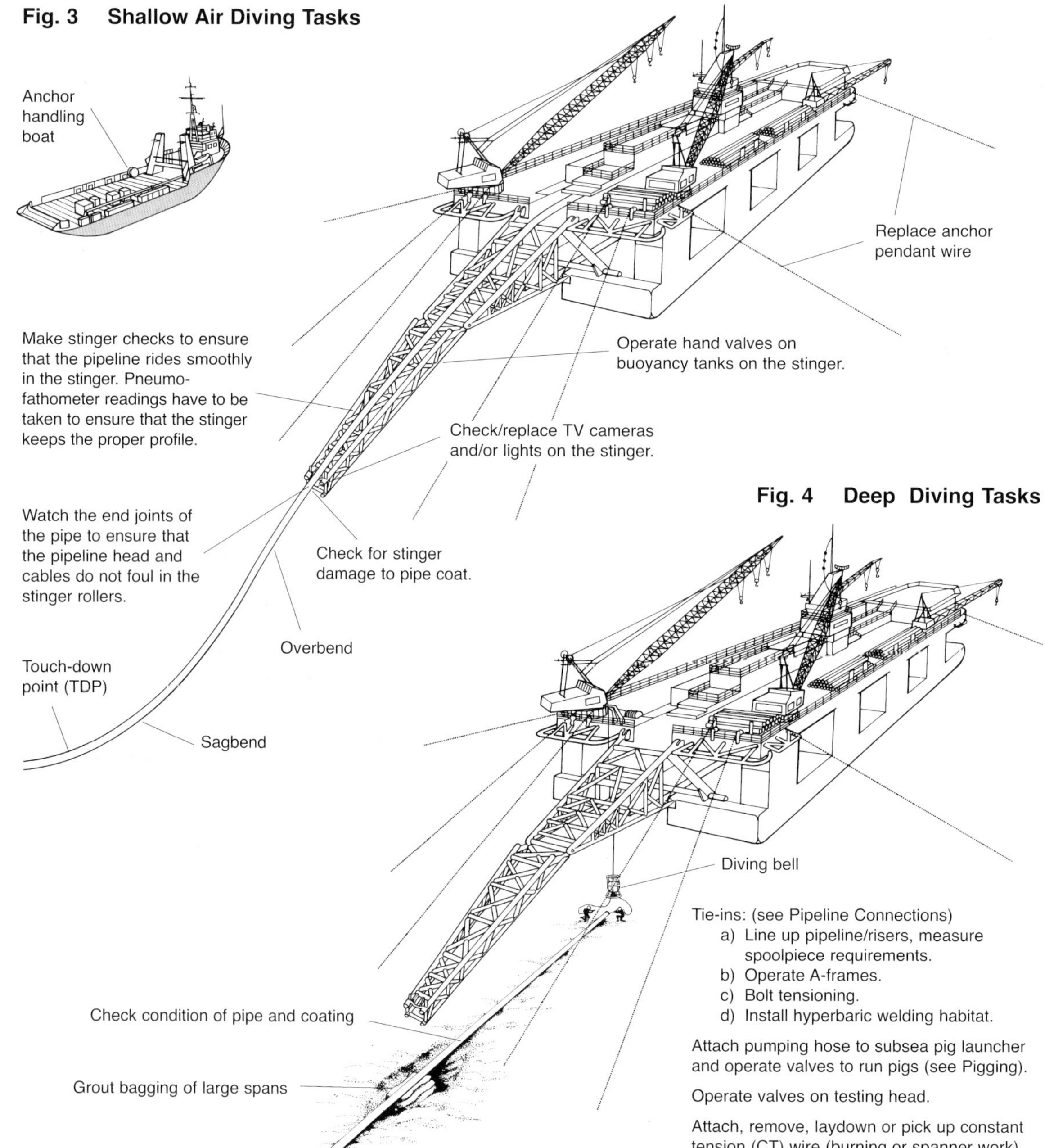
Anchor handling boat
Replace anchor pendant wire
Make stinger checks to ensure that the pipeline rides smoothly in the stinger. Pneumo-fathometer readings have to be taken to ensure that the stinger keeps the proper profile.
Operate hand valves on buoyancy tanks on the stinger.
Check/replace TV cameras and/or lights on the stinger.
Watch the end joints of the pipe to ensure that the pipeline head and cables do not foul in the stinger rollers.
Check for stinger damage to pipe coat.
Overbend
Touch-down point (TDP)
Sagbend
Diving bell
Tie-ins: (see Pipeline Connections)
a) Line up pipeline/risers, measure spoolpiece requirements.
b) Operate A-frames.
c) Bolt tensioning.
d) Install hyperbaric welding habitat.
Attach pumping hose to subsea pig launcher and operate valves to run pigs (see Pigging).
Operate valves on testing head.
Attach, remove, laydown or pick up constant tension (CT) wire (burning or spanner work)
Check condition of pipe and coating
Grout bagging of large spans

Fig. 4 Deep Diving Tasks

Fig. 5 Removal or attachment of constant tension wire

The cable which lifts or lowers the pipe to the seabed may be removed or replaced at the pulling head. Extreme caution must be exercised by divers when cutting the laydown wire as there can be over 100 kips (100,000lb force) tension on it.

Fig.6 Stinger valve operation

Opening and shutting specific valves to adjust buoyancy and catenary. Just because the diver has been told a certain valve is open or shut he should not assume that it is so and should check for himself. Always carry a wrench.

Fig. 7 TV camera replacement

Removal and replacement of CCTV camera(s) on stinger.

Fig. 8 Valve operation

Valves at the testing (pull or laydown) head are opened or closed to flood or dewater the pipe.

Fig. 9 Typical arrangements of diving equipment on the stern of a laybarge

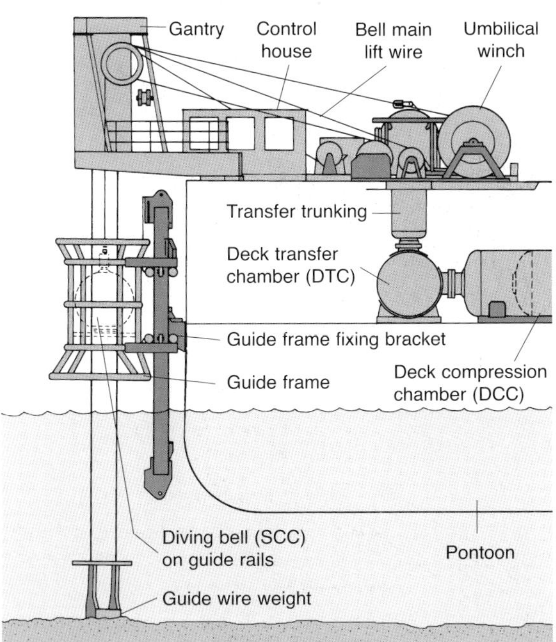
Gantry
Control house
Bell main lift wire
Umbilical winch
Transfer trunking
Deck transfer chamber (DTC)
Guide frame fixing bracket
Guide frame
Deck compression chamber (DCC)
Diving bell (SCC) on guide rails
Pontoon
Guide wire weight

LAYBARGES – OPERATIONAL SAFETY

1. In rough weather, diving on the stinger can be very dangerous. If a swell is running the diver may be drawn in and get caught between the rollers and the pipe if he gets too close. The diver's umbilical may be similarly trapped. Consequently the diver should stay outside the stinger, especially in poor weather. If a tide is running the diver should swim along the lee side to keep his umbilical away from the stinger. The saying, "The stinger sucks you in before it spits you out" should be remembered.
2. The decision to wear scuba in place of umbilical supplied UBA should be carefully considered. The diver should always wear an inflatable lifejacket if he uses scuba. In the UK, the use of scuba requires exemption from certain regulations to be given prior to use.
3. Fins should always be worn when diving around a stinger.
4. All valves on a stinger or on a pipe must be treated with the greatest caution.
5. The barge should not be moved whilst divers are working on the stinger. If this is not feasible the diver must stay well clear of the stinger during movements.
6. If decompression stops are required either in the water or as surface decompression a swift means of recovery from the water is necessary such as a diving basket or wet bell.

1.5 TRENCHING BARGES

Trenching barges are also known as 'jet' or 'bury' barges. Their function is to excavate a trench for a pipe or cable in order to protect the pipe or cable from damage and to stabilise it on the seabed. The depth of the trench required can vary from as little as 0.5m to 5m (1–15ft) depending on the area such as shipping lanes or anchorage grounds. The infilling of the trench is normally left to the natural movements of the seabed. The amount of infilling that eventually occurs varies according to the area and the nature of the seabed. The sleds used to produce the trench differ considerably in design depending on seabed conditions and the policy of the operator. They may use high pressure water jets with air-lifts, water extruder or a proprietary ploughing system.

The diving tasks are associated with checking the physical characteristics of the trench, the status of the pipe and sled, setting the sled and assisting with any problems which may arise.

Fig. 1 Typical trenching barge

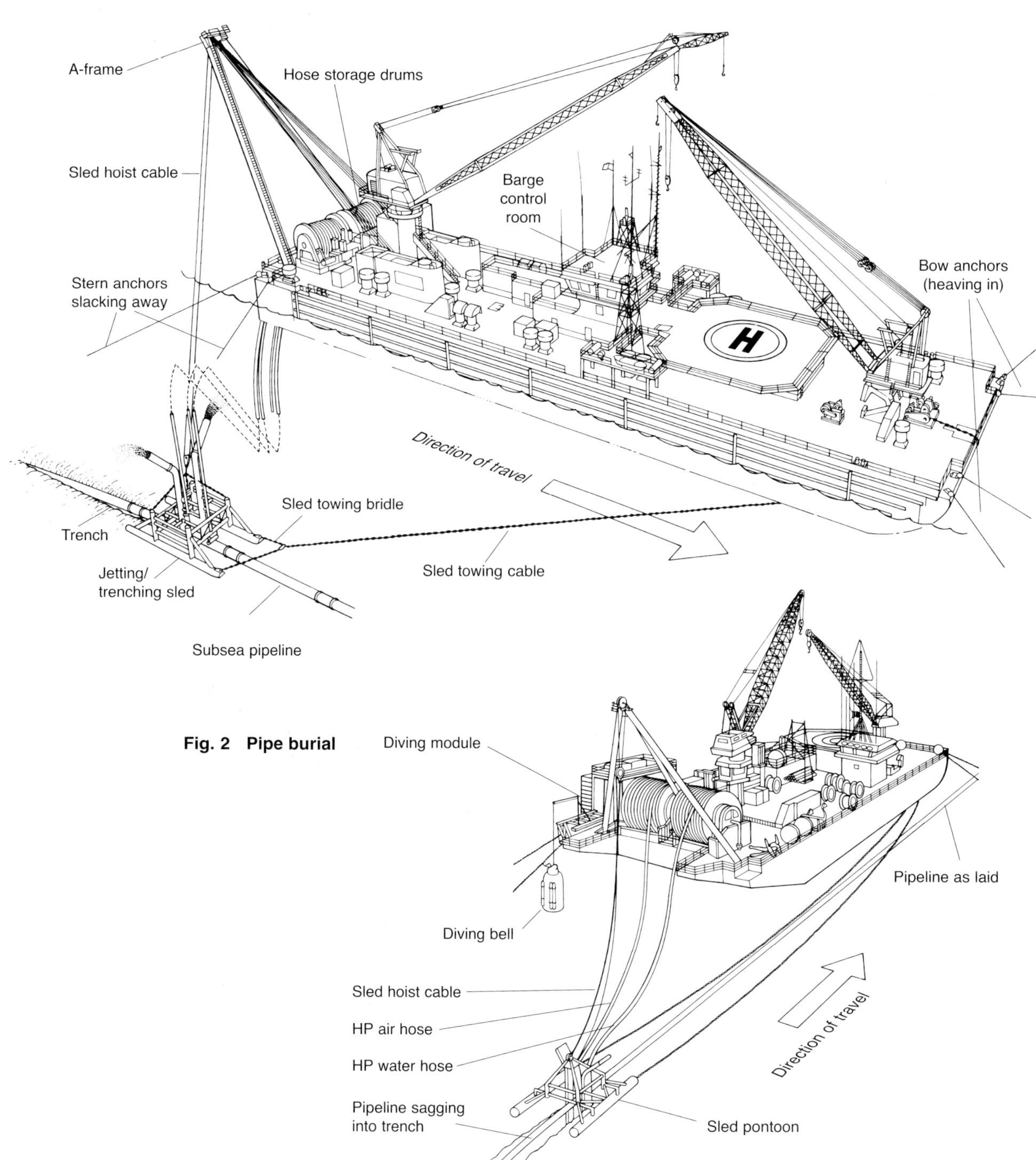
A-frame
Hose storage drums
Sled hoist cable
Barge control room
Stern anchors slacking away
Bow anchors (heaving in)
H
Direction of travel
Sled towing bridle
Trench
Jetting/ trenching sled
Sled towing cable
Subsea pipeline
Diving module
Pipeline as laid
Diving bell
Sled hoist cable
HP air hose
HP water hose
Direction of travel
Pipeline sagging into trench
Sled pontoon

Fig. 2 Pipe burial

Typical diving procedure

The following procedure provides an example of how the diving may be carried out on a jet barge. There may be variations between different diving companies and barge operators.

SETTING THE SLED

When diving in the saturation mode the jet sled may be lowered to within 4.5m (15ft) of the bottom. A diving bell would then be lowered with a guide wire attached to the sled until the bell is 6m (20ft) above the sled. The diver locks out and checks the location of the diving bell in relation to the sled. The diver then locates the pipeline and directs the barge to move until the sled is directly over the pipeline.

When the movement of the barge has subsided the diver positions himself at the rear of the sled and, after checking that his diving umbilical is clear of and above the lower pontoon, he slowly directs the lowering of the sled over the pipeline. The diver can lower the sled in zero visibility by standing at the rear of the sled with his feet straddling the pipeline and holding on to the rear air lifts as the sled is slowly lowered over the pipeline. Once the sled is set the position of the pipeline in the sled must be checked. Checks should be made of:

- The front and rear rollers.
- The towing bridle, for possible fouling.
- The position of the pontoons in relation to the natural bottom.

Fig. 3 Diving tasks on a trenching sled

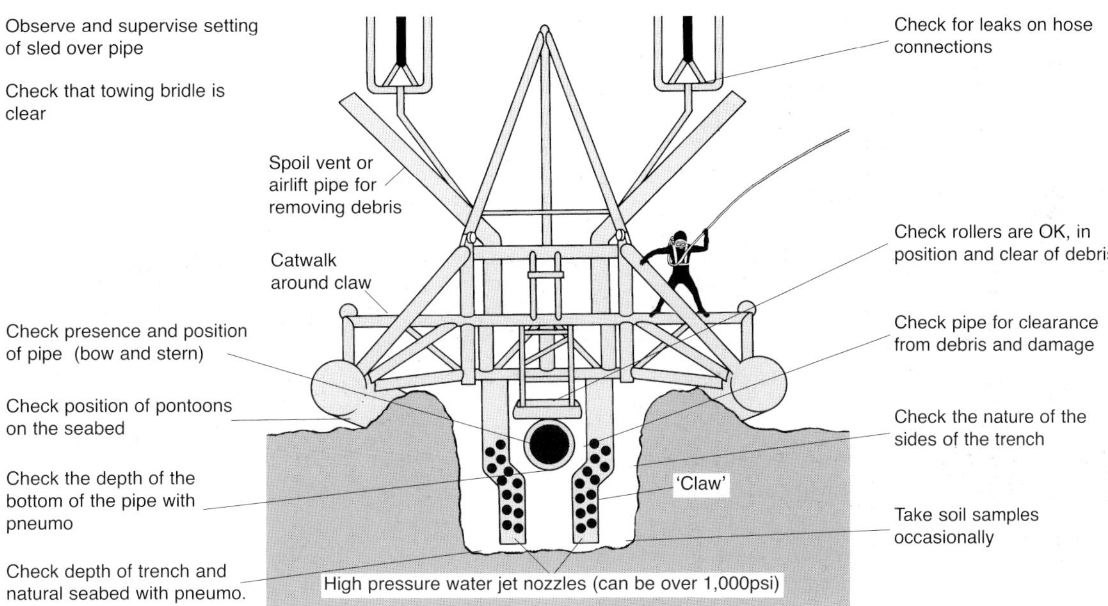
Observe and supervise setting of sled over pipe
Check that towing bridle is clear
Spoil vent or airlift pipe for removing debris
Catwalk around claw
Check presence and position of pipe (bow and stern)
Check position of pontoons on the seabed
Check the depth of the bottom of the pipe with pneumo
Check depth of trench and natural seabed with pneumo.
Check for leaks on hose connections
Check rollers are OK, in position and clear of debris
Check pipe for clearance from debris and damage
Check the nature of the sides of the trench
'Claw'
Take soil samples occasionally
High pressure water jet nozzles (can be over 1,000psi)

Fig. 4 Checking depth of trench
Diver places pneumo at base of trench for surface readout.

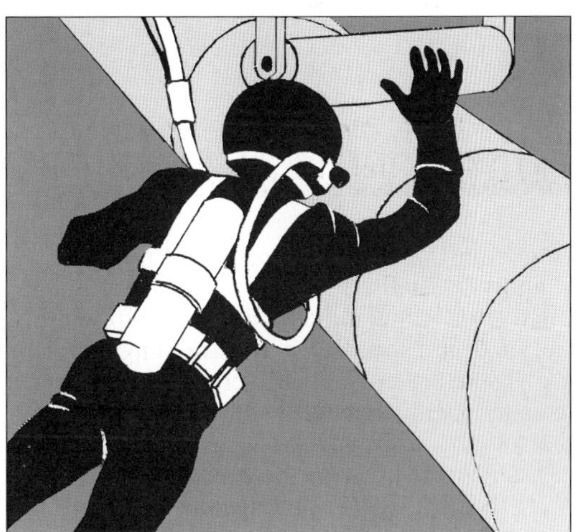

Fig. 5 Checking rollers
Diver feels position of rollers on the pipe to ensure their proper functioning and positioning.

CHECKING THE SLED

Before any dive is made it is imperative that the barge foreman shuts down the jetting pressure and air lifts because of the dangers from the high pressure water jets, heavy duty air lifts and because voice communication with the diver would be impossible over the roar of the water jets.

Once the water and air supplies to the jet sled have been secured the bell is lowered to within about 10m (30ft) of the bottom and the diver can be required to check the following:

1. Natural bottom depth, by pneumo.
2. Elevation of the pipe.
3. Elevation of the trench bottom under the pipe at the stern roller.
4. Position of the pipe relative to the rear of the sled.
5. Position of pontoons on the seabed and the orientation relative to the pipeline.
6. Position of the pipe relative to the bow of the sled.
7. Check that the towing bridle is clear.
8. Condition of the pipeline (cracks in the concrete coating, etc), if visibility allows.
9. Take a soil sample.
10. Pipeline elevation in the trench, well to the stern of the trench.

TRENCH BARGES – OPERATIONAL SAFETY

BEFORE DIVING the diver should:

1. Make himself completely familiar with the type of jet sled being used before going underwater. He should be able to draw a picture of the sled from memory and be able to identify every part of it. As much time as possible should be spent learning the way around the sled whenever it is on the surface because visibility will normally be zero on the bottom.
2. Be able to identify and memorise any danger areas such as the moving parts, cables, rollers, etc. He must learn how to locate himself by touch alone so as to be able to avoid danger areas and must take special care to keep his fingers clear.
3. Learn how to use his own body as a unit of measure so that he can give useful measurements in poor visibility (see Fig. 14, page 104). Useful lengths of measurement, for example, would include knowing his own height, the length from elbow to finger tip, and the distance between his thumb and little finger on his outstretched hand.
4. Ensure that the sled is at a standstill and that power is shut down (including jetting pressure and air lifts).
5. Use a helmet (as opposed to a Band Mask) for head protection.

UNDERWATER, the diver should:

1. Pay special attention to his umbilical at all times to ensure that it does not become damaged or entangled.
2. Use down-lines and swim-lines wherever possible to provide direction and range in poor visibility.
3. Always work in the lee of the sled if there is a current running.
4. Use the catwalk on the sled, if provided.
5. Never get under a sled which is being lowered.
6. Be able to give approximate measurements in zero visibility by using his own body as a means of measurement.

1.6 DYNAMICALLY POSITIONED VESSELS

Diving from Dynamically Positioned (DP) vessels is a highly specialised type of diving. It requires a detailed knowledge of the mode of operation of the vessel and its specific station-keeping arrangements. There are unique and very important safety aspects involved. The following is an introduction to the subject.

Divers should familiarise themselves with the layout of their vessel including the position and number of thrusters, the relative positions of the diving moonpool, work station(s), taut wire A-frame(s), cranes etc. The position of the thrusters should be marked on the vessel's hull above the water line, on deck and ideally also on bulwarks or handrails.

A DP vessel maintains its position by computer-controlled operation of its propellers and thrusters. The computer monitors the vessel's position using reference systems (see Fig. 1) which can include:

- Taut wire (vertically to the sea bed or horizontally to a fixed structure).
- Artemis (using surface microwave antenna).
- Hydroacoustic Position Reference (HPR) using seabed, acoustic transponders.
- Differential Global Positioning System (DGPS) using satellites and a terrestrial reference.

For diving operations, the vessel must be using at least three independent position referencing systems and at least two of these must be of different types. Under good conditions and with all three referencing systems on line, it can be acceptable to move the vessel while the divers are out of the bell. The following two systems are especially relevant to the diver.

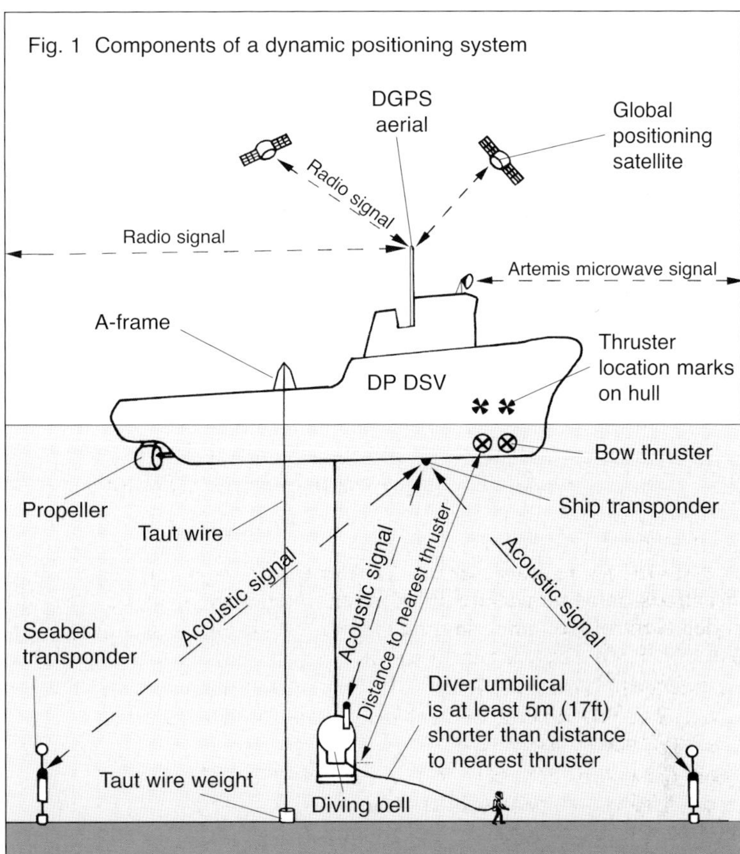
DGPS aerial
Global positioning satellite
Radio signal
Radio signal
Artemis microwave signal
A-frame
Thruster location marks on hull
DP DSV
Bow thruster
Propeller
Ship transponder
Taut wire
Acoustic signal
Acoustic signal
Distance to nearest thruster
Acoustic signal
Seabed transponder
Diver umbilical is at least 5m (17ft) shorter than distance to nearest thruster
Taut wire weight
Diving bell
Fig. 1 Components of a dynamic positioning system

Taut wire system

This consists of a constant tension wire connected to a weight lowered to the sea bed and supported from an A-frame. Sensors in the pulley-head detect any change in the wire's angle or length of wire paid out. They are usually positioned near the centre of the vessel to minimise the effects of pitch and yaw. The taut wires must be carefully protected from anything that may deflect them (such as an ROV umbilical) otherwise the computer could receive misleading information.

It is important for a diver to be able to identify the taut wire and its weight. The diver can familiarise himself with what it looks like before mobilisation/deployment. The taut wire weight is several hundred kilograms and is usually painted white. The wire can be marked with fluorescent tape or light sticks.

The vessel may move in steps by lifting and replacing the taut wire ('walking the taut wire').

Hydroacoustic Position Reference system (HPR)

An array of transponders may be placed on the sea bed around the dive site. Divers may be required to place some of the transponders. An additional transponder may be attached to the diving bell. These communicate with a transponder under the vessel's hull to give the position information. It is important that no gas should be vented that could interfere with the acoustic signals between the transponders. This includes the use of air bags and air tools. The noise generated by high pressure water jetting equipment can also interfere with these systems.

Divers may be required to recover the transponders on completion of a diving operation.

DP Footprint

While operating under its DP system, a vessel does not remain in a perfectly stationary position. It is normal for the vessel to move about slightly, within a certain limited boundary. The limit of this boundary is called the vessel's 'footprint'. The better the DP system is working, the smaller the footprint. Various factors can degrade the footprint including interference with position-fixing systems, thruster wash from other vessels, changing wind and waves etc. The diver must take this into account particularly during lifting and lowering operations.

DP alerts

If there is a failure of the DP system, the vessel may move unexpectedly including:

- change of heading
- excursion
- drive off

In order to safeguard the divers, the vessel operator provides at least three DP alert levels to the Diving Supervisor to indicate the status of the vessel's DP system. These are indicated by green, yellow and red lights in the Dive Control (as well as on deck, in saturation control, ROV control room etc). Every diving operation will have its own specific contingency plans for the various levels of alert.

a) GREEN, CONSTANT
This is the normal operational status. The DP equipment is working adequately and within safe working limits.
Action: The divers have no extra restrictions on their operational capabilities.

b) YELLOW, FLASHING (this is accompanied by an audio alarm)
There is a degraded operational status. One or more of the components of the DP system has failed. Safe working limits have been exceeded or an excursion of heading or position is likely but will not be critical.
Action:
- The Diving Supervisor will instruct the diver to move to a safe location. This could be the bell weight, bell or basket.
- As far as practicable, the diver should make safe any work or items of equipment that could pose a hazard.
- After consultation with the DP Operator, the Diving Supervisor will decide whether or not to abort the dive. If there are any doubts, he should abort the dive and recover the divers.

c) RED (this is accompanied by an audio alarm)
This is the emergency status. There is, or will be a loss of position.
Action: The Diving Supervisor will order the immediate recovery of the divers into the diving bell or basket, bearing in mind any hazards posed by downlines, subsea structures etc.

Umbilical handling

This is of critical importance when working from a DP vessel. It is essential that the diver, standby diver and tender make themselves fully aware of the Dive Plan and Procedures for umbilical handling specific to their vessel.
The bell diver's umbilical must be physically limited/restrained in length. The length must be no longer than 5 metres (17ft) short of any hazard such as the nearest thrusters. The standby diver's umbilical must be 2m (6ft) longer than the diver's so that he can always reach the diver.
There must be a diagram in the Dive Control, DP Control and other relevant areas clearly showing the location of the bell and divers in relation to the worksite. The diagram should include:

1. A thrusters-to-bell configuration showing the bell at various depths at 10m (33ft) increments together with the distances to the nearest thrusters(s). This is the distance from the centre of the bell trunking to the nearest possible moving part of the thruster envelope.
2. All other hazards which the main or excursion umbilicals must not reach, including propellers, intakes, etc.
3. The position of any nearby mooring lines.

The diver's umbilical should be kept as short as possible and should be either neutrally or negatively buoyant. It should be marked at least every 10 metres (33ft).
Many companies use a colour-coded system of umbilical marking. The example shown in Fig. 2 uses a turn of red tape for every 5m (17ft) and a turn of black tape at every 10m (33ft). It is a good idea to ensure that the different coloured tapes are also different widths so that the diver can more easily distinguish between them in poor visibility.

Fig 2. Example of an umbilical marking system

Length metres	Black tape No of turns	Red tape No of turns	
5	-	1	
10	1	-	
15	1	1	
20	2	-	
25	2	1	
30	3	-	
35	3	1	
40	4	-	
45	4	1	
50	1 broad turn		

See page 167, 'Lifting Operations from DP Vessels' for information on orientation and familiarisation.

1.7 PIPELINE CONNECTIONS

Subsea pipeline connections are mainly carried out during the construction phase of an offshore development. Occasionally, at a later date, extra connections may be made or maintenance and repairs carried out. Commonly used subsea pipeline connections or 'tie-ins' include:
- Tie-in of a pipeline to a platform riser.
- Mid-line tie-ins between two or three pipelines (end-to-end or T-pieces).
- Tie-in of new step-out wells/manifolds
- 'Hot taps' (attaching pipes to already operating pipes).
- Placing a valve box in an existing pipeline.
- Repair of a damaged pipeline.
- Replacing flexible hoses on SPMs.

There are many methods of making underwater pipeline connections. Those commonly used include:
- Flanged connections.
- Hyperbarically welded connections.
- Mechanical connections

Regardless of the method used to connect two pipelines (or a pipeline to a riser), it is first necessary to take some accurate measurements (see Fig. 1). These will include the stand-off distance between the

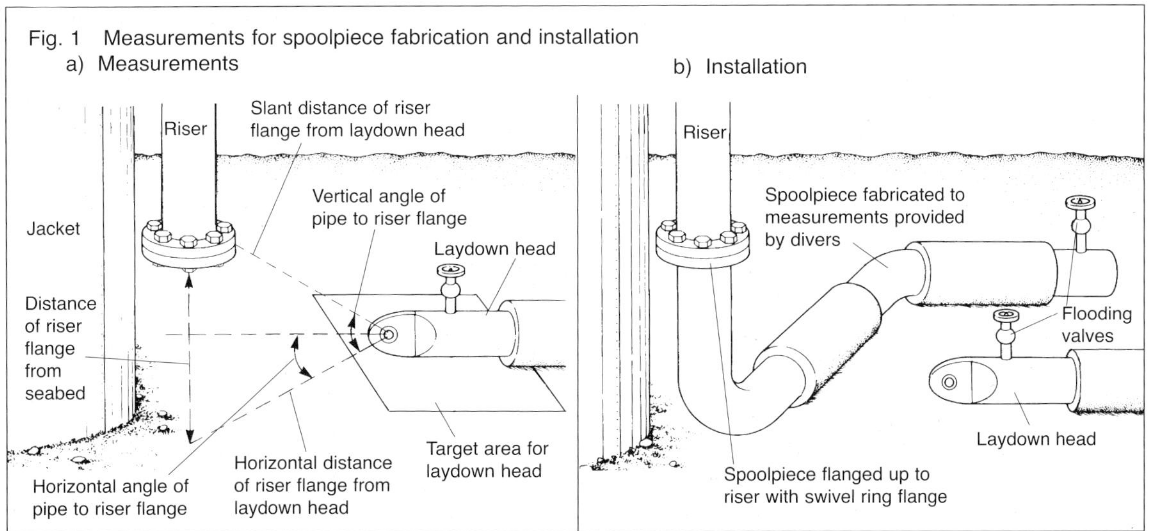
a) Measurements
Riser
Slant distance of riser flange from laydown head
Jacket
Vertical angle of pipe to riser flange
Laydown head
Distance of riser flange from seabed
Horizontal angle of pipe to riser flange
Horizontal distance of riser flange from laydown head
Target area for laydown head
b) Installation
Riser
Spoolpiece fabricated to measurements provided by divers
Flooding valves
Laydown head
Spoolpiece flanged up to riser with swivel ring flange

Fig. 1 Measurements for spoolpiece fabrication and installation

two ends to be connected as well as their relative angles to each other in azimuth (plan view) and vertically (in elevation). The methods used to measure these parameters are called 'metrology'.

Metrology

TRANSPONDERS

This is the most commonly used system and involves the use of acoustic transponders. In this method a number of transponders are placed in a specific array on the seabed, usually by an ROV. The ROV, carrying its own transponder, is then positioned at the various points to be measured enabling the survey team onboard to take the necessary readings in order to fabricate a tailor-made spoolpiece.

TAUT WIRE SYSTEM

Another method uses taut wires and protractors. Fig. 2 shows a typical flange-mounted two-protractor system with tensioning winch. The wire is connected to a similar second unit called the 'anchor protractor' (without a winch facility) which is fixed to the end of the other pipe. After the two units have been secured to the pipe flanges the wire between them is tensioned up using the hand-operated winch. Once the correct tension is achieved the two swivelling protractors are locked securely in position with lock nuts. The diver can use tape to mark the cable where it emerges from the swivelling arm to record the length of wire deployed. The units are then taken to the surface where the angle and distance measurements can be carefully recorded.
From these measurements a spoolpiece can be constructed to exactly fit between the two flanges.

DUMMY SPOOL

A dummy spool is a telescopic length of pipe fitted with articulated flanges at each end. The two flanges are bolted in place and then all their joints (including the central joint between the booms) are locked into position. The dummy spool is then recovered to the surface and the measurements recorded by the engineer. The disadvantages of this method are that it is time-consuming, relies on having a dummy spool of the right size (flanges and length) and that the positions, and the angles may be disturbed during its recovery.

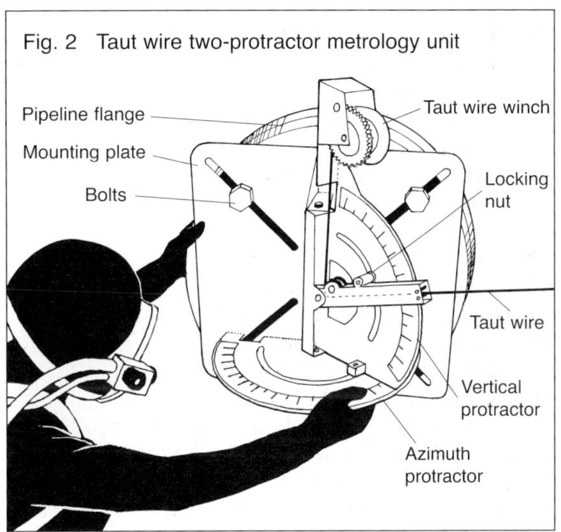
Pipeline flange
Mounting plate
Bolts
Taut wire winch
Locking nut
Taut wire
Vertical protractor
Azimuth protractor

Fig. 2 Taut wire two-protractor metrology unit

1. Flanged connections

Flanged pipeline connections are the most common method of pipeline connection used worldwide.

TYPES OF FLANGES

Flanges come in an assortment of types depending on the operational design requirements (see Fig. 3).

TYPES OF FLANGE FACINGS

The most commonly found flange facing offshore is the raised face ring joint facing (see Fig. 4c). This is because it is the best for high pressures and temperatures.

TYPES OF FLANGE BOLT (see Fig. 5)

Stud bolts are much more commonly used on flanges than machine bolts. Stud bolts have the advantage that they are more easily removed if corroded.

Fig. 3 Flanged pipeline connections

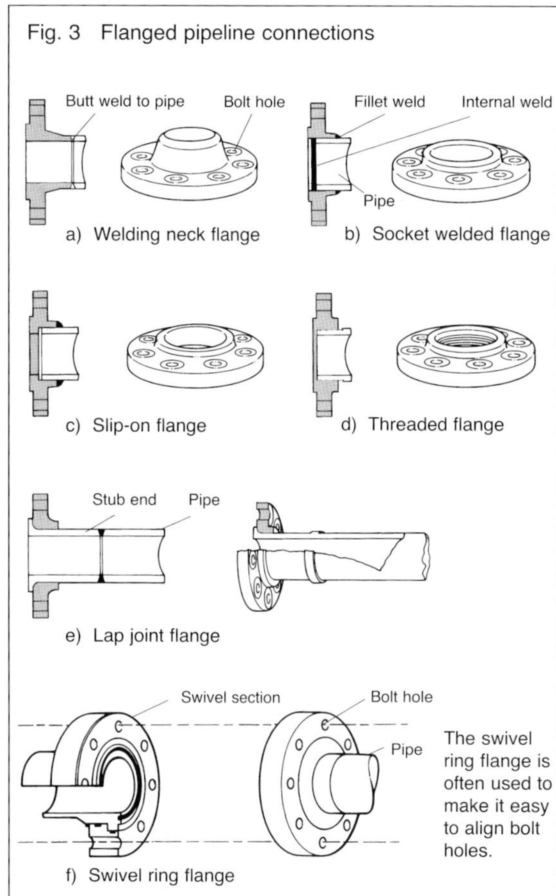
Butt weld to pipe
Bolt hole
Fillet weld
Internal weld
Pipe
a) Welding neck flange
b) Socket welded flange
c) Slip-on flange
d) Threaded flange
Stub end
Pipe
e) Lap joint flange
Swivel section
Bolt hole
Pipe
The swivel ring flange is often used to make it easy to align bolt holes.
f) Swivel ring flange

Fig. 4 Flange facings

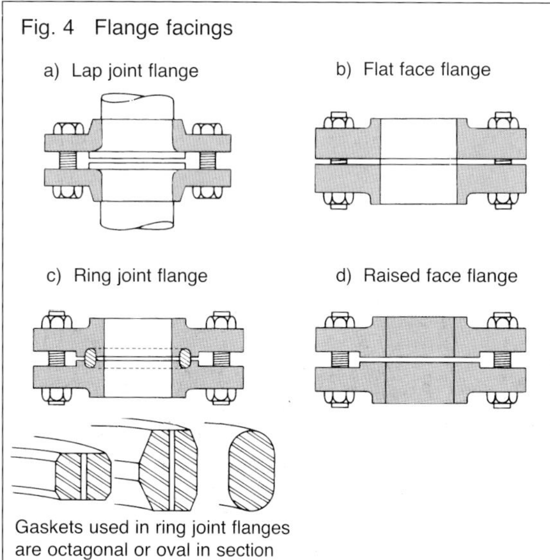
a) Lap joint flange
b) Flat face flange
c) Ring joint flange
d) Raised face flange
Gaskets used in ring joint flanges are octagonal or oval in section

Fig. 5 Flange bolts

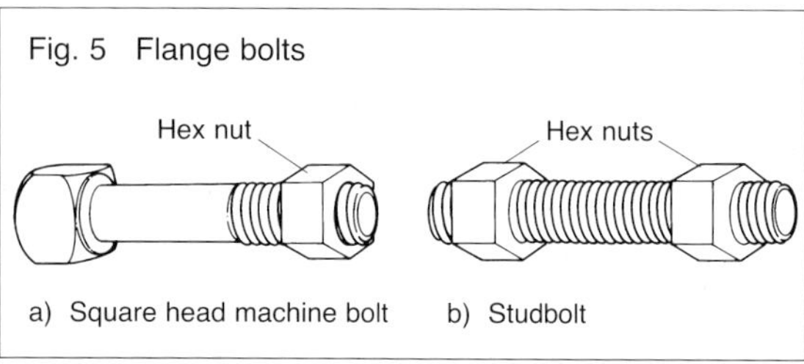
Hex nut
Hex nuts
a) Square head machine bolt
b) Studbolt

TYPES OF FLANGE GASKETS

Raised face flanges take ring gaskets and flat-faced flanges take full face gaskets. Gasket materials include compressed asbestos and spiral wound, asbestos-filled metal. The latter is particularly useful if the flange has to be repeatedly made and unmade such as in SPM hose changes. The gasket separates cleanly and may be re-useable.

Examples of gasket materials and their applications are given in Fig. 6.

Fig. 6 Gasket materials and applications

Gasket material	Application
Synthetic rubbers	Water, air.
Vegetable fibre	Oil.
Synthetic rubbers with cloth insert	Water, air.
Solid Teflon	Chemicals.
Compressed asbestos	Most applications.
Carbon steel (CS)	High pressure fluids.
Stainless steel (SS)	High pressure and/or corrosive fluids.
Spiral wound:	
SS/Teflon	Chemicals.
CS/Asbestos	Most applications.
SS/Asbestos	Corrosive fluids.
SS/Ceramic	Hot gases.

FLANGING OPERATIONS

The following example describes a procedure for carrying out a pipeline tie-in to a riser using flanged connections. A tie-in is the connecting of a pipeline to another pipeline or riser or well head. A spool-piece is used to close the gap between the riser and the as-laid pipeline. Spools usually have one right angled elbow to absorb any expansion or contraction in the pipeline.

The riser would either terminate vertically (see Fig. 1) or horizontally after a 90-degree elbow. It will be terminated with a fully bolted blind flange. Fitted on the flange is a caged/protected quarter-turn valve for pressure equalisation/checking. The newly laid pipeline is laid in a target box and fitted with either a lay-down head or a pig launcher/receiver. After the metrology has been completed, the spool piece fabricated and brought in, the lay-down head/launcher/catcher recovered, and the pipeline blanked, the divers will ensure that the as-laid pipeline and riser are flooded.

The greatest care must always be taken to protect the diver from the danger of differential pressures in pipes and spools.

The spool is lowered to the seabed by crane and landed as close as possible to the alignment position. Before the spool is moved by the divers both ends are secured, normally to the pipeline and the riser, but sometimes to dead-man-anchors (DMA). This is to ensure that when lift is applied the spool will not be carried to the surface in an uncontrolled manner. The metal blind flanges are removed from both ends of the spool and the riser after everything has been flooded. They are replaced with perforated wooden flange protectors tied loosely into position.

Lift bags are attached to the spool, ensuring that the rigging is of the correct type, the dump lines are in working order and the inverter lines are secured. The inverter line can be secured to the spool (so if primary rigging breaks, the lift bag will just invert and then come to rest close by). Alternatively it can be secured to a DMA. Once the spool has been correctly floated, it will be very easy to move. A single chain-pull is more than enough to bring even big spools into position. Spools of up to 12-inch diameter can usually be brought together by hand. Various tools are available to assist in final flange alignment (see 'Flange connection tools' below). Before the flange faces are brought together, the protectors are removed and a video survey of the flange faces undertaken.

Starting at the riser connection, bolts are usually installed from the 3 o'clock position down to 6 o'clock and round to the 9 o'clock position. They can be hand-drawn or lightly spannered up to leave enough room to lower the gasket/AX ring in. The gasket will then have to be inspected and the serial number recorded by the supervisor. After inserting dye sticks and inhibitor inside the pipe, the gasket is installed. The remainder of the bolts are installed and tightened up using spanners. The diver should check that the flange spacing is even at the four clock positions during the final closing. Finally the bolt tensioning procedure is carried out (see Bolt Tensioning Procedures below). When finished, the flange gap at the 4 clock positions should be re-checked. The other end of the spool can then be worked on. With the riser end now tied in, the divers will need to use much more effort to move the spool.

The as-laid pipeline has to be floated and the angle of presentation of the flange has to be adjusted. This is done by attaching liftbags at various points including at the 'Break Over Point'. This is the point at which the pipeline can be lifted and the end droop down rather than lift up (the topside engineer usually provides this information). Alternatively, pipe-handling frames may be used. These can be fitted with chain hoists or, for large pipes, they can be fitted with hydraulic rams. The adjacent flanges are brought to the same height, and level in elevation view. Using a correctly placed DMA, the spool can then be pulled into alignment (in plan view). The flanges can be brought together using a chain-pull and choked strops, or a chain-pull and lacing wire (tirfors can be used but chain-pulls are easier). Before the flange faces are brought fully together, the protectors are removed and a video done of the flange faces.

The stud bolts are then inserted. One of the flanges will be a swivel flange which can be rotated to allow the bolt holes to be aligned. Sometimes podger bars are required if the alignment is not spot on. If all the bolts cannot be put in, then the flange alignment is probably out in which case the alignment will need to be adjusted. When the lower half of the bolts are in, dye sticks are placed inside the pipe and this should be videoed. Then the installed gasket is videoed. The rest of the bolts are inserted, spannered up and finally tensioned up (see Bolt Tensioning Procedures below).

OPERATIONAL SAFETY – FLANGING

1. Before removing blind flanges, ensure the pressure has been equalised on both sides.
2. When operating the equalisation valves, stay well clear of the intakes.
3. Safe rigging and handling of the lift bags is essential (see Section 3.8b, Buoyant Lifting, p. 170).

FLANGE CONNECTION TOOLS

In order to achieve the high bolt tensions required, some sort of hydraulic tool is commonly used, such as impact wrenches, torque wrenches and bolt tensioners.

a) *Impact wrenches* (see Fig. 7). These are useful bolt-tensioning tools. They may be air or hydraulically-powered. They tend to be used for smaller nuts and lower torque as the diver has to provide the reaction force. The tool can weigh 3–20 kg (6–44 lb) with hydraulic pressures up to about 150 bars. The smaller tools can be held in one hand but the heavier, two-handed versions require special rigging arrangements for handling them. The number of impacts per minute varies from 180–1150, producing torques from 190–163 Nm (140–1200ft lb).

Fig. 7 Hydraulic Impact Wrenches

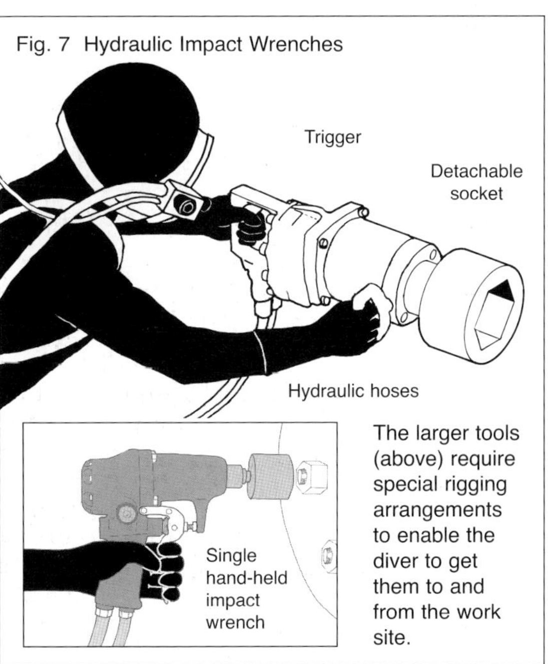
Trigger
Detachable socket
Hydraulic hoses
Single hand-held impact wrench
The larger tools (above) require special rigging arrangements to enable the diver to get them to and from the work site.

Extreme care should be taken when using impact wrenches as a poorly protected socket locking pin can cause serious hand injuries.

b) *Torque wrenches* (see Fig. 8) are usually hydraulically-powered with powers up to 350–450 bars. They provide a constant force on the nut which increases until the required bolt tension is reached. The wrenches usually have a range of heads to suit different sized nuts. A variety of reaction devices can be used to suit different flange configurations. The wrench sizes range from 3–36kg (6–80lb) in weight. The torque range can be from 203–150,000Nm (150–110,000ft lb). Special rigging arrangements may be necessary to deploy the heavier tools to a diver.

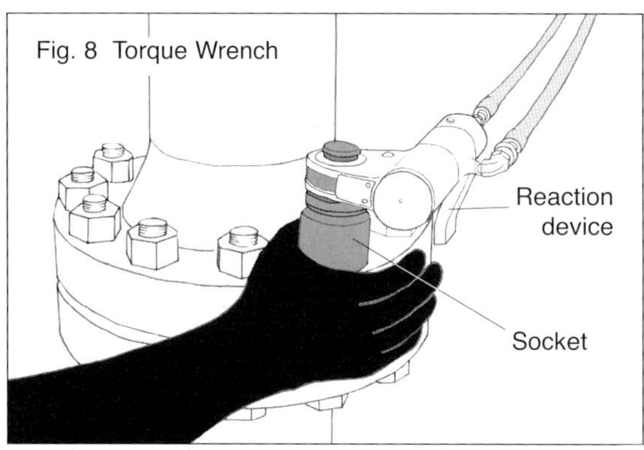
Reaction device
Socket
Fig. 8 Torque Wrench

c) *Bolt tensioners* (see Fig. 9) consist of a series of hydraulically-operated bolt stretchers which simultaneously stretch the bolts around a flange by exactly the same amount. When the bolts are held in elastic tension the nuts can be hand-tightened by the diver.
When the hydraulic pressure is released the bolts contract elastically leaving the required tension in the bolt.

BOLT TENSIONING PROCEDURES
This is an introduction to the procedures and special training is required before a diver can carry out this task.
There are several different types of hydraulic bolt tensioners available but all are designed to be connected up in series. After the surface supply hydraulic hose is connected to the last jack in line the hydraulic force is applied simultaneously to all the jacks in series. The hydraulic force pushes out the jack rams against the reaction nuts. This stretches the bolts which are then held in elastic tension. The nuts can then be hand-tightened by the diver by placing a small bar into the holes in the nut faces and turning a sixth of a rotation at a time. Each one-sixth rotation of the nut flats is counted and recorded by the supervisor. When the pressure is released the bolts contract elastically leaving the required tension in the bolt.

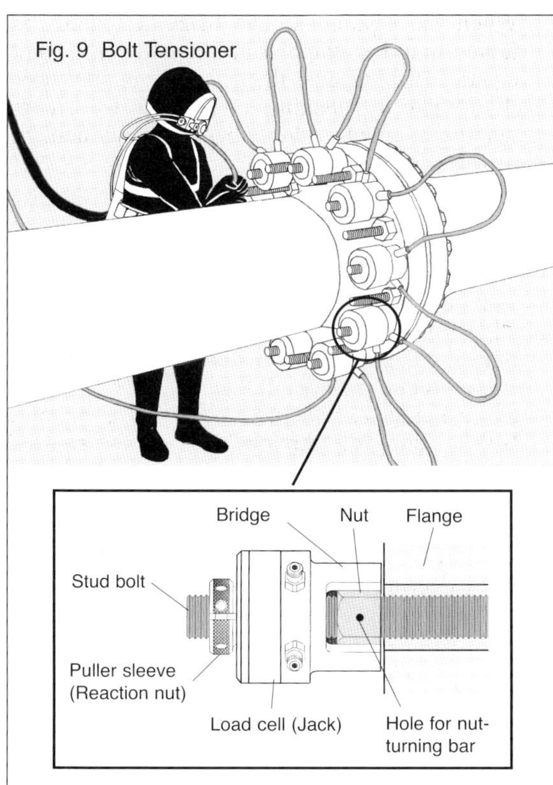
Bridge
Nut
Flange
Stud bolt
Puller sleeve (Reaction nut)
Load cell (Jack)
Hole for nut-turning bar
Fig. 9 Bolt Tensioner

Bolt tensioning can be done in two ways, either 50% (50/50) or 100%. The 50% method is illustrated in Fig. 9. Here only half the bolts (every other one) are tensioned.
Once the 'odds' are done (bolts 1, 3, 5, 7, 9, 11, etc) the jacks are repositioned on the 'evens' which are then tensioned up. When the 'evens' have been done, the 'odds' have to be re-tightened to complete the procedure. This method takes longer than the 100% procedure and is only used when the access to the flange is restricted and all the long bolt ends have to come out on the same side of the flange.
The preferred method is the 100% way, when the long ends of the bolts are staggered either side of the flange. This allows the diver to fit a jack on every bolt. The jacks are connected together by whips. This can be done by a series of cross-overs (1 to 2, 2 to 3 etc) when the whips cross the flange from one bolt to the next. Alternatively, the whips can follow the jacks around one side of the flange, cross over and complete the circuit on the other side.
The circuit is tested with a pressure of 1,000 psi. The diver only has to check the last jack in the line. If that is 'tight' then all the ones before it must also be tight. Full pressure is then applied and the nuts tightened up. The pressure is then released. Usually a second pressurisation is given to double check the nuts are fully tightened. If any nuts needed further tightening then the repressurisation cycle is repeated once more.

When the equipment has been derigged, the flange may be wrapped in cling film and duct taped. This means that if the gasket fails fluorescent dye leaking out through the flange will be trapped under the cling film and be readily visible to divers or an ROV.

d) Flange alignment tool

Flanges must be perfectly aligned before the stud bolts can be inserted. A variety of techniques are available to assist with the alignment. One example is illustrated in Fig. 10. In this example the diver fits the alignment tool into a bolt hole on one flange and stabilizes the tool using the drop leg at at the back of the tool. By ratcheting the threaded bolt at the front of the tool (which sits on the edge of the other flange) the diver uses the tool to push one flange downwards while simultaneously pulling the other upwards until the flanges are perfectly aligned, ready to be bolted together.

Fig. 10 Flange alignment tool

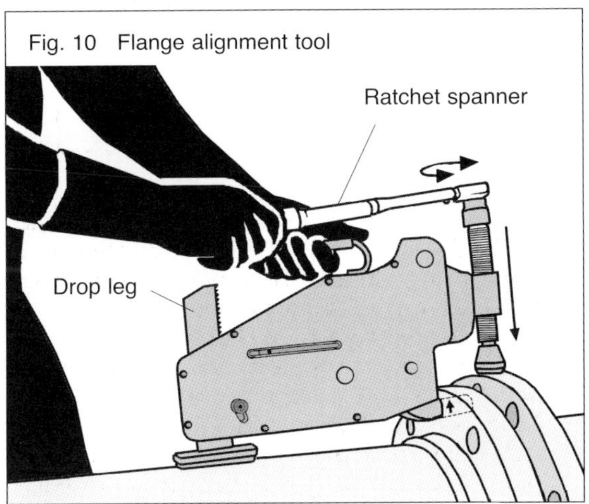
Ratchet spanner
Drop leg

e) Flange puller

When large pipes need to be flanged together they may need to be pulled together before the stud bolts can be introduced. When a pipe spool is first lowered to the sea bed the crane is used to position the spool as close as possible to its final position.

If the adjacent flanges are a long way apart and a lever chain hoist or tirfor cannot be used, hydraulic flange pullers can be used to bring them together (see Figs. 11 and 12). One or both pipes may be supported by lift bags or pipe handling frames to assist in the operation. Flange pullers are not normally needed for small diameter pipes. They are usually used for 24 to 48-inch diameter pipes where chain hoists or tirfors may be inadequate.

Flange pullers are normally installed in pairs (see Fig. 11) when flanges are between 1–2m (3–6ft) apart. The diver operates the hydraulic control handles on each puller alternately as necessary to achieve alignment.

Fig. 11 Diver operating flange pullers to align pipes

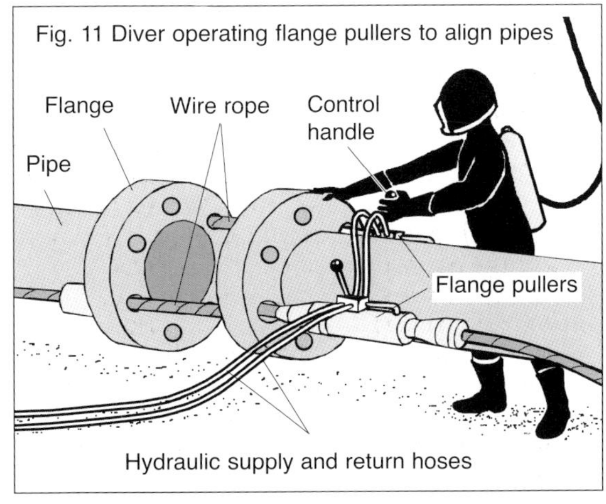
Flange
Wire rope
Control handle
Pipe
Flange pullers
Hydraulic supply and return hoses

Fig. 12 Wire rope flange puller

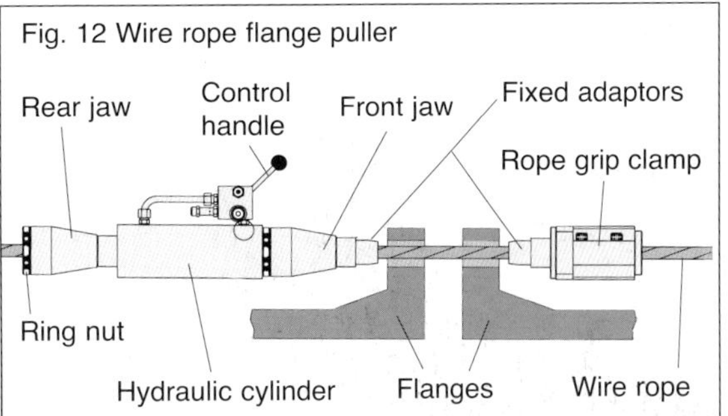
Rear jaw
Control handle
Front jaw
Fixed adaptors
Rope grip clamp
Ring nut
Hydraulic cylinder
Flanges
Wire rope

High tensile low rotation wire rope is passed through the assembly. On the forward stroke the rear jaw grips the rope pulling it through the cylinder. On the return stroke the rear jaws are released and the front jaws are activated preventing the rope from being pulled back through the cylinder. The loose end of the rope can be attached directly to the object being pulled or a rope grip clamp can be used (as shown).

Two types of puller are available: wire rope puller (see Fig. 12) and bar puller. The most commonly used is the wire rope system.

f) Removal of tensioned bolts

Tensioned bolts may be removed in one of five ways:

1. Manually, using a flogging spanner and a large hammer.
2. With a hydraulic nut splitter. This requires a single hydraulic downline (as in tensioning equipment). This method is mostly used when the nut and bolt are corroded.
3. With a bolt-tensioning jack. Normally only one is used at a time but with connecting whips more can be used. The jack is mounted on the bolt with the reaction nut as usual, but with 1cm (1/2 in) of slack (or a jack showing about 1cm of travel on its ram). Hydraulic pressure is then applied to the jack, stretching the bolt. The diver can then slacken the nut back. When the hydraulic pressure is released the residual tension in the jack will

force the ram into the jack leaving the bolt loose. Failure to leave slack in the jack will result in the diver not being able to remove the jack at the end of the procedure.

4. By ultrathermic cutting. This requires a skilful burner and often results in a damaged flange.
5. Manually, using mechanical cutting, saws and grinders.

g) *Flange splitter*
When a section of pipe needs to be removed it can be difficult to break open a flanged joint. Several types of tools are available to achieve this. Care must be taken to avoid damaging the flange faces and this will affect the choice of tool. An example is shown in Fig. 13.

Fig. 13 Flange splitter

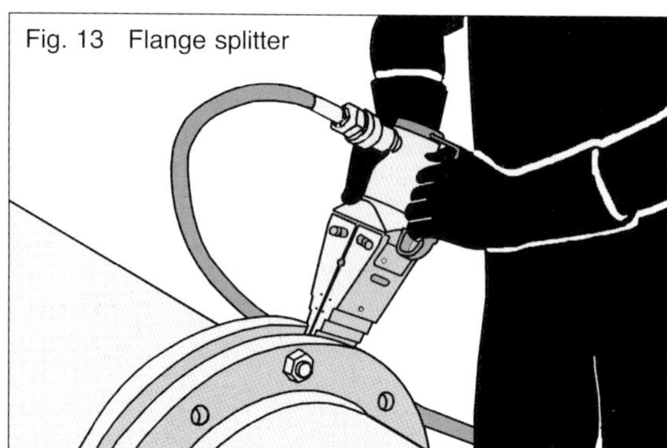

2. Hyperbaric welded connections

Hyperbaric welding carried out inside a dry habitat is sometimes used offshore. The welds can be of the highest quality and the results, therefore, can have the greatest reliability.
There is a considerable amount of diving involved in the preparation for hyperbaric welding on a pipe. The following procedure is a rough generalisation of a pipeline riser tie-in aimed at providing some idea of the diving tasks involved.

1. After the pipcline has been set down with its lay-down head in the target area, divers may be needed to remove the constant tension cable.
2. Accurate measurements can then be made between the riser flange and the pipe to determine the final dimensions of the tie-in spool-piece (or pieces). Depending on the distances involved, these measurements can be produced using either a template, a taut wire system or an acoustic transponder (see Metrology, page 21).
3. The spool is fabricated to the required size and configuration. It is lowered to the seabed and manoeuvred into position using surface cranes or davits and diver-operated tirfors (or equivalent).
4. At this stage the spoolpiece may need to be flooded, if it was sent down sealed and dry. Diver-operated valves are provided for this purpose.
5. The riser-to-spool flange is then connected, sometimes only loosely to allow a small swivelling capability on a swivel ring flange.
6. The ends of the pipe are then carefully cut to allow them to be brought into line ready for the arrival of the alignment frame.
7. Oxy-arc cutting and some prior seabed excavation by water jetting may be required to provide access.
8. Various handling systems can be used to manoeuvre the pipe into position including:
   - 'H' frames: Static and walking-type.
   - Subsea cranes.
   - Tirfors and dead man anchors.
   - Surface cranes and/or davits.
   - Air bags.
9. Once in line, guide wires are attached to the pipes to guide the descending pipeline alignment frame and welding habitat down over the ends of the pipes.
10. The alignment frame is lowered to the seabed (see Fig. 14). A combination of CCTV from ROVs and direct diver supervision can be used for the lowering operation.

Fig. 14 Installation of habitat and alignment frame

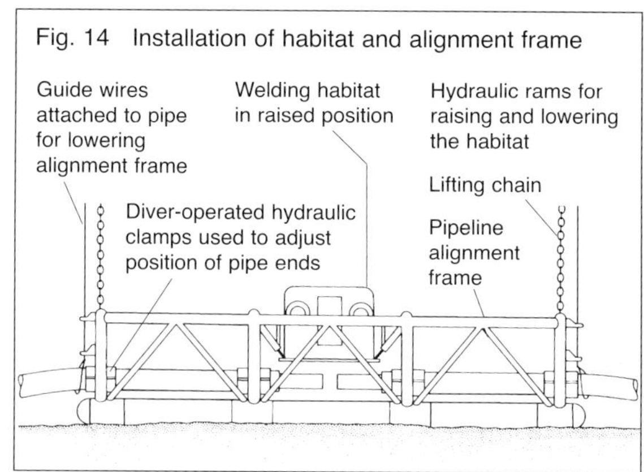
Guide wires attached to pipe for lowering alignment frame
Welding habitat in raised position
Hydraulic rams for raising and lowering the habitat
Lifting chain
Diver-operated hydraulic clamps used to adjust position of pipe ends
Pipeline alignment frame

11. Divers operate the hydraulic pipeline clamps to bring the pipe ends into a suitable position to allow the lowering of the habitat.
12. The habitat is lowered into position. In smaller systems the habitat may be separate from the main alignment frame. The access to the habitat can also vary between companies. The bell may mate directly with the habitat for a 'dry transfer' or the welder/divers may have to carry out a'wet transfer' by locking out of the bell, swimming across to the habitat and locking into it (see Fig. 15).
13. Once the habitat is positioned over the pipe ends the diver installs the door seals (see Fig. 16).
14. Stopper pigs are placed inside the pipe ends and inflated to seal off the inside from the habitat (see Fig. 17).
15. With the door and pipe seals made good, the habitat can be dewatered by blowing down with the appropriate gas mix. The actual gases used

Fig. 15 Alignment frame and transfer bell

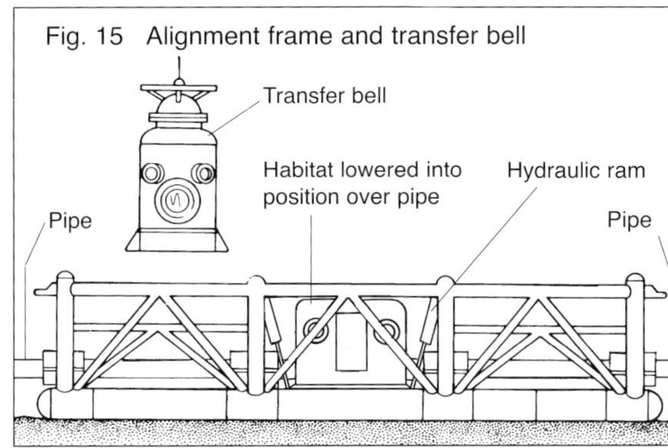
Transfer bell
Habitat lowered into position over pipe
Hydraulic ram
Pipe
Pipe

Fig. 16 Typical door seal inside a hyperbaric welding habitat

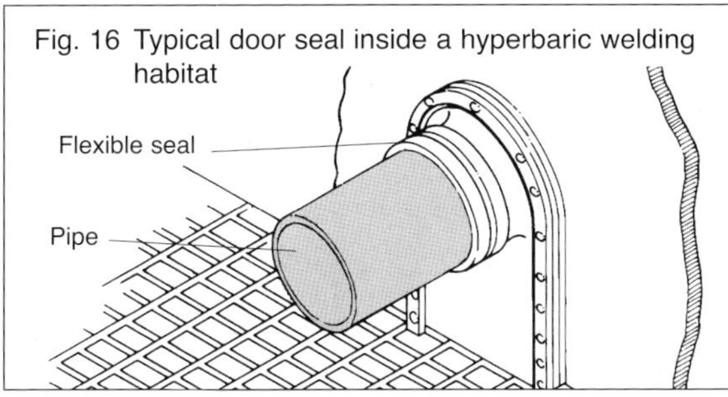
Flexible seal
Pipe

Fig. 17 Inserting a stopper pig into the pipeline in preparation for hyperbaric welding

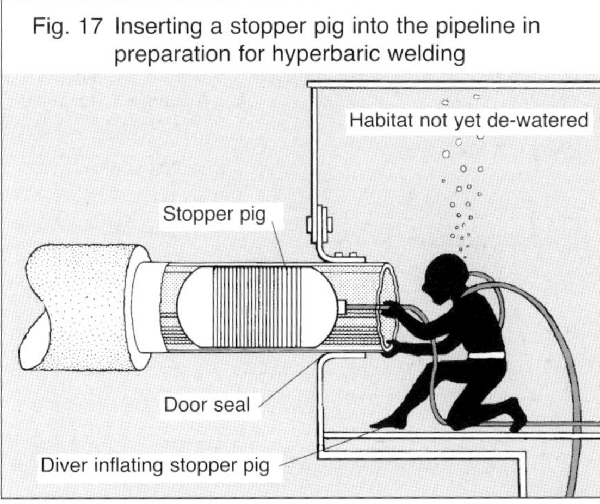
Habitat not yet de-watered
Stopper pig
Door seal
Diver inflating stopper pig

for this can vary between diving companies from breathable to unbreathable. In the latter case the welders have to wear special masks while inside the habitat.

16. The next phase consists of welding preparation and the specialised welding procedure itself, including the installation of a pup piece to close the gap (see Fig. 18).
17. The pipe ends are bevelled, demagnetised, pre-heated and MMA, MIG or TIG welded.
18. Following the welding there is a radiographic examination to check the integrity of the pipe connection.
19. Once the weld is confirmed as meeting the design specification the exposed pipe metal is wrapped with bitumen tape.
20. The habitat is then flooded and recovered by reversal of the installation procedure.

Fig. 18 Installation of a pup piece
a) Sealing pipeline in preparation for positioning pup piece
b) Aligning pup piece
c) Welding pup piece in position

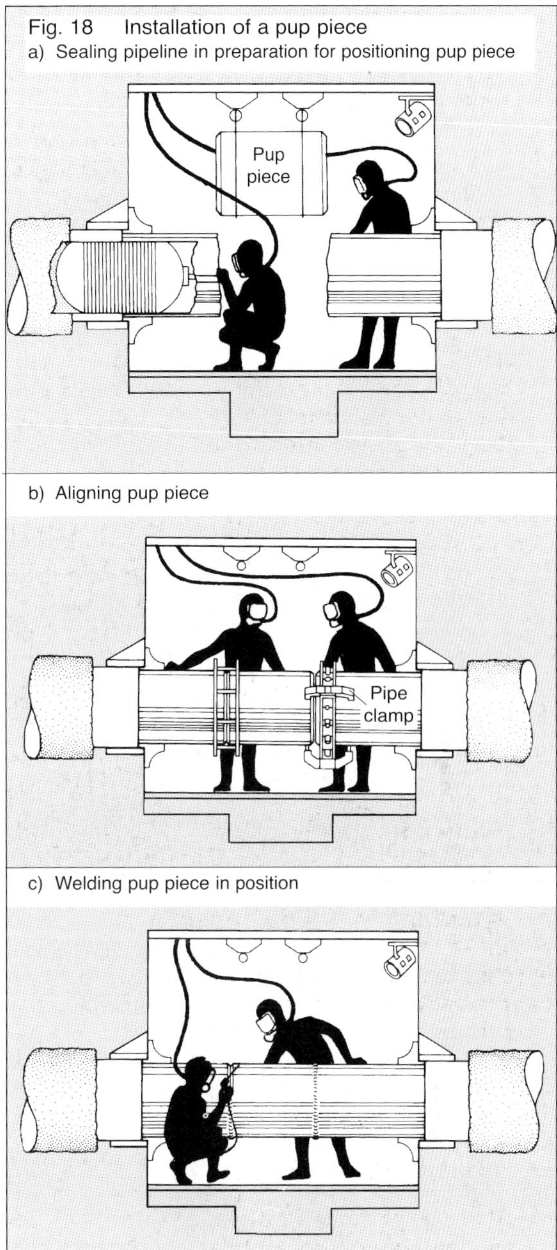
Pup piece
Pipe clamp

3. Mechanical Connections

'FLEXIFORGE' PIPELINE CONNECTOR

The Flexiforge Connector is a means of attaching a flange to the end of a pipe (see Figs. 19 and 20).

It incorporates the principle of cold forging the pipe into the flange body.

The diver places the Flexiforge connector on the end of a pipe and inserts into it a hydraulically actuated forging tool (see Fig. 21). This rotates and expands until its rollers mould the pipewall into a plastic state. As the rollers continue to expand the pipeline is forged into complete contact with the specially designed grooves of the end connector.

The result is that the pipe has been stressed into the plastic range but the connector has been stressed only into the elastic range. The residual

stresses make the end connector function like a steel rubber band.
The forging process is controlled from the surface and takes about one minute per inch diameter of the pipe. On completion, the diver checks the pressure integrity of the seal via an annulus test port.

CAMERON PIPELINE CONNECTOR
The Cameron connector is a mechanical connector (see Figs. 22 and 23). The system uses hydraulic actuators to minimise the physical effort of the diver on the seabed. They are easy to operate and provide several reference points for the diver to assure the alignment and position of the hub before connection and pressure testing begins. In addition, the actuator performs the following functions:

- Leads the connection assembly down the guide-wires to the tie-in base on the seabed.
- Moves the hubs together.
- Locks the collet fingers around the two hubs and energises the AX metal seal ring.
- Disconnects and supports tie-in assembly if retrieval of equipment is required.

1. The hydraulically-operated actuators are positioned over the collet connectors at each end of the tie-in assembly and attached to it by means of resealable shoes and swing clamps.
2. Guidewires are passed through the guide funnels on the actuators, from the guide pins on the seabed to the surface support vessel. Motion compensators on the surface are used to keep these lines tight throughout the operation.
3. The actuators and tie-in assembly are lowered down the guidewires to a close alignment with the hubs of the pipeline on the seabed.
4. When they have landed on the support base and alignment is verified, a control valve in the actuator is operated by a diver (or by remote control) and a hydraulic mechanism moves the mating hubs together.

Fig. 19 Flexiforge cold forging tool

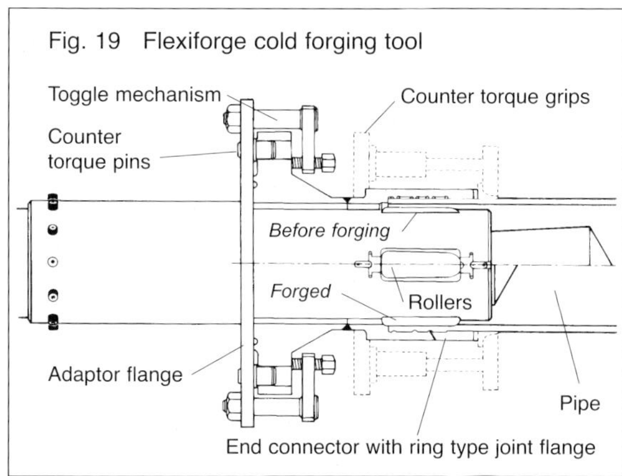
Toggle mechanism
Counter torque grips
Counter torque pins
Before forging
Forged
Rollers
Adaptor flange
Pipe
End connector with ring type joint flange

5. The diver operates a second lever which actuates another hydraulic piston set to move a metal sleeve forward in order to lock the collet fingers around the mating hubs and load the metal seal. The pipeline hubs are now face-to-face.
6. Once a pressure test on the AX seal has been carried out, the actuator is released from the collet connector and retrieved to the surface.

MORGRIP CONNECTOR
Morgrip connectors comprise a centre section housing and one or more gripping segments on

Fig. 22 Cameron collet connector

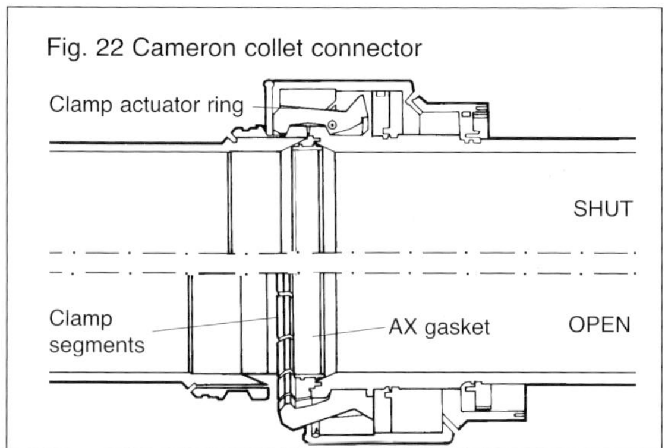
Clamp actuator ring
SHUT
Clamp segments
AX gasket
OPEN

Fig. 23 Cameron in-line riser connection

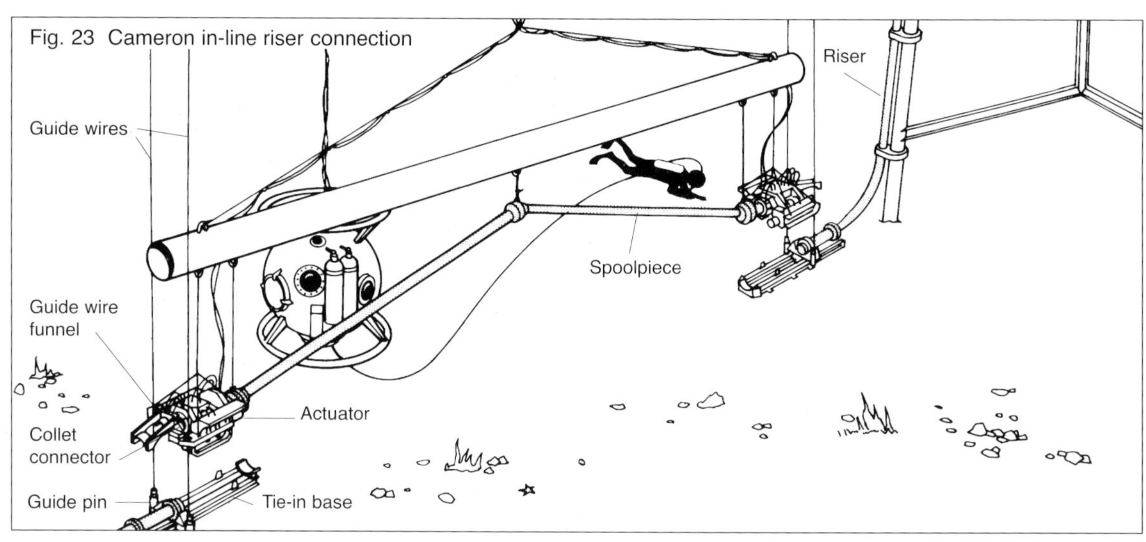
Riser
Guide wires
Spoolpiece
Guide wire funnel
Actuator
Collet connector
Guide pin
Tie-in base

Fig. 20 Flexiforge pipe end connector

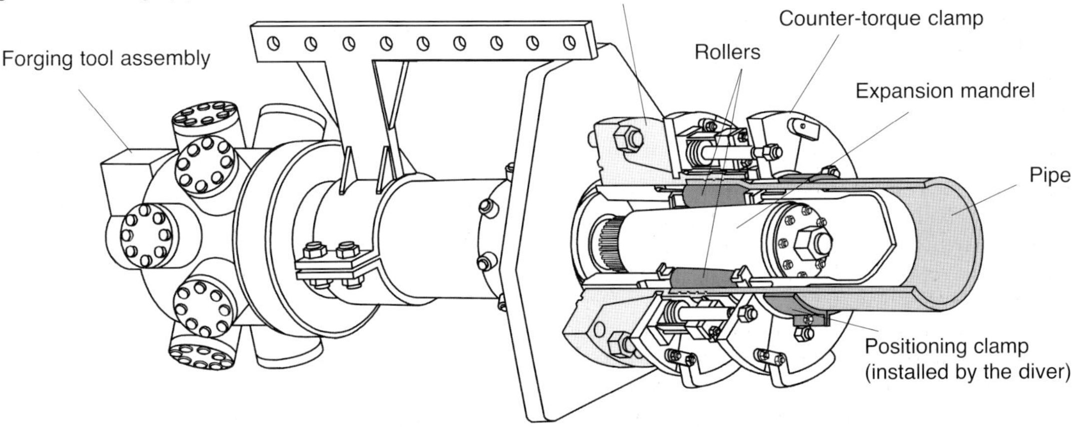

Flexiforge Connector
Counter-torque clamp
Forging tool assembly
Rollers
Expansion mandrel
Pipe
Positioning clamp (installed by the diver)

The forging tool and and Flexiforge connector are bolted together for easy installation by the diver. The connector fits over the outside of the pipe end and the end of the forging tool stabs into the end of the pipe. The counter-torque clamp keeps the connector from rotating during installation. After forging is complete the diver removes the three bolts from the connector flange and the forging tool is recovered to the surface.

Fig. 21 Installing the Flexiforge connector

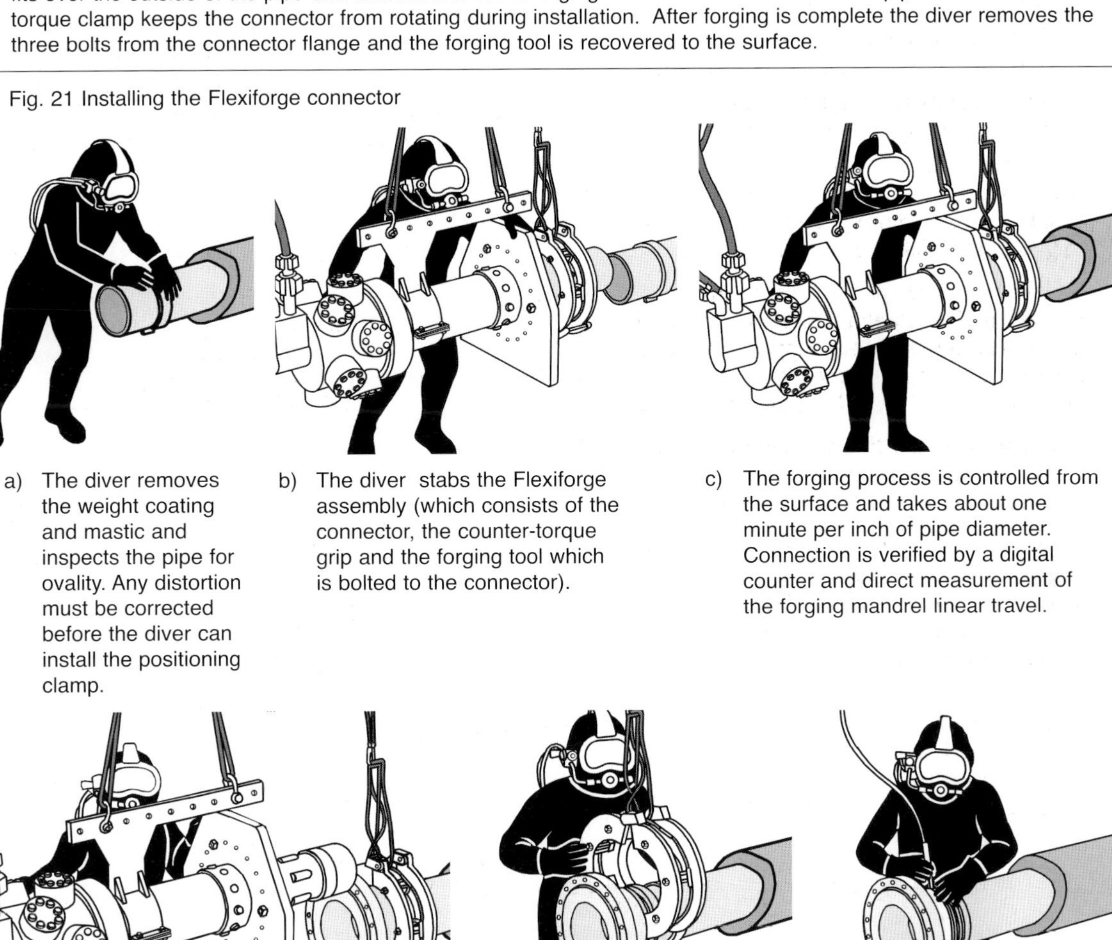

a) The diver removes the weight coating and mastic and inspects the pipe for ovality. Any distortion must be corrected before the diver can install the positioning clamp.

b) The diver stabs the Flexiforge assembly (which consists of the connector, the counter-torque grip and the forging tool which is bolted to the connector).

c) The forging process is controlled from the surface and takes about one minute per inch of pipe diameter. Connection is verified by a digital counter and direct measurement of the forging mandrel linear travel.

d) The diver unbolts the forging tool from the connector and the tool is recovered to the surface.

e) The diver releases the counter-torque clamp which is retrieved to the surface and then recovers the position clamp.

f) The diver tests the metal-to-metal seal using the annulus test port.

either side of the centre section. (The number of gripping segments used depends on the pressure rating of the connector). Each gripping section houses a series of spring-loaded ball bearings which are positioned around the inside of the segment (see Fig. 24).

Before installing the connector, both ends of pipe must be cleaned of all surface coatings. The required number of gripping segments are then slid over the end of each pipe. A centre section housing is then placed over the pipe joint, between the gripping segments. Tightening the stud bolts draws all the segments together causing the ball bearings to roll. At the same time, the seals are compressed swaging the ball bearings into the surface of the pipe. Because the ball bearings move independently of each other they are capable of compensating for small imperfections in the pipe's surface and diameter, thereby providing a sound mechanical seal.

Fig. 24 Morgrip connector

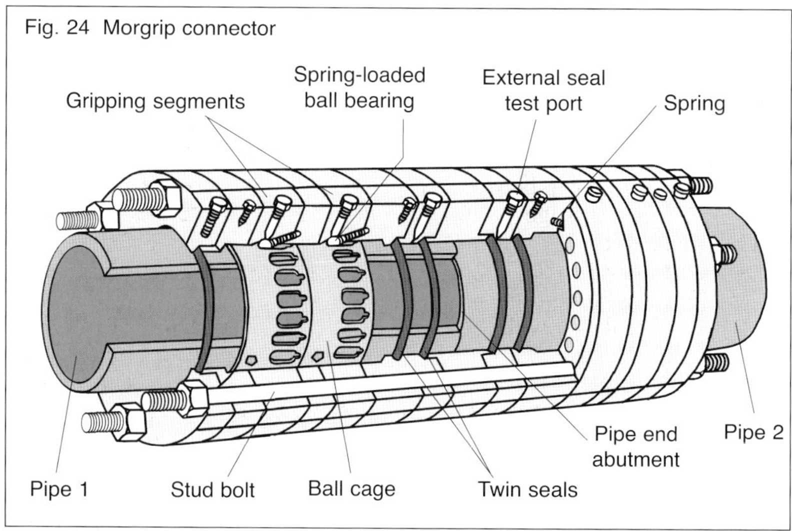
Gripping segments
Spring-loaded ball bearing
External seal test port
Spring
Pipe end abutment
Pipe 2
Pipe 1
Stud bolt
Ball cage
Twin seals

SMART FLANGE CONNECTOR

Smart Flange connectors (see Fig. 25) are available in all sizes from 1½" to 48". A seal is created by tensioning the stud bolts which activates a piston which, in turn, compresses an elastomeric seal onto the pipe.

Before installation the damaged part of the pipe is cut and removed. The end where the Smart Flange is to be installed must be cut clean, without any burrs. The diver may also bevel the end of the pipe to help the Smart Flange slide easily onto the pipe.

The area of the pipe which is to be fitted with the connector must be cleaned to bare metal (including removal of anti-corrosive material or paint. The diameter and ovality of the pipe should then be measured to ensure compatibility with the flange specifications.

Before fitting the Smart Flange, excess grease, dirt and debris should be removed from inside the flange, especially around the seals.

The flange is then fitted onto the pipe ensuring that the pipeline rests against the top lip of the piston. The groove for the ring type joint is cleaned and the RTJ inserted, adding a small amount of adhesive if necessary.

When the spool section is lowered, the diver aligns the bolt holes using two drift (line-up) pins or two oversized-diameter bolts inserted in the 3 and 9 o'clock positions. When all the other bolts are inserted in place, the drift pins (or oversized bolts) are replaced with the correct-sized bolts. The bolt

Fig. 25 Smart Flange connector

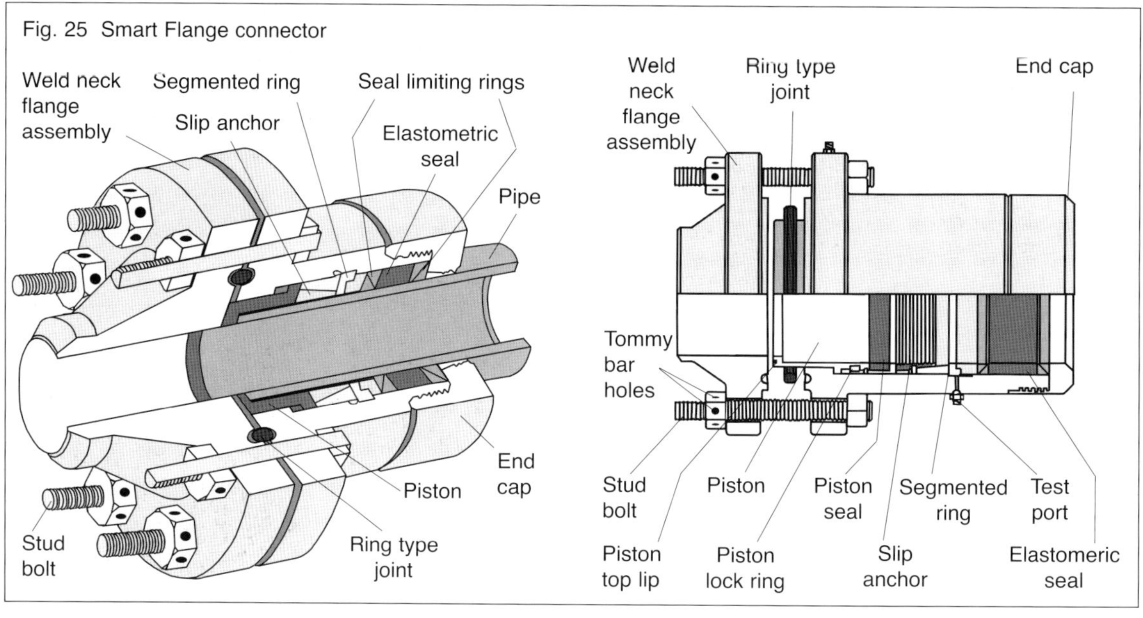
Weld neck flange assembly
Segmented ring
Slip anchor
Seal limiting rings
Elastomeric seal
Pipe
End cap
Piston
Ring type joint
Stud bolt
Weld neck flange assembly
Ring type joint
End cap
Tommy bar holes
Stud bolt
Piston
Piston seal
Segmented ring
Test port
Piston top lip
Piston lock ring
Slip anchor
Elastomeric seal

threads and nut faces are lubricated, and finger-tightened. The bolt-tensioner is activated until the gap between the mating flanges complies with the manufacturer's recommendations (the gap is measured using a feeler gauge). Sometimes it may be necessary to over-stress the bolts in order to achieve the correct gap between the flanges.

When the Smart Flange is correctly installed the diver fits an appropriate hose connector and hose to the test port to enable the integrity of the seal to be tested. On completion the hose and fitting are removed and replaced with a suitable plug.

GRIP AND SEAL MECHANICAL COUPLING

The 'Gripper' mechanical coupling provides a metal-to-metal sealed flowline connection (see Fig. 26). The grip and seal is installed by stud tensioning by the diver.

HYDROBALL/HYDROCOUPLE CONNECTORS

The external set HydroBall/HydroCouple connector is sealed at the pipe ends and at the ball-and-socket connection (see Fig. 27).

Fig. 26 Gripper connection

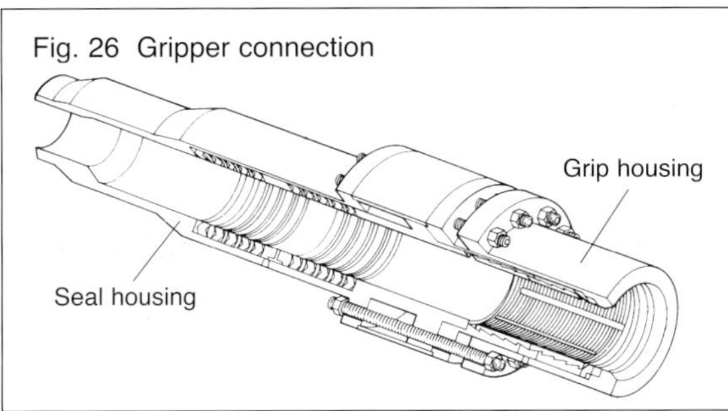
Grip housing
Seal housing

Fig. 27 HydroCouple and HydroBall connectors

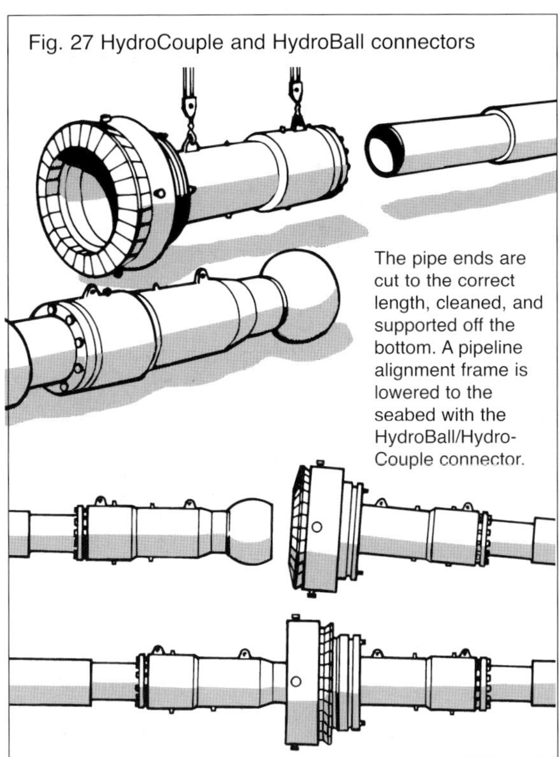
The pipe ends are cut to the correct length, cleaned, and supported off the bottom. A pipeline alignment frame is lowered to the seabed with the HydroBall/Hydro-Couple connector.

The HydroCouple connector is set and sealed onto the pipe end from the surface. The pressure of the fluid forces bi-directional slips against the inner and outer diameters of the connector and the pipe ensuring a positive and permanent connection. That same pressure seats packers to seal the space between the connector and the pipe.

The ball-and-socket portion of the connector uses a mechanical setting procedure. The ball half is moved into the socket and locked in place with lugs. Seals are then set around the machined surface of the ball to complete the connection.

Every seal is then tested through the use of ports and the pipeline can then be put on stream. The completed connection maintains full pipeline diameter so that pigs and spheres can pass through easily.

4. Weldball connector (see Fig. 28)

The Weldball connector is a combination 'welded' and 'mechanical' connector. It utilises sleeved ball and socket halves to allow welded pipeline connections at up to 10° misalignment and 30cm (12in) or one pipe diameter of end gap. Under special circumstances these design parameters can be exceeded.

The connection is made using an underwater welding procedure that differs from other underwater welding in that the welder works in the wet but welds in the dry through the bottom of a transparent chamber called a Hydrobox. The 'box' may be made in virtually any shape, as required for a particular job.

Fig. 28 Weldball connector

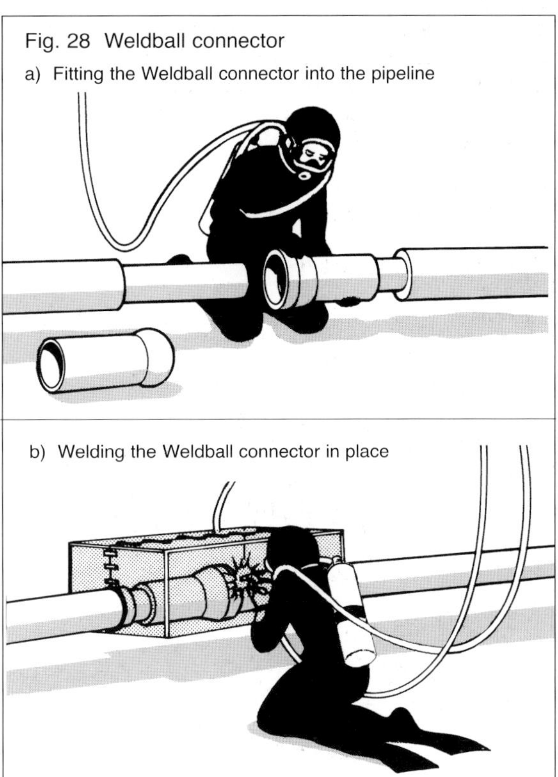
a) Fitting the Weldball connector into the pipeline
b) Welding the Weldball connector in place

In use it is sealed around the weld area and the water is evacuated from it with an inert gas. The diver is then able to perform standard metal inert gas welding in the dry, holding the gun inside the box.
A riser-to-pipeline connection for example would be carried out as follows: The ball half of the connector is welded onto the riser before it is put in place. Underwater welders then place the socket on the pipeline end, fit it to the ball half and fillet weld it into place in the dry area inside the Hydrobox.

Pigs and Pigging

A 'pig' is a device designed to fit snugly inside a pipeline (see Fig. 29). Pigs carry out a variety of tasks such as cleaning, gauging and proving, separating products, inspecting and recording pipeline interiors, and plugging.
Pigs are so-called because of the squealing sound the first pigs used to make when in operation.
The diver may be involved in pigging operations either opening or shutting pipe valves during flooding or dewatering a section of the pipe, or in tracking and locating a pig.

PLUGGING, ISOLATION OR STOPPING PIGS
These are highly specialised pigs used to isolate a section of pipe, such as for cutting out a damaged or corroded length.
Typically the pig is pumped along the pipe at between 1–3m/sec. The pig is stopped at a predetermined point along the pipe by an electronic or acoustic signal. This could involve a special antenna system previously placed on or alongside the pipe at the desired stop location. Once at the required location, signals are sent to the pig to anchor itself and make a pressure-tight seal against the pipe wall. These pigs may be left at their locations for several months while the maintenance work is carried out on the isolated pipe length.
When the work is complete, signals can be sent to the pig to make it release its grip. Then it can be

Fig. 29 Examples of commonly used pigs

Sphere

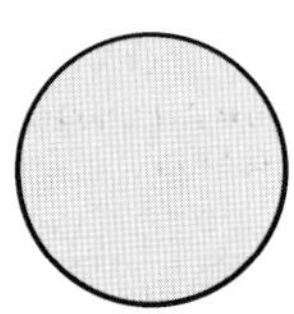

For sealing and occasionally for removing solids. It is normally filled with water/glycol and can be inflated to the optimum pipeline diameter. It can negotiate 'zero radius bends' and roll freely making it ideal for complex pipeline configurations.

Cleaning Pig

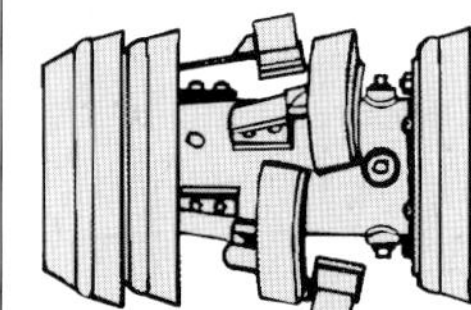

For use in pre-commissioning and on-stream cleaning of oil, refined product and gas pipelines. Carbon or stainless steel twin brushes.

Wirebrush Pig

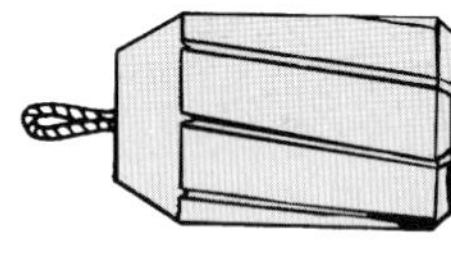

For cleaning and displacing dry sediment. Heavy duty steel wire brush strips are bonded helically to a polyether-based urethane body.

Separating Pig

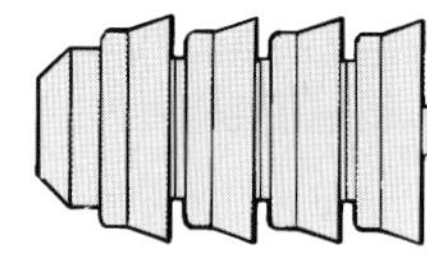

For use as a product interface or for the evacuation of liquids. Replaceable polyurethane cups are mounted on a tubular steel body.

Soft foam Pig

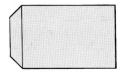

For expelling liquid residue, swabbing and drying. It is a polyether-based methane body with a polyurethane elastomer skin.

Gauging Pig

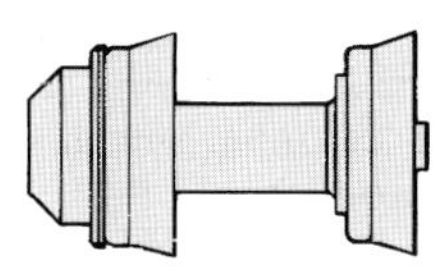

For use in pre-commissioning of pipelines and to prove that the inside of the pipe is circular without excessive weld penetration or debris. Two polyurethane driving cups around a steel body.

Scraper Pig

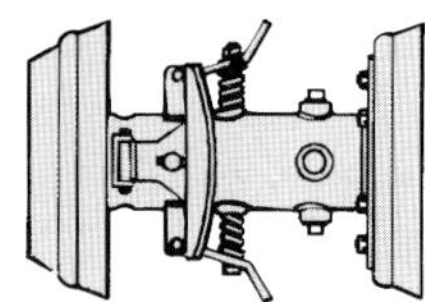

For the removal of hard scale, corrosion and wax deposits. A series of hardened face, profiled scraper blades are mounted on spring-loaded pivot arms around the body.

Mandrel Pig

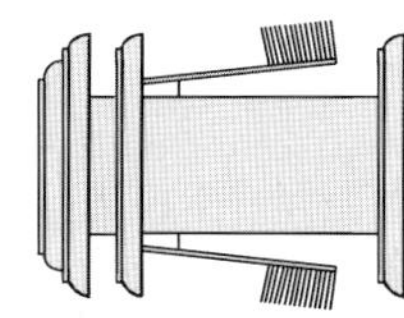

For cleaning. Made from several components which can be reconfigured as required. For hard deposits, wire brushes or scraper blades may be used; elastomer 'plough' blades are used for soft materials.

Inspection Pig

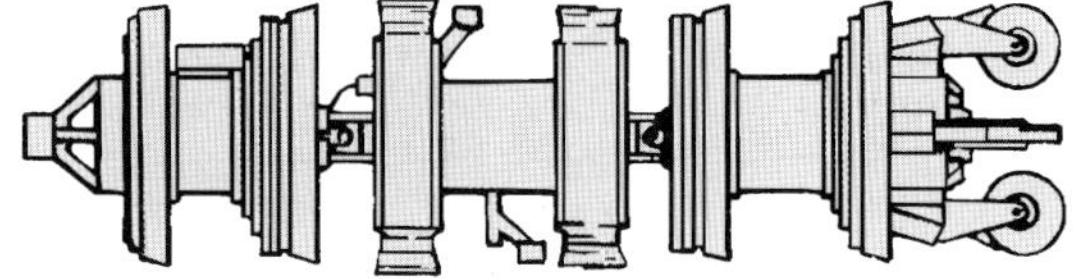

For the inspection of internal corrosion, external inspection and cathodic protection inspection. It consists of a drive section in the forward part, a combined magnetiser/transducer in the centre and electronic amplifiers and recorders in the rear.

Fig. 30 Pig Launcher/Start-up Head

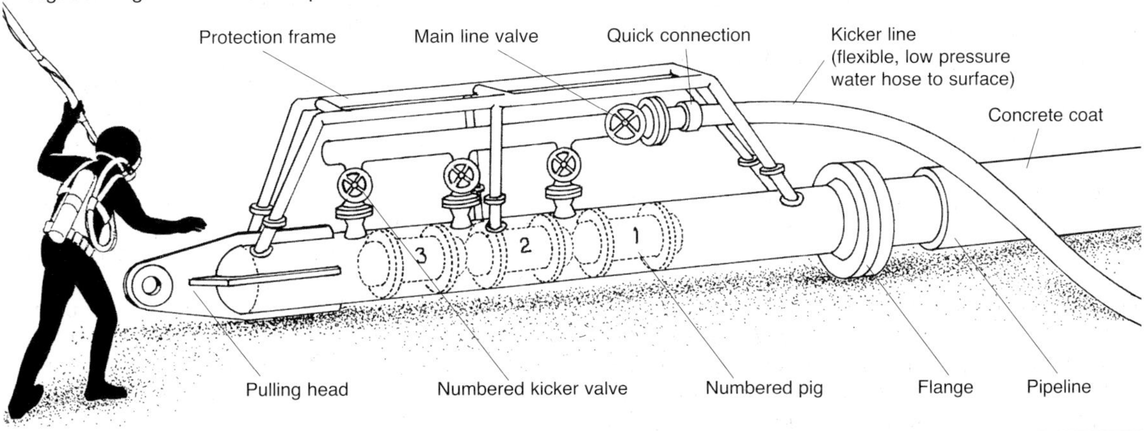

Protection frame
Main line valve
Quick connection
Kicker line (flexible, low pressure water hose to surface)
Concrete coat
Pulling head
Numbered kicker valve
Numbered pig
Flange
Pipeline

pumped back up the pipe and the pipe recommissioned.

PIG TRAPS AND PIGGING STATIONS
Pig traps are used for inserting pigs into a pipeline, then launching, receiving and finally removing them from the pipeline.
Often during construction, and sometimes for maintenance and inspection purposes, temporary traps and 'pig catchers' may be installed. These may be anything from simple spool pieces with branch connections or vents fabricated on site, to complex portable units such as laydown heads which may be designed to launch multiple pigs (Fig. 30).
All pigging operations will be special situations using specially designed systems and procedures.
Diver tasks include opening and closing valves (eg the kicker valve and main line valve) and monitoring a pig signaller to check for the passage of a pig.

PIG SPEED
Pigs must run at their optimum performance speed which is preset by the manufacturers. Speeds range from 1 to 10 mph (0.5 to 4m/sec) although many gauging pigs can perform at much higher velocities. Utility pigs, however, must run at the same velocity as the pipeline product.
For routine, conventional use in on-stream pipelines, pigs generally operate at 2–10mph (1–5m/sec) in liquid pipelines and 5–15mph (2–7m/sec) in gas pipelines.
During construction or commissioning, pig speeds will vary according to the maker's recommendations.

Pipeline Bends and Lateral Connections

Pipeline bends and branches can present a problem for pigs. Whether or not a pig can travel around a bend depends on the type of the pig and the sharpness of the bend.
Bends are commonly seen at the lower ends of risers, near subsea structures and in expansion spool pieces. A pipeline bend is described by the radius of curvature of its centre line relative to the nominal pipe diameter (Fig. 31). The smallest is a one-diameter bend ('D') and is known as a short radius elbow. Other common sizes are 1½D, 3D and 5D.
Pigs may have to pass through a lateral pipeline connection or even stop at a connection in order to isolate a section of the pipe. A lateral pipeline connection describes any pipeline connection that is not at 90°).

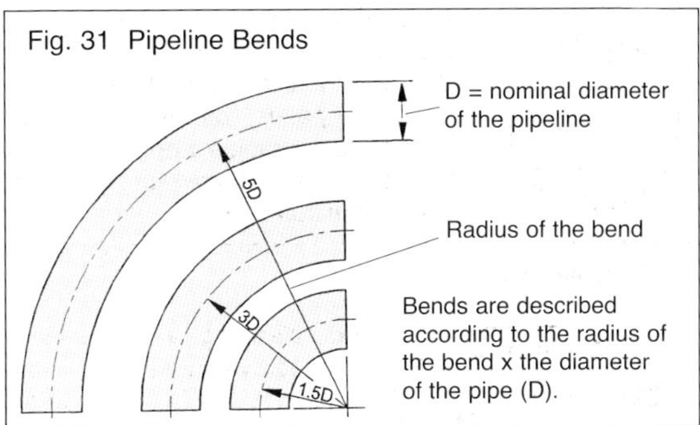
D = nominal diameter of the pipeline
5D
3D
1.5D
Radius of the bend
Bends are described according to the radius of the bend x the diameter of the pipe (D).
Fig. 31 Pipeline Bends

Pipeline Valves

The most common types of valves divers are likely to meet are conduit gate valves and solid bored ball valves (see Fig. 32). Both of these types are suitable for pigging operations. When operating a valve, special attention must be paid to ensure that the valve is fully opened or closed fully to its stops.

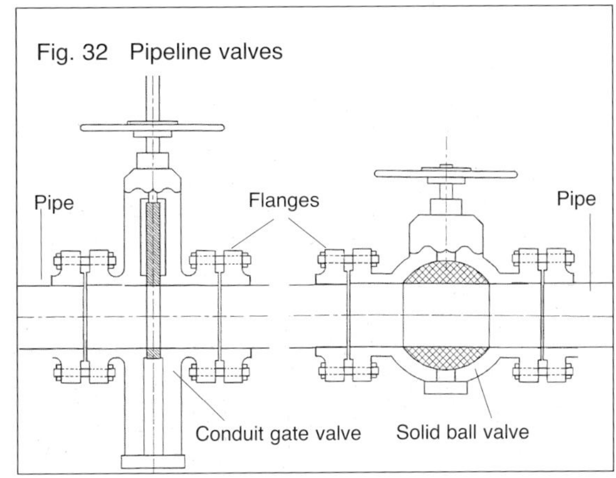
Pipe
Flanges
Pipe
Conduit gate valve
Solid ball valve
Fig. 32 Pipeline valves

1.8 PIPELINE STABILISATION

There are several ways in which pipelines can be stabilised (see Figs. 1 and 2).

Mattresses

1. *Frond mattresses* replicate the effects of seaweed and cause sand to be deposited rather than swept away. They are transported in a roll, laid out and secured to the seabed using a jack hammer to secure anchors into the seabed.
2. *Concrete Mattresses* are made from concrete blocks linked together by rope to form a mattress. They provide a versatile pipeline protection system (Fig. 2a). The flexibility allows the mattress to spread the load and comply with the pipeline formation. This is especially useful at pipeline bends and junctions (Fig. 2b).
   Mattresses may be laid on the seabed prior to the installation of a spool piece and further mattresses then laid on top of the installed spool piece.
3. *Combination Mattresses* are formed by attaching frond mats to the top of ordinary concrete mattresses. They are deployed in the same way as normal concrete mats with a cover holding the fronds down. Once the mat is in position the cover is pulled off to activate the fronds.

Diver Tasks

Diver tasks include:

a) Observation of the landing of the mattress and providing guidance instructions to the surface crane driver.
b) Rotation and alignment of the mattress using tag lines prior to its landing (see Fig. 2a).
c) Release of lifting strops from mattress after landing.

Fig. 1 Pipeline stabilisation techniques

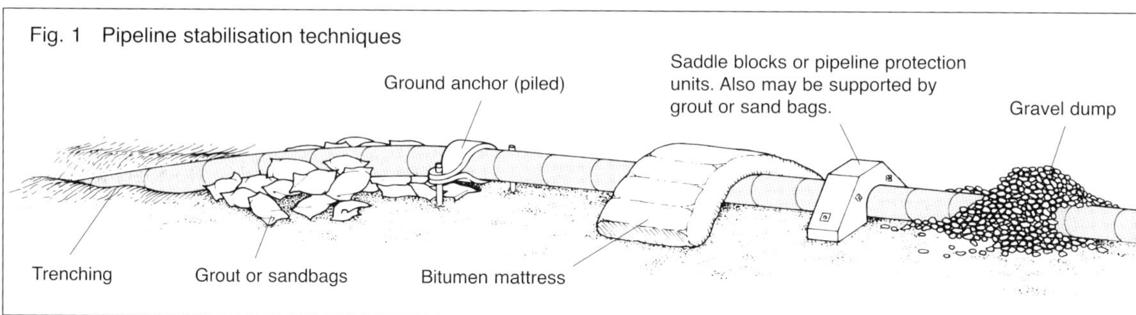
Ground anchor (piled)
Saddle blocks or pipeline protection units. Also may be supported by grout or sand bags.
Gravel dump
Trenching
Grout or sandbags
Bitumen mattress

Fig. 2 Concrete block mattress

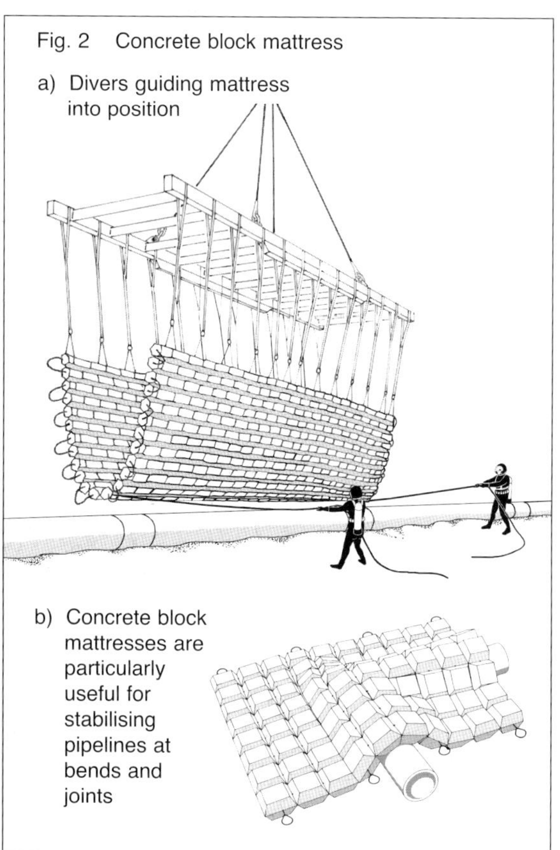

a) Divers guiding mattress into position

b) Concrete block mattresses are particularly useful for stabilising pipelines at bends and joints

PIPELINE STABILISATION
OPERATIONAL SAFETY

1. The lowering of the mattress is weather sensitive. Large vertical heave motions can be a hazard to the diver.
2. Long tag lines should be provided to allow divers to remain well clear of the lowered mattress.
3. Large vertical movement of the mattress near the sea bed can cause a suction effect beneath it within its close vicinity.
4. Keep diver and his umbilical well clear of landing zone of mattress.
5. Beware vertical heave movement of the spreader frame when mattress has been landed and whilst the divers are releasing lifting strops. If necessary use long slings or strops to keep frame well clear of divers.
6. The central concrete blocks can be painted white to assist the divers to align the centre of the mattress over the pipe.
7. Good voice communications is required between the crane operator and the divers to ensure a safe lowering operation.
8. Refer also to Crane Operations, page162.

1.9 OFFSHORE PRODUCTION SYSTEMS

Fixed Platforms

Fixed platforms are used extensively offshore in oil production in water depths down to about 300m (1,000ft). Beyond this depth other systems are used (see Fig. 5). Fixed platforms can provide a drilling base, production/processing facility, personnel accommodation, communications and logistic storage and transport facilities.
The design of a platform installation will depend on a number of factors: depth of water, size of field, high or low production, prevailing sea state, nature and contour of sea bottom, production costs and capital requirements. Production drilling can be conducted from a variety of structures.

There are four categories of fixed platforms (see Figs. 1 and 2). They are listed below in order of increasing capacity:

1. *Caisson Well Guard*. This is the minimum structure and is suitable only for a single well in shallow water and sheltered location.
2. *Well Protector Platform*, a three- or four-legged structure over one or more wells connecting flowlines to a nearby production platform. Some of these are found in the southern North Sea but this design is no longer much used.
3. *Simple Production Platform* which collects the flowlines from surrounding wells in a widely scattered field.

   All of the above platforms provide controls for existing flowlines.
4. *Self-Contained Drilling/Production Platforms*. These are capable of handling as many as 25–30 conductors and can drill deviated wells in the surrounding field. They can process and separate oil from gas, water and debris. These larger platforms are usually restricted to depths down to 300m (1,000ft) and can weigh in excess of 20,000–30,000 tonnes.

Multi-platform systems can be created where platforms, each with a specific function, can be interconnected to provide the individual supports for drilling, production and accommodation. This has safety advantages and also allows the drilling to start sooner (see Fig. 3).

STEEL PLATFORMS

Fixed platforms are usually constructed of steel in the form of a four- to eight-legged framework called a jacket. The topside modules are fixed to the top of this structure at a height dictated by the anticipated sea states and tidal levels. These steel structures are fabricated ashore and towed out to the well site either on a barge or supported by their own buoyancy. When accurately positioned (siting can be accurate to 2m/6ft), the structure is deballasted and set down. The jacket is then secured to the seabed by a series of steel piles.

CONCRETE PLATFORMS

Concrete is also used to fabricate production platforms but differ from steel in that they are gravity

Fig. 1 Examples of simple fixed platforms

a) Caisson well guard

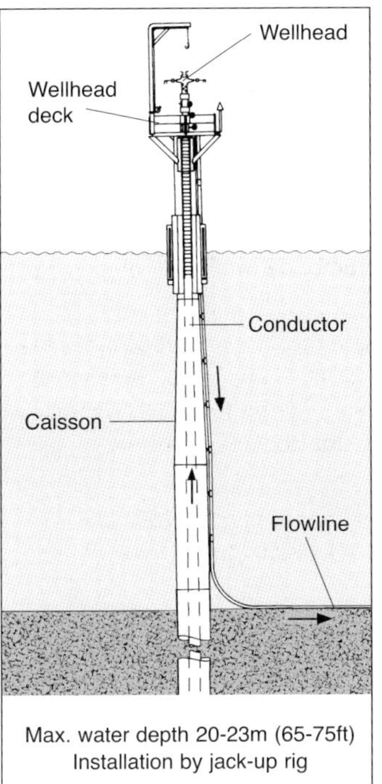
Wellhead
Wellhead deck
Conductor
Caisson
Flowline

Max. water depth 20-23m (65-75ft)
Installation by jack-up rig

b) Well protector platform

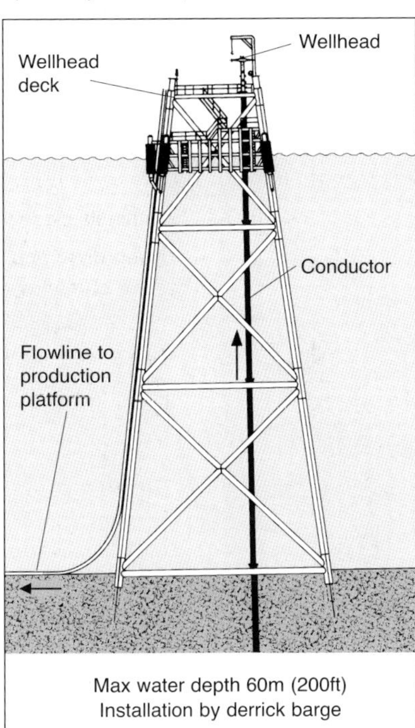
Wellhead
Wellhead deck
Conductor
Flowline to production platform

Max water depth 60m (200ft)
Installation by derrick barge

c) Production platform

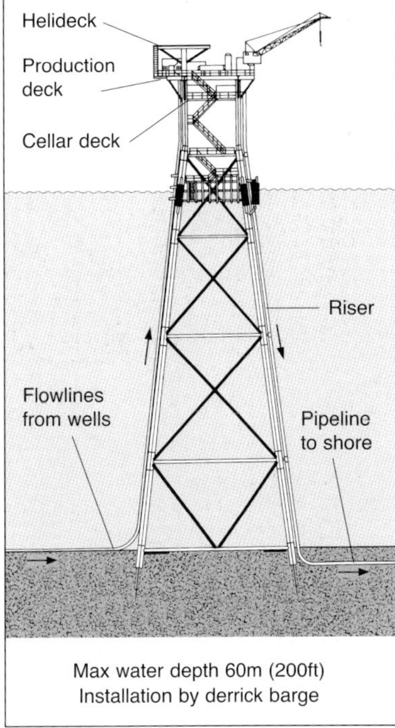
Helideck
Production deck
Cellar deck
Riser
Flowlines from wells
Pipeline to shore

Max water depth 60m (200ft)
Installation by derrick barge

Fig. 2 Typical Self-contained Drilling/Production platform

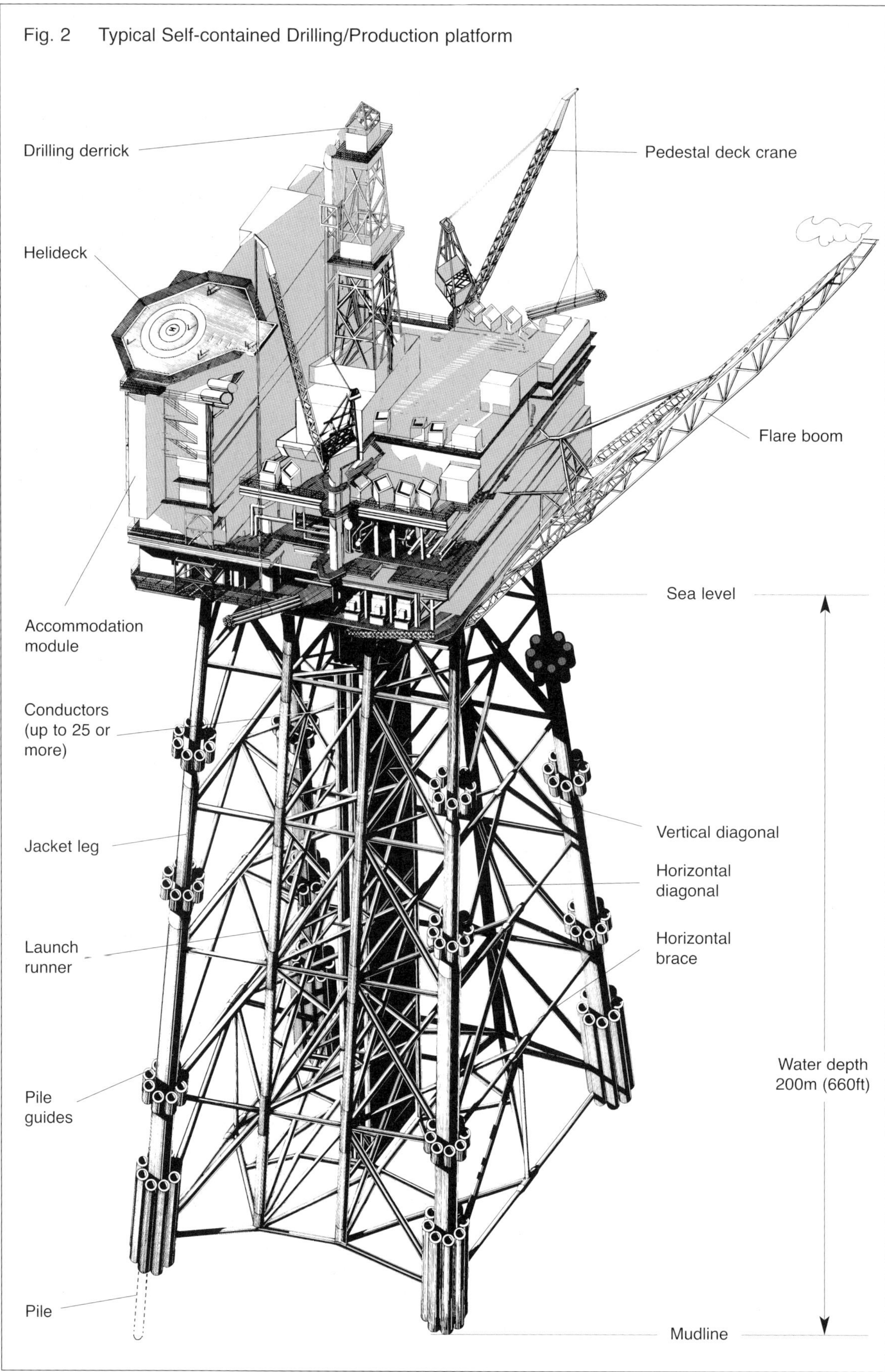
Drilling derrick
Pedestal deck crane
Helideck
Flare boom
Sea level
Accommodation module
Conductors (up to 25 or more)
Vertical diagonal
Jacket leg
Horizontal diagonal
Horizontal brace
Launch runner
Water depth 200m (660ft)
Pile guides
Pile
Mudline

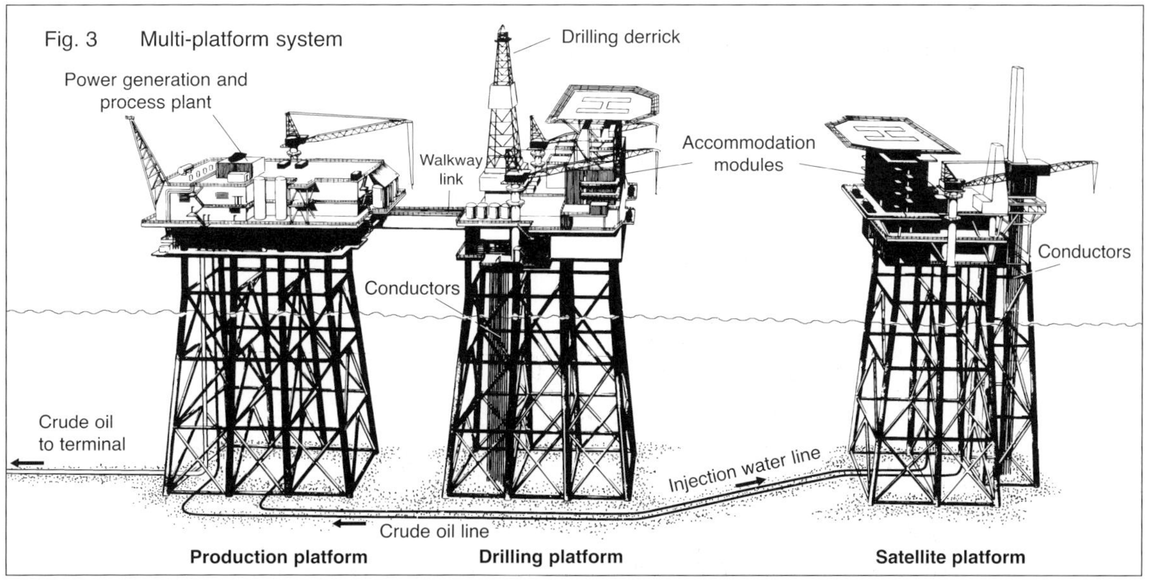
Drilling derrick
Power generation and process plant
Walkway link
Accommodation modules
Conductors
Conductors
Crude oil to terminal
Injection water line
Crude oil line
Production platform
Drilling platform
Satellite platform

Fig. 3 Multi-platform system

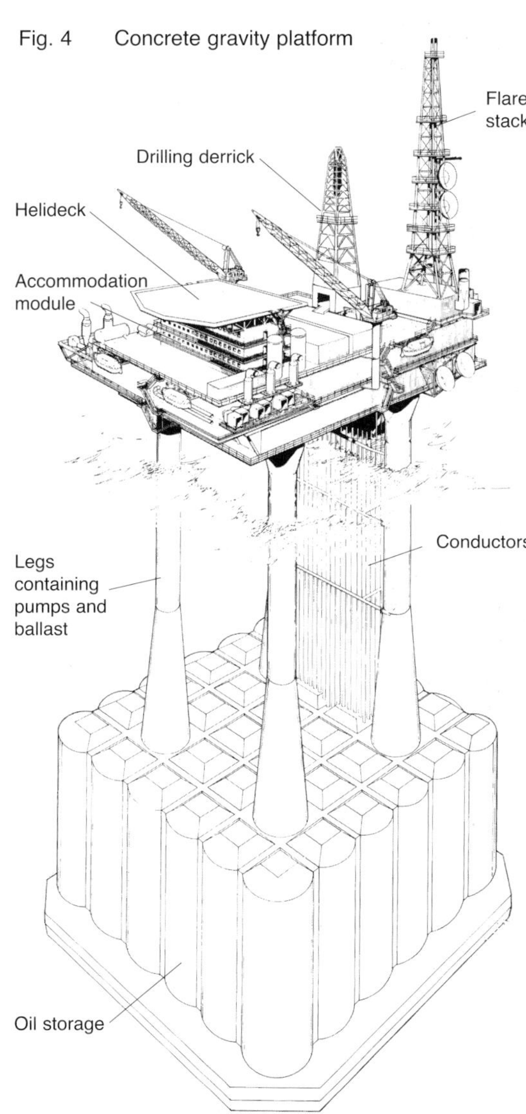
Flare stack
Drilling derrick
Helideck
Accommodation module
Conductors
Legs containing pumps and ballast
Oil storage

Fig. 4 Concrete gravity platform

Gravity structures require no piling and remain in position by virtue of their own weight.

structures. They depend on their mass for stability and immobility. Ballast tanks built into the base can be either flooded with seawater or used as storage tanks for oil. The major concrete structures are found in the northern North Sea (see Fig. 4).

While steel and concrete platforms are commonly used on the Continental Shelf a variety of different types of structures are used in very deep water (see Fig. 5). Some of these are discussed below.

Compliant Platforms

These are fixed platforms which, although compliant, their movement is minimised to avoid undue strain on the seabed well connections.

Surface, lateral movement may be in the region of up to 10m (33ft) depending on the relationship between the natural period of the waves and the platform period.

1. GUYED TOWER PLATFORMS
   This is a fixed platform designed for deep water locations. It is a compliant steel jacket supported in a single, weight-bearing foundation on the seabed. The stability of the structure is maintained by guylines secured to the seabed by anchor piles (see Fig. 6a).

2. TENSION LEG PLATFORM
   An alternative compliant, fixed platform design for deepwater locations. It consists of a semi-submersible unit fixed in position by vertical, tensioned cables secured to piled anchors on the seabed directly below (see Fig. 6b).

Floating Production Systems

FPSOs (Floating Production Storage and Offloading) systems are used in the deepest offshore locations. They are very large vessels which receive, process and store oil offshore in preparation for transfer to shore by oil tankers (see Fig. 7). Oil from the reservoir travels up through the production wells and flows into a series of

Fig. 5 Examples of typical deepwater production systems.

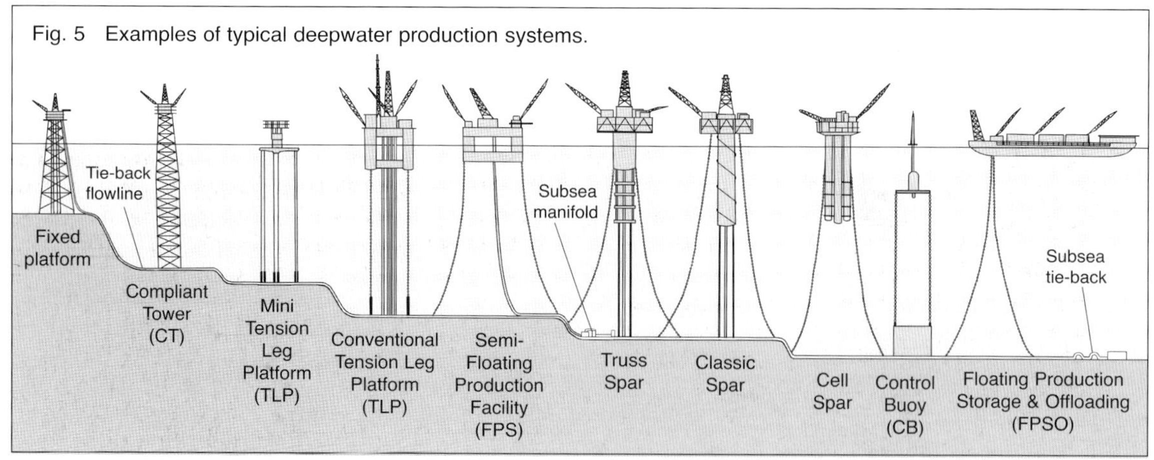
Tie-back flowline
Fixed platform
Compliant Tower (CT)
Mini Tension Leg Platform (TLP)
Conventional Tension Leg Platform (TLP)
Semi-Floating Production Facility (FPS)
Subsea manifold
Truss Spar
Classic Spar
Cell Spar
Control Buoy (CB)
Floating Production Storage & Offloading (FPSO)
Subsea tie-back

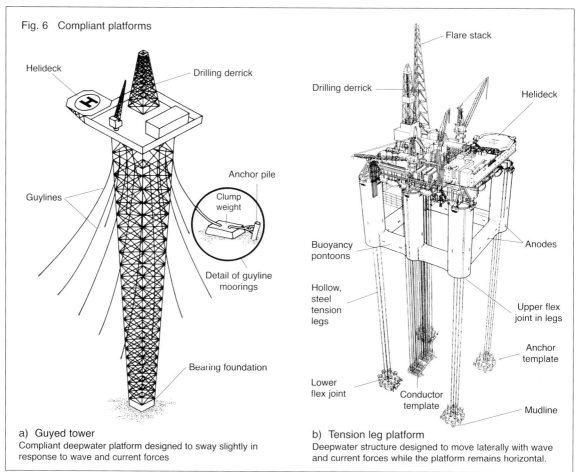

Fig. 6 Compliant platforms

a) Guyed tower
Compliant deepwater platform designed to sway slightly in response to wave and current forces

b) Tension leg platform
Deepwater structure designed to move laterally with wave and current forces while the platform remains horizontal.

production valves and piping at the wellhead, known as the 'christmas tree' (Fig. 10). The oil is then sent through pipelines on the seabed to a subsea manifold (Fig. 11) which directs the oil to the FPSO.

At the FPSO the oil is first processed and then stored in large tanks in the hull. 'Shuttle' oil tankers arrive on a regular basis to off-load the oil from the FPSO and take it to shore. Transfer of the oil normally takes place from the stern of the FPSO. It takes about 24 hours to fill the shuttle tanker.

Guidebases

Guidebases are structures which are lowered to the seabed from the drilling rig to act as a guide for the drill string and later, for installing the blow-out preventer. The casing around the drillhole in the seabed terminates at the guide base (see Fig. 8). The BOP is latched onto the casing at the guidebase. Several production wells may be drilled alongside each other. So two or more guidebases may be installed together. When several guidebases are

Fig. 7 A typical deepwater floating production system

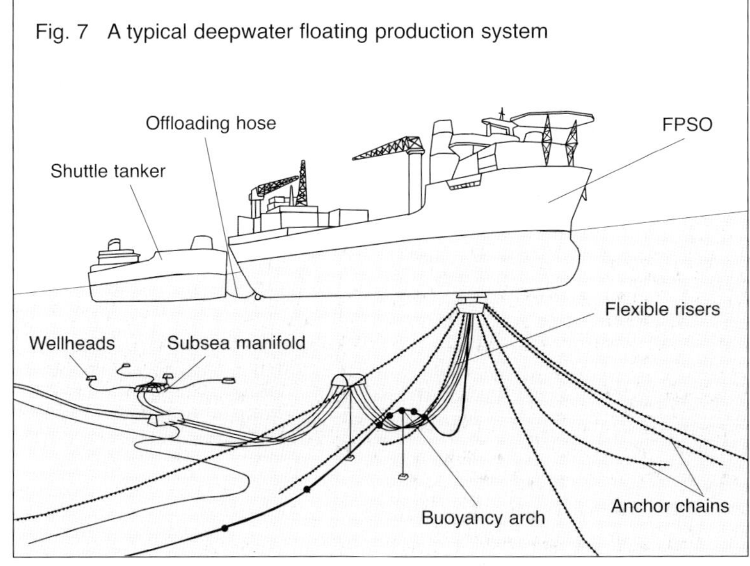
Offloading hose
Shuttle tanker
FPSO
Flexible risers
Wellheads
Subsea manifold
Buoyancy arch
Anchor chains

installed together they are grouped on a template (see Fig. 9).

Subsea Wellheads

Wellheads, also referred to as 'christmas trees' are mounted on production guidebases and control the production of oil or gas from the well (see Fig. 10). They can also be used for water injection.

A wellhead can be directly connected to a subsea manifold or connected to other wellheads in a 'daisy chain' configuration. Groups of wellheads can also be mounted together on a subsea template.

Subsea Well Templates

These are structures which are sometimes placed on the seabed and through which production wells are drilled by a jack-up or semi-submersible drilling rig (see Fig. 9). A platform is then placed over the template and the risers connected up.

Tie-back

When a marginal field is connected to an existing field, the operation is called a Tie Back. This involves the installation of one or more remote wellheads on the marginal field. These can be single or multiple remote wells tied into a jacket, either directly or through a subsea manifold.

Diving work on these wellheads and manifolds

Fig. 8 Guidebase

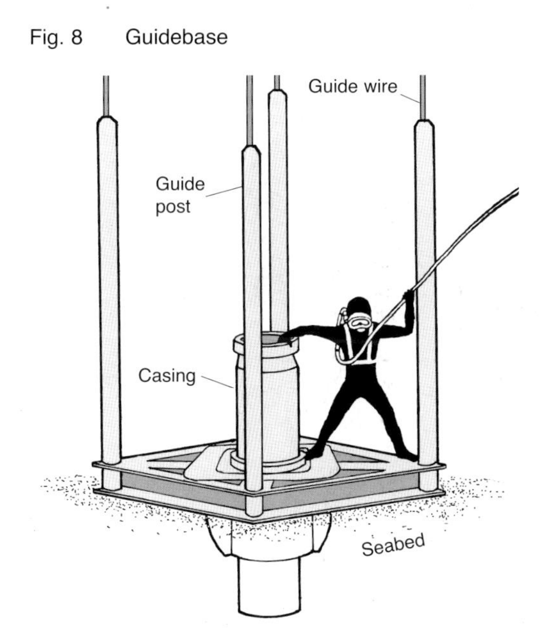
Guide wire
Guide post
Casing
Seabed

Fig 9 Guidebases and Templates

Production guidebases can be in one, two or three-slot versions

Subsea templates are combinations of four or more guidebases in pre-fabricated units

Fig. 10 Typical subsea wellhead

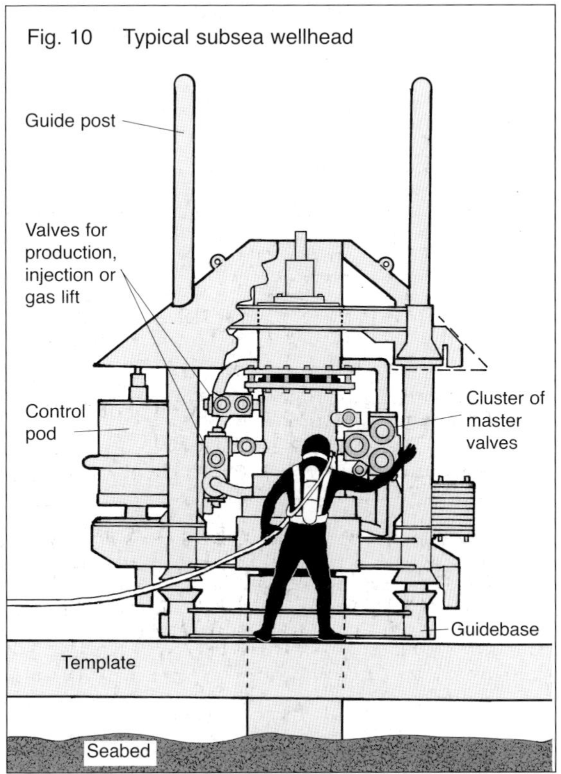
Guide post
Valves for production, injection or gas lift
Control pod
Cluster of master valves
Guidebase
Template
Seabed

includes their installation and maintenance. Before any work is done on a wellhead, it is essential to confirm that the diver is on the correct wellhead. Working on the wrong wellhead not only endangers the diver but may cause substantial damage to the wellhead.

DIVER TASKS

a) Installation

For the installation of joining and closing of flowline spools, refer to Section 1.7, Pipeline Connections. Every wellhead has an electrical/hydraulic control umbilical which connects it to the controlling jacket, either directly or via a subsea manifold.

The manifold is normally positioned so that the subsea umbilical terminal unit (SUTU) is very close to the panel to which it will be connected. The diver's job is to connect the hydraulic and electrical 'jumpers.' Once these are connected the commissioning engineer will run tests to ensure that all functions operate correctly before the well is made live. Occasionally some functions may not operate properly; this may be due, for example, to mis-labelling of the hydraulic and electrical connectors, or malfunctioning of the choke or subsea control module (SCM).

b) Maintenance

Typical maintenance tasks include changing over the choke module or the SCM (subsea control module). Both these modular units are delicate, but relatively easy to work with.

Before work commences, a landing area is prepared (eg, pallet or sandbags) close to the location of the change-out onto which the replacement units will be lowered.

Most wellheads and manifolds are protected by top and side panels which the diver will have to remove to gain access to the units which are to be replaced. The panels should be put on a hard surface (such as a concrete mattress) to prevent them from getting coated in mud.

The diver will then conduct the valve closures and isolation checks necessary to remove the unit. Only when it is safe to proceed can the diver remove the old unit. The unit can be lifted directly by crane vessel (weather permitting), by wellhead davit (if fitted) or by using lift bags.

The new unit is then lowered onto the prepared landing area. Once disconnected from the crane rigging, the unit is lifted into position using the wellhead davit or lift bag. After installing the new unit, it is tested to ensure that it is working correctly before the diver replaces the protective panels.

Subsea Manifolds

These can be massive structures up to 35m long x 6m high (115ft x 20ft) (see Fig. 11). Diver tasks include tying-in new wellheads and general maintenance such as valve status checks. It is important to note that when using torque wrenches, it is essential to use the correct setting for each valve to prevent causing damage to the valve.

Fig. 11 A typical subsea manifold

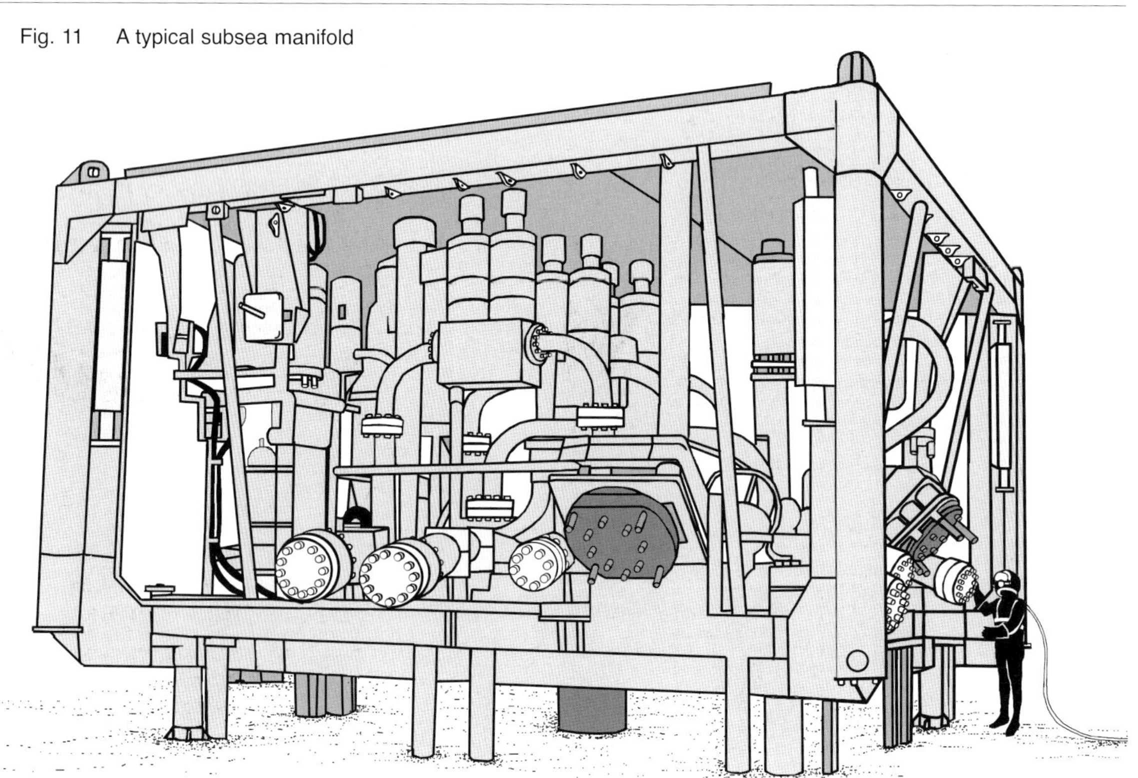

1.10 SINGLE POINT MOORING (SPM) SYSTEMS

An SPM (also known as a SBM (single buoy mooring) or SPBM (single point buoy mooring) is a large mooring facility for loading/unloading petroleum products. It is specially designed to enable tankers to be moored to them just by the bow. One or two flexible product lines can be connected to the tanker for delivering the oil products.

Applications of SPMs

1. In shallow water: To export or import crude oil or oil products from onshore/offshore fields or a refinery via some form of storage system. These installations are often multiple and the loss of one buoy may not be too serious in terms of lost production. These buoys usually accept ordinary world trade oil tankers.
2. In deep water: To take oil straight from the oil field(s) via the production platform. They are not limited by depth and are often used in smaller oil fields, in remote locations, or where production does not justify the expense of a pipeline to the shore. The loss of this buoy is much more serious as the oil production may have to stop as soon as the buoy is shut down. These installations usually have dedicated tankers which need little or no assistance in mooring to the buoy.

Divers are heavily involved in the installation, operation and maintenance of shallow-water SPMs most of which are moored within air-diving range although some, for example in the North Sea, require mixed gas diving to reach the lower hoses and seabed manifolds.

Types of SPMs

a) The most common type of single point mooring is the catenary anchor leg mooring (CALM). (The shape of the curve taken by the anchor chain between the stopper and the seabed is called a catenary). There are now well over 200 operating around the world in water depths from under 15m (50ft) to over 65m (200ft) and capable of handling tankers ranging in size from less than 50,000 dead weight tons (dwt) to the giant VLCCs (very large crude carriers) exceeding half a million dwt.
Other less common types, used mainly where the CALM might show certain disadvantages, are:

b) Single anchor leg mooring (SALM), shallow and deep water types (see Fig. 1).

c) Vertical anchor leg mooring (VALM) of which only a few have been installed (see Fig. 2).

d) Single point mooring tower (SPMT) of which there are two types:
   1. The jacket type, in which a jacket is piled to the seabed on top of which is a turntable carrying the mooring gear and pipework.
   2. The spring pile. There is no underbuoy hose system. Risers are steel pipes housed within the structure.

e) Exposed location single buoy mooring (ELSBM) (see Fig. 3). The mooring hawser and the cargo handling hose are stored on large diameter drums when the berth is unoccupied.

f) Articulated loading platform (ALP) (see Fig. 4). The ELSBM and ALP are designed for the extreme conditions of the North Sea often in water depths exceeding 90m (300ft).

Fig. 1 SALM (Single anchor leg mooring)

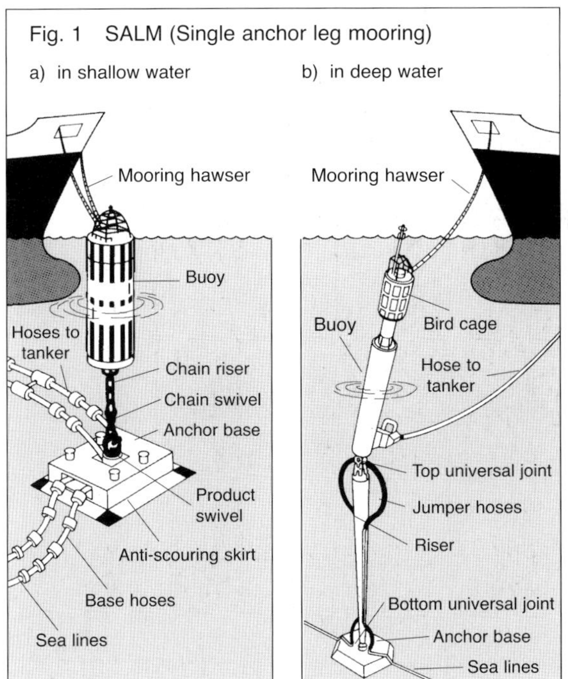
a) in shallow water
b) in deep water
Mooring hawser
Mooring hawser
Buoy
Hoses to tanker
Chain riser
Chain swivel
Anchor base
Product swivel
Anti-scouring skirt
Base hoses
Sea lines
Buoy
Bird cage
Hose to tanker
Top universal joint
Jumper hoses
Riser
Bottom universal joint
Anchor base
Sea lines

Fig. 2 VALM (Vertical anchor leg mooring)

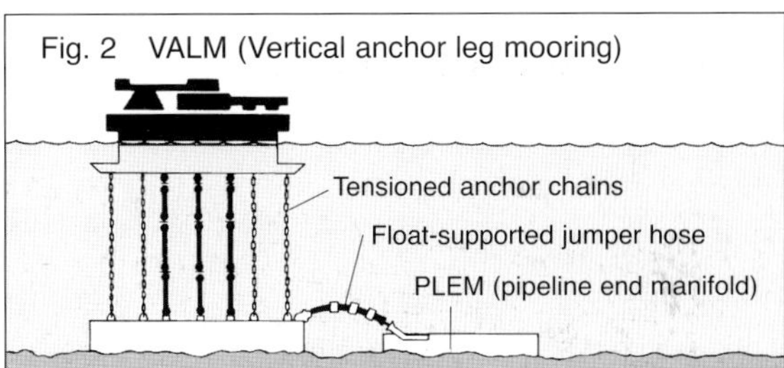
Tensioned anchor chains
Float-supported jumper hose
PLEM (pipeline end manifold)

Fig. 3 ELSBM (Exposed location single buoy mooring)

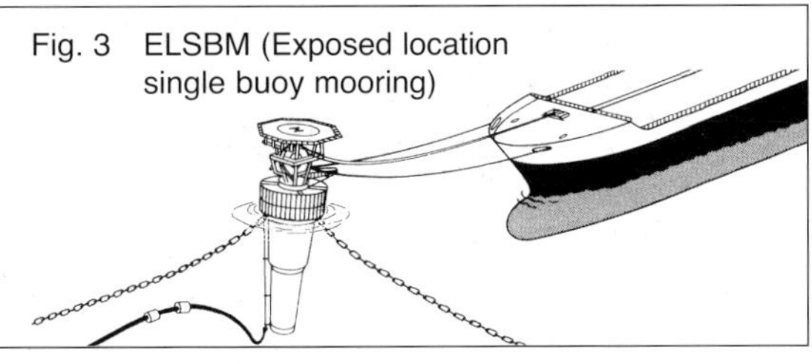

Fig. 4 ALP (Articulated loading platform)

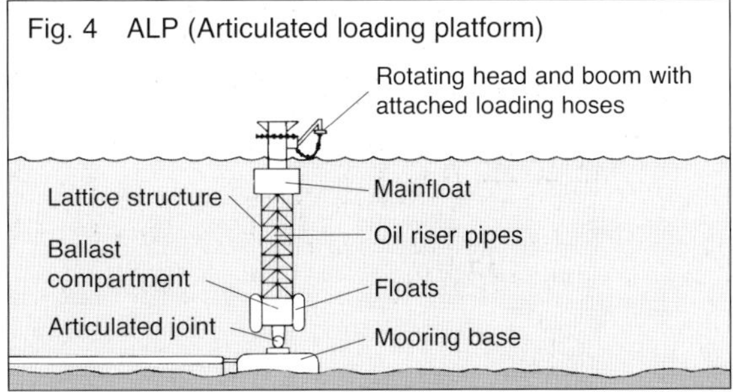
Rotating head and boom with attached loading hoses
Mainfloat
Lattice structure
Oil riser pipes
Ballast compartment
Floats
Articulated joint
Mooring base

The CALM

THE MOORING SYSTEM

The mooring system consists of a number of anchor chains laid radially from the buoy. Earlier buoys had eight anchor legs arranged in four pairs, the usual standard is now six.

The size or weight of the chain depends on the size of ship which the terminal has been designed to handle. It may vary from 6.5–10cm (2½–4"). To prevent the chain from reaching a fully tensioned state causing shock loads and, in extreme cases, breakage, the size and length are chosen such that the last 27m (90ft) remains on the bottom under the maximum horizontal movement load.

Each leg is some 340–370m (1,100–1,200ft) long and is attached to either an anchor, a driven pile or a drilled and grouted pile depending on the nature of the seabed and the required holding power.

When the buoy is installed the anchor chains are accurately pre-tensioned to ensure that the buoy is in the correct position. The mooring load applied by the tanker causes the buoy to move horizontally, lifting chain from the seabed on the side opposite to the applied mooring force until the system again comes into equilibrium.

SUBMARINE HOSE SYSTEMS

There are three systems:

1. *Chinese lantern*, in which the configuration is achieved by separate attachment of submarine floats (see Fig. 6a). Hose strings are separate. Two or three are usual; four are uncommon but possible.
2. *Lazy-S*, in which the correct configuration is obtained by adjusting the buoyancy of tanks or by submarine floats (see Figs. 6b and c). Hose strings are parallel and usually connected together all along their lengths. Two to three hose strings are common and occasionally there may be four or more.
3. *Steep-S*, in which the configuration is achieved with one buoyancy tank of the appropriate size which is blown dry after installation (Fig. 6d). The modified Steep-S permits the use of this system in shallow water.

Fig. 5 Arrangement of anchors on an SPM

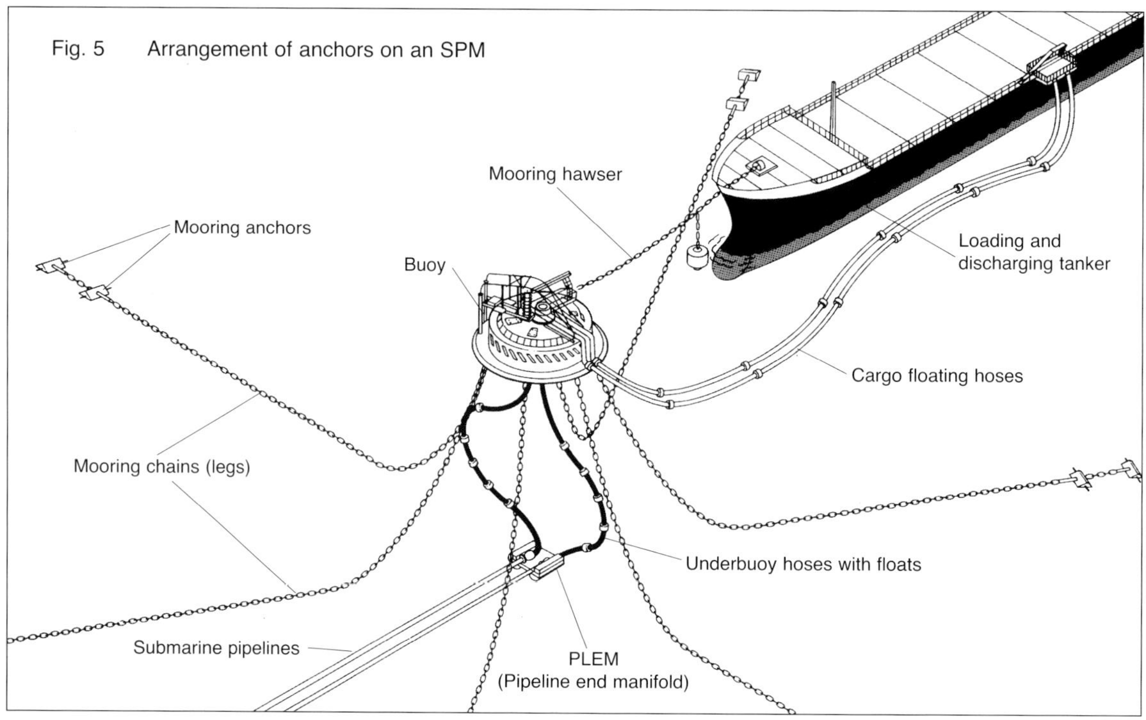
Mooring hawser
Mooring anchors
Buoy
Loading and discharging tanker
Cargo floating hoses
Mooring chains (legs)
Underbuoy hoses with floats
Submarine pipelines
PLEM
(Pipeline end manifold)

Fig. 6 Submarine hose systems

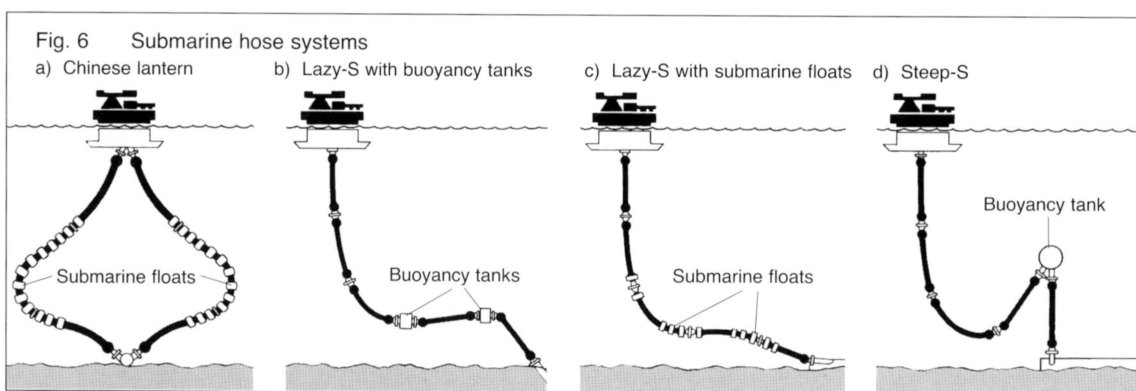
a) Chinese lantern
b) Lazy-S with buoyancy tanks
c) Lazy-S with submarine floats
d) Steep-S
Submarine floats
Buoyancy tanks
Submarine floats
Buoyancy tank

FLOATING HOSE SYSTEMS

Floating hoses are now almost always the integral floating type in which a jacket of buoyant material is built onto the main carcass.

All floatation material is compressible to a degree and if any part of a floating hose system is pulled below the surface the hydrostatic pressure will cause the material to compress causing a reduction in volume and thus buoyancy. The affected section will become negatively buoyant and progressively pull the rest of the hose string below the surface until it is lying on the seabed attached only by the flange connection at the outboard end of the pipearm. This is known as 'auto-submersion' and usually commences with a hose not fully floated which loses its additional support buoy (ie, a half-float rail hose). It can also occur if the first hose off the buoy breaks at the flange, which can happen in heavy weather. The first situation has been overcome by the introduction of the bar-bell or dumb-bell hose.

Some brands of hose are more prone to these problems than others depending on the type of material used for the buoyancy jacket. The other likely sources of trouble are the Y-piece reducer and concentric reducers sometimes found in floating hose systems. The tank around the Y-piece reducer should always be filled with a closed cell polyurethane foam and concentric reducers should always be fitted with some additional buoyancy. This in itself is vulnerable and needs frequent and regular inspection and repair.

Fig. 7 Typical floating hose arrangement

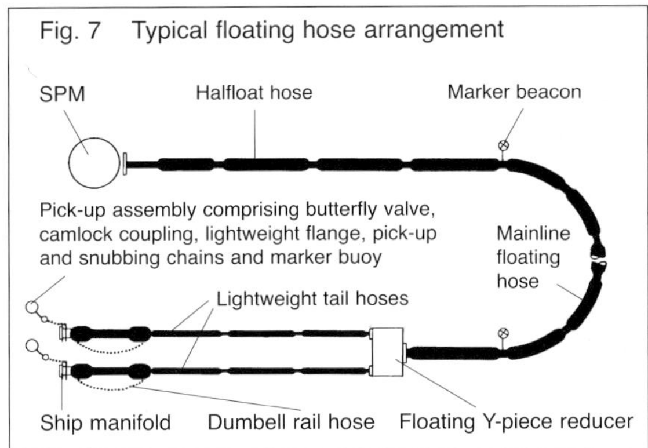
SPM
Halfloat hose
Marker beacon
Pick-up assembly comprising butterfly valve, camlock coupling, lightweight flange, pick-up and snubbing chains and marker buoy
Mainline floating hose
Lightweight tail hoses
Ship manifold
Dumbell rail hose
Floating Y-piece reducer

The complete tail and rail hose assembly can often be changed with ease and these together with the first hose off the buoy require a lot of attention.

At a busy terminal not too far offshore, it is often simpler to have a replacement string made up ashore ready to tow off. The string should require only one connection to be unbolted and remade.

Diver Tasks on a CALM

INSTALLATION TASKS

1. Placing the PLEM (pipeline end manifold – see Fig. 8) and flanging-up with submarine pipelines.
2. Installing the anchor chains into the buoy hawser pipes and chain stoppers. Checking chain angles and adjusting as and when necessary.
3. Installing the submarine hoses on the PLEM and buoy. On modern buoys the latter is done in the dry or in waist-deep water in the buoy's centre well. On older buoys the flanges are in the water underneath the buoy and the work is very weather sensitive.
4. Installing a ship's mooring system. This is usually the last item to install. The systems vary greatly and can be very heavy duty.
5. Operating subsea valves. The testing and commissioning will include checks for leaks on the PLEM valves, hose strings under the buoy and deck hoses.

Theses tasks will include:

a) Use of surface winches and cranes.
b) Rigging, including using tirfors, pull-lifts, chain-hoists, strops and spreaders.
c) Flanging, including impact wrenches (air or hydraulic), spanners, hammers and placing gaskets.
d) Burning, using oxy-arc above and below water.
e) Welding, possibly on various locking tabs on monkey face plates.

WARNING: When using arc cutting or welding on an SPM beware of the risk of fire, explosion and damage to the bearing carriage through arcing. Always ground to the job.

Fig. 8 PLEM (Pipe Line End Manifold)

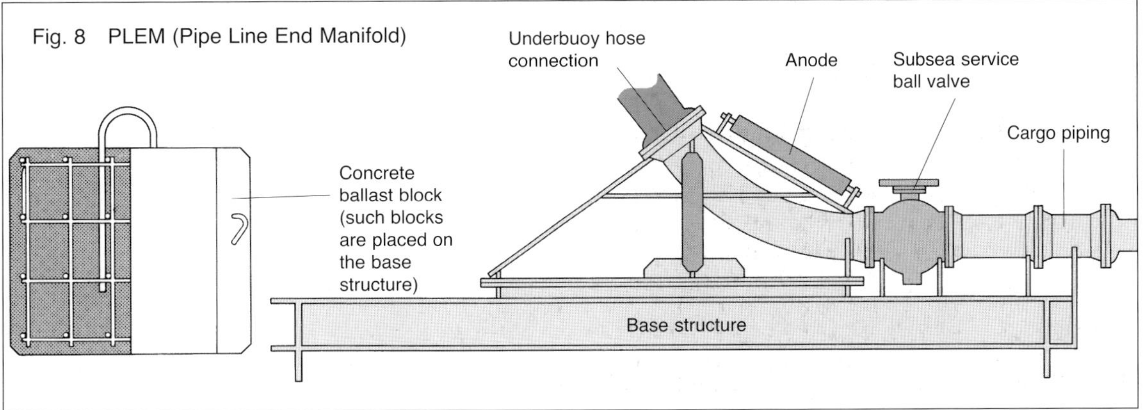
Underbuoy hose connection
Anode
Subsea service ball valve
Cargo piping
Concrete ballast block (such blocks are placed on the base structure)
Base structure

Fig. 9 Typical Inspection programme for an SPM

SPMs need to be inspected at regular intervals – specific tasks are associated with each inspection period. In addition to the general inspection tasks, the manufacturer's manual should be consulted for specific details. All repairs and adjustments must be carried out as necessary. Divers normally provide both topside and underwater maintenance services.

Pre-installation

Most of these tasks are carried out above water.

1. With the equipment at normal working pressure, check for oil leaks/spillage.
2. Inspect the following for signs of damage or fouling:
   a) The buoy
   b) Hawsers
   c) Pick-up lines
   d) Floating hoses
3. Check that the following are undamaged and working properly:
   a) Lights
   b) Telemetry systems
   c) Hatches

Weekly

Most of these tasks are carried out above water.

1. All of the above plus
2. Lubricate all components as specified in the manufacturer's maintenance manual.
3. On a CALM:
   a) Check centre well for contamination.
   b) Open bearing cavity drain plugs.
   c) Pull out rod to drain any accumulated water.
4. Check buoy fendering for damage (diver).

Monthly

1. Inspect mooring equipment. Help lift onto deck for inspection.
2. Check floating hose sections for underwater damage.
3. Monitor valve actuator test underwater. Operate hydraulic power pack to test valve actuator as necessary. Observe test from bottom under PLEM protective cover. Make video recording if required.
4. Measure configuration of subsea hose. Adjust floatation collars as required to re-align to normal configuration.

Quarterly

1. Make video/photographic record of marine growth prior to removal.
2. Remove marine growth from subsea hoses using scrapers.
3. Clean floatation collars, flanges and hydraulic umbilical clamps using HP water jet.
4. Make video/photographic record of structures after removal of marine growth.

Six-monthly

This is the most extensive inspection

1. Check position of SBM and PLEM.
2. Measure chain angles and adjust if necessary.
3. Ensure anchor chains and chain stoppers are secure.
4. Check wear on chain links.
5. Hoses:
   a) Inspect floating hose to check for underside damage
   b) Inspect underwater hoses for damage.
6. Measure subsea hose configuration and correct if necessary by adjusting floatation collars.
7. Inspect underwater part of buoy/skirt for damage.
8. Check and measure level of PLEM base.
9. Check valve actuator functions on all valves.
10. Ensure all flange bolts on PLEM are secure.
11. Ensure all bolts of subsea hose flange connections are secure.
12. Check umbilical hydraulic hose bundles and fittings.
13. Anodes:
    a) Inspect and clean all anodes.
    b) Check effectiveness of cathodic protection system.
14. Inspect all paintwork for damage.
15. Any other work as specified in the manufacturer's maintenance manual.

10 yearly Entire buoy to be dry-docked for service and maintenance.

Hose change After a period specified by the manufacturer, subsea hoses need to be replaced.

MAINTENANCE TASKS

SPMs need to be inspected at regular intervals. A typical inspection programme is shown in Fig. 9.

1. Marine tasks

Divers may be required to assist with the surface activities on an SPM. These can include the following:

a) Dressing the berth. Arrange for the mooring equipment and floating hose-strings to be properly laid out in readiness for the incoming tanker.

b) Mooring/unmooring assistance. The handling of hawsers on and off the tanker.

c) Hose handling assistance. Bring the ends of the floating hose strings into a position alongside the tanker, near the manifold connection to be hooked on the tanker derrick. When disconnecting, the hose ends need to be unhooked and streamed out clear of the tanker propeller.

2. Non-diving maintenance tasks

Divers may be required to carry out planned maintenance of the SPM and the diving company may have to provide the power tools, hydraulics, water etc. Typical tasks are shown in Fig. 10.

SPMs – OPERATIONAL SAFETY

1. Special care is needed to avoid suffocation risk inside buoy compartments. This can be caused by de-gassing oil or inert gas pockets. Do not enter any compartment which has not been ventilated for a long time even if it had not contained any oil or gas. Never work on your own.
2. Special care is also needed due to the explosion risk from de-gassing oil, especially if using oxy-arc or other hot cutting equipment. Make sure that permission is sought and given before using hot tools. Remember to earth to the job and not to the hull of the buoy. Smoking is prohibited.
3. Avoid the use of spark-producing tools if there is a risk of explosive gases.
4. Always turn off the fog-horn (if fitted) while working onboard.

3. Diving tasks:

These tasks are divided into three types:

1. Surface diving work: around the structure of the buoy.
2. Mid-water work: on the submarine or under-buoy hoses.

Fig. 10 Non-Diving maintenance tasks on an SPM (Imodco example)

Inspect the exterior of the floating hose string and the mooring hawsers and all accessories for any signs of wear or damage. Lubricate the hawser attachments and thimbles.

Check buoy security and ensure that all hatches and doors are closed and the rotating assembly is unobstructed.

Inspect all painted surfaces and repair and replace as necessary.

Check operation of light and fog horn.

Remove the mooring hawsers from the water. Dry the lines. Scrape off all sea growth. Inspect all components and repair, replace, represerve and lubricate as necessary.

Check the pipe arm clamps and tighten the clamp bolts as necessary to compensate for Teflon pad wear. (Not all buoys).

Lubricate all arm connector hinge pins.

Check all pipe arm expansion joints and all pipe flange joints for leaks. Tighten flange bolts or replace gaskets as necessary.

Stores compartment:
a) Check and clean bilge pump.
b) Check inventory of onboard spares, inspect, represerve and repack.
c) Change out compressed air cylinders as necessary.

New hose string make-up. Change out floating hoses as necessary. Hydrostatic testing. Vacuum testing.

Inspect all wheel assemblies and their mounting bolts. Tighten bolts as necessary. Lubricate all wheel assemblies, pumping grease until it is observed coming out of the seals on each wheel.

Winch:
a) Inspect, exercise and lubricate the chain tensioning winch.
b) Inspect the wire rope, exercise the winch, represerve the wire rope with a suitable lubricant.

Exercise all cargo valves.

Check all battery boxes for proper voltage output. Change batteries as necessary.

Sound all non-foamed compartments for leakage or condensation and pump out as necessary.

Check the (M)PDU for seal leakage.

Check operation of all watertight hatches and doors, lubricate hinges and dogs, change gaskets if necessary.

Inspect the buoy hull and rotating assembly for signs of structural weakness or damage.

Inspect fenders. Replace as necessary.

Inspect the wheel track for signs of wear.

Fig. 11 Diving Tasks on an SPM (Imodco)

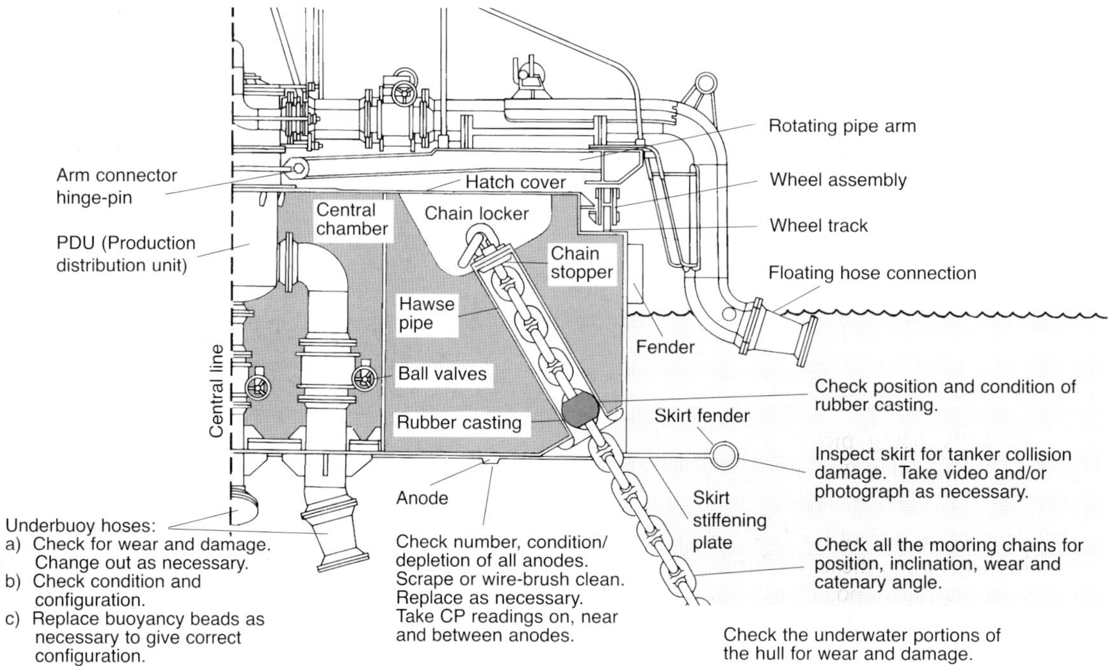

Arm connector hinge-pin
PDU (Production distribution unit)
Central line
Central chamber
Hatch cover
Chain locker
Chain stopper
Hawse pipe
Ball valves
Rubber casting
Anode
Fender
Skirt fender
Skirt stiffening plate
Rotating pipe arm
Wheel assembly
Wheel track
Floating hose connection
Check position and condition of rubber casting.
Inspect skirt for tanker collision damage. Take video and/or photograph as necessary.
Check all the mooring chains for position, inclination, wear and catenary angle.
Check the underwater portions of the hull for wear and damage.
Underbuoy hoses:
a) Check for wear and damage. Change out as necessary.
b) Check condition and configuration.
c) Replace buoyancy beads as necessary to give correct configuration.
Check number, condition/ depletion of all anodes. Scrape or wire-brush clean. Replace as necessary. Take CP readings on, near and between anodes.

3. Seabed diving work: on the PLEM, pipe and anchor moorings.

Diving tasks around the buoy structure are illustrated in Fig. 11. Care must be taken to avoid injury and over-exertion during rough sea conditions.

1. SURFACE DIVING TASKS

a) *Chain angle and measurement.*
The chain catenary angle is measured immediately beneath the buoy using a protractor or inclinometer supplied by the manufacturer.
The handbook of basic data and drawings, also supplied by the manufacturer, should specify the angle and make clear whether it is measured from the vertical or the horizontal axis, as this can vary from one manufacturer to another.
Serious errors can occur if the original protractor has been lost or damaged and if a locally made replacement has the scale reversed or wrongly marked so that it reads the opposite. If the angles are too steep the whole system will be 'sloppy' and movements greater than designed. If the angles are too shallow then the system will be too 'stiff' and loads will exceed the design limits.
The protractor should look like the one illustrated in Fig. 12b. It is designed to show the angle between the chain and the horizontal and should be hooked to the chain as close to the stopper as possible.

Fig. 12 Measuring chain angles

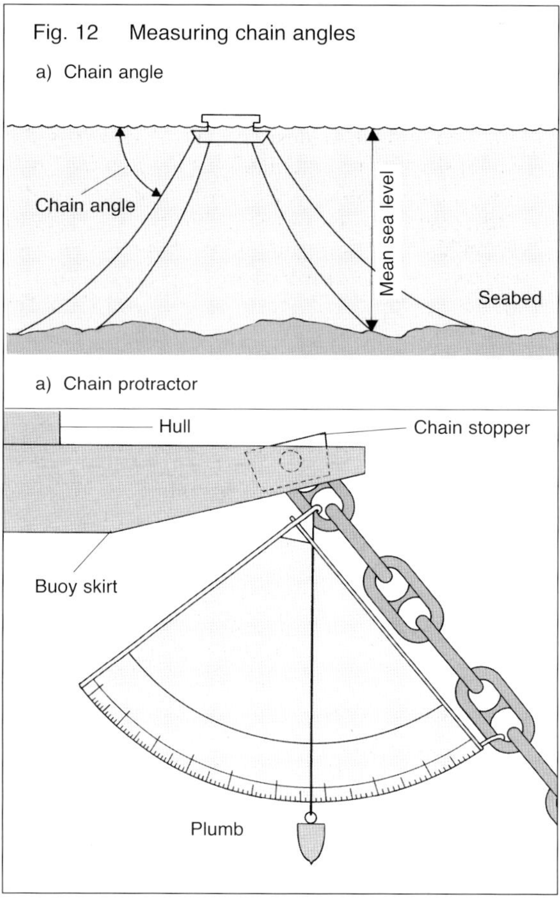

a) Chain angle
Chain angle
Mean sea level
Seabed
a) Chain protractor
Hull
Chain stopper
Buoy skirt
Plumb

b) *Chain wear measurement.*
Anchor chains wear most at two places:
1. At the link in the chain stopper (see Fig. 13). The maximum tension in a catenary occurs at the point of suspension.
2. Along the length of each chain where it makes contact with the seabed. Because of the motion of the buoy, chain in this area is

Fig. 13 Chain stopper

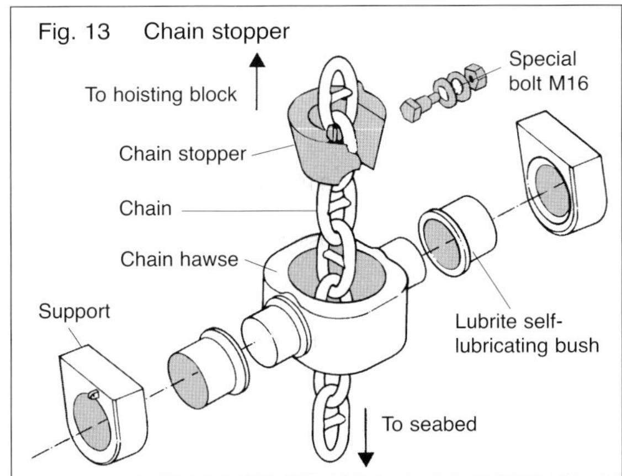
To hoisting block
Chain stopper
Chain
Chain hawse
Support
Special bolt M16
Lubrite self-lubricating bush
To seabed

constantly being picked up and laid down and this, coupled with the abrasive nature of the seabed material, causes wear.

Frequent inspection of the links on the stoppers will indicate when these need to be changed. It is sometimes possible to reverse this particular 'shot' or shackle of the chain if the wear has taken place towards one end. (A shot or shackle is 27m (90ft) in length). Two types of joining shackle are to be found in making up the required lengths of anchor chains: lugged and lugless ('Kenter') shackles where this has to pass through the chain stopper (see Fig. 14). There are minor differences between the Imodco and SBM designs one of which is the chain stopper arrangements. In the Imodco buoy each chain passes through a hawse pipe in the hull (see Figs. 11 and 14). The chain is held in a latch at the top end of the hawse pipe and chafing at the lower end is prevented by a rubber casting. All these points need frequent inspection.

In the SBM design (also produced by McDermott where it is called the 'swivel top') the chain stoppers are located in the skirt and consist of bucket-shape steel casting (which is in two parts

Fig. 14 Joining shackles

a) Lugged joining shackle — Dovetail chamber, Lead pellet, Bolt, Tapered pin, Lug

b) Lugless (Kenter) joining shackle — Stud, Dovetail chamber, Pin, Lead pellet

The four parts of the shackle fitted together

Note arrows facing each other

NB: It is essential to ensure that all the old lead is cleared out of the dovetail chamber before hammering in a new lead pellet. Use the point of a sharp spike.

bolted together around the chain) housed in a trunnion mounting frame allowing movement in the vertical plane.

The Blue Water Terminals buoy has a similar arrangement. Each stopper is carried in trunnions at the ends of a six-legged spider which is carried in the lower end of the central column. The buoyant hull, which is free to rotate around a column, carries the tanker mooring attachment and the floating hose connection.

c) *Buoy position measurement.*
Another aid to check the buoy position depends on the configuration of the underbuoy hoses.
If these are of the Chinese lantern type the buoy is vertically over the PLEM or seabed manifold and a plumb-bob dropped from the centre of the underside of the buoy is a useful aid (see Fig. 15).
With the Lazy-S underbuoy hose system (see Fig. 16) the installation crew may have used a datum – usually a concrete block with a staff on the seabed. The drawing and/or handbook should specify the distance between a mark on the manifold and the position on the seabed vertically below the centre of the buoy.
All measurements should be taken in calm

Fig. 15 Example of a sketch produced from diver's measurements of Chinese lantern

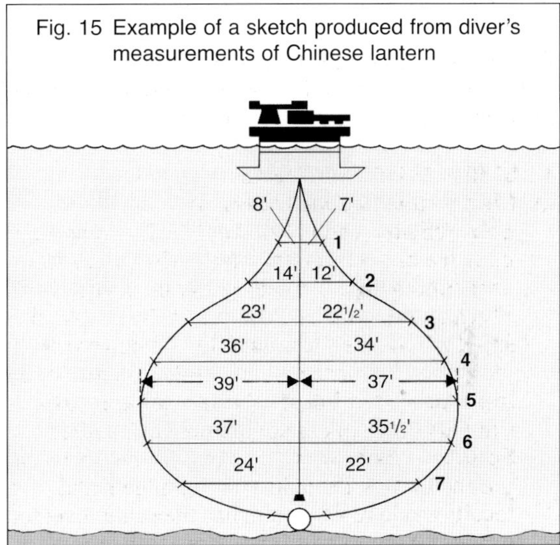
8'
7'
1
14'
12'
2
23'
22½'
3
36'
34'
4
39'
37'
5
37'
35½'
6
24'
22'
7

Fig. 16 Measurement of Lazy-S hose system

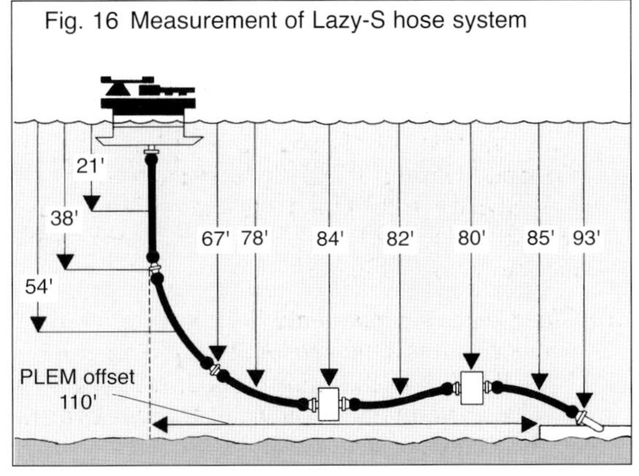
21'
38'
54'
67'
78'
84'
82'
80'
85'
93'
PLEM offset
110'

conditions and, ideally, at mean sea level. If adjustments to the chain are necessary the handbook and drawings will detail how to rig the buoy derrick and operate the winch.
Pulling up a chain shallows the angle, increases the tension and tends to move the buoy in the direction of that chain. It has the same effect on the chain diametrically opposite, so work on opposite pairs of anchors and not 'around the clock'.

2. MID-WATER DIVING WORK

a) *Check and adjustment of configuration of hoses.* Whichever system is adopted, before any adjustments are made the initial configuration must be measured and drawn as accurately as possible. To get a true representation of the configuration this task is best carried out at low, slack water with no wind. The following procedures are examples.

1. Chinese Lantern (Fig. 15)
A plumb line is dropped from the centre of the underside of the buoy. The line can be marked every 3m (10ft) or so with a metal or plastic tag. Two divers are necessary – one on the plumb line and one on the hose string to take a series of measurements of the horizontal distance from the plumb line to the midpoint of each hose and each flange connection, recording the depth on the plumb line at each point. Ideally, these measurements should be taken in calm conditions at slack water. From them a rough sketch is produced as in Fig. 15 which should later be drawn accurately to scale on squared paper.
Removal of floats is largely common sense and practice. If there is a hose company representative present, take his advice.
Do not move more than two floats at a time and allow the system adequate time to settle, particularly with new hoses which will be quite stiff for the first few days in service.
Repeat the above procedure until the recommended configuration is achieved and then produce and file an accurate diagram for future reference.

2. Lazy-S (with floats or tanks)
Here only one diver is necessary and if the procedure is not hurried, depths can be recorded from the pneumo gauge. Since the water depth and PLEM offset should be known from measurement the diagram in Fig. 16 can be produced.
When installing a new system of this type, the buoyancy tanks will contain just sufficient ballast water to give them a negative buoyancy and will be supported by the crane via a spreader bar. The strings cannot be removed until the hose system is connected to the PLEM and buoy and the buoyancy of the tanks adjusted to their approximate position. Final adjustment consists of altering the ballast in the Lazy-S system with floats. Adjustments are made by removing or repositioning individual floats. After allowing time for the system to settle after the final adjustment has been made, a record of the configuration should be made, drawn to scale and filed for future reference.

Fig. 17 Measurement of Steep-S hose system

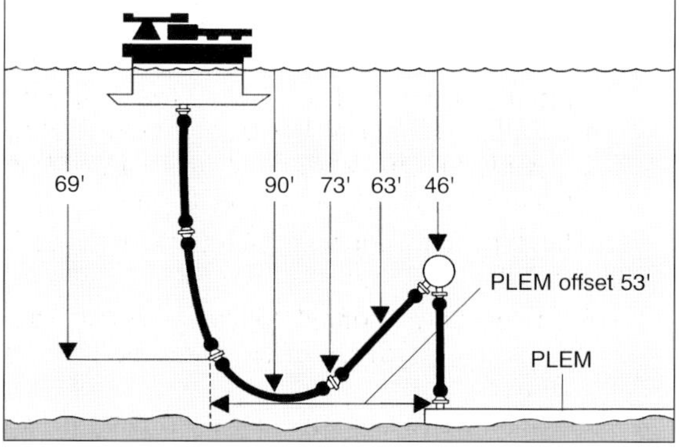

69'
90'
73'
63'
46'
PLEM offset 53'
PLEM

3. Steep-S and Modified Steep-S
In these systems no adjustments are possible and, if correctly designed, neither should they be necessary. For installation, the tank is flooded and, after hook-up, blown dry. However, it is equally important to measure and record the configuration as shown in Fig. 17.
Since all submarine hose systems are water-filled after installation or a hose change, and since the initial configuration is made in this condition, some change is to be expected when oil is introduced into the system. The earliest opportunity of checking the oil-filled configuration should be taken and an accurate diagram made for comparison with the water-filled configuration.

b) *Installation and Change-out of hoses.*
The Chinese lantern is the simplest system to install since each hose string is handled separately. If it becomes necessary to change one hose in a string it will usually be easier to remove the whole string, change the hose on the surface and re-install rather than attempt to change a hose underwater.
The same procedures apply to the Lazy-S or to the Steep-S configurations.
With a single hose system of these types complete removal, change-out on the surface and re-installation is the obvious answer. With twin and multiple hose systems other procedures apply and each can only be assessed on its own merits. When faced with this problem the following points should be considered.

1. Weather and sea conditions, depth of water, underwater visibility and currents.
2. Distance from the onshore operating base.

(All types of hose strings and systems have been towed from shore assembly to the installation for distances up to 240km (150 miles). It is often easier to remove a complete system, rebuild it onshore, tow-out and reinstall). Submarine hoses float when full of air without any additional buoyancy. Use lightweight flanges to blank-off ends.

3. The type and capacity of crane or derrick available.
4. Number of personnel to carry out all the necessary duties. Local availability if required.
5. Availability of suitable pad eyes on both the buoy and PLEM to rig the necessary tackles. Extra securing points can be provided by bolt-on clamps.

Example of an underbuoy hose change

a) Flange-up of hose and PLEM (see Fig. 18)
When replacing an underbuoy hose the bottom flange is normally made up (at least partially) before the underbuoy flange is made up.

Fig. 18 Changing an underbuoy hose

a) Initial alignment

To air tugger
Guide wire in 12 o'clock position
Hose
Padeye
PLEM
Coiled and bulldogged wires at 3 o'clock and 9 o'clock positions

b) Final alignment

To air tugger
Pipe
Hose
Tirfor
Padeye
PLEM
Wire rope threaded through 8 and 9 o'clock positions on flanges

Fig. 19 Replacement of gasket at underbuoy hose/PLEM

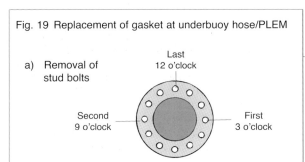

a) Removal of stud bolts

Last 12 o'clock
Second 9 o'clock
First 3 o'clock

b) Holding flanges in place

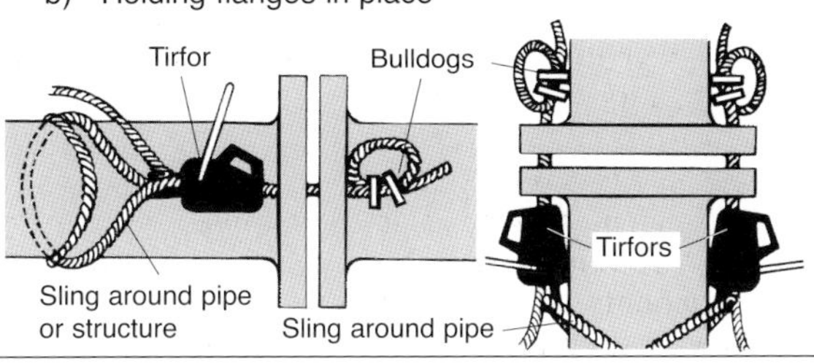
Tirfor
Bulldogs
Tirfors
Sling around pipe or structure
Sling around pipe

c) Slackening off stud bolts

Flange
Loosen bolts to 2 turns of thread
Stud bolt

d) Re-alignment of flanges using tolerance pins

Flange
Close tolerance pin in flange

Replacing a gasket

If recently installed, the gasket will probably be easily extracted intact and only half the bolts will need to be removed. Slacken the other half. Remove and tighten them up. Make sure the nut is flush with the end of the bolt to prevent fouling/jamming.

If the installation is an old one, it will probably be necessary to break the flange completely. The following procedure is an example.

First remove the 3 o'clock and 9 o'clock stud bolts (see Fig. 20a).

Two tirfors are then rigged with their wires going through the bolt holes and terminating in a small loop with bulldog clips to prevent them being pulled back through (see Fig. 20b).

These tirfors must then be tensioned up.

Slacken off the bolts and arrange the 12 o'clock nut taking care to avoid any subsequent movement of the hose flange.

Always have the 12 o'clock bolt as the last to undo to reduce the risk of injury due to flange movement. Slacken off the tirfors to get at the gasket. Remove the gasket and check the flange faces carefully for any damage. Clean as necessary.

Fit the new gasket.

Tension up tirfors to re-align the flanges. Use close tolerance pins/podgers and hammer to help with the final line-up.

Replace the bolts and move the pins as necessary.

Avoid the use of a hammer on the bolts.

Remove the tirfor and wire and install the last two bolts.

At all times take care to avoid hands, arms, umbilical, etc from getting trapped between flanges, especially if working in bad visibility.

The procedure for manoeuvring and aligning the flanges is basically the same as for the gasket change-out (see Fig. 19). The initial closing in of the hose flange is achieved using a guide wire rigged from the surface.

The 3 o'clock and 9 o'clock wires are prepared and stowed on the hose flange prior to submergence. They are uncoiled and rigged via the PLEM flange when the final alignment is required. The diver must be careful to avoid injury during the lowering of the hose especially if the visibility is poor. A knotted tag-line on the hose flange can give the diver an indication of its approach. If the sea surface is rough, the flange can be moving violently and great care is then required to avoid collision, entrapment and entanglement.

b) Flange-up under the buoy (see Fig. 20)
This is also similar to the previous arrangement. The hose is paid out from the diving support vessel and then winched in below the buoy.
The winches or tirfors on the buoy make the final alignment.

Fig. 20 Flanging up under the buoy
a) Hose winched in below the buoy

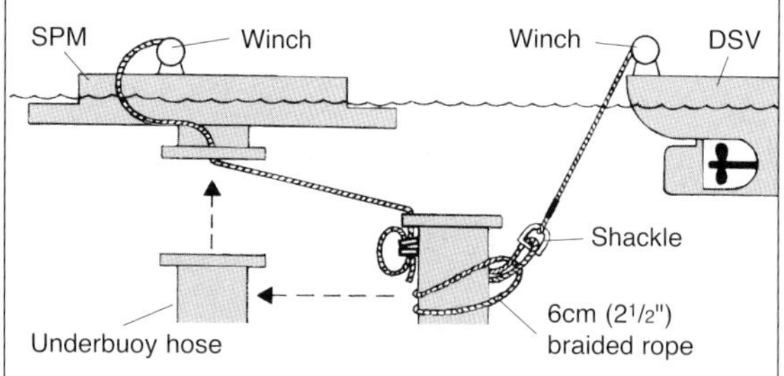

b) Final alignment

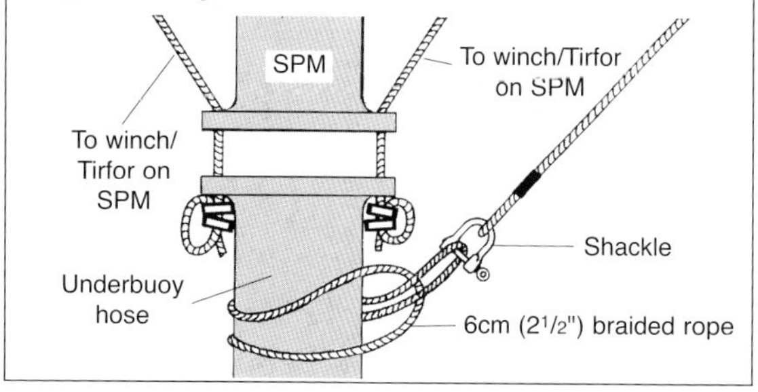

For the Lazy-S system with submarine floats the 'controlled sink' method can be used in which both ends of each string are closed off with blind flanges equipped with a 5cm (2in) valve through which the seawater can be admitted (see Fig. 21c). When the lower end reaches the area of the PLEM the flange is removed and further control exercised by operating the valve on the top end. Both Lazy-S and Steep-S systems can be installed even in the absence of large crane facilities. After assembly and pressure-testing the tank(s) is (are) flooded until just negatively buoyancy such that the depth can be controlled by a lightweight tackle during connection to the PLEM. When the top end has been connected to the buoy the tank(s) is (are) ballasted accordingly.

3. SEABED DIVING WORK

Tasks on the Pipeline End Manifold (PLEM)

1. Valve operations
These are undertaken according to client requirements.

2. Hydraulic valves
Only a little work is normally required.
   a) Stab hydraulic line into the open and close sockets to test the actuator. Observe/feel the indicator to check action.
   b) If difficult, check the ball valve in the socket and hose connector. Purge if necessary.
   c) Check that the blank caps are secure over the connector on the valve before and after operation.

3. Hand-operated valves
   a) If the valve handle has been removed, take a wheel down to turn the valve. If a wheel is not available on site, use a hydraulic tool.
   b) Clean the shaft.
   c) Place the wheel/tool on the spindle. Turn to fully shut or open as required. Make sure that the valve is fully home.
   d) Test by unwinding slightly and retightening.
   e) Check (see/feel) that the indicator has moved as expected. Take care because sometimes the indicators can jam and sheer off and not function normally.
   f) If appropriate, check with surface control that the pipe pressure confirms the correct valve operation.

4. Control system
   a) Replacement of HP hydraulic hoses.
   b) Installation of bypass hydraulic hoses.

5. Piles
   a) Check anodes. Replace if required.
   b) Check for scour. Infill if necessary.
   c) Check for any other damage.

6. Cathodic protection
   a) Take readings on and near the anode, possibly on the continuity strap, for example, on elbows near the PLEM.
   b) Make visual checks and calliper checks on the anodes to assess the rate of depletion.

7. Pipeline to PLEM connection
Can be a flange, or hydroball type, or a Cameron connector, etc.
   a) Check for leaks.

8. Debris around PLEM and pipeline
   a) Check and remove debris, as necessary.

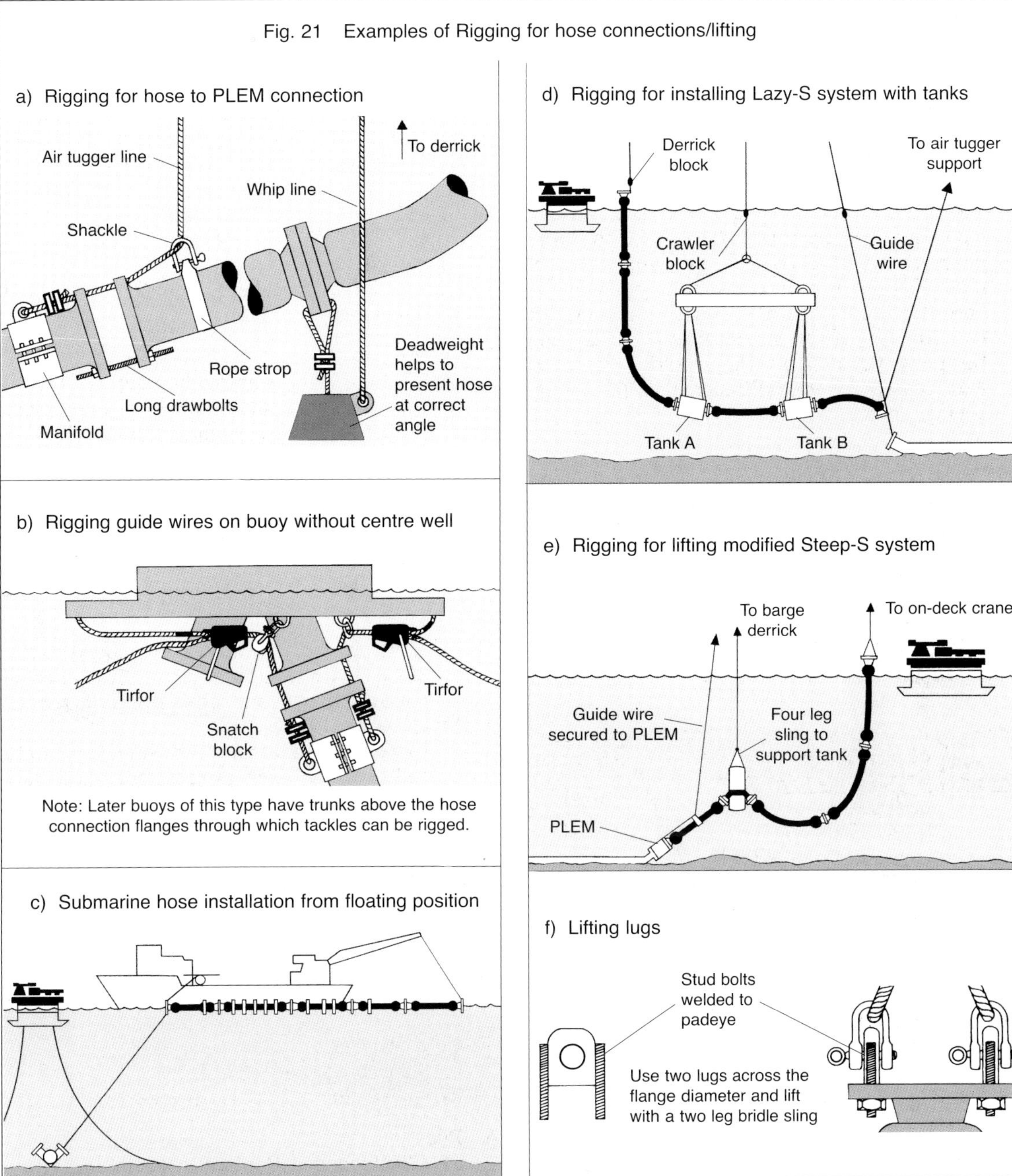
Fig. 21 Examples of Rigging for hose connections/lifting
a) Rigging for hose to PLEM connection
Air tugger line
To derrick
Whip line
Shackle
Rope strop
Deadweight helps to present hose at correct angle
Long drawbolts
Manifold
d) Rigging for installing Lazy-S system with tanks
Derrick block
To air tugger support
Crawler block
Guide wire
Tank A
Tank B
b) Rigging guide wires on buoy without centre well
Tirfor
Tirfor
Snatch block
Note: Later buoys of this type have trunks above the hose connection flanges through which tackles can be rigged.
e) Rigging for lifting modified Steep-S system
To barge derrick
To on-deck crane
Guide wire secured to PLEM
Four leg sling to support tank
PLEM
c) Submarine hose installation from floating position
f) Lifting lugs
Stud bolts welded to padeye
Use two lugs across the flange diameter and lift with a two leg bridle sling

PLEM TASKS – OPERATIONAL SAFETY

1. In poor visibility the tender must make sure that the diver's umbilical has the absolute minimum of slack to avoid entanglement.
2. For the same reason, if there is a current the diver should ensure that he remains downstream of the main activity. It is often convenient for the diver to locate himself on a downstream anchor chain to observe and supervise the flange alignment and closing operations.
3. The area between two flanges is a danger area. The diver should never put his hand or fingers in between two flanges.
4. In any flanging operation, particularly when removing blind flanges, the diver must take the greatest care to avoid the danger of differential pressure between the inside and outside of the pipe.

1.11 PIPELINE INSPECTION

Pipeline inspection is carried out by divers and remotely operated vehicles (ROVs) and is part of the routine offshore inspection and maintenance programme. Inspection requirements include those of the owners, certifying authorities, insurance companies and governmental bodies.

Pipeline inspection data are very important and the highest possible standards of inspection are essential. Figs. 1 to 6 help to identify pipeline features and indicate the type of data that may be required by an oil company client.

Pipeline inspection tasks are shown in Figs. 4 and 6 however they are discussed in greater detail in Section 2, 'Inspection Diving'.

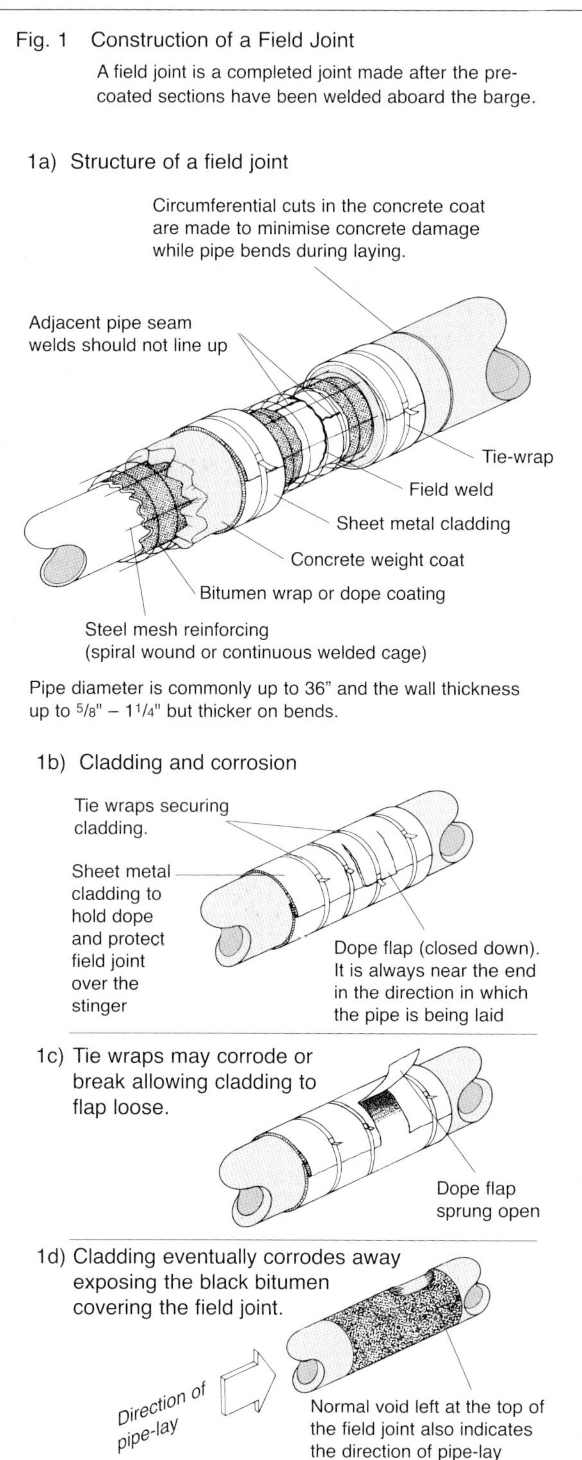
1a) Structure of a field joint
Circumferential cuts in the concrete coat are made to minimise concrete damage while pipe bends during laying.
Adjacent pipe seam welds should not line up
Tie-wrap
Field weld
Sheet metal cladding
Concrete weight coat
Bitumen wrap or dope coating
Steel mesh reinforcing (spiral wound or continuous welded cage)
Pipe diameter is commonly up to 36" and the wall thickness up to 5/8" – 1 1/4" but thicker on bends.
1b) Cladding and corrosion
Tie wraps securing cladding.
Sheet metal cladding to hold dope and protect field joint over the stinger
Dope flap (closed down). It is always near the end in the direction in which the pipe is being laid
1c) Tie wraps may corrode or break allowing cladding to flap loose.
Dope flap sprung open
1d) Cladding eventually corrodes away exposing the black bitumen covering the field joint.
Direction of pipe-lay
Normal void left at the top of the field joint also indicates the direction of pipe-lay

Fig. 1 Construction of a Field Joint

A field joint is a completed joint made after the pre-coated sections have been welded aboard the barge.

Fig. 2 Pipeline terminations
(see also Pig traps, Pigs and Pigging, Section 1.7)

a) Blind flange.

b) Pulling head or lay-down head.

c) Laydown head with internal valve(s).

d) Laydown head with external valve(s). The valves may be protected by a shroud or frame. There may be an extension tube on the inlet/outlet to deflect water or air away from the diver.

e) Net fitted to open flanged end to catch pigs.

f) Caged or recessed bleed valve with flange.

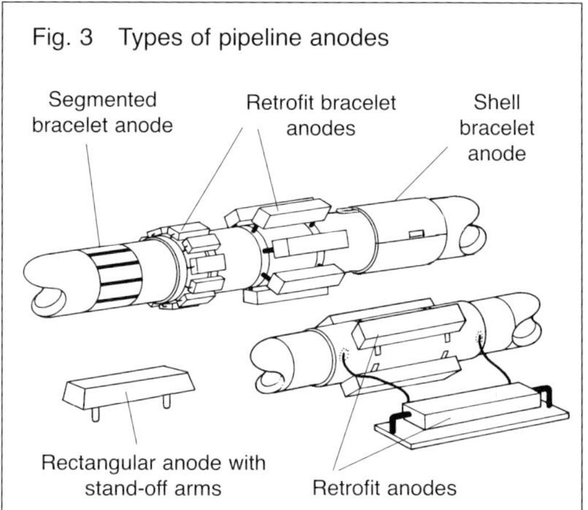
Segmented bracelet anode
Retrofit bracelet anodes
Shell bracelet anode
Rectangular anode with stand-off arms
Retrofit anodes

Fig. 3 Types of pipeline anodes

Fig. 4 Pipeline stabilisation techniques

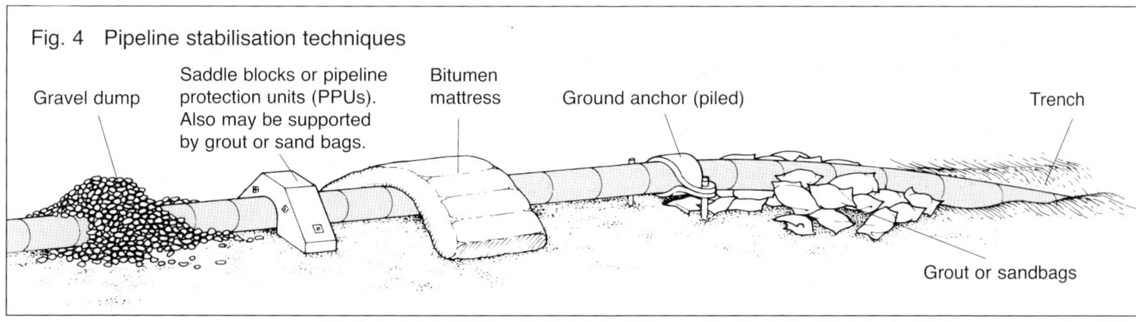

Gravel dump
Saddle blocks or pipeline protection units (PPUs). Also may be supported by grout or sand bags.
Bitumen mattress
Ground anchor (piled)
Trench
Grout or sandbags

Fig. 5 Pipeline inspection tasks

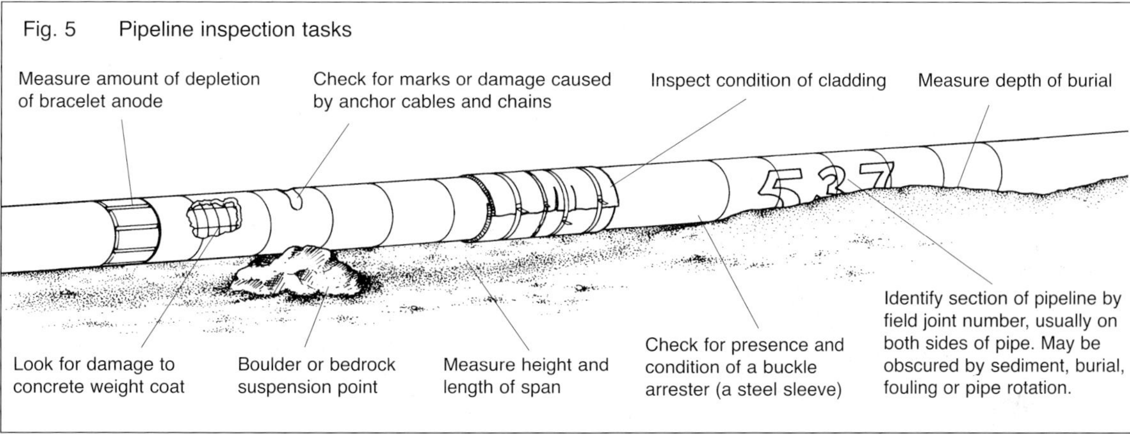

Measure amount of depletion of bracelet anode
Check for marks or damage caused by anchor cables and chains
Inspect condition of cladding
Measure depth of burial
Look for damage to concrete weight coat
Boulder or bedrock suspension point
Measure height and length of span
Check for presence and condition of a buckle arrester (a steel sleeve)
Identify section of pipeline by field joint number, usually on both sides of pipe. May be obscured by sediment, burial, fouling or pipe rotation.

Scouring

The dimensions and position of scours need to be estimated accurately. This is needed to assess the movement of scours and whether the size of the scour is increasing (by comparing with previous surveys). Scours should only be so-called when the seabed drops to the bottom point of the pipe, as opposed to the 'scallop' effects often noticed against the side of the pipe (see Fig 7). The scallop effect is not as important as scour. Differentiation between the two is required on any report or video commentary.

Fig. 7 Seabed scour and scallop effect

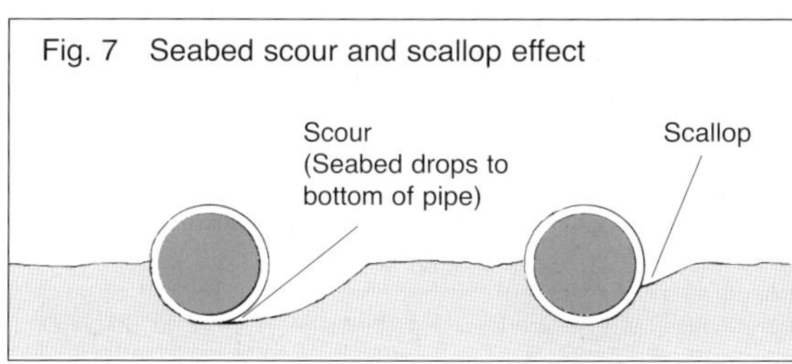

Scour (Seabed drops to bottom of pipe)
Scallop

Fig. 6 Characteristics of a trench

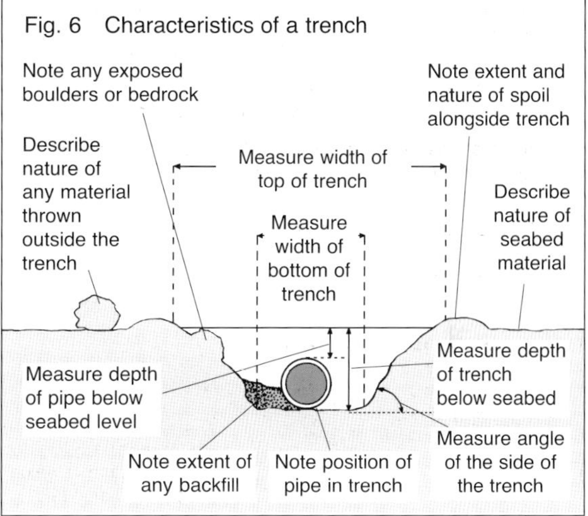

Note any exposed boulders or bedrock
Note extent and nature of spoil alongside trench
Describe nature of any material thrown outside the trench
Measure width of top of trench
Measure width of bottom of trench
Describe nature of seabed material
Measure depth of pipe below seabed level
Measure depth of trench below seabed
Measure angle of the side of the trench
Note extent of any backfill
Note position of pipe in trench

Spans

Estimate dimensions as accurately as possible, if necessary in field joints and pipe lengths (see Fig. 8). Detailed coverage is required to enable comparison with previous work, to assess whether the span has got larger or smaller.

Fig. 8 Span inspection

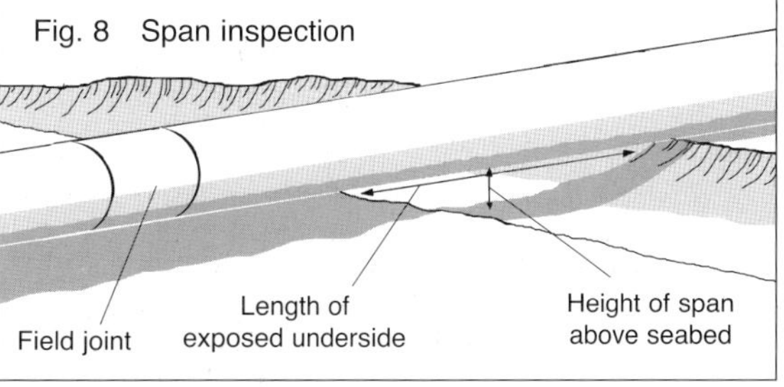

Field joint
Length of exposed underside
Height of span above seabed

Pipeline damage

Accurate dimensions are required of any damage down to the bare pipe metal. The term 'pipe damage' must not be used lightly. It applies only to the pipe metal itself, not to the concrete coat. For guidance on the inspection of concrete structures and pipe coating, see Fig. 9. The terminology relating to concrete construction is illustrated in Fig. 10.

Fig. 9 Visual inspection guide for concrete-coated pipelines (see also Section 10)

This guide is to assist divers in the inspection of offshore concrete structures. A complete classification of concrete defects is given the *American Concrete Institute Code 201*, and HMSO publication, *Typical blemishes visible on the surface of concrete underwater (OTH 87 261)*. The accuracy of recording features will depend on the class of inspection.

Divers should attempt to describe defects fully so that their significance, related to structural integrity can be assessed by engineers. Careful visual observation is needed because it can be difficult to distinguish between defects and normal features. For example, thin wire could be mistakenly identified as a crack or white paint as sulphate attack.

1. CRACKS: An incomplete separation into one or more parts with or without space between. Caused by a force sufficient to rip concrete apart.

Feature	Description	Cause	What to record
Corrosion cracks	Most likely to occur in the splash zone or where cover is low. Usually follows line of reinforcement.	Corrosion of reinforcement. Corrosion products are larger than the initial volume of steel giving rise to bursting forces.	Length, width, orientation, surface deposits, location. Covermeters are available to measure the cover and position of reinforcement.
Thermal cracking	Most likely to occur in storage cells.	Restricted expansion or contraction of concrete.	Length, width, orientation, location.
Structural overload	From impact most likely to occur in splash zone and cell roofs. Distribution of cracks is important for structural analysis.	Excessive applied force, eg impact, environmental.	Length, width, orientation, location.
Pattern cracking	Pattern found by interconnection of cracks.	Differential volume change between surface and internal concrete.	Area covered, location, width.
Shrinkage cracking	Possibly in unprestressed concrete. Can form even distribution over the surface.	Concrete curing.	Length, width, orientation, location.

2. CONCRETE LOSSES: Loss of concrete section formed after construction.

Feature	Description	Cause	What to record
Pop out	Shallow, typically conical depressions in the concrete surface.	Development of localised internal pressure, eg expansion of aggregate particle.	Diameter, depth, location.
Spall	Fragment detached from mass. Depression formed exposing aggregate not covered by laitence (see Fig. 10).	Corrosion of reinforcement or application of applied force.	Exposed reinforcement, complete dimensional survey, location.
Delamination	A form of 'spall' except that the fragment breaks away in a sheet. Thickness of sheet varies from 5-100mm but often to depth of reinforcement.	Corrosion of reinforcement or applied force.	Exposed reinforcement, complete dimensional survey, location.
Chemical attack	Softening of concrete surface possibly white surface appearance.	Sulphate attack.	Area covered, depth, location.
Erosion	Possibly due to particles in fast moving seawater.	Abrasion of concrete surface.	Area covered, depth, location.

3. SURFACE DEPOSITS

Feature	Description	Cause	What to record
Exudation	A liquid or viscous gel-like material discharged through a pore, crack or opening in the surface.	Reaction between the alkali in the cement and the aggregate.	Extent of area covered, thickness, whether hard or soft, location.
Incrustation	A crust or coating generally white in appearance.	Leaching of lime from the cement.	Extent of area covered, thickness, whether hard or soft, location.
Rust stains	Brown stains on the concrete surface.	Corrosion of embedded steelwork.	Extent of area covered, location.

4. CONSTRUCTION FEATURES: Visible surface features not generally considered as defects.

Feature	Description	Cause	What to record
Construction joint	Usually marked on construction drawings. Distinguishable from cracks since they are more continuous and a smoother line.	Placing fresh concrete on hardened concrete.	Location, if not marked on drawing.
Panel joint	Slight honeycombing and grout wedges a few millimetres wide are sometimes associated.	Marks formed by the joints in formwork.	

Fig. 9 continued overleaf

Fig. 9 (continued)

5. CONSTRUCTION DEFECTS: Defects formed on the concrete surface during construction. (see also p. 262)			
Defect	Description	Cause	What to record
Tearing	Similar in appearance to horizontal cracks on slip formed walls. Normally discontinuous from about 100mm (4") to several metres long.	Adhesion of the concrete to slip form shutters as they are jacked up.	Width, length, measurable depth, location.
Honey-combing	Voidage between coarse aggregate.	Vibration of concrete insufficient to give complete compaction.	Area covered, estimate of voids as a percentage, location.
Voidage	Non-designed recess in concrete.	Debris left in shutters.	Length, width, depth, location.
Cold joint	Similar appearance to crack. Distinguished by close examination as line is smooth, not jagged, as if ripped apart. Line is not continuous and rarely straight.	Lack of vibration between concrete layers.	Location, orientation, length.

Fig. 10 Typical section through a concrete wall to illustrate the terminology of concrete construction.

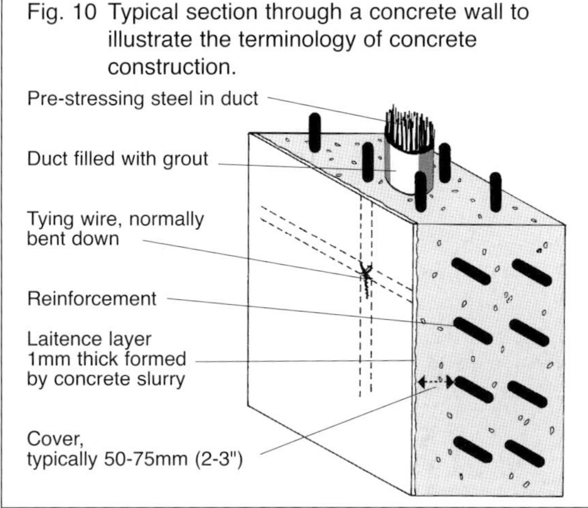
Pre-stressing steel in duct
Duct filled with grout
Tying wire, normally bent down
Reinforcement
Laitence layer 1mm thick formed by concrete slurry
Cover, typically 50-75mm (2-3")

Debris (see Fig. 11).

1. Items of interest are those found essentially within 3m (10ft) of pipe.
2. Large items such as 45 gallon oil drums should be noted, but not small tins, etc.
3. Cables and ropes are important. Their positions and dimensions must be given.
4. Fishing nets. Give dimensions of large pieces and rolls but ignore small pieces of under 1m (3ft) diameter.
5. Rocks and boulders should be mentioned but only attach importance to those in excess of 1m (3ft) diameter.
6. Note the condition of pipeline cladding. It can be a rusty covering on field joints or be lying on the seabed beside the pipeline.

Fig. 11 Debris identification

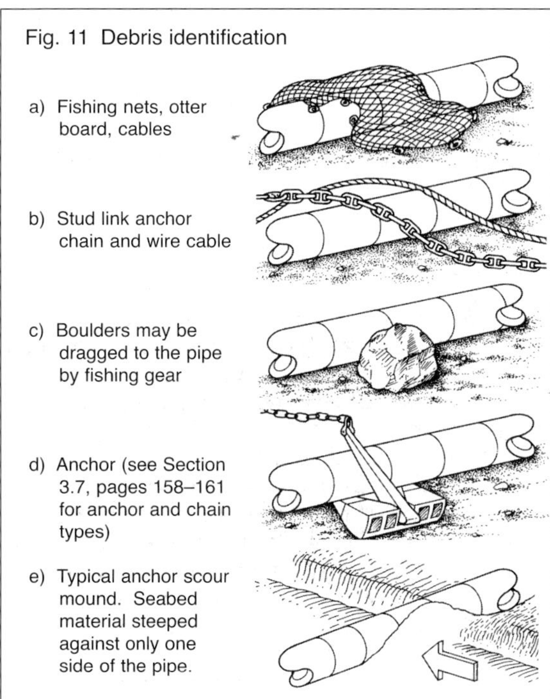
a) Fishing nets, otter board, cables
b) Stud link anchor chain and wire cable
c) Boulders may be dragged to the pipe by fishing gear
d) Anchor (see Section 3.7, pages 158–161 for anchor and chain types)
e) Typical anchor scour mound. Seabed material steeped against only one side of the pipe.

Reporting

Great importance is attached to technical accuracy, detail and standardisation of format and terminology.

NATURE OF THE SEABED

When reporting on the nature of the seabed it is useful to use standardised terminology as illustrated in Fig. 12.

PIPELINE INSPECTION – OPERATIONAL SAFETY

1. Always be aware of the dangers of differential pressure when working on pipelines and valves. There is a possibility of being sucked onto and into valves and pipes when pressure differentials are rapidly altered.
2. Take care to avoid contact with high concentrations of corrosion inhibitor, oxygen scavenger and dyes which may escape from the pipe. Special care should be taken to avoid contact between these substances and hot water suits and to avoid the possibility of contaminating the interior of the bell.

VIDEO RECORDING

The following would form an introduction to an inspection record such as a video recording in order to assist in future data retrieval and cross-referencing. Every separate tape should carry such an introduction, at least as an audio heading.

Fig. 12 Characteristics of the the seabed

It is helpful to use standardised terms when describing the seabed. The following system is adopted internationally.

Boulder. A detached rock mass, rounded (or otherwise modified by abrasion). Minimum size is 255mm (10") diameter.

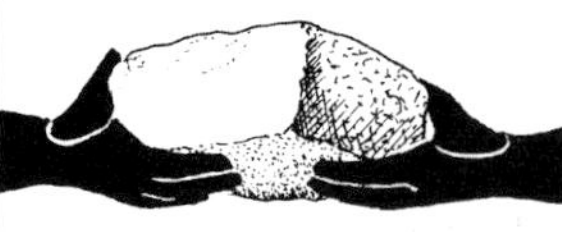

Block. Same size as a boulder but an angular fragment showing little or no abrasion.

Cobbles. Similar to boulders but smaller. Size ranges from 65 to 255mm ($2^1/_2$ – 10").

Pebbles. Rock fragments, rounded or otherwise abraded by the water, ice or wind. Size ranges from 5-5mm ($^3/_8$ – $2^1/_2$ ").

Granules. Small rock fragments 2 – 4mm ($^1/_{16}$ – $^1/_8$ ") in diameter.

Sand. An aggregate of mineral or rock grains between 0.6 and 2mm in diameter.

Silt. Sediment consisting of particles ranging in size from 0.004 – 0.6mm.

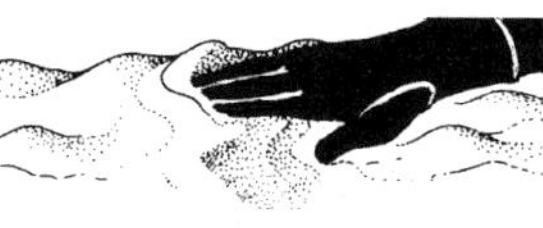

Clay. Sediment with particle sizes of less than 0.004mm diameter.

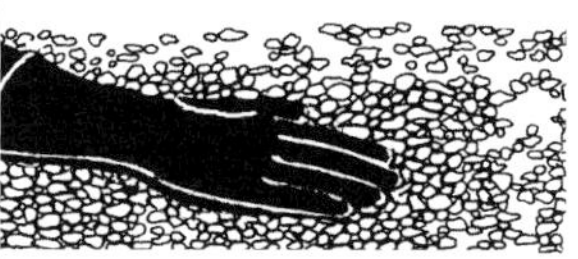

Gravel. Unconsolidated accumulation of pebbles, cobbles or boulders. Referred to as pebble-gravel, cobble-gravel, etc as appropriate.

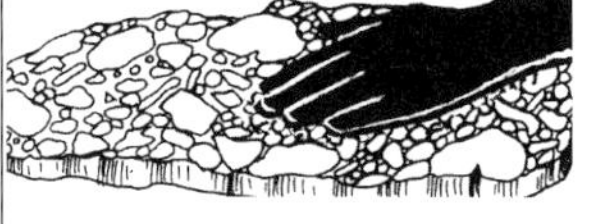

Conglomerate. Consolidated equivalent of gravel and likewise is called pebble-, cobble-conglomerate, etc as appropriate.

Rubble. Unconsolidated accumulation of angular rock fragments coarser than sand.

Such information can be presented on a video recording using any of the following methods:

- Electronic character generator
- On a chalk board
- On a dry wipe board
- On a notice board with removable letters/figures.
- As a voice recording.

Title items should include:

a) Name of project.
b) Name of client.
c) Name of inspection company.
d) Name of surface support vessel.
e) Name and designation of inspection equipment (submersible, ROV, diver).
f) Name of pilot/observer/diver.
g) Date: day, month, year.
h) Time: 24 hour clock.
i) Video tape number.
j) Dive number.
k) Geographical location, eg:
   - North Sea
   - UTM co-ordinates or latitude and longitude
   - mile post or chainage.
   - any relevant chart reference numbers.
l) Pipe start and finish location.
m) Pipe diameter.

Video records are greatly improved if an electronic character generator provides data in real time during the recording on:

a) Date and time.
b) Gyro compass heading of vehicle (if applicable).
c) Depth.
d) CP readings, etc.

Additional information can also be added at a later stage when editing tapes, for example, arrows indicating areas of interest.

THE COMMENTARY

Before diving:

1. Familiarise yourself with client drawings so that you can refer to them as appropriate.
2. Familiarise yourself with the client's terminology and use it as appropriate.

Underwater:

3. Speak clearly and slightly slower than normal.
4. Be brief.
5. Be positive.
6. Avoid saying 'er . . .' and 'um . . .'.
7. Don't be afraid of repetition.
8. Never be flippant.
9. Never swear.
10. Be as informative as possible.
11. If the TV is black and white, describe colours.
12. Always comment on anything unusual.

Remember, All that the onshore engineer has to refer to is the video tape commentary. Make sure it is accurate and not ambiguous.

From time to time go through the tapes made by you and ask yourself:

- Is what I am saying relevant?
- Is it informative?
- Is the picture I am showing clearly demonstrating what I am saying?
- Is the microphone too close or too far away?

Use your self-criticism constructively to improve your recording technique.

PROCEDURAL ADVICE

1. Leave one minute of tape free at the start of each tape for later addition of titles.
2. Tape changes should be at field joints or other readily identifiable points. Stop so that the field joint is in the frame at the end of one tape and at the start of the next. If this is impractical, arrange for the next tape to start at an identifiable point already covered at the end of the previous tape.
3. Describe burial depths using the following terms:
   a) Pipe lying firmly on the seabed.
   b) Pipe $^1/_4$, $^1/_2$, or $^3/_4$, buried.
   c) Pipe fully buried.
   d) Pipe suspended by 5cm (2"), 10cm (4"), etc

.

STILL PHOTOGRAPHY

Try to take stills with the video running, even if the tape is not to be presented to the client. On the video commentary mention where you are when taking a still. This will establish exactly where and when the photo was taken. Give full details of the still: what it is, its position, which side of the pipe it is on, the photo number, film size (35mm or 70mm), the gyro axis of the camera and the depth. The observer can also log these details.

A checklist of items which need to be recorded or described in any survey is given in Fig. 13.

Example of inspection procedure for underwater pipelines damaged by anchor cables

Although this example relates specifically to anchor damage many of these activities can be used in other types of inspection. It is essential that divers, supervisors and NDT personnel know exactly what the procedure will be before commencing the survey.

To facilitate the data collection and to make reporting as fast and as accurate as possible the senior NDT supervisor should have a clear idea of the final reporting format very soon after sighting the damage area. The report should include details of the type and frequency of instrument calibration.

1. *Location, identification and marking*

a) Position bell over the damaged area (assuming there is no danger from any pipe contents reaching the bell and contaminating the bell atmosphere). Take accurate surface position fix. Record field joint numbers on either side of the damaged pipe.

Fig. 13 Items which may be included in a general pipeline inspection video or written report.

- Orientation of pipe
- Depth
- Current direction and speed
- Nature of seabed, note changes
- Identify which side of pipe is being inspected
- Condition of weight coat
- Field joint condition
- Field joint numbers
- Presence of buckle arresters
- Condition and type of anodes
- Spans, length and height
- Nature of trench
- Burial status
- Anchor mounds in seabed
- Cable marks/damage to pipe
- Cable marks on seabed
- Debris:
  - identification
  - description
  - location
- Damage:
  - weight coat
  - reinforcing wire
  - bitumen wrap
  - pipe metal
- NDT data:
  - corrosion potential readings*
  - MPI
  - ultrasonics*
  - radiography
- Leak detection:
  - dye
  - bubbles
  - scouring of seabed
  - water/plankton movement
  - rust marks
  - product
- Pig tracking

*On bare metal: ultrasonic thickness measurement and cathodic protection. If specially required, expose metal at field joint. CP may be required on nearest anode.

b) Install a labelled marker pole
c) Establish upstream/downstream directions.

2. *General area survey*

a) Carry out a video survey in the immediate vicinity of the damaged area to a radius of about 20m (66ft) and include footage of the damage (Fig. 14).

Fig. 14

b) Record the position of any anchor chains or wires, debris, etc and the direction of chains, trenches, scour, scars, etc.
c) Record the position of any field joints and any anodes or buckle arresters within the survey area.

3. *General inspection and surface preparation*

a) Take still photographs of the damaged area of pipe and any significant findings resulting from the general area survey (Fig. 15a).

Fig. 15a

b) If the sediment and/or marine growth is heavy, remove it using a fan jet (Fig. 15b). Note if there is any surface corrosion on the exposed steel.

Fig. 15b

c) Mark the four clock positions around the damaged area with the 12 o'clock position on the up-stream side of the damage (Fig. 15c).

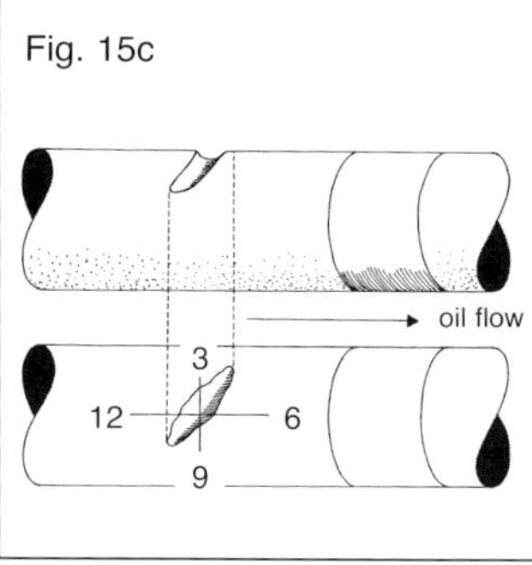
oil flow
3
12
6
9
Fig. 15c

d) Take still photographs from each position at about 45° to the damaged plane (Fig. 15d).
The stand-off distance will be determined by the dimensions of the damage but each photograph should cover the whole area of interest. Take low-level stills along the plane of the damage to give indication of groove depth and profile.

Fig. 15d

e) Remove all weight and corrosion coating up to 100mm (½") into sound coating (Fig. 15e). Remove wire re-inforcing. Clean to parent metal.

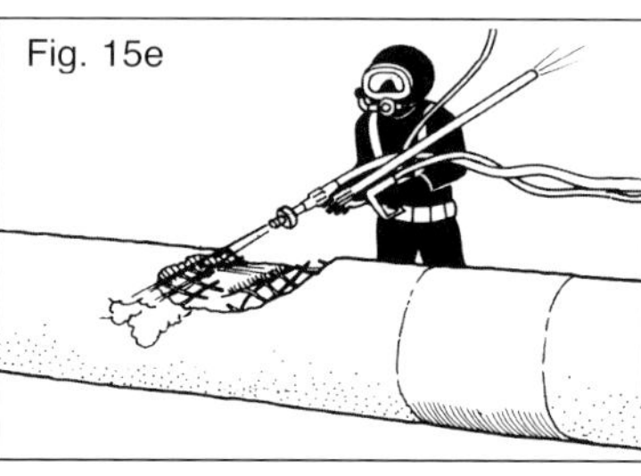
Fig. 15e

f) Make a moulding of any metal surface indentation with Ephopen or similar (Fig. 15f). Ensure that the orientation is marked on the moulding.

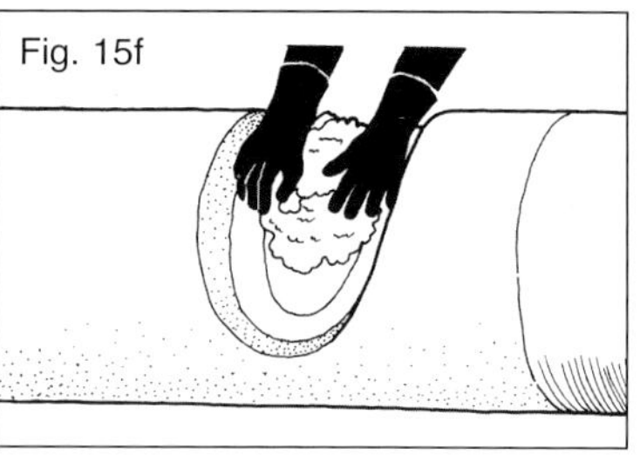
Fig. 15f

g) Photogrammetry. Adjust the camera by taking six photographs of the frame from at least two different angles, determined by the photo-technician. These will depend upon visibility, size, etc. Align the camera probes at 90° to the plane of damage and take three 45° either side of the perpendicular (Fig. 15g). Take a further six of calibration frame on completion.

Fig. 15g

4. *Non destructive testing (NDT)*

a) Use hand tools to flush any burr type defects to assist the probe-to-metal contact (Fig. 16a).

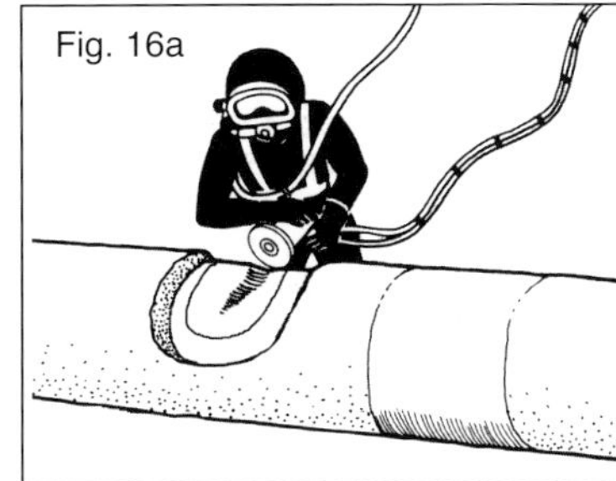

Fig. 16a

b) Carry out MPI (see Fig. 16b).

Fig. 16b

c) Locate the deepest point of damage with a pit gauge and scribe a straight line passing over the point and in the direction of the gauge or dent. Scribe a second line through that point in the direction of the pipe axis. Mark off 10mm (or 1/2") increments on each line the full length of the damaged area (Fig. 16c).

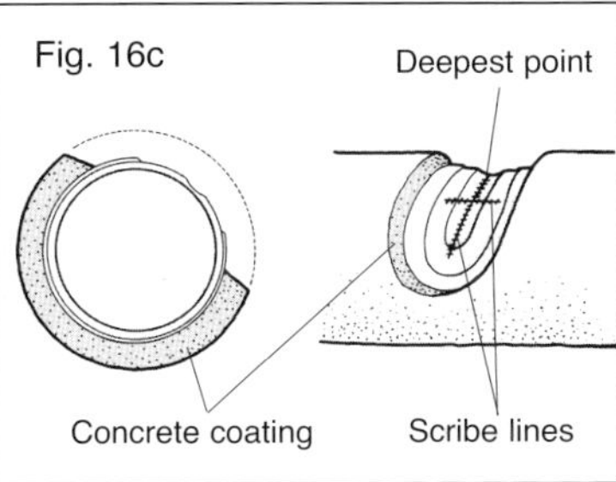
Deepest point
Concrete coating
Scribe lines

Fig. 16c

d) Take still photographs of the grid (Fig. 16d).

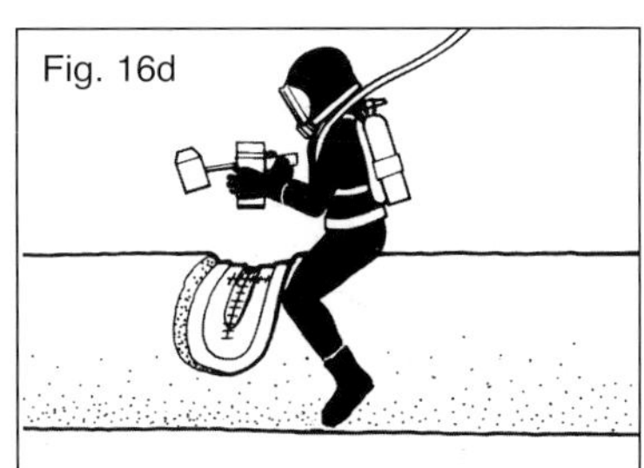

Fig. 16d

e) Take ultrasonic wall thickness measurements of each grid point using, for example, a compression probe. Readings to be continued into damaged parent plate on each axis to give a check reading on a parent plate thickness.

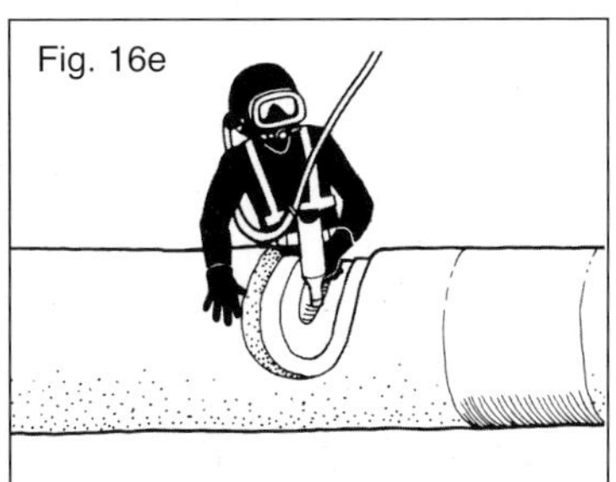

Fig. 16e

f) Take CP potential readings. One reading for each half m^2 ($1/2\ yd^2$) of exposed steel will suffice. Take a reading from a standard zinc anode before and after bare metal readings.

Fig. 16f

1.12 SHIPWORK

This drawing of a typical cargo ship shows the approximate position of various underwater fittings that might require the services of a diver. No two vessels are exactly alike, so the diver would need to consult the ship's plans for the exact position, location and type of all fittings. Classification societies, such as Lloyds Register, Bureau Veritas, etc, issue their own rules for their classification in-water surveys. These precisely detail the diver tasks required.

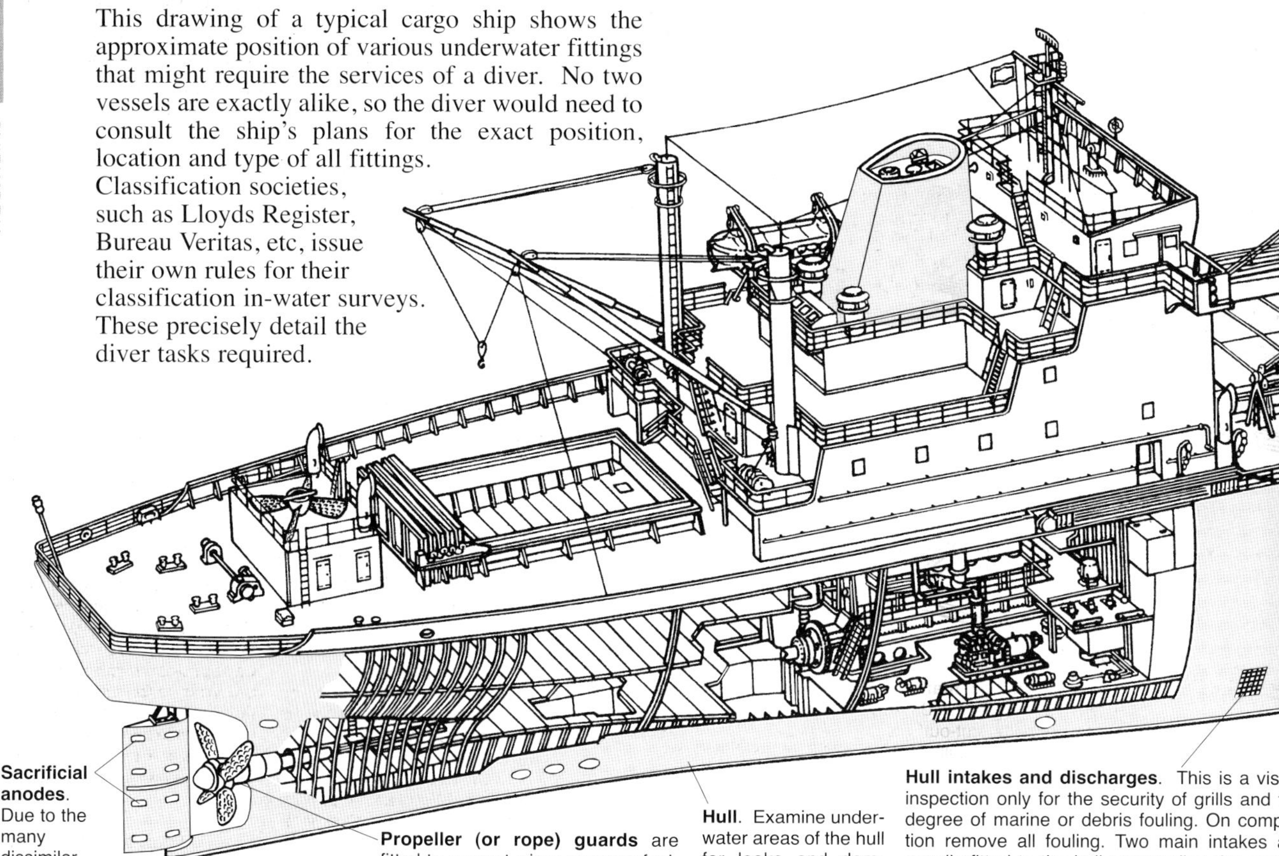

Sacrificial anodes. Due to the many dissimilar metals around the stern a number of sacrificial anodes may be fitted. Check each anode as in 'Rudder, stock and bearings' section 'e', below.

Propeller (or rope) guards are fitted to prevent wires or ropes fouling the propeller. They are circular plates which cover the gap between the aft end of the propeller shaft and the forward face of the propeller.

Hull. Examine underwater areas of the hull for leaks and damage. Look for pockets of trapped air under a flat-bottomed hull and measure their depth.

Hull intakes and discharges. This is a visu inspection only for the security of grills and t degree of marine or debris fouling. On comp tion remove all fouling. Two main intakes a usually fitted to the hull surrounding the engi room – one high and one low. There may many more intakes and discharges elsewhere the hull. The senior engineer on watch must told that divers are at work.

Preparing to work on a ship's bottom

SHIP'S CREW'S RESPONSIBILITIES

Before the diver enters the water:

1. The senior engineer on watch must ensure that the main engines are shut down and the shaft brakes are on with warning signs displayed in the engine room and on the bridge. Beware, there is a tendency for some propellers to turn, even when the engine may be in neutral. This is particularly true of steam turbine engines while cooling down.
2. Because of the possible suction effects on divers working on main inlets, the circulating pumps must be stopped and the main inlet and discharge valves shut. Overboard discharges are to be secured.
3. Sonar equipment should not be energised and their power switches should be tagged to that effect.
4. The stabiliser breaker must be opened and a warning board affixed to it.
5. If an impressed current cathodic protection system is fitted, it must be switched off.
6. International flag 'A' should be flown and the deck officer kept acquainted with the progress of the diving operations.
7. The Harbour and Berthing Master should also be informed of the diving operations.

DIVING TEAM'S RESPONSIBILITIES

1. The Diving Supervisor must be aware of the state of the tide, especially the depth of water beneath the ship's bottom on the ebb.
2. The underwater staging and bottom lines must be securely and properly rigged for the work.
3. If diving is from a boat, it must be moored so that it cannot break adrift while the diver is down. If diving is in tidal waters, both boat and underwater stages must be secured so that they do not drift.
4. The diver can be negatively buoyant so as to increase his purchase when using tools underwater.
5. The diver should be fully briefed in exactly what he is required to do and should be shown any relevant ship's plans or fitting diagrams.
   Care must be taken when using older ship drawings. They are often wrong and may not show post-manufacturing modifications – eg, inlets may be in different positions.
6. All tools likely to be required for the task should be ready at the work site.
7. It is often difficult for the diver to be sure that he has reached exactly the right fitting, especially when there are several similar ones close together. There are various ways of guiding him, for example: air can be

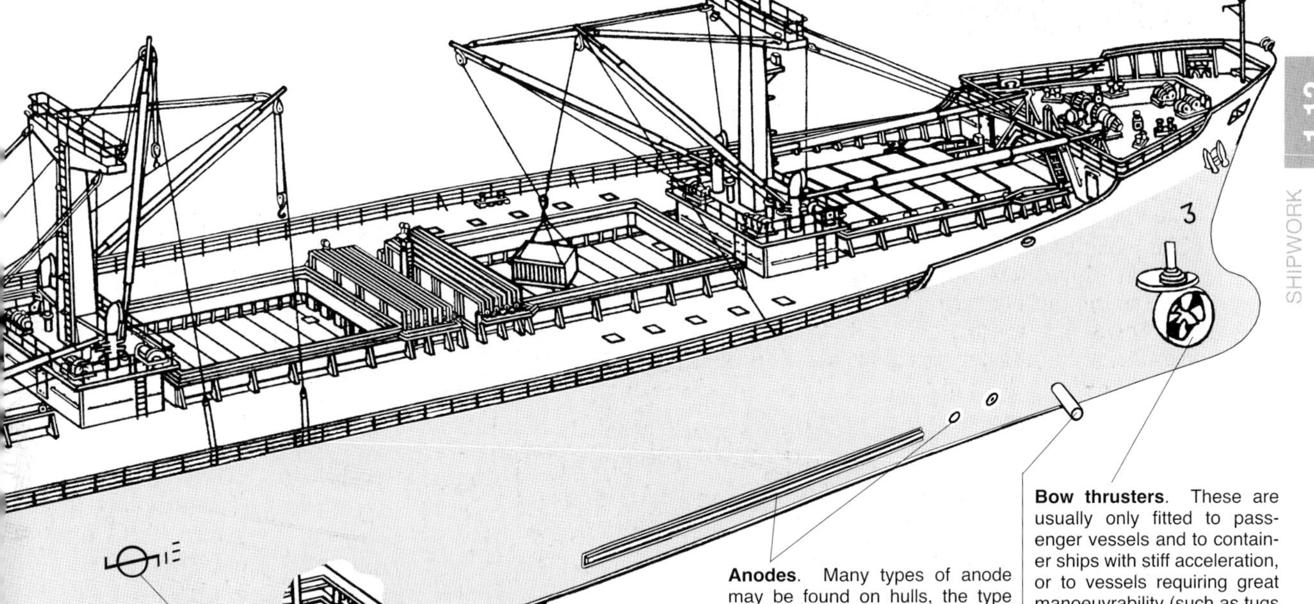

Load line markings, ie Lloyd's Register, Bureau Veritas, etc, are normally 'cut-out' steel markings welded onto the hull. These marks are usually situated slightly above the water line depending on the trim. Marks are welded bead, not plate. Check for any sign of failing welds allowing marks to fall off or for any sign of damage.

Bilge Keel. Check for security, broken welds, condition of sacrificial anodes, physical damage or distortion.

Double bottoms are rows of cellular boxes each side of the keel and running along two thirds of the hull. They act as a second ship's bottom in case of damage and are often filled with fuel or water.

Fin stabilisers (not illustrated). Check travel to port and starboard. Hydroplane to full dive then mark ship's side with crayon at the trailing edge, the full rise and neutral positions. Measure distance from centre mark to top and bottom marks.

Anodes. Many types of anode may be found on hulls, the type fitted depends on the protection required. These may vary from sacrificial anodes for external cathodic protection to impressed current systems.

Marine growth needs to be removed periodically because the friction it causes reduces the ship's speed. It can also cause corrosion by breaking through the protective anti-fouling. Check and report on percentage coverage, thickness, density and nature, especially around intakes close to discharges where hot fluids will encourage rapid growth. Marine growth cleaning is usually done with divers using brush carts.

Bow thrusters. These are usually only fitted to passenger vessels and to container ships with stiff acceleration, or to vessels requiring great manoeuvrability (such as tugs or DP vessels). Usually it is a 'tunnel' right through the bow section with a propeller inside. Some thrusters are fitted with grills on openings which must be kept clear of fouling. Check propeller as for stern – welds, debris and any loose packing gland material. Most bow thrusters may be entered from inside the hull for inspection.

Log. Retractable electronic device. Check free movement – extended and retracted; measure protrusion if necessary; check for damage, corrosion and marine fouling.

pumped through an outlet to produce bubbles as a guide; someone inside the ship, close to the fitting can tap on the hull with a hammer.

8. The tender must remain constantly alert in case the diver should fall off a stage.

Rudder, Stock and Bearings (see Fig.1)

Starting at the top, inspect:

a) *Rudder stock*. Check for cracks and connection to rudder for loose or missing bolts or nuts.

b) *Upper support housing*. Look for obvious wear, loose or missing bolts or nuts, the security and effectiveness of locking devices and any missing components. The space between the upper bearing gland and rudder should be free of debris.

c) *Top portion of rudder*. Check for missing filling plugs, corrosion and damage.

d) *Inspection plates*. Check for security of all bolts or nuts, and that no gasket material is hanging loose or parts of gaskets are missing.

e) *Sacrificial anodes* (Fig. 2). Check for degree and coverage of pitting. Measure pits and report average depth and maximum depth of pitting. Check and report percentage waste.

Take circumferential and one length measurements to compare with the original (as new) size. Check if securely attached. Check securing lugs for corrosion or if in good condition.

Check and report if anodes are secured by bolts, welded lugs or any other means.

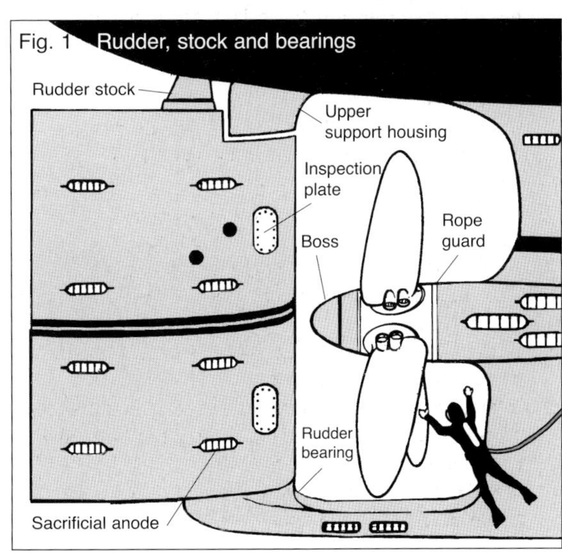
Rudder stock
Upper support housing
Inspection plate
Boss
Rope guard
Rudder bearing
Sacrificial anode

Fig. 1 Rudder, stock and bearings

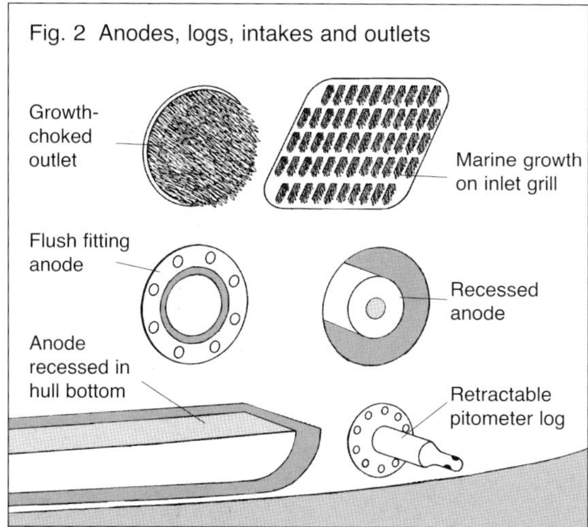
Growth-
choked
outlet
Marine growth
on inlet grill
Flush fitting
anode
Recessed
anode
Anode
recessed in
hull bottom
Retractable
pitometer log

Fig. 2 Anodes, logs, intakes and outlets

f) *Lower portion of rudder.* Check plugs, lower inspection plate(s), anodes and lower bearing. NOTE: If rudder can be moved, with the diver on the propeller shaft (ensuring that both the diver and his umbilical are well clear of movement), the rudder should be set amidships and the position checked for alignment; then hard to port/starboard and the full travel checked and measured in degrees, if possible. Measure rudder tracking edge to prop boss when rudder is hard to port and hard to starboard.

g) *Rudder bearings.* Check rudder bearing clearances. Measure with feeler gauges at 3 o'clock and 9 o'clock positions, then 6 and 12 o'clock positions.

Propeller and Shafting (see Fig.1)

a) Check boss for damage, locking devices and that no significant gap exists in any joints.

b) Check each blade for chipping, cracks, distortion, 'polishing.' If any damage has occurred, take detailed measurements of all dimensions of any damage. Report with a sketch and carefully note which blade it is on in that particular position.

c) If variable pitch, check each blade's securing flange, nuts and locking devices. Check that no debris, ie wire rope, nylon, etc, has intruded on the fittings. With the diver well clear of the propeller but within good visibility range, check each blade as it is 'feathered'. Then turn from full-ahead position to full-astern. Measure this angle if practicable.

d) Report on all blades in sequence.

e) Check ropeguard for security, fixtures and securing bolts and locking devices. Check that no line or wire rope has entered the gap between the guard and the propeller. The propeller (or rope) guards are circular plates that cover the gap between the aft end of the propeller shaft and the forward face of the propeller. They are designed to prevent wires or ropes fouling the propeller.

f) If A-brackets are fitted, check for damage and any cracks, particularly the welds or attachment devices to both hull and shaft housing.

g) Clear ropes and debris and check main stern gland(s) for wear or damage.

h) Check all bearings and shafts for oil leaks.

i) *Bronze propeller blades – emergency repairs.* Do not use burning gear because the cut quality is very poor. For best results use a hydraulic cutting disc. On a four-bladed propeller, if one blade tip is repaired, the opposite blade tip will have to be equally cut to restore symmetry and balance and to prevent vibration. Three- or five-bladed propellers would require all the blades to be cut. A template needs to be made to ensure that the cut profile on each blade is accurately reproduced.

j) *Stem gland replacement.* The diver applies 'Denso' or equivalent tape around the shaft where it leaves the hull and packs it tightly to produce a temporary seal. When engineers have replaced the gland, the diver must remove the tape completely.

Hull cleaning and Prop polishing

A vessel's efficiency is significantly reduced if its hull and propellers become rough. Surface roughness can be caused by marine growth, mechanical damage or cavitation erosion. The resultant effect is increased drag and fuel consumption and, in the case of the propeller, increased torque, decreased thrust, and increased load on propulsion machinery for a given speed.

Surface roughness can be assessed using the Rubert Gauge which grades roughness from A (new finish) to F (very rough). The diver feels the surface of the propeller and assesses the roughness by comparing it to a Rubert Gauge. Several readings should be taken on both sides of the propeller blade (see Fig. 3).

Fig. 3 Assessing roughness of propeller blade

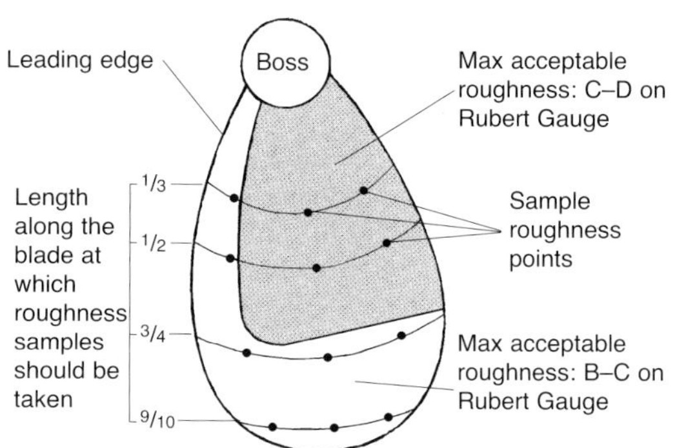
Leading edge
Boss
Max acceptable
roughness: C–D on
Rubert Gauge
Length
along the
blade at
which
roughness
samples
should be
taken
1/3
1/2
3/4
9/10
Sample
roughness
points
Max acceptable
roughness: B–C on
Rubert Gauge

Ideally the entire surface of the propeller blades should be polished but where this is not possible a 75% benefit can be gained by polishing the outer half and leading edges of the blades.

Hull cleaning and propeller polishing should be carried out regularly as part of a planned maintenance programme (ideally every 4–6 months). In-water hull cleaning can be carried out manually, with small hand-held polishers or, in the case of large vessels, by specialist machines which can be remotely or diver-operated (see Fig. 4).

Repairs to damaged hull

In some cases a wet weld can be acceptable to the insurance company. Otherwise, a caisson has to be built to surround the damaged area. The caisson is guided into place by a diver. When it is de-watered, the hydrostatic pressure is normally enough to secure it in position. Concrete is then pumped into the void from inside the vessel. This temporary repair is normally satisfactory to the insurance company until the vessel can be dry-docked for a permanent repair.

Thrusters

Many new vessels have jet thrusters instead of propellers. These are extremely powerful jet engines which suck water in through forward grilles and blast it out through ports in the stern.
Extreme care must be taken during any diving work on such vessels to ensure that the thrusters cannot be turned on at any time while divers are in the vicinity.
The stern area on these vessels is very complicated and the diver must rely on induction by experienced personnel in order to learn and confidently perform the individual diver tasks.

Fig. 4 Propeller polishing and hull cleaning

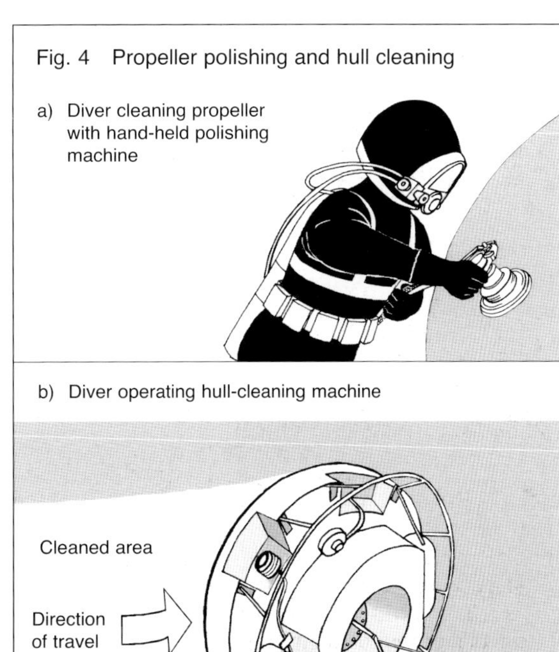
a) Diver cleaning propeller with hand-held polishing machine
b) Diver operating hull-cleaning machine
Cleaned area
Direction of travel
Hull

1.13 DOCKS AND HARBOURS

Docks, ports and harbours have strict administrative regimes.
The Dock/Harbour Master is responsible for safety aspects including all vessel movements, tidal and water conditions within his area of jurisdiction. There will probably be pre-existing conditions for calling emergency services and possibly the provision of in-house emergency services. There may be controlled access to specific sites.
Close co-operation with the relevant Dock/Harbour Master is essential. This includes clear voice communication using, for example, VHF radio links.

DIVER TASKS

The standard tasks for divers working in docks include:

1 Inspection of damage to dock walls.
2 Inspection of gates and sills.
3 Debris removal.
4 Video inspection of ship propellers.
5 Maintenance of sluices including replacement of spear rods in sluice pits.
6 Recovery of lost cargo and containers.
7 Recovery of miscellaneous lost items including various vehicles.

OPERATIONAL SAFETY

Specific hazards in docks and harbours can include:
- Locks and Weirs
- Underwater sluices
- Water outfalls and intakes
- Sewage
- Chemicals
- Noise from Pile-driving and breaking concrete
- Vessel movements

1. A Permit to Work system must be used.
2. Ensure a safe means of entry and exit for the diver to/from the water.
3. Establish good voice communications with the Dock Master.
4. Wear appropriate PPE (personal protection equipment) if there is a possible water pollution hazard.
5. Isolate sluice operating machinery as necessary.
6. Be aware of dangers associated with differential pressures.
7. When working in confined spaces, ensure that there is enough space to allow the safe recovery of an unconscious diver.
8. Fly the diving flag, Alpha.

Fig. 1 Construction of a dock gate

a) Structure of a typical mitre gate

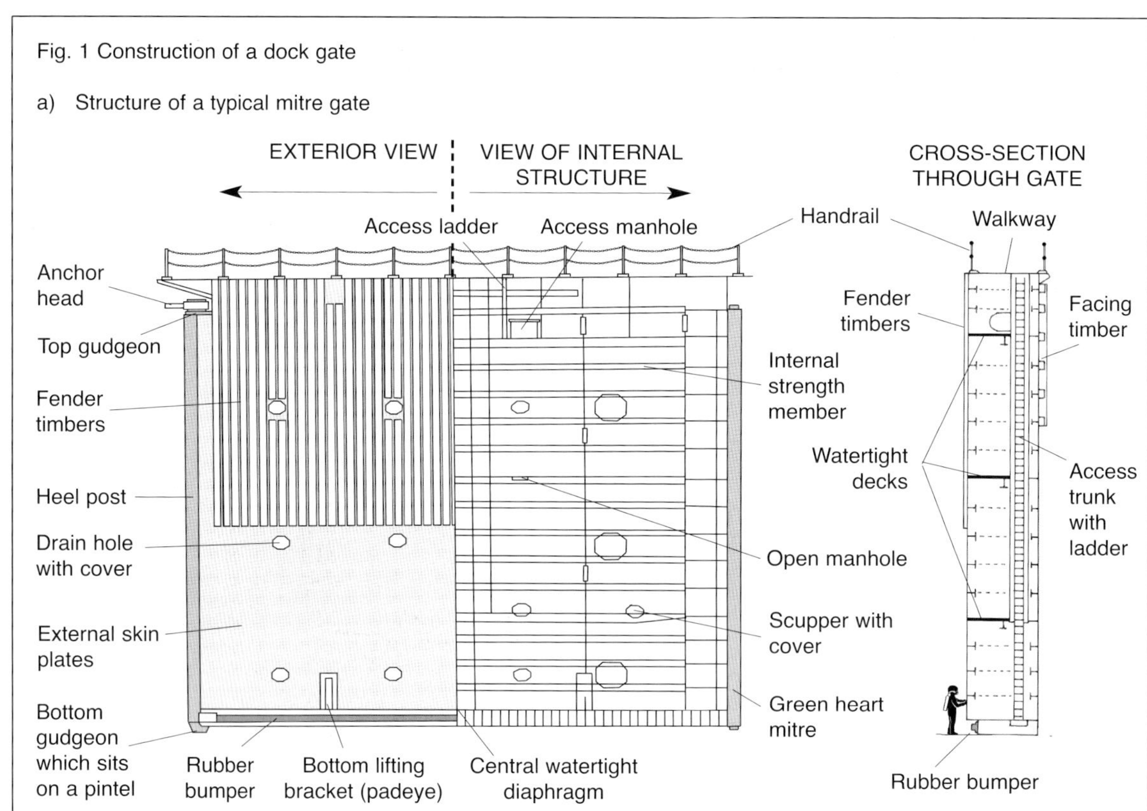
EXTERIOR VIEW
VIEW OF INTERNAL STRUCTURE
CROSS-SECTION THROUGH GATE
Access ladder
Access manhole
Handrail
Walkway
Anchor head
Top gudgeon
Fender timbers
Heel post
Drain hole with cover
External skin plates
Bottom gudgeon which sits on a pintel
Rubber bumper
Bottom lifting bracket (padeye)
Central watertight diaphragm
Fender timbers
Internal strength member
Watertight decks
Open manhole
Scupper with cover
Green heart mitre
Facing timber
Access trunk with ladder
Rubber bumper

b) Construction of Pintel (or Pivot)

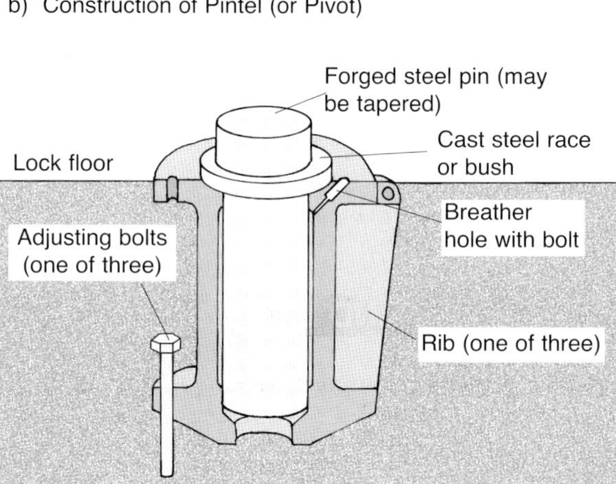
Forged steel pin (may be tapered)
Cast steel race or bush
Lock floor
Breather hole with bolt
Adjusting bolts (one of three)
Rib (one of three)

Mitre gates

These are common on most docks and locks and range enormously in size. A typical mitre gate is shown in Fig. 1a. The smaller gates may be fitted with sluices but larger locks usually have culverts fitted with their own sluices.

The gates are pivoted, top and bottom. At the top, a gudgeon (or journal) on the gate turns within a collar fixed to the lock head. At the bottom, a gudgeon sits in a pintel (or pivot) (see Fig. 1b) which is fixed in the lock floor.

When the gates are closed, they press on, and seal against meeting posts in the side walls and a mitre sill along the bottom of the lock.

c) Construction of Sill (plan view)

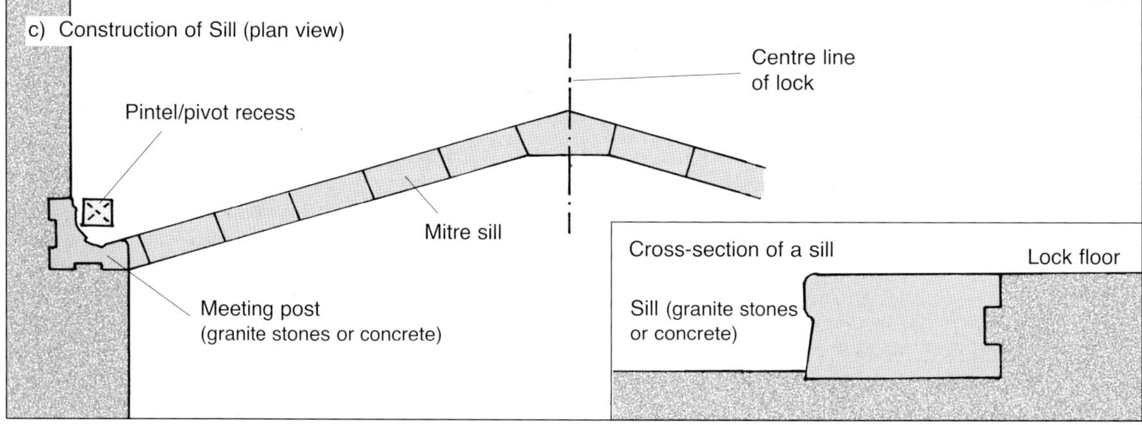
Centre line of lock
Pintel/pivot recess
Mitre sill
Meeting post (granite stones or concrete)
Cross-section of a sill
Lock floor
Sill (granite stones or concrete)

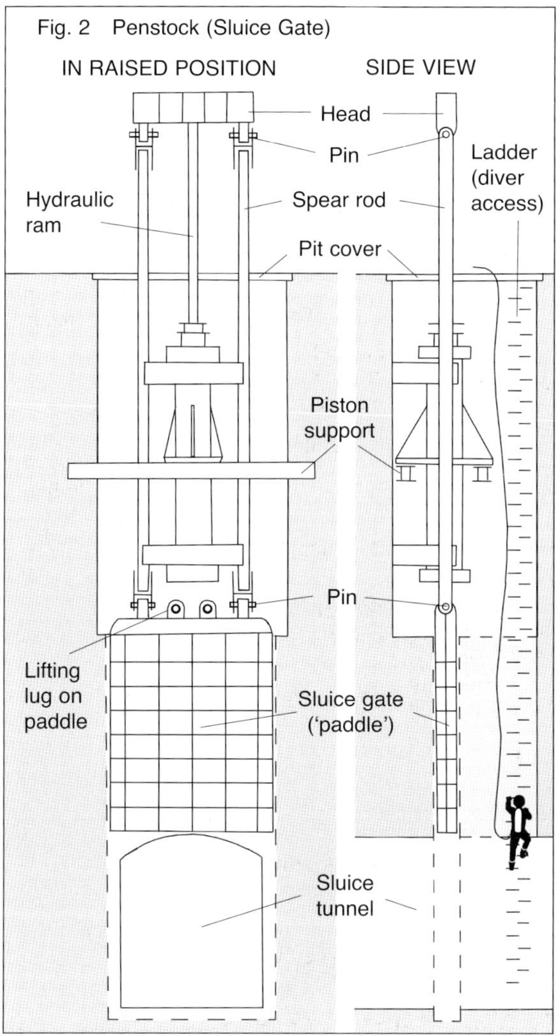
IN RAISED POSITION
SIDE VIEW
Head
Pin
Ladder
(diver
access)
Hydraulic
ram
Spear rod
Pit cover
Piston
support
Pin
Lifting
lug on
paddle
Sluice gate
('paddle')
Sluice
tunnel
Fig. 2 Penstock (Sluice Gate)

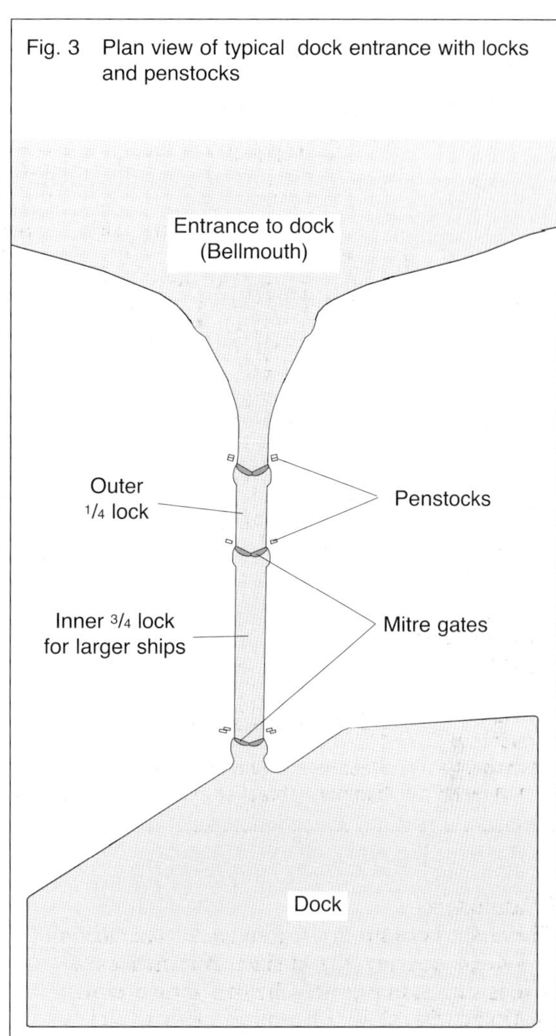
Entrance to dock
(Bellmouth)
Outer
1/4 lock
Penstocks
Inner 3/4 lock
for larger ships
Mitre gates
Dock
Fig. 3 Plan view of typical dock entrance with locks and penstocks

1.14 WEIRS AND LOCKS

Weirs and locks are used in rivers and canals for controlling water levels.

Weirs

Weirs are used to control the flow or level of the water, or to measure its flow. They are used in rivers and canals to raise the upstream water level. This can be in order to divert flow into canals, to assist the water supply by pumping, to create a head of water for hydraulic power or to maintain a required depth of water for navigation. Weirs can range from low walls across streams to the slipway crests of high dams.

The simplest weir is a fixed-crest structure, much like a dam, over which the water flows (see Fig. 1). Weirs can be constructed out of earth or rock, concrete, faced with 'Armourflex' or built on steel piling, in which case the face of the weir foundation would be vertical. They can be of various designs and are described by their profiles as:

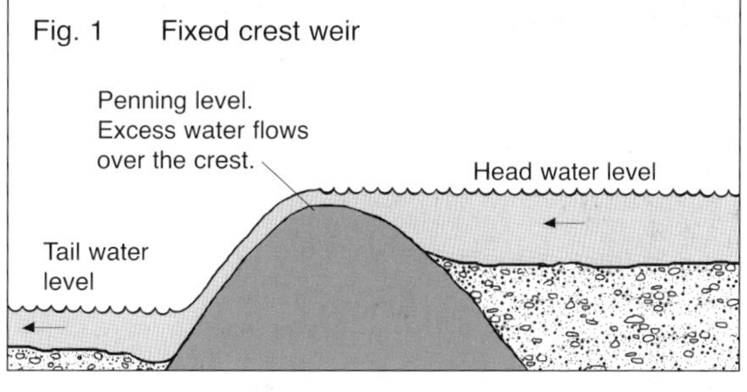
Penning level.
Excess water flows
over the crest.
Head water level
Tail water
level
Fig. 1 Fixed crest weir

1. *Sharp-crested weirs* – formed of metal plates and used for precise measurement of flow.
2. *Triangular profile weirs* – used for precise measurement of flow.
3. *Trapezoidal profile weirs* have flat upstream and downstream slopes and a narrow horizontal crest formed by the gate sill. They are often used in gated controls and barrages.

4. *Broad-crested weirs* – extensively used for flow measurement and for proportional distribution of flow at dividing points in irrigation systems.
5. *Free-nappe profile weirs* – widely used for overflow spillway crests.

A variation on the fixed crest weir is the labyrinth weir which is designed so as to increase the effective length of the crest, thereby allowing more water to flow over it (see Fig. 2).

Fig. 2 Labyrinth weir, plan view

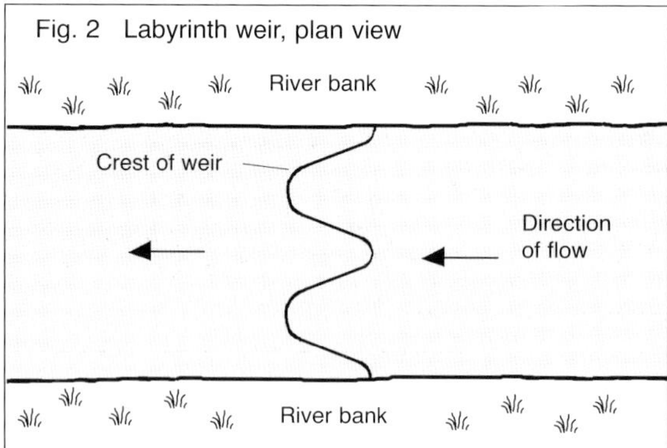
River bank
Crest of weir
Direction
of flow
River bank

The main disadvantage of the fixed crest weir is that it cannot control the water level in the river at times of very high water. Since excess water can only flow over the top of the weir, whenever the depth of the water over the top of the weir becomes higher than the river bank, the river will 'burst its banks'.
To run off water more quickly and with more control it is necessary to run the water through the base of the weir. The greater the upstream head of water, the faster it will flow through. Thus, gates are needed in order to control the level of water in the river by either opening the gates to let excess water through at times of high water or by closing the gates at times of lower flow in order to prevent the upstream reach from emptying out.

GATES
Gates are placed in weirs, open channels or closed conduits to control the flow of water. Their sills can be level with the river bed or on a low weir crest. There are several types of gates in common use:

1. *Vertical lift gate*
   This is the simplest form of gate. It is supported by guides in slots at the side walls of the conduit. They may have sliding contact with the guides or wheels (fixed-wheel gates) or a moving train of rollers (Stoney gates). They may have seals at the sides and, in the case of orifices or closed conduits, also at the top. In general they close onto steel sills with an inset compressible seal if required.
   There are various methods of raising and lowering these gates, from rack and pinion to chain or wire on a winch. If the gate is not 'driven' down (as it is with the rack and pinion method) but relies on gravity, rollers are often incorporated to reduce friction on bearing surfaces. Otherwise the gate may not run smoothly into the shut position and the pressure of the higher water on the upstream side or debris can prevent the gate from shutting.
   If rollers are not incorporated into the design, gates are often dropped off a slip to build up enough momentum out of the water to overcome this friction and shut correctly. This method is not foolproof and gates sometimes have to be jacked down.
   A variation of the simple vertical gate is the 'buck gate' (see Figs. 3–5). To reduce the height of the structure out of the water gates are often in two parts which either hinge or overlap in the stowed position when clear of the water.
   In operation, the lifting gear first lifts the buck. When the top of the buck meets the lip on the top both buck and top come up together. When in the 'stowed' position they are hung on a hook and/or slip (see Fig. 4). To shut the gate the chain or the wire is run off the winch drum, the slip is knocked off, both halves fall together until the top meets the stop and the buck carries on falling, hopefully into the fully shut position. Sometimes this doesn't happen leading to the dangerous position shown in Fig. 5 where the top is in the correct, shut position but the buck is not. In this example the gate is not divable due to the dangerously large opening. Trench sheeters would be necessary to seal an opening of this size. As a general rule diving should not be permitted when openings are greater than about 2cm (3/4").

Fig. 3 Main components of a buck gate

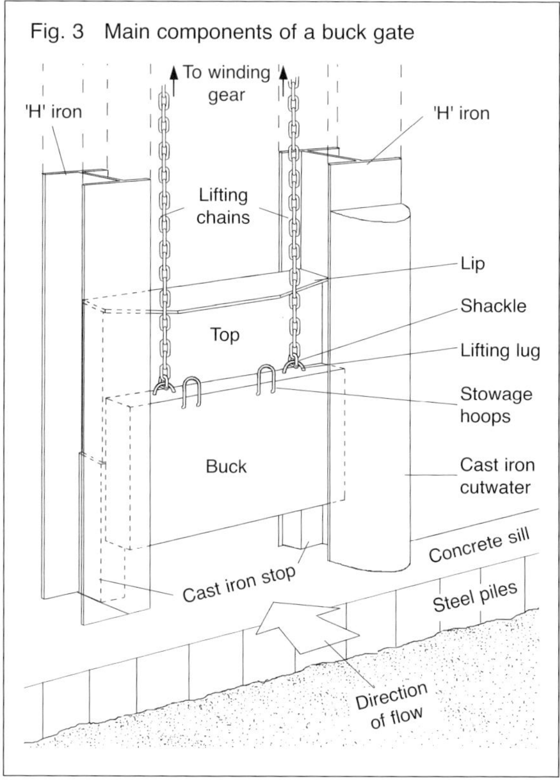
To winding
gear
'H' iron
'H' iron
Lifting
chains
Lip
Shackle
Top
Lifting lug
Stowage
hoops
Buck
Cast iron
cutwater
Concrete sill
Cast iron stop
Steel piles
Direction
of flow

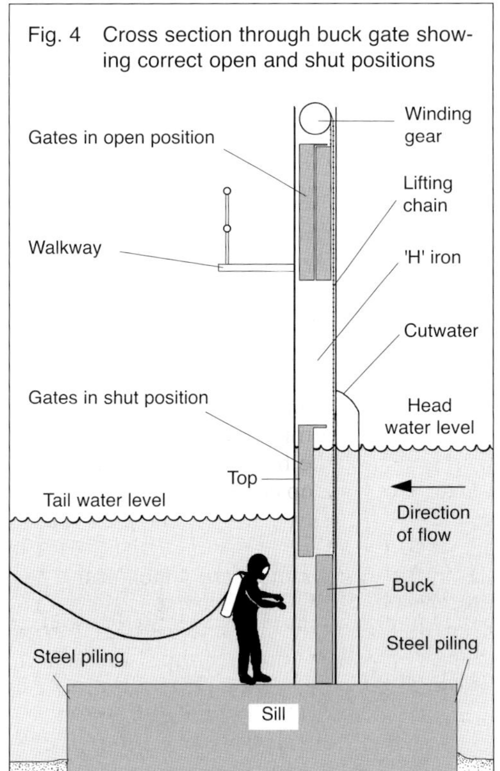
Gates in open position
Winding gear
Lifting chain
Walkway
'H' iron
Cutwater
Gates in shut position
Head water level
Top
Tail water level
Direction of flow
Buck
Steel piling
Steel piling
Sill
Fig. 4 Cross section through buck gate showing correct open and shut positions

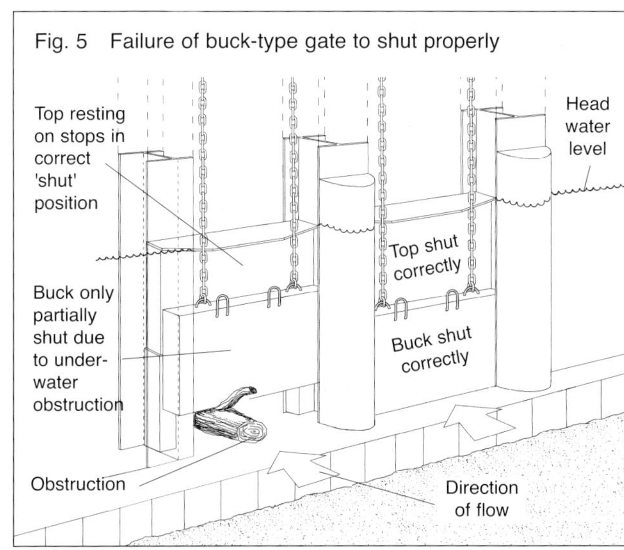
Top resting on stops in correct 'shut' position
Head water level
Top shut correctly
Buck only partially shut due to under-water obstruction
Buck shut correctly
Obstruction
Direction of flow
Fig. 5 Failure of buck-type gate to shut properly

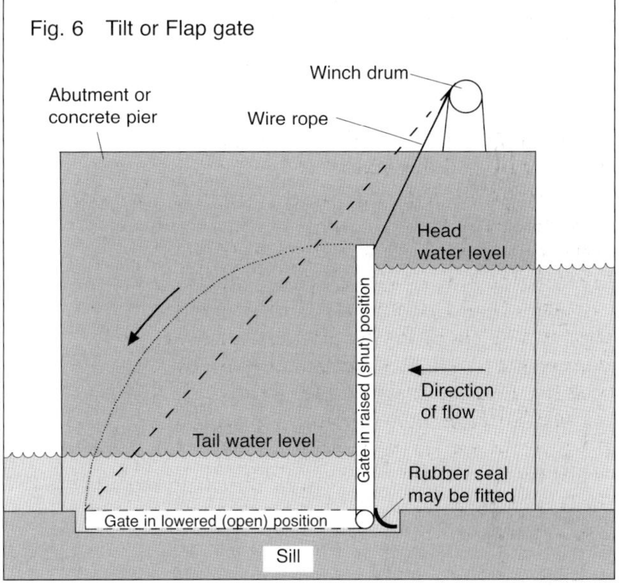
Winch drum
Abutment or concrete pier
Wire rope
Head water level
Gate in raised (shut) position
Direction of flow
Tail water level
Rubber seal may be fitted
Gate in lowered (open) position
Sill
Fig. 6 Tilt or Flap gate

Care must be taken to check that both gates are fully closed. When the top part of the gate is in the shut position it can give the misleading appearance that the whole gate is shut. Before diving it is essential to know the true state of the gates.

2. *Tilt gate (also called Hinged Leaf, Bascule or Flap gate)*
Another simple type of lock gate is the tilt gate, (see Fig. 6). They are hinged at the bottom and may be used for river regulation with water spilling over them. They are sometimes used for crest control where water depth is not great. In Europe hydraulically-operated tilt gates are often used for regulating upstream water levels. Gates hinged at the top are also used where the whole assembly is retractable in order to allow the passage of ships.
They have the advantage of allowing floating debris to pass at small openings. Hinged gates may be made to open automatically by a simple mechanical device when the upstream water level rises to a given height.

3. *Radial Gate (also called Tainter gate)*
Radial, or tainter, gates are widely used for both weir and orifice control in spillways and may sometimes be used in pressure conduits. They are cylindrical in shape and are supported on cross members spanning between two radial arms which rotate on short axles extending from the side walls or piers. They are simple, reliable and low cost. Because they do not need powerful actuators, even quite large gates can be operated manually if required (for example, in the event of a power failure). They do not have side slots. Side seals are of the sliding type and the gates close onto a steel sill. The top of the gate may consist of a hinged flap which can be lowered to allow floating debris to pass downstream.
Variations of the radial gate are shown in Fig. 7. Some radial gates pivot halfway along the arms with counterweights further along the arms. The variable crest radial gate, shown in Fig. 7b, is a relatively recent variation. This type of gate allows the gate to be lowered to allow water to spill over the crest of the gate or it can be lifted like a normal radial gate.
The sills at the bottom of lifting or radial gates are usually metal-to-metal between the gate edge and a

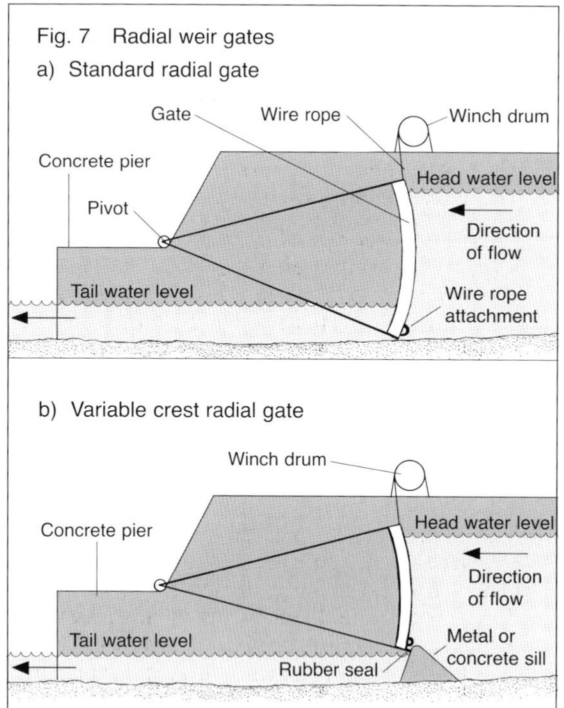
Gate
Wire rope
Winch drum
Concrete pier
Pivot
Head water level
Direction of flow
Tail water level
Wire rope attachment
Winch drum
Concrete pier
Head water level
Direction of flow
Tail water level
Metal or concrete sill
Rubber seal
Fig. 7 Radial weir gates
a) Standard radial gate
b) Variable crest radial gate

steel sill set in the floor. A rubber seal, inset flush into the floor, can sometimes provide a better seal. Side and top seals can be metal-to-metal, although rubber strips are often used.

Most weirs incorporate a mixture of different types of gates. For example, a weir may have a 100m (330ft) fixed crest overfall, 14 variable crest radial gates, 2 flap gates and 2 large vertical gates known as 'roller sluices'.

4. *Drum and Sector gates*
   These are crest gates which open downwards retracting into a recess in the crest. They are known as drum gates when they are hinged on the upstream side, and sector gates when hinged on the downstream side (see Figs 8a and b). The gate is sealed at both the hinge and gate seat. The upper edge of the gate can be shaped to suit the weir profile when fully open.
   The level of the gate is controlled by the pressure of water beneath it. They can be arranged to operate automatically by the upstream water level.

5. *Inclined Lift gate*
   These are similar in many respects to vertical lift gates but operated on sloping tracks.
   They are sometimes used for guard or emergency purposes at intakes in earth or rock-fill dams the track being laid on the upstream face of the dam.

6. *Segmental gate*
   These are rotated to lower them into a recess in the bed and are particularly suited for waterways used by ships. Special arrangements are needed to maintain the recess clear of debris.

7. *Bear Trap gate*
   These gates have long been used in Europe and USA for regulating river flow. They form a low 'A' shape when raised with upstream and downstream leaves forming the two legs. The leaves are hinged at the bottom and have seals at the hinges and the apex. The gate is raised by admitting water under pressure from the headwater. When lowered the upstream leaf overlaps the downstream leaf and both fold flat.

8. *Roller gate*
   Roller gates have been used for river regulation. They consist of a roller with a toothed wheel meshing with an inclined toothed rack at each end. The gate is rotated by a chain and accordingly moves up and down the racks.

9. *Cylinder or Ring gate*
   Used as crest gates on bellmouth spillways and for bottom outlets. Bottom outlet gates are lifted from above to open them. Others can be opened by lowering them vertically into a recess in the weir crest, and are controlled by water pressure.

VALVES

Valves are used to control the water flow or pressure in pipes or conduits. For operational and safety reasons the diver should be familiar with the

Fig. 8 Drum and Sector gates

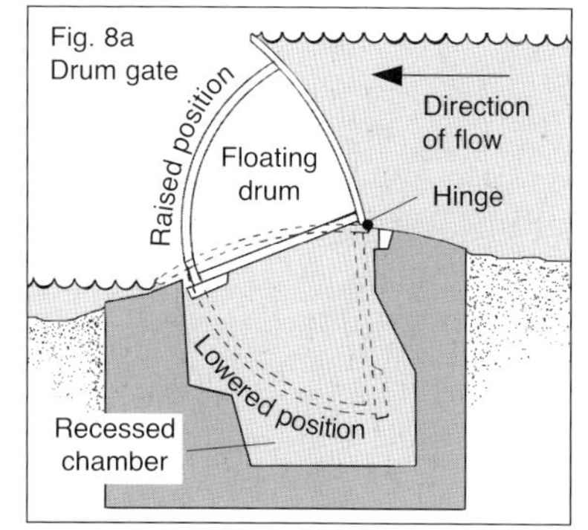
Raised position
Floating drum
Direction of flow
Hinge
Lowered position
Recessed chamber
Fig. 8a Drum gate

Drum and Sector gates retract into recessed chambers in the ground.

Drum gates are hinged on the upstream side (Fig. 8a) and Sector gates on the downstream side (Fig. 8b).

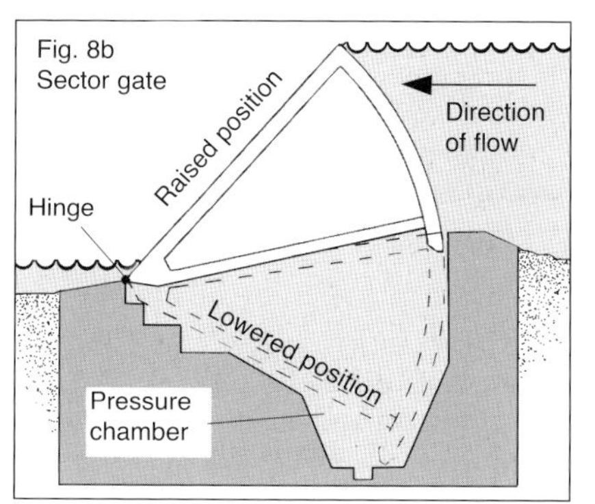
Raised position
Direction of flow
Hinge
Lowered position
Pressure chamber
Fig. 8b Sector gate

various types of valves that may be used on locks and weirs.

A service valve is usually protected by an upstream gate or guard valve which can be closed to isolate the service valve. This prevents leakage and allows maintenance or repair of the service valve to be undertaken. Valves may be 'in-line' or 'terminal' depending on whether they are located within a length of pipe or at its end.

1. *Gate or Sluice valve*
   In their simplest form these consist of a sliding leaf in a valve body with side slots – thus resembling a vertical lift gate, with operating rod sealed to contain the pressure. The sealing contact is metal-to-metal and the leaf is usually wedge-shaped (see Fig. 9).
   Gate valves are not suited for regulation except at low or moderate pressures. A bypass is usually provided to balance pressures but a valve for guard or emergency duty may have to close under unbalanced pressure. Advantages of the gate valve include simplicity of design and low head loss when fully open. One of the disadvantages is the considerable power needed to operate the valve under unbalanced heads.

Fig. 9 Gate valve (or Sluice valve)

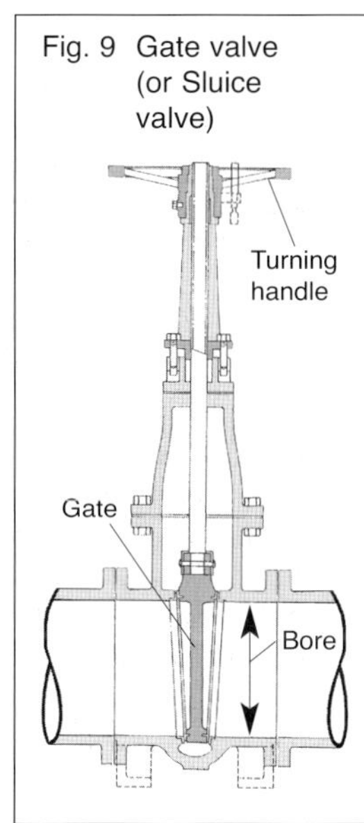
Turning handle
Gate
Bore

2. *Butterfly valve* (see Fig. 10)
   Although these are widely used as guard or isolating valves, under low or medium pressure conditions they can be used for regulation. A blade or disc inside the valve is mounted on a shaft or two stub axles and is hydraulically rotated. When fully-opened the blade still partially obstructs the flow resulting in down-stream turbulence and loss of head pressure.

Fig. 10 Butterfly valve

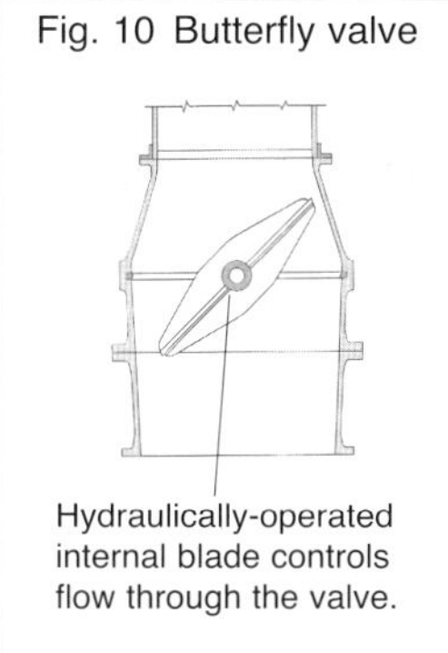
Hydraulically-operated internal blade controls flow through the valve.

3. *Spherical, Ball or Rotary Plug valve*
   Used for guard and on/off duties. They consist of an internal sphere through which is a hole the same size as the conduit. When the ball is rotated 90° the flow is either turned on or off.
4. *Needle valve*
   These are used for precise flow control. They have a needle or tapered plunger which moves axially within an orifice forming part of the valve body.
5. *Tube and Hollow Jet valve*
   These resemble needle valves.
6. *Fixed cone-sleeve valve*
   Also known as Howell-Binger valves, these are commonly used in free discharge terminal applications and pressure relief for turbines.
7. *Submerged Sleeve valve*
   Consisting of an internal sleeve which slides over a perforated cylinder, these are located in stilling wells as terminal regulators.

TASKS ON WEIRS

1. Visual inspection of abutment and foundation structure up and down-stream of the gates.
2. Check for and damage caused by scouring on downstream side. Identify any damage found.
3. Repair as necessary, eg filling voids with grout or welding re-inforcing plates over any separated piles.
4. Visual inspection of the gates.
5. Metal thickness measurements on gates using 'D' meters.
6. Visual inspection of lifting gear. Replace any parts as necessary.
7. Removal of obstructions/debris from under gates.
8. Replacement of seals.
9. Fitting a dam where work has to be carried out in dry conditions.
10. Replacement of damaged or missing 'stops' on buck weirs.

WEIRS – OPERATIONAL SAFETY (see also Operational Safety for Dams and Reservoirs)

GENERAL: When diving operations are to be undertaken on structures where the water levels vary or where there is a significant flow past or through the structure (such as at dams, weirs, locks etc) this differential pressure poses a major risk to the diver in the water. Even a small pressure head on the high-pressure side of a structure can trap a diver in a situation from which he cannot escape. A one-metre head of pressure, for example, will create a pressure of 1 tonne per square metre. A hole large enough for a hand, arm or hose to enter is large enough to trap and pin someone securely. It is not the depth of water that necessarily determines the extent of suction, it is the discharge elevation compared to the water level that counts.

Where possible, the water levels to either side of the structure should be equalled, for example, when inspecting lock gates operate the lock to equal the levels across the gate to be inspected. Where this

continued . . .

continued . . .

cannot be achieved on an unknown structure the first inspection should be carried out on the low pressure side since this will cause the diver to be swept away from the structure if there are any significant flows or leakage. The dive on the high pressure side, if necessary, must only be carried out after a careful review of the risk assessment including an umbilical management plan.

1. Gain control of the weir.
2. Ascertain the state of the weir. Never take anybody's word for it. Check:
   a) The position and condition of the gates. Do not rely on the position of the top of the gate. Some gates (buck gates) are in two halves. The top half may be shut while the lower half may still be open.
   b) The depth of water.
   c) The current. The current at the dive site must be checked carefully before allowing any diving to take place. If in doubt, always check from the downstream side (where the water is usually shallow) to avoid the danger of being trapped.
3. Once the weir is in the required state, isolate the power and retain keys and/or fix padlocks. Affix a notice stating 'Do not operate – divers working'.
4. Variable crest gates may need to be suspended in the shut position using portable winches.
5. Open or leaking weir gates:
   a) Seal any partly open gates with plastic drainpipe, sandbags, timbers or trench sheeters, preferably placed from the surface.
   b) When diving on the upstream side of a gate, the diver's umbilical must be tended from upstream to avoid the umbilical being drawn through any small leaks in the gates. This normally means that diving must take place from a vessel.
6. Partly drawn weirs:
   Always work on shut gates, away from drawn ones.

Locks

In order to enable boats to negotiate a weir, a lock must be built alongside.

A lock is a section of the river enclosed by two sets of gates. A typical example of a lock is illustrated in Fig. 11. The gates are opened or closed to fill or empty the lock as required thus enabling a vessel to negotiate the different levels of the river (see Fig. 12). The lock gates rely on the water pressure from upstream to keep the gates firmly closed.

There is very little variation in the type of lock gates. Some smaller locks on canals have single gates and 'guillotine' gates can also be found. These lift completely out of the water allowing water craft to pass beneath them.

All locks work the same way and vary only in the way the locks are filled or emptied.

Gate sluices or culvert sluices may be used to control the flow of water through locks. Gate sluices are shown in Fig. 11. An example of the location of culvert sluices is shown in Fig. 13.

CULVERTS

On canals culverts are fairly small (around 600mm/2ft square). On a large river lock some culverts can be about 1m (3ft) in diameter and fill the lock through a series of small holes (150mm/6") in the floor of the lock. On larger locks there can be multiple entrances and exits (say, 9) between a lock and a large culvert of say 1.5m (5ft) in diameter.

Fig. 11 Typical lock system

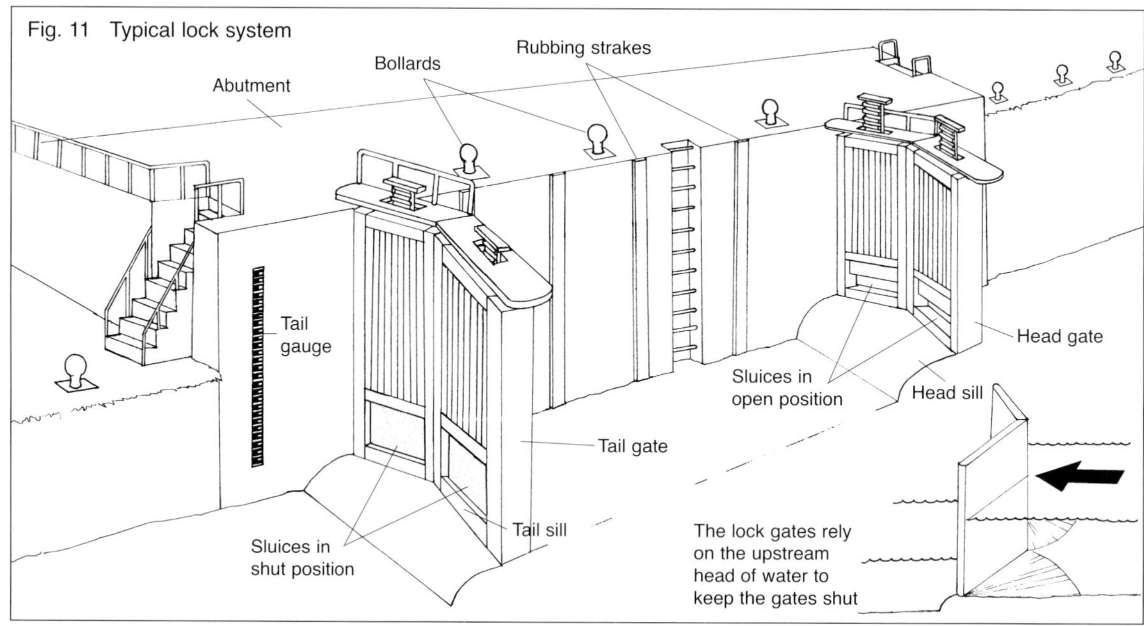
Rubbing strakes
Bollards
Abutment
Tail gauge
Head gate
Sluices in open position
Head sill
Tail gate
Tail sill
Sluices in shut position
The lock gates rely on the upstream head of water to keep the gates shut

Fig. 12 How a lock operates - vessel moving upstream (Reverse procedure for vessel moving downstream)

a) Tail gate open, vessel enters lock.

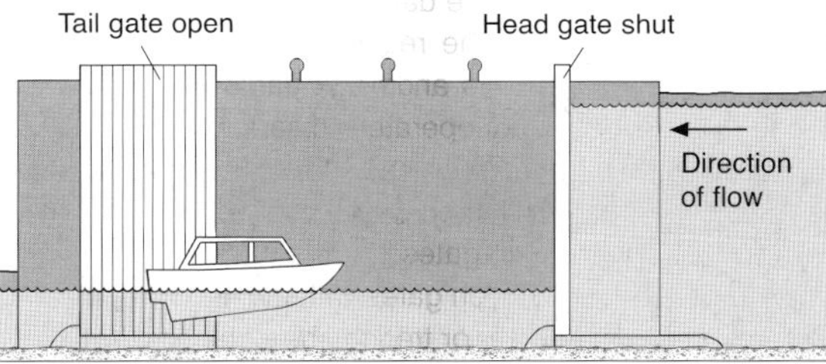
Tail gate open
Head gate shut
Direction of flow

b) Both gates shut. Sluices opened in head gate. Lock fills with water from upstream reach.

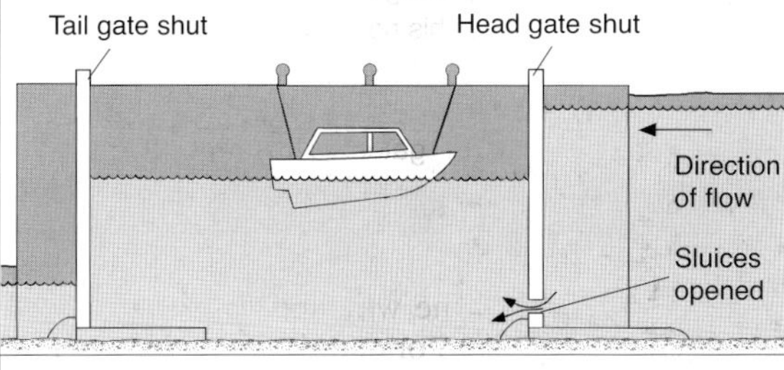
Tail gate shut
Head gate shut
Direction of flow
Sluices opened

c) Water level in lock equalises with upstream level. Head gates can be opened. Vessel moves out of lock.

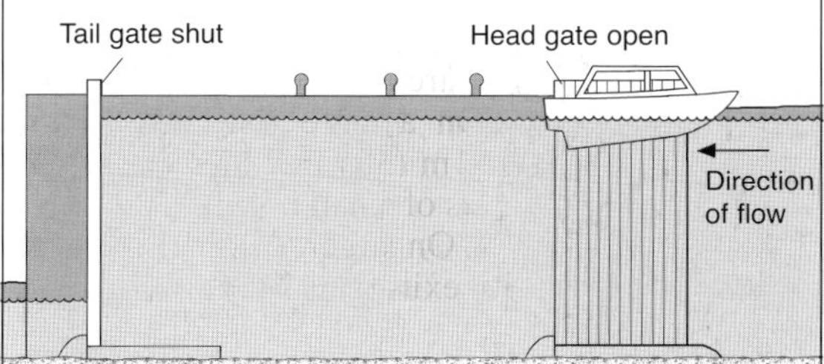
Tail gate shut
Head gate open
Direction of flow

Fig. 13 Plan view of culvert sluices incorporated into a lock gate system

Sluice gate
Culverts
Sluice gate
Lock gates
Direction of flow

Whether or not a diver can enter a culvert depends on its size and related safety considerations. Combinations of gate and culvert sluices can also be found. Some canals, for example, favour culvert sluices at the head of the lock and gates at the tail end of the lock.

TASKS ON LOCKS

Diver tasks are similar to those on weirs, plus:

1. Removal of silt from around gates using air-lift.
2. Repair of sluice gear as necessary: eg, broken iron-work or sluice doors.
3. Repair hydraulic systems as necessary.
4. Inspect and repair gates as necessary.
5. Inspect and repair damage to sills as necessary.

LOCKS – OPERATIONAL SAFETY

The potential dangers of diving on locks and weirs cannot be over-emphasised. Always treat them with respect and never dive without first thoroughly investigating the situation.

See general safety advice in 'Operational Safety on Weirs'.

1. Consult as necessary with the relevant navigation authority before commencing diving operations.
2. Gain control of the lock.
3. Ascertain the state of the lock. Check:
   a) The position and condition of gates and sluice gates.
   b) The depth of water.
4. Shut off power to all gates before diving starts.
   a) Attach a sign warning that the controls should not be operated because divers are at work.
   b) Never leave the controls unattended. Some systems can still be operated using battery power, even though the electrical power source has been switched off. A responsible person, in direct contact with the Diving Supervisor, should remain as sentry.
   c) Consider securing the gates shut with chain and padlock.
   d) Where it is possible for the controls at the other end of the lock to affect the gate being worked on, a responsible person must also be placed there to prevent interference with the controls. Warning notices are not enough.
   e) Where the power has to be left on (for example, when repairing sluice gear, the diver might need it to be moved) extra care must be taken to ensure that the controls are not interfered with. Some computerised systems, for example, do not allow independent operation of head and tail sluice gates. Opening one will automatically open the other. An irreversible series of actions can be started at the press of a button.
5. If working on head gates with sluices shut (even if the tail gates and sluices are shut), beware because enough water can leak out of a full lock to cause a pressure difference and endanger a diver should the head gate sluices be opened.
6. If working with gates open it will be necessary to prevent craft attempting to enter the lock. It may be necessary to place ropes or other craft, etc to block the entrance.
7. Place warning signs a fair distance both up and downstream of the lock so vessels are aware of the impending delay.

1.15 SPILLWAYS, RESERVOIRS AND DAMS

1. Spillways

Spillways are the means by which surplus water is removed from a reservoir. They protect a dam and embankments from damage by over-topping. There are several different types of spillway:

a) ORIFICES
These are usually rectangular, horizontal tunnels fitted with a radial gate to control water flow (see Fig. 1)

b) BELLMOUTH, SHAFT AND CLOSED CONDUIT SPILLWAYS
Also called Morning Glory spillway because of its resemblance to the shape of the flower of the same name (see Fig. 2), this type of spillway is usually an overflow weir, circular in plan (although some are multi-sided) opening into a vertical shaft. The shaft leads to a tunnel or culvert through high ground with its outfall in the downstream river. The weir may be fitted with gates or siphons. Since the base of the bellmouth can be damaged by heavy debris (such as ice or logs) falling into it, steel or cast-iron linings are sometimes provided.

c) OTHER TYPES
Other types of spillway include Chute and Siphon spillways.

Fig. 1 Orifice spillway

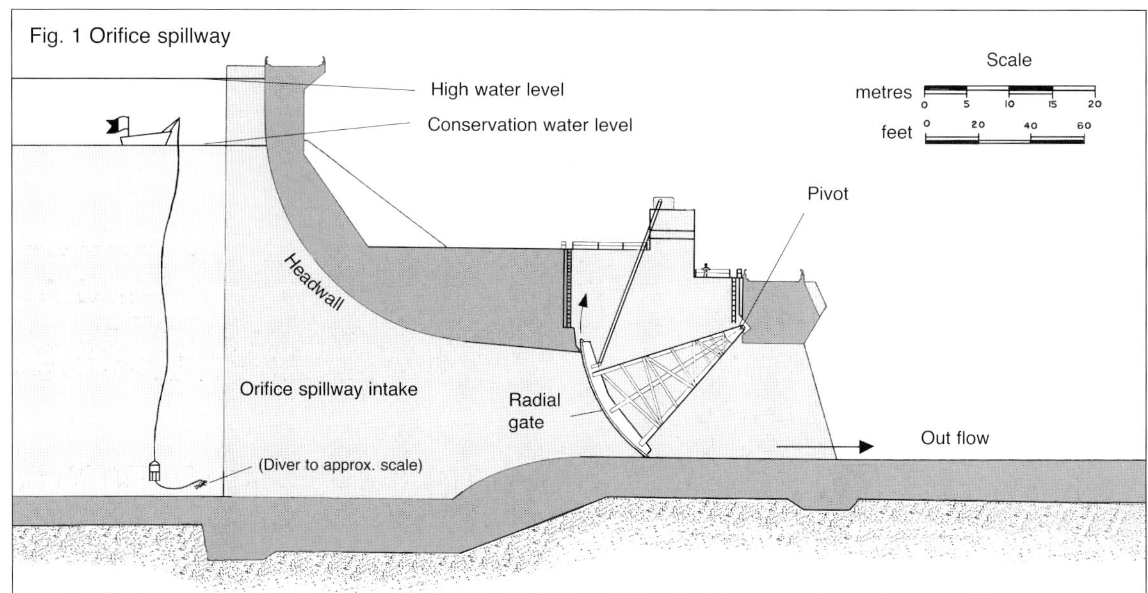
Scale
metres
0
5
10
15
20
feet
0
20
40
60
High water level
Conservation water level
Pivot
Headwall
Orifice spillway intake
Radial gate
Out flow
(Diver to approx. scale)

Fig. 2 Bellmouth or Morning Glory spillway

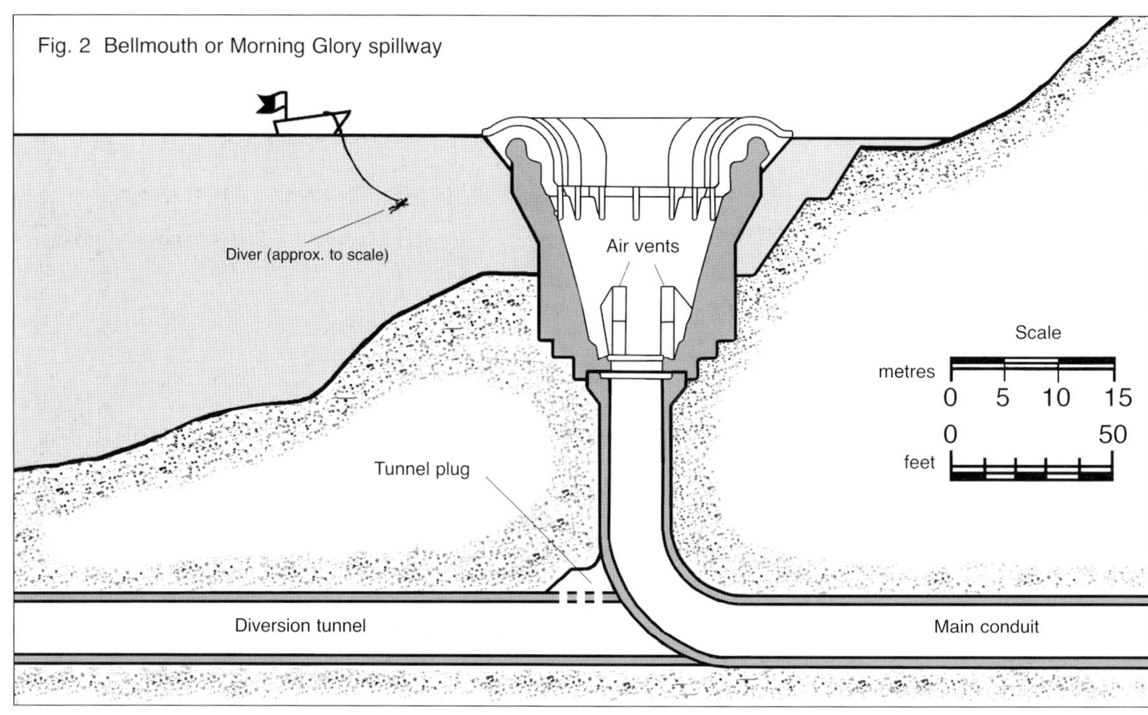
Diver (approx. to scale)
Air vents
Scale
metres
0
5
10
15
0
50
feet
Tunnel plug
Diversion tunnel
Main conduit

2. Reservoir intakes (see Fig. 3)
Intake designs vary according to the type of the dam and the purpose of the supply. The flow velocity may be low and against a back pressure, as for example in intakes for domestic water supply, and into penstocks for power generation, or it may be high, for example in spillways and into diversion tunnels during construction. If the dam is concrete, the intakes may be located in the dam structure. Where the dam is constructed of rockfill or earth, a separate intake structure may be built leading to a tunnel or a free-standing draw-off tower may be provided, sometimes combined with a shaft spillway. One or more free-standing towers may exist where draw-off is required at several levels, such as for domestic water supply (see Fig. 4). In such cases a bottom draw-off or 'scour' sluice is generally included. This is opened at intervals to

Fig. 3 Reservoir intake

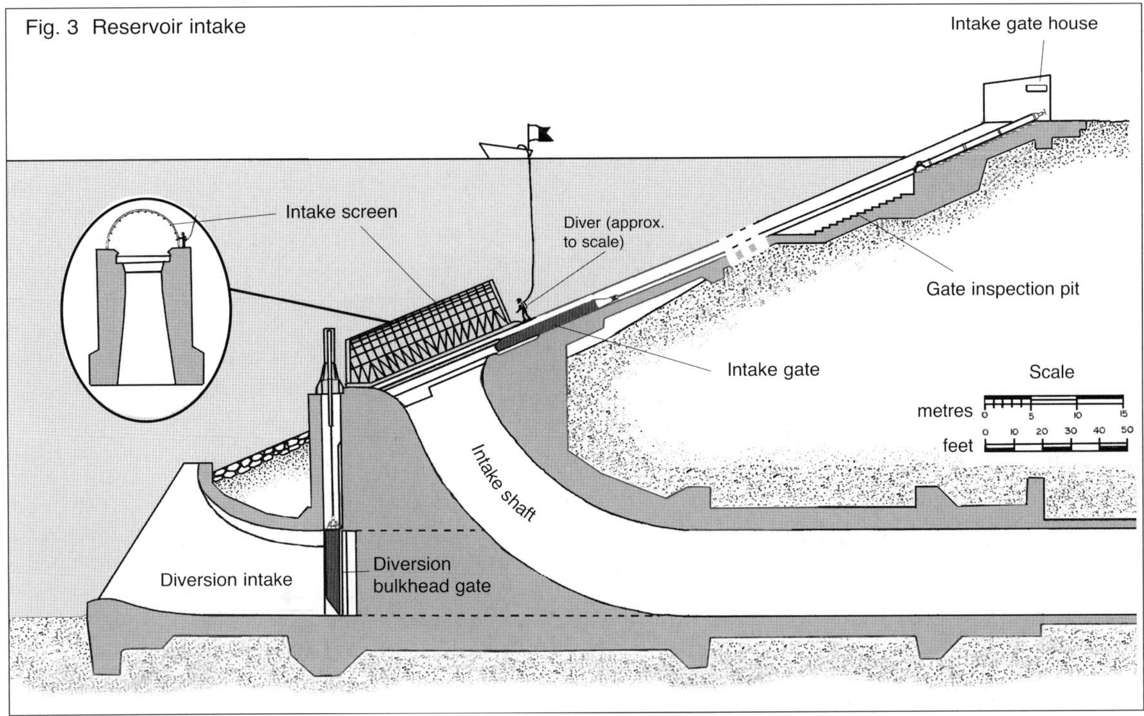
Intake gate house
Intake screen
Diver (approx. to scale)
Gate inspection pit
Intake gate
Scale
metres
0 5 10 15
0 10 20 30 40 50
feet
Intake shaft
Diversion intake
Diversion bulkhead gate

Fig. 4 Draw-off Tower

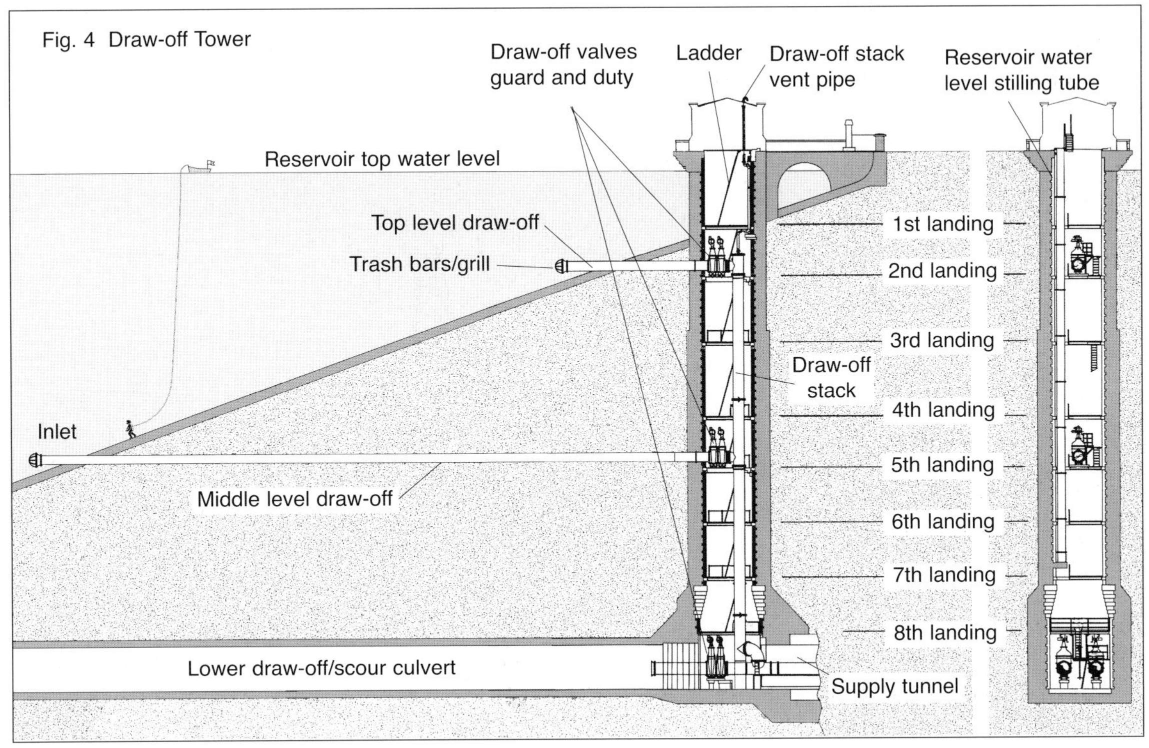
Draw-off valves guard and duty
Ladder
Draw-off stack vent pipe
Reservoir water level stilling tube
Reservoir top water level
Top level draw-off
Trash bars/grill
1st landing
2nd landing
3rd landing
Draw-off stack
4th landing
5th landing
6th landing
7th landing
8th landing
Inlet
Middle level draw-off
Lower draw-off/scour culvert
Supply tunnel

prevent sediment from building up a deposit in the immediate vicinity of the lowest draw-off supply. Deep intakes are less susceptible to obstruction by ice and floating debris but access to the screens for cleaning may be more difficult.

SCREENS

Screens, or trash racks, are devices which are fitted to intakes to prevent debris from entering. They are generally in the form of a cage or grill with the bars 2-20cm (1-8 in) apart. They are commonly used at hydro-electric power plants, pumps and water treatment works. Log booms may also be fitted upstream to trap floating debris. Screens require periodic cleaning.

COMPENSATOR DRAW-OFF AND VALVE

In addition to the usual draw-off piping and valves, there may be a compensator draw-off, which provides access for fish up and down stream. It is normally kept open. These systems should be checked whenever diving operations are planned.

SCOUR PROTECTION

Water flowing at great velocity has considerable erosive power, even on hard rock. Scours can appear downstream of stilling basins, jetties, groynes and where there are structural obstructions in the flow. There are several methods of providing protection against scour and may require divers to install and maintain them:

a) Boulders
b) Rip-rap or Pitching of quarried stone is often used. It may be hand-packed on side slopes to ensure their stability.
c) Derrick stones are too heavy to be placed by hand. They are individually placed, usually on an underlay or graded rip-rap.
d) Concrete blocks of various sizes and shapes. They are often used where suitable stone is not available or too costly. Specially shaped units are often used for coastal protection and river channel works.
e) Gabions are wire crates containing boulders or broken stone and are used to provide temporary protection against erosion.

   The wire crates can be made from galvanised or plastic-coated wire to protect it from corrosion. The stone filling is usually same-size pieces of rock selected for its density and durability. Gabions can be filled at the surface and craned into position, guided by a diver. A special lifting frame is used to avoid damage to the gabion baskets.

   They can be wired together to form an apron. Gabion mattresses are generally laid over a geotextile membrane which prevents the substrata exuding into the gabion, but is permeable to allow free drainage.
f) Asphalt. This is used where a smooth protective cover is required.
g) Sheets of nylon and other synthetic materials can provide a filter layer over sand. They form thin mattresses and have pockets filled with cement grout. They are used for side slope protection.
h) Flexible formwork is a scour protection scheme which can vary in size and thickness. The diver installs the mattress and then inserts the concrete delivery hose, monitoring as the mattress is pumped full.
i) Brushwood fascine mattresses are willow twigs bound together in bundles and formed into longitudinal and lateral layers bound together. They are weighted with stones and sunk into place.

TASKS ON DAMS AND RESERVOIRS

1. Repair and inspection of pumps and control gear.
2. Inspection and repair of structural elements.
3. Silt and debris clearance within control structures and from debris screens.
4. Inspection and repair within culvert systems including gate valves.
5. Inspection of dam faces to check for localised leakages or seepage flows.
6. Guiding placement of gabion baskets and mattresses for scour protection.
7. Connecting, monitoring and disconnecting concrete supply hoses to anti-scour mattresses.

DAMS AND RESERVOIRS – OPERATIONAL SAFETY

1. Hold a pre-dive safety meeting and ensure that all personnel associated with the diving operations attend (including the client).
2. Create a Risk Analysis to identify and assess all potential hazards before diving commences. The Dive Supervisor should work closely with the dam operators in this regard.
3. Consult plant engineering drawings but do not rely too heavily on them – many are not up-to-date. Ask staff from the Engineering and Operational departments to identify areas of potential risk.
4. Always respect pressure heads. (See General advice in 'Operational Safety on Weirs').
5. Identify all possible openings that could have a potential pressure head differential. These can be absolutely anything that opens into a dam forebay and discharges at a lower level, eg

continued . . .

continued . . .

turbine intakes, bypass systems, diversions intakes, penstocks, cooling water intakes, fill valves, etc.

6. Ensure that the necessary safety precautions are in place when diving in tunnels or pipes where there is no clear route to the surface.
7. In the UK, beware of the risk of unexploded mines in reservoirs. During the Second World War many UK reservoirs were seeded with mines to prevent landings by amphibious aircraft. Not all the mines have been recovered.
8. Include a 'permit to work' system within the dive plan to ensure that all mechanical plant is locked down before commencing diving operations.
9. If there is any doubt about procedures a dive supervisor must make absolute provision to protect the divers. If necessary, pull fuses out of hoist/pump controls, dismantle valves or place a person on guard at the controls so that they cannot be turned on or off.
10. Use multiple redundancy safety points when possible so that failure at one point is backed up by other safeguards.
11. Divers should approach all openings and valves with extreme caution. If possible, always check from downstream first. If there are any leaks, diving cannot be permitted.
12. Never presume that openings are completely closed – a good seal cannot be presumed simply because openings have been closed at the surface. A seal can fail due to a very small amount of interference. Mechanical gate indicators have been known to indicate 'closed' when the gate was slightly open. Hydraulically-controlled gates should also be suspect unless there is a positive way to measure closure.
13. The valve closest to the diver's work site (and any additional valves that can isolate the diver's work site) should be closed.
14. Take extra care when working where man-made structures meet the natural bottom. Some dams leak and it is not always evident from the surface.
15. The diver should never go head-first into a pipeline of less than 42-inch (107cm) in diameter. His first priority must be given to his ability to get back out of the pipe.
16. The diver should keep his hands and fingers well clear of the gate valve.
17. A Safety Diver must be present at the entrance to a pipe to tend the working diver's umbilical at that point.
18. When working inside a stone or brick culvert, consideration must be given to the structural integrity of the roof. If there is a risk of instability, a breathing system should be used that does not release air at the diver (see, for example, the 'Dirty Harry' system, Section 5.3, page 237).
19. When working near spillages it may be necessary to erect a barrier, such as netting, to prevent boats or divers being washed over the spillway.
20. Many reservoirs are at significant altitude. In such cases, allowance must be included in the decompression procedures.
21. The water temperature is likely to be very cold (4°C/32°F) so good, thermally-insulated clothing is required.
22. Most depth gauges, including pneumogauges, will be calibrated for sea water which is more dense than fresh water. Care must therefore be taken when interpreting actual depth from such gauges. The diver in fresh water will be deeper than indicated on a seawater-calibrated gauge.This principle must also be observed during decompression stops.
23. The lighter density of fresh water must be taken into account when making any buoyancy calculations. The maximum buoyancy of a lifting bag will be less in fresh water than in salt water.

1.16 OUTFALLS

Outfalls discharge effluent into the sea, estuaries or rivers. Typically they discharge: storm water, sewage, power station cooling water, industrial waste and atomic waste.

Most outfalls are small diameter (less than 2ft/600mm), open-ended, single outlet pipes which discharge at or above low water. Medium diameter outfall pipes (2–4ft/600–1200mm) can be much longer (up to 4km/2.5miles or more), ending in deeper water and may be partially or completely buried). Hatch boxes are inspection points which can be located at several points along a long outlet pipe. A concrete cover may be placed over a steel manhole at each hatch box.

The design of an outfall depends on the nature of the effluent it is discharging, its location and the nature of the immediate environment. A variety of protective measures can be provided to avoid risk

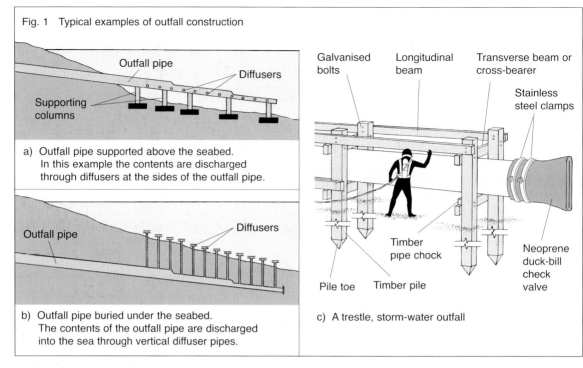

Fig. 1 Typical examples of outfall construction

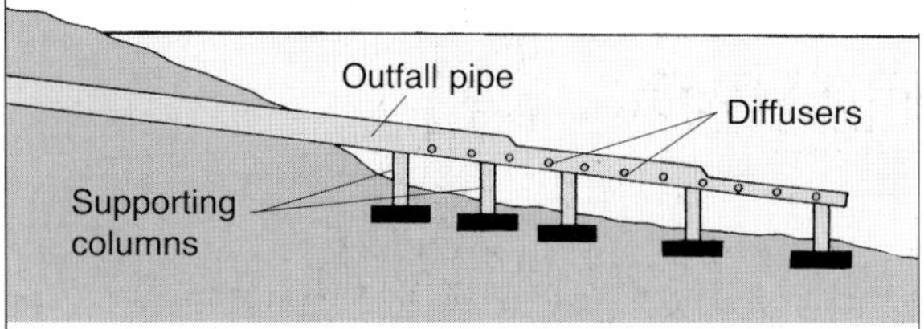

Outfall pipe
Diffusers
Supporting columns

a) Outfall pipe supported above the seabed. In this example the contents are discharged through diffusers at the sides of the outfall pipe.

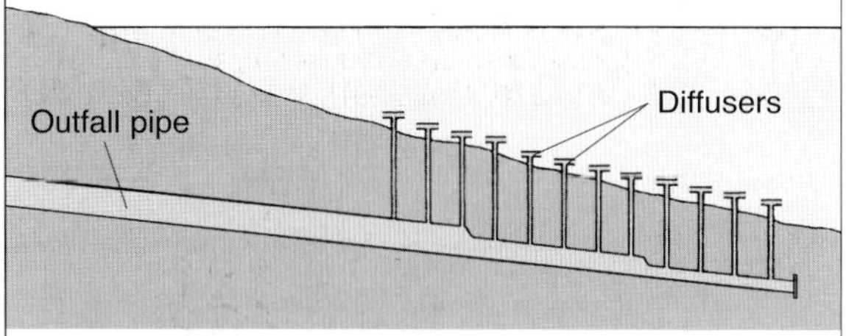

Outfall pipe
Diffusers

b) Outfall pipe buried under the seabed. The contents of the outfall pipe are discharged into the sea through vertical diffuser pipes.

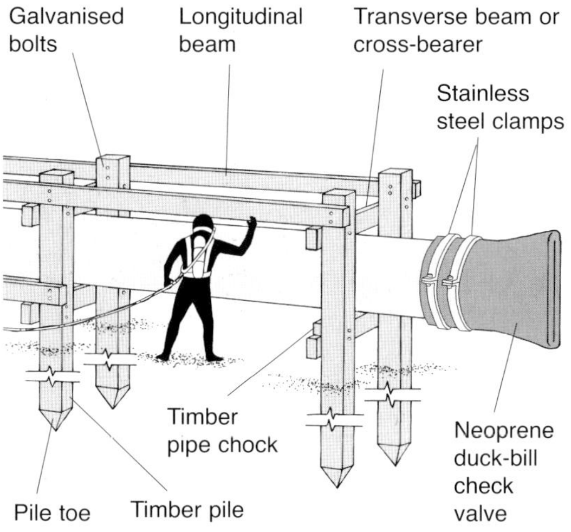

Galvanised bolts
Longitudinal beam
Transverse beam or cross-bearer
Stainless steel clamps
Timber pipe chock
Neoprene duck-bill check valve
Pile toe
Timber pile

c) A trestle, storm-water outfall

of damage. These include burial, specially designed concrete structures, gravel dumping, grout bags and cages (see Figs. 1 and 2a–2e).

The end of the outfall may be marked and protected by a dolphin (see Fig. 3).

Diffusers

To encourage the dissipation of the effluent into the surrounding water, outfalls often have diffusers at their distal ends The number and design of the diffusers varies widely (see Fig. 2).

Diffusers may also have non-return check valve systems to prevent the ingress of sediments, animal growths etc. They can include simple flap or lift valves. An example is the 'duck-bill' diffuser (see Fig. 2b). It can be constructed of neoprene and designed such that it opens when effluent flows out but closes automatically as soon as the flow stops. A 'pepper-pot' diffuser is one where there are several exits for the effluent on the end of a diffuser pipe. Each hole may have deflectors which direct the effluent flow downwards. This has a scouring effect which assists in preventing the diffuser from silting up.

Hydraulics

The hydraulic characteristics of an outfall show how it is performing. This involves regular monitoring of the flow and head at the outfall which can reveal changes in headloss (see Fig. 4).

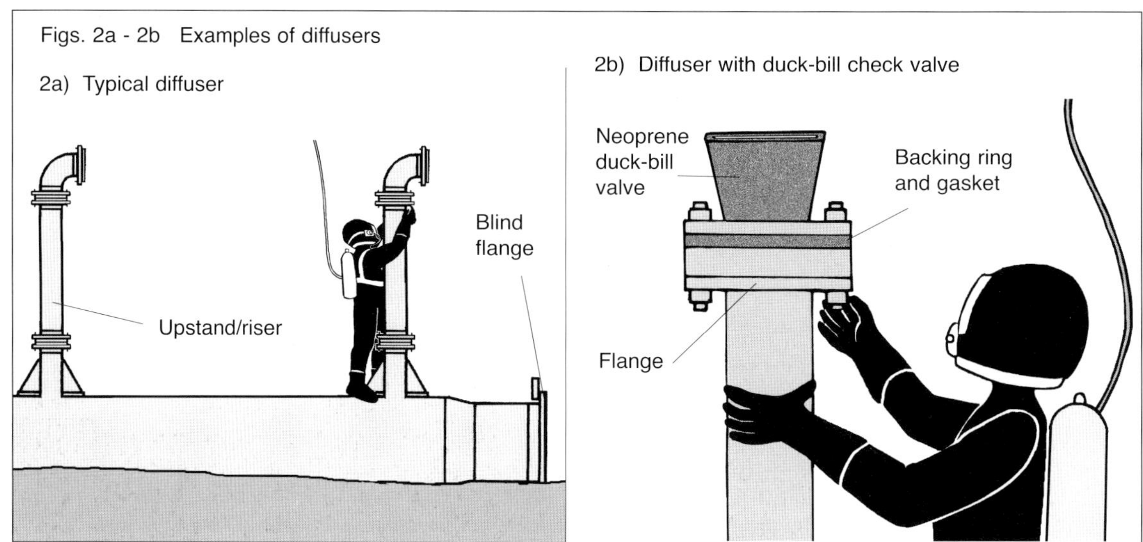
Upstand/riser
Blind flange
Neoprene duck-bill valve
Backing ring and gasket
Flange

Figs. 2a - 2b Examples of diffusers

2a) Typical diffuser

2b) Diffuser with duck-bill check valve

Figs. 2c – 2e Examples of diffusers

2c) Concrete-protected diffuser

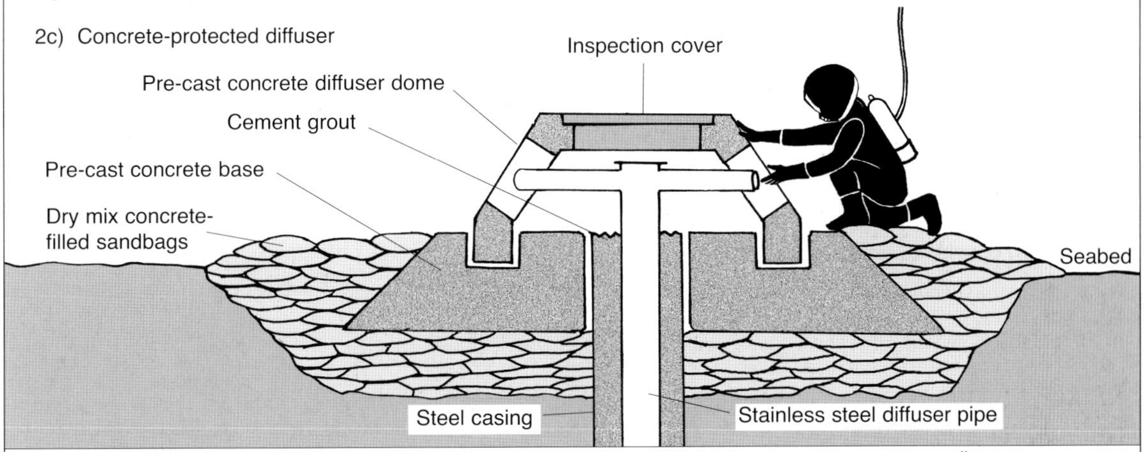

Inspection cover
Pre-cast concrete diffuser dome
Cement grout
Pre-cast concrete base
Dry mix concrete-filled sandbags
Seabed
Steel casing
Stainless steel diffuser pipe

2d) Rubble-protected diffuser

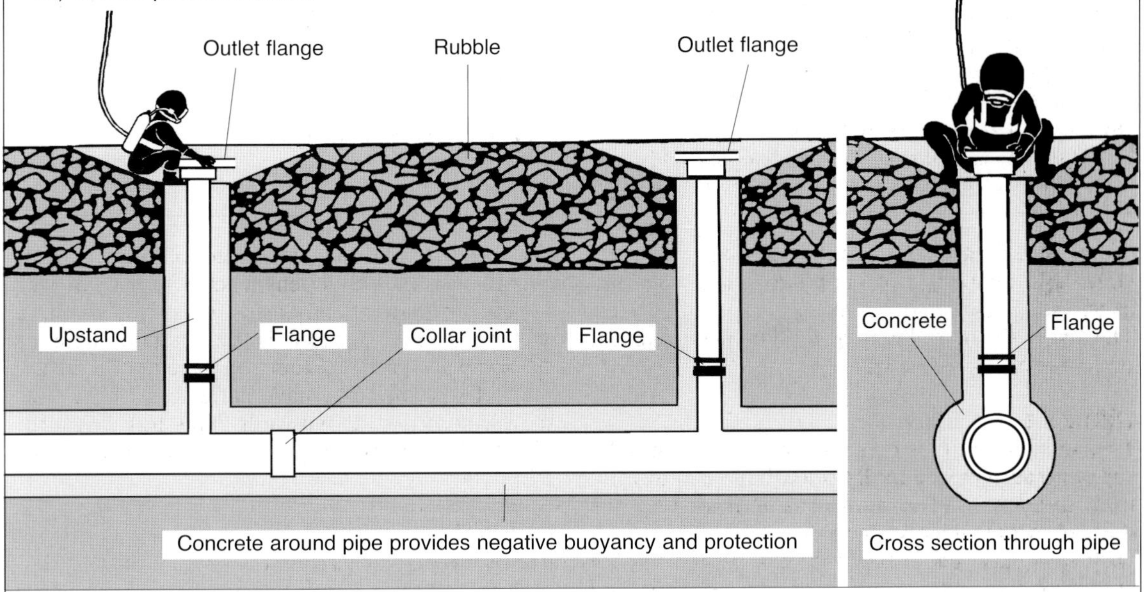

Outlet flange
Rubble
Outlet flange
Upstand
Flange
Collar joint
Flange
Concrete
Flange
Concrete around pipe provides negative buoyancy and protection
Cross section through pipe

Typical example: 20 diffusers about 4m (approx 15ft) apart. Total length 80m (260 ft).

2e) A caged diffuser

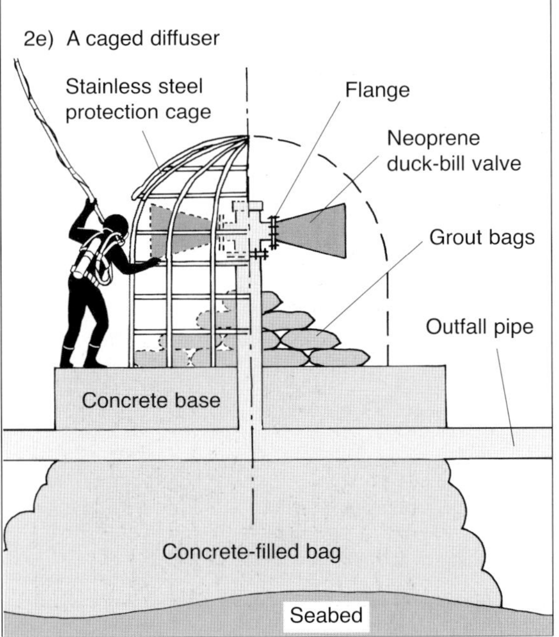
Stainless steel protection cage
Flange
Neoprene duck-bill valve
Grout bags
Outfall pipe
Concrete base
Concrete-filled bag
Seabed

Fig. 3 Outfall discharge with dolphin

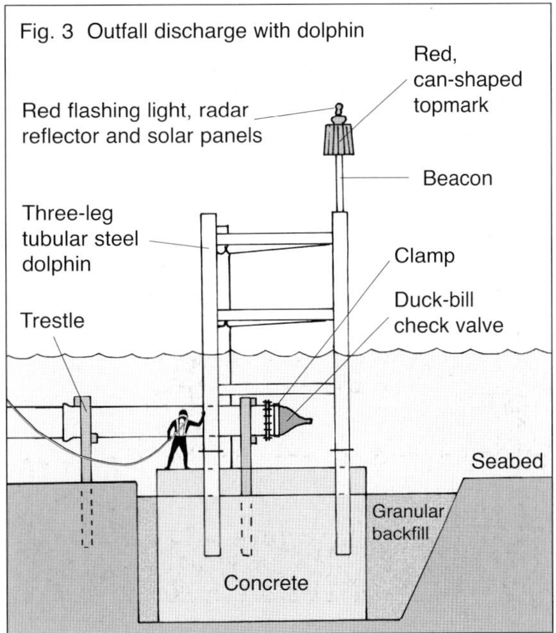
Red, can-shaped topmark
Red flashing light, radar reflector and solar panels
Beacon
Three-leg tubular steel dolphin
Clamp
Duck-bill check valve
Trestle
Seabed
Granular backfill
Concrete

Fig. 4 Monitoring outfall hydraulic performance

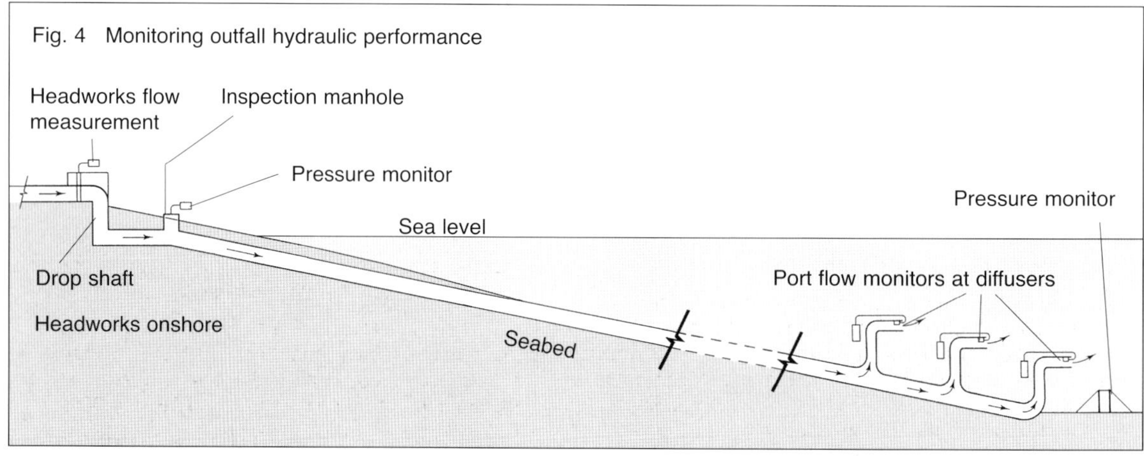
Headworks flow measurement
Inspection manhole
Pressure monitor
Sea level
Pressure monitor
Drop shaft
Port flow monitors at diffusers
Headworks onshore
Seabed

Changes in headloss can indicate damage to the pipe or a blockage. Types of flow recorders include standing wave flumes coupled with level measurements, magnetic flowmeters and ultrasonic flowmeters. The head/depth recorders include ultrasonic depth recorders, float recorders and pressure transducers. A tidal gauge near the outfall also provides important information.

DIVER TASKS

1. Check structural integrity.
   a) External inspection of pipe and diffuser.
   b) Internal inspection of pipeline and diffuser.
   c) Check cathodic protection (on steel outfalls).
2. Survey of outfall for later extension or modification.
   a) Hydrographic survey of outfall route.
   b) Measurement of pipework and other parts.
   c) Measurement and survey of any damage.
3. Check of hydraulic performance.
   a) Measurement of driving head.
   b) Measurement of total flow.
   c) Measurement of port flow.
   d) Initial dilution measurement.
4. Survey of environmental performance.
   a) Ecological survey.
   b) Secondary dispersion survey.
   c) Water movement survey.
   d) Water chemistry survey.
   e) Biological study.
   f) Sediment movement survey.

INSPECTION EQUIPMENT

1. TV video camera.
2. Still camera.
3. Cleaning: scraper, wire brush, power brush, grit blaster, HP water jet, grinder.
4. Measurement: tape, rule, pit gauge, profile gauge.
5. Ultrasonic thickness measurement.
6. Cathodic protection.
   – Proximity system (see Fig. 5).
   – Contact system (see Fig. 6).

Fig. 5 Cathodic protection (proximity system) using trailed electrode and connection to pipe to measure electrode pipe potential

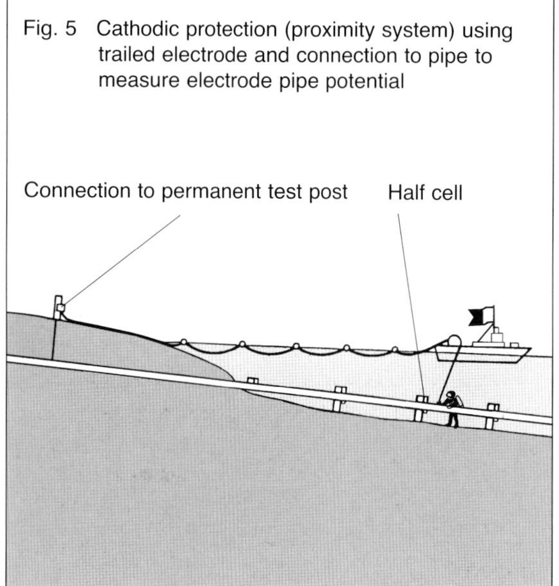
Connection to permanent test post
Half cell

Fig. 6 Diver measuring CP potential (contact system) on outfall pipe.

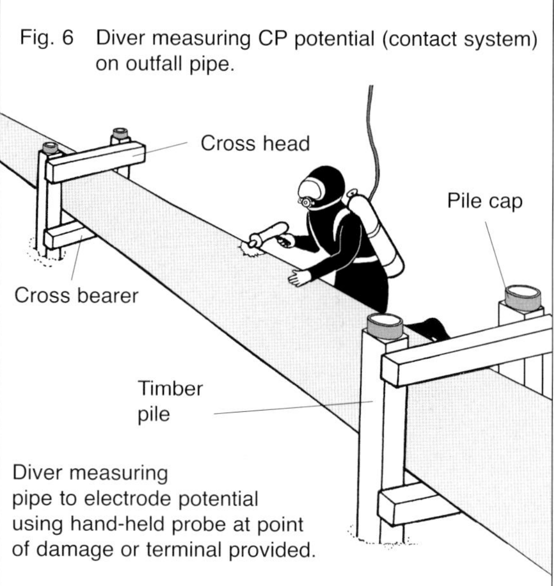
Cross head
Pile cap
Cross bearer
Timber pile
Diver measuring pipe to electrode potential using hand-held probe at point of damage or terminal provided.

MATERIALS THAT MAY REQUIRE INSPECTION
1. Concrete – pipe, weightcoat, diffuser.
2. Steel – pipe, fittings, diffuser, rebar etc.
3. Cast iron – pipe, fittings, saddles etc.
4. Ductile iron – pipe, fittings etc.
5. Phosphor bronze – fittings etc.
6. Plastics – pipe, diffuser, gaskets.
7. Wood – piles.

OUTFALLS – OPERATIONAL SAFETY

1. A Permit to Work system must be used.
2. The outfall and any related pumps must be certified to be completely shut off prior to any diving operation. The power supply of electrically operated valves must be isolated. On manually operated valves, either the valve wheel should be taken off and kept by the diving supervisor or the valve should be locked shut and the key kept by the supervisor. Large signs must be placed warning that relevant valves must not be touched due to diving operations.
3. Any residual flows must be stopped by insertion of a penstock or reliable stop log device.
4. A detailed hydraulic analysis must be carried out prior to any diving operation. For example, a vacuum can develop downstream of the closure valve on a falling tide which can break and cause a sudden outflow of water.
5. Only surface supplied equipment with emergency bail-out and good voice communications should be used when working inside a pipe. No SCUBA equipment should be used.
6. The design of the diver's harness and umbilical attachments should allow feet-first recovery when the diver cannot be turned.
7. The bail out cylinder should be as small as possible while providing enough gas to allow the diver to reach safety, plus a safety margin (typically 1 minute/10m (33ft) length of umbilical).
8. Diver entry should not be allowed into pipeline diameters of less than 1m (3ft). Entry distance should not be more than 100m. Total excursion from the surface should be no more than 120m (393ft).
9. When working inside an outfall, an additional diver should be placed at the entry point to assist with handling the working diver's umbilical.
10. The diving supervisor and tender(s) should know the diver's actual location at all times.
11. All umbilicals should be marked at intervals to indicate their length.
12. The dive team should have enough divers to be able to recover an unconscious diver.
13. The recovery of an incapacitated diver should be a preplanned and rehearsed method.
14. The adjacent access point in the direction of the survey should also be opened where possible to assist emergency diver recovery.
15. In recently dredged or steep-sided excavations and trenches, be aware of possible slope failure and provisions should be made for diver safety.
16. Be aware of normal safety requirements when working in shallow, tidal water, currents, exposed location and poor visibility

1.17 SHEET PILES

Sheet piling is used to form walls to retain, for example, water or soil as in a quay wall. Such walls may also be used as temporary works, acting to exclude water (cofferdams) or to serve as permanent formwork for concrete (as in bridge pier foundations). The piles are driven into place using a simple drop hammer or vibrating driver. Each pile interlocks with the one previously driven by means of a 'jaw' or 'clutch,' running the full length of the pile. The clutches are normally free to slide, but piles are often pitched and driven in pairs, after first welding the clutches together, for increased strength and for ease of handling.

Sheet piles are of two basic types:
1. U-type: with the jaw at the sides (see Fig. 1)
2. Z-type: with centre jaw (see Fig. 2) – generally a higher strength.

Fig. 1 Side-interlocked U-type sheet piles

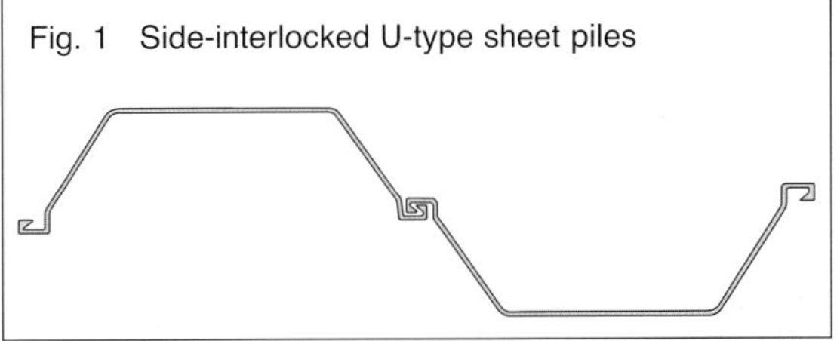

Fig. 2 Centrally-interlocked Z-type sheet piles

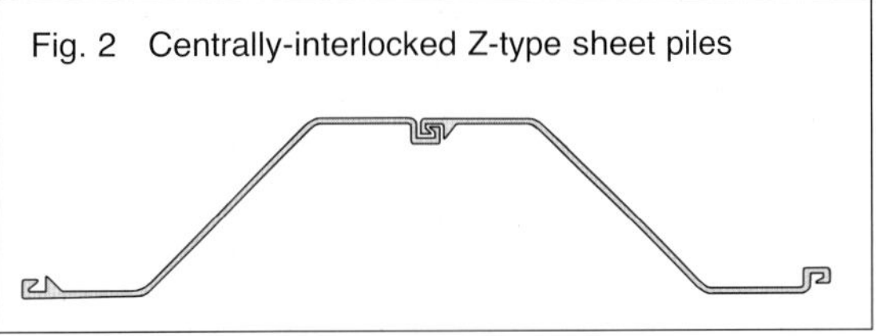

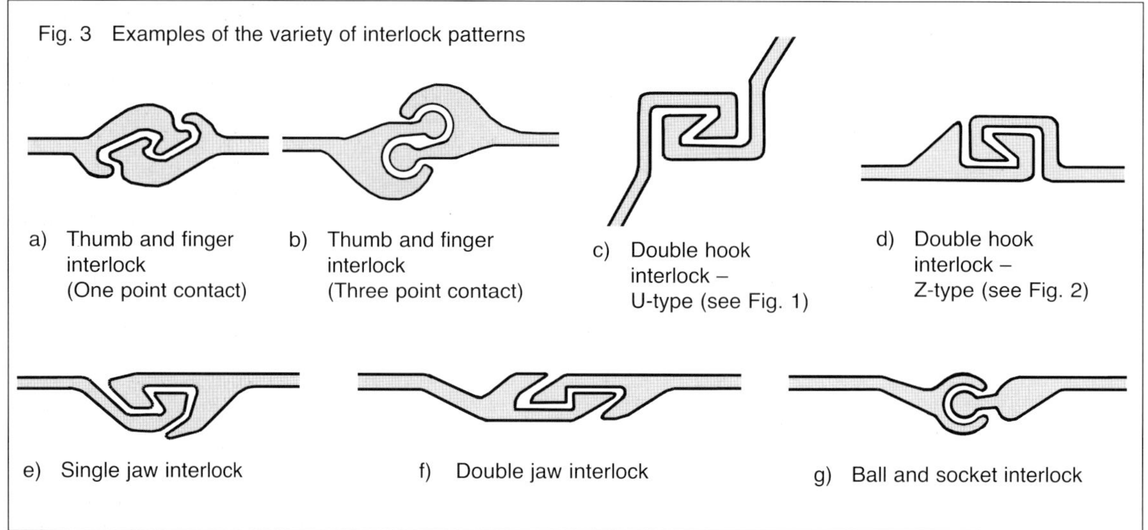
a) Thumb and finger interlock (One point contact)
b) Thumb and finger interlock (Three point contact)
c) Double hook interlock – U-type (see Fig. 1)
d) Double hook interlock – Z-type (see Fig. 2)
e) Single jaw interlock
f) Double jaw interlock
g) Ball and socket interlock

Fig. 3 Examples of the variety of interlock patterns

The U-type section is typified by, and often described as a 'Larssen pile'. Z-type piles include and are described as 'Frodingham piles' or 'frods' and there are several variants produced by Krupp, Hoesch, etc.

A variety of interlocking patterns exist which include those illustrated in Fig. 3.

Specially rolled or fabricated piles may be found at wall corners or junctions. Other pile types include tubular piles with welded-on clutches, or modified standard sections such as universal beams with patent clutch connectors. Sheet pile sections will also be found paired up or plated, to produce box pile sections.

For most applications, simply driving the pile does not provide adequate or efficient structural capacity and some form of horizontal support, or tie-back, is provided at or near the top of the piles (see Fig. 4). For a retaining (or quay) wall, this typically takes the form of steel tie rods. In order to distribute the tie rod loads across the sheet piles, a horizontal beam or 'waling' is usually provided. This may be back-to-back channel or universal beam sections. This waling section is sometimes on the front of the wall but more commonly on the back, or buried side. The tie rods will usually project through the wall, with a threaded end, nut and washer plate. Some lighter designs use only tie rods and washer plates, and no waling. The other end of the tie rods may be anchored into rock, or to another buried sheet pile anchor wall, some way distant from the 'active zone' of the main wall.

In some cases, the tops of the sheet piles may be cast into a concrete cope beam and the support is provided at this level, either by cast-in tie rods or by the deck slab itself.

In cofferdams, walings typically form a horizontal frame which may be cross-braced or corner braced to strengthen the whole structure.

Stresses are concentrated where the tie-back is fixed to the sheet pile wall, with the potential for local overstress damage or aggravated corrosion.

Modes of failure of piles

1. OUT OF INTERLOCK/DECLUTCHED
   The piles remain in line but have become separated.
2. DECLUTCHED AND ROTATED
   The piles have separated and one has rotated around its longitudinal axis.
3. DEFORMED
   The piles have separated and one has been bent out of shape.

Modes of failure of interlocks

1. OPENING CAP
   The interlock has separated but no damage or deformation has occurred.
2. DEFORMED INTERLOCK
   The interlock has separated and one or both sides have become deformed.
3. PARTIALLY TORN OFF INTERLOCK
   The interlock has separated and one or both sides of the interlock have lost part of its material.

Diving Tasks

1. Cleaning of sheet piling prior to pouring of concrete. This ensures the concrete adheres to the steel piles.
2. Attaching drilling tubes to prepare for grouted anchors.
3. Inspection including:
   - Visual inspection for damage, corrosion, clutch failure, condition of tie rod ends, condition of cathodic protection anodes.
   - Ultrasonic thickness measurement of pile.
   - Cathodic protection electrical potential levels.
4. Repairs, including welding.

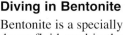

Fig. 4 Sheet pile wading and tie rods.

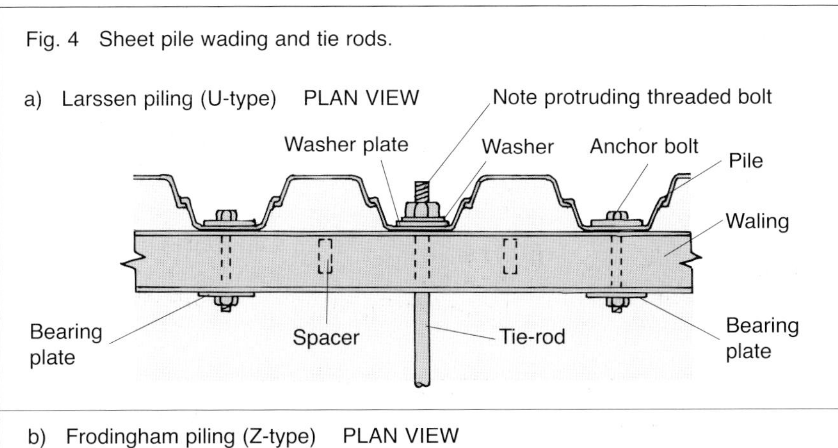
a) Larssen piling (U-type) PLAN VIEW
Note protruding threaded bolt
Washer plate
Washer
Anchor bolt
Pile
Waling
Bearing plate
Spacer
Tie-rod
Bearing plate

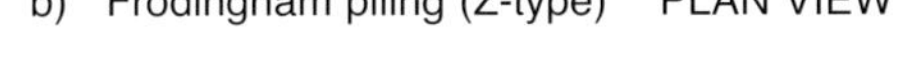
b) Frodingham piling (Z-type) PLAN VIEW

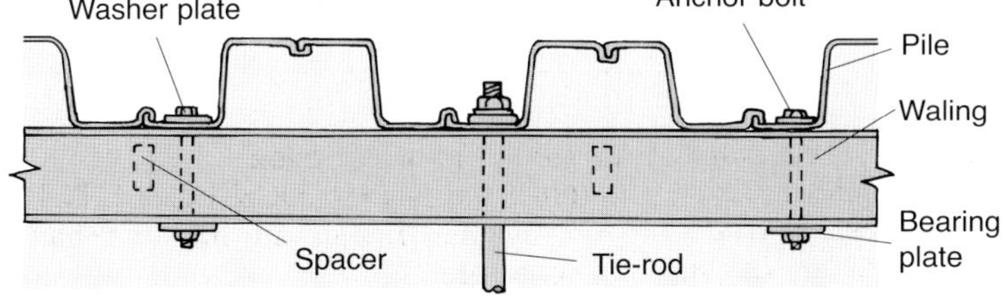
Washer plate
Anchor bolt
Pile
Waling
Bearing plate
Spacer
Tie-rod

ELEVATIONS

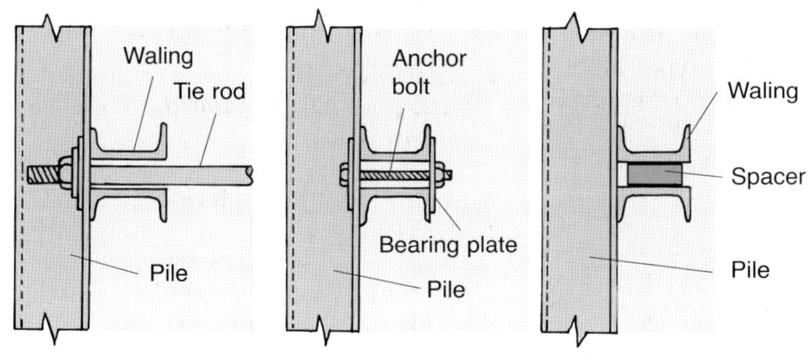
Waling
Tie rod
Pile
Anchor bolt
Bearing plate
Pile
Waling
Spacer
Pile

Landward view to show waling fixed to piles

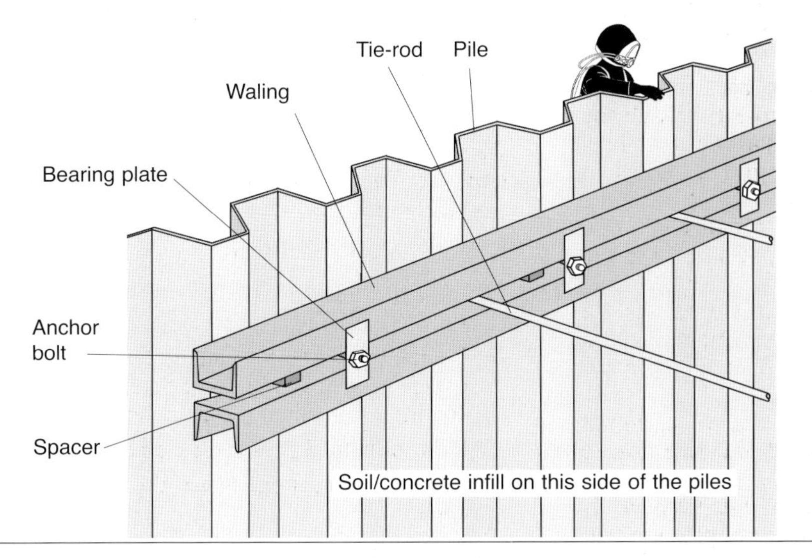
Tie-rod
Pile
Waling
Bearing plate
Anchor bolt
Spacer
Soil/concrete infill on this side of the piles

Diving in Bentonite

Bentonite is a specially dense fluid used in the hydrocarbon and civil engineering industries. Its density is such it is equivalent to that of sea bed material. It is made of a mixture of chemicals, some of which are toxic. Its exact density can be adjusted to meet the requirements in any particular application. These applications range from filling and supporting the walls of trenches, shafts and tunnels.

Occasionally, divers are required to dive in this liquid. Visibility will be zero and the diver will require substantially greater weight to be able to sink in it. Because of the toxic nature of the fluid, the diver must be completely protected from any contact whatsoever with it. This includes using a breathing system that prevents any ingress of fluid (see section 5.3). This system should also be one that does not vent air into the fluid because this can cause a reduction in the density of the fluid with the loss of its supporting properties. A trench wall, for example, could collapse under such circumstances.

A further consequence of the high density of the liquid is that the diver will be exposed to pressures significantly greater than those at equivalent depths in water. This must be taken into account when calculating any decompression requirements.

Inspection Diving Techniques

2.1 INSPECTION DIVING

Following the construction and installation phases of a structure and for the ensuing lifetime of the structure, there follows the phase of inspection, maintenance and repair (IMR). The inspection activities discussed in this section relate exclusively to 'certification (and other integrity assurance) inspections.' Exploration wellhead inspection tasks are discussed in Section 1.

Inspection is a complex subject some aspects of which involve theories and formulae beyond the scope of this book. More detailed information may be obtained from other sources such as underwater inspection training course notes.

Inspection diving is a diver task traditionally applied to exploration wellhead diving and has been based almost exclusively on visual methods such as photography, video and the diver's own eyes.

However, the emergence of certification requirements for fixed production structures in some areas has meant that the requirements for inspection of a high quality has been established. To cater for this, the traditional tasks and methods are now supplemented by additional specialised activities which include:

- Non-destructive testing (NDT) of nominated areas.
- Corrosion damage inspection.
- Cathodic protection surveys: anode inspection and electrical potential measurement.
- Marine growth inspection and removal.
- Debris inspection (and removal).
- Scour and stability inspections.

The basic reason for inspection is to help assess the structural integrity of a structure. It must be remembered that inspection is a data-gathering task only and does not normally include interpretation of the data. Diver inspectors are not expected to interpret structural integrity from the inspection data that they gather.

The various inspection activities have a basic logical order. Some tasks have to be done prior to cleaning while others must be done afterwards. For example, most NDT cannot be performed before cleaning while, obviously, a marine growth survey cannot be performed afterwards.

Once this is understood the various inspection requirements of a client can be arranged so as to create the most efficient inspection programme. In general terms, programmes are arranged so as to perform:

1. A general initial survey before any cleaning to see if there is any obvious damage or problem.
2. General tasks such as seabed surveys, marine growth surveys and corrosion inspection.
3. Appropriate underwater cleaning.
4. Critical inspection tasks in likely areas in relation to less obvious (or even invisible) defects. The most important of these is cracking. This critical inspection is to detect defects and then, if found, to measure them accurately.

Planning

Planning of inspection programmes is very important. Ineffectual and inapplicable schemes are costly.

Careful initial planning will ensure that no unnecessary activities are allowed to intrude.

The most efficient intervention method should be selected whether by vehicle or diver. If by diver, whether vertical or horizontal working should be the most advantageous.

The selection of equipment most appropriate to the specific tasks can greatly increase efficiency and this is especially important with photography, video and NDT. However, where alternative techniques are possible, particularly in the case of NDT, cost effectiveness must not be allowed to interfere with the validity of the tests. There is no value in expenditure for testing that merely goes through the motions.

Inspection programme planning must be based on experience and awareness of both the underlying engineering objectives and the available resources and capabilities.

Typical inspection programme

Fig. 1 summarises a typical planned inspection programme together with reasons for each activity, items to be inspected and the commonly used methods. Although this programme is typical, individual programmes may emphasise different aspects according to the client's particular needs.

INSPECTION DIVING – OPERATIONAL SAFETY

1. Most diver inspection is carried out in the air diving range. Special care is needed with umbilical handling, especially where there is a swell, current and/or bad visibility.
2. Certain NDT techniques (such as radiographic work) introduce specific hazards. The very greatest care must be taken in handling any radioactive materials. The set procedures must be followed to the letter.
3. Impressed current anodes can have dangerously high electrical voltages. Care must be exercised in avoiding getting too close to such anodes. If necessary, power to the anodes should be switched off while divers are operating in their vicinity.
4. Certain cleaning techniques (such as high pressure water jetting) introduce special hazards. The 'dead-man' handles must never be tied off. Never point the jetting gun towards any part of your body or at another diver.

Fig. 1 GENERALISED SUMMARY OF INSPECTION ACTIVITIES

Category		Activity/summary	Principal reasons	Items to be inspected	Methods used
VISUAL INSPECTION	General	Examine the entire structure to detect and note obvious damage such as dents, buckles, tears, missing items, etc Visual and physical checks	To discover structural weakening To record any loss of design redundancy allowances	- Boat bumpers, fenders, etc - All legs, braces and other structural members. - Splashzone coatings - Pitting corrosion - Riser clamps - Surface of anodes	Diver's eyes Photography CCTV Sketches Measurements Documentation
VISUAL INSPECTION	Seabed survey* – Debris	Debris survey to detect and record all metallic and other debris	To record debris which can: - divert corrosion protection away from the structure towards the debris - cause a hazard to divers and ROVs	Seabed to a nominated distance from the structure	
VISUAL INSPECTION	Seabed survey* – Scour abrasion	Scour abrasion survey to record: - soil levels - evidence of rocking, etc - integrity of scour prevention devices	To record any possible movement and instability of the structure To identify any associated structural stresses	Pipelines, piles, legs and horizontal members, etc at the mudline	
MARINEGROWTH SURVEY*		Measure the thickness of the marinegrowth Plot distribution patterns Distinguish between soft and hard growths	To assess marinegrowth Excess marinegrowth attached to a structure can: - Induce unacceptable physical loads to a structure by adding deadweight load and/or increasing wave loading - Provide interference to divers	Mainly the splashzone Hard growth zone (normally El 30ft+ to -60ft) Possibly some other locations in special circumstances	Measurements of thicknesses Mapping of patterns Photography CCTV Sampling/specimens
CORROSION INSPECTION		Assess the integrity of the protection systems by: - checking coatings - measuring dimensions of sample anodes - checking electrical continuity of anodes - taking CP potential readings Determine if any corrosion damage is evident by: - measuring the steel thicknesses - measuring the depths of corrosion pits	To assess effectiveness of corrosion prevention systems by: - measuring the effectiveness of the systems - providing data to help plan the anode replacement schedule To ensure that the material corrosion losses have not: - exceeded the design allowances - reduced the material thicknesses below an acceptable level	Nominated/random areas Nominated/random anodes All (or most) anode connections - continuity straps Nominated areas - normally 4 cardinal points around the legs (at node levels) and risers/conductors Worst detected examples of pitting corrosion	Physical checks Size measurements CP potential readings Ultrasonic thickness readings Pit gauges or pit moulds
CLEANING		General removal of marinegrowth fouling Special cleaning to 'bright metal' for the close and critical inspections	To remove excess loadings To prepare for close visual and NDT inspection by removing all matter including marinegrowth, paint or bituministic coatings, corrosion products, scale, etc	Splashzone areas All nominated welded joints in preparation for - close visual inspection - critical (NDT) inspection - critical defect sizing	- Hand tools (wire strops, brushes) - Mechanical power tools (pneumatic and/or hydraulic) - High pressure water jet - Low pressure water jet with grit entrainment
CRITICAL INSPECTION	Close visual inspection	Rapid scan detection to detect visible cracking defects	Cracking defects may compromise the safety of a structure Cracking can result from: - continual and/or cyclic stresses causing fatigue cracking - physical impact, eg from a vessel, dropped pile or similar	Nominated high stress, low-fatigue node joints Known or suspected defects Previous repairs	Diver's eyes Close-up photography Close-up CCTV Any appropriate NDT method including: - MPI - Electro-magnetic interrogation
CRITICAL INSPECTION	NDT insp.	Rapid scan detection to detect cracking defects invisible to the human eye			
CRITICAL INSPECTION	Further inspection	Detail defect sizing to establish the dimensions of any crack defects detected by Close Visual and NDT inspection	To enable engineers to better understand the defect and to: - decide whether or not a repair is necessary - enable an appropriate repair method to be developed	Nominated relevant defects detected by close visual and/or NDT inspection	Appropriate NDT Photogrammetry Ultrasonics

* may be carried out concurrently with general visual inspection

2.2 VISUAL INSPECTION

The bulk of inspection data is derived from visual inspection techniques.

Visual inspection is used to inspect structures for obvious damage such as missing parts, dents, buckles and tears and to observe and record underwater conditions and features.

Underwater visual inspection is carried out by the human eye, still photography and closed circuit television (often referred to as CCTV or video). These methods are used in conjunction with verbal and written reports from the underwater inspector, who may be a diver or ROV pilot.

Still photography and CCTV are frequently used together as each has its own advantages. Still photography provides the necessary high definition required for detailed analysis while video, although it has poorer resolution, provides a continuous, real-time image of events that can be monitored by surface engineers and recorded for later viewing. A typical example might be during a pipeline survey: the diver or ROV pilot would follow the pipeline with a TV camera and whenever high definition details are required, a still camera would be used.

It must be remembered that visual inspection can only detect visible defects. While this seems obvious, cracking defects can be very difficult to find by visual methods (although once found they may then be able to be 'seen') and may indeed be invisible to the naked eye or camera. Detection of cracks is discussed in Section 2.8, NDT Inspection.

Close visual inspection

Close visual inspection is an important component of the 'critical' stage of most inspection programmes. There are two principal forms: the use of the human eye from close quarters, whether or not in conjunction with NDT inspection, and the production of close-up photographs in order to study small details in high definition enlargements (see Section 2.3). Close-up video recording may also be used in some circumstances providing that the video camera has an adequate close-focus capability.

The human eye

The human eye is invaluable in locating and identifying areas of interest, to place and use specialist equipment and for observing and making assessments on a continual basis. It would be very difficult to perform any sort of inspection without the human eye. However, it has its limitations as well as advantages (see Fig. 1).

The value of observation by the human eye is largely dependent on a log of what the eyes have seen. For this reason it is essential that inspectors should provide continual verbal commentary for recording, for subsequent analysis and correlation with photographic and videographic records.

As a result of these factors, the diver's eyes are used for initial surveys to first identify and locate areas of interest and then to place specialist equipment.

Underwater problems

There are four factors which are responsible for all the optical problems of underwater visual inspection: visibility, lighting, refraction and filtration.

1. VISIBILITY

Visibility is dependent on the amount of suspended particles and algae in the water between the viewing point and the subject and upon the strength, type and position of the source of light.

Visibility does not necessarily correlate to the amount of light and lack of visibility may not mean that it is dark. Low visibility conditions are like being in a fog. Regardless of whether it is night or day in a fog (dark or light), the addition of light can sometimes hinder seeing.

As regards the sediment and algae matter in the seawater, the best visibility is often just before or just after slack water after a period of calm. It should be remembered that slack water is not always at high or low water and it is important to avoid disturbing the seabed and surrounding area.

To get the best photographic and video results the lens-to-subject distance should be kept to a minimum – never more than one-third of the ambient visibility distance.

There are many ways of overcoming bad visibility when one cannot wait until the conditions are right. Known as 'clear water systems' they are simple to operate and depend upon the ingenuity of the photographer. One example might be when a close-up of a weld is required in 15cm (6") visibility. Squashing a transparent plastic bag filled with clean tap water between the camera and the weld would produce a reasonable result. Another solution might

Fig. 1 The Human Eye - Advantages and Disadvantages

ADVANTAGES	DISADVANTAGES
Stereo capability	Requires human presence
Colour capability	No permanent record is produced
Connected to the reasoning logic of the human brain	May have defects
Adapts to a wide range of ambient light conditions	Has no capability to enlarge images
Requires no extraneous instrumentation to be bought, carried or maintained	Adjusts slowly to low light conditions (cannot compete with low-light CCTV)
Requires no external power requirements	Does not always assess what it sees
Intrinsically hazard-free	No remote or third-party viewing
Versatile	Has difficulty in assessing size and distance
	Sensitive to damaging irradiations (eg, from welding)

be to construct an enclosure around the subject and pump clear water into it to replace the turbid water. Most of these techniques are really only suitable for close-up work.

2. LIGHTING – AMBIENT LIGHT

The lower the sun is in the sky the more light reflects off the surface of the water and, therefore, the less light passes through into the water. Providing that the sun is high enough in the sky to penetrate the surface, available light from the sun is normally adequate for human eye and video inspection at shallow depths, say up to 10m (33ft). Wave motion will also deflect the sun's rays off the surface, while some reflection may occur from the bottom.

With an increase in depth, daylight and colour diminish rapidly due to absorption and filtration and some form of artificial illumination becomes necessary. This can be provided by fixed lights for human eye and video inspection or, in the case of still photography, by electronic flash. Ambient light is not appropriate for most underwater photography. For the inspection of large areas, ie structural inspection, available light is preferred because it gives a more even illumination. However, available light is not normally adequate for most offshore video and photographic requirements.

Fixed lights and electronic flash give good illumination but are restricted to relatively small areas.

3. REFRACTION

When light passes from any transparent medium to another (for example sunlight passing from air to seawater) the differences in optical densities affect

Fig. 2 The effect of water on reflection, refraction and filtration of light.

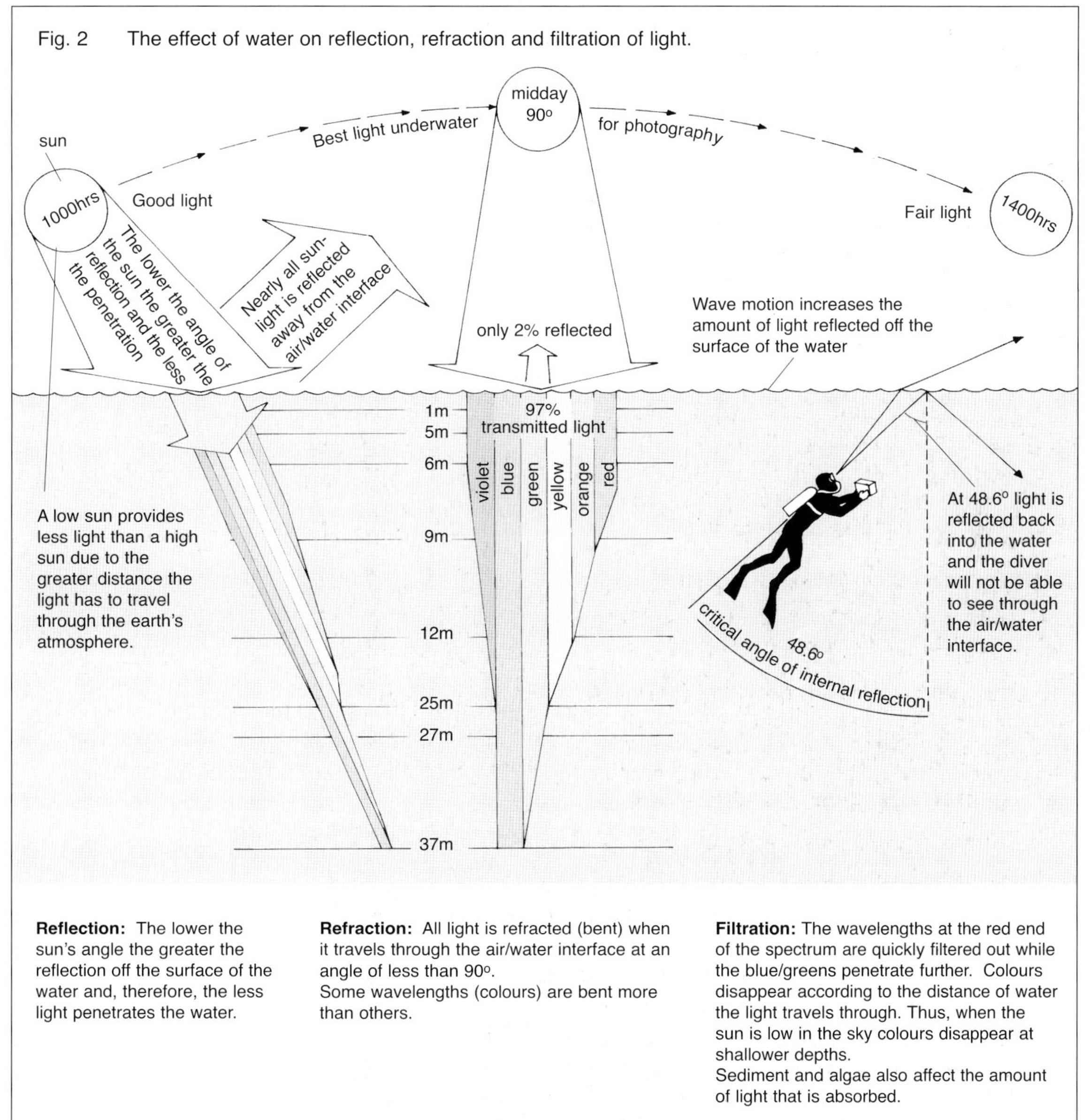
sun
1000hrs
Good light
Best light underwater
midday
90°
for photography
Fair light
1400hrs
The lower the angle of the sun the greater the reflection and the less the penetration
Nearly all sunlight is reflected away from the air/water interface
only 2% reflected
Wave motion increases the amount of light reflected off the surface of the water
1m
5m
97%
transmitted light
6m
violet
blue
green
yellow
orange
red
9m
12m
25m
27m
37m
A low sun provides less light than a high sun due to the greater distance the light has to travel through the earth's atmosphere.
At 48.6° light is reflected back into the water and the diver will not be able to see through the air/water interface.
48.6°
critical angle of internal reflection

Reflection: The lower the sun's angle the greater the reflection off the surface of the water and, therefore, the less light penetrates the water.

Refraction: All light is refracted (bent) when it travels through the air/water interface at an angle of less than 90°.
Some wavelengths (colours) are bent more than others.

Filtration: The wavelengths at the red end of the spectrum are quickly filtered out while the blue/greens penetrate further. Colours disappear according to the distance of water the light travels through. Thus, when the sun is low in the sky colours disappear at shallower depths.
Sediment and algae also affect the amount of light that is absorbed.

the light velocities and, according to Snell's Law, three things happen.

i) The light both reflects from and penetrates the seawater.
ii) The light is refracted (ie bent) (See 'Optics', page 91).
iii) Some individual wavelengths (ie colours) bend more than others.

The degree of these effects is entirely dependent on the light's angle of incidence to the water surface.

4. FILTRATION

Seawater acts as a progressive colour filter with its own colour cast and degree of absorption. The greater the distance that light travels through water the more density the colour filter has and the greater the filtration effect. Even in clear water, at depths in excess of 10m (33ft) most of the colour has been filtered out.

The exact colour of this filter depends on the location, time of day, and the suspended and dissolved matter in the water. But in general terms the filtration colour is cyan (blue) in appearance due to the progressive absorption of the red end of the spectrum (see Fig. 2).

All seawater contains varying amounts of sediment and algae etc; the greater the concentrations, the more turbid the water. In shallow coastal waters, dyes dissolved from suspended particles usually tint the sea with yellow which, added to the existing cyan, makes the sea appear green.

At a certain depth the dyes cancel out the water colour filter absorbing all the blue light as well as the red and other colours. So, although the water may be clear, very little light will get through it. In other words, the filtration effect of the water reduces the amount of light available in the water (which has already been reduced at the air/water interface) and eventually it will absorb all the colours until no light remains at all.

To put back the colour and light that have been lost it is necessary to use some form of supplementary lighting; fixed lights for human eyes and video inspection and electronic flash for still photography. When colour values are important to colour photography and video recording, the diver should place a colour card (guide) within the picture area for subsequent analysis and comparison.

2.3 STILL PHOTOGRAPHY

Still photography is invaluable to underwater inspection for topside analysis by engineers. It is a relatively simple and economical means of securing high definition permanent records from which engineers can obtain a great deal of information. However, in order to achieve its potential, it is necessary to recognise the inherent capabilities and limitations of still photography and to understand the problems of the seawater environment.

Advantages and limitations of still photography

ADVANTAGES:

- High detail (good resolution) possible.
- Relatively inexpensive.
- Magnification of images. Small detail possible.
- Stereo photography available.
- Colour capability.
- Large film loadings.
- System controls can be simplified/pre-set.
- Easy, low-cost duplication of records.
- Digital data recording on photographs.
- Critical measurements in three planes.

LIMITATIONS:

- For best results (for offshore-related work), artificial lighting is preferable in most conditions.
- No real-time remote viewing and no real-time record of movement.
- Moderate skill required.
- Requires identification data in each photograph.
- Requires a chemical process before results are available (except with digital photography).
- Success of results cannot be determined until after film processing or digital printing.
- Difficulties in interpretation where black and white film is used.

Underwater digital photography

Digital photography has several advantages over conventional photography:

- A phototechnician and darkroom are not required.
- Pictures can be reviewed subsea by the diver.
- Viewing is almost instantaneous.
- After uploading dissemination is easy.
- Pictures can be e-mailed directly to land-based engineers quickly with no loss in quality.
- Printing is a simple easy process.
- Reprints are quick and inexpensive although good quality paper is required for good results.

Photographic constraints

The environmental problems of visibility, sufficient light and colour casts discussed in Section 2.2 produce specific limitations for underwater photography all of which are related to lighting. Low levels of available light and associated colour saturation problems will be eliminated by correct application of artificial light sources.

The lack of the correct colour light causes two main problems: a level of darkness which results in contrast problems, and false colours (or colour casts).

CONTRAST/BRIGHTNESS

Contrast (ie, the brightness range) is the relationship between the brightest and darkest points within the overall picture. When there is a great difference between them the contrast is said to be high (or 'crisp') and when there is little difference the contrast is low (or 'muddy'). Image quality is directly related to good (high) contrast. Brightness may be described as an illumination level and there can be a range of light levels from one area in a photograph to another. While this would appear to provide good contrast, it may look disappointing in the finished photograph. However, this is not a problem of contrast, but one of poor lighting.

There are a number of reasons for low image contrast:

1. The subject itself may lack contrast (ie all of it may be shades of one colour, or all white or all black, etc). This is known as 'subject contrast' and although different can affect 'image contrast.'
2. There is insufficient light illuminating the subject.
3. The photographic image has been underexposed or overexposed. (It must be remembered that under-exposure does not necessarily mean that the subject was not adequately lit; it could be that much of the light could not penetrate the sediment within the water between the subject and the camera).
4. The film has been over or underdeveloped.
5. A combination of the above in particular numbers 3 and 4 above.

In underwater terms, subject contrast problems may lie in photographing an area of corrosion. For example, high contrast would exist where there is a bright flared reflection from a bare metal surface which is against a totally unlit seawater background. Should a photograph have a low contrast which is not caused by subject contrast, it is likely that there has not been enough light reaching the film (assuming that the processing has been correct).

In underwater photography contrast is best controlled by correctly lighting the subject (see 'Type of Lighting' and 'Placement of Lighting' below). However, some compensation is possible during processing (see 'Choice of Film').

FALSE COLOUR

The manufacturers of colour film assume that the light to be used will be either of two types: sunlight or flash (colour temperature of approximately 5500°K); or tungsten/quartz floods (3200°K).

There are several reasons commonly responsible for false colour in photographs taken underwater:

a) Incompatibility of light source and film type. For example, tungsten-type film should not be used with an electronic flash, or daylight-type film with fixed continuous lights.
b) The light became filtered (assuming that the correct type of light was used). Filtering can occur due to the effect of seawater or by reflection off a large non-white surface. It affects both tungsten and daylight film.
c) No filter, or the wrong filter, was used to correct the light source.
d) Faulty colour processing.
e) Use of 'tired,' over-used chemicals in processing.

All of these can be controlled. Assuming that the processing is correct, the principal remedy for false colour is to ensure that the light suits the film being used and the underwater conditions. That is, that there is enough light and that only minimal filtration is allowed to occur by having the camera and the light source close to the subject (see 'Placement of Lighting' below).

BACK SCATTER

Back scatter is a problem of lighting. It results from the light reflecting off suspended particles in the seawater and back into the camera. (In principle, this is similar to the effect of car lights in fog).

To avoid back scatter the flash should be mounted to the side of and well in front of the camera so as not to light the seawater in front of the camera (see 'Placement of Lighting' below).

Other problems

The photographic problems of refraction and optics are dealt with in 'Camera Optics and features' , p. 89.

Identification board

When taking photographs, the photographer should always include an identification board. In addition to the standard information (scale, name, date, location, etc) the board should include 3–6cm (1–2in) strips of red, green and blue electrical insulation tape (for colour comparison). Colour matching is carried out during the print processing to ensure that the subject is the correct colour.

The essentials of lighting

Available light underwater is not an ideal source for the reasons previously mentioned, ie, it is variable, low in contrast, renders colour incorrectly, etc.

Ideally, correct lighting should be:

a) Strong enough to provide high contrast image without extra enhancement of the medium, ie push processing film image or enhancement of the video.
b) Evenly spread over the required area.
c) The correct colour temperature for the film or video camera being used.

The technical quality of a photograph is directly related to the quality of light forming the image. In broad terms, the more light the better the quality. While there can, in theory, be too much light, this is rarely a practical problem underwater. The main underwater lighting problem relates to the placement of the light.

Before defining the essentials of correct lighting, it should be remembered that detail should be visible in both the brightest and the darkest low light areas. Even if an underwater photograph is sharply focused and has bright saturated colours, it is not a good photograph for engineering purposes unless detail can be seen in it.

Every light casts shadows and the brightness range (ie the contrast gradient) between the brightest areas and the darkest shadows may be in the order of 20:1. However, the latitude of most photographic emulsions is not as wide, typically about 15:1 to 17:1. If detail is to be seen in the highlights and the shadows of the film, additional light must illuminate the shadow areas. This is the reason that some photographers use more than one light. They use a main (prime) light with one or more modelling (fill-in) lights at a 3:1 relationship, that is to say, the main light is three times brighter than the secondary one. While 3:1 would be difficult to attain underwater, the principle is worth pursuing.

Using more than one light source will give fine detail and even lighting but may produce flat working results. In some circumstances a single light source may be preferred if surface texture is required.

TYPE OF LIGHTING

There are two types of artificial light sources used underwater – fixed lamps and electronic flash. Fixed lamps are usually available to the diver or vehicle but may be of mixed colour temperatures: some have a yellow bias, others a green. Some of these may be adequate for video but not for still photography. As fixed lamps require external power, are bulkier and heavier, involve the use of exposure meters and are significantly lower powered, so there is little benefit in their use for underwater still photography except in certain specialised applications.

Electronic flashguns, sometimes called 'strobes' (see Glossary below), should always be used for the following reasons:

1. They provide the appropriate power necessary.
2. They have the correct colour temperature for daylight film.
3. They are compact and easily carried.
4. They are inexpensive.

Electronic flashguns should not be kept in saturation chambers as prolonged exposure to a heliox environment can lead to helium entering the xenon gas-filled strobe rendering it useless.

POSITIONING THE LIGHT SOURCE

The placement of additional lighting is important and is frequently the difference between a good and bad photograph – particularly underwater. However, a compromise is often necessary between what is ideal and what is possible.

There are two points to bear in mind:

1. In order to reduce the volume of seawater between the subject and the lens the diver needs to take his photographs from as close to the subject as practicably possible.
2. In order not to light the seawater (sediment/algae) in front of the lens he needs to offset the light from the camera axis. Unfortunately, this tends to light only one side of the subject. The closer the light to the camera, the more severe is the problem. The previous recommendation for the use of more than one flash substantially reduces the problems of uneven lighting.

The following principles for positioning lights should always be considered:

1. For all work:
   a) Keep the flash unit(s) offset from the lens axis wherever possible so as not to light the water in front of the camera lens, thereby inducing back scatter.

Glossary of Standard Terms

Acceptance angle This is the angle at the lens described by the limits of the subject recorded on the film. It is also referred to as the angle of the lens. Standard lenses usually have an angle of 45° to 50°.

ASA American Standards Association (see Film Speed).

Colour temperature This is a way of describing the quality of white light. It is expressed in degrees Kelvin (°K).

F-number This is a numerical indication of the size of the aperture in a lens. The number is derived from an arithmetic relationship between the diameter of the aperture and the focal length of the lens. A lens in which the widest possible aperture has a low f-number is called a 'fast' lens whereas a lens with a relatively high f-number is called a 'slow' lens.

Film speed Film speed is measured by several alternative standards including ISO (International Standards Organisation) and ASA (American Standards Association). The higher the ISO or ASA number, the faster the speed of the film.

Focal length This is the distance between the optical centre of the lens and the film when the lens is focused at infinity.

ISO International Standards Organisation (see Film Speed).

Negative film This film is used to produce positive prints, either colour or black and white.

Refractive index The ratio of the speed of light in a vacuum to its speed in any given medium.

Reversal film This is a positive film which makes colour slides.

SLR camera Single lens reflex camera. This is a camera where the viewer views the shot through the same lens that the photograph is taken. There is no parallax error between the viewed shot and the photographed shot.

Strobe Also known as an electronic flash. A flash of very short duration produced by an electronic discharge through a tube containing an inert gas such as xenon.

Wide angle lens A lens with a short focal length and a wide acceptance angle.

   b) If necessary utilise a 'barn door' principle.
   c) Ensure that the unit's angle of illumination is adequate for both the subject size/flash position and the camera lens acceptance angle.

2. For close-up work:
   (For subjects of say 5–50cm (2–20") in size.
   a) Where the camera is close to the subject it is important to keep the illumination as even as possible across the subject. Therefore:
      – when using one flash unit: keep the unit a reasonable distance back from the subject.
      – when using two flash units: place the units closer, ensuring that the distances from the subject are equal.
   b) Ensure that a shadow of the camera is not cast onto the subject.
3. For medium and distance work (for subjects of say 50–150cm (20–60") in size:
   a) Keep the flash unit(s) in front of the camera plane (about 25–30cm (9–12") wherever possible.
   b) Ensure that the flash unit(s) do not intrude into the field of view.

Camera optics and features

There is as yet no one camera that is ideal for all underwater situations. There are specialist cameras that can do one job really well and there are others which can be adapted to do many tasks moderately well. Selection of a camera system will depend on its particular features and its suitability to the work objectives. However, there is one subject common to all cameras – the optics.

UNDERWATER OPTICS

As previously stated, when light passes from one medium to another it is refracted (bent). Underwater photography involves using light that passes through three different media. From the water it passes through multiple glass and air interfaces. Lens manufacturers make all necessary air/glass corrections but some manufacturers of underwater cameras may not have fully considered the corrections necessary for the water/air/glass interfaces. For any given camera front, different focal length lenses will produce differently scaled images of the same subject from the same distance. A wide angle lens will cover a large area and objects in it will appear small. A telephoto lens will cover a small area and objects will appear large. Most formats have a standard lens which gives an angle of view similar to that of the human eye. The angle of view of a lens is termed the acceptance angle.

Specific focal lengths for any given angle vary with the size of the camera format. However, should a lens be encapsulated for underwater use, the design of the port can significantly change the acceptance angle. Considering that seawater has a different refractive index to air and glass (ie 1.33 against nearly 1.0 and anything between 1.5 and 1.8) anticipated angles of acceptance can be changed significantly.

Such uncorrected underwater optics will, for example, change a 35mm lens (63°) at infinity to a 50mm lens on a 35mm format (47°) at close focus. This means that the image will be about one third larger and in order to picture the whole subject, a greater distance must be put between the camera and the subject. This introduces unnecessary attendant problems of lower contrast, less light and colour, visibility losses and significantly less depth of field, making focusing more difficult.

OPTICAL CORRECTIONS

The solution to the problem is quite simple. The refraction can be reduced by the use of a domed port instead of a flat port. For full underwater correction an Ivanoff corrector is required (see Fig. 1).

Fig. 1 The effects of refraction on the angle of view

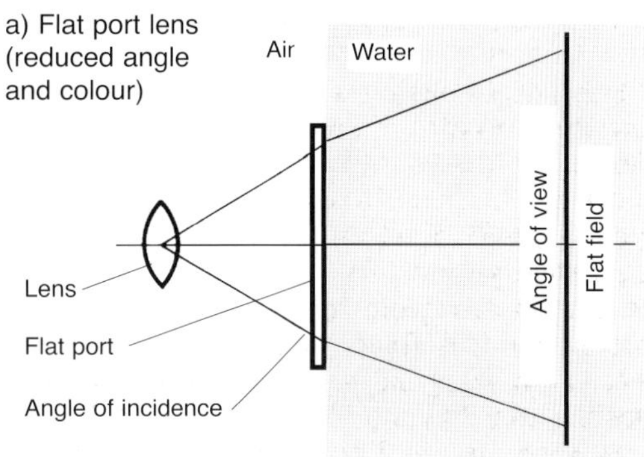
a) Flat port lens
(reduced angle
and colour)
Air
Water
Lens
Flat port
Angle of incidence
Angle of view
Flat field

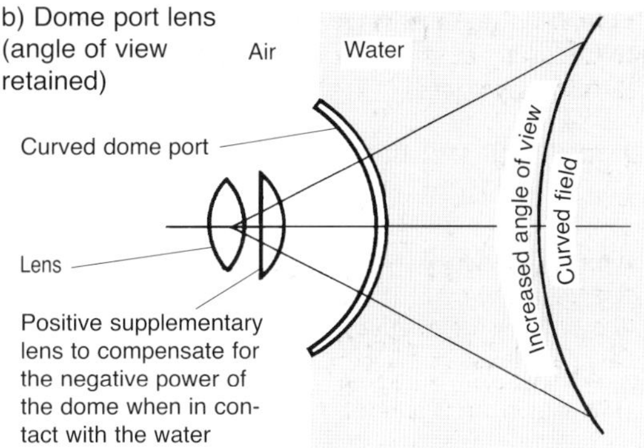
b) Dome port lens
(angle of view
retained)
Air
Water
Curved dome port
Lens
Positive supplementary
lens to compensate for
the negative power of
the dome when in con-
tact with the water
Increased angle of view
Curved field

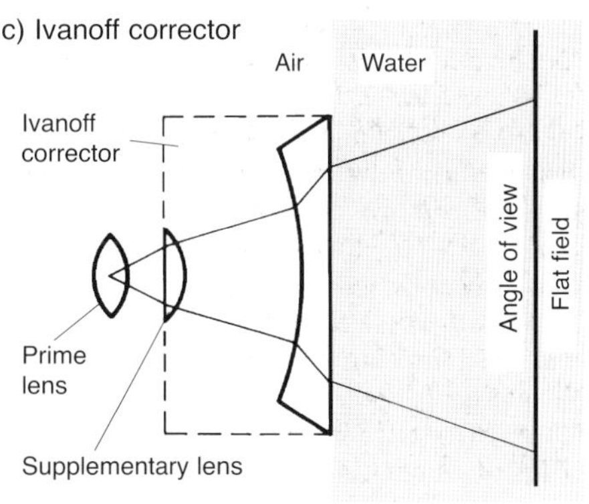
c) Ivanoff corrector
Air
Water
Ivanoff
corrector
Prime
lens
Supplementary lens
Angle of view
Flat field

ANGLES OF VIEW

The angle of view of a lens will determine the stand-off distance necessary to cover a given subject. As the seawater is the main degrading factor, it is important to reduce the amount of the water between the subject and the lens by reducing the stand-off.

Standard lens: Most subjects for underwater inspection would be in the order of 1–2m (3–6ft) in size and up to a maximum of 3m (10ft). Should a standard lens be used the subject is often too large to fit into the viewfinder. To enable it to fit, it would be necessary to go further away from the subject – thereby increasing the stand-off distance and hence reducing the quality of the photograph.

Telephoto (long focus) lens: These have limited applications in conventional underwater photography.

Wide-angle lens: These are most suitable underwater because they provide the maximum image from the shortest stand-off distance. In addition they are usually close-focusing and have a large depth of focus. The most useful lenses for underwater have an angle of acceptance of about 92°–63° (ie 21–35mm focal lengths in 35mm format and 38–50mm in 6 x 6cm format).
There is a disadvantage in that the wide angle lenses distort perspective. Objects closer to the lens will appear to be much larger in relation to things further away.
Many of the qualities of a wide angle lens are thrown away when the lens is placed behind a flat port in an underwater housing which reduces the angle of acceptance of the lens. A corrected port, or a specially designed underwater lens is the best answer.

Close-up or Supplementary lens: These are convenient in that they can be fitted and removed underwater from Nikonos and certain similar cameras. They may be useful for closer focusing distances than can be managed by the use of close-up lenses for, say, magnifications of 1:0.4 and greater, but they do need an exposure allowance.

Macro lens: These are designed for close-ups of small objects and are satisfactory behind a flat port. These lenses focus down to close distances and are often used with extension tubes. They are usually of a 50mm focal length or longer but can be used only with SLR cameras in housings.

CHOICE OF FILM – Colour or black and white

Colour film is used in nearly all underwater photographic inspection work because there is so much more information to be obtained from it than from black and white film. Modern colour films now have greatly increased speeds. For general inspection colour film may be up-rated.
Black and white film is only used for special purposes where colour would be irrelevant or if higher resolution is required.

Compared to black and white film, colour has some disadvantages:

1. *Narrow latitude*
   Latitude is the film's tolerance to under- and over-exposure. Colour negative film can tolerate ± two f-stops while colour reversal film can only handle ± half an f-stop. A wide latitude film is best underwater where exposure is uncertain. Colour negative film allows some colour correction at the printing stage.
2. *Bracketing*
   To ensure the photograph has the correct exposure, bracketing can be used. This is a simple procedure. For example, with colour negative film (which has a latitude of ± 2 f-stops) the first picture is taken at the estimated correct exposure, then a further two pictures are taken, one 2 f-stops above and the other 2 f-stops below the original.
3. *Greater precision required in processing*
   Colour processing must be carried out to close temperature tolerances and the time interval of each stage carefully controlled.
   In low light conditions the effective ISO (International Standard Organisation, formerly called ASA) value of the colour film may be increased up to four times but this would require special processing. Black and white films are available that can be up-rated to as much as 3200 ISO with little quality loss. Care would have to be taken in the processing not to lose shadow. detail. The newly introduced dye-coupled black and white films combine extreme speed with high resolution and low granularity. Examples of these films are Agfa Vario XL and Ilford XPI.
   The film speed may be up-rated by extending the first developer times. As a general guide, the first developer time should be multiplied by one third for every one stop increase in film speed.

   For example:

Normal first developer time		=	6 min.
1 stop increase	= 6 x 1/3	=	8 min.
2 stop increase	= 8 x 1/3	=	10½ min.

FILM SPEED

Films are made for specific purposes. Their sensitivity is rated at speeds between 25 and 2750 ISO. Slow films, 25 to 125 ISO, are fine-grained and the resolution is high. This is especially important if there is to be considerable enlargement of the photographs. Unless available light is sufficient, slow-speed film should be used.

THE END PRODUCT

When taking photographs the prime consideration should be "what ultimately is going to be done with the information obtained?" Many of the pictures taken underwater are processed on site so that the original transparencies can be seen by the client or engineers to guarantee results without delay.

Reversal films (which produce transparencies) tend to be used for this reason.

There are two ways of presenting the finished product:

1. *Reversal*: The original film is developed to become a positive transparency which can be viewed by projection. Colour prints may be produced from the transparency by means of a reversal paper. The results tend to be rather contrasty, losing detail in the highlights and/or the shadow areas in the print. On the other hand, this sort of print can achieve a high degree of resolution.
2. *Negative*: Negative film has a wider latitude, is cheaper and initially quicker to process than reversal film. Its comparative disadvantages are that the original film has to be converted to a positive print or to a transparency before it can be viewed. The print, however, can be of a superior quality to a conventional reversal print and cheaper to produce. Transparencies can be readily and inexpensively reproduced as photographic prints. Negative film is probably the most suitable for recording data.

MONO OR STEREO PHOTOGRAPHY

Mono photography requires only one camera with a single lens and is the simplest way of producing good quality still reproductions. Most black and white or colour still photography will be mono but stereo reproduction is becoming more popular in inspection specifications.

Stereo photography is a technique for producing three-dimensional photographic images by simultaneously taking two photographs of the same subject from slightly different camera positions. The resulting prints have to be viewed in a special viewer. Stereo images would be produced when the maximum amount of visual assessment is required. For instance, a dent in a tubular bracing would be more apparent and possibly only obvious in a stereo image. The combination of stereo and colour can provide topside personnel with information which cannot be achieved by mono alone. Stereo photography is not to be confused with photogrammetry, which is described below and is a technique employed when accurate measurement is required.

PHOTOGRAMMETRY

Photogrammetry is a form of stereo photography from which measurements of all three dimensions can be obtained – length, breadth and thickness. The technique is being increasingly used in offshore inspection, particularly for evaluating and monitoring corrosion and damaged areas. Photogrammetry differs from stereo photography mainly in the provision of a Reseau plate in the film plane. This holds the film flat and superimposes accurate register marks on the film to aid the analysis of the results.

The photographic stage is only the first part of the photogrammetric process. The photographs must be observed in a special machine to identify the points that have to be measured. The output from this machine must then be further processed by a computer to obtain the results of the type required and to introduce corrections for the inherent optical distortions present in every camera as well as for the refractive index of water.

The drawings made from these results can show measurements of discrete points, dimensions, profiles, etc. Where a part of a structure is damaged and needs to be repaired the use of photogrammetry can lead to the manufacture of a piece that will exactly fit damaged area.

The use of photogrammetric cameras is dependent on the correct photographic procedures and computations being made available. With a correctly designed system even an untrained diver can obtain results that can be used for photogrammetric measurements.

Photogrammetry has the following advantages over conventional measuring techniques:

1. It is a non-contact measuring technique so there is little or no interference with the subject.
2. It allows underwater measurement of objects that are difficult to measure by other techniques due to their shape, size or physical position. Complex subjects may require photographic coverage from several positions.
3. The total effort does not increase proportionally with the number of points to be measured.
4. The amount of information provided is very high compared to other measuring techniques.
5. The data acquisition and data processing stages are separate.
6. The data acquisition is fast, limited only to the time taken to photograph the subject. The saving in offshore time is considerable.
7. The data are stored in permanent form. Measurements can be taken at any time in the future of any part of the subject, thus avoiding the costly remobilisation of an ROV or diving spread should additional measurements be needed.
8. The results may be presented in a number of ways as separate points, dimensions, contour maps, cross-section, or even as volumes. Reporting may be tailored to the exact needs of the job.
9. It is a very precise technique with an accuracy of 1:1000 (subject stand-off distance to accuracy) which is equivalent to 0.1mm in a one square metre field of view. This precision is only obtainable with correct use of suitable equipment.

2.4 CLOSED CIRCUIT TELEVISION (CCTV)

Monochrome CCTV systems

Underwater CCTV, particularly when used with wide-angle lenses give better overall images than can be perceived by the diver. Typically, twice the diver's angle of view can be achieved. The tonal compression and the ability to alter the contrast and intensity at the surface monitor combine to give this effect.

CCTV systems run on a low voltage supply of between 9 and 18 volts and the output is a video signal out. Systems standards for the UK are 625 lines, 50 cycles; and for the USA, 525 lines, 60 cycles.

Some systems incorporate an audio channel into the umbilical which may be used for a diver communication link with the surface.

A variety of lighting systems are available. The quality of the lighting for CCTV is important. The type of lamp used is of secondary importance. Soft, even, wide-angle illumination is required for TV cameras.

Picture interference on CCTV can be introduced from many different sources, for example: platform supplies and radio interference. These and others can be minimised by the use of an independent supply such as batteries or voltage or frequency stabilisers. ROVs present a different problem which might be solved either by transmitting the umbilical signal as a radio frequency (rf) or digitally.

The majority of underwater CCTV systems use standard Vidicon tubes. The larger sizes, around 25mm (1"), are mostly mounted on submersibles. The smaller sizes 20mm ($^{2}/_{3}$") and below are mounted on the diver's helmet or are hand-held.

A Vidicon requires a lot of light compared with silicon diode (SiD) systems.

The SiD systems can be used without supplementary lighting at greater depths and are suitable in turbid water where there is a lot of back-scatter which might be a problem with additional lighting.

A silicon intensified target (SIT) system is designed for depths where there is little ambient light. Back-scatter problems are minimised because only a low power light source is required. A SIT can produce excellent results with a weak diver's torch covered with a diffusing material such as a handkerchief. SIT cameras can record images at light levels as low as 0.0005 foot candles while maintaining a horizontal resolution of 300+ lines.

Colour CCTV systems

To date, CCTV colour cameras have been land cameras fitted into underwater housings.

As stated previously, the amount of extra information provided by colour is considerable, even though the picture may be less sharp or lack some detail.

There are three basic types of colour video cameras:

1. Single tube cameras.
2. Three tube cameras.
3. CCD (charge coupled device) cameras.

Single tube cameras use a tube which has red/green and blue vertical stripes on the face plate which give three separate signal colours. They are limited in resolution because of the shaved face plate. Typical resolution is between 200 and 350 TV lines. Three-tube cameras use a beam-splitting system and three separate tubes to record the red/green and blue separate images. The resolution is then similar to a black and white image given by equivalent tubes, ie between 300 and 500 lines. The average 600 lines per frame on TV compares favourably with the 3600 lines per frame resolved by a still camera. However, since the colour can present so much more information than monochrome, it is not significant.

The characteristics of a single tube camera are:

1. It is electronically simple.
2. It is compact, which makes it capable of being fitted into a small underwater housing, a significant factor in underwater equipment.
3. It does not have the image restriction problems of a three-tube camera and does not go out of register.

The characteristics of a three-tube camera are:

1. It incorporates three tubes, each dedicated to an individual colour: red, green and blue.
2. It has a good image quality, superior to the single tube. It should be said, however, that a top quality single tube is equal to the lower end of the three-tube range.
3. It is complex. One particular result of this complexity is that registration of the tube images are prone to drift, either electronically or because of physical damage, the result of which is an overall degradation of quality. Image drifting is a problem with three-tube cameras and a qualified technician is needed to regularly re-register these cameras.
4. It is more expensive than a single tube camera.

The sensitivity of CCTV colour systems is about the same as the Vidicon monochrome cameras. The amount of light required and most of the other problems encountered with a Vidicon are similar. Colour systems, in common with Vidicons, require a reasonable level of light and low lighting contrast range (about 3:1). Although they will not automatically compensate for red or blue light, it is possible to adjust for minor colour differences.

NOTE: Colour correction of a high order can be achieved but it is important that any modification of the colour imaging characteristics of CCTV cameras used underwater is carried out by experienced personnel.

If inexperienced manipulation of the electronic functions is carried out, the resulting images can result in all the benefits of colour being thrown away. Colour CCTV cameras can produce a satisfactory image on a black and white monitoring screen but not the other way around.

Thalium iodide, sodium and mercury discharge lighting are not suitable for colour TV. Tungsten halogen or straight tungsten lighting is required.

Many applications are especially suitable for colour TV apart from inspection: offshore construction, salvage, marine fouling identification and marine environmental studies to name but a few.

Stereo CCTV systems

These are only used in highly specialised applications.
All the advantages of stereo in still photography apply equally to a CCTV stereo system. Miniaturisation has made it possible to mount two CCTV cameras alongside each other on a single fixed mount. The spatial impression given to the observer greatly enhances the information presented. Stereo is particularly useful in inspection work, differentiating between corrosion and dirt and other damage to structures.
Where the camera is mounted on an ROV which operates a manipulator, the stereo system is a considerable advantage in gauging distance by giving a sense of depth. Unfortunately, stereo video is difficult to record because stereo CCTV recorders do not yet exist. However, the main benefit of stereo is to facilitate real-time dexterity and information.

Applications for stereo TV are listed below:

1. Positioning tasks using manipulators or other systems.
2. Precise control of ROVs.
3. Inspection and video tape documentation (diver or ROV).
4. Enhanced optical search and detection.
5. Subsea equipment positioning and drilling and production operations.
6. Mating of structures in offshore construction.
7. Internal pipeline inspection.

2.5 GENERAL SURVEY INSPECTION

Seabed surveys

Tide and current movement around the base of a structure or pipeline may produce shifting of the seabed levels. Scour may leave portions of a structure (particularly leg bases) or a pipeline unsupported, resulting in the movement, rocking, displacement, or even rupture of the structure or pipeline. Scour prevention devices, such as artificial seaweed mats can effectively prevent or control scouring problems but regular seabed inspections are still required to check their continued effectiveness.

Debris surveys

Debris means any material that should not be there such as lost fishing nets, anchor cables, wire ropes, girders and scrap material dropped over the side from offshore platforms and vessels.
Debris is a serious problem, not only because it may create a hazard to divers and ROVs but also because it can interfere with corrosion protection systems and may even cause fretting wear and resultant accelerated corrosion.
For these reasons debris surveys are essential in order to locate and record the position of all debris so that it may later be removed efficiently and safely.

Marinegrowth surveys

Marinegrowth can jeopardise the safety of a structure by increasing not only the weight of the structure itself, but also its surface area which means that the impact of waves and currents is increased. Every offshore structure has a limit to the amount of weight and wave loading that it can safely endure. If marinegrowth becomes excessive important equipment may have to be removed from the deck or the structure may become unsafe. Regular surveys are needed to help determine when the removal of marinegrowth will be necessary.
Such surveys need to measure the thickness of the growth on the structure that is affected and whether the growth is 'soft' or 'hard' as each type has different significance due to different weights per volume. Section 9 deals with the identification of commonly found types of marine growth.

2.6 CORROSION INSPECTION

Corrosion surveys are essential to any inspection programme. Because steel and water are a very corrosive combination much attention is directed to the problem (See Section 3.1, 'Corrosion Prevention', for a full explanation, and Fig. 1 for an illustration of the corrosion reaction).
There are many different types of corrosion, each produced by different causes. They may occur alone or simultaneously.

Fig. 1 The corrosion reaction

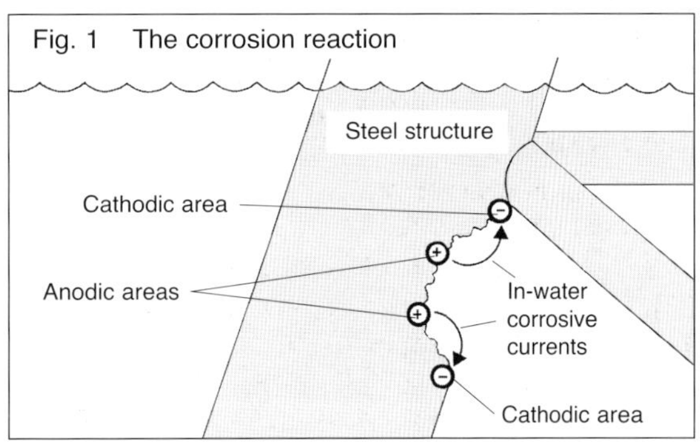
Steel structure
Cathodic area
Anodic areas
In-water corrosive currents
Cathodic area

Types of corrosion include:

1. Galvanic corrosion (dissimilar metals in close proximity) (See Fig. 2).
2. Fretting corrosion (See Fig. 3).
3. Stress corrosion and fatigue (See Fig. 4).
4. Biological corrosion (See Fig. 5).
5. Erosion corrosion (See Fig. 6).
6. Crevice and concentration cell corrosion (Fig. 7).
7. Hydrogen attack and embrittlement, etc.

The two types of galvanic corrosion that are of the most interest to the diver are 'general corrosion' (an even loss of metal) and 'pitting corrosion' (localised areas of concentrated metal loss (see Fig. 8).

Fig. 2 Galvanic corrosion between dissimilar metals

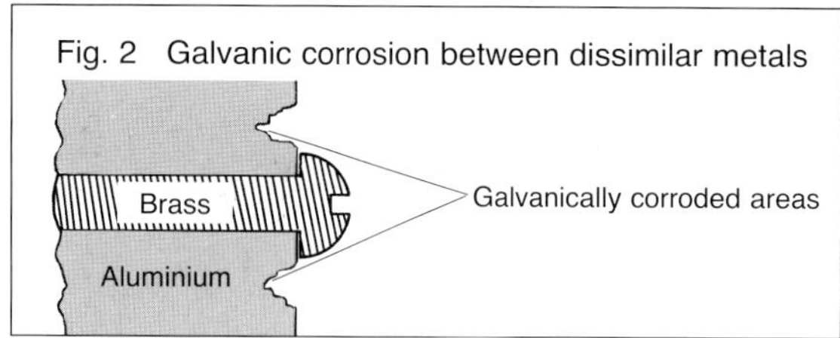
Brass
Aluminium
Galvanically corroded areas

Fig. 3 Fretting corrosion due to rubbing between two corrosive metals

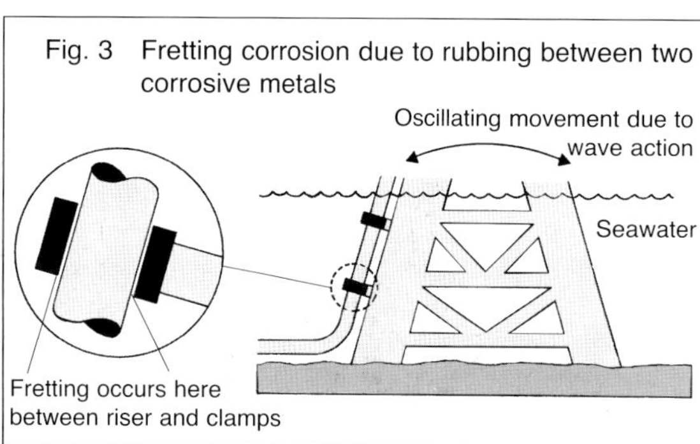
Oscillating movement due to wave action
Seawater
Fretting occurs here between riser and clamps

Fig. 4 Corrosion fatigue

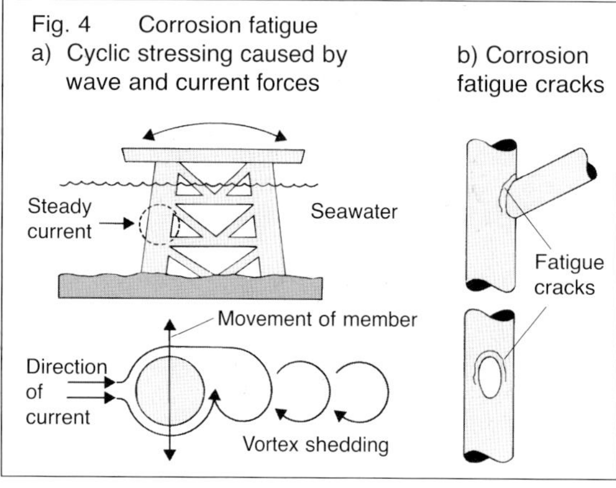
a) Cyclic stressing caused by wave and current forces
b) Corrosion fatigue cracks
Steady current
Seawater
Fatigue cracks
Movement of member
Direction of current
Vortex shedding

Fig. 5 Biological corrosion

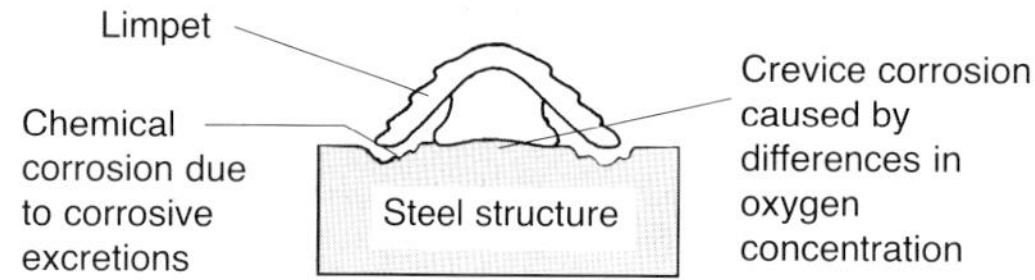
Limpet
Chemical corrosion due to corrosive excretions
Steel structure
Crevice corrosion caused by differences in oxygen concentration

Fig. 6 Erosion corrosion

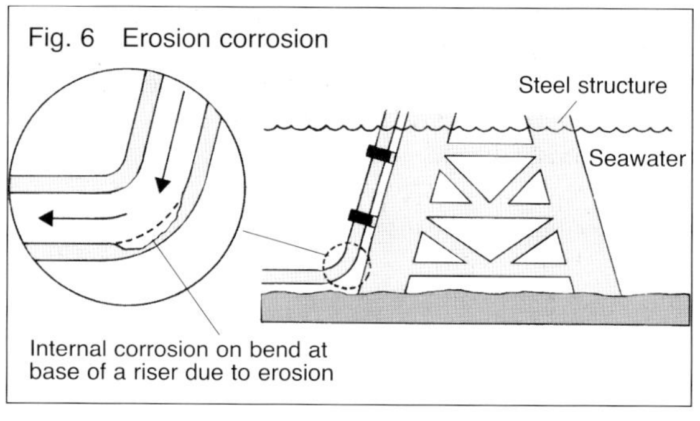
Steel structure
Seawater
Internal corrosion on bend at base of a riser due to erosion

Fig. 7 Crevice corrosion of metals in an electrolyte

a) Due to variations in metal ion concentrations

Electrolyte – Area of low ion concentration

Area of high ion concentration

b) Due to an oxygen concentration cell

Area of low oxygen concentration

Electrolyte – Area of high oxygen concentration

Fig. 8

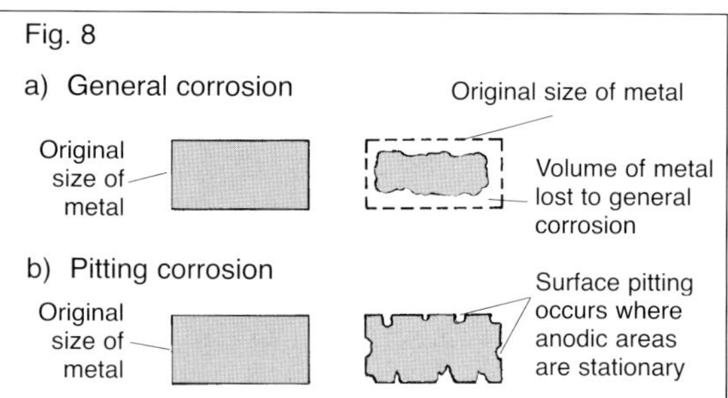
a) General corrosion
Original size of metal
Original size of metal
Volume of metal lost to general corrosion
b) Pitting corrosion
Original size of metal
Surface pitting occurs where anodic areas are stationary

There are two main ways of dealing with corrosion problems:

1. To design and build-in an extra thickness of steel as a corrosion 'allowance'. This is normally about 20–30mm (3/4–1 1/4in) extra thickness built into those parts of the structure that are in the splash zone.
2. To attempt to prevent corrosion. The main protection methods are cathodic protection and protective coatings which are described in Section 3.1, Corrosion Prevention.

Corrosion inspection has three important objectives:

1. To find out if the corrosion protection systems are actually working by checking to ensure that:
   a) Any coating is intact.
   b) Any coating remains bonded to the steel.
   c) The anodes are still in place.
   d) The electrical circuit still exists between the anode and structure (check continuity strap).
   e) The electrical potential between the structure and the seawater is adequate by comparison against a reference half-cell indication, using a CP meter.

2. To find and measure corrosion damage by:
   a) Measuring the thickness of steel for general corrosion, using ultrasonic thickness meters, commonly called 'D' meters.
   b) Measuring the extent and depth of pitting corrosion using pit gauges (see Fig. 9).
   c) Visually measuring fatigue cracks using a crack width ruler (see Fig. 10). See also Critical Sizing Methods in 'NDT Inspection'.

3. To help plan the maintenance of corrosion protection systems by:
   a) Measuring the dimensions of anodes to find the rate of corrosion and thereby estimate the remaining life of an anode.
   b) Assessing the condition of the protective coating to find out if/when maintenance is required.

Fig. 9 Gauge used to measure the length and depth of pitting corrosion

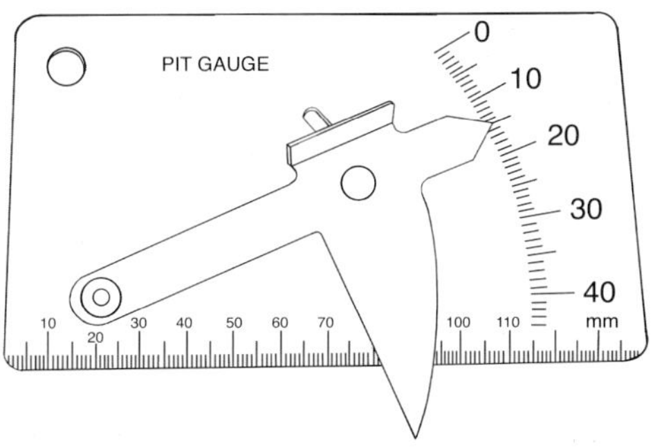
PIT GAUGE
0
10
20
30
40
mm
10
20
30
40
50
60
70
100
110

Fig. 10 Example of a ruler used by divers to make visual assessments of crack widths.

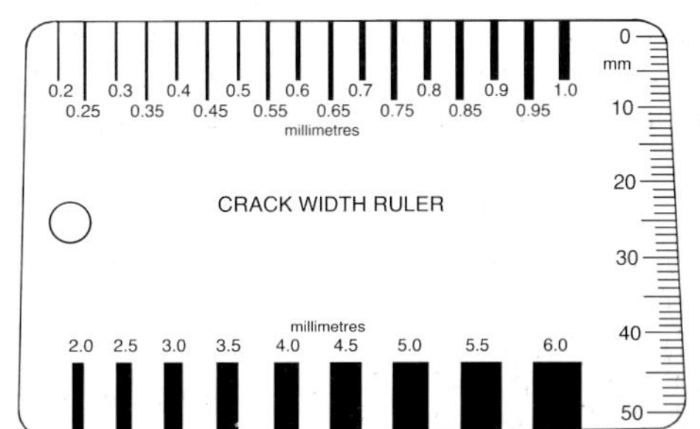
0.2 0.3 0.4 0.5 0.6 0.7 0.8 0.9 1.0
0.25 0.35 0.45 0.55 0.65 0.75 0.85 0.95
millimetres
CRACK WIDTH RULER
millimetres
2.0 2.5 3.0 3.5 4.0 4.5 5.0 5.5 6.0
0
mm
10
20
30
40
50

2.7 UNDERWATER CLEANING

Cleaning is performed for one of three reasons:

1. To remove excessive marine growth.
2. To prepare a surface for close visual and critical (NDT) inspection. Removal of marine growth is normally sufficient but critical NDT inspection requires the removal of everything (including paint, coatings, scale, etc) from the metal surface to leave a bright metal surface.
3. To unblock a seawater intake.

Cleaning methods range from the slow, simple and inexpensive to the fast, complex and expensive. A summary of cleaning methods and their applications is given in Fig. 2, overleaf.

CHIPPING HAMMERS

Chipping hammers can be air (pneumatic) or hydraulically-powered tools. The larger, two-handed versions can weigh up to 12kg (26lb) and deliver over 2,000 blows per minute (see Fig. 1a). They require a hydraulic supply of 25–35 l/min (0.8–1.2 ft^3/min) at 105–140 bars. The smaller, one-handed tools are commonly used as weld flux chippers (see Fig. 1b). These can be easily converted into needle scalers. The small pneumatic chippers can be powered by compressed air at 280–425 l/min (10–15 ft^3/min).

Operation of hydraulic hammers

1. Install the appropriate tool bit for the job.
2. Place the bit firmly against the surface to be broken.

Fig. 1 Chipping hammers

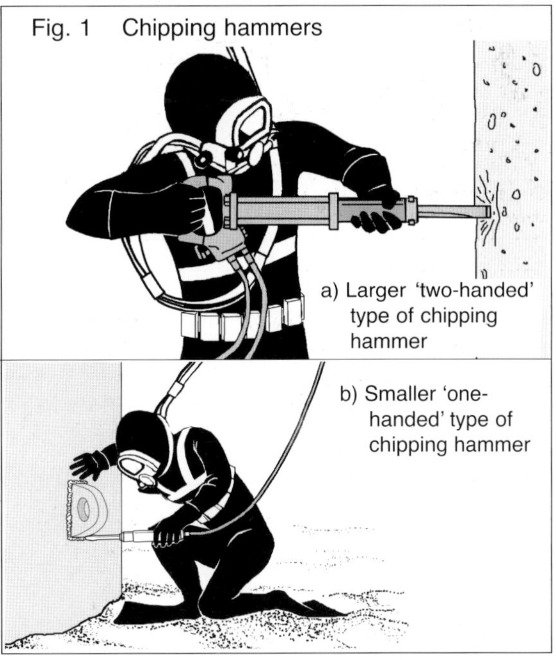
a) Larger 'two-handed' type of chipping hammer
b) Smaller 'one-handed' type of chipping hammer

3. Partially depress the trigger to start the chipper at slow speed. Adequate down pressure is important.
4. Fully depress the trigger as necessary to increase the speed.
5. When the tool bit breaks through the job or becomes bound, release the trigger and reposition the tool bit.

Fig. 2. Summary of cleaning methods

CLEANING METHOD				GENERAL MARINEGROWTH REMOVAL	SPECIAL CLEANING FOR CLOSE AND CRITICAL (NDT) INSPECTION: AIR RANGE WORK	SPECIAL CLEANING FOR CLOSE AND CRITICAL (NDT) INSPECTION: GAS RANGE WORK
Hand tools	Wire strops			Excellent, fast, inexpensive.	Not suitable	
Hand tools	Wire brushes			Not suitable (very slow)	Not suitable (very slow)	
Power mechanical tools	Brushes and grinders Chipping hammers Needle guns			Not suitable (very slow)	Not suitable (makes defect worse, eg peening of its edges)	
LP water jets	HP water (alone)		Flow requirements HP water: to 1030 bars at 45 lpm* (15,000 psi at 12 gpm*).	Excellent, fast and effective, but comparatively very expensive.	Not recommended (slower than with grit entrainment and requires much higher pressures, hence more costly).	
LP water jets	LP water + grit entrainment	Dry grit	LP water: to 240 bars at 45 lpm (3,500 psi at 12 gpm). Air supply: Approximately: 10 bars at 3.4 m^{3}pm (150 psi at 120 ft^{3}pm).	Effective, very commonly used	Optimum method Fastest and most efficient; lowest (non-manual) cost	Possible (Slurry better due to dry sand problems)
LP water jets	LP water + grit entrainment	Wet slurry	Slurry: to 310 bars at 30 lpm (4,500 psi at 8 gpm).	Effective, very commonly used.	Adequate (Dry method is much simpler and cheaper)	Optimum method Fastest and most efficient; lowest (non-manual) cost.
Air grit-blasting	Air and grit. (Shallow water only)			Effective and inexpensive	Good finish	Not applicable

6. To start, break an opening (hole) in the centre of the job surface. Once this hole is started, crack portions of the material into the original opening. Continue in a spiral pattern around the original hole.
7. The bite or width of the broken material will vary with the strength and thickness of the material and the amount of reinforcement wire or rebar. Harder material and more reinforcing wire or rebar will need smaller bites. The bites can then be increased until the broken piece becomes too large for efficient handling.

HAMMERS - OPERATIONAL SAFETY

1. Always follow the manufacturer's instructions.
2. Do not force a small chipper to do the work of a heavy duty chipper.
3. Keep the tool bit sharp for maximum performance.
4. Do not use bits that have chipped or rounded tips.
5. Never operate a chipper without a tool bit installed or without holding it against the work surface.
6. Only trained personnel should carry out any repairs on the tool.
7. Ensure hose couplers are wiped clean before connection to hoses.
8. The hydraulic circuit control must be in the 'OFF' position when coupling or uncoupling.

8. The tool can stick when too large a bite is taken. The tool bit drills into the material without breaking it up.
9. Tools require preventive maintenance after every use underwater.
10. In cold weather, preheat the hydraulic oil at low engine speed. Normally oil temperature should be at or above 10°C (50°F) before use.

NEEDLE GUNS

These are air-powered tools used for cleaning metal surfaces, often to prepare a weld for inspection. The needles, which can have chisel, flat or pointed heads, are vibrated at a rate of about 2400 blows per minute. They are very effective against hard scaling

Fig. 3 Diver using needle gun to clean weld

or corrosion but may not be suitable for cleaning surfaces in preparation for detailed crack detection because the needles can deform the surface metal and obscure very small cracks.

Needle guns can weigh from 1.5–6kg (3–13lb) and operate on an air supply of 6 bars (see Fig. 3).

The needle heads can be interchanged with heads that replace the needles with a variety of chisels. Long-reach versions are also available extending the length of the tool to 1–2m (3–6ft).

HIGH PRESSURE WATER JETTING

High pressure water jets provide the most effective underwater cleaning technique. It is, however, comparatively expensive because the cost is directly related to the pressure used. The cost of the operation can be significantly reduced by a reduction of the pressure requirement or by the addition of an abrasive (sand or grit) to the water, either dry or as a wet slurry. An example of a jetting gun system is illustrated in Fig. 4.

When using an abrasive the water pressure can be reduced. For example, pressures up to 1030 bars (15,000 psi) are employed when using HP water alone, whereas pressures of only 140–420 bars (2,000–6,000 psi) at the gun can give excellent results when abrasives are used. The addition of abrasives improves efficiency and provides faster operation.

High pressure water jets can also be used for cutting timber or concrete.

HP WATER JETTING - SAFETY

The high pressure water jetting gun is a potentially dangerous tool and needs handling with great care. All divers using such equipment must be trained in its use.

Equipment:

1. A strong guard should be fitted around the trigger to prevent inadvertent operation.
2. a) The retrojet cover should be long enough to prevent damage to the diver's equipment.
   b) This should also include a handle/shield to prevent self-inflicted injury.
3. The diffuser tube on the retrojet should be secure and checked before use.
4. Abrasives can interfere with other equipment such as suit inflation valves, etc. Care should be taken to clean all equipment after every dive.
5. The diving supervisor should always be in direct contact with the technician running the pumps who should be standing by his pump while it is running. It is imperative that clear communications exist at all times between the supervisor, the pump technician and the diver.
6. At no time should there be more than one diver working in an area where jetting is taking place
7. The diver should wear a helmet in preference to a mask. Jetting is noisy.
8. The gun must never be lowered to the diver or returned to the surface with the power on.
9. The signal to start the high pressure water supply should not be given by the diver until he is ready to start jetting.

(continued . . .)

Fig 4 An underwater abrasive slurry jetting gun and containerised unit

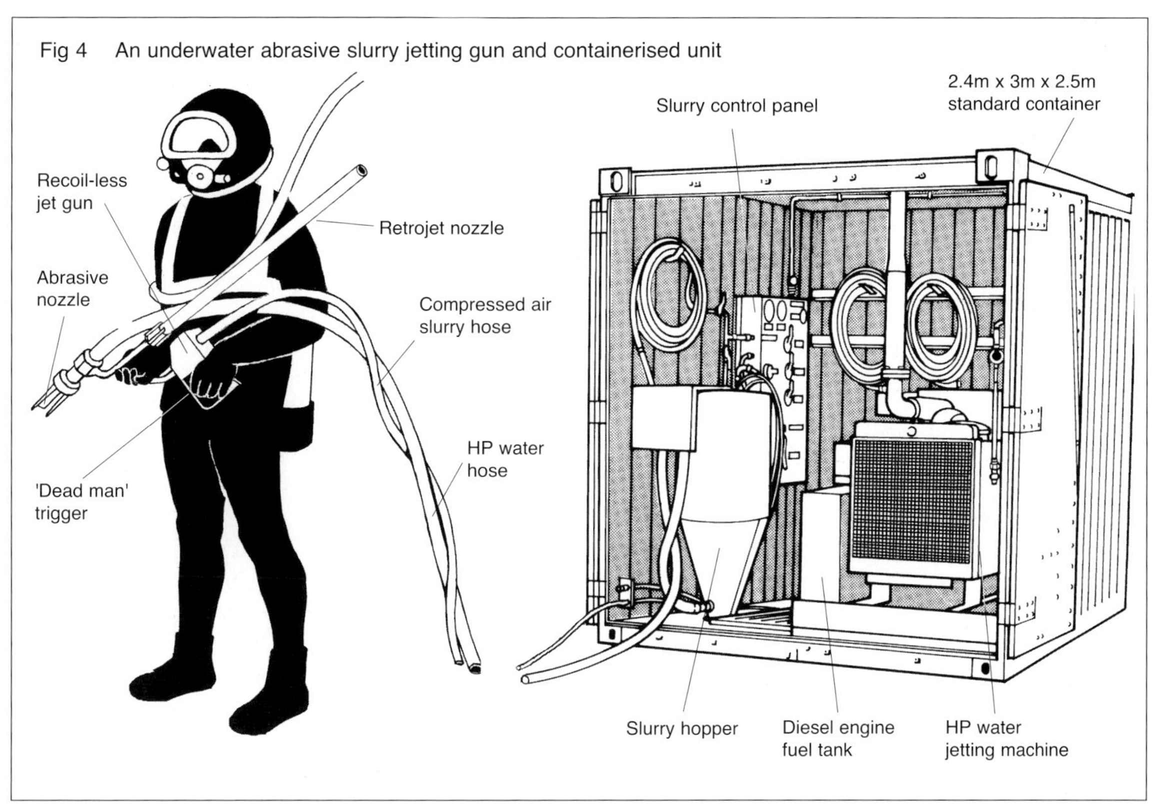
Recoil-less jet gun
Abrasive nozzle
'Dead man' trigger
Retrojet nozzle
Compressed air slurry hose
HP water hose
Slurry control panel
2.4m x 3m x 2.5m standard container
Slurry hopper
Diesel engine fuel tank
HP water jetting machine

(continued . . .)

10. High pressure should be supplied only when requested by the diver.
11. Under no circumstances should the diver rig the operating trigger in order to maintain an open position.
12. Care should be taken when working from a DP vessel - the noise from the water jet can interfere with acoustic positioning systems.
13. The working pressure of the compressor must not exceed that of the guns and the hoses.
14. Any injury from water jetting can be very serious and medical aid must be called for immediately. The jet can carry infection deep into the body and the casualty's conditions can deteriorate rapidly in a few hours. See section 12.1, 'First Aid' for treatment of injuries.

2.8 NDT INSPECTION

The harsh marine environment and the high loads imposed on offshore installations can result in the formation of defects underwater. These defects start as minor flaws and, if not discovered at an early stage, may develop into dangerous faults. The role of the NDT diver/technician is to provide information on those defects, or lack of them, so that the underwater condition of the structure can be assessed by the topside engineers.

Any inspection method which does not destroy the item under test is an NDT method. Visual inspection and photography are recognised NDT methods. Serious defects are, however, not always visible and some other means of detection is required. One of the oldest methods, radiography, shows the appropriateness of the name 'non-destructive': a diver having an X-ray of his chest is being tested by NDT. A radiograph can be made of steel (or anything else) and, under appropriate circumstances, can graphically show the internal defects without destroying the article.

NDT was initially developed on land installations. However, underwater NDT is now established as a valid engineering discipline. This has largely been due to the certification requirements for offshore production installations. However, NDT requires considerable skill in operation and experience in interpretation. Hence the need for NDT qualifications.

The purpose of NDT

The prime purpose of NDT is to confirm that there are no defects in an inspected area. Assurance of structural integrity does not come from knowing that there is a crack but from knowing that there are no cracks. For example, a new weld is radiographed to attest that it has no defects. If, however, defects are discovered, the radiographer must be able to recognise them in order to prevent the defective weld from being passed as clean.

Each NDT technique may be applied wrongly, resulting in invalid data so it is important that an

Fig. 1 NDT methods: A summary of suitability and use underwater.

Technique	Application	Suitability underwater
Visual inspection	Surface condition of all materials at low cost. Always primary method of inspection.	***
Magnetic particle inspection	Surface and near surface defects on ferromagnetic materials only. To detect and monitor fatigue cracks.	***
Magnetographic tape	As for MPI.	**
Ultrasonics	Thickness testing. Laminations and other planar defects such as cracks. Volumetric defects.	*** *** *
Radiography	Volumetric defects (provides permanent records). Planar defects.	*** *
Corrosion potential measurement	Metallic components immersed in an electrolyte. (See section 3.1)	***
Structural monitoring: - Vibration analysis - Acoustic emission	Gross structural defects. Nature and location of defects on a structure.	** not suitable

KEY: *** very suitable ** possible * sometimes possible

NDT technologist specifies the correct technique for a particular inspection. A certain technique may be chosen to examine an area because that technique may have proved successful elsewhere. Use of invalid NDT may well find defects, but it may miss more important ones.
Within the NDT process of seeking to report no defects, indications of possible defects may be found which must be confirmed, they must be repaired and re-tested so that a report can be issued attesting that the inspected item now has no significant defects.

NDT in practice

Underwater practices are constantly changing. Consequently, the following information is intended to help divers gain a general understanding of the subject rather than to give detailed instructions.
There are more than 50 NDT methods, none of which can be universally applied to all problems. Each has its own advantages, disadvantages and applications. Apart from being used to discover defects, visible and invisible, they may also size them.
Defect sizing, ie measuring the length, breadth and height, is more demanding than defect detection in terms of both time and cost. Care is needed to select which NDT method should be applied. For this reason it is advisable to consider NDT practice under two main categories:

1. RAPID SCANNING METHODS which include magnetic particle inspection, compression wave ultrasonics, electromagnetic interrogation, radiography and AC potential drop methods. Although these methods are referred to as 'rapid', most rapid scan methods can take a considerable time to perform. However, they are rapid compared to the inspection times required when sizing methods are employed.
2. CRITICAL SIZING METHODS including shear-wave ultrasonics and AC potential drop methods.

Rapid scanning methods

1. MAGNETIC PARTICLE INSPECTION

MPI is sometimes known as MPCD (magnetic particle crack detection) and can only be applied to ferrous metals. It is based on the fact that where a magnetic field exists within a ferrous metal, the magnetic flux (lines of force) will jump over and concentrate at any discontinuity in the metal. This is known as 'flux leakage' and occurs because one side of the crack acts as a north and the other side as a south pole (See Fig. 2).
Thus magnetisable particles are attracted even to the edges of a hairline crack and bridge the gap, forming a concentration along the length of the defect. When this concentration can be seen it reliably indicates an otherwise invisible crack.
For underwater MPI to be successful the following three conditions must exist:

1. There must be adequate magnetic flux in the metal being tested.

Fig. 2 Diagram of flux leakage

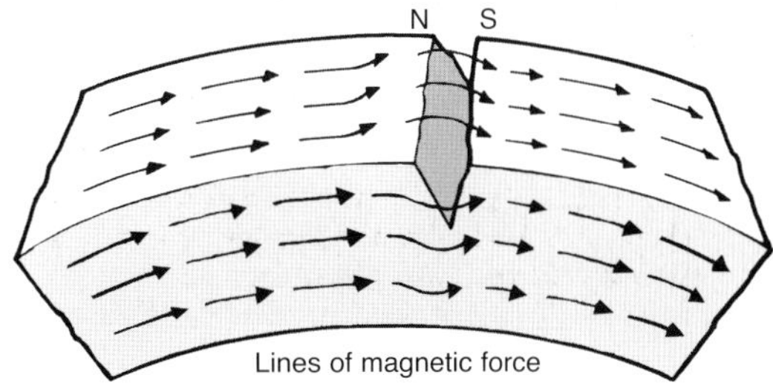
N
S
Lines of magnetic force

2. Suitable ferrous particles must be applied and allowed to be attracted by the flux leakage.
3. The particles must be appropriately illuminated

a) Provision of magnetic flux
A magnetic field may be created within the metal by applying either a magnet or an electric current. Currents may be passed either through the metal itself by the use of prods, or close to the metal through an insulated coil or conductor (see Fig. 3). These are called 'current flow techniques'.

Fig. 3 Creating a magnetic field

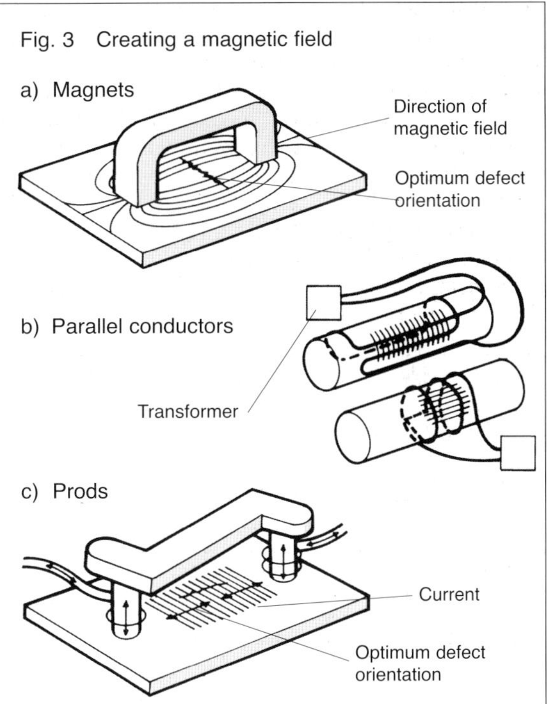
a) Magnets
Direction of magnetic field
Optimum defect orientation
b) Parallel conductors
Transformer
c) Prods
Current
Optimum defect orientation

Flux path techniques involve the passing of magnetism into the steel under test from either a permanent or an electro-magnet. Each technique has limitations and inappropriate usage may invalidate the test results.
Important aspects of flux provision are that the flux

i) is applied into the steel (not merely in its vicinity)
ii) is neither too little nor too much (between 7,200 and 12,000 gauss, 0.72–1.2 Tesla).

a.

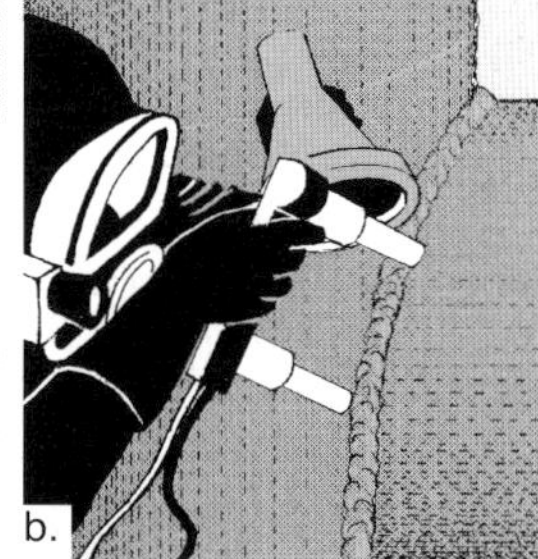
b.

c.

Fig. 4 Magnetic particle inspection in practice

a. Diver using the magnet technique

b. Diver using prods across a weld

c. Diver using the insulated coil technique

iii) direction is appropriate for the direction of the defect being sought (the two directions should, ideally, be perpendicular to one another).

The strength of the magnets or currents to be used depends on the permeability of the steel, ie its ability to be magnetised and specific values for each test must be determined from a relevant Standard or Specification.

b) Particle indicators

Having established the magnetic field, each ferrous particle is highlighted with fluorescent dye. Under the influence of the magnetic field the particles concentrate along the edges of any defect that may exist. In order to see this concentration the fluorescent-coated particles must be irradiated using ultraviolet light in dark ambient light conditions (less than 10 lux). The fluorescent particles must also be maintained in suspension by constant agitation of the ink. The irradiation requires wavelengths in excess of 3,500 Ångstroms (350 nanometres) and the light intensity on the testpiece should not be less than 1,000 W/cm^2 and no more than 3,000 W/cm^2. Viewing and interpretation can then take place.

MPI is a very reliable crack-detection method but only under the following conditions:

i) The correct technique is selected for a particular job.

ii) The correct procedure is complied with throughout the test.

iii) The diver inspector performing the test is adequately trained, qualified and experienced.

Until such time as techniques are developed to enable the transmission of the details of leakage field distributions, accurate interpretation is totally in the hands of the diver inspector. He should take care to avoid the following conditions which may reduce the reliability of the MPI test:

- Not having sufficient concentration of magnetic particles in the ink.
- Insufficient output from the ultraviolet light.
- Using light of the wrong wavelength.

2. COMPRESSION WAVE (CW) ULTRASONICS

CW ultrasonics is primarily used in underwater corrosion surveys to measure the thickness of metal. Very high frequency sound waves (2.5–6 MHz) are applied at right angles to the metal testpiece surface via a hand-held probe (see Figs. 5 and 6). The sound waves travel through the metal and reflect off the back wall. The time taken for the sound waves to return to the probe is measured and since the rate at which sound travels is known, this measurement can be used to determine the thickness of the metal. The data are displayed on either a cathode ray tube screen ('A' scan) or a digital readout on a diver-carried unit. Digital meters are simple to use and are accurate when used appropriately and correctly.

3. ELECTRO-MAGNETIC DETECTION

EMD is based on detecting the change of permeability and polarity, a condition which occurs where there is any defect in metal (see Fig. 7).

Fig. 5 Compression wave ultrasonics for measuring wall thickness

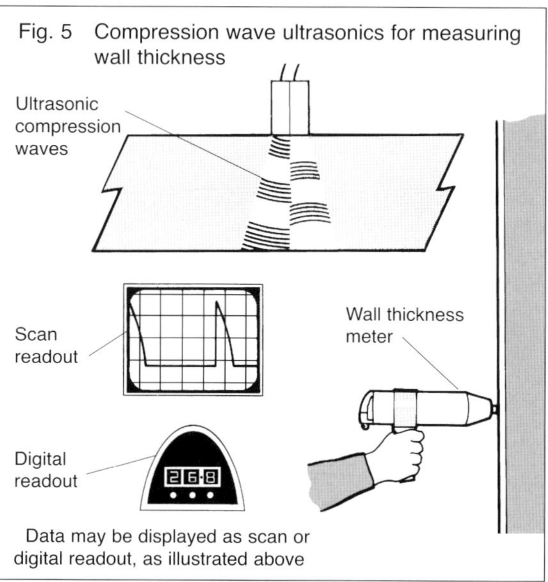
Ultrasonic compression waves
Scan readout
Wall thickness meter
Digital readout
268

Data may be displayed as scan or digital readout, as illustrated above

Fig. 6 Diver measuring wall thickness with a hand-held digital readout gauge

Fig. 7 Principle of the EMD method

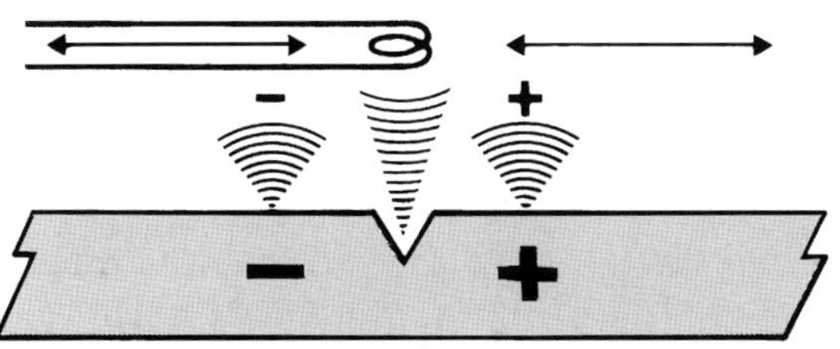
-
+
-
+

Compared to other NDT methods, it requires less preparatory surface cleaning and less operator skill, training and expertise.

4. RADIOGRAPHY
A serious weakness of radiography is its poor ability to detect cracks. Its use underwater is therefore of limited value. It is, however, sometimes used to assess blockages in pipelines or to detect internal corrosion of pipelines.
It operates on the same principle as X-rays. A radiographic photosensitive plate is placed on one side of the pipeline while the unit that emits the radiographic rays is placed opposite it on the other side of the pipe (see Fig. 8). The diver exposes the isotope in the unit and moves away while the rays travel through the pipeline to expose the film. After sufficient time for a correct exposure he returns to re-shield the isotope. He returns the equipment to the surface where the film is developed and viewed. Great care is required in the safe handling of the radioactive source.

Critical sizing methods

Critical sizing methods should provide accurate data regarding defect dimensions, position and orientation. Existing methods are very good for determining the length of surface-breaking defects but are questionable regarding measurement of defect depth and determining subsurface orientation. The best available methods are shearwave ultrasonics and AC drop methods (see Figs. 9–13). The former is used to determine the position and depth of a sub-surface crack, while AC drop methods may be able to measure the depth of some surface-breaking cracks.

Fig. 8 Radiographic pipeline inspection. Gammagraphy used in pipeline survey and inspection

Isotope
Gamma rays
Film
Section through pipe

1. SHEARWAVE ULTRASONICS
'Shearwave' indicates the ultrasound is introduced into the metal testpiece at an angle (usually 30°–70°) and it is therefore often known as 'angle working.' The frequencies used are normally around the 5 MHz level. Shearwave ultrasonics are mainly used for flaw detection in welds and parent materials.

Fig. 9 How an ultrasonic flaw detector works

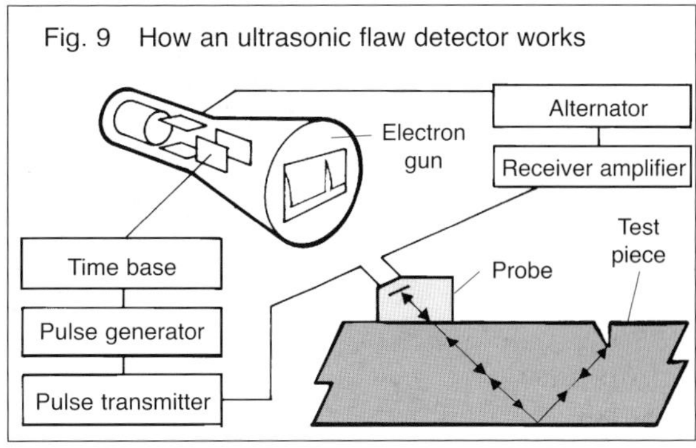
Alternator
Electron gun
Receiver amplifier
Test piece
Probe
Time base
Pulse generator
Pulse transmitter

Fig. 10 Application of ultrasonic flaw detection equipment

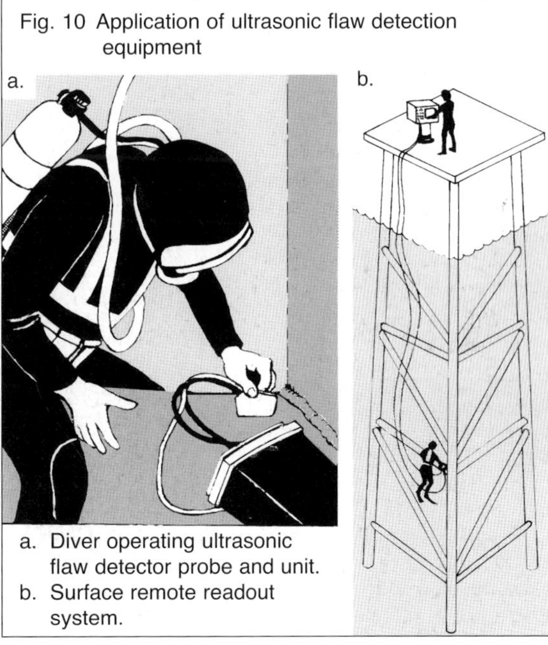
a.
b.

a. Diver operating ultrasonic flaw detector probe and unit.
b. Surface remote readout system.

Fig. 11 An example of a readout from an underwater shearwave and ultrasonic flaw detector

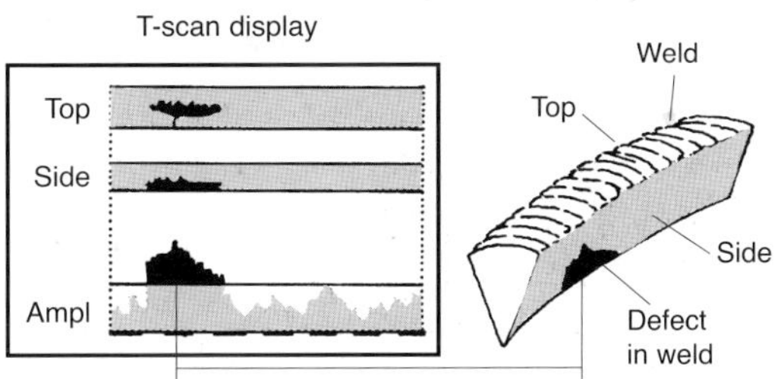
T-scan display
Top
Side
Ampl
Weld
Top
Side
Defect in weld

Fig. 12 Diver observing SVC 'P' scanner travelling along a pipeline

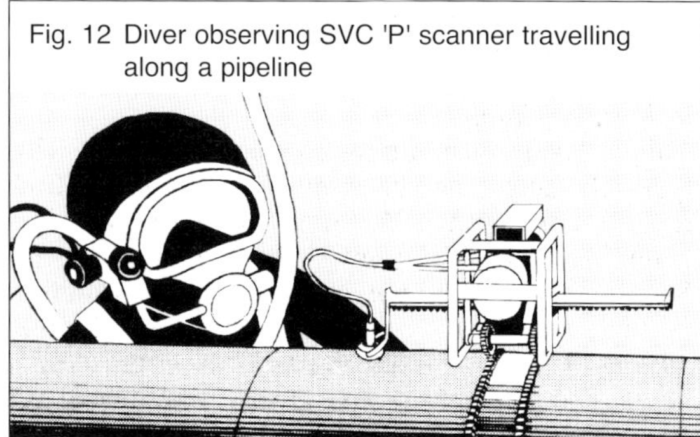

Fig. 13 Diagram to show operation of AC drop method

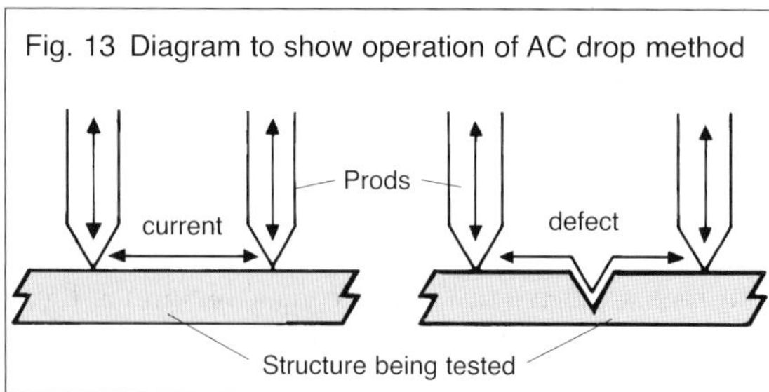
Prods
current
defect
Structure being tested

The operator has a choice of manual or automated application – the latter being more valuable underwater. Manual application requires considerable training and skill and is difficult enough on land. The underwater environment only compounds the problems. Useful results can only be obtained if quality controls on the operator's skill and technique are of the highest order.
Automated computer-controlled use has, however, considerable potential underwater, especially for use on circumferential butt joints. The Danish SVC 'P' scan system appears to be the most effective system currently available (see Fig. 11). Current techniques however are not yet sufficiently advanced to be able to cope with crack detection on the more complex structures of node joints.

2. AC DROP METHODS (AC-D)
Although it can be used as a rapid scanning method, AC-D may be more valuable as a means of defect sizing.
AC-D methods are used to measure the depth of surface-breaking cracks (see Fig. 13). AC-D operates on the 'skin' effect of AC electrical currents, ie currents travel mainly along the surface (skin) of the metal. The distance that a current travels between two contact points is measured. Should a crack exist along this path the distance travelled will increase by the distance up and down both faces of the crack. From this data the depth of the crack can be calculated.

Taking measurements underwater

ESTIMATING MEASUREMENTS
When a diver has to take measurements in poor visibility without the aid of any instruments, it helps if he can use his own body as a reference. Memorising certain body measurements can help the diver make meaningful estimates underwater (see Fig. 14).

Fig.14 Useful body measurements

Memorising the measurements of parts of his own body can help a diver to estimate the length of objects and distances between objects in poor visibility underwater.

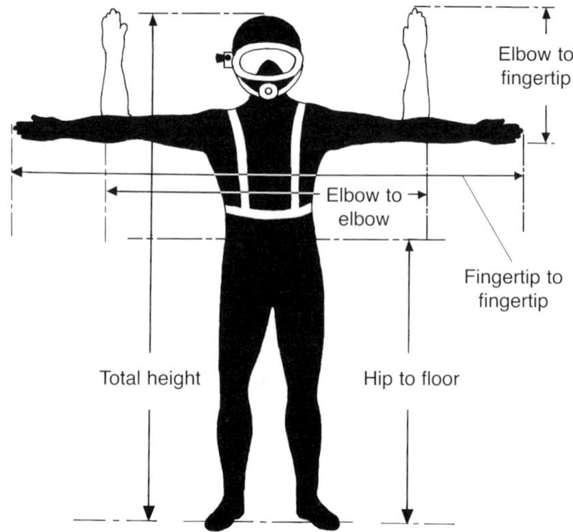
Elbow to fingertip
Elbow to elbow
Fingertip to fingertip
Total height
Hip to floor

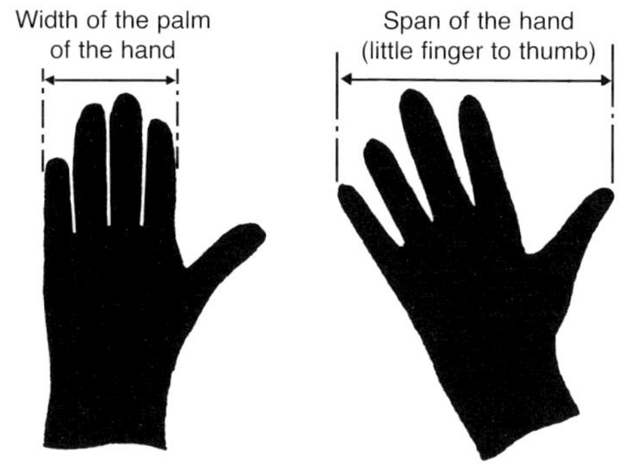
Width of the palm of the hand
Span of the hand (little finger to thumb)

TAKING FINE MEASUREMENTS
a) *Calipers*
One of the simplest ways of taking a measurement underwater is to use a caliper. They can measure internal and external dimensions and can be firm-jointed or spring (see Fig. 15)

Fig. 15 Types of caliper

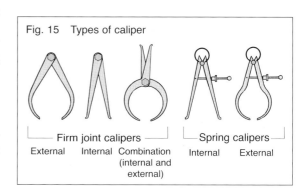

Firm joint calipers			Spring calipers	
External	Internal	Combination (internal and external)	Internal	External

Fig. 16 Reading a measurement using calipers

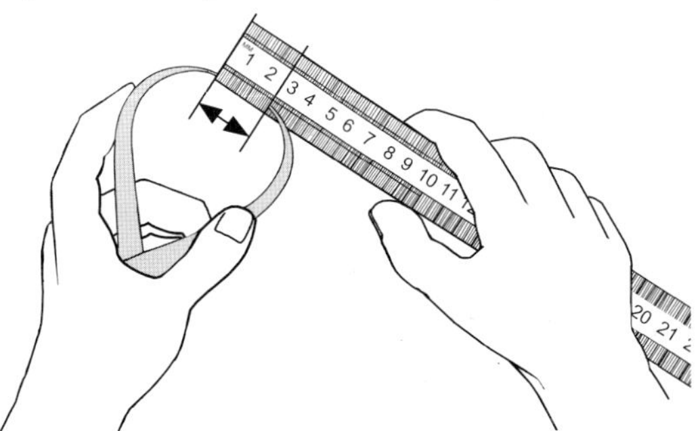

External calipers: One leg against the outside edge of the ruler; the other on the face of the ruler. Measure between the points of the caliper legs.

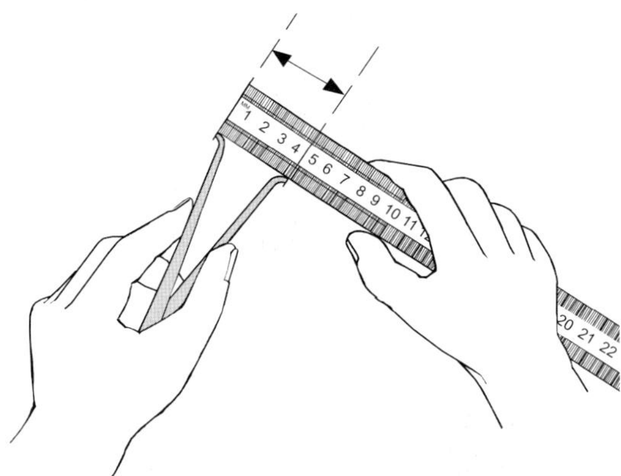

Internal calipers: Both legs against the long edge of the ruler. Measure from outside edge to outside edge of caliper legs.

Firm-jointed calipers should be set to a width slightly more (or less, if taking an internal measurement) than required for the item to be measured. One leg should be held against the item and the other gently tapped until it makes contact with the item being measured.
Before taking a reading, remove the caliper and re-present it to the item to make sure that the caliper has not moved and that the legs still make light contact with both surfaces. Although it is easy to use calipers, it may be difficult to measure the gap against a rule underwater. In such cases the caliper may have to be returned to the surface taking care not to disturb it in the process.

b) *Vernier Gauge*
This is a very accurate measuring instrument. This type of gauge can be used for measuring both lengths and angles. The most common type is a 'ruler' for measuring length as shown in Fig.17. Some can read down to 0.025mm (1/1000in) without the need for a magnifying glass. Vernier gauges are commonly incorporated in caliper devices for measuring lengths, as well as internal and external diameters. Because vernier gauges are precision instruments, they can be a little delicate. Great care is needed in handling them to avoid causing any damage.

HOW TO USE A VERNIER GAUGE
The caliper or sliding gauge is first set to the measurement being taken. Care must be taken to ensure that the gauge does not move again before the measurement has been read. Sometimes there is a clamping mechanism to ensure there is no further movement.
The measurement is then read off the main scale. In the example in Fig. 17, this reads just over 20 units, say millimetres, or more precisely, somewhere between 20 and 21. To find the next place of decimal measurement, namely tenths of a millimetre, look along the vernier gauge to find which one of the divisions lines up with any of the divisions on the main scale. In this case, it is 5. This means 5 tenths of a millimetre. So the total length measured is exactly 20.5 millimetres.

Fig. 17 Vernier gauge

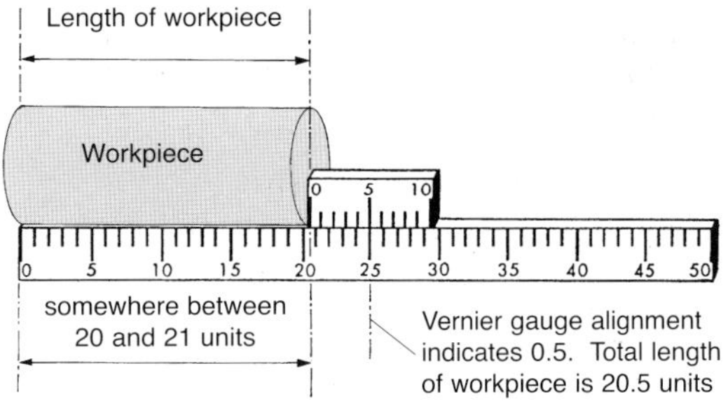
Length of workpiece
Workpiece
0 5 10
0 5 10 15 20 25 30 35 40 45 50
somewhere between 20 and 21 units
Vernier gauge alignment indicates 0.5. Total length of workpiece is 20.5 units

2.9 INSPECTION QUALIFICATIONS

As inspection is a major diver activity offshore it is to the advantage of everyone in the diving industry for divers to have a sound training and a recognised qualification.
Qualifications are, however, only of real value when they are supported by a track record of supervised practical training and experience.
The normal inspection qualification process involves a balance of:

1. Formal training (theoretical and practical).
2. Ideally, a period of supervised practical experience.
3. Formal examination (theoretical and practical).

The most widely accepted inspection qualification system for divers is CSWIP – the Certification Scheme for Welding and Inspection Personnel. As far as the UK is concerned, the Health and Safety Executive (HSE), in its evaluation of safety cases, regards CSWIP certification as a demonstration of the competence of inspection personnel. Verification bodies like Lloyds Register and DNV, which operate worldwide, also recognise CSWIP.

Alternatives to CSWIP for diver inspectors exist. For example, Lloyds Register offer their own approval scheme in countries where CSWIP is not easily accessible. Employer-based schemes, for example, conforming to the American Society of Non-Destructive Testing TC-1A Specifications, are also available.

Fig. 1 summarises the position regarding NDT and Inspection certification. Further information can be obtained from *www.cswip.com*.

Fig. 1 Overview of NDT and inspection certification bodies worldwide

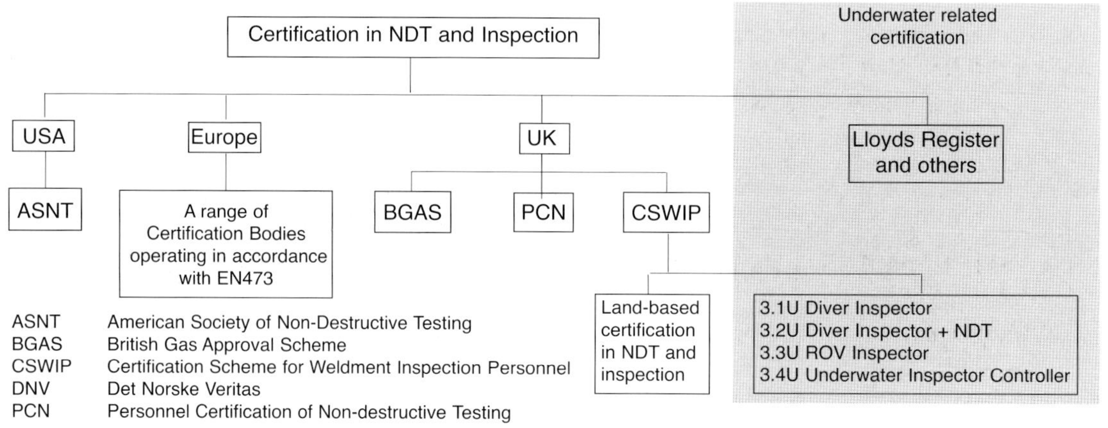
Certification in NDT and Inspection
Underwater related certification
USA
Europe
UK
Lloyds Register and others
ASNT
A range of Certification Bodies operating in accordance with EN473
BGAS
PCN
CSWIP
Land-based certification in NDT and inspection
3.1U Diver Inspector
3.2U Diver Inspector + NDT
3.3U ROV Inspector
3.4U Underwater Inspector Controller
ASNT American Society of Non-Destructive Testing
BGAS British Gas Approval Scheme
CSWIP Certification Scheme for Weldment Inspection Personnel
DNV Det Norske Veritas
PCN Personnel Certification of Non-destructive Testing

Applied techniques

3.1 CORROSION PREVENTION

Electrolytic Corrosion

A solution which conducts electricity is known as an electrolyte. Seawater is an electrolyte and is considered as such in this section.

When two different metals are submerged together in seawater, an electrochemical reaction occurs which produces a potential (or voltage difference) between them (see Fig. 1a). This can also occur between different parts of a single piece of metal where a potential difference can be created due to localised variations in temperature, stress, fabrication (eg mill scale, or slag inclusions in steel), or the environment (eg marine growth or variable silting) (see Fig. 1b).

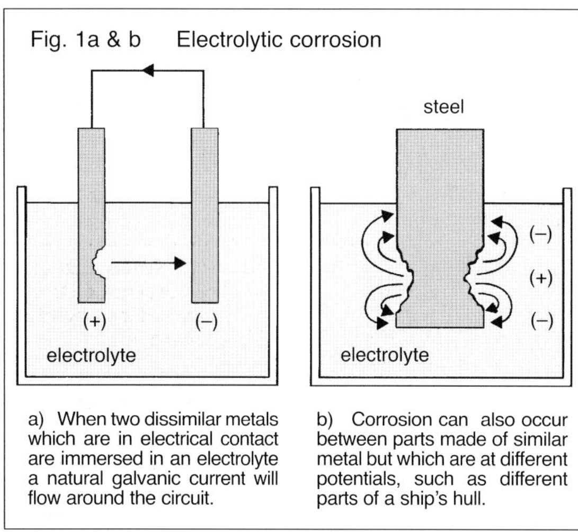
steel
(+)
(–)
electrolyte
(–)
(+)
(–)
electrolyte

Fig. 1a & b Electrolytic corrosion

a) When two dissimilar metals which are in electrical contact are immersed in an electrolyte a natural galvanic current will flow around the circuit.

b) Corrosion can also occur between parts made of similar metal but which are at different potentials, such as different parts of a ship's hull.

This potential difference causes a current to flow through the metal from an area with a positive potential to another more negative area. The circuit is completed when the current leaves the metal and returns to the first area via the seawater. In simple, practical terms, areas where this circulating current leaves the metal are corroded. Potential at these points moves in a positive direction and they are called ANODIC areas. Similarly, areas where the current enters the metal from the electrolyte are protected from corrosion. Their potential moves in a negative direction so they are called CATHODIC areas.

Corrosion protection techniques

Corrosion protection is based on the elimination of the anodic areas. Five main techniques are used.

1. Selection of materials.
2. Protective coatings.
3. Cathodic protection.
4. Corrosion inhibitors.
5. Insulation.

1. SELECTION OF MATERIALS

Since it is the dissimilarity between metals that produces the electrochemical process that leads to corrosion, the use of compatible metals is the first step in corrosion prevention since this results in low potential differences and hence low corrosion rates. This is particularly important for structures consisting of many components.

It should be appreciated that this reaction is not limited to steel – any metal will tend to behave in a similar way if immersed in an electrolyte. Fig. 2 shows the order in which various metals tend to corrode. It is called the GALVANIC SERIES and is determined from the natural potentials of each metal relative to the others.

Fig. 2 Galvanic series of metals and alloys

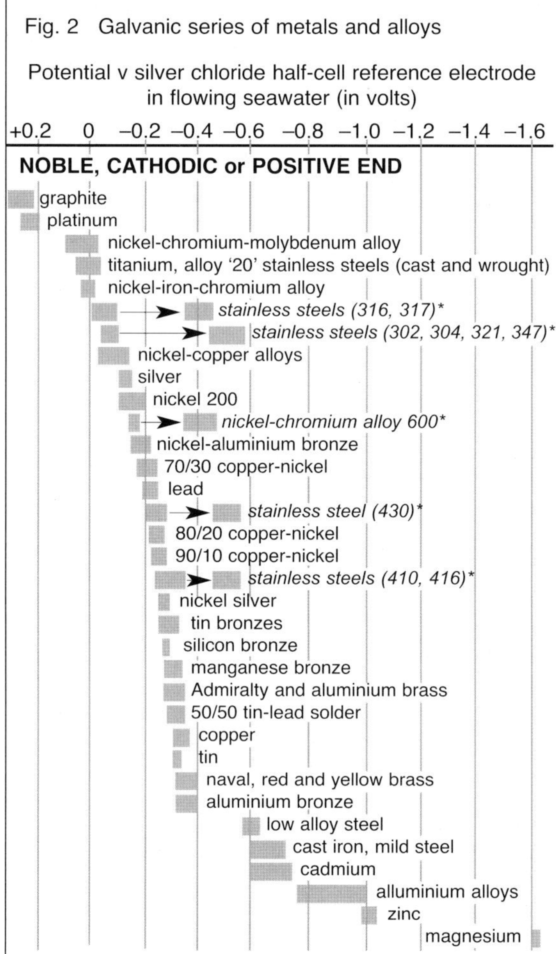
Potential v silver chloride half-cell reference electrode in flowing seawater (in volts)
+0.2 0 –0.2 –0.4 –0.6 –0.8 –1.0 –1.2 –1.4 –1.6
NOBLE, CATHODIC or POSITIVE END
graphite
platinum
nickel-chromium-molybdenum alloy
titanium, alloy '20' stainless steels (cast and wrought)
nickel-iron-chromium alloy
stainless steels (316, 317)*
stainless steels (302, 304, 321, 347)*
nickel-copper alloys
silver
nickel 200
nickel-chromium alloy 600*
nickel-aluminium bronze
70/30 copper-nickel
lead
stainless steel (430)*
80/20 copper-nickel
90/10 copper-nickel
stainless steels (410, 416)*
nickel silver
tin bronzes
silicon bronze
manganese bronze
Admiralty and aluminium brass
50/50 tin-lead solder
copper
tin
naval, red and yellow brass
aluminium bronze
low alloy steel
cast iron, mild steel
cadmium
alluminium alloys
zinc
magnesium
BASE, ANODIC OR NEGATIVE END

*The alloys shown in italics may become active; both passive *(left)* and active *(right)* voltage ranges are shown. Stainless steel is covered by a very thin skin of oxide (or corrosion product) on the surface of the steel. This oxide film insulates and protects the surface. However, the oxide film can be broken down by voltage stress causing stainless steel to corrode rapidly when in contact with the wrong metal. Once it has started corroding, it becomes active and moves much further down the galvanic series.

The galvanic series lists metals in order of their electrical potential in an electrolyte, such as seawater. Any metal closer to the anodic (active) end of the series will tend to corrode to 'protect' any other above it in the series. For example, zinc in contact with mild steel will corrode to 'protect' the steel;

while mild steel in contact with cast iron will corrode to protect the cast iron and so on up the series.

Care must be taken when using stainless steel. Normally mild steel, for example, would act to protect the stainless steel from corrosion. The significance of this can be shown by the example of a mild steel cover secured by stainless steel bolts. The cover will corrode rapidly around the bolts (where it is in contact with the stainless steel).

2. PROTECTIVE COATINGS

The main aim of a coating is to provide an electrically insulating cover to the metal which will prevent discharge of current. To be effective it must be a good insulator, be well bonded to the metal and must maintain these properties for many years. Unbonded coatings which allow water to penetrate behind them are a corrosion hazard which can be most difficult to detect.

Coatings for subsea service must be highly chemical-resistant and offer long term protection because of the high cost and difficulty of replacing them.

Insulating coatings consist of various plastics and epoxies, either in the form of tapes or as coatings of various thicknesses. Typical of these are the epoxy-phenolic coats, zinc-rich primers, polyamide epoxies and urethanes. Metal and concrete coatings are encountered regularly in offshore work.

A casing of monel metal is sometimes placed around the members of offshore installations, in the splash zone. This is to give physical protection to the structure in the most corrosive area where the metal alternates between being wet in air and being fully submerged. Regular coatings normally suffer extensive mechanical damage in this area and atmospheric corrosion is very rapid in the wet conditions.

Concrete coatings are also frequently used on offshore pipelines. They act as weight coatings to overcome the buoyancy of the line and to ensure that it stays in place on the seabed. The concrete is applied over an epoxy or bitumen coating which provides the corrosion protection. However, if the concrete weight coat and bitumen coating is damaged, a severely corrosive galvanic cell is produced between the encased steel and any exposed steel.

3. CATHODIC PROTECTION

Another method of eliminating the anodic area is to overcome the discharging current by introducing a separate source of current of such polarity as to ensure the structure receives current over its entire surface area. By doing this, the potential of the structure becomes more negative, or more cathodic; hence the term 'cathodic protection'.

Cathodic protection can be achieved by the use of either of two different types of anode: sacrificial and impressed current. Figs. 3 and 4 provide a comparison of the two types.

1. Sacrificial Anodes

To protect a steel structure, a more active metal than the steel (such as zinc) is selected from the galvanic

Fig. 3 Sacrificial and Impressed Current Systems compared

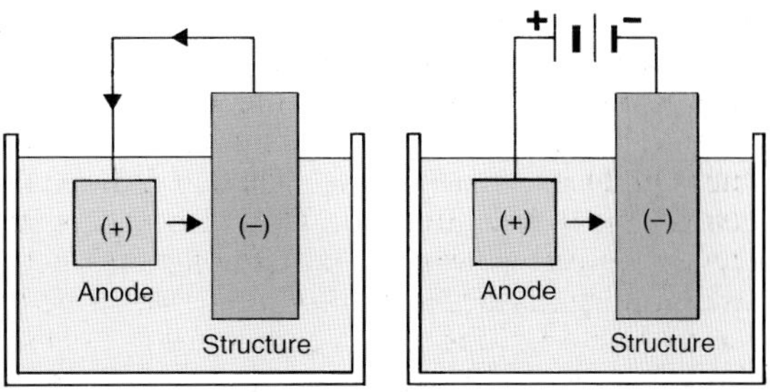
+
−
(+)
(−)
Anode
Structure
(+)
(−)
Anode
Structure

a) Sacrificial Anode system which makes use of the difference in potential between metals in an electrolyte to create a current.

b) Impressed Current system where the current is provided by an external DC source.

Fig. 4 Comparative Aspects of the Two Types of Cathodic Protection System

Cathodic Protection system	Advantages	Limitations
SACRIFICIAL ANODE	Power supply is not required. Little supervision required once installed. Does not cause interference to other structures in the vicinity.	Protection is limited and depends on the total surface area of the anodes. Very heavy – design of structure must be able to support them. Difficult to replace after permanent failure or at the end of their working/design life. May cause excessive drag on structural members. Consumable and may need replacement in due course.
IMPRESSED CURRENT	Saving in weight and drag. Provided the power is available, protection may be increased to any desired value as long as the anode material can still operate. Integral monitoring systems can easily be built.	The power source must be connected to the structure correctly. If the power fails, protection is lost. Too much power can be applied which may damage paint coatings, increase fatigue crack growth and cause hydrogen embrittlement. The electrical cables must be well protected; damage to them will result in failure of the system. The system must be continuously monitored. Higher voltages are a possible hazard to divers.

series and is placed in contact with the steel below water level. As a result of the electro-chemical difference, current flows from the active metal, through the seawater, to the steel. (There is no external power source. See Fig. 3a). Thus the active metal becomes anodic and corrodes while the steel becomes cathodic and is protected. This type of anode is frequently called 'sacrificial' since it becomes depleted and sacrifices itself to protect the metal to which it is attached. Examples of typical sacrificial anodes are shown in Fig. 5.

Fig. 5 Typical sacrificial anodes

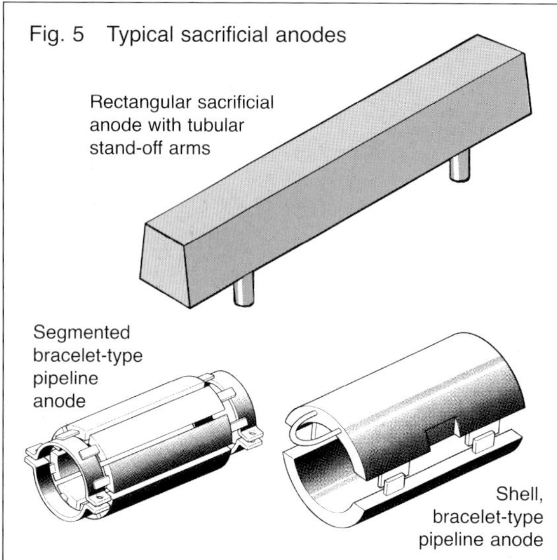
Rectangular sacrificial anode with tubular stand-off arms
Segmented bracelet-type pipeline anode
Shell, bracelet-type pipeline anode

The most commonly used metals for this type of anode are magnesium (in freshwater), and zinc and aluminium (in seawater).

All metals corrode at known rates so their life expectancy can be estimated and maintenance replacement programmes specified in order to ensure that new anodes are installed before the old ones are entirely corroded away.

Typically a large platform anode can produce around 4 amps DC at about 0.25V (power level 1W). The current is only transmitted over relatively short distances.

2. *Impressed Current Anodes*

Impressed current anodes have the same overall effect as sacrificial anodes except that they require an external power source to create the electrical circuit (see Figs. 3b and 6). Because of this an anode material with the lowest possible corrosion rate is used. Lead-silver-antimony alloys or, either titanium or platinum with a very thin niobium covering are the most commonly used materials.

The typical operating power for a single impressed current anode may be around 50 amps, 20V DC (1,000W). Thus high power levels can be achieved with few anodes and large areas can be covered.

4. CORROSION INHIBITORS

These are chemical systems, normally only used as additives to water in closed systems or in

Fig. 6 Impressed Current Systems

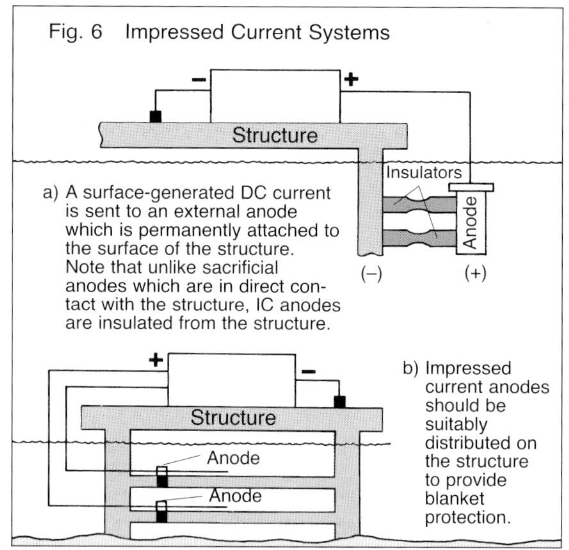
–
+
Structure
Insulators
Anode
(–)
(+)
a) A surface-generated DC current is sent to an external anode which is permanently attached to the surface of the structure. Note that unlike sacrificial anodes which are in direct contact with the structure, IC anodes are insulated from the structure.
+
–
Structure
Anode
Anode
b) Impressed current anodes should be suitably distributed on the structure to provide blanket protection.

circulating water systems in refineries etc. Diver involvement is, therefore, rare.

Corrosion inhibitors of many types are used depending on the application and the metal to be protected. However, they fall into two main categories:

1. Where a protective film is deposited onto the surface of the structure, pipes, etc, out of the liquid.
2. Where the chemicals in the inhibitor react on the surface of the steel and with the steel itself to form a protective skin in a similar way to the oxide layer on stainless steel.

Corrosion inhibitors are commonly seen in new spoolpieces when being installed. The spools are sent down filled with an inhibiting gel to which fluoroscene (harmless to divers) has been added. This protects the inner surface area of the spoolpiece when it is flooded with seawater. The spool is then mechanically connected to the rest of the structure and is protected by system anodes.

5. INSULATION

A galvanic cell such as, for example, a zinc anode on a steel ship's hull, will only experience current flow if a very low resistance contact exists for the current return path. This is made deliberately in the case of an anode by welding the anode's steel core directly to the steel hull. Other cases may not be so beneficial. For example, the cast iron body of a valve bolted directly onto a steel pipeline. With no protection, the pipeline steel will become anodic to the cast iron valve and will corrode. Corrosion due to this cell can be prevented by insulating the flanges on each side of the valve. It is more common, however, to apply a cathodic protection system which will tend to equalise the potentials of the two metals, both at a protective level.

Corrosion Rate

Because anodic (or active, corroding) areas are those where the current is passing from the metal into the electrolyte (seawater), the higher the current level, the more rapid will be the corrosion. The rate of corrosion can be defined in terms of current flow and a typical figure is that for steel: 1 amp flowing for 1 year will remove approximately 10kg of steel. Although this is a relatively low current level, 10kg of steel represents a large amount of metal to be removed from a pipewall and could constitute a major leak.

According to Ohm's Law, current level is equivalent to voltage divided by resistance. Therefore, high voltage (or low resistance) will cause high current and rapid corrosion. It should be noted, however, that high voltage in this context will still be extremely low – in most cases less than one volt.

The specific resistance, or resistivity of the water is the electrical resistance of a 1 cm (2/5 in) cube of water measured between two opposite faces of the cube and is normally stated as Ohm/cm. This provides a means of measuring the corrosivity of water and the levels given in Fig. 7 are generally accepted.

Fig. 7 Typical Resistivities and Current Densities of Bare Steel

0–2,000 Ohm/cm	=	severely corrosive
2,000–10,000 Ohm/cm	=	moderately corrosive
10,000+ Ohm/cm	=	unlikely to be corrosive

Ocean Area	Resistivity (Ohm/cm)	Current Density (milliAmp/m^2)
North Sea	30	130–180
Gulf of Mexico	20	65
Australia (south)	20	130
West Africa	20	85–130
Indonesia	19	65
Gulf of Persia	15	110
Buried pipelines	70–100	50
Saline mud	70–100	11–30
Estuarine water	750–1,000	–

Diver Tasks

These are generally associated with the installation and monitoring of a cathodic protection system.

1. INSTALLATION OF SACRIFICIAL ANODES

A sacrificial cathodic protection system design first identifies the total tonnage of anodic material required for a specified life. This tonnage is then subdivided into individual anodes, each of which produces a proportion of the total current required for protection. The actual current produced by an anode depends on a number of factors the most significant of which, in seawater, are the dimensions and shape of the anode.

Thus the designer calculates the optimum quantity and size of the anodes and then specifies their location to achieve the most even current distribution.

The diver then fits the anodes by welding, clamping or bolting them to the structure.

2. INSTALLATION OF IMPRESSED CURRENT SYSTEMS

There are two significant differences between sacrificial and impressed anode systems:

1. The impressed current anode system requires a DC power source.
2. Impressed current anodes may be remote from the structure and connected to it by electrical cables.

The power source, such as a transformer-rectifier, will be mounted out of the water while the anodes will be permanently below water. Thus, the cable connection between the transformer-rectifier and the anode must, inevitably, run through the 'splash zone' and be subject to wave action. Fixing of conduits, etc, must take this into account when mounting impressed current anodes on a structure. An assembly, or array, of impressed current anodes may also be located on the seabed remote from the protected structure (see Fig. 8). This is mainly pre-assembled above water and lowered directly into position.

Retro-fitting of anodes is a common diver task.

Fig. 8 Typical pattern of installing remote impressed current anodes on a structure

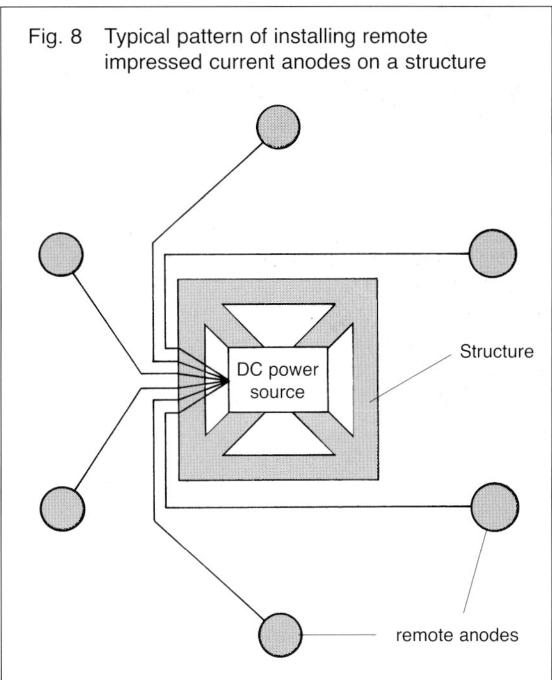
DC power source
Structure
remote anodes

3. MONITORING

a) Permanent monitoring systems

Permanent reference electrodes are installed to enable periodic measurements to be made at designated positions on a structure and these may be used with either type of cathodic protection system.

A reference electrode is an electrical conductor which is placed on a structure in order to measure the level of protection that is being provided by the corrosion protection system.

They work by utilising the electro-chemical reaction between two metals in an electrolyte. A selected metal surrounded by a saturated solution of its own salts, for example, a silver electrode in a silver chloride paste, is placed near the metal, say steel, to be monitored. Silver chloride is commonly used since, because the silver chloride paste is saturated, the silver electrode can be considered to be in a stable and unchanging environment. In contrast, the steel structure is subject to all of the normal variations and stresses that it will encounter in its working situation. Therefore, if the voltage between the steel and the silver is measured it can be assumed that any change in this voltage level is the result of the changing effect of the environment upon the steel. Thus the voltage is a direct indication of the corroding or protected condition of the steel.

The other most common type of reference electrode used in submerged applications is high purity zinc which, for most practical purposes, has a stable voltage when directly immersed in seawater. This means that it can be assembled into a much more rugged electrode unit and is often favoured for this reason.

Fig. 10 gives some typical electric potentials developed in protected and unprotected metals.

Fig. 10 The expected range of potentials in sea water of the most common metals used in marine installations

Metal	Potential with reference to the silver/silver chloride half cell
Unprotected iron/ steel	–400 to –650 mV
Cathodically protected iron and steel	–800 to –900 mV
Zinc	–1,000 to –1 ,050 mV
Monel	–50 to –150 mV

Reference electrodes are normally connected by cables to a monitoring control panel above water and, as in the case of impressed current systems, these cables must be suitably installed and protected.

b) Diver monitoring

Even where permanent reference electrodes are installed a diver may be required to take CP readings at specified positions on an underwater structure. This is usually done using a hand-held probe (see Figs. 11 and 12). The diver can either record the readings from the probe and report them to the surface or, where recording equipment is installed at the surface, the readings can be transmitted directly to the surface monitors (see Fig. 12b).

Fig. 11 A diver inspector taking cathodic protection potential measurements using a typical corrosion meter

Voltmeter display

Stainless steel probe

0·15

half cell bathycorrometer

Steel structure

Fig. 12 Corrosion level measurement with a silver chloride half cell meter and probe.

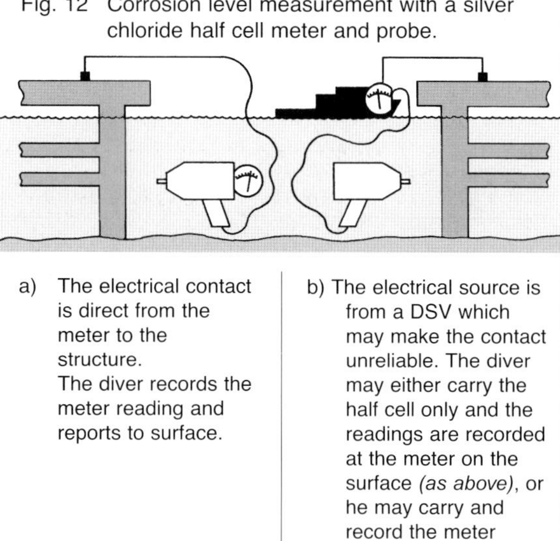

a) The electrical contact is direct from the meter to the structure. The diver records the meter reading and reports to surface.

b) The electrical source is from a DSV which may make the contact unreliable. The diver may either carry the half cell only and the readings are recorded at the meter on the surface *(as above)*, or he may carry and record the meter readings himself *(as in Fig. 12a)*.

3.2 UNDERWATER CUTTING

No cutting plant or equipment should be used by untrained personnel. Serious injury or death may result from improper use of cutting equipment.
There are two categories of underwater cutting: 'hot' cutting and 'cold' cutting.
In order to reduce risk to the diver, cold cutting techniques should be used in preference to hot cutting techniques wherever possible.

'HOT' CUTTING TECHNIQUES
There are four main 'hot' cutting processes generally in use:

1. Oxy-arc (carbon and tubular steel electrodes).
2. Exothermic cutting (Kerie Cable and Broco Rods).
3. Gas cutting (Oxy-hydrogen torch).
4. Shielded metal arc (SMA), also known as Manual metal arc (MMA).

1. Oxy-arc cutting

Oxy-arc is probably the most widely used underwater cutting technique. It easily cuts plain and low carbon steel. Examples of typical equipment used in oxy-arc cutting are shown in Figs. 1 and 2.
Oxy-arc cutting is a process which exploits the chemical reaction between oxygen and the base ferrous metal at very high temperatures. This heat is initiated and maintained by an electric arc between the electrode and the base metal and by the chemical reactions in the work and the electrode itself. In other words, a spot on the base metal is made hot by the electric arc which is formed between the base metal and the tip of the hollow tubular cutting electrode. Preheating is instantaneous, a jet of oxygen is directed at the pre-

Fig. 1 Typical arrangement for underwater arc cutting equipment

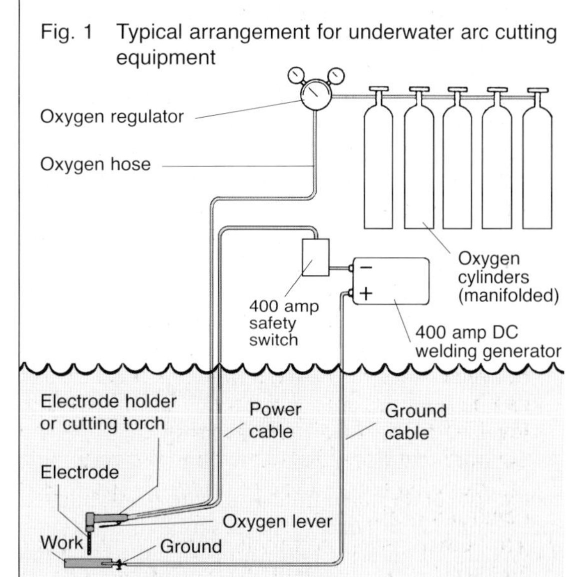
Oxygen regulator
Oxygen hose
Oxygen cylinders (manifolded)
400 amp safety switch
−
+
400 amp DC welding generator
Electrode holder or cutting torch
Power cable
Ground cable
Electrode
Oxygen lever
Work
Ground

Oxy-Arc cutting Equipment

The equipment used for oxy-arc cutting and shielded metal arc cutting is basically the same as for Shielded Metal Arc welding.

1. DC welding generator
2. Oxygen supply
3. Oxygen coupler
4. Oxygen regulator
5. Ground (earth) plate
6. Work or base metal
7. Knife switch or electrical contact
8. Cutting electrode
9. Cutting torch and spares
10. Cable connector
11. 400 amps cable (supply and return)
12. Oxygen supply hose
13. Scraper or wire brush

Fig. 2 Some commonly used underwater oxygen arc cutting torches

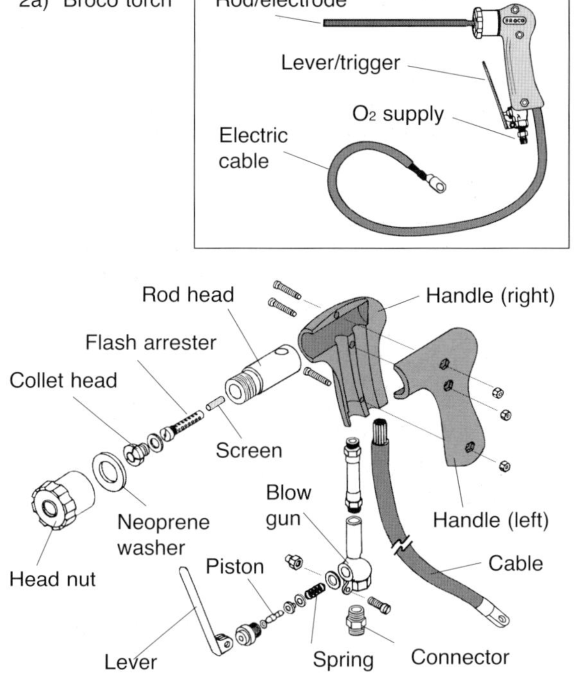
2a) Broco torch
Rod/electrode
Lever/trigger
O_2 supply
Electric cable
Rod head
Handle (right)
Flash arrester
Collet head
Screen
Blow gun
Handle (left)
Neoprene washer
Piston
Cable
Head nut
Lever
Spring
Connector

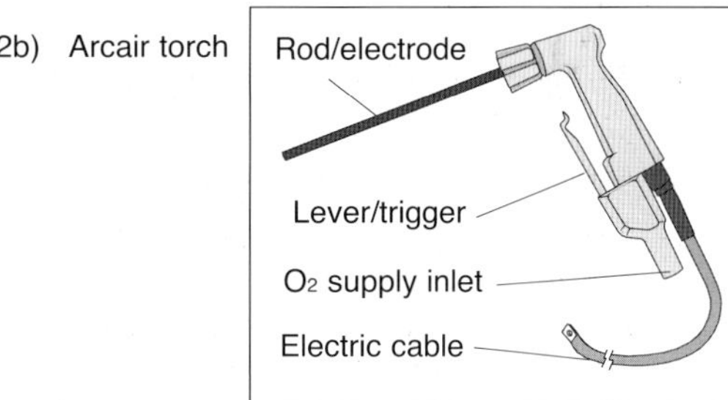
2b) Arcair torch
Rod/electrode
Lever/trigger
O_2 supply inlet
Electric cable

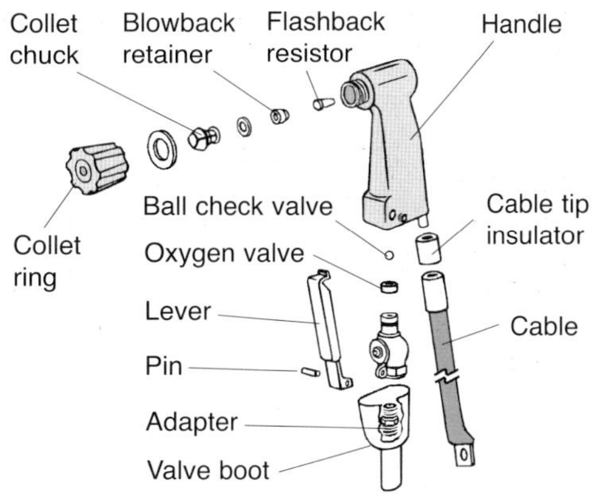
Collet chuck
Blowback retainer
Flashback resistor
Handle
Ball check valve
Cable tip insulator
Collet ring
Oxygen valve
Lever
Cable
Pin
Adapter
Valve boot

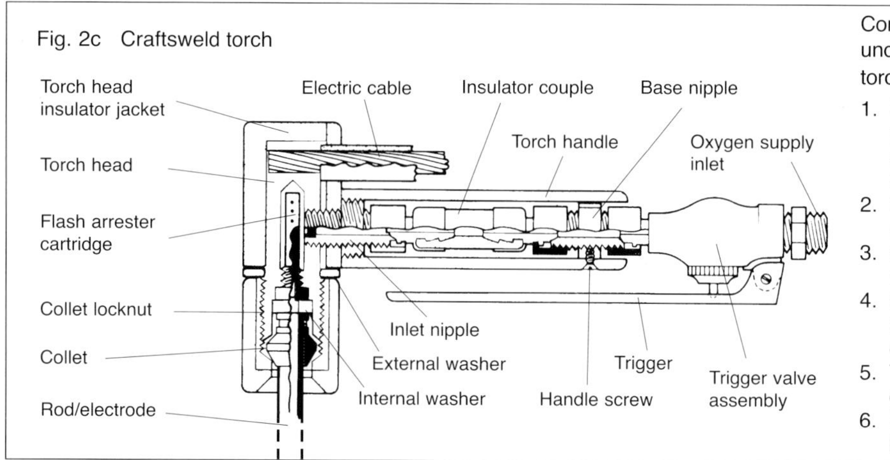
Torch head insulator jacket
Electric cable
Insulator couple
Base nipple
Torch handle
Oxygen supply inlet
Torch head
Flash arrester cartridge
Collet locknut
Collet
Rod/electrode
Inlet nipple
External washer
Internal washer
Handle screw
Trigger
Trigger valve assembly
Fig. 2c Craftsweld torch

Common problems with underwater oxy-arc cutting torches

1. Worn or damaged collet possibly causing poor electrical contact or an oxygen leak.
2. Worn or damaged blow-out preventer or spring.
3. Sealing washers need replacement.
4. Oxygen valve/torch seized up through corrosion.
5. Torch insulation broken down.
6. Poor electrical contact between cable and torch.

heated spot at the same time as the arc is established and cutting commences. In practice the oxygen flow is turned on prior to forming an arc so that the oxidized steel will be blown away from the line of the cut, thus preventing fusion between rod and metal and possible sealing of the tip when using steel electrodes. For the same reason the oxygen flow is maintained for a short period after breaking the cutting arc.

FACTORS IN PLANNING OXY-ARC CUTTING OPERATIONS

1. Check the sea state, tidal state, rate and direction of tidal stream and weather forecast.
2. Check visibility underwater.
3. Setting up the equipment:
   a) Determine the amperage which depends on the length of the cables, the depth of the worksite and the thickness of the plate to be cut. An amperage of between 300 and 500 amps would be required. Excess cable should be laid out in straight lines or snaked out in large U's because coiling reduces the electrical efficiency of the burning.
   b) Set a low voltage (between 60 and 90V DC at straight polarity (electrode negative).
   c) The electrode cable should be connected to the negative terminal at the electric supply generator.
   d) A safety switch or contact should be fitted in the negative lead.
   e) Make sure there is an adequate supply of commercial grade oxygen (99.5% pure). You will need a manifold to connect the cylinders if more than one is used and to minimise interruptions due to cylinder change.
   f) The oxygen regulator should be set to provide a pressure of 4–6.8bar (60–100psi) above ambient pressure.
   g) Electrodes
      – Select the type of electrode from carbon, tubular steel or ultrathermic electrodes.
      – Inspect the condition of the electrodes. Ensure that the flux coating is intact. Reject damaged electrodes.
      – All electrodes must be suitably waterproofed and insulated.
      – Ultrathermic electrodes may need an adaptor to fit some torches.
4. Provide a steady stage or platform from which to cut. If nothing else is available use magnetic holds.

PROCEDURE

Confirm the agreed diver instructions prior to diving, for example to turn on the electrical power supply to the torch, diver says "Make it hot" and for "off": "Make it cold".

1. *Grounding the work*
   Before starting electric-arc cutting on conductive material, a ground cable must be attached to the work piece.
   a) The materials (torch, ground cable and electrodes) can be taken to the worksite by the diver or can be lowered to him on arrival.
   b) The diver must first clean a part of the workpiece in front of him (using a wire brush or scraper) until it is shiny clean.
   c) The diver attaches the cable to the cleaned area using a C-clamp ensuring that there is enough slack in the cable to prevent it from being pulled loose. To prevent this happening, the clamp may be tack welded to an approved location near the workpiece.
   d) During the cutting procedure, the diver may need to reposition the clamp from time to time to ensure that he does not become part of the electrical circuit.
   e) The ground (earth) plate should be connected to the positive terminal of the electrical supply.
2. The diver should ensure that he is in a suitable position to start cutting, including the offset position of his head in relation to the cut.
3. He must ensure that his umbilical, torch hose and power cable are clear of the work area.
4. *Cutting*. The diver should:
   a) Flush the torch with oxygen and maintain the flow.

b) Place the tip of the electrode in contact with the work and call for current.
c) When the arc is established the pre-determined oxygen pressure is released and the metal is pierced. The diver holds the electrode at 90° to the workpiece and keeps it in constant contact with the workpiece while he is cutting.
If difficulty is experienced in striking the arc or maintaining the cut, the torch should be again flushed with oxygen as a matter of routine before resuming the cut.
d) Changing the electrode: When the electrode has burned down to 5cm (2in), stop the cut and order "make it cold". Keep the torch near the cutting position until the Supervisor confirms that the electricity has been turned off. Tap the electrode twice on the workpiece to confirm that the current is off. Only then change the electrode.

5. Ensure a clean line of cut. Where neatness of the cut is important a cutting template is useful. On a pipeline, it is often useful to wrap a strap or rope around the pipe so that the outline can be followed. On more complex structures a cutting template may be designed for the job.

6. When cutting through thick steel it will be useful to have some tool, such as kitchen knife, to push all the way through the cut to check for bridging.

7. Gases from the torch and cutting process can accumulate in a void and cause a violent explosion. Never allow gas pockets to accumulate from the cutting process. Take special care to evaluate the risk of gas pockets being formed. Gas pockets can form:
   - in mud/soil behind or beneath a steel structure.
   - under the concrete coating on a steel pipe.
   - in annular spaces in well suspension or pile guiding structures.
   - under flat structures such as a ship's hull.
   - inside an enclosed space such as a tubular structure, tank or pipe.
   - inside thick metal being cut.

8. Before cutting into an enclosed space a vent hole must be cut in the upper part to allow trapped and cutting gases to escape. When cutting the vent hole be careful of any pressure differential between the inside and outside. If it is possible that a flammable gas exists on the other side, a cold cutting technique should be used to cut the vent hole.

9. Blow-backs (small explosions) can be caused when cutting in or near a pipe due to the ignition of hydrocarbons, paint or bitumastic coatings and some light alloy materials such as in sacrificial anodes. The greater the depth, the more violent the explosions.

Two types of electrode are commonly used with oxy-arc cutting:

1. Carbon electrodes
Carbon electrodes are usually 20.3cm (8") long and 9.5mm (3/8") in diameter. These electrodes have the following characteristics.
a) Cutting technique is simple.
b) Economy. They oxidize more slowly than the other types of rod and therefore will cut a more linear plate per rod on plate up to 25mm (1") thick. The average speed is 0.3m/min on 12.7mm plate (1ft/min on 1/2" plate).
c) Relatively cheap. They are half the price of tubular steel.
d) Limited cutting at one pass on plate over 25mm (1") thick unless the cut is opened up.
e) Poor insulation, unless plastic coated.
f) They break easily.

2. Tubular steel electrodes
These widely-used burning electrodes are of tubular steel, usually 35cm (14") long and 8mm (5/16") OD, with a bore of approximately 3mm (1/8").
Their characteristics are:
a) Cutting technique is simple.
b) Can cut up to 51mm (2") metal at one pass.
c) Cutting is very rapid, depending on the metal thickness, oxygen pressure, water depth, current and operator skill. Average cutting speed is 0.7m/min on a 12.7mm plate (27" on 1/2" plate).
d) Neat trim cuts are produced.
e) The power requirement is within 400 amps.
f) They have a short burning life.

2. Exothermic cutting

Exothermic cutting will burn through almost anything, including reinforced concrete.
This technique is relatively simple and cuts rapidly but it consumes large volumes of oxygen.

1. BROCO ULTRATHERMIC ELECTRODES
Ultrathermic electrodes differ from tubular steel electrodes in construction being composed of seven thin rods inside a steel tube. One of the seven rods is a special alloy which will burn independently once an arc is struck and oxygen is flowing through the tube. It is about 46cm (18") long and comes in two diameters: 9.5mm (3/8") and 6.3mm (1/4").

Ultrathermic electrodes have the following characteristics:
a) Cutting technique is simple.
b) They allow electrical cut-off. The electrodes will go on burning if the oxygen flow is maintained so provision should be made for the rapid isolation of the oxygen supply.
c) Cutting is performed as rapidly as tubular cutting electrodes.
d) They may be used for cutting both ferrous and non-ferrous metals.
e) The power requirement is only about 150 amps which allows a much smaller and lighter welding set – light enough to be carried by one man.

(A typical 400 amps set can weigh as much as half a ton).

f) The electrodes are costly.

g) Their burning life underwater is about 1 minute.

2. INDUSTRIAL THERMIC LANCES

The thermic lance is a steel tube, 3.2m (10.5ft) long by 9.5mm ($^3/_8$") diameter packed with a number of mild steel rods (see Fig. 3).

Fig. 3 Typical thermic lance holder

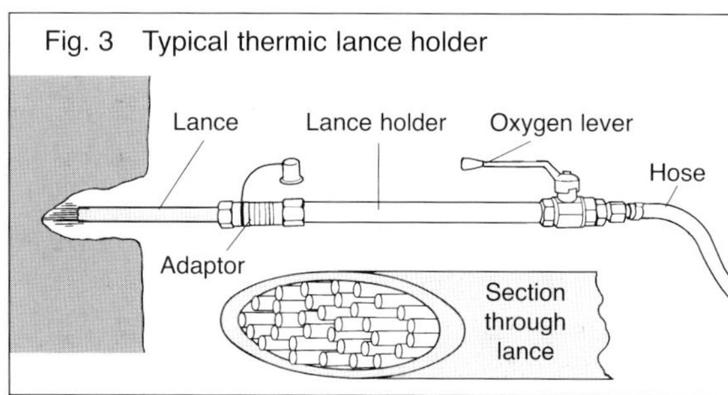
Lance
Lance holder
Oxygen lever
Hose
Adaptor
Section through lance

Due to the very high temperatures produced the lance will burn through almost anything – steel, nonferrous metals, rock and concrete – but the risk of explosion makes the cutting of nonferrous metals highly dangerous.
One of its special applications underwater is to cut holes in reinforced concrete. It is difficult to handle because of its length and it has a high rate of oxygen consumption. One lance will burn for 6 minutes.

3. KERIE CABLE

A development from the thermic lance is the Clucas Thermic-Arc System which operates on the same principle but instead of a rigid bar, the consumable agent is 30m (100ft), 12mm ($^1/_2$") or 6mm ($^1/_4$") diameter flexible, plastic-covered cable of high tensile steel wire. It is called Kerie Cable. Fig. 4 illustrates typical equipment layout for underwater cutting using Kerie cable.

Its advantages are its ease of handling and its average burning time of nearly one hour. Kerie Cable will burn at a rate of 27m (89ft) per hour, ie 0.5m (18") per minute. The electrical circuit is used only for igniting the thermic cable and is not used during the actual burning. For safety reasons the temperature of Kerie Cable is reduced to 2,700°C which prevents it from cutting nonferrous metals. The cut is broader than that of carbon or tubular steel electrodes.
The selection of cable depends on the thickness of the metal being cut. 30m (100ft) of 12mm ($^1/_2$") cable will provide 45 minutes of continuous cutting and consume approximately 3 oxygen cylinders at 0–18m depth (0–60ft).
Typical oxygen consumption would be as follows: 3 x 6794 litre cylinders of oxygen consumed for every 30m depth when set to a surface pressure of 27 bar + ambient pressure (in this case +4 bars).
That is, in imperial units: 3 x 240ft^3 cylinders of oxygen will be consumed for every 100ft depth when set to a surface pressure of 400psi + ambient pressure (in this case +59psi).

PROCEDURE

1. After the striker plate is secured at the work site, the cable should be pressurised and passed down to the diver. The cable needs to be pressurised sufficiently to overcome hydrostatic pressure and to exclude water from entering the cable bore.
2. On reaching the work site the diver calls for gas pressure to be increased. It takes about 20 seconds for the oxygen pressure to build up along the full length of the cable.
3. The tender then increases oxygen pressure to correct over-bottom pressure. When the diver sees an increase in the bubbles escaping from the cable end, he calls for "switch on".
4. The Supervisor closes the knife switch and confirms 'switch on' enabling the diver to ignite

Fig. 4 Exothermic arc cutting equipment

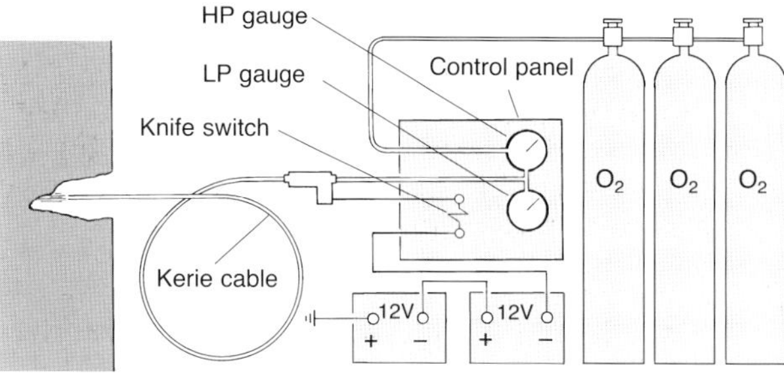
HP gauge
LP gauge
Knife switch
Control panel
Kerie cable
12V
12V
+ –
+ –
O_2
O_2
O_2

Exothermic Arc Cutting Equipment

1. Oxygen supply.
2. Three-cylinder oxygen manifold.
3. Control panel/unit.
4. a) 30m length of 12mm Kerie Cable, or
   b) 15m of 6mm Kerie Cable, or
   c) a number of 3.5m thermic lances.
5. 30m extension lead.
6. One or two 12V batteries.
7. Wire wool for surface ignition.
8. Heavy duty wire cutters.
9. Insulating sleeves.

Kerie cable control panel

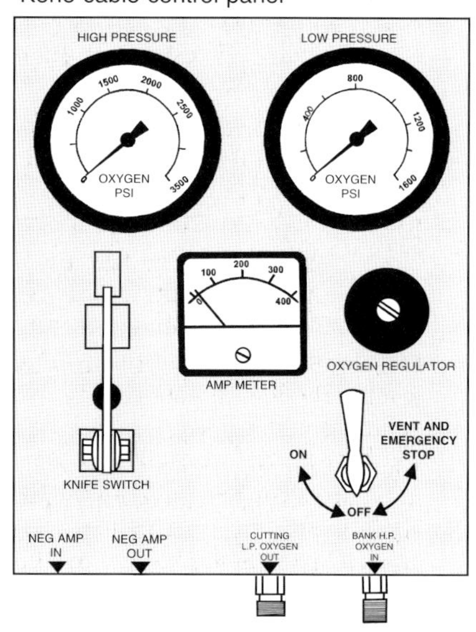
HIGH PRESSURE
LOW PRESSURE
OXYGEN PSI
OXYGEN PSI
AMP METER
OXYGEN REGULATOR
KNIFE SWITCH
ON
OFF
VENT AND EMERGENCY STOP
NEG AMP IN
NEG AMP OUT
CUTTING L.P. OXYGEN OUT
BANK H.P. OXYGEN IN

OXY-ARC AND EXOTHERMIC CUTTING – OPERATIONAL SAFETY

1. Make sure that you have chosen the best cutting technique. Cutting nonferrous metals is always dangerous as with any hot cutting process. It may be preferable to use explosives or cold cutting techniques.
2. The diving station and the area immediately around it must be free of combustible and explosive materials.
3. Make certain that all electrical connections are securely made before starting operations.
4. Ensure that all cable connections and metallic parts are properly insulated.
5. Make certain that the electrical supply is earthed before starting operations, ie, earth the frame of the welding set.
6. The topside electricity switch must be rigidly mounted. It should be located where it cannot be accidentally knocked or vibrated shut. The action of the switch lever falling down should break the circuit.
7. The safety switch should be kept open at all times except when directed by the diver/cutter to close it.
8. The electrical current must never be on except when the diver is actually cutting or has the torch poised ready to start.
9. Before the gun is sent underwater, the correct polarity can be confirmed by immersing the gun and the earth clamp in a bucket of seawater. With the electric current on, a small tail of 'fizzing' bubbles should be emitted from the end of the rod.
10. The diver's dress and voice communications must be in perfect working order.
11. It is strongly recommended that divers should wear a full helmet apparatus when cutting underwater.
12. The diver should always wear the appropriate tinted eye shield in front of the mask/helmet.
13. The diver should always wear adequate rubber gloves to electrically insulate himself. They should be secured at the wrist to prevent slag entering.
14. The diver must never hold the cutting torch so that it points towards him.
15. The diver should make certain that he positions the earth so that he cannot accidentally become part of the circuit when he stands between the earth and the electrode. He must never turn his back on the earth connection.
16. The diver should position himself to the side of the cutting area and not directly in front of it. This will minimise any effects of blow-backs or explosions.
17. The diver must never let his hand get closer than 10cm (4 in) from the tip of the electrode.
18. The collet washer should be changed out if oxygen 'leaks' out from around the top of the rod or gun.
19. The diver should not cut into a compartment or void space without first making sure that there are no explosive or flammable substances on the other side.
20. Care should be taken to vent inflammable gases generated by the arc. Gases may become trapped in an enclosed compartment or void space during electric cutting. Oxy-arc cutting produces hydrogen. Hydrogen is also a hazard when cutting in habitats or hyperbaric enclosures on or above the sea or river beds, especially in mud, where trapped methane gas can cause explosions.
21. The diver should take care to ensure that the pieces of metal cut from the work do not fall on him or his umbilical. He should cut carefully so as to prevent dropping slag or molten metal from falling on him.
22. The diver must always be closely tended. The diver umbilical, torch oxygen supply and electricity supply cable should be kept well clear of the work area.
23. The diver must never take the cutting gun back to the bell for repairs. It must always be sent back to the surface.
24. The torch should never be passed from the water to the tender unless the power is off.
25. Divers must never surface while the power is on.

the torch by touching the tip of the cable to the striker plate. (The ammeter shows a reading as the diver tries to ignite the torch and falls back to zero when ignition is successful).

5. The diver confirms ignition by announcing, "I have ignition" and the Supervisor then opens the knife switch, isolating the electrical circuit.
6. Cutting begins when the ignited tip of the cable is brought in contact with the workpiece. The cable should be kept in constant contact with the workpiece and at right angles to it.
7. To stop cutting the diver calls for "gas off" but should continue to rub the cable against the work to prevent the molten plastic coating from covering the inner wire core thus preventing it from being able to be reignited.
8. Only in an emergency should the cable be extinguished by turning the switch to the 'Vent' position since this floods the cable to extinguish the flame and therefore makes it difficult to relight it underwater.

KERIE CABLE CUTTING – SAFETY

1. The 3m (10ft) HP manifold which connects the oxygen cylinders with the panel must *never* be substituted. It is specially designed to insulate the manifold by preventing any returning electrical current from travelling up the steel-braided hose to the oxygen cylinders.

(cont . . .)

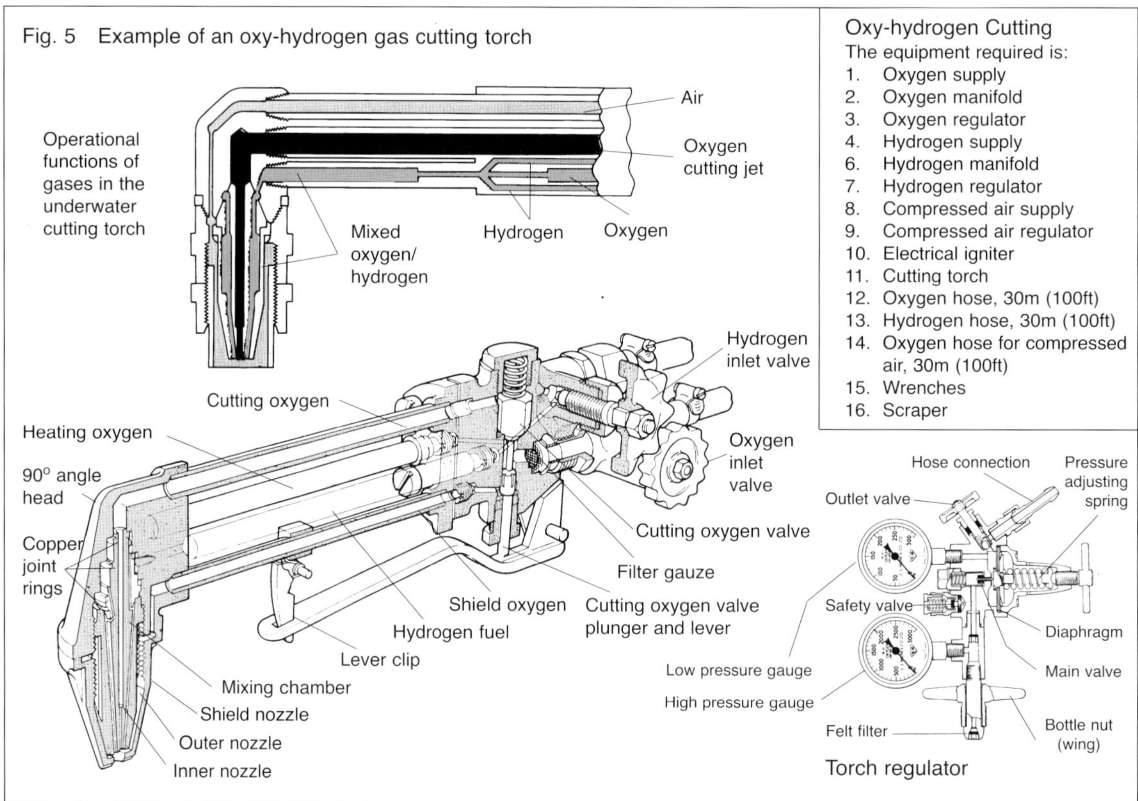
Operational functions of gases in the underwater cutting torch
Air
Oxygen cutting jet
Mixed oxygen/ hydrogen
Hydrogen
Oxygen
Hydrogen inlet valve
Cutting oxygen
Heating oxygen
90° angle head
Oxygen inlet valve
Copper joint rings
Cutting oxygen valve
Filter gauze
Shield oxygen
Cutting oxygen valve plunger and lever
Hydrogen fuel
Lever clip
Mixing chamber
Shield nozzle
Outer nozzle
Inner nozzle
Oxy-hydrogen Cutting
The equipment required is:
1. Oxygen supply
2. Oxygen manifold
3. Oxygen regulator
4. Hydrogen supply
6. Hydrogen manifold
7. Hydrogen regulator
8. Compressed air supply
9. Compressed air regulator
10. Electrical igniter
11. Cutting torch
12. Oxygen hose, 30m (100ft)
13. Hydrogen hose, 30m (100ft)
14. Oxygen hose for compressed air, 30m (100ft)
15. Wrenches
16. Scraper
Hose connection
Pressure adjusting spring
Outlet valve
Safety valve
Diaphragm
Main valve
Low pressure gauge
High pressure gauge
Felt filter
Bottle nut (wing)
Torch regulator

Fig. 5 Example of an oxy-hydrogen gas cutting torch

(continued from previous page)

2. Before commencing operations the Supervisor should establish an 'Emergency Off' procedure to be implemented in case of emergency.
3. The Supervisor must stay within reach of the control panel during the entire cutting operation.
4. The Supervisor must ensure that the diver has the correct over-bottom pressure at all times.
5. In an emergency the diver can call for the cable to be extinguished immediately by calling "emergency off". The Supervisor will then turn the valve to the 'vent' position.
6. The cutting operation must stop immediately if communication with the diver is lost. It should not recommence until communications are restored.
7. The diver must not force or poke the cable into the material being cut since this will cause blow-back.
8. The diver should keep his hands at least 15cm (6in) clear of the tip of the burning cable.

3. Oxy-hydrogen gas cutting

Gas cutting uses an oxy-hydrogen cutting torch rather than with a cutting electrode. The very high heat required for cutting is generated by burning hydrogen gas in the presence of oxygen. For safety reasons, when cutting at depths greater than 7.5m (25 ft) oxy-hydrogen is often used in preference to oxy-acetylene. Oxy-acetylene is not suitable for underwater cutting.

A jet of compressed air is blown through a cylindrical tube around the torch tip (see Fig. 5). The pressure of the air and gas creates a gas pocket around the oxy-hydrogen flame. The flame may be lit and adjusted before descending underwater or may be struck underwater using a striker plate.

A typical arrangement of the equipment used in oxy-hydrogen cutting is shown in Fig. 6.

Fig. 6 Typical equipment arrangement for oxy-hydrogen underwater cutting equipment

4. Shielded Metal Arc (SMA) also known as Manual Metal Arc (MMA)

Shielded metal arc cutting is a simple process that uses stick-type electrodes (although almost any waterproofed, mild steel electrodes will do). It can cut steels which are resistant to corrosion and

Fig. 7 Comparison of some characteristic features of cutting processes	OXY-ARC Electrode		EXOTHERMIC			SMA/ MMA	OXYGEN-HYDROGEN
	Carbon	Tubular	Ultra-electrode	Thermic lance	Kerie Cable		
Cuts ferrous metals	✓	✓	✓	✓	✓	✓	✓
Cuts nonferrous metals			✓	✓		✓	
Cuts non-metals				✓	✓		✓
Cuts oxidization/corrosion-resistant materials						✓	
Cuts laminated plating	✓	✓	✓	✓	✓	✓	✓
Cuts all standard thicknesses	✓	✓	✓	✓	✓	✓	✓
Cuts rapidly			✓	✓	✓		
Cuts neatly and precisely	✓	✓	✓				✓
Needs experience/skill						✓	✓
Easy to handle	✓	✓	✓		✓		
Requires oxygen	✓	✓	✓	✓	✓		✓
Requires fuel gas							✓
Requires electrodes	✓	✓	✓			✓	
Instant start	✓	✓	✓	✓	✓	✓	
Requires preheating							✓
Burns after current switch off			✓	✓	✓		
Electric shock hazard	✓	✓	✓			✓	
Explosion hazard	✓	✓	✓	✓	✓	✓	✓
Protective clothing should be worn	✓	✓	✓	✓	✓	✓	✓

When selecting which process to use other factors also need to be taken into account, such as: operating conditions; available equipment, its weight and bulkiness; and the training and experience of operators.

oxidization and nonferrous materials. It can also be used where no oxygen is available.
SMA relies on the intense heat of the arc to cut the metal. The heat melts a localised area of metal forming a small molten pool. Since the surrounding water rapidly cools the molten metal, the pool will not flow enough to allow a good cut to be made. The tip of the electrode must therefore be constantly moved about to push the molten metal out of the cut. The materials and equipment needed for SMA cutting are the same as those used in SMA welding. The four main 'hot' cutting methods are compared in Fig.7.

'COLD' CUTTING TECHNIQUES
A wide range of underwater hydraulic cutting tools is available. Some typical examples are illustrated

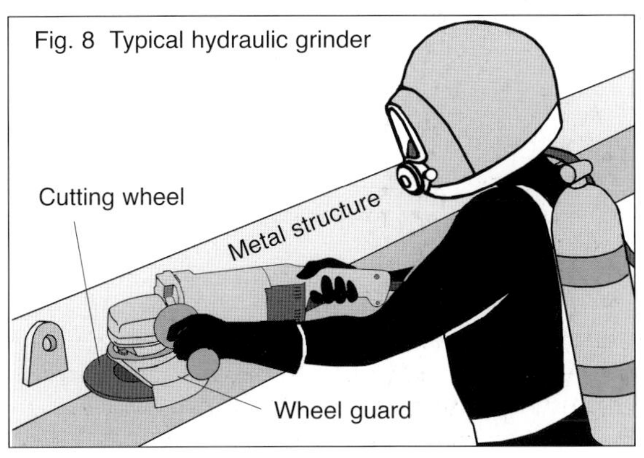
Cutting wheel
Metal structure
Wheel guard
Fig. 8 Typical hydraulic grinder

GRINDERS – OPERATIONAL SAFETY

1. Divers should receive training in the use of the tool before using it operationally.
2. Follow manufacturer's instructions.
3. Always hold the tool firmly with both hands.
4. Do not operate the tool if damaged in any way.
5. Inspect wheels for damage before installation.
6. Do not operate the tool without the wheel guard.
7. Never reverse the wheel rotation by reversing the oil flow direction.
8. The diver should ensure he is in a secure and safe position before operating the tool.
9. Do not inspect or clean the tool while the hydraulic power is still on.
10. Do not start the wheel while it is in contact with any surface.
11. Keep the rotating wheel well clear of the body and equipment.
12. Make sure the wheel has stopped before putting the tool down.
13. Do not store or transport the tool with a wheel installed.
14. Ensure the hose couplers are clean before connecting the hoses.
15. Ensure that the hoses are securely connected to the hose couplers before energising the hydraulic power source.
16. Ensure the hoses are connected to the correct couplers.

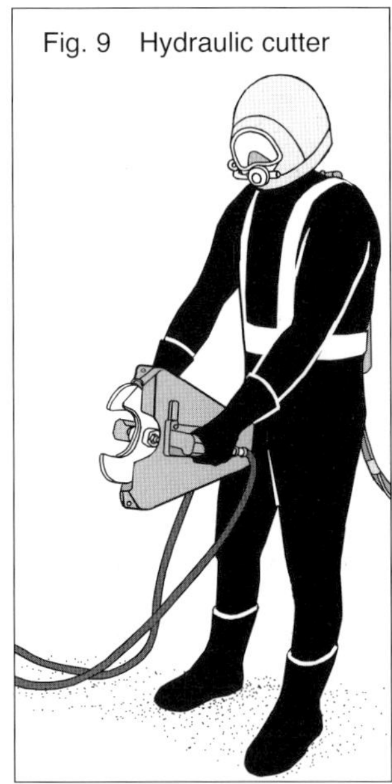
Fig. 9 Hydraulic cutter

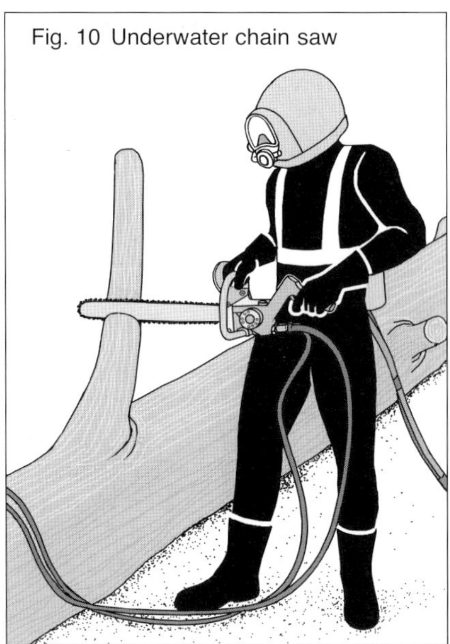
Fig. 10 Underwater chain saw

Fig. 11 Hydraulic hammer drill

in Figs 8–12. All require careful cleaning and maintenance after every use. Refer to the relevant manufacturer's manual for handling and maintenance procedures.

Hydraulic grinder

Hydraulic grinders are general purpose cutters. They are particularly effective in cutting through metal structures (see Fig. 8). Tools used for underwater operations should be specially designed for immersion. Because grinders develop torque and can jerk violently against a solid surface, divers must ensure that they are in a safe, stable and secure position before operating the tool.

There is a risk of abrasive cutting discs breaking when used underwater. The adhesive used in the discs can degrade when in contact with water. The dive project plan should ensure that only dry discs which have not been underwater before should be used. Only enough discs to carry out the work on each dive should be taken underwater.

Hydraulic hammer drill

This drill is not suitable for drilling steel or wood. A typical example is shown in Fig. 11.

Operation

1. Always follow the manufacturer's instructions.
2. Install the appropriate drill bit for the job and lock it in position.
3. Wipe the hose couplers clean before attaching the hydraulic hoses.
4. Connect the return hose first and disconnect it last to minimise/avoid trapped pressure within the tool.
5. Make sure the hoses are connected to the correct couplers.
6. Move the hydraulic circuit control valve to the 'ON' position to operate the tool.
7. The rotation of the drill bit can be reversed by rotating a lever on the lower part of the tool.
8. The tool is in 'neutral' when the lever points upwards.
9. The speed of the tool is increased the further the lever is rotated either side of the vertical.
10. Adjust the speed to suit the job.
11. Usually the best position for the lever is half-way between vertical and horizontal.
12. Squeeze the trigger partially to start the drill. The piston will cycle at a low rate to make it easier for the drill bit to enter the job surface. Fully depress the trigger as necessary to complete the work.
13. Adequate down pressure is important.
14. Pull the drill bit out of the job periodically with the bit still rotating to clear the hole.
15. If the drill bit binds in the hole, reverse the rotation direction to help backing out the drill.
16. Keep the drill bit centred in the hole.
17. The tool requires preventive maintenance after every use underwater.
18. In cold weather, preheat the hydraulic oil at low engine speed. Normally oil temperature should be at or above 10°C (50°F) before use.

HAMMER DRILLS – OPERATIONAL SAFETY

1. Divers should receive training in the use of the tool before using it operationally.
2. Follow the manufacturer's instructions.
3. The diver should ensure he is in a secure and safe position before operating the tool.
4. Do not inspect or clean the tool while the hydraulic power is still on.

(continued . . .)

(continued . . .)

5. Ensure that the hoses are tightly connected to the hose couplers before energising the hydraulic power source.
6. Never rest the tool on your foot.
7. Never point the tool at anyone.
8. Never start the tool while it is laid down.
9. Never 'ride' the tool with one leg over the handle.

Hydraulic nut splitter

When it is impossible to remove a nut by conventional unscrewing, the final option is to split it open. This is achieved using a hydraulic nut splitter. Control of the splitting blade can be conveniently maintained by the use of a hydraulic hand pump (see Fig. 12).

Fig. 12 Hydraulic nut splitter

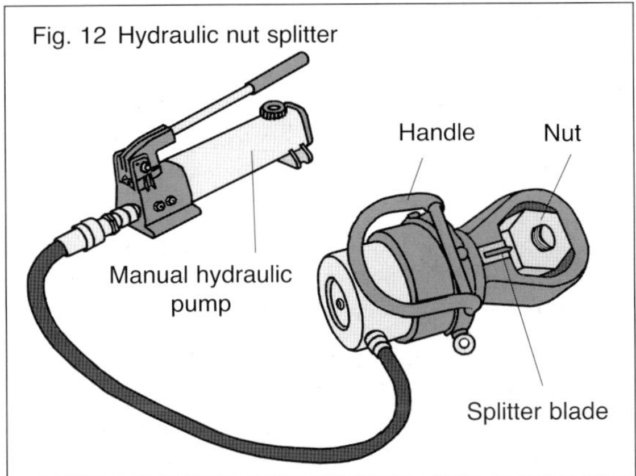
Handle
Nut
Manual hydraulic pump
Splitter blade

Splitter blades can fracture and occasionally need replacing. Always ensure that the blade is in the correct position before applying pressure. The blade has a few millimetres of leeway in its slot, but if the blade is not set to 100% cover the nut, even excessive force may not split the nut. In this case the splitter will have to be repositioned to cut a new flat on the nut.

High pressure water with grit entrainment

A jig is installed over the area to be cut. A nozzle travels on a track along the line of cut and it is controlled hydraulically from the surface. The unit can have a TV camera positioned close to the nozzle. The operation is very quick and produces a neat, clean cut.

HP WATER WITH GRIT ENTRAINMENT
OPERATIONAL SAFETY

1. Because the operation is very noisy, the diver must wear a hard hat to reduce the noise and to aid communication.
2. When the unit is operating the diver must keep well clear to avoid possible limb or equipment damage.

Diamond-wire cutter (Fig.13)

This tool can be used to cut pipe. It can be installed by either divers or ROV.

A tool to cut 36-inch pipe, for example, would be over 2m high, nearly 2m wide and 1m long (6ft x 6ft x 3ft) and weigh over 400kg (880lb) in air.

For diver installation, it is lowered by crane together with its hydraulic power hose(s). The divers can guide the final positioning of the tool over the pipe. When the tool is in place, the pipe clamps are activated from the surface.

When the drive jig is started, a wire (which is made up of diamond-impregnated collars) runs over 2–4 pulleys which are progressively lowered until the moving diamond-wire makes contact with the pipe and starts to cut.

The diver must keep well clear during cutting operations (say, 5m (16ft) away) from where he can report the progress of the cut. The operation is easy to set up and quiet. It can cut contaminated pipeline and can be achieved without a diver present.

Fig. 13 Diamond-wire cutter

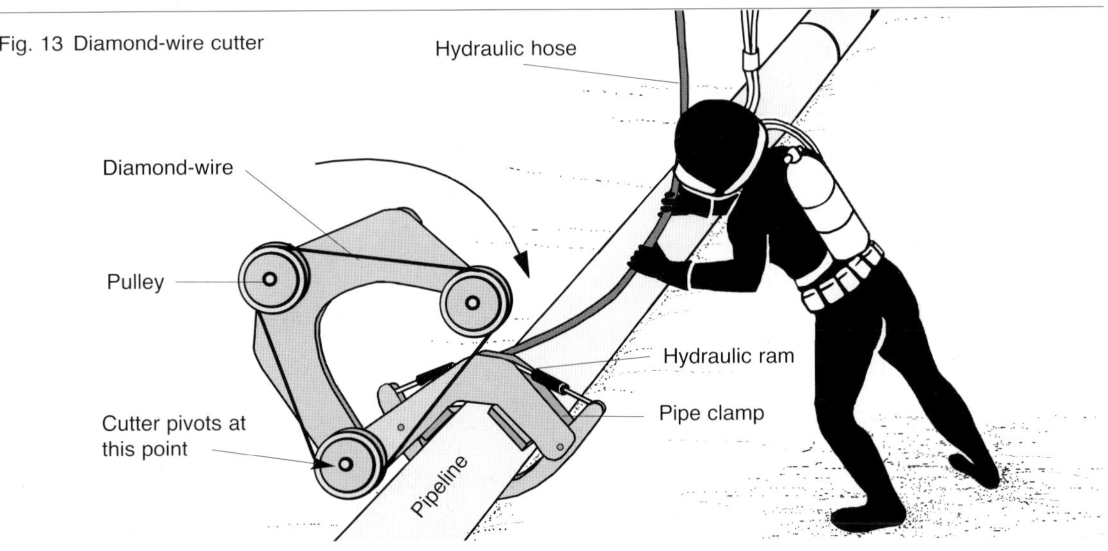
Hydraulic hose
Diamond-wire
Pulley
Hydraulic ram
Pipe clamp
Cutter pivots at this point
Pipeline

3.3 UNDERWATER WELDING

There are two basic arc welding processes:

1. Flux shielded arc welding.
Typically, this is manual metal arc welding in which short, flux-coated electrodes are used. The electrode is burnt and consumed in the process providing the metal necessary to fill the weld. This method is the most widely used and is known as manual metal arc (MMA) in the UK or shielded metal arc welding (SMAW) in USA. A typical layout of equipment is shown in Fig. 1.

Fig. 1 Typical layout for MMA welding equipment

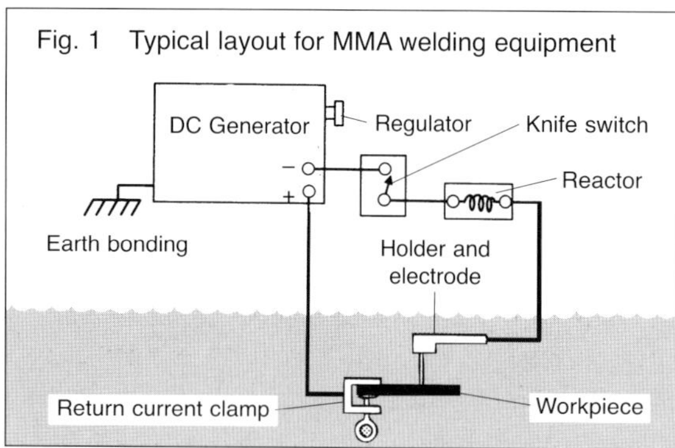
DC Generator
Regulator
Knife switch
Reactor
Earth bonding
Holder and electrode
Return current clamp
Workpiece

Underwater wet welding most commonly uses negative polarity, ie: the cable from the electrode holder is attached to the negative (straight polarity) side of the circuit, and the cable from the earth clamp is attached to the positive terminal (reverse polarity) side of the circuit. Reversing the polarity causes electrolytic corrosion of the metallic parts of the electrode holder and diver's equipment.

2. Gas shielded arc welding.
Typically, this is when an arc is struck between a non-consumable tungsten electrode and the workpiece. This is known as tungsten inert gas welding (TIG) in the UK or gas tungsten arc welding (GTAW) in the USA. Filler material in the form of a bare metal rod is added into the molten pool by the welder-diver.
An alternative method is where an arc is struck between a consumable bare metal wire electrode fed from a reel into the weld pool. This is known in the UK as metal inert gas welding (MIG) and in USA, as gas metal arc welding (GMAW).
Typical equipment layouts are shown in Fig. 2.

There are two main categories of underwater welding – wet welding and dry welding. There are two sub-categories of dry welding: hyperbaric and one-atmosphere welding. All three types are described below.

1. Wet Welding:
Manual Metal Arc (MMA) or
Shielded Metal Arc Welding (SMAW).
This method uses basically the same equipment as surface welding but with insulated torch and cable

Fig. 2 Gas Shielded Arc welding equipment

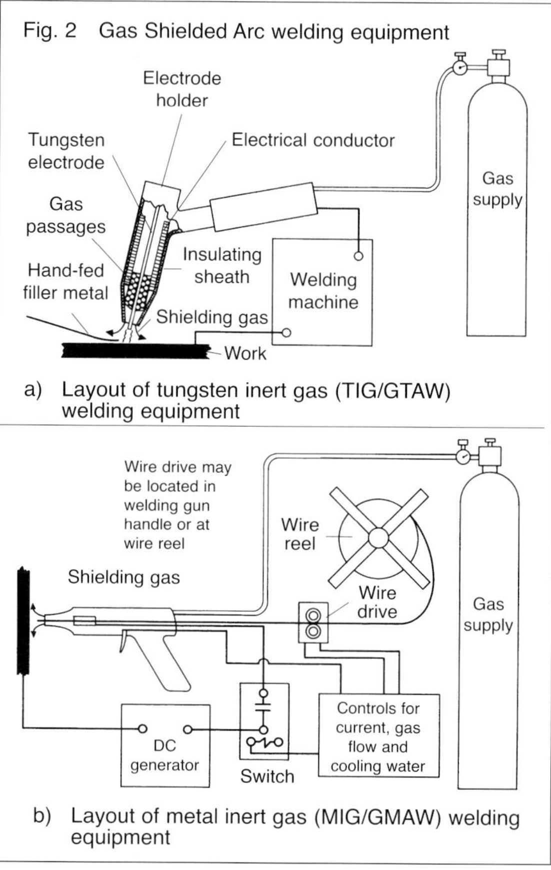
Electrode holder
Tungsten electrode
Electrical conductor
Gas supply
Gas passages
Insulating sheath
Hand-fed filler metal
Welding machine
Shielding gas
Work
Wire drive may be located in welding gun handle or at wire reel
Wire reel
Shielding gas
Wire drive
Gas supply
Controls for current, gas flow and cooling water
DC generator
Switch

a) Layout of tungsten inert gas (TIG/GTAW) welding equipment

b) Layout of metal inert gas (MIG/GMAW) welding equipment

joints and with special waterproof electrodes. Underwater electrode holders must not be used for surface work; they are designed to be water-cooled and will rapidly overheat if used topside.
Although wet welding was once considered inferior to surface welding, technological developments have enabled good quality wet welds to be achieved to internationally recognised standards.
Manual metal arc welding is the most widely used wet process and is carried out by creating an electric arc between a flux-covered metal electrode and the workpiece (see Fig. 3). The heat developed by the arc results in the melting of the parent metal

Fig. 3 Manual metal arc welding (MMA/SMAW)

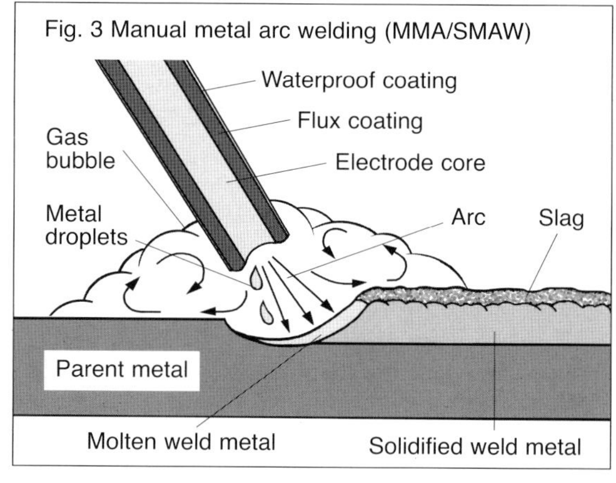
Waterproof coating
Flux coating
Gas bubble
Electrode core
Metal droplets
Arc
Slag
Parent metal
Molten weld metal
Solidified weld metal

parts, the core wire and the flux covering. Under the action of the arc the flux decomposes into gas which shields the molten metal from the surrounding water. Current flow forces droplets of molten metal from the core of the electrode to cross the arc to the weld pool (thus enabling overhead welding to be carried out). The main metallurgical problem with all wet welding methods is the high rate of cooling of the molten weld pool. To counteract this the flux coating on the electrode forms a layer of slag over the weld metal which not only helps reduce the rate of cooling but also helps to smooth the face of the weld. (The terminology of a weld is shown in Fig. 4). The various types and positions of welds are shown in Figs. 5–6.

Before welding commences, the workpiece needs to be prepared. In addition to cleaning, joint faces need to be bevelled prior to welding. The various types of bevel are illustrated in Fig. 6.

There are two main wet welding techniques:

1. The 'stringer,' 'touch' or 'drag' technique where a constant contact is maintained between the electrode covering and the work. The electrode is dragged across the work and pressure applied by the welder-diver so that the weld metal is deposited in a series of beads or strings. The technique is ideal for fillet welding and suitable for most underwater work.
2. The 'manipulative' or 'weave' technique in which the welder holds a constant arc which he controls by manoeuvring the electrode, but does not apply pressure to it. Beads can be applied with a significant weave but this technique calls for an expert and experienced operator.

Some common problems and their possible causes are illustrated in Fig. 7.

Fig. 4 Terminology of a weld

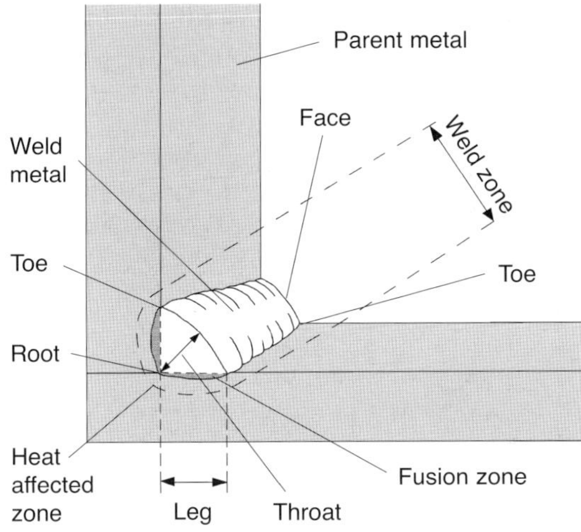
Parent metal
Face
Weld zone
Weld metal
Toe
Toe
Root
Heat affected zone
Leg
Throat
Fusion zone

Fig. 5 Basic wet welding positions

a) Flat
b) Horizontal/ Vertical
c) Vertical down
d) Overhead

Fig. 6 Terminology of welds, joints and grooves

a) Types of welds

Fillet weld, Groove weld, Bead weld, Plug weld

b) Types of joints

Butt, Lap, Tee, Corner, Edge

c) Types of grooves for pre-weld preparation of joints

Square, Single J, Single bevel, Double bevel, Single U, Single V

Fig. 7 Common welding defects and possible causes.
In simple terms: the current affects the penetration; the voltage affects the shape of the profile.

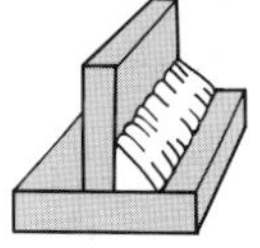
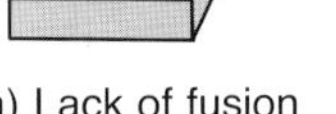

a) Lack of fusion
Cause:
- Electrode angle <30° or >45°
- Travelling too fast
- Low current
- Poor cleaning
- Arc deflection

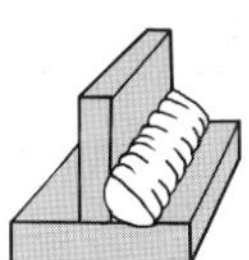

b) Lack of penetration
Cause:
- Electrode angle <30° or >45°
- Electrode too large
- Low current
- Welding over gaps

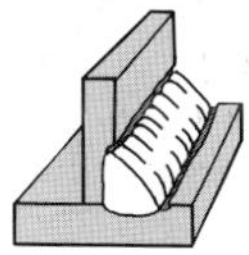

c) Undercutting
Cause:
- Electrode angle <30° or >45°
- Inadequate access to joint
- Arc too long
- Voltage too high
- Wrong electrode
- Travel speed too slow

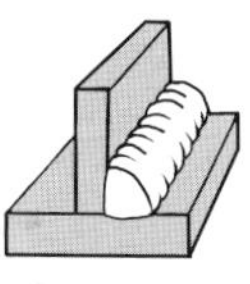

d) Convex fillet weld
Cause:
- Poor bead placement
- Travel speed too slow
- Low current
- Low voltage

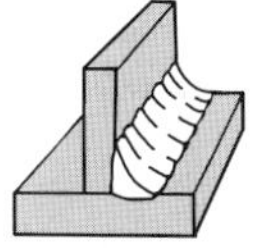

e) Concave fillet weld
Cause:
- Amps too high
- Travelling too fast
- Voltage too high

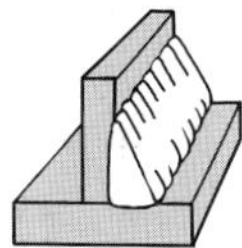

f) Unequal leg length
Cause:
- Poor bead placement
- Voltage too high
- Wrong electrode
- Travel speed too slow

Operational Factors

There are at least five main factors that need to be taken into consideration when wet welding. A shortfall in any one of these can make it difficult to produce a good quality wet weld.

1. PERSONNEL
   Training, skill and 'on-the-job' experience are essential in order to produce the highest quality wet welding.

2. EQUIPMENT
   Most of the equipment required for underwater wet welding is the same as that used for conventional welding used above water. However, there are some important modifications and additions:
   a) An isolation switch (circuit breaker or knife switch) must be included in the system.
   b) Welding cables and connections used underwater must be fully insulated.
   c) The electrode holder must be designed for underwater use and an appropriate visor must be used.
   d) Rubber insulating gloves are essential.

   Fig. 8 lists the basic minimum equipment requirements for underwater wet welding.

Fig. 8 Recommended minimum equipment requirements for underwater wet welding

1. DC welding generator, inverter or rectifier with minimum upper limits of 350 amps and 65 OCV.
2. DC circuit breaker (twin pole, single action, 400 amps minimum).
3. Voltmeter/ammeter or clamp meter
4. Welding cables (50mm^2 minimum).
5. Dinze-type connectors throughout.
6. Secure ground/earth connector.
7. Underwater electrode holder (commonly known as a 'stinger').
8. Appropriate electrodes.
9. Electrode quiver.
10. Chipping hammer and wire brush.
11. Die/peanut grinder and burrs.
12. Insulating rubber gloves/diving dress.
13. Appropriate flip-up welding shield c/w 8 or 9 glass.
14. Hat-mounted lighting.

Underwater visibility and lighting:
The diver must be able to clearly see the arc and the results of the weld. Hat-mounted lighting is strongly recommended, even in good visibility.

Supplementary equipment:
1. Grit blasting or jetting equipment.
2. Power tools (eg, wire brush, chisels, angle grinder).
3. Fitting-up equipment (eg, clamps, screw dogs, wedges).
4. Rigging and associated equipment.
5. Staging, if required.

Welder stability:
Never try to weld while free-swimming – use a stage.

3. ELECTRODES
   The correct choice of electrode is essential. Conventional water-proofed surface electrodes rarely produce a high quality wet weld underwater and can be difficult to use, prolonging the welding time and causing frustration/fatigue to the diver-welder. Use only a good quality electrode designed for underwater use.
   The most commonly used underwater electrode is a 3.2mm ferritic electrode with a normal current range of 120–180 amps, depending on the job and position. 2.5mm electrodes are frequently used with austinitic stainless or nickel electrodes with currents as low as 80 amps. 200–300 amps may be used with 4mm electrodes. Electrodes larger than 4mm are not recommended for underwater use since the arc density drops with larger sizes.

4. MATERIALS
   a) Carbon steels: Wet welding is most commonly carried out on carbon steel. Some carbon steels are not easily wet-weldable and suffer from hydrogen embrittlement, high hardness and prone to cracking along the heat-affected zone or fusion boundary. Thorough testing by the completion of wet-welding procedures should be carried out to ensure the weldment meets the required quality or specification.
   b) Low carbon, low alloy, mild steels: These are wet-weldable but production methods or older materials may cause problems depending on their chemistry. The carbon content has the most significant effect on the weldability of the material, irrespective of its type or grade; however it is not the only element to be taken into consideration. The CE (carbon equivalent), which takes into account all the siginificant elements, should be used to assess the weldability of the material.
   c) Stainless steel: It is not uncommon to weld stainless steel underwater, particularly in the nuclear industry. Generally these stainless steels are in the 300 range and can be wet-welded relatively easily, providing the correct electrode is used to avoid centre-line cracking in the weld.
   d) Unknown materials: Where critical or load-bearing welds are required on unknown materials (and the original material or mill sheets are unavailable) a chemical analysis should be made of the materials to be welded. Then a welding procedure or similar test should be qualified on equivalent materials prior to production welding.

5. ENVIRONMENT
   a) Good visibility is essential to achieve high quality underwater wet welding; visibility less than 0.5m (19in) generally results in deterioration of the weld quality.
   b) Strong water currents can affect the weld by washing away the protective gases generated

by the degradaton of the flux during the welding process.

c) *Swell or wave conditions* can also wash away these gases, as well as impair the welder-diver's ability to maintain stability.

d) *Contaminated water* may adversely affect the diver and the properties of the weld.

e) *Maintaining the welder-diver's body temperature* is essential for prolonged periods of welding to prevent loss of concentration.

Wet welding Codes and Specifications

To enable control of the quality of welding and welders, it is normal practice to follow a Code or Specification. These Codes and Specifications detail the essential variables to be recorded, testing requirements and acceptance criteria. The American Welding Institute's *D3.6M: 1999 Specification for Underwater Welding* is universally used on the majority of projects. An ISO Standard (which closely complies with AWS D3.6) is currently being developed. Always check the latest specification applicable.

The AWS D3.6 specification was first published in 1983 and has been revised several times since then. It is intended to provide a choice of weld quality on a 'fitness for purpose' basis. It covers all the welding methods discussed in this chapter and sets out four classes of welds (identified as Class A, B, C or O) which can be broadly defined as follows:

- *Class A welds:* Comparable with above-water welds by virtue of specifying comparable properties and testing requirements.
- *Class B welds:* For less critical applications, where lower ductility, greater porosity and larger discontinuities can be tolerated.
- *Class C welds:* For applications where load-bearing is not a primary consideration and which satisfy lesser requirements than Class A, B and O.
- *Class O welds:* For applications which must meet the requirements of another Code or Specification.

2. Dry welding:

a) Dry hyperbaric welding

This method uses either the semi-automatic or the manual metal arc welding processes. Welding is carried out at ambient pressure in a dry environment. The weld area can be enclosed in three ways:

a) FULL-SIZED HABITAT. An open-bottomed chamber enclosing the whole area, the welder and his equipment; it is filled with an appropriate gas mixture at ambient pressure (see Fig. 9). The welder-diver may be dressed in lightweight diving equipment or he may change headgear into a surface-type breathing apparatus and coveralls. The habitat may have pipe-handling frames attached or they may be separate.

There are two methods of diver access to welding habitats:

1. *Dry transfer* where the diving bell mates with the habitat and divers climb through, directly into the habitat (see Fig. 9).
2. *Wet transfer* where the diving bell is lowered alongside the habitat and the divers exit the bell in the usual way entering the habitat via a lock.

In addition to the pipeline connection habitat, other types of application include:

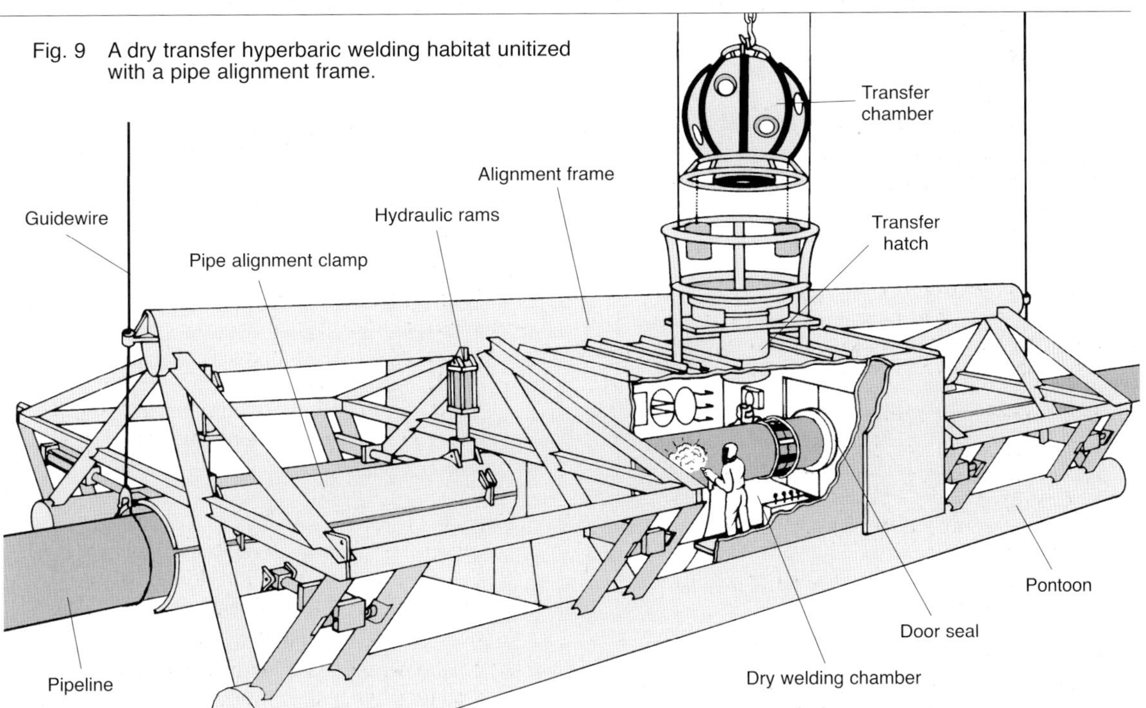
Transfer chamber
Alignment frame
Guidewire
Hydraulic rams
Transfer hatch
Pipe alignment clamp
Pontoon
Door seal
Pipeline
Dry welding chamber

Fig. 9 A dry transfer hyperbaric welding habitat unitized with a pipe alignment frame.

Fig. 10 Habitat for ship's bottom repair

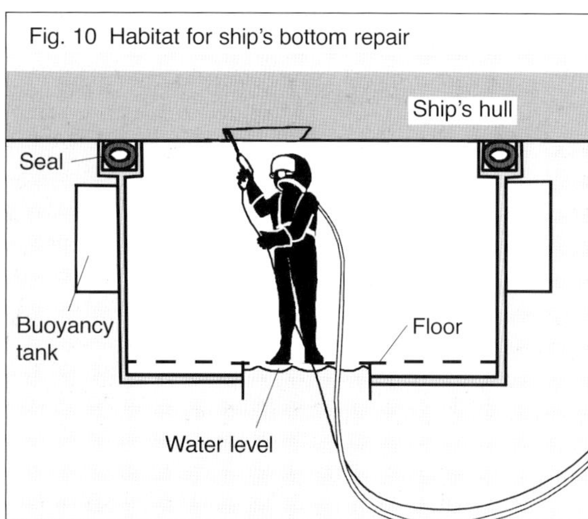
Ship's hull
Seal
Buoyancy tank
Floor
Water level

Fig. 11 Habitat for vertical face repair

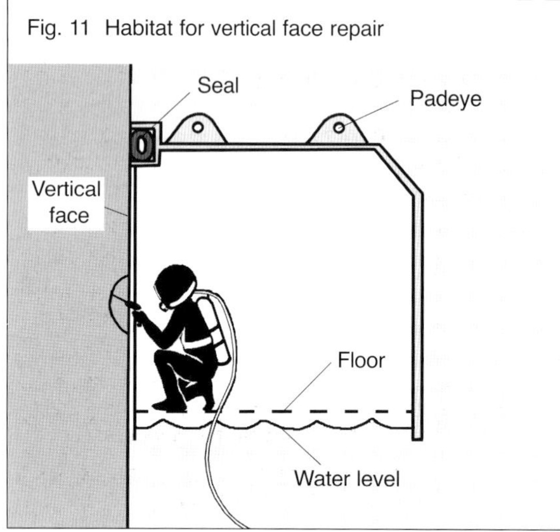
Seal
Padeye
Vertical face
Floor
Water level

– ships' bottom (Fig. 10).
– vertical face repair (Fig. 11).
– vertical, steel tubular repairs (Fig.12).

b) MINI-HABITAT. A small chamber enclosing the weld and the upper half of the welder-diver's body (see Fig. 13). The water in the chamber is displaced by an inert gas or by air and the welding is performed by one of the two processes referred to above.

c) PORTABLE DRY BOX. This encloses the weld area only (see Fig. 14).
Metal inert gas (MIG) or gas metal arc (GMAW) is normally used. A gas is introduced to displace the water in the box, usually an argon mixture. The box is transparent. The diver works from outside the box, in the water, and reaches into the opening on the underside of the box. A vent in the top of the box helps to clear the welding fumes.

b) Dry, one-atmosphere welding

In this method the welder-diver is transported by a one-atmosphere transfer submersible to an

Fig. 12 Habitat for vertical steel tubular repair

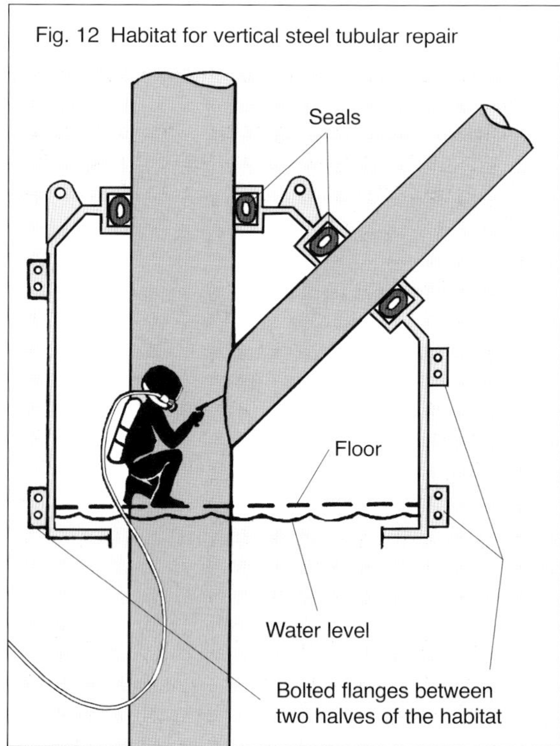
Seals
Floor
Water level
Bolted flanges between two halves of the habitat

Fig. 13 A sectional welding mini-habitat placed around a pipeline

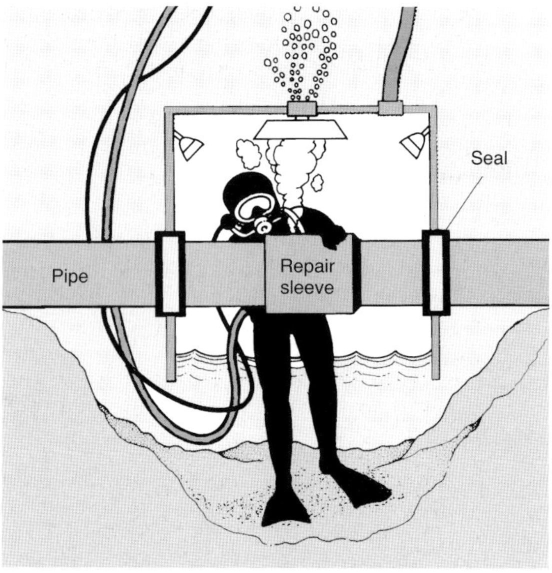
Seal
Pipe
Repair sleeve

Fig. 14 Portable dry box

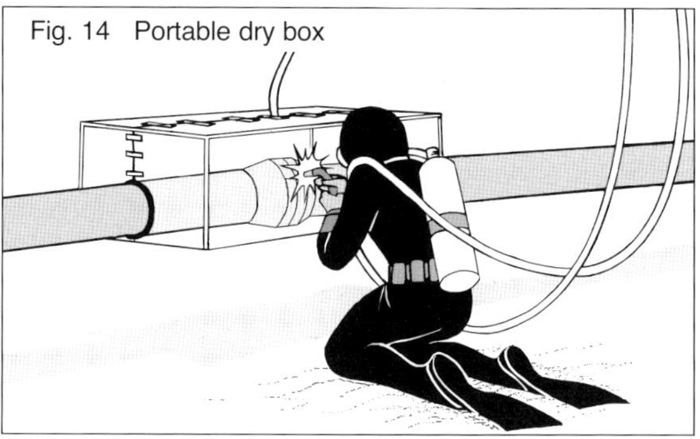

underwater chamber in which the environment is maintained at one atmosphere (see Fig. 15). Water sealing can be a problem with this method.

In terms of process, dry hyperbaric welding and one-atmosphere welding are the same except that dry hyperbaric welding is conducted under pressure.

Fig. 15 A one-atmosphere fully-enclosed welding habitat

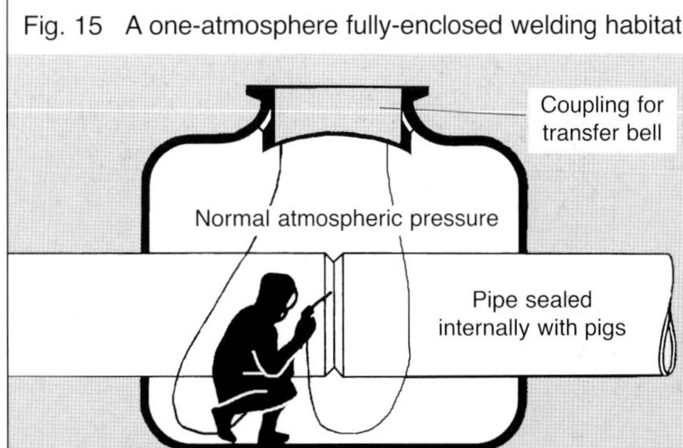
Coupling for transfer bell
Normal atmospheric pressure
Pipe sealed internally with pigs

UNDERWATER WELDING OPERATIONAL SAFETY

1. *Environmental considerations*
   a) Ensure that environmental conditions are safe. Check the sea state, state of the tide, rate and direction of the tidal stream and the weather forecast.
   b) Check that there is adequate visibility underwater, especially where there might not be a groove to follow in the workpiece.
2. *Equipment*
   a) The electrical power source must be insulated.
   b) The welding machine frame must be earthed before starting any operation.
   c) Ensure that all electrical connections are clean and securely made.
   d) Ensure that all cables are undamaged and fully insulated. Protect topside cables from damage. To reduce inductance they need to be snaked or flaked out rather than coiled. Do not lay them on top of each other.
   e) Ensure that the welding generator is of the correct type. For MMA a constant current (CC) machine is used; for MIG welding a constant voltage (CV) machine is required.
   f) Determine the amperage, which is dependent on the size of the rod/electrode. The larger the rod, the higher the amperage – usually 200–300 amps.
   g) Set the correct voltage values on the welding set for the type of work and depth:
      i) overhead welding (in this case *only*, the polarity is reversed and the amperage is reduced).
      ii) vertical-up welding.
      iii) down-hand welding.

Fig. 16 Voltage drop in power supply cables

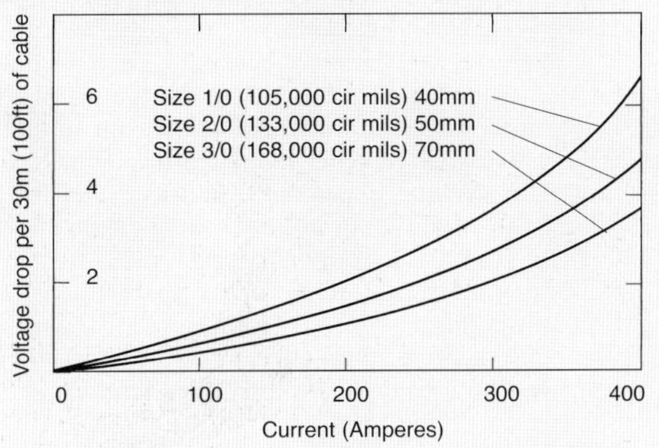
Voltage drop per 30m (100ft) of cable
6
4
2
Size 1/0 (105,000 cir mils) 40mm
Size 2/0 (133,000 cir mils) 50mm
Size 3/0 (168,000 cir mils) 70mm
0
100
200
300
400
Current (Amperes)

   h) Adjust voltage for operating depth [10V per 30m (100ft)]. (See Fig. 16).
   i) In wet welding the current should be off at all times except when actually welding. The tender should never close the circuit unless specifically directed by the diver-welder.
3. *Torch and Electrodes*
   a) Use only torches specifically made for underwater use, especially when wet welding.
   b) Check that the torch and all joints in the cable are properly insulated, especially when wet welding.
   c) Check that the correct electrodes are being used.
   d) Check that the electrodes are waterproofed and stored in a container to keep them dry until required. Never use damaged electrodes.
   e) Ensure that the correct polarity has been selected for the job specifications.
   f) Wash and dry the electrode holder each day after use.
4. *The Diver-Welder*
   a) Ensure that a steady stage or platform is provided from which the welding can take place.
   b) Do not start to weld unless you are certain that there is no hazardous material nearby which may be affected by the heat generated.
   c) Always wear gloves. Rubber gloves should be worn to insulate your hands, especially when wet welding. For dry hyperbaric welding, leather or asbestos gloves are preferred to protect your hands from the heat of the welding arc.
   d) Always use the appropriate grade of welding filter to protect your eyes.
   e) Ensure that your diving suit is undamaged. Insulate any internal metal parts. If wearing a hot water suit, wear a rubberised undersuit.
   f) Secure the ground (earth) clamp to the work. This is especially important when welding together pipelines each of which may have different magnetic polarities, making it necessary to earth them in more than one place.

(continued . . .)

(continued . . .)

g) Position the earth so that you cannot accidentally get between the electrode and the workpiece, thus becoming part of the secondary circuit, especially when wet welding.

h) Only change or tighten the electrode when it is cold and there is no current in the circuit.

i) Never point the electrode holder towards yourself.

j) Do not allow the electrode to touch any part of your suit or body.

k) Inspect metallic parts of your diving equipment for signs of electrolytic corrosion.

l) When working in an enclosed area make certain that no escaped gases are being trapped nearby underwater, especially when wet welding.

5. *Working on Structures and Pipelines*
   - Repairs to structures:

a) With regard to supply boat landings, debris and dumping cement, etc, observe precautions as for other diving operations.

b) No ROVs are to approach the work site without prior consultation with the Diving Supervisor, especially when wet welding.

- Pipeline tie-ins or repairs:
  1a and 1b above apply, plus the following:

a) Valves and by-passes at both ends of the pipeline and any interconnecting pipeline systems must be shut and locked.

b) Where possible, risers should be drained to sea level and pig traps etc, opened.

c) Platform and shore terminal personnel must be strictly instructed not to undertake any actions which could result in a variation of pressure in the pipeline being worked upon.

d) No pressure tests are to be performed on any interconnected pipelines during hyperbaric welding operations.

e) The electrical neutrality of the pipeline is to be maintained at all times.

f) No operations which can result in abnormal noise or vibration being transmitted down the pipeline can be permitted without full consultation with the Diving Supervisor (eg, drilling operations, piling, etc).

g) No nearby marine operations are to be undertaken which could conceivably result in distortion of the alignment of the pipe(s), for example, anchor movements and positioning of pipeline covers.

3.4 UNDERWATER CONCRETING

Concrete sets as a result of a chemical reaction, not by drying out. When prepared correctly, it sets underwater just as quickly as it would in air, as long as it is not disturbed during setting.

When poured underwater, it can suffer from leaching out of some of the cement content unless the proper procedures and precautions are followed. Concrete cannot be poured, for example, in fast-running water unless a cofferdam is used. Even where there is little or no current certain precautions need to be taken both in the proportions used in the mix and in the pouring procedure.

To prevent the concrete from spreading too much it can be set into steel shutters or walls built up of bagged concrete. This has the added advantage of protecting the concrete from potential scour damage. Shutters are normally used where the shape and level of the concrete is important – the diver achieves the final shape by rough screeding the concrete underwater. Shutters are not used where the shape of the mass of concrete is not critical (eg, where the only function is to provide a hard base for a structure). In these cases the concrete is allowed to adopt its own angle.

In all cases a consistent supply of concrete which has a sufficiently high cement content to cater for the inevitable loss through leaching, is essential to the success of the job.

Pouring Concrete

Before concrete can be poured it is essential that the site is cleared of all unsuitable material using any suitable method, such as diver-directed grab, suction pipe or air lift. If the site is likely to silt up again rapidly, the concrete should be poured as soon as possible after clearing the site.

There are two main ways of pouring concrete underwater: by tremie or by skip.

1. TREMIE

A tremie is a steel tube. At the topside end is a hopper into which the concrete is poured (see Fig. 1). The diver directs the lower end to deliver the concrete to where it is needed underwater.

The diameter of the tremie should be 5–6 times greater than the maximum size of the aggregate being used. The concrete should be mixed so that it is very workable in order to enable it to flow easily down the pipe and spread out over a wide area (up to 2.5m (8ft) radius). If a larger area needs to be covered it is generally better to use more than one tremie, or to repeat the process several times at different points.

The equipment required consists of a tremie tube, a receiving hopper, a supporting structure/crane and a crane skip or pump. The tremie tube is normally segmented to enable it to be adjusted to suit the

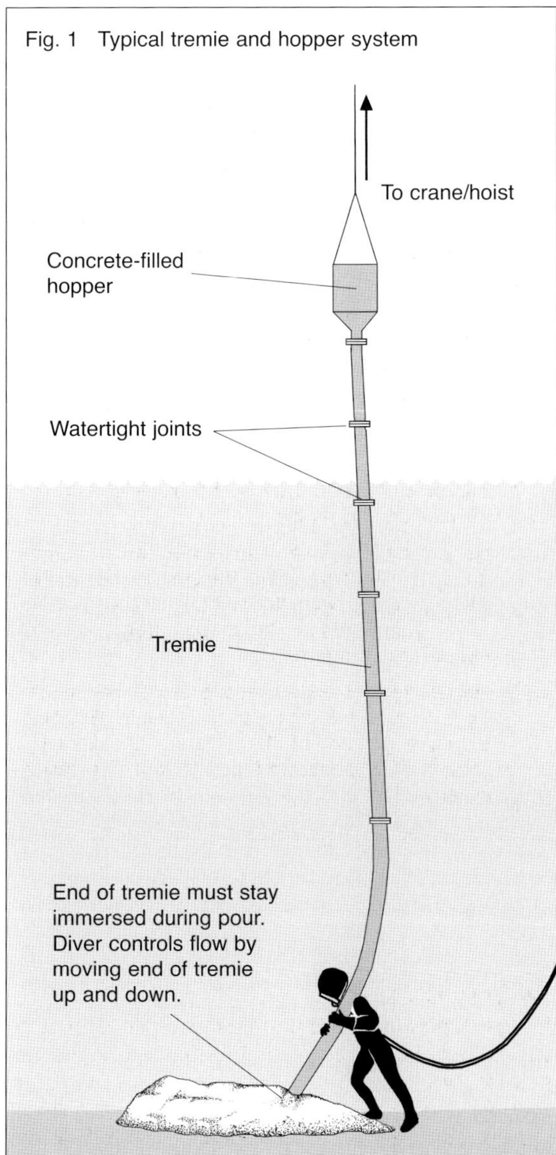
To crane/hoist
Concrete-filled hopper
Watertight joints
Tremie
End of tremie must stay immersed during pour. Diver controls flow by moving end of tremie up and down.

Fig. 1 Typical tremie and hopper system

working depth. Both the hopper and tremie tube are suspended from a crane or overhead structure and are fed with concrete from either a crane skip or pump.

Before the pouring commences the tremie tube is set hard down on the work site. A travelling plug may then be set into the hopper outlet. As concrete is poured into the hopper it forces the plug down the tremie tube thereby displacing the water from the tube and preventing the concrete from falling directly through the water. When the plug reaches the bottom, the tremie tube is raised slightly to allow the plug to be forced out. The concrete flows out in all directions, including upwards. To encourage the concrete to flow outwards, the end of the tremie tube should continue to be slightly raised without lifting it clear of the concrete mass. If the end of the tube is removed from the concrete mass (by accident or attempting to clear a blockage), the concrete in the pipe will rush out, losing its cement content as it mixes with water, and disturbing any unset concrete all of which may need to be removed before the operations can recommence.

A successful pour requires a continuous supply of concrete at the correct consistency and should not be interrupted for more than 10 minutes.

Where large volumes of concrete are to be poured the usual method is by direct pumping. The diver directs the pouring of the concrete by manoeuvring the end tube. Slightly raising and lowering the tube controls the rate of flow. The tip of the tube should be kept below the surface of the poured concrete by, say, about 15cm (6in). When one layer of concrete has been poured (from 30cm–2m (1–7ft) deep) the diver can immediately retrace his path pouring the next layer directly over the previous one.

A vibrator may be used to help level the concrete.

When the required height of concrete has been poured the tremie tube should be cleared and, if another area needs to covered, it should be relocated and the process repeated. If for any reason the tremie tube has to be made shorter, proper provision must be made to support the lower lengths of the tube while the necessary adjustments are made.

2. SKIP

An alternative to the tremie tube is a bottom-opening skip (see Fig. 2). The skip has a fitted canvas cover to protect the concrete during the lowering phase and an enveloping metal shroud which prevents the wet concrete from suddenly surging out when the doors are opened in the bottom of the skip. The shroud is designed to allow the concrete to flow only when the skip is raised slowly off the bottom.

Loaded skips must be lowered and raised slowly to avoid disturbing the concrete contents – especially when entering the water, approaching the bottom and when raising the skip for pouring.

Fig. 2 Examples of bottom-opening skips

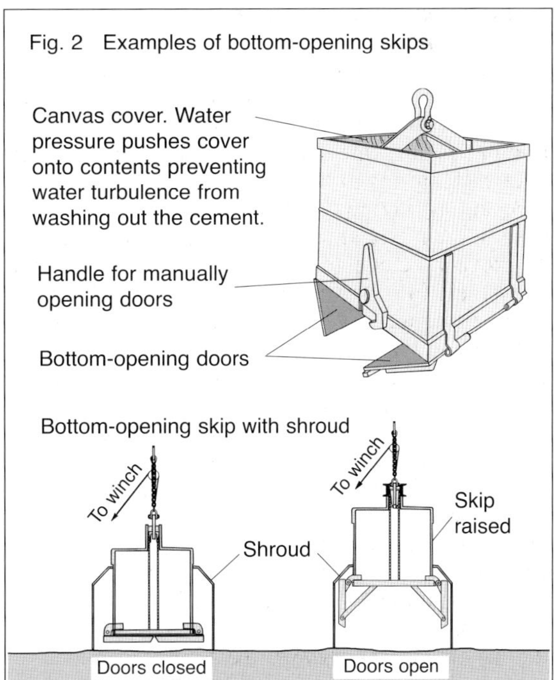
Canvas cover. Water pressure pushes cover onto contents preventing water turbulence from washing out the cement.
Handle for manually opening doors
Bottom-opening doors
Bottom-opening skip with shroud
To winch
To winch
Shroud
Skip raised
Doors closed
Doors open

UNDERWATER CONCRETING 3.4

Skips may be opened manually on site or by a surface operator. In both cases it is helpful to have a diver direct the skip into position.

Because skip pouring is intermittent, tremie-poured concrete is usually faster, and more homogeneous. Skips, however, are often used for thin pours and where a screeded finish is required.

Concrete usually has various additives, including curing compounds. When it cures underwater, the top 1–2cm (1/2–3/4in) suffers from 'laitence' (ie, the concrete breaks out of its mixture and the ingredients separate). Before the next 'lift' is poured, the laitence needs to be removed using a small airlift, LP waterjet or even by brushing it aside. 'Lifts' are limited in depth since the weight of too much liquid concrete can push out lower shuttering (even 45-tonne concrete blocks).

Shuttering

There are two types of shuttering that can be used for concrete work: temporary and sacrificial.

1. Temporary shuttering is removed after the concreting is completed. It is commonly made of steel.
2. Sacrificial shuttering remains in place and becomes a permanent fixture. It is usually provided in the form of concrete blocks of various sizes (eg 2 or 4 tonne). Dry grout-filled bags can be used when a small-volume pour is to be contained.

Shutters are placed by divers and sealed using dry grout-filled bags or 'Speed-crete.'

Sealing of shuttering is essential before any pour begins. If the shuttering should leak or a structural failure occur during a pour, not only will the concrete be washed but it may also harden where it is not wanted. This hardened concrete may, therefore, need to be removed before the concrete work can resume.

Divers place the grout-filled bags into any cracks or joints around the shuttering. The grout reacts with the water and hardens, stopping any leaks of the concrete when the pouring begins. Shuttering may be back-filled with rock to strengthen the structure and reduce the amount of concrete required for the pour. Whether or not this method is adopted depends on the engineering constraints of the job. Repair or reinforcing of a harbour or sea wall often uses sacrificial concrete blocks for shuttering. The shuttering is back-filled with rock before the concrete is poured. In this way the concrete block shutters become part of the repair structure.

Temporary shuttering is used to contain the concrete until it has hardened enough to allow the shuttering to be safely removed. The size of the pour determines whether a single or multi-piece shutter is used. This type of shuttering is commonly used for concreting the locking keys of two caissons. In this instance shuttering is placed on either side of the keys and secured in place with 'divvy bars.' The base and any joints are sealed with grout-filled bags or Speed-crete prior to the pour.

Placing and sealing of shuttering is considerably more difficult in low or nil visibility conditions where the diver will have to rely on feel alone to successfully complete his task.

The diver may be required to dive inside the shuttering to be able to seal it successfully. This can be particularly hazardous for the diver in respect of access and egress – especially if divvy bars are being used to secure the shuttering. Good communications with the diver are essential at all times.

Glossary

Divvy bar. A divvy bar is a steel rod with a very coarse thread onto which a large wing-nut is threaded. The wing-nuts are then tightened to secure the shuttering in place for the pour. The divvy-bar is passed through a sacrificial plastic tube which is placed between the shutters so that the bars can be removed after the pour.

Pug is a cement mixture similar to Speed-crete but with a longer curing time. It is made by preparing a paste made from mixing water with Portland Cement or underwater grout. It is used by divers to plug cracks/holes through which the poured concrete might escape.

'Speed-crete' is a quick-curing grout that is mixed in small quantities and sent down to the diver to spread into the joints and gaps in the shutter work. Dry 'Speed-crete' powder is mixed with a small quantity of water to form a paste-like consistency. It is then immediately sent down to the diver as it has a very rapid setting time. The process may be repeated many times before the diver has successfully sealed the shutter work. Where greater time is needed, pug should be used.

UNDERWATER CONCRETING – OPERATIONAL SAFETY

1. The physical nature of pouring concrete requires attention to be paid to good manual handling practice.
2. The delivery pipe must be properly inspected and maintained between operations in order to avoid the possibility of bursting.
3. For safety and operational reasons it is essential to maintain good voice communication between the diver and the diving supervisor at all times
4. Concrete is alkaline. This can cause irritation and rashes. Divers should wear protective clothing or shower frequently between pours.
5. Cement dust can collect in the diving equipment, helmet, etc. All equipment should be washed regularly.

3.5 EXPLOSIVES

Theory

An explosion is a chemical reaction during which the original material is rapidly converted into a gas so that pressures of about 50,000 bars and temperatures of about 3,000°C are created. This reaction is called detonation. It can travel at speeds from 1,500m/sec to 9,000m/sec through the explosive material. Slower reactions are propagated by thermal conduction and radiation and are known as deflagration.

Underwater, the reaction forms a sphere of gas which displaces the surrounding water at speeds greater than sound (approximately 1,500m/sec in water) and produces an intense pressure wave. As the gas expands, so its pressure drops.

The most important phenomenon associated with underwater explosions is the initial shock wave and associated peak pressure and impulse (see Fig. 1).

Fig.1 Underwater detonation

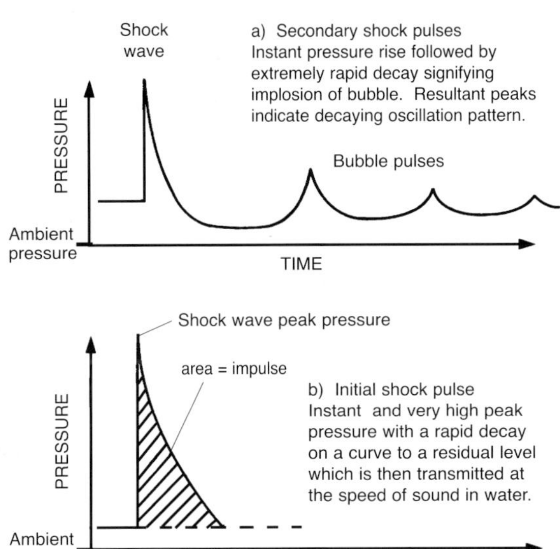
Shock wave
a) Secondary shock pulses
Instant pressure rise followed by extremely rapid decay signifying implosion of bubble. Resultant peaks indicate decaying oscillation pattern.
Bubble pulses
PRESSURE
Ambient pressure
TIME
Shock wave peak pressure
area = impulse
b) Initial shock pulse
Instant and very high peak pressure with a rapid decay on a curve to a residual level which is then transmitted at the speed of sound in water.
PRESSURE
Ambient pressure
TIME

This initial shock wave is caused by the detonation wave travelling through the explosive and precedes the subsequent pressure increase caused by the gaseous products of the shock wave reaction.

The second phenomenon associated with underwater explosions is the action of the sphere of gas between detonation and venting to the surface.

This sphere of gas alternately expands and collapses in a series of rapid cycles. The bubble oscillates for up to 10 cycles, creating diminishing secondary pressure pulses and is attracted towards rigid boundaries rather than to a free surface. The effect of this bubble must be taken into account when planning underwater explosions.

Applications

Before undertaking any operations involving explosives all necessary permissions must be in place. In the UK, a valid Police Explosives Licence or Certificate is required in order to purchase, store or use explosives.

Many underwater tasks can be most efficiently carried out by the use of explosives.

Typical applications include:

- Fragmentation of rock pinnacles, bedrock, hard coral and conglomerates prior to dredging.
- Cutting or clearing of trenches for cables and pipelines in rock, conglomerates and soft sediments.
- Breaking and scattering wrecks and obstructions.
- Dismantling of seabed structures prior to their recovery, eg wellheads, platforms, anchor chains, etc.
- Repair and maintenance tasks such as pipeline weight coat removal, pipeline venting, removal of marine growth, cleaning of areas prior to inspection and explosive welding and swaging.

Types

Most commercial explosive is nitro-based and is available with high or low detonating velocities.

Low explosives, such as cordite and gunpowder burn at rates of up to 300m/sec. High explosives detonate at 3,000–9,000m/sec and develop large amounts of energy which produce a shattering effect known as 'brisance.'

High explosives which are used almost exclusively underwater, are of two types:

1. PRIMARIES, such as fulminates and lead azide, which can be easily detonated by heat, friction or shock. They are mostly used in detonators and require careful handling.

2. SECONDARY explosives are more stable, have much greater strength and, being safe to handle and transport, are used as main charges. All need a detonator to initiate them.
   The most stable types may also require boosting by a commercial PETN booster (about 14.5gm (1/2oz) is usually sufficient) or by taping a dozen short strands of sealed detonating cord around the detonator; a single strand of cord is not enough.

Techniques

DRILLING AND BLASTING

The most economic method of using explosives is to insert and tamp the charge into a pre-drilled hole. This is most suitable when the bench height (the thickness of rock to be removed) is more than 2m (6ft).

For small operations a hand-held rock drill is sufficient. A template should be used by the diver to ensure that the holes, which should be plugged as they are drilled, are correctly spaced. Drilling should never be undertaken closer than 2m (6ft) to a charged hole.

Drilling of multiple holes can also be carried out from the surface using one or more drill heads. Here the diver's role is confined to assisting with the lining up of the drill(s) and to the laying and wiring of the charges.

Where an overburden is likely to cause problems, the drill is passed through an outer casing which penetrates the sediment and the surface of the base

Explosives Recommended for Underwater Use				
Product	Description	Depth limitation	Duration of immersion	Velocity of detonation
Special gelatine (90%) Special gelatine (80%)	Nitroglycerine medium strength gelatinous explosive obtainable in various cartridge sizes or bulk packing.	Down to 6m	A few days	2,500m/sec to 5,000m/sec
Subgel Fortex	High density strength nitroglycerine-based explosives.	Down to 46m	Several weeks	5–6,000 m/sec
Plaster gelatine	Nitroglycerine high strength gelatinous putty.	Down to 45m	Several weeks	6,300 m/sec
Submarine blasting	Nitroglycerine high strength, high density, rubber-like explosive. Cannot be moulded.	In excess of 300m	Several weeks	7,500 m/sec
PETN Plastic explosive 1509	PETN and plasticiser high density medium sensitivity explosive. High brisance.	No limit	Several months	8,400 m/sec
RDX Plastic explosive PE4, C4, T4	High brisance, stable explosive. Suitable for shaped charge operations.	No limit	Several months	8,700 m/sec
Nitromethane (sensitised)	Liquid propellant-based explosive, requires sensitising with an amine. Can be used for shaped charge operations but PETN and RDX are better.	No limit if sealed in a container	Requires sealed container	6,300m/sec
Hydrazine Astrolite	Liquid propellant-based explosive sensitised with appropriate nitrate compound; difficult to handle unless purchased in twin bottle mixer packs (Astro-Pak).	No limit if sealed in a container	Requires sealed container	8,700 m/sec
Cast explosives Pentolite RDX/TNT	Pourable mixture of TNT and PETN 50/50. More stable than Pentolite.	Unlimited	Unlimited	7,400 m/sec
Slurry explosives Methylamine Nitrate (man)	Special slurries can be used in trenching charges.	25m	Unlimited	Up to 6,200 m/sec
Detonating cord	Waterproof coated cord with an explosive filling (PETN, RDX, HMX).	Dependent on cord size	Ends have to be sealed	6,500 m/sec to 8,200 m/sec depending on cord size and explosive type.

Fig. 2 Drilling a charge hole

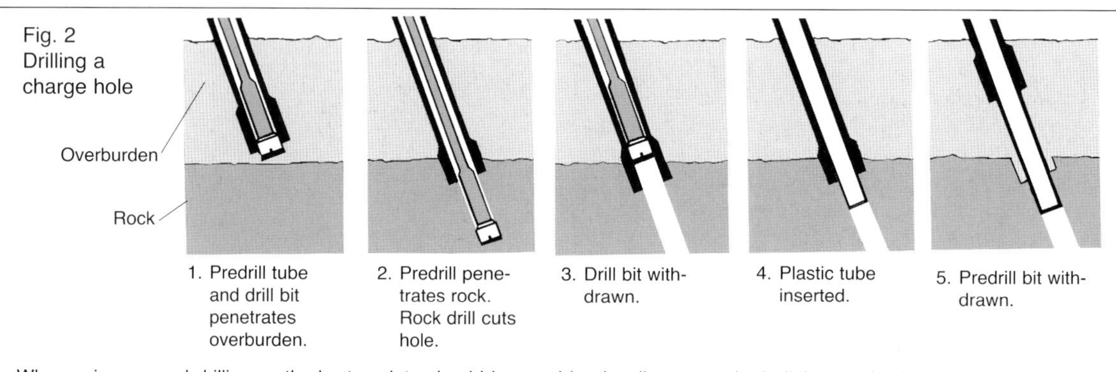
Overburden
Rock
1. Predrill tube and drill bit penetrates overburden.
2. Predrill penetrates rock. Rock drill cuts hole.
3. Drill bit withdrawn.
4. Plastic tube inserted.
5. Predrill bit withdrawn.

When using manual drilling method a template should be used by the diver to assist in lining up the holes. Holes should be plugged as they are made and drilling should never be carried out closer than 2m (6ft) from charged drill holes.

rock; the charge is then loaded directly from the surface and the risk of the hole filling is eliminated.

CALCULATION OF CHARGES

Calculation of charges is usually the responsibility of an explosives expert rather than a diver. However, as a rough guide, about 1kg/m^3 of low velocity underwater explosive should ensure good fragmentation and allow for misfires; this can be reduced by 10% if the holes are drilled at an angle of 3:1.

In general, about two thirds of a hole is filled with explosive. Spacing between the holes will depend on the charge concentration while the depth of drilling should equal the bench height plus the hole spacing.

BULK BLASTING/PLASTER SHOOTING

This involves the use of bulk explosives to break up submarine rock or to create trenches in silt and sand. It is best used in depths of 8m (26ft) or more because it relies on the head of the water to tamp down the charge and because it can produce high levels of waterborne shock and vibration. A typical pattern would involve 22kg (50lb) charges spaced at 2m (6ft) intervals (see Fig. 3).

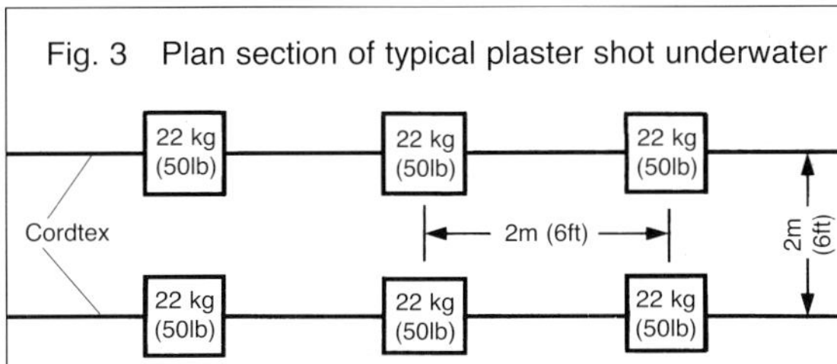
22 kg (50lb)
Cordtex
2m (6ft)
2m (6ft)

Fig. 3 Plan section of typical plaster shot underwater

A trench through soft material can be blasted by using a single line of boreholes. Approximately 0.5kg (1lb) of explosive per 75cm (30") centres should give a trench 1m (3ft) deep by 2m (6ft) wide at the mudline (see Fig. 4a).

An alternative method, which enables a trench to be blasted in one operation, is to attach charges to a weighted rope. Initiation is effected by high strength detonating cord threaded through the top of the charges (see Fig. 4b).

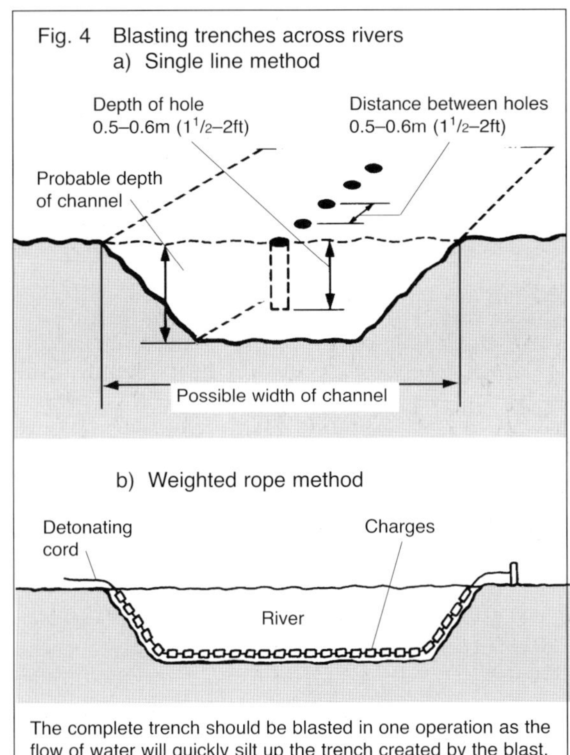
a) Single line method
Depth of hole
0.5–0.6m (1½–2ft)
Distance between holes
0.5–0.6m (1½–2ft)
Probable depth of channel
Possible width of channel
b) Weighted rope method
Detonating cord
Charges
River

Fig. 4 Blasting trenches across rivers

The complete trench should be blasted in one operation as the flow of water will quickly silt up the trench created by the blast.

SHAPED CHARGES

An alternative to drilling and blasting or plaster shooting to break up bedrock or to create an underwater trench is to use shaped trenching charges. They are particularly effective if a cut of 2m (6ft) or less is required or if the water depth restricts drilling/blasting or plaster shooting. The charge is held in a container with a sealed conical inner liner which directs the explosive force downwards (see Fig. 5). It is, however, important that any overburden should be cleared away to ensure optimum effect.

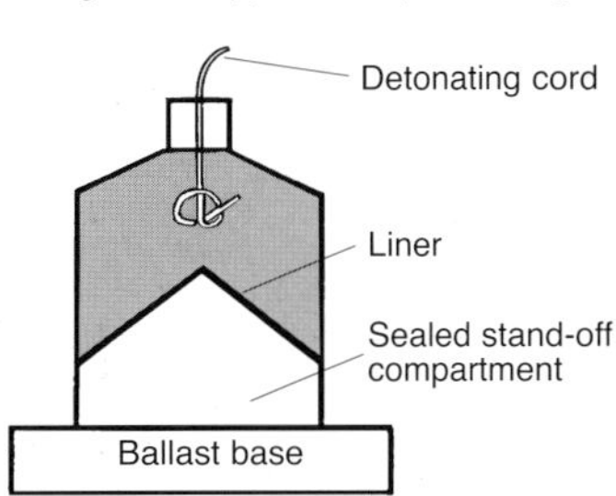
Detonating cord
Liner
Sealed stand-off compartment
Ballast base

Fig. 5 A typical shaped charge

Depending on the rock material, charges are usually spaced 1–2m (3–6ft) apart. For small operations, charges can be loaded by hand. Large operations require a recoverable laying frame holding 30–90 charges. Diver assistance may be required. Shaped charges are normally deployed under the supervision of an explosives engineer.

CUTTING CHARGES

Most of the specialised cutting charges now available are normally used under expert supervision.

A simple cutting charge can be made by sealing a length of copper pipe at both ends and forming a saddle of high velocity explosive, such as PE4, along its length. About 170–225gm per 30cm (6–8oz per foot) of 13mm bore pipe will cut up to 1.6cm (⅝") of mild steel. Alternatively, proprietary products such as 'Flexicut' can be used (see Fig. 6).

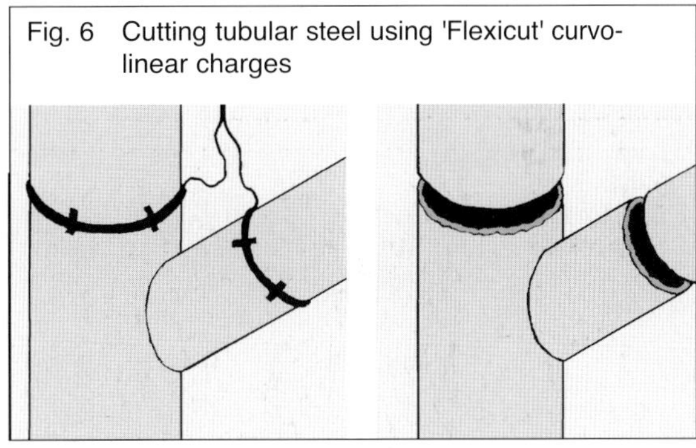

Fig. 6 Cutting tubular steel using 'Flexicut' curvolinear charges

LIQUID EXPLOSIVES

If the charge case has not been supplied by the manufacturer it is important that his directions be followed exactly. Some explosives are not compatible with steel. And the charge must be made up in strict compliance with the stated specifications.

WELLHEAD REMOVAL

Most charges which are used to simultaneously cut several strings of casings for wellhead removal, work by creating a 'collision effect.' That is, a column of explosive is simultaneously initiated from both ends sending detonation waves from each end which converge at the centre of the charge.

For most applications approximately 34kg (75lb) of high density explosive is sufficient. For a 9⅝" (24cm) casing a container about 7¾" (18cm) in diameter by 46" (117cm) long will be required. For 13⅜" (35cm) the dimensions should be about 11½x22" (29x56cm). The container, which need not be waterproof, should be designed so that the explosive can be initiated simultaneously from both ends with EBW (Exploding Bridgewire) detonators and boosters or by other special fusing mechanisms. The charge is lowered in its container into the well casing from the surface supported by a T-piece and slung between guide wires (see Fig. 7).

Fig. 7 Explosive wellhead recovery system

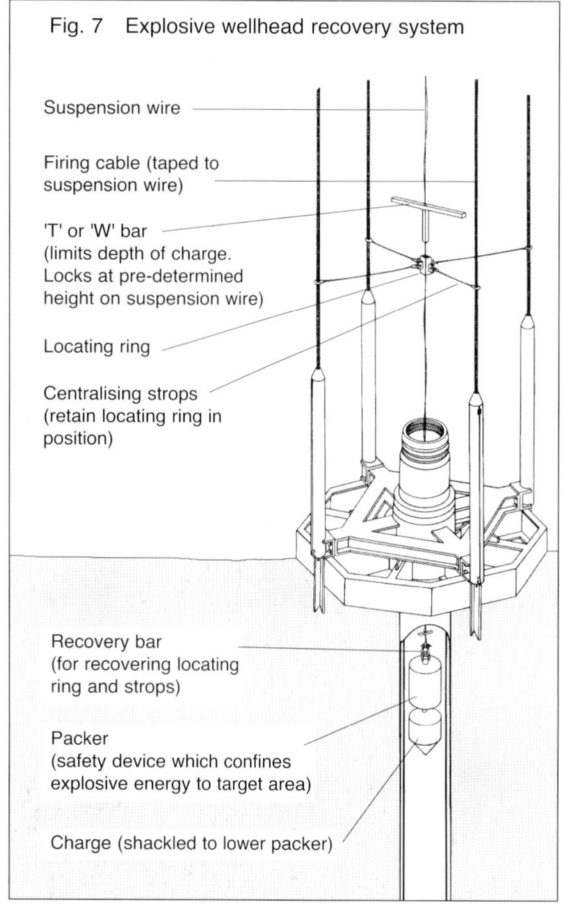
Suspension wire
Firing cable (taped to suspension wire)
'T' or 'W' bar (limits depth of charge. Locks at pre-determined height on suspension wire)
Locating ring
Centralising strops (retain locating ring in position)
Recovery bar (for recovering locating ring and strops)
Packer (safety device which confines explosive energy to target area)
Charge (shackled to lower packer)

The depth at which the charge is placed will depend on the lifting gear available on the recovery vessel – a casing cut 6m (20ft) below the mudline will typically demand a pull of 91.5 tonnes (90 tons) to remove it.

Initiation

Conventional detonators contain a primary explosive which is sensitive to both shock and friction and they can therefore create a hazard when handled underwater or in atmospheric diving systems. For most surface use, detonators that offer safety features are recommended.

There are two types of detonator: plain and electric.

1. PLAIN. Designed to be fired by spark from a safety fuse. When supplied with the fuse already fitted these are known as capped fuses and usually have a bean pole connector for use with the plastic igniter cord. Alternatively they may be supplied with a separate fuse for use for single-shot firing or for charges linked with detonating cord.
   Conventional detonators are available with resistors built into the circuit to increase the initiating voltage requirements: typically two 25 ohm resistors are introduced to produce an overall detonator resistance of at least 50 ohms.

2. ELECTRIC. Particularly suitable for use underwater, these are safer since they allow greater control over initiation. Instantaneous and time delay types are available.
   Electric detonators are also available which do not contain primary explosives, for example Exploding Bridgewire (EBW) which uses a special gold filament bridgewire in contact with a secondary explosive (see Fig. 8). Initiation is through rapid application of energy (3000 volts, 1,000 amps) from a special firing control system (capacitor discharge). The bridgewire vaporises so rapidly that the secondary explosive charge is detonated.

Fig. 8 Standard and EBW detonators

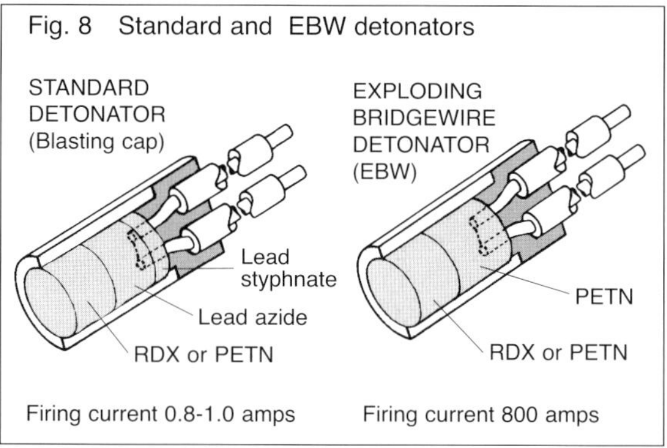
STANDARD DETONATOR (Blasting cap)
Lead styphnate
Lead azide
RDX or PETN
Firing current 0.8-1.0 amps
EXPLODING BRIDGEWIRE DETONATOR (EBW)
PETN
RDX or PETN
Firing current 800 amps

Another type of detonator that contains no primary explosives is the EFI (Exploding Foil Initiator). A necked metal foil acts as the bridgewire. This foil is in contact with an insulating flier material. The foil is vaporised by a high current pulse generated by a similar method to that of the EBW. The vaporisation of the foil causes the flier to accelerate and impact with sufficient energy to cause a secondary explosive (such as HNS) to initiate.

Conventional 1 ohm or 50 ohm detonators are relatively easily initiated by static, other sources of voltage or electro-magnetic radiation. Therefore, radio silence must be enforced before handling these types of detonator. The capacitor discharge EBW or EFI detonating systems are radio frequency-attenuated and are normally considered safe for use without enforced radio silence. There are other RF-attenuated electric detonating systems available

which use electronic circuits such as transformers or integrated circuits to prevent inadvertent initiation by static, radio frequency or other electrical power sources.
The point from which the charge is initiated has an important effect on efficiency. The explosive should always be placed between the detonator and the area where the effect is required. A cone- or prism-shaped charge initiated from the apex is more efficient than a cylindrical charge (see Fig. 9).

Fig. 9 Diagram to show how the placing of detonators and the form of the explosive affects the work of a charge.

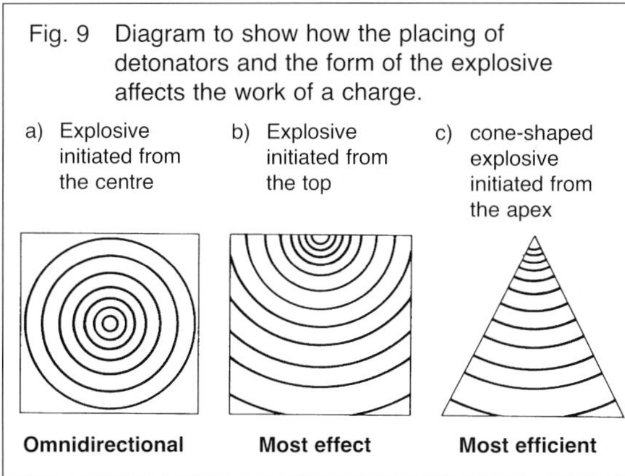
a) Explosive initiated from the centre
b) Explosive initiated from the top
c) cone-shaped explosive initiated from the apex
Omnidirectional
Most effect
Most efficient

FIRING CIRCUITS
Many operations involve the simultaneous firing of several charges. For most applications a simple series circuit (Fig. 10a) is sufficient. The parallel series circuit (Fig. 10b) reduces the possibility of misfires but it is not normally employed with an exploder where more than three detonators are used because of the large currents required. In this event mains firing is advisable.
For very large rounds the parallel series (Fig. 11c) circuit is normally used with mains firing. For proper distribution this should be in the form of a closed loop (Fig. 11a) or a reverse ladder (Fig. 11b).

Dangers to divers from explosions (see also Section 12.12, page 309)

Explosions underwater have several important differences from those in air. Water is much less yielding than air because it is about 800 times more dense and about 10,000 times less compressible than air. As a result, the lethal range for any given charge is three times further underwater than in air.

Fig. 10 Electrical circuits for simultaneous shotfiring

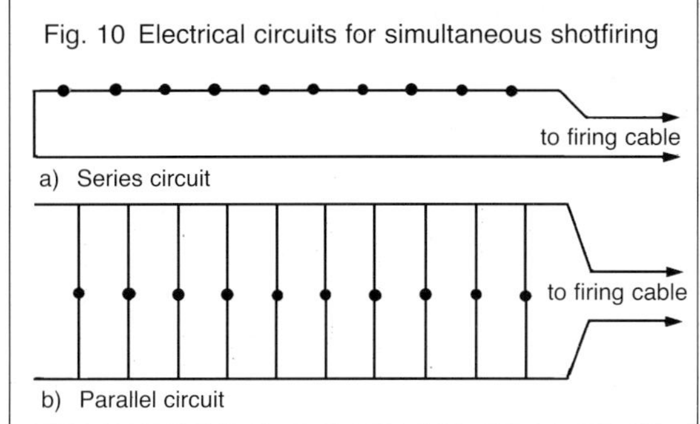
to firing cable
a) Series circuit
to firing cable
b) Parallel circuit

INJURIES TO DIVERS FROM EXPLOSIONS
The shock wave and bubble pulses generated by an underwater explosion can cause significant to fatal injuries. The main injuries involve haemorrhage into and rupture of air-containing organs such as the lungs, large bowel and ears. The brain can also be directly affected. The 'water-ram effect' can also injure the lungs and upper part of the liver.

EXPLOSIONS IN A FREELY SUSPENDED CHARGE
Factors that contribute to injuries include:

a) A shock wave – this lasts only about one millisecond and travels at the speed of sound in water, about 1,500 m/sec (4,900 ft/sec).
b) Subsidiary pulses – these are caused by reflections of the shock wave from a structure or the surface.
c) Water displacement – this is a 'ram-effect' of the water, especially at close range, which moves rapidly to-and-fro as the shock wave passes by.
d) Bubble pulses – the bubble caused by the expanding gas of the explosion reaches a diameter of about 25 times the size of the original explosive solid. The bubble collapses and re-expands several times producing pulses of pressure.

EXPLOSIONS IN ROCK UNDER WATER
Explosions in boreholes in rock prior to dredging have different effects. The shock wave peak pressure can be reduced by 95%, however the duration is increased tenfold. The rise time increases to about a millisecond and the impulse can be reduced by 70%. No bubble pulses occur. As a result, whilst pulmonary injuries can be expected, there is probably a reduced risk of injury from shearing of body tissues.

THE EFFECT OF DIVER DEPTH
When an impulse from an explosion is reflected down from the water surface, it tends to cancel out incoming impulses. As a result, the nearer to the surface a diver may be, the more protected he will be from impulses. The shallower, the safer.

Fig. 11 Mains firing circuits

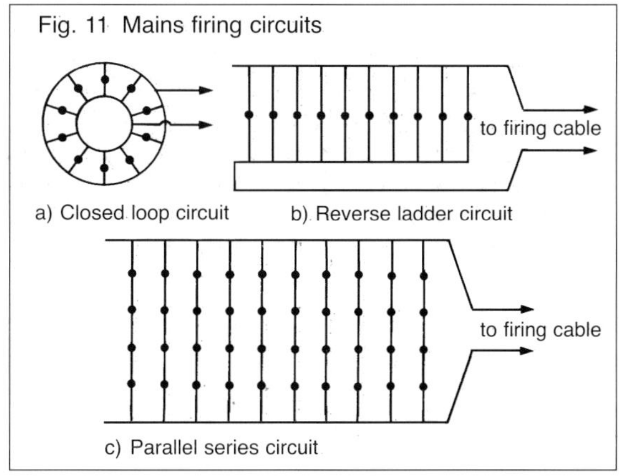
to firing cable
a) Closed loop circuit
b) Reverse ladder circuit
to firing cable
c) Parallel series circuit

SAFE STAND-OFF DISTANCES FOR DIVERS

Many factors can reduce the safe distance from an underwater explosion, such as reflection of the shockwave from structures or the surface. These can cause a funnelling or focussing of the shock wave and impulses. The estimates in Fig. 12 are, therefore, for rough guidance only and refer to a diver in open water not exceeding 50m (165 ft) depth.

Fig. 12 Estimated safe stand-off distances for divers

Charge weight		Stand-off distance		
kg	lb	m	ft	yd
10	22	600	1970	650
20	44	750	2460	820
30	66	900	2950	985
40	88	1050	3445	1150
50	110	1200	3937	1315

EXPLOSIVES – GENERAL SAFETY

Always remember:

- **Explosives are safe, until you forget that they are dangerous.**
- **Ensure all necessary permits/licences are in place before commencing operations.**
- **Only appropriately qualified personnel should handle or use explosives.**
- **Don't trust your memory. Always refer to the safety guides or to the manufacturer's instructions, where appropriate.**
- **Explosives should never be placed underwater without the direct supervision of the diving supervisor, acting with the advice of an explosives expert.**

The following rules should always be observed:

1. Basic explosive, without firing caps, is a fire hazard. Never smoke anywhere near explosives or detonators. There must be no naked lights in the vicinity. Ensure that sparks cannot be created in the work area.
2. Never stow explosive in rusty steel cans. Nitro-glycerine can be absorbed by the rust which then becomes hypersensitive to shock or friction.
3. Protect all explosives from sub-zero temperatures. Most become extra sensitive and, therefore, dangerous when frozen.
4. Never touch an explosive that looks wet or is weeping liquid. It may be dangerously unstable.
5. Never drag or throw explosives. Always treat them with care.
6. Don't leave detonating cord lying around.
7. Never leave explosives unattended.
8. Keep the work area free of unnecessary personnel.
9. Don't allow untrained personnel to handle explosives.
10. Never use steel for tamping explosive. Use wood or nonferrous metal.
11. Water transmits explosive shock waves more efficiently than air. Even a small charge can affect a diver at distances of over 1.5km (1 mile).
12. Explosives should never be detonated until all divers are clear of the water and all vessels are in safe locations.

DETONATORS, etc – SAFETY PRECAUTIONS

1. **DETONATORS AND FIRING CAPS.**
   These provide the greatest hazard. Always handle them with care. An exploding detonator can kill.

a) Never stow detonators with bulk explosive.

b). Always keep detonators in their cases until they are required for use.

c) Only one person should handle detonators.

d) Consult the safety guide to radiation frequency hazards before you handle detonators.

e) Ensure all mobile telephones, radio and radar transmitters are switched off before handling detonators or primed charges.

f) Ensure that the ends of detonators and firing leads are shorted together when not in use.

g) Check all the firing cables and detonators with a safety ohmeter before connecting up.

h) Always use proper dynamo exploders for initiating charges.

i) Secure all firing cables before placing detonators. If the leads are jerked from a detonator it could fire.

j) Place all detonators in a safe place before testing.

k) Never work near power cables or electric meters. They can cause electrostatic hazards.

l) Never work in an electric, thunder or sand storm.

(Detonators safety, continued...)

m) When operating from small boats a buoy should mark the position of the charge. Another buoy should be laid up or down tide of the charge area to enable the boat to be moored and the engine stopped to avoid electrical interference.

n) Some types of detonators can be accidentally initiated by stray electrical charges caused by:

- *Lightning.* At the first sign of lightning, all detonators should be removed and placed in secure storage and the area cleared of personnel.
- *Static Electricity.* This can be generated by snow, dust storms and other atmospheric conditions as well as by moving parts of machinery. For safety, shot-firing cable should be laid carefully and all detonator leads should be shorted and earthed. Leads should not be unearthed and connected up until everything is ready for firing. Earth yourself before handling detonators.
- *Stray Electric Currents.* All machinery and metal structures should be properly earthed.
- *Galvanic Action.* Electric currents can be created by the joining of two dissimilar metals. To avoid this hazard always use a non-metallic tool for loading shot holes and do not mix metals in charge cases.
- *Electro-magnetic radiation.* Any transmitting device can set off a detonator. For safety, the following minimum distances should always be observed:

Mobile communications equipment	10m (33ft)
Transmitters up to 1kW	300m (984ft)
Transmitters up 1–10kW	1km (0.6 mile)
Transmitters 10–100kW	7.4km (4.6 miles)
Transmitters 100–1,000kW	10km (6 miles)

2. DETONATING WIRE and FIRING CABLES

a) Detonator wires should not be unwound until they are ready for use.

b) Twin firing cables should always be used and the ends of the leads kept together and not splayed so that they can form a dipole.

c) The firing cable should be secured to the detonating cord before the detonator is attached and both should be tied off to ensure that no strain can be placed on the cable or the charge pulled out of position – a detonator can be accidentally fired if the leads are jerked from it.

d) The firing cable should be laid directly away from any source of radiation, such as a transmitter.

e) The cable should never be suspended.

f) All spare lead wires should be firmly taped over.

g) The cord should be securely taped to a small rope for its full length to prevent kinks and sharp angles which will cause misfires.

h) Where the cord is to be taken round an angle it is advisable to pass it through a length of spare hose or tape several strands of sealed detonating cord around the angle to the main firing line.

i) When running fuses or firing cables from underwater to the surface, always leave enough slack to deal with tidal changes and surface swell.

3. DETONATING CORD CARE

Remember that detonating cord is an explosive. It can be fired by a sharp blow.

4. MISFIRE PROCEDURES

In the event of an electrical misfire:

a) Retest the circuit with an ohmeter. If it appears complete attempt to fire again using a different initiation source.

b) If this is unsuccessful wait for 30 minutes, recover the charge and inspect all joints. Internal breaks will sometimes show only when the firing cable is under tension.

c) Replace all charges with new ones.

d) Do not attempt to remove a detonator from a charge.

3.6 EXPLOSIVE TOOLS

One form of velocity power tool is an explosively-actuated gun which instantaneously drives a solid or hollow bolt into steel plate above or below water. The projectile is driven by the explosive energy of a cartridge which can be varied for the amount of penetration desired and the thickness of the plate. Main uses are the rapid attachment of steel plates, splinter boxes etc, the construction of cofferdams and the attachment of eye plates and other fixtures for lifting and salvage purposes.

Cox Submarine Bolt-driving and Punching Gun (see Fig. 1)

This is a low-maintenance, explosively-actuated gun which drives special steel alloy, threaded bolts at high velocity into steel plate up to 25mm (1") thick. The plate requires no previous preparation. It is equally effective above and below water and will operate at any depth.

The bolts are of special 100-ton tensile steel with a shearing strength of 10 tons per bolt. They can be used for the attachment of steel plates and wooden patches, for securing bolts, for replacing faulty rivets, to attach lifting bolts and in cofferdam work. Also available are hollow bolts which incorporate a seal removable from the operating side of the structure. The hollow bolts create conduits through which various materials can be supplied. For

Fig. 1 Cox Submarine Bolt driving and Punching Gun – Assembly for firing

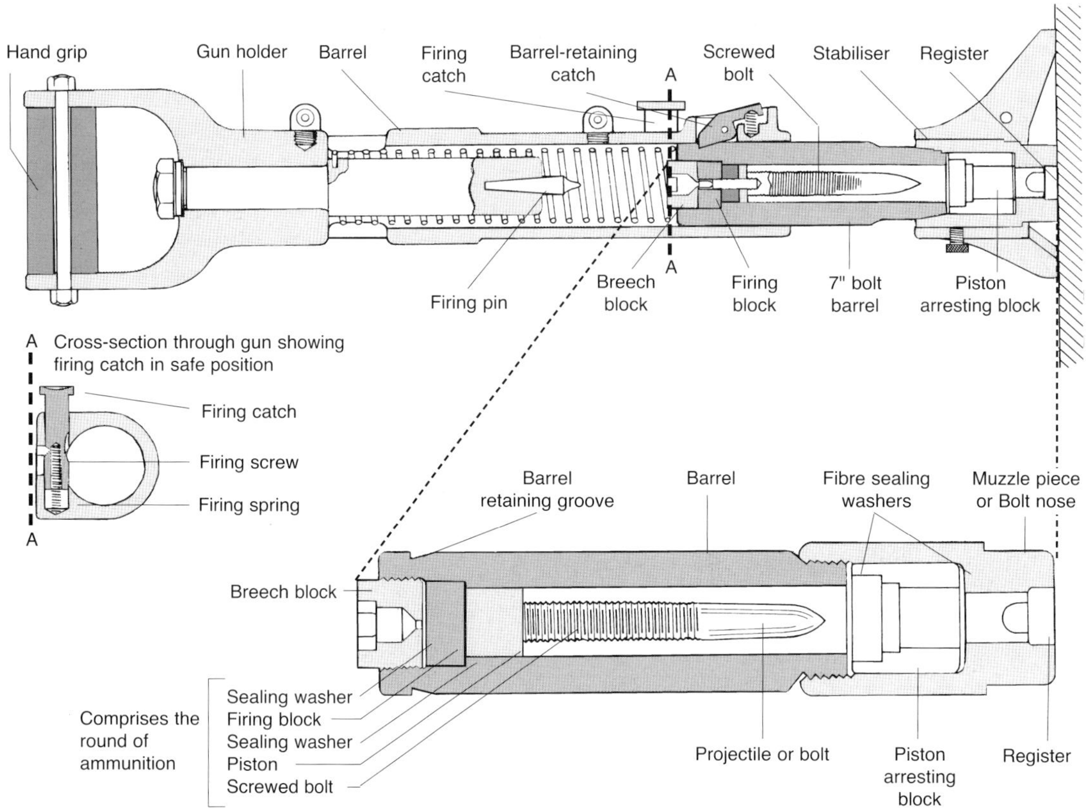

Hand grip
Gun holder
Barrel
Firing catch
Barrel-retaining catch
A
Screwed bolt
Stabiliser
Register
Firing pin
Breech block
A
Firing block
7" bolt barrel
Piston arresting block
A Cross-section through gun showing firing catch in safe position
Firing catch
Firing screw
Firing spring
A
Barrel retaining groove
Barrel
Fibre sealing washers
Muzzle piece or Bolt nose
Breech block
Comprises the round of ammunition
Sealing washer
Firing block
Sealing washer
Piston
Screwed bolt
Projectile or bolt
Piston arresting block
Register

example, they can be used to supply breathing air or compressed air for lifting. They can also be used as a means of introducing electrical circuitry, or for supplying external foam or carbon dioxide gas lines for extinguishing fires.

The gun is a heavy tool to handle and has a powerful recoil. It can be tiring to use, especially when many shots are fired. The handling of the gun should be carefully planned before diving. Consider using a line to sling the gun from the surface.

The diver should brace himself properly to accommodate the recoil.

He should take special care to achieve good alignment, especially when he becomes tired after firing several shots. The better the alignment, the less the recoil. Poor alignment will result in a heavy recoil as well as the risk of the bolt failing to penetrate and ricocheting off the plate.

Tornado T6U Amphibious Cartridge Hammer (see Fig. 3)

The Tornado T6U is an explosively-actuated hammer designed to fire threaded studs or rivets into naval quality steel plate up to 25mm (1") thick. It consists of two parts, a hand set and a barrel assembly which can be changed to allow it to be used above water. A blank safety cartridge is loaded into the breech together with the appropriate fastener. After taking up the safety pressures the tool is then fired.

Fig. 2 Operation of Cox Bolt Gun

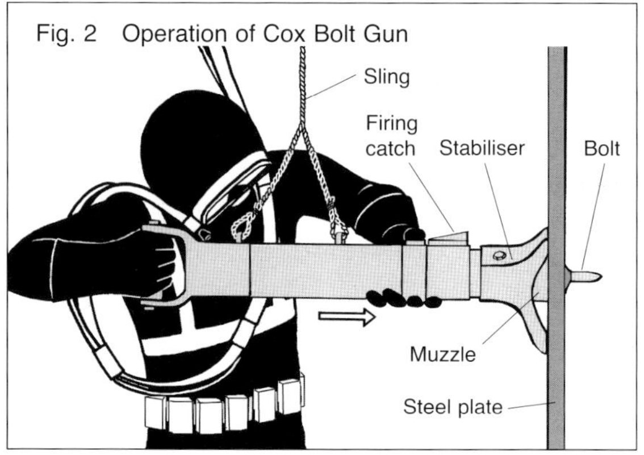
Sling
Firing catch
Stabiliser
Bolt
Muzzle
Steel plate

The hammer may be used to fix steel plates onto steel or concrete surfaces underwater, to fix eyebolts to lift large submerged objects, to fix demolition charges to piers, etc.

OPERATION

1. Select a cartridge and stud together with the appropriate barrel suitable for the thickness of steel. There are two sizes of bore for underwater use: 5/16" and 3/8".

   1/4" bore is only used above water.
2. If possible, test penetration by firing a test shot into the same thickness of steel out of the water using the T6 front section for above-water use

Fig. 3 Tornado T6U Underwater Hammer

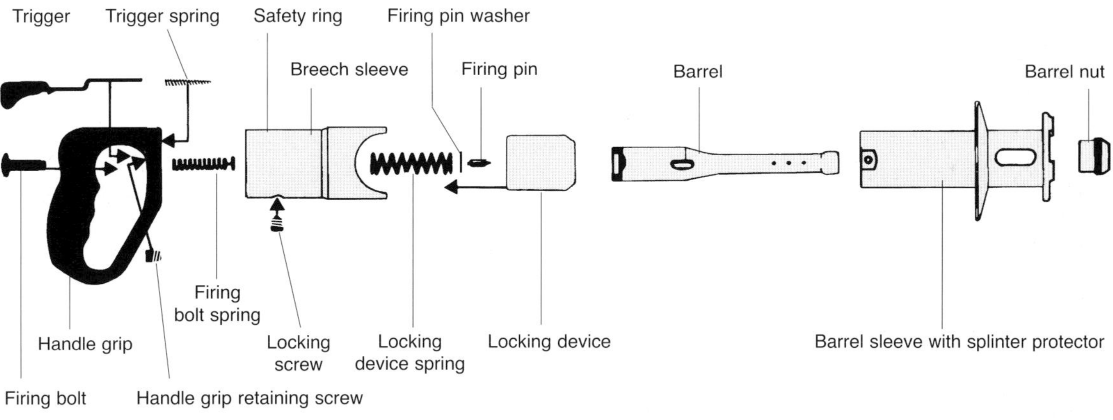
Trigger
Trigger spring
Safety ring
Firing pin washer
Breech sleeve
Firing pin
Barrel
Barrel nut
Firing
bolt spring
Handle grip
Locking
screw
Locking
device spring
Locking device
Barrel sleeve with splinter protector
Firing bolt
Handle grip retaining screw

with its yellow splinter shield. With correct penetration the full shaft should be embedded leaving the threaded portion proud. Adjustments can be made by positioning fasteners in the breech to allow more space (less penetration) or less space (more penetration) between the stud and cartridge.

3. Insert the stud into the barrel.
4. Insert the cartridge into the breech.
5. Close and lock the breech by turning the handgrip to the right.
6. Lower the gun to the diver in the water.
7. Before firing check what is on the other side of the steel plate. Make sure that it does not present a problem.
8. Place the muzzle at right angles to the surface.
9. Push the hammer firmly against the surface to take up the full safety pressure. Where a firm standing is not available, the diver may need extra weights in order to enable him to exert this pressure. Always keep hands behind the protective shield.
10. Squeeze the trigger while maintaining firm contact with the surface.
11. A final adjustment to the penetration may be necessary because of the effect of depth.
12. Reload. It is preferable to reload on the surface especially if the water is murky. This is because debris may enter the breech and cause the hammer to misfire.

    Two or three guns may be used in rotation to ensure fast continuous fixing.
13. After use wash parts separately in B05 oil using washing tanks provided. Allow to dry for 15 minutes. Do not wipe. B05 oil is reusable after settlement.

MISFIRES

If the gun fails to fire check that it is at right angles to the surface and that the full safety pressure has been taken up. If it still misfires return the hammer to the surface to be reloaded.

If the hammer has to be reloaded underwater:

a) Wait 1 minute before opening the breech.
b) Check that the cartridge has been struck correctly.
c) If struck, let the cartridge slip out of the breech. If it does not, eject it by pushing a ram-rod down the muzzle pointing the muzzle away from the body.
d) If not struck, check the firing pin and change it if broken.
e) Never attempt to remove a damaged cartridge any other way.

If the hammer repeatedly misfires strip the tool completely. Check all components for damage and replace as necessary. Thoroughly clean and wash in B05 oil.

TORNADO HAMMER – OPERATIONAL SAFETY

1. Always assume the hammer is loaded until proved otherwise.
2. Never point the hammer at anyone or any part of the body.
3. Use only 5/16" and 3/8" studs underwater.
4. Do not fix through thin, non-resistant material.
5. Do not exceed the recommended charge. If too large a charge is used the bolt can fire completely through the plate.
6. Do not fix nearer to the edge than 5cm (2") in concrete and 2cm (3/4") in steel.
7. Do not exert pressure on the muzzle of a loaded hammer except when firing.
8. Do not drop a loaded hammer.
9. Always fix at right angles to the work surface – good alignment is essential.
10. Make sure that there is nobody anywhere near the area of the bolt on the other side of the plate.

3.7 RIGGING a) PULLING AND LIFTING TOOLS

Whenever a diver joins a new diving operation it is a good idea for him to visit the rigging store to familiarise himself with the operation of the various types of tools he is likely to have to use underwater.

PULLING AND LIFTING TOOLS

The diver has a choice of pulling and lifting tools from ratchet lever hoists to chain hoists and trolleys. They have many underwater applications including the accurate positioning of awkward loads such as heavy riser clamps.

1. Tirfor (also called Griphoist, Greifzug)

Among the most commonly used is a pulling and lifting tool called a 'Tirfor' (see Fig. 1). It is hand-operated with unlimited rope travel. Tirfors are designed for land use but with additional care and maintenance can be successfully used underwater. Several different models of Tirfor are available from lightweight to heavy duty (see Fig. 2). They can be used for any lifting and pulling job within the rated capacities of the machines. They are particularly useful for longer pulls and higher lifts than can be done with other equipment due to the fact that any length of rope can be used.

Tirfors work by pulling directly on the rope, the pull being applied by means of two pairs of jaws which exert a grip on the rope in proportion to the load being lifted or pulled. The Tirfor works by a 'hand-to-hand' principle, like a man pulling a rope, ie, while one hand pulls the other one moves forward to grip and pull in its turn (see Fig. 3). The two hands represent the two pairs of jaws of the Tirfor alternately gripping and releasing the rope.

Fig. 3 The Tirfor Principle

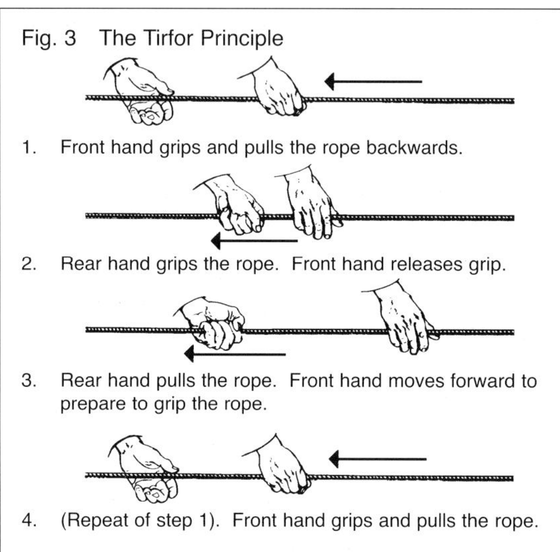
1. Front hand grips and pulls the rope backwards.
2. Rear hand grips the rope. Front hand releases grip.
3. Rear hand pulls the rope. Front hand moves forward to prepare to grip the rope.
4. (Repeat of step 1). Front hand grips and pulls the rope.

RIGGING A TIRFOR (see Fig. 4)

1. Lubricate generously before use.
2. Uncoil the special Tirfor wire rope in a straight line to prevent loops, untwisting of strands or kinks from forming when under tension (see Fig. 8).

Fig. 1 Tirfor

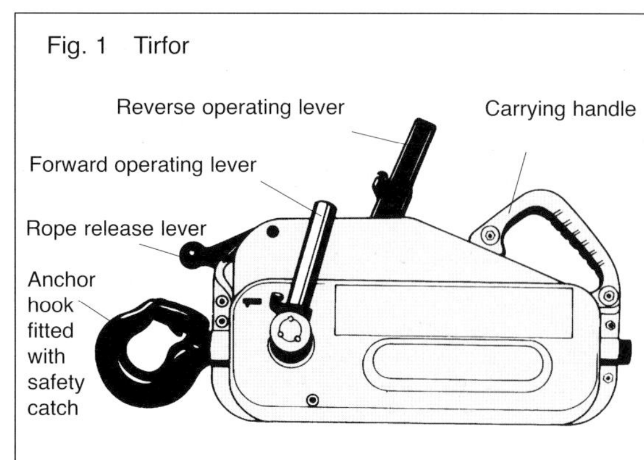
Reverse operating lever
Carrying handle
Forward operating lever
Rope release lever
Anchor hook fitted with safety catch

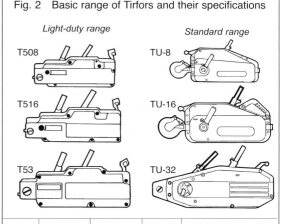

Fig. 2 Basic range of Tirfors and their specifications

Light-duty range
Standard range
T508
TU-8
T516
TU-16
T53
TU-32

Model	SWL Lifting[2] capacity		SWL Pulling[3] capacity		Weight of Tirfor including handle		Tirfor wire rope[1] diameter		Tirfor wire rope[1] min. breaking strain	
	tonnes	tons	tonnes	tons	kg	lb	mm	in	tonnes	tons
T508	0.5	0.49	8	7.9	7.4	16	8.3	3.3	4.8	4.7
T516	0.9	0.89	1.6	1.5	13.7	30	11.5	4.5	8.15	8
T53	1.9	1.87	3.2	3.1	26	57	16	6.4	16.8	16.5
TU-8	0.5	0.49	8	7.9	9.2	20	8.3	3.3	4.8	4.7
TU-16	0.9	0.89	1.6	1.5	20	44	11.5	4.5	8.15	8
TU-32	1.9	1.87	3.2	3.1	29	64	16	6.4	16.8	16.5

1 Standard length 20m (66ft). Other lengths available on request.
2 with a Factor of Safety 5:1
3 with a Factor of Safety of 3:1

3. With the left hand push in and maintain pressure on the release catch 'C' (see Fig. 4a). With the right hand, pull the rope release lever 'P' away from the hook until it is vertical.
   Release catch 'C'. Continue to pull back on lever 'P' until it locks into position. Both sets of jaws are now open.
4. With the machine placed on the ground, insert the fused and tapered end of the wire rope at the rope guide 'A' (see Fig. 4b). Push the rope through the Tirfor until it emerges at 'B'.
   Anchor the machine and the cable hook with the correct slings. Ensure that safety catch 'C' is closed.
6. Pull the wire rope by hand until the rope becomes tight on the load (see Fig. 4c).

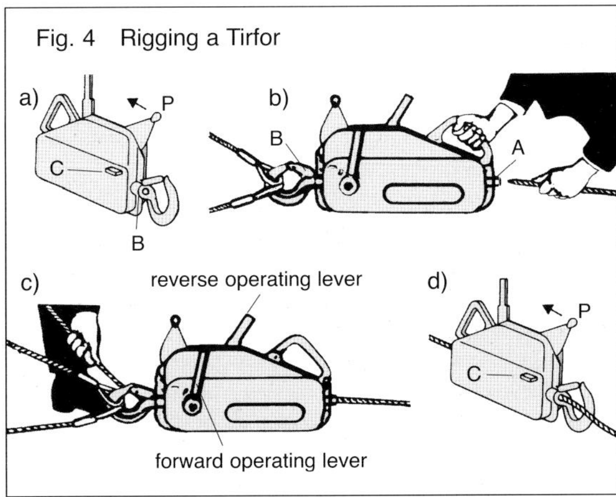
a)
P
C
B
b)
B
A
c)
reverse operating lever
forward operating lever
d)
P
C

Fig. 4 Rigging a Tirfor

7. To engage the machine on the rope, ease the rope release lever 'P' away from the hook. Press and maintain pressure on the release catch 'C' on the side of the machine. Allow lever 'P' to travel slowly back to its original position (see Fig. 4d). Release catch 'C'.
8. The rope is now firmly fixed between the jaws of the machine. To operate the machine, put the operating handle on the forward operating lever and lock it into position by twisting. Move the handle to and fro. The rope will move through the machine on both forward and backward strokes of the lever.

OPERATING THE TIRFOR

Forward motion is obtained by maintaining a to-and-fro motion of the Forward Operating Lever (see Fig. 1). The rope progresses towards the hook-end of the Tirfor and thus pulls or lifts the load.
Reverse motion is obtained by moving the Reverse Operating Lever (see Fig. 1) to-and-fro. The rope moves through the Tirfor away from the hook end thus lowering the load.

PULLING (see Fig. 5)

Anchor the Tirfor by its hook using a sling or a chain to any fixed point, pad eye or support column, etc.
For horizontal pulling, or for angles of up to 45°, secure the anchor hook about 15cm (6") above the ground. For angles between 45° and 90° the recommended height above the ground is 60cm (2ft).

LIFTING (see Fig. 6)

There are several ways of using a Tirfor as a lifting machine:

a) The machine can be anchored by its hook to a fixed point above the load and the load lifted toward the machine (see Fig. 6a).
b) The machine can be anchored directly to the load and the rope hook anchored directly above it. In this case the rope remains static and the machine and load climb the rope (see Fig 6b).
c) The most popular use is to anchor the machine by its hook to a fixed point as near to the seabed or deck as possible and to take the rope over a pulley fixed directly above the load. This system is convenient for the diver and keeps him away from the danger of the load (see Fig 6c).

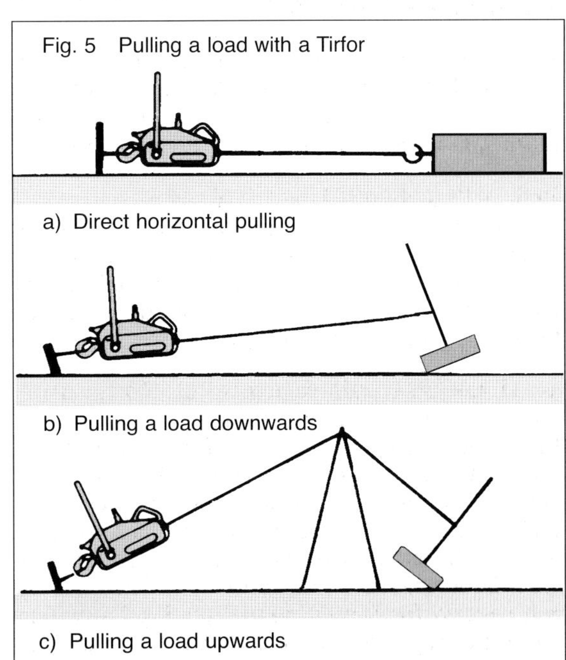
a) Direct horizontal pulling
b) Pulling a load downwards
c) Pulling a load upwards

Fig. 5 Pulling a load with a Tirfor

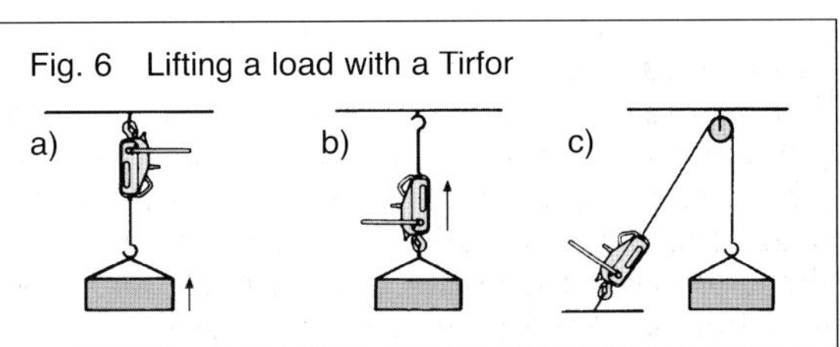
a)
b)
c)

Fig. 6 Lifting a load with a Tirfor

USING SHEAVE BLOCKS

Sheave blocks are used to increase the pulling (or lifting) power capacity of the Tirfor (see Fig. 7). When using multi-sheave blocks always ensure that the blocks are suitable for the total load to be lifted and that the top anchorage for the combination is sufficient to carry the total load of the machine, the

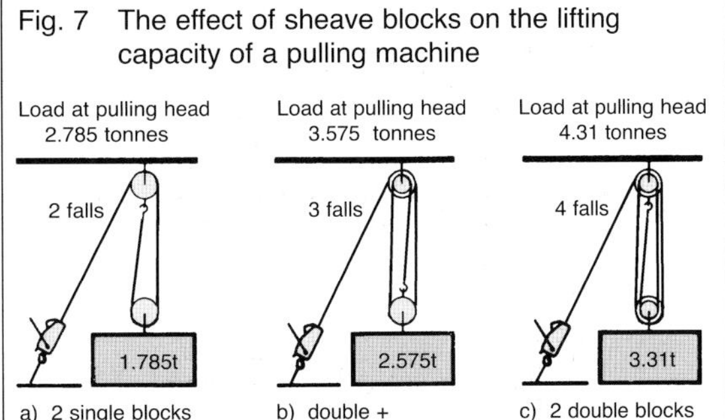
Load at pulling head
2.785 tonnes
Load at pulling head
3.575 tonnes
Load at pulling head
4.31 tonnes
2 falls
3 falls
4 falls
1.785t
2.575t
3.31t
a) 2 single blocks
b) double +
a single block
c) 2 double blocks

Fig. 7 The effect of sheave blocks on the lifting capacity of a pulling machine

In each of these examples a pull of 1 tonne is exerted on the pulling rope.

In a) a pull of one tonne will enable the pulling machine to lift 1.785 tonnes, in b) 2.575 tonnes and in c) 3.31 tonnes.

The lifting capacity is directly related to the number of falls (working ropes). Very simply, 2 falls = approx. 2 x capacity; 3 falls = 3 x capacity, and so on.

tension in the lead rope, the weight of the blocks and the load to be lifted.
The Factor of Safety (FoS) for lifting is 5:1 and for pulling, 3:1. So for example, in Fig. 7c where the load at the pulling head is 4.31 tonnes, the anchor fixture must have a SWL of at least 4.31 tonnes and a breaking strain of 21.55 tonnes (5 x 4.31).

MAINTENANCE AND LUBRICATION

Lubrication should be carried out at regular intervals to ensure that all the rope gripping mechanisms are working freely. Before putting a machine into service lubricate generously and again each time before use.
A lack of lubricant sometimes brings about a condition known as 'pumping', ie as the operating handle is pulled down the machine climbs up the rope about 2.5cm (1") but when the operating handle is moved up again the machine moves down the same distance. It must be stressed that while this situation is inconvenient it is not dangerous as there is no risk of the machine releasing its load and slipping. The normal procedure is then to lower the machine back to the ground using the reverse operating lever which is unaffected by the 'pumping' action of the forward operating lever. The Tirfor should then be thoroughly lubricated with a good quality gear oil (grease for underwater application) and it should recommence working normally.
After use the Tirfor must be washed in fresh water to remove all the sea water and then re-lubricated. If the machine is very dirty or clogged it should be soaked in paraffin, diesel or some proprietary cleansing fluid such as Jizer, then lubricated again. If the Tirfor cannot be washed and greased immediately after being brought to the surface it may be temporarily stored submerged in diesel fuel oil. Excess lubrication cannot cause the wire to slip. Greases and oils containing additives such as molybdenum disulphide must not be used in these machines. NOTE: If extended periods of submersion are anticipated, the Tirfor should be regarded as consumable since sea water will cause corrosion.

TIRFOR WIRE ROPE

The Tirfor steel wire rope supplied with the machine is designed and manufactured specially for use with the Tirfor and no other rope should be used. Ordinary wire ropes deform under the pressure of the jaws causing the machine to malfunction.
Wire rope should be inspected regularly. Damaged rope should not be used.

1. Wire rope should be reeled and unreeled in a straight line to prevent loops or kinks.
2. Kinked rope will not work in the Tirfor. For this reason never use the rope as a sling (ie passing the rope around an object and then hooking onto the rope again). Always use a separate wire rope sling.
3. The wire rope outlet of the machine should not be obstructed. The rope must be able to pass freely to prevent it being forced back into the unit.
4. Ensure that the end of the wire which is to be fed through the Tirfor is tapered and free from burnt metal beads or free wire strands which will not allow the wire to pass through.
5. Avoid subjecting the wire rope to abrasion by rubbing over sharp edges. Be sure that the wire rope is wiped clean before inserting it into the machine.
6. To avoid unlaying the strands, never allow a loaded rope to rotate.
7. Never use rope that has been subjected to fire, corrosion or exposed to electric current.
8. For longer life and better performance the wire rope should be regularly cleaned and lubricated.

Fig. 8 Examples of damaged wire rope or cable

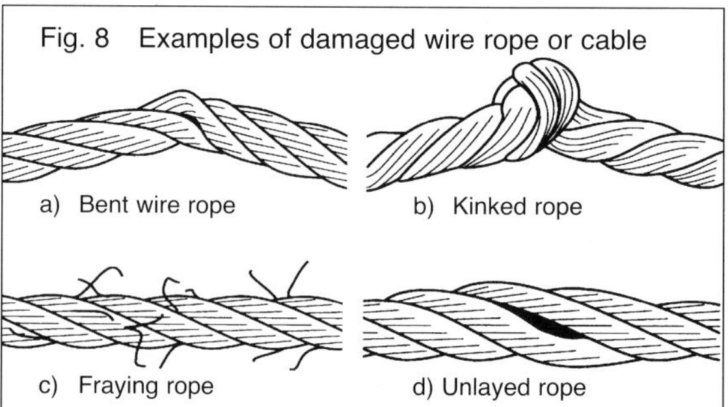
a) Bent wire rope
b) Kinked rope
c) Fraying rope
d) Unlayed rope

TIRFOR – OPERATIONAL SAFETY

1. Use only cable designed for use with the machine.
2. Ensure that the lifting or pulling effort to be exerted is within the rated capacity of the machine.
3. Ensure that both the anchor sling and the anchorage are of sufficient strength to hold the load.
4. Make sure that the machine anchoring sling is long enough to enable the machine to be comfortably used.
5. Ensure that there are no obstructions around the machine which could prevent the rope, machine and anchor from operating in a straight line.
6. Always check the operation of the machine including the feeding of the wire rope and its smooth running before sending it underwater.
7. Ensure that the forward and reverse levers can move freely at all times.
8. Never use a cheater pipe for extra leverage. Change to a larger unit.
9. If the machine is to be lowered to the worksite from the surface, the rope release lever should be tied down to prevent its accidental operation.
10. Never operate the forward and reverse levers at the same time.
11. Never anchor the machine by the tip of its hook.
12. When used underwater, try to arrange the working location of the machine to be near a good anchorage point for the diver to pull against. Pulling is always easier than pushing.

Lubricants containing graphite additives or molybdenum disulphide must not be used.

2. **Ratchet Lever Hoists** (Figs. 9 and 10)
These are usually the preferred pulling/hoisting tools for underwater use. There are many types of ratchet lever hoists. In all cases, before use, it is essential to ensure that the reverse mode works properly, that the load is not too great for the tool's rated capacity and that the chains are not kinked.

3. **Chain Hoists and Trolleys**
Not all trolleys can be used underwater. Most are designed to be suspended from fixed girders. However, they are commonly encountered on platforms or on shore.

Fig. 11 compares the Tirfor to ratchet lever and chain hoists.

Fig. 9 Ratchet lever hoist with link chain

Typical range of lifting capacities: 750–9,000kg

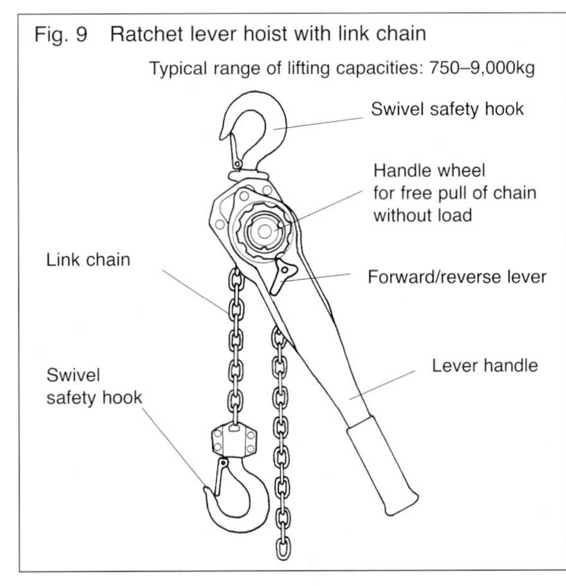
Swivel safety hook
Handle wheel for free pull of chain without load
Link chain
Forward/reverse lever
Swivel safety hook
Lever handle

Fig. 11 Choice of Pulling Machine – Tirfor compared to Ratchet Lever and Chain Hoists

	TIRFOR	RATCHET LEVER OR CHAIN HOISTS (Roller chain and Link chain)
APPLICATION	Used for long distance movement of object and where the distance between the pulling points may not be accurately known.	Used for moving objects relatively short distances and when the starting distance between two points is fairly accurately known.
OVERLOAD	If overloaded can fail in the seized mode requiring cutting away. Some models are fitted with a shear pin. Reverse operation still possible. It may also fail by gradually allowing the cable to slip through.	Can fail by breaking of the chain. Ratchet wheel mechanism may fail but load can remain safely held.
LOAD CAPACITY	Tends to be used for smaller pulling loads.	Normally used for relatively heavy pulling loads.
SIZE	Bulkier than equivalent strength ratchet hoist.	Smaller than Tirfor of equivalent strength.
OPERATION	a) Better control of smaller movements due to continuous pull over fractions of a stroke. b) Operation requires dexterity and mental concentration. This can be a problem especially in bad visibility.	a) Minimum distance of a pulling movement is limited to the length of link of the chain or to the ratchet movement. This could be between 5mm and 10mm depending on capacity. Smaller stroke movements are not possible unless blocks are used. b) Simpler mode of operation than Tirfor. Therefore easier to use in bad visibility and under the effect of nitrogen narcosis in deep air diving. Also less likely to be incorrectly used.
CONSTRUCTION	Uses a separate handle which needs to be carried by the diver, potentially committing the another hand. To avoid the danger of loss it is advisable to attach the handle to the machine by a short chain.	One-piece construction – no parts to fall off or get lost.
ROPE/CHAIN	Cable feeds freely through the machine but damaged cable will jam.	a) Roller chain feeds more easily than link chain but can jam due to seized or corroded links. Sensitive to sideways bending. b) Link chain can get tangled and jam machine. Can be a problem in bad visibility.
MAINTENANCE	Needs normal maintenance to avoid corrosion and seizing.	Needs normal maintenance to avoid corrosion and seizing of links.

Fig. 10 Ratchet lever hoist with roller chain

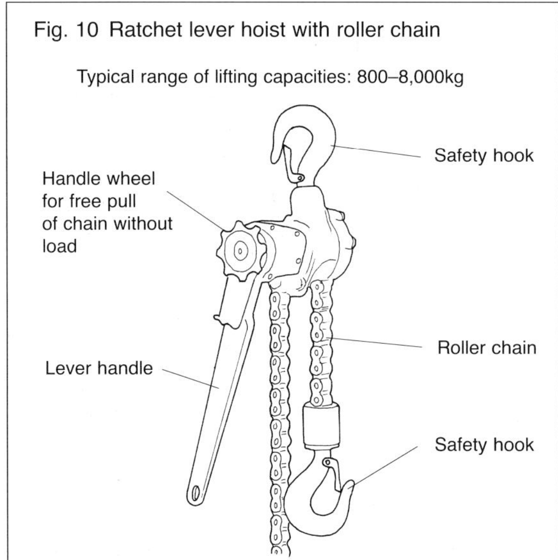
Typical range of lifting capacities: 800–8,000kg
Safety hook
Handle wheel for free pull of chain without load
Roller chain
Lever handle
Safety hook

Ratchet Tie Downs

These are commonly used on trucks to secure loads. Divers can use them as 'come-alongs' or to securely bind objects together. Their advantages include:

- Strength (1000–5000kg/2,000–11,000lb versions available).
  Pulling power can be increased by using them in association with a sheave block system.
- Light weight.
- Cheap (they are mass-produced).
- Consumable (cheapness means they can be discarded if showing any signs of corrosion or damage etc).
- Simple to operate.
- Slack can be taken in easily.
- Tension can be released easily.
- Reliable and safe to use.
- Can be used in either 'come-along' or encapsulating modes (see Fig. 12).

Disadvantages include:

- Winching distance limited to how much belt can be rolled onto the drum. If longer winching distances are required, two units may be used alternately.
- Not normally designed for underwater use, therefore fresh water wash and careful maintenance are required.

Fig. 12 Ratchet tie-down

a) in Come-along mode

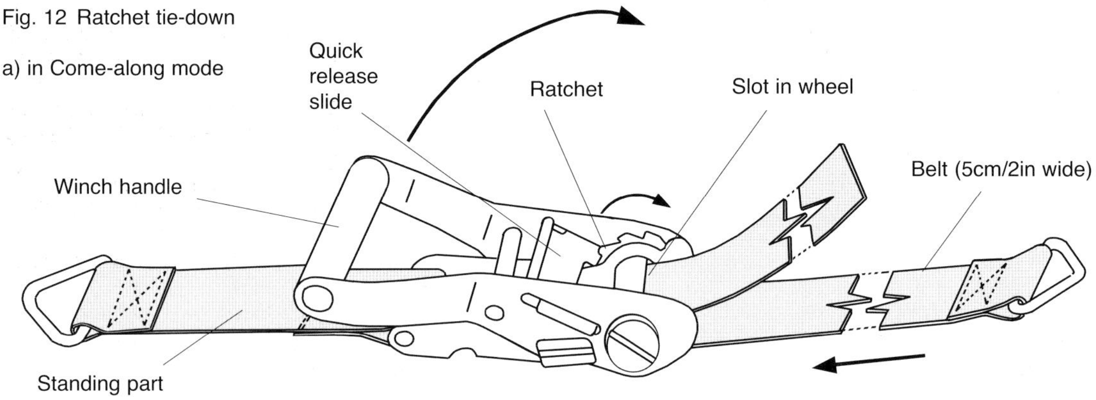

Quick release slide
Ratchet
Slot in wheel
Winch handle
Belt (5cm/2in wide)
Standing part

b) in Encapsulating mode

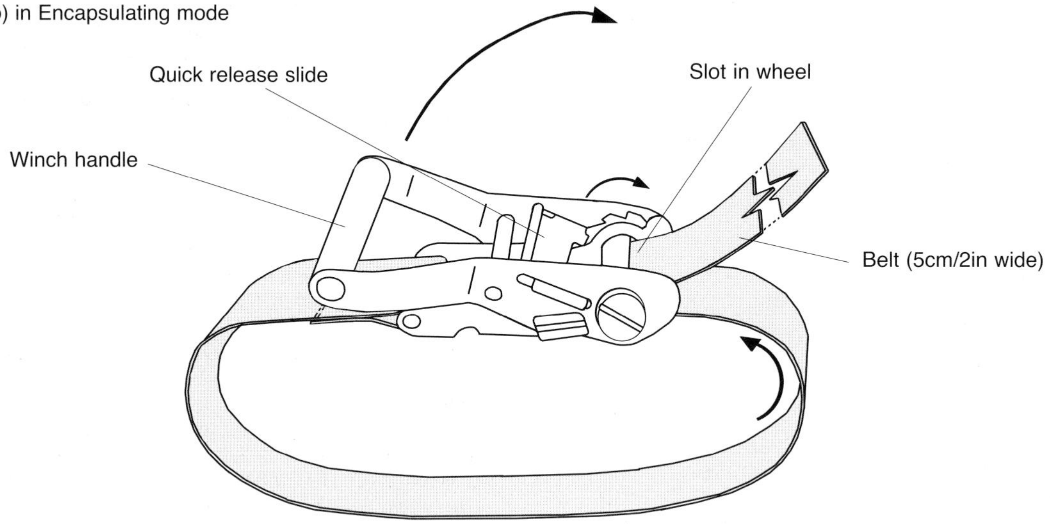

Quick release slide
Slot in wheel
Winch handle
Belt (5cm/2in wide)

b) PURCHASES AND TACKLES

Rigging for hoisting, pulling or hauling heavy objects consists of a purchase (which is a mechanical device to increase power or force by means of blocks or pulleys rove with a rope or chain) or by levers, ratchets or gears. There are many such devices available: traditional block and rope tackle, jacks, come-alongs, lever hoists and hand winches. Most of these can be operated manually, hydraulically or electrically. The types used underwater are mainly manual systems.

The choice of the equipment to be used depends on:

- The availability of equipment.
- The weight of the object to be handled.
- The size and physical nature of the object.
- The distance the object has to be moved.
- The rated power of the equipment.
- Access (enough room to operate the equipment).

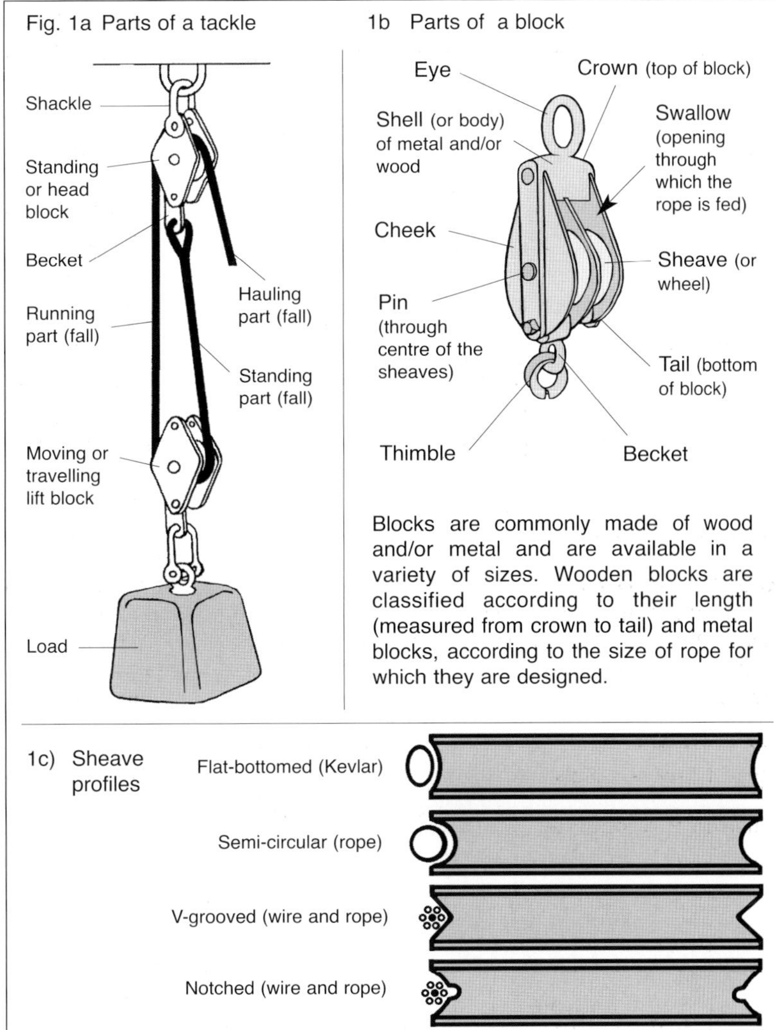
Fig. 1a Parts of a tackle
Shackle
Standing or head block
Becket
Running part (fall)
Hauling part (fall)
Standing part (fall)
Moving or travelling lift block
Load
1b Parts of a block
Eye
Crown (top of block)
Shell (or body) of metal and/or wood
Swallow (opening through which the rope is fed)
Cheek
Sheave (or wheel)
Pin (through centre of the sheaves)
Tail (bottom of block)
Thimble
Becket
1c) Sheave profiles
Flat-bottomed (Kevlar)
Semi-circular (rope)
V-grooved (wire and rope)
Notched (wire and rope)

Blocks are commonly made of wood and/or metal and are available in a variety of sizes. Wooden blocks are classified according to their length (measured from crown to tail) and metal blocks, according to the size of rope for which they are designed.

Traditional Tackle

A tackle (see Fig. 1) consists of a rope rove through two or more blocks in such a way that a pull applied to its hauling part is increased by an amount determined by the number of sheaves in the blocks and the way in which the rope is rove through them.

The gain in the power is equivalent to the number of parts (of rope) which enter and leave the moving block of the tackle, depending on whether or not the tackle is rigged to advantage or disadvantage (see Fig. 2).

A single block used for a straight lift (a single whip) imparts no mechanical advantage because the block does not move.

As its name implies, a tackle rigged to advantage provides the most efficient use of power.

Fig. 2 Tackle rigged to advantage (b) and disadvantage (a)

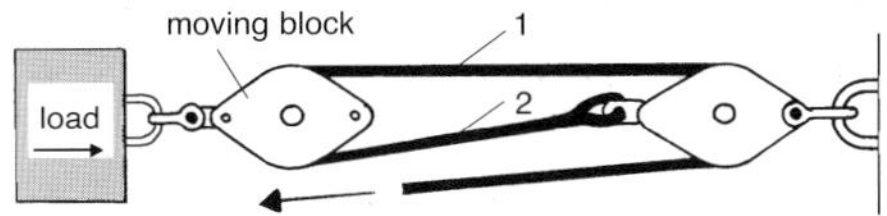
moving block
1
2
load

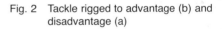

a) Disadvantage (pulling in the opposite direction to the load movement). The gain is 2:1

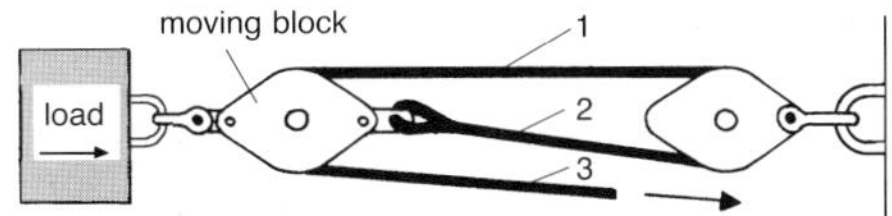
moving block
1
2
3
load

b) Advantage (pulling in the same direction of the load movement). The gain is 3:1

Gain in power is equivalent to the number of parts of rope which are attached to, enter or leave the moving block.

In a) two parts go through the moving block. Therefore the gain is 2:1. In b) three parts go through and/or are attached to the moving block. Therefore the advantage is 3:1

Mechanical Advantage

The amount by which the pull on the hauling part is multiplied by the tackle is called its mechanical advantage (MA) and, if friction is disregarded, this is equal to the number of parts of the fall at the moving block. For example, in Fig. 3 there are two moving parts at the moving block, therefore the MA is 2 and, disregarding friction, a pull on the hauling rope would hold a weight of 2 x 51kg, ie 102kg. For the same reason, in order to raise the

Fig. 3 Mechanical advantage and velocity ratio

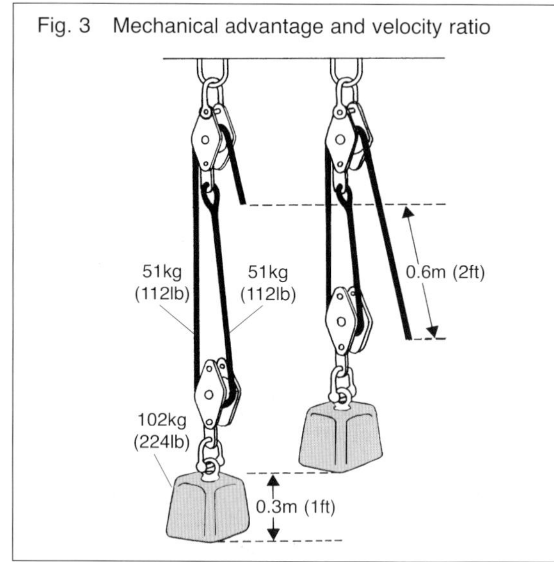
51kg
(112lb)
51kg
(112lb)
0.6m (2ft)
102kg
(224lb)
0.3m (1ft)

load 0.3m (1ft) each working part will need to be shortened by 0.3m. Since there are two working parts, a pull of 2 x 0.3m on the hauling part will lift the load 0.3m (see Fig. 3).

Mechanical advantage is gained only at the expense of the speed of working.

It should be remembered that friction in the bearings of the sheaves reduces the mechanical advantage by about one tenth of the weight to be hoisted for each sheave of the tackle.

Fig. 4 Reeving of tackle blocks – various combinations

a) Two-part falls (single and single) Used for pulling more than hoisting.

b) Three-part falls (double and single) A luff, usually of 8cm (3") in size or greater.

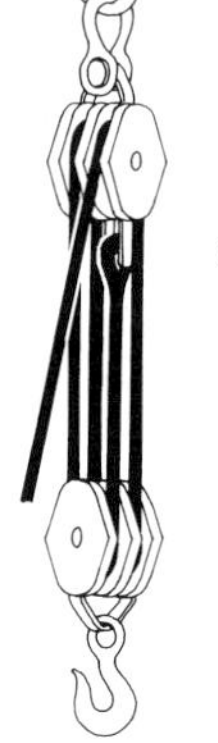

c) Runner (double and double. VR = 4) A useful general purpose tackle often called a two-fold purchase.

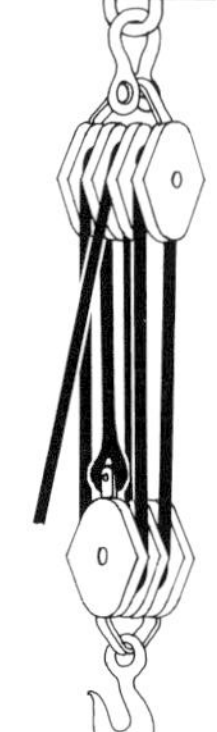

d) Five-part falls (triple and double. VR = 5) This is often used in boats' falls.

Fig. 5 Examples of Tackles in Common Use

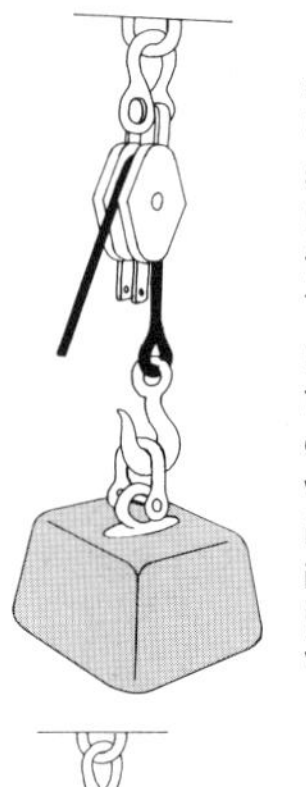

a) Single whip
Used for lifting simple light loads from a fixed position. The pull required to hoist the load is equal to its weight. No advantage is gained.
MA = 0
VR = 0

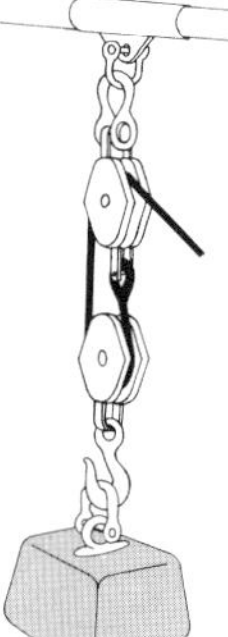

b) Double Whip (disadvantage)
Used in hoisting light loads which have swung to another position. Cannot be rove to advantage.
MA = 1.67
VR = 2

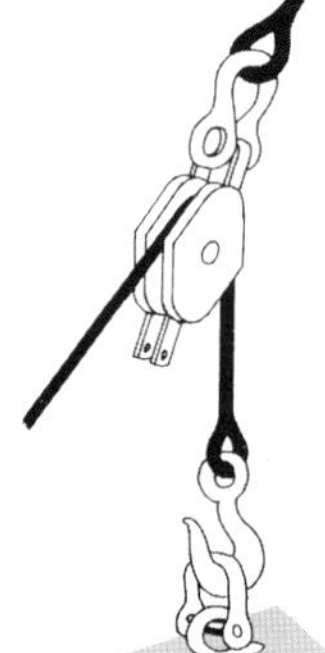

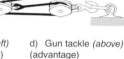

c) Runner *(left)* (disadvantage)
Used for tensioning halyards and guy ropes. There is only a slight mechanical advantage.
MA = 1.8
VR = 2

d) Gun tackle *(above)* (advantage)
Used for pulling a load only. Not for hoisting. Can be reeved either to advantage or disadvantage.
MA = 2.5 (A) 1.67 (D)
VR = 3 (A) 2 (D)

e) Luff (disadvantage)
With this single and double block the MA is an improvement on the double whip.
MA = 3.08 (A) 2.3 (D)
VR = 4 (A) 3 (D)

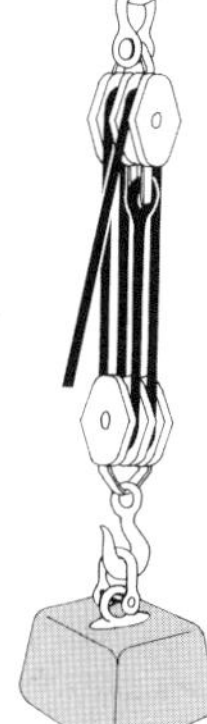

f) Two-fold purchase (disadvantage)
Two double blocks considerably improve the MA. A widely used tackle.
MA = 3.57 (A) 2.26 (D)
VR = 5 (A) 4 (D)

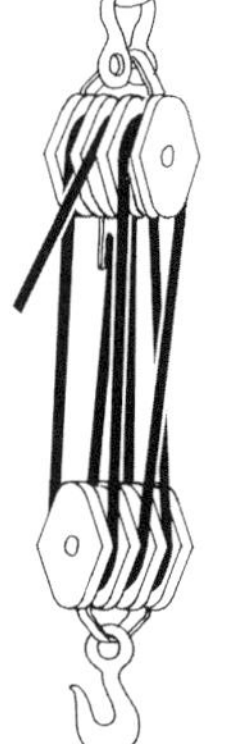

g) Three-fold purchase (disadvantage)
Two treble blocks give greatly increased lifting power. These are mainly used for boats' falls.
MA = 4.37 (A) 3.75 (D)
VR = 7 (A) 6 (D)

MA = mechanical advantage (includes frictional losses) VR = velocity ratio A = advantage D = disadvantage

The pull required to hoist a given weight is equal to the weight divided by the MA. Conversely, the weight which can be hoisted can be found by multiplying the pull by the MA.
Note that all the sheaves in a set of blocks will rotate at different rates – the ones nearest the lead line turning the most. Consequently the sheaves nearest the lead line wear out fastest.
Many combinations of tackle can be used, such as two tackles rigged together, or blocks with multiple sheaves (see Fig. 4).

Velocity Ratio

The ratio between the distance moved by the hauling part and that moved by the moving block is called the velocity ratio (VR) and is always equal to the number of parts of the fall at the moving block (see Fig. 5). The difference between MA and VR = the amount of friction.

Reeving Tackle Blocks

Before using purchases and tackles always ensure that the blocks, ropes and shackles are within the safe working load for the weight.

In reeving a pair of tackle blocks one of which has more than two sheaves, the hoisting rope should lead from one of the centre sheaves of the upper block. When so reeved the hoisting strain comes on the centre of the blocks and they are prevented from toppling (which would damage the rope by cutting across the edges of the block shell).
To reeve by this method the two blocks should be placed so that the sheaves in the upper block are at right angles to those in the lower on, as shown in Fig 4, c and d. Start reeving with the becket, or standing part of the rope.
It is good practice to use a shackle block as the upper one of a pair and a hook as the lower one. A shackle is much stronger than a hook of the same size and the strain on the upper block is much greater than the one on the lower one. The lower block supports only the load whereas the upper block carries the load as well as the hoisting strain. A hook is more convenient on the lower block because it can more readily be attached or detached from the load.

3.7 RIGGING c) RIGGING FITTINGS

Among the many varieties of rigging equipment there are special fittings for each particular application. Fittings particular to ropes and slings are discussed in those sections (Sections 3.7d and e). This section deals with a selection of other fittings likely to be used by a diver.
All rigging fittings should be checked before use to ensure that they are of adequate strength to cope with the job and must suit the rope or chain being used.

Shackles

Shackles are made of wrought iron, mild steel or forged alloy steel. They are coupling links for joining chains to wires or ropes, or to a fitting. Shackles are more secure than hooks and should always be used between a tension member and a load.
Although there are specialised shackles for every purpose there are two main types: straight (or 'D') shackles and bow shackles (see Fig. 1).
The size of a shackle is determined by the diameter of the metal in the bow section.
The safe working load (SWL) can be found in the tables supplied by the manufacturer and is often stamped on the shackle itself. Proof load = twice the SWL. Min. breaking strength = 4–6 times the SWL.

OPERATIONAL CONSIDERATIONS

For the diver there are several advantages in using a safety shackle with a nut and pin. Once the bolt is rammed home the load is secure and the diver will not have to take the weight while he is screwing on

Fig. 1 Types of Shackles

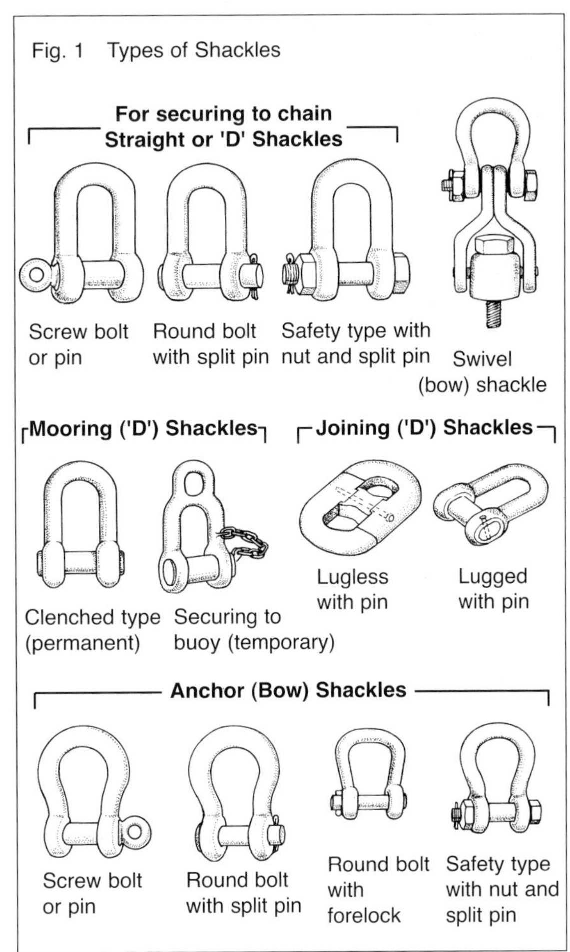
For securing to chain
Straight or 'D' Shackles
Screw bolt or pin
Round bolt with split pin
Safety type with nut and split pin
Swivel (bow) shackle
Mooring ('D') Shackles
Joining ('D') Shackles
Clenched type (permanent)
Securing to buoy (temporary)
Lugless with pin
Lugged with pin
Anchor (Bow) Shackles
Screw bolt or pin
Round bolt with split pin
Round bolt with forelock
Safety type with nut and split pin

the nut. A safety shackle bolt is secure from coming undone and is therefore safer. It can be made even more secure by inserting a pin or wire through the hole in the bolt.

Fig. 2 Parts of a shackle

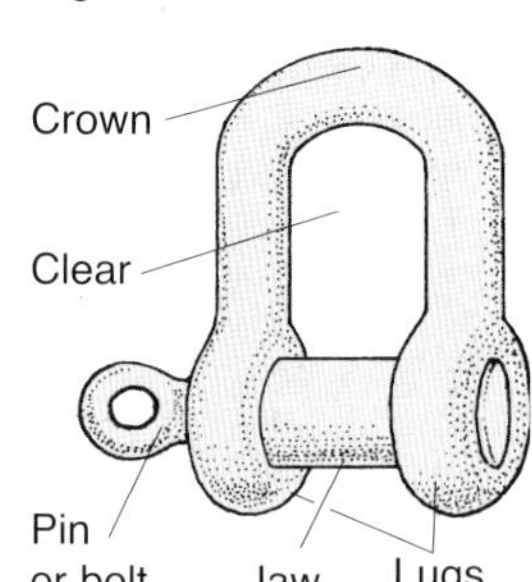
Crown
Clear
Pin
or bolt
Jaw
Lugs

Before going underwater the diver should ensure that he takes the right tool for loosening shackle bolts. Shackles should be carefully greased before being taken underwater to ensure easy operation.

Many companies operate a regular inspection and certification programme for their rigging. The shackles etc, once tested, are painted with a coloured stripe corresponding to a time-frame in which that item will be 'certified for use'. After or near to the end of that time-frame the items should be returned to the base or testing house for re-certification.

SHACKLES – OPERATIONAL SAFETY

1. Always check that the shackle is rated for the load weight.
2. Never use a shackle that is worn or damaged (see Fig. 3).
3. Never pull a shackle at an angle. Not only might this pull the lugs apart, it will also greatly reduce the shackle's lifting capacity (see Fig 4a and b).
4. Always centralise the load on the bolt (see Fig. 4b). Pack with spacers if necessary.
5. Never substitute an ordinary bolt for a missing shackle pin (Fig. 4e).
6. When working with rigging under tension, the diver and his umbilical must be well clear.

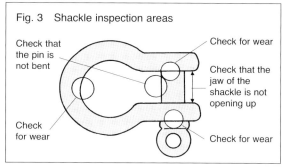

Fig. 3 Shackle inspection areas

Check that the pin is not bent

Check for wear

Check for wear

Check that the jaw of the shackle is not opening up

Check for wear

Fig. 4 Correct and Incorrect ways of using a Shackle

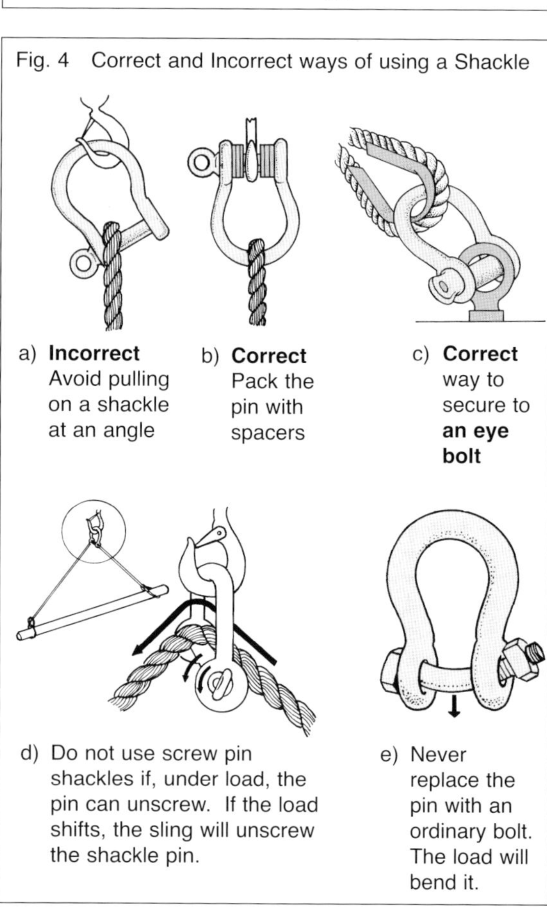
a) **Incorrect** Avoid pulling on a shackle at an angle
b) **Correct** Pack the pin with spacers
c) **Correct** way to secure to **an eye bolt**
d) Do not use screw pin shackles if, under load, the pin can unscrew. If the load shifts, the sling will unscrew the shackle pin.
e) Never replace the pin with an ordinary bolt. The load will bend it.

Hooks

Hooks are generally not as strong as equivalent-sized shackles. Only hooks with safety hooks should be used; if none are available the hook should be moused using wire or line (see Fig. 5c).

Fig. 5 Hooks

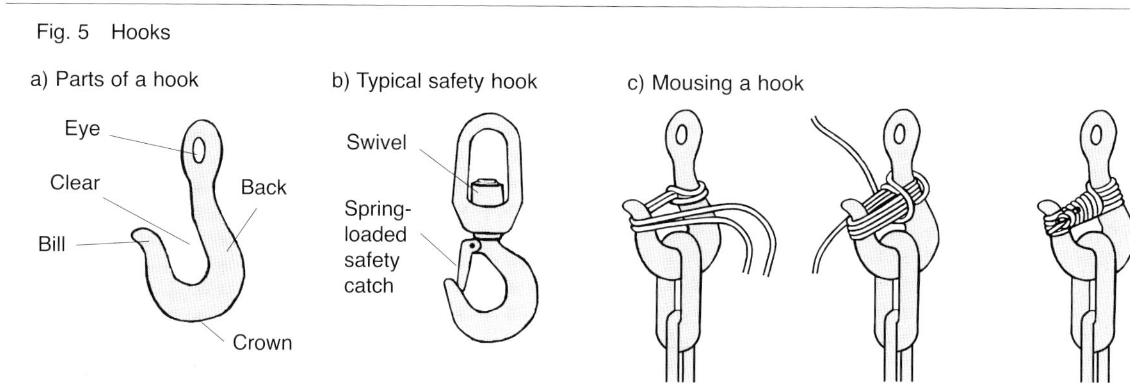
a) Parts of a hook
Eye
Clear
Back
Bill
Crown
b) Typical safety hook
Swivel
Spring-loaded safety catch
c) Mousing a hook

Carabiner Hooks and Links (Fig. 6)

These are usually small and commonly used for attaching an object or tools to the diver.

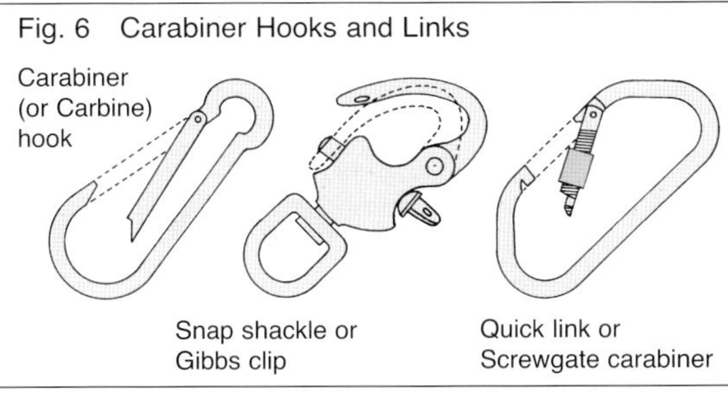
Carabiner
(or Carbine)
hook
Snap shackle or
Gibbs clip
Quick link or
Screwgate carabiner
Fig. 6 Carabiner Hooks and Links

Magnets

Magnets can be used to provide divers with hand-holds and reference points on steel structures such as sheet piling or ships' hulls. They may also be used, as appropriate, to assist with suspending heavy tools, rigging and to recover lost steel items. The more powerful magnets are provided with release devices to allow the diver break the magnetic attraction (see Fig. 7).

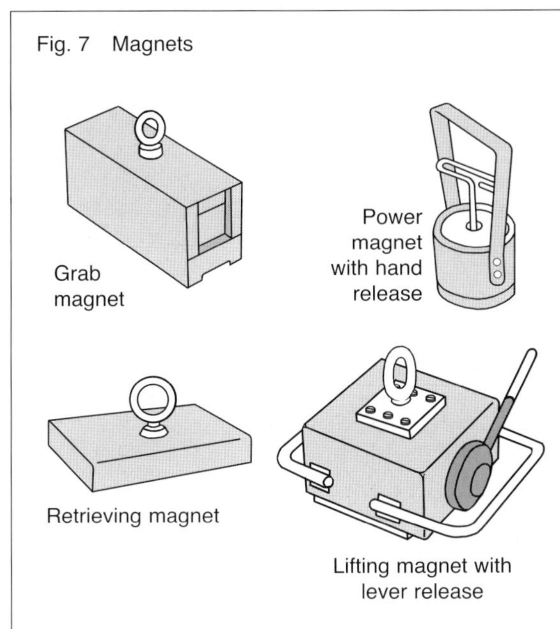
Grab
magnet
Power
magnet
with hand
release
Retrieving magnet
Lifting magnet with
lever release
Fig. 7 Magnets

Rope clamps ('climbers' or 'ascenders')

These are commonly used by rock climbers to establish hand-holds on a rope whilst climbing (see Fig. 8). A diver can easily hook an ascender onto a shot rope, slide it up or down to the desired point and jam it onto the rope. It can be easily released by pushing upwards and using the thumb to hold back the sprung cam.

Typical applications include:

- Securing a diver to a shot rope to carry out an inspection task.
- Securing a diver to a shot rope to carry out a decompression stop.
  The ascender/handle can be conveniently attached to the diver's harness by a short rope and snap shackle/ carabiner (see Fig. 8).
- To attach a tool to a shot line.

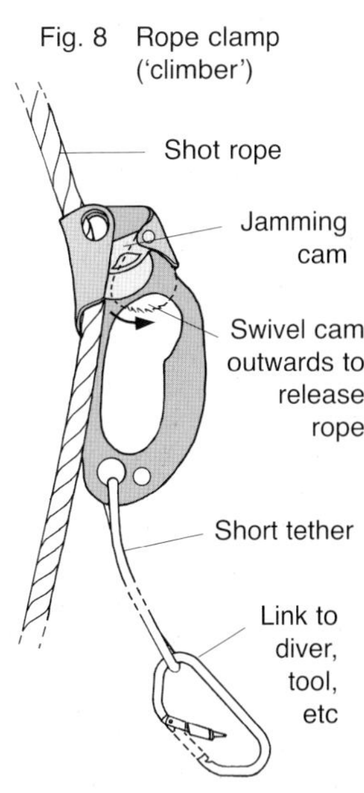
Shot rope
Jamming
cam
Swivel cam
outwards to
release
rope
Short tether
Link to
diver,
tool,
etc
Fig. 8 Rope clamp ('climber')

Turnbuckles

Sometimes called rigging or bottle screws, turnbuckles are used to adjust the length or tension of rigging (see Fig. 9). The end fittings are selected to suit the particular application. If there is any vibration, the end fittings should be locked to the body to prevent loosening.

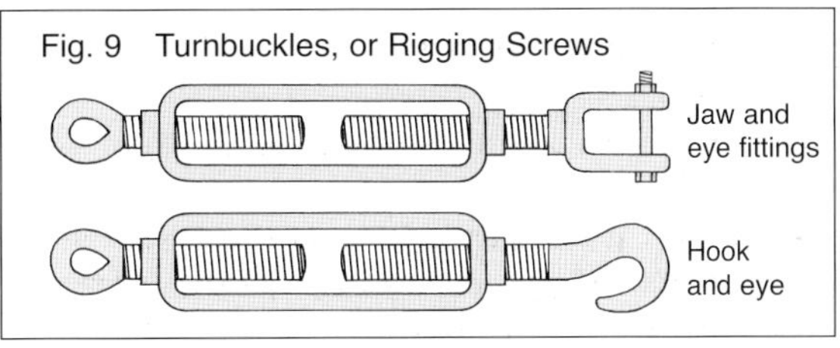
Jaw and
eye fittings
Hook
and eye
Fig. 9 Turnbuckles, or Rigging Screws

Thimbles

Thimbles are made of galvanised gunmetal or mild steel and are used as linings to eye splices to reduce the wear from an attached shackle. They also greatly increase the strength of the eye. Thimbles are usually teardrop-shaped but some are round or solid according to their purpose (see Fig. 10).

Chain fittings

A selection of hooks, shackles and fittings designed for use with chain is shown in Fig. 11.

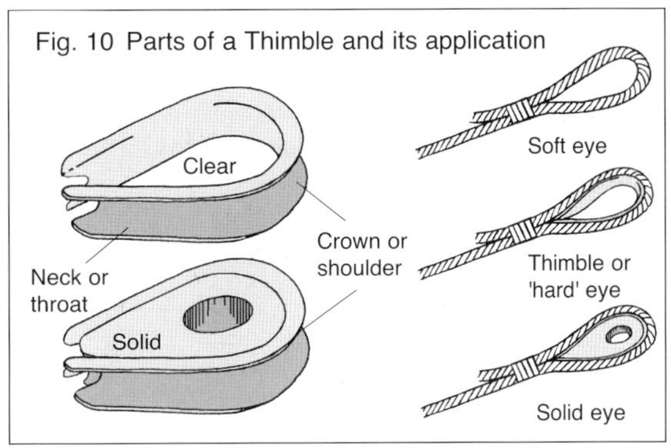
Clear
Neck or
throat
Crown or
shoulder
Solid
Soft eye
Thimble or
'hard' eye
Solid eye
Fig. 10 Parts of a Thimble and its application

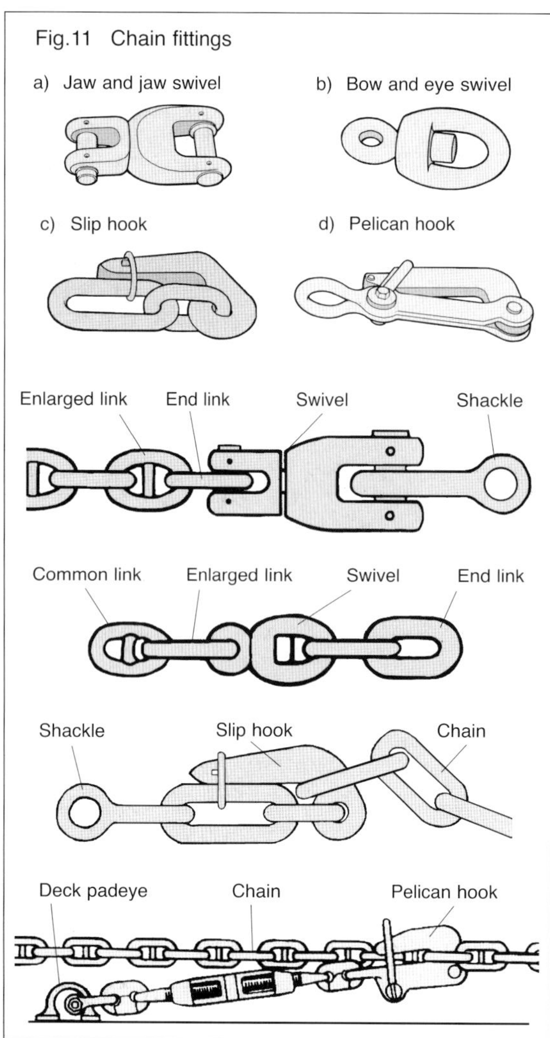
Fig.11 Chain fittings
a) Jaw and jaw swivel
b) Bow and eye swivel
c) Slip hook
d) Pelican hook
Enlarged link
End link
Swivel
Shackle
Common link
Enlarged link
Swivel
End link
Shackle
Slip hook
Chain
Deck padeye
Chain
Pelican hook

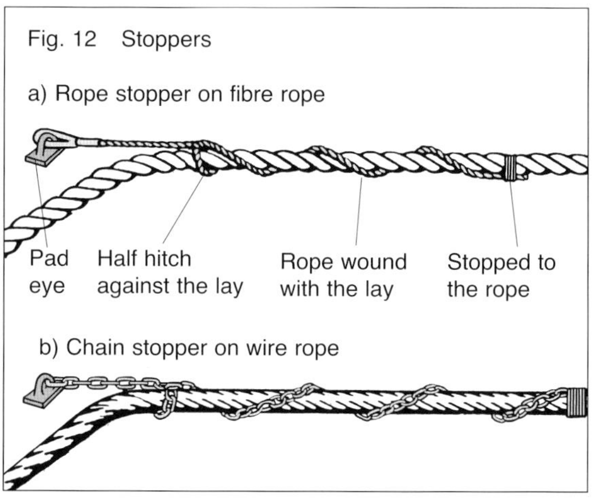
Fig. 12 Stoppers
a) Rope stopper on fibre rope
Pad eye
Half hitch against the lay
Rope wound with the lay
Stopped to the rope
b) Chain stopper on wire rope

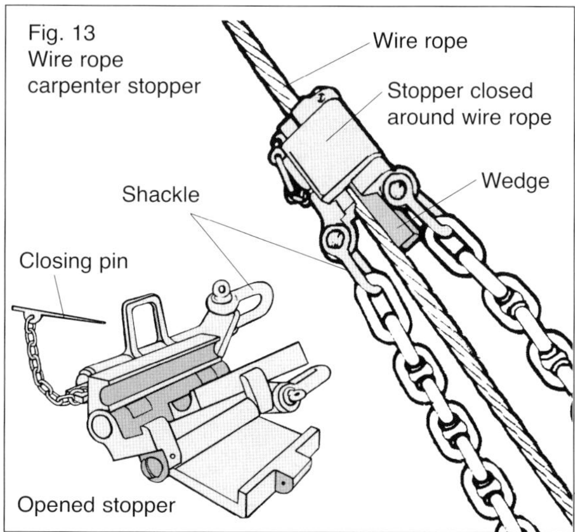
Fig. 13 Wire rope carpenter stopper
Wire rope
Stopper closed around wire rope
Wedge
Shackle
Closing pin
Opened stopper

Fig. 14 Spreader Bar and Equaliser Beam

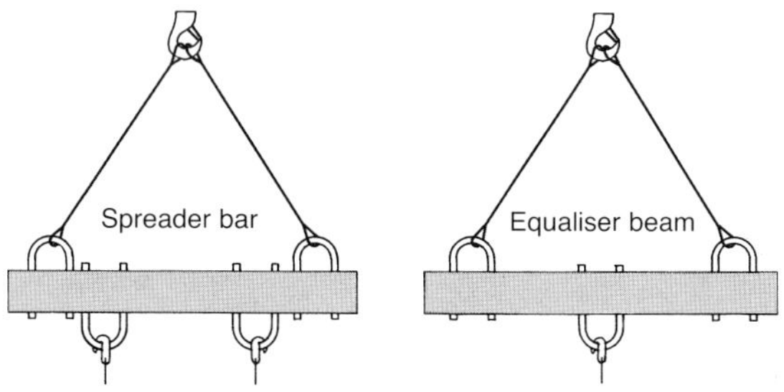
Spreader bar
Equaliser beam

Stoppers

Stoppers are used to temporarily take the strain off a rope under tension, to enable it to be adjusted or secured. A length of rope is first secured to a pad-eye or similar, the free end is half-hitched around the rope under strain (against the lay) and then wrapped around the rope in the same direction as the lay, the free end is whipped to the rope under strain (see Fig. 12). Both fibre ropes and chains may be used as stoppers.

A Carpenter's stopper (see Fig. 13) is used only on wire rope. It consists of a metal block which is closed around the wire rope; a wedge is pushed hard into the block against the rope so that when any strain is put on the rope, it is pulled through the stopper drawing the wedge deeper into the stopper, jamming the rope.

Spreader Bars and Equalising Beams

These are used to prevent long loads from tipping during lifting and to avoid the use of low sling angles (see Section 3.7e, Slings). Be sure to check that the bar is of appropriate strength and material for the load.

3.7 RIGGING d) FIBRE AND WIRE ROPES

Fibre Ropes

Fibre ropes may be divided into two main types:

1. NATURAL ROPES are constructed of overlapped vegetable fibres twisted together into yarns and again into strands and finally into 3–4 stranded hawser laid rope. They are made from manila, sisal or hemp. Manila is the strongest and most durable. They are negatively buoyant.

2. SYNTHETIC FIBRE ROPES are replacing natural fibres in the marine environment. In general synthetic fibres are stronger and lighter, rot-resistant and do not stiffen when wet or frozen. They are more elastic and shock-resistant, are longer lasting and easier to handle. However, they do have a low melting point so care should be taken where there is a lot of friction. Unlike natural fibres, individual synthetic fibres are manufactured to run the entire length of a rope.

The important features of the different types of synthetic fibres are shown in Fig. 1.

Synthetic fibre ropes may be hawser laid or 8–16 strand plaited or braided. Braided lines consists of a braided core enclosed in a braided sheath and is the strongest form of nylon rope. It has the advantage that it will neither twist nor kink (see Fig. 2).

The elasticity and slipperiness of synthetic ropes may make conventional knots and bends unreliable. It is often better to use a climber's or angler's knot to secure free ends with an extra hitch or tuck. Each diver will have his own preferences but those shown in Fig. 3 can be useful.

Synthetic ropes may be spliced but it may be complicated if there are many strands. There are many connectors and terminations available which offer a more practical solution.

It is important to remember that rope loses some of its strength according to how it is used.

Knots (loops, turns and locking crosses) will cause the rope to lose approximately 55% of its strength. Hitches (a knot tied around an object) lose 25% strength. Bends (two ropes tied together) lose 50% of the rope strength. Kinks lose 30% and splices 10%. All rope is described by its diameter, in millimetres.

Fig. 1 Characteristics of Synthetic Fibres

Fibre and Trade names	Characteristics
NYLON Perlon, Enkalon *Density 1.14 (sinks)*	The strongest of the synthetic fibres. Good resistance to abrasion and weathering. Extensively used for towing because of its elasticity.
POLYESTER Dacron, Terylene *Density 1.38 (sinks)*	Almost identical to nylon except that it has little elasticity. Its low stretch properties make polyester ideal for lifting. It has good electrical insulating properties which makes it useful when working near power lines.
POLYPROPYLENE Ulstron, Nelson, Prolene *Density 0.91 (floats)*	Not as strong as nylon or polyester and has a relatively low melting point. Lightweight and buoyant. Extensively used for mooring and spring lines. Good electrical insulating properties.
POLYETHYLENE Courlene, X3 *Density 0.95 (floats)*	Similar to polypropylene. Good electrical insulating properties.
BLENDS	Many combinations of the above are made to suit particular applications.
ARAMID POLYAMIDE Kevlar, Kexlon *Density 1.44 (sinks)*	Can have the same strength as wire rope at one-fifth the weight. It is corrosion free, lasts longer and is cheaper than wire rope.

Fig. 2 Construction of synthetic fibre ropes

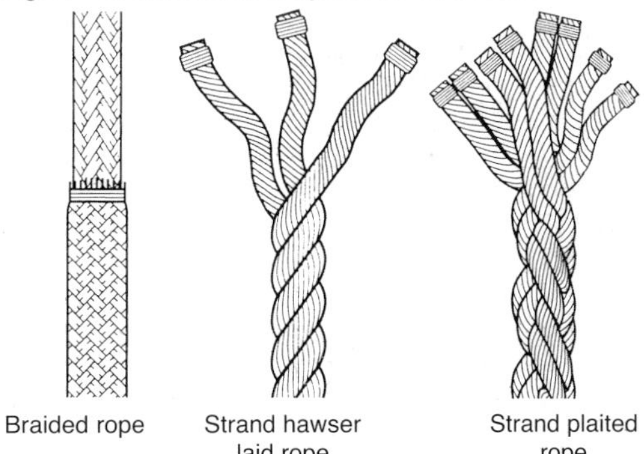
Braided rope
Strand hawser laid rope
Strand plaited rope

STOWING ROPE

Unused rope should always be tidily stowed away. To reduce twisting and tangling, the rope should be properly coiled. First lay the rope straight out for its entire length and stretch to remove any kinks. Holding one end of the rope in the left hand, pull the rope towards you using your right hand. Loop the rope in a clockwise direction into your left hand. To counteract the twist in the loop, use your right hand to roll the rope half a turn before placing the rope into your left hand (see Fig. 4).

Once the rope has been coiled it can be stowed away in one of six ways.

1. With the coiled rope in the left hand, the last length of free rope can be wrapped around the coil and the tail of the rope passed through the 'eye' where the hand holds the rope (see Fig. 5a).
2. If the rope has no free end, the last few coils should be wrapped around the coiled rope; the last length is looped and passed through and over the 'eye' at the top of the coil (see Fig. 5b).
3. It can be coiled on the ground and tied at 12, 3, 6 and 9 o'clock positions.
4. It can be 'poured' into a container. It will come out as it went in. The container must not be disturbed if the rope is to remain untangled.
5. If a rope is to be paid out quickly, it can be faked down, ie, it is laid down backwards and forwards in long straight lengths.
6. It can be laid in 'figure-of-eights'.

Fig. 3 Commonly used Knots, Bends and Hitches

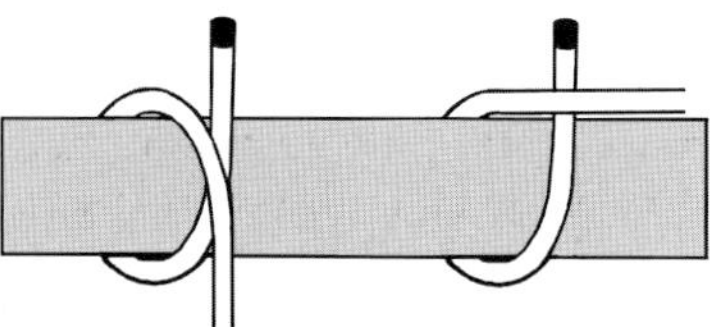

Round turn Half hitch
Turns and hitches are used in various combinations to make up many of the most commonly used rigging knots.

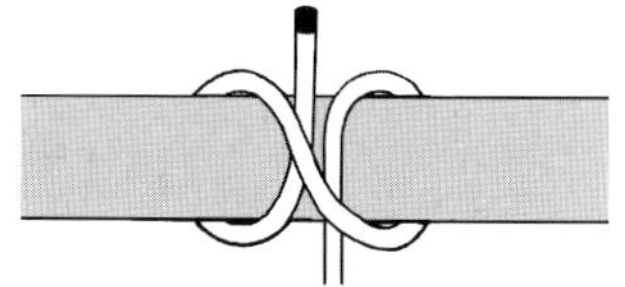

Clove Hitch
For temporarily making fast to a spar or stanchion. Non-jamming. May slip.

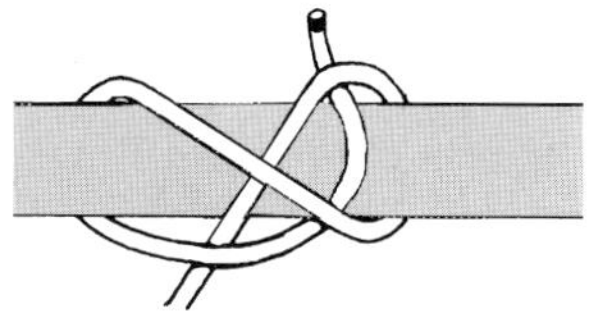

Constrictor Knot
For securing tools or lines to pipes. More secure than clove hitch. Self-jamming.

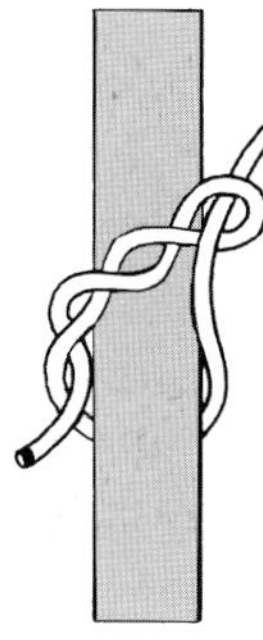

Timber Hitch
for vertical lifts or towing long objects. Self-jamming.

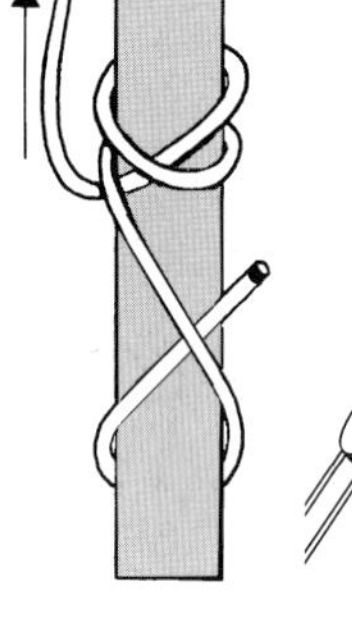

Rolling Hitch
For securing to slippery cylindrical surfaces or a rope to a wire. Or use a strop. Will not slide. Self-jamming.

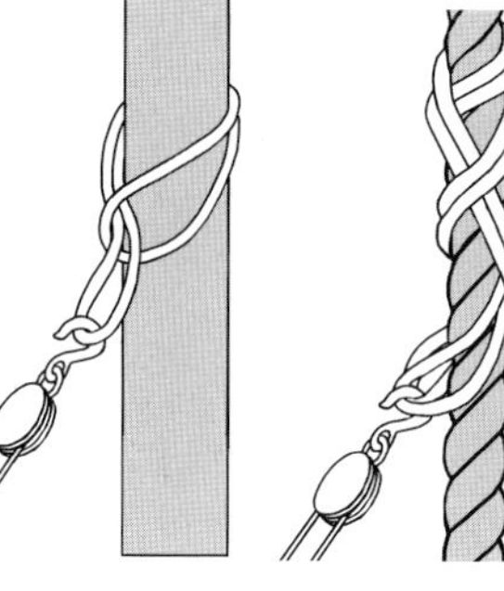

Strops
A strop is a ring of rope or wire rope. For a strong, sideways pull on a spar, apply as above left. To strop a rope, apply as above right. Chain may be used for stropping wire rope. Will not slip. Self-jamming.

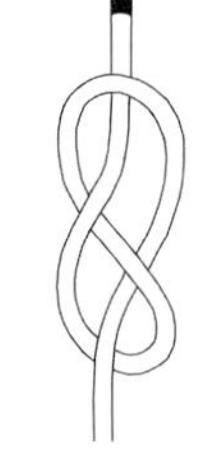

Figure of Eight
To prevent a rope unreeving through an eye or block.

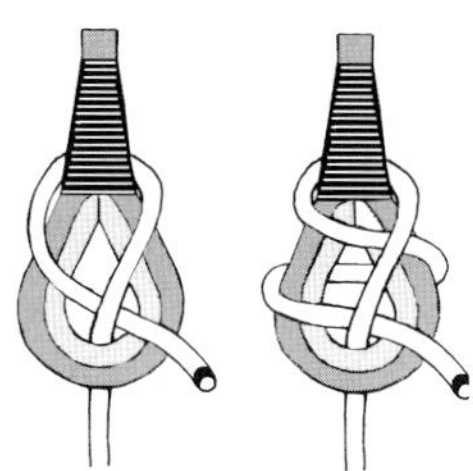

Sheet Bend and Double Sheet Bend
Also used for joining different sized ropes.

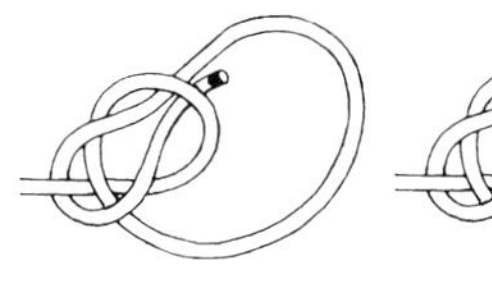

Bowline and Double Bowline
The most versatile of all knots. Ideal for lifelines. Non-jamming. Will not slip.

Round turn and 2 half hitches
For securing to anchors and shackles. Never jams.

Fisherman's Bend
For securing to anchors and shackles. Self-jamming. Will not slip.

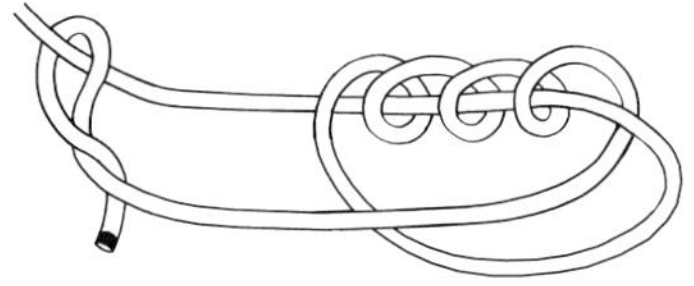

Tarbuck Knot
A lifeline knot. Self-jamming.

Fig. 4 Coiling a right hand hawser-laid rope

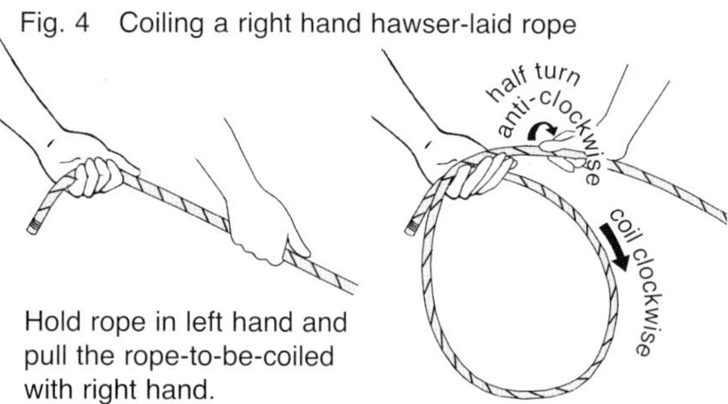
half turn anti-clockwise
coil clockwise

Hold rope in left hand and pull the rope-to-be-coiled with right hand.

Coil rope in clockwise direction. Half-turn each coil anti-clockwise before placing in left hand.

Wire Ropes

There is a wide variety of wire ropes, each of which has been made to withstand the demands of a particular task.
Wire rope is used for both standing and running rigging for which the requirements are different. Standing rigging is made of minimum stretch wire whereas running rigging needs to be flexible.
The characteristics of a wire rope depend on:

1. GRADE OF WIRE
   Wire rope is manufactured in grades signifying degrees of strength, toughness, abrasion and corrosion resistance. A commonly used grade is

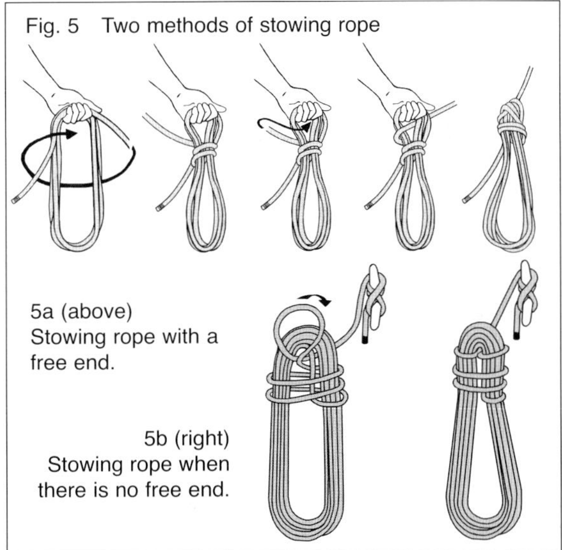
5a (above)
Stowing rope with a free end.
5b (right)
Stowing rope when there is no free end.
Fig. 5 Two methods of stowing rope

Grade 160 (16.6 tonnes force/cm^2, 102 tons force/in^2).

2. NUMBER AND PATTERN OF WIRE IN A STRAND
A single wire is a long slender solid rod.
A strand is made up of several wires twisted around a central wire. The number of wires in a strand affects the rope's flexibility and resistance to both bending fatigue and abrasion. The greater the number of wires the more flexible the strand. Most ropes consist of seven strands: a central core with six strands winding helically around it (see Fig. 6).

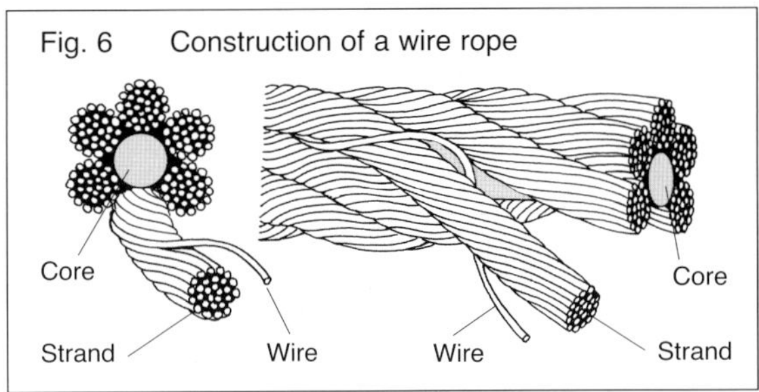
Core
Strand
Wire
Wire
Core
Strand
Fig. 6 Construction of a wire rope

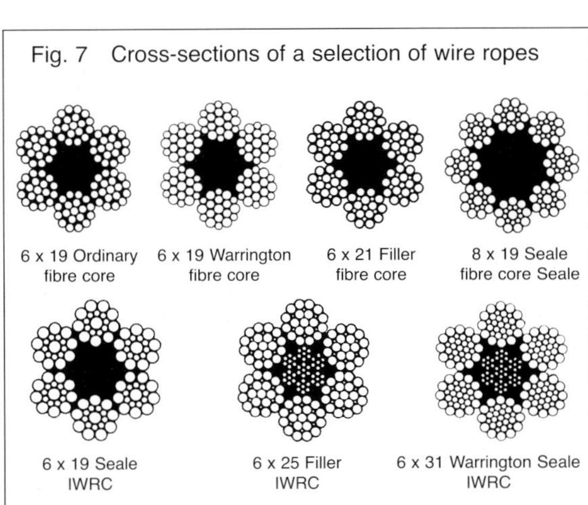
6 x 19 Ordinary fibre core
6 x 19 Warrington fibre core
6 x 21 Filler fibre core
8 x 19 Seale fibre core Seale
6 x 19 Seale IWRC
6 x 25 Filler IWRC
6 x 31 Warrington Seale IWRC
Fig. 7 Cross-sections of a selection of wire ropes

The construction specification of a wire rope is indicated by the number of strands and the number of wires in each strand (see Fig. 7).
The wires in the strands may all be the same size or a mixture of sizes. Amongst the many variations of these, the most commonly used are the 19 and 31 wire strand ropes. In wire rope the strands are usually twisted around a hemp core. Steel wire cores are used when additional strength and low stretch properties are needed.
Strands are classed according to their shape: round, flattened or concentric strand ropes and locked coil ropes (see Fig. 8). Most are round strands.

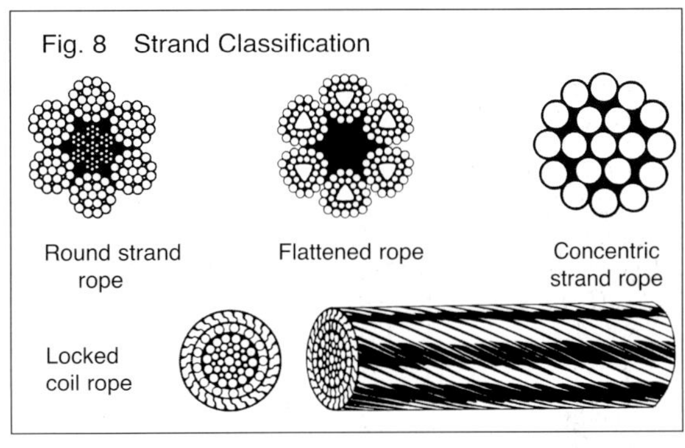
Round strand rope
Flattened rope
Concentric strand rope
Locked coil rope
Fig. 8 Strand Classification

3. TYPE OF LAY
The rope lay is the direction of rotation of the wires and the strands – clockwise (right) or anticlockwise (left) (see Fig. 9). Lay affects flexibility and wear. In regular lay ropes the wire in the strands are laid one way while the strands are laid the opposite way. This lay offers good resistance to kinking and twisting and makes them easy to handle.
In Lang's lay ropes, both the wire and the strands are laid in the same direction. Lang's lay ropes have greater resistance to abrasion and are very flexible but liable to kinking.
Unless otherwise stated the standard rope is a right, regular lay.

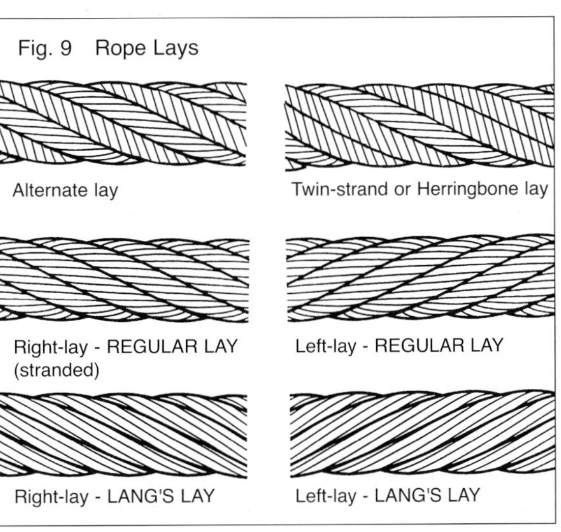
Alternate lay
Twin-strand or Herringbone lay
Right-lay - REGULAR LAY (stranded)
Left-lay - REGULAR LAY
Right-lay - LANG'S LAY
Left-lay - LANG'S LAY
Fig. 9 Rope Lays

4. PREFORMING
Preforming a rope is a manufacturing process which shapes the wires and strands so that they tend not to straighten out when cut (see Fig. 10).

Fig. 10 Preformed and non-preformed rope

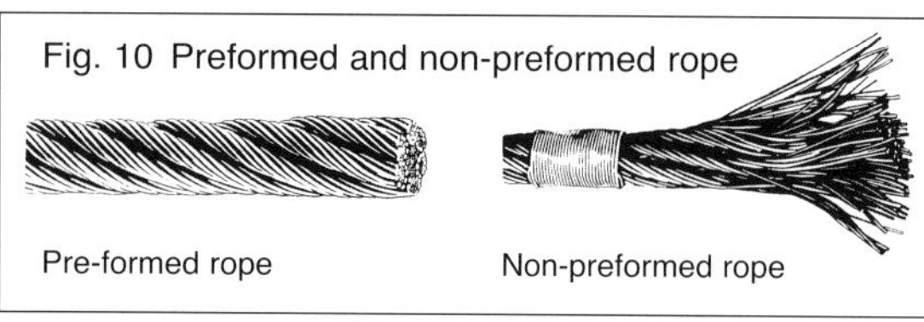
Pre-formed rope
Non-preformed rope

5. TYPE OF CORE
Cores form the heart of a rope around which the strands are laid and prevent them from jamming against each other when flexing. Cores may be of fibre or wire. Wire cores stretch less and are stronger but are less resilient and less resistant to shock than fibre cores.

SIZE
The size of a wire rope is its length measured in metres and its diameter in millimetres. The diameter of wire rope is always measured at the widest part of the rope (see Fig. 11).

Fig. 11 Measuring the diameter of a rope

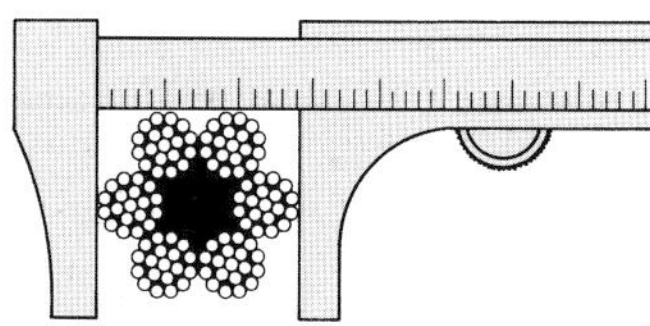

The best way to measure rope is to use a caliper gauge. Always measure at the widest point. To be certain, take several measurements.

SAFE WORKING LOAD (SWL)
The load on a wire rope should only be a fraction of its breaking load. This fraction is called the Factor of Safety (FoS) and varies between 5 and 8 according to whether or not the rope is used for carrying personnel.
The SWL is derived by dividing the minimum breaking strain of the rope by the Factor of Safety (see Fig. 12).

Care of Wire Rope

Wire rope used in the marine environment must be specially designed to withstand corrosion caused by salt water. This is normally done by using galvanised steel wire and by impregnating a fibre core with a special lubricant. Although wire rope looks indestructible, a programme of periodic inspections is necessary. Wire rope in constant service must be inspected weekly with a thorough examination every month. A wire rope inspection report should be logged by a competent person who will give an indication of when a rope should be taken out of service. The kind of defects which an inspector would look for include signs of abrasion, wear, fatigue, corrosion, kinking and evidence of incorrect reeving.

Fig. 12 To find the Safe Working Load of a Rope

$$\text{Maximum SWL} = \frac{\text{Min. breaking strength of the rope*}}{\text{Factor of Safety}}$$

Factor of Safety (FoS) varies from 3 to 8 depending on how the wire rope is being used. For example, when pulling it can be 3:1, lifting 5:1 and if carrying personnel, 8:1.

EXAMPLE
If the wire rope catalogue gives the breaking strength of the rope as 10 tonnes, and the FoS is 5, then

$$\text{Maximum SWL} = \frac{10 \text{ tonnes}}{5} = 2 \text{ tonnes}$$

* The minimum breaking loads are found in the manufacturer's rating tables or in BS 302. If the manufacturer quotes the breaking strength, that figure must be divided by the Factor of Safety to get the SWL.

When a rope is considered to be unfit for service it must be destroyed, not just discarded.
Wire ropes used in diving systems and operations may be subject to periodic examination and testing procedures laid down by industry associations such as IMCA (International Maritime Contractors' Association).

UNREELING AND UNCOILING WIRE ROPE
When unreeling or uncoiling rope for installation on a winch drum, care must be taken to avoid kinks developing. This normally requires the rope to be drawn from a rotating reel or by rolling the coil of rope along the ground. If the rope is simply lifted from a static coil it will develop kinks and twists which can cause serious damage to the rope when it is placed onto a winch drum.

SPOOLING WIRE ROPE
It is important to spool wire rope correctly onto a drum to avoid the rope criss-crossing and overlapping when tension is let off. If this does occur, the rope can be crushed and flattened when the tension is re-applied. When the rope is correctly spooled, it will tend to hug together and maintain an even layer, even when the tension is let off. This helps to protect the rope from damage.
The factors which must be taken into account before spooling wire rope on a drum are whether the rope is right or left lay, whether the spooling starts from the left or the right of the drum, and whether the rope is spooled over the top of the drum (overwind) or underneath (underwind) (see Fig. 13).

FLEET ANGLE
The fleet angle is the angle between the centre line of a sheave and the rope at its greatest excursion to the left or right of a winch drum. The greater this angle, the greater will be the wear and tear on the rope due to abrasion unless a special spooling

Fig. 13 Spooling wire rope onto a drum

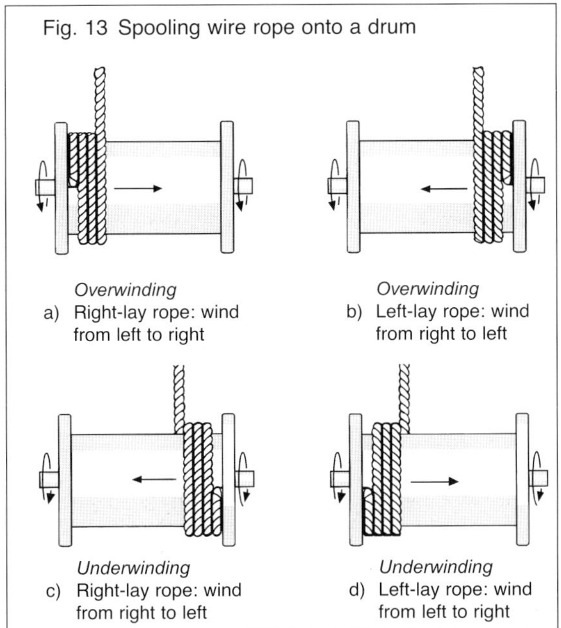
Overwinding
a) Right-lay rope: wind from left to right
Overwinding
b) Left-lay rope: wind from right to left
Underwinding
c) Right-lay rope: wind from right to left
Underwinding
d) Left-lay rope: wind from left to right

system is fitted on the winch. The abrasion is caused by the rope chafing on the drum, the sides of the sheave groove, or other turns of the wire rope. The damage caused in this way reduces the life of the rope. In the absence of a special spooling system, and to minimise this damage and wear, the fleet angle (see Fig. 14) for a plain-faced drum should not exceed 1.5° and for a grooved drum 2.5°.

Fig. 14 Fleet angle

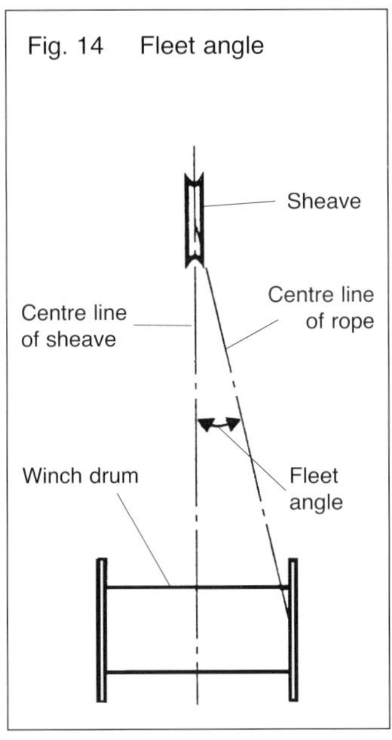
Sheave
Centre line of sheave
Centre line of rope
Winch drum
Fleet angle

End fittings and connections

Splicing of wire rope is best left to professional riggers. The average diver is more likely to use the special fittings available. Care must be taken to ensure that the fittings are of the correct load rating (SWL) and installed correctly.

END FITTINGS

• *Swaged socket* attachments are used on permanent types of installations such as pendants. The steel sleeve is hydraulically compressed over the rope (see Fig. 15). They are 100% efficient. They are not suitable where there is much movement as ropes tend to crack at the socket entry.

Fig. 15 End fittings

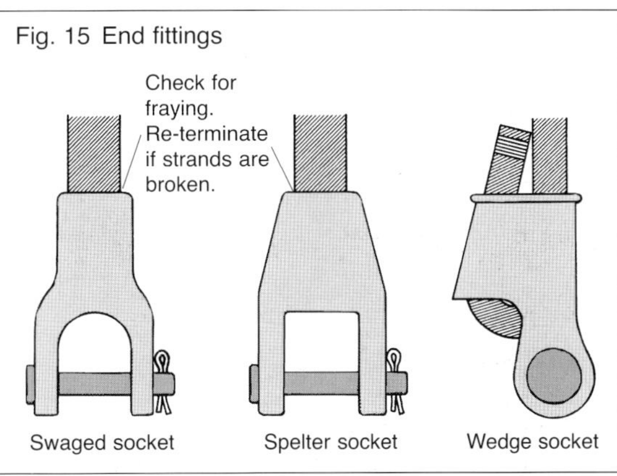
Check for fraying.
Re-terminate if strands are broken.
Swaged socket
Spelter socket
Wedge socket

• *Zinc (spelter) sockets* are the most reliable of terminal fittings made by setting the rope in molten zinc in a white metal capping. 100% efficient.

• *Wedge sockets* are simple and easy devices for anchoring a wire rope and can be just as easily detached. They are 70% efficient. Care must be taken to prevent the wedges being forced out.

CONNECTIONS

The most common method of making an eye or attaching a wire rope is with cable or Crosby clips (U-bolt and saddle type) or with 'fist grips' (double integral saddle-and-bolt type). U-bolt clips must always be fitted with the U-bolt section on the dead or short end of the rope and with the saddle on the long end (see Fig. 16). Three to four clips should be used depending on the diameter of the rope; they should be spaced at approximately three times the circumference of the rope.

Fig. 16 Wire rope connections

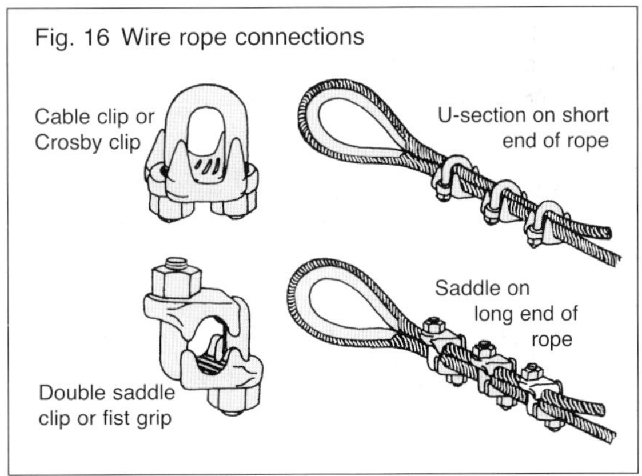
Cable clip or Crosby clip
U-section on short end of rope
Saddle on long end of rope
Double saddle clip or fist grip

Clips should never be used to join two ropes together. Connectors are the weakest point in the system and are probably the largest single known cause of mooring failures. They should always be suspected in failures from unknown cause.

Another way of making an eye in wire rope is to use a Talurit connector (see Fig. 17). The wire rope is threaded through the ferrule to form a loop. The ferrule is then placed in a hydraulic press where it is swaged onto the rope. Ferrules are available in various sizes to suit different sizes of wire rope. Their alloy construction means that if they are used for extended periods underwater, the ferrule will corrode in much the same way as a sacrificial anode, protecting the wire rope.

Fig. 17 Talurit eye connections

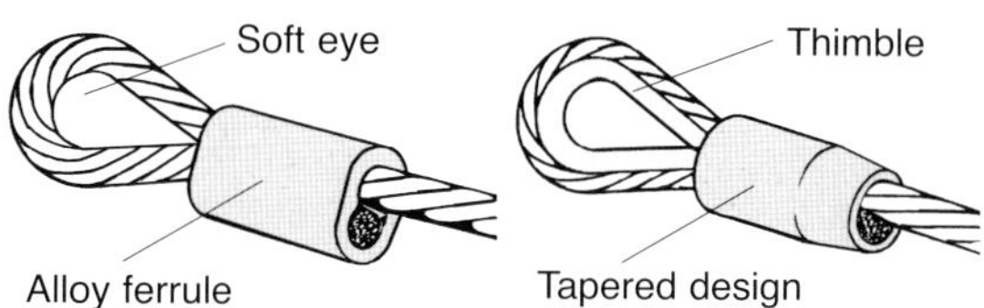
Soft eye
Thimble
Alloy ferrule
Tapered design

3.7 RIGGING e) SLINGS

Slings for attaching a purchase to a load come in many different types and materials. It is important to use a specific configuration of legs and to position them correctly around the load. The aim is to keep the centre of gravity as low as possible. The misuse of slings is a frequent cause of accidents. Slings must be of more than sufficient strength to lift the load. The safe working load (SWL) may be found in the manufacturer's SWL table.

All these points are important because in any lifting operation it is essential that the load is rigged so that it is stable. A stable load is one in which the centre of gravity is directly below the main hook and below the lowest point of attachment of the slings.

The centre of gravity of an object is that point at which the object will balance. The entire weight is concentrated at this point. A suspended object will therefore always move so that its centre of gravity is below the point of support. The hook must always be directly above this point. A load which is slung above and through the centre of gravity will be stable and will not slide out of the slings. In practice, the centre of gravity is determined by judgement, or by cautious trial and error methods, lifting a little at a time. For crane signals see page 169, Section 3.8a.

The angle between the legs of the sling and the load has a great effect on the stress imparted by the load. The lesser the angle, the more tension the legs have to bear. As a general rule the angle at the load should be kept greater than 45°. Avoid angles below 30° as this would considerably increase the load on each leg (see Fig. 1). In practice the angle at the *hook* between the slings is limited to between 0° and 120°.

The most common configurations of slings and their specific applications are shown in Fig. 2.

There are many other uses for slings apart from lifting loads.

Slings are made of many different materials such as wire rope, synthetic fibres, chain, etc. The load will determine the choice of sling.

WIRE ROPE SLINGS are widely used for specific applications underwater because of their great strength and stability. They are usually used in multiple sling assemblies (bridles). Wire rope has considerable reserves of strength in the case of a failure. However, it is often forgotten that wire rope needs care and maintenance. Kinks must be avoided

Fig. 1 Effect of sling on load angle

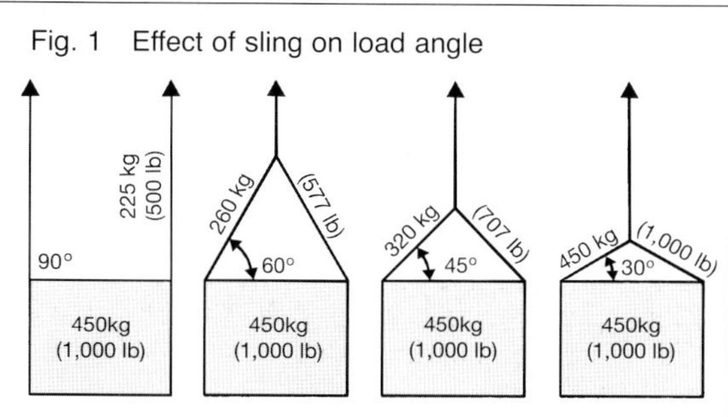
90°
225 kg (500 lb)
450kg (1,000 lb)
260 kg (577 lb)
60°
450kg (1,000 lb)
320 kg (707 lb)
45°
450kg (1,000 lb)
450 kg (1,000 lb)
30°
450kg (1,000 lb)

As the angle at the load decreases, the strain on the sling increases.

Fig. 2 Hoisting Hitches

a) Bridle hitches – for hoisting objects that have lifting lugs or attachments.

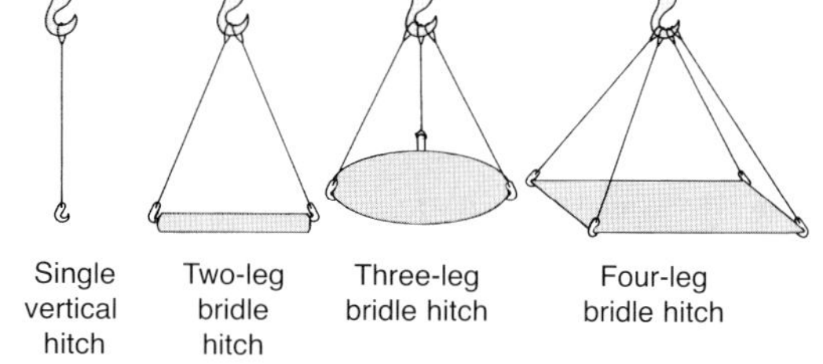
Single vertical hitch
Two-leg bridle hitch
Three-leg bridle hitch
Four-leg bridle hitch

b) Basket hitches – for hoisting objects which can be balanced

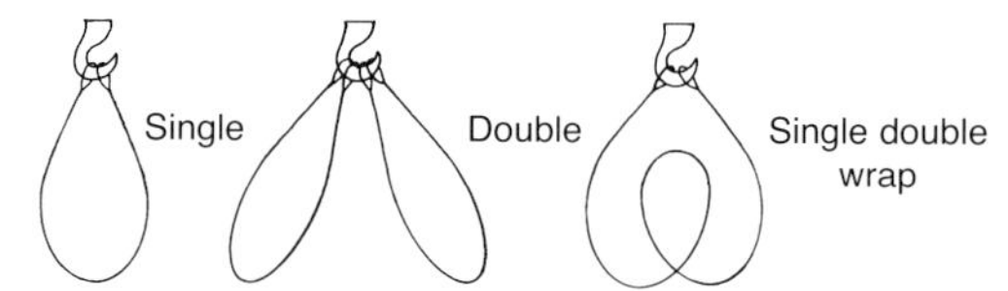
Single
Double
Single double wrap

c) Choker Hitches – not suitable for loose bundles from which material may fall

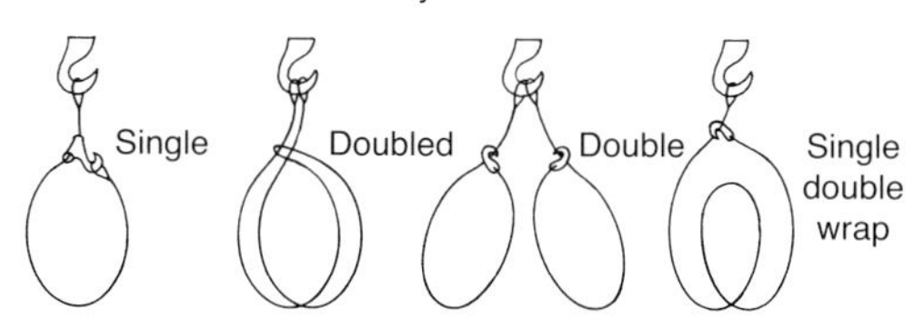
Single
Doubled
Double
Single double wrap

d) Endless or Grommet Sling

These can be used in many configurations. This example is in the choker hitch configuration. Always ensure that the splice in the rope is clear of the load or hook.

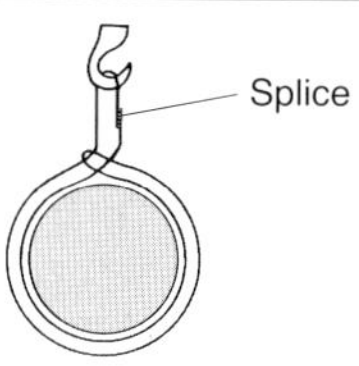
Splice

and attention must be paid to ensure that it is not used beyond its safe working life. The SWL is usually stamped on the collar.

FIBRE ROPE SLINGS are pliant and grip a load well without damaging its surface. They are only used for light loads and are rarely used underwater.

NYLON ROPE SLINGS are stronger than fibre rope slings. They are occasionally used between a chain choker and the crane hook to impart a moving force to an object – such as when picking up a pipe to line up two flanges. The stretch in nylon can usefully act as a shock-absorber between the diving support vessel and the load when there is a lot of swell.

SYNTHETIC WEB SLINGS (Fig. 3) are used extensively underwater and have several advantages:

- They are not affected by moisture.
- Being flexible, they mould to the shape of the load.
- They are non-sparking and can be safely used with explosives.
- They minimise twisting and spinning.
- They are easier and faster to use than wire.
- They do not get broken strands that cut hands and tear equipment.
- When wrapped around a member or pipe they will not damage it.
- It is much easier to load out a work basket with a selection of SWL and lengths.
- All strops are manufactured in a colour which indicates its SWL: Purple = 1 tonne; Green = 2 tonne; Yellow = 3 tonne; Red = 5 tonne; Brown = 10 tonne.

If using a web strop in any configuration other than

Fig. 3 Two types of synthetic slings

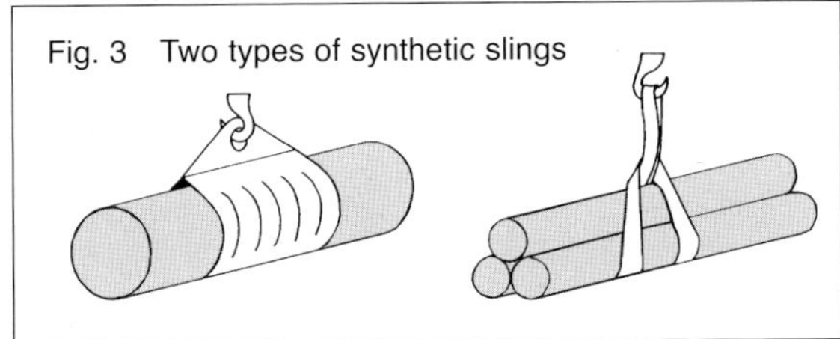

standard, ie choked around a pipe, look at the manufacturer's tag as it may change its SWL. For example, if you choke it, the SWL is halved.
The best way to store nylon rope slings in order for them to be ready for immediate deployment is to concertina them, secure with with duct tape and mark them with their SWL (in tonnes) and length (in metres) with a permanent marker, eg: 3Te, 10m.

CHAIN SLINGS are the strongest of all types of sling and need minimal maintenance. They are referred to as 'brothers.' A single brother has one leg; a pair of brothers has two legs; a triple brother has three legs and a double brother has four legs. All brothers must have a master link. A length of chain without a master link is not a brother. Some have a safety hook (usually locking) instead of a shackle at the end.

Chain is very hard wearing and is the safest type of sling for lifting. Chain has a better grip on cylindrical surfaces than wire rope and should be used when slipping might occur. A good example of chain use is when lining up two flange bolt holes. A chain sling would be most effective in imparting a rolling force to the pipe. Chain should be used when rigging has to pass over rough surfaces or sharp edges.

Fig. 4 Terminology of slings

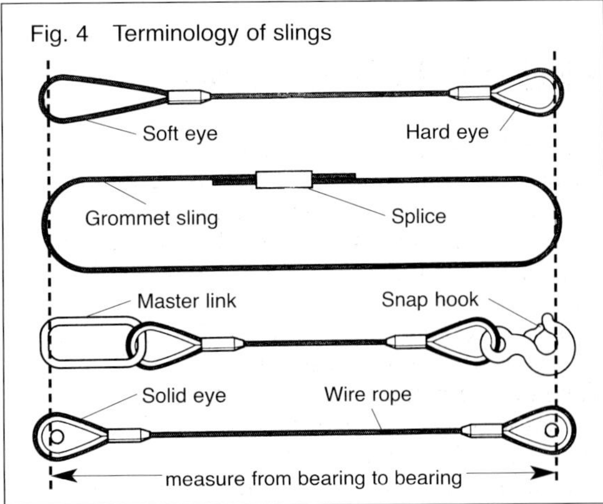
Soft eye
Hard eye
Grommet sling
Splice
Master link
Snap hook
Solid eye
Wire rope
measure from bearing to bearing

Fig. 5 Terminology of multiple leg sling assemblies

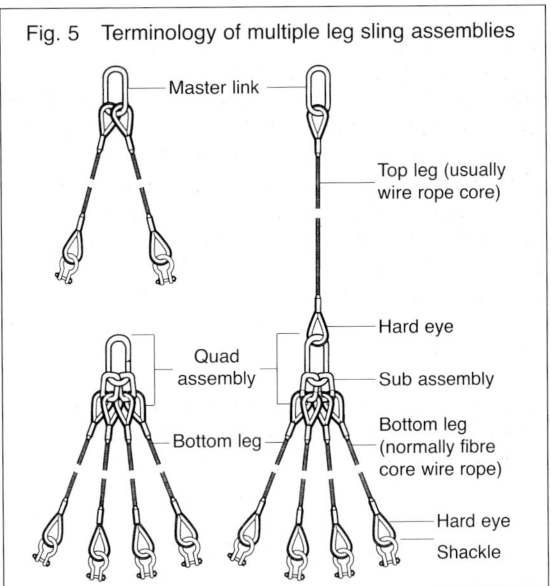
Master link
Top leg (usually wire rope core)
Hard eye
Quad assembly
Sub assembly
Bottom leg
Bottom leg (normally fibre core wire rope)
Hard eye
Shackle

Hooks on Slings

Open hooks are not generally used underwater because of their tendency to become unhooked. Snap hooks or shackles are more reliable. There are some rules about using hooks:

1. With a 2-leg bridle hitch the hooks should point outwards when picking up a load. The exception is when lifting a joint of pipe inwards, as in Fig. 6a.
2. With choker hitches, the bill of the hook should always point downwards. When picking up a joint of pipe with a double choker hitch the hooks should point down and outwards (see

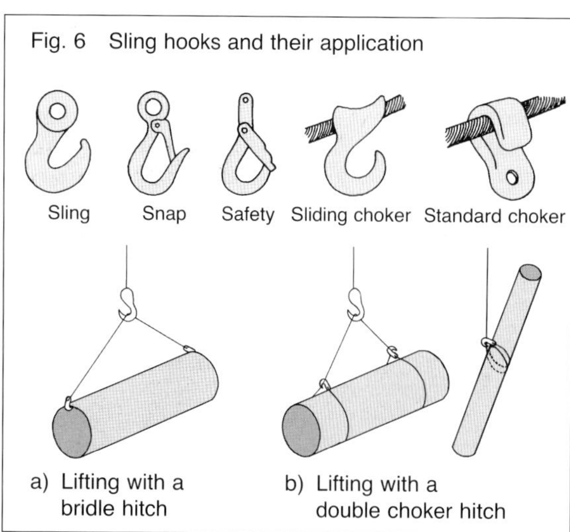
Sling
Snap
Safety
Sliding choker
Standard choker
a) Lifting with a bridle hitch
b) Lifting with a double choker hitch
Fig. 6 Sling hooks and their application

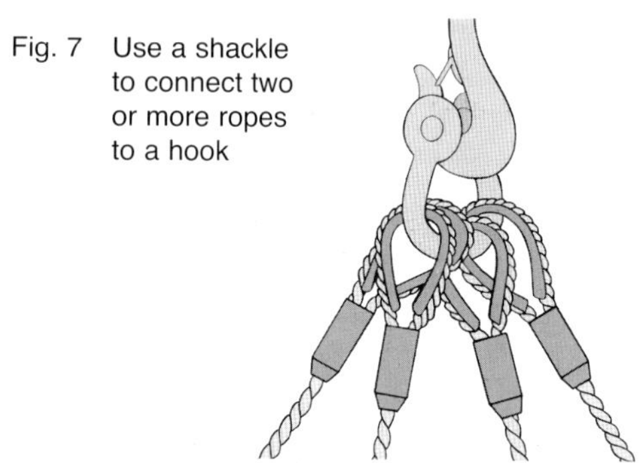
Fig. 7 Use a shackle to connect two or more ropes to a hook

Fig. 6b). As a general rule hooks must point down on vertical lifts.

3. Try to centre a crane hook as near as possible over a load.
4. Use a shackle whenever two or more ropes are to be placed over a hook (see Fig. 7)

SLINGS – OPERATIONAL SAFETY

1. Inspect all lifting gear regularly. Do not use damaged or worn equipment.
2. Destroy defective equipment so that others can not inadvertently use it.
3. Determine the load weight before lifting.
4. Find out the SWL of the equipment being used. Do not exceed it.
5. If a sling is run over a hook or shackle, its SWL will be reduced.
6. Make sure that the wire rope has a safety factor of at least 5. That is, the rope or sling should not be used for loads greater than one fifth of the breaking strain.
7. Avoid sharp bends, kinks, pinching or crushing.
8. Keep the hoist well clear of power lines at all times in order to avoid the risk of electrocution.
9. Watch the weather. Wind and swell can affect the control of a hoist.
10. Extreme caution should be exercised in temperatures below freezing to ensure that no equipment is shock-loaded.

3.7 RIGGING f) ANCHORS

There is an appropriate anchor for every type and size of vessel or installation, depending on the particular function the anchor is required to perform, the nature of the seabed where the anchor will be used, and the prevailing weather conditions. The seabed may be categorised into three types as far as anchors are concerned:

1. Mud or silt, which offers little resistance to forces.
2. Sand, which provides good holding for specifically designed anchors.
3. Rock, where only the deadweight anchors will hold although occasionally a fluke will catch.

The holding power of an anchor is its efficiency expressed in terms of holding power per pound of its own weight. This is greatly affected by the fluke/shank angle, depending on the relationship between the flukes to the length of the shank and to the tripping palm or stock stabiliser which turns the anchor to its correct burial position. The holding power of an anchor in sand can reach 35 times its own weight, but only about twice its weight in mud. The essentials for good holding power are the reliable opening of the flukes at the tripping palm areas and good fluke design to maximise deep penetration and stability.

Fig. 1 Parts of an anchor

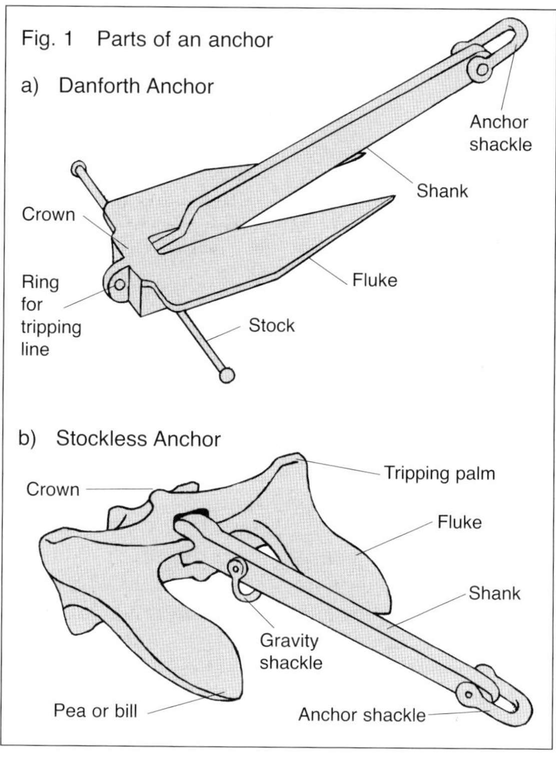
a) Danforth Anchor
Anchor shackle
Shank
Crown
Fluke
Ring for tripping line
Stock
b) Stockless Anchor
Crown
Tripping palm
Fluke
Shank
Gravity shackle
Pea or bill
Anchor shackle

The flukes will penetrate the seabed according to their design and the nature of the bottom. As an approximate guide, the angle of penetration (fluke/shank angle) should be as follows:

- in mud, approximately 50º.
- in sand, approximately 30º.
- hard to variable seabed, approximately 45º.

Drag is the distance required for the anchor to be pulled over the bottom before attaining any holding power. An anchor will drag if it is of a type unsuitable for that particular sea bottom or if insufficient cable is laid out.

Originally ships' anchors were only required to hold a vessel in shallow water in the event of a propulsion or steering gear failure. It is the weight of the chain, not the anchor, that moors them. The anchor is only a 'nail' in the seabed to stretch out the chain. The general rule is for the weight of the laid-out chain to be six times the weight of the anchor.

To function properly the anchor ought to be as nearly horizontal as possible as this position tends to drive the flukes into the seabed. To ensure this horizontal position the seamanlike practice is to lay out a length of anchor cable or wire at least three times the depth of the water. The ship's bow turns into the wind/tide and rides to a long sloping catenary.

Characteristics of Anchor Types

Anchors can be broadly classified into 3 groups:

1. DRAGGING ANCHORS rely on their weight and, to some degree, on hooking or suction to the seabed for their holding power (Fig. 2).

Fig. 2 How a Stockless dragging Anchor holds

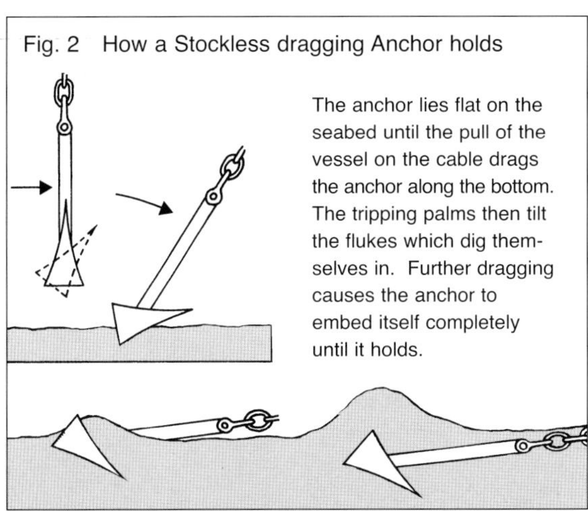
The anchor lies flat on the seabed until the pull of the vessel on the cable drags the anchor along the bottom. The tripping palms then tilt the flukes which dig themselves in. Further dragging causes the anchor to embed itself completely until it holds.

This type of anchor and anchor chain has a resistance to drag equal to its own weight in sandy soils. On a clay bottom its resistance is about 30% and on mud it is even less. Dragging anchors would be unacceptable for use with a pipelay or derrick barge.

Representative types of dragging anchors include clump, mushroom, fisherman or kedge, and stockless.

2. BURIAL ANCHORS do not rely on weight but depend on the withdrawal resistance of their large flukes.

The early stockless anchors were unstable and tended to turn the anchor so that the flukes pointed upwards and did not bite into the seabed so stockless anchors were developed with stabilising stocks protruding through the head or crown. Unfortunately these have the disadvantage that the pendant wire is easily fouled around the stock. Dropping could sometimes bend or break it. If a burial anchor such as a Danforth falls onto hard bottom, the results will probably be as shown in Fig. 3b.

Fig. 3 Fluke penetration

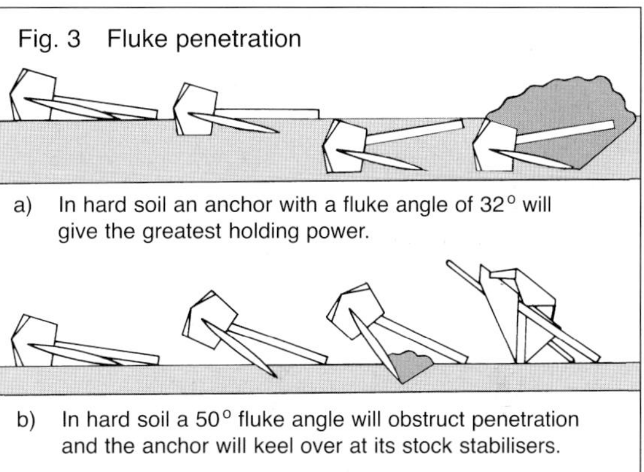

a) In hard soil an anchor with a fluke angle of 32° will give the greatest holding power.

b) In hard soil a 50° fluke angle will obstruct penetration and the anchor will keel over at its stock stabilisers.

Should it fall onto soft bottom however, it may behave as in Fig. 4. At first its heavy head will make it sink with the flukes pointing upwards but as soon as a horizontal pull is exerted, the anchor will slide up on the flukes. The small tripping area on a Danforth could result in the flukes not turning around.

To overcome these problems a new generation of stockless anchors has been developed such as the Flipper-Delta anchor (see Fig. 5).

Fig. 4 Behaviour of a Danforth burial anchor in a soft bottom

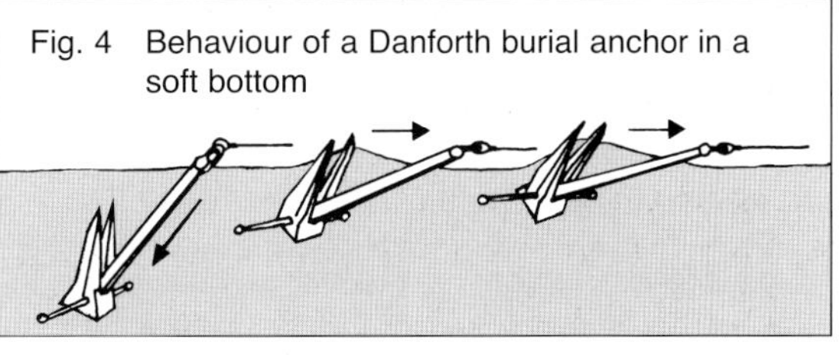

Fig. 5 Behaviour of a Flipper Delta anchor in a soft bottom

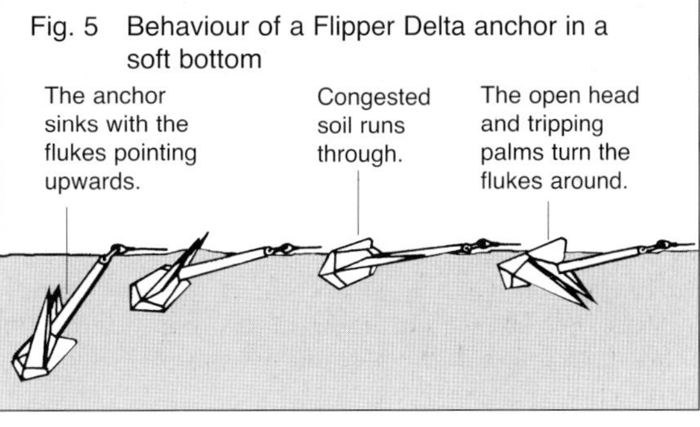
The anchor sinks with the flukes pointing upwards.
Congested soil runs through.
The open head and tripping palms turn the flukes around.

Anchoring systems in use offshore have quite separate requirements from ships' systems and may be divided into two aspects:

1. For fixed installations, such as a guyed tower, capable of withstanding the most severe environmental conditions and requiring that the integrity of the structure may be safely maintained by direct permanent contact with the seabed. Systems commonly in use are piled or gravity anchors.
2. For mobile installations, such as semi-submersibles, SPMs, DSVs, or pipelay barges where the environmental criteria would allow operations to continue (Fig. 6).

Fig. 6 Typical mooring arrangement for semi-submersible vessels

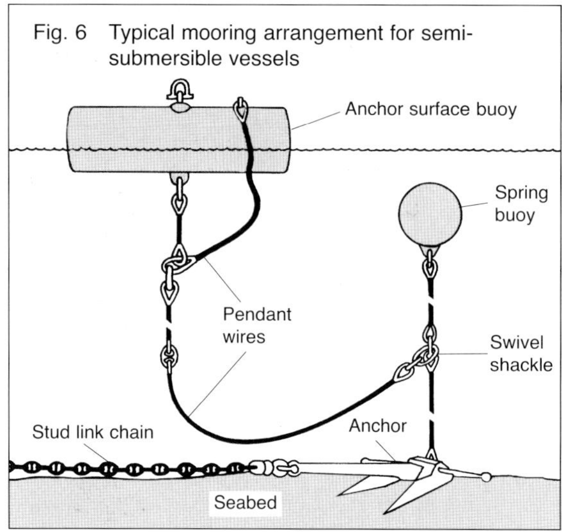
Anchor surface buoy
Spring buoy
Pendant wires
Swivel shackle
Stud link chain
Anchor
Seabed

Mobile systems incorporate special anchors, chain cables and wires tensioned by dedicated winches such that the installation can be securely moored in all conditions. This is known as a marine system but it should be appreciated that the mode of working a mooring system for a semi-submersible is entirely different from that for a ship.

The increased depth of water (up to 610m/2,000ft), the inability to turn into the wind to face the prevailing weather and the lack of compensating catenary effect all require different design approaches. These would involve the design of the anchors, a much longer scope of wire, increased horsepower on the winches and a planned geometry of layout.

It should be noted that, regardless of whether or not an installation is classed as a ship, if it is involved in mineral exploitation in the UK waters it is, by definition, an offshore installation and therefore must comply with HSE requirements.

3. EMBEDMENT ANCHORS are a form of burial anchor which penetrate into the seabed by means of an explosive/hydrostatic/pneumatic charge.

Pendant (or Pennant) Wires and Buoys

To facilitate breaking out mooring anchors, a pendant wire is secured to the crown of the anchor and located by means of a surface marker buoy. These pendant wires may be of a considerable length dictated by the water depth. Because of the tide's rise and fall, the pendant may slacken and foul its own anchor. Supporting the pendant on a spring buoy reduces fouling and chafing.

Chasers (see Fig. 7)

Pendant buoys have a habit of getting lost. Fitting a chaser around the mooring line eliminates the need for them. To lay the anchor the chaser is positioned around the shank near the crown and is towed out from the installation by the anchor handling boat. At the planned site it is lowered to the seabed by the pendant wire. To recover the anchor the same procedure is followed: the handling boat tows the chaser out to the anchor until it is arrested by the anchor crown when it can be broken out and raised.

Anchor Cradles or 'racks'

Mooring anchors on installations are usually stowed on cradles or racks protruding from the side (Fig. 8). The transfer of the anchor, chaser and pendant to the anchor handling boat is more easily accomplished from the cradle. Another method is to use davits.

Fig. 7 Use of a chaser and chain depressors

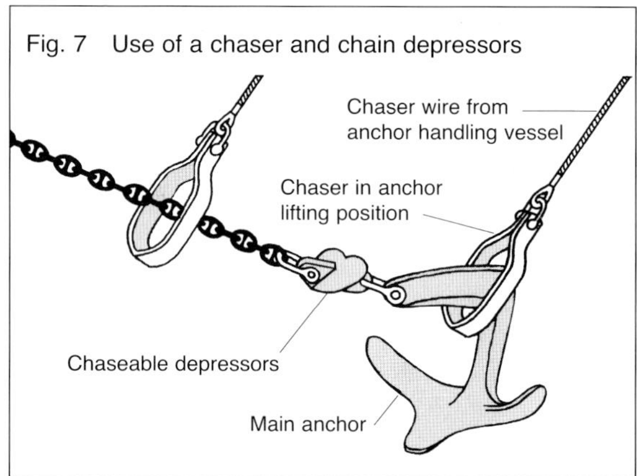
Chaser wire from anchor handling vessel
Chaser in anchor lifting position
Chaseable depressors
Main anchor

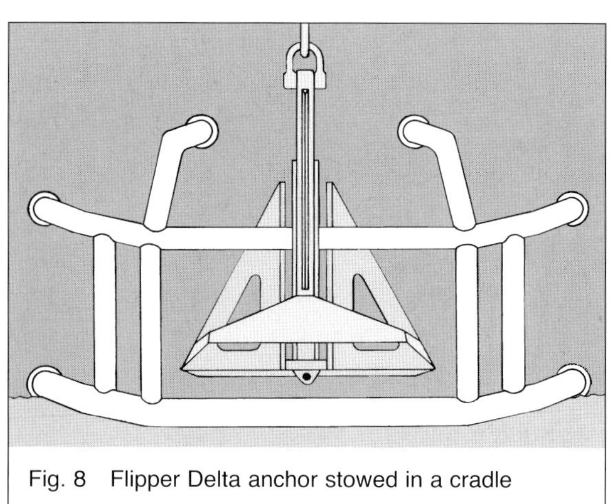

Fig. 8 Flipper Delta anchor stowed in a cradle

	ANCHOR CHARACTERISTICS	TYPICAL EXAMPLES
DRAGGING ANCHORS	Clump types are simply weights, consequently effective in all grounds.	CLUMP
	Stock anchors with small fluke area and stabilisers at the front and the shank.	STOCK, or KEDGE, MOORING ANCHOR
	Anchors with a square shank, not stock stabilisers, the stabilising resistance being built into the fluke design. Efficient in sand and heavy mud but drags on soft mud, shingle or shell.	US NAVY STOCKLESS, BEIJERS, UNION
BURIAL ANCHORS	Anchors with extremely short, thick stabilisers hinged at the rear and relatively short, more or less square shanks. Not efficient in soft mud.	AC14, STOKES, SNUGSTOW
	Anchors with hinge and stabilisers at the rear and with relatively long shanks and stabilisers. Suitable for all bottoms and for sand and mud if allowed to settle.	DANFORTH, MOORFAST, STATO, BOSS.
	Anchors with large hollow flukes, hinged near the centre of gravity and with relatively short shank and stabilisers. Effective in all bottoms, especially on soft ground.	STEVIN/STEFIX, STEVMUD, FLIPPER-DELTA.
	Anchors with 'elbowed' shank giving deep penetration. Effective in all grounds.	BRUCE, BRUCE TS, HOOK, CQR.
	Anchors with ultra penetration and high holding power. Particularly effective in soft ground.	DELTA, KITE, WISHBONE (STEVPRIS).
EMBEDMENT ANCHORS	Anchors with ultra penetration, high holding power to fluke weight ratio. Usually a single fluke attached to a long pendant. Does not rely on cable weight. Suitable in hard bottom.	OMC TENSIONS PILE, PEA (PROPELLANT EMBEDMENT ANCHOR), REA (RAFOSS EXPLOSIVE ANCHOR).

Types of ships' anchors

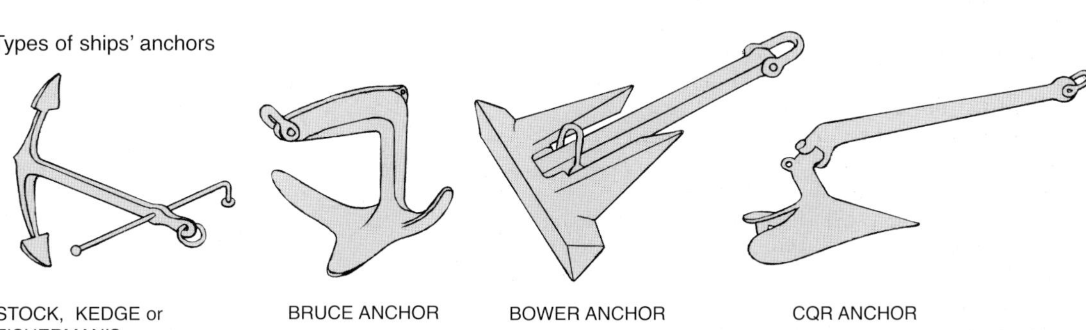

STOCK, KEDGE or FISHERMAN'S ANCHOR

Fisherman's kedge, stock anchors. A common type for small craft. Good holding but awkward to stow.

BRUCE ANCHOR

BOWER ANCHOR

Bower or stockless, Admiralty, AC anchors. For larger vessels.

CQR ANCHOR

CQR plough type, Bruce and Danforth anchors are widely used in yachts and small to medium-sized craft.

a) CRANES and LIFTING DEVICES

Cranes

Crane operations can introduce significant hazards. Appropriate regulations and codes of practice should be complied with.

Crane types can be described in various ways:

1. Mobility
   a) *Stationary*.
   b) *Mobile*. These cranes may be on tracked or wheeled vehicles (Figs. 1 and 2). As well as lifting and swivelling, mobile cranes can move loads from place to place. Outriggers and sea fastenings improve stability. They are particularly sensitive to vessel movements, dynamic loading and weather factors. Special care must be taken when operating them afloat including considerations of vessel stability. It is common practice to halve the maximum lift of a mobile crane when used afloat.
2. Boom type
   a) *Lattice boom*. A common type of crane, lattice boom cranes are both strong and lightweight (Figs. 1 & 3).
   b) *Telescopic boom*. An hydraulically-operated, telescopic boom crane which is often found on mobile cranes (Fig. 2).
   c) *Knuckle boom ('cherry-picker')* (Fig. 4). Knuckle boom cranes reduce or eliminate the length of lifting wire between the tip of the jib and the load. This reduces the tendency of the load to swing: an important consideration when operating at sea.

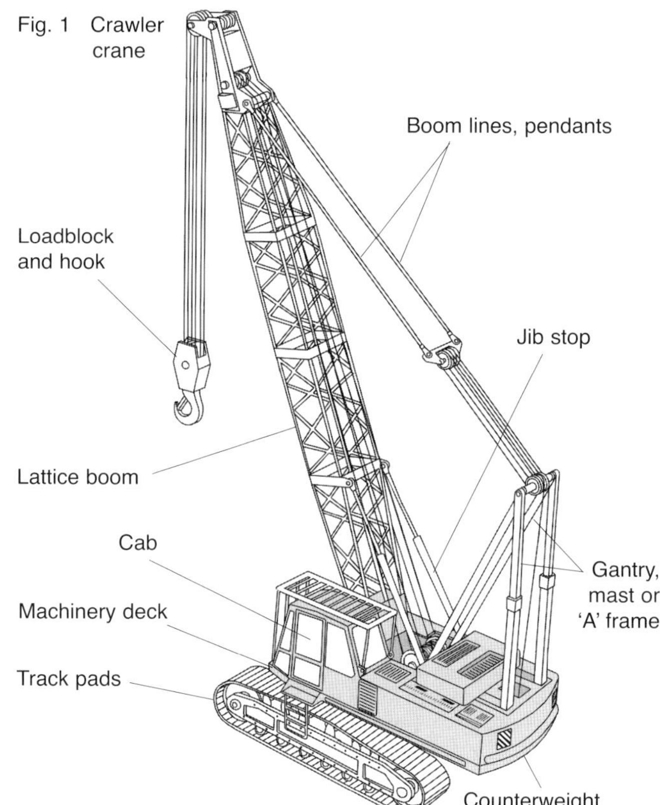
Boom lines, pendants
Loadblock and hook
Jib stop
Lattice boom
Cab
Gantry, mast or 'A' frame
Machinery deck
Track pads
Counterweight
Fig. 1 Crawler crane

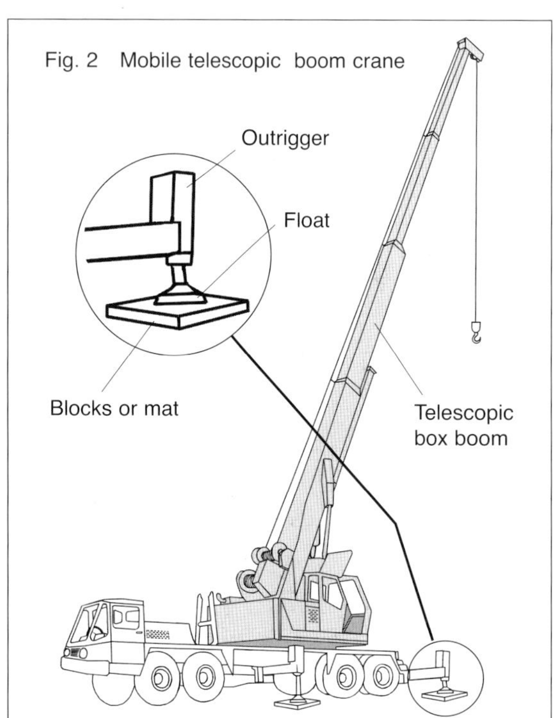
Outrigger
Float
Blocks or mat
Telescopic box boom
Fig. 2 Mobile telescopic boom crane

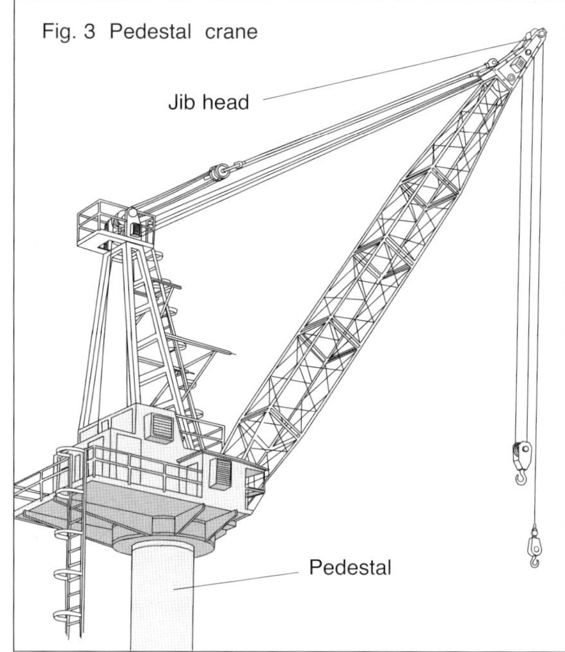
Jib head
Pedestal
Fig. 3 Pedestal crane

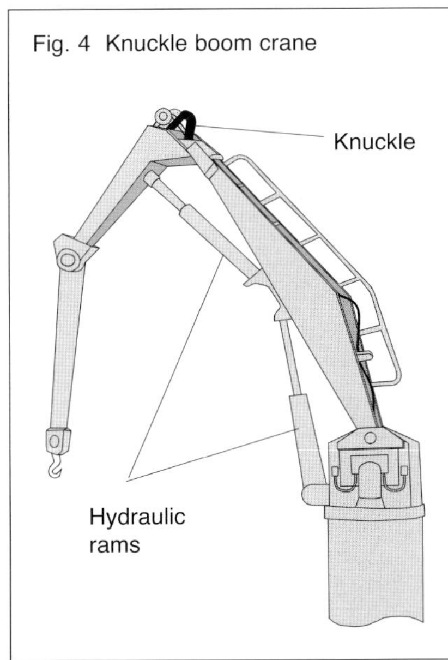
Knuckle
Hydraulic
rams
Fig. 4 Knuckle boom crane

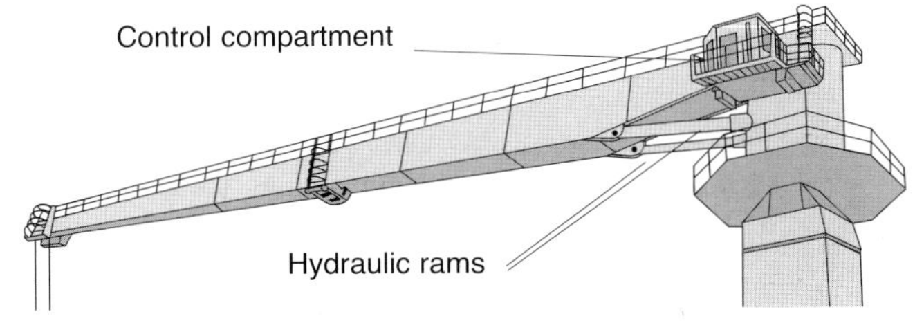
Control compartment
Hydraulic rams
Fig. 5 Box boom crane

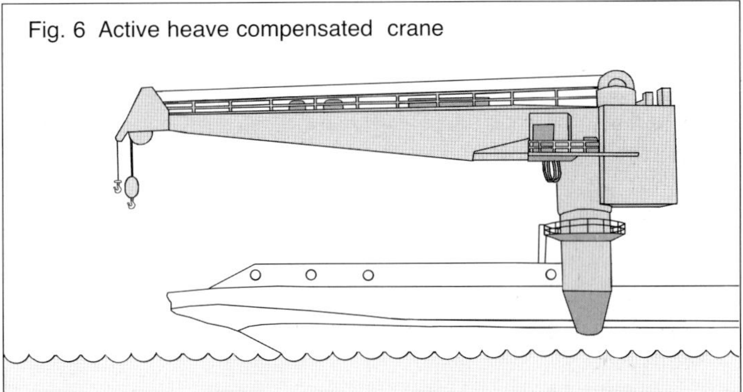
Fig. 6 Active heave compensated crane

d) *Box boom* (Fig. 5). A robust and reliable crane, this type of crane is commonly used offshore. The boom is resistant to collisions with swinging loads. Box boom cranes may have telescopic heads (as in Fig. 2).

3. Other identifying features, include:
   a) *Slewing*.
   b) *Pedestal*. These cranes (see Figs 3–6) are fixed, slewing cranes and are commonly seen on offshore vessel installations.
   c) *Heave compensated*. Heave compensated cranes (Fig. 6) incorporate an active heave compensation system which raises and lowers the load out of phase with the vessel's heave. The effect is that the load in suspension remains relatively stationary while the vessel and crane move up and down. This is particularly useful when moving loads underwater near a fixed structure or the sea bed and where divers may be operating.
   d) *Constant Tension* is where the load is landed and the tension in the wire is kept constant so that the load will not lift off the bottom regardless of the movement of the vessel (eg, as in a DP DSV taut wire weight). This is a useful safety feature when divers are working near a load.

4. Other types of crane:
   a) *Trolley on runway beam* (Fig. 7). These can be powered or manually-operated. Their use will be restricted on vessels where the vessel's movement can induce movement of the trolley and/or the load.

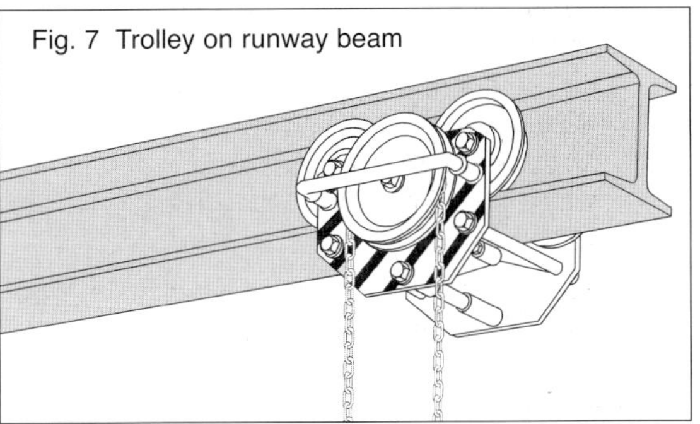
Fig. 7 Trolley on runway beam

   b) *Overhead ('gantry travelling')* (Fig. 8). These are mainly used onshore. When they operate on rails located at deck level they should be provided with audible and visual warnings which alert everyone in the area when the crane is travelling. Where they are in transit afloat or in preparation for storm conditions, they should be tied back to the installation.

SAFETY FEATURES

In addition to the safety features mentioned in the crane descriptions above, cranes should be fitted with a Rated Capacity Indicator (RCI) which gives the crane driver details of the actual/permissible loads (at the appropriate radius) and the movement over the working area where the load is lifted or set down. The greater the radius of the load, the lower the maximum lift capacity of the crane (see Fig. 9) and the greater the vertical movement caused by a rolling vessel (see Fig. 10). It is helpful to have a duplicate of the RCI in Dive Control so that it can be monitored by the Diving Supervisor.

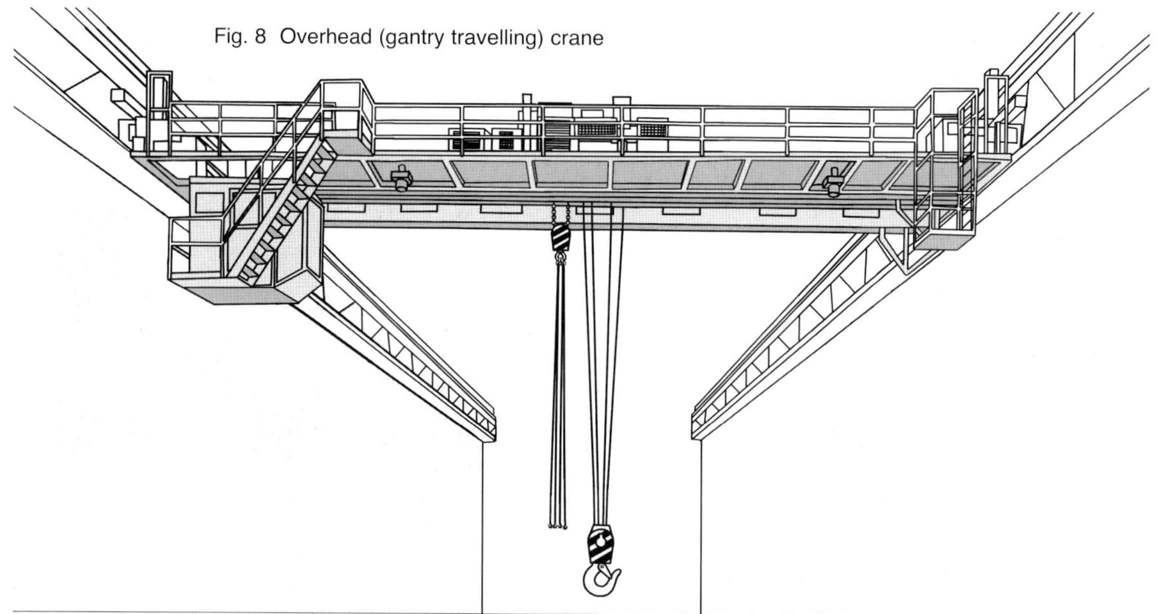
Fig. 8 Overhead (gantry travelling) crane

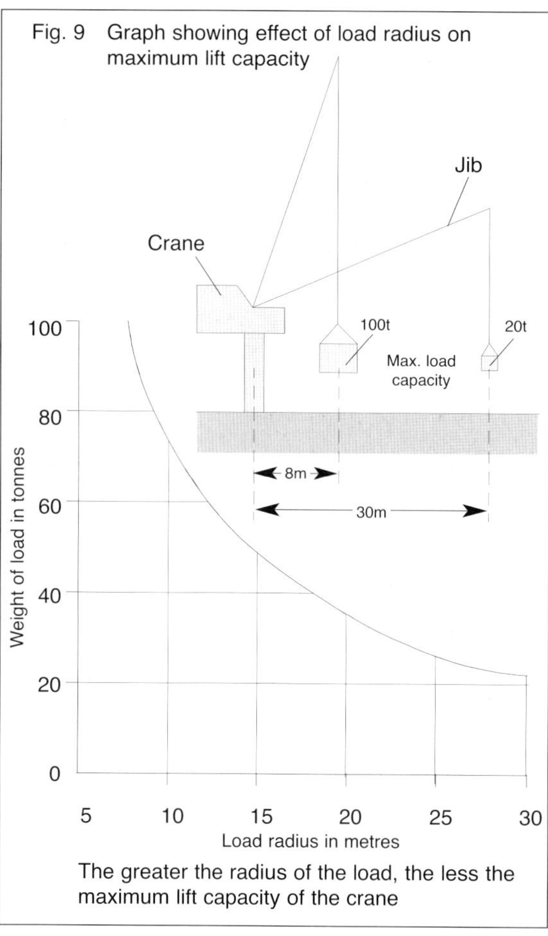
Crane
Jib
100t
20t
Max. load capacity
8m
30m
Weight of load in tonnes
100
80
60
40
20
0
5
10
15
20
25
30
Load radius in metres
Fig. 9 Graph showing effect of load radius on maximum lift capacity

The greater the radius of the load, the less the maximum lift capacity of the crane

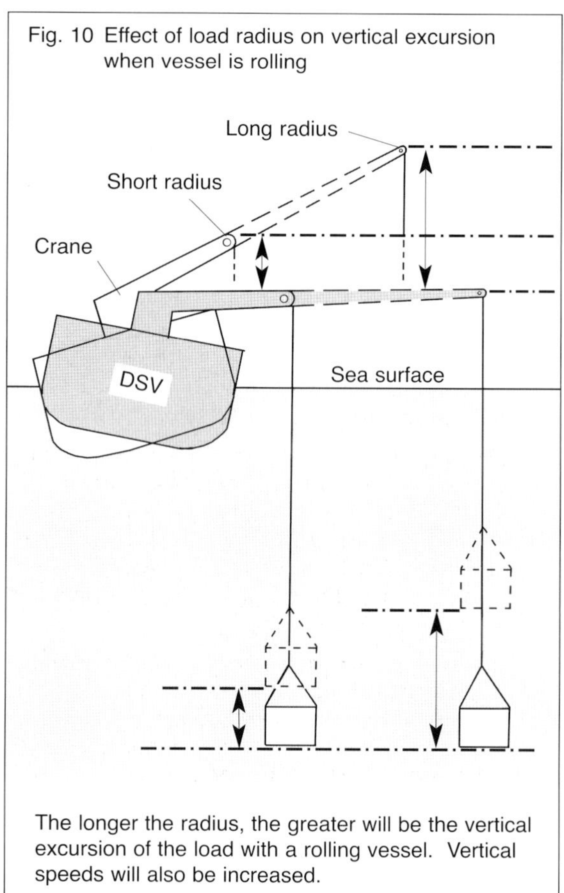
Long radius
Short radius
Crane
DSV
Sea surface
Fig. 10 Effect of load radius on vertical excursion when vessel is rolling

The longer the radius, the greater will be the vertical excursion of the load with a rolling vessel. Vertical speeds will also be increased.

Derricks

Derricks are stationary hoisting machines. There are three main types.

1. GIN POLE DERRICKS. These are the simplest form of derrick comprising of pole (or mast) secured by four guy ropes. A pulley at the top of the pole provides the lifting arrangement.
2. SHEER LEG DERRICKS. These derricks have two crossed masts, joined at the top and secured by two guy lines.

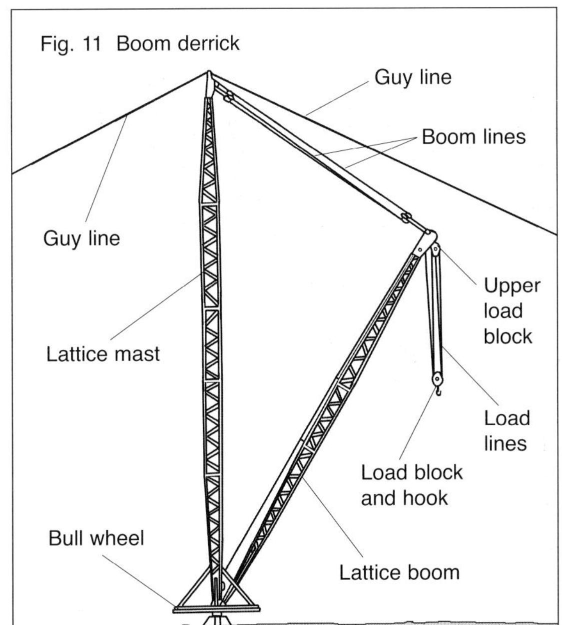
Guy line
Boom lines
Guy line
Upper load block
Lattice mast
Load lines
Load block and hook
Bull wheel
Lattice boom
Fig. 11 Boom derrick

3. BOOM DERRICKS. A boom derrick has a long boom or pole which is hinged at the bottom of the mast base. A cable attached to the top of the mast supports the boom (see Fig. 11).

Davits

Davits are normally used for handling small boats, including lifeboats, into and out of the water.

They can be simple devices (as in Fig. 12) or scaled down versions of various types of cranes including knuckle or telescopic booms.

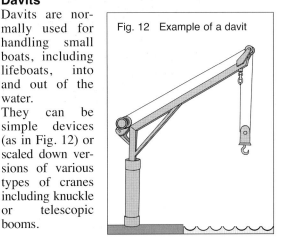

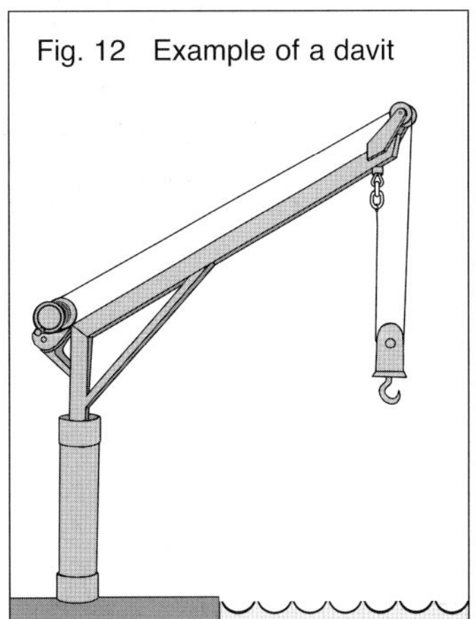
Fig. 12 Example of a davit

CRANES - OPERATIONAL SAFETY

Personnel and Maintenance:

1. There should be a person in overall charge of the lifting operation eg: Shift Supervisor, Base Manager, Project Engineer, Deck Foreman. He must be competent to perform the duties which will include the production of a risk assessment for the lifting operation(s).
2. The Competent Person in charge of a lifting operation must ensure the equipment used is certified, fit-for-purpose and visually checked for defects etc before it is used.
3. The Competent Person should approve a Lift Plan for each lifting operation. This should include step-by-step instructions for the lift, the equipment required and the activities assigned to each team member. The lift plans can be generic or load-specific. It should be discussed with all members of the team at a Toolbox Meeting.
4. There should always be a competent Banksman or Signaller positioned so that he has an unrestricted view of the load and crane operator in order to be able to give load manoeuvring instructions to the Crane Operator via hand signals or radio.
5. The condition and safety of the lifting equipment should be thoroughly checked at regular intervals by a competent person.
6. There should be a visual and, if necessary, also a function check of the lifting equipment by a competent person at intervals between the 'thorough examinations.'
7. The Slinger/Load Handler who attaches/detaches the loads on/from the lifting equipment must be a competent person.
8. Every member of the team has the responsibility to stop the lifting operation at any time if they believe the operation is unsafe.

Moving a load:

1. The signaller must check that the area is clear before lowering a load.
2. The signaller must never give the signal to lift until he has clearance from the person slinging the load.
3. Nobody must ride on a load.
4. Slings should not be attached to bands, strops or fastenings on packages unless they are specifically designed for lifting.
5. Protect slings and edges against abrasion with strips of softwood or other suitable material.
6. Always use four-legged slings on trays or pallets and fix a net if necessary to stop items falling off.
7. Always use the correct slings with spreaders on long loads.
8. Always first 'test lift' awkward loads, like pipework, to check for stability.
9. Always raise and lower loads smoothly and lower them immediately if the load shows signs of slipping.
10. Never lift a load over personnel.
11. Never get underneath a load.
12. Never leave unattended winches or cranes with loads slung.

Winches

Winches may be powered by hydraulics, compressed air or electricity. They are rated for either 'general' or 'people-carrying' use (see Fig. 13).

A winch driven by compressed air (air tugger) can be very noisy. The noise can be reduced by attaching a suitable hose to the winch exhaust; the other end of the hose can be placed underwater.

Fig. 13 General and man-riding winches

The operator's side of a winch should always be covered with a steel mesh guard.

General utility winch
This kind of winch should never be used for moving personnel.

Man-riding winch

WINCHES - OPERATIONAL SAFETY

Appropriate regulations and codes of practice should always be complied with when operating winches.

General utility winches

1. The winch-operating lever should automatically return to neutral when released.
2. Automatic brakes should be fitted so that they apply whenever the operating lever is returned to neutral or if there is loss of power to the drive control system.
3. These winches should never be used for lifting people.

Man-riding winches

These winches are specially designed for lifting people.

1. They should be clearly marked 'Suitable for lifting people' or 'Suitable for man-riding'.
2. A second independent brake should be provided for use if the automatic brake fails. This brake should be manually operated unless it is completely independent of the automatic braking systems.
3. The winch must also be able to lower the carrier in a controlled manner in an emergency or if there is loss of power.
4. The rope should be automatically spooled onto the winch drum to prevent bunching.
5. A safety test should be carried out at the beginning of each mobilisation by operating the man-riding winch with a maximum test load.
6. The lifting wire should have a safety factor of 8 to 1 (ie, a safety factor of 4 to 1 plus a 2g factor to take dynamic loading into account).

Chain hoists and lever hoists (Fig 14)

These are not usually made for marine applications so they need to be regularly checked to ensure that they can be safely used underwater.

Fig. 14 Typical chain hoists

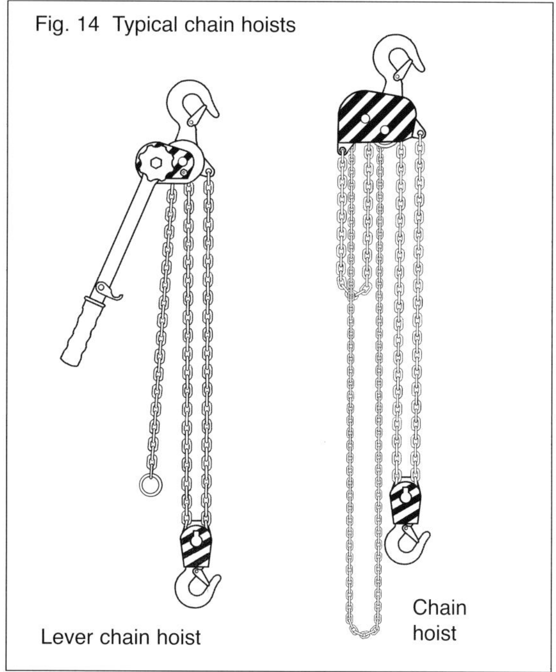
Lever chain hoist
Chain hoist

HOISTS - OPERATIONAL SAFETY

1. Regularly check for corrosion.
2. Only appropriate lubricants should be used.
3. The Safe Working Load (SWL) should be permanently marked on the hoist.
4. The anchor point for suspending the hoist must be of adequate strength.
5. They should never be used for lifting people.
6. There must be an automatic braking system which allows the smooth lowering of the load.
7. Manually-operated hoists should never be power driven.
8. Only people experienced in their use and rigging should operate hoists.

Hooks and hook blocks (Fig. 15)

The Safe Working Load (SWL) should be legibly marked on every hook, identifiable with an in-date test document. Hooks should be fitted with an effective safety latch or mechanism which ensures that slings or pennant wires are positively held captive under all operating circumstances. Every hook block should carry a non-removable plate showing its SWL and other technical information. Simple spring-loaded safety catches can be unreliable. A positive latching arrangement such as a cargo hook is preferable.

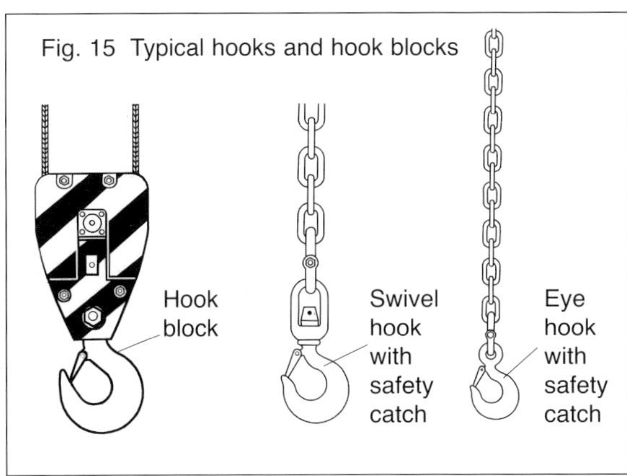
Hook
block
Swivel
hook
with
safety
catch
Eye
hook
with
safety
catch
Fig. 15 Typical hooks and hook blocks

Work baskets

Work baskets are often used to lower heavy tools and equipment to the diver (Fig. 16). They come in many sizes and may be moved by crane, A-frame or tugger winch.

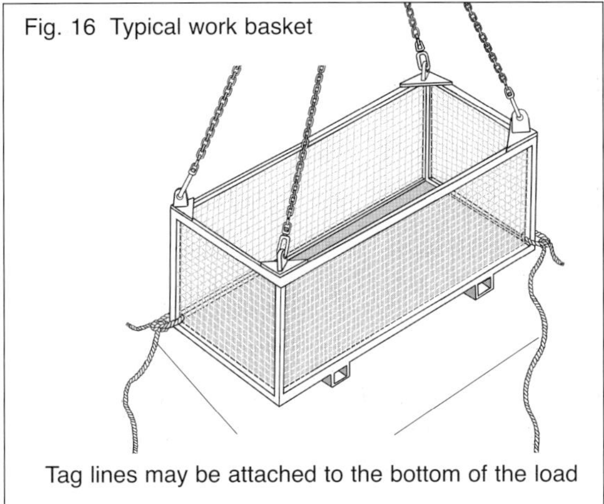
Fig. 16 Typical work basket

Tag lines may be attached to the bottom of the load

Tag lines are usually attached to the lowest point on a load to help handlers to control the load and land it correctly. Topside tag lines on large loads can run around a strong point such as a bollard or cleat to increase control.

Underwater, divers may use tag lines on large loads such as a concrete mattresses, where placement and orientation are important. The tag lines can be weighted and illuminated by strobes or light sticks.

Lifting operations from DP vessels

MOVING THE LOAD

When diving from a DP DSV, there are two ways of moving a subsea load: by moving the crane and keeping the vessel still, or by moving the vessel and keeping the crane still. If the diver is armed with a compass it is often easier and quicker to move the vessel with a single compass direction and distance command. When diving from a barge which is kept in position using 4, 8 or 12 anchor winches, it can be faster and easier to move loads by crane than to reposition the vessel.

ORIENTATION FAMILIARISATION

In all lifting operations from DP vessels it is essential that the diver is aware of his position in relation to the vessel and its heading. This is especially important in low visibility.

Underwater crane lifts normally start near a vessel's work station so that the diver can easily locate the crane wire. After that, the lift may be moved to a different location which the diver can locate in relation to the start position by directions from the start position.

The orientation systems that are to be used should be agreed beforehand, ie vessel orientation (forward/aft/port/starboard) and/or compass bearings.

The following suggestions can help to develop a sense of direction and orientation when operating from a DSV's diving bell:

1. At mobilisation, walk the jetty alongside the vessel and also the DSV's deck noting the position and layout of:
   a) Cranes and other lifting devices.
   b) Work station(s) on the side of the ship where work baskets and/or equipment may be lowered to divers.
   c) The DP taut-wire davits.
   d) The diving moonpool(s).
   e) ROV launch point.
2. Examine the diving bell and note:
   a) The number of lights.
   b) The positions of lights.
   c) The pattern of the lights in relation to the fore and aft orientation of the ship.
3. Examine the bell weights and guide wire configuration relative to the vessel. The bell guide weights can be marked up to show fore and aft, port and starboard.
4. Before a dive, examine a plan of the area to build up a mental picture of the work site. Learn the compass orientation of everything on the site. The position of the ship should be indicated on the plan so the diver can work out where he will be landing. The plan and any relevant paperwork can be laminated so that the diver can take it with him to the work site.
5. When locked out of the bell, the diver can ask for particular lights to be turned off/on to help with orientation

LANDING THE LOAD

On deck the most important consideration is to bring the load quickly under control so that it can be safely landed.

Underwater, load swing is reduced by the sea and for loads under 2 tonnes divers can often push or pull the load slightly to get it to the desired location or orientation. Much larger loads can be manoeuvred by a diver if their negative buoyancy is reduced by the addition of air bags.

DP FOOTPRINT

A footprint is the area around a central set point in

which a DP vessel will move in a controlled manner. Shallow water, lack of wind or current, or extreme weather conditions will all affect the dynamic positioning system and so the area of the footprint will vary according to the vessel itself, the operating depth, sea state and weather conditions. It is important for divers to appreciate the extent of the footprint of a DP DSV because a load which is being lowered down to them will swing horizontally within the footprint area as it follows the movement of the DSV.

HANDLING LOADS UNDERWATER
OPERATIONAL SAFETY

1. The ends of diver tag lines should be weighted (polypropylene and other synthetic ropes float).
2. Tag lines should be long enough to enable divers to get hold of the load well before it arrives (up to 10m below the load). They should normally be attached at or near the bottom of the load. Divers should always position themselves at a safe distance from the load when using tag lines.
3. Locating the load underwater:
   a) Light sticks may be attached to the side or bottom of the load and to the ends of tag lines to enable the diver to locate them easily underwater.
   b) Strobe lights may also be used. They are often located just above the crane hook. They should be mounted with the lens pointing downwards.
4. Before the load is landed divers must ensure that their umbilicals are clear to the bell; if necessary, the bellman should pull in any excess. In poor visibility, one diver may have to manage the umbilicals while the other lands the load.
5. Surface waves and/or swell may cause the load to heave or lift off the bottom. In such situations divers should stay well clear and be aware of any possible suction effect near and below the load.
6. Allow for the delay in the load coming to rest after the crane has stopped swinging. This depends on the depth and any current. The deeper the depth the longer it takes for the load to come to rest.
7. When diving from DP vessels divers must inform the Diving Supervisor and DP Operator *before* deflating lift bags and using airlifts or other air-emitting tools since the air can interfere with the acoustic dynamic positioning of the vessel.
8. If divers are lifting a load which is close to a critical structure, they should watch the vessel footprint and instruct topside to position the crane so that it pulls away from the structure.

Personnel Carriers

These are designed to protect people who are using them from being crushed, trapped, being struck, or from falling (see Fig. 17).

Fig. 17 Personnel carrier

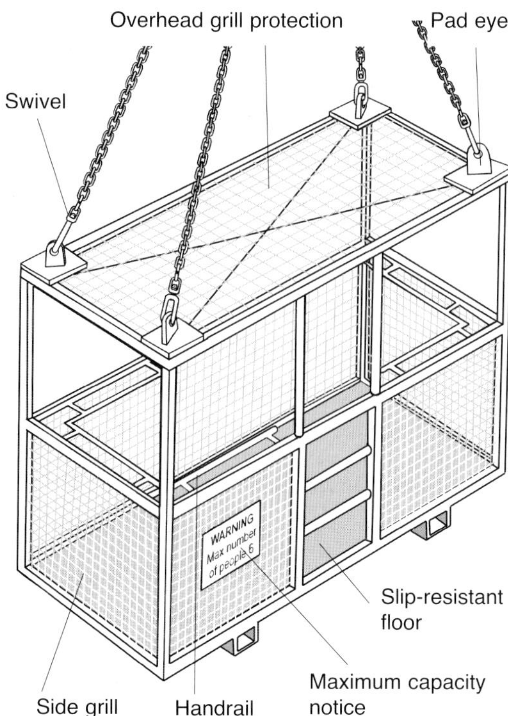
Overhead grill protection
Pad eye
Swivel
WARNING
Max number of people 6
Slip-resistant floor
Maximum capacity notice
Side grill
Handrail

A basket or open-bottom bell, used in support of surface-supplied diving, should be capable of carrying at least two divers in an uncramped condition.

DIVING BASKETS AND OPEN BELLS
OPERATIONAL SAFETY

1. Only man-rated lifting equipment can be used.
2. All equipment is required to be inspected regularly and kept in-date in accordance with an appropriate regime.
3. A conspicuous sign should show the Safe Working Load (SWL) and the maximum number of people that it can carry.
4. There should be a drop bar, chain or gate at the entry/exit point to prevent divers falling out.
5. The door must have a positive closure device.
6. Suitable head protection and internal hand holds should be provided.
7. Wire ropes for man-riding must have a safety factor of 8, ie: the total load must not exceed one eighth of the rope's breaking strain.
8. The hoisting arrangement must prevent spinning or tipping.
9. Tag lines should be used as appropriate.
10. There should always be an alternative method of diver recovery in the event of any failure of the basket or bell system.
11. Appropriate regulations and codes of practice should always be complied with.

Crane operator signals

Crane operations are potentially dangerous and clear communication between the crane operator and ground personnel is essential at all times. Radio communication may be used but hand signals are preferred and are commonly used (see Fig. 18).

In some areas or organisations, only qualified personnel may give crane signals. Where no such restrictions apply, anyone may be asked to act as the signaller and so it is advisable for all on-site personnel to be familiar with crane operator hand signals.

Since regional differences may occur, it is important to agree which signals are to be used before operations commence.

> CRANE OPERATIONS – OPERATIONAL SAFETY
>
> 1. Before operations commence, all on-site personnel should be made familiar with signals to be used, especially the emergency stop signal. The following audible signals may be given by the crane operator:
>   - 3 horn blasts: crane reversing
>   - 2 horn blasts: crane moving forward
>   - 1 horn blast: crane stopping
>
> *continued . . .*

Fig. 18 Some commonly used hand signals used in UK and USA

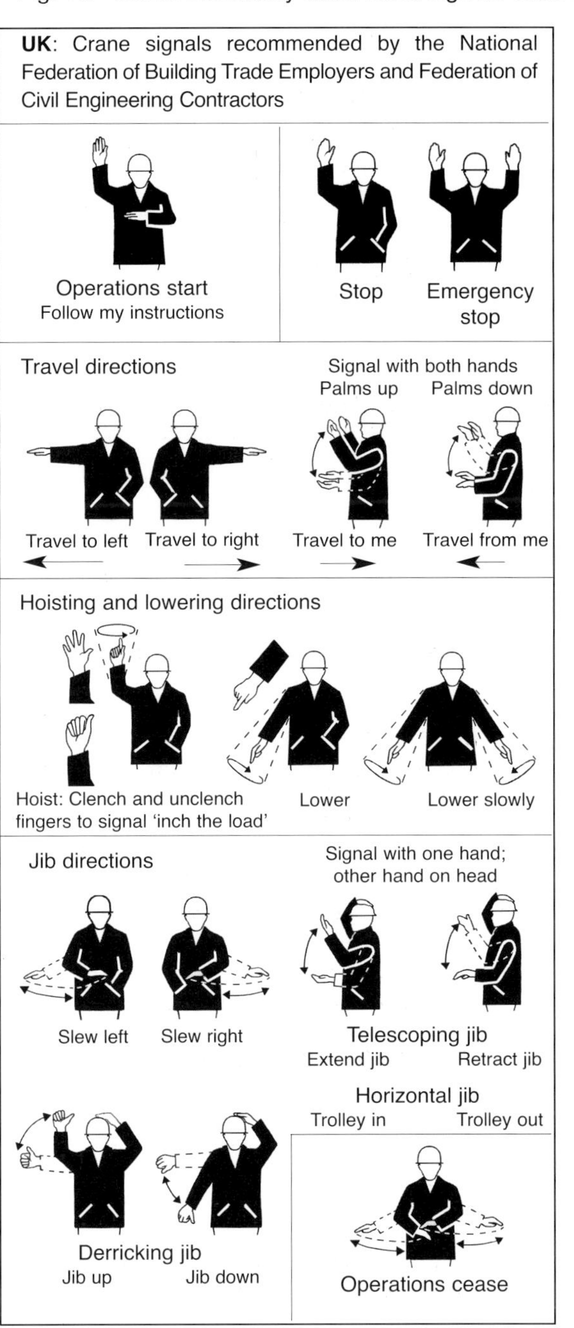

UK: Crane signals recommended by the National Federation of Building Trade Employers and Federation of Civil Engineering Contractors
Operations start
Follow my instructions
Stop
Emergency stop
Travel directions
Signal with both hands
Palms up
Palms down
Travel to left
Travel to right
Travel to me
Travel from me
Hoisting and lowering directions
Hoist: Clench and unclench fingers to signal 'inch the load'
Lower
Lower slowly
Jib directions
Signal with one hand; other hand on head
Slew left
Slew right
Telescoping jib
Extend jib
Retract jib
Horizontal jib
Trolley in
Trolley out
Derricking jib
Jib up
Jib down
Operations cease

USA: Basic crane hand signals recommended by the US Occupational Safety and Health Administration (OSHA).
Hoisting and lowering directions
Hoist
Lower
Hoist slowly
Lower slowly
Boom directions
Raise boom
Lower boom
Extend boom (thumbs out)
Retract boom (thumbs in)
Tap head
Tap elbow
Swing left
Swing right
Use main hoist
Use whip line
Travel directions
Move both tracks
Move left track only
Move right track only
Bridge travel 'Push' in direction of travel
Circle forearms: towards body = move forwards
away from body = move backwards
Hold everything
One hand holds the other
Stop
Emergency stop

continued . . .

2. There should be only ONE designated signaller at a time. He should wear something which makes him easily identifiable and must stand in clear view of the crane operator at all times. He must watch the load at all times and ensure that it is kept clear of any hazard that might endanger either the load or personnel.
3. The crane operator will take directions only from the designated signaller except in the case of an emergency stop (which can be given by anyone).
4. When radio communication is used, hands-free, voice-activated headsets are preferred. Special precautions should be taken:
   a) Once lifting operations have started, *constant* communication must be maintained with the crane operator, eg "Slowly down, slow, slow, slow ...". If the crane operator needs to talk to the signaller he should give one blast of the horn to instruct the signaller to unkey the mike so that the operator can talk to the signaller.
   b) Ensure that there are no explosive devices in the vicinity which may be activated by the radio transmission.
   c) Use a secure frequency which will be free from any distracting chatter.
   d) Make sure that there are no other radios nearby operating on the same frequency.
   e) Try to avoid transmitting near other electronic devices which may cause radio interference.
   f) Use agreed terminology, eg boom or jib, slew or swing, hoist or raise, etc.
   g) Directions (left/right) should always be given according to the *crane operator's* left or right.
   h) When directing the crane operator to swing the crane right or left, approximate length of swing should be given.

3.8 LIFTING OPERATIONS b) BUOYANT LIFTING

Marine Wreck Law

The basis of wreck law is that property lost at sea remains the property of the owner. In the UK, any wreck material recovered (which may be part of the hull, fixtures and fittings, cargo or personal possessions from any shipwreck, aircraft or hovercraft) must be reported to the Receiver of Wreck if it comes from UK territorial waters, or is landed in the UK. Wreck material should be reported within 28 days of recovery. Failure to do so is a criminal offence.

Wreck law exists to ensure that owners and salvors are both treated fairly. The owner is given the opportunity of having their property returned, on payment of a salvage award to the salvor. The salvage award is calculated according to a number of aspects of each salvage operation and cannot exceed the value of the material salved.

To reduce risk to the salvor, it may be advisable to ascertain ownership and where possible to enter into an agreement prior to any salvage operation. Where there is no prior agreement between owner and salvor, any salvage operation is 'voluntary', ie the risk is entirely the salvor's.

Material recovered must be declared to the Receiver of Wreck, whose duty it is to undertake research into the ownership of the wreck. The owner of a wreck has one year in which to prove ownership to the satisfaction of the Receiver. Wreck material which is unclaimed after one year automatically becomes the property of the Crown. In such instances it falls to the Receiver of Wreck to dispose of the property on behalf of the Crown, and to ensure the payment of an appropriate salvage award to the salvor.

Where wreck material is of particular historical significance, the Receiver would, in the first instance, offer the material to a suitable museum, with the sale price providing the salvage award.

Any wreck lying in UK territorial waters is subject to salvage, unless it is protected under specific legislation. Wrecks which are protected under legislation usually require a licence from the Secretary of State, which would authorise specific activities, eg access, survey or excavation etc.

Lifting Methods

A sunken object may be lifted off the seabed in various ways depending largely on its size and weight, its structural integrity, its flotation capacity and degree of stiction.

Common methods are:

1. Lifting with a floating crane or from salvage pontoons equipped with multiple winches. This method requires slings to be passed either underneath the sunken object or attached to suitable points on it.
2. Attaching lifting bags to anchorage points on the object, underslings or placing them inside the object.
3. Closing the main compartments of the object to make them airtight and then filling them with a gas or a liquid that is lighter than water. If an air-tight seal is impossible the compartments can be filled with a very light flotation material such as expanded polystyrene.

Preparing to Lift a Sunken Object

Lifting operations are potentially hazardous.

Before any operation can take place the following areas of concern must be fully understood:

1. Identification of the object. In the case of a shipwreck, the availability of the ship's plans can be of enormous help in calculating the centre of gravity, details of fixings, capacity of compartments and displacement weight.
2. The exact location of the sunken object and its attitude on the seabed.
3. The depth of the water. This will govern both the amount of air needed to provide buoyancy and the bottom time of the divers.
4. The nature of the seabed, in particular its load-bearing capacity which might cause sinking resulting in stiction and the need to provide a break-out force.
5. The degree of stiction and the level of break-out force required can often be difficult to determine. Consequently, the lift may need a prolonged period of tension to initiate and sustain movement of the load. On a large, heavy lift, fathometers may be placed at strategic points on the load to indicate the initial movement.
6. The amount of burial or overburden of the object including sand or mud that may be inside it. It may be necessary to remove this material by air lifts or water jets before attempting to lift.
7. The condition of the object including:
   - verification of material(s) of which it is made.
   - its structural strength and integrity.
   - its stability, submerged or afloat.
   - its seaworthiness and its water-tightness.
   - the structural integrity of the attachment points* to which lifting strops may have to be attached.
8. Suitability of the proposed method of lift based on the above. Underwater repairs or reinforcement may need to be made before attempting to start lifting.
9. In the case of vessels it may be desirable to remove cargo and fuel before attempting to lift.
10. Tidal and weather information:
    - times and heights of high and low water.
    - range of tide.
    - rate and direction of tidal streams.
    - forecast weather conditions and sea state.
11. The stability and integrity of the salvaged object when at (or near) the surface.
12. The law relating to wreck and salvage. In the UK it is *The Merchant Shipping Act, 1995* which requires all wreck material to be reported to the Receiver of Wreck in order to settle questions of ownership and salvage.

*suitable lifting points on a vessel may include: prop shafts, rudder posts, A-frames, derrick and engine mountings, anchor windlasses, cargo winches, gantries and on steel vessels: portholes, hawser pipes and scupper holes.

Planning the Lifting Procedure

1. Select the best method of lifting based on full consideration of all of the items listed above.
2. Make a complete plan of action involving precise briefings and the establishment of a good underwater communications system.
3. Establish the number and duties of personnel required.
4. Carry out a risk assessment to check the safety of divers, surface crew and any third parties, such as members of the public.
5. Make arrangements for:
   - the safe recovery and landing of the object.
   - the avoidance of splash zone damage.
   - the safe disposal of the object.
   - the preservation of the object to avoid deterioration in air.

Every operation has its own particular difficulties and large scale lifting can involve complex calculations. For example, when selecting suitable attachment points, note that the centre of gravity and centre of buoyancy are not necessarily the same point: The CENTRE OF GRAVITY depends on the distribution of mass in the object. CENTRE OF BUOYANCY depends on the volume distribution of the object in the water. These calculations are complicated and often better left to specialists.

Theory

The successful application of buoyancy methods requires an understanding of the physics involved, ie: the interaction between weight, volume, density and pressure.

ATMOSPHERIC PRESSURE is the air pressure at sea level and is expressed as bar or psi (pounds per square inch). At sea level atmospheric pressure is taken as 1 bar or 14.7psi.

HYDROSTATIC PRESSURE is the pressure of water acting at any given point underwater. It increases at a uniform rate of 1 bar for every 10m of water depth (or 14.7psi for every 33ft). At any given depth hydrostatic pressure is very slightly greater in salt water than in fresh water (due to the slightly greater density of salt water) but for practical purposes the above figures can be applied in most cases.

ABSOLUTE PRESSURE is the sum of the atmospheric pressure and hydrostatic pressure at any given point underwater. Absolute pressure may be expressed as 'atmospheres absolute' (ata) or pounds per square inch (psi).

GAUGE PRESSURE. It is important to note that the pressure recorded on a depth gauge registers hydrostatic pressure not absolute pressure.

BOYLE'S LAW. In basic terms Boyle's law states that (as long as temperature remains constant) as the pressure of a gas increases, the volume decreases in direct proportion (and vice versa). So, for example,

if you double the pressure, you halve the volume. In calculations, always use the absolute pressure.
In practical terms this means that as a submerged, air-filled container rises to the surface the volume of gas will increase. Provision should be made for the expanding air to escape or the ascent will accelerate.

ARCHIMEDES' PRINCIPLE states that any object wholly or partially immersed in a liquid experiences an upthrust equal to the weight of the liquid displaced, ie, objects tend to weigh less when immersed in water (see Fig. 1).

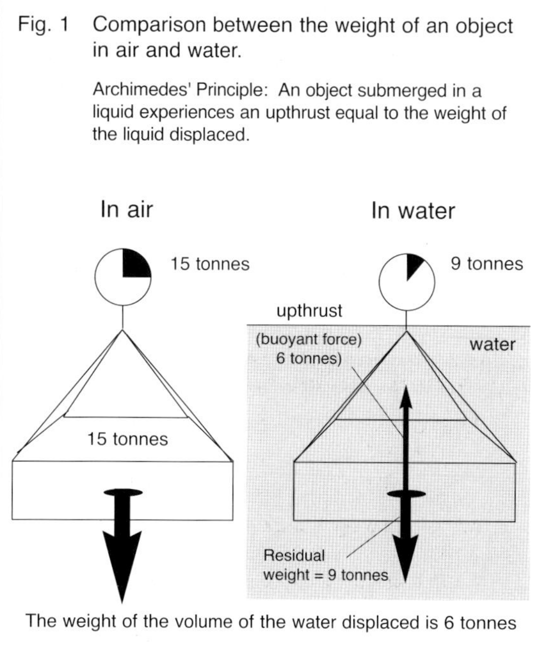
In air
In water
15 tonnes
9 tonnes
upthrust
(buoyant force)
6 tonnes)
water
15 tonnes
Residual
weight = 9 tonnes

Fig. 1 Comparison between the weight of an object in air and water.

Archimedes' Principle: An object submerged in a liquid experiences an upthrust equal to the weight of the liquid displaced.

The weight of the volume of the water displaced is 6 tonnes

The difference between the weight of an object in air and the weight of the water it displaces will tell you how buoyant the object is when immersed. If the object is heavier than the water it displaces it will sink; if lighter, it will float.
The upwards force (buoyant force) of the water depends on its density (see Fig. 2). Seawater (1,025kg/m^3) is denser than freshwater (1,000kg/m^3) and therefore provides greater buoyancy. In practical terms this means that objects immersed in seawater will need slightly less buoyancy to be raised than if they were in fresh water.

Calculations to Raise a Submerged Object

To calculate the weight of a fully submerged object you will need to know its weight in air and the weight of the volume of water it displaces when submerged. The difference between the two will give you the submerged weight of the object (see Example 1, below).
Caution: Always take care to use compatible units. Don't mix metric and imperial measures. Also, if the volume is given in cubic *metres*, the density should be in kilograms per cubic *metre*.

Fig. 2 Table of Density of Selected Materials (at 20°C, 68°F)

Material	Density per m^3 (in kg)	Density per ft^3 (in lb)
Aluminium	2,700	169
Asbestos	2,003–2,804	125–175
Asphalt	1,105–1,506	69–94
Basalt	2,400–3,100	150–194
Brass, yellow (high)	8,470	529
Brass, red (cast)	8,700	544
Brick, common	1,794	112
Bronze	8,715	544
Cadmium	8,690	540
Cement, (set)	2,700–3,000	169–188
Chalk	1,900–2,800	118–175
Chromium	7,150	449
Clay (wet)	2,643–3,124	165–195
Coal, anthracite	1554	97
Coal, bituminous	1346	84
Cobalt	8,860	556
Coke	1,000–1,700	62–105
Concrete masonry	2,323	145
Copper ore	4,197	262
Copper	8,960	560
Cork	256	16
Ebony	1,110–1,330	69–83
Gasoline (petroleum)	660–669	41–42
Glass, common	2,400–2,800	150–175
Gold	19,320	1208
Granite	2,640–2,760	165–173
Gravel	1,602–1,922	100–120
Ice (at 0°C, 32°F)	917	57
Iron, cast	7,874	492
Iron ore, Haematite (loose)	2,403	150
Kerosene	800	51
Lead	11,350	709
Limestone	2,675–2,739	167–171
Magnesium	1,738	109
Manganese	7,300	456
Marble	2,600–2, 840	160–177
Mercury	13,534	846
Monel	8471	529
Nickel	8,902	556
Nitrates (loosely piled)	1,602	100
Oils, mineral	929	58
Paper	700–1,150	44–72
Petroleum, crude	881	55
Platinum	2,145	134
Porcelain	2,300–2,500	143–156
River mud	1,442	90
Rubber, hard	1,190	74
Sand	1,442 - 1,602	90–100
Sandstone	2,140–2,360	134–147
Silver	10,500	656
Slate, shale	2,595–3,284	162–205
Steel, mild	7,860	485
Steel, stainless	8,020	501
Styrofoam	16	1
Tar, bituminous	1,202	75
Tin	7,298	456
Titanium	4,507	282
Tungsten	19,300	1,206
Water, fresh (at 0°C, 32°F)	1,000	62.4
Water, fresh	998	62
Water, sea	1,025	64
Zinc	7,133	445

The density of a material is its weight per unit volume which can be expressed in kg/m^3 or lb/ft^3. Lead is so dense that its weight is not significantly affected underwater, whereas aluminium will lose about 38% of its weight underwater. The diver will lose almost 100% of his weight underwater because the body's density is nearly the same as that of water.

EXAMPLE 1

To calculate the weight of an object totally immersed in seawater.

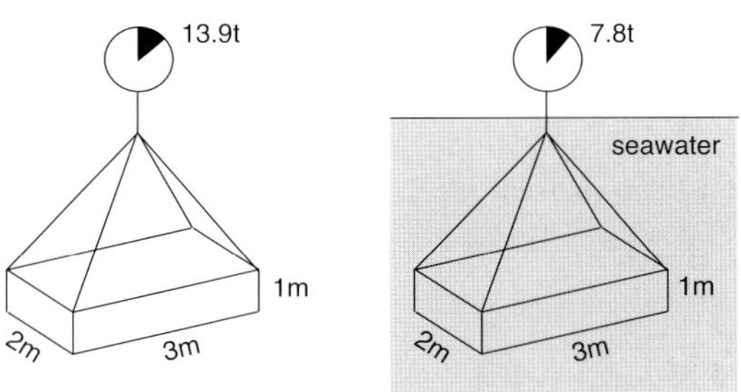
13.9t
7.8t
seawater
1m
2m
3m
1m
2m
3m

A concrete block measures 1m x 2m x 3m.

$W_{sub} = W_{air} - W_w$

(Submerged weight = weight in air – weight of displaced water)

In metric units	*In imperial units*

1. To find the weight of the object in air you will first need to find the volume of the object:
   V = l x w x d
   (Volume = length x width x depth)

In metric units	In imperial units
V = 1m x 2m x 3m	V = 3.2ft x 6.4 ft x 9.6ft
= 6m³	= 196.6ft³

2. Then calculate its weight in air using the formula:
   $W_{air} = V_o \times \rho_o$
   (Weight in air = volume of object x density of object) (in this case, concrete – refer to Fig. 2 for density of concrete)

In metric units	In imperial units
W_{air} = 6m³ x 2323*kg/m³	= 196.6ft³ x 145*lb/ft³
=13,938 kg	= 28,493.5lb
=13.938 tonnes	= 12.72 (long) tons

3. Then calculate the weight of the seawater displaced:

In metric units	In imperial units
Weight of 6m³ of seawater	(Weight of 190.5ft³ seawater)
= 6 x 1,025*kg/m³	= 196.6 x 64*lb/ft³
= 6,150kg	= 12,582lb
= 6.15 tonnes	= 5.62 (long) tons

4. Finally, subtract the weight of the water from the weight of the object in air:

In metric units	In imperial units
= 13.938 – 6.15 tonnes	=12.72– 5.62 tons
= 7.788 tonnes	= 6.71 (long) tons

Therefore, the submerged weight of this concrete block is approximately 7.8 tonnes (or 6.71 tons).

Useful conversion data

To convert units shown in first column to those in the other columns, multiply by the number given

Mass	Tonne	Long ton	Short ton	kg	lb
Tonne**	-	0.984	1.102	1,000	2,205
Long ton	1.016	-	1.120	1,016.05	2,240
Short ton	0.907	0.893	-	5	2,000
kg	0.001	0.0009842	0.001102	-	2.205
lb	0.000453	0.000446	0.0005	2.20462	-

**1 metric tonne of crude oil = approx. 1.16 kilolitres or 1.16m³

*from Fig. 2

Sunken objects, however, are rarely conveniently cuboid and so their volume may be difficult to ascertain. In such cases the weight of the object can be determined by finding its displacement using the formula: Displacement = Weight in air ÷ Density of material) and then subtracting the weight of the displaced water from the weight in air (see Example 2).

EXAMPLE 2

To calculate the weight of a steel vessel totally submerged in seawater.

1. First estimate the weight of the vessel based on engineering drawings, builder's notes, etc taking into account any alterations that have been made since its construction. In this case let us assume a weight of 8 tonnes (7.87 tons).
2. Then calculate its displacement:

   First convert tonnes to kg, or tons to lbs:

In metric units	*In imperial units*
8 x 1000 = 8,000kg	7.87 x 2,240 = 17,628.8lb

   Then find the displacement using the formula:
   $D = \frac{W_{air}}{\rho_o}$
   (Displacement = weight in air ÷ density of material)
   (in this case steel – refer to Fig. 2 for density of steel)

In metric units	In imperial units
$D = \frac{8,000}{7,860^*}$	$D = \frac{17,628.8}{485^*}$
= 1.02m³	= 36.35ft³

3. Now find the weight of the seawater displaced:
   $W_w = D \times \rho_w$
   (Weight of seawater = Displacement x density of seawater)

In metric units	In imperial units
W_w = 1.02 x 1,025*	W_w = 36.35 x 64*
= 1,045.5kg	= 2,326.4lb

4. Therefore, the submerged weight of the vessel is:
   $W_{sub} = W_{air} - W_w$
   (Submerged weight = weight in air – weight of displaced water)

In metric units	In imperial units
W_{sub} = 8,000 – 1,045.5	W_{sub} =17,628.8 – 2,326.4
= 6,954.5kg	=15,302.4lb
= 6.9 tonnes	=6.82 (long) tons

Lifting Calculations

Once the submerged weight of an object is established a lifting container should be chosen that is sufficiently large to overcome the weight of the object and slowly raise it to the surface. Too large a container will result in a rapid, unstable and dangerous ascent. In the case of Example 2, lifting containers with a combined capacity slightly in excess of 6.9 tonnes (6.83 tons) would be required to raise the vessel. For a safe, controlled ascent choose a lifting force no more than 20% greater than the submerged weight of the object being raised.

Since air weighs virtually nothing compared with an equal volume of water, its lifting capacity more

or less equals the weight of the water it displaces. In other words, 1m³ (35ft³) of air will lift 1 tonne. However, it is necessary to subtract the weight of the lifting container† from the lifting capacity of the air. Thus the true lifting capacity of an air-filled container is found by subtracting its weight from the weight of the water it displaces (ie, Lifting Capacity (LC) = weight of displaced water – weight of container).
If purpose-built air bags are used, the real lift capacity is already provided, in which case it is not necessary to subtract the weight of the air bag.

EXAMPLE 3
To calculate the lifting capacity in seawater of a 55-gallon (0.208m³) oil drum which weighs 9.07kg (20lb).
(55 gallons = 7.35ft³).

$LC = W_w - W_c$
(Lifting Capacity = weight of displaced water – weight of container).

In metric units	*In imperial units*

1. First find the weight of the displaced seawater:
$W_w = V_w \times \rho_w$
(Weight of displaced seawater = volume x density)

= 0.208m³ x 1,025*kg/m³	= 7.35 x 64*lb/ft³
= 213.2kg	= 470.4lb

2. Therefore, LC = 212.99kg (4704lb) – weight of the container.

= 213.2 – 9.07kg	= 4,704 – 20lb
= 204kg approx	= 450.4lb

Air Lift Bags

There are two main types of air lift bag: open-bottomed, parachute-shaped bags and sealed, barrel- or pillow-shaped lifting bags (see Fig. 3). They are available in a wide range of sizes with varying lift capacities. To ensure a successful operation it is essential to choose the correct type and size for each job. The wrong choice may not only mean a failed job but may also pose considerable risk to personnel. The size and number of bags used may be affected by the number of safe lifting points available.

The main factors affecting choice are:

1. The amount of buoyancy required.
2. Whether a vertical lift or static buoyancy is needed.
3. The depth of the operation.
4. The degree of control required.

PARACHUTE-TYPE LIFTING BAGS
These are versatile, easy to use and provide maximum lift for weight of the bag. They are the only type that should be used where an ascent is planned. They are open-bottomed, balloon-shaped bags with a single attachment point to ensure stability and ease of use. They should be fitted with a restraining line at or near the crown; the restraining line should be attached to an independent anchor during lifting operations so that the lift bag can be inverted and the air released in the event of a dangerous situation arising. They should also be fitted with a dump valve which can be operated by a diver by means of a dump line (see Fig. 4).
Bags of 300kg and more have lift harnesses built into the skin of the bag; smaller bags have strops attached at the bottom edge. The minimum factor of safety for bags and webbing strops is 5:1 and 7:1 of their safe working load respectively.

SEALED/ENCLOSED LIFTING BAGS
Sealed lifting bags are characteristically stable and, because of their cylindrical shape, are ideal for shallow water operations. They can be attached outside or inside the object being raised. They are ideal for reducing the draught of a vessel, long tows (such as pipeline and cable float-outs), vessel/vehicle recovery, emergency flotation and pontoons. Commonly used examples are shown in Fig. 3b.
A built-in harness is designed to maintain the bag in

Fig. 3 Examples of commonly used lifting bags
a) Parachute type lifting bags

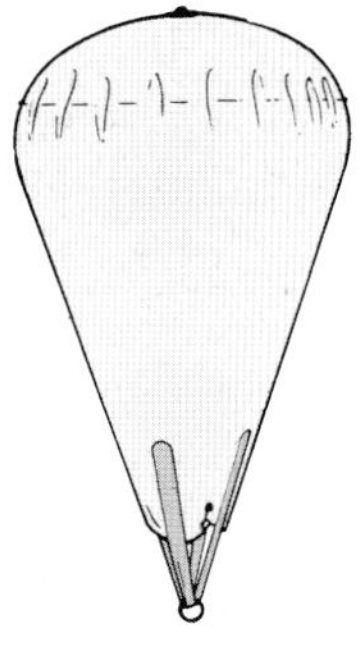

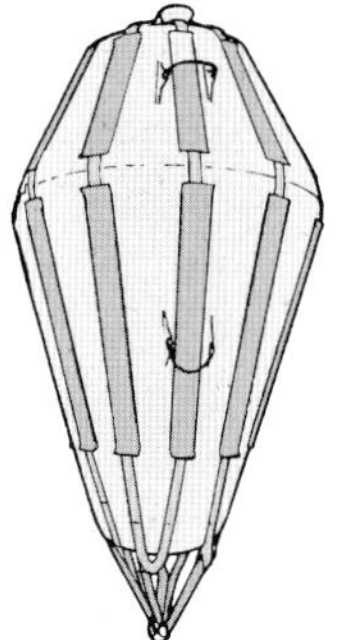

b) Enclosed/Sealed-type lifting bags

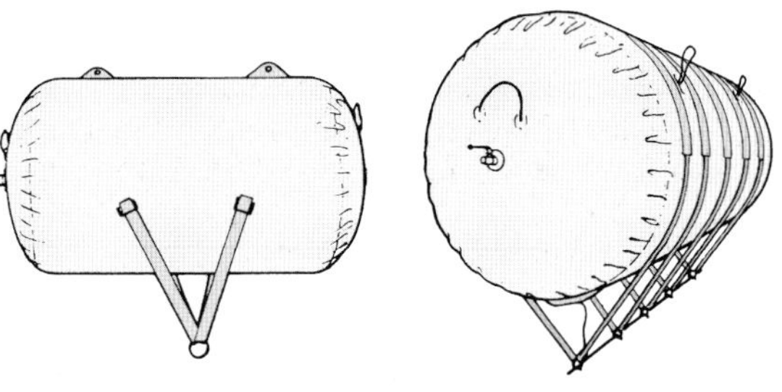

† Strictly speaking, this should be the submerged, flooded weight of the container. This may be negligible in buoyancy aids of light construction such as bags.
*from Fig. 2

Fig. 4 Typical parachute lift bag rigging arrangement for moving a pipeline.

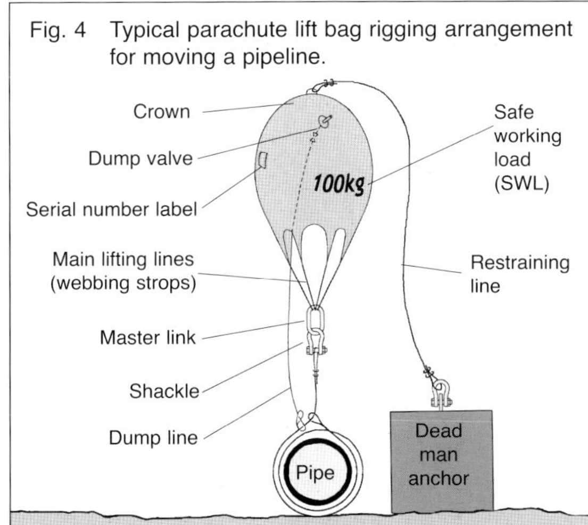
Crown
Dump valve
Serial number label
Main lifting lines
(webbing strops)
Master link
Shackle
Dump line
100kg
Safe
working
load
(SWL)
Restraining
line
Pipe
Dead
man
anchor

a horizontal position thus ensuring maximum lift and stability; however, stress bars may be needed (especially for larger models) to ensure an even distribution of the load.

Enclosed lifting bags incorporate pre-set pressure relief valves to avoid over-pressurisation and operate at approximately 2psi above ambient pressure.

They should not be used where an ascent is planned and must never be rigged in a vertical position.

Air requirements for lifting bags are given in Fig. 5.

Practical Considerations

There is no standard formula for a successful lift – each case is different although the general considerations given in this chapter will need to be applied to every case.

Many jobs may require pre-lift preparation including jetting around the base of the object to assist break-out, attaching sound lift points to the object, etc.

Some lifts may need to be carried out in several stages, readjusting the lifting containers between each stage.

A controlled ascent is vital to a successful lift.

Beware of leaking bags and subsequent loss of buoyancy. When inflated, check all bag dump valves for leaks.

Using Air Lift Bags

Since gas expands as it rises, buoyancy can increase and so the speed of ascent can increase unless air is released. An ascent rate of no more than 1m/sec (3ft/sec) should be aimed for.

Where a break-out force is required at least 150% of the estimated lifting requirement should be applied.

The choice and positioning of lifting containers will vary according to whether or not a break-out force (for semi-submerged objects) is required, how sound the structure is and whether sealed containers or open-bottomed lift bags are used.

Because parachute-type lift bags are open-bottomed they allow expanding gas to escape from the bottom during ascent. They are commonly used in all types of underwater recovery work, especially in deep water. Because of the danger of air loss at the surface, it may be advisable to use buoyancy just to reduce the in-water weight of the object and control the ascent by use of a crane lift.

Care and Maintenance of Air Lift Bags

Air lift bags are a major piece of lifting equipment and require careful maintenance.

All lifting equipment should comply with the appropriate code of practice relating to the initial and periodic examination, testing and certification of diving plant and equipment.

Before commencing operations ensure that:

1. Serial numbers match on all components.
2. The certification of the air bag is valid and in date.
3. The bag, strops and stitching are sound.
4. The pressure relief and dump valves are clean and operational.
5. (On parachute-type bags) The dump and restraining lines are properly attached; are easily identifiable from each other and from other lines; and are long enough to be attached to an anchor point (restraining line) or safely operated by a diver (dump line).
6. If using a spreader bar, it must be properly certified, be in date and have an appropriate safe working load.

After completing operations

1. Wash the bags in fresh water. Remove oil and grease.
2. Check dump and relief valves; clean, dry and dust with French chalk.
3. Check for damage: fully spread out parachute type bags. Reinflate enclosed bags. Dry out.
4. Check strops and fittings.
5. Log any damage.
6. Get all damage repaired.
7. Log all repairs.
8. When repaired, roll up (do not fold) and store in a clean, dry place.

AIR LIFT BAGS – OPERATIONAL SAFETY

1. Before starting the lifting operation check and double check all lifting calculations.
2. Ensure that tides, weather and sea state conditions are safe to work in.
3. Formulate a definite plan of operation. Inform all members of the team. Work as a co-ordinated team.
4. Ensure that all rigging is in good condition, within test dates and free of kinks.
5. Ensure that:
   a) the bags are sound (they should be inspected approximately every 6 months.
   b) there is enough air available to fill the number of bags required. (Amount of air required = the total displacement of all the bags multiplied by the absolute pressure at the depth of the object).

(continued . . .)

Fig. 5 LIFTING BAG AIR REQUIREMENTS AT SELECTED DEPTHS

LIFTING BAGS		DEPTH												
lifting capacity	displacement	ata	1	2	3	4	5	6	7	8	9	10	25	50
kg	m^3	m	0	10	20	30	40	50	60	70	80	90	240	490
lb	ft^3	*ft*	*0*	*33*	*66*	*99*	*132*	*165*	*198*	*231*	*264*	*297*	*825*	*1650*
50	0.05	m^3	0.05	0.1	0.15	0.2	0.25	0.3	0.35	0.4	0.45	0.5	1.25	2.5
110	*1.75*	ft^3	*1.75*	*3.5*	*5.3*	*7.1*	*8.8*	*10.6*	*12.4*	*14*	*16*	*17.7*	*44*	*88*
100	0.10	m^3	0.1	0.2	0.3	0.4	0.5	0.6	0.7	0.8	0.9	1.0	2.5	5.0
220	*3.5*	ft^3	*3.5*	*7*	*10.3*	*13.7*	*17.2*	*20.6*	*24*	*27.5*	*30.9*	*34.3*	*85.7*	*177*
250	0.25	m^3	0.25	0.5	0.75	1.0	1.25	1.5	1.75	2.0	2.25	2.5	6.25	12.5
550	*8.8*	ft^3	*8.8*	*17.7*	*26.5*	*35.3*	*44*	*53*	*61.8*	*70.6*	*79.5*	*88*	*221*	*442*
500	0.50	m^3	0.5	1.0	1.5	2.0	2.5	3.0	3.5	4.0	4.5	5.0	12.5	25.0
1100	*17.7*	ft^3	*17.7*	*35.3*	*53*	*70.6*	*85.7*	*106*	*124*	*142*	*159*	*177*	*442*	*883*
1000	1.0	m^3	1	2	3	4	5	6	7	8	9	10	25	50
2200	*35.3*	ft^3	*35.3*	*70.6*	*106*	*141*	*177*	*212*	*247*	*283*	*318*	*353*	*883*	*1766*
1500	1.5	m^3	1.5	3.0	4.5	6.0	7.5	9.0	10.5	12.0	13.5	15.0	37.5	75.0
3300	*53*	ft^3	*53*	*106*	*159*	*212*	*265*	*318*	*371*	*424*	*477*	*530*	*1324*	*2649*
2000	2.0	m^3	2	4	6	8	10	12	14	16	18	20	50	100
4400	*70.6*	ft^3	*70.6*	*142*	*212*	*283*	*353*	*424*	*494*	*565*	*636*	*706*	*1766*	*3532*
3000	3.0	m^3	3	6	9	12	15	18	21	24	27	30	75	150
6600	*106*	ft^3	*106*	*212*	*318*	*424*	*530*	*636*	*742*	*848*	*954*	*1059*	*2649*	*5297*
5000	5.0	m^3	5	10	15	20	25	30	35	40	45	50	125	250
11000	*177*	ft^3	*177*	*353*	*530*	*706*	*883*	*1059*	*1236*	*1413*	*1589*	*1766*	*4415*	*8823*
10000	10.0	m^3	10	20	30	40	50	60	70	80	90	100	250	500
22000	*353*	ft^3	*353*	*706*	*1059*	*1413*	*1765*	*2119*	*2472*	*2825*	*3178*	*3532*	*8823*	*17658*
20000	20.0	m^3	20	40	60	80	100	120	140	160	180	200	500	1000
44000	*706*	ft^3	*706*	*1413*	*2119*	*2825*	*3532*	*4238*	*4944*	*5650*	*6357*	*7063*	*17658*	*35316*
35000	35.0	m^3	35	70	105	140	175	210	245	280	315	350	875	1750
77000	*1236*	ft^3	*1236*	*2472*	*3708*	*4944*	*6180*	*7416*	*8652*	*9888*	*11124*	*12360*	*30901*	*61802*

Cubic feet: All values over 100 are given to the nearest whole number

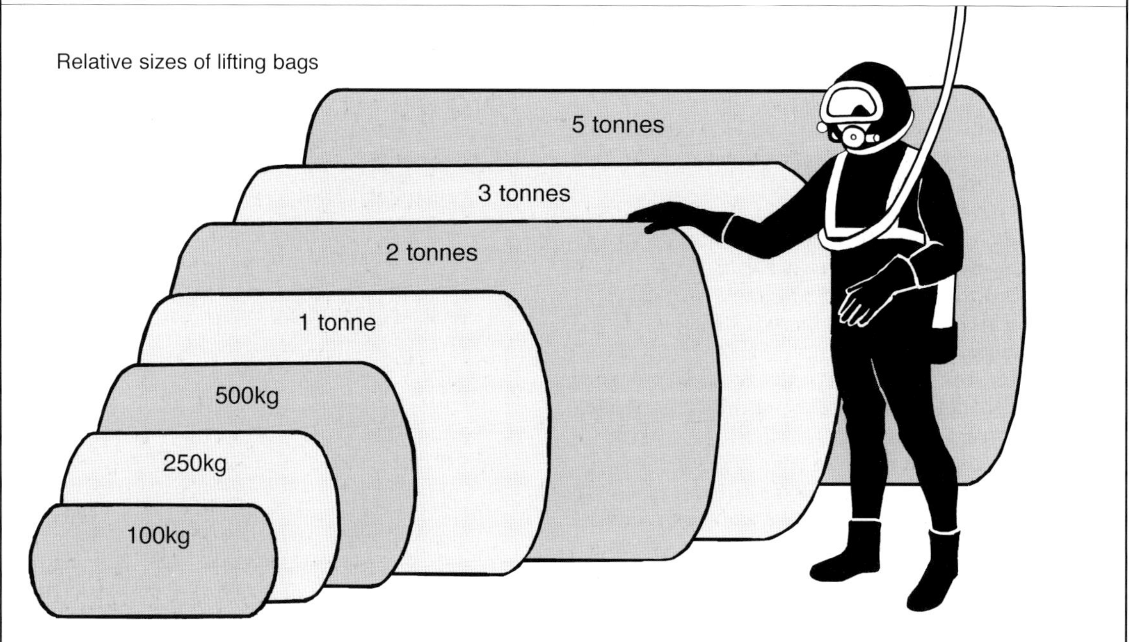
5 tonnes
3 tonnes
2 tonnes
1 tonne
500kg
250kg
100kg

Relative sizes of lifting bags

(continued . . .)

6. Always use the minimum lift capacity required otherwise the lift may be too rapid and become unstable. No more than 0.5-1m/sec (2-3ft/sec) is recommended.
7. Ensure that the object to be lifted does not exceed the safe working load (SWL) of the tackle. Check documentation. Take into consideration snatch-loads, especially when the object is on the surface and subject to wave motion.
8. Ensure that:
   a) the bags are securely attached to safe lifting points.
   b) the bags and air lines to them are free from restriction so that all bags can be fully inflated.
   c) the restraining line on parachute-type lifting bags is securely tied to a dead man anchor.
9. If divers are in the water no inflation or deflation should take place until:
   a) the position of each diver is known and confirmed and each diver knows the position of all other divers.
   b) all diver umbilicals and other lines are confirmed clear.
10. Once the bags are attached, partially inflate the bags to test:
   a) even distribution.
   b) secure attachment.
   c) there are no snags or tangles after deployment.
   Only when these are established should you proceed with full inflation.
11. The inflation hose should not be tied off to the bag during inflation.
12. Bags should be inflated in an appropriate sequence to avoid undue stress on the object and to prevent tipping it.
13. Depending on the requirements, fill each bag to two-thirds or to capacity before starting to fill the next one. Check bags for leaks, especially at the dump valves.
14. Take care to ensure that air never gets into the bell and contaminates the atmosphere.
15. Divers should never position themselves beneath the object being raised. Divers should remain well clear of lifting lines while the object is being raised.
16. All personnel must be kept clear of rigging under strain.
17. Be prepared for lifted structures to break up, especially if the object has been submerged for some time.
18. Be ready to control the object immediately upon surfacing. Stability can easily change at this moment.
19. Make sure that totally enclosed lifting bags remain horizontal throughout the operation. If towing, do not exceed 2–3 knots (depending on sea state).
20. After every operation clean, dry, inspect and repair any damage to lift bags that incurred during the operation.

3.9 AIR LIFTS AND DREDGES

An air lift consists of a low pressure compressor, a discharge pipe, a foot piece (or air chamber) and an air hose. The foot piece is directed, by the diver, at the material to be lifted from under water. The other end of the discharge pipe is held at the surface (see Fig. 1). Air is pumped from the surface down the air hose to the submerged foot piece where it is injected into it. As the air rises up the discharge pipe it draws water (and suspended material) up the pipe, discharging it at the surface.

An air lift can be used to excavate a hole or trench on the sea bed and to lift mixtures of water, gravel, sand, mud, grain or similar loose material from ships' holds during salvage operations. It can also be used, for example, to help release a stranded vessel by clearing away the sand or mud from one side.

The amount of liquid that can be lifted varies according to the diameter of the air lift, the operating depth of the pipe, the air pressure and volume used and the discharge head.

Discharge pipes can range from 5–35cm (2–14") depending on the nature and amount of work required (see Fig. 2). The air chamber is located approximately 50–75cm (20–30") from the end of the pipe. Sometimes considerable experimentation is needed to determine the amount of air required to operate

Fig. 1 Air lift operations

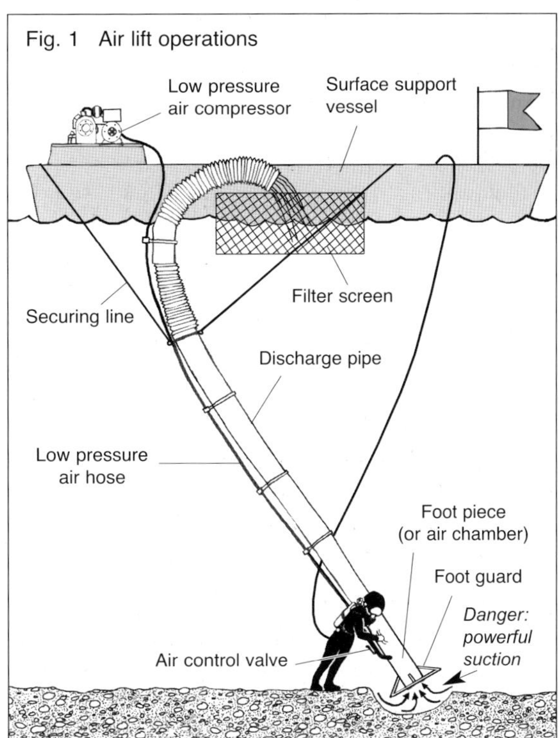
Low pressure air compressor
Surface support vessel
Filter screen
Securing line
Discharge pipe
Low pressure air hose
Foot piece (or air chamber)
Foot guard
Danger: powerful suction
Air control valve

Fig. 2 Guide for selecting discharge pipes and air lines

Diameter of discharge pipe		Diameter of compressed air pipe		Water flow per minute		Air flow per minute	
cm	*in*	cm	*in*	litres	*gallons**	cu m	*cu ft*
7	*3*	1	*0.5*	155-235	*50-75*	0.4-1	*15-40*
10	*4*	2	*0.75*	284-473	*90-150*	0.5-1.8	*20-65*
15	*6*	3	*1.25*	662-1420	*210-450*	1.4-5.5	*50-200*
25	*10*	5	*2.00*	1892-2839	*600-900*	4.2-11	*150-400*

*US gallons

the lift efficiently and the amount of weight that needs to be added to the discharge pipe to prevent it from floating upwards when the air is introduced. The suction begins almost immediately the air is turned on. The success of the operation depends on selecting the correct size and power required for the job. For example, extremely delicate work (such as archaeological excavations) could require the use of a small lift (5cm/2") and low power. The diver can also control the power by adjusting the air supply valve.

Underwater visibility may be reduced if the discharge material drifts back across the work site and may cause the work to be temporarily aborted. To avoid dumping the airlifted materials back onto the site it may be necessary to transport this material away from the site. A long horizontal pipe floating on the surface can be used. Use should be made of local factors, such as currents, when deciding where to lay this floating pipe. It may be necessary to attach a water jet pump to the pipe to help move the material through it.

A high pressure water jet can be incorporated with the air lift to help break up the excavated material (see Fig. 3). In such a system 10–30 tonnes (11–33 short tons) of material per hour can be discharged up to 60m (200ft) distance away. There is usually a choice of different suction pipes and jetting configurations to suit varying requirements.

Air lifts rely on the head of water to work efficiently. The greater the head of water, the greater the suction power. Extra care must be taken at depths greater than 10m (33ft) to ensure that the diver or his equipment does not become entrapped.

Fig. 3 Air lift with jetting nozzle

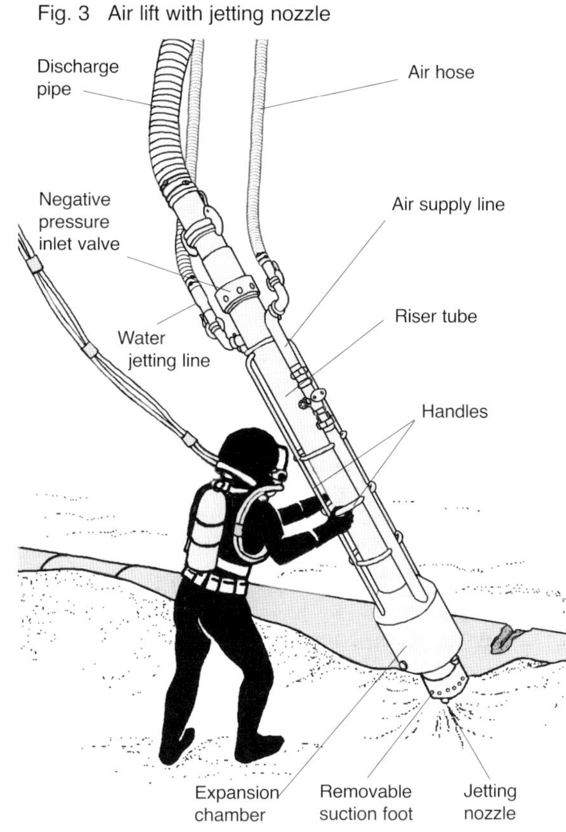
Discharge pipe
Air hose
Negative pressure inlet valve
Air supply line
Riser tube
Water jetting line
Handles
Expansion chamber
Removable suction foot
Jetting nozzle

Fig. 4 Suction ejector

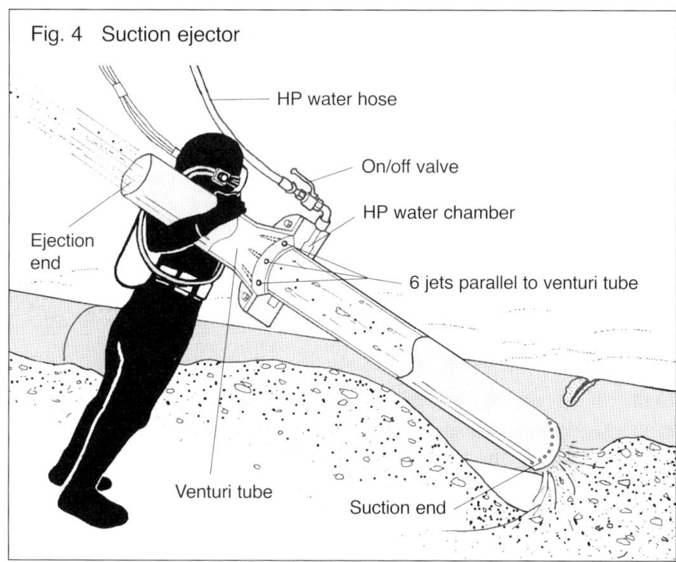
HP water hose
On/off valve
HP water chamber
Ejection end
6 jets parallel to venturi tube
Venturi tube
Suction end

Suction ejector

In shallow water, where air lifts are less effective, venturi suction systems should be used (see Fig. 4).

In this system the suction up the discharge pipe is produced by high pressure water jets which are directed up the inside of the pipe. Since it does not use air, its effectiveness is independent of the water depth and it has no depth limitation. The suction force can be increased by several ejectors in series.

Maximum high pressure water flow rates can be between 150–210 l/min (5–7 cu ft/min) at pressures between 150–210 bars. Up to 150 tonnes (165 short tons) per hour of sand of silt can be excavated by this method.

In all dredging operations divers should ensure that they do not excavate steep-sided trenches which may collapse and bury them (see Fig. 5).

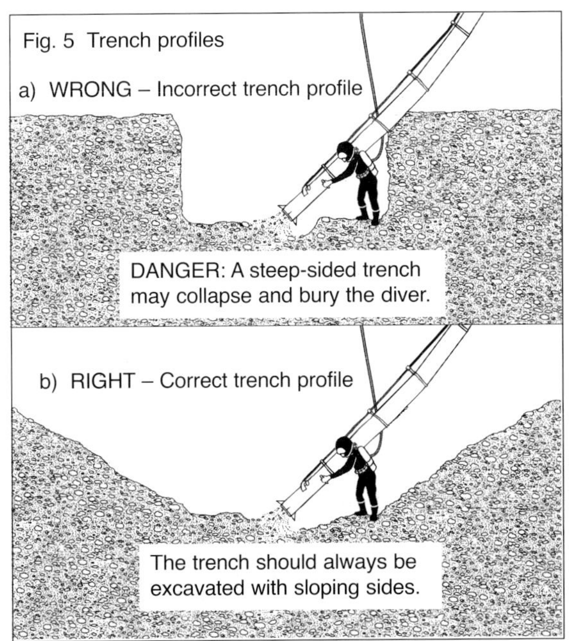
a) WRONG – Incorrect trench profile
DANGER: A steep-sided trench may collapse and bury the diver.
b) RIGHT – Correct trench profile
The trench should always be excavated with sloping sides.
Fig. 5 Trench profiles

AIRLIFTS AND DREDGES OPERATIONAL SAFETY

1. The amount of suction at the end of the discharge hose is considerable. The diver must ensure that he does not have any loose equipment hanging from his harness which could be sucked into the airlift.
2. There should be a quarter-turn air-control valve for emergency shut-off within easy reach of the diver. It should be checked to ensure that it is working properly before commencing operations.
3. The discharge pipe can suddenly increase its buoyancy if the bottom end becomes blocked introducing the danger of the pipe floating upwards out of control. Provision should be made to prevent this happening by, for example, tying off the bottom end of the foot piece to a suitable anchoring point on the sea bed.
4. Good voice communication with the diver is essential to reduce the potential danger to the diver and to ensure co-ordination between surface and diver operations. It is also important since it enables the diver to call for emergency shut-off of the inflation air supply if necessary.
5. If a trench is being excavated the diver should ensure that the sides are sloping to avoid the danger of the trench wall collapsing on him (see Fig. 5).
6. Underwater visibility may be reduced if the discharge material drifts back across the work site increasing the risk of entanglement, etc. The diver must, therefore, be prepared to return to the surface in poor visibility conditions.

Dredgehog, diver-operated dredging system

The Dredgehog dredging system consists of a motive water hose, a central jet pump, a discharge hose, a suction hose and a diver-held ring jet suction head (see Figs. 6–8). The system is deployed and operated from a DSV. It is lowered to

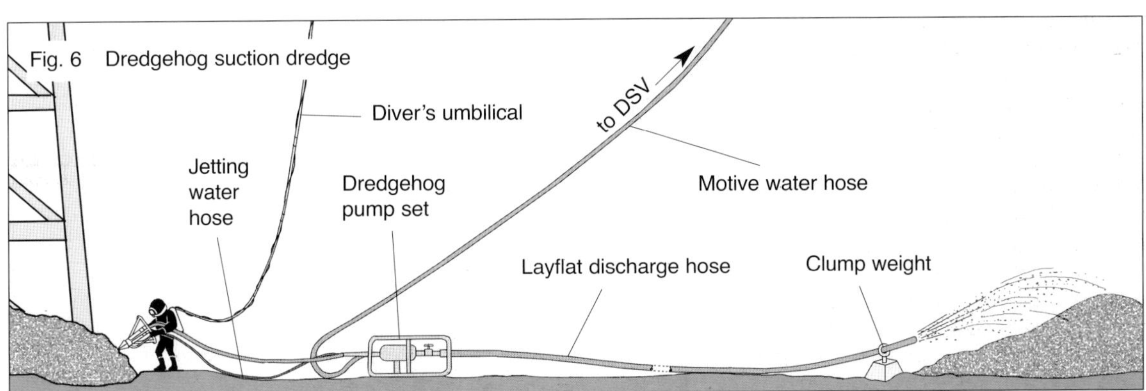
Diver's umbilical
to DSV
Jetting water hose
Dredgehog pump set
Motive water hose
Layflat discharge hose
Clump weight
Fig. 6 Dredgehog suction dredge

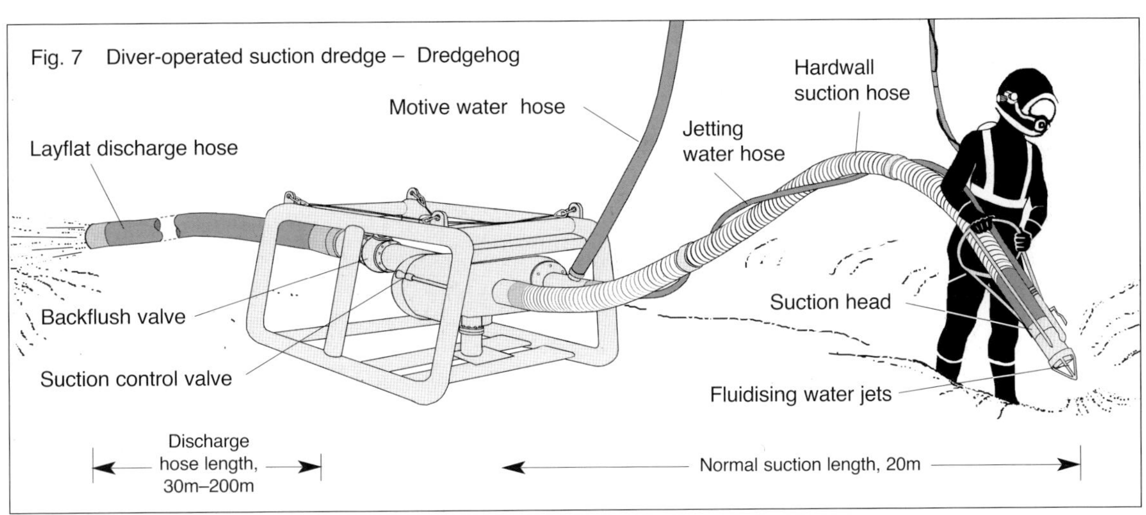
Motive water hose
Hardwall suction hose
Jetting water hose
Layflat discharge hose
Backflush valve
Suction control valve
Suction head
Fluidising water jets
Discharge hose length, 30m–200m
Normal suction length, 20m
Fig. 7 Diver-operated suction dredge – Dredgehog

the seabed and positioned as close as possible (within 20m/66ft) to the work area to minimise the required suction pipe length. At the seabed, the diver connects the motive water hose which may be lowered by a downline. He then lays out and stabilizes the discharge hose using weights or pins and pulls the suction hose towards the dredging area. Floats can be attached to the suction hose to increase ease of handling.

When the diver is ready to start work he asks for the topside pump to be started and carries out an initial check of the system before starting to dredge. For optimum efficiency the diver should keep the suction head continually immersed in the material to be dredged.

The suction head (Fig. 8) includes a disintegration nozzle and fluidising jets for breaking down heavy/stubborn material. A diver-operated valve enables the diver to fine tune the suction to ensure that it is not too powerful. An average dredging rate is about 15–20m^3 (530–700ft^3) per hour.

Typical tasks include muck dredging/desilting, rock lifting, pipelaying/trenching, cell top cleaning, cofferdam construction, subsea mineral extraction and shaft sinking/tunnelling.

DREDGEHOG – OPERATIONAL SAFETY

1. The motive water hose must always be deployed away from the DSV's thrusters.
2. Good communications are required at all times to allow the diver to call for the pump to be turned on and off as required.

Fig. 8 Suction head – Dredgehog system

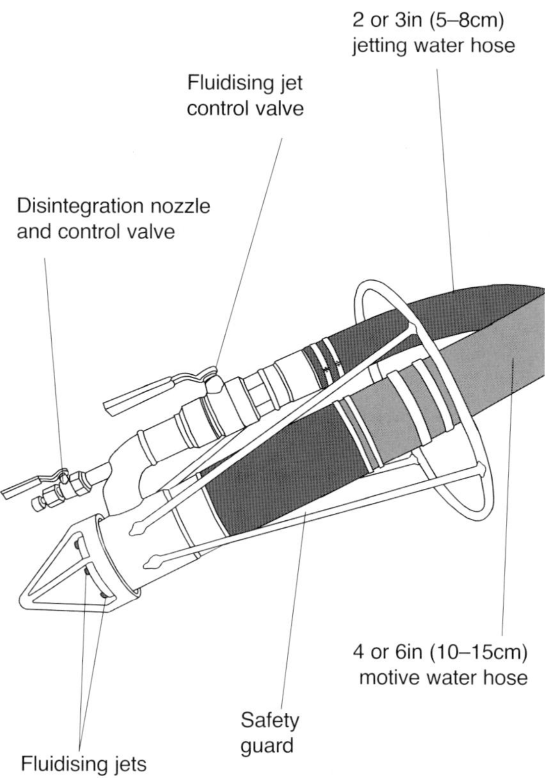
2 or 3in (5–8cm)
jetting water hose
Fluidising jet
control valve
Disintegration nozzle
and control valve
4 or 6in (10–15cm)
motive water hose
Safety
guard
Fluidising jets

3.10 ENGINEERING DRAWINGS

The interpretation of mechanical drawings relating to the installation and inspection of subsea structures is an important part of a diver's work. Finding the correct drawing relating to a particular aspect of a subsea structure is often a time consuming job. It is therefore necessary to understand the way in which the drawings of any platform or subsea installation are organised. A system of drawings is often referred to as a family tree and usually has a master drawing number.

A typical family tree of drawings for a subsea structure appears in a simplified form in Fig. 1.

The detailed drawing for any part of a subsea structure usually has its own drawing number and can be found by reference to the drawing list.

Every drawing or print should contain a panel showing the technical details of the drawing. This panel is normally found in the lower right hand side of the sheet and might contain the following information:

– Title of drawing.
– Name of the owner.

Fig.1 Typical family tree of drawings for a subsea structure

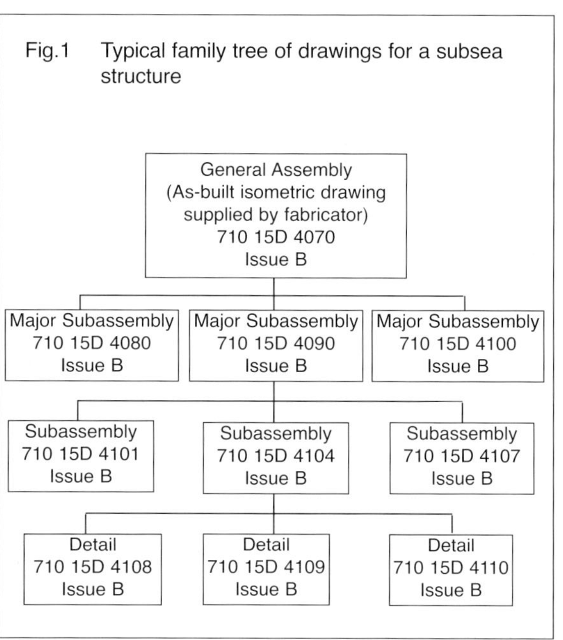
General Assembly
(As-built isometric drawing
supplied by fabricator)
710 15D 4070
Issue B
Major Subassembly
710 15D 4080
Issue B
Major Subassembly
710 15D 4090
Issue B
Major Subassembly
710 15D 4100
Issue B
Subassembly
710 15D 4101
Issue B
Subassembly
710 15D 4104
Issue B
Subassembly
710 15D 4107
Issue B
Detail
710 15D 4108
Issue B
Detail
710 15D 4109
Issue B
Detail
710 15D 4110
Issue B

- Location of the project.
- Project or contract number.
- Drawing number.
- Number of drawing sheet; there can be several drawings against one drawing number.
- Revision number.
- Date on which the drawing was issued or revised.
- Scale.
- Key plan, showing geographical orientation.
- Projection.
- Notes. These might specify details such as the units in which dimensions are stated, mechanical tolerances, materials, etc.
- Legend: explanation of symbols.

A typical drawing panel is shown in Fig. 2.

Fig. 2 Typical drawing panel

Orientation/ Key plan Notes Projection Legend			
REVISIONS	Drawn by	TITLE OF DRAWING	PROJECT or CONTRACT No.
ISSUE or REVISION No. date	DATE Checked by		DRAWING No.
Revised by date	date	Name of owner	
APPROVALS date date date	Scale	Location of project	REVISION No. SHEET of

Additional information which may appear on a drawing (generally in the overall drawing list legend) can include 'type of steel', 'type of welds', 'extent of reinforcing' and 'finish'.

The units in which the dimensions are shown on drawings vary. The units are usually defined on the drawing and different units can be used for different parts of the structure, ie: dimensions of tubular sections can be expressed in millimetres while figures for elevations can be given in metres on the same drawing.

Most mistakes during construction occur when dimensions on drawings are not properly defined, or are misinterpreted.

Care must be taken to distinguish early conceptual drawings from 'Approved for construction' drawings. When a drawing is modified it is given a new issue number. Changes in issue are recorded on both the family tree and appear on the drawing as a number or letter against the word, 'Issue'. The issue number of every drawing should be checked before use against the current build standard of the structure. Always use the latest issue.

Master drawings, ie the originals, are usually kept ashore. Photocopies, dye-line prints, or facsimile copies can be made for use offshore.

Prints should always be folded in such a way that the title block and drawing number remain visible. Drawing sheets should be handled by the borders and should not be left in strong sunlight otherwise they will fade.

The 3 types of platform drawings which will most commonly be encountered by a diver are as follows:

1. ISOMETRIC DRAWING. This is a perspective drawing or three-dimensional view (Fig. 3c). For it a diver can identify:
   - the position of pile guides.
   - orientation of nodes and weldments.
   - position of risers.
   - number and identification system used for jacket legs.
   - location of horizontal and diagonal support bracings.
   - relative sizes and positions of the various parts.

2. ELEVATION DRAWING, or side view (Fig. 3a). These usually provide information about the depth at various points on the structure. This is generally given as a figure in metres, prefixed by the word, 'Elevation' (EL) and either a plus or minus sign depending on whether the location is above or below the surface. Depths shown in this way are normally referred to as Lowest Astronomical Tide (LAT). Care must be taken to avoid any confusion as sometimes the elevation figures refer to height above the seabed rather than the depth below the LAT.

3. PLAN DRAWING, or top view looking vertically down on a structure (Fig. 3b).
   Because of the height and shape of structures, it is usual practice to have a large number of separate plan drawings made at various levels on the structure. These different plan drawings are defined by reference to the elevation at which the drawing was made, eg: 'Plan view at –30.000' means that the drawing depicts a horizontal section of the platform 30m below the Lowest Astronomical Tide.

Using drawings for Inspection

A primary aspect of any underwater inspection is to check that the actual structure conforms to the as-built isometric drawings and to note any discrepancies.

Very often it is useful to make one's own working sketch of a particular part of the structure for reference purposes underwater. Since components such as bracing joints and nodes involve structures running in different directions, the sketch must have a reference to a directional axis, eg: Leg D, Node 6, looking north. The terminology of a typical node is shown in Fig. 4.

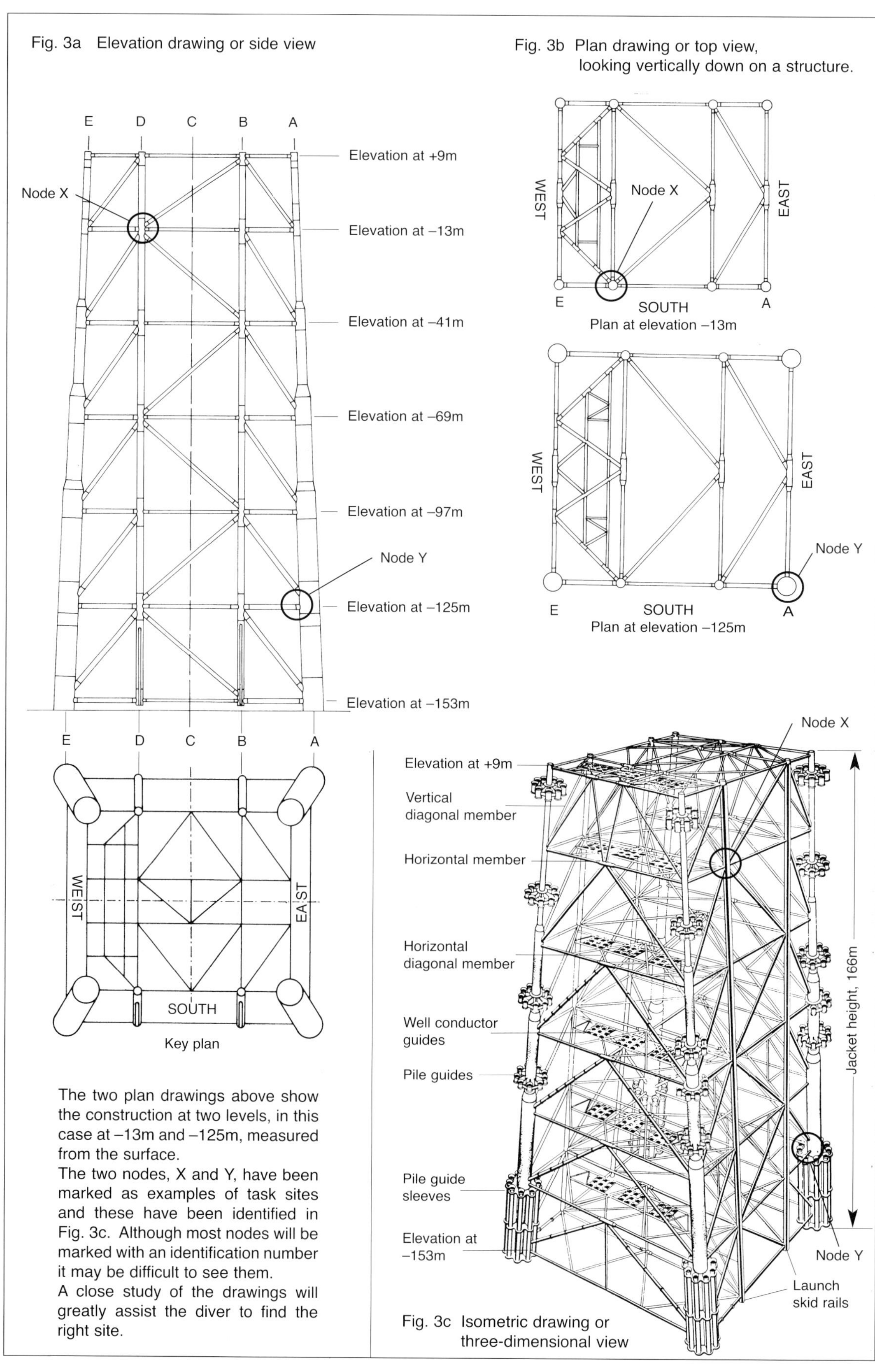

E
D
C
B
A
Node X
Elevation at +9m
Elevation at –13m
Elevation at –41m
Elevation at –69m
Elevation at –97m
Node Y
Elevation at –125m
Elevation at –153m
WEST
EAST
SOUTH
Key plan
WEST
Node X
EAST
SOUTH
Plan at elevation –13m
WEST
EAST
Node Y
SOUTH
Plan at elevation –125m
Node X
Elevation at +9m
Vertical diagonal member
Horizontal member
Horizontal diagonal member
Well conductor guides
Pile guides
Pile guide sleeves
Elevation at –153m
Jacket height, 166m
Node Y
Launch skid rails

Fig. 3a Elevation drawing or side view

Fig. 3b Plan drawing or top view, looking vertically down on a structure.

Fig. 3c Isometric drawing or three-dimensional view

The two plan drawings above show the construction at two levels, in this case at –13m and –125m, measured from the surface.
The two nodes, X and Y, have been marked as examples of task sites and these have been identified in Fig. 3c. Although most nodes will be marked with an identification number it may be difficult to see them.
A close study of the drawings will greatly assist the diver to find the right site.

Fig. 4 Terminology of a node

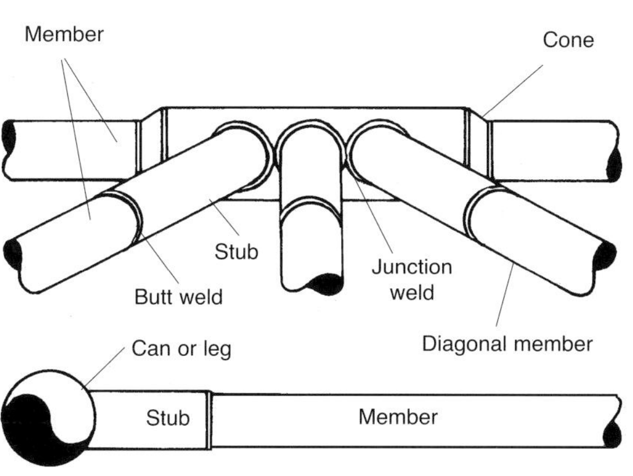
Member
Cone
Stub
Butt weld
Junction weld
Diagonal member
Can or leg
Stub
Member

Special symbols

A large variety of symbols are used to indicate special features on engineering drawings. The details of welds, for example, can be shown on some drawings. Fig. 5 shows some of the welding symbols recommended in British Standard 499.

Fig. 5 BS499 welding symbols

Weld	Symbol	Illustration
Fillet		l, T
Square butt		T, g
Single V butt		α, T, g
Double V butt		α, T
Single U butt		α, t, T, g
Double U butt		α, g, T
Single bevel butt		α, T, g
Double bevel butt		α, T
Single J butt		α, t, T
Double J butt		T
Edge		
Seal		
Sealing run		
Backing strip		
Spot	N, d, S	
Seam	d	
Mashed seam		before, after
Stitch		
Mashed stitch		
Projection	N, VPS, St	
Flash	L	
Butt	L	
Stud	N, C	
Full penetration butt weld		

α Angle
C Centre distance
d Diameter
g Width of groove
ι Leg length
L Upset travel

N Number
S Spacing
T Thickness of parent metal
t Depth of groove in parent metal
WPS Weld Procedure Sheet

Submersibles

4.1 SUBMERSIBLES

The difference between a submarine and a submersible is one of autonomy, of size and independence from surface support. Whereas a submarine carries its own fuel to recharge its batteries, a submersible relies on a support ship for its power requirements. Almost all submarines have been designed for military purposes, while submersibles have been designed mainly for commercial use.

There are two basic types of submersible used in underwater work: manned submersibles and unmanned remotely operated vehicles (ROVs). Each is a part of a fully integrated system: vehicle, surface support vessel, handling gear, logistic and maintenance support.

The applications of the two systems can be complementary and are often overlapping. Determining factors are: safety of personnel, economics, deck-loading and space limitations, operating depths, duration of dives, visibility, current and other environmental conditions, urgency and complexity of the task, and the user's operating policies. The choice between using one type rather than the other does not always fall into an either/or category. Sometimes both are used together, or even with divers.

Apart from construction work, the most important and frequent underwater tasks offshore are:

1. Inspection and NDT.
2. Simple repair.
3. Repair of modules in situ.
4. Equipment salvage.
5. Debris clearance.
6. Measurements and alignment.
7. Structural repair.
8. Wellhead and subsea valve alignments, workovers and maintenance.

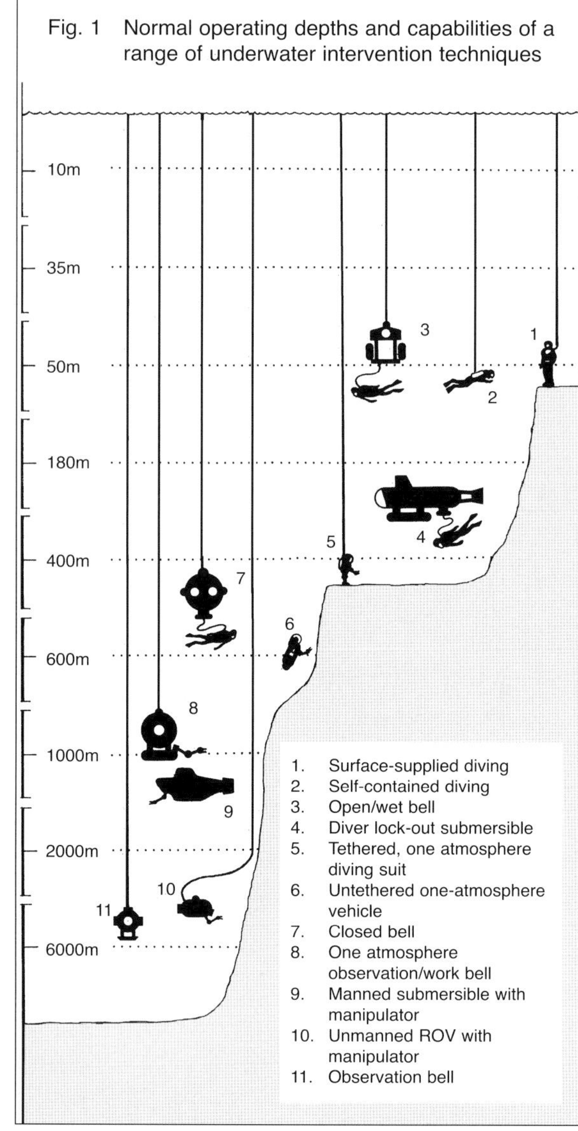
10m
35m
50m
180m
400m
600m
1000m
2000m
6000m
1
2
3
4
5
6
7
8
9
10
11
1. Surface-supplied diving
2. Self-contained diving
3. Open/wet bell
4. Diver lock-out submersible
5. Tethered, one atmosphere diving suit
6. Untethered one-atmosphere vehicle
7. Closed bell
8. One atmosphere observation/work bell
9. Manned submersible with manipulator
10. Unmanned ROV with manipulator
11. Observation bell

Fig. 1 Normal operating depths and capabilities of a range of underwater intervention techniques

Diving support services and life support systems are most affected by increased operational depths and grow significantly with size and cost. The cost of supporting divers at hyperbaric pressures exceeding 15 atmospheres is expensive. Offshore exploration depths are approaching both physical and economical barriers to the use of man in the sea. The alternatives to deep hyperbaric diving are manned one-atmosphere systems and unmanned remotely operated systems which involve the redesign of subsea installations to make up for their lack of dexterity.

The capabilities of man versus submersible are compared in Fig. 2 (not all the systems in the table are capable of performing the ten functions listed).

It evaluates diver alternative work systems and shows that although man-in-the-sea is best, it is more costly and at greater risk at depth.

Fig. 2. Diver and Submersible capabilities compared

RATING: 1 2 3 4 5 → better

Method of intervention				Visual inspection	Photography	CCTV	NDT	Seabed survey	Debris clearance	Salvage	Manipulative tasks	Mid-water operations	Vertical excursions	Large area coverage	Safety of personnel	Payload
MANNED	ADS	Walking		3	2	2	2	2	3	2	3	1	1	1	4	1
		Thrusters		4	2	2	2	2	3	2	3	4	5	2	4	1
	1-at tethered, 1-man sub			4	3	2	2	3	3	3	2	4	5	3	4	2
	1-at tethered, observation bell			4	4	3	2	3	3	3	3	4	5	3	4	4
	1-at untethered, multi-man sub			4	4	5	2	5	3	3	2	4	5	5	4	5
ROV	TETHERED	Free-swimming	Large	4	4	4	2	5	3	3	2	4	5	5	4	5
			Small	3	3	2	1	3	–	–	–	4	5	4	5	1
		Bottom-crawling		2	3	3	2	4	2	2	3	–	–	4	5	5
		Towed		1	1	2	–	4	–	–	–	3	4	5	5	5
	Untethered, free-swimming			1	1	1	–	3	–	–	–	2	3	2	5	3
Diver				5	5	5	5	2	5	5	5	5	2	3	1	1

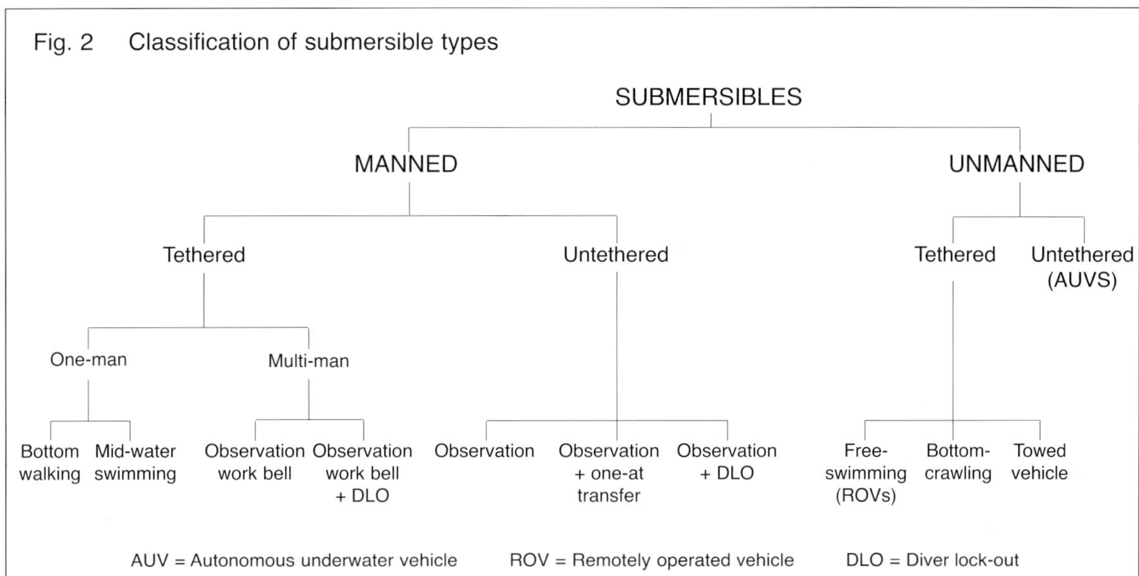
SUBMERSIBLES
MANNED
UNMANNED
Tethered
Untethered
Tethered
Untethered (AUVS)
One-man
Multi-man
Bottom walking
Mid-water swimming
Observation work bell
Observation work bell + DLO
Observation
Observation + one-at transfer
Observation + DLO
Free-swimming (ROVs)
Bottom-crawling
Towed vehicle
AUV = Autonomous underwater vehicle
ROV = Remotely operated vehicle
DLO = Diver lock-out
Fig. 2 Classification of submersible types

Manned submersibles

Manned submersibles can be categorised into five main groups.

1. ONE-ATMOSPHERE, TETHERED ONE-MAN SUBMERSIBLES
   a) Atmospheric Diving Suits (ADS)
   One-man crew, one-atmosphere, human-powered and/or thruster-powered, with a surface tether and hard wire communication line.
   b) One-atmosphere, one-man submersible
   One-man crew, one-atmosphere, electrically-powered from the surface and with emergency batteries, some mid-water capability from thrusters. Some also capable of ROV operations.

2. ONE-ATMOSPHERE, TETHERED OBSERVATION/WORK BELLS
   a) Two-man crew, battery-powered, electro-mechanical lift line for TV and communications, horizontal thrusters. Some have advanced manipulators.
   b) Two or three-man crew, electrically-powered from surface, fixed reversible thrusters, emergency battery power, advanced manipulators.

3. ONE-ATMOSPHERE, UNTETHERED SUBMERSIBLES
   Two or three-man crew, self-powered by batteries and independent of movement from the support ship. Range limited only by the power supply's endurance

4. DIVER LOCK OUT VEHICLES
   Two or three-man crew, one-atmosphere control section with adjoining separate lockout chamber for two or three divers.
   a) Battery-powered.
   b) Surface umbilical for power.

5. ONE-ATMOSPHERE TRANSFER VEHICLES
   For transferring personnel in and out of underwater chambers including rescue from a sunken submarine.
   a) Specifically constructed.
   b) Modified diver lockout submersibles.

Unmanned Submersibles

Unmanned submersibles fall into four main groups:

1. FREE-SWIMMING, TETHERED VEHICLES
   Commonly called remotely operated vehicles (ROVs). Surface umbilical-powered for use in mid-water or on the seabed. Controlled from the surface or a manned submersible.
   a) Small observation vehicles, commonly called 'eyeball' ROVs. Several are capable of simple NDT work.
   b) Larger survey vehicles which can undertake varied tasks from pipeline survey to BOP work. Commonly called 'work-class' ROVs.

2. BOTTOM-CRAWLING VEHICLES
   There are several heavy duty bottom-crawling tethered vehicles built to carry out a variety of tasks such as pipeline surveys, visual TV inspection, debris clearance and cable burial. Because of their weight and stability these tractors can perform tasks outside the capabilities of a submersible or ROV, such as operating in strong currents or lifting heavy loads.

3. TOWED VEHICLES
   Powered and propelled by a surface support ship via an umbilical.

4. UNTETHERED VEHICLES
   Commonly called autonomous underwater vehicles (AUVs). Self-powered from batteries. Pre-programmed or surface-controlled by acoustics (telemetry).

4.2 MANNED SUBMERSIBLES

The use of manned submersibles in the offshore industry has been declining since the 1970s largely due to the complexity of their handling/operating systems and the high cost of manning and insuring them. They require life-support systems that are complex, expensive and indispensable. Their time-on-bottom can be limited by weather, sea state and human endurance. The launch and recovery of most submersibles also requires the specialised equipment of a dedicated support vessel. Submersibles are particularly vulnerable when passing through the air/water interface. Depending on the spread, a sea state of 4–6 is about their limit.

Despite the advantages of being untethered and of having person(nel) onboard who can make real-time observations and decisions in reaction to changing situations, they have been largely supplanted by ROVs which are less costly and less complicated to operate.

Since ROVs lack the manual dexterity of the diver, sophisticated mechanical arms and tools have been attached to work class ROVs and many fittings on subsea equipment have been redesigned to accommodate them – simpler valving on well-heads, for example.

Manned submersibles are now mainly used in the tourist industry and for scientific marine research. Although many are now decommissioned, divers may encounter similar examples and so they are briefly described below.

Manned submersibles can be categorised into five main groups:

1. One-man, one-atmosphere, tethered submersibles

Designed to operate in depths from 100m to 300m (330–1,000ft) they are mainly used for search and identification in limited areas for objects such as sunken ships, downed aircraft, etc. Their interaction with diving is often restricted to providing emergency back-up facilities for diving spreads.

a) ATMOSPHERIC DIVING SUIT
These are bottom-orientated, tethered suits with armoured bodies and flexible limbs. Thrusters may be fitted to provide a mid-water working capability. *eg: Jim, Newt suit* (Fig. 1).

b) ONE-ATMOSPHERE, TETHERED, ONE-MAN SUBMERSIBLE
Self-propelled inspection system, similar to the ADS but without legs. It can hover mid-water or anchor itself. Articulated arms are equipped with manipulators. Depending on the model it can be battery or umbilical powered and operate in either vertical or horizontal mode. *eg: Mantis, Wasp, Spider* (Figs. 2 and 3).

2. Multi-man, one-atmosphere, tethered submersibles

OBSERVATION/WORK BELLS
Unlike conventional diving bells, observation bells usually have some degree of independent movement and the crew are maintained at atmospheric pressure.

Fig. 1 Atmospheric diving suits

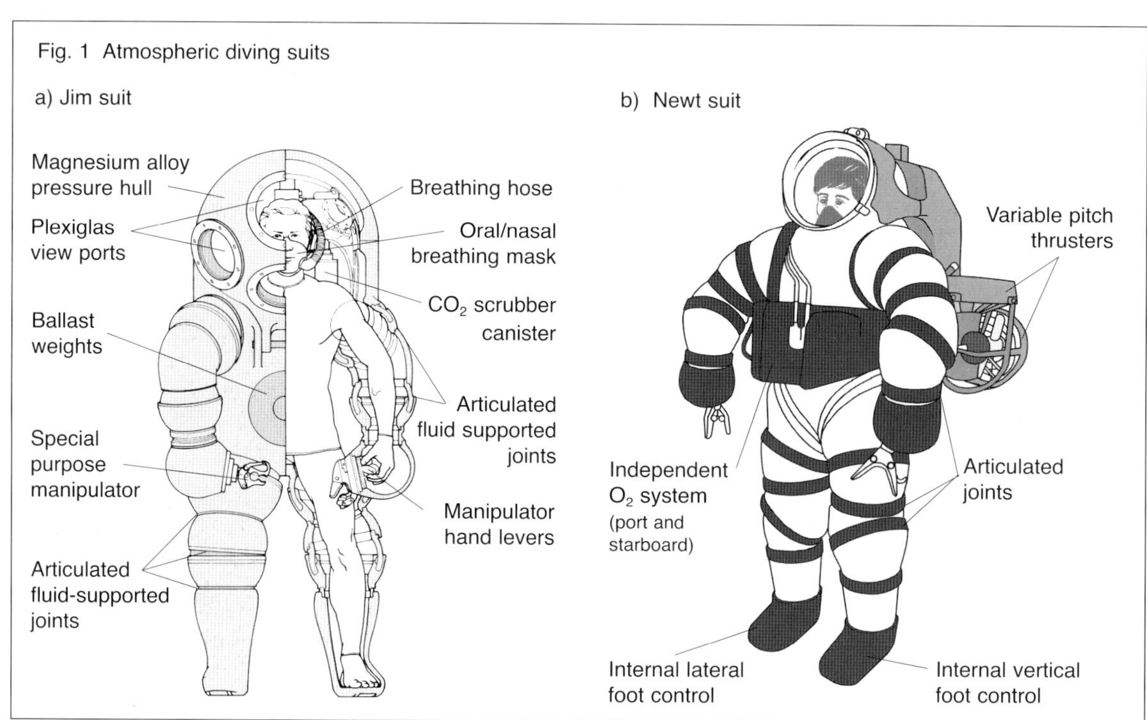
a) Jim suit
Magnesium alloy pressure hull
Plexiglas view ports
Ballast weights
Special purpose manipulator
Articulated fluid-supported joints
Breathing hose
Oral/nasal breathing mask
CO_2 scrubber canister
Articulated fluid supported joints
Manipulator hand levers
b) Newt suit
Variable pitch thrusters
Independent O_2 system (port and starboard)
Articulated joints
Internal lateral foot control
Internal vertical foot control

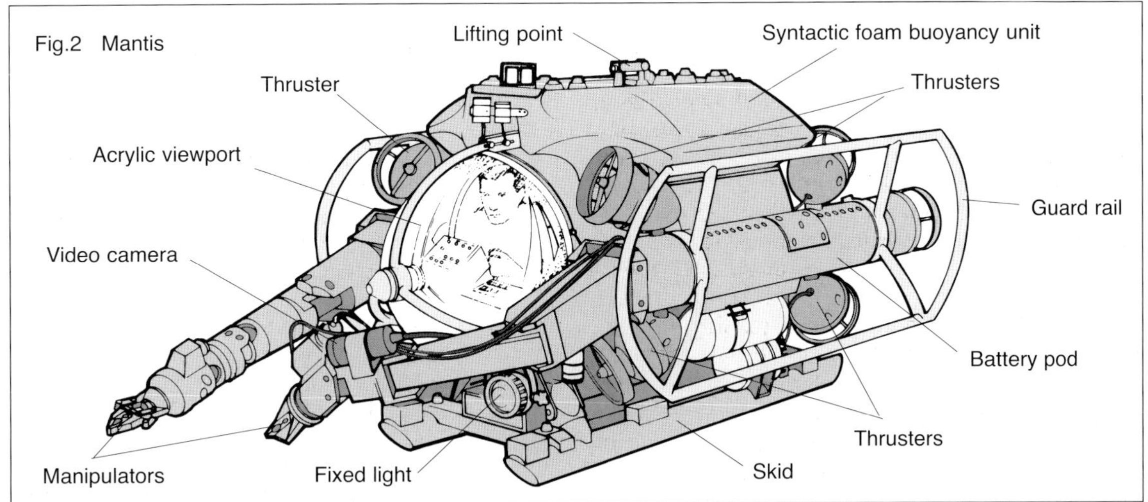
Fig.2 Mantis
Lifting point
Syntactic foam buoyancy unit
Thruster
Thrusters
Acrylic viewport
Guard rail
Video camera
Battery pod
Thrusters
Manipulators
Fixed light
Skid

They may have manipulators and may be connected to submersible compression chambers. They are usually launched and recovered through a moonpool on a dedicated vessel. Although these craft may run off vessels fitted with diving spreads, the only likely diver requirement would be in a rescue situation or for surface swimming if the bell is forced to surface away from its handling system. *eg: ARMS* (Fig. 4).

3. One-atmosphere, untethered submersibles

Operating from a dedicated support ship these vessels are battery-powered, carry manipulators and can carry a crew of 2–4. Used for survey and inspection, some are also capable of carrying out NDT tasks around platforms and other structures. Diver/swimmer involvement is limited to occasional launch and recovery support. *eg: Pisces* (Fig. 5), *LR2*(Fig. 6).

4. Diver Lock-out submersibles (DLOs)

These combine the versatility, endurance and hardware capabilities of the manned submersible with the manual dexterity of the diver. DLO submersibles can be used in a variety of modes such as seabed lockout, mid-water lookout while fixed to a structure, one-atmosphere transfer and submarine rescue. They have two pressure hull sections one of which is maintained at one-atmosphere and the other can be brought to ambient pressure. One of the chief advantages of the DLO submersible over the other systems is mobility. Divers can be transported to the work-site which can be any distance away from the support vessel and they can observe and plan their work before entering the water. The submersible's underwater navigation systems can position it at ±2m with respect of the surface. The divers can be directly monitored by a supervisor who remains in the submersible. The DLO submersible provides a high level of diver

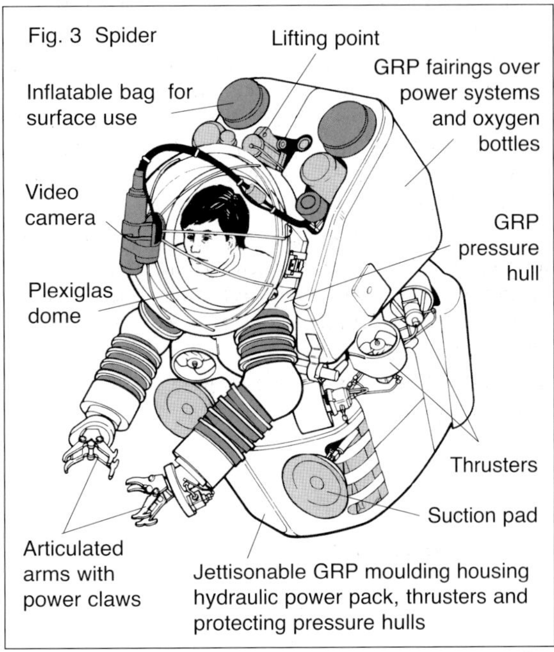
Fig. 3 Spider
Lifting point
GRP fairings over power systems and oxygen bottles
Inflatable bag for surface use
Video camera
GRP pressure hull
Plexiglas dome
Thrusters
Suction pad
Articulated arms with power claws
Jettisonable GRP moulding housing hydraulic power pack, thrusters and protecting pressure hulls

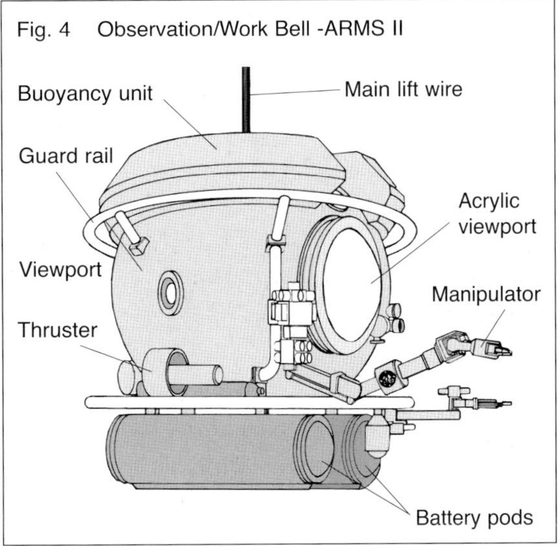
Fig. 4 Observation/Work Bell -ARMS II
Buoyancy unit
Main lift wire
Guard rail
Acrylic viewport
Viewport
Manipulator
Thruster
Battery pods

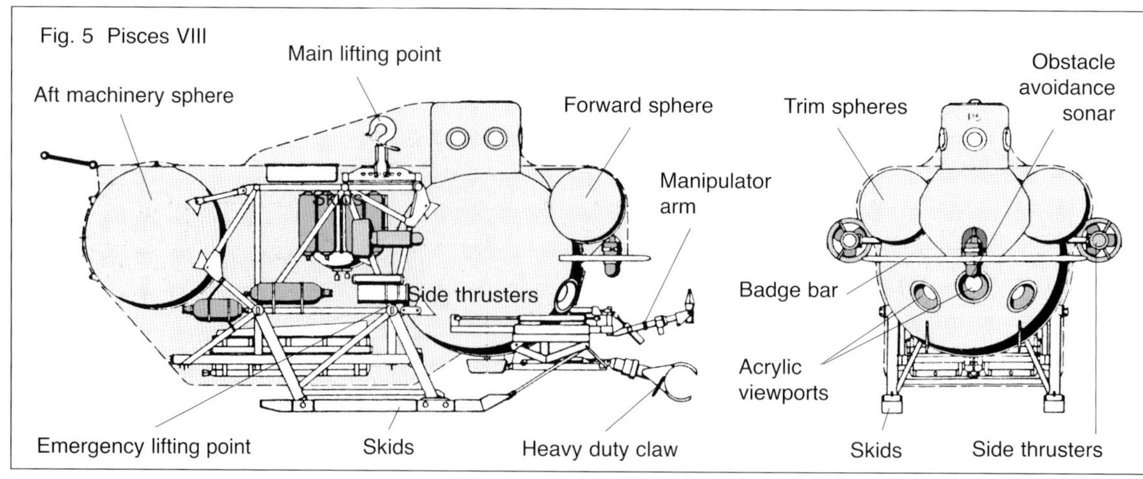
Main lifting point
Aft machinery sphere
Forward sphere
Trim spheres
Obstacle avoidance sonar
Manipulator arm
Side thrusters
Badge bar
Acrylic viewports
Emergency lifting point
Skids
Heavy duty claw
Skids
Side thrusters

Fig. 5 Pisces VIII

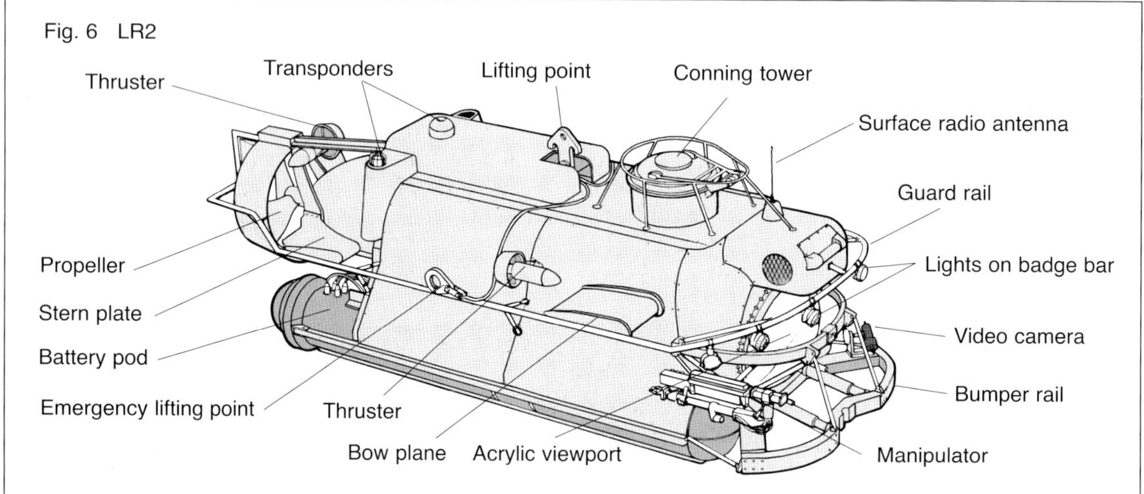
Thruster
Transponders
Lifting point
Conning tower
Surface radio antenna
Guard rail
Propeller
Lights on badge bar
Stern plate
Video camera
Battery pod
Bumper rail
Emergency lifting point
Thruster
Bow plane
Acrylic viewport
Manipulator

Fig. 6 LR2

safety and rescue. Variable buoyancy tanks enable the pilot to compensate for its divers' movements. Some DLO submersibles can be used as hyperbaric lifeboats in emergencies. The main limitation of DLO submersibles is their limited power for supplying the thrusters, diver heating and electronic instrumentation, etc.

Mainly used for underwater pipeline or rig maintenance, search and recovery operations and underwater operations with hydraulic tools. DLO submersibles are generally run from dedicated support ships with built-in transfer locks and DCCs (deck compression chambers). *eg: Taurus* (Fig. 7), *DSRV, LS 200 12* (Fig. 8).

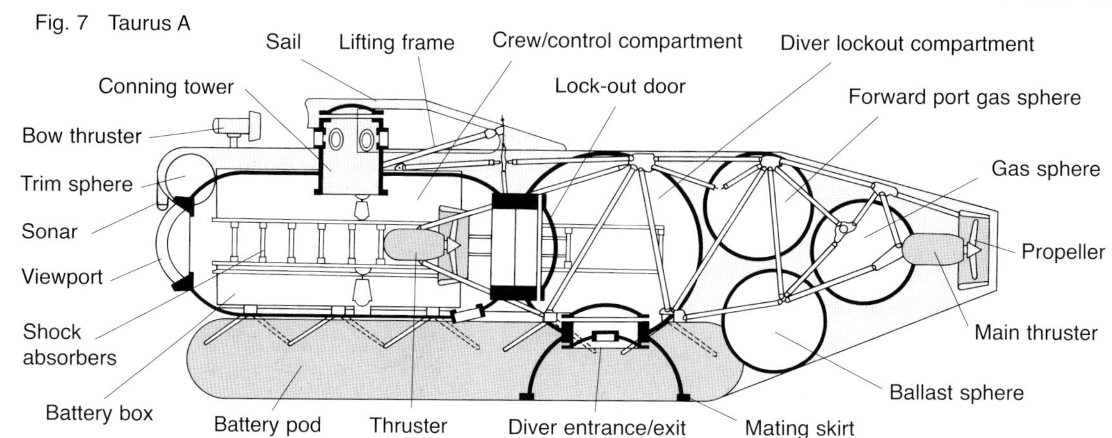
Sail
Lifting frame
Crew/control compartment
Diver lockout compartment
Conning tower
Lock-out door
Forward port gas sphere
Bow thruster
Gas sphere
Trim sphere
Sonar
Propeller
Viewport
Shock absorbers
Main thruster
Ballast sphere
Battery box
Battery pod
Thruster
Diver entrance/exit
Mating skirt

Fig. 7 Taurus A

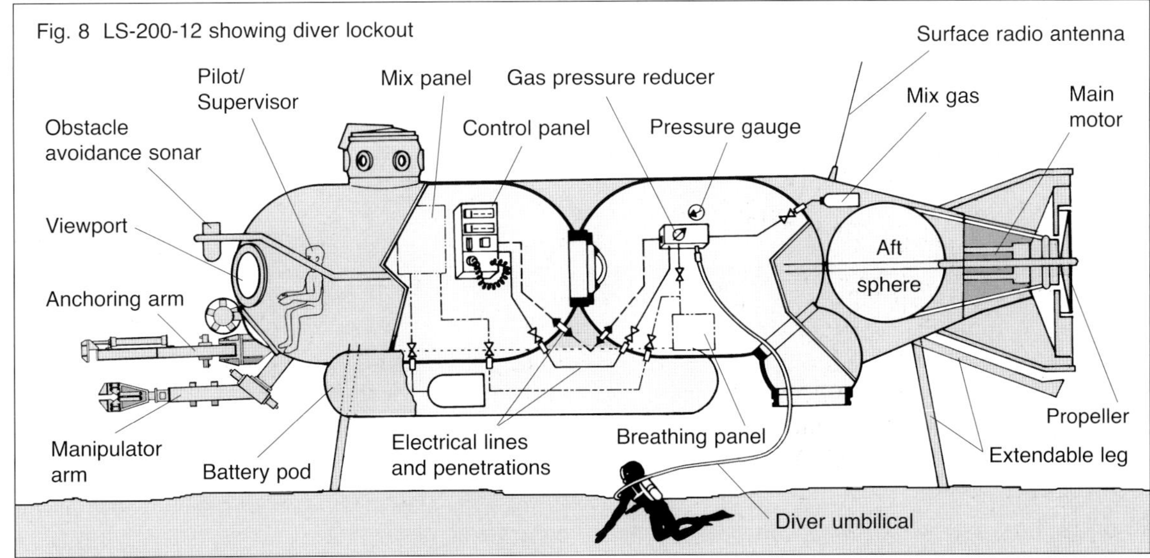
Surface radio antenna
Pilot/
Supervisor
Mix panel
Gas pressure reducer
Mix gas
Main
motor
Obstacle
avoidance sonar
Control panel
Pressure gauge
Viewport
Aft
sphere
Anchoring arm
Propeller
Manipulator
arm
Battery pod
Electrical lines
and penetrations
Breathing panel
Extendable leg
Diver umbilical
Fig. 8 LS-200-12 showing diver lockout

5. **One-atmosphere transfer submersibles**
Medium to small submersibles with both a dry transfer and a diver lookout facility. Two compartments, both at atmospheric pressure: one compartment for the pilot/observer and the other – a diver lockout or dry transfer compartment with medical lock. Battery-powered with manipulators and an array of other equipment. *eg: PC 1801* (Fig. 9).

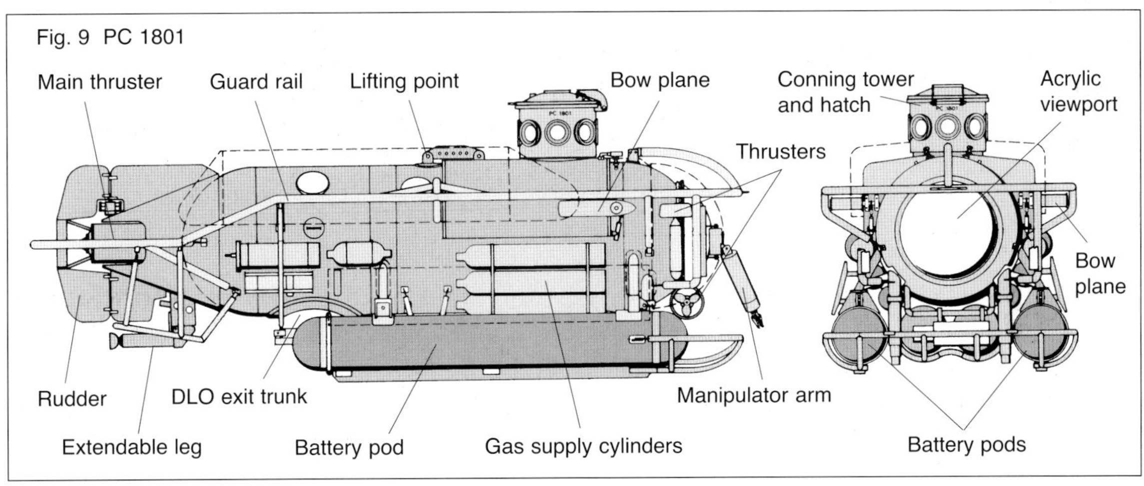
Main thruster
Guard rail
Lifting point
Bow plane
Conning tower
and hatch
Acrylic
viewport
Thrusters
Bow
plane
Rudder
DLO exit trunk
Manipulator arm
Extendable leg
Battery pod
Gas supply cylinders
Battery pods
Fig. 9 PC 1801

4.3 UNMANNED SUBMERSIBLES

The high cost of putting a person into the water either as a diver or in a manned submersible including all his attendant support, has contributed to the development of the ROV (remotely operated vehicle).
The development of ROVs has been accelerated by exploration and production moving into deeper water, well beyond the depth at which divers can safely work.
ROVs are built in many different forms and sizes depending on the tasks they are required to perform. The advantages of ROVs are their unlimited operational endurance at the work site and their ability to perform in hazardous areas. There is also a considerable economy in not having to provide life-support systems and safety provisions.
ROVs have many industrial, military and research applications and can be used for:

1. *Inspection and maintenance*. Locating and checking the condition of structures and performing simple maintenance tasks.
2. *Monitoring*. Observation/measurement of tasks.
3. *Exploration drilling support*. Observation of wellhead systems, positioning of drill string, changing seals and operating valves.

4. *Survey*. The measurement and sampling of bottom features.
5. *Diver assistance*. Support of other diver activities.
6. *Search and identification*. The location and identification of objects on the sea floor.
7. *Installation and retrieval*. Assistance with installation of fixed structures and the retrieval of objects.
8. *Cleaning*.

There are four main categories of ROV:
1. Free-swimming, tethered vehicles.
2. Bottom-crawling, tethered vehicles.
3. Towed vehicles.
4. Autonomous underwater vehicles (AUVs).

All are rapidly-evolving systems. The following examples include some early systems which are used to illustrate the different categories of ROVs.

1. Free-swimming, tethered vehicles

This category comprises the majority of ROVs ranging from the small eyeball ROVs (Fig. 1) to work-class ROVs as large as trucks (Fig. 2).

Free-swimming ROVs are integrated systems consisting of an underwater vehicle, a deployment unit and a control station on the support vessel. No two systems are the same. Each one is designed for a specific task. The vehicle carries the necessary equipment such as lights, video cameras and manipulator(s). All vehicles have their own means of propulsion by thrusters but they are tethered to the support ship which supplies the electric power.

In strong currents, drag on the tether can cause manoeuvring difficulties. To reduce this drag some vehicles are deployed from an underwater 'garage' or tether management system lowered to the operating depth by a deployment unit on the support vessel. The control station supplies the power to the vehicle and a control display monitors the vehicle's movements which are directed by a pilot using a hand controller. The ROV's endurance is limited only by that of the surface operator(s).

The tethers on free-swimming ROVs can easily become entangled in underwater obstructions. In most cases the CCTV on free-swimming ROVs does not provide three-dimensional viewing which would help avoid this problem and can improve the ROV's ability to carry out complex manipulative tasks.

There are two groups of free-swimming, tethered ROVs: Observation/survey ROVs, and Work class ROVs (WROVs).

a) OBSERVATION VEHICLES

Commonly referred to as 'eyeball' ROVs, the smallest of these is little more than a tethered free-swimming camera. They are highly manoeuvrable and are usually fitted with lights, and video and possibly a still camera (see Fig. 1). Their small size makes them easily transportable and particularly suitable for inspection in areas inaccessible to large vehicles.

Observation ROVs are commonly used to monitor divers at work in the offshore industry. They provide the Diving Supervisor with good visual supervision of the diver.

Fig. 1 Example of an observation ROV (Hyball)

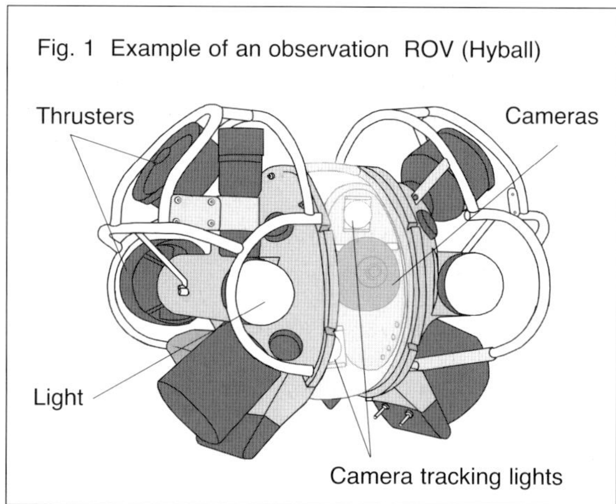
Thrusters
Cameras
Light
Camera tracking lights

Diver-related tasks
1. Observe a diving bell approaching a guide-wire weight to ensure that it avoids contact.
2. Illuminate a work site to guide divers coming from the bell.
3. Observe divers at work from a distance, from, say, 5–10m (15–33ft).
4. Observe and illuminate crane loads on the way down to an underwater worksite.
5. Illuminate a crane load that has been landed at an underwater worksite.
6. Fix and record the location of items for 'as-built', 'as-found' and 'as-left' surveys using an onboard mini-beacon.
7. Make a video record of work done by divers.

b) WORK CLASS VEHICLES

These range in size from the size of a small car to huge deep-sea ROVs the size of trucks. They are

Fig. 2 Example of a work class ROV (Scorpio)

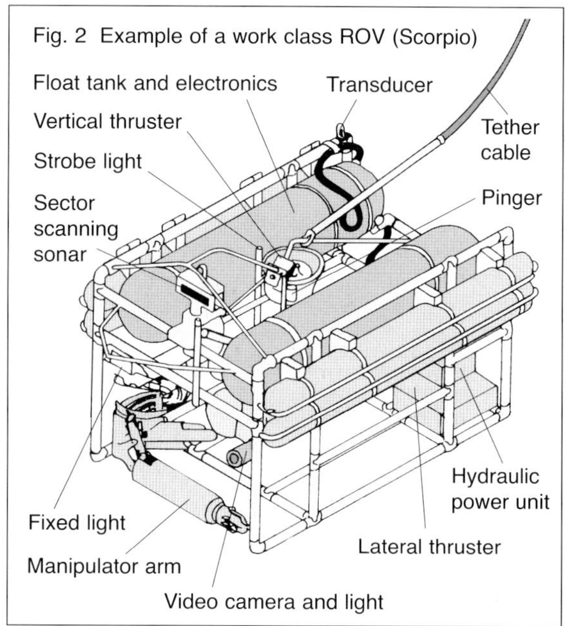
Float tank and electronics
Transducer
Vertical thruster
Tether cable
Strobe light
Pinger
Sector scanning sonar
Hydraulic power unit
Fixed light
Lateral thruster
Manipulator arm
Video camera and light

powered via a cable from the support vessel and usually have four or more thrusters (see Fig. 2).

Many are built to order and are equipped according to client requirements. Standard equipment normally includes sonar, video camera(s), manipulator(s), data recording equipment and underwater navigation transponder. They are widely used for exploration drilling support and pipeline inspection.

Typically, a standard work class ROV is at least 100 shaft horse power, weighs about 3 tonnes (in air), has a payload of about 200kg (440 lb) and some can operate to depths of 2000–3000m (6500–9800 ft) or more. Most work class ROVs convert surface-supplied electrical power into hydraulic power which is used for propulsion and tool operation. These vehicles, known as 'hydraulic work class' ROVs, usually have two manipulators as well as several outlets for additional hydraulic tools, sensors, tracking devices and survey equipment. They are the most capable and stable class of ROV and are widely used in the offshore oil/gas industry as well as for salvage operations, cable maintenance, deep scientific research and submarine rescue support.

Some work class ROVs use direct electric propulsion. Not only is this more efficient than converting electric power to hydraulics but it is also more reliable and enables considerable weight reductions to be made to the ROV.

Work class ROV operating systems

Work class ROVs can either be free-swimming or operated using a tether management system.

A free-swimming system has four main components (Fig. 3a):

1. Workshop/Storage area containing maintenance tools, spare parts and accessories.
2. Control module containing system power transformer, surface controls, inter-site communications, etc.
3. Launch and recovery system comprising: ship's crane or 'A' frame, lift wire and umbilical handling equipment.
4. The ROV itself.

Compared to other operating systems, free-swimming systems are less expensive, less complicated to deploy and control (useful for live

Fig. 3 Typical work class ROV operating systems

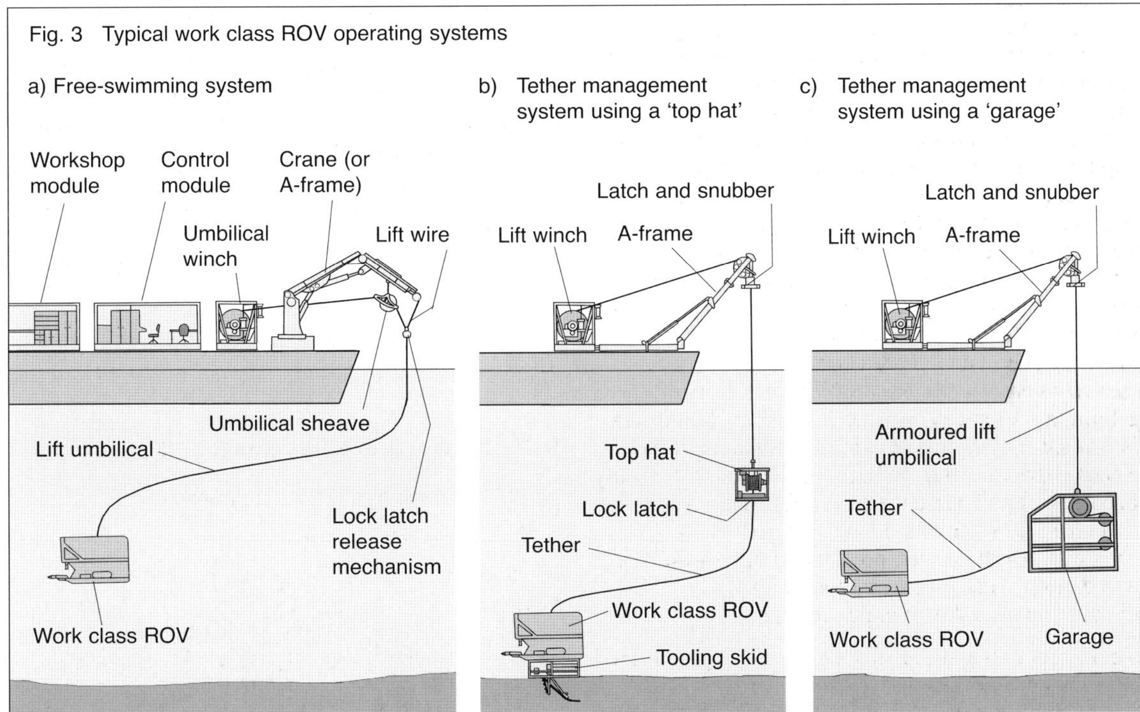
a) Free-swimming system
b) Tether management system using a 'top hat'
c) Tether management system using a 'garage'
Workshop module
Control module
Crane (or A-frame)
Umbilical winch
Lift wire
Umbilical sheave
Lift umbilical
Lock latch release mechanism
Work class ROV
Latch and snubber
Lift winch
A-frame
Top hat
Lock latch
Tether
Work class ROV
Tooling skid
Latch and snubber
Lift winch
A-frame
Armoured lift umbilical
Tether
Work class ROV
Garage

Control module contains power transformer, power distribution unit (PDU) and control system.

Launch and recovery system (LARS) comprises winch, crane or A frame, lift wire and, in the case of a tether management system, a top hat or garage.

Umbilical winch and the **crane or A-frame** are rated to launch and recover the ROV up to sea state 6.

Umbilical sheave accommodates the minimum bend radius of the umbilical.

Lock latch release mechanism hydraulically releases the lock latch when the ROV is in the water (and the weight is taken off the umbilical) enabling the pilot to take control of the ROV.

Tooling skid enables the ROV to be fitted with tools required for the specific task (in this example a cable burial and water jetting tool is illustrated).

Latch and snubber secures the recovered ROV and enables it to be swung onto the deck of the vessel.

boat operations, ie when the vessel follows the ROV) and because they do not need tether management equipment, they weigh less and occupy less deck space.

In addition to the equipment required for a free-swimming system, a tether management system utilises either a 'top hat' or 'garage' to launch and recover the ROV (see Figs. 3b/c). The ROV is installed into the top hat or garage and lowered to the working depth. It is then released and the tether is paid out to enable the ROV to be flown to the work site. On completing the task, the ROV returns and to the top hat/garage before being recovered to the surface.

A tether management system enables the ROV to be rapidly deployed to depth with reduced interference from currents and also provides an opportunity to park the ROV between jobs, if required.

Compared to the top hat system, using a garage provides:

- Greater stability during launch and recovery.
- Easier subsea docking.
- Less chance of tether damage during docking.
- Less operator experience required.
- Ability to park on seabed (sea state permitting).

Compared to the garage system, the top hat system is more compact and since the dimensions of the ROV are not critical to docking with the top hat, the ROV can be customised for the task by adding extra tools as required.

2. Bottom-crawling tethered vehicles

Heavy duty, bottom-crawling, tethered vehicles are designed to carry out trenching tasks on fibre optic cables, telephone cables and flowlines and to lift heavy loads. They come in many forms including racked and wheeled versions. An example of a wheeled version is shown in Fig. 4. Because of their weight these vehicles are normally stable and can perform heavy-duty tasks outside the range of ROVs or submersibles such as operating in strong currents or lifting heavy loads.

The vehicles can be fitted with still and video cameras, lights, sonar, sub-bottom profiler, trench profiler and CP probe. They are normally launched by winch from an 'A' frame on the support vessel or platform from which they are also monitored and remotely operated. The whole system includes the underwater vehicle, its handling equipment, a power generator and control cabin.

Fig. 4 Example of a bottom-crawling vehicle fitted with cable burial tool

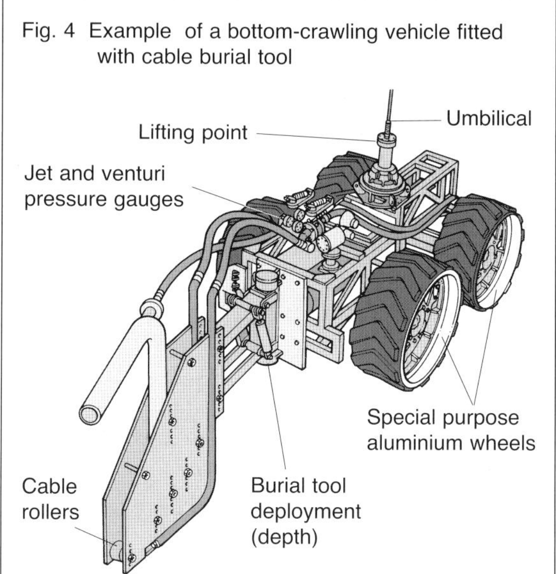
Lifting point
Umbilical
Jet and venturi pressure gauges
Special purpose aluminium wheels
Cable rollers
Burial tool deployment (depth)

DIVERS WORKING WITH ROVs – OPERATIONAL SAFETY

Before commencing operations:

1. Operational procedures must be set up in advance and only changed with proper authority. (During diving, the diving supervisor must have authority over the ROV team).
2. All members of both the diving and ROV teams should be aware of all potential hazards:
   a) entanglement of wires/umbilicals
   b) ROV collision or thruster injury to divers
   c) ROVs are a potential electrical shock hazard
3. Emergency diving procedures should be understood by all ROV personnel.

During diving/ROV operations:

1. Only experienced ROV pilots should be used when divers are in the water.
2. The diving supervisor must have authority over the ROV supervisor or pilot while divers are in the water.
3. There must be direct communication between the diving supervisor and the ROV supervisor or pilot at all times. The diving supervisor should have a monitor which shows him what the ROV pilot sees.
4. During diving the ROV should only be deployed or recovered with the authority of the diving supervisor.
5. The current should be continuously monitored to assess the risk of the ROV or garage becoming entangled with the bell or diver's umbilical.
6. Care must be taken to avoid the ROV tether becoming entangled with:
   a) the diver's umbilical.
   b) the diving bell umbilical, hoist and guide wires.
   c) the ship's DP taut-wire system or seabed transponder.
7. An ROV pinger must not be used as a ship's DP reference while divers are in the water.
8. If a diver is used to recover a trapped ROV the electrical power to the ROV must first be turned off.
9. If the ROV loses orientation the pilot must inform the diving supervisor immediately.
10. The ROV should always stand off unless given permission by the diving supervisor to move in.
11. Ideally, the diver should be the first to leave the work site.

3. Towed vehicles

Towed vehicles are designed for specific tasks in deep-sea monitoring and seabed survey work with particular emphasis on deep-sea mining. Towed vehicles are easier to operate for visual surveys than ROVs. Power to operate the instrumentation (such as video cameras and sonar) is supplied from the support vessel via a tether.

4. Autonomous underwater vehicles

AUVs are untethered, self-propelled vehicles. Tether cables from ROVs to their support vessels are restrictive and a potential hazard as they often become twisted or fouled, sometimes even severed. Because of the risk of tether cable entanglement, some tasks are therefore better suited to untethered vehicles. AUVs are used in surveying roles in oceanography, oil, gas and mineral industries and in military mine countermeasures.

Advantages of AUVs include:

a) Almost silent operation (useful for surveying fish stocks, etc)
b) low vibration (useful in researching ocean physics)
c) Under-ice operations (they can follow the sea–ice interface)
d) Terrain-following (useful when operating at a fixed height off the seabed is important)
e) Low radius turns (towed vehicles and ships need high radius turns).

Since many AUVs are custom-built for specific projects a wide variety of designs exist (see Fig. 5).

Fig. 5 Examples of AUVs

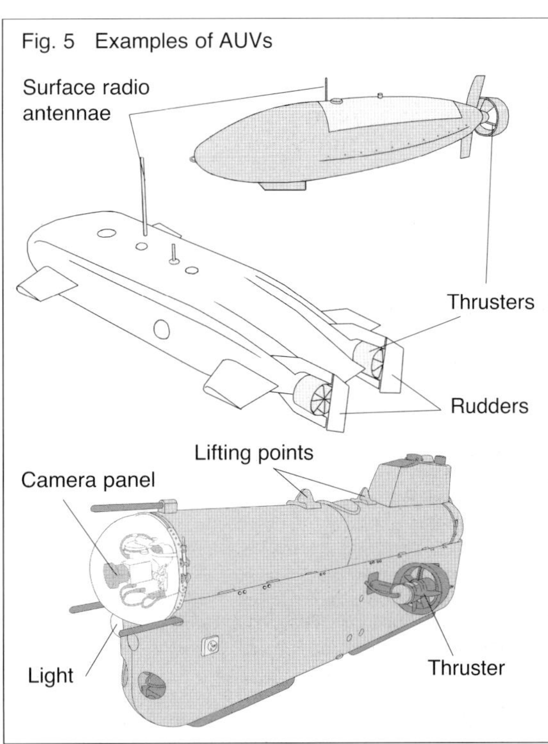
Surface radio antennae
Thrusters
Rudders
Lifting points
Camera panel
Light
Thruster

INSTRUMENTATION

AUVs normally carry state-of-the-art acoustic and inertial navigation systems. Positioning data can also be obtained by surface hops to obtain GPS fixes. Task-orientated instrumentation is highly variable and specific to the task. This equipment can be limited by the payload and power capacity of the AUV.

4.4 SUBMERSIBLE ANCILLARY EQUIPMENT

Except for the very specialised or lightweight submersibles, electronic and hydraulic instrumentation and equipment can be fitted to submersibles to suit any specific work to be done. Most will carry some form of lighting and CCTV for monitoring, remote direction control and data collection. Many will be fitted with a mechanical arm (manipulator) and some with special hydraulic tools such as cable-cutter or jetting gun. The electronic instrumentation might include underwater navigation systems, sonar and various NDT, surveying and measuring instruments.

Navigation systems

Radio techniques used by surface vessels do not work underwater. Instead, dead reckoning (calculating distances from a known position), inertial or underwater sound (acoustic) systems are employed. The latter can be used by both surface and subsea craft. Acoustic techniques can be combined in various ways to form communication systems, telemetering systems, control and positioning systems.

If an array of transponders is placed in known positions on the seabed, submersibles can determine their position relative to them. Acoustic systems are classified by their baselines (see Figs. 1 and 2):

a) Short baseline (SBL) (5–20m/15–60 ft)
b) Super short baseline (SSBL) (0.5m/1½ ft)
c) Long baseline (LBL) (20m/60 ft)

Sonar systems

Sonar stands for 'sound and ranging' and is the detection of objects underwater by sound waves. There are many specialised applications, such as:

a) *Echo-sounder.* Establishes the depth of water by measuring the time taken for a vertical sound pulse to reach the bottom and to be reflected back to the source.
b) *Sector scan.*
   i) A continuous-sweep sonar to locate objects or for obstacle avoidance (OAS).
   ii) a continuous transmission frequency modulator (CTFM).

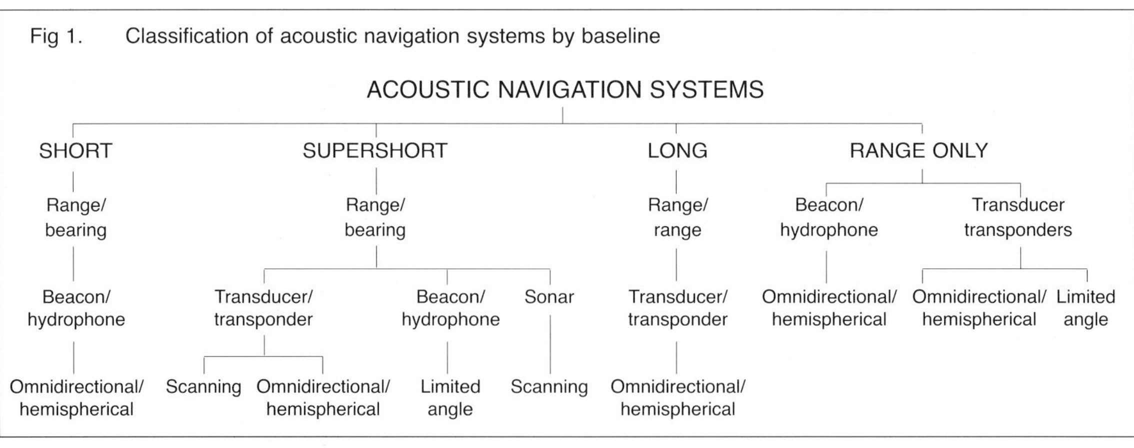
ACOUSTIC NAVIGATION SYSTEMS
SHORT
Range/ bearing
Beacon/ hydrophone
Omnidirectional/ hemispherical
SUPERSHORT
Range/ bearing
Transducer/ transponder
Scanning
Omnidirectional/ hemispherical
Beacon/ hydrophone
Limited angle
Sonar
Scanning
LONG
Range/ range
Transducer/ transponder
Omnidirectional/ hemispherical
RANGE ONLY
Beacon/ hydrophone
Omnidirectional/ hemispherical
Transducer transponders
Omnidirectional/ hemispherical
Limited angle

Fig 1. Classification of acoustic navigation systems by baseline

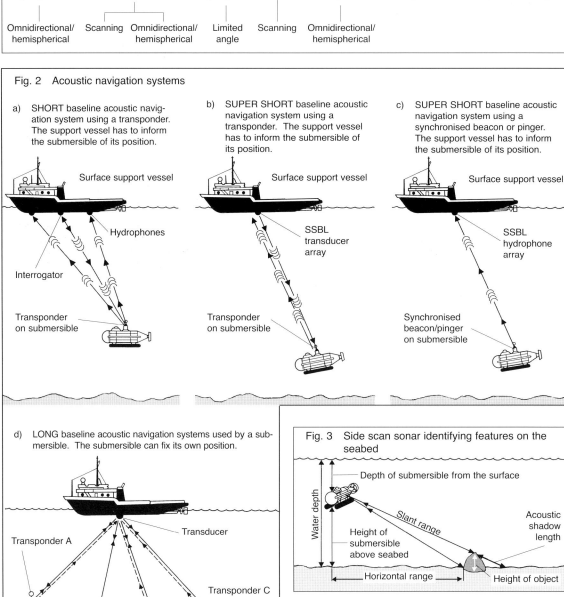

Fig. 2 Acoustic navigation systems

a) SHORT baseline acoustic navigation system using a transponder. The support vessel has to inform the submersible of its position.

Surface support vessel
Hydrophones
Interrogator
Transponder on submersible

b) SUPER SHORT baseline acoustic navigation system using a transponder. The support vessel has to inform the submersible of its position.

Surface support vessel
SSBL transducer array
Transponder on submersible

c) SUPER SHORT baseline acoustic navigation system using a synchronised beacon or pinger. The support vessel has to inform the submersible of its position.

Surface support vessel
SSBL hydrophone array
Synchronised beacon/pinger on submersible

d) LONG baseline acoustic navigation systems used by a submersible. The submersible can fix its own position.

Transducer
Transponder A
Transponder C
Echo sounder
Transponder B

Fig. 3 Side scan sonar identifying features on the seabed

Depth of submersible from the surface
Water depth
Slant range
Acoustic shadow length
Height of submersible above seabed
Horizontal range
Height of object

c) *Side scan sonar.* Fan-shaped sound beams provide a continuous shadow-graph of the surrounding ocean floor (see Fig. 3).

d) *Sub-bottom profiler.* Traces a reflection profile of the strata beneath the sea bottom such as sedimentary rock layers forming the sub-bottom structure.

e) *Pinger/locater.*
Trainable receiver used to determine the direction of an underwater sound source such as a submersible might use to locate a pinger on the seabed.

f) *Scan trench profile sonar.*
Provides transversal profiles of a pipe trench by combining a high resolution scanning sonar with a very accurate echo-sounder (see Fig. 4).

g) *Through-water communications.*
Acoustic signals are modulated into speech in much the same way as in radio telephony.

Fig. 4 Sector scanning trench profiler

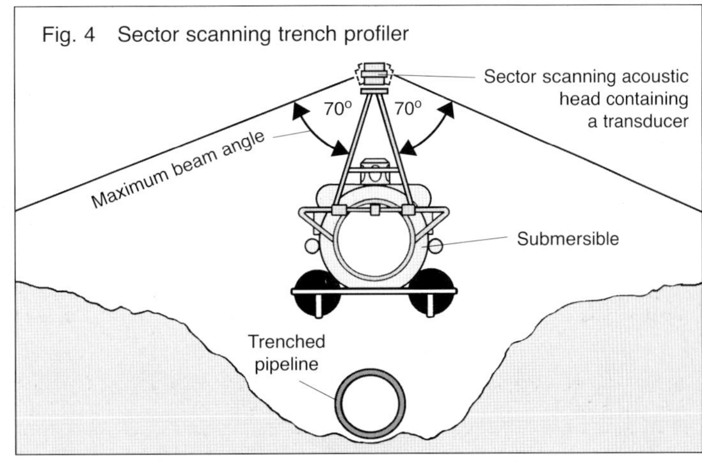
Sector scanning acoustic head containing a transducer
70°
70°
Maximum beam angle
Submersible
Trenched pipeline

Terms commonly used in acoustic systems

Acoustic release
A method of releasing a positively-buoyant package from its sinker on the seabed using sound pulses.

Hydrophone
A device for converting underwater sounds into electrical signals. A fixed or directional receiver capable of detecting an underwater noise source.

Pinger
A battery-powered device which transmits continuous sound pulses through the water.

Responder
Like a transponder but with power and time trigger signal passed by umbilical – not acoustically transmitted or battery-supplied.

Temperature and salinity meter
Gauge for measuring seawater temperature and salinity for use in calculating sound velocity.

Transducer
A device for converting electrical signals into sound and vice versa.

Transponder
A receiver/transmitter which will transmit a sound pulse through water on receipt of a suitably coded acoustic signal from another source.
Most transponders on the seabed are positively-buoyant and are fitted with a coded acoustic release for recovery. The source of the original signal can measure the range from the transponder by computing the time taken by the transmission.

Velocimeter
An acoustic device for measuring the speed of sound in water.

Operational Diving Equipment

5.1 DIVING SYSTEMS

Diving systems can be divided into two types: air or mixed gas. The mixed gas types can be further subdivided into bounce diving systems and saturation diving systems. There is, however, a considerable overlap between these techniques.
A saturation diving system is made up of six main components (see Fig. 1):

1. Diving bell
2. Bell handling and dive control.
3. Deck compression chamber complex.
4. Chamber control.
5. Life support equipment.
6. Hyperbaric lifeboat.

1. Diving bell

A variety of designs exists according to the individual requirements of the manufacturer, operator and the task.
A bell may be a two or three-man unit, the latter is usually used for construction tasks requiring two divers working together out of the bell. It may be bottom-mating locking onto the top of a transfer chamber. It may have a rollover bottom-mating facility which connects with the side of a transfer chamber or it may be side-mating using a second trunking-and-door arrangement on the side of the bell. There are many variations of bell construction and the diver should familiarise himself thoroughly with the bell and its handling system before use. A typical bell is illustrated in Fig. 2.

2. Bell handling and dive control

The dive control station is the normal location of the diving supervisor during the dive. It is usually positioned alongside the launching point for the bell to allow easy control of the launch and recovery. The various ways in which the bell can be launched are illustrated in Fig. 3.
The diving bell may be launched over the side of a vessel or through a dedicated moonpool. To launch over the side an extendable A-frame gantry or davit may be used to hoist the bell clear of the vessel (see Figs. 3a-c). In the moonpool arrangement, the bell usually has a specially built handling system for the particular vessel (see Fig. 3d).
A means of increasing the foul weather bell handling capability is provided by use of a bell cursor. The cursor may be 'active' or 'passive.' The passive cursor may be a heavy weight secured on vertical rails and can be attached to the bell (see Fig. 4). It is lowered by additional winches and allows the bell to sink steadily through the air/water interface. The bell is released from the weight near the bottom of the vessel where the water movement is not so great.
The 'active' cursor may have a similar means of restraining the bell against a vertical rail system. It would have, in addition, an active drive system to move the bell up and down the rails. Cursor systems are usually seen in dedicated DSVs (diving support vessels) with moonpools.

Fig. 1 Major components of a saturation diving system

Deck compression chamber complex
Bell mating flange
Chamber light
Deck compression chamber
Deck transfer chamber
Deck compression chamber
Sanitation unit
Entrance lock
Chamber control
Helium recovery unit
Bell and diver hot water
Air compressor
Emergency generator
Gas conditioning unit
Gas storage
Gas mixing unit
Life support equipment

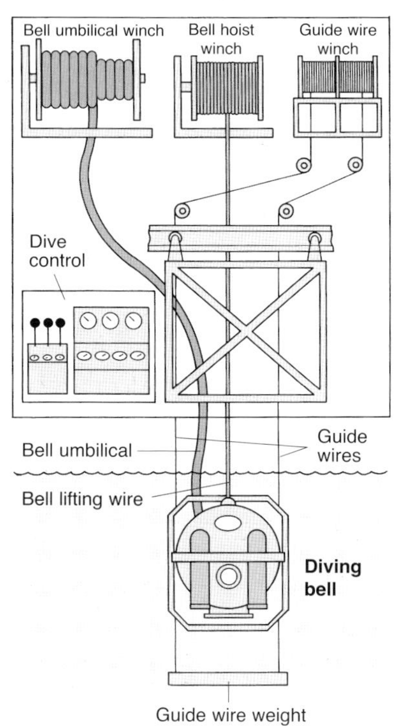

Bell handling system
Bell umbilical winch
Bell hoist winch
Guide wire winch
Dive control
Bell umbilical
Guide wires
Bell lifting wire
Diving bell
Guide wire weight

Fig. 2a) Typical open diving bell

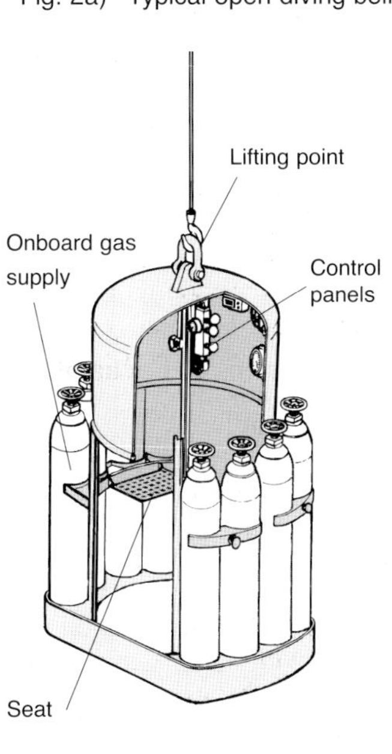
Lifting point
Onboard gas supply
Control panels
Seat

b) Typical layout of a mixed gas diving bell

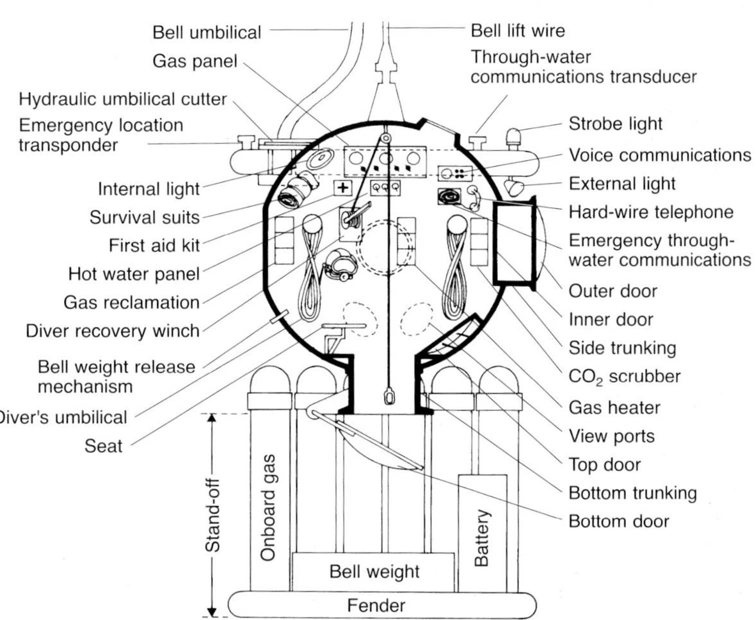
Bell umbilical
Gas panel
Hydraulic umbilical cutter
Emergency location transponder
Internal light
Survival suits
First aid kit
Hot water panel
Gas reclamation
Diver recovery winch
Bell weight release mechanism
Diver's umbilical
Seat
Bell lift wire
Through-water communications transducer
Strobe light
Voice communications
External light
Hard-wire telephone
Emergency through-water communications
Outer door
Inner door
Side trunking
CO2 scrubber
Gas heater
View ports
Top door
Bottom trunking
Bottom door
Stand-off
Onboard gas
Bell weight
Battery
Fender

Fig. 3 Bell launching systems

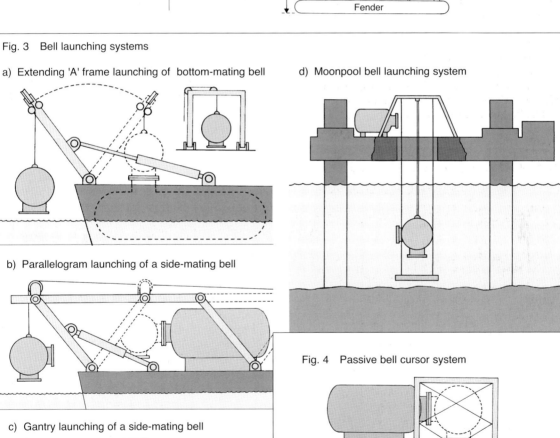

a) Extending 'A' frame launching of bottom-mating bell

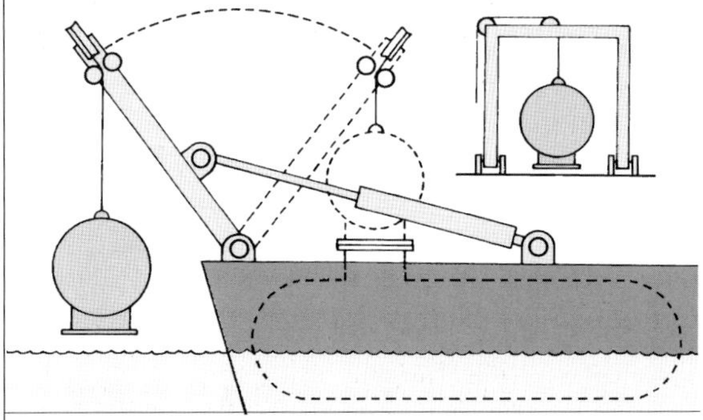

b) Parallelogram launching of a side-mating bell

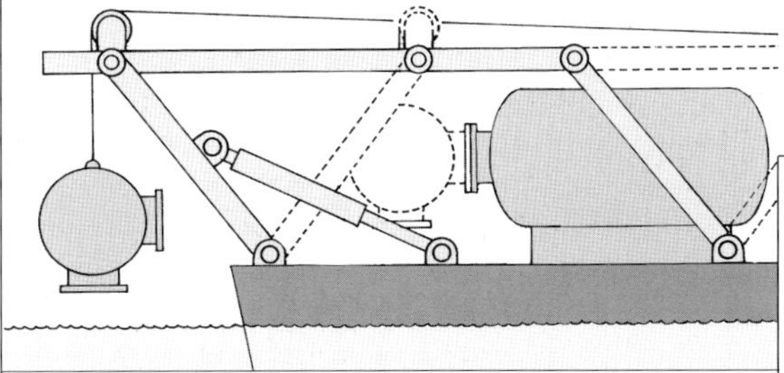

c) Gantry launching of a side-mating bell

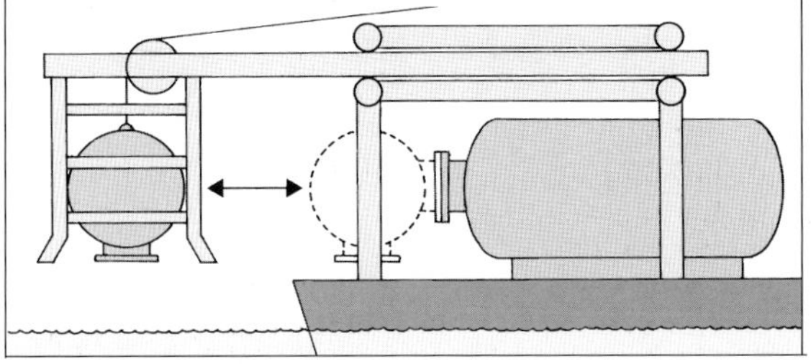

d) Moonpool bell launching system

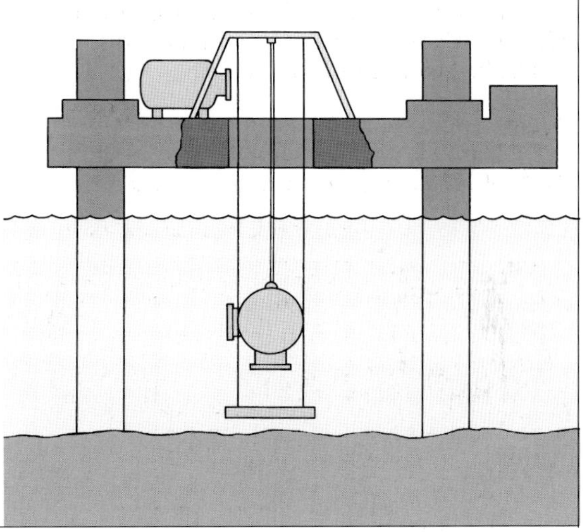

Fig. 4 Passive bell cursor system

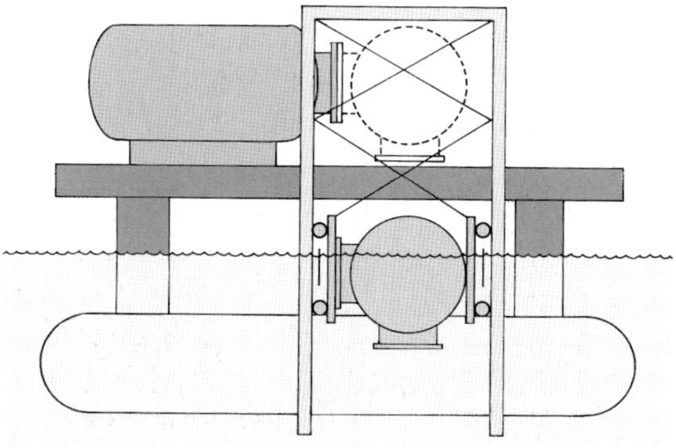

Most moonpools are fitted with an aeration system. When the weather is rough or the vessel is heaving, this can be switched on. A network of large pipes delivers a volume of air to the bottom of the moonpool. The effect is to lower the density of the water, making the bell appear to be heavier and therefore less susceptible to bouncing in the heave.

BELL DIVING OPERATIONS

Bells may be used for routine diving in the following ways:

a) One-atmosphere observation dive.
b) Shallow air lockout dive.
c) Shallow air (nitrox) saturation dive.
d) Deep mixed gas (heliox) bounce dive.
e) Deep mixed gas saturation dive.

The procedure for the main types of diving is summarised and illustrated in Figs. 5a–d.

3. Deck compression chamber complex

The chamber complex may consist of up to five or more interconnecting chambers depending on the size of the task for which it is built. The chambers themselves may be subdivided internally by pressure bulkheads or simple partitions.

The various locks provide sleeping, eating, showering, changing, toilet and storage facilities. One chamber, called the transfer chamber, receives the bell. It is used to store wet clothing, for kitting up and de-kitting, showering and provides toilet facilities.

Smaller 'hand locks' allow the transfer of food and small items in and out of the main chambers. Nothing should be passed into a chamber without first notifying chamber control and checking that it is safe to do so.

4. Chamber control

This is the main base of the chamber operator or saturation technician and is the central point of life support control for all chambers and the bell. Chamber control includes the following functions:

a) Regulation of all chamber compression and decompression procedures.
b) All routine gas analysis for the bell, chambers and gas banks.
c) All voice communications with chamber occupants.
d) Regulation of gas mix in chamber, its temperature and humidity control.
e) Control of handlocks including transfers of meals and materials.
f) Control of all chamber electrics.
g) Control of any entertainment facilities such as radio, tape cassettes/CDs, film, etc.
h) Control of sanitation unit.

5. Life support equipment

The life support equipment tends to be grouped together for convenience. The exception is normally any oxygen handling equipment which should be located well away from areas of possible oil contamination, high temperatures, electrics and poor ventilation.

Figs. 5a–b Some typical diving systems compared

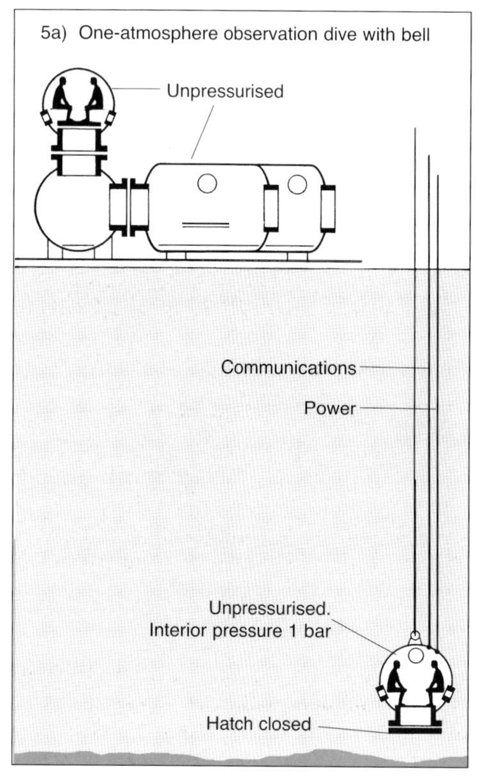
5a) One-atmosphere observation dive with bell
Unpressurised
Communications
Power
Unpressurised.
Interior pressure 1 bar
Hatch closed

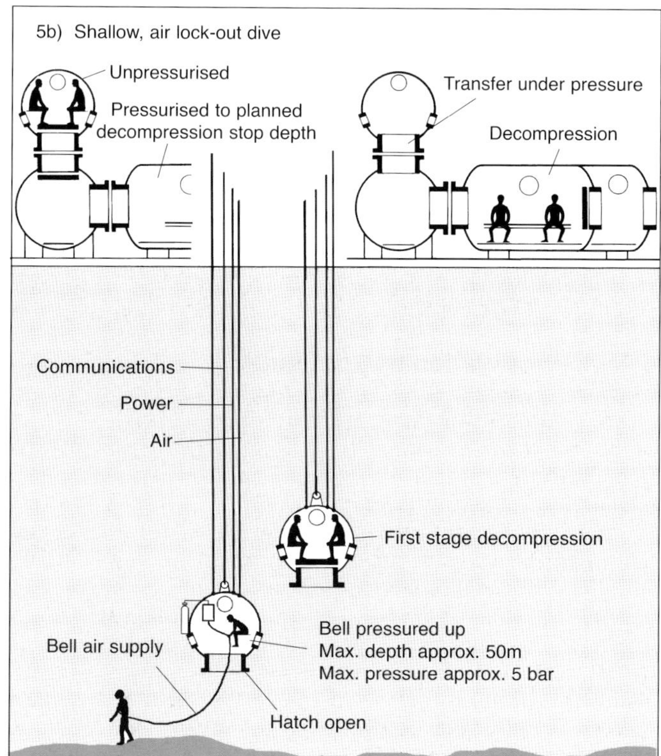
5b) Shallow, air lock-out dive
Unpressurised
Pressurised to planned decompression stop depth
Transfer under pressure
Decompression
Communications
Power
Air
First stage decompression
Bell air supply
Bell pressured up
Max. depth approx. 50m
Max. pressure approx. 5 bar
Hatch open

Fig. 5c) Mixed gas bounce dive

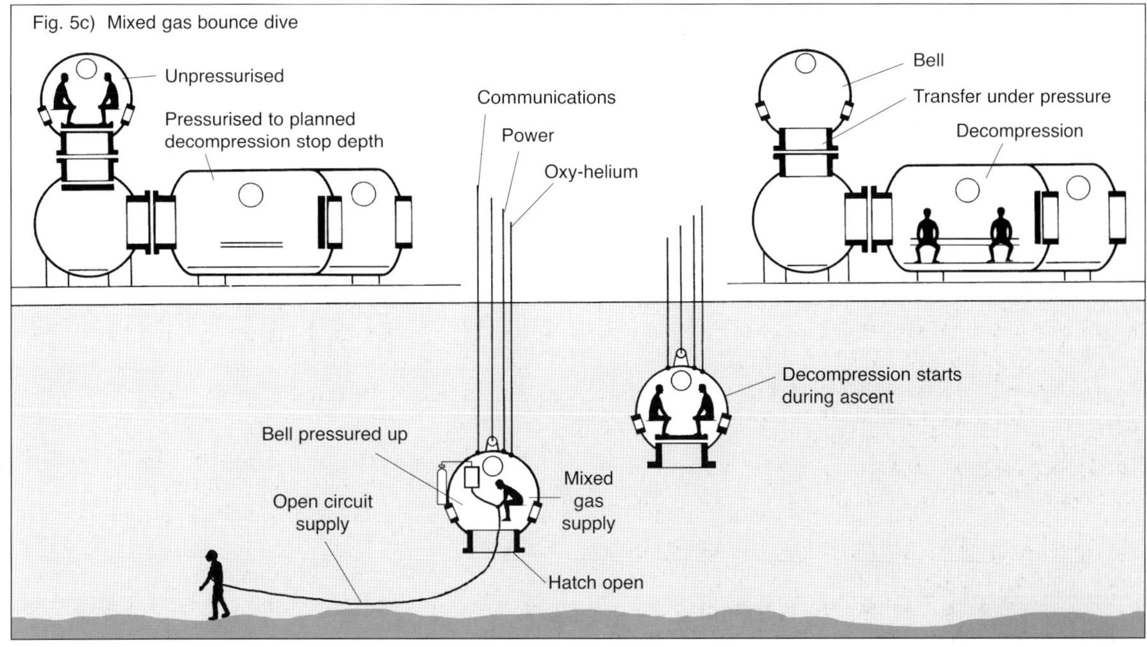
Unpressurised
Pressurised to planned decompression stop depth
Communications
Power
Oxy-helium
Bell
Transfer under pressure
Decompression
Decompression starts during ascent
Bell pressured up
Open circuit supply
Mixed gas supply
Hatch open

Fig. 5d) Deep, mixed gas saturation dive

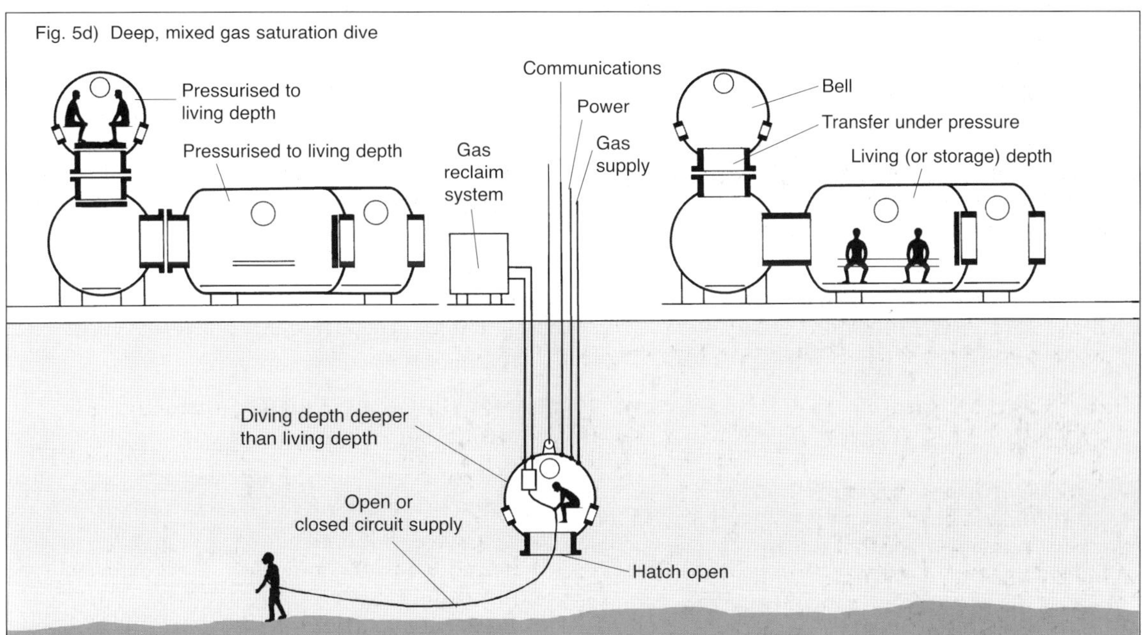
Pressurised to living depth
Pressurised to living depth
Gas reclaim system
Communications
Power
Gas supply
Bell
Transfer under pressure
Living (or storage) depth
Diving depth deeper than living depth
Open or closed circuit supply
Hatch open

Chamber operation and life support

Chamber operators (life support technicians) are responsible for maintaining the internal environment of the compression chambers in a healthy condition. This involves constant maintenance of the correct oxygen level, keeping the carbon dioxide level to a minimum and controlling the temperature and humidity. It also includes management of the compression and decompression phases. This is a very technical and responsible position requiring a high professional standard essential for the maintenance of the health of the divers.

The following information provides general guidelines only and company procedures should always take precedence.

TIME AND DEPTH CONTROL

Time

Accurate timing is always necessary and should be kept to the nearest second if possible, although the nearest minute is adequate. Control clocks, either digital or analogue, should be synchronised to local time by telephone or radio time checks. If a ‘dive time’ or ‘running time’ is used, be sure to record time of day as well.

Depth gauges

Pneumatic analogue or transducer digital depth gauges require frequent calibration checks. For diving beyond 250 msw, the relative density to which a gauge system is calibrated becomes increasingly important. In practice, many have adopted a standard for msw where 10 msw is exactly equivalent to 1 bar. Legislation in several countries lays down standards for the frequency and accuracy of gauge calibration.

CHAMBER GAS MANAGEMENT

Gas Composition

Air Saturation

Chamber gas should be kept as close as possible to the normal composition of atmosphere air unless company procedure dictates a different arrangement. The normal composition of air and the suggested acceptable tolerance ranges are shown in Fig. 6.

Fig. 6. Chamber gas tolerances

Gas	Normal % of air by volume	Suggested acceptable tolerances
Oxygen	20.946%	20–22%
Nitrogen	78.084%	78–80%
Carbon dioxide	0.033%	less than 0.005 bar
Relative humidity	50–60% preferred	50–80%

Oxy-Helium Saturation

Oxygen	0.2–0.6 bar. Tolerance of ±0.01 bar.
Nitrogen	Less than 0.10 bar. Above 0.8 bar should be considered as Trimix.
Carbon dioxide	Less than 0.005 bar
Helium	Remainder
Relative humidity	50–60% preferred. 50–80% tolerated (may be lower tolerance for depths greater than 300 msw)

Oxy-Helium-Nitrogen (Trimix) Saturation

As for 'Oxy-helium saturation' except that the nitrogen content is specified either as a percentage of the volume or a constant partial pressure.

If percentage, then ±0.5% should be achieved.

If partial pressure, ±0.1 bar should be achieved.

Oxygen Control

Very strict control of the oxygen levels must be maintained for several reasons.

1. To provide for the diver's bodily requirements.
2. To avoid hypoxia.
3. To avoid oxygen toxicity.
4. To maintain the effectiveness of the decompression schedule.
5. To minimise fire hazard.

Company procedure will specify the required levels of oxygen to be maintained at the various stages of a dive. For any particular depth, different levels of oxygen may be specified for:

a) The DCC (deck compression chamber) when at living depth or during decompression.
b) BIBS (built-in breathing system) for therapeutic purposes.
c) The diver's breathing supply during DLO (diver lockout).
d) The bail-out gas supply.

Oxygen must be carefully added to the DCC to maintain the correct levels. Special care must be taken to ensure good mixing of the oxygen and that all fire hazard precautions are taken. The chamber oxygen should never exceed 25% by volume. The rate at which oxygen will be required will depend on the number of divers and their levels of physical activity, as shown in Fig. 7.

Fig. 7 Amount of oxygen used up by a diver in relation to the level of work

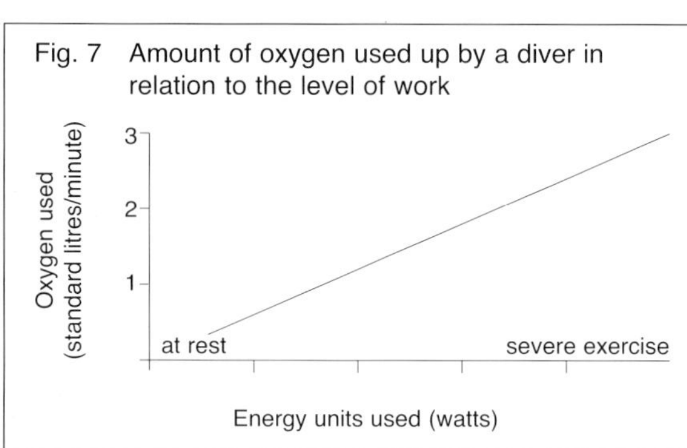
Oxygen used (standard litres/minute)
3
2
1
at rest
severe exercise
Energy units used (watts)

In general, raised partial pressures of oxygen can have advantages including:

a) Faster decompression times.
b) Reduced incidence of bends.
c) Greater tolerance to sudden loss of gas supply.
d) Higher percentages for more accurate monitoring at depths greater than 300m (1,000ft) when the percentage becomes very low.

But upper limits are imposed because:

a) Oxygen poisoning can occur.
b) An increased fire hazard may arise at depths shallower than 50m (165ft).
c) Tolerance to the higher oxygen levels that may be required for therapeutic procedures will be reduced.

Fig. 8 shows how the length of exposure to high oxygen partial pressures must be reduced in the higher range to avoid oxygen poisoning.

Fig. 8 Limits of oxygen in breathing gas

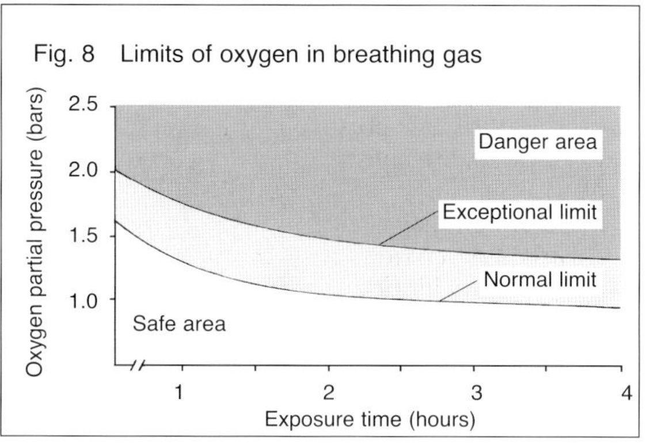
Oxygen partial pressure (bars)
2.5
2.0
1.5
1.0
Danger area
Exceptional limit
Normal limit
Safe area
1
2
3
4
Exposure time (hours)

Carbon Dioxide Control

Carbon dioxide must be kept at very low levels for the comfort and safety of the divers.

The DCC carbon dioxide level should normally be kept below 5mb while a slightly higher level of 10mb may be accepted for shorter periods spent, say, in the diving bell. If the level exceeds 50mb then BIBS or ora-nasal carbon dioxide scrubbers should be used by the divers until the level returns to normal.

Fig. 9 shows how a small increase in the carbon dioxide level can rapidly cause a dangerous situation.

Fig. 9 Limits of carbon dioxide in breathing gas

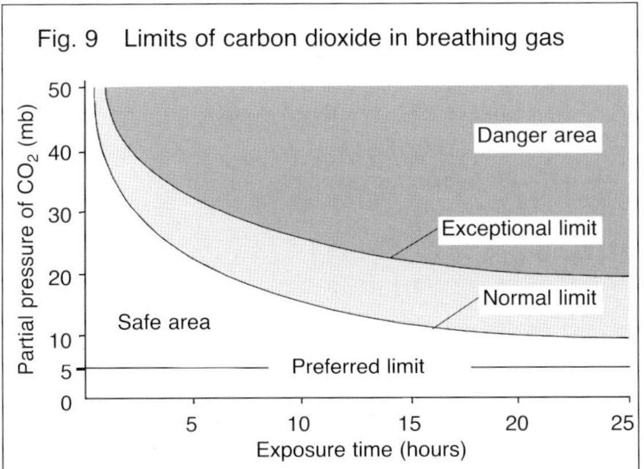
Partial pressure of CO_2 (mb)
50
40
30
20
10
5
0
Danger area
Exceptional limit
Normal limit
Safe area
Preferred limit
5
10
15
20
25
Exposure time (hours)

Gas Contaminants

Most life support gas analysis is concerned with monitoring only oxygen and carbon dioxide. However, other gases can sometimes appear. These can be highly toxic even at very low levels and therefore tests should be made to reduce the risk of such occurrences. These tests can be carried out using chemical colour-indicating tubes or electronic instrumentation.

As a rough guide, the following sources of contaminants and their relative degrees of toxicity should be appreciated.

Sources of Toxic Gases

Overheating or burning of electrical insulation and other materials

Overheating can cause smoke without fire. The chemicals in the smoke and fumes can be highly poisonous. They affect the eyes, lungs and skin. When absorbed into the blood stream they can attack the nervous system and quickly incapacitate the diver. Only very small quantities may be required to incapacitate. Slightly larger amounts can be fatal.

Just a few of the poisonous gases which can be formed are listed below:

Ammonia	NH_3
Carbon dioxide	CO_2
Carbon monoxide	CO
Hydrogen chloride	HCl
Hydrogen cyanide	HCN
Hydrogen fluoride	HF
Nitrogen dioxide	NO_2
Sulphur dioxide	SO_2

Some of the materials in a diving system that can produce these gases include PVC, ABS, polystyrene, polyester, polyurethane, phenol-formaldehyde, wool, silk, acrylics, rubber, nylon, PTFE.

Gases produced from electrical arcing

Apart from ozone and oxides of nitrogen most of these products are not a problem in the short term. But a long term exposure could be a problem.

Task-orientated contaminants

Contaminant gases can appear in a diving system via the diving bell. These can appear if divers return to the bell with contaminated equipment/suits, or if the bell is located over:

- an area of seabed which is degassing.
- a diver using oxy-arc equipment.
- a welding habitat.
- an open pipeline end.

All these sources can and should be avoided with proper diving practice.

Some additional gases which can appear are:

Acetone	CH_3COCH_3
Acetylene	C_2H_2
Benzene	C_6H_6
Ethylalcohol	C_2H_5OH
Hydrogen	H_2
Hydrogen sulphide	H_2S
Methane	CH_4
Oxygen	O_2
Other hydrocarbons	
Various halogens	

Fig. 10 gives the relative toxicity of some example gas contaminants. Note the low concentrations.

Fig. 10. Relative toxicity of selected gas contaminants

Gas	SURFACE EQUIVALENT VALUES		
	Concentration which will produce rapid death (ppm)	Concentration tolerable for a short time (ppm)	Threshold limit value (ppm)
NH_3	*	*	25
CO	4,000–5,000	400–500	50
HCl	1,000–2,000	50–100	5
HCN	100–300	*	10
HF	50–250	*	3
H_2S_2	800–1,000	20	10
NO_2	200–700	*	5
SO_2	400–500	50	5

* No information available

TEMPERATURE CONTROL

Chamber temperature levels are adjusted according to diver comfort requirements. As the depth increases the comfortable temperature range narrows to plus or minus 1°C at around 300m (1,000ft) (see Fig. 11).

Great care is required not only to maintain comfort but also to avoid the danger of both overheating (hyperthermia) and overcooling (hypothermia). Emergency procedures are required to cater for the accidental occurrence of both conditions.

The temperature of inspired breathing gas of a diver in the water also becomes increasingly important as

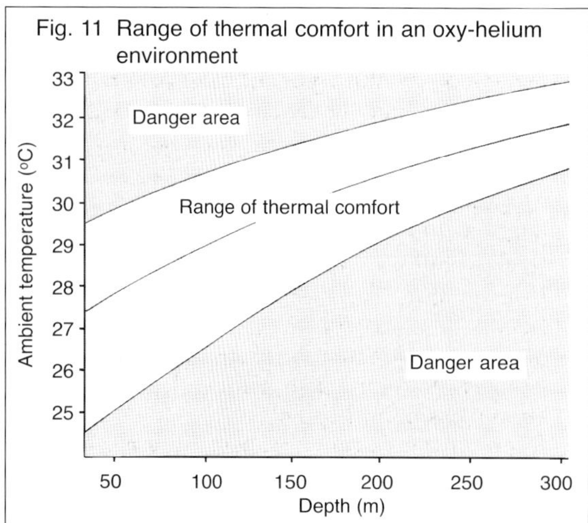
Fig. 11 Range of thermal comfort in an oxy-helium environment
Ambient temperature (°C)
33
32
31
30
29
28
27
26
25
Danger area
Range of thermal comfort
Danger area
50
100
150
200
250
300
Depth (m)

depth increases. UK Regulations require special gas heating to be provided for the diver at 150m (480ft) and deeper. Fig. 12 shows the minimum inspired temperature for oxy-helium, based on US Navy data. Diver suit heating is required by UK Regulations at 50m (165ft) and deeper.

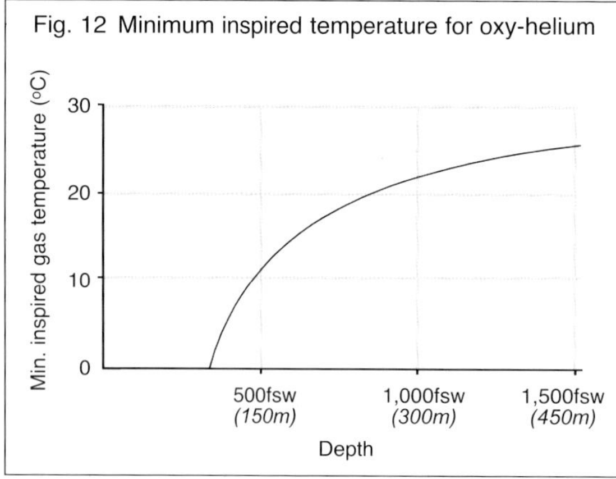
Fig. 12 Minimum inspired temperature for oxy-helium
Min. inspired gas temperature (°C)
30
20
10
0
500fsw
(150m)
1,000fsw
(300m)
1,500fsw
(450m)
Depth

HUMIDITY CONTROL

Chamber gas should be kept between about 50% and 60% relative humidity. Prolonged periods outside this range can cause respiratory problems.

A high atmospheric humidity will reduce a diver's tolerance to ambient temperature changes and increase the risk of infections.

The main problem with controlling humidity is keeping it down. Apart from the use of dehumidifiers, care must be taken by the divers within the DCC to avoid unnecessary increases in humidity. This includes:

a) Keeping wet equipment from the bell separate from the DCC.
b) Draining the bilge and drying the wet pot after showering.
c) Regularly checking the DCC bilges for water and draining as necessary.
d) Draining condensates in main chambers, daily.

USE OF MEDICAL AND EQUIPMENT LOCKS

If equipment is being locked in or out, the following rates may be used:

- Compression rate 20m (65ft)/min
- Decompression rate 40m (130ft)/hr

Medical samples such as blood should be decompressed at rates specified by a medical doctor.

When hot food is being transferred into the chamber, the faster the compression the better. Otherwise, the compression rate of food is not critical. Some rules include:

- Bottle tops should be removed or pierced.
- Cereal and biscuit packets should be unsealed.
- Food should not be stored in the chamber for hygiene reasons.

The chamber operator must keep very strict control of every item that is locked into the chamber. He must examine every item and check:

a) Is it a fire risk?
b) Is there a toxicity risk?
c) Is there a health risk?
d) Is there a risk of explosion on decompression?
e) Will it withstand the pressure (implosion)?
f) Will it withstand the rate of compression (implosion)?

EMERGENCY PROCEDURES

Loss of pressure

Causes:

1. Failure of O-rings or seals.
2. Failure of valve casings, fittings or pipe runs.
3. Cracked or damaged portholes.
4. Incorrect valve operation.

When pressure loss occurs the operator should endeavour to re-establish and maintain depth using the appropriate mix gas on-line because if helium is used in such a circumstance a risk of hypoxia may occur due to reduced PO_2 levels.

It is advisable that a treatment gas (10% or 20% oxygen) should be on-line in saturation control ready for immediate use in the event of a sudden pressure loss. It also allows the controller to have the necessary gas on-line to deal with any case of decompression sickness which may occur.

Slow pressure loss

Frequently caused through worn or damaged seals in handlock mechanisms or worn door or hatch seals. Where the cause of pressure loss is known and unlikely to require drastic action such as an evacuation of the chamber, then the leak should be rectified as soon as convenient.

Rapid pressure loss

Whatever the cause this must be considered as a serious problem as there is a decompression risk when the pressure cannot be maintained. If the fault cannot be rectified immediately then the chamber must be evacuated and surfaced until the fault is repaired and further pressure tests have been carried out to the diving superintendent's satisfaction.

BIBS gas must be on-line for immediate use in the event of the partial pressure of oxygen dropping below the acceptable limits and if it cannot immediately be made up.

Avoidance of loss of pressure
Regular maintenance and visual inspection of valves and door seals will minimise the risk of mechanical or seal failures. Before O-rings are fitted it must be ascertained that they are of the correct size and type for the task they have to perform. When removing O-rings care must be taken to avoid scratching the seating with the tool and causing a leak.
Particular attention must be paid to the operation of handlocks, flush valves and drain valves. Before operation of the valves takes place visual and, where possible, direct voice communication should be made between the tenders outside and the divers inside the chamber. None of these functions should be carried out without first checking with the saturation controller. This is particularly critical when decompression is in progress.

FIRE IN A CHAMBER
Causes:
1. Spontaneous ignition with high ppO_2 content.
2. Spontaneous combustion of hydrocarbon-based materials under pressure.
3. Failure of electrical insulation.
4. Sparks from metal-to-metal impact.

Fires may be of the 'slow burn or smouldering' type or of the spontaneous 'flash fire or explosion' type. Whichever the type or cause, any fire is a serious problem in a chamber.
The slow burn type of fire may occur without the divers being immediately aware of its presence and may produce toxic gases to which the divers may succumb before danger is realised. If the oxygen content is high enough, a slow fire may develop into a sudden flash fire.
A sudden flash fire will usually result in severe burns to personnel, hypoxia and, as already stated, a danger from toxic gases produced from the burning material.
If fire occurs the chamber must be evacuated instantly. The divers may enter an adjacent lock or HRV (hyperbaric rescue vessel) and breathe on BIBS if necessary. Most complexes are now fitted with fire-drenching systems which operate automatically (and occasionally manually) from the control area. All oxygen and electrical supplies to the affected chamber must be turned off.
If the fire is not of great intensity then it may be possible for the divers in the chamber to put on their BIBS masks and extinguish the fire themselves.
The manually-operated fire extinguishers inside the chamber may first be operated by one of the divers in the chamber – usually the last man out – and only if this does not expose him to harm.

FIRE IN SATURATION CONTROL ROOM or OUTSIDE THE CHAMBER
In the event of this type of fire occurring, the following steps may be taken to regain control:
1. Saturation controller and other personnel to don breathing apparatus.
2. Isolate all oxygen and electrical supplies but maintain chamber communication.
3. Inform the diving superintendent and Dive Control of the situation.
4. Inform the divers in the chamber and, if necessary, put divers on the BIBS system.
5. Attempt to extinguish fire with locally-sited appliances until help arrives.
6. Keep chambers cool by hosing down with cold water paying particular attention to oxygen lines and gas lines.
7. Prepare to transfer divers into the HRV or by bell to another diving vessel with a compatible bell system.

CHAMBER HEATING FAILURE
When there is more than one chamber the DCC heating supplies to each chamber are usually cross-connected in case one should fail.
If emergency heaters are fitted within the chamber they should be switched on.
Extra blankets and 'woolly bears' may also be provided.
In a multi-chamber set-up, there could be a possibility of transferring the divers to a functional chamber while repairs are carried out.
If a fault cannot be corrected quickly the divers should be decompressed.

CHAMBER COOLING FAILURE (TROPICS)
If the chamber is exposed to the sun, a tarpaulin should be rigged over the chamber to provide shade. The chamber should be kept hosed down. As much ice as possible should be locked into the chamber. If the fault cannot be repaired quickly, the divers should be decompressed.

Oxygen boosters
Industrial gases are delivered under high pressure. When gas is decanted off the cylinders, the pressure progressively drops off as it is used up. If more high pressure gas is needed from the same bank, boosters will be required to recompress the gas. For example, low pressure gas cannot be transferred into a high pressure quad unless it is boosted higher than the pressure of the receiving gas supply.
In diving terms oxygen boosters are mainly used to mix gases and to transfer gas from a low pressure to a high pressure store.
Since oxygen under pressure can be particularly dangerous, oxygen boosters are specially designed to avoid the risk of explosion. Stringent maintenance procedures must be carried out according to the manufacturer's instructions.
Other precautions include the use of special inert lubricants such as Voltalef, Fomblin and Brayco

greases/fluids. They are not affected by the oxygen and also provide some corrosion protection. Utmost caution is recommended when handling these lubricants at high temperatures since vapours may be given off which can irritate the skin and are toxic if inhaled. Smoking should be prohibited. Cigarettes should not be taken into an area where these lubricants are being handled because they can absorb the toxic vapours.
There are two types of oxygen booster commonly used offshore: diaphragm-type and piston-type.

DIAPHRAGM-TYPE OXYGEN BOOSTERS
The electrically-driven, water-cooled boosters are of the diaphragm type (see Fig. 13). The flexing metal diaphragm separates the piston from the gas being handled and this sealed construction allows for higher pressures and eliminates contamination by lubricants. The most commonly used type incorporates a single stage compressor capable of handling all diving gases including pure oxygen. The booster's capability allows slight overpressure filling to compensate for the pressure drop when the gas cools down after transfer. They are usually available in a wide range of pressure and volume capacities to suit the application and can be single or two-stage boosters.

Fig. 13 Diaphragm compressor head (Corblin's)

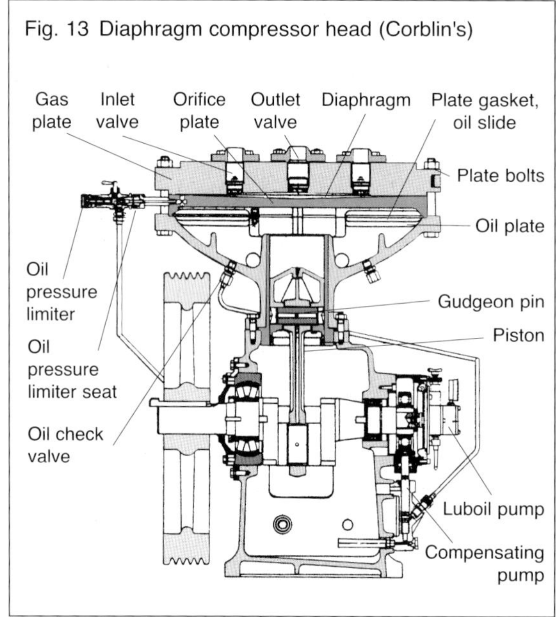
Gas plate
Inlet valve
Orifice plate
Outlet valve
Diaphragm
Plate gasket, oil slide
Plate bolts
Oil plate
Oil pressure limiter
Oil pressure limiter seat
Oil check valve
Gudgeon pin
Piston
Luboil pump
Compensating pump

PISTON-TYPE OXYGEN BOOSTERS
The piston-type boosters are air-driven, air-cooled and piston-operated (see Fig. 14). Two stage boosters with a compression ratio of 15:1 are normally selected to achieve the pressures needed for diving gas handling. These piston-type boosters consist of a large-area, reciprocating, air-driven piston directly coupled by a connecting rod to a small-area gas piston. The air drive section includes a cycling spool and pilot valves which provide continuous reciprocating action when compressed air is supplied to the air drive inlet. Conventional industrial, shipboard or contractor-type compressed air sources are normally used for power. The gas piston operates in a high pressure gas barrel. The end cap of each gas barrel contains the high pressure gas inlet and outlet and their associated check valves. The intervening two chambers are vented to atmosphere. This design prevents air-drive contamination from entering the gas stream.
Cooling is provided by directing the cold exhausted drive air through a jacket surrounding the gas barrel and also through an intercooler on the interstage line. All motive power and controls are pneumatic with no electrical connections. The inlet cylinder pressure and outlet receiver pressure are continually monitored by a pneumatic control package which stops the booster automatically when the desired outlet or minimum inlet pressure is reached, which means that they can be left unattended while in operation.

Fig. 14 Air-driven, piston-type gas booster (Haskel's)

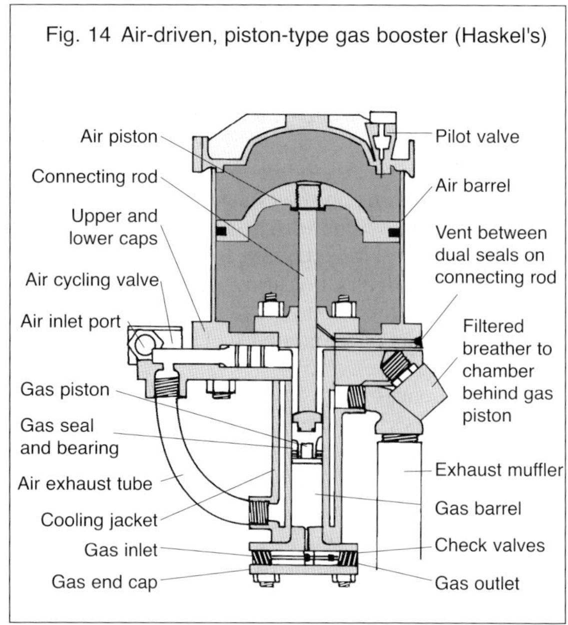
Air piston
Connecting rod
Upper and lower caps
Air cycling valve
Air inlet port
Gas piston
Gas seal and bearing
Air exhaust tube
Cooling jacket
Gas inlet
Gas end cap
Pilot valve
Air barrel
Vent between dual seals on connecting rod
Filtered breather to chamber behind gas piston
Exhaust muffler
Gas barrel
Check valves
Gas outlet

Gas analysis and purity standards

Breathing gas standards have to be rigorously maintained. The presence of very small amounts of certain contaminants can be fatal. Furthermore, as depth increases, so does the partial pressure exposure to contaminants – permissible percentages become very small. In saturation diving, the possible build up of gaseous impurities in the chambers due to contamination or inadequate ventilation becomes a major concern. Consequently the accuracy of breathing gas analysis takes on a very important role.

GAS ANALYSIS
Oxygen and carbon dioxide are the main gas components measured in a diving system. Future diving methods, procedures and techniques may require a wider range of analysis to encompass other possible toxic impurities. Hyperbaric welding is a special

example because of the gases generated by the welding process.

Analysis equipment
There are two broad categories of analysis equipment: single component analysers (which monitor, for example, the levels of oxygen, carbon dioxide or moisture in the environment) and multi-component analysers which can be modified to meet the individual requirements of application, components and concentrations. Infra-red spectro-photometers, which can provide visual display and printed records of component concentrations fall into this latter category.
The constituents of a gas mixture may be varied and therefore may be required to be analysed by different methods. The main commercial diving gas suppliers use a combination of mass spectrometer, infra-red spectrophotometry and gas chromatography to ensure that the gas purity meets the required standards.
A variety of instruments is available. Most of these maintain a constant visible read-out of the various gas concentrations in the chambers. Some systems are fitted with sophisticated electronic instruments which, at the flick of a switch, can show the gas content either as a partial pressure or as a percentage. Many of these can leave the oxygen levels preset so that automatic oxygen injection is carried out by the instrument without manual assistance from the operator.
Most gas monitoring instruments are mounted on or adjacent to the control panel in the saturation system control room. The gas from the chamber is fed to the instruments using the same operating principle as depth gauges. Gas flow to the instruments is regulated according to the manufacturer's recommendations.
All monitors should be calibrated daily against a known calibration gas usually stored or fed into the saturation control room. Methods of calibration are always contained in the instrument handbooks supplied by the makers.
Analytical instruments for hyperbaric monitoring cover a wide range. They depend on the type and concentration of components to be measured. The main factors to be considered when selecting such instruments should be:

a) Compatibility with the environment in which it will be used.
b) Simplicity of operation.
c) Accuracy of measurement.
d) Repeatability of measurement accuracy.
e) Response time to components being measured.
f) Suitability for constant monitoring.
g) Compatibility with electrical supply at the work place.
h) Emergency power requirements.
i) Robustness, reliability and maintenance requirements.

The offshore industry requires a rugged, fast, accurate and stable instrument. By meeting the criteria stated above the instruments can provide the necessary safeguards to the diver.

STANDARDS
Every country has its own purity standards for air and some countries have standards for mixed gas. As an example, a summary of the international standards for breathing air is shown in Fig. 15. Since standards are constantly under review, always check the local/national authority for current requirements.

United Kingdom
Breathing gases should be blended from pure gases and the mixing process should not add any impurities at concentrations likely to cause toxic or other harmful effects when breathed continuously under pressure.

Fig 15. Summary of international standards for breathing air (for selected components). *Maximum* limits.

	UK		Europe	USA	Canada	Australia/NZ
	BS 4275, 1997 general use	BS EN 12021, 1999 diving use	EN 12021, 1999	ANSI/CGA G-7.1 OSHA–Grade E	Z180-1-M85, 1985	AS/NZS 1715, 1994
Oxygen (% by vol)	20-23%	21±1%	21±1%	20-22%	19.5-22%	19.5-22%
Carbon monoxide	5ppm	15 ppm	15 ppm	10 ppm	5 ppm	10 ppm
Carbon dioxide	500ppm	500 ppm	500 ppm	500 ppm	500 ppm	<800 mg/m^3
Oil mist	0.5 mg/m^3	0.5 mg/m^3	0.5 mg/m^3	5 mg/m^3	1 mg/m^3	1 mg/m^3
Solid particulates	10% OEL*	<LTEL**	<LTEL**	not specified	1 mg/m^3	not specified
Pressure dewpoint	5°C below lowest likely temperature.	5°C – 11°C below lowest temperature.	5°C –11°C below lowest temperature.	10°F below lowest anticipated temperature.	5°C below system.	100 mg/m^3
Odours	None odour/taste.	No significant odour/taste.	No significant odour.	No pronounced odour.	None	No pronauseous odour.

*OEL = occupational exposure limit. **LTEL = long term exposure limit.

Air standards (BS EN 12021):

Purity – oxygen	21% ± 1% volume
Maximum permissible contaminants:	
Carbon dioxide (CO_2)	500 ml/m³
Carbon monoxide (CO)	15 ml/m³
Lubricants (droplets or mist)	0.5 mg/m³
Odour	no significant
Water – at compressor outlet	25 mg/m³
– cylinder pressures <40bar	not specified
– cylinder pressures 40–200bar	50 mg/m³
– cylinder pressures >200bar	35 mg/m³

A risk assessment should be carried out to establish if any other contaminants should be tested for in addition to those specified above. In all cases all contaminants should be kept as low as possible (preferably less than 10% of UK occupational exposure limits (OELs) which can be found in the government publication EH40, which is up-dated annually). EH75/2 provides OELs for hyperbaric conditions.

It should be noted that the limits specified above are generally 10% of UK OELs, except for CO which would be 3.5ml/m³ if calculated as 10% OEL. Ideally, a target level below 3.5ml/m³ should be aimed for; a limit of 15 ml/m³ is permissible but consideration must be given to depth (pressure) of use and period of exposure. If pressure and time corrections are made, air with 15ml/m³ CO contamination can be breathed for all depths and durations recommended by the HSE for air diving, without exceeding the OEL for CO. For other dive profiles, specific calculations should be made if CO levels exceed 3.5ml/m³.

To ensure accurate analysis, air quality should be tested at least once every three months and more frequently if air quality cannot be assured.

Mixed gas standards:

UK legislation relating to gas standards includes *The Control of Substances Hazardous to Health* (SI 2002/2677) and the related Approved Code of Practice. Occupational Exposure Limits are defined in EH40 (which is up-dated annually) and, for hyperbaric conditions, see EH75/2.

Oxygen	99.5%
Maximum permissible contaminants:	
Nitrogen (N_2)	0.1%
Argon (Ar)	0.4%
Hydrocarbons	3 ppm
Methane	25 ppm
Carbon dioxide (CO_2)	5 ppm
Carbon monoxide (CO)	1 ppm
Moisture (H_2O)	25 ppm
Nitrogen	99.5%
Maximum permissible contaminants:	
Oxygen (O_2)	50 ppm
Hydrocarbons	1 ppm
Carbon dioxide (CO_2)	1 ppm
Carbon monoxide (CO)	1 ppm
Moisture (H_2O)	25 ppm
Helium (He)	99.97%
Maximum permissible contaminants:	
Oxygen (O_2)	50 ppm
Hydrocarbons	1 ppm
Carbon dioxide (CO_2)	1 ppm
Carbon monoxide (CO)	1 ppm
Moisture (H_2O)	25 ppm

Oil mist should not be present. However, if detected after pumping, the level of contaminant should not exceed 1mg/m³. The percentage of error in the mixture should be restricted to plus or minus 5% of the minor component.

United States of America

There are many standards relating to the purity of compressed gases used for breathing purposes. The most widely accepted are those established by the Compressed Gas Association (CGA). Commodity specifications for breathing gases and be found in CGA documents G–4.3 (oxygen), G–5.3 (helium), G–7.1 (respirable air), G–9.1 (helium) and G10.1 (nitrogen).

Gases are graded according to use. CGA Grade E is specified as suitable for diving on compressed air.

a) Air: Respirable air standards (Grade E):

Oxygen (by volume)	20-22%
Maximum permissible contaminants:	
Carbon dioxide (CO_2)	500 ppm
Carbon monoxide (CO)	10 ppm
Oil/mist/particulates	5 mg/m³
Hydrocarbons as methane	25 ppm
Water vapour, dewpoint	≤ 50°F, or 10°F below expected coldest temperature
Noxious or pronounced odour	none

Air purity tests should be carried out every 6 months by means of samples taken at the connection to the distribution system. Non-oil lubricated compressors need not be tested for oil mist.

The US Navy specifies the following standards for gases used in diver's breathing mixes:

b) Oxygen:	*Type I**	*Type II**
Oxygen (% by volume)	99.5%	99.5%
Maximum permissible contaminants:		
Carbon dioxide (CO_2)	10ppm	5ppm
Hydrocarbons:		
as methane	50 ppm	25 ppm
as ethane and others	6 ppm	3 ppm
Nitrous oxide	4 ppm	2 ppm
Acetylene	0.1 ppm	0.005 ppm
Ethylene	0.4 ppm	0.2 ppm
Refrigerants	2 ppm	1 ppm
Solvents	0.2 ppm	0.1 ppm
Water vapour,	7 ppm	7 ppm
or by dewpoint	≥ –83°F	≥ –83°F
Noxious/pronounced odour	none	none

* Breathing gases are classified as follows: Type I: gaseous, Type II: liquid; Class 1: Oil-free, Class 2: Oil-tolerant

c) Nitrogen (Class I, Type I and Type II)

	A	B	C
	Grades		
Nitrogen (% by volume)	99.5	99.5	99.5
Oxygen (% by volume)	0.05	0.5	0.5
Moisture (water vapour, mg/l)	0.02	0.02	†
Total hydrocarbons (ppm)	50	50	50
Odour	none	none	none

(† not a limiting characteristic)

d) Helium

Helium (% by volume)	99.997%
Maximum permissible contaminants:	
Oxygen	3 ppm
Nitrogen and Argon	5 ppm
Neon	23 ppm
Hydrogen	1 ppm
Hydrocarbons (as methane)	1 ppm
Moisture (water vapour)	7 ppm
Dew point	≤ –78°F

'Safety to Life' calculations

With the growth in 'nitrox' and 'technical diving' divers are increasingly required to undertake 'safety to life' calculations about their diving gases and dive profiles. Such calculations might include:

a) Converting gas percentage to partial pressures (and *vice versa*).
b) Determining maximum safe depth.
c) Calculating Equivalent Air Depth (EAD) for decompression procedures.
d) Determining safe flow rates and gas mixtures for gas rebreathers.

These calculations can be determined by a variety of means:

1. *Mathematical formulae*. Formulae and equations have been traditionally used to make these calculations. However, they can be complex and a small error can have dire consequences for the health and safety of the diver.
2. *'Look up' tables*. These replace the use of mathematics and are generally easy to use. However, they can only present a limited range of variables at specific values. To be accurate, a large number of tables may be required.
3. *Computers*. Many user-friendly, pre-programmed calculators or computers are available which, providing they are used correctly, can provide accurate solutions. However, it is a costly option to equip all divers and trainees with such devices and for some it may be prohibitively expensive.
4. *Nomograms*. Nomograms are two-dimensional diagrams which represent a mathematical equation. They are simple, easy to use (even in harsh marine environments), inexpensive, durable and do not require the user to have a mathematical aptitude.

NOMOGRAMS

Nomograms are two-dimensional diagrams with graduated axes representing the variables in the equation (see Figs. 16–18). The axes can be straight or curved depending on the equation or method of construction.

To perform the calculation a further line (index line) is superimposed onto the nomogram so that it intersects with each of the axes at the required value of the variable. The related values can then be read directly from the nomogram at the points at which the lines intersect.

Example 1

To calculate gas control in gas rebreather systems four variables have to be taken into account:

1. Percentage of inspired oxygen.
2. Percentage of oxygen in gas mixture.
3. Gas mix flow rates.
4. Oxygen consumption by the diver.

The relationship between these four variables can be worked out by using the following formula:

$$\%O_2insp = \left(\frac{(\%O_2mix \times 0.01 \times flow) - VO_2}{(flow - VO_2)}\right) \times 100$$

where $\%O_2insp$ = percentage O_2 in breathing circuit
$\%O_2mix$ = percentage oxygen in gas mix
flow = gas mix flow rate, in litres/min
VO_2 = O_2 consumed by diver, in litres/min

To a non-mathematician using this formula may be a daunting challenge. A small mistake could lead to the wrong gas mix being used resulting in the diver losing consciousness underwater from hypoxia (insufficient oxygen) or hyperoxia (excess oxygen) with a potentially fatal outcome.

Fig. 16 shows how this equation can be represented as a nomogram and how it can be used in calculation. In this case the variables are represented by straight lines. Note that the percentage of oxygen in the gas mix is given on a set of three lines, each representing a different value of oxygen consumption.

Using this nomogram the percentage of oxygen in the breathing circuit, for example, can be found by drawing a line between the known values of the other variables. If, for example, the gas mix contains 40% oxygen and the flow rate is 15 litres per minute and the diver's oxygen consumption is 2 litres per minute it is possible to draw a line (index line) connecting these three values. If it is extended it will intersect with the scale representing percentage of oxygen in the breathing circuit. The point at which it intersects will provide the value of percentage of oxygen in the breathing circuit. In this case 31% (see Fig. 16).

Similarly, nomograms can be designed to facilitate calculations relating to EAD (equivalent air depth) for dive decompression requirements (see Fig. 17) and for calculating safe limits of partial pressure of oxygen (see Fig. 18).

In some cases acceptable ranges cannot be fitted onto a single printed sheet. Curving the scales, however, can solve this problem and at the same time present clear, accurate, easy to use scales for all variables. Such nomograms are called 'circular.' Figs. 17 and 18 are examples.

Example 2
To calculate equivalent air depth (EAD) for decompression procedure when using nitrox mix.

For a diver at a given depth, breathing a given nitrox mixture, his equivalent air depth will be that depth at which the diver would have to be whilst breathing air, in order to experience the same nitrogen partial pressure. This is his equivalent air depth (EAD). Knowing the EAD enables the

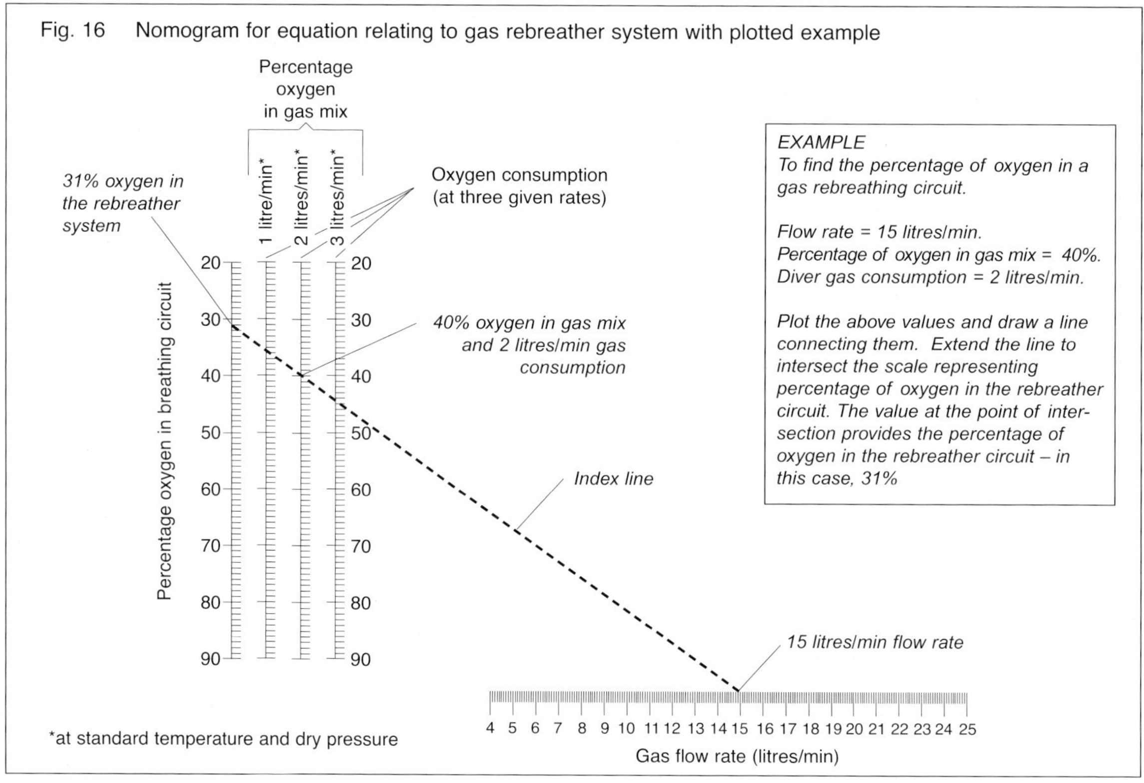
Percentage oxygen in gas mix
1 litre/min*
2 litres/min*
3 litres/min*
31% oxygen in the rebreather system
Oxygen consumption (at three given rates)
Percentage oxygen in breathing circuit
20
30
40
50
60
70
80
90
40% oxygen in gas mix and 2 litres/min gas consumption
Index line
15 litres/min flow rate
4 5 6 7 8 9 10 11 12 13 14 15 16 17 18 19 20 21 22 23 24 25
Gas flow rate (litres/min)
*at standard temperature and dry pressure
EXAMPLE
To find the percentage of oxygen in a gas rebreathing circuit.
Flow rate = 15 litres/min.
Percentage of oxygen in gas mix = 40%.
Diver gas consumption = 2 litres/min.
Plot the above values and draw a line connecting them. Extend the line to intersect the scale representing percentage of oxygen in the rebreather circuit. The value at the point of intersection provides the percentage of oxygen in the rebreather circuit – in this case, 31%
Fig. 16 Nomogram for equation relating to gas rebreather system with plotted example

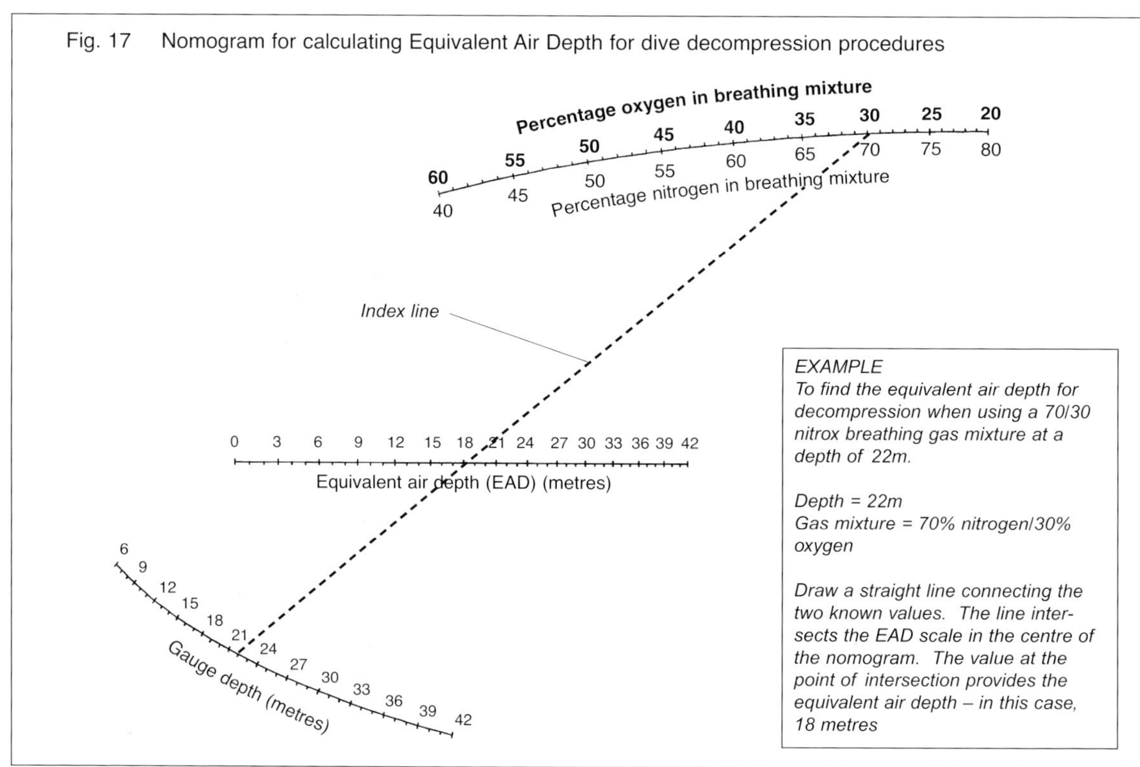
Percentage oxygen in breathing mixture
60 55 50 45 40 35 30 25 20
40 45 50 55 60 65 70 75 80
Percentage nitrogen in breathing mixture
Index line
0 3 6 9 12 15 18 21 24 27 30 33 36 39 42
Equivalent air depth (EAD) (metres)
6 9 12 15 18 21 24 27 30 33 36 39 42
Gauge depth (metres)
EXAMPLE
To find the equivalent air depth for decompression when using a 70/30 nitrox breathing gas mixture at a depth of 22m.
Depth = 22m
Gas mixture = 70% nitrogen/30% oxygen
Draw a straight line connecting the two known values. The line intersects the EAD scale in the centre of the nomogram. The value at the point of intersection provides the equivalent air depth – in this case, 18 metres
Fig. 17 Nomogram for calculating Equivalent Air Depth for dive decompression procedures

decompression procedure to take place using air decompression tables.
The nomogram in Fig. 17 has been designed to enable the calculation of EADs and shows a plotted example.

Example 3
To determine the relationships between inspired partial pressure of oxygen, percentage of oxygen in breathing mixture and dive depth.
Dalton's Law of Partial Pressures can be used to determine these relationships. The Law states that 'in a mixture of gases, the pressure exerted by one of the gases is the same as it would exert if it alone occupied the same volume.' In diving this can be complicated because the total pressure of a gas mixture increases with depth.
The nomogram illustrated in Fig. 18 illustrates Dalton's Law and relates it to the limits of partial pressure of oxygen. From this, several useful calculations can easily be made, such as:

a) Finding the partial pressure of oxygen for a dive using a given breathing mixture at a given depth.
b) Finding how much oxygen is in the breathing mixture at a given partial pressure of oxygen at a given depth (see examples plotted in Fig. 18).

The above three examples relate to the three selected nomograms given as examples in this section. Several other diving-related nomograms have been constructed which can be used, for example, for determining safe diving depths of gas mixtures, safe gas flow for semi-closed circuit gas rebreathers, identification of appropriate nitrox decompression schedules and unit pulmonary toxicity dose (UPTD). All employ the same principles and ease of use.

ADVANTAGES AND LIMITATIONS OF USING NOMOGRAMS

1. Advantages

a) User does not need formal mathematical skills.
b) Can be used in stressful environments where it may be difficult to carry out complex calculations.
c) Requires no specialist equipment to use.
d) Can be used in situations where electronic aids cannot be used.
e) Cheap and easy to produce.
f) Easily reproduced for diver training. (Note: some photocopiers distort images. Make 'check' calculations to assess the validity of copies).
g) Infallible calculation system providing the index line is drawn accurately.
h) Quick calculation procedure enables user to easily check and double check accuracy.
i) Safety limits can be easily marked on the nomogram. Discontinuing scales beyond margins of safety provides instant alerts and prevents nomograms being used to make potentially dangerous calculations (see Fig. 18).

2. Disadvantages

a) Poor resolution of the scaled lines can provide less accurate results. Line scales and intercepts must be of high enough resolution to allow acceptable accuracy for the calculation being made.
b) Limiting the range of values (for safety reasons) can reduce the flexibility of the nomogram.

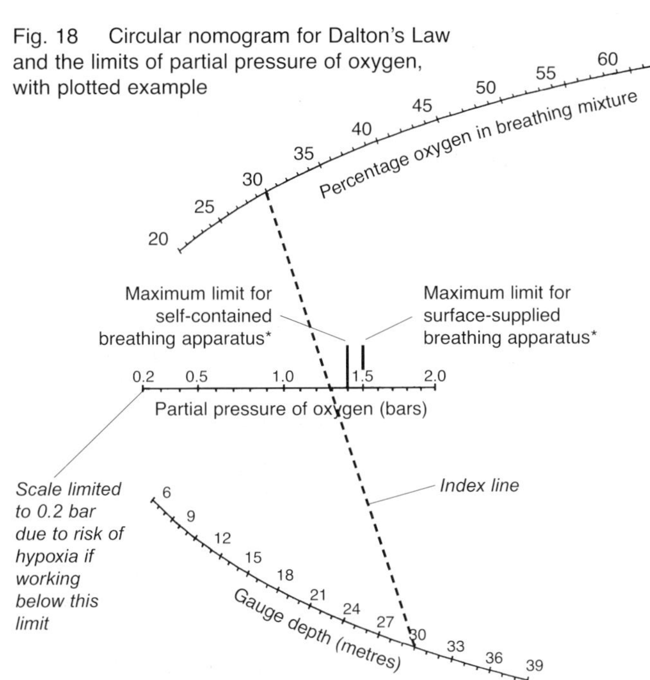
20
25
30
35
40
45
50
55
60
65
70
75
80
Percentage oxygen in breathing mixture
Maximum limit for self-contained breathing apparatus*
Maximum limit for surface-supplied breathing apparatus*
0.2
0.5
1.0
1.5
2.0
Partial pressure of oxygen (bars)
Scale limited to 0.2 bar due to risk of hypoxia if working below this limit
Index line
6
9
12
15
18
21
24
27
30
33
36
39
Gauge depth (metres)

Fig. 18 Circular nomogram for Dalton's Law and the limits of partial pressure of oxygen, with plotted example

EXAMPLES

1 *To find PO_2 at 30m using a 30% oxygen breathing gas mix.*
Depth = 30m
Percentage of oxygen in gas mix = 30%.
Plot the above values and draw a line connecting them. The line intersects the PO_2 scale in the centre of the nomogram. Note the value at the point of intersection – in this case, 1.3 bars.

2. *To find the percentage of oxygen in the breathing mixture when working at 30m with a PO_2 of 1.3 bars.*
Depth = 30m
PO_2 = 1.3 bars
Draw a line to connect the two known values and extend the line to intersect the line scale representing percentage of oxygen in the breathing mixture. Note the value and the point of intersection – in this case, 30%.

**UK Health and Safety Executive (HSE) partial pressure of oxygen limits*

5.2 DIVING HELMETS AND MASKS

Band masks differ from helmets in that the former make a water-tight seal around the face only, whereas helmets keep the diver's head completely dry as the gas seal is made by a neck seal.
In most band masks and helmets there are two alternative systems for breathing: a steady flow of gas, or by a demand regulator. Most divers breathe through the demand regulator and maintain a slight steady flow to keep the face plate clear.
The emergency gas supply is an independent system. Helmets fitted with umbilicals which provide a continuous supply of air divide into two groups: heavyweight or lightweight. The distinction between the two is that the lightweight helmets are usually not integral with the diving dress. Examples of heavyweight helmets are the Siebe Gorman 12-bolt and the Divex M2000 helmets. The Superlite series of helmets is typical of the lightweight helmets.
The choice between wearing a helmet or a mask usually depends on several factors. These include

- The type of diving dress worn.
- The depth, how much swimming is involved.
- What type of work the diver is required to do.
- Whether or not the water is polluted.
- Whether or not the diver's head needs to be kept dry.

The relative merits of each type of headgear are compared in Fig. 1.
The depth of the diving operation can also influence the choice of equipment. Masks are commonly worn in shallow water diving because they are relatively light and easy to put on. However, should the diver become unconscious and fall in such a way as to dislodge his mask the face seal may be broken, flooding the mask. This would not occur when wearing a helmet which would retain an intact seal under any circumstances.
The nature of the dive task will also dictate which type of equipment to use. Should the job entail a lot of swimming, as in pipeline inspection, a mask is preferable since it is easier to swim in than a helmet. Although it is difficult to look upwards when wearing a helmet, the diver should wear a helmet when working inside structures because of the protection it provides. However, many masks can be fitted with a head protector.
Communications are considerably better in a helmet as opposed to a mask. A helmet is to be preferred in polluted water as the ears and skin are not exposed to the water.
In many helmets an air deflector prevents the faceplate from misting up. Where this is not available, a light smear of some liquid soap, such as Prell, on the inside of the faceplate makes an effective demisting agent.
On balance, a helmet is safer than a mask in most diving operations.

Fig. 1. Helmets and bandmasks compared

Helmets
1. Keeps the head dry and decreases the risk of ear infections, especially in saturation diving.
2. Reduces risk of infection when diving in polluted waters.
3. Provides integral physical protection to the head.
4. Can provide better voice communications than masks.
5. Better suited to gas recovery systems.
6. Can provide a stable platform for head-mounted TV camera/light.
7. Some divers find helmets more comfortable to wear for long dives, especially in saturation.

Band masks
1. Smaller than helmets and lighter to wear.
2. Allows for greater mobility of the head than if wearing a helmet.
3. Easier to swim in than a helmet.
4. Some types can be quicker to put on than helmets.
5. Requires less assistance to put on.
6. Allows the use of the hot water hood to keep the head warm.
7. Usually cheaper.

Maintenance
Regular maintenance of all diving equipment is essential for the safety and comfort of the diver. Hygiene is also important if the equipment is being used by different divers. The following points should be taken into consideration when forming a maintenance plan.

1. The routine maintenance of both masks and helmets consists mostly of washing in clean, fresh water after use – perhaps with a mild disinfectant. If using disinfectant, always dilute it with fresh water – never use it neat.
2. Avoid letting water enter orifices such as the emergency gas inlet.
3. When wearing a helmet, the neck dam should be inspected for tears or holes. The head cushion or lining should be secure and any chin strap adjusted to suit the individual diver.
4. The diver should always be fastidious about checking the communication system and all moving parts such as the main gas supply handle, the nose-clearing device and the regulator adjustment knob. Most important of all to check is the non-return valve on the air intake.
5. A monthly routine should include:
   a) Detailed inspection of the regulator.
   b) Lubrication of all 'O' rings and rubber components with silicon grease.
   c) Check that the non-return valve is working properly.

The following pages show the main components of, and describe the controls of some of the more widely used helmets and masks. It should be noted that these are constantly being modified and some parts are interchangeable.

a) KIRBY MORGAN SUPERLITE 17A/B

This positively buoyant helmet weighs 24 lb (10.9 kg) and weights of 1–3lb (approx. 0.5–1.4kg) can be added according to diver preference. It consists of two parts: the neck dam yoke and the helmet. The diver puts on the neck dam with the attached yoke hingeing into place. The neck clamp is then slipped up onto the helmet and locked. A special neck dam is available for cold water and hot water suits. Most of the breathing equipment parts on the front of the Superlite are interchangeable with the KM 18 masks. The only difference between the 17A and 17B models is that in the 17A the umbilical passes down in front of the diver, whereas in the 17B it passes backwards over the diver's shoulder.

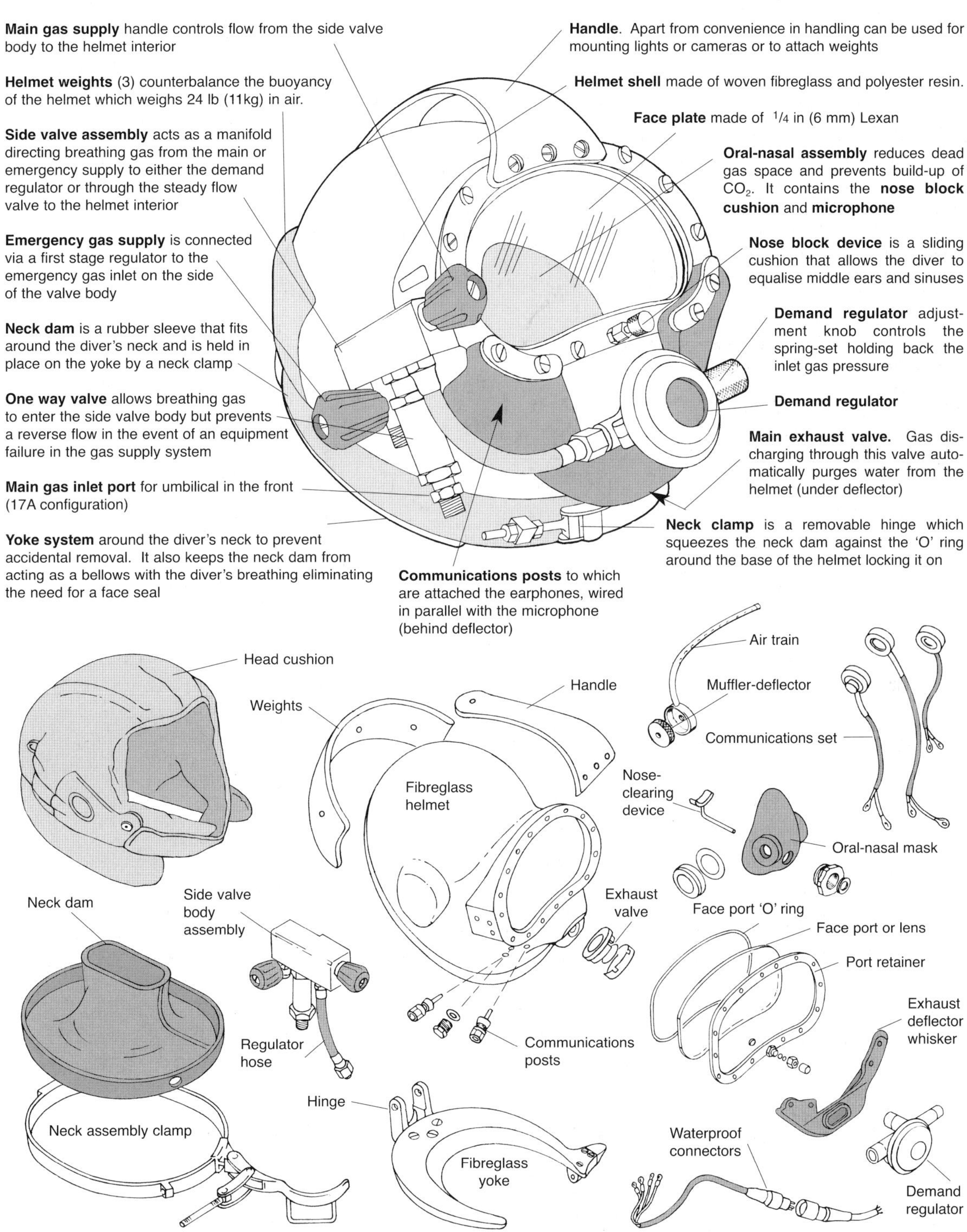

Main gas supply handle controls flow from the side valve body to the helmet interior
Helmet weights (3) counterbalance the buoyancy of the helmet which weighs 24 lb (11kg) in air.
Side valve assembly acts as a manifold directing breathing gas from the main or emergency supply to either the demand regulator or through the steady flow valve to the helmet interior
Emergency gas supply is connected via a first stage regulator to the emergency gas inlet on the side of the valve body
Neck dam is a rubber sleeve that fits around the diver's neck and is held in place on the yoke by a neck clamp
One way valve allows breathing gas to enter the side valve body but prevents a reverse flow in the event of an equipment failure in the gas supply system
Main gas inlet port for umbilical in the front (17A configuration)
Yoke system around the diver's neck to prevent accidental removal. It also keeps the neck dam from acting as a bellows with the diver's breathing eliminating the need for a face seal
Handle. Apart from convenience in handling can be used for mounting lights or cameras or to attach weights
Helmet shell made of woven fibreglass and polyester resin.
Face plate made of 1/4 in (6 mm) Lexan
Oral-nasal assembly reduces dead gas space and prevents build-up of CO_2. It contains the **nose block cushion** and **microphone**
Nose block device is a sliding cushion that allows the diver to equalise middle ears and sinuses
Demand regulator adjustment knob controls the spring-set holding back the inlet gas pressure
Demand regulator
Main exhaust valve. Gas discharging through this valve automatically purges water from the helmet (under deflector)
Neck clamp is a removable hinge which squeezes the neck dam against the 'O' ring around the base of the helmet locking it on
Communications posts to which are attached the earphones, wired in parallel with the microphone (behind deflector)
Head cushion
Weights
Handle
Fibreglass helmet
Air train
Muffler-deflector
Communications set
Nose-clearing device
Oral-nasal mask
Neck dam
Side valve body assembly
Exhaust valve
Face port 'O' ring
Face port or lens
Port retainer
Exhaust deflector whisker
Regulator hose
Communications posts
Hinge
Neck assembly clamp
Fibreglass yoke
Waterproof connectors
Demand regulator

5.2 DIVING HELMETS AND MASKS

b) KIRBY MORGAN SUPERLITE 17C

Based on the helmet shell design of the SuperLite 17A/B, the SuperLite 17C incorporates the helmet neck ring design of the SuperLite 27 and 17K for improved ease of use.
Other modifications include the redesign of the side block to allow the umbilical to pass over the diver's shoulder in the 'B' configuration and the addition of two mounting brackets on either side of the handle. For improved comfort and security of fit the head/chin cushions and helmet weights have also be redesigned and the adjustable neck pad on the locking collar enables the diver to 'custom tailor' the fit to his own requirements.

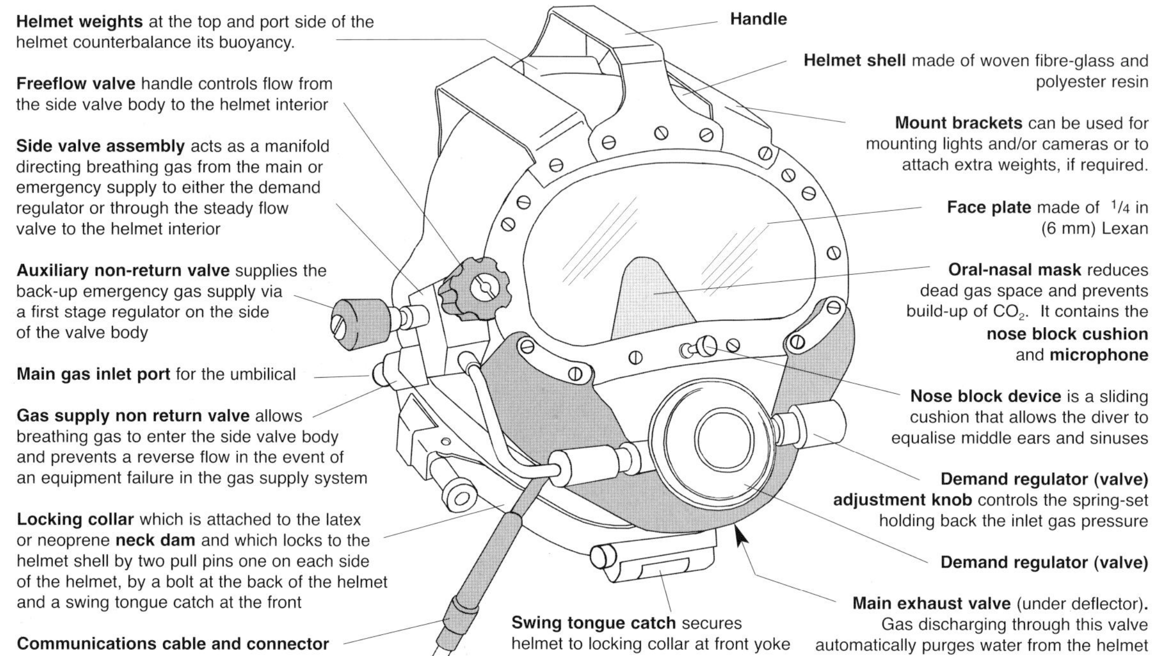
Helmet weights at the top and port side of the helmet counterbalance its buoyancy.
Freeflow valve handle controls flow from the side valve body to the helmet interior
Side valve assembly acts as a manifold directing breathing gas from the main or emergency supply to either the demand regulator or through the steady flow valve to the helmet interior
Auxiliary non-return valve supplies the back-up emergency gas supply via a first stage regulator on the side of the valve body
Main gas inlet port for the umbilical
Gas supply non return valve allows breathing gas to enter the side valve body and prevents a reverse flow in the event of an equipment failure in the gas supply system
Locking collar which is attached to the latex or neoprene **neck dam** and which locks to the helmet shell by two pull pins one on each side of the helmet, by a bolt at the back of the helmet and a swing tongue catch at the front
Communications cable and connector
Swing tongue catch secures helmet to locking collar at front yoke
Handle
Helmet shell made of woven fibre-glass and polyester resin
Mount brackets can be used for mounting lights and/or cameras or to attach extra weights, if required.
Face plate made of 1/4 in (6 mm) Lexan
Oral-nasal mask reduces dead gas space and prevents build-up of CO_2. It contains the **nose block cushion** and **microphone**
Nose block device is a sliding cushion that allows the diver to equalise middle ears and sinuses
Demand regulator (valve) adjustment knob controls the spring-set holding back the inlet gas pressure
Demand regulator (valve)
Main exhaust valve (under deflector). Gas discharging through this valve automatically purges water from the helmet

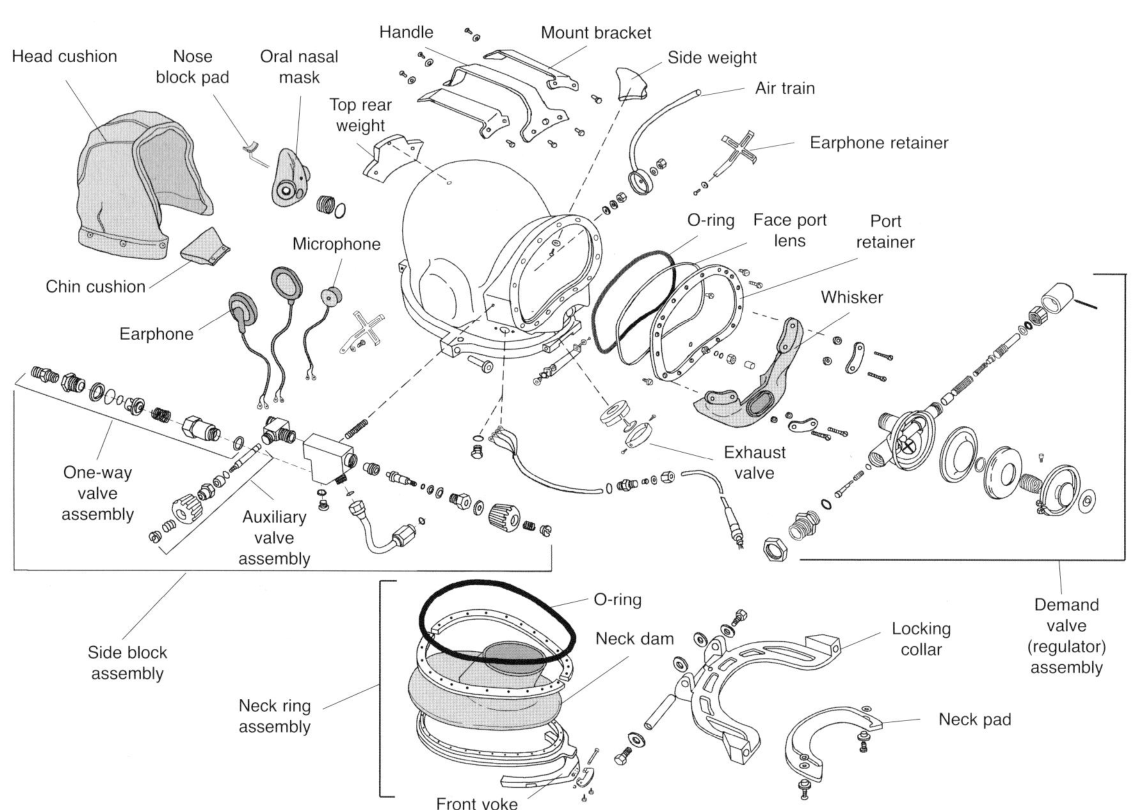
Handle
Mount bracket
Head cushion
Nose block pad
Oral nasal mask
Top rear weight
Side weight
Air train
Earphone retainer
Microphone
Chin cushion
Earphone
O-ring
Face port lens
Port retainer
Whisker
One-way valve assembly
Auxiliary valve assembly
Exhaust valve
Side block assembly
O-ring
Neck dam
Locking collar
Demand valve (regulator) assembly
Neck ring assembly
Neck pad
Front yoke

c) KIRBY MORGAN SUPERLITE 17K, 27 and 37

The Superlite 17K incorporates the locking and communications systems of the SuperLite 27 onto a larger fibreglass shell of the 17A/B model. A large tube, adjustable demand regulator/valve provides easy breathing gas flow during peak work periods.
The SuperLite 27 has been designed to conform to European standards and differs from the 17K only in the design of the exhaust/water dump valve and the top weight (see exploded drawing below).
The 37 model has a tri-valve exhaust system which has less breathing resistance than earlier models and helps to prevent back-flow, making it suitable for diving in contaminated environments.

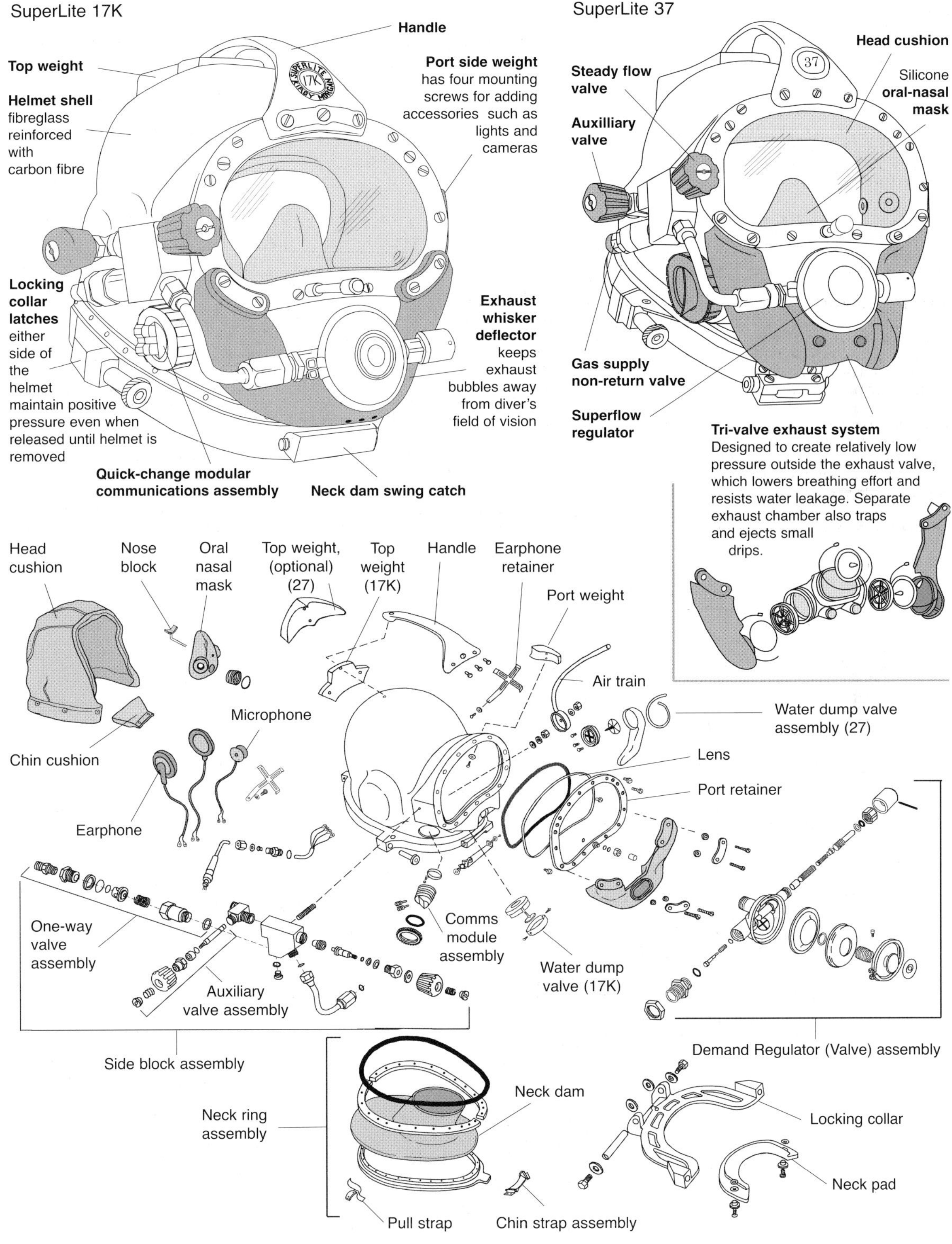
SuperLite 17K
Handle
Top weight
Port side weight has four mounting screws for adding accessories such as lights and cameras
Helmet shell fibreglass reinforced with carbon fibre
Locking collar latches either side of the helmet maintain positive pressure even when released until helmet is removed
Exhaust whisker deflector keeps exhaust bubbles away from diver's field of vision
Quick-change modular communications assembly
Neck dam swing catch
SuperLite 37
Head cushion
Steady flow valve
Silicone oral-nasal mask
Auxilliary valve
Gas supply non-return valve
Superflow regulator
Tri-valve exhaust system
Designed to create relatively low pressure outside the exhaust valve, which lowers breathing effort and resists water leakage. Separate exhaust chamber also traps and ejects small drips.
Head cushion
Nose block
Oral nasal mask
Top weight, (optional) (27)
Top weight (17K)
Handle
Earphone retainer
Port weight
Air train
Water dump valve assembly (27)
Microphone
Chin cushion
Lens
Port retainer
Earphone
One-way valve assembly
Comms module assembly
Water dump valve (17K)
Auxiliary valve assembly
Side block assembly
Demand Regulator (Valve) assembly
Neck dam
Neck ring assembly
Locking collar
Neck pad
Pull strap
Chin strap assembly

d) KIRBY MORGAN SUPERLITE 47

The Superlite 47 has a breathing system, oral-nasal mask and water ejection system which provides the diver with a very dry helmet with excellent work-of-breathing performance. It is ideal for diving in contaminated environments.

The helmet consists of two major assemblies: the upper helmet shell/helmet ring assembly, and the lower neck dam/neck-ring assembly. The upper helmet ring houses the latch catches and provides protection for the bottom part of the helmet. It also contains the chin support and neck pad, both of which can be adjusted to ensure a secure, custom fit. The helmet is configured to receive the umbilical over the shoulder in the 'B' configuration.

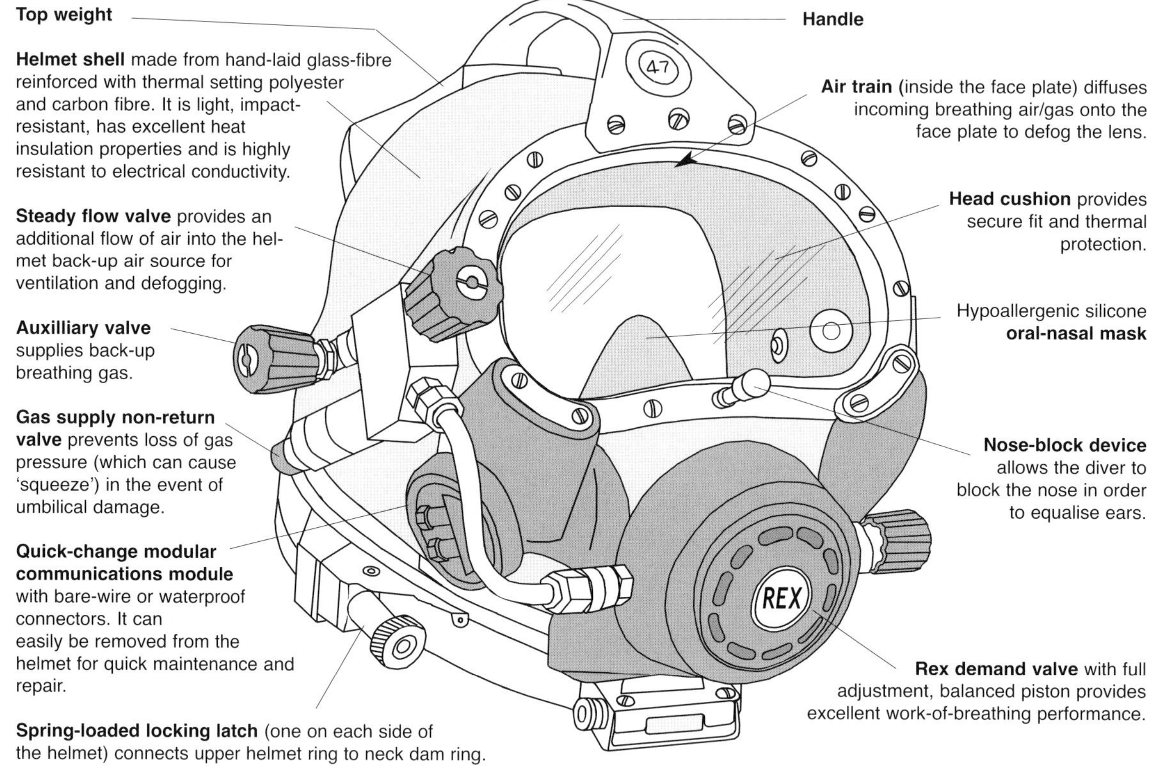
Top weight
Helmet shell made from hand-laid glass-fibre reinforced with thermal setting polyester and carbon fibre. It is light, impact-resistant, has excellent heat insulation properties and is highly resistant to electrical conductivity.
Steady flow valve provides an additional flow of air into the helmet back-up air source for ventilation and defogging.
Auxilliary valve supplies back-up breathing gas.
Gas supply non-return valve prevents loss of gas pressure (which can cause 'squeeze') in the event of umbilical damage.
Quick-change modular communications module with bare-wire or waterproof connectors. It can easily be removed from the helmet for quick maintenance and repair.
Spring-loaded locking latch (one on each side of the helmet) connects upper helmet ring to neck dam ring.
Handle
47
Air train (inside the face plate) diffuses incoming breathing air/gas onto the face plate to defog the lens.
Head cushion provides secure fit and thermal protection.
Hypoallergenic silicone **oral-nasal mask**
Nose-block device allows the diver to block the nose in order to equalise ears.
REX
Rex demand valve with full adjustment, balanced piston provides excellent work-of-breathing performance.

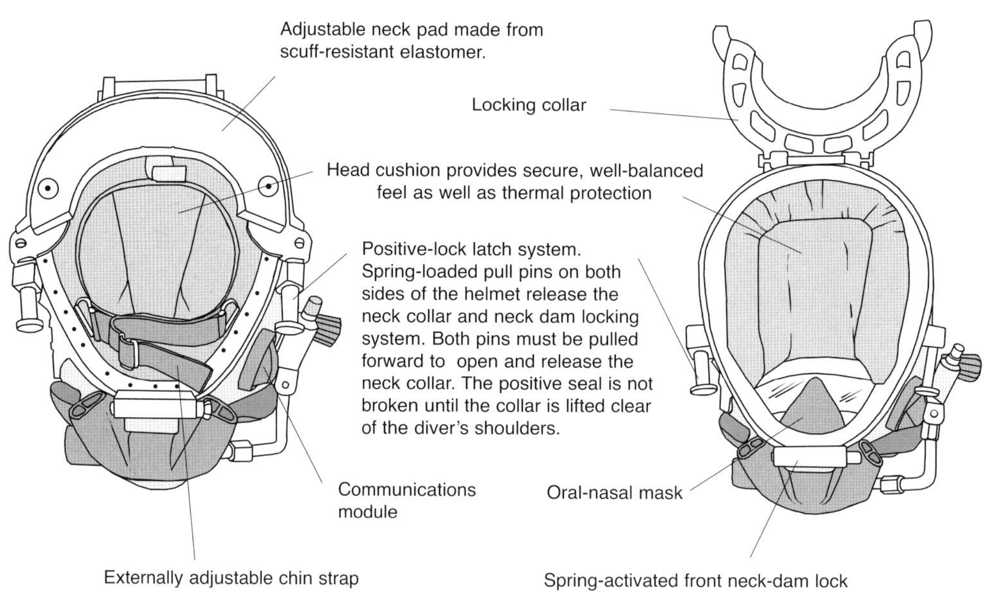
Adjustable neck pad made from scuff-resistant elastomer.
Locking collar
Head cushion provides secure, well-balanced feel as well as thermal protection
Positive-lock latch system. Spring-loaded pull pins on both sides of the helmet release the neck collar and neck dam locking system. Both pins must be pulled forward to open and release the neck collar. The positive seal is not broken until the collar is lifted clear of the diver's shoulders.
Communications module
Oral-nasal mask
Externally adjustable chin strap
Spring-activated front neck-dam lock

e) KIRBY MORGAN BANDMASKS (KMB) 18 AND 28

For use in mixed gas and shallow water diving. The standard configuration of the side block receives the umbilical over the shoulder (in the 18A model the umbilical passes in front of the diver).

The main difference between the 18 and 28 models concerns the mask frame (fibreglass in the 18 model and injection-moulded plastic in the 28). They each use slightly different regulators (demand valves), there is a small difference in face port size and in the design of the exhaust body.

The 18 has a 'comfort insert' on the interior of the face seal/cushion to make the face seal more comfortable; this is not required in the 28.

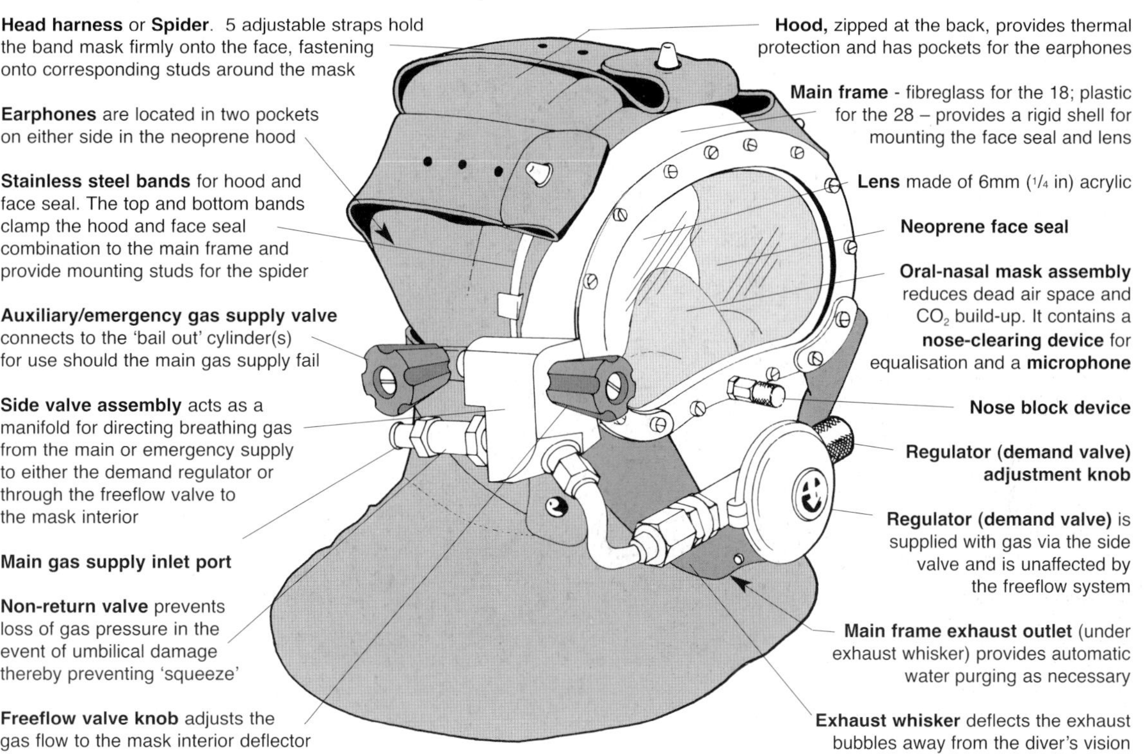
Head harness or **Spider**. 5 adjustable straps hold the band mask firmly onto the face, fastening onto corresponding studs around the mask
Earphones are located in two pockets on either side in the neoprene hood
Stainless steel bands for hood and face seal. The top and bottom bands clamp the hood and face seal combination to the main frame and provide mounting studs for the spider
Auxiliary/emergency gas supply valve connects to the 'bail out' cylinder(s) for use should the main gas supply fail
Side valve assembly acts as a manifold for directing breathing gas from the main or emergency supply to either the demand regulator or through the freeflow valve to the mask interior
Main gas supply inlet port
Non-return valve prevents loss of gas pressure in the event of umbilical damage thereby preventing 'squeeze'
Freeflow valve knob adjusts the gas flow to the mask interior deflector
Hood, zipped at the back, provides thermal protection and has pockets for the earphones
Main frame - fibreglass for the 18; plastic for the 28 – provides a rigid shell for mounting the face seal and lens
Lens made of 6mm (1/4 in) acrylic
Neoprene face seal
Oral-nasal mask assembly reduces dead air space and CO_2 build-up. It contains a **nose-clearing device** for equalisation and a **microphone**
Nose block device
Regulator (demand valve) adjustment knob
Regulator (demand valve) is supplied with gas via the side valve and is unaffected by the freeflow system
Main frame exhaust outlet (under exhaust whisker) provides automatic water purging as necessary
Exhaust whisker deflects the exhaust bubbles away from the diver's vision

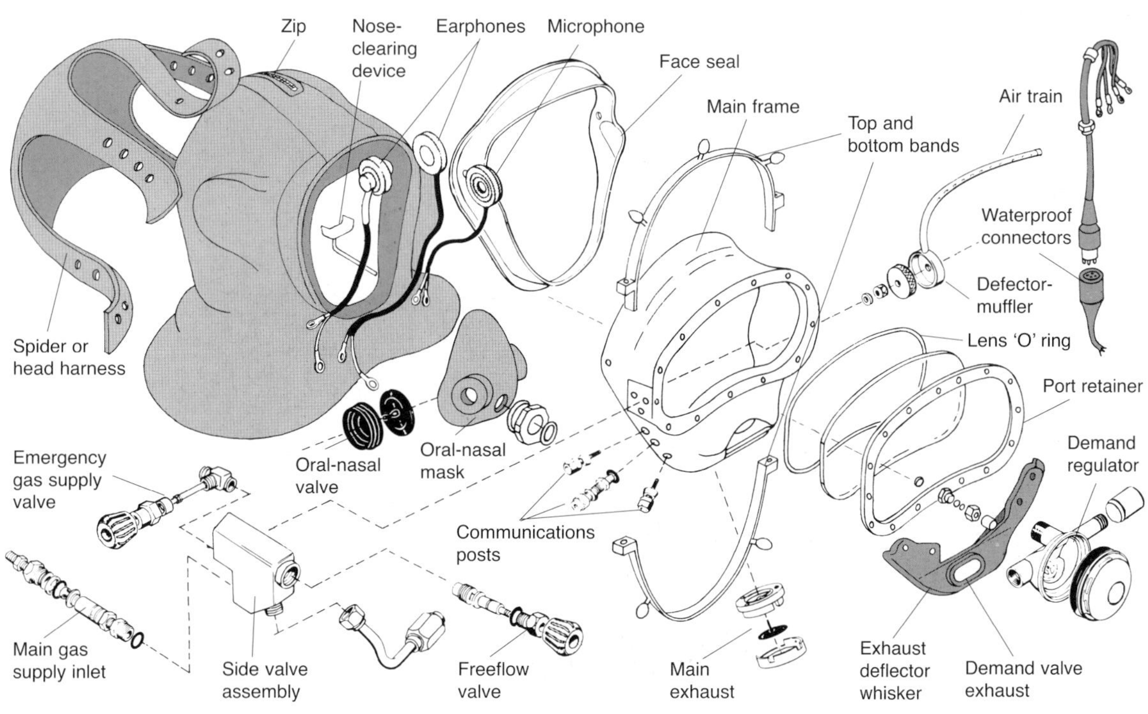
Zip
Nose-clearing device
Earphones
Microphone
Face seal
Main frame
Top and bottom bands
Air train
Waterproof connectors
Defector-muffler
Lens 'O' ring
Port retainer
Demand regulator
Spider or head harness
Emergency gas supply valve
Oral-nasal valve
Oral-nasal mask
Communications posts
Main gas supply inlet
Side valve assembly
Freeflow valve
Main exhaust
Exhaust deflector whisker
Demand valve exhaust

f) KIRBY MORGAN EXO-26 FULL FACE MASK

Designed for use with both scuba and surface-supplied diving, this lightweight mask can help to reduce jaw and neck fatigue on long dives.
The harness is secured by automatic-locking fixed buckles and is removed using quick-release buckles. The external frame sits slightly away from the diver's face to enable communication and breathing equipment to remain in place without discomfort.

An optional hard shell is available to enable accessories (eg lights, cameras) to be added.
The communications configuration varies from model to model according to the type of system installed. The original/basic version does not have communications or oral-nasal mask/nose block as standard. Models with the EXO-BR regulator are CE (Europe) and US Navy approved.

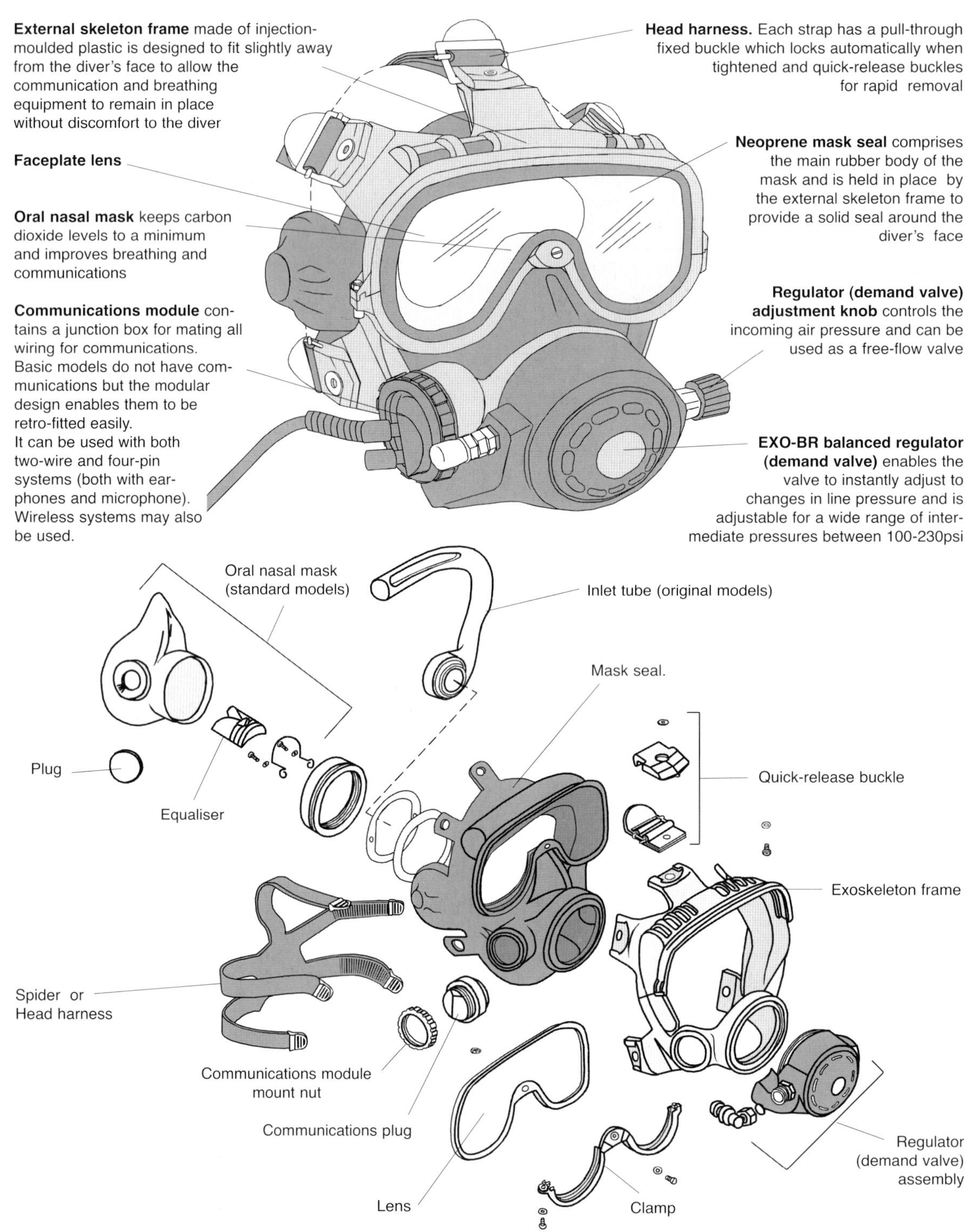
External skeleton frame made of injection-moulded plastic is designed to fit slightly away from the diver's face to allow the communication and breathing equipment to remain in place without discomfort to the diver
Faceplate lens
Oral nasal mask keeps carbon dioxide levels to a minimum and improves breathing and communications
Communications module contains a junction box for mating all wiring for communications. Basic models do not have communications but the modular design enables them to be retro-fitted easily. It can be used with both two-wire and four-pin systems (both with earphones and microphone). Wireless systems may also be used.
Head harness. Each strap has a pull-through fixed buckle which locks automatically when tightened and quick-release buckles for rapid removal
Neoprene mask seal comprises the main rubber body of the mask and is held in place by the external skeleton frame to provide a solid seal around the diver's face
Regulator (demand valve) adjustment knob controls the incoming air pressure and can be used as a free-flow valve
EXO-BR balanced regulator (demand valve) enables the valve to instantly adjust to changes in line pressure and is adjustable for a wide range of intermediate pressures between 100-230psi
Oral nasal mask (standard models)
Inlet tube (original models)
Mask seal.
Plug
Equaliser
Quick-release buckle
Exoskeleton frame
Spider or Head harness
Communications module mount nut
Communications plug
Lens
Clamp
Regulator (demand valve) assembly

g) KIRBY MORGAN SUPERMASK M48

Lightweight modular full face mask which allows quick and easy adaptation to both self-contained and surface-supplied breathing systems. The modular mouthpod is removable (see Fig. 1b below) enabling the diver to buddy-breathe, use a snorkel/octopus or to perform an in-water gas switch.

With the flexible, silicone pod sealed to the mask the diver can quickly place the regulator mouthpiece into his mouth or dive with it free of the mouth for communications (see Fig. 2 below). With the mouthpiece in the regulator may be used without the pod being sealed to the mask. The mask can also be used for surface-supplied diving using different pod configurations to enable both open circuit and rebreather use. It can also accept various wireless communications configurations.

Fig 1. SuperMask M48

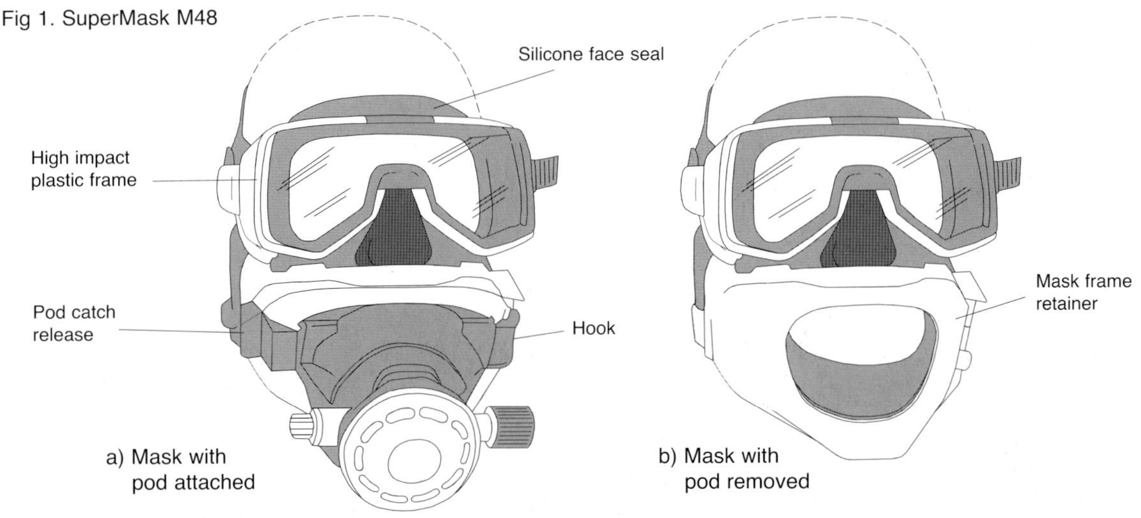
Silicone face seal
High impact plastic frame
Pod catch release
Hook
Mask frame retainer
a) Mask with pod attached
b) Mask with pod removed

Fig. 2 The mask allows the diver the choice of breathing with or without a mouthpiece

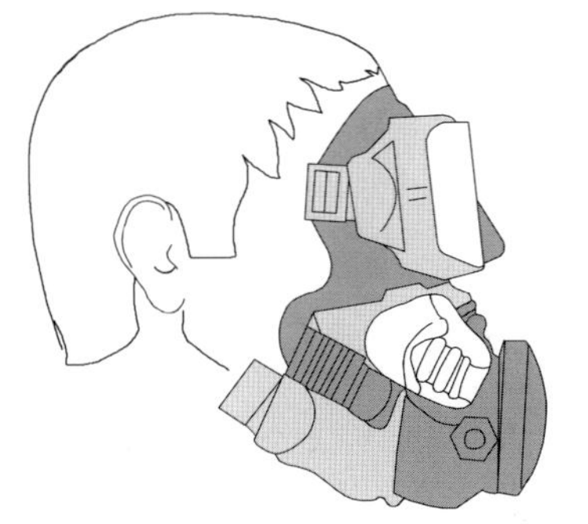

a) With the mouthpiece in the pod does not have to be sealed to the mask.

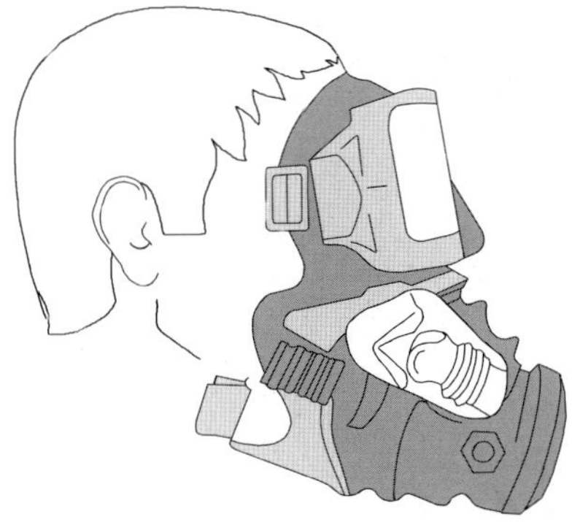

b) With the pod sealed to the mask the diver can choose not to use the mouthpiece in order to speak.

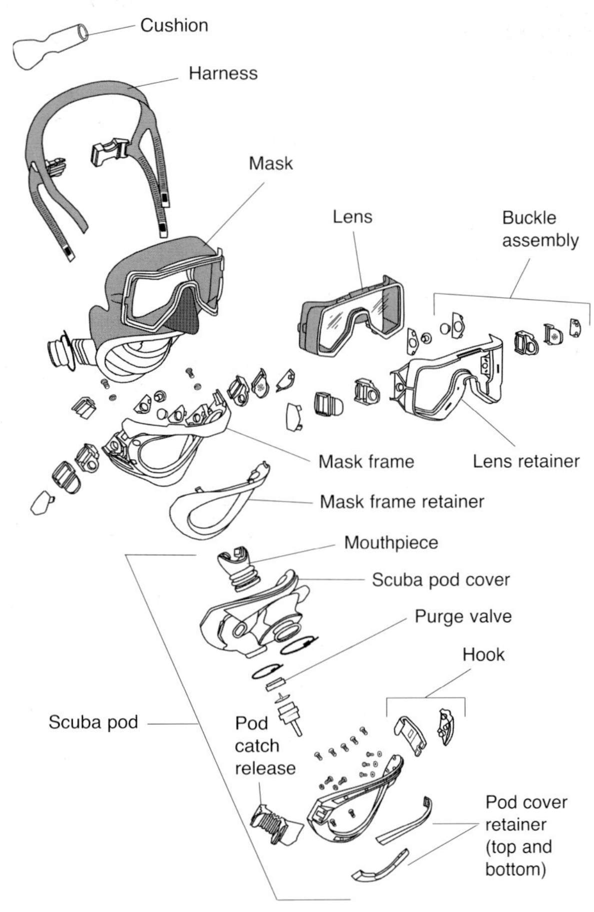
Cushion
Harness
Mask
Lens
Buckle assembly
Mask frame
Lens retainer
Mask frame retainer
Mouthpiece
Scuba pod cover
Purge valve
Hook
Scuba pod
Pod catch release
Pod cover retainer (top and bottom)

h) GENESIS DIVING HELMET

The Genesis diving helmet is made of glass-reinforced resin and has a larger than average view port which provides the diver with an excellent field of view. It has a balanced regulator valve which can be adjusted according to variations in umbilical pressure. It can deliver very high gas flow and has exceptionally good breathing-effort performance.

A drain valve, below the regulator, removes any excess moisture from the breathing gas making the helmet very dry and, therefore, ideally suited for diving in contaminated water.

The helmet is available with either a single or double exhaust. Both models have full CE approval (EN 250:1993/2000) to 60 metres (188 feet) and also meet the standards of NPD/DEn guidelines, DIN 58642:1998 and NAWR standards.

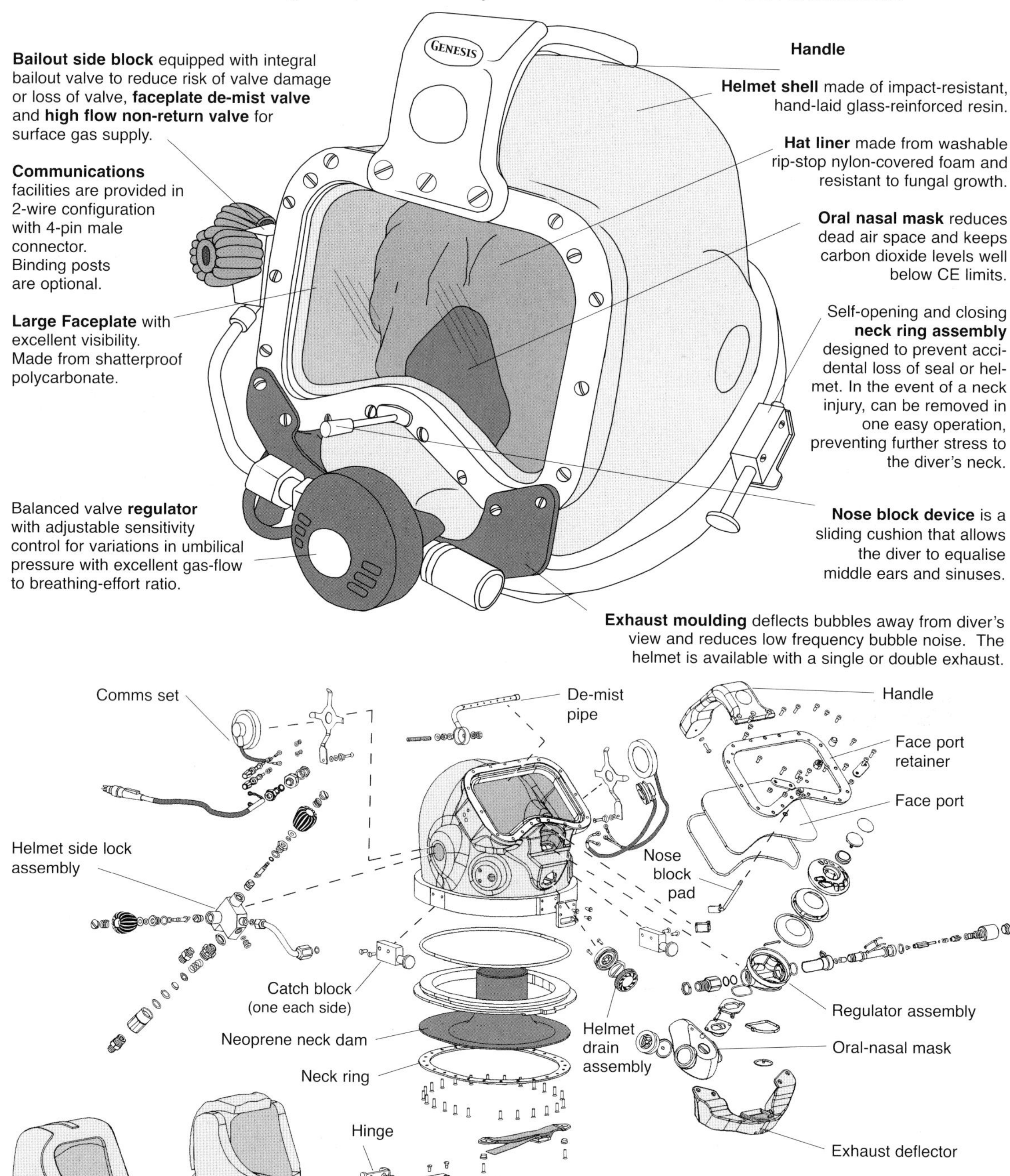

GENESIS
Bailout side block equipped with integral bailout valve to reduce risk of valve damage or loss of valve, **faceplate de-mist valve** and **high flow non-return valve** for surface gas supply.
Communications facilities are provided in 2-wire configuration with 4-pin male connector. Binding posts are optional.
Large Faceplate with excellent visibility. Made from shatterproof polycarbonate.
Balanced valve **regulator** with adjustable sensitivity control for variations in umbilical pressure with excellent gas-flow to breathing-effort ratio.
Handle
Helmet shell made of impact-resistant, hand-laid glass-reinforced resin.
Hat liner made from washable rip-stop nylon-covered foam and resistant to fungal growth.
Oral nasal mask reduces dead air space and keeps carbon dioxide levels well below CE limits.
Self-opening and closing **neck ring assembly** designed to prevent accidental loss of seal or helmet. In the event of a neck injury, can be removed in one easy operation, preventing further stress to the diver's neck.
Nose block device is a sliding cushion that allows the diver to equalise middle ears and sinuses.
Exhaust moulding deflects bubbles away from diver's view and reduces low frequency bubble noise. The helmet is available with a single or double exhaust.
Comms set
De-mist pipe
Handle
Face port retainer
Face port
Helmet side lock assembly
Nose block pad
Catch block (one each side)
Neoprene neck dam
Neck ring
Helmet drain assembly
Regulator assembly
Oral-nasal mask
Exhaust deflector
Hinge
Swing collar assembly
Helmet foam set
Helmet liner

i) OMEGA DIVING FULL FACE MASK

Built to the same standards as the Genesis diving helmet, the Omega mask has an impact-resistant frame made of hand-laid, glass-reinforced resin and a neoprene spider and hood.
It has a larger than average viewport made of shatter-proof polycarbonate which provides the diver with an excellent field of view.

Like the Genesis diving helmet, the Omega mask can deliver very high gas flow and has an excellent breathing-effort performance.
It is available in a single exhaust model and has full CE approval to 60m (188ft) and meets all the following standards: EN 250:1993/2000; DIN 58642:1998; NAWR and NPD/DEn guidelines.

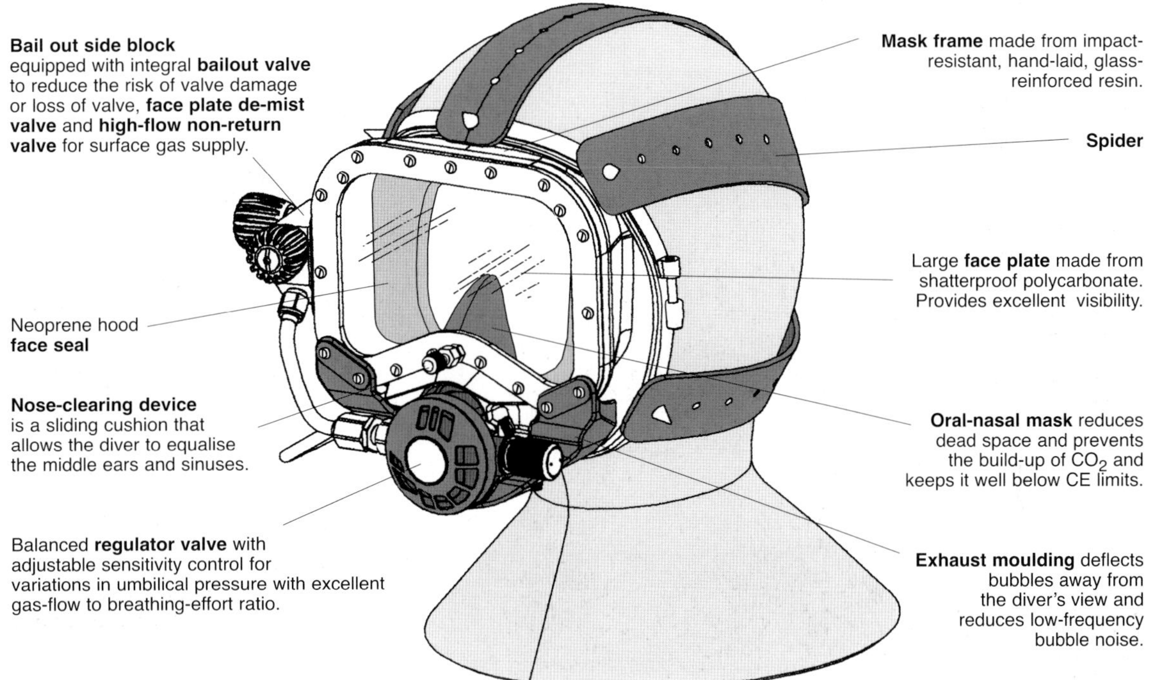

Bail out side block equipped with integral **bailout valve** to reduce the risk of valve damage or loss of valve, **face plate de-mist valve** and **high-flow non-return valve** for surface gas supply.
Neoprene hood **face seal**
Nose-clearing device is a sliding cushion that allows the diver to equalise the middle ears and sinuses.
Balanced **regulator valve** with adjustable sensitivity control for variations in umbilical pressure with excellent gas-flow to breathing-effort ratio.
Mask frame made from impact-resistant, hand-laid, glass-reinforced resin.
Spider
Large **face plate** made from shatterproof polycarbonate. Provides excellent visibility.
Oral-nasal mask reduces dead space and prevents the build-up of CO_2 and keeps it well below CE limits.
Exhaust moulding deflects bubbles away from the diver's view and reduces low-frequency bubble noise.

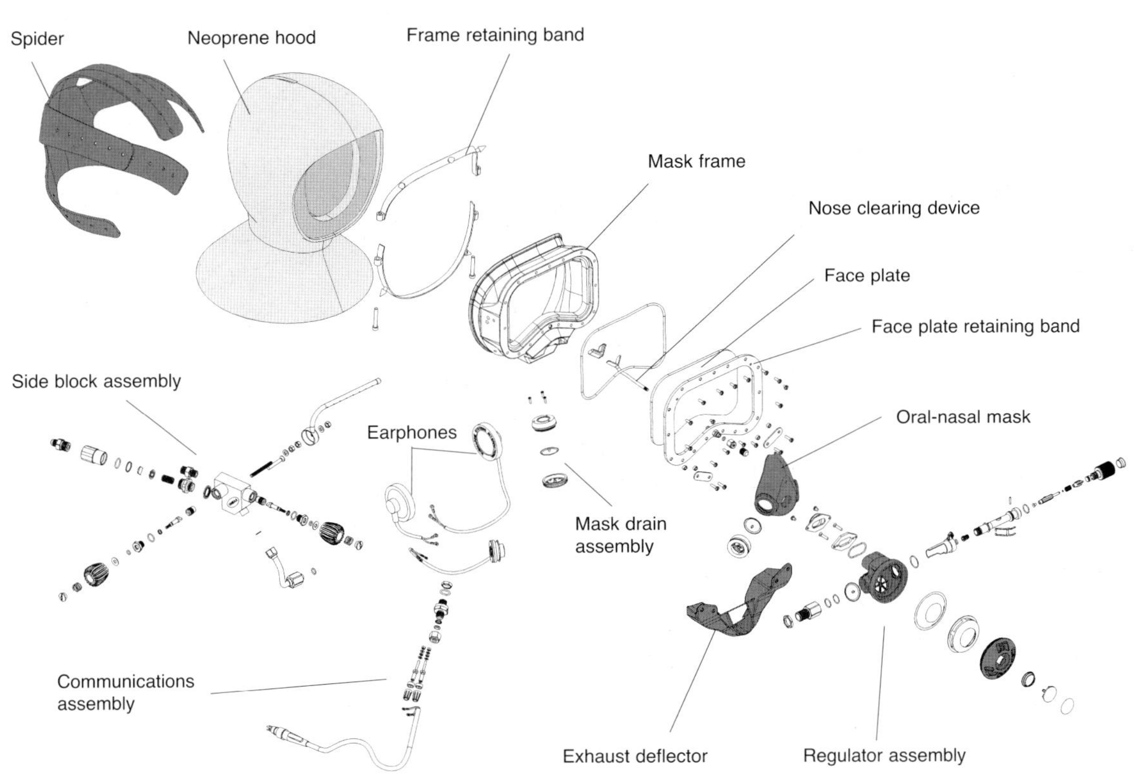

Spider
Neoprene hood
Frame retaining band
Mask frame
Nose clearing device
Face plate
Face plate retaining band
Side block assembly
Earphones
Oral-nasal mask
Mask drain assembly
Communications assembly
Exhaust deflector
Regulator assembly

j) DIVEX FREEFLOW AIR HELMET (AH-5)

Because this freeflow helmet has no oral-nasal mask or air-demand breathing system, it allows the diver complete freedom to move his head within the helmet, communications are clearer than via an oral-nasal system and breathing resistance is negligible, even when the diver is working strenuously.

The helmet is designed to be used either with its own neck-seal or can be locked directly into a drysuit. When locked into a drysuit it provides excellent protection for diving in polluted waters and for nuclear diving operations. It also allows the diver to control his buoyancy by adjusting the helmet's valves.

The helmet is used with a jocking harness to secure the helmet in a comfortable position.

It is CE certified.

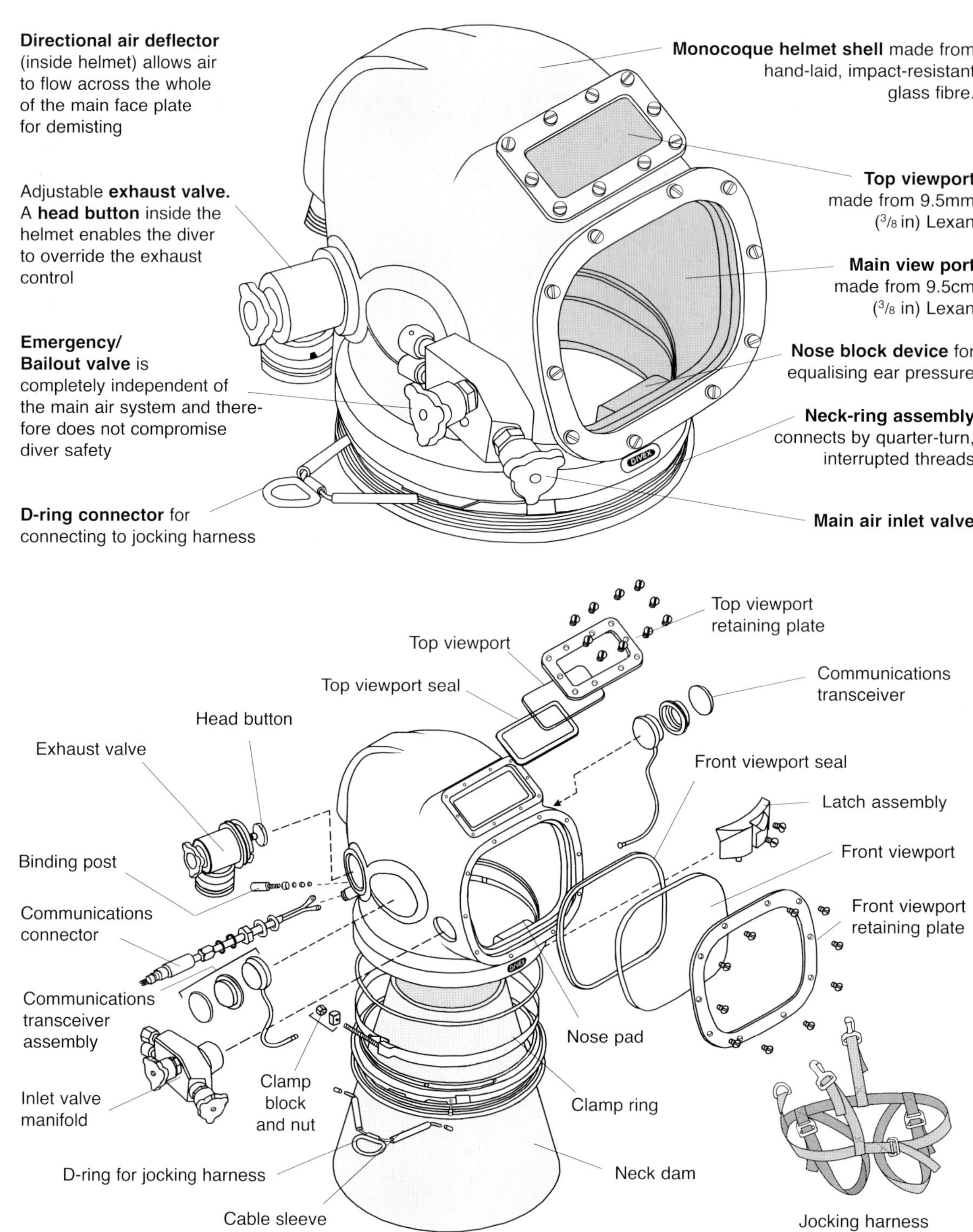
Directional air deflector (inside helmet) allows air to flow across the whole of the main face plate for demisting
Adjustable **exhaust valve.** A **head button** inside the helmet enables the diver to override the exhaust control
Emergency/ Bailout valve is completely independent of the main air system and therefore does not compromise diver safety
D-ring connector for connecting to jocking harness
Monocoque helmet shell made from hand-laid, impact-resistant glass fibre.
Top viewport made from 9.5mm (3/8 in) Lexan
Main view port made from 9.5cm (3/8 in) Lexan
Nose block device for equalising ear pressure
Neck-ring assembly connects by quarter-turn, interrupted threads
Main air inlet valve
DIVEX
Top viewport retaining plate
Top viewport
Top viewport seal
Communications transceiver
Head button
Exhaust valve
Front viewport seal
Latch assembly
Front viewport
Binding post
Front viewport retaining plate
Communications connector
Communications transceiver assembly
Nose pad
Clamp block and nut
Inlet valve manifold
Clamp ring
D-ring for jocking harness
Neck dam
Cable sleeve
Jocking harness

k) DIVEX FREEFLOW AIR HELMET (AH-3)

This lightweight, free-flow helmet is a modification of the Divex AH-2.

It is designed to be fitted either with its own neck seal or locked directly into a drysuit, making it an ideal helmet for use in contaminated water.

Because it has no oral-nasal mask, head movement is unrestricted. An air-silencer ensures that free-flow noise is kept to a minimum. The absence of an air-demand system also means that breathing resistance is zero, even when the diver is working strenuously. All of these features contribute to providing exceptionally clear communication with the diver.

The main and emergency air supplies are completely independent of each other and are controlled by two separate valves on the helmet control manifold. Buoyancy is controlled by adjusting the helmet valves.

The helmet is used with a jocking harness.

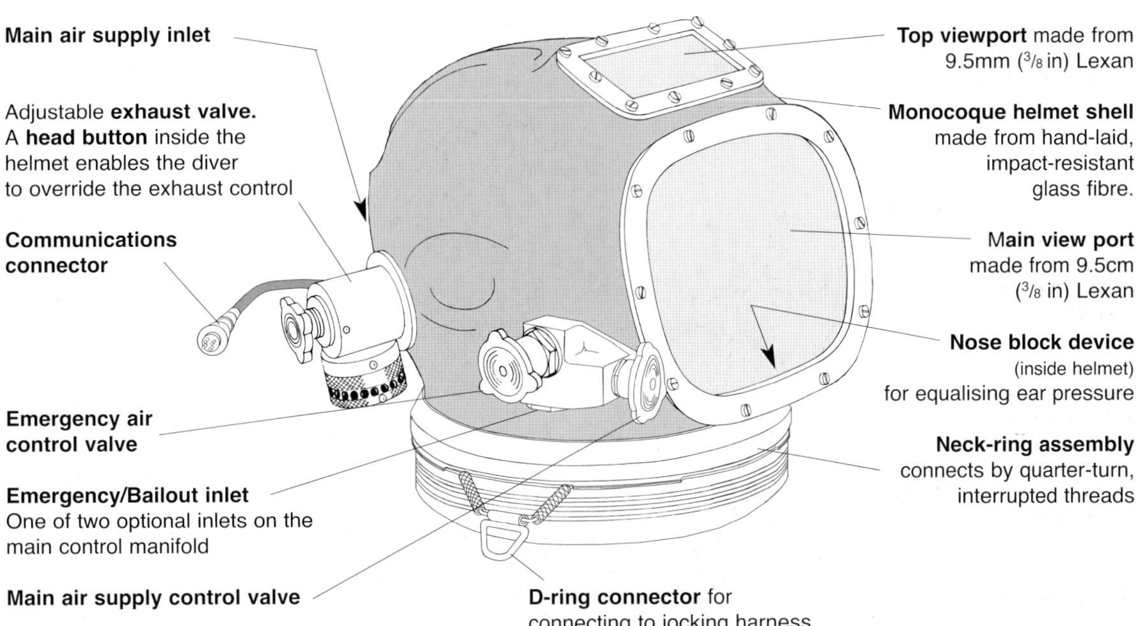
Main air supply inlet
Adjustable **exhaust valve.** A **head button** inside the helmet enables the diver to override the exhaust control
Communications connector
Emergency air control valve
Emergency/Bailout inlet One of two optional inlets on the main control manifold
Main air supply control valve
D-ring connector for connecting to jocking harness
Top viewport made from 9.5mm (3/8 in) Lexan
Monocoque helmet shell made from hand-laid, impact-resistant glass fibre.
Main view port made from 9.5cm (3/8 in) Lexan
Nose block device (inside helmet) for equalising ear pressure
Neck-ring assembly connects by quarter-turn, interrupted threads

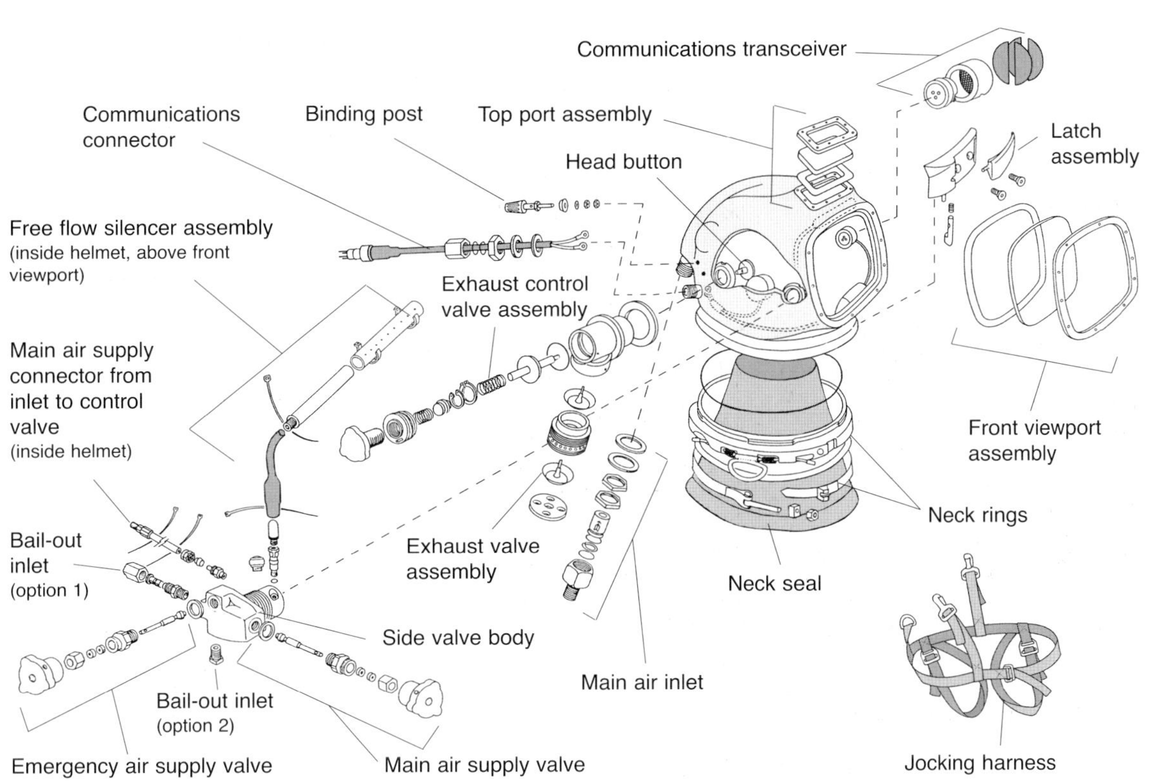
Communications transceiver
Communications connector
Binding post
Top port assembly
Head button
Latch assembly
Free flow silencer assembly (inside helmet, above front viewport)
Exhaust control valve assembly
Main air supply connector from inlet to control valve (inside helmet)
Front viewport assembly
Neck rings
Bail-out inlet (option 1)
Exhaust valve assembly
Neck seal
Side valve body
Main air inlet
Bail-out inlet (option 2)
Emergency air supply valve
Main air supply valve
Jocking harness

l) DIVEX AIR HELMET (AH-2)

A distinguishing feature of this lightweight buoyant helmet is the two ports. The front port provides excellent vision for normal tasks while the top port permits vision when the diver is required to crawl, swim, guide descending equipment and when ascending or re-entering a bell or chamber. The helmet can be fitted to a standard dry suit with a special breastplate or used with its own neoprene neck seal for diving with a dry suit, wet suit, hot water suit or boiler suit (jockey system available). The neck ring assembly has an external annular groove permitting attachment to certain dry suits. It has a freeflow system with an automatic exhaust and two-way communications but no oral-nasal mask.

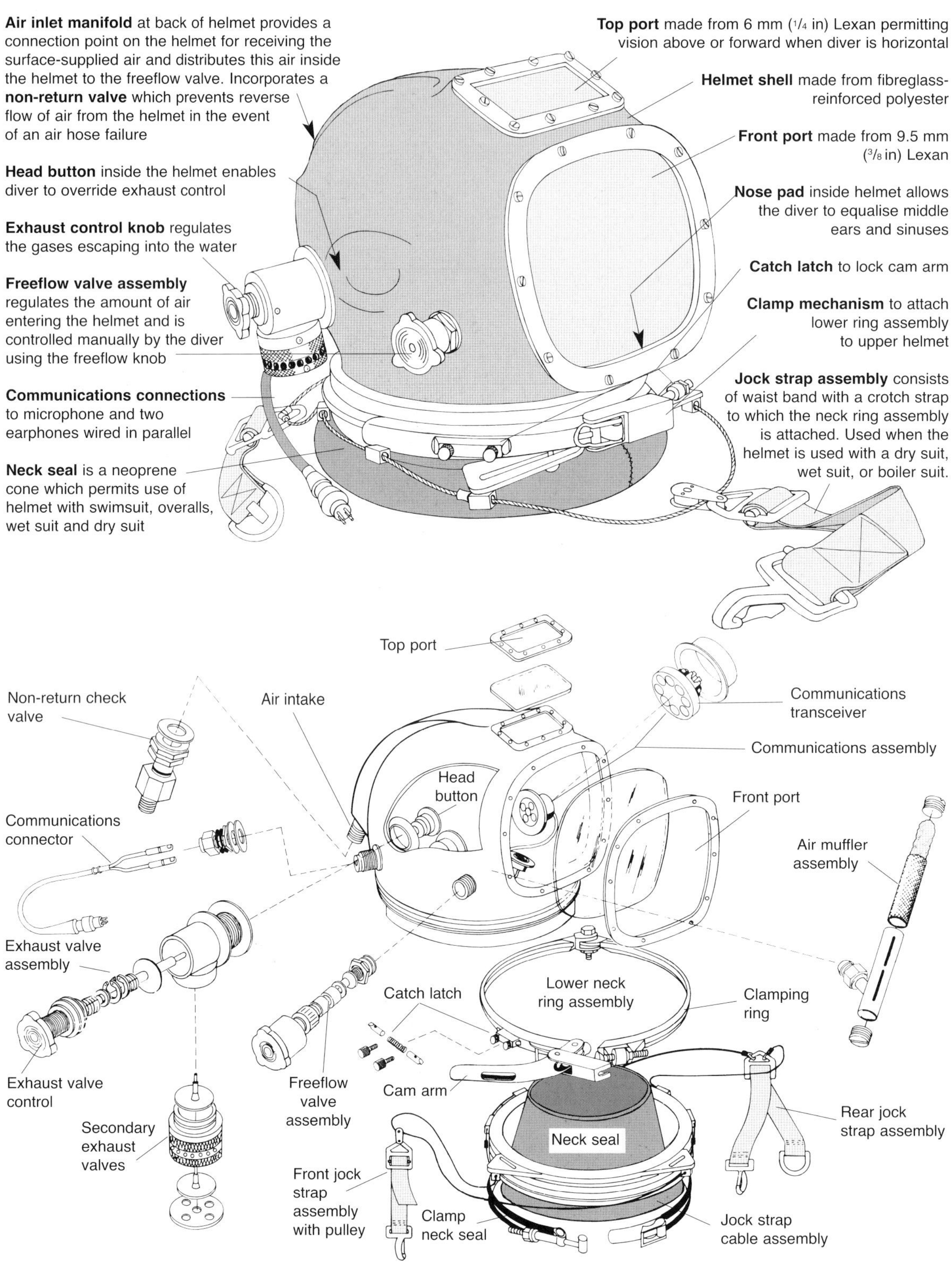
Air inlet manifold at back of helmet provides a connection point on the helmet for receiving the surface-supplied air and distributes this air inside the helmet to the freeflow valve. Incorporates a **non-return valve** which prevents reverse flow of air from the helmet in the event of an air hose failure
Head button inside the helmet enables diver to override exhaust control
Exhaust control knob regulates the gases escaping into the water
Freeflow valve assembly regulates the amount of air entering the helmet and is controlled manually by the diver using the freeflow knob
Communications connections to microphone and two earphones wired in parallel
Neck seal is a neoprene cone which permits use of helmet with swimsuit, overalls, wet suit and dry suit
Top port made from 6 mm (1/4 in) Lexan permitting vision above or forward when diver is horizontal
Helmet shell made from fibreglass-reinforced polyester
Front port made from 9.5 mm (3/8 in) Lexan
Nose pad inside helmet allows the diver to equalise middle ears and sinuses
Catch latch to lock cam arm
Clamp mechanism to attach lower ring assembly to upper helmet
Jock strap assembly consists of waist band with a crotch strap to which the neck ring assembly is attached. Used when the helmet is used with a dry suit, wet suit, or boiler suit.
Top port
Non-return check valve
Air intake
Communications transceiver
Communications assembly
Head button
Front port
Communications connector
Air muffler assembly
Exhaust valve assembly
Lower neck ring assembly
Catch latch
Clamping ring
Exhaust valve control
Freeflow valve assembly
Cam arm
Secondary exhaust valves
Neck seal
Rear jock strap assembly
Front jock strap assembly with pulley
Clamp neck seal
Jock strap cable assembly

m) DIVEX ULTRAJEWEL 601 HELIUM RECLAIM HELMET

This helmet consists of a Kirby Morgan Superlite 17 fitted with an Ultrajewel 601 helium reclaim regulator. The Ultrajewel regulator is a combination of the Ultraflow balanced demand valve and the Jewel two-stage reclaim valve. When used with the Gasmizer helium system, gas consumption is typically reduced by 90% or more.

The equipment is rated to 450 metres (1,475ft).

The helmet can operate in open-circuit mode if required. (This is also the fail-safe mode).

To change to closed-circuit mode, the diver opens a quarter-turn valve on the side of the helmet and closes the Jewel push-turn overpressure exhaust valve. In closed-circuit mode it provides excellent voice communications since it eliminates bubble noise and reduces breathing noise to a minimum.

The Ultrajewel helmet is commonly used in contaminated diving operations as part of the 'Dirty Harry' surface-supplied, return-line exhaust, life support system. In this system the diver's respiratory system is isolated and therefore kept free from potential contamination by removing the diver's exhaled gas to the surface where it is 'dumped'.

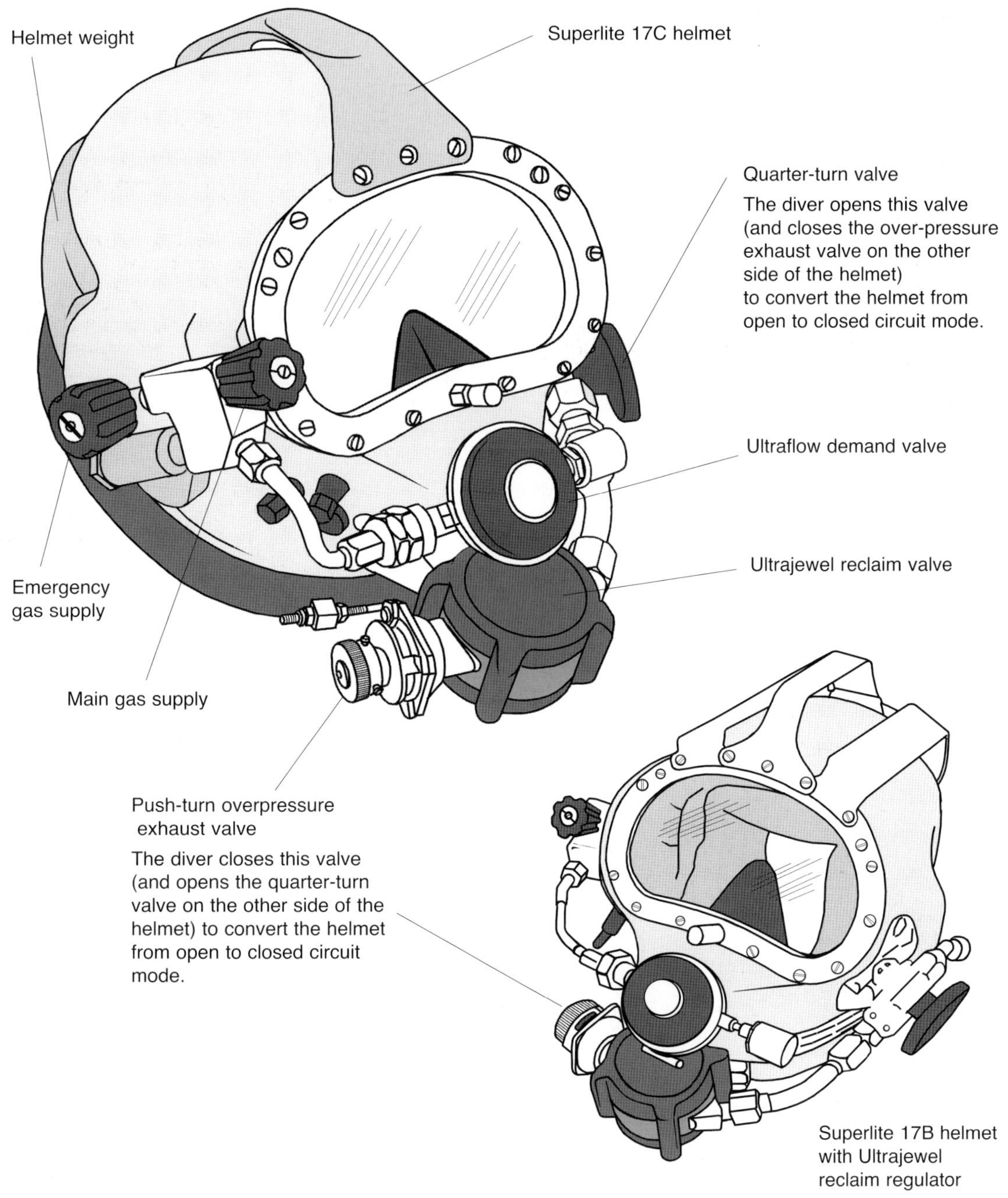

Helmet weight
Superlite 17C helmet
Quarter-turn valve
The diver opens this valve (and closes the over-pressure exhaust valve on the other side of the helmet) to convert the helmet from open to closed circuit mode.
Ultraflow demand valve
Ultrajewel reclaim valve
Emergency gas supply
Main gas supply
Push-turn overpressure exhaust valve
The diver closes this valve (and opens the quarter-turn valve on the other side of the helmet) to convert the helmet from open to closed circuit mode.
Superlite 17B helmet with Ultrajewel reclaim regulator

n) AQUADYNE DMC-7 HELMET

The distinctive feature of this neutrally-buoyant helmet is its adjustable head pads. The pads are integral with the helmet and are adjusted by each diver to his own head and neck size eliminating the need for additional pads or parts. Adjustment can be made underwater to improve comfort during long dives.

Air or mixed gas is supplied through a demand regulator and/or flow valve.

The regulator has an external adjustable orifice so it does not require disassembly to keep in fine tune. The helmet exhausts through the tee on the demand regulator and water escapes through the purge valve on the helmet.

Two alternative communication connections are provided: binding posts and Marsh-Marine. The helmet has earphones and a microphone wired in parallel.

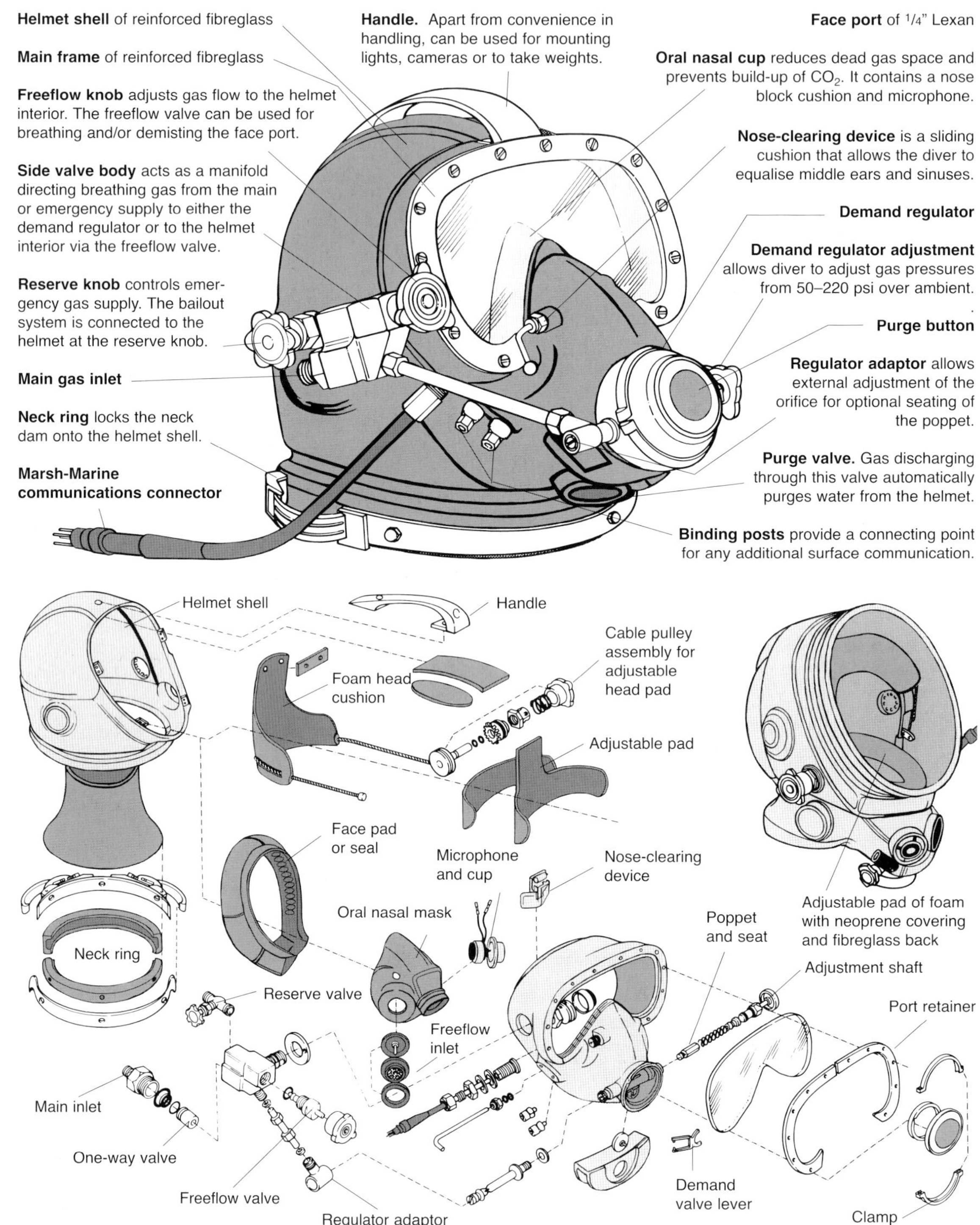
Helmet shell of reinforced fibreglass
Main frame of reinforced fibreglass
Freeflow knob adjusts gas flow to the helmet interior. The freeflow valve can be used for breathing and/or demisting the face port.
Side valve body acts as a manifold directing breathing gas from the main or emergency supply to either the demand regulator or to the helmet interior via the freeflow valve.
Reserve knob controls emergency gas supply. The bailout system is connected to the helmet at the reserve knob.
Main gas inlet
Neck ring locks the neck dam onto the helmet shell.
Marsh-Marine communications connector
Handle. Apart from convenience in handling, can be used for mounting lights, cameras or to take weights.
Face port of 1/4" Lexan
Oral nasal cup reduces dead gas space and prevents build-up of CO_2. It contains a nose block cushion and microphone.
Nose-clearing device is a sliding cushion that allows the diver to equalise middle ears and sinuses.
Demand regulator
Demand regulator adjustment allows diver to adjust gas pressures from 50–220 psi over ambient.
Purge button
Regulator adaptor allows external adjustment of the orifice for optional seating of the poppet.
Purge valve. Gas discharging through this valve automatically purges water from the helmet.
Binding posts provide a connecting point for any additional surface communication.
Helmet shell
Handle
Foam head cushion
Cable pulley assembly for adjustable head pad
Adjustable pad
Face pad or seal
Microphone and cup
Nose-clearing device
Oral nasal mask
Neck ring
Reserve valve
Freeflow inlet
Poppet and seat
Adjustable pad of foam with neoprene covering and fibreglass back
Adjustment shaft
Port retainer
Main inlet
One-way valve
Freeflow valve
Regulator adaptor
Demand valve lever
Clamp

o) AQUADYNE MASKS DM-5 AND DM-6

The Aquadyne mask is a flexible system which can be surface-supplied with air or mixed gas. Both the DM-5 and DM-6 and masks can be converted easily to a DMC-7 helmet. Depending on the diver's needs and workload the mask's air intake can be freeflow or demand.

A contoured face seal bonded to the mask opening provides padding for the diver's face, forming the watertight seal. Comfort and sealing is achieved through proper adjustment of the rubber harness which secures the mask to the diver's head. Excessive tension on the head harness adjustment straps results in discomfort to the diver without improving the face seal.

Two-way communications consist of a microphone and an earphone and are wired in parallel, thereby preventing the failure of one unit from affecting the performance of the other. The DM-6 mask is exactly the same as the DM-5 but with two earphones instead of one which are housed in pockets in the neoprene hood.

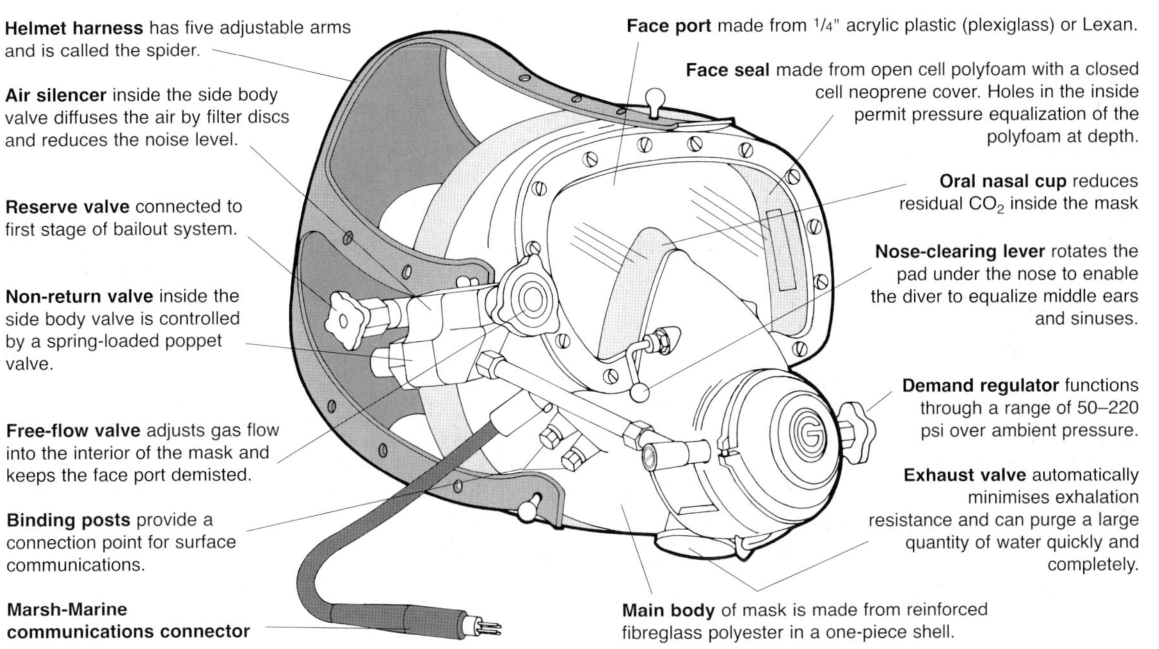
Helmet harness has five adjustable arms and is called the spider.
Air silencer inside the side body valve diffuses the air by filter discs and reduces the noise level.
Reserve valve connected to first stage of bailout system.
Non-return valve inside the side body valve is controlled by a spring-loaded poppet valve.
Free-flow valve adjusts gas flow into the interior of the mask and keeps the face port demisted.
Binding posts provide a connection point for surface communications.
Marsh-Marine communications connector
Face port made from 1/4" acrylic plastic (plexiglass) or Lexan.
Face seal made from open cell polyfoam with a closed cell neoprene cover. Holes in the inside permit pressure equalization of the polyfoam at depth.
Oral nasal cup reduces residual CO_2 inside the mask
Nose-clearing lever rotates the pad under the nose to enable the diver to equalize middle ears and sinuses.
Demand regulator functions through a range of 50–220 psi over ambient pressure.
Exhaust valve automatically minimises exhalation resistance and can purge a large quantity of water quickly and completely.
Main body of mask is made from reinforced fibreglass polyester in a one-piece shell.

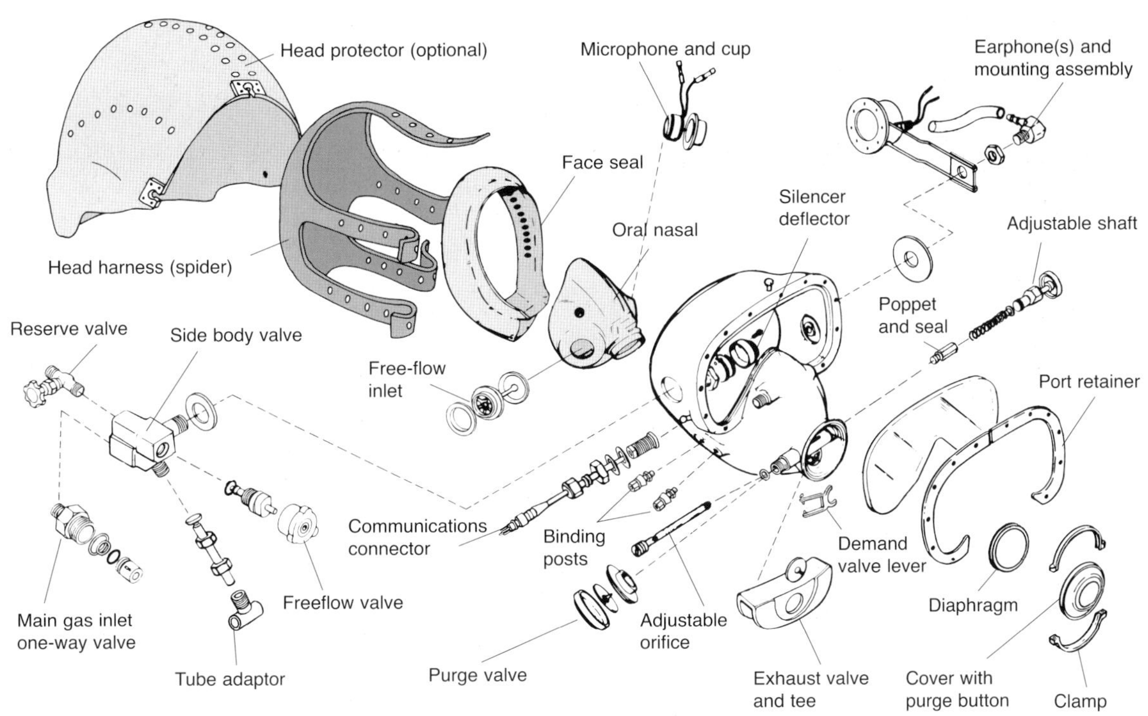
Head protector (optional)
Microphone and cup
Earphone(s) and mounting assembly
Face seal
Oral nasal
Silencer deflector
Adjustable shaft
Head harness (spider)
Poppet and seal
Reserve valve
Side body valve
Free-flow inlet
Port retainer
Communications connector
Binding posts
Demand valve lever
Main gas inlet one-way valve
Freeflow valve
Adjustable orifice
Diaphragm
Tube adaptor
Purge valve
Exhaust valve and tee
Cover with purge button
Clamp

p) DESCO AIR DIVING HAT

The Desco freeflow helmet has a tinned, heavy, spun copper shell with brass fittings, a large window of 3/4 in (19mm) acrylic and an adjustable leather-lined foam internal liner.
It weighs 34lb (15.5kg) is rugged and easy to assemble/disassemble and can be put on and taken off without the need for assistance from a tender.
The adjustable exhaust valve enables the diver to adjust buoyancy underwater. It provides maximum protection for air diving in contaminated water.
The helmet can be used with the neoprene neck dam or with any diving suit equipped with a Desco yoke which then attaches to the helmet's neck ring insert in lieu of the neck dam. The neck ring insert mates to the base neck ring of the helmet with two gaskets which form an air and water-tight seal.
The post-1993 models have double one-way exhaust valves which incorporate two seals to prevent possible water leakage back into the helmet through the exhaust outlet.
The helmet also as a distinctive double air intake elbow with the two non-return valves, one for the surface supply, the other for bail-out system.

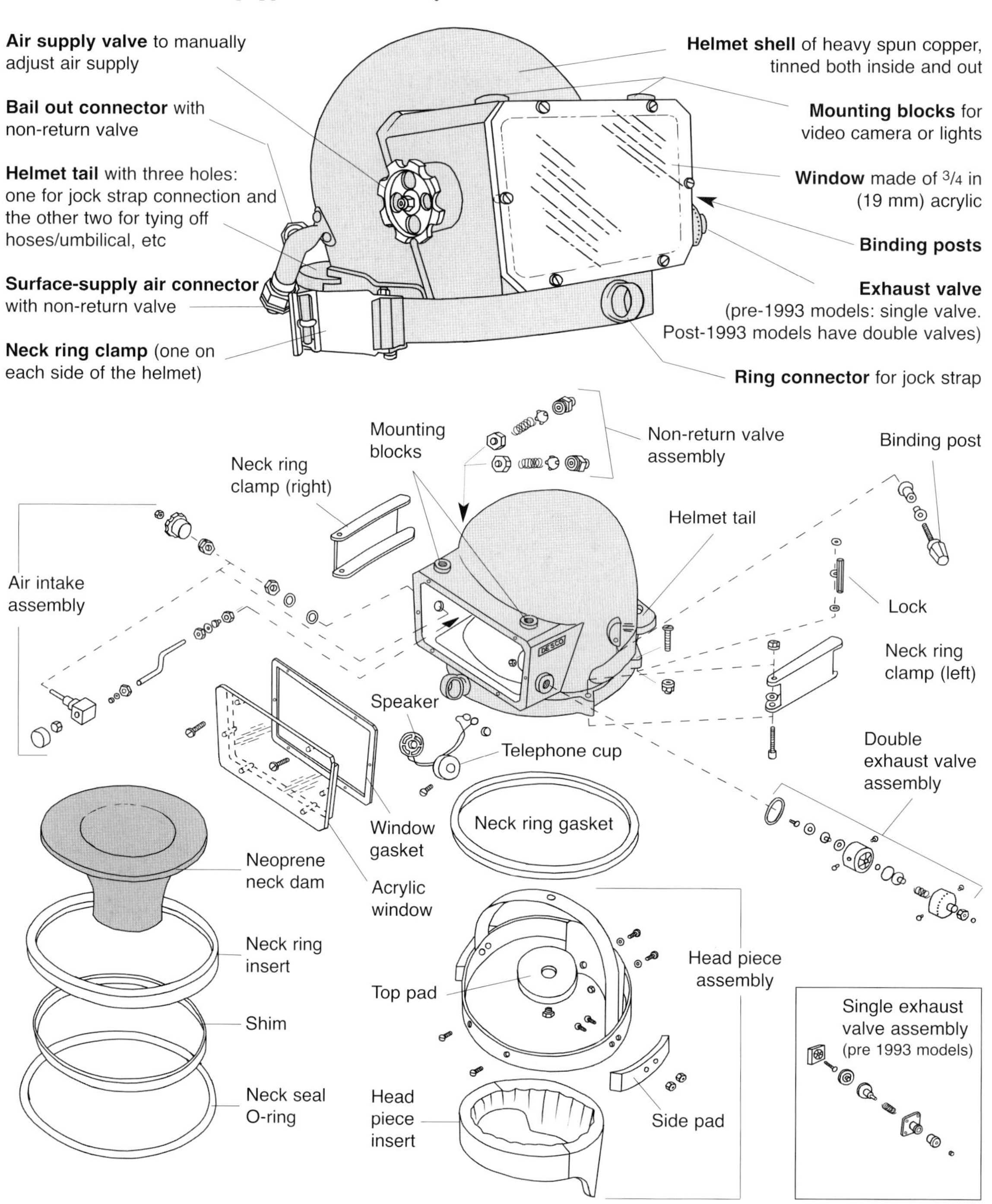
Air supply valve to manually adjust air supply
Bail out connector with non-return valve
Helmet tail with three holes: one for jock strap connection and the other two for tying off hoses/umbilical, etc
Surface-supply air connector with non-return valve
Neck ring clamp (one on each side of the helmet)
Helmet shell of heavy spun copper, tinned both inside and out
Mounting blocks for video camera or lights
Window made of 3/4 in (19 mm) acrylic
Binding posts
Exhaust valve (pre-1993 models: single valve. Post-1993 models have double valves)
Ring connector for jock strap
Mounting blocks
Neck ring clamp (right)
Non-return valve assembly
Binding post
Helmet tail
Air intake assembly
Lock
Neck ring clamp (left)
Speaker
Telephone cup
Double exhaust valve assembly
Window gasket
Neck ring gasket
Neoprene neck dam
Acrylic window
Neck ring insert
Top pad
Head piece assembly
Shim
Single exhaust valve assembly (pre 1993 models)
Neck seal O-ring
Head piece insert
Side pad
DESCO

q) DESCO DIVING MASK

Made of compression-moulded rubber and bonded to a rigid brass frame this compact, lightweight mask is used for shallow water diving in uncontaminated water and confined spaces.

Air is delivered to the mask via a non-return valve and air control valve mounted on the right side of the mask. The air flows over the inside of the face plate preventing it from misting up. Air is exhausted from the mask by a one-way rubber disc valve on the left side of the mask.

The five adjustable straps hold the mask firmly in position and minimize the risk of accidental dislodgement. However, the quick-release buckles allow the mask to be quickly and easily removed should it become necessary.

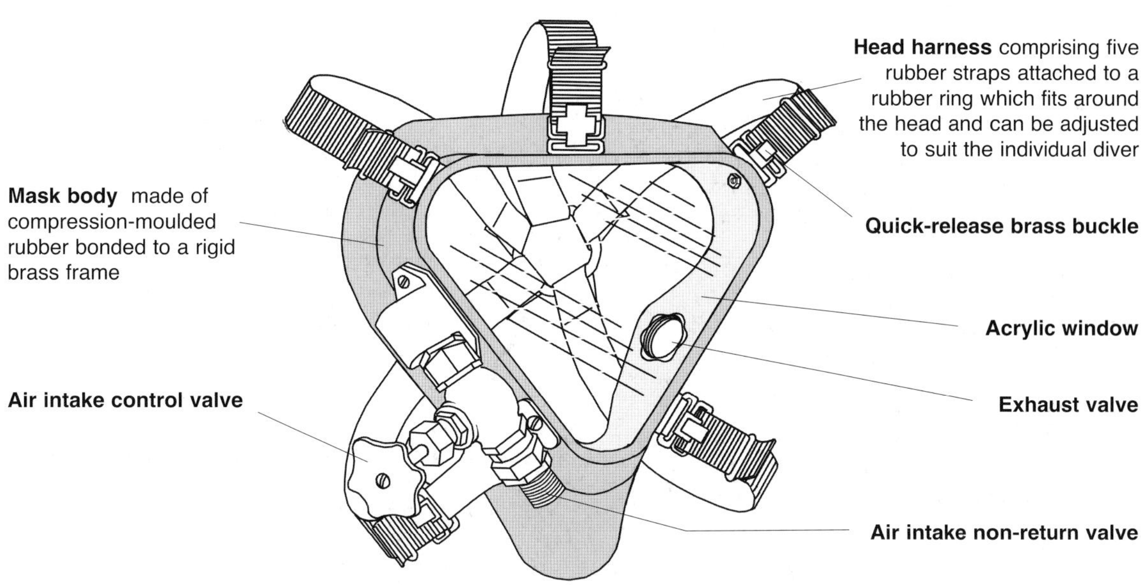
Head harness comprising five rubber straps attached to a rubber ring which fits around the head and can be adjusted to suit the individual diver
Mask body made of compression-moulded rubber bonded to a rigid brass frame
Quick-release brass buckle
Acrylic window
Exhaust valve
Air intake control valve
Air intake non-return valve

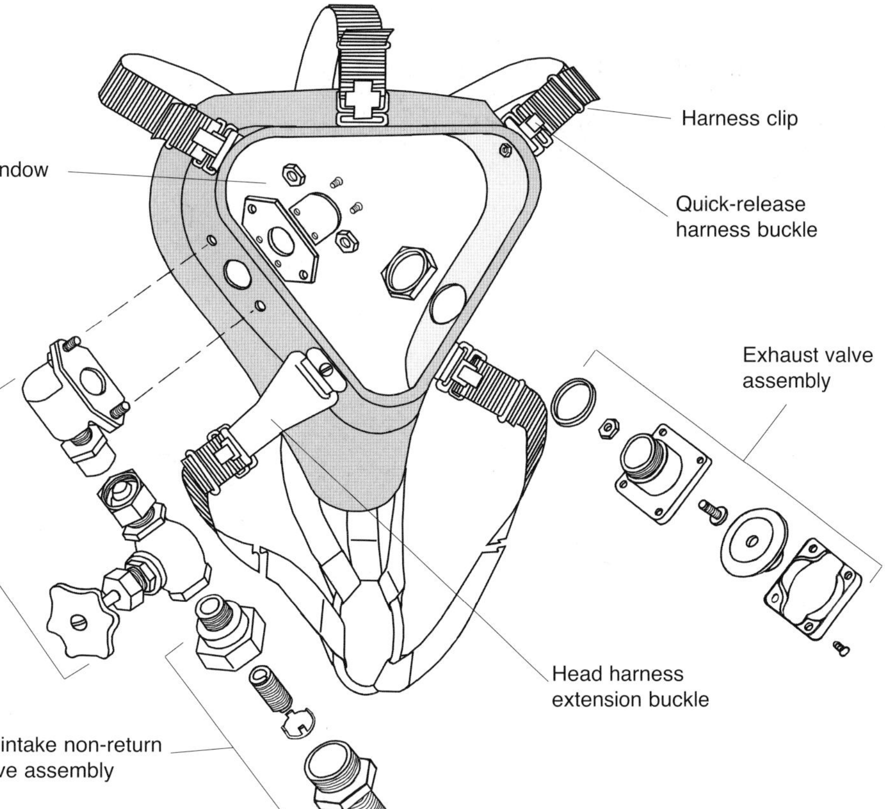

Harness clip
Acrylic window
Quick-release harness buckle
Exhaust valve assembly
Air intake control valve assembly
Head harness extension buckle
Air intake non-return valve assembly

r) AGA DIVATOR MASK

Aga developed a positive pressure mask for work in toxic atmospheres such as firefighting and rescue operations. The diving version is available in a sport-diving version with a yellow colour-coded breathing valve, and a professional version where the valve is an integral part of the face mask. The professional diving version is particularly suitable for cutting and welding in an underwater habitat as it eliminates the risk of inhaling toxic gases. In an emergency it can be donned very quickly by the bell diver. The mask has a flat visor to prevent optical distortion. To avoid disturbing reflections but still let in light the sides of the visor may be matted on the inside using fine glass paper. There is a nose-clearing device for equalising pressure. The positive pressure should always be turned on underwater to automatically drain the mask should it become dislodged.

The mask is easy to put on and can be worn with most types of diving dress. Communications are optional extras and are usually in the form of a microphone and a mastoid transmitter.

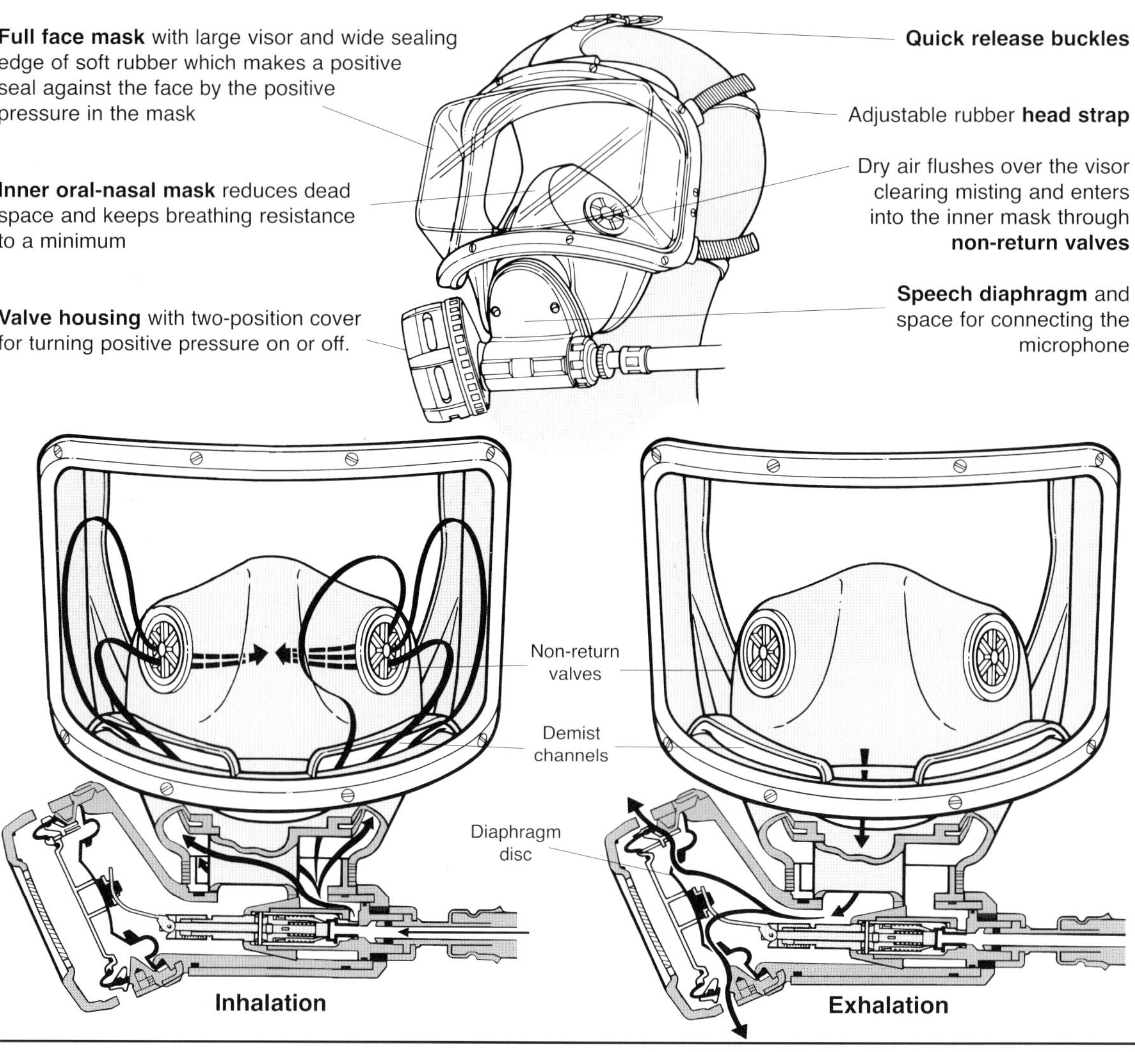
Full face mask with large visor and wide sealing edge of soft rubber which makes a positive seal against the face by the positive pressure in the mask
Quick release buckles
Adjustable rubber **head strap**
Inner oral-nasal mask reduces dead space and keeps breathing resistance to a minimum
Dry air flushes over the visor clearing misting and enters into the inner mask through **non-return valves**
Valve housing with two-position cover for turning positive pressure on or off.
Speech diaphragm and space for connecting the microphone
Non-return valves
Demist channels
Diaphragm disc
Inhalation
Exhalation

Inhalation

Switching on the positive pressure causes the diaphragm disc to press on the lever and open the air supply. On inhalation, air passes into the breathing valve and mask through the demist channels flushing across the visor and is drawn through the non-return valves of the inner mask, escaping through the exhalation valve into the positive pressure chamber. The chamber is closed to any leakage of air, in or out, by the diaphragm disc and the positive pressure diaphragm tightened against the valve housing by the inner diaphragm ring.

When the pressure in the chamber, mask and breathing valve has risen to approximately 300Pa (or 300N/m^2, or 300x10^{-5} bar) the spring pressure on the diaphragm disc is counteracted pressing it outwards. The lever then ceases to operate the inlet valve and the air supply is shut off.

Exhalation

During exhalation the pressure in the chamber rises to above 300Pa which causes the diaphragm disc to be pressed further outwards, engaging the inner diaphragm ring together with the positive pressure diaphragm and the outlet is opened to allow exhaled air out. When the exhalation cycle is over the inner diaphragm ring and diaphragm edge shut off the outlet and the whole procedure is repeated in the next breath.

Maintenance

The mask should only be cleaned with a detergent with a pH value of less than 10 and which does not contain Perborate. Liquid Fenom, Ajax and Extol are recommended by Aga.

s) MILLER 400 SERIES HELMET

This lightweight neutrally-buoyant helmet is made entirely from metal. The helmet shell is bronze and all the valves, hardware and fasteners are made of stainless steel or nickel-plated brass.

The helmet moves with the diver's head because it is secured with an internal adjustable padded neck strap. The jam-proof, locking neck ring can be adjusted on all four external cams for an effective watertight seal and can be matched to almost any type of diving suit. It has an optional bronze face guard and a flip-up welding shield.

There are two alternative breathing systems: one is freeflow, the other is by demand regulator. It is available with three different demand regulators: Miller, KMB-10 with Miller adaptor and a Miller-10 (KMB-10 valve in a Miller regulator). It has two adjustable exhausts – one on the helmet and one on the regulator and has an optional bailout elbow.

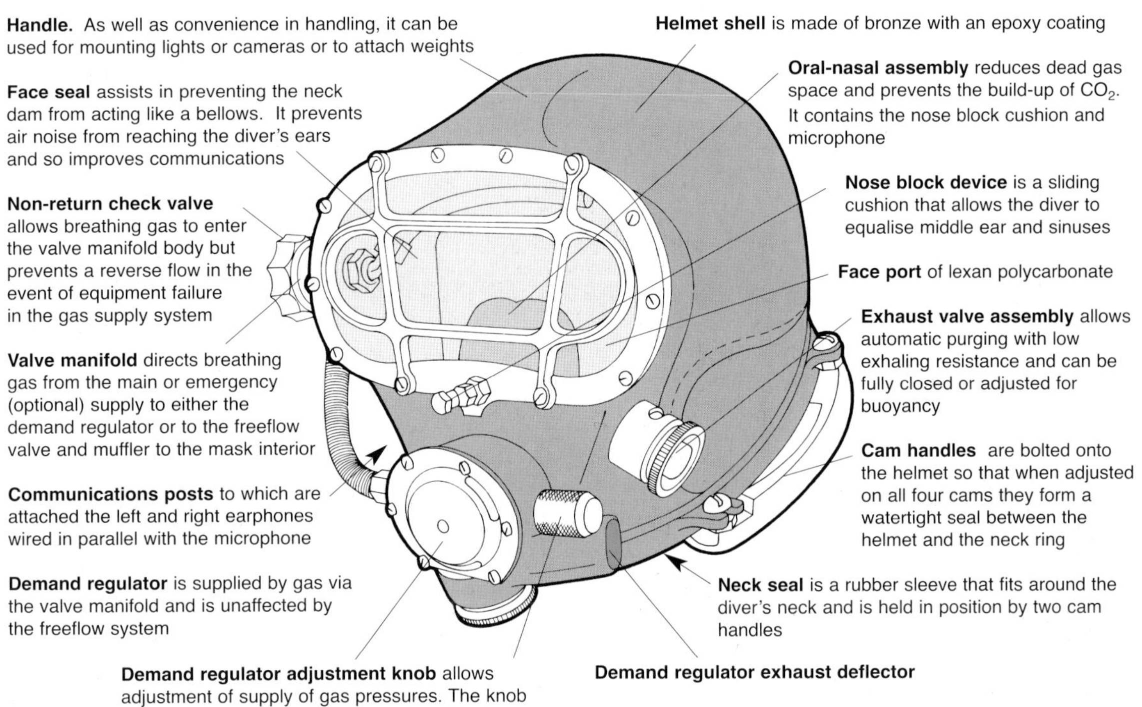

Handle. As well as convenience in handling, it can be used for mounting lights or cameras or to attach weights
Face seal assists in preventing the neck dam from acting like a bellows. It prevents air noise from reaching the diver's ears and so improves communications
Non-return check valve allows breathing gas to enter the valve manifold body but prevents a reverse flow in the event of equipment failure in the gas supply system
Valve manifold directs breathing gas from the main or emergency (optional) supply to either the demand regulator or to the freeflow valve and muffler to the mask interior
Communications posts to which are attached the left and right earphones wired in parallel with the microphone
Demand regulator is supplied by gas via the valve manifold and is unaffected by the freeflow system
Demand regulator adjustment knob allows adjustment of supply of gas pressures. The knob can also provide a freeflow through the regulator
Helmet shell is made of bronze with an epoxy coating
Oral-nasal assembly reduces dead gas space and prevents the build-up of CO_2. It contains the nose block cushion and microphone
Nose block device is a sliding cushion that allows the diver to equalise middle ear and sinuses
Face port of lexan polycarbonate
Exhaust valve assembly allows automatic purging with low exhaling resistance and can be fully closed or adjusted for buoyancy
Cam handles are bolted onto the helmet so that when adjusted on all four cams they form a watertight seal between the helmet and the neck ring
Neck seal is a rubber sleeve that fits around the diver's neck and is held in position by two cam handles
Demand regulator exhaust deflector

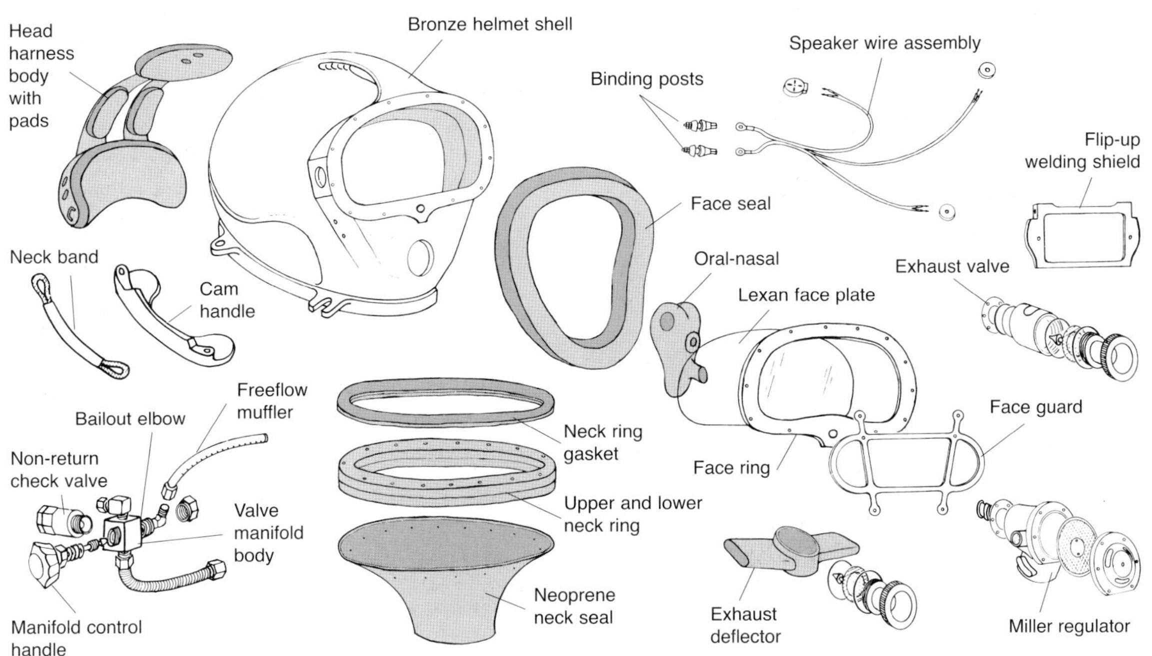

Head harness body with pads
Bronze helmet shell
Binding posts
Speaker wire assembly
Flip-up welding shield
Face seal
Neck band
Cam handle
Oral-nasal
Lexan face plate
Exhaust valve
Freeflow muffler
Bailout elbow
Non-return check valve
Neck ring gasket
Face guard
Face ring
Valve manifold body
Upper and lower neck ring
Neoprene neck seal
Manifold control handle
Exhaust deflector
Miller regulator

5.2 DIVING HELMETS AND MASKS

t) RATCLIFFE HELMET (RAT HAT)

The 'Rat Hat' derives its name from its designer Bob Ratcliffe and was produced for the exclusive use of Oceaneering International.

It is positively-buoyant by about 2–3lb (1kg). Different sized head liners, a chin strap and jock strap keep the helmet in place on the diver's head. Both the emergency and operational breathing gases are connected to a manifold on the back of the helmet. The manifold directs gas either to the freeflow valve or to the demand regulator system.

There are two different neck ring assemblies: one for dry suit diving (seldom used) and one for wet suit/hot water suit diving. The wet suit neck ring can also be used when wearing a Unisuit.

The microphone and earphone are connected by a Marsh-Marine connector to the diver's umbilical.

The helmet can be fitted with such options as a hot water breathing gas heater, a thermal regenerator breathing gas heater, a helium reclaim valve and a lamp mounted on the handle.

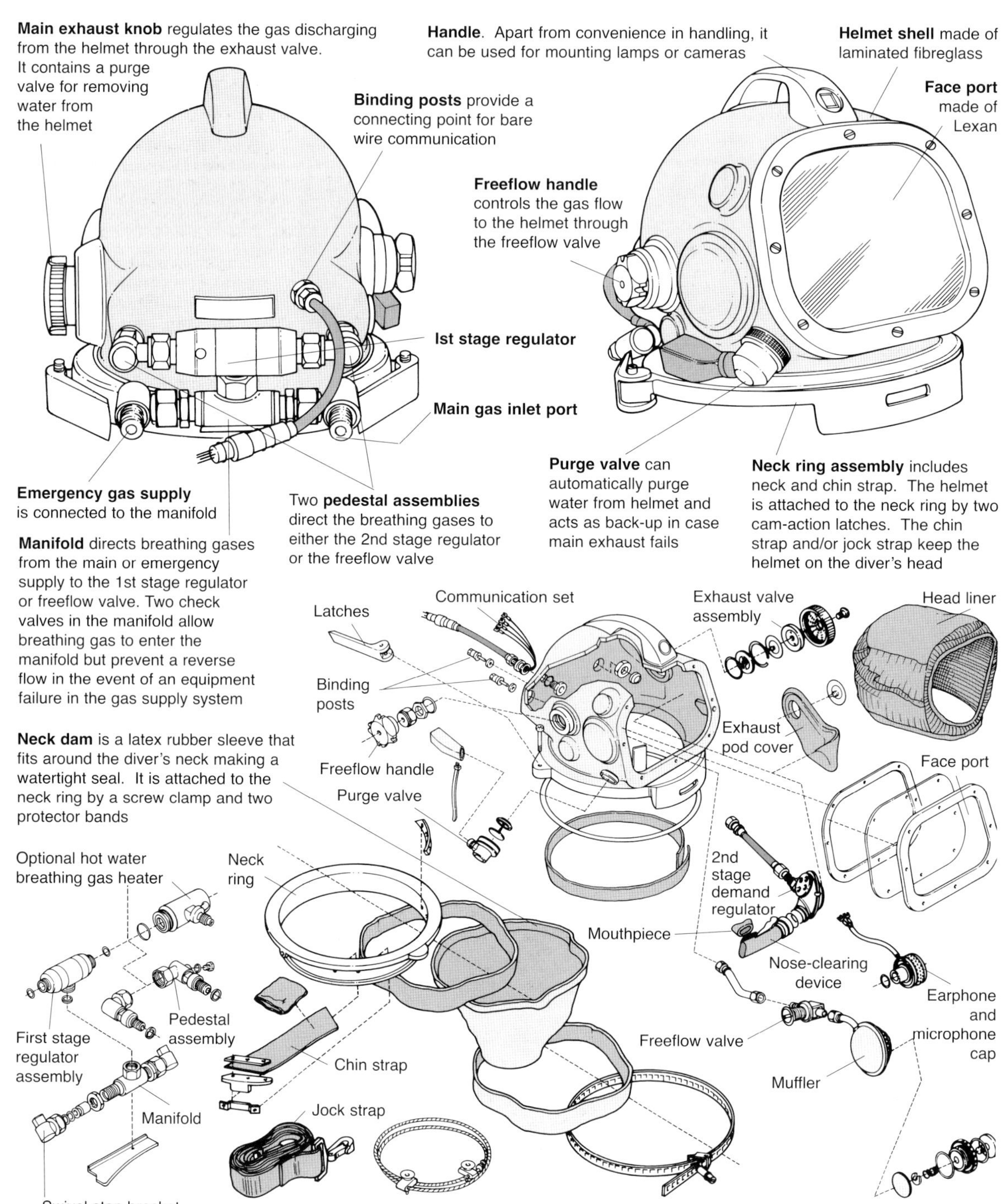
Main exhaust knob regulates the gas discharging from the helmet through the exhaust valve. It contains a purge valve for removing water from the helmet
Handle. Apart from convenience in handling, it can be used for mounting lamps or cameras
Helmet shell made of laminated fibreglass
Face port made of Lexan
Binding posts provide a connecting point for bare wire communication
Freeflow handle controls the gas flow to the helmet through the freeflow valve
Ist stage regulator
Main gas inlet port
Emergency gas supply is connected to the manifold
Two **pedestal assemblies** direct the breathing gases to either the 2nd stage regulator or the freeflow valve
Purge valve can automatically purge water from helmet and acts as back-up in case main exhaust fails
Neck ring assembly includes neck and chin strap. The helmet is attached to the neck ring by two cam-action latches. The chin strap and/or jock strap keep the helmet on the diver's head
Manifold directs breathing gases from the main or emergency supply to the 1st stage regulator or freeflow valve. Two check valves in the manifold allow breathing gas to enter the manifold but prevent a reverse flow in the event of an equipment failure in the gas supply system
Neck dam is a latex rubber sleeve that fits around the diver's neck making a watertight seal. It is attached to the neck ring by a screw clamp and two protector bands
Latches
Communication set
Exhaust valve assembly
Head liner
Binding posts
Exhaust pod cover
Freeflow handle
Purge valve
Face port
Optional hot water breathing gas heater
Neck ring
2nd stage demand regulator
Mouthpiece
Nose-clearing device
Earphone and microphone cap
Pedestal assembly
First stage regulator assembly
Chin strap
Freeflow valve
Muffler
Manifold
Jock strap
Swivel stop bracket

u) DIVEX AIR HELMET (SWINDELL)

The Divex 2000 Air Helmet was originally developed by George Swindell and manufactured by Advanced Diving Equipment and Manufacturing Company. Beckman Instrument Company later joined Advanced and later still Divex Limited took over so the helmet is variously known as a Swindell, Advanced, Beckman or Divex helmet. It is constructed from lightweight fibreglass which is electrically non-conductive so the helmet can be worn when cutting or welding underwater. Because the diver's head is kept dry by a neck seal it can be worn with any dry or wet suit.

The helmet is positively buoyant and therefore is worn with a jock strap assembly. A special breast plate can be supplied for use with the standard dry suit and in this configuration the diver must be careful to avoid a blow-up.

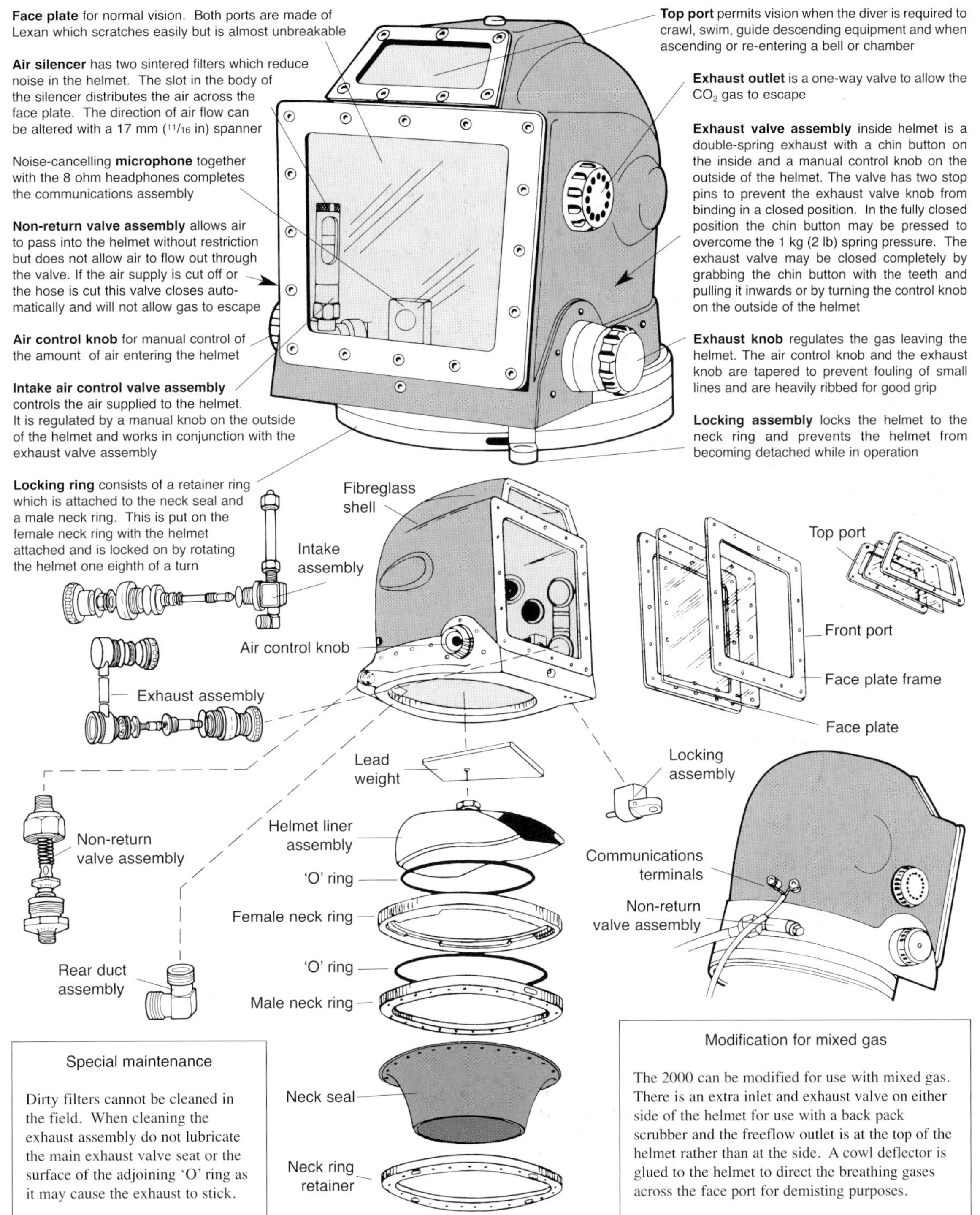
Face plate for normal vision. Both ports are made of Lexan which scratches easily but is almost unbreakable
Air silencer has two sintered filters which reduce noise in the helmet. The slot in the body of the silencer distributes the air across the face plate. The direction of air flow can be altered with a 17 mm (11/16 in) spanner
Noise-cancelling **microphone** together with the 8 ohm headphones completes the communications assembly
Non-return valve assembly allows air to pass into the helmet without restriction but does not allow air to flow out through the valve. If the air supply is cut off or the hose is cut this valve closes automatically and will not allow gas to escape
Air control knob for manual control of the amount of air entering the helmet
Intake air control valve assembly controls the air supplied to the helmet. It is regulated by a manual knob on the outside of the helmet and works in conjunction with the exhaust valve assembly
Locking ring consists of a retainer ring which is attached to the neck seal and a male neck ring. This is put on the female neck ring with the helmet attached and is locked on by rotating the helmet one eighth of a turn
Top port permits vision when the diver is required to crawl, swim, guide descending equipment and when ascending or re-entering a bell or chamber
Exhaust outlet is a one-way valve to allow the CO_2 gas to escape
Exhaust valve assembly inside helmet is a double-spring exhaust with a chin button on the inside and a manual control knob on the outside of the helmet. The valve has two stop pins to prevent the exhaust valve knob from binding in a closed position. In the fully closed position the chin button may be pressed to overcome the 1 kg (2 lb) spring pressure. The exhaust valve may be closed completely by grabbing the chin button with the teeth and pulling it inwards or by turning the control knob on the outside of the helmet
Exhaust knob regulates the gas leaving the helmet. The air control knob and the exhaust knob are tapered to prevent fouling of small lines and are heavily ribbed for good grip
Locking assembly locks the helmet to the neck ring and prevents the helmet from becoming detached while in operation
Fibreglass shell
Intake assembly
Air control knob
Exhaust assembly
Top port
Front port
Face plate frame
Face plate
Lead weight
Locking assembly
Non-return valve assembly
Helmet liner assembly
'O' ring
Female neck ring
Communications terminals
Non-return valve assembly
Rear duct assembly
'O' ring
Male neck ring
Neck seal
Neck ring retainer

Special maintenance

Dirty filters cannot be cleaned in the field. When cleaning the exhaust assembly do not lubricate the main exhaust valve seat or the surface of the adjoining 'O' ring as it may cause the exhaust to stick.

Modification for mixed gas

The 2000 can be modified for use with mixed gas. There is an extra inlet and exhaust valve on either side of the helmet for use with a back pack scrubber and the freeflow outlet is at the top of the helmet rather than at the side. A cowl deflector is glued to the helmet to direct the breathing gases across the face port for demisting purposes.

v) SIEBE GORMAN 12-BOLT HELMET

The famous Siebe Gorman standard helmet has been developed directly from an original Siebe helmet first introduced in 1840. The original design was so sound and functional that it is the direct ancestor of today's deep sea diving outfit.

The all-metal, positively-buoyant helmet is worn with a standard dry suit to which it is attached by a 12-bolt corselet, so care must be taken to avoid a blow-up.

The front window is removable. A protective faceplate can be added when cutting or welding. The helmet is freeflow with two exhausts: a spitcock and a regulating exhaust valve.

Its main advantages include the protection it provides to the diver in polluted waters, the large internal volume which acts as a built-in air reserve, and when well-maintained, it will last indefinitely. The major disadvantage is that it is heavy and bulky.

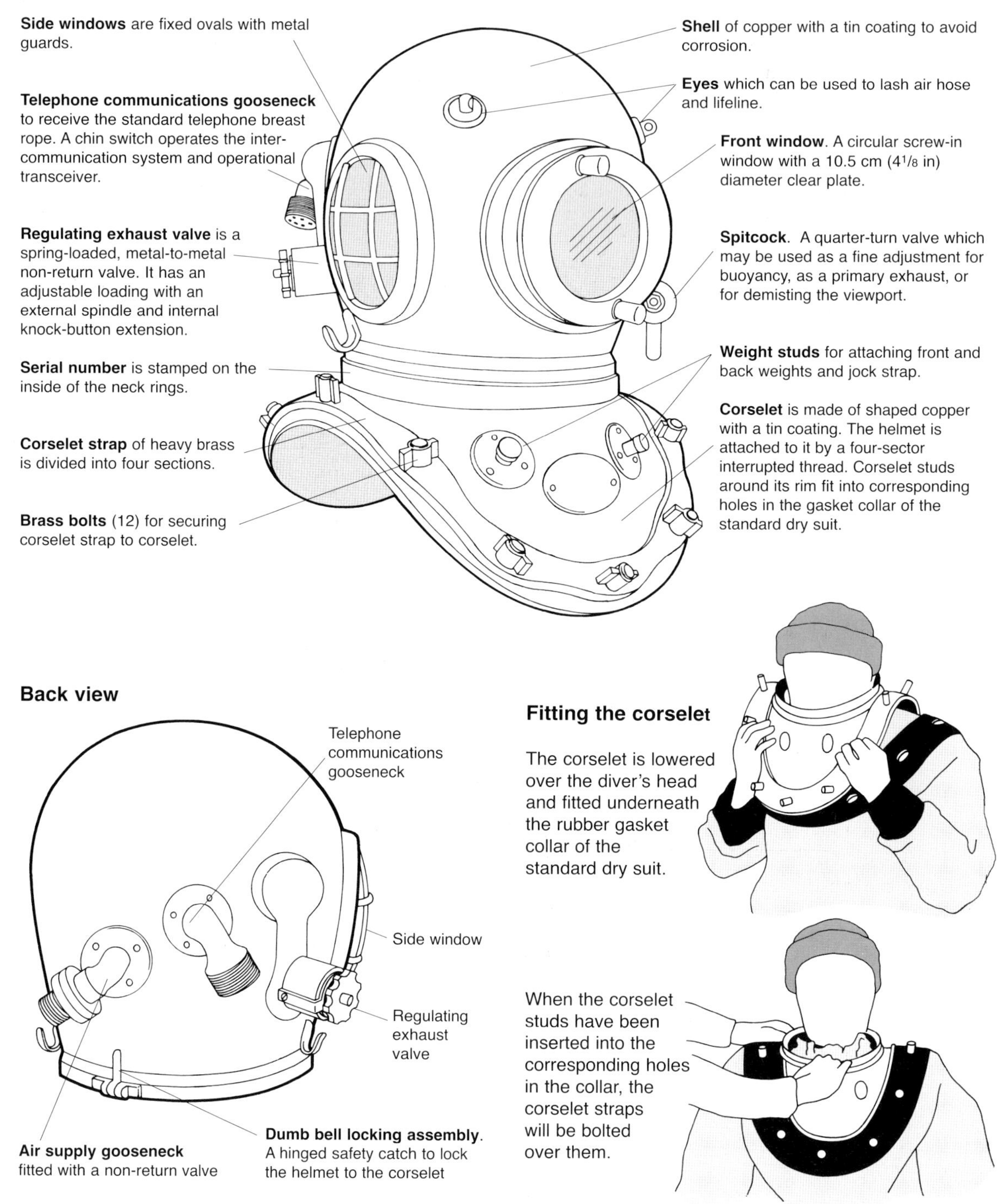
Side windows are fixed ovals with metal guards.
Telephone communications gooseneck to receive the standard telephone breast rope. A chin switch operates the inter-communication system and operational transceiver.
Regulating exhaust valve is a spring-loaded, metal-to-metal non-return valve. It has an adjustable loading with an external spindle and internal knock-button extension.
Serial number is stamped on the inside of the neck rings.
Corselet strap of heavy brass is divided into four sections.
Brass bolts (12) for securing corselet strap to corselet.
Shell of copper with a tin coating to avoid corrosion.
Eyes which can be used to lash air hose and lifeline.
Front window. A circular screw-in window with a 10.5 cm (4 1/8 in) diameter clear plate.
Spitcock. A quarter-turn valve which may be used as a fine adjustment for buoyancy, as a primary exhaust, or for demisting the viewport.
Weight studs for attaching front and back weights and jock strap.
Corselet is made of shaped copper with a tin coating. The helmet is attached to it by a four-sector interrupted thread. Corselet studs around its rim fit into corresponding holes in the gasket collar of the standard dry suit.
Back view
Telephone communications gooseneck
Side window
Regulating exhaust valve
Air supply gooseneck fitted with a non-return valve
Dumb bell locking assembly. A hinged safety catch to lock the helmet to the corselet
Fitting the corselet
The corselet is lowered over the diver's head and fitted underneath the rubber gasket collar of the standard dry suit.
When the corselet studs have been inserted into the corresponding holes in the collar, the corselet straps will be bolted over them.

Contaminated water breathing equipment

When diving in contaminated water, it is essential that the breathing system and associated equipment must isolate the diver completely from the water. Standard open-circuit equipment does not guarantee, for example, that there will be no influx of contaminated water back through exhaust valves. If contaminated water reaches the mouth, nose or lungs of the diver, then a serious risk to health can result. One system that offers this protection is 'Dirty Harry' from Divex (see Fig. 1).

In the 'Dirty Harry' system, the diver's exhaust gas is returned to the surface by his umbilical where it is vented to atmosphere (not in the water). This means that if the diver is working inside a culvert there is no risk of rising air de-stabilising stone or brickwork above him which might otherwise fall on top of him. The surface-venting exhaust is achieved by means of the Ultrajewel 601 Exhaust Reclaim Regulator which is fitted to a Superlite 17 helmet (see page 227). It is used in conjunction with a Diver Panel, Exhaust Control Panel and a Dirty Harry Drysuit fitted with a special sealing arrangement. The dry suit material options include polyurethane, butyl trilaminate or natural rubber and the choice depends on the nature of the contaminants.

Since the standby diver requires the same protection in contaminated water, the 'Dirty Harry' system is built for two-diver operation.

Secondary life support system

The endurance of the bell-diver's bail-out breathing apparatus is of critical importance. The use of open circuit systems becomes inadequate at the deeper end of the diver's range. Consequently, a rebreather system becomes essential. The Divex SLS is one of the most commonly used (see Fig. 2).

Features include:

- Standard semi-closed operation.
- The counterlung is located on the upper chest to minimise work of breathing.
- The counterlung is deployed by pulling a rip-cord on the harness, which also initiates the gas supply.
- Mouthpiece facility inside the oral-nasal mask which is brought into position by the rotation of an interface valve on the helmet.

Fig. 1 Schematic drawing of 'Dirty Harry' diving system

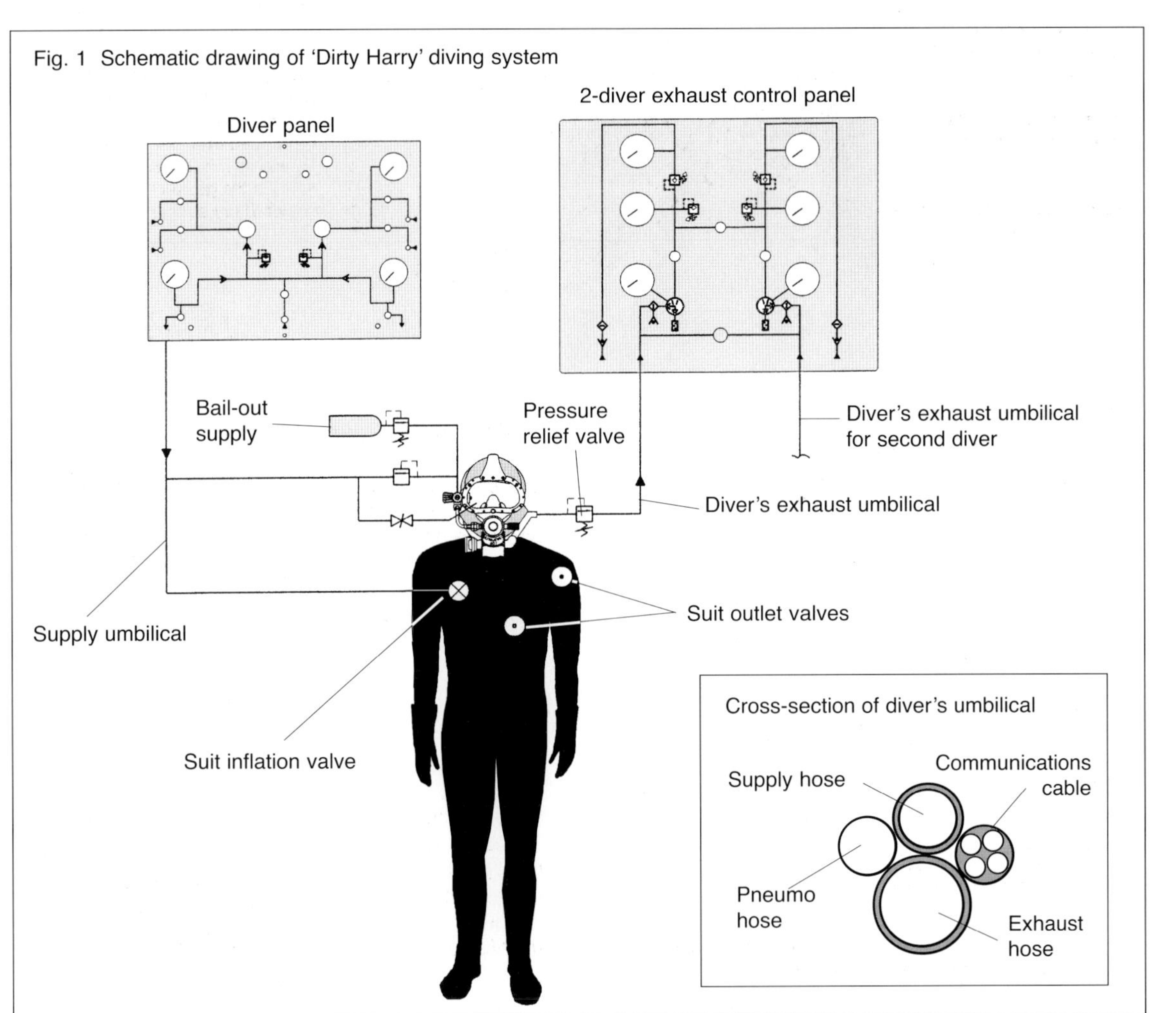
Diver panel
2-diver exhaust control panel
Bail-out supply
Pressure relief valve
Diver's exhaust umbilical for second diver
Diver's exhaust umbilical
Supply umbilical
Suit outlet valves
Suit inflation valve
Cross-section of diver's umbilical
Supply hose
Communications cable
Pneumo hose
Exhaust hose

Fig. 2 Secondary Life Support (SLS) system

a) SLS system

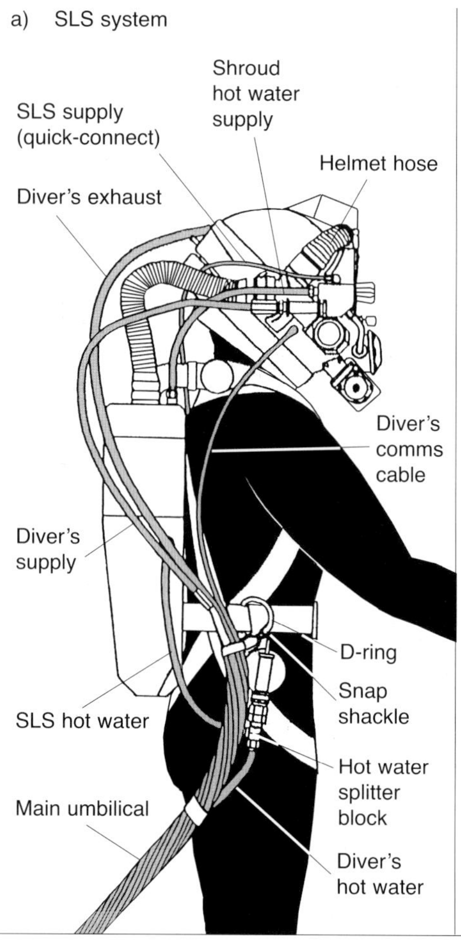
Shroud
hot water
supply
SLS supply
(quick-connect)
Helmet hose
Diver's exhaust
Diver's
comms
cable
Diver's
supply
D-ring
Snap
shackle
SLS hot water
Hot water
splitter
block
Main umbilical
Diver's
hot water

b) Schematic drawing of SLS system

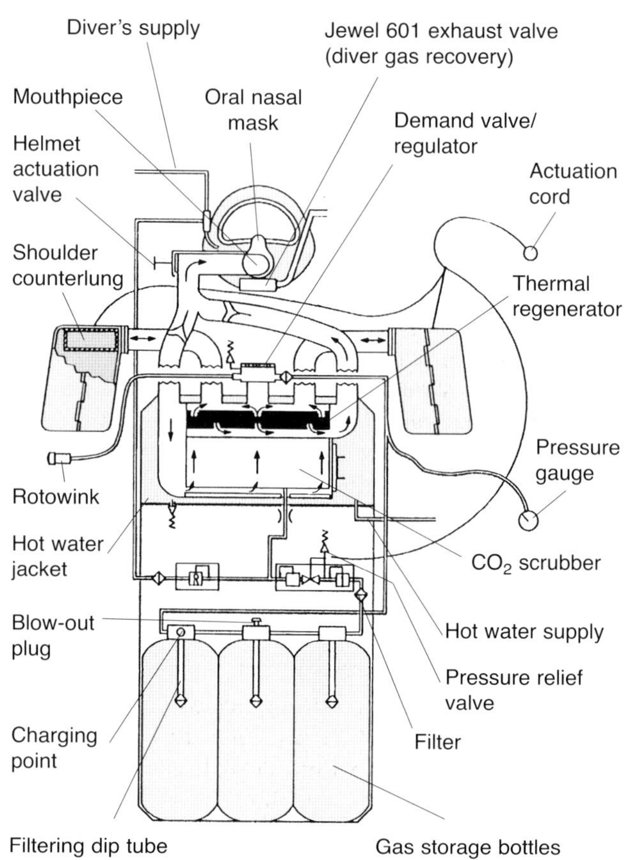
Diver's supply
Jewel 601 exhaust valve
(diver gas recovery)
Mouthpiece
Oral nasal
mask
Demand valve/
regulator
Helmet
actuation
valve
Actuation
cord
Shoulder
counterlung
Thermal
regenerator
Pressure
gauge
Rotowink
Hot water
jacket
CO2 scrubber
Blow-out
plug
Hot water supply
Pressure relief
valve
Charging
point
Filter
Filtering dip tube
Gas storage bottles

Fig. 3 Divex SLS endurance

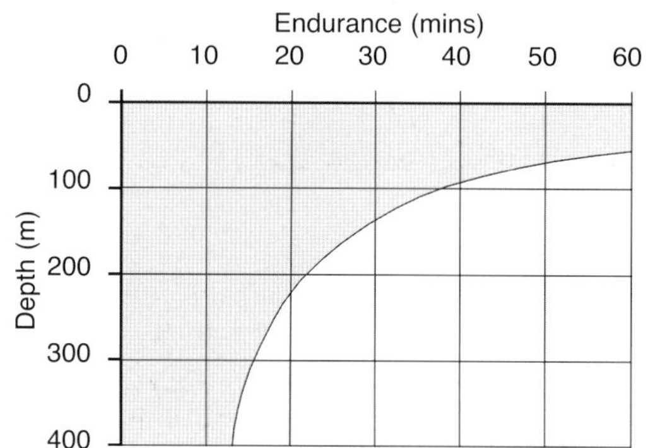
Endurance (mins)
0
10
20
30
40
50
60
Depth (m)
0
100
200
300
400

Graph showing the effect of depth on the length of time the Secondary Life Support system can be safely used.
For example: at 400m (1,300ft) the SLS can be used for no more than about 15 minutes.
At 200m (650ft) the dive must be limited to approximately 20 minutes. At 50m (150ft), the SLS can be safely used for over an hour.

Gas reclaim systems

Saturation diving to depths in excess of 50m (165ft) requires a helium-oxygen breathing mixture. Helium, however, is expensive and supply arrangements can be difficult, especially in remote areas or where bad weather conditions prevail.

Furthermore, during extended diving operations, very large volumes of gas are used which, if used in open circuit, can exhaust the limited supply that can be carried onboard a DSV.

A closed-circuit gas recovery system can save about 80–85% of these costs by recovering the helium that would otherwise be vented into the water and by reconstituting it for re-use. It also reduces the amount of helium required to be transported and stored, thus saving on deck space and reducing deck weight. A further benefit is that, since the gas is re-cycled, in situations where gas-carrying capacity is limited, excursion times can be considerably extended before the gas has to be recharged.

Gas reclaim systems are used to recover/recycle both the gas breathed by the divers while out of the bell as well as the gas exhausted from the compression chambers during decompression.

An example of a diver gas reclaim system is the Divex Electric Gasmizer (see Fig. 4). This consists of five basic components:

1. THE CONTROL CONSOLE which is located in Dive Control and is operated by the diving supervisor. This includes control of the electric gas booster start/stop, oxygen injection, diver supply pressure, exhaust hose pressure and make-up gas addition.

2. THE INTERNAL BELL EQUIPMENT which maintains the optimum negative pressure in the diver's exhaust hose, removes water and provides automatic shut-down should the diver's gas supply be interrupted. It also scrubs the bell atmosphere. A two-stage water trap is provided for easy drainage.

3. THE EXTERNAL BELL EQUIPMENT which includes a high flow check-valve and an external water trap.

4. THE GAS BOOSTER. This is electrically-driven, non-lubricated, water-cooled, two-stage gas booster which can support two divers down to a depth of 500msw (1,650fsw) by supplying 150 actual litres (5.3cu ft) per minute at all depths.

5. THE REPROCESSING UNIT which is bulkhead-mounted. It is silent-running, includes high-pressure carbon dioxide scrubbing, moisture removal by condensation and a volume tank to store reprocessed gas.

Fig. 4 'Gasmizer' gas reprocessing system

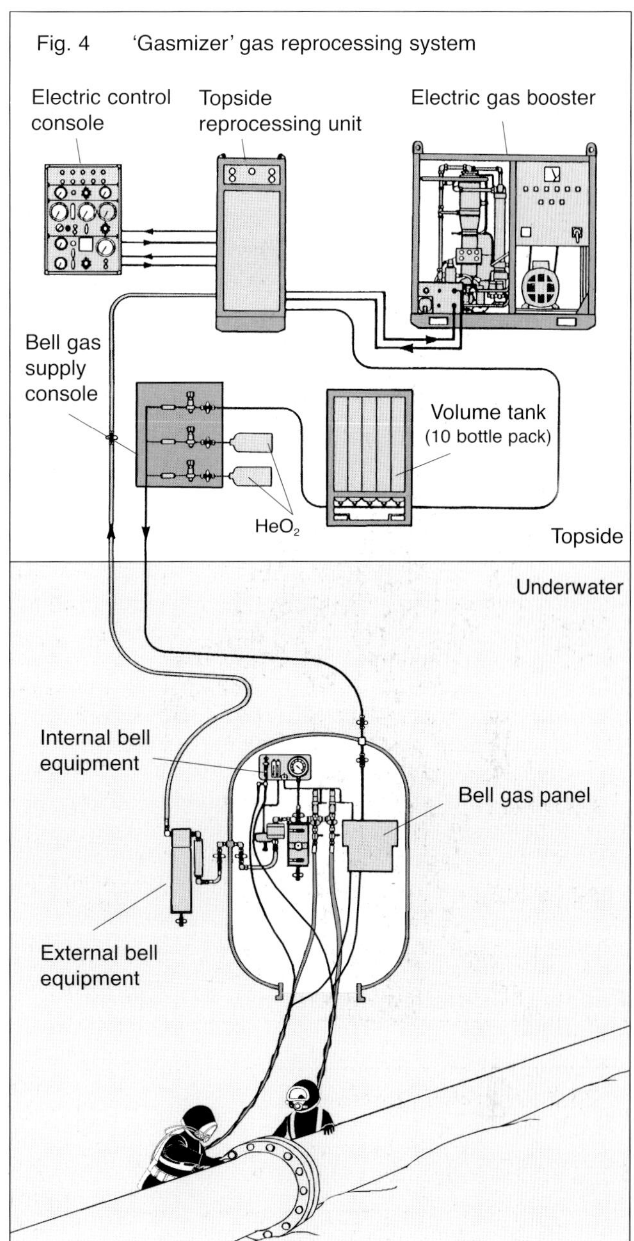
Electric control console
Topside reprocessing unit
Electric gas booster
Bell gas supply console
Volume tank (10 bottle pack)
HeO_2
Topside
Underwater
Internal bell equipment
Bell gas panel
External bell equipment

5.4 THERMAL PROTECTION

Proper thermal protection is imperative for divers working in cold water since it increases efficiency and prevents hypothermia. It is especially important on deep dives when breathing oxy-helium since the danger of hypothermia is increased due to the pressure of the working depth and the breathing mix used. The pressure compresses the normal insulating material of the suit (eg, foamed neoprene) rendering it ineffective, while oxy-helium rapidly conducts heat away from the diver's lungs and body, especially when it is under pressure. (Helium conducts heat at a rate 6 times that of air).

The main aim for any form of thermal protection is to maintain as normal the body's core and skin temperatures (see Sections 12.5 & 12.6) so the diver can work at maximum efficiency. Thermal protection can be divided into three categories:

1. Operational.
2. Emergency.
3. Combined operational and emergency.

1. OPERATIONAL THERMAL PROTECTION

Operational thermal protection is used from day to day in any normal working situation. There are 2

Fig. 1 Types of thermal protection

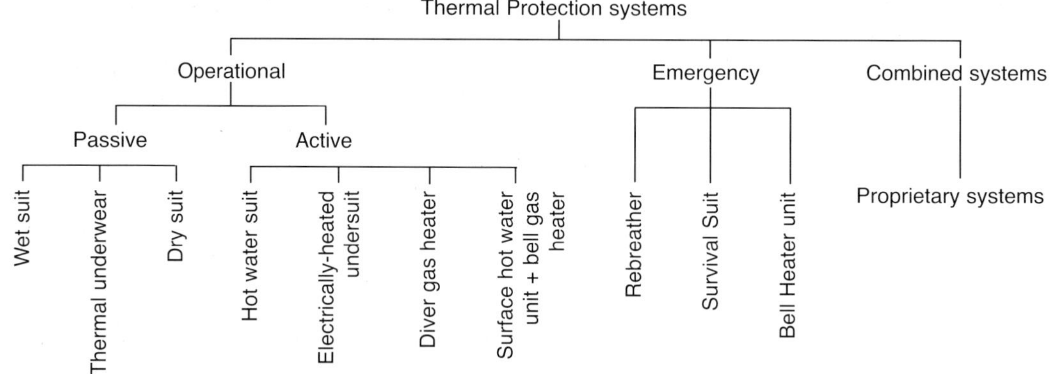
Thermal Protection systems
Operational
Emergency
Combined systems
Passive
Active
Wet suit
Thermal underwear
Dry suit
Hot water suit
Electrically-heated undersuit
Diver gas heater
Surface hot water unit + bell gas heater
Rebreather
Survival Suit
Bell Heater unit
Proprietary systems

types of operational thermal protection: Passive and Active (see Fig. 1).

Passive thermal protection relies on the insulation, either of the air/water trapped inside the suit, or of the suit itself. Active protection means that heat is supplied to the diver. In both cases the objective is to reduce the diver's normal heat loss to a rate the body can comfortably tolerate and control.

When active protection is used, especially in hot climates, care must be taken to avoid hyperthermia. The recommended maximum body temperatures to avoid hyperthermia are shown in Section 12.6.

Apart from the main aim stated above, other considerations such as keeping the diver mobile, giving him free use of his hands and being as unencumbered as possible are major factors affecting the design of operational protection equipment.

Passive Operational Thermal Protection Systems

a) WET SUIT

A close-fitting garment worn next to the diver's skin. Water enters the suit at its edges, cuff, neck, etc, and is retained against the wearer's skin by the close fit of the suit.

Material:

Closed-cell, expande-foam neoprene – a synthetic rubber-like material full of minute 'closed cells' of nitrogen gas. These cells are not interconnected and the material does not soak up water.

Design variations:

One piece trousers (with optional long-john extension to cover the chest), jacket, hood, bootees and gloves. Neoprene thickness varies from 4mm–8mm, nylon-lined or unlined.

Thermal protection:

The minute closed cells of nitrogen gas within the neoprene form an insulating later. The diver's body heats the film of water between the diver's skin and the wet suit and so assists in providing insulation.

Potential thermal protection problems:

The pressure of water at depth compresses the gas-filled neoprene. At 20m (65ft) a diver's wet suit is about half its original thickness and its insulation quality is also approximately halved. Flushing (the action of pumping out of the layer of water between suit and skin) can occur if the suit is too loose or if there are too many tears. It is initiated by the frequent flexing of the body particularly at the waist and reduces thermal protection to almost zero. With age, neoprene cells develop inter-connections, lose gas and soak up water, reducing their thermal protection capacity. Wet suits are not as effective in air. Divers can often get very cold on the way to and from a dive if the air temperature is low and especially if there is a wind chill factor.

Other considerations:

- Fit: A good fit is important. Too loose allows flushing; too tight restricts blood circulation, movement and breathing.
- Buoyancy: Because of the gas trapped in the wet suit, it is very buoyant. to compensate for this a weight belt has to be worn. The pressure of water at depth compresses the gas-filled neoprene resulting in a loss of buoyancy. This poses a potential buoyancy problem as a diver who is weighted for neutral buoyancy on the surface will become negatively buoyant at depth and this may lead to problems during controlled ascent. Care should be taken to determine the optimum level at which a state of neutral buoyancy should be achieved. This can be overcome by using an buoyancy compensating device (BCD).

Advantages:

1. Relatively inexpensive.
2. Relatively lightweight – easy to transport.
3. Easy to repair.
3. If punctured, continues to provide thermal protection and buoyancy.
5. Comfortable to wear.
6. Easy to swim in.
7. Little care and maintenance required.
8. Urination does not cause loss of efficiency.

Disadvantages:

1. Good fit is essential:
   - Flushing can occur if the suit is too loose or there are too many holes or zips.

– Aural barotrauma can occur if the hood is too tight; flood with water before diving.
2. Compresses with depth which reduces thermal protection. Not effective below 12°C (39°F).
3. Little thermal protection if there is a wind chill factor.
4. Loses buoyancy with depth.

b) THERMAL UNDERWEAR

Used under a dry suit when conditions are cold.

Material:
Flameproof wool, synthetic fibres, or foamed neoprene.

Design variations:
One piece; separate pants and jacket; some with feet enclosed; often with such extras as double zipper, boots and gloves.

Thermal protection:
The gas trapped in the material provides an insulating layer. The thickness of this insulating layer can be controlled by dry suit inflation and deflation facilities.

Potential thermal protection problems:
When heliox is used the gas trapped in the fibres does not provide a layer of insulation as helium rapidly conducts heat away from the divers, especially when it is under pressure.

Other considerations:
Foamed-neoprene underwear can be used when using hot water suits, both for added protection and for a back-up in case of malfunction.

Advantages:
1. Protection can be varied to suit the conditions.
2. Rugged and easy to repair.
3. Inexpensive enough for every diver to own one, so fit and cleanliness is the individual diver's responsibility.

Disadvantages:
1. When wet, loses most of its thermal protection.
2. Attention must be paid to maintenance to ensure personal hygiene.

c) DRY SUIT

The diver is intended to remain dry in these suits, which have seals around the cuffs and neck and/or face. Thermal underwear is usually worn underneath, either to provide insulation, as a protective layer, or to soak up sweat. In all cases gas must be able to flow into the suit because, under pressure, the gas in the suit is compressed until the suit is squeezed against the body. This is painful, restrictive and causes loss of buoyancy.

Material:
Rubberised canvas (for use with standard helmets), foamed-neoprene, reinforced rubber or various synthetic materials.

Design variations:
There are four types of dry suits: Standard, Unisuit, Conventional Dry and Constant Volume types.
1. The Standard suit (canvas/rubber) is connected directly to the helmet by a breastplate so the air flows from the helmet into the suit.
2. The Unisuit is a sung fitting foamed-neoprene suit with inflation/deflation facilities on the suit.
3. The Conventional Dry suit is a loose-fitting, strong, thin skin with suit deflation/inflation facilities on the suit.
4. The Constant Volume suit automatically maintains a constant volume with the suit regardless of the depth of the diver.

Thermal protection:
The main thermal protection comes from the layer of gas trapped between the diver's skin, the thermal underwear and the suit. This layer can be increased or decreased with suit inflation/deflation facilities or, in the case of the standard suit with the helmet's intake/exhaust facilities. When the suit is made from foamed-neoprene, the material also provides thermal protection from the layer of 'closed cells' of nitrogen.

Potential thermal protection problems:
When used with heliox the dry suit's thermal protection is reduced as the heliox does not provide an insulating layer but rather conducts the diver's body heat away into the surrounding water. Consequently, the dry suit is usually only used for diving in shallow cold waters up to 50m (165ft).

Other considerations:
BLOW UP. A most important aspect of the use of any dry suit is to learn to avoid a blow-up. This is when the suit inflates and forces the diver into an uncontrolled ascent. the suit pressure can, in some cases, completely immobilise the diver. Special care is therefore required to use the suits properly and to know the appropriate ways of dumping suit gas quickly. Any special dump valves must be carefully maintained and protected (from sand, for example) during a dive.

Advantages:
1. Thermal protection can be varied to suit the conditions.
2. Can be very rugged.
3. Can protect the diver in polluted or infected water.
4. Fit is not so critical.

Disadvantages:
1. If punctured, there is a loss of thermal protection, possibly some buoyancy and the dive may need to be aborted.
2. Blow-up possible.
3. Urination leads to discomfort and loss of insulation.
4. Requires careful maintenance/repair.

Active Thermal Protection Systems

a) HOT WATER SUIT (see Fig. 2)

Widely used in commerical diving, it is a loose--fitting suit with tubing to distribute the heated water around the inside of the suit. It has a control manifold so the diver can regulate the amount and distribution of hot water. It usually includes gloves and boots and should be worn with protective undersuit to avoid scalding in case of malfunction.

Material:
Foamed-neoprene insulation material with double-sided nylon lining.

Design variations:
A one-piece suit which usually includes gloves and boots. The mixed-gas suit can include a heated hood. The hot water can either vent through the arm, leg and neck seal (open circuit and most common system) or recirculate (closed circuit) to the heater unit to be re-warmed. This is used in special applications such as DLO submersibles.

Thermal protection:
Hot water is produced at the surface and transferred, either directly or via the diving bell, through insulating tubing to the diver for use in his hot water suit. The circulation of the warm water around the diver's body creates an active insulation barrier which allows the diver to easily maintain a normal body temperature and normal blood circulation. The hot water sacrifices its heat to the environment in place of the heat that would otherwise be drained from the diver's body. The diver himself is still losing metabolic heat from his body to the water in the suit. However, he is losing heat slowly enough for his body to sustain the heat loss comfortably. The hot water around the diver should not fall below 32°C (90°F) or hypothermia can result. Nor should it rise above 45°C (113°F) or the diver can be burned.

Fig. 2 Hot water suits

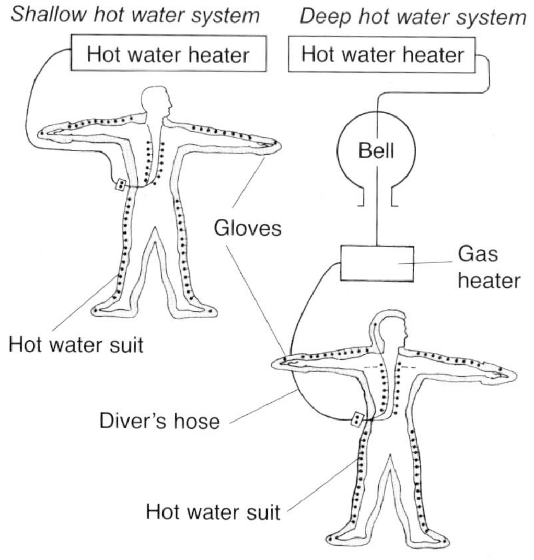

Shallow hot water system
Deep hot water system
Hot water heater
Hot water heater
Bell
Gloves
Gas heater
Hot water suit
Diver's hose
Hot water suit

For hot water suits, specially-insulated umbilicals are required to carry the hot water to the diver. Even so, heat loss from the umbilical can make controlling the temperature of the diver difficult, especially during deep dives.

Potential thermal protection problems:

- Fit: This is important – a suit which is too tight will prevent the hot water in the suit from circulating freely. The manufacturers usually recommend 2.5cm (1in) between the diver's body and the inside of the suit. A reduced circulation means the heat will not be distributed evenly throughout the suit and the diver will experience both hot and cold spots.
- Swimming: The average suit will hold 13–22 litres (3–5 gallons) of water. When a great deal of swimming is needed, this can become a hindrance. If for this reason the volume of water in the suit is reduced, the flow rate and the injection temperature must be carefully readjusted.
- Injection temperature: The injection temperature of hot water into the suit should be carefully controlled as the diver is often not aware of a gradual changes in the water temperature. In the initial stages of both hyper- and hypothermia, the diver is often unaware of his deteriorating condition.
- Heater unit: Care should be taken to ensure that the heater unit is compatible with the hot water suits and length and type of the umbilicals used.

Other considerations:
The water temperature within the suit is affected by:

- the injection temperature of the water entering the suit.
- the rate at which the water flow enters the suit.
- the amount of water in the suit.
- the exchange rate within the suit (which is obtained by dividing the number of litres/gallons of water in the suit by the rate of flow of water entering the suit).
- the insulation of the suit material.
- the depth and temperature of the water.
- the amount of surrounding water which gets into the suit, causing inefficiency.

Advantages:

1. Safe, comfortable, effective.
2. Diver is able to regulate the amount of thermal protection.

Disadvantages:

1. Can be difficult to swim in.
2. In DLO submersible operations, special consideration should be given to the efficiency of heat conservation.
3. In some open circuit suits constriction can cause burning.

b) DIVER GAS HEATING

Upon inhalation the body attempts to bring the vapour content of the inhaled gas up to 100% and bring the temperature up to that of the deep core temperature. If the gas is cold and dry it will take heat from the body to accomplish this. In air diving, because the diver is at a relatively shallow depth the gas is not very dense. As air is not a good conductor of heat, this is not a major problem. Helium, however, has six times the thermal conductivity of air and is only breathed at depths where it will be very dense. Consequently, if the diver breathes cold, oxy-helium he loses an enormous amount of body heat whenever he exhales. This can cause inefficiency of operation and can bring on hypothermia. For dives deeper than 150m (500ft) the diver's gas is usually heated to reduce this loss of body heat.

Hot water from the hot water suit supply is used to heat the breathing gas by means of a splitter block which is attached to the hot water suit inlet connection. It divides the hot water flow between the suit and breathing gas heating system. (see Fig. 4).

Fig. 4 Diver gas heating

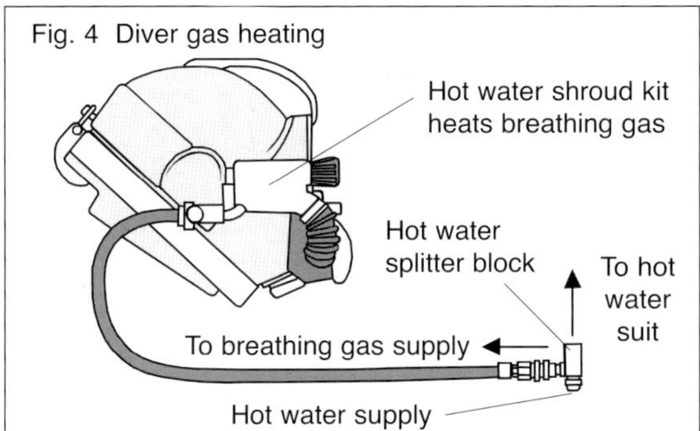
Hot water shroud kit
heats breathing gas
Hot water
splitter block
To hot
water
suit
To breathing gas supply
Hot water supply

Material:
Non-corrosive metals and plastic hose connections.

Design variations:
A deep diving version supplies more hot water to provide greater heating of heliox at depths greater than 200m.

Thermal protection:
Hot water circulates around and heats up the diver's breathing gas as it enters the helmet.

Potential thermal protection problems:
Any malfunction in the diver's hot water supply can affect the gas heating.

Other considerations:
As the diver goes deeper the gas inhalation temperature needs to be increased to maintain a safe body temperature (see Fig. 5).

Advantages:
1. Safe and effective.
2. Little care and maintenance is required.

Disadvantages:
1. No emergency back-up is available if the umbilical supply is lost.

Fig. 5 Minimum inspired gas temperatures

Depth		Minimum temperature	
m	ft	°C	°F
150	490	6	42
200	655	16	60
250	820	22	71
300	985	26	78
350	1150	28	83

c) ELECTRICALLY HEATED UNDERSUIT (EHS)

Rarely used in commercial diving. Light underwear (ie, long johns, etc) may be worn underneath the EHS as it is more practical to wash than the suit. A dry suit should be worn on top. Wearing thermal underwear between the EHS and the dry suit increases the efficiency of the thermal protection.

Material:
Electric heating wires on a woollen material or proprietary conducting material.

Design variations:
1. One-piece suit. Heating element extends over the whole body including the feet and up as far as the base of the neck but not over the shoulders where the weight of the helmet corselet might compress it against the skin. Gloves are designed to function when wet. The suit is run from low DC voltage. Although normally dry, the heated suit is safe even when flooded and will still provide a good measure of thermal protection in this condition.
2. Part-body cover, eg trunk only.

Thermal protection:
The EHS uses an electrical heating element to actively heat the diver.

Potential thermal protection problems:
Care must be taken to hang up the suit after use. It should never be turned on unless the suit is being worn as this might damage the heating element. Misuse may lead to the diver suffering burns. One electrical element in the suit should never overlap with another.

Other considerations:
The EHS is mainly used by military divers. For offshore use its main advantages would be in manned submersibles where there is already an electric power source aboard the submersible and where the need to reduce the size of the umbilical is of paramount importance.

Advantages:
1. Very efficient for heat produced.
2. Small heater unit required for maximum heat production.
3. Smaller umbilicals than hot water suits.
4. More effective than open circuit suits at greater depths.
5. More versatile for setting up at remote sites where hot water equipment is too cumbersome to install.

Disadvantages:

1. Diver does not receive as much heat as with hot water suits.
2. As four layers are needed for thermal protection, the diver's mobility can be reduced and care is needed in dressing.

d) SURFACE HOT WATER HEATER UNIT (SHU) AND BELL GAS HEATER (BGH)

The Surface Heater Unit (SHU) is placed in the ship or platform and should be near the diving spread. It is an important part of the diving system and its location on the ship/platform should be taken into consideration when the diving system is placed. The bell gas heater (BGH) is usually attached outside the bell.

Material:
Non-corrosive metals.

Design variations:
The SHU produces hot water which may be provided by steam from the ship's supply, propane, diesel or electrical immersion systems. An insulated umbilical delivers this hot water to the bell gas heater. Other variables, such as fresh or salt water, depth of operation and number of divers using the heating, determine the selection of the heater. Some companies custom-build heaters to fit the power source and may provide a back-up heat supply as a safety feature. The most popular heating method is by electricity to heat water at the surface. Bell gas heaters can also affect the choice of carbon dioxide adsorbent.

Thermal protection:
In surface-supplied diving the surface heater unit provides hot water directly to the diver for use in hot water suits and diver gas heaters. When a diving bell is used the surface heater unit sends the hot water to the bell. This hot water is used to heat the bell's breathing gases, the diver's hot water and his breathing gases.

Potential thermal protection problems:
If the design of the heater is inadequate, fluctuations within the system can occur and the diver can suffer burns. If the heater unit is unable to cope with the number of divers using the system, it may fail to heat the divers adequately, leading to hypothermia. Care should therefore be taken to provide a heater capable of providing controlled heat for the maximum number of divers likely to use the system.

Advantages:

1. Safe, simple, effective.
2. Rugged.
3. Good redundancy of heat/power supplies can be built in.
4. Excellent track record.

Disadvantages:

1. If the heater failed, the dive would have to be terminated.
2. Training is required to properly maintain the unit.
3. The diver can be unaware of slow temperature changes.

2. EMERGENCY THERMAL PROTECTION

A surface-supplied diver suffering from hypothermia would be brought to the surface and treated. However, when a bell is used it may not be possible to retrieve the diver to the surface since, in the worst possible case, the bell's umbilical would be severed. Consequently emergency equipment should be carried in the bell. The bell is already crowded with equipment so size is a major consideration for any emergency equipment.

There are three main types of emergency thermal protection:

a) Rebreather.

b) Survival suit.

c) Bell heater unit.

a) REBREATHER

When a diver breathes cold oxy-helium under pressure he loses body heat whenever he exhales. In an emergency, where all heating to the bell is lost, this can quickly incapacitate the diver leading to hypothermia and eventually death. Under most bottom conditions, divers without protection could be incapacitated in only a few hours.

Thermal protection:
A rebreather acts as a 'heat exchanger.' The diver exhales into the rebreather which picks up the heat and moisture from the expired breath. This then warms and moistens the next inhalation. To avoid carbon dioxide build-up a passive scrubber is needed. Ordinary CO_2-adsorbing agents are inefficient at low temperatures so either Sodalime or Sodasorb must be used.

Other considerations:
The CO_2 adsorbent can form a caustic solution if the rebreather gets wet and, although it can provide some thermal protection, the rebreather can lose much of its effectiveness.
Oxygen deficiency can occur if the rebreather is deep inside a sleeping bag (part of the survival suit) with no ventilation.
A combination of CO_2 build-up and oxygen deficiency can occur when the diver's breathing is shallow (due to hypothermia) and the rebreather's CO_2 adsorbent is almost used up. When the adsorbent is almost used up the 'dead space' can increase by almost 50%. Dead space is the portion of an exhaled breath which is rebreathed in the next breath. If the diver is severely hypothermic, or in a deep sleep, he may become hypoxic.
CO_2 build-up can occur when the CO_2 adsorbent is used up. However, this alerts the diver by stimulating breathing, so it is not a major problem.
Despite the potential problems it is much more dangerous to be without a re-breather than to risk the associated difficulties.

b) SURVIVAL SUIT

At low temperatures the diver loses heat, not only from exhaling, but also from his body, unless he is wearing protective clothing. Pressure renders foamed-neoprene suits ineffective as it compresses the material. In a helium environment, the helium will diffuse into the gas spaces of the neoprene. Other protective materials, such as goose down, are inadequate when wet. When helium is used its heat-conducting properties make normal insulating materials ineffective. There are two types of survival suits: passive and active.

Passive survival suits are designed to reduce body heat loss in a wet, helium, pressurised environment. Thermal protection is provided by the material from which the suit is made. These suits vary in design, however all cover the diver's entire body from head to feet. Only the nose and mouth are uncovered to allow the diver to breathe.

Passive survival suits or rebreathers on their own do not provide sufficient thermal protection to avoid hypothermia. In an emergency, both systems may be used (together with other survival equipment such as rations, mattress, towel, stowage bag, etc).

Active survival suits use emergency heater units to heat the suit using either hot water or an electrically-heated undersuit. They can also be used as operational suits. However, unlike normal operational suits, they are extremely efficient with low power consumption. The heater units required to heat these emergency suits are extremely small in comparison with the surface heater units and are usually carried aboard the bell.

The same suit is used both operationally and in an emergency. Two power sources are used – a surface power source (for operational use) and an emergency power supply affixed to the bell or submersible (for emergency use). In an emergency, active survival suits offer little or no protection if the emergency power supply is not fitted to the bell.

c) BELL HEATER UNIT

In the worst possible case, power and hot water supplies to the bell would be lost, so normal bell heater units would not function. An emergency heater unit may be incorporated into the layout of the bell for use in such situations. There are two types of emergency heater unit: chemical and electrical.

Chemical units produce an exothermic reaction (give off heat) when seawater is added. The seawater is then pumped through a heat exchanger equipped with blowers.

Electrical units are battery cells which, with the addition of seawater, generate heat or power. When heat is generated, the seawater surrounding the battery unit is pumped through a heat exchanger equipped with blowers. When power is generated this can be used to heat the bell or submersible.

Some emergency heater units only operate if the heater is upright. If the umbilical breaks, the bell will not necessarily fall to the bottom in an upright position. Careful consideration should, therefore, be given to placement of the heater unit in the bell.

Fig. 6. Typical active bell survival suit

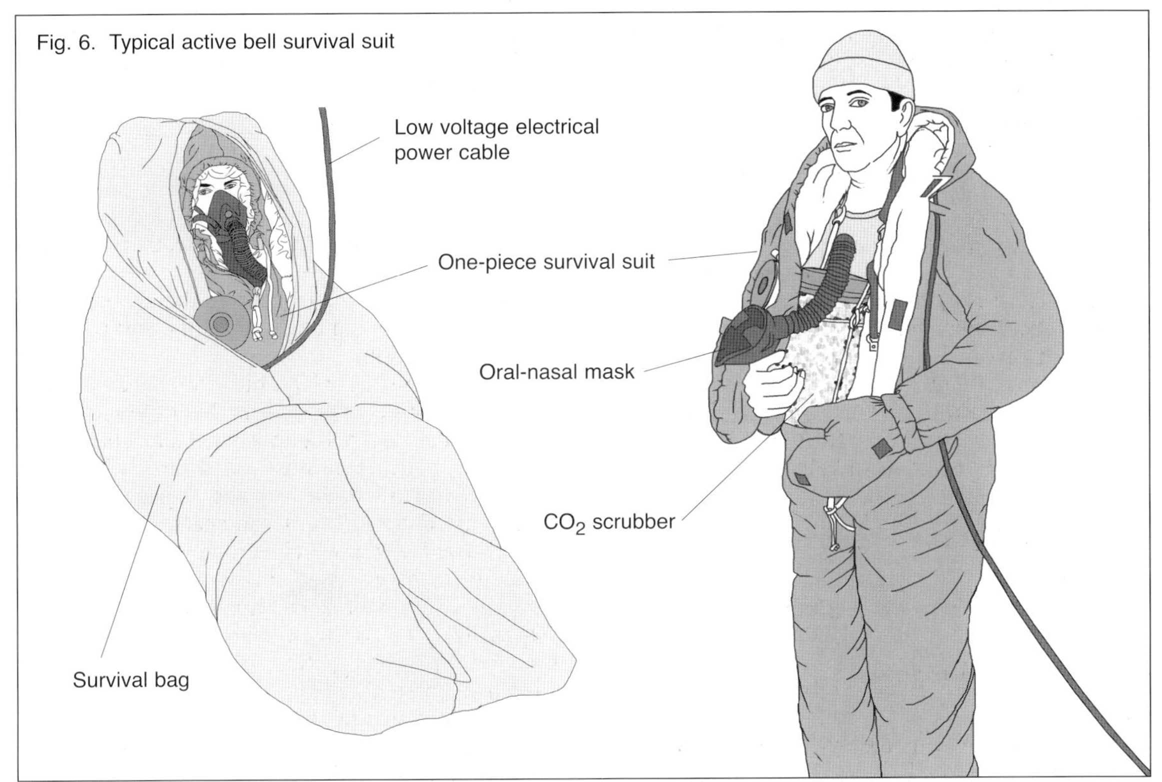
Low voltage electrical power cable
One-piece survival suit
Oral-nasal mask
CO_2 scrubber
Survival bag

3. COMBINED OPERATIONAL AND EMERGENCY THERMAL PROTECTION

Active thermal protection systems, which have both operational and emergency capabilities, are available for bells and submersibles.
Two examples are the Divematics and Société Eca systems.

DIVEMATICS SYSTEM

A pump, especially designed to maximise heat output circulates and heats the seawater used in the system. The pump, which is affixed to the bell or submersible, is powered by electricity from the surface and circulates the water through the hot water suits and diver gas heaters. In an emergency, when the supply is severed, an ethane gas heater unit (also affixed to the bell or submersible) provides an alternate power source. The emergency heater unit is activated from inside the bell or submersible.
A closed-circuit hot water suit and a diver gas heater actively protect the diver. The hot water in the suit sacrifices its heat and reduces the diver heat loss so that the diver can function safely and efficiently. Since the suit is closed-circuit, the diver remains dry, thus reducing the possibility of skin infection and irritation. The diver's breathing gases are actively heated by the hot water so that the heat loss from breathing is kept to a minimum.

SOCIETE ECA SYSTEM

The system is powered by a bell or submersible-mounted molten salt storage unit. Molten salts are chosen for their high energy storing capabilities. The storage unit is electrically-charged on the surface and then disconnected from the onboard circuit. The storage unit is linked with a heat exchanger and the molten salts give up their heat to the seawater which circulates through the diver gas heaters and hot water suits.
A specially-designed low flow rate suit and diver gas heater actively protect the diver. The suit, which is open-circuit, has a flow rate of 1–2 litres/min (compared to 5–8 l/min with most other open-circuit hot water suits). The hot water sacrifices its heat so that the diver's body temperature remains stable. The two layers of 4mm neoprene also provide some passive insulation. The diver's gas is actively heated by the hot water so that heat loss from breathing is kept to a minimum.
The combined system of thermal protection is designed to maximise space and equipment when providing operation and emergency thermal protection. Consequently, it would be inadvisable to mix parts of the system with other equipment without first checking with the manufacturers.
Because the systems are fitted to the bell or submersible, the equipment is in constant use and should be maintained in good working condition.
The hot water umbilical is only from the bell or submersible to the diver so it is easier to control the diver's hot water temperature and heat loss from umbilical is reduced to a minimum. A lower injection temperature can be used which increases the efficiency of operation.

Advantages:

1. Both operational and emergency capabilities are available.
2. Reduces heat loss through umbilicals.
3. It is independent of the surface.
4. Very efficient heat production.
5. More efficient at greater depths than surface-supplied hot water suits.

Disadvantages:

1. Limited storage capacity in submersibles.
2. Any serious malfunction can halt diving operations.

SECTION SIX
Communications

SECTION SEVEN
Navigation and Buoyage

SECTION EIGHT
Cylinder Identification

SECTION NINE
Marine Fouling

SECTION TEN
Concrete Blemishes

6.1 RADIO TELEPHONY (RT)

Radio telephony is the method of communication used between vessels and the shore. A vessel or platform can be connected to the worldwide telecommunications network via the Coast Station Ratio Telephony Service. RT is used widely by offshore installations to nearby ships or aircraft, or to the nearest shore radio station for onward relay (as the range is short).

RT is transmitted by voice over radio circuits, usually in plain language but can be by ICS (International Code of Signals) where language difficulties are encountered.

A 'simplex' arrangement is where one party only can transmit at any one time. A 'duplex' type of communication is like an ordinary telephone arrangement when both parties can talk at the same time and can, therefore, interrupt each other.

There are four ranges of frequency:

1. Long range high frequency (HF) worldwide service. (In the UK this is conducted through Portishead Radio).
2. Medium frequency (MF) which has a range of about 200 miles.
3. Very high frequency (VHF) which has a range limited to little more than line of sight between aerials and 55–65 kilometres (35–40 miles) between coastal shipping and coastal radio stations. It is the system most used by offshore installations.
4. UHF (ultra high frequency) is occasionally used in place of VHF to avoid interference in busy areas. UHF is suitable for walkie-talkies.

VHF call procedure

Before you start make sure that you know:

a) How to operate the radio/telephone.
b) To whom you are speaking.
c) On what frequency to transmit.
d) And be prepared for any likely questions.

Call procedure:

a) Turn on your receiver to Channel 16 and listen before calling. If the channel is engaged wait until it is free.
b) Transmit the name or call sign of the station that you are calling (up to three times only).
c) Transmit the words, "This is," followed by the name or call sign of your own station (up to three times only).
d) When contact is established:
   - transmit your own name or call sign once.
   - nominate your working channel/frequency (not Channel 16) and ensure that the receiving station has that particular channel facility.
   - transfer to your chosen working frequency. *Note*: Many offshore companies have their own channels.
   - Transmit, "Do you hear me? Over."
   - Wait for response, "I hear you loud and clear/weak but clear/loud but distorted," etc).
   - Deliver message.

e) Use the phonetic alphabet (see Fig. 1) for spelling difficult or unusual words.
f) Use prowords (see Table 2) wherever possible.
g) If you require an answer or continuation with the conversation, end your transmission with, "Over." If you do not require an answer or continuation say, "Out."
   Note: "Over and out" is contradictory and should never be used.
h) On completion of transmission return the radio channel selector to 16.

VHF operating technique

a) Always give precedence to distress calls or urgent calls.
b) Do not jam channels with unnecessary conversation.
c) Avoid interrupting.
d) Avoid swearing.
e) Try not to say, "um" or "er" between phrases.
f) Speak steadily and at a medium speed.
g) Always keep your mouth close to the microphone.
h) Speak only slightly louder than normal conversation.
i) Pitch your voice slightly higher than normal.
j) Use prowords where possible.

Prowords (procedure words) are short words or phrases that make conversation by radio telephone clearer. A selection of some important and commonly use prowords is given in Fig. 2.

Fig. 1 Phonetic alphabet and numerals

Alphabet
(place emphasis on emboldened syllables)

A	Alfa	**AL**FAH	N	November	NOV**EM**BER
B	Bravo	**BRAH**VOH	O	Oscar	**OSS**KAR
C	Charlie	**CHAR**LEE	P	Papa	**PAH**PAH
D	Delta	**DELL**TAH	Q	Quebec	KEH**BEK**
E	Echo	**ECK**OH	R	Romeo	**ROW**MEEOH
F	Foxtrot	**FOKS**TROT	S	Sierra	SEE**AIR**RAH
G	Golf	**GOLF**	T	Tango	**TAN**GO
H	Hotel	HOH**TEL**	U	Uniform	**YOU**NEEFORM
I	India	**IN**DEEAH	V	Victor	**VIK**TAH
J	Juliet	**JEW**LEE**ETT**	W	Whiskey	**WISS**KEE
K	Kilo	**KEE**LOH	X	X-ray	**ECKS**RAY
L	Lima	**LEE**MAH	Y	Yankee	**YANG**KEE
M	Mike	**MIKE**	Z	Zulu	**ZOO**LOO

Numerals
(apart from call signs and grid references, all figures should be preceded by the word, "Figures")

0	**ZEE**RO	5	**FIVE**-ER
1	**WUN**	6	**SICK**SER
2	**TOO**	7	**SEH**VEN
3	THUH-**REE**	8	**ATE**
4	**FOW**-ER	9	**NINE** -ER

Fig. 2 Prowords (procedure words)

Proword	Use or meaning
MAYDAY (3 times)	The **distress** signal. Request for immediate assistance. Used when threatened by grave or imminent danger. Your call sign and position are of vital importance and should always follow the phrase, "Mayday, mayday, mayday."
PANPAN (3 times)	The **urgency** signal. Used for a message concerning the safety of a ship or person. If you require medical assistance ask your coast guard radio station for 'Medico Service' and you will be connected to the casualty department of a local hospital (no charge).
SECURITÉ (3 times) *(pronounce Say-cure-ee-tay)*	The **safety** signal. Mostly used to transmit important navigational or meteorological warnings. (Usually originate onshore).
Acknowledge	Have you received and understood this message?
Affirmative	'Yes' or 'Permission granted.'
All after . . .	To identify part of a message. For example, "repeat all after . . ."
All before . . .	To identify part of a message. For example, "repeat all after. . ." Used in conjunction with other words.
All stop	Stop the action and wait for further instructions.
Break	Separation between address, text, signature, etc of a dictated telegram.
Come up	Lift (on a winch or crane).
Come down	Lower (on a winch or crane).
Confirm	My version is . . . Is that correct?
Correct	You are correct.
Correction	Cancels the word or phrase just sent or indicated.
Easy	Lift or lower slowly (on a winch or crane) 'Slowly' is also used.
Go ahead	Proceed with your message.
How do you read?	Can you understand what I am saying?
I read back	In response to 'read back.' The message already sent is repeated (usually for confirmation).
I say again	Used by the sender when conditions are bad to emphasize the important areas, or when a repetition is requested.
I spell	Used when spelling out a word or abbreviation. Use the phonetic alphabet (see Fig. 1).
Negative	'No' or 'Permission not granted.'
Net message	Message for all stations.
Out*	Transmission is over and no reply is expected.
Over*	Transmission is over but a reply is expected.
Read back	Please repeat the whole message.
Roger	Message received and understood.
Say again	Used by the receiver when requiring the whole message to be repeated.
Silence *(pronounce See-lonce)*	All stations maintain a radio silence and await direction.
Silence fini *(pronounce See-lonce fee-nee)*	Silence is lifted.
Slowly	Lift or lower slowly (on a winch or crane) 'Easy' is also used.
Speak slower	Speak more slowly.
Standby	Wait for another message.
Verify	Confirm the accuracy of your last message.
Wait	The station requires to consider the reply to a transmission. 'Wait' followed by a number indicates the time (in minutes) required to consider.
Wilco	I have understood your message and will carry out the instructions. (Must only be used after verification of the instructions by repeating them).

* Note: The combination "over and out" is contradictory and should never be used.

6.2 DIVER VOICE COMMUNICATIONS

Voice communication by underwater telephone is the primary source of diver/surface communication. Line pull signals serve as a back-up. Direct diver-to-diver conversations are possible without apparatus where both divers are using helmets. By touching the helmets together an acoustic connection is made and the divers are able to talk to each other. Standard visual hand signals also supplement diver-to-diver communications.

There are four main types of voice communication systems:

1. *Through-water acoustic system.*
   Consists of a microphone, amplifier, power supply and transducer. It transduces speech into the water through an underwater loudspeaker. The signal is picked up by a hydrophone or by nearby divers.

2. *Through-water amplitude modulated (AM) system.*
   Consists of a microphone, amplifier, power supply modulator and underwater transducer. In this system a carrier wave is modulated by the speech signal and can be understood only by a diver or tender with a receiver and modulator.

3. *Hardwire system.*
   Similar to a telephone: consists of a microphone, a cable through which the signal is transmitted and a receiver. This system requires an umbilical and is the most commonly used system for surface-supplied and diver lockout communications.

   Hardwire systems are of three kinds:

   i) The original intercommunication system consisting of an amplifier, a diver's reproducer and a combination lifeline/amplifier cable operated by a surface tender controlling tender-to-diver or diver-to-diver communications by switching.

   ii) Another DIS (diver intercommunication system – sometimes called DUCS (diver underwater communication system) is similar to the above except that it is a party line system in which any diver may speak to another without switching. DIS I and DIS II are used mostly with hard-hat equipment.

   iii) DIS III is a surface/underwater system between the tender and up to three divers in surface-supplied helmets or masks and includes voice correction (unscrambling) circuitry to compensate for speaking in an oxy-helium atmosphere.

4. *Non-acoustic wireless system.*
   An electric field, a voice-actuated microphone and carried on the back. It is designed for diver-to-diver communications with a range of only 30–60m (100–200ft). It can also be used for diver-surface or surface-surface communications.

Procedure

GENERAL

1. After establishing contact, communications often open with a readability check. The standard phrase is "How do you read?" The reply is usually given as "loud and clear," "broken," "distorted" or "faint."

2. If all crew members are familiar with the system, the standard readability scale is more precise:

   1: Unreadable.

   2: Readable but with difficulty.

   3: Readable now and then.

   4: Readable.

   5: Perfectly readable.

   The response to "How do you read?" would be, for example, "Reading you strength 4."

3. On a multinational worksite agree communications language procedure before the operation starts. Have written aide-memoires at each communications site.

4. Only speak if it is necessary. If you don't have anything to say, don't say it!

5. Speak clearly, at a steady pace and at normal volume.

6. Never assume that a message has been received. Repeat it until you get a response.

7. If you want a message repeated say, "Say again."

8. A message which needs to be repeated should be repeated using the same words. When it is obvious that the repeats are not being understood you should say, "Rephrasing message" and say the message again in a different way.

9. If a message is failing to get through and you suddenly need to say something different indicate the change of subject by saying, "Cancel that last" before giving a new, different message.

10. When acknowledging a message it is better to repeat back the message, or a summary of it, rather than just saying, "Roger." 'Roger' on its own does not indicate that the message has been received correctly.

11. In general, the worse the communications link and the more important the message the more essential it is that you check that your message has been correctly understood.

12. When there has been a pause in the conversation identify yourself and the person to whom you are talking at the start of the next message.

13. Use the standard words and phrases correctly. If in doubt, use plain English.

14. Let the other person know when you have finished speaking, usually by saying "over."

15. Have a procedure to deal with communications breakdown. In most cases you will carry out the last instruction received and then stop the operation. Alternative methods of communication can then be used.

16. Complete recordings should be made of all dives including pre-dive checks and blow-down. The recordings should be retained until it is clear that no problems were met during or after the dive.

17. Tapes of incidents or accidents should be carefully removed (to prevent them from being over-recorded) and stored in a secure place pending investigation.

SURFACE-TO-DIVER

18. Topside should pay attention to the diver's breathing rhythm. Try not to talk over loud diver inhalation noises.

19. Break long messages into short sections the length of one breath or shorter. This is because the diver may have to shut off his air to hear you. Gas recovery systems, which have no exhaust noises, are much quieter.

20. The telephone operator should not talk to the diver whenever power is applied or when cables are moving because it prevents the diver from warning the surface of any problems.

DIVER-TO-SURFACE

21. Keep each message as simple as you can, especially on the diver-to-surface links which are particularly difficult.

22. Arrange your diving tasks so as to avoid long periods of continuous talking since it reduces breathing efficiency.

Language

BEFORE GOING UNDERWATER:

1. Mark and label tools and equipment with sizes and/or reference numbers before use so as to avoid making mistakes and wasting time.

2. Agreed names should be developed and used for tools, components, positioning and other aspects of the diver's work. If possible these names and words should be three syllables long as they are the easiest words to understand.

UNDERWATER:

1. Use the phonetic alphabet wherever it is needed.

2. Always use the word 'zero.' Do not use 'nought,' 'oh' or 'nothing.'

3. Use metric measurements whenever possible and always say what units you are using, eg, "six metres."

4. Avoid using fractions where possible. If you have to use a fraction repeat it in a different way, eg : "one sixth, that is, one over six."

5. For all 'teen' numbers repeat in a different way, eg "thirteen, that is, one three."

6. For all 'tens' repeat in a different way, eg "thirty, that is, three zero."

7. Be specific. Don't add endings such as, '...ish.' Say "red" not "reddish."

Factors which can improve diver voice communications intelligibility

1. SYSTEM DESIGN
   a) High quality, robust components.
   b) Compatibility of components.
   c) Good acoustics including:
      – mask/helmet design.
      – elimination of noise from electrical interference, vibration and explosives.

2. REDUCTION OF AMBIENT NOISES FROM:
   a) diver exhaust gas.
   b) diver free-flow.
   c) task noises from sources such as: air-driven tools, hydraulic tools, gas escape, water escape, surface machinery, vibrations, explosives.
   d) marine animals.
   e) pingers and transponders.
   f) surface vessel noises, especially DP vessels.

3. PERSONNEL
   Divers and tenders should ideally speak the same language, with similar regional accents and have no speech impediments.

4. LANGUAGE
   Personnel should be trained in and be familiar with the use of standard vocabulary, prowords and procedures (see 'Radio Telephony', p. 248).

6.3 DIVER HAND SIGNALS

These signals are a selection of hand signals widely used throughout the diving industry. Regional variations exist and so, before diving, check that everyone is using the same code.

Signals should be given slowly, deliberately exaggerated and acknowledged if understood. At night the diver should illuminate his signalling hand by a torch held in his other hand.

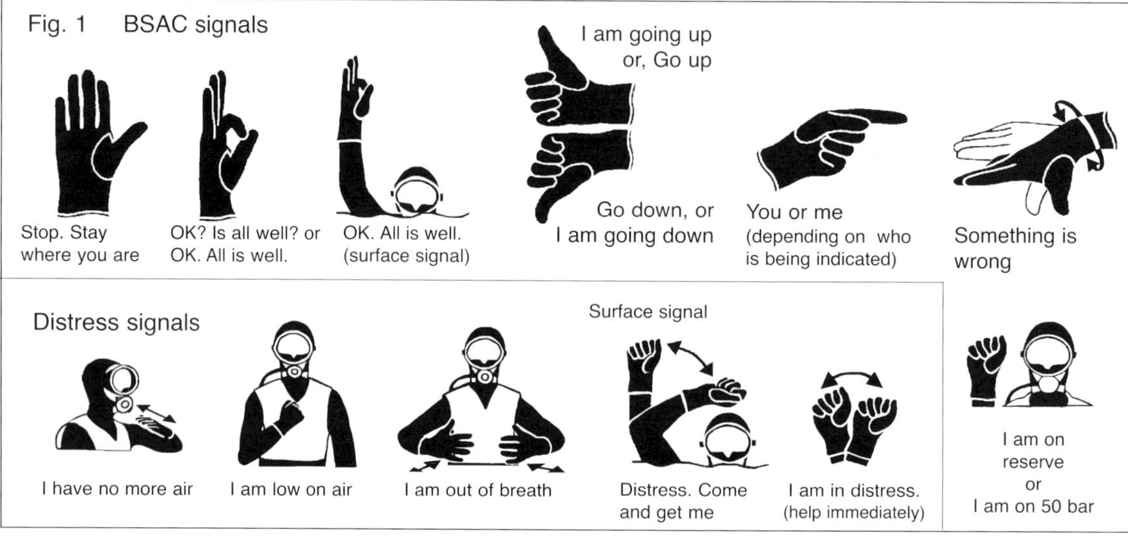
Fig. 1 BSAC signals
Stop. Stay where you are
OK? Is all well? or OK. All is well.
OK. All is well. (surface signal)
I am going up or, Go up
Go down, or I am going down
You or me (depending on who is being indicated)
Something is wrong
Distress signals
I have no more air
I am low on air
I am out of breath
Surface signal
Distress. Come and get me
I am in distress. (help immediately)
I am on reserve or I am on 50 bar

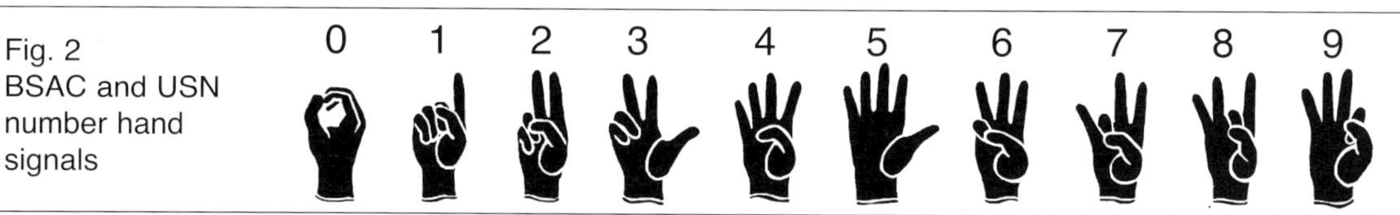
Fig. 2 BSAC and USN number hand signals
0 1 2 3 4 5 6 7 8 9

Fig. 3 US Navy signals

(gloved hand)

Stop

I am OK.

Are you OK?

I am OK. (at a distance, on the surface)

Something is wrong

What time? What depth?

Level off, or How deep?

You lead. I'll follow

Slow down. Take it easy.

Which direction?

Go that way.

Go down. I am going down.

Go up. I am going up.

Distress signals

Help. Pick me up. (surface signal)

I am out of air.

I need to buddy breathe.

I am cold.

I have ear trouble.

Something is wrong. (Night signal, at a distance.)

6.4 DIVER ROPE SIGNALS

There are a number of situations where a diver should be in physical contact with his partner or his tender by means of a rope. Such situations might include a low visibility search or a failure of the telephone link.

Care should be taken to keep lines free from possible entanglement. If a lifeline gets fouled, or has turns around the shot rope, it may be impossible to get signals through.

In order that the diver can feel the signal, any slack must first be taken up; then the line should be pulled firmly and decisively. Most signals are acknowledged by repeating the signal. Never assume a message has been received without acknowledgement. If the acknowledgement is not properly received, the message should be sent again. Persistent lack of confirmation means there is a problem: there may be too much slack in the rope, the rope may be fouled or the diver may be in trouble. Act immediately to resolve the problem.

The Royal Navy and US Navy use their own codes of signals. If rope signals are to be used it is essential that the diver and tender agree on which system is to be used *before* the dive starts.

Royal Navy rope signals (see Fig. 1)

All signals are to be preceded by one pull to attract attention and the signal itself should not be made until the diver has responded.

Rope signals are called either 'pulls' or 'bells' according to how they are sent. Pulls are long steady pulls. Bells are short, sharp tugs similar to striking a ship's bell and are given in pairs.

US Navy line-pull signals

Lines must be kept free of slack while line-pull signals are in operation. All signals, except 4+4+4 pulls, must be acknowledged immediately. Every 2–3 minutes the tender should send a single pull to ensure that the diver is OK. The diver must return the signal to indicate the he is alright. Failure of the diver to respond must be treated as an emergency and the standby diver should investigate immediately.

Only three signals do not need to be answered immediately. Diver signals, 'Haul me up' and 'Haul me up immediately' are answered by initiating the action; the Tender signal, 'Come up' is answered by the diver only when he is ready to leave the bottom.

Fig. 1. Royal Navy rope signals

a) General signals

Signal	From tender	From diver
1 PULL	To call attention. Are you OK?	To call attention. I am OK. Arrived at or have left bottom.
2 PULLS	Am sending down a rope	Send down a rope.
3 PULLS	You have come too far. Go down slowly till I stop you.	I am going down.
4 PULLS	Come up.	May I come up?

b) Emergency signals

Signal	From tender	From diver
SUCCESSION OF PULLS (more than 4)	Emergency signal. Come up immediately.	Pull me up. Pull me up immediately.
4 PULLS + 2 BELLS	Come up. Hurry up. Come up – surface decompression.	I want to come up. Assist me up.
4 PULLS + 5 BELLS	Come up on your SMB?	May I come up on my SMB?
SUCCESSION OF 2 BELLS	–	Am fouled and need assistance.
SUCCESSION OF 3 BELLS	–	Am fouled but can clear myself.

c) Direction and working signals

Signal	From tender	From diver
1 PULL	Search where you are.	Hold on. Stop
2 BELLS	Go to end of distance line.	Pull up.
3 BELLS	Face shotline, then go right.	Lower.
4 BELLS	Face shotline, then go left.	Take up slack. Give me slack.
5 BELLS	Come in to your shotline.	Have found/started/completed work.

Fig. 2. US Navy line-pull signals

a) General signals

Signal	From tender	From diver
1 PULL	Are you OK? Stop (if descending).	I am OK. Stop (if descending). I am on the bottom.
2 PULLS	Am going down. You have come up too far – go down till we stop you.	Lower. Give me slack.
3 PULLS	Stand by to ascend.	Take up my slack.
4 PULLS	Come up.	Haul me up.
2 + 1 PULLS	I understand. Talk to me.	I understand. Talk to me.
3 + 2 PULLS	Ventilate.	Give me more air.
4 + 3 PULLS	Circulate.	Give me less air.

b) Emergency signals from diver*

Signal	From tender	From diver
2 + 2 + 2 PULLS	–	I am fouled and need diver assistance.
3 + 3 + 3 PULLS	–	I am fouled but can clear myself.
4 + 4 + 4 PULLS	–	Haul me up immediately.

c) Searching signals

Signal	From tender	From diver
7 PULLS	Searching signals starting/stopping now.	I am starting/stopping searching signals now.
1 PULL	Stop and search where you are.	I am stopping and searching where I am.
2 PULLS	Move away (if given slack); Move back (if strain taken up).	I am moving away from the shot weight.
3 PULLS	Face umbilical and go right.	I am facing the shot weight and going right.
4 PULLS	Face umbilical and go left.	I am facing the shot weight and going left.

* All emergency signals must be answered except 4+4+4 pulls

6.5 RADIO TELEGRAPHY (WT)

Radio telegraphy is no longer widely used but is included here for reference only. As it is sent in Morse it requires a skilled operator. It is very fast, precise and capable of being transmitted over long distances. It was employed mostly for ship-to-ship or ship-to-shore transmissions.

WT can use any of four services: Long range WT for onward transmission to any ship or station via a main national radio station; medium range transmissions via one of several local stations, medium range radio telegram service and for weather and navigational broadcasts.

Sending morse requires a great deal of skill and practice to get the right rhythm and spacing. If a dot is taken as the unit of time, the correct spacing is as follows:

Dot = 1 unit; Dash = 3 units;

Space between each dot or dash in a letter =1 unit

Space between each letter or symbol = 3 units

Space between each word or group = 7 units.

By whatever method Morse is sent, it must be remembered that a dash is three times the length of a dot and that there must be a slight pause between each letter – otherwise, for example, EE would be read as I, or AE as R. The pause between each word must be even more pronounced.

ALPHABET			NUMERALS
A · –	J · – – –	S · · ·	1 · – – – –
B – · · ·	K – · –	T –	2 · · – – –
C – · – ·	L · – · ·	U · · –	3 · · · – –
D – · ·	M – –	V · · · –	4 · · · · –
E ·	N – ·	W · – –	5 · · · · ·
F · · – ·	O – – –	X – · – –	6 – · · · ·
G – – ·	P · – – ·	Y – · – –	7 – – · · ·
H · · · ·	Q – – · –	Z – – · ·	8 – – – · ·
I · ·	R · – ·		9 – – – – ·
			0 – – – – –

6.6 LIGHT SIGNALS

Light signals can have the same meaning as flags in the International Code of Signals (ICS) but are transmitted by lamp light using Morse Code. Messages can be sent in plain language but there are a variety of procedure signals which can save time. The ICS can be understood in nine languages.

- Single letter signals are urgent, important or frequently used.
- Two letter signals are general signals.

Light signals are particularly effective for attracting the attention of specific recipient and can be seen by day as well as by night.

Procedure

A signal by flashing light comprises the following:

1. *The call*. This may be either the general call (AA AA AA, etc) if it is required to attract the attention of all stations within the sight or of a station whose identity is not known. The call is repeated until response is made in the form of the answering signal, TTT, etc.
2. *The identity*. The transmitting station then makes 'DE' followed by its identity signal or name. This is repeated back by the receiving station which then signals its own identity signal.
3. *The text*. This may consist of plain language or code groups the latter being preceded by the signal 'YU'. The receiving station acknowledges the receipt of each word or code group by the letter 'T'.
4. *The Ending*. The transmitting station indicates the end of the signal with letters 'AR' which are acknowledged by the receiving station with 'R' meaning 'received.'

Table 1. Procedure Signals for Light Signalling

	Sign	Morse symbol	Meaning
Only used when sending Morse by light.	AA AA AA repeat until answered	·–·– ·–·–	Call up
	TTTTTT repeat until answered	– – – –	Answering signal
	T	–	Word received
	AAA	·– ·– ·–	Full stop or decimal point
	EEEEEEE	· · · · · · · · · ·	Erase
Used when sending Morse by light or other methods.	DE	–·· ·	From
	RPT	·–· ·––· –	Repeat signal
	AA	·– ·–	All after
	AB	·– –···	All before
	WA	·–– ·–	Word or group after
	WB	·–– –···	Word or group before
	BN	–··· –·	Word or group between
	AR	·– ·–·	Message ends
	AS	·– ···	Waiting signal or period signal
	C	–·–·	Affirmative – YES
	R	·–·	Received
	YT4	–·–– – ····–	I cannot read your morse signalling lamp
	YU	–·–– ··–	Am going to communicate by International Code

6.7 FLAG SIGNALS

Flag signals are used by ship or shore authorities where a continuous message is displayed for general information in daylight only. The International Flag Code uses 26 alphabet flags, 10 numeral pennants, an answering pennant and 3 or 4 substitute (or repeater) pennants. Each alphabet flag represents a letter of the alphabet and most also have a specific meaning. Substitute flags are used to repeat letters or numerals that precede them thereby making it unnecessary to carry extra sets of flags. There are three substitute pennants; a fourth sub is used by NATO and other western navies.

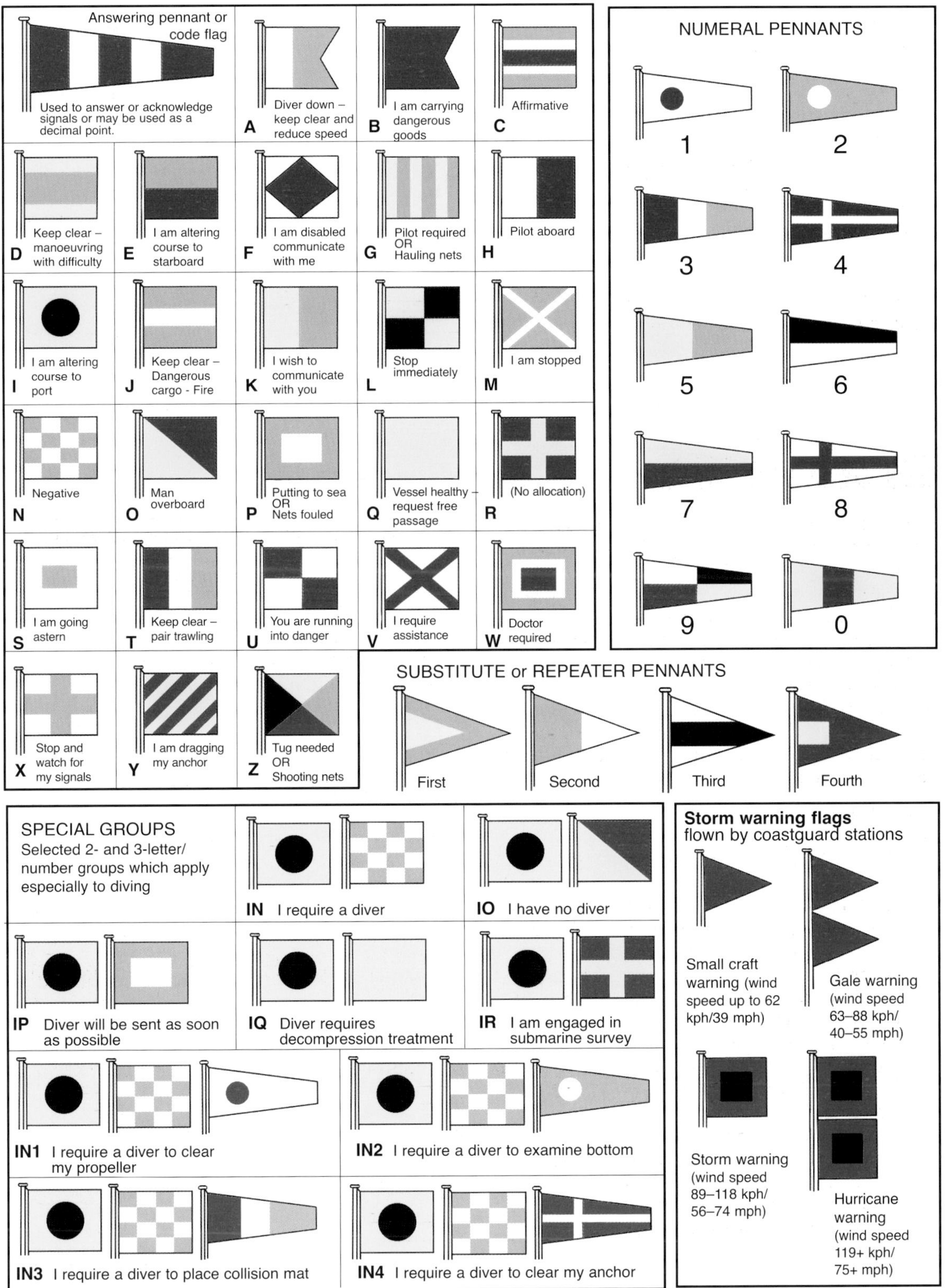

Answering pennant or code flag
Used to answer or acknowledge signals or may be used as a decimal point.
A Diver down – keep clear and reduce speed
B I am carrying dangerous goods
C Affirmative
D Keep clear – manoeuvring with difficulty
E I am altering course to starboard
F I am disabled communicate with me
G Pilot required OR Hauling nets
H Pilot aboard
I I am altering course to port
J Keep clear – Dangerous cargo - Fire
K I wish to communicate with you
L Stop immediately
M I am stopped
N Negative
O Man overboard
P Putting to sea OR Nets fouled
Q Vessel healthy – request free passage
R (No allocation)
S I am going astern
T Keep clear – pair trawling
U You are running into danger
V I require assistance
W Doctor required
X Stop and watch for my signals
Y I am dragging my anchor
Z Tug needed OR Shooting nets
NUMERAL PENNANTS
1
2
3
4
5
6
7
8
9
0
SUBSTITUTE or REPEATER PENNANTS
First
Second
Third
Fourth
SPECIAL GROUPS
Selected 2- and 3-letter/ number groups which apply especially to diving
IN I require a diver
IO I have no diver
IP Diver will be sent as soon as possible
IQ Diver requires decompression treatment
IR I am engaged in submarine survey
IN1 I require a diver to clear my propeller
IN2 I require a diver to examine bottom
IN3 I require a diver to place collision mat
IN4 I require a diver to clear my anchor
Storm warning flags flown by coastguard stations
Small craft warning (wind speed up to 62 kph/39 mph)
Gale warning (wind speed 63–88 kph/ 40–55 mph)
Storm warning (wind speed 89–118 kph/ 56–74 mph)
Hurricane warning (wind speed 119+ kph/ 75+ mph)

6.8 DISTRESS AT SEA

There are a number of emergencies that the diver may be faced with and which will demand immediate action on his part. Diving Superintendents will have worked out procedures for dealing with diving emergencies before they happen and many operating companies have their own instructions. Every diver should be familiar with these and be prepared to apply them the moment things start to go wrong. Chaos often attends disaster and at such times it is easy to make the wrong decisions.

Distress is critical, life-threatening circumstances from which the victims are unable to extricate themselves and therefore need immediate assistance.

Some examples of distress at sea might include the collapse of a structure, the collision of two ships, an uncontrollable blow-out followed by a fire, the ditching of a helicopter. In all such events the first call for help would probably be by radio telephone (RT). The signal also might be given by radio telegraphy (WT) by the transmission of an alarm signal followed by SOS in morse code. A third method might be by visual signals (see Fig. 1).

Search and rescue (SAR) organisation

Coastal radio stations in the UK keep watch on the international distress frequency which is 2182 kHz MF on the radio telephone and 500 kHz by radio telegraphy. Most ships and coastguard radio stations keep watch on Channel 16, 156.8 MHz.

Most maritime countries maintain a life-saving service for anyone in distress. Around the UK coast and between latitudes 45°N to 61°N and as far west as longitude 30°W, HM Coastguard will normally co-ordinate and initiate search and rescue measures. To be effective, a MAYDAY call must be accompanied by the victim's position and, if possible, the nature of the distress and the aid required. Failure to provide these details may greatly reduce the chances of being found.

Good communications are essential and of great importance in order to keep the rescue under control.

There are some fundamental rules for surviving distress:

1. Try to stay with the boat or wreckage so that you can be spotted more easily. Keep together.
2. If obliged to swim in cold water, keep exertion to a minimum to conserve heat and energy.
3. If being rescued by a helicopter, abandon any support or craft that could endanger the helicopter. Allow the winch wire to dip (earth) in the sea before touching it. Never secure the winch wire to a boat or structure.
4. Use flares sparingly and only when they are likely to be seen.
5. Never give up hope. Many a rescue has been successful after all chances have apparently faded.

Fig. 1 Visual distress signals

A rocket parachute red light flare

A hand-held red light flare

Rockets/shells firing red stars

Orange coloured smoke

Flames on a vessel

Square flag above or below a ball

Article of clothing flown as a flag

Raising and lowering of arms

Ensign hoisted upside down

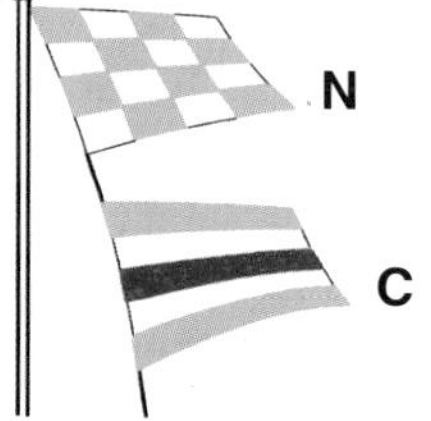
N
C
ICS flags NC

ASSISTANCE SIGNALS

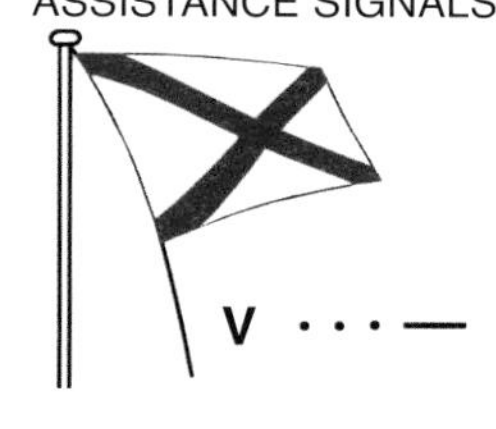
V · · · —
I require assistance

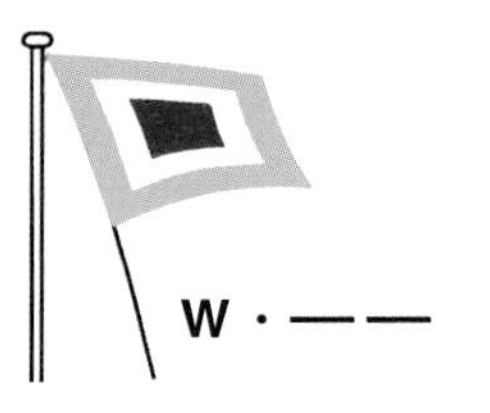
W · — —
I require medical assistance

7 NAVIGATION AND BUOYAGE

Navigation buoys are used to mark the approximate position of underwater features such as obstructions. In order to standardize worldwide buoyage, the IALA Maritime Buoyage System is used. The meaning of any buoy is defined by its colour, shape and topmark (during daylight) and by the colour and rhythm of its light at night. The same marks are used worldwide except for lateral (channel) marking buoys. For this reason the IALA system is divided into two regions: A and B (see Fig. 1).

Fig. 1 World Map showing IALA Maritime Buoyage System Regions A & B

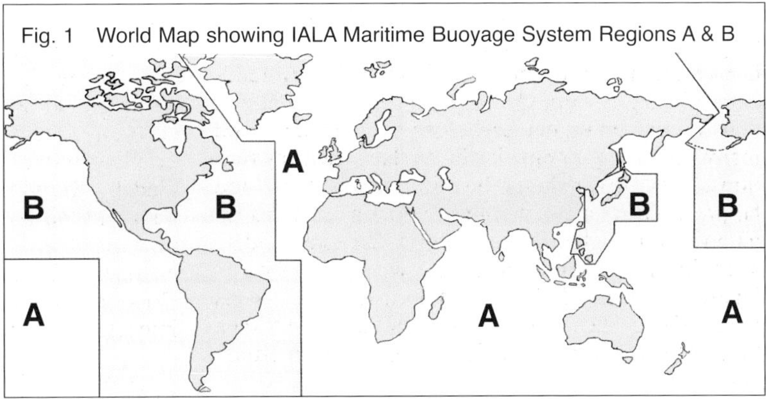

A
B
B
B
B
A
A
A

In general region A uses the UK system of buoyage and Region B the US system. The main difference between the two regions relates to the colour of the lateral marks.

Lateral marks are used in conjunction with a direction of buoyage to indicate the sides of a channel when approaching a harbour, river or estuary from seaward. In both regions can-shaped buoys indicate the port side of the channel and cone-shaped buoys, the starboard side. However, in Region B starboard marks are red and port marks green and vice versa in Region A (See Fig. 2). Other marks are the same in both regions (see Figs. 3 and 4).

Fig. 2 Lateral (Channel) marks

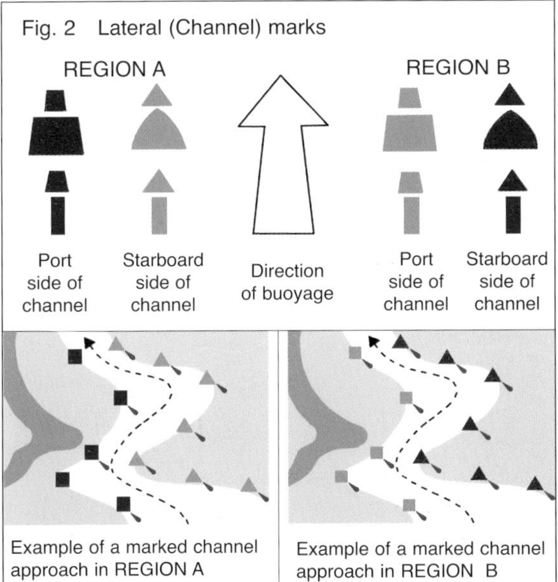

REGION A
REGION B
Port side of channel
Starboard side of channel
Direction of buoyage
Port side of channel
Starboard side of channel
Example of a marked channel approach in REGION A
Example of a marked channel approach in REGION B

Fig. 3 Other marks

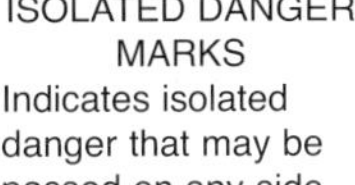

ISOLATED DANGER MARKS
Indicates isolated danger that may be passed on any side.

SAFEWATER MARKS
Indicates navigable water all around that position.

SPECIAL MARKS
Indicates a special feature referred to on the chart.

Isolated danger marks indicate isolated dangers of limited size which have navigable water all around them. They are usually pillar or spar-shaped and black with one or more horizontal bands. They may have a white light which emits two flashes at approximately every 5–10 second intervals.

Safe water marks indicate navigable water all around their position (eg. mid-channel marks). They are spherical or pillar-shaped with red and white vertical stripes and may have a white light flashing in isophase (equal length on/off), occulting (longer on than off), one flash every 10 seconds, or Morse A (• —).

Special marks are used to indicate an area or feature referred to on nautical charts (eg cable/pipeline marks, military or recreation zone marks). The buoy (which can be any shape) is yellow. It is surmounted by a cross-shaped topmark and may have a yellow light.

Cardinal marks indicate safe water 45° either side of the compass point they represent (see Fig. 4). For example, a north mark indicates danger south of the mark and safe passage northward of the mark in the quadrant NW to NE.

Fig. 4 Cardinal marks

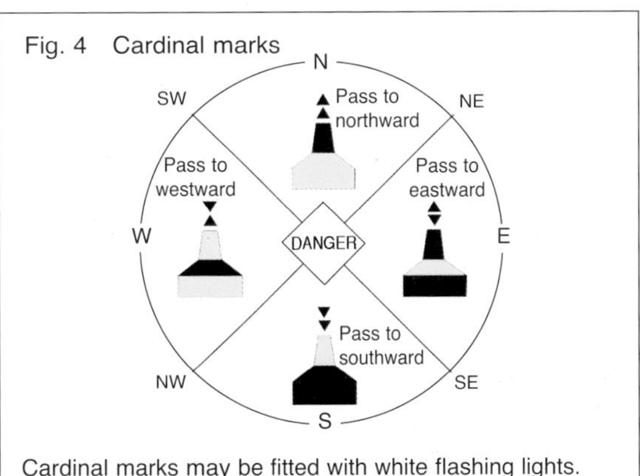

N
SW
NE
Pass to northward
Pass to westward
Pass to eastward
W
E
DANGER
Pass to southward
NW
SE
S

Cardinal marks may be fitted with white flashing lights.
The rhythm of flashes identifies each mark:
North: constant quick or very quick flashing.
East: 3 flashes every 5 or 10 seconds
South: 6 flashes + 1 longer flash every 10 or 15 seconds.
West: 9 flashes every 10 or 15 seconds

Fig. 5 Navigation lights and daymarks displayed at sea

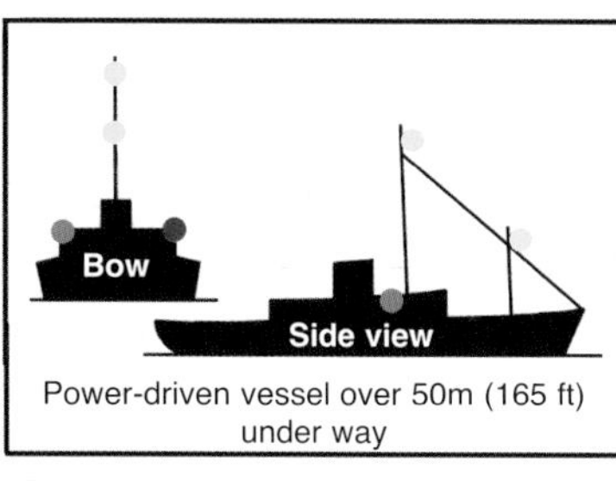
Bow
Side view
Power-driven vessel over 50m (165 ft) under way

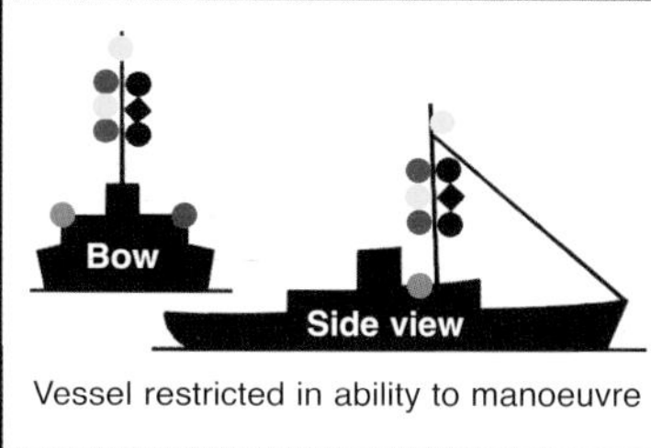
Bow
Side view
Vessel restricted in ability to manoeuvre

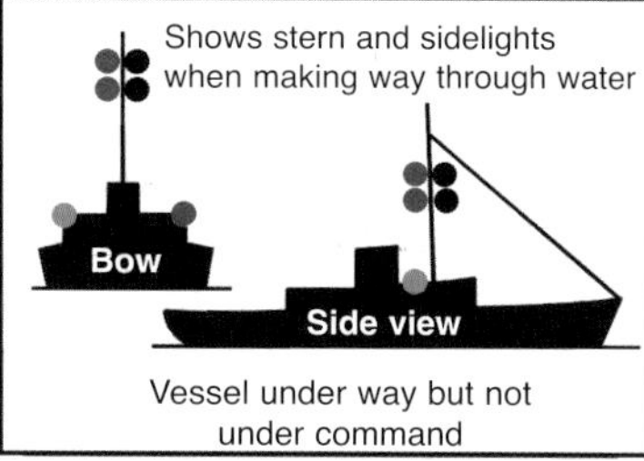
Shows stern and sidelights when making way through water
Bow
Side view
Vessel under way but not under command

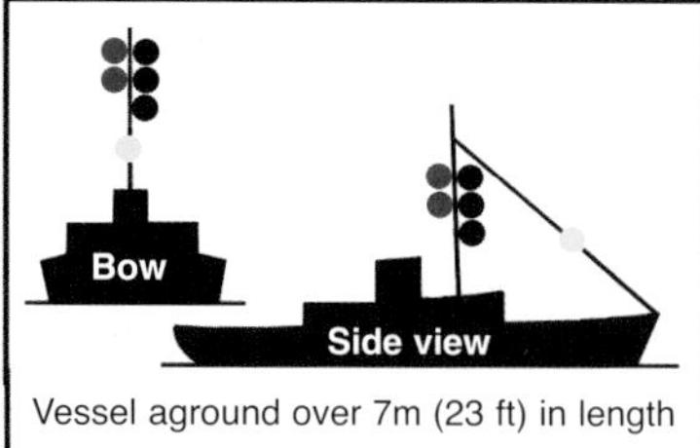
Bow
Side view
Vessel aground over 7m (23 ft) in length

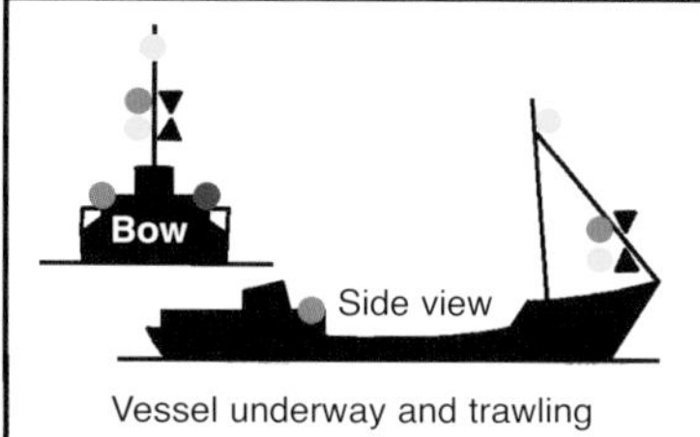
Bow
Side view
Vessel underway and trawling

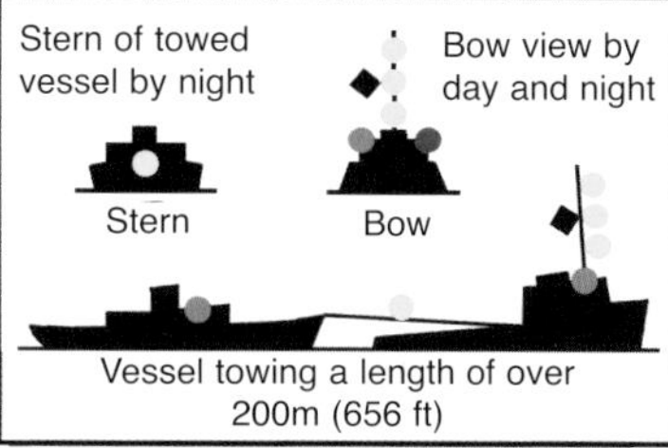
Stern of towed vessel by night
Bow view by day and night
Stern
Bow
Vessel towing a length of over 200m (656 ft)

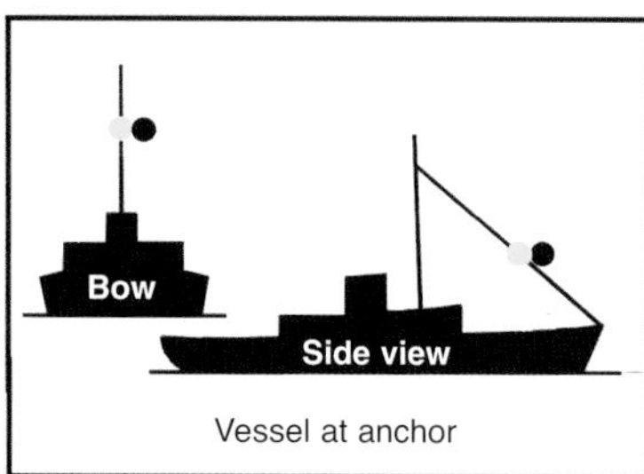
Bow
Side view
Vessel at anchor

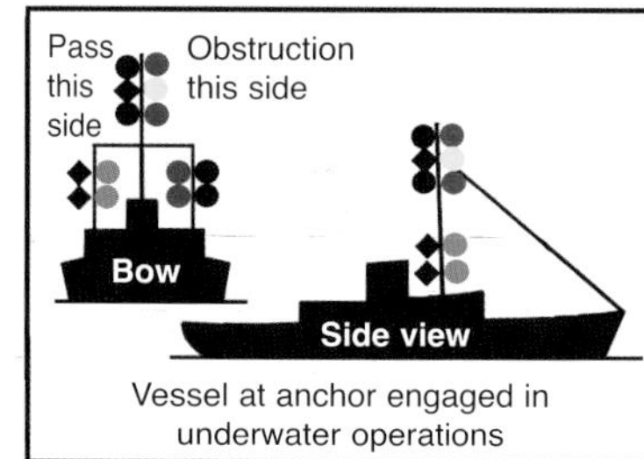
Pass this side
Obstruction this side
Bow
Side view
Vessel at anchor engaged in underwater operations

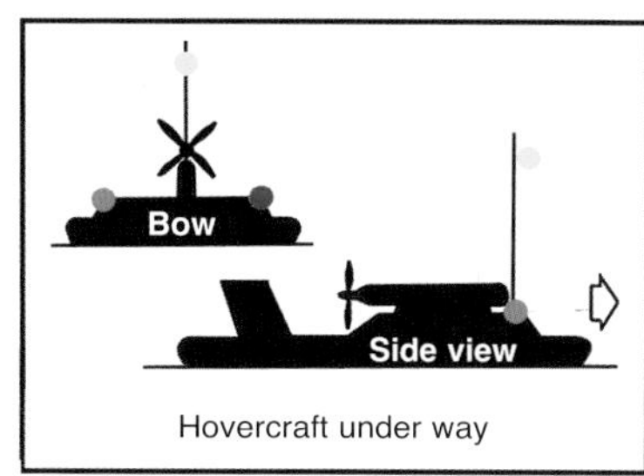
Bow
Side view
Hovercraft under way

Charts

Charts contain a wealth of information essential to divers and vessel operators. The symbols and abbreviations used in Admiralty Charts are fully illustrated and explained in Chart Number 5011. Fig. 6 below shows a small selection of these.

Many countries have now standardised their symbols and abbreviations in accordance with the International Hydrographic Organization (IHO). Modern Admiralty charts use the metric system while older charts will still be in fathoms and feet. The USA uses fathoms and feet.

Fig. 6 A small selection of Admiralty Chart symbols. Refer to Chart 5011 for full list and details.
Reproduced from Admiralty Chart 5011 by permission of the Controller of Her Majesty's Stationery Office and the UK Hydrographic Office (www.ukho.gov.uk).

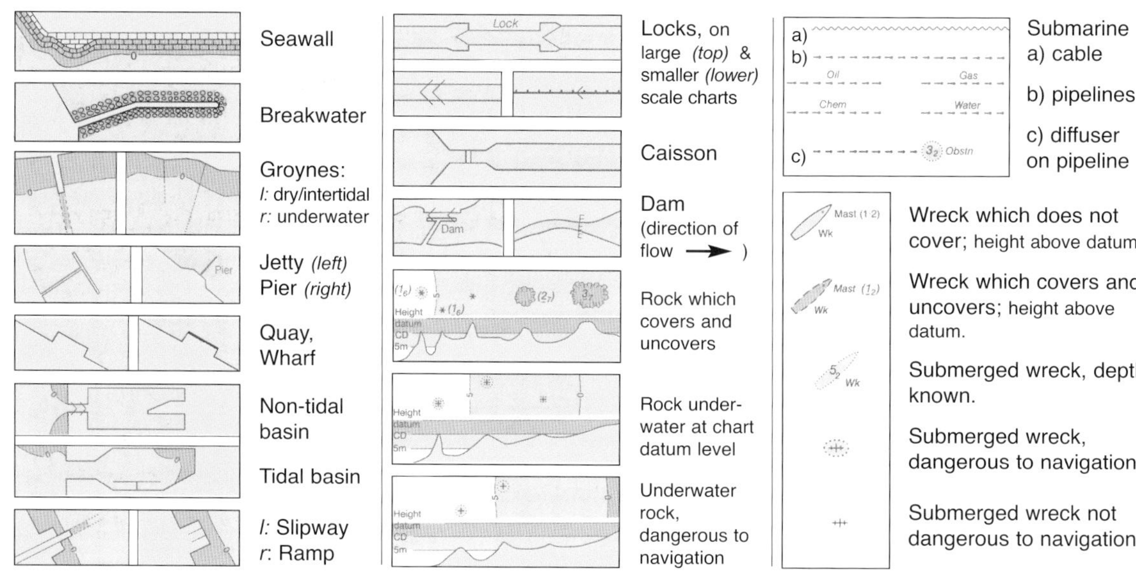
Seawall
Breakwater
Groynes:
l: dry/intertidal
r: underwater
Pier
Jetty *(left)*
Pier *(right)*
Quay,
Wharf
Non-tidal basin
Tidal basin
l: Slipway
r: Ramp
Lock
Locks, on large *(top)* & smaller *(lower)* scale charts
Caisson
Dam
Dam (direction of flow →)
Height
datum
CD
5m
Rock which covers and uncovers
Rock under-water at chart datum level
Underwater rock, dangerous to navigation
a)
b)
Oil
Gas
Chem
Water
c)
Obstn
Submarine
a) cable
b) pipelines
c) diffuser on pipeline
Mast
Wk
Wreck which does not cover; height above datum.
Wreck which covers and uncovers; height above datum.
Submerged wreck, depth known.
Submerged wreck, dangerous to navigation.
Submerged wreck not dangerous to navigation.

8 CYLINDER IDENTIFICATION

Compressed gas cylinders are identified by colour and labelling. The labelling is the primary means of identification – the colour is only a guide.

Cylinder labelling consists of two parts a hazard diamond and an information panel.

The hazard diamond indicates the degree of hazard of the contents. If more than one diamond is required they should be affixed slightly overlapping with the primary risk diamond uppermost (Fig. 1).

Fig. 1 Examples of hazard diamonds

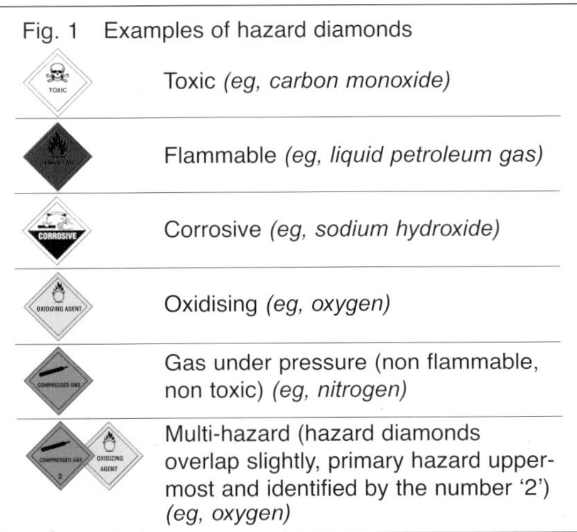
Toxic *(eg, carbon monoxide)*
Flammable *(eg, liquid petroleum gas)*
CORROSIVE
Corrosive *(eg, sodium hydroxide)*
Oxidising *(eg, oxygen)*
Gas under pressure (non flammable, non toxic) *(eg, nitrogen)*
Multi-hazard (hazard diamonds overlap slightly, primary hazard uppermost and identified by the number '2') *(eg, oxygen)*

The panel must contain the proper name and chemical formula of the contents. If variable mixes are used the percentage volume of each gas must be shown. The label may also include other information such as risk and safety information, and details of the company or organisation that filled the cylinder (see Fig. 2).

For refilled cylinders, a fill tag should be securely attached indicating contents (including volume percentages of gases), pressure, maximum operating depth, name of the filler, date of fill and, in case it should become detached, the cylinder serial number.

Colour coding

Until 2001 there was no European convention on the colour coding of medical or industrial gas cylinders. In 2001 the European standard (EN 1089-3) established a colour code with the aim of attaining full harmonisation of colour coding across Europe.

Colour coding applies solely to the shoulder (curved part at the top) of the cylinder. The body may be any colour that does not conflict with the colour on the shoulder.

Some gases have been assigned specific colours (see Fig. 3). Where a gas does not have a specific colour the shoulder is coded according to its properties as in Fig. 4.

Calibration gases (for gas analysis equipment) are stored in pink cylinders.

Fig. 2 Typical cylinder label

Product and chemical formula
Company name/logo
Space for additional information
Heliox He/O2
Company logo
Risk and safety information relating to the contents of the cylinder
Company name and address
COMPRESSED GAS
2
Any additional information and identification numbers
Company phone number
Space for additional information
Hazard diamond
Company information

Fig. 3 Cylinder colours for selected gases commonly used in the diving industry.

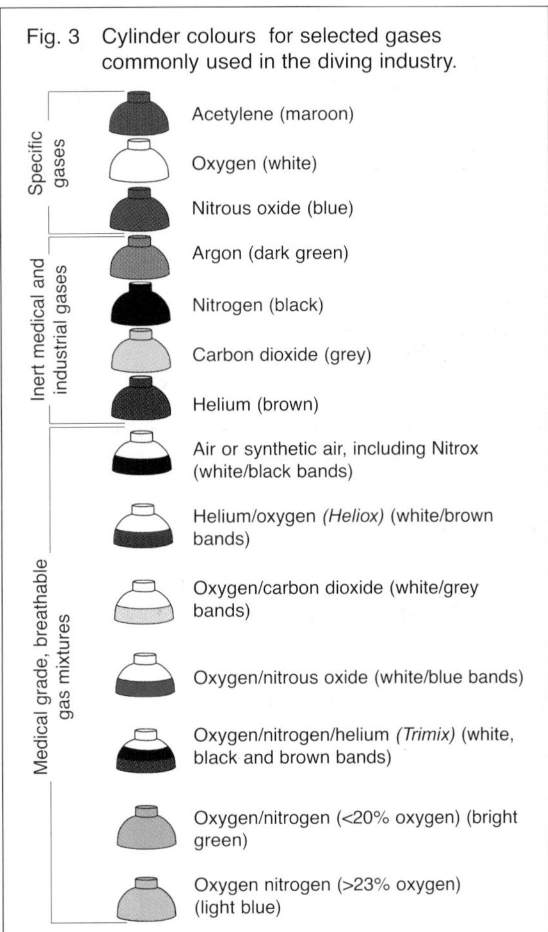
Specific gases
Acetylene (maroon)
Oxygen (white)
Nitrous oxide (blue)
Inert medical and industrial gases
Argon (dark green)
Nitrogen (black)
Carbon dioxide (grey)
Helium (brown)
Medical grade, breathable gas mixtures
Air or synthetic air, including Nitrox (white/black bands)
Helium/oxygen *(Heliox)* (white/brown bands)
Oxygen/carbon dioxide (white/grey bands)
Oxygen/nitrous oxide (white/blue bands)
Oxygen/nitrogen/helium *(Trimix)* (white, black and brown bands)
Oxygen/nitrogen (<20% oxygen) (bright green)
Oxygen nitrogen (>23% oxygen) (light blue)

Fig. 4 Cylinder shoulder colour coding for non-specified gases

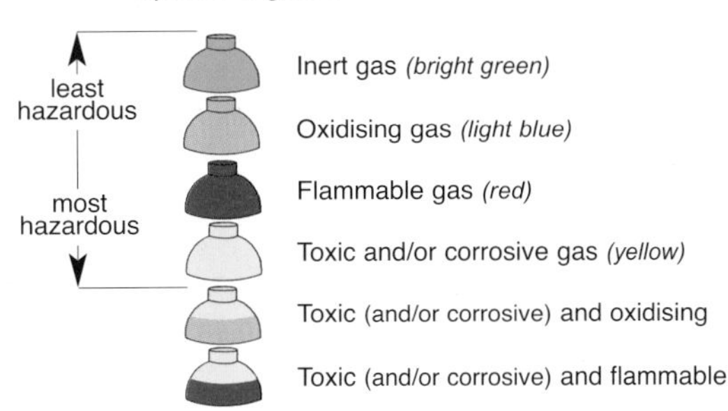
least hazardous
most hazardous
Inert gas *(bright green)*
Oxidising gas *(light blue)*
Flammable gas *(red)*
Toxic and/or corrosive gas *(yellow)*
Toxic (and/or corrosive) and oxidising
Toxic (and/or corrosive) and flammable

9 MARINE FOULING

An underwater structure provides an ideal site for marine growth colonisation. Marine growth increases the size and weight of the structure causing it to suffer greater waveloading and current forces. To maintain its safety it is necessary to assess the extent and nature of the marine growth. Local variation in the type and density will occur according to environmental conditions. For example, the warmth derived from the hot products in the risers can encourage local growth.

Fig. 1 Seaweeds

Seaweeds are present on most structures on sunlit surfaces less than 15m (50 ft) deep. Annual species such as the green ribbon-like and dull, feathery seaweeds (Fig. 1a) may grow up to 15cm (6 in) in length during the summer months. Perennial (living for more than 2 years) seaweeds, such as kelp (Fig. 1b) are slower to colonise but may grow to 50–150cm (1 1/2–5 ft).

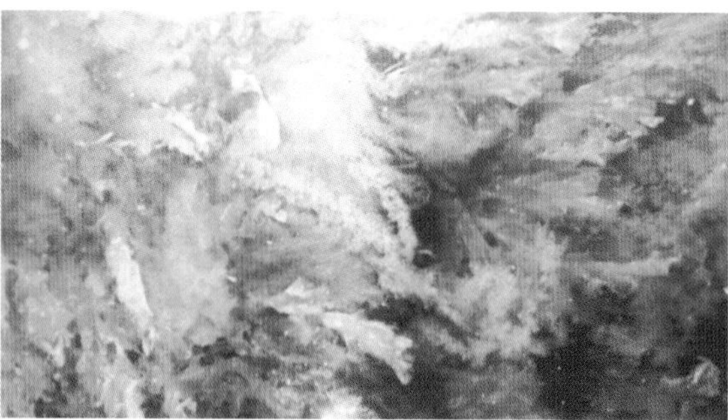

1a) *Ulva lactuca* (green); *Polysiphonia* (dull red)

1b) Kelp: *Laminaria hyperborea*

Fig. 2 Mussels

Mussels grow most densely on the upper surfaces of horizontal members of the structures in the 0–20m (0–65 ft) depth range. Mussel shells on offshore structures are smooth, glossy, brown or black in contrast to the abraded blue-black shells of inshore mussels (Fig. 2a). In sunlit areas mussels themselves bear an overgrowth of filamentous red and green seaweeds up to 15cm (6 in) long like those in Fig. 2b. Fig. 2c shows a typical mussel bed about 4cm (1 1/2 in) thick composed of mussels up to 5cm (2 in) long.

2a) Mussels: *Mytilus edulis*

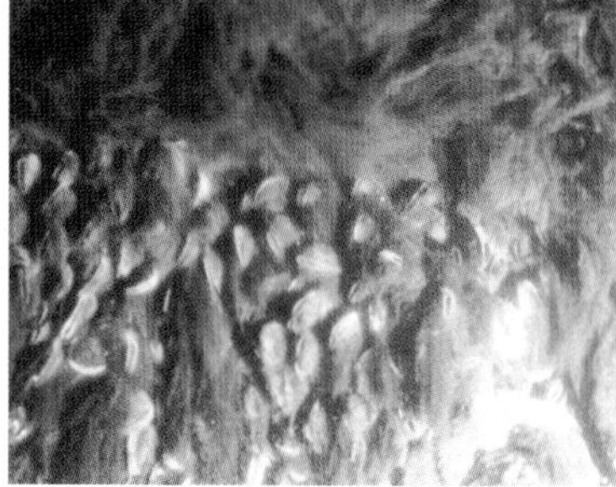

2b) with seaweeds: *Polysiphonia; Ectocarpus*

2c) with kelp: *Laminaria digitata*

Fig. 3 Tubeworms

Fig. 3a shows a dense cover of solitary tubeworms forming a brittle, calcareous (chalky) layer 0.5–1.5cm (1/2 in) thick. The colonial tubeworms shown in Fig. 3b are often present at depths greater than 50m (165 ft). Individual tubes are only 0.5mm wide and 4–7mm long but colonies form dense cone-shaped growths. They form colonies up to 50cm (20 in) in diameter and 20cm (8 in) high. Another form is a thin, spreading, disc-shaped colony. Discs may be 10–40cm (4–15 in) in diameter. In Fig. 3c they have almost joined together to form a layer approximately 1cm (1/2 in) thick.

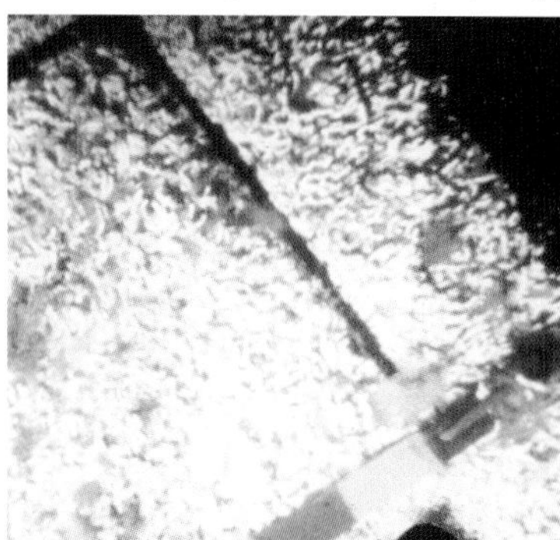

3a) Tubeworm: *Pomatoceros triqueter*

3b) Colonial tubeworm: *Filograna implexa*

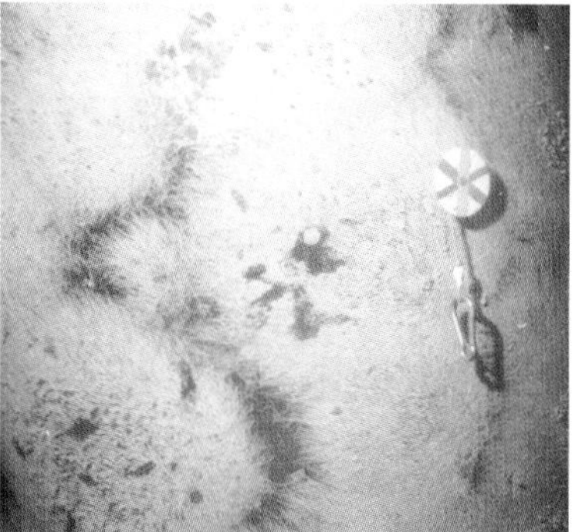

3c) Colonial tubeworm: *Filograna implexa*

Marine growth can be described as either hard or soft. Hard growths include mussels, barnacles, hard corals and calcareous tube worms. Soft growths include anemones, sponges, soft corals, kelps, sea squirts, etc. It is important to be able to differentiate between these two groups since they will affect the engineering stress calculations and also the choice of cleaning method used to remove them. Marine fouling makes it difficult to apply NDT and inspection techniques. It can often take much longer to remove the marine growth than to carry out the inspection. Figs. 1–9 below show some common varieties of marine growth found on underwater structures in the North Sea.

Fig. 4 Soft coral
Often found over the initial hard fouling layer of tubeworms or barnacles. These individuals are 3–12 cm (1–5 in) high and range in colour from white to pale yellow or deep orange.

Dead men's fingers: *Alcyonium digitatum*

Fig. 5 Anemones
Present on most structures, particularly deeper than 30m (100 ft) Fig. 5 shows a typical dense cluster of individuals 8–15cm (3-6 in) long. Colour ranges from palest yellow through orange to reddish brown.

Plumose anemones: *Medridium senile*

Fig. 6 Hydroids
These plant-like, colonial organisms called hydroids are the principal members of the layer of soft growth found on most structures offshore. Many, like those in Fig. 6a are often confused with seaweed, but individuals such as those in Fig. 6b are more easily recognised by their large pink 'heads'. These varieties are typically 4-6cm (1 1/2-2 in) long.

6a) Hydroids: *Bougainvillia Ramosa*

6b) Hydroids: *Tubularia larynx*

Fig. 7 Barnacles
Various species of barnacles are found at different depths. A typical cluster is shown below. These are 2–3cm (1in) in diameter and 3–4cm (1–1 1/2 in) long.

7 Deep water barnacle: *Balanus hameri*

Fig. 8 Sponges
Encrusting sponges may be recognised on some structures. Size and shape are variable. The surface pattern and holes of the breadcrumb sponge, shown below, are readily recognisable.

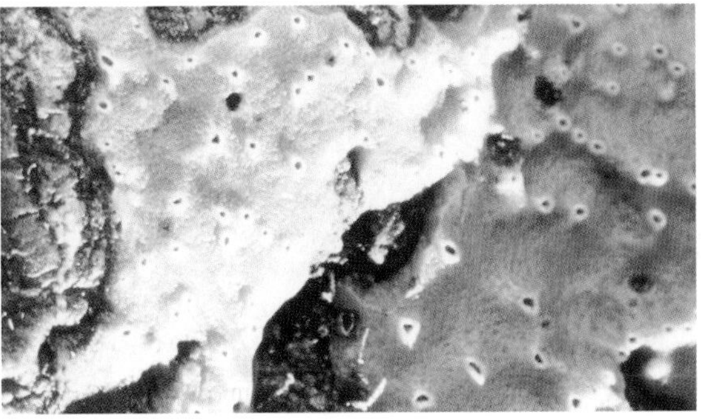

Fig. 9 Sea squirts
Sea squirts are abundant in regions free from silt. These individuals are 4–6 cm (1 1/2–2 in) long growing over a background of solitary tubeworms.

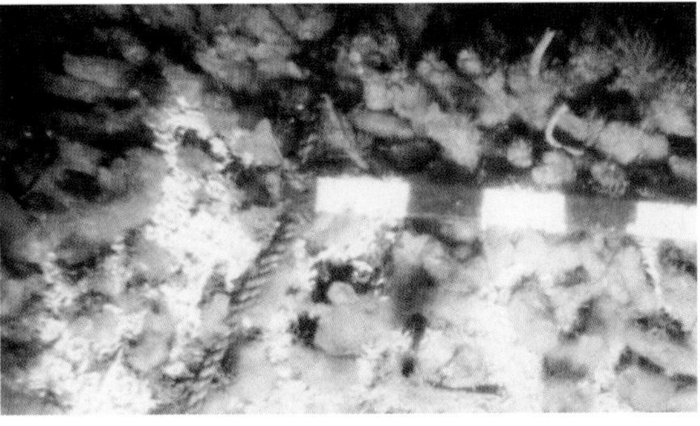

10 CONCRETE BLEMISHES

(see also Fig. 9, Section 1.11, pp 54-55)

Identifying concrete defects requires care. It can also be complicated by repairs, surface treatments and stains, etc which may make harmless surface features look like damage or faults. There are two main types of concrete blemish:

1. Those resulting from the construction of the concrete, such as slip-formed ridges, shuttering marks, grout runs, tie-rod holes, blowholes, etc.
2. Post-construction marks/damage, such as rust, water jetting marks, impact damage, abrasion, epoxy peeling, etc.

Not all blemishes indicate damage to underlying concrete; they may be superficial. Accurate identification improves with experience. The table and photographs below represent a tiny selection of some commonly found concrete blemishes.

Main feature of blemish	Possible cause
Grooves, channels, rebates, ridges	Slip-formed ridges (vertical or horizontal); shuttering marks, construction joint between two pours (ridge or channel); hardened grout over-flows.
Cracks, flaking, peeling, separation	Epoxy coat peeling, superficial impact, spalling, structural cracks, grout sheets.
Stains, runs, drips, deposits	Slip-formed ridges, grout runs, exudation (white seepage from construction joints), stains.
Holes, depressions, voids	Built-in objects (tie-rods, sockets), popouts, aggregate bridging, honeycombing, superficial impact, spalling, blowholes.
Strips, bands, patches, coatings	Slip-formed vertical drags, surface sealants/paint, rust, small repairs (infills).
Nuts, bolts, plates, beams	Surface attachments and in-built items (bolts, plates, sockets, etc).
Lines, marks, streaks	Slip-formed ridges/grooves, shutter markings, stains, rust, exudation (white marks), water-jetting marks, structural cracks, grout sheets.
Surface texture: Smooth Rough	Smooth: Ply shuttering marks, small repairs, infills, sealants/paint, abrasion. Rough: Plank shuttering, grout runs, honeycombing, superficial impact, spalling, exudation, construction joint.

200mm

1. Construction joint: fairly straight surface line formed between successive pours of concrete. May be slightly ridged or depressed.

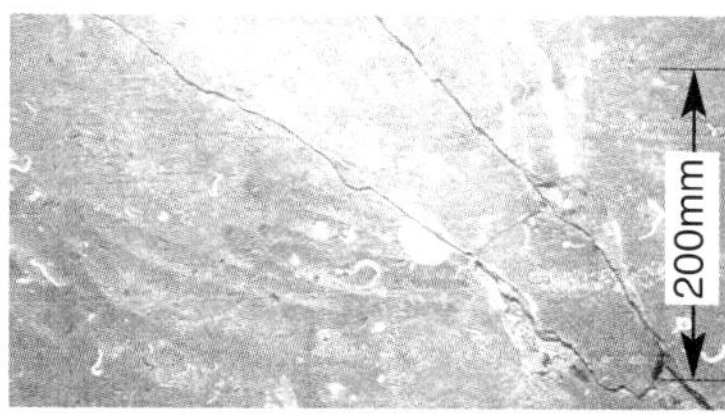
200mm

2. Structural cracks formed by movement of the structure. Note marks made by water jetting on left side of image.

150mm

3. Honeycombing caused by inadequate compaction during construction or lack of fine material. Note shuttering plank marks.

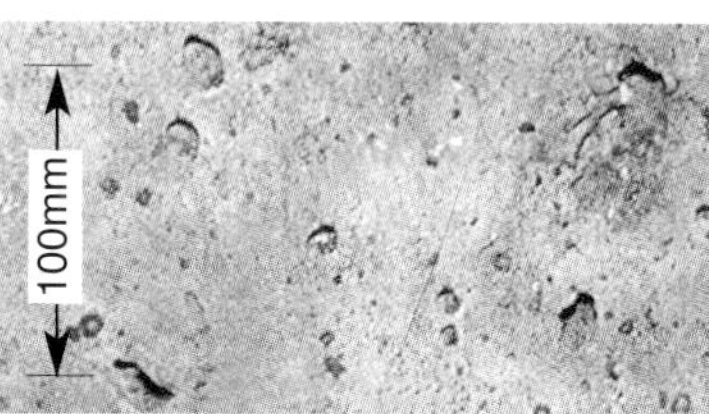
100mm

4. Blowholes: Small round holes less than 10mm across, formed when small airpockets get trapped behind shutter during construction. Popouts are similar, but conical.

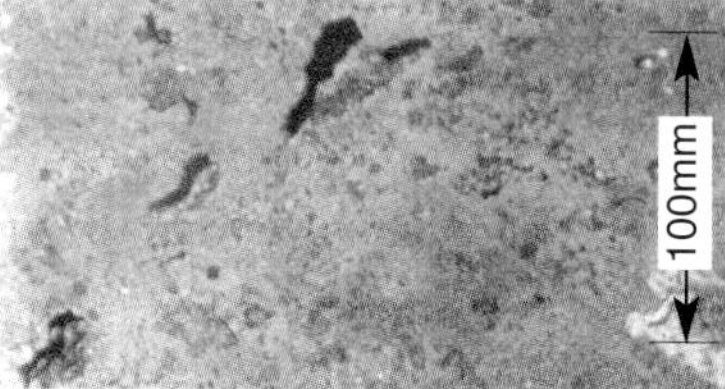
100mm

5. Aggregate bridging: Irregular holes 10–20mm across with coarse aggregate at the top. Caused by slight variations in concrete mix.

100mm

6. Rebate formed at construction joint for flexible sealant. Bitumastic sealant runs out if not properly bonded to the concrete.

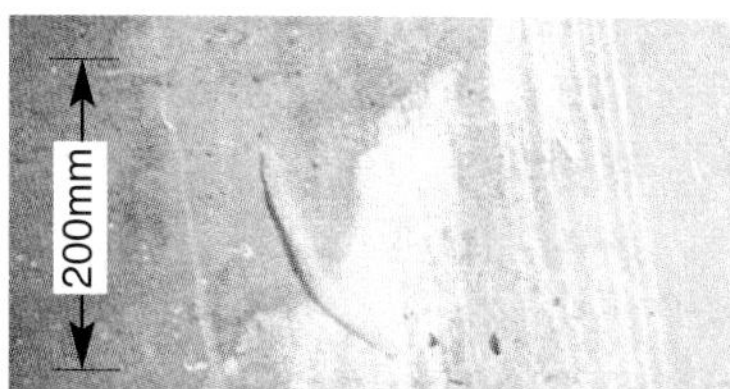
200mm

7. Exudation: White salt deposits seeping from joint or crack formed when water flows through crack. May be above or below the crack.

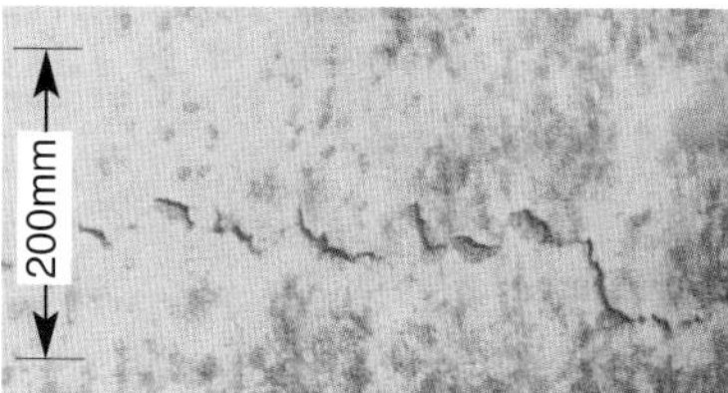
200mm

8. Grout over-run caused by concrete or grout overlapping previous pour. Over-runs may be lifted or detached, exposing the construction joint.

200mm

9. Built-in redundant plate (square plate with circle at centre). Ridge at extreme left is caused by slight misalignment of shuttering.

Weather and the Sea

The diver needs to understand something about the weather since it limits many of his activities.
The area covered by an individual forecast may include an area as big as 130,000 square kilometres (50,000 square miles), but the weather conditions within that area may vary considerably in different parts of it.

The offshore diver is in a unique position to observe the weather regularly and to be able to make quite accurate forecasts based on what he can see, his built-up experience and the available information.
Weather is wind and wind is sea state. The more the diver knows about these three, the safer and more effective will be his diving.

11.1 WEATHER

Weather is the result of the interaction of many phenomena, including solar energy input, temperature, wind and humidity. The key factor, however, is that hot air rises.

The sun heats the Earth's surface which, in turn, warms the air immediately above it causing it to rise. However, not all parts of the earth's surface receive the same amount of heat of the sun. Areas nearer the equator usually receive the most direct sunlight and therefore tend to be hotter than areas nearer the poles where the sun's rays have to travel further and through a thicker section of the atmosphere (see Fig. 1a).

The amount of sunlight received also varies during the year according to the position of the Earth in relation to the sun. Because the Earth's axis is 'tilted' at 23½°, as it moves around the sun different latitudes are closer to the sun at different times during the orbit, and therefore receive more heat at those times. The result is the seasons (see Fig. 1b). When the northern hemisphere is closer to the sun it is summer in the northern hemisphere (and winter in the southern hemisphere) and vice versa.

Fig. 1 The effect on the Earth of it's rotation around the sun

1a) Areas nearer the equator receive most direct sunlight and are therefore hotter than the poles where the sun's rays have further to travel. Latitude also governs the length of daytime and the amount of heat received from the sun at different times of the year.
In this diagram it is winter in the northern hemisphere and summer in the southern hemisphere.

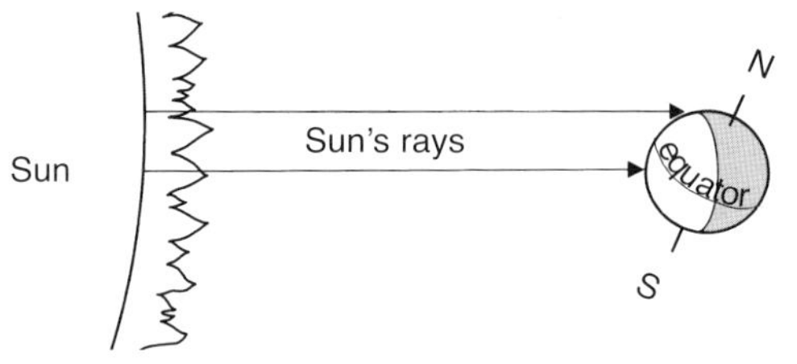

Sun
Sun's rays
N
equator
S

1b) The seasons are the direct result of the way in which the earth is aligned in relation to its orbit. The Earth's axis through the poles, is at 23½° tilt to the plane of its orbit. The Earth takes approx. 365 days to orbit the sun during which time different parts of the Earth are closer to the sun at different times. When the northern hemisphere is closer to the sun it is summer in the northern hemisphere (and winter in the southern hemisphere) – and vice versa when the southern hemisphere is closer to the sun. In this diagram the seasons shown are those of the northern hemisphere.

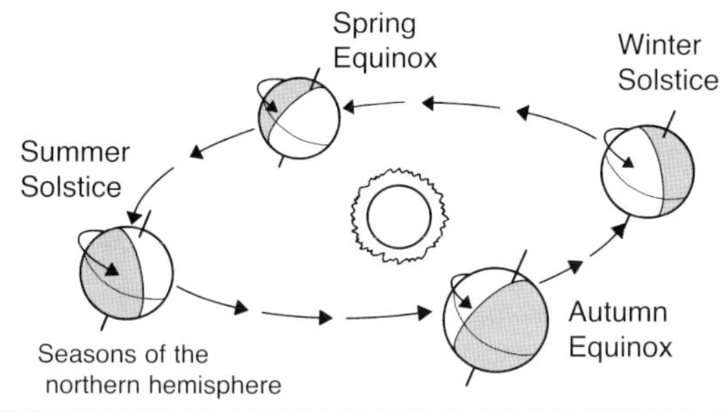

Spring Equinox
Winter Solstice
Summer Solstice
Autumn Equinox
Seasons of the northern hemisphere

General circulation of the atmosphere

The amount of heat received by the atmosphere varies with latitude, resulting in coolness in the polar regions and warmth at the equator. This temperature difference causes related variations in atmospheric pressure. Warm air from the equatorial region rises and travels towards the poles where it cools and descends. Considered on a global scale, low pressure areas occur where warm air rises and high pressure areas occur where cooler air descends. Like all natural forces that seek to establish an equilibrium, air tends to move from areas of high pressure to areas of low pressure. This movement is called wind. If the Earth were not rotating, sinking air over the poles would move directly to the equator (see Fig. 2a).

Because the Earth rotates it imparts a rotational motion to any moving object on its surface. The Earth rotates from west to east. This causes the winds blowing from the equator to seem to curve towards the west (see Fig. 2b). This is known as the Coriolis Effect and it results in the formation of 6 belts of prevailing winds: the North-East and South-East Trade winds, the Prevailing Westerlies in temperate latitudes and the Polar Easterlies (see

Fig. 2 General circulation of the atmosphere

2a) General circulation for a non-rotating Earth

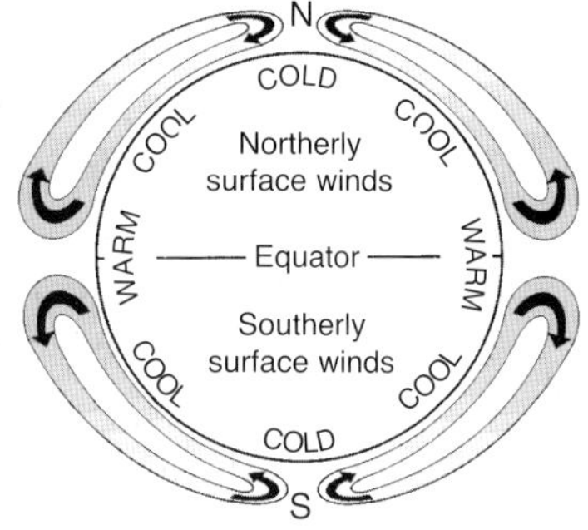

N
COLD
COOL
COOL
Northerly surface winds
WARM
Equator
WARM
Southerly surface winds
COOL
COOL
COLD
S

2b) General circulation for the rotating Earth

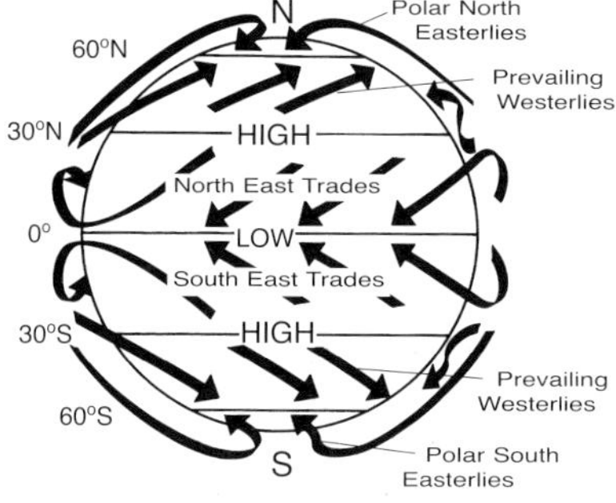

N
Polar North Easterlies
60°N
Prevailing Westerlies
30°N
HIGH
North East Trades
0°
LOW
South East Trades
30°S
HIGH
Prevailing Westerlies
60°S
S
Polar South Easterlies

2c) Speed of the eastward movement of the Earth's surface at given latitudes, and direction of air currents.

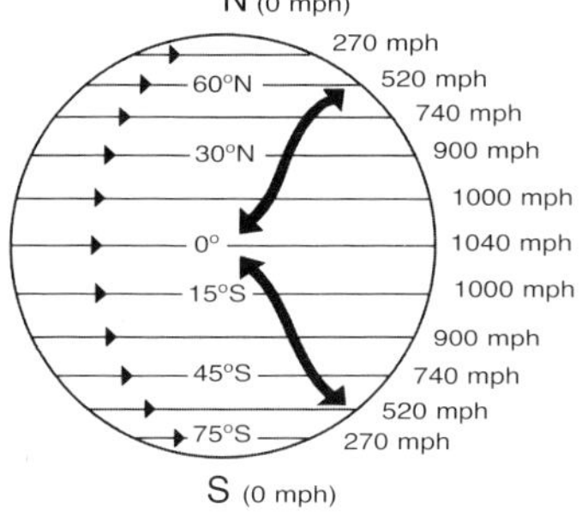

N (0 mph)
270 mph
60°N
520 mph
740 mph
30°N
900 mph
1000 mph
0°
1040 mph
15°S
1000 mph
900 mph
45°S
740 mph
520 mph
75°S
270 mph
S (0 mph)

Fig. 2b) (Note: winds are always described by the direction *from* which they are blowing).
The Earth's rotation also affects the speed of the wind over the Earth's surface (see Fig. 2c).

Pressure systems

The Polar Easterlies and Prevailing Westerlies meet at the Polar Front. As the two air masses move past each other they create eddies called cyclones and anticyclones. Cyclones swirl inwards towards a centre of low pressure and move anticlockwise in the northern hemisphere and clockwise in the southern hemisphere. (These cyclones should not be confused with tropical storms of the same name). Anticyclones are the reverse: they swirl outwards around a centre of high pressure and turn clockwise in the northern hemisphere and anticlockwise in the southern hemisphere.
Cyclones (low pressure systems) tend to bring cloudy, wet weather and are followed by anticyclones (high pressure systems) which tend to bring drier weather and light winds.
The differing pressures are shown on 'weather maps' by concentric ring patterns called isobars which are formed by joining points of equal pressure.
In temperate regions weather systems move in a west to east direction, and the cloud types indicate weather activities. However, in tropical and subtropical regions (0–30° north and south) most systems move in an east to west direction and are generally shallow and indeterminate. They do not carry frontal systems like the temperate weather systems but usually have an 'easterly wave' area of less fine weather, sometimes with heavy thundery conditions. The exceptions to this are the hurricanes and tropical storms (also known as cyclones). These are slow-moving, usually no more than 5–12 knots, but have intense cyclonic circulations of winds of 100 knots or more, heavy thundery rain and very rough seas. The swell will often advance rapidly well to the west of such a system so that divers should keep in touch with their nearest meteorological service for adequate warning of its approach.

Air masses

Air masses are very large bodies of air (up to 13 million sq km (5 million sq miles) that form over areas of relatively constant temperature. They take on the temperature and humidity characteristics of the area they cover – eg maritime (moist) or continental (dry) and polar (cold) or tropical (warm). They are usually described by a combination of these two characteristics, eg: polar maritime (see Fig. 3).

AIR MASSES OF NORTH WESTERN EUROPE

The North Sea lies between latitude 50°N and 65°N close to an interface between low and high pressure air masses. Cool air from higher latitudes and warm air from lower latitudes are brought together in a broad band which stretches across the Atlantic Ocean from the eastern United States to north-west Europe. Along this band warm air pushes into the cold, setting up a pattern of large depressions moving eastward. Such depressions bring a variety of weather, mostly unsettled. Whether they arrive in the North Sea depends on whether they are deflected by the positions of the Azores or Polar Highs. The Azores High pushes them north towards Iceland and the Polar High steers them south towards the Bay of Biscay. Highs such as these are slow moving and usually cause settled weather for several days.

Fig. 3 Air masses which influence the weather of north-west Europe – characteristics and origins

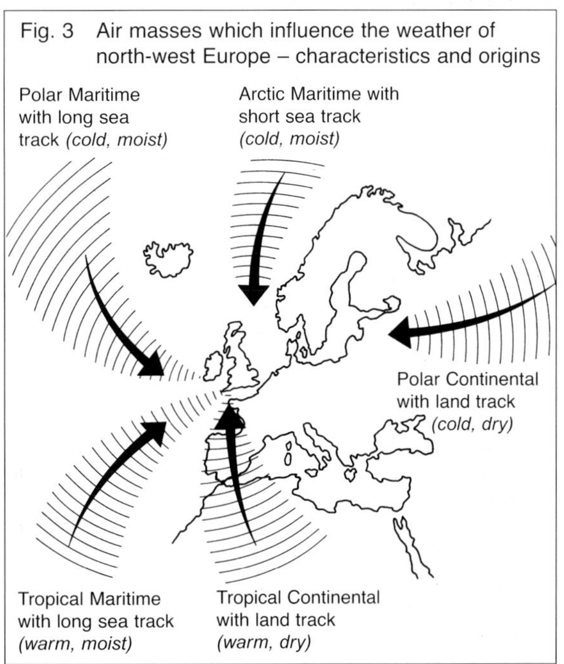
Polar Maritime
with long sea
track *(cold, moist)*
Arctic Maritime with
short sea track
(cold, moist)
Polar Continental
with land track
(cold, dry)
Tropical Maritime
with long sea track
(warm, moist)
Tropical Continental
with land track
(warm, dry)

Fronts

When air masses of differing temperatures meet, fronts are formed. There are 2 main types of front: warm and cold. A warm front occurs when warm air is the moving force; a cold front forms when the colder air mass is advancing (see Fig. 4).
Because warm air rises it will climb over (or be pushed up by) an adjacent mass of colder air, depending on whether it is overtaking or being overtaken. When warm air overtakes colder air, it rises up over the colder air and a warm front develops at the boundary between the two air masses (Fig. 4a). When cold air overtakes warmer air, it undercuts the warmer air, forcing it upwards and a cold front is formed (Fig. 4b).
Fronts are driven along by pressure systems. Cold fronts tend to move faster than warm fronts and bring sudden weather changes. Warm fronts bring more gradual change. Because cold fronts move about twice as fast as warm fronts, they occasionally catch them up forming what is known as an 'occluded front' (see Figs. 4c and d).
Occluded fronts usually occur at altitude and may be either 'warm occluded' or 'cold occluded.' Both are represented in the same way on a weather map.

Fig. 4 Fronts – cross-section and plan views

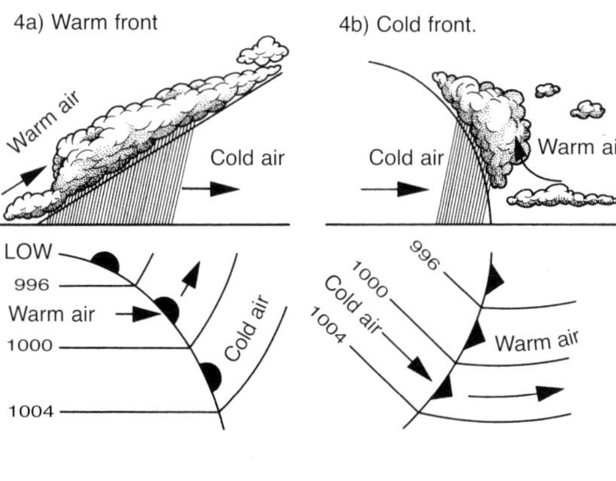
4a) Warm front
Warm air
Cold air
LOW
996
Warm air
1000
1004
Cold air
4b) Cold front.
Cold air
Warm air
996
1000
1004
Cold air
Warm air

a) Warm air advances and rises over a mass of colder air. Warm fronts usually bring light, steady rain and following warmer weather.

b) Cold air advances and pushes under a mass of warmer air. Cold fronts usually bring heavy rain and following colder weather.

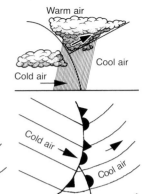

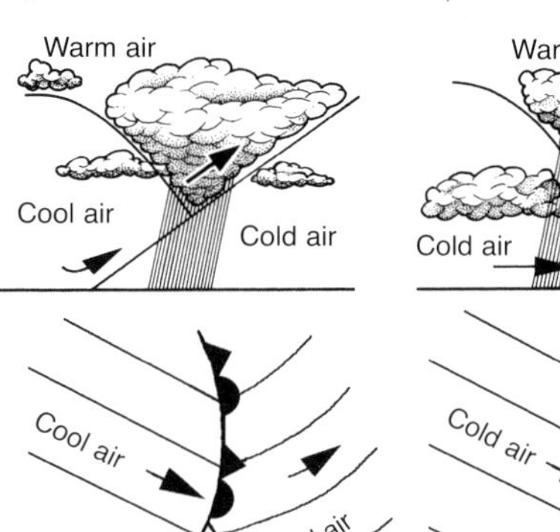
4c) Warm front occlusion.
Warm air
Cool air
Cold air
Cool air
Cold air
Warm air
4d) Cold front occlusion.
Warm air
Cool air
Cold air
Cold air
Cool air
Warm air

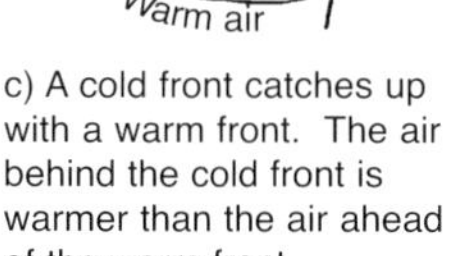

c) A cold front catches up with a warm front. The air behind the cold front is warmer than the air ahead of the warm front.

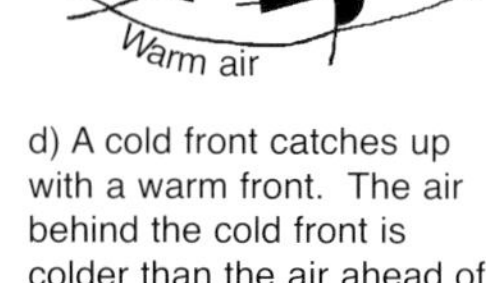

d) A cold front catches up with a warm front. The air behind the cold front is colder than the air ahead of the warm front.

Because warm air cools and forms clouds, fronts are often readily identified by associated banks of cloud. Fig. 5 shows the typical profile of a warm front and the type of cloud that might be expected to be found in terms of distance, and time from the arrival of the front. For a cold front the profile would slope backwards.

Cloud types

As warm air rises it cools and its water vapour condenses to form clouds. The moisture content of air varies according to its temperature and the surface over which it travels before it is forced to rise. The higher the temperature of the air the more moisture it can contain. However, a warm air mass over land will not pick up as much moisture as a similar air mass over the sea. Thus a warm wind blowing onshore generally carries more moisture than a wind blowing off the land onto the sea. Because of the moisture content and temperature variations of our atmosphere, clouds follow the movement of air masses and thus clouds can provide an indication of these movements. The many varieties of cloud make it possible to extract much more information than just the direction (and perhaps speed) of the air mass.

Clouds can be categorised into three main groups:

1. Low cloud – bases from sea level up to 2km (7,000ft): stratus, nimbostratus, cumulus, cumulonimbus.
2. Medium level cloud – bases from 2km up to 8km (25,000ft): altostratus, altocumulus.
3. High cloud – bases from 5km up to 13km (16,000–45,000ft): cirrus, cirrostratus, cirrocumulus (see Fig. 5).

The base levels tend to sink below their lower limits in winter and in higher altitudes.

Fig. 5 Cloud types in relation to a warm front (A cold front profile would slope backwards)

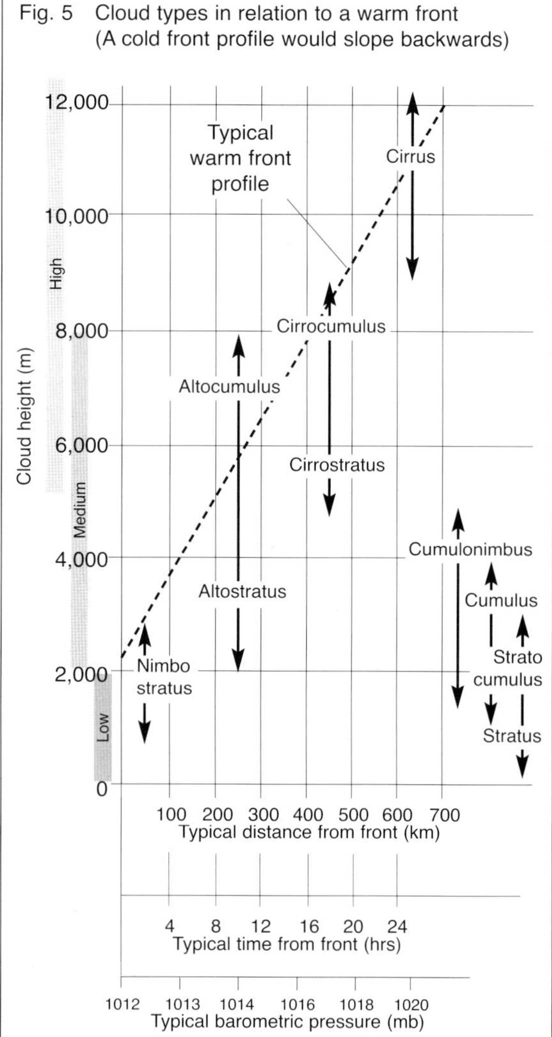
Cloud height (m)
12,000
10,000
8,000
6,000
4,000
2,000
0
High
Medium
Low
Typical warm front profile
Cirrus
Cirrocumulus
Altocumulus
Cirrostratus
Cumulonimbus
Altostratus
Cumulus
Strato cumulus
Nimbo stratus
Stratus
100 200 300 400 500 600 700
Typical distance from front (km)
4 8 12 16 20 24
Typical time from front (hrs)
1012 1013 1014 1016 1018 1020
Typical barometric pressure (mb)

Cloud types can also be divided into three classifications according to their appearance:

1. Layer clouds (stratiform)
2. Heaped clouds (cumuloform)
3. Feathery clouds (cirroform)

'Alto' used with a cloud means medium level and 'nimbus' means rain-bearing. Cloud sub-types can be more precisely specified by combinations of these names, eg: altostratus, cumulonimbus, cirro-cumulus, etc (see Fig. 6).

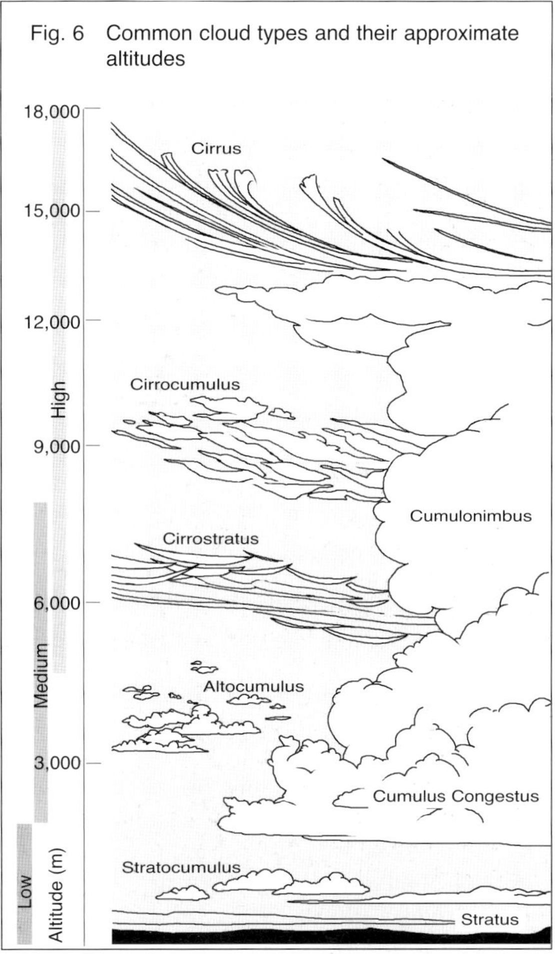
18,000
15,000
12,000
9,000
6,000
3,000
High
Medium
Low
Altitude (m)
Cirrus
Cirrocumulus
Cumulonimbus
Cirrostratus
Altocumulus
Cumulus Congestus
Stratocumulus
Stratus
Fig. 6 Common cloud types and their approximate altitudes

Winds

Wind is caused by temperature differences between one area and another, which in turn give rise to pressure differences. The pressure difference over a unit distance is known as the pressure gradient – the steeper the gradient the stronger the wind.

There are three main types of wind:

1. Trade winds – permanent oceanic winds which blow in the same direction most of the year.
2. Seasonal winds – regular winds, such as the monsoons of the Indian Ocean, which depend on the declination of the sun, the season and the pressure distribution.
3. Winds associated with individual weather systems.

The direction of a wind is the point *from* which it is blowing, ie a south-westerly wind blows from the south-west towards the north east.

Wind speed is measured in knots using an anemometer and its force is classified in the Beaufort Scale (see pages 271–272). When estimating wind force and speed from an offshore structure it should be remembered that at platform height (which could be 50m (165 ft) above sea level), the wind will probably be stronger than at the surface.

As a general rule in the northern hemisphere, if the observer stands with his back to the wind the area of lowest barometric pressure will lie to his left, the highest to his right.

Wind is said to 'back' or 'veer' when it changes direction. In the northern hemisphere a backing wind blows in an anti-clockwise direction, ie north through east, and south through west. A veering wind is the opposite and in the northern hemisphere is often a sign of approaching bad weather.

LOCAL WINDS

Offshore and onshore breezes

Land heats up and cools down faster than the sea. In summer the sun warms up the land faster than the sea. Warm air rises off the land and is replaced by cooler air off the sea causing an onshore breeze. At night, as the land cools to below sea temperature, the effect is reversed, producing an offshore breeze.

At the end of the summer the land will cool down more rapidly than the sea, ie, the sea will be warmer than the land. This causes warmer air to rise off the sea creating offshore cloud. A change in wind direction towards the shore, or the warming up of the land creating an onshore sea breeze will draw the clouds towards the land and showers might be expected to migrate inland.

Coastline clouds over the land indicate that the air is unstable over the land and stable over the sea. If the wind should blow offshore, cloud may migrate over the coast.

Fog

Fog results from the condensation of water vapour due to the high humidity of the air. It is usually caused by the cooling of the air.

Sea fog is sometimes formed when warm air moves over a cold sea surface (advection fog) and may be due to a change of wind or a cold sea current. If the air mass above the sea is warmer than the land it is approaching, the increased moisture that it is carrying will form fog when it cools on reaching land. This is known as 'Haar' on North Sea coasts. In the same way, warm moist air crossing a warm land mass will be cooled and form fog when it reaches the cold sea.

11.2 WEATHER FORECASTS

When trying to forecast the approaching weather by watching the changing cloud formations it is important to note the sequence of the changes. A pattern of weather watching should be established. Temperature and humidity, wind speed and direction (especially high-altitude estimates), and barometric pressure are all valuable considerations likely to increase the accuracy of the forecast.

The pattern of differing barometric pressures is the most important factor in producing a 'weather map' (properly known as synoptic chart). Differing pressures are shown on these charts by contours called 'isobars' which are lines joining points of equal barometric pressure. In general, the higher the latitude the more unsettled and unpredictable will be the weather. Diving operations in the Persian Gulf, the Gulf of Guinea, the Gulf of Mexico and around the coasts of Indonesia are each subject to quite different constraints. Close to the equator weather conditions tend to remain the same for much longer periods.

Forecast sources

NAVTEX

Marine safety information is broadcast to shipping every 4 hours via the international NAVTEX service (satellite and 518 kHz). NAVTEX is an automated, direct-printing service which can be programmed to receive specified messages for nominated areas of passage.

The world's ocean areas are divided into 16 NAVareas (or METareas) for which designated countries are responsible for provision and co-ordination of meteorological and navigational warnings and information (Fig. 1).

Each Metarea is divided into named zones and detailed, up-to-date information is provided for each zone by the national organisation responsible for that Metarea. The zones of Metarea I are shown in Fig. 2.

The UK example is used as an illustration of the services available.

In the UK the Met Office provides comprehensive marine weather information including reports by fax, telephone, mobile phone and on the internet.

INTERNET

The UK Met Office website, *www.metoffice.com*, provides detailed marine weather information for the UK including surface pressure charts, satellite

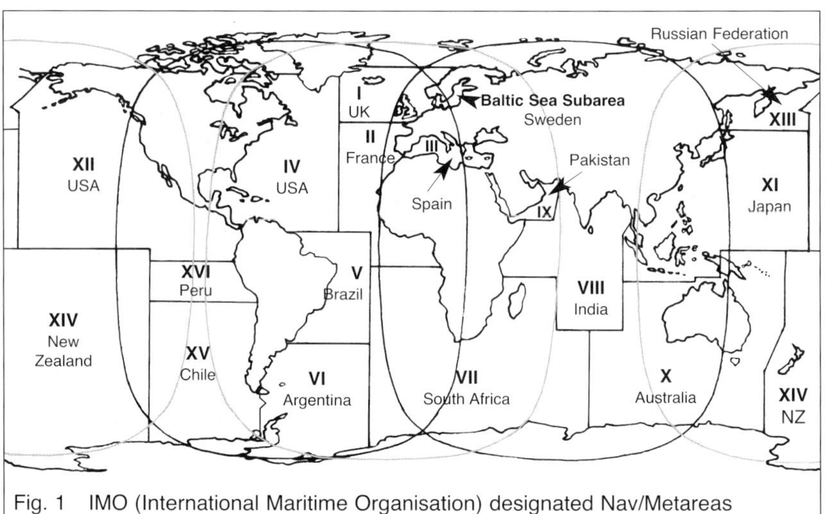

Russian Federation
I
UK
II
France
III
Spain
Baltic Sea Subarea
Sweden
XIII
Pakistan
IX
XII
USA
IV
USA
XI
Japan
XVI
Peru
V
Brazil
VIII
India
XIV
New Zealand
XV
Chile
VI
Argentina
VII
South Africa
X
Australia
XIV
NZ

Fig. 1 IMO (International Maritime Organisation) designated Nav/Metareas

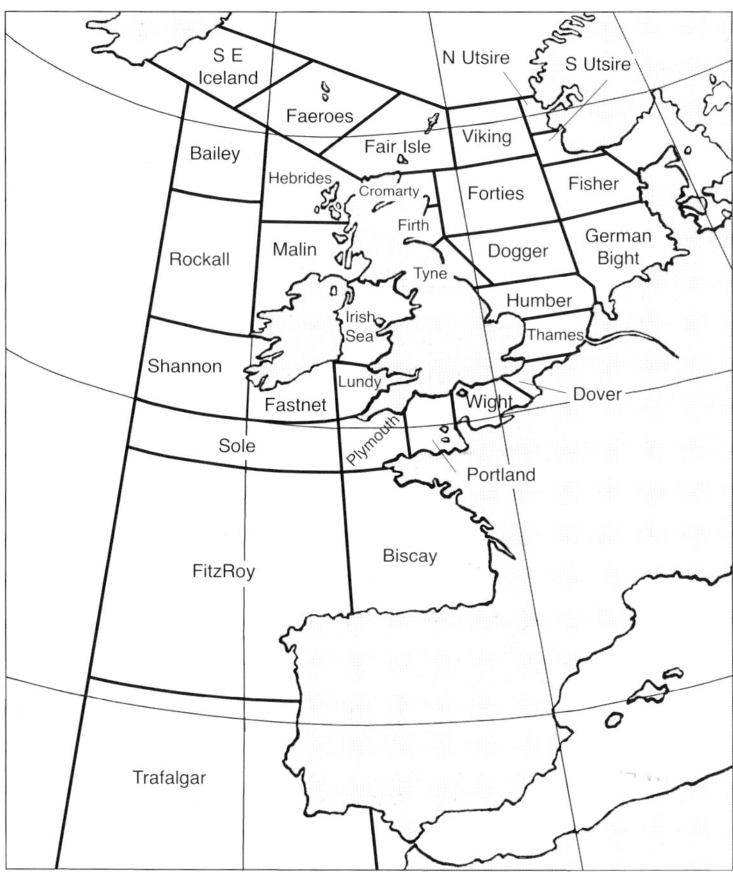

S E Iceland
N Utsire
S Utsire
Faeroes
Fair Isle
Viking
Bailey
Hebrides
Cromarty
Forties
Fisher
Firth
Malin
Dogger
German Bight
Rockall
Tyne
Humber
Irish Sea
Thames
Shannon
Lundy
Dover
Fastnet
Wight
Plymouth
Sole
Portland
Biscay
FitzRoy
Trafalgar

Fig. 2 UK Met Office Shipping Forecast Areas

images, inshore and planning forecasts, severe weather warnings and reports on real-time coastal conditions. The standard reporting and forecasting height is 10m (33ft) above sea level. Links with meteorological organisations worldwide provide up-to-date information on weather conditions for any location in the world.

FAX
Daily forecasts for inshore areas and two- to five-day forecasts for UK Shipping Areas and for the western Mediterranean are available by fax from the Met Office. Inshore forecasts are up-dated at 0700hr and 1900hr daily.

TELEPHONE
Recorded information for UK inshore areas and planning forecasts (updated at 0800hr and 1900hr) are available by telephone. A telephone consultancy service is also available where the user can talk directly to a forecaster.

MOBILE PHONE
Text messaging to all mobile phone networks is available by subscription. Information can be requested for specified inshore forecasts (issued at 0500hr and 2300hr daily), customised exact location forecasts for the next 6 hours (up-dated hourly), gale warnings, real-time coastal reports and shipping reports (updated at 0001hr, 0500hr, 1100hr and 1700hr daily).

Fig. 3 Typical surface pressure chart

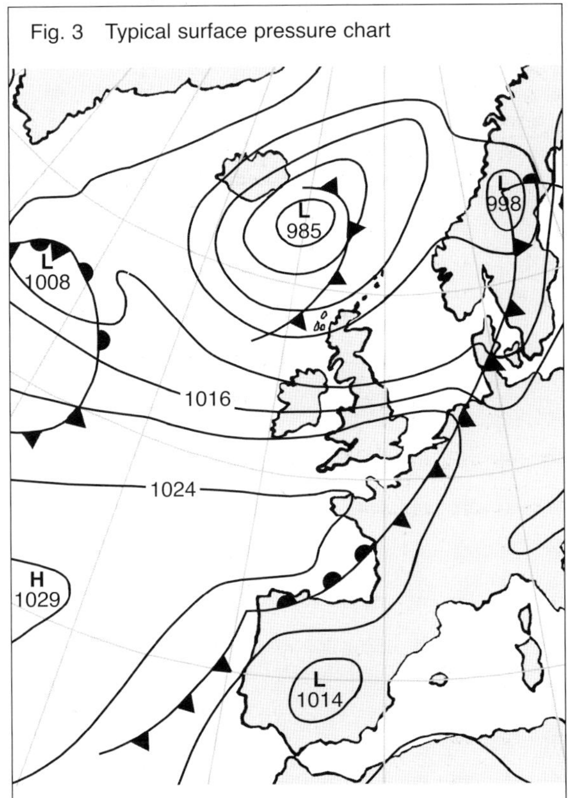
L
985
L
998
L
1008
1016
1024
H
1029
L
1014

In NW Europe the prevailing westerly winds drive fronts eastwards bringing rain. Warm fronts bring warmer air; cold fronts bring colder air. Winds blow clockwise around high pressure areas and anticlockwise around low pressure areas. Isobars close together indicate strong winds.

RADIO
The Met Office bulletins for UK shipping areas (Fig. 2) are broadcast on BBC Radio 4 long wave (198 kHz/1515 m) at 0048hr, 0536hr, 1201hr and 1754hr daily. Radio 4 VHF (92-94 kHz) also broadcasts the 0048hr and 0536hr bulletins daily and the 1754hr bulletin on weekends only).

Forecasts are given in the following order:
1. Gale warnings.
2. General synopsis.
3. Forecasts for shipping areas.
4. Reports from selected coastal stations (at 0048hr and 0536hr only).

Gale warnings are broadcast on BBC radio at the first opportunity after receipt. 'Imminent' means that it can be expected within 6 hours; 'soon', between 6 and 12 hours and 'later', after 12 hours. Visibility is described as 'fog' (<1000m); 'poor' (1000m–2 nautical miles); 'moderate' (2–5nm) and 'good' (more than 5nm).
Local radio stations also broadcast weather information for local coastal waters at various times during the day.
UK Coastguard stations provide regular 4-hourly forecasts for shipping on Channel 16, MF (via 2182 kHz), NAVTEX and VHF. The VHF service includes an additional forecast for local inshore waters. Gale warnings are broadcast on receipt.

Specialised Forecasting Services

In addition to the free and publicly available information, it is possible to obtain customised weather reports from the Met Office on a commercial basis.
Subscribers to the UK Met Office's services can receive customised information covering a specified location, such as an individual offshore installation, and can include details of expected winds, weather, visibility, sea and swell for the next 24 hours. The information can be provided by phone, fax, internet and text messaging, as required.

Weather Charts

When planning weather-sensitive activities such as diving it is important to know what the conditions will be like on site at the proposed time of the dive. It is a good idea, therefore, to keep a record of weather forecasts. These can be written down and may be tape-recorded if necessary. It is useful to have to hand a reference map of the area of interest, with prominent features marked.
Surface pressure charts provide a good visual summary of developing weather conditions and can help predict likely developments. Forecast charts are available from the Met Office website, *www.metoffice.com* and can be valuable in helping to plan diving operations. Fig. 3 shows a typical weather chart for N W Europe.

11.3 SEA STATE

Waves

Sea state is the result of weather conditions. The friction between the wind and the sea surface slows the wind and the energy produced becomes a wave. Waves at sea travel in the same general direction as the wind which causes them, although the water itself makes little forward progress. Waves can be compared to a stretched out rope which is given an upward flick – a wave travels along the rope which itself does not move forward (Fig. 1).

As a wave undulates past, each particle describes a circular path. The circles diminish as they descend from the surface (Fig. 2). In deep water its effect is felt to a depth equal to about half the wave length.

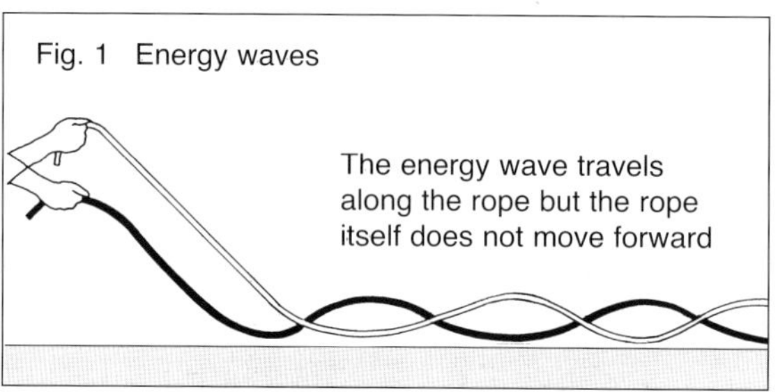
The energy wave travels along the rope but the rope itself does not move forward
Fig. 1 Energy waves

For example, a wavelength of 20m (66ft) may cause turbulence down to 10m (33ft).

In shallow water the surface wave energy cannot be absorbed in this way and breakers result.

Much of the measurable properties of a wave, such as its length, height, shape and speed may be changed by the nature and situation of the wave. The only relationship is that wave speed is equal to the wave length divided by the period.

There is a common belief that every seventh wave is larger than the rest. There is no 'law' about this but it can sometimes happen when two nearby wave trains mix together. The pattern arising from several waves becomes complex because of the many and varied influences on them. However, considered generally, some useful predictions can be made.

When a wind of constant velocity blows for a long time across an ocean unaffected by other wave trains, the waves will reach their maximum size. In such conditions the average wave height (in metres) will be equal to half the wind speed (in knots). The largest waves will attain a height of 2.5m (8ft) for every 10kt of wind. A strong wind of 50kt (Beaufort Scale Force 9) has been known to produce a largest storm wave of some 12m (40ft) high.

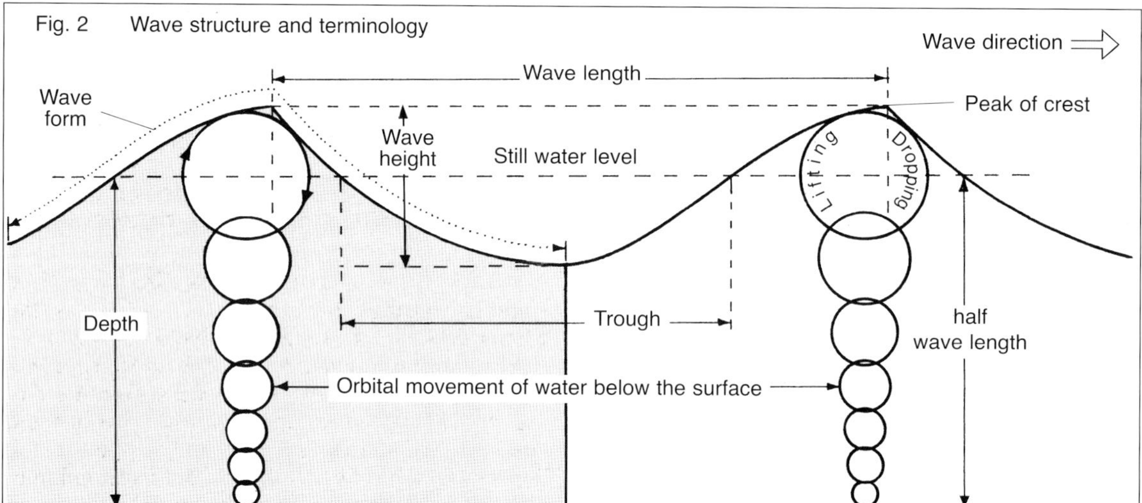
Wave direction
Wave length
Wave form
Peak of crest
Wave height
Still water level
Lifting
Dropping
Trough
Depth
half wave length
Orbital movement of water below the surface
Fig. 2 Wave structure and terminology

Wave Form. The curve of the surface of the sea seen in elevation. Any one wave form extends from a point on a wave surface (such as the crest) to the equivalent point on the next wave.

Wave length. The horizontal distance between one wave crest and the next along the line of wave advance.

Wave height. The vertical distance from trough to crest on one wave form.

Maximum wave height. The greatest wave height measured over a ten-minute period.

Significant wave height. The average height of the largest one third of all waves recorded over a ten-minute period.

Wave Speed. The speed at which the wave form is moving relative to the undisturbed body of water. It is measured horizontally in the direction of the wave advance.

Still Water Level. The level which a body of water will assume when unaffected by wave forms.

Wave Train. A succession of waves proceeding as a group in a given direction.

Period of a wave. The time interval between the passing of two successive crests or troughs.

Swell. Slow, regular, rolling, non-breaking wave movement caused by past wind or distant wind.

Fetch. The distance over which the wind has blown before reaching a given point.

Wave Climate. Average wave conditions for any locality for any time of the year

Recording data

The standard reporting units are the knot (kt), the second (sec), the foot (ft), metre (m) and nautical mile (nm). World Meteorological Organisation reports are coded in half metres of wave height.
When measuring wave height observers should note that the fore-shortening effect of looking down from the deck of a vessel or structure is considerable. Eye-ball estimates can be very inaccurate. A convenient scale should be marked on one or more legs of the structure to aid accurate assessment. Although significant wave height is defined as the average height of the largest one third of all waves recorded over a 10-minute period, it should be noted that a close approximation can be obtained by recording the highest wave in any two-minute period.

Sea and Swell

For those working on or below the surface of the sea the most important aspect of the weather is likely to be its effect on the surface of the sea. Apart from the tides and currents, all the sea's activities are the result of the effect of the wind. It affects the sea in three different ways:

1. By the speed of the wind.
2. By the length of time the wind has been blowing.
3. By the distance that the wind has blown over the water (ie, the fetch).

Locally-produced disturbances are called 'seas' and are different from remotely-produced ones called 'swells' (Fig. 3). Swells may be the product of a past wind or a weather system from across the ocean.
A cross-swell is caused by a fresh swell being formed from a different direction from the residual swell. The result can produce a most uncomfortable motion which may complicate shallow water operations.

Fig. 3 Wind generation of waves, seas and swell

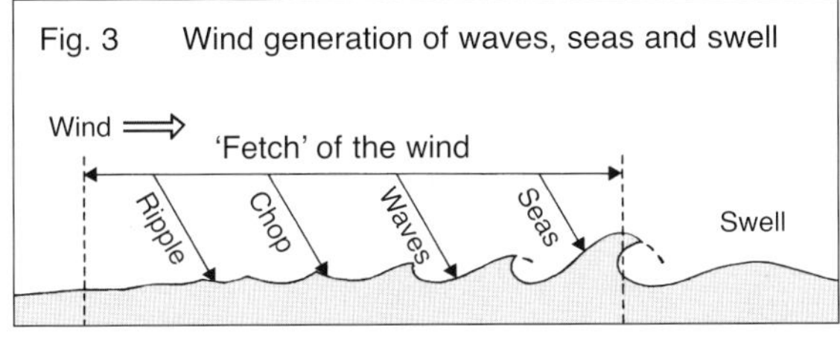
Wind
'Fetch' of the wind
Ripple
Chop
Waves
Seas
Swell

Wind-driven currents

The wind also causes the sea surface to move as a current. The direction of this wind-driven surface current is not the same as that of the wind but is at an angle of 45° to it (Fig. 4). In the northern hemisphere it is 45° to the right of the wind direction, while in the southern hemisphere it is 45° to the left. This effect is due to the earth's rotation and is called the Coriolis effect.
The strength of the wind-driven current lessens with increasing depth. Also the direction of travel turns progressively away from the direction of the wind. For example, at 11m (36ft) the current direction is 90° to the wind direction. This spiralling change of direction is known as the Ekman Spiral (Fig. 4) and its effect becomes more marked with increasing distance from the equator. Except in very shallow water the surface current speed is equivalent to approximately 3% of wind speed. It decreases, however, at a rate which depends on the stability of the entire water column, the length of time the wind has been blowing, the fetch and the size of the waves present.

Fig. 4 The Ekman Spiral

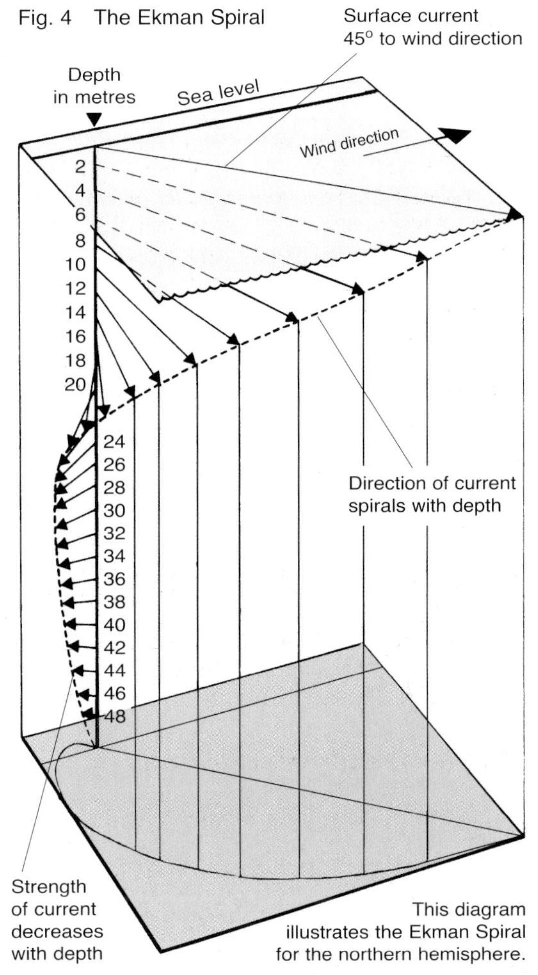
Surface current
45° to wind direction
Depth
in metres
Sea level
Wind direction
2
4
6
8
10
12
14
16
18
20
24
26
28
30
32
34
36
38
40
42
44
46
48
Direction of current
spirals with depth
Strength
of current
decreases
with depth
This diagram
illustrates the Ekman Spiral
for the northern hemisphere.

Sea State Tables

Sea states are normally expressed in tabular form and usually correspond quite closely to the Beaufort Wind Scale which uses sea state conditions to assess the strength of the wind. It should *not* be used in reverse, ie, to report sea state. The Beaufort Scale refers to the sea condition in a fully arisen sea. This can take hours to achieve in any wind condition. Sea State Scales describe actual sea conditions at the time of the observation. There are several different Sea State Scales in use. It is therefore important to specify the scale being used when quoting any particular sea state value. Fig. 5 compares two widely used sea state scales with the Beaufort Wind Scale.

Fig. 5 US Navy and RN Sea State Scales compared with the Beaufort Wind Scale

Description of sea state	Average wave height ft	m	**Beaufort Wind Scale**		Wind Speed kt	**US Navy Sea State Scale**		**Royal Navy Sea State Code**	
Sea like a mirror	0	*0*	**0**	Calm	0-1	**0**	Calm	**0**	Calm (glassy)
Ripples without crests	0.10	*0.03*	**1**	Light air	1-3	**1**	Light airs to Light breeze	**1**	Calm (ripple)
Small, smooth wavelets	0.37	*0.1*	**2**	Light breeze	4-6			**2**	Smooth (wavelets)
Large wavelets, scattered white caps	2	*0.6*	**3**	Gentle breeze	7-10	**2**	Gentle breeze	**3**	Slight
Small waves, frequent white caps	3.5	*1*	**4**	Moderate breeze	11-16	**3**	Moderate breeze	**4**	Moderate
Moderate waves, many white caps, some spray	6	*1.8*	**5**	Fresh breeze	17-21	**4**	Fresh breeze	**5**	Rough
Large waves, extensive foam crests, some spray	9.5	*3*	**6**	Strong breeze	22-27	**5**	Strong breeze	**6**	Very rough
Heaped-up sea, foam starts to be blown in streaks	13.5	*4*	**7**	Near gale	28-33	**6**	Moderate gale	**7**	High
Moderately high waves, spindrift, spray affects viz.	18	*5.5*	**8**	Gale	31-40	**7**	Fresh gale		
High waves, dense foam streaks, sea starts to roll	23	*7*	**9**	Severe gale	41-47	**8**	Strong gale to Whole gale	**8**	Very high
Very high waves, sea appears white	29	*8.8*	**10**	Storm	48-55				
Exceptionally high waves, dense foam, frothy crests	37	*11.3*	**11**	Violent storm	56-63	**9**	Storm to Hurricane	**9**	Phenomenal
Sea completely white with driving spray	45+	*13+*	**12**	Hurricane	64+				

11.4 TIDES AND TIDAL STREAMS

Tides

Tides are periodic vertical movements of the sea and tidal streams are its horizontal movements resulting from the tides. Both are caused by the attraction of the moon and sun.

The result is that the tidal range varies from small (neap tides) to large (spring tides) (see Fig. 1).

In operational terms, underwater visibility can be better at high water when clearer water is brought in by the incoming tide.

Some important terms which are used to describe various tidal levels are shown in Fig. 2.

Tides are of little concern to the offshore deep water diver as the rise and fall is usually insignificant to diving operations. To the inshore or shallow water offshore diver, however, determining the height and duration of the tide at a given time and place may be of great importance, for example, when repairing the piles of a pier or salvaging a sunken object. For this information it is necessary

Fig. 1 Tidal ranges

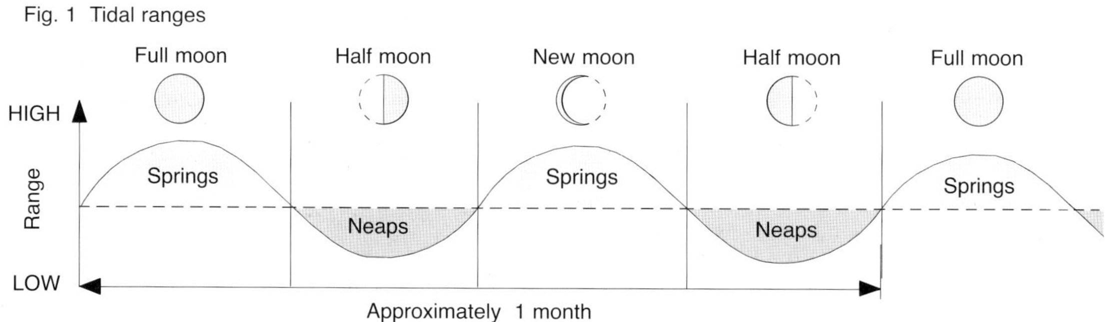
Full moon
Half moon
New moon
Half moon
Full moon
HIGH
Range
Springs
Springs
Springs
Neaps
Neaps
LOW
Approximately 1 month

Neap tides have longer slack water periods and less strong tidal streams.
Spring tides have shallower water at low water and higher at high water and provide greater lift height for tidal lift operations.

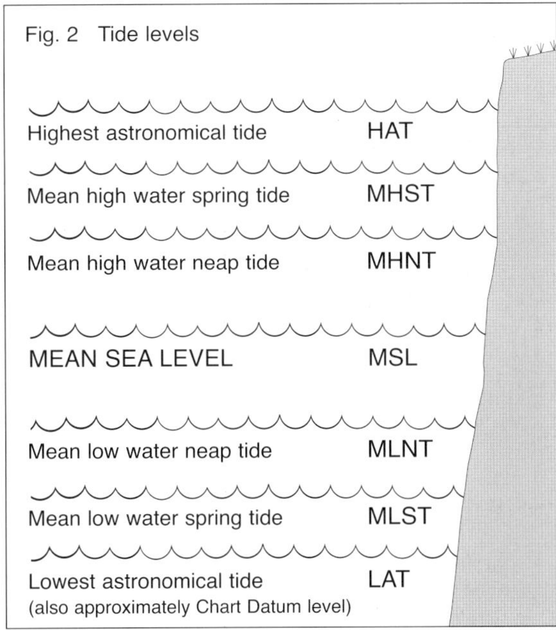
Highest astronomical tide HAT
Mean high water spring tide MHST
Mean high water neap tide MHNT
MEAN SEA LEVEL MSL
Mean low water neap tide MLNT
Mean low water spring tide MLST
Lowest astronomical tide LAT
(also approximately Chart Datum level)
Fig. 2 Tide levels

to find the time of the next high or low water at the nearest standard or secondary port and to extrapolate the exact details by a simple calculation. High water times and heights may be obtained from the Admiralty Tide Tables or most nautical almanacs.
Tidal stream information normally refers only to the surface water layer.

EFFECT OF WIND ON TIDES

The sea level tends to be raised in the direction in which the wind is blowing and lowered in the direction from which it is blowing. A strong southerly wind blowing in the North Sea, for example, may cause lower low waters in the Thames Estuary. Strong winds may also have the effect of advancing or delaying the time of high water by as much as 1 hour.
When a wind blows in the opposite direction to the tide a rough, choppy sea is generated.

Tidal Streams

Tidal streams are a horizontal movement of water which usually flow in one direction for a known period of time and then return along much the same path for another period. The two periods may not be the same.
Tidal stream direction depends on the direction of the flood tide and usually it flows the opposite way on the ebb. Slack water is the time of change of flow from one direction to its opposite. Although this often coincides with high or low water, it need not necessarily be so.
The greatest rate of rise or fall, and consequently the fastest tidal stream, occurs half way through the tide in open water. The 'Twelfths Rule'(Fig. 3) is used to estimate the amount of rise or fall in each of the 6 hours of ebb and flow. The bigger the range, the faster the tidal stream. Tidal streams are strongest during spring tides and weakest during

Fig. 3 The Twelfths Rule

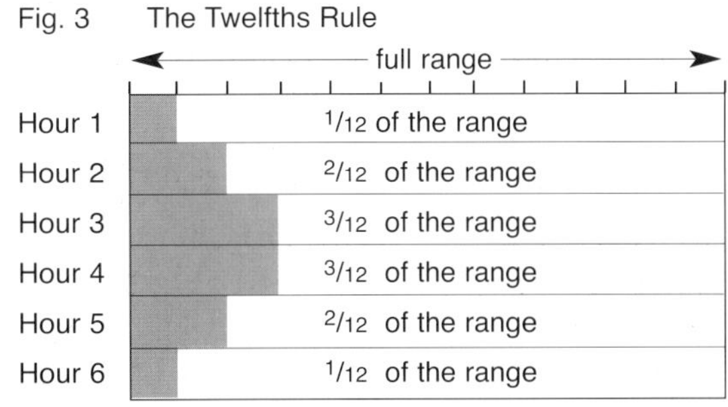
full range
Hour 1 1/12 of the range
Hour 2 2/12 of the range
Hour 3 3/12 of the range
Hour 4 3/12 of the range
Hour 5 2/12 of the range
Hour 6 1/12 of the range

neaps and are usually strongest in inshore areas.
The velocity or rate of the stream is influenced by the shape of the adjoining land and the configuration of the bottom. For example, tidal streams can increase in speed round headlands and in narrow channels. Fig. 4 illustrates the tidal streams of the North Sea. In the southern North Sea strong streams are caused by the funnel effect of the English Channel. As a result of these strong streams dive times are considerably restricted, usually between 45 minutes and an hour). In the northern North Sea, north of latitude 56ºN, tidal streams are not so affected and dive times are only limited by diver endurance levels.
Tidal streams on the bottom in deep water often differ in strength and direction from those on the surface. Information on bottom tidal streams and currents can often be obtained from the client's records. However, in some areas information may only be built up from practical experience.
Tidal streams concern all divers in the sea because they can affect working capacity and safety. Any stream in excess of 1kt will make underwater swimming difficult, especially when hauling an umbilical. In streams in excess of 1kt the diver may have to wear additional weights or find some shelter from the main force of the stream.

Determining the Rate and Direction of Tidal Streams

Tide tables, which provide diurnal high and low water times for given ports, can be found in almanacs, newspapers and on the internet. The UK Hydrographic Office website (www.ukho.gov.uk) provides tidal information for 6,000 ports worldwide for 7–14 days in advance. Long-range (annual) tide tables can also be purchased for individual ports. There is also a wide range of tide prediction software which can provide useful long-term predictions for a large number of ports.
There are two ways of determining the rate and direction of the tidal stream *at the surface* in any area (in each case, the time of local high water must be known):

1. Refer to an appropriate tidal atlas.
2. Using a local chart, find the tidal stream diamond nearest to the dive site. Note the letter in the diamond and find the information that relates to it by referring to the tidal stream table positioned near the edge of the chart (See Fig. 5).

Fig. 4 Tidal streams in the North Sea

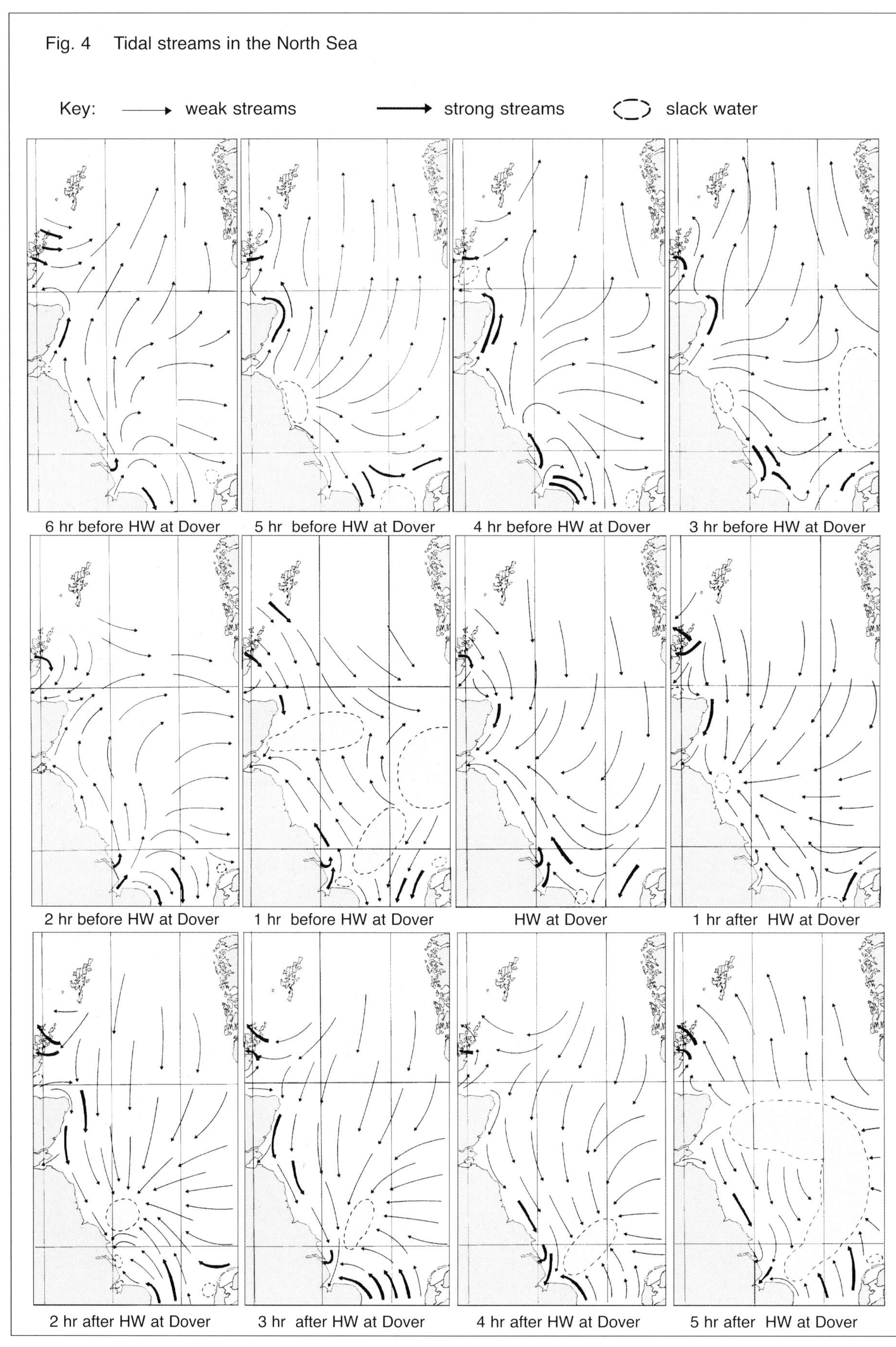
Key: weak streams
strong streams
slack water
6 hr before HW at Dover
5 hr before HW at Dover
4 hr before HW at Dover
3 hr before HW at Dover
2 hr before HW at Dover
1 hr before HW at Dover
HW at Dover
1 hr after HW at Dover
2 hr after HW at Dover
3 hr after HW at Dover
4 hr after HW at Dover
5 hr after HW at Dover

Fig. 5 Typical chart showing tidal stream diamond and related information as it would appear on a nautical chart.

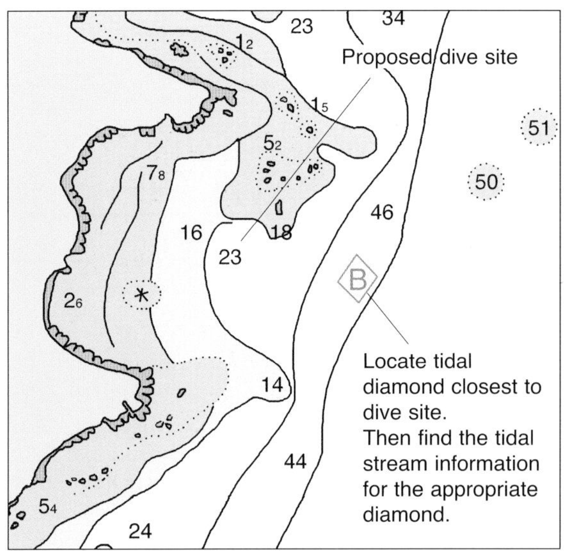
Proposed dive site
B
Locate tidal diamond closest to dive site.
Then find the tidal stream information for the appropriate diamond.
23
34
51
50
46
16
23
14
44
24

In this imaginary example, diamond B is closest to the proposed dive site. Refer to Column B of the tidal stream table on the chart which provides data on direction and speed of the current, at hourly times in relation to the high water mark for a given local port.

KEY				
Hours	◇ Geographical Position	B 55° 26'36N 5° 26'02W		
	hr	Direction of streams (degrees)	Rates at spring tides (knots) kt	Rates at neap tides (knots) kt
Before HW 6	–6	201	1.0	0.5
Before HW 5	–5	309	0.1	0.0
Before HW 4	–4	006	1.0	0.5
Before HW 3	–3	011	1.4	0.7
Before HW 2	–2	015	1.5	0.8
Before HW 1	–1	022	1.5	0.7
High Water	0	028	1.2	0.6
After HW 1	+1	030	0.5	0.2
After HW 2	+2	202	0.4	0.2
After HW 3	+3	196	1.2	0.6
After HW 4	+4	195	1.7	0.9
After HW 5	+5	197	1.6	0.8
After HW 6	+6	202	1.2	0.6

Determining Slack Water using Charts and Tide Tables

The following example is based on the information shown in Fig. 5, above.

Having found the chart diamond nearest to the dive site, use the tidal stream table (in this case, column B) to find where the current is least. In this case it at 5 hours before high water (see –5 hours: 0.0 on neaps; 0.1 on springs). The second lowest speed is at 2 hours after high water (see +2: 0.2 on neaps; 0.4 on springs).

Slack water at the dive site can be calculated by subtracting 5 hours from (or adding 2 hours to) the time of high water at the designated port. A local tide table or almanac will provide the high water times at the port for the relevant day. The most suitable time of day (either 5 hours before or 2 hours after HW) can then be chosen for diving operations. Since UK tide tables are usually written in GMT, remember to make adjustments for British Summer Time (or equivalent) if necessary.

Once the time of slack water has been established, it is advisable to check the rate of the current either side of slack water to calculate the safest time to dive.

In this instance, assume that 2 hours after HW is the most suitable time and that the day falls in a period of neap tides. From the chart data (in Fig. 5) it can be seen that current speed is 0.2kt one hour after HW but leaps to 0.6kt 3 hours after HW (see +1 and +3 for rates at neap tides). The best time to start diving is, therefore, 1 hour after HW.

Currents

Currents in the sea are not the same as tidal streams. Currents are different in that they are an onward flow of water, not an oscillating one. They are of two types:

1. Ocean currents, which include regular horizontal movements of water in one direction, such as the Gulf Stream.
2. Weather-generated currents. These are usually the result of meteorological conditions such as wind, or the geographical nature of the adjacent land and the sea bottom. The speed of a wind-generated current is usually about 3% of the wind speed. A Force 7 wind (28–33kt), therefore, will generate a surface current of about 1 knot; a Force 5 wind (17–21kt) will generate a current of about 0.6 knots.

DIVING IN CURRENTS AND TIDAL STREAMS

IMCA (The International Marine Contractors Association) has drawn up a list of suggested restrictions on working in tidal streams and currents (see Fig. 6). Since conditions vary enormously, the restrictions should be applied flexibly, taking into account diver feedback and operational requirements.

GULF OF MEXICO

The range of tides in this area is small (on average 0.6m/2ft) and the tides have a marked diurnal inequality – ie, one high water of the day is much higher than the other. Tidal streams in general are weak and in many places there is only one stream a day running for about 12 hours continuously in one direction. As a general rule the streams offshore set to the northward and westward on the rising tide and vice versa on the falling tide.

Comparatively strong currents tend to predominate in the Gulf. The main current is the Equatorial which circuits the Gulf in three main branches before flowing out to become the Gulf Stream.

Fig. 7 shows the general current circulation throughout the year. To a very large extent the flow of water within this area is very variable and dependent on the prevailing winds.

INDIAN OCEAN

Prevailing winds can have a significant effect on surface currents. The monsoon winds of the north

Indian Ocean dramatically change the direction of surface currents twice a year (Fig. 8).

Fig. 6 Suggested restrictions on working in currents and tidal streams.

Current *(knots)*	Surface-supply in mid-water	Surface-supply on bottom	Bell or Wet Bell in mid-water	Bell or Wet Bell on bottom
0 – 0.8	1	1	1	1
0.8 – 1.0	3	2	1	1
1.0 – 1.2	4	3	2	1
1.2 – 1.5	5	4	3	2
1.5 – 1.8	5	5	4	3
1.8 – 2.0	5	5	5	4
over 2	5	5	5	5

Key:

1	Normal work
2	Light work
3	Observation only
4	Consult and reconsider. The diving supervisor should consult divers and others as necessary about how best to proceed.
5	Do not dive unless pre-planning has taken into account the presence of high current from the early stages of the project. Special solutions involving equipment, techniques and procedures should have been evolved to overcome (or protect the diver from) the effects of current and provide contingencies for foreseeable emergencies.

Specialist information

Specialist advice and published oceanographic inform-ation or numerical data relating to the marine environment can be obtained from marine research establishments such as the Marine Information Advisory Service (MIAS) at the Southampton Oceanography Centre, UK (*www.soc.soton.ac.uk*).

The Centre can advise on any location worldwide and can provide customised information for specific sites.

Such information can include, for example, details of bottom-currents for a particular pipeline inspection area for a given period. Inshore tidal data can be processed to provide local tidal stream atlases for port operations. Specific information on the nature of the seabed, its structure and strength of bottom currents can be provided to assist in submersible operations and/or the installation of subsea structures.

Fig. 7 Prevailing surface currents, Gulf of Mexico

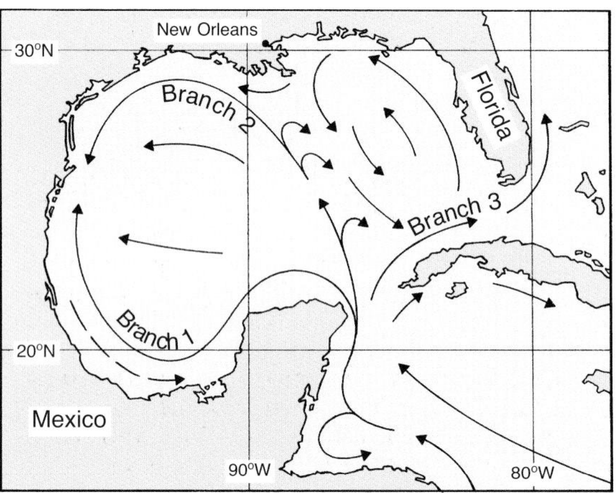
New Orleans
30°N
Florida
Branch 2
Branch 3
Branch 1
20°N
Mexico
90°W
80°W

General surface current circulation throughout the year

Branch 1.
Mean rate: 1/2–1 1/2 kt increasing with southerly winds in summer.

Branch 2.
Mean rate: 1 kt increasing with easterly winds, decreasing with westerlies.

Branch 3.
Mean rate: 1–1 1/2 kt. There is a westerly set off the delta.

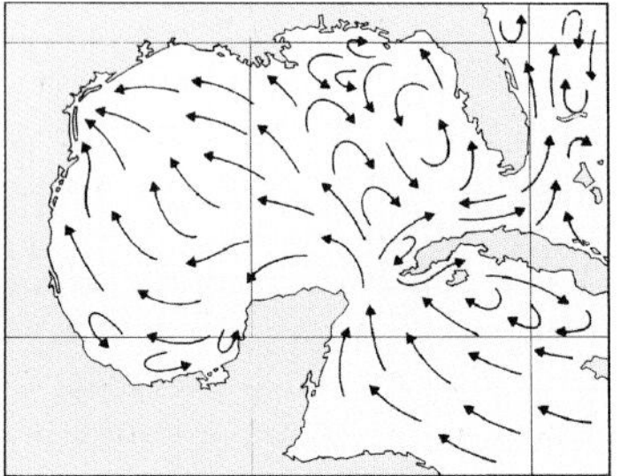

Winter (January, February, March)

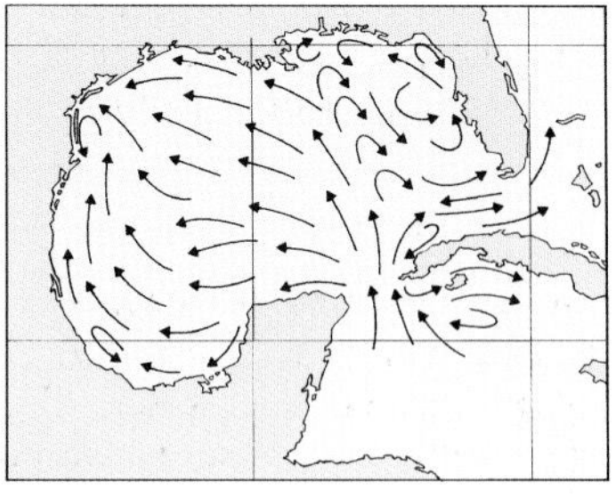

Spring (April, May June)

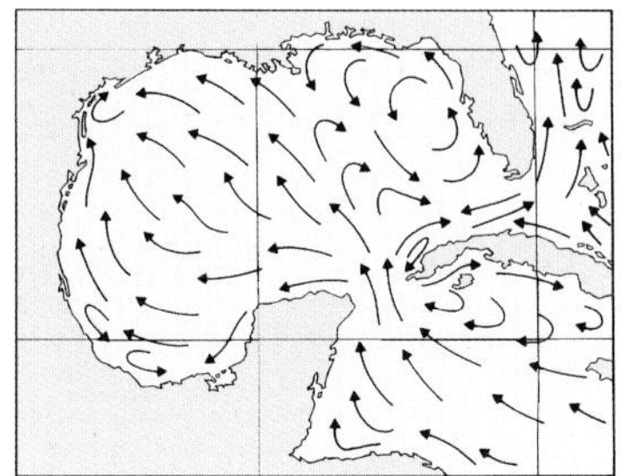

Summer (July, August, September)

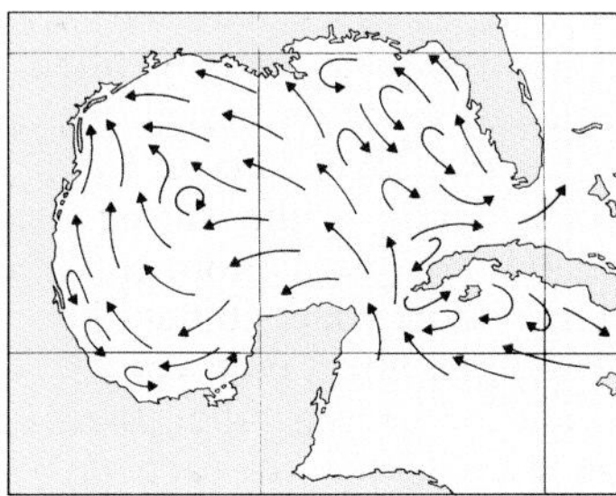

Autumn (October, November, December)

Fig. 8 General direction of main surface currents in the Indian Ocean

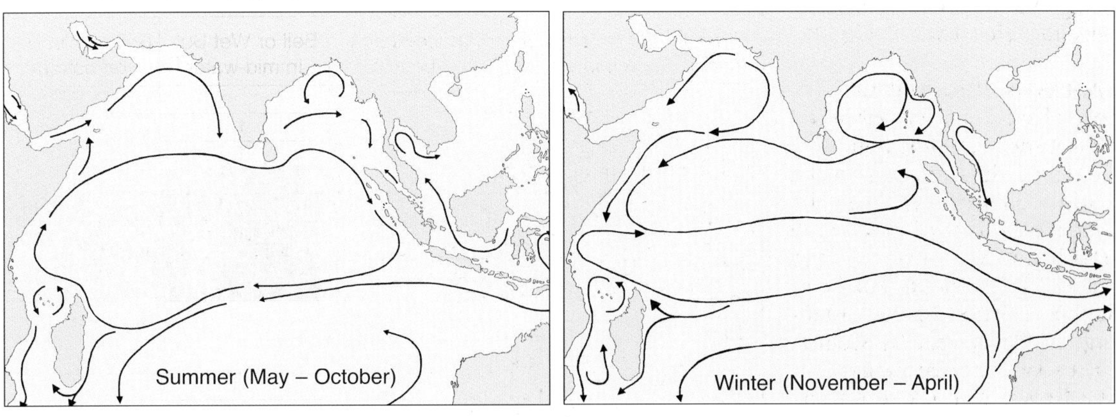
Summer (May – October)
Winter (November – April)

The North Indian Ocean is the only ocean where the surface current pattern changes twice a year (due to the influence of the monsoon winds). The south-westerly summer monsoon winds drive surface currents northwards along the coast of Somalia and thence clockwise around the northern ocean. By November the south-westerly winds cease and are replaced by the north-easterly monsoon which reverses the pattern and surface currents circulate in a generally anti-clockwise direction in the northern part of the ocean.

11.5 TEMPERATURE, THERMOCLINES AND HALOCLINES

Temperature

Water temperature is a significant factor in diving since it can influence the type of equipment used and, possibly, the duration and safety of the dive.
Because the temperature at the surface of the sea is affected by the air temperature, the sea temperature can range from sub-zero at the poles up to 27°C (80°F) at the equator (Figs. 2a & b). The deeper one goes the less the temperature varies until eventually a depth is reached where it can be constant all year round (Fig. 1).
There can be a sandwich-like layering of cold and warm water masses. The warmer layers lie on top of colder layers which get colder as the depth increases. Because the lowering temperatures make each layer denser than the one above it, each layer rests stably upon the one below. There is little mixing.

Fig. 1 Average temperature variation of the North Sea at selected depths

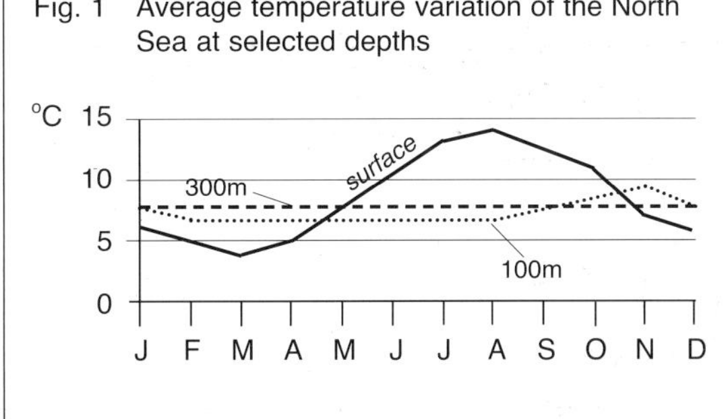
°C
15
10
5
0
300m
surface
100m
J F M A M J J A S O N D

At the surface, the sea temperature varies markedly throughout the year. At 100m (330ft) depth the variation is less pronounced. At 300m (985ft) depth the temperature of the sea remains constant throughout the year.

Thermoclines

The boundaries between the layers of different water temperatures are called thermoclines. These may occur at any level and the temperature may vary from layer to layer by as much as 7°C (20°F). Thus, even if the surface conditions indicate a warm dive, the bottom conditions could result in a much shorter and colder dive.
The other effect on divers is currents. The layers of water between the thermoclines can move independently of each other so that a freely descending diver may drift in several different directions on his way down.
It is important to note that the direction of the current on the surface is not necessarily the same as the current near the sea bed. Consequently, if the direction of the current is to be used for navigation purposes (eg, in order to keep close to the divers) it must be determined according to the direction on the *bottom*, not the surface.

Haloclines

Different layers of water can also be formed by differences in water salinity. A mass of fresh water can form a layer over denser salt water. The boundaries between such layers are called haloclines. As with thermoclines, these layers can be moving in different directions causing the diver to drift in different directions on his way to the bottom. There may also be a significant difference in visibility between layers of different salinity.

Fig. 2 Isocrymes and Isotheres.

Fig. 2a - Isocrymes – Coolest surface sea temperatures (irrespective of month when it occurs)

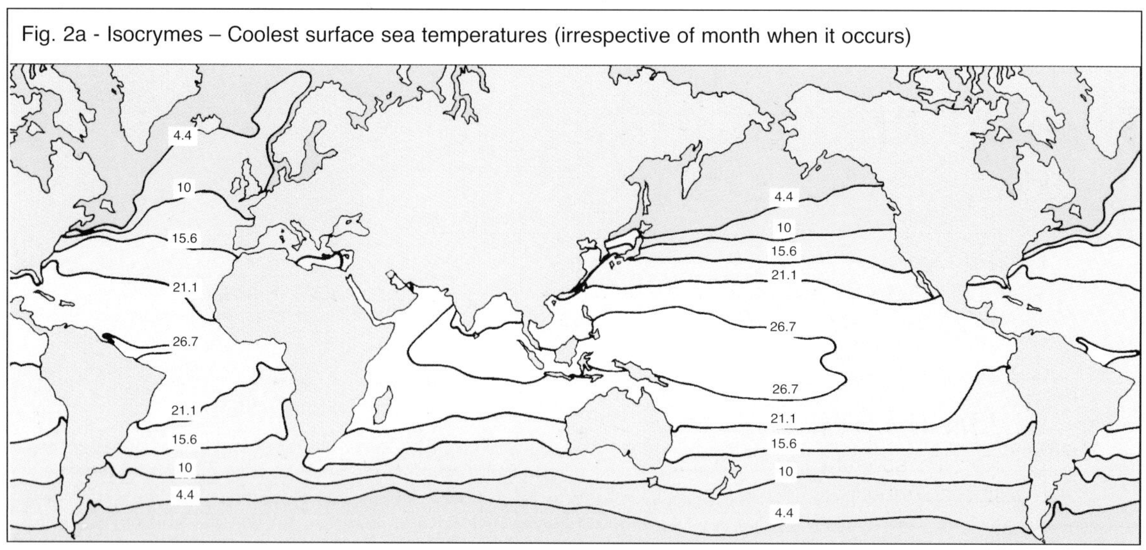
4.4
10
15.6
21.1
26.7
21.1
15.6
10
4.4
4.4
10
15.6
21.1
26.7
26.7
21.1
15.6
10
4.4

Fig. 2b - Isotheres – Warmest surface sea temperatures (irrespective of month when it occurs)

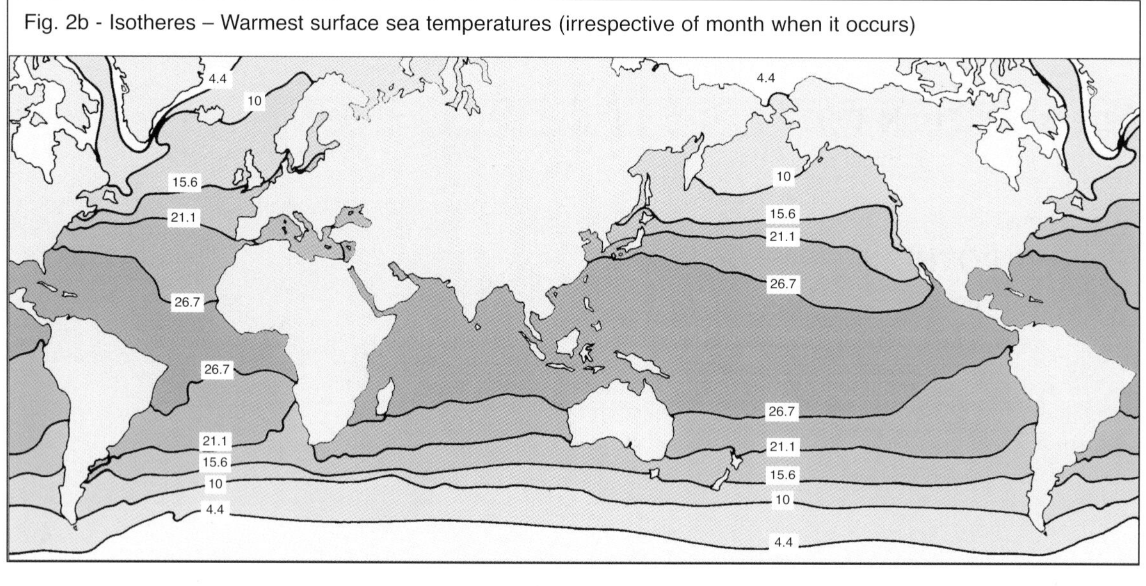
4.4
10
15.6
21.1
26.7
26.7
21.1
15.6
10
4.4
4.4
10
15.6
21.1
26.7
26.7
21.1
15.6
10
4.4

Health and Safety

12.1 FIRST AID

This section addresses a variety of types of accidents. However, it should be remembered that accidents are most commonly the result of slips, trips and falls.

The first aid described in this book is limited to the treatment of diving accidents including the treatment of injuries while under pressure. It is assumed that little or no first aid equipment is to hand. When treating an unconscious diver remember that unconsciousness may be due to a variety of reasons. Some important examples are shown in Fig. 1. (Remember that near-drowning may complicate or mask other injuries).

In all cases of rescue, the basic guidelines are:

1. Remove victim from danger.
2. Check breathing.
3. Check pulse (if no breathing).
4. Stop major bleeding.
5. Treat for shock.
6. Treat any other conditions.
7. Summon expert medical advice.

1. Remove victim from danger

This will usually mean remove victim from the water.

2. Check breathing

First extend the victim's airway. In a bell it may be dark and there may be excessive noise and vibration so use the 'feel and listen' method by placing your cheek over the victim's open mouth to check if he is breathing.

3. Check pulse

If breathing is absent, check the pulse. A victim's pulse may be weak, erratic or very slow and so may be difficult to feel. When searching for a victim's pulse allow at least 10 seconds to find it. The wearing of a neck-dam may make it difficult to feel the diver's carotid (throat) pulse (Fig. 2). Alternatives include the wrist or auricular pulse (small flap in front of the entrance to the ear).

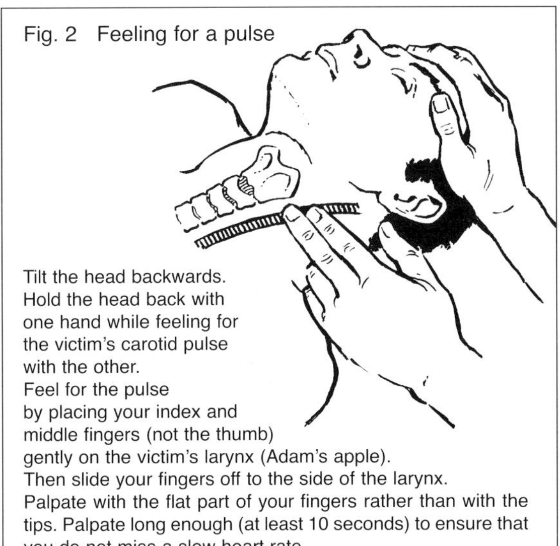

Fig. 2 Feeling for a pulse

Tilt the head backwards.
Hold the head back with one hand while feeling for the victim's carotid pulse with the other.
Feel for the pulse by placing your index and middle fingers (not the thumb) gently on the victim's larynx (Adam's apple).
Then slide your fingers off to the side of the larynx.
Palpate with the flat part of your fingers rather than with the tips. Palpate long enough (at least 10 seconds) to ensure that you do not miss a slow heart rate.

Fig. 1 Examples of possible causes of unconsciousness in a diver

Remember that unconsciousness may be due to more than one of these causes.

1. Hypoxia/anoxia (insufficient oxygen in breathing gas).
2. Asphyxia/drowning.
3. Arterial gas embolism.
4. Carbon dioxide poisoning.
5. Serious decompression sickness (type II), severe central nervous system (CNS) or cardio-respiratory involvement.
6. Hyperoxia (acute oxygen poisoning: too much oxygen in breathing gas).
7. Inert gas narcosis (only significant on air at depths greater than 80m/260ft).
8. Hypothermia (body cooling).
9. Hyperthermia (body overheating)
10. Toxic gas contamination of breathing gas, eg carbon monoxide, consequences of underwater processes such as gases associated with welding/cutting, epoxy-resin gases, decomposing organic matter gases.
11. HPNS (high pressure nervous syndrome, 'microsleep', but only at depths over 300m/1000ft).
12. Head injury.
13. Psychological factors such as fainting.
14. Electrocution.
15. Unassociated medical problems such as diabetes, brain haemorrhage or heart attack.

4. Stop major bleeding

Apply direct pressure to the bleeding point. In most cases the best treatment for staunching an external wound is to apply a pressure pad on the wound itself. The origin of the bleeding should be exposed but unless the bleeding is very severe or inaccessible leave the victim's suit on.

HOW TO APPLY A PRESSURE PAD (see Fig. 3)

a) If practicable, elevate the bleeding site above the level of the heart.
b) Apply pressure over the wound with the hands until a pad is available.
c) Replace hands with a pressure pad. It doesn't matter what the pad is made of, but ideally it should consist of a sterile dressing, a self-

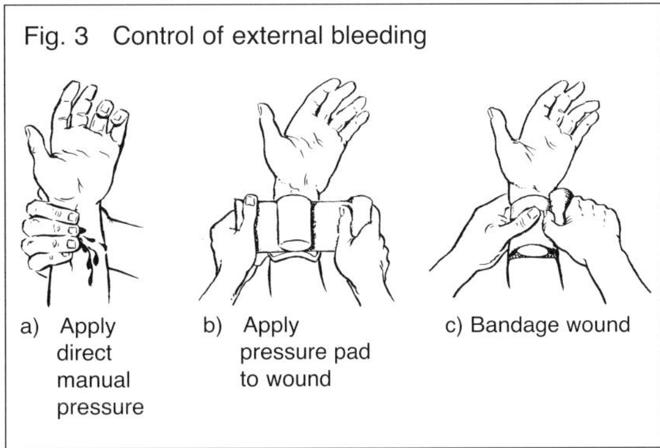

Fig. 3 Control of external bleeding

a) Apply direct manual pressure
b) Apply pressure pad to wound
c) Bandage wound

adhesive elastic bandage strip and a semi-rigid styrene block over the pad. An elastic bandage wrapped over the block applies pressure against the wound and stops bleeding.

HOW TO APPLY A TOURNIQUET

Only use a tourniquet if bleeding cannot be stopped by applying a pressure pad.

a) Place the tourniquet close to the wound and between the heart and the wound.
b) Make a record of the time.
c) Loosen the tourniquet for ten seconds every 20 minutes.

5. Treat for shock

Any serious injury causes shock. It is the result of a loss of blood or a drop in blood pressure causing decreased circulation. Shock and fright are not the same thing.

a) Symptoms of shock (not all may be present):
   - weak and rapid pulse.
   - trembling.
   - cold clammy skin.
   - pale ashen skin.
   - low blood pressure.
   - thirst.
   - sometimes, cyanosis (blueish appearance of the skin, especially lips and fingernails).

b) Treatment
   - Victim should be reassured and made to lie down.
   - Keep victim quiet and warm but do not overheat.
   - If conscious, victim may be given a warm drink, but not alcohol.
   - Do not massage his limbs.
   - Except in the case of chest and head injuries, it may help to elevate the legs.
   - Administer oxygen if necessary.

6. Treat special conditions

Divers are constantly injuring their hands because of the nature of the work and the tools they use. Low temperatures will have a numbing effect which will cause less efficient handling of tools. It is even possible to be unaware of an injury. Many of these will be burns from cutting and welding. Treatment is to seek medical aid promptly.

One particular type of injury that deserves special attention is that caused by high pressure water jets which are used, primarily for cleaning surfaces in preparation for NDT work. Superficial damage to the skin may appear trivial and give little indication of the extent of the injury and the damage to deeper tissue beneath. On site, first aid is confined to dressing the wound. The victim should be observed for the next few hours for developing symptoms. In the event of fever, pain or a rising pulse rate occurring before medical advice is available, give a course of antibiotics.

Drowning

Drowning is basically asphyxia due to immersion in a liquid and is the fatal termination of a sequence of preventable events. Among the many causes of drowning, the most common is hypothermia.

The victim of immersion both inhales and swallows water, however in the majority of cases comparatively little water enters the lungs. Whether it does or not, the result is the same: breathing stops. Drowning is lung damage and failure of oxygen transfer; it is unimportant whether immersion occurs in fresh or salt water. Death usually occurs within about 8 minutes. Occasionally survival may be prolonged by profound hypothermia. People have recovered after being totally immersed and without breathing for 40 minutes. In all cases of drowning attempts to restore respiration must be commenced without delay. Even though a survivor of near-drowning may appear to have recovered he should not be allowed to go home since possible complications may rapidly develop during the next few days.

Resuscitation

The basic technique of rescue from drowning is called cardiopulmonary resuscitation (CPR). The treatment is always the same although the technique may vary with the expertise of the rescuer and the equipment available. CPR can be a lengthy treatment but is a critical life-saving skill required in the recovery of an unconscious diver (see flow charts on the following two pages).

For convenience, resuscitation can be divided into three phases:

Phase 1 Basic life support (BLS), known as the ABC of lifesaving (see Fig. 4).

Phase 2 Advanced life support (ALS) which is the restoration of spontaneous breathing and circulation by trained personnel only. This involves the insertion of a tube into the throat to control the airway, the administration of drugs and the use of defibrilation equipment.

Phase 3 Prolonged life support (PLS) which is long-term resuscitation involving intensive care in a hospital.

Phases 2 and 3 are beyond the scope of this book.

COMMON PITFALLS

When attempting resuscitation be aware of the following three common pitfalls:

1. The airway is often not properly extended so that air passes into the victim's stomach instead of into his lungs. The rescuer will know this is case if the victim's stomach bulges. This may cause vomiting so be prepared to tilt the victim's head down and onto the side.
2. The rescuer often makes himself dizzy if he ventilates too fast. EAR should not exceed 12 breaths a minute.

RESCUE OF AN UNCONSCIOUS SURFACE-SUPPLIED DIVER

Practical intervention by a standby diver from the surface can take place only down to a limit of 75m

UNDERWATER

Descend down victim's lifeline. Grasp victim firmly – assess the situation – drop his weight belt. Vent victim's freeflow and check that he has gas. Assist to surface.

ON THE SURFACE

Support on surface and secure victim in basket, holding him firmly. Remove his helmet/mask. Open airway by tilting back his head. Maintain open airways.

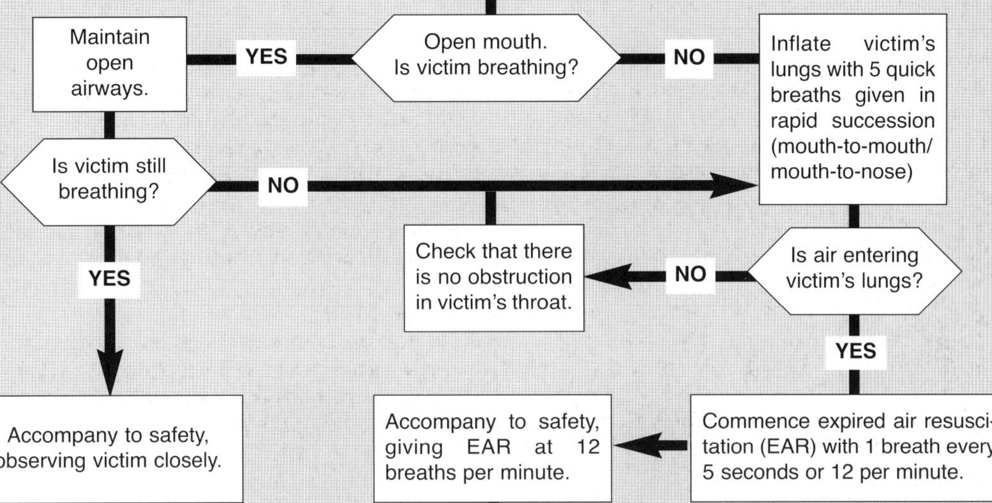

Maintain open airways.
YES
Open mouth. Is victim breathing?
NO
Inflate victim's lungs with 5 quick breaths given in rapid succession (mouth-to-mouth/ mouth-to-nose)
Is victim still breathing?
NO
YES
Check that there is no obstruction in victim's throat.
NO
Is air entering victim's lungs?
YES
Accompany to safety, observing victim closely.
Accompany to safety, giving EAR at 12 breaths per minute.
Commence expired air resuscitation (EAR) with 1 breath every 5 seconds or 12 per minute.

REMOVE VICTIM FROM THE WATER

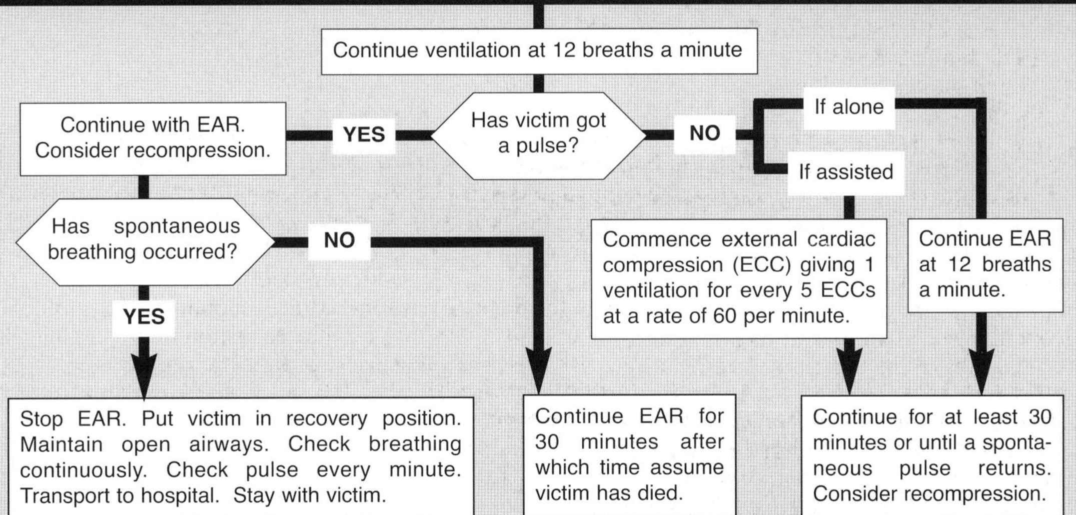

Continue ventilation at 12 breaths a minute
Continue with EAR. Consider recompression.
YES
Has victim got a pulse?
NO
If alone
If assisted
Has spontaneous breathing occurred?
NO
YES
Commence external cardiac compression (ECC) giving 1 ventilation for every 5 ECCs at a rate of 60 per minute.
Continue EAR at 12 breaths a minute.
Stop EAR. Put victim in recovery position. Maintain open airways. Check breathing continuously. Check pulse every minute. Transport to hospital. Stay with victim.
Continue EAR for 30 minutes after which time assume victim has died.
Continue for at least 30 minutes or until a spontaneous pulse returns. Consider recompression.

If victim develops cardiac or respiratory arrest with no obvious reason for collapse

PUT VICTIM INTO COMPRESSION CHAMBER

Do not interrupt resuscitation for more than 5 seconds while lifting victim into deck compression chamber head first. Diagnose whether victim is suffering from gas embolism or decompression sickness. If in doubt assume gas embolism and treat accordingly.

RESCUE OF AN UNCONSCIOUS BELL DIVER

When a diver becomes unconscious out of a bell or does not respond for whatever reason, it must be assumed that he is not breathing or not breathing sufficiently.

UNDERWATER

Bring victim back into the bell either by pulling him in on his umbilical or by a bell excursion. Should the victim's gear snag on the bell hatch coaming, a twist on his umbilical may free it. Remove his weight belt.

Vent victim's freeflow valve. If no bubbles, close it and switch to emergency bail-out supply.

Snapshackle lifting device to victim's harness so that he can be hoisted vertically through trunking. Raising the water level in the bell helps both rescuer and victim to get back inside but sometimes it is more convenient to leave the victim partially immersed in water when initiating resuscitation. Take off his helmet or mask.

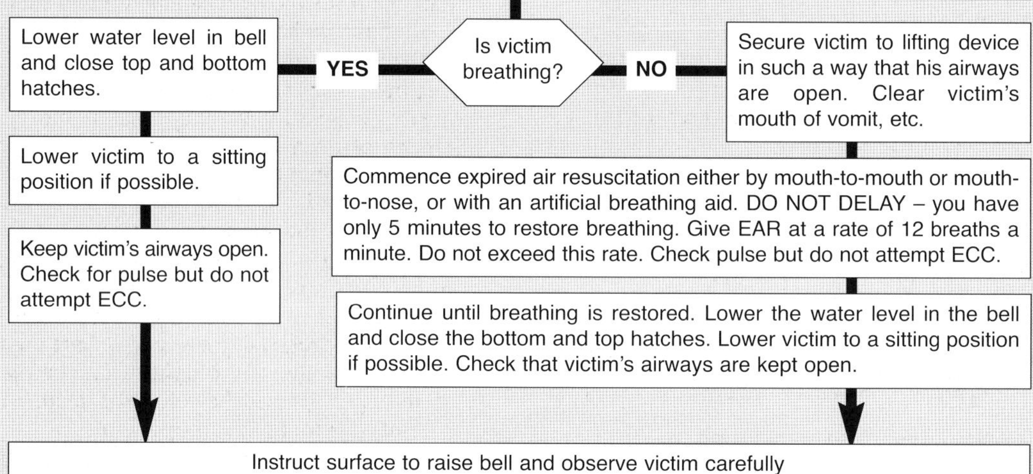

Is victim breathing?
YES
Lower water level in bell and close top and bottom hatches.
Lower victim to a sitting position if possible.
Keep victim's airways open. Check for pulse but do not attempt ECC.
NO
Secure victim to lifting device in such a way that his airways are open. Clear victim's mouth of vomit, etc.
Commence expired air resuscitation either by mouth-to-mouth or mouth-to-nose, or with an artificial breathing aid. DO NOT DELAY – you have only 5 minutes to restore breathing. Give EAR at a rate of 12 breaths a minute. Do not exceed this rate. Check pulse but do not attempt ECC.
Continue until breathing is restored. Lower the water level in the bell and close the bottom and top hatches. Lower victim to a sitting position if possible. Check that victim's airways are kept open.

Instruct surface to raise bell and observe victim carefully

ON THE SURFACE – REMOVE VICTIM FROM BELL

Victim and rescuer transfer from bell to a DCC. Lift victim into chamber head first. Do not interrupt resuscitation for more than 5 seconds while lifting victim into chamber, head first.

PUT VICTIM INTO COMPRESSION CHAMBER

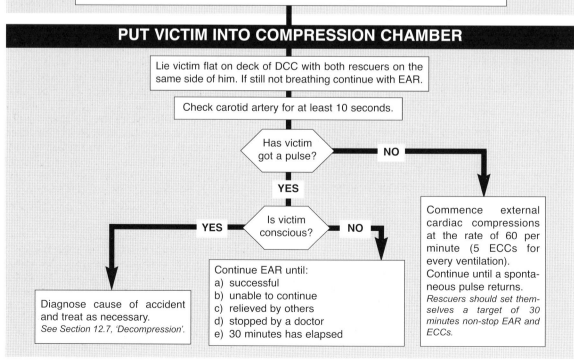

Lie victim flat on deck of DCC with both rescuers on the same side of him. If still not breathing continue with EAR.

Check carotid artery for at least 10 seconds.

Has victim got a pulse?

NO

Commence external cardiac compressions at the rate of 60 per minute (5 ECCs for every ventilation). Continue until a spontaneous pulse returns. *Rescuers should set themselves a target of 30 minutes non-stop EAR and ECCs.*

YES

Is victim conscious?

YES

Diagnose cause of accident and treat as necessary. *See Section 12.7, 'Decompression'.*

NO

Continue EAR until:
- a) successful
- b) unable to continue
- c) relieved by others
- d) stopped by a doctor
- e) 30 minutes has elapsed

Fig. 4 Basic Life Support (BLS)
also known as the ABC of lifesaving:
A = Airway; B = Breathing; C = Circulation

a) Airway

i) With head forward the tongue obstructs the airway

ii) Tilt the head backwards to clear the airway

iii) Lift the neck and support the jaw to get better control of opening the mouth

b) Breathing - expired air resuscitation (EAR)
Give 12 breaths per minute

i) Mouth-to-mouth. Head tilted by supporting neck.

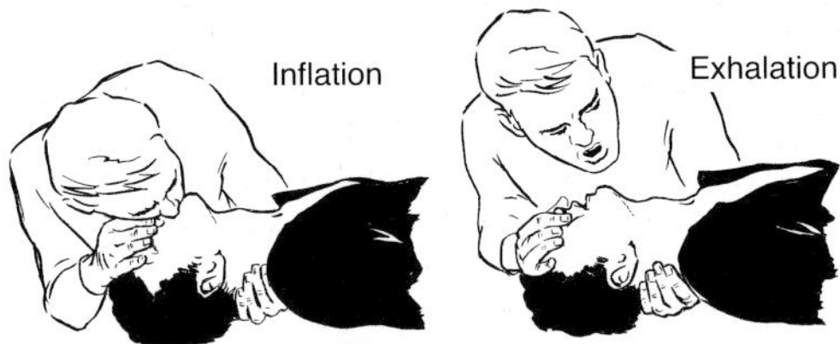
Inflation
Exhalation

ii) Mouth-to-nose. Head tilted by supporting chin .

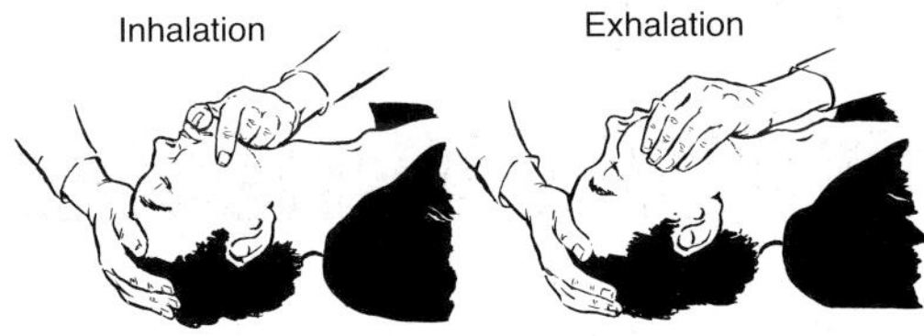
Inhalation
Exhalation

c) Circulation - external cardiac compression (ECC)

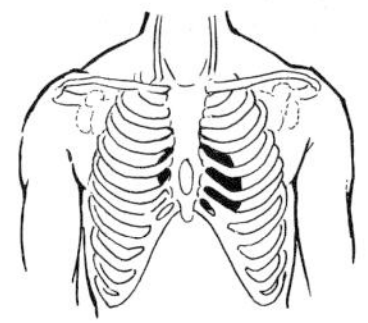

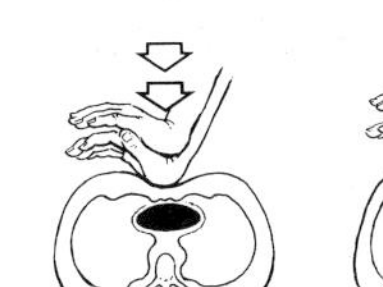

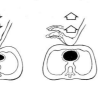

i) Identify the pressure point. Feel for lower end of breastbone and move about 4cm ($1\frac{1}{2}$ in) above it.

ii) Use the heels of both hands. Keep arms straight and keep hands off the rib cage. Press down approximately 4–5cm ($1\frac{1}{2}$–2 in). Press and release 60 times per minute.

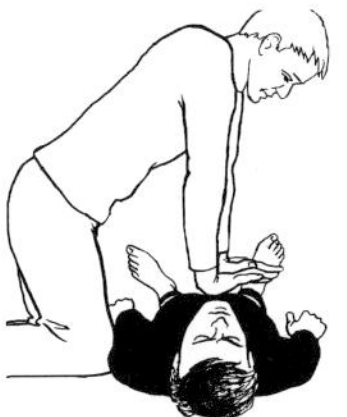

iii) ECC given by one operator

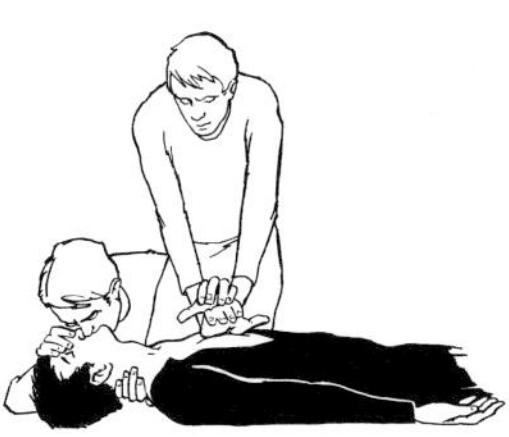

iv) ECC given by two operators. EAR and ECC given simultaneously

3. The rescuer giving ECC must maintain an uninterrupted steady rhythm with the other rescuer giving EAR. One ventilation should be given with every 5 ECCs (at a rate of 60 per minute) without interrupting the rhythm of the compressions.

Points to remember when rescuing a victim of drowning.

1. Speed in commencing EAR is essential. Unconsciousness will result from depriving the brain of oxygen for more than 30 seconds. An absolute deprivation of oxygen (anoxia) for more than 3 minutes may result in brain damage followed by death although survival up to 40 minutes has been recorded.
2. Immersion victims usually suffer from respiratory arrest before cardiac arrest (which is the opposite of what happens in most other modes of death). In many immersion victims the heart continues to beat although breathing has stopped, making ECC unnecessary. Therefore, concentrate on ventilation.
3. Be prepared to have to force open the victim's mouth. Victims of drowning often clench their teeth. Use the 'crossed-finger' manoeuvre for moderately relaxed jaws and 'finger-behind-the-teeth' method for a tightly clenched jaw. A solid object placed between the teeth to one side of his mouth will keep it open.
4. 50% of victims will vomit during resuscitation. Constantly check that the airways remain clear.
5. Victims of near drowning may or may not have water in their lungs. You can check this by putting your ear on the back of the victim's chest at the bottom part of the chest wall and listen.
6. The treatment of wounds takes second place to resuscitation except in the case of a severe haemorrhage.
7. A drowning victim's pulse may be weak, erratic or very slow. When searching for a victim's pulse allow at least 10 seconds to find it.
8. When performing ECC a square wave sequence should be adopted. That is, depress the sternum (breast bone) 4–5cm ($1\frac{1}{2}$–2in) for half a second (50% of the cycle) then release rapidly and wait for another half a second (the other half of the cycle) to let the heart fill with blood.
9. The use of artificial airways is only effective if the rescuer is trained to use them. There are many to choose from starting with the simple S-shaped plastic airway tube, to an oesophageal obturator airway.
10. Cardiopulmonary resuscitation, if done effectively, is exhausting. It is recommended that the rescuers set themselves a half-hour target to re-establish breathing, otherwise the rescuers themselves may become in need of medical assistance. The decision to stop resuscitation should be left to a qualified person. Efforts may reasonably be discontinued however after a minimum of half an hour if the

victim remains without a pulse. An exception may be made for a victim that has been immersed in very cold water, in which case CPR should be continued for at least one hour.

11. If CPR is successful arrange the victim into the recovery position (see Fig. 5).
12. Following recovery never relax your vigilance. Stay with the victim, observe him closely and be ready to furnish medical staff with details of the accident. Admission to hospital is mandatory for all drowning victims. If water has entered the lungs the victim may drown, even after a successful rescue, or his lungs may suddenly react and fill up with his own body fluids. Many victims have died days after an apparently successful recovery.

NOTE:

1. ECC is not recommended in the diving bell because of the practical limitations with space and positioning of the victim. Therefore concentrate on EAR.
2. The rescuer should be alert for symptoms of hypothermia: shallow, slow breathing, mental confusion, heart rate decrease, unconsciousness.
3. If the victim is shivering, EAR will not be necessary since it indicates that the victim has a pulse and is breathing.

Fig. 5 Recovery position

a) Flex victim's leg which is closest to you.
b) Take victim's hand which is closest to you and put it under his buttocks.

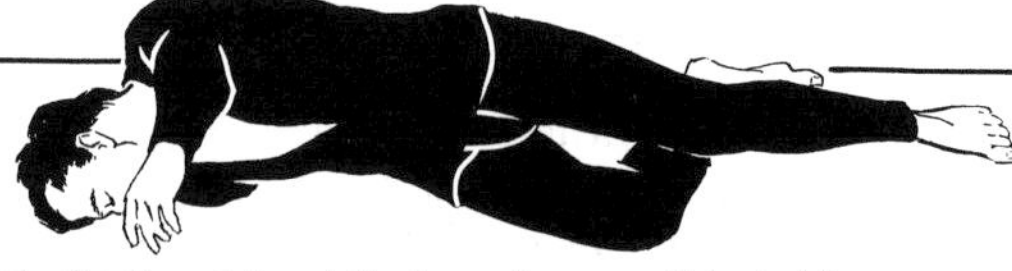

c) Gently roll the victim towards you until he is lying on his side.

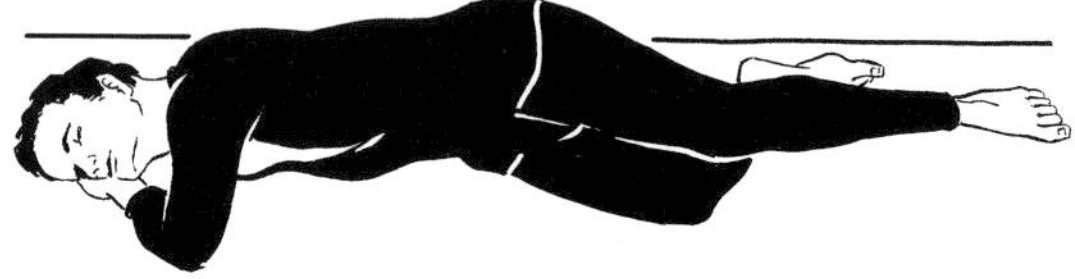

d) Tilt his head backwards keeping his face low.
e) Put his upper hand under his lower cheek to maintain head tilt and to prevent him from rolling onto his face. The other arm behind his back prevents him from rolling backwards.

Jellyfish stings

Jellyfish stings, North Atlantic

1. First ask the victim about his general well-being or reaction to the sting. If there is any concern at all, seek medical advice.
2. Pour vinegar gently over affected area. Do not rub in. Keep area wet with vinegar. Cool with ice pack covered with dry plastic for 10–15 minutes. Repeat if required. For persistent redness or swelling, use high potency steroid ointment or cream. Xylocaine cream can help relieve persistent pain.
3. Severe local reaction, or general reaction, requires urgent medical attention. Adrenaline injection, oral steroids or oral or injectable antihistamines, should be used immediately, if available.
4. Do not wash area with fresh water. This can make undischarged, microscopic stinging cells fire off. If needed, use salt water.
5. Do not rub the affected area.
6. Do not leave the victim alone because a delayed allergic reaction might develop.

12.2 CHAMBER HYGIENE AND DIET

Chamber hygiene is of paramount importance to the health and safety of divers undergoing pressurization, particularly in saturation. Divers should be aware of the potential hazards to their health that simple exposure to pressure may present. To maintain a habitable environment within a chamber, oxygen and carbon dioxide concentrations, temperature and especially humidity must be kept within the following limits:

1. *Oxygen content*: The partial pressure of oxygen must lie between 0.25 and 0.5ata (250–500mb or 3.65–7.35psi). The percent by volume should never exceed 25%.
2. *Carbon dioxide content*: The partial pressure of carbon dioxide should not exceed 0.005ata (5mb or 0.75psi).
3. *Temperature* must be between 75°F and 85°F (24°C–30°C) and/or as directed by the chamber occupants.
4. *Humidity* should be between 60% and 75% relative humidity.

Infection

Viruses, bacteria and fungi are microscopic organisms of which there are many types. Many are capable of causing infections in humans; they can destroy tissues and produce poisonous products within the body.

Some bacteria, however, are actually necessary for the body functions and occur normally within and on the human body. Others are controlled by the body's protective mechanisms.

Three common ways of contracting an infection are:
1. Direct physical contact with an infected person or surface.
2. Inhaling infective organisms from an infected person.
3. Eating contaminated food.

There are four common categories of disease that particularly concern divers in chambers.
1. Internal disorders such as gastro-enteritis.
2. Fungal infections such as athlete's foot.
3. Outer ear infections such as *otitis externa*.
4. Respiratory infections such as colds.

Because of the confined nature of the chamber environment, great attention must be given to a preventative (prophylactic) hygiene regime. Such a regime could be considered in two parts:
1. Personal hygiene.
2. Chamber hygiene.

1. Personal Hygiene

A high standard of hygiene is essential.

BEFORE ENTERING A CHAMBER
1. You should not be suffering from any kind of infection whatsoever. Any disorder, or even a suspected oncoming disorder, must be reported to the diving supervisor and, if necessary, be given clearance by a diving doctor before recommencing diving.
2. You should shower immediately before entering a chamber and don clean clothes.

INSIDE A CHAMBER
3. Shower at least once per day. Shower before and after each bell run.
4. Do not use strong or aggressive detergents or soaps that might irritate the skin and allow an infection to become established. Use soap in the shower only once in every 24 hours so as not to remove the skin's natural oils and defences. Do not share soap.
5. Armpits and crotch should be regularly cleaned and dried.
6. Avoid, or limit, shaving if the skin is irritated.
7. Nails should be kept short.
8. Use only your own personally marked towels and bed linen. Towels should be passed out of the chamber immediately after showering. Bed linen should be changed regularly, usually every 3 days, but daily if there is an infection in the chamber.
9. The shower area should be drained quickly after use and the floor dried.
10. Change your clothing every day after showering.
11. Divers should not share diving gear (undersuit, suit, headliner) or chamber headsets.
12. Helmet oral-nasal mask and nose block pads can be removed after each bell run and locked out for washing, disinfection and drying. Suits, etc, should be cleaned and dried on the surface between dives.
13. Pay regular visits to a dentist. Brush teeth thoroughly at least twice a day.
14. You should apply prophylactic (preventative) ear-drops and maintain a meticulous regime.
15. All minor injuries must be treated immediately. Persistently cut or scratched skin and small wounds need careful cleaning and covering. The attendant should wear disposable gloves when tending to a wound. Waste from cleaning and dressing a wound should be placed in plastic bags for prompt lock-out.

2. Chamber hygiene.

1. The chamber should be cleaned thoroughly every day using a suitable disinfectant.
2. Chambers may be swabbed to check for infection. Areas and items that may be swabbed include the toilet, sink, walls, sump, shower heads, ECU drip tray, helmet liners, suits, bedding and headsets. The frequency of swabbing should be specified in the company manual. If a chamber gas reclaim system is used, the reclaim bag should also be swabbed on a regular basis.
3. The only practical method of disinfecting a chamber is by chemical means.
   A suitable disinfectant must be:
   a) Unaffected by pressure
   b) Non-toxic.
   c) Non-allergic.
   d) Non-volatile.
   e) Non-inflammable.
   f) Non-corrosive.
   g) Odourless, if possible.

   Dichlorophen is such a chemical, trade-named 'Panacide M'. When diluted by a factor of 1:2000 by volume, it is used to scrub the whole chamber complex and as it dries it deposits a film which inhibits bacterial growth. 'Panaclean' is 'Panacide' mixed with detergent which, when diluted 1:100 by volume in water is used for the physical cleaning of the inside of the chamber before disinfection with 'Panacide'. (See Fig. 1). Other products include 'Tego 103G', 'Tego 2000' and 'Trigene'.
4. A suitable disinfectant should be poured into the toilet bowl after use.
5. Chamber sumps must be kept dry. They should be drained of any cleanser, but not actively cleansed or disturbed.
6. Internal ECU systems must be drained frequently.
7. Rubbish must be sent out of the chamber every day.
8. Unused food and drink should be locked out without delay.
9. Any spillage of blood, vomit or diarrhoea must be cleaned up immediately and thoroughly using disposable gloves and paper towels. Soiled materials must be placed in plastic bags for immediate lock-out. Affected surfaces must be washed and disinfected.
10. All chamber laundry should be washed in a dedicated washing machine at the highest suitable temperature.

Fig. 1 Examples of how to achieve the required dilutions

PANACIDE		PANACLEAN
1:1000 in clean fresh water	1:2000 in clean fresh water	1:100 in clean fresh water
Panacide + water *(millilitres and litres)*	Panacide + water *(millilitres and litres)*	Panaclean + water *(millilitres and litres)*
1 ml + 1 l	1 ml + 2 l	1 ml + 0.1 l
0.3 ml + 0.3 l	0.3 ml + 0.6 l	0.3 ml + 0.03 l
2.4 ml + 2.4 l	2.4 ml + 4.8 l	2.4ml + 0.24 l
12 ml + 12 l	12 ml + 24 l	12 ml + 1.2 l

COMPARATIVE MEASURES			
dilution	Litres	US Gallons	UK gallons
	PANACIDE/WATER		
1:1000	1 ml x 1.0	1 cm³ x 0.26	1 cm³ x 0.22
	0.3ml x 0.3	0.3 cm³ x 0.08	0.3 cm³ x 0.07
	2.4 ml x 24	2.4 cm³ x 0.63	2.4 cm³ x 0.53
	12 ml x 12	12 cm³ x 3.17	12 cm³ x 2.64
1:2000	1 ml x 2	1cm³ x 0.53	1 cm³ x 0.44
	0.3 ml x 0.6	0.3 cm³ x 0.16	0.3 cm³ x 0.13
	2.4 ml x 4.8	2.4 cm³ x 1.27	2.4 cm³ x 1.06
	12 ml x 24	12 cm³ x 6.34	12 cm³ x 5.28
1:100	1 ml x 0.1	1 cm³ x 0.026	1 cm³ x 0.022
	0.3 ml x 0.03	0.3 cm³ x 0.008	0.3 cm³ x 0.007
	2.4 ml x 0.24	2.4 cm³ x 0.063	2.4 cm³ x 0.053
	12 ml x 1.2	12 cm³ x 0.317	12 cm³ x 0.264

Disinfection routine

Panaclean/Panacide is used as an example in the following disinfection routine, however any suitable disinfectant may be used. Avoid skin contact when using disinfectants. Use disposable gloves.

BEFORE PRESSURIZATION

1. Scrub the chamber with 'Panaclean' (1:100).
2. Disinfect the chamber with 'Panacide' (1:2000).
3. Mattresses and bedding which have been washed should have had a final rinse in 'Panacide' (1:1000).
4. A container of 'Panacide' solution (1:2000) may be placed in the transfer trunking prior to locking on the bell or, alternatively, a 10 litre container of neat 'Panacide' together with a 10ml syringe could be passed through the medical lock for use during saturation. (See Fig. 1 for dilution requirements).
5. Urine spilt outside the pan or on the toilet seat must be wiped up immediately.

DURING PRESSURIZATION

6. Washbasins and toilets should be washed with 'Panacide' (1:2000) every 24 hours.
7. Pour a small amount of the 'Panacide' solution into the toilet bowl each time it is used and just prior to flushing.
8. Wipe over the medical lock door, tables, seats and deck plates daily.
9. Wipe down chamber bulkheads every 3–4 days.
10. Be meticulous in cleaning up spilt food.
11. It is recommended that bedding is changed every 48 hours (unless it has been rinsed in 'Panacide' when it can be extended to 72 hours).
12. Used clothing and towels must be placed in a plastic bag and passed out through the lock.

AFTER DECOMPRESSION

13. When the chamber is unpressurized 'Panacide' (1:2000) should be left on all surfaces with the door closed for at least 12 hours.
14. Diving suits and hoods should be soaked in 'Panacide' (1:2000) for at least 12 hours.

BIBS equipment

Visually check the BIBS masks, hoses and their fittings that are to be installed in the chamber. The masks and lines should be oxygen cleaned then tested and disinfected with 'Panacide' (1:2000) before fitting. Enclosing the equipment in a plastic bag ensures that it stays free of dust.

Oral-nasal masks and the linings of helmets should be sterilised from time to time in a solution of Hycalin or similar disinfectant.

Diet in chamber

There are two basic considerations affecting the choice of foodstuff entering the chamber.

1. To maintain a healthy diet (see 'Keeping Fit').
2. To avoid introducing a fire risk (see 'DCC operation'). Certain substances, for example sugar, (especially if finely ground), butter, oils, etc, can introduce a major fire hazard and should therefore not be locked into a chamber. This also applies to certain powder-based medications and alcoholic solutions.

Remember that the saturation diving environment is ideal for the growth of bacteria because of the high temperatures and humidities; the atmosphere is totally enclosed and constantly recirculated by the life support system. All this means that each man is exposed to any infection that may be present. Any diver who contracts an infection in a chamber should report it immediately. Failure to do so could mean that the entire team in the chamber stands to lose good health and income and even, perhaps, job prospects.

Items that should never be locked into a DCC under pressure include:

- Butter.
- Oil (such as salad dressings).
- Sugar in fine powders. (If sugar is required in drinks it should be dissolved in the drink before it is passed into the chamber).
- Alcohol.
- Drugs, other than those provided. (When passing medication into a chamber loosen the tops of the bottles first).
- Thermos flasks.

12.3 EAR INFECTIONS

Infection of the outer ear passage (external auditory meatus), *Otitis Externa*, familiarly known as 'Singapore Ear,' is very common among swimmers and divers in tropical waters, some people being particularly prone to it. It is also the commonest single cause of unfitness in saturation divers. No preventative (prophylactic) treatment of the ears can be guaranteed to be 100% effective because of the enclosed atmosphere of the compression chambers in which divers spend so much time.

A real physical effort is required with regard to personal hygiene. No one should enter a chamber with any kind of ear or skin infection, however slight.

Prevention of infection

The following procedures must become a regular routine for every day of a saturation dive. These preventative measures have no chance of success otherwise.

1. Ensure that the ears are clean and dry. Dry the outside of the ears with a towel. Do not push anything inside the ears. Avoid using ear buds.
2. Start applying ear drops 24 hours before each dive and then apply each morning and evening of the saturation as well as after each dive or shower.
3. Swabs are sometimes taken from the divers 24 hours before pressurisation and the use of preventative ear drops would be started at this time.

Ear infections

There are two types of ear infection and they can be identified only in a laboratory. One type is due to *pseudomonas aeruginosa* and known as 'Pyo.' The other is due to gram negative bacilli and known as 'gram negative not Pyo.'

Divers suffering from Pyo must be removed from saturation as soon as possible. Divers with other ear infections may continue in saturation although this is undesirable.

Treatment of infection

Irritation or pain in the ears is the symptom of an infection. Take swabs of both ears of the affected diver and of the ears of all others in the chamber. Send all swabs to a laboratory for analysis.

Inform a doctor of the situation.

Apply 3–4 ear drops, either acetate in a 2% acetic acid solution, 5% aluminium acetate, or Otic Domeboro solution ear drops. The drops should be used for a timed minute in each ear, twice daily and following each dive or shower.

Severe infections will require antibiotic drops such as a mixture of polymixin and gentamicin but should only be taken under medical supervision.

There may be severe pain which can be treated with a pain-killer such as Distalgesic (co-proximal), 1 or 2 tablets up to 4 times a day.

Curative treatment drops for ear infections should *not* be used as a preventative measure (see 'Applying Ear Drops' below). Begin treatment only when there is a positive indication, ie significant ear pain and/or confirmation of infection from the results of the laboratory bacteriological studies.

Preventative treatment drops must stop before any curative treatment drops can be applied.

Use curative treatment as recommended by medical advice. If this is not possible use polymixin/gentimicin ear drops. Use Otosporin only if pain is very severe.

The proper use of curative ear drops, while simple, is not a trivial matter. Treatment must be supervised and carried out with close attention to detail.

APPLYING EAR DROPS

1. To avoid cross-infection, label all ear-drop bottles (two for each person) with the name of the diver and which ear (right or left). One bottle should be used for each ear and this rule must be rigorously observed.
2. The head should be tilted to one side and three drops allowed to fall into the ear canal. The dropper must not touch the ear or anything else. It is often easier for someone other than the patient to administer the drops. Do not exceed the stated dose as toxic side effects may occur. The head should be kept tilted to one side for at least 30 seconds while the tragus (the small cartilaginous lump in front of the ear) is massaged with a circular motion. Repeat for the other ear.
3. Repeat this procedure four times daily (every 6 hours) for seven full days, even if the symptoms disappear. Discard any remaining drops after this time.
4. Do not keep drops for more than 3 weeks at 30°C (86°F) (saturation environment) or more than 5 months at 4°C (39°F). Do not put in a freezer.

Fig. 1 Parts of the ear

External ear consists of outer, fleshy part (auricle) and canal leading to eardrum

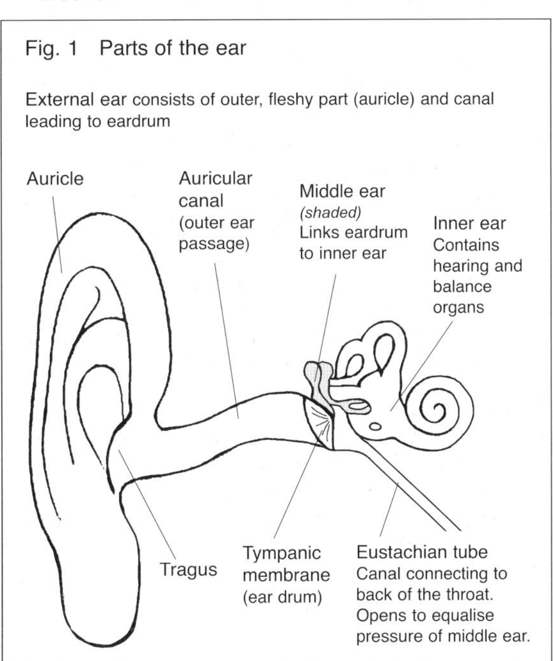
Auricle
Auricular canal (outer ear passage)
Middle ear (shaded) Links eardrum to inner ear
Inner ear Contains hearing and balance organs
Tragus
Tympanic membrane (ear drum)
Eustachian tube Canal connecting to back of the throat. Opens to equalise pressure of middle ear.

5. Paracetamol may be taken as a painkiller (do not exceed 2 tablets every 6 hours). Beware of masking pains that may be due to decompression sickness. If divers develop any other symptoms other than ear pain while under treatment, seek immediate medical advice.
6. Ear swabs must not be taken during treatment. Results during this time are misleading. At the end of the course of treatment, drops should not be used for a further 2 days. Ear swabs may be taken on the third day. If these swabs are clear a cure can be assumed. If the infection persists seek medical advice.
7. Repeated infections in a DCC require investigation. Check that the DCC is not contaminated.
8. Oral-nasal masks and the linings of helmets should be sterilized regularly in a solution of Hycalin or similar development.

12.4 HEALTH IN THE TROPICS

Due to the high heat and humidity in the tropics special care must be taken to help ensure healthy working conditions.

It is always wise to carry an anti-diahorreal such as 'Imodium' or 'Arret' and to take it in accordance with the manufacturer's instructions as soon as there is any looseness of the bowels.

Prompt treatment is the path to a rapid relief of symptoms in most cases. But there are several possible causes of diahorrea, some of them dangerous. If symptoms persist and are accompanied by considerable pain professional help must be sought.

A rare but potentially lethal cause of diarrhoea is the Red Tide produced by microscopic organisms called dinoflagellates and transmitted to humans by eating infected shellfish. The first symptoms are usually a tingling around the mouth and hands followed by numbness and limb weakness and signs of neurological incoordination. First-aid consists of getting the patient to vomit as soon as the symptoms are recognised.

Diet

1. Avoid drinking local water. Do not use ice cubes in drinks. These will be made from local water. When ordering bottled water make sure that it is opened in front of you. Already-opened bottles may have been refilled with local water.
2. Avoid eating salads and fresh fruits as they can harbour micro-organisms that cause diarrhoea.
3. Avoid eating all forms of shellfish.

Ears

After diving wash your ears with fresh water to flush out the salt water and any microscopic organisms and debris that may be present in the sea-water. Dry your ears but never push anything into the outer ear canals. (See 12.3, 'Ear Infections', p. 289).

Tropical diseases

Before travelling, find out if the destination is a high risk area for tropical diseases such as Malaria, Yellow Fever and Cholera (see 15.1, 'Time and Travel', page 335) and take the appropriate medical precautions.

There are many types of malaria, each requiring a different medical regime. Follow the medical instructions strictly.

Try to avoid getting bitten by mosquitoes:

1. Avoid places with lush tropical vegetation and standing water.
2. Use insect repellant on exposed skin and wear long-sleeved shirts and long trousers especially at dusk and at night.
3. Use sprays, fumigants and other repellents in your room as required. Apply the insecticide half an hour before going to bed and keep the windows and doors closed.
4. Use a mosquito net over the bed.
5. If bitten, try not to break the skin at the area of the bite. Don't scratch it. A minor lesion can quickly become infected in the tropics.

Cuts

If your skin is cut, even slightly, there is a high risk of serious infection.

1. Bathe the wound or scratch with sterile water. Apply an aerosol antiseptic powder and keep it dry. For example, Cicatrin powder is very easy to apply accurately. It can be very gently massaged into the wound and the excess wiped away.
2. A coating of Vaseline or collodion 'New Skin' can protect a damaged area if you have to get back into the water.
3. Always wear something on your feet in the tropics to prevent unnecessary injury (such as coral cuts and burns).
4. Wounds from sea urchin spines should be soaked in a mild acid such as vinegar or even urine. This dissolves the fine barbs on the spines which prevents them from being pulled out. After 30 minutes soak the area with oil to lubricate the spines and help the body reject them.

Sunburn

Sunburn can lead to many problems including weakness, feverishness and stomach problems. Use the appropriate factor sun screen. Keep covered up as much as possible, especially your head and neck.

Dehydration

Dehydration significantly increases the risk of decompression illness. Drink plenty of bottled water. In desert conditions drink at least 6 litres of bottled water per day. Avoid spending long periods in the sun. Remember long air flights, alcohol consumption and diarrhoea cause dehydration.

12.5 HYPOTHERMIA

Hypothermia is the condition of a person when the deep body temperature is abnormally low. It is usually associated with immersion in cold water.

But it is important to know that a deep diver can become hypothermic when breathing cold heliox even though his skin temperature is kept high.

When body temperature first falls below the normal level (37°C, 98.4°F) the body will try to prevent a further fall and try to return to normal by increasing heat production (by shivering), and by reducing heat loss (by restricting blood flow to the skin and limbs).

If the skin temperature falls below 10°C (50°F) (due to, say, immersion in cold water) the blood vessels lose the ability to restrict the blood flow. They relax and the skin becomes red. At this time the body loses control of heat retention by the skin.

Only when these preventative measures fail does the body progress from merely 'being cold' towards true 'hypothermia.'

Heliox gas is a good conductor of heat. The thermal conductivity of helium is six times that of air and at pressure it is also quite dense. Deep divers therefore can lose body heat via their breathing gas as well as from the body surface. This can be minimised while in the water by heating the respiratory gas to a suitable temperature. The chamber gas will also require to be maintained at elevated temperatures (see 'Temperature control,' page 205).

Signs and symptoms (see Fig. 1)

1. SHIVERING. The degree of shivering increases as the body temperature falls to about 35°C (95°F). If the body temperature continues to fall, the shivering decreases and disappears and the muscles become stiff.
2. CONFUSION AND DISORIENTATION. The victim becomes irrational and confused. Logical thinking and the ability to take corrective action are lost.
3. SWITCH-OFF PHENOMENON. It is impossible to communicate with the victim and he is unable to listen or pay attention to even the simplest instructions.
4. AMNESIA. The victim will have no recollection of events while his body is at or below this temperature.
5. CARDIAC ARRHYTHMIAS. The heartbeat becomes irregular and inefficient and the danger of heart failure is considerably increased.
6. SEMI-CONSCIOUSNESS. The victim is unable to perform any useful action.
7. UNCONSCIOUSNESS. The victim is rigid and unconscious.
8. VENTRICULAR FIBRILATION. Heart failure. Recovery from this stage is unlikely and would require specialist medical equipment and supervision.
9. DEATH. A seriously hypothermic victim may have no detectable signs of life. The only way to discover if the victim has died is to observe for signs of life (pulse, breathing) during re-warming.

Survival times

The thermal insulation provided by diving suits offers a major advantage where accidents result in divers drifting on the surface for long periods (see Fig. 2). This has a most important effect on the requirement for subsequent search and rescue operations which would need to be maintained much longer than in conventional 'man overboard' situations. This length of time should be a minimum of 48 hours.

When drifting for long periods in the sea it is most important to retain the mask if possible, in order to keep water from entering the eyes.

Fig. 1 Symptoms and signs in acute hypothermia

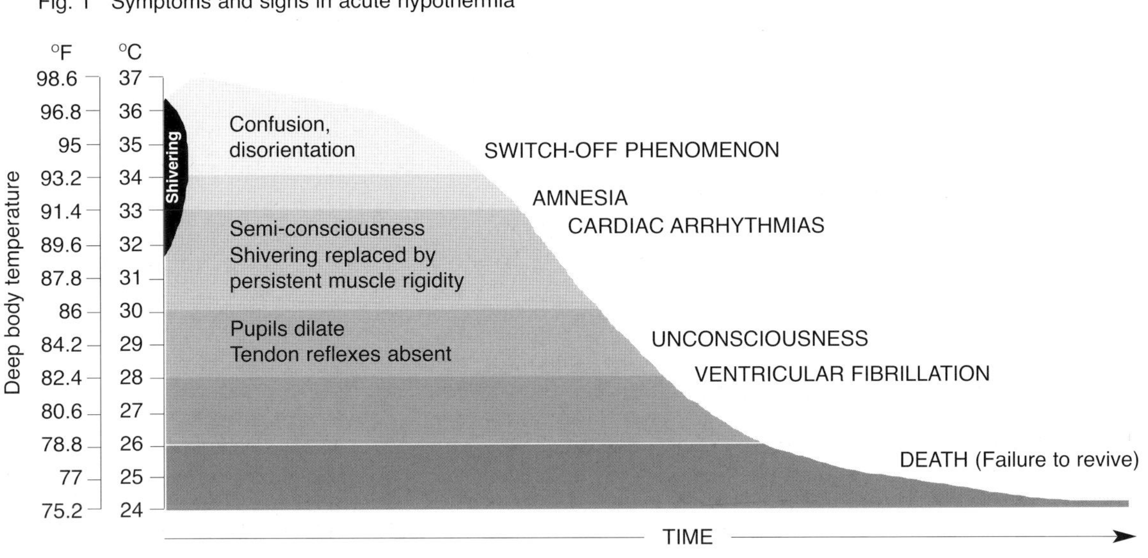

°F
°C
98.6
96.8
95
93.2
91.4
89.6
87.8
86
84.2
82.4
80.6
78.8
77
75.2
37
36
35
34
33
32
31
30
29
28
27
26
25
24
Deep body temperature
Shivering
Confusion, disorientation
SWITCH-OFF PHENOMENON
AMNESIA
CARDIAC ARRHYTHMIAS
Semi-consciousness
Shivering replaced by persistent muscle rigidity
Pupils dilate
Tendon reflexes absent
UNCONSCIOUSNESS
VENTRICULAR FIBRILLATION
DEATH (Failure to revive)
TIME

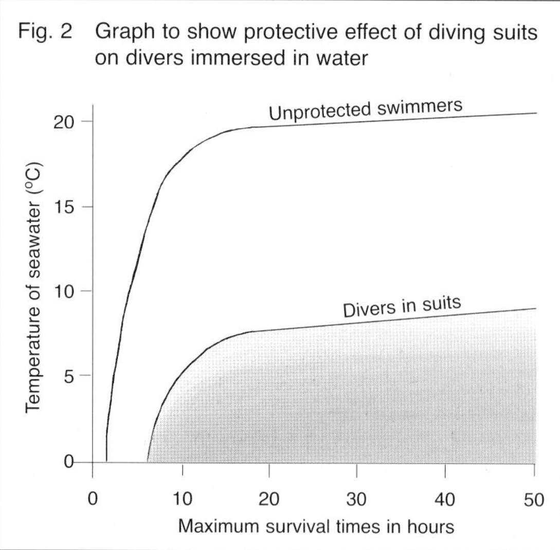
Unprotected swimmers
Divers in suits
Temperature of seawater (°C)
20
15
10
5
0
0
10
20
30
40
50
Maximum survival times in hours

Fig. 2 Graph to show protective effect of diving suits on divers immersed in water

It should be remembered that the chilling effect on the wet-suited diver in an open boat in a cold wind can be considerably greater than while he was in the water (see Fig. 3). Special precautions should be taken to provide protection against a long exposure to cold wind, especially following a dive.

Methods of revival

If the deep body temperature falls below 35°C (94°F) the body will lose progressively the ability to shiver. At this stage the body's active protective mechanisms are beginning to fail. Remember therefore, that a cold person who is not shivering could actually be seriously hypothermic.

1. If the deep body temperature is between 34°C and 37°C (93–98°F) and the victim is fully conscious, immerse the victim in a hot bath at 40°C (104°F). The water temperature should then be rapidly increased to 45°C (113°F), stirring continuously to avoid burning.
2. A large tot of spirits (such as rum) may be given while in the bath; because of its dilationary effect on the capillaries it speeds up the heat absorption. The alcohol also blocks ventricular fibrillation which is usually the cause of death in hypothermia.
3. If the deep body temperature is below 33°C (91°F) and the victim is unconscious or semi-conscious, maintain the victim in a horizontal position, maintain ventilation and assist circulation where necessary. Gradually re-warm. Summon medical assistance.

It is important to note that it is normal for deep body temperature to continue to fall, perhaps by several degrees more (the afterdrop) during the initial phase of re-warming. Special care of the patient must be taken during this time because the ensuing rapid circulatory changes can jeopardise the victim.

Protection from hypothermia

To protect a diver against hypothermia it is recommended that:

1. Skin/head temperatures do not fall below 25°C (77°F), nor local temperatures below 20°C (68°F).
2. Net respiratory loss should be no more than 175W.
3. Net body heat loss should be no more than 12kJ/kg (3.3Wh/kg) of body weight, assuming a starting core temperature of 37°C. (98°F).
4. Deep core temperature should not fall below 35.5°C (96°F).
5. Limb temperature should be greater than 15°C (59°F) to be able to work usefully and greater than 10°C (32°F) to prevent pain.

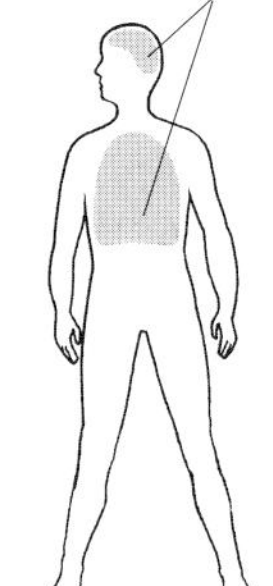
Deep core temperature

PROTECTIVE EQUIPMENT

1. DIVING SUITS. UK regulations require divers to be provided with appropriate personal protective

Fig. 3 Equivalent wind chill temperature charts – in degrees Fahrenheit (left) and in degrees Celsius (right)

TEMPERATURE (°F)	Wind speed. (miles per hour) 5	10	15	20	25	30	35	40
40	35	30	25	20	15	10	10	10
35	30	20	15	10	10	5	5	0
30	25	15	10	5	0	0	-5	-5
25	20	10	0	0	-5	-10	-10	-15
20	15	5	-5	-10	-15	-20	-20	-20
15	10	0	-10	-15	-20	**-25**	**-30**	**-30**
10	5	-10	-20	**-25**	**-30**	**-30**	**-35**	**-35**
5	0	-15	**-25**	**-30**	**-35**	**-40**	**-40**	**-45**
0	-5	-20	**-30**	**-35**	**-45**	**-50**	**-50**	**-55**
-5	-10	**-25**	**-40**	**-45**	**-50**	**-55**	**-60**	**-60**
-10	-15	**-35**	**-45**	**-50**	**-60**	**-65**	**-65**	**-70**
-15	-20	**-40**	**-50**	**-60**	**-65**	**-70**	**-75**	**-75**
-20	**-25**	**-45**	**-60**	**-65**	**-75**	**-80**	**-80**	**-85**
-25	**-30**	**-46**	**-65**	**-75**	**-80**	**-85**	**-90**	**-95**

In cold windy weather divers on the surface may become very chilled by the movement of cold air over exposed skin.

These charts show the decrease in air temperature caused by an increase in wind velocity (°F, mph left; °C, k/hr right).

Winds above 40 mph (64 km/hr) have little additional effect.

Shaded figures indicate greatest danger. (Flesh may freeze within 1 minute).

TEMPERATURE (°C)	Wind speed. (km per hour) 8	16	24	32	40	48	56	64
4	2	-1	-4	-7	-9	-12	-12	-12
2	-1	-7	-9	-12	-12	-15	-15	-17
-1	-4	-9	-12	-15	-17	-17	-21	-21
-4	-7	-12	-17	-17	-21	-23	-23	-26
-7	-9	-15	-21	-23	-26	-29	-29	-29
-9	-12	-17	-23	-26	-29	**-32**	**-34**	**-34**
-12	-15	-23	-29	**-32**	**-34**	**-34**	**-37**	**-37**
-15	-17	-26	**-32**	**-34**	**-37**	**-40**	**-40**	**-43**
-17	-20	-24	**-34**	**-37**	**-43**	**-46**	**-46**	**-48**
-21	-23	**-32**	**-40**	**-43**	**-46**	**-48**	**-51**	**-51**
-23	-26	**-37**	**-43**	**-46**	**-51**	**-54**	**-54**	**-57**
-26	-29	**-40**	**-46**	**-51**	**-54**	**-57**	**-60**	**-60**
-29	**-32**	**-43**	**-51**	**-54**	**-60**	**-62**	**-62**	**-65**
-32	**-34**	**-46**	**-54**	**-60**	**-62**	**-65**	**-68**	**-71**

equipment and those working deeper than 150m (490 ft) must have gas heating.

2. DIVING BELLS. Provision for a minimum life support endurance of 24 hours, including protection from hypothermia, should be made in the equipping of diving bells to cater for the accidental disconnection of the bell from the surface support.

3. PROTECTIVE DEVICES AND EQUIPMENT. See 'Thermal Protection,' page 239.

12.6 HYPERTHERMIA

Hyperthermia (heat stroke) occurs when a body is unable to lose the heat which it produces and/or when it is forced to absorb heat from its surroundings. The raising of the body temperature by more than 2°C (4.4°F) above normal (ie, from 37°C to 39°C/98.6–102°F) produces a serious condition. A further increase as far as 41°C (106°F) results in an emergency condition and the temperature must be lowered quickly to prevent permanent brain damage or death.

The body is less capable of surviving an increase in temperature than a reduction of the same order. Damage to the body caused by hyperthermia can be irreversible and is therefore more serious than the more recoverable effects of hypothermia.

In hot, humid climates, and especially when the compression chamber is on deck, the heat from the sun combined with the heat produced during pressurisation can lead to extremely high temperatures within the chamber. The conductivity of oxy-helium is six times that of air and if the humidity in the chamber is high (more than 85%) the diver will not lose heat by sweating. The victim will then be absorbing heat without losing any and hyperthermia will result. The danger is greater for overweight people.

Signs and symptoms

Rise in body temperature.
Skin extremely dry and hot.
Weakness and/or sudden collapse.
Convulsions.
Dilated pupils.
Extremely rapid and feeble pulse.
Breathing – deep at first, then shallow and rapid.

Methods of Revival

It is imperative that the following points are fully understood. A lack of understanding can lead to fatalities caused by hyperthermia. In the event of a diver showing signs of hyperthermia:

1. Lower the chamber temperature.
   In hot climates any compression chamber on deck should be protected from the sun by an awning. It can be kept cool by covering it with a blanket or sacking and by dowsing it with cold water since evaporation has a cooling effect. If necessary and possible, the outside of the chamber may be packed with ice, particularly on top.
   Flush the chamber with the appropriate gas mix. Gas from a high pressure source is cooled as its pressure reduces on entering the chamber.
2. Lower the body temperature as quickly as possible by bathing the victim in cold water or, if possible, by completely immersing the body. Sponge the head and neck with the same cool water. The victim must drink copious fluids. A weak solution of salt water (1 teaspoon of salt per quart (1 litre) of water) is beneficial.
   Since clothing reduces the cooling effect of sweating, remove all clothing.
   If the victim is in a deck compression chamber, ice may be passed through the medical lock. In an emergency, stop compression immediately and decompress as soon and as quickly as safety allows.
   The victim should be examined by a physician.

Protection from hyperthermia

To protect a diver against hyperthermia it is recommended that:

1. Skin temperature should not exceed 42°C (107°F).
2. Deep core temperature should not be greater than 39°C (102°F).
3. The inspiration temperature of dry gas should not exceed 35°C (95°F).

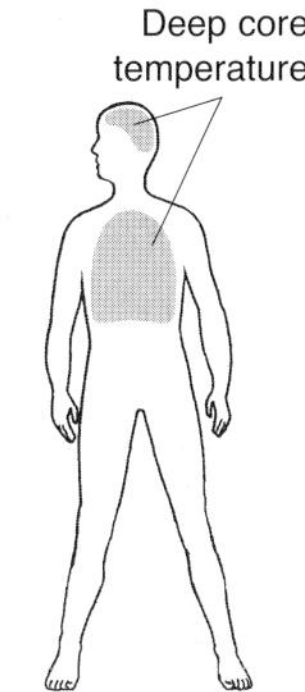
Deep core temperature

12.7 DECOMPRESSION

Decompression is a drop in pressure which may occur either:

a) when climbing to altitude in an aircraft or going up a mountain (ie, atmospheric pressure reduces to sub-atmospheric pressure), or
b) when ascending to the surface after a dive (raised pressure returns to sea level or atmospheric pressure).

The importance of decompression lies in the effect it has on the inert gas dissolved in the body.

Types of decompression

A BOUNCE DIVE, whether on air or mixed gas, is where the bottom time is limited to no more than about one hour to avoid the diver's tissues becoming saturated.

A SATURATION DIVE is a dive of unlimited bottom time made possible by the diver's tissues becoming completely saturated with inert gas in a submersible compression chamber (SCC) or DCC before and during the dive.

STAGE DECOMPRESSION is a technique, used mostly in air diving, of bringing the diver safely back to the surface without suffering decompression sickness by ascending in a series of programmed stages.

SURFACE DECOMPRESSION is where a diver omits shallow in-water stops, surfaces and is decompressed after being recompressed in a deck compression chamber (DCC) to beyond the depth of his last stop within five minutes of leaving that stop.

MIXED GAS DECOMPRESSION The term 'mixed gas' refers to any breathing medium other than air. Mixed gas might consist of an oxygen/nitrogen mixture (in different proportions to atmospheric air) or of a mixture of oxygen with any other inert, non-toxic gas, such as helium. Air is sometimes used in phases of a mixed gas dive.
There are two main reasons for breathing mixed gas instead of air on dives deeper than 50m (165ft). One is that the partial pressure of oxygen becomes toxic at such depths. The other is that nitrogen narcosis impairs diver performance severely.
Mixed gas diving is a complex operation requiring detailed planning, specialised equipment and extensive surface support. Mixed gas operations require their own decompression tables according to whether they are scuba or surface-supplied and whether helium/oxygen or nitrogen/oxygen is used.

OMITTED DECOMPRESSION is when a diver has neglected to carry out the required decompression procedure, either by ascending too rapidly or by missing decompression stops due to an emergency such as an exhausted air supply or bodily injury. The diver should be recompressed to depth, as appropriate. Consider any illness during or after this procedure as a recurrence.

IN-WATER DECOMPRESSION should be avoided except in the most favourable circumstances.

DECOMPRESSION SICKNESS (DCS) occurs when a diver is subjected to reduced environmental pressure sufficient to cause the formation of bubbles from the inert gases dissolved in his tissues. If the elimination of gas by the blood flowing through the lungs is inadequate to parallel the rate of reduction of the ambient pressure, the super-saturation of gas in the tissues will cause the gas to come out of solution in the form of bubbles. Bubbles collecting in the blood stream may block circulation, while those in the tissues will distort the tissues as the bubbles arise, wherever they may be – in the joints, muscles, bones, nerves, etc. Recognition of the symptoms of DCS, which may occur up to 36 hours after a dive has ended, is very important.

Factors affecting decompression

FLYING AFTER DIVING
To avoid the risk of decompression sickness by flying after having dived, it is best to wait for 24 hours. Fig. 1 shows the rules that apply for normal commercial aircraft. These rules do not apply to very low flying aircraft (less than 300m/1000ft) such as a helicopter transporting a decompression victim to a compression chamber.

Fig. 1 Altitude restrictions – flying after diving	**Time before flying at cabin altitude***	
Total time under pressure	610m (2000ft)	240m (8000ft)
No-stop air diving. Less than 60 minutes within previous 12 hours.	2 hours	4 hours
All other air diving. Less than 4 hours.	12 hours	12 hours
Air or Nitrox saturation. More than 4 hours. *Caution: Experience in this range is extremely limited.*	24 hours	48 hours
Mixed gas diving (diver on air at sea level). Following return to to atmospheric pressure after heliox and trimix bounce and saturation diving.	12 hours	12 hours

*normally 1500–3000m (4900–9900ft) for commercial aircraft.

DIVING AT ALTITUDE
When air diving at altitudes of less than 100m (330ft) above sea level, no adjustments to the decompression tables will be necessary. Higher than 100m, where surface pressure is less than 1 bar absolute, the adjustments shown in Fig. 2 should be added to the actual dive depth in order to find the effective depth.

Fig. 2 Required adjustments when diving at altitudes higher than 100m (330ft)	
Altitude	Correction
Under 100m (330ft)	no adjustment necessary
100-300m (330-1,000ft)	add 1/4 of actual depth
300-2000m (1,000-6,600ft)	add 1/3 of actual depth
2000-3000m (6,600-10,000ft)	add 1/2 of actual depth

Decompression stops should always be calculated for sea water as a safety precaution.
For oxy-helium diving at altitude consult special Buhlmann tables (compiled by Professor Albert Buhlmann, Zurich University, 1983).

Signs & symptoms of decompression illness

Decompression *illness* is a collective term used to cover decompression *sickness* (bends, DCS) and pulmonary barotrauma (burst lung). There are two types of decompression illness. For all practical purposes, all or any of them should be regarded as requiring emergency action. Symptoms appear usually within 6 hours after surfacing but can be delayed up to 36 hours afterwards.

Type I decompression illness is represented by joint pains and skin rashes which are defined as 'mild'. Type II is serious and dangerous and usually involves either the central nervous system or pulmonary effects, such as air embolism.
Symptoms such as those due to clearance failure of a middle ear or sinus, or an escape of air from a tear in the lungs (pulmonary barotrauma) can occur during or immediately after an ascent. Symptoms due to bubbles of gas in the bloodstream or tissues (the bends) may occur during or up to 36 hours after ascent, though most occur within one hour.
A summary of symptoms is shown in Fig. 3.

TYPE I (MILD)

These are often described as 'mild', which is not always necessarily true. Symptoms include:

a) *Pain*, which is the most frequent symptom. It is deep and usually felt in or near a joint and can become progressively worse until it is unbearable. It is important to distinguish between this and a muscle or joint sprain which is usually painful to the touch and swollen or discoloured.

b) *Itching*. A typical example of decompression sickness might begin with itching or burning of a particular part of the body. It may spread and later reduce. The skin also has a tingling sensation.

Fig. 3 Symptoms of decompression illness

Symptom	Type	Common and/or Technical name	Urgency	Action
Discomfort or slight pain in a limb.	I	Niggle	Vigilance.	Observe. Possibly recompress.
Rash. Itching.	I	Skin bend. Pruritis. Mild decompression sickness.	Vigilance.	Observe. Possibly recompress.
Deep pain in joint.	I	Bend. Hit. Decompression sickness.	Urgent.	Recompress.
Localised soft swelling.	I	Oedema. Lymphatic bend.	Vigilance.	May need recompression.
Swelling in neck with crackling under the skin.	I	Interstitial emphysema. Surgical emphysema.	Non urgent.	Observe. Do *not* recompress.
Pins and needles. 'Woolliness' of feet.	II	Bend. Spinal bend. Serious decompression sickness.	Very urgent.	Recompress. Consult nearest diving doctor.
Excessive tiredness. General 'unwellness'.	II	Bend. Decompression sickness.	Very urgent.	Probably recompress. Consult nearest diving doctor.
Unconsciousness. Headache. Difficulty with vision or speech.	II	Bend. Cerebral bend. Serious decompression sickness. Air embolism.	Extremely urgent.	Recompress. Send for nearest diving doctor.
Unsteadiness. Dizziness. Nausea. Vomiting.	II	Staggers. Cerebral bend. Vestibular bend/hit. Vertigo. Serious decompression sickness.	Extremely urgent.	Recompress. Send for nearest diving doctor.
Pain in the chest. Difficulty breathing. Shortness of breath. Coughing; Blue colour.	II	Pneumothorax. Chokes.	Extremely urgent.	Give oxygen. Recompress for chokes only. Send for nearest diving doctor

c) *Skin appearance.* The skin may occasionally show a blotchy, mottled rash or red spots of varying size. It can sometimes look like marble.
d) *Fatigue.* This is an important symptom and may precede serious problems.

TYPE II (SERIOUS)
These are often called 'serious' symptoms but all decompression symptoms should be managed as serious. Type II, however, are extremely urgent and dangerous. Symptoms are much more random than for Type I and are easily confused with those of gas embolism. In both cases immediate treatment by recompression is indicated. Symptoms include:

a) *Shock, nausea* and *hearing difficulties.*

b) *Abdominal pain,* which is frequently followed by:

c) *Weakness, paralysis or numbness* of the limbs. Sensory and muscular changes of a scattered nature affecting one or more limbs are the most common signs. It is quite easy to be misled when an obvious and painful symptom masks another which may develop into a more serious symptom later. For example, a joint pain may seem dominant, diverting attention from some patch of numbness that demands a more vigorous approach.

d) *Dizziness* frequently occurs.

e) *Chest pain.*

f) *Shortness of breath.*

g) *Extreme fatigue.*

h) *Collapse* and *unconsciousness.*

Diagnosing decompression illness

A major problem with divers is that they tend to ignore mild symptoms of decompression sickness that may develop into a more serious problem later on. Initial misdiagnosis is, therefore, a common problem in the management of diving accidents.

To minimize the likelihood of overlooking serious symptoms of decompression sickness or gas embolism, an attending diving doctor should give a neurological examination which usually takes about 30 minutes and requires certain diagnostic equipment and training to interpret the results. However, since a diving doctor is rarely at the scene of a diving accident a preliminary four-minute neurological evaluation has been developed which requires no equipment and can be carried out by non-medical persons (see Fig. 4). The results can then be communicated to a diving doctor.

The information from this check list will help the doctor to make a fast and accurate decision without actually examining the diver himself.

Treatment of decompression illness where there is no compression chamber on site

If there is no hyperbaric chamber on site, divers suspected of having serious DCS should be given oxygen immediately and placed in the

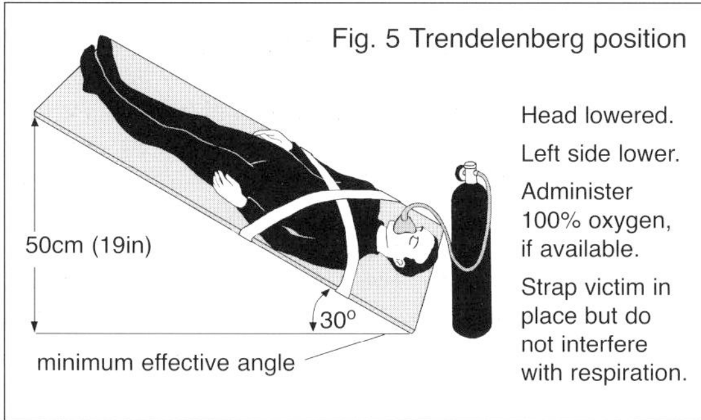
Head lowered.
Left side lower.
Administer 100% oxygen, if available.
Strap victim in place but do not interfere with respiration.
50cm (19in)
30°
minimum effective angle
Fig. 5 Trendelenberg position

Trendelenberg Position (see Fig. 5). If a Hyperlite hyperbaric stretcher (or equivalent) is available, hyperbaric oxygen treatment can be started immediately while the patient is transported under pressure, to the treatment centre (see Fig. 6). In any case, the victim should be transferred immediately to the nearest suitable hyperbaric chamber.

Contact the authority controlling the chamber and request that it be made available. If no chamber is available locally, telephone the RN Duty Diving Medical Officer on 07831 151523; in Scotland, call 01224 681818.

In the USA, anyone needing emergency help should call the USN Experimental Diving Unit in Panama City (904) 230 3100 or Divers Alert Network (DAN), (919) 684 8111. (Confirm telephone numbers in advance – they may change).

Despatch the patient by the quickest available means – if by air, at a pressure equivalent to less than 300m (1000ft) altitude.

If a Hyperlite hyperbaric stretcher is not available, oxygen should be administered to the victim during transport, if possible. Entonox, a nitrous oxide analgesic, should *not* be administered by the ambulance crew as it makes the bends worse.

The victim should be accompanied by another diver fully conversant with the details of the accident (preferably his companion or the diving supervisor) and, if possible, a diving doctor. A careful note should be made of the deepest depth and the duration of the dive.

Decompression procedures

The diving company which employs the diver is responsible for determining the decompression procedures, which may be derived from several sources: US Navy, Royal Navy (UK), other navies, diving company in-house, and diving consultant.

Decompression procedures will cover both air and mixed gas diving and therapeutic recompression requirements.

The US Navy and Royal Navy tables are freely available while those of proprietary sources such as the diving companies, specialist consultants or other navies tend to be confidential, though not necessarily any better.

The most widely used procedures in the professional diving field worldwide are provided by the US Navy.

Fig. 4 Initial Neurological Examination by Non-Medical Personnel

NOTE: When interpreting the results of this examination, try to ascertain whether the abnormalities are the result of the diving disorder and not the result of a previous disorder. For example, some divers may have hearing impairment caused by working near noisy equipment. If in doubt assume it is decompression illness.

Mental condition or status
As very little interference is required to impair functioning of the higher mental faculties, test for subtle signs of decompression illness by observing:

1. *Orientation*
   Time (the first function to go), eg, 'What day is this?'
   Place (the next function to go), eg, 'Where are you?'
   Person (severe impairment), eg, 'What is your name?'
2. *Memory*
   Immediate (test with recalling a series of numbers)
   Recent (recall events of within the last 24 hours)
   Remote (recall background)
3. *Mental function*
   Test by using serial 7's. Subtract 7 from 100; then 7 from the answer and so on. If an error is repeated, eg, 93, 80, 83, 80, 73, 70, etc, there is a condition called perseveration that usually indicates impairment.
4. *Level of consciousness*
   Watch for any fluctuation
5. *Seizures*
   These are obvious.

Cranial nerves (nerves that come directly from the brain).
Test one side versus the other side.

1. *Sense of smell (olfactory nerves)*
   Test with coffee, for example, one nostril at a time. Do not delay if appropriate material for this test is not available.
2. *Sight (optic nerve)*
   Hold up fingers for the diver to count. Test one eye at a time.
3. *Eye movement (oculomotor, trochlear and abducens nerves)*
   Have the diver's eyes follow your finger as you move it up and down, and left to right.
4. *Chewing (trigeminal nerves)*
   Can the teeth be clenched? Feel the jaw muscles on both sides simultaneously.
5. *Mouth (facial nerves)*
   Can the diver smile? Can both corners of the mouth be lifted simultaneously?
6. *Hearing (auditory nerves)*
   Test one ear at a time by whispering or rubbing your fingers together approximately 2cm (3/4 inch) away from the ear.
7. *Talking (glossopharyngeal, vagus nerves)*
   Check for gagging and proper pronunciation of words.
8. *Shoulder muscles (spinal accessory nerves)*
   Have the diver shrug his shoulders while you press down on them. Note any weakness on one side.
9. *Tongue (hypoglossal nerves)*
   Can the diver stick his tongue out straight? Does it move to one side?

Sensory nerves

1. *Sharp versus dull* (check one hand versus the other)
   Using sharp and dull objects see if the diver can distinguish between them by testing:
   a) back of the hand
   b) base of the thumb
   c) base of the little finger.

Motor nerves (nerves that operate the muscles)

1. *Muscle strength*
   Have the diver grip two of your fingers with each hand. Is the strength the same in each hand?
   With the diver sitting or lying down, place your hands on the legs just above the ankles and press down lightly. Have the diver try to raise his legs. Is the strength equal in both legs?
2. *Range of motion*
   Check normal movement of both arms and legs.
3. *Muscle tone*
   Check if the muscles are spastic (in a state of contraction) or flaccid (totally relaxed).

Muscle co-ordination (cerebellar function)

1. *Point in space*
   Can the diver touch your finger held in front of his nose?
2. *Finger to nose*
   Can the diver move a finger from touching your finger to the tip of his nose and repeat the motion?
3. *Gait*
   Walking gait – check for rubber legs, staggering and unsteadiness. Tandem gait – walking heel to toe.
4. *Balance*
   Have a diver stand straight, feet together, arms folded in front and eyes closed.

Reflexes

1. *Basic reflexes* (check both sides with a blunt instrument).
   biceps knee forearm ankle triceps
2. *Babinski reflex*
   Run a blunt object up the sole of the foot. If the toes curl down towards the sole of the foot a normal Babinski reflex is present. If nothing happens no conclusion can be drawn. But if the toes flex backwards, upwards and spread this is a reliable sign of probable spinal involvement.

Language problem

1. *Aphasia (speech impairment)*
   Check for misplaced words and incorrect word order.

Although there is usually little time in which to examine the diver, especially under pressure in a deck compression chamber, do not skimp on the examination. In all cases of doubt treat the diver by recompression. If you are not sure that he is completely free from serious symptoms, use the longer decompression table. Time and air are cheaper than joints and brain tissue.
For a comparative summary of symptoms of both decompression sickness and gas embolism see Fig. 1, page 300.

Youngblood and Clarke, 1978

Fig. 6 Hyperlite portable hyperbaric stretcher and treatment system

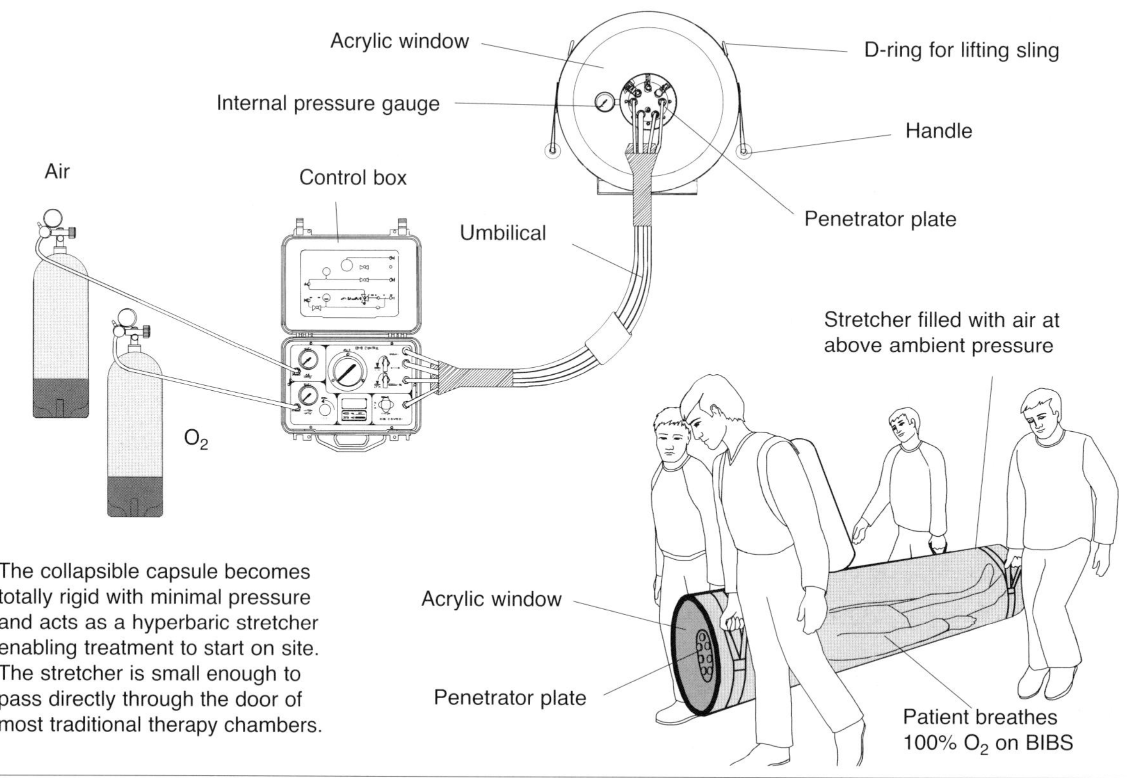
Acrylic window
Internal pressure gauge
D-ring for lifting sling
Handle
Air
Control box
Umbilical
Penetrator plate
Stretcher filled with air at above ambient pressure
O_2
The collapsible capsule becomes totally rigid with minimal pressure and acts as a hyperbaric stretcher enabling treatment to start on site. The stretcher is small enough to pass directly through the door of most traditional therapy chambers.
Acrylic window
Penetrator plate
Patient breathes 100% O_2 on BIBS

Due to the large number of these tables and since they and their associated therapeutic recompression tables are constantly under review they are not reproduced in this Handbook. However, they are available directly from their sources.

Notes on decompression tables

It is important to use the corresponding advice on repetitive diving, diving at altitude and flying after diving consistent with the source of the decompression table. If changing between tables from different sources, perhaps due to a change of diving company, it is extremely important to learn the new procedure in full detail. This is because there can be basic differences between the procedures. Notable examples include whether the excursion time between two stops is taken out of the stop being left or the stop being approached, and what gas mixed/partial pressures are routinely used for operational and therapeutic purposes.

If there is a choice of whose tables to use, bear in mind the following:

- What gases are available?
- What DCCs are available?
- How available are the DCCs?
- What medical support is available?
- Which procedure is the most conservative?
- Is a conservative table needed, because of, say, very cold conditions, hard work, lack of medical and therapeutic support?
- Are tables metricated to match charts?
- Which authority can advise you?

Post-treatment restrictions

Divers who have been carrying out a decompression involving stops should remain in the vicinity of a deck compression chamber for 8 hours following an air dive and for 5 hours following a heliox dive, including saturation.

Divers surfacing after therapeutic treatment are to be kept close to a chamber for 6 hours and within 1 hour's travelling time for the next 18 hours.

Mild cases with successful treatment are not to be allowed to dive for 24 hours and no deeper than 10m for an additional 2 days. In serious cases the examining doctor would normally consider a lay-off of 7 days after a complete recovery.

If any signs of decompression sickness persist the diver should be re-examined before diving.

After all the above intervals a diver may travel by boat without further restriction or fly by helicopter not higher than 300m (1000ft). It is advisable to wait for at least 12 hours after an air or heliox dive prior to flying.

RECOMPRESSION – SAFE PRACTICE RULES

ALWAYS . . .

1. Treat an unconscious patient for gas embolism or serious DCS unless the possibility of such a condition can be ruled out without question.
2. Follow the treatment tables accurately.
3. Maintain accurate timekeeping and recording.
4. Maintain the normal descent and ascent rates.
5. Have a qualified tender in the chamber at all times during recompression.
6. Check the patient's condition before and after coming to each stop and during long stops.
7. Examine the patient thoroughly at depth of relief or treatment depth.
8. Use air tables only if oxygen is not available.
9. Maintain oxygen usage within the time and depth limitations.
10. Be alert for oxygen poisoning if oxygen is used.
11. Observe the patient for at least 6 hours after treatment for recurrence of symptoms.
12. Maintain a well-stocked medical kit at hand.
13. Observe oxygen fire hazard rules.

NEVER . . .

1. (Diver) Fail to report symptoms early.
2. Fail to treat doubtful cases.
3. Permit any shortening or other alteration to the tables except under the direction of a trained Diving Medical Officer.
4. Let the patient sleep between depth changes or for more than one hour at any one stop.
5. Permit the use of oxygen below 60 feet (18m).
6. Allow personnel in the chamber to assume any cramped position which may interfere with complete blood circulation
7. Wait for a bag resuscitator. Use mouth-to-mouth immediately if breathing ceases.
8. Break rhythm during resuscitation.

NOTE: The utilisation of a helium/oxygen breathing medium is an option to be considered at the discretion of the cognizant medical officer as determined by the circumstances of the individual case.

Notes on oxygen toxicity.

1. At the first sign of oxygen poisoning the supervisor should instruct the attendant to remove the patient's oxygen mask to allow the patient to breathe the chamber air.
2. The tender should try to protect a convulsing patient's tongue and prevent the patient from harming himself.
3. If ascending, halt the ascent and maintain depth.
4. The tender should wait for 15 minutes after all symptoms of oxygen poisoning have subsided before resuming oxygen treatment.
5. Treatment should recommence at the point of interruption on the treatment table.
6. If the symptoms of oxygen toxicity occur for a second time repeat items 1–5 above. If necessary, and on the advice of a diving medical officer, a different treatment table can be employed, starting from the same depth.
7. If the symptoms occur for a third time contact a diving medical doctor as soon as possible for advice on modifying oxygen breathing periods.

12.8 BURST LUNG (PULMONARY BAROTRAUMA)

Burst lung is the result of pressure damage to the lungs brought about by excess differential pressures causing tearing of the lung tissue. It may occur from compression but it is usually a decompression injury.

Pulmonary barotrauma (or burst lung) is the cause of unconsciousness immediately following or within 10 minutes of an important decompression. It is usually caused when a diver ascends through the water holding his breath. It is a very real risk if the diver abandons his breathing set and returns to the surface by a free ascent. It can also be caused by local retention of gas in a diver who is exhaling correctly during ascent. This may be due to a chronic or recent chest illness. If, for any reason, the expanding air in the chest cannot escape it will rupture the lung membranes and can pass into the blood circulation and/or into the tissue between the lungs, heart and rib cage.

There are 3 presentations of pulmonary barotrauma:

1. INTERSTITIAL EMPHYSEMA sometimes called MEDIASTINAL EMPHYSEMA
   The gas may escape upwards into the central tissues within the chest cavity and appear under the skin in the neck and/or around the heart. A voice change is quite common if the gas extends into the neck (tinny quality). It is from this site that the gas may cause pneumothorax and respiratory distress.

2. PNEUMOTHORAX
   The gas can escape through the alveolar walls track back to the root of the lungs and end up between the lung sac and the chest wall. This causes the lung to collapse and can lead to respiratory distress and hypoxia.

3. ARTERIAL GAS EMBOLISM
   This is where expanding gas in the lungs enters the blood stream (pulmonary veins) via the damaged tissue. If these bubbles in the bloodstream find their way into the brain circulation arteries they may block the oxygen supply and cause brain damage. More rarely, the bubbles may cause the sudden cessation of heartbeat and breathing by direct blockage of the coronary arteries or by a reflex from the brain. Gas embolism is a major cause of death in diving. It can be complicated by decompression sickness if the tissues are pre-loaded with dissolved gas.

There may be more than one of the above conditions present at the same time. Any diver who has obtained a breath from any source at depth and who becomes unconscious at the surface should be assumed to be suffering from gas embolism.

Signs and symptoms

It is easy to confuse the symptoms of gas embolism with those of serious decompression sickness. Both are caused by gas bubbles. If no differentiation can be made between the diagnosis of decompression sickness and gas embolism, treat as if it is gas embolism. By far the most common symptom is chest pain.

Note: Any abnormal situation that starts within 10 minutes of the accident should be treated as a gas embolism no matter how shallow the depth. Any doubt about the correct diagnosis must be resolved in favour of the victim – treat as for gas embolism.

Fig.1 Diagnosis of decompression sickness (DCS) and pulmonary barotrauma

Summary of probable meaning of various presentations. Note: any abnormality that occurs after a dive should be treated as DCS unless proved otherwise.

Key: Probable (dark shading); Possible (light shading)

SYMPTOMS and SIGNS		Decompression Sickness: Mild (Type I)		Decompression Sickness: Serious (Type II)		Pulmonary Barotrauma		
		Skin	Pain-only	CNS	Chokes	Arterial gas embolism	Pneumothorax	Mediastinal emphysema
Pain	back			Possible				Probable
	neck						Possible	Possible
	chest			Possible	Probable			
	stomach			Probable				
	arms/legs		Probable					
	shoulders		Probable					
	hips		Probable					
Coughing/pain on breathing					Probable			
Unconsciousness				Probable	Possible	Probable	Possible	
Shock				Possible	Possible	Possible		
Vertigo				Probable		Probable		
Visual difficulty				Probable		Probable		
Nausea/vomiting				Probable		Possible		
Speech difficulty				Possible		Possible		
Hearing difficulty				Probable		Possible		
Lack of balance				Probable		Probable		
Numbness		Possible		Probable		Probable		
Weakness			Possible	Probable		Probable		
Swollen neck				Probable		Probable		
Shortness of breath				Possible		Possible	Possible	Possible
Cyanosis				Possible	Probable	Possible	Probable	Possible
Skin changes		Probable			Possible	Possible	Possible	Possible
'Cellophane' crackling under skin							Probable	
Bloody, frothy sputum								Probable
Paralysis							Possible	Possible
Irregular pulse							Possible	

1. SYMPTOMS OF INTERSTITIAL EMPHYSEMA
   - Pain under the breastbone or elsewhere in the chest.
   - Shortness of breath; difficulty in breathing.
   - Feeling of fullness in the neck area,
   - Crackling sensation on the skin, like crumpled cellophane, particularly near the front of the neck just above the collar bone.
   - Change in sound of the voice.

2. SYMPTOMS OF PNEUMOTHORAX.
   - Bloody, frothy sputum.
   - Shortness of breath – rapid shallow breathing.
   - Pain anywhere in the chest, especially when breathing in, and made worse by deep breathing.
   - Coughing.
   - Swelling of the neck veins.
   - Cyanosis (blueness) of the fingertips, lips and earlobes.
   - Irregular pulse.
   - The pneumothorax that normally accompanies pulmonary barotrauma is usually found by X-ray and is seldom troublesome.

3. SYMPTOMS OF ARTERIAL GAS EMBOLISM.
   - Chest pain.
   - Visual disturbances; sometimes even blindness.
   - Dizziness.
   - Weakness or paralysis, usually one-sided.
   - Numbness and tingling; usually one-sided.
   - Headache,
   - Sudden unconsciousness, often on surfacing.
   - Confusion, stupor.
   - Cessation of breathing.
   - Bloody, frothy sputum (quite rare).
   - Respiratory distress (rare).

Pulmonary barotrauma without arterial gas embolism is quite rare and accounts for only 10% of pulmonary over-inflation. However, careful examination and observation are vital.

Treatment

1. INTERSTITIAL EMPHYSEMA (IE)
   If diagnosis is uncertain, recompress as for gas embolism. Treat as for pneumothorax but in IE the needle is less likely to be ineffective. The therapeutic decompression will be a slow procedure requiring very close medical supervision.

2. PNEUMOTHORAX.
   If diagnosis is uncertain, recompress as for gas embolism. Pneumothorax does not usually require recompression for itself. However, if recompression is needed for concurrent embolism, manifestations of pneumothorax will be improved. Recompression is useful if symptoms are serious (eg, pneumothorax of both sides) and if no hollow needle is available to remove trapped air.
   If the victim is under pressure stop any further decompression. Treatment can include administering oxygen-rich mixtures at appropriate depths. If breathing is very impaired, or in order to continue a decompression. A suitably skilled person can withdraw most of the entrapped gas by inserting a hollow needle into the affected part.

3. ARTERIAL GAS EMBOLISM
   This is extremely urgent and very serious. Immediate recompression in a deck compression chamber is required.
   As victims are often also near-drowning victims, CPR may have to be initiated. The chances of recovery decreases rapidly with each minute lost in getting the victim under pressure.

12.9 HIGH PRESSURE NERVOUS SYNDROME (HPNS)

High pressure nervous (or neurological) syndrome can occur at depths over 200m (660ft) when breathing helium/oxygen mixtures. It is probably caused by the pressure itself and not by the gas. HPNS is the major limiting factor in very deep diving – at present around 670m (2200ft).

Signs and symptoms

- Tremors of the hands. Studies in animals have shown that tremors are followed by convulsions, coma and death. If the convulsion stage is reached, even with immediate decompression, death may result.
- Jerky movements of the limbs.
- Dizziness.
- Nausea.
- Decreased alertness.
- Tendency to sleep if the diver does not stay active.
- There are also changes in the electrical activity of the brain.

Ways to avoid/reduce the effects of HPNS

1. For dives of about 1 hour duration at depths of less than 200m (660ft), use a compression rate of 30m/min (100ft/min).
2. For dives over 200m (660ft), use a compression rate of less than 3m/min (10ft/min). Ideally it should be 1m/min (3ft/min).
3. Compression stops at various levels reduce the severity of the HPNS symptoms and allow deeper dives.
4. Symptoms may be reduced by adding small quantities of nitrogen to the breathing mixture, enabling deeper dives and more rapid compressions.

12.10 HYPOXIA AND ANOXIA

Hypoxia means a reduced amount of oxygen. Anoxia means a total lack of oxygen (and is unusual). Both conditions can result in death or decreased efficiency of the body.

Causes of hypoxia

Continuing life depends on the combined reactions of the heart, blood and lungs.

If the heart stops, the body will use up all the oxygen left in the tissues and then die of anoxia. If the heart is not strong enough to pump sufficient blood around the body, various parts will suffer from hypoxia. If the blood volume is decreased because of bleeding, the amount of oxygen that can be carried around the body will be reduced and, again, the body will suffer. Some substances, such as carbon monoxide, can poison the blood and prevent the carriage of oxygen.

If the interchange of gases in the lungs is interfered with, either because breathing has stopped or because the breathing gas cannot reach the lungs, the body will continue to use the oxygen which remains in the bloodstream, further reducing the blood's oxygen. The skin will take on a blue-grey tinge, particularly noticeable at the lips, earlobes and fingernail beds, characteristic of cases of hypoxia. If normal breathing is not restored, or if resuscitation is not applied, the body will suffer from a lack of oxygen and die. Hypoxia will also occur if the breathing gas in the lungs does not contain sufficient oxygen for the body's needs.

Different parts of the body vary in their sensitivity to hypoxia and, therefore, the time it takes to cause damage from which they cannot recover. The cells of the brain are most sensitive and if the heart stops the brain is likely to be irrevocably damaged within 4 minutes. Other tissues are much more resistant and can tolerate an oxygen debt. A muscle, for example, will eventually recover its full strength and function even if its blood supply has been stopped for as much as 30 minutes.

Signs and symptoms of hypoxia

It is almost impossible to detect the onset of these in oneself, especially during a dive. It is more likely that they would cause a change in behaviour in the diver that would be noticed by the buddy diver, supervisor or tender. They include:

- Tiredness.
- Headache.
- 'Drunkenness,' over-confidence.
- Unconsciousness in or under the water.
- Unconsciousness after surfacing, possibly from a free ascent.
- Strong breathing efforts.
- Blueness of lips, ear-lobes and fingernail beds.

Treatment of hypoxia

If normal breathing is not present, restore normal breathing by applying EAR (expired air resuscitation also referred to as 'mouth-to-mouth'). Apply pure oxygen or a high oxygen mix as appropriate. Treat for shock and get medical help. Keep the victim under observation.

Avoidance of hypoxia

1. Use the correct gas mixture for each particular range of depths.
2. Check and double check (by analysis) oxygen levels in gas banks before use.
3. As far as possible, avoid the use of pure helium for mixing on dive sites. Try to use heliox mixtures for mixing. This reduces the risk of accidental use of pure helium in breathing circuits.
4. Ensure efficient mixing of gases during oxygen make-up in life-support systems.
5. Carefully monitor the bell oxygen level during long lock-outs.
6. Consciously control efficient breathing whilst diving.
7. Keep talking to a minimum when wearing a mask or helmet.
8. When using closed circuit or semi-closed circuit breathing equipment, avoid rapid ascents, especially near the surface, and comply strictly with the manufacturer's operating rules.

Some useful medical terms

Bradycardia Slow heart beat.

Cyanosis A bluish discoloration of the skin resulting from insufficient oxygenation of the blood.

Dyspnoea Difficulty in breathing.

Expiratory reserve The amount of air that can be exhaled out of the lungs after normal expiration.

Hypercapnoea Undue amount of carbon dioxide in the blood causing over-activity in the respiratory centre.

Hyperpnoea Increased ventilation.

Normoxic A breathing gas mixture that supplies the diver with a 'normal' partial pressure of oxygen (about 0.21 ata) at any specific depth.

Residual nitrogen A theoretical concept that describes the amount of nitrogen remaining in a diver's tissues after a hyperbaric exposure.

Residual nitrogen time Time (in minutes) added to actual bottom time for calculating the decompression schedule for a repetitive dive, based on the concept of residual nitrogen.

Residual volume The amount of air left in the lungs after a maximal expiratory effort.

Tachycardia Excessive rapidity of the heart beat.

Tidal volume The amount of air breathed in and out of the lungs during normal respiration.

Vital capacity Maximal volume of air which can be expired after maximal inhalation.

12.11 GAS HAZARDS

The nature of diving often exposes the diver to a variety of gases which must be handled with due care and attention to avoid risk to diving personnel. The following commonly encountered risks are discussed here:

1. Oxygen poisoning
2. Oxygen handling
3. Nitrogen narcosis
4. Carbon monoxide poisoning
5. Carbon dioxide poisoning
6. Hydrocarbons degassing.
7. Hydrogen sulphide poisoning
8. Epoxy resin degassing

1. Oxygen poisoning

There are two basic types of oxygen poisoning: acute and chronic. 'Acute' means short-term effect, while 'chronic' means a long-term effect.

ACUTE OXYGEN POISONING

Acute oxygen poisoning occurs when a particularly high concentration of oxygen appears in the blood and the brain. This is brought about by breathing a gas mixture with a particularly high partial pressure of oxygen. The danger arises whenever the partial pressure of oxygen exceeds 1.6 bars. Under ideal conditions, such as in the comfort of a chamber, 2 bars can be tolerated for many hours. This figure reduces towards 1.6 bars whenever additional stresses are incurred, such as physical exercise, cold (hypothermia) and carbon dioxide. The limits for nitrox and heliox diving are shown in Fig. 1.

Fig. 1 Oxygen partial pressure limits for nitrogen/oxygen scuba and surface-supplied helium/oxygen mixed gas diving.

Exposure times *(mins)*	Normal exposure *(bar)*	Exceptional exposure *(bar)*
30	1.6	2.0
40	1.5	1.9
50	1.4	–
60	1.3	1.8
80	1.2	1.7
100	–	1.6
120	1.1	1.5
180	–	1.4
240	1.0	1.3

Maximum oxygen partial pressure = 6 bar

Certain types of closed circuit breathing equipment automatically change the oxygen concentration in the breathing gas mixture as the diver varies his depth, thus maintaining a constant and safe partial pressure of oxygen.

Oxygen poisoning does not occur immediately the diver is exposed to a high partial pressure. There is a delay or 'latent period' while the oxygen gradually builds up in the brain. Logically the higher the partial pressure of oxygen (due to a greater depth or a richer gas mixture), the shorter the latent period.

Unfortunately it is impossible to predict the latent period reliably, or even an individual diver's susceptibility to acute oxygen poisoning. Both susceptibility and latency vary widely from individual to individual and from day to day. Certain broad generalisations can be made in some cases. For example, it is known that fatigue, stress, hard work, carbon dioxide concentration, cold water, hangover and poor physical condition increase susceptibility and reduce the latency to acute oxygen poisoning.

The following is a list of possible symptoms of acute oxygen poisoning which may be experienced by a diver:

a) Twitching of lip and other facial muscles.
b) Dizziness (vertigo).
c) Feeling sick (nausea).
d) Unusual tiredness.
e) Disturbances of breathing such as overbreathing (hypernoea), temporary stoppage (apnoea) or difficulty in breathing (dyspnoea).
f) Unusual mental state, eg euphoria
g) Disturbances of sight, eg tunnel vision
h) Unconsciousness and general convulsions similar to a major (*grand mal*) epileptic fit.

By far the most dangerous symptoms to the divers are unconsciousness and convulsions since each condition could easily lead to losing a mouthpiece or mask and drowning. The other symptoms may or may not occur prior to the convulsions and experience shows that in the case of divers, there is most often no warning whatever before convulsive seizure and unconsciousness interrupts their dive.

OXYGEN CONVULSIONS

There are three distinct phases experienced by the unsuspecting diver. A diver succumbing to oxygen convulsions would first become unconscious and enter the 'tonic phase' which lasts about 30 seconds to 2 minutes. During this phase the diver arches backwards as all his voluntary muscles contract simultaneously and completely, his body becoming quite rigid. Following immediately after the tonic phase is the 'clonic phase' which is the familiar convulsive phase. In this phase the diver jerks violently and spasmodically perhaps for 2–3 minutes. As the clonic phase subsides the diver passes into a relaxed though exhausted and unconscious stage called the 'post-convulsive depression'. Once this series has begun there is no means of stopping the natural progression to the post-convulsive stage.

The rescuer should return the victim to air-breathing or back into the bell as soon as possible and then support him until he can be laid in a comatose position and allowed to 'sleep it off' and recover. Once the victim is returned to breathing air (or lower PO_2) he may or may not have another convulsion. He should slowly recover consciousness over a period of 5–30 minutes after returning to air-breathing but he should not be regarded as having revived since he will be in an exhausted state, mentally confused and likely to become unconscious or fall asleep without warning.

No permanent neurological injury would be expected to have occurred as a direct cause of one or two convulsions. However, the violent muscular contractions which occur during the tonic and clonic phases are so complete (a condition that would never occur in normal life) that the forces exerted occasionally tear muscle tissue, tear tendons from bones or even break the bones to which the tendons are attached.

If the victim regained consciousness shortly after returning to air-breathing there is often a strong desire to fall asleep. This is beneficial as long as he can be kept warm and safe from further accidents. When he re-awakens he should be talked to calmly, reassuringly and in simple terms. Warm clothing should be provided as soon as possible. He will not have any recollection of his previous experience (amnesia) from the time he became unconscious, or perhaps even shortly before that.

It is important to note that the victim automatically holds his breath during the tonic phase and consequently, it would be dangerous to bring him to the surface (or decompress him) during this brief period due to the danger of pulmonary barotrauma (burst lung). Even though it would be more difficult to surface a convulsive body than a rigid one, it is much safer to wait for the onset of the clonic (or convulsive) phase before ascending. However, the tonic phase is rarely noticed underwater. The rescuing diver's attention will probably be first drawn by the convulsions, so it is unlikely that the rescuer would have to wait before surfacing with the victim.

CHRONIC OXYGEN POISONING

This form of poisoning can be suffered at a lower partial pressure of oxygen than that which produces acute oxygen poisoning and the time taken to the onset of symptoms is much longer. This particular type shows itself initially as soreness of the chest. As the lungs themselves become further irritated by the high level of oxygen a condition develops similar to pneumonia with congestion, coughing and considerable discomfort.

More pertinent to the diver would be the case of mixed gas and saturation dives in which case the diver is exposed to a high-pressure gas environment for days or even weeks. Thus if the oxygen partial pressure of the gas were too high the diver would be a likely candidate for chronic oxygen poisoning. The condition is even more likely during therapeutic schedules where higher than normal oxygen partial pressures are deliberately used.

If 100% oxygen is breathed at atmospheric pressure (that is, at a partial pressure of 1 bar) the irritation would probably be experienced within 24 hours. However, breathing 60% oxygen at atmospheric

Fig. 2 KP value table *(KP = oxygen tolerance units/minute)*

ppO_2 (bars)	KP	ppO_2 (bars)	KP	ppO_2 (bars)	KP
0.50	0.00	1.34	1.54	2.18	2.74
0.51	0.03	1.35	1.56	2.19	2.76
0.52	0.05	1.36	1.57	2.20	2.77
0.53	0.08	1.37	1.59	2.21	2.78
0.54	0.10	1.38	1.60	2.22	2.80
0.55	0.13	1.39	1.62	2.23	2.81
0.56	0.16	1.40	1.63	2.24	2.83
0.57	0.18	1.41	1.65	2.25	2.84
0.58	0.21	1.42	1.66	2.26	2.85
0.59	0.23	1.43	1.68	2.27	2.87
0.60	0.26	1.44	1.69	2.28	2.88
0.61	0.28	1.45	1.71	2.29	2.90
0.62	0.30	1.46	1.72	2.30	2.91
0.63	0.32	1.47	1.74	2.31	2.92
0.64	0.34	1.48	1.75	2.32	2.94
0.65	0.37	1.49	1.77	2.33	2.95
0.66	0.39	1.50	1.78	2.34	2.96
0.67	0.41	1.51	1.80	2.35	2.98
0.68	0.43	1.52	1.81	2.36	2.99
0.69	0.45	1.53	1.83	2.37	3.00
0.70	0.47	1.54	1.84	2.38	3.01
0.71	0.49	1.55	1.86	2.39	3.03
0.72	0.51	1.56	1.87	2.40	3.04
0.73	0.52	1.57	1.89	2.41	3.05
0.74	0.54	1.58	1.90	2.42	3.07
0.75	0.56	1.59	1.92	2.43	3.08
0.76	0.59	1.60	1.93	2.44	3.09
0.77	0.60	1.61	1.94	2.45	3.11
0.78	0.61	1.62	1.96	2.46	3.12
0.79	0.63	1.63	1.97	2.47	3.13
0.80	0.65	1.64	1.99	2.48	3.14
0.81	0.67	1.65	2.00	2.49	3.16
0.82	0.69	1.66	2.01	2.50	3.17
0.83	0.70	1.67	2.03	2.51	3.18
0.84	0.72	1.68	2.04	2.52	3.20
0.85	0.74	1.69	2.06	2.53	3.21
0.86	0.76	1.70	2.07	2.54	3.23
0.87	0.78	1.71	2.08	2.55	3.24
0.88	0.79	1.72	2.10	2.56	2.25
0.89	0.81	1.73	2.12	2.57	3.27
0.90	0.83	1.74	2.13	2.58	3.28
0.91	0.85	1.75	2.15	2.59	3.30
0.92	0.86	1.76	2.16	2.60	3.31
0.93	0.88	1.77	2.18	2.61	3.32
0.94	0.90	1.78	2.19	2.62	3.34
0.95	0.92	1.79	2.21	2.63	3.35
0.96	0.93	1.80	2.22	2.64	3.36
0.97	0.95	1.81	2.23	2.65	3.38
0.98	0.97	1.82	2.25	2.66	3.39
0.99	0.98	1.83	2.26	2.67	3.40
1.00	1.00	1.84	2.28	2.68	3.41
1.01	1.02	1.85	2.29	2.69	3.43
1.02	1.03	1.86	2.30	2.70	3.44
1.03	1.05	1.87	2.32	2.71	3.45
1.04	1.06	1.88	2.33	2.72	3.47
1.05	1.08	1.89	2.35	2.73	3.48
1.06	1.10	1.90	2.36	2.74	3.49
1.07	1.11	1.91	2.37	2.75	3.51
1.08	1.13	1.92	2.39	2.76	3.52
1.09	1.14	1.93	2.40	2.77	3.53
1.10	1.16	1.94	2.42	2.78	3.54
1.11	1.18	1.95	2.43	2.79	3.56
1.12	1.19	1.96	2.44	2.80	3.57
1.13	1.21	1.97	2.46	2.81	3.58
1.14	1.22	1.98	2.47	2.82	3.60
1.15	1.24	1.99	2.49	2.83	3.61
1.16	1.26	2.00	2.50	2.84	3.62
1.17	1.27	2.01	2.51	2.85	3.64
1.18	1.29	2.02	2.53	2.86	3.65
1.19	1.30	2.03	2.54	2.87	3.66
1.20	1.32	2.04	2.56	2.88	3.67
1.21	1.34	2.05	2.57	2.89	3.68
1.22	1.35	2.06	2.58	2.90	3.70
1.23	1.37	2.07	2.60	2.91	3.71
1.24	1.38	2.08	2.61	2.92	3.72
1.25	1.40	2.09	2.63	2.93	3.74
1.26	1.42	2.10	2.64	2.94	3.75
1.27	1.43	2.11	2.65	2.95	3.76
1.28	1.45	2.12	2.67	2.96	3.77
1.29	1.46	2.13	2.68	2.97	3.78
1.30	1.48	2.14	2.69	2.98	3.80
1.31	1.50	2.15	2.70	2.99	3.81
1.32	1.51	2.16	2.72	3.00	3.82
1.33	1.53	2.17	2.73		

pressure (partial pressure of 0.6 bar) for an indefinite period appears to result in no ill effects to most people.

When increased pressures of oxygen are used in the treatment of more serious diseases such as severe decompression sickness or gas gangrene, it may be reasonable to accept a greater degree of pulmonary toxicity in order to treat the illness. The primary requirement of any therapy is that the treatment is not worse than the disease. The degree of pulmonary oxygen toxicity which produces a 10% decrease in lung vital capacity is associated with coughing and pain in the chest on deep inspiration. This degree of impairment of the lungs has been shown to be reversible within a few days. However, symptoms and signs of toxicity can increase for a few hours following the ending of the high oxygen exposure. Greater oxygen exposure may not be reversible.

A system of assessing and predicting the possible complications of chronic oxygen poisoning has been devised which uses values of 'unit pulmonary toxic dose' (UPTD) or 'oxygen tolerance unit' (OTU). This system can be a useful and worthwhile guide but it should not be regarded as infallible.

The formula is as follows: UPTD = t x KP

where t = time of exposure (in minutes) and KP is a constant to each partial pressure of oxygen (pO_2) in bars. (Note: KP values are sometimes referred to as OTUs per minute).

To work out the UPTD use the table in Fig. 2.
A UPTD of 615 produces no symptoms at all.
A UPTD of 1425 can produce symptoms of congestion and a 10% reduction in lung vital capacity. This is regarded as the upper safe limit.

OPERATIONAL SAFETY – OXYGEN HANDLING

1. All materials that come into contact with HP oxygen must be carefully selected. Stainless steel fittings should be avoided. Brass, copper and tungum should be used wherever possible.
2. Rigid piping should be used in preference to flexible whips wherever possible. Avoid sharp bends in oxygen piping. If flexible whips are used, keep them as short as possible, use the minimum number of inter-connectors and protect them from damage.
3. Pipework should be protected from any form of damage, especially from objects being dropped on it.
4. Any gas containing 25% or more oxygen should be treated as if it is pure oxygen.
5. Oxygen and O_2-mixes in excess of 25% should be in pipes separate from other pipework.
6. Oxygen should be piped at low to medium pressure rather than high pressure.
7. The pressure should be reduced immediately at the oxygen bank to 40 bar (590 psi) or less before being transferred.
8. Decanting should be the main system of transferring oxygen. Pumping should be used as little as possible.
9. A buffer, medium pressure oxygen bank near the deck compression chambers can be helpful if there is a long pipe run from the HP bank. It provides continuity of supply while changing over HP banks or in the event of a failure somewhere along the pipe run.

   Check valves and isolation valves are required upstream of the medium pressure bank.
10. Never use quarter-turn ball valves in HP oxygen lines since they can cause too rapid a pressure-up with consequent heating effect and fire risk. Quarter-turn valves may be used as emergency isolation valves in low to medium pressure oxygen lines.
11. Only slow pressure-up HP oxygen compatible valves should be used.
12. Always open an oxygen valve slowly.
13. HP oxygen banks should be stored in open air safe areas. They should be well secured against movement during poor weather conditions offshore.
14. HP oxygen banks should be well protected from any form of damage.
15. HP oxygen banks should be separate from other HP gas banks and any fire-risk materials.
16. The area around the HP oxygen banks pipework and fittings should be clean and free of oil and grease.
17. All pipework or end-fittings should be sealed or blanked carefully to avoid contamination when not connected up.
18. Any pipework or related fittings which have been (or are suspected of being) contaminated and are likely to carry oxygen should be cleaned very carefully.
19. If compressed air has been allowed into piping or fittings which are likely to carry oxygen, assume they are oil-contaminated and clean as necessary.
20. The cleaning of oxygen pipework and fittings can be done using special solvents. If possible, avoid using toxic solvents such as trichlorethylene (a typical toxic degreasant) and always ensure complete drying after cleaning.
21. Rigorously observe gas colour codes.
22. The gas mix should be checked on receipt and re-checked immediately before connecting to a supply system.
23. In fighting an oxygen fire, give priority to sealing off the source of the oxygen.
24. Absolutely no smoking or naked flames should be allowed near oxygen systems.

Note: Section 12.2 (Chamber Hygiene) lists substances that must never be brought into contact with high pressure oxygen (page 288).

2. Oxygen handling

Oxygen, especially at pressure, vigorously supports burning and explosion. Metal, clothing and flesh can burn like paper. Oils and grease will ignite spontaneously in the presence of high pressure oxygen. Assume everything will burn in HP oxygen.

Develop a healthy respect for oxygen and keep an acute awareness of the danger of fire and explosion. The properties of oxygen should be understood and the greatest care must be taken when handling it.

3. Nitrogen narcosis

This is a state of stupor experienced by a diver due to the introduction of nitrogen under pressure into his body tissue at too high a rate. Narcosis dulls the senses and is most likely to occur when compressed air is used as a breathing gas. This is one of the factors limiting the use of compressed air to shallow dives. It is occasionally met by divers involved in nitrox (oxygen and nitrogen mixtures) or in trimix (oxygen, helium and nitrogen mixtures). The effect is very similar to that of drinking alcoholic drinks. Symptoms may manifest themselves at depths of 28m (90 ft) or deeper.

It is important to realise that there are two different effects of narcosis on the mental activities of the diver:

1. *Personality change*: This is a potentially very serious effect but only affects some divers. A normally careful and disciplined diver may become totally carefree and undisciplined with disastrous results. This is important to watch for, especially in inexperienced divers. Generally speaking, such individuals should not be allowed to dive deep on air.
2. *Reduced mental ability:* There is a progressive reduction in thinking ability as divers go deeper on air. This affects every diver without exception. It is usually not noticeable until it is necessary to work out a task such as setting up a camera – only then does it become apparent.

   As the depth increases it can become impossible to work out even simple tasks. For this reason the supervision of deep air divers must be close. The diver must be carefully briefed and, if necessary, his job rehearsed. The amount of on-site thinking and decision-making required of the diver must be kept to a minimum.

   If any important diver observations need to be recorded, they should be done during, rather than after the dive. This is because the memory is also reduced in capability by nitrogen narcosis.

While experience will help overcome both these effects of nitrogen narcosis it will never eliminate them. So the problem must always be treated with the greatest respect.

Regular diving tends to reduce the severity of nitrogen narcosis.

Certain other aspects of diving can greatly increase the effects of nitrogen narcosis and should be avoided wherever possible. These will include:

- Heavy exercise and high CO_2 levels.
- Inefficient breathing equipment.
- Cold.
- Bad visibility
- Fear.
- Hangover.
- Poor physical condition.

SIGNS AND SYMPTOMS

- Personality changes.
- Dizziness.
- Apparent drunkenness or general euphoria.
- Loss of co-ordination.
- Numbness of the lips.
- Tunnel vision.

The only way to avoid nitrogen narcosis is to return to shallower water and lower pressure. Nitrogen narcosis disappears immediately on such action and leaves no after-effects.

4. Carbon monoxide poisoning

Carbon monoxide (CO) can, very occasionally, contaminate a diver's air supply, usually because of the exhaust fumes from a petrol/diesel engine being drawn into the compressor intake.

Carbon monoxide is particularly dangerous because it is virtually undetectable in very small concentrations and as little as 0.00001 bar absolute (0.02 psi) can kill a diver. One of the dangers of breathing contaminated air is that on the surface it can easily be undetected. As the diver's water depth increases the partial pressure of the CO can rise to lethal levels. Divers who smoke will already have a high concentration of CO in their blood making them more sensitive to the contaminated air.

The effect on the body is to cause hypoxia, except that in CO poisoning the blood does not turn blue in colour. The skin remains an apparently healthy colour while the body is being robbed of its oxygen. This is because the CO is taken up by the red blood cells in preference to the oxygen and the result is to make the blood cells appear bright red.

SYMPTOMS

In any diving situation the first noticeable effect of CO poisoning is likely to be diver unconsciousness. It is therefore unlikely that any of the less serious symptoms will be noticed beforehand. They include:

- Dizziness, headache and tiredness.
- Staggering, mental confusion, slurred speech.
- Flushed lips and cheeks.
- Nausea and vomiting.
- Unconsciousness.
- Coma and death.

TREATMENT

The victim should breathe pure oxygen or a high percentage of oxygen, preferably under pressure. The high pressure of oxygen speeds up the elimination of CO from the blood and pushes extra oxygen into simple solution in the blood.

Fig. 3 Carbon Monoxide Treatment Table

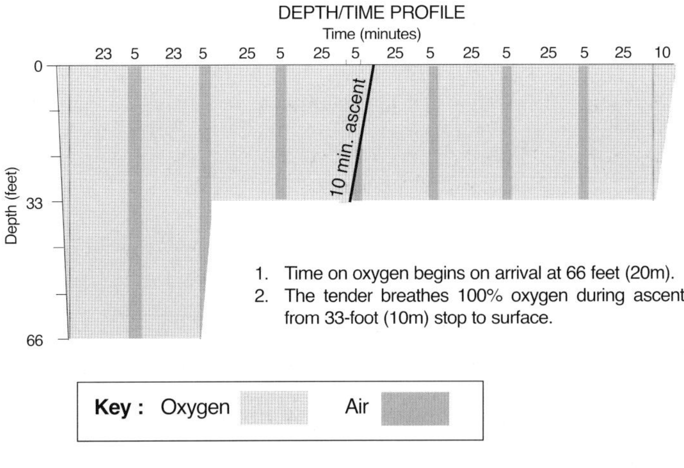
DEPTH/TIME PROFILE
Time (minutes)
23 5 23 5 25 5 25 5 25 5 25 5 25 5 25 10
Depth (feet)
0
33
66
10 min. ascent
1. Time on oxygen begins on arrival at 66 feet (20m).
2. The tender breathes 100% oxygen during ascent from 33-foot (10m) stop to surface.
Key : Oxygen
Air

Depth (m)	Depth (ft)	Stop Time (min)	Media	Elapsed Time (hr:min)
20	66	23	oxygen	0:23
20	66	5	Air	0:28
20	66	23	oxygen	0:51
20-10	66-33	5	Air	0:56
10	33	25	oxygen	1:21
10	33	5	Air	1:26
10	33	25	oxygen	1:51
if symptoms relieved:				
10-0	33-0	10	oxygen	2:01
if symptoms not relieved, extend as required as follows:				
10	33	5	Air	1:56
10	33	25	oxygen	2:21
10	33	5	Air	2:26
10	33	25	oxygen	2:51
10	33	5	Air	2:56
10	33	25	oxygen	3:21
10	33	5	Air	3:26
10	33	25	oxygen	3:51
0-0	33-0	10	Air	4:01

Fig. 3 illustrates an example of a treatment schedule for a severe case of CO poisoning. Treatment should be administered with the greatest urgency.

PREVENTION

CO poisoning is easily preventable and should never happen. The entry of CO into the air supply can be the result of negligence on the part of the compressor operator and can be avoided by good maintenance and sound operational practice of the compressors.

4. Carbon dioxide poisoning

Carbon dioxide (CO_2) is a waste product of the body that is eliminated through the lungs. The body monitors the CO_2 level in the blood and regulates the breathing rate based on this information. A rise in the CO_2 level will cause an increase in the depth and rate of breathing (hypercapnoea). If it continues to rise this may cause a headache and breathlessness increases until confusion occurs. In extreme cases consciousness is lost.

Anything that prevents normal breathing efficiency can cause CO_2 poisoning. Examples include:

- Over exertion.
- An inefficient demand valve.
- A large dead space in the breathing circuit.
- Restricting clothing or harness.
- Inefficient or exhausted CO_2 scrubber in a re-breathing set or life-support unit.
- Inadequate or badly-sited CO_2 scrubber in a bell or chamber.
- Improper use of a free-flow helmet, such as too low a setting for the free-flow rate, or too much shutting-off of the free-flow for better voice communication.

SYMPTOMS

A partial pressure of 20mb of CO_2 in the lungs causes little disturbance to the diver. Levels of 50mb will cause breathlessness and a feeling of discomfort. An increase of up to 100mb will cause a marked increase in breathing effort with mental confusion and headaches. Levels in excess of 100mb will be accompanied by marked mental effects leading to unconsciousness. Higher levels will cause convulsions, unconsciousness and eventually death.

PREVENTION

It is not as easy as it may seem to notice the problem of CO_2 poisoning in oneself. If, however, it is recognised, the following action should be taken:

1. Stop any physical exertion immediately.
2. Ensure a stable position and relax the body as much as possible. Try to remain calm.
3. Concentrate on regaining controlled breathing.
4. Flush the mask or helmet with air.
5. Do not attempt talking until a stable breathing rate has been established.
6. Breathe deeply – not in shallow, rapid breaths.
7. If breathing on an inefficient demand valve take long, slow, deep breaths. Avoid sucking hard. Use the free-flow.
8. If on a closed or semi-closed breathing set change to an open circuit as soon as possible.

5. Hydrogen sulphide poisoning

Hydrogen sulphide (H_2S) is a dangerous gas that can be released from the crude oil or the gas produced by drilling operations. It smells strongly of rotten eggs so can be easily detected in small concentrations. But the sense of smell adapts rapidly and after a short while the smell may seem to have disappeared. However, the H_2S may not have gone. H_2S is very poisonous, even in small quantities and great care should be taken to avoid exposure to it. Over 1000ppm at atmospheric pressure can kill instantaneously.

SIGNS AND SYMPTOMS

- Smell of rotten eggs that 'disappears' quickly.
- Irritation of the eyes and lungs.
- Dizziness, headache, nausea, vomiting.
- Loss of consciousness.
- Death.

SAFETY – HYDROGEN SULPHIDE POISONING

Wherever there are hydrocarbons there is a potential risk from H_2S poisoning. The risk is greatest in confined spaces. The following pre-cautions will help reduce the risk of H_2S poisoning:

1 Avoid contaminating diving equipment with crude oil.
2. Avoid bringing equipment and materials contaminated with crude oil into a diving bell.
3. Avoid locating a diving bell over an area of gassing.
4. If in doubt go onto BIBS or breathing mask/ helmet immediately.
5. Be particularly careful when first entering a confined space such as an SPM compartment. In such cases never work alone.
6. If a contaminated atmosphere is suspected, carry out gas tests such as the use of chemical indicator tubes before attempting to breathe the atmosphere.

6. Hydrocarbons degassing

The bell atmosphere can become contaminated by vaporisation of hydrocarbons brought back to the bell on the divers' suits and/or umbilicals. Because of the relatively small internal volume of the bell, just small amounts of vaporised gas can quickly produce a dangerously high concentration. The effect on the divers inside the bell is the rapid onset of anaesthesia, and can be fatal. Instruments (such as Analox) can detect the presence of these noxious hydrocarbon gases in the bell before they reach dangerous levels. Bell divers would need to go on to BIBS or other masks immediately any such contamination is detected.

7. Epoxy resin degassing

Epoxy resins are commonly used underwater to provide protective coatings and for making various types of repairs such as on concrete.

During the curing phase of some resins, gases can be given off which are potentially very harmful. The risk concerns the possibility of causing cancer and increases if the exposure to the contamination is over a long period. This may occur if the gases appear in a compression chamber with its closed-circuit life-support system because these harmful gases are not removed by ordinary scrubbing systems.

SAFETY – EPOXY RESIN DEGASSING

1. Avoid contaminating diving equipment and clothing with the resin.
2. Avoid bringing equipment and materials contaminated with the resin into a bell or chamber.
3. Carefully follow the manufacturer's operating instructions.

8. High pressure gas handling

Gas handling is a skilled procedure. Poor gas handling can cause injuries and fatalities.

The hazards include:

- Explosion by fire.
- Clamps on doors opening under pressure.
- Hose ends whipping under pressure.
- Supply of the wrong gas mixture.
- Blindness or deafness caused by a blast of high pressure gas.
- Hearing impairment due to regular exposure to the noise of venting gas.

Only personnel nominated by the diving supervisor should be allowed to handle gas. Procedures must be laid down and followed at all times. Although responsibility for gas may be delegated to the life support supervisor, the diving supervisor should make regular checks of the system.

OPERATIONAL SAFETY – GAS HANDLING

1. HANDLING:

a) Never drop cylinders or allow them to strike each other violently. Avoid dragging, rolling or sliding them even for a short distance. They should be moved by a suitable hand truck.
b) Never operate any valve or carry out any operation on the gas system without checking with the diving supervisor or life support supervisor.
c) On some installations, a 'Hazardous Operations work permit' may be needed when transferring gas through flexible hoses.
d) Never connect a supply without analysing the gas at the quad before connection. On a worksite where both mixed gas and air diving operations are taking place, the gas supply from the HP air quads must be analysed before connection.
e) *Never* put a gas on-line without analysing it at the control panel – regardless of labelling.
f) Never put a gas on-line to the diver without an on-line oxygen analyser with an audio alarm.
g) Always use correct fittings.
h) *Hoses*:
   - Always check that the hoses are correctly rated for the task, that they are the correct length and free from dirt and rust.
   - Check the condition of all hoses and fittings before use. Hose end fittings which show fatigue cracks should be replaced.
   - Tie hose end connections to a strong point to prevent whipping in the event of a fitting failure.
   - Route all hoses safely.
i) *Valves*:
   - Open all valves slowly at arm's length, looking away from the valve. When the valve is fully open, close it by half a turn. This leaves the valve handle free to move, clearly indicating that it is open.
   - Never over-tighten valves in the closed position. This will cause damage to the seats.
   - When venting gas, wear ear defenders to prevent long term damage to hearing.

2. STORAGE:

a) Cylinders may be stored in the open but in such cases should be protected against extremes of the weather and to prevent rusting, from the dampness of the ground. In areas where extreme temperatures are prevalent cylinders should be stored in the shade.
b) Store filled cylinders horizontally or vertically with the valve upwards. Never store a cylinder upside down.
c) For long-term storage, leave a slight positive pressure in the cylinder.
d) Do not store full and empty cylinders together. Serious suckback can occur when an empty cylinder is attached to a pressurised system.

(cont . . .)

(continued . . .)

e) Never place cylinders where they might be subjected to a temperature higher that 52°C (125°F). A flame should never come in contact with a compressed gas cylinder.

f) Never place cylinders where they might become part of an electrical circuit. When electric arc welding, precautions must be taken to prevent striking an arc against a cylinder.

g) The valve protection cap should be left on each cylinder until it has been secured against a wall or bench or placed in a cylinder stand and is ready to be used.

h) All cylinders must be correctly marked. Colour coding alone is not sufficient and a system of labelling must be used which precisely indicates the contents of each cylinder. Labelling should show the types and percentages of the gases it contains, with the oxygen percentage given first. Regardless of colour coding and labelling, all gas must be analysed before connection.

i) Air and mixed gas quads should be stored in separate areas to minimise the risk of wrong connections.

j) Single cylinders must be fixed securely either in an upright or horizontal position. If one falls over, the pillar valve could be broken off, releasing the HP gas and propelling the cylinder like a rocket and the valve like a bullet.

3. MAINTENANCE

a) Keep paintwork in good condition. Touch up damaged areas with suitable primers and paints, preferably air-drying. When removing old paintwork do not use heat or chemical strippers on any type of cylinder. When repainting do not use paints that require stoving for longer than 30 minutes at temperatures greater than 150°C (302°F).

b) Never fill to a pressure greater than the working pressure stamped on the cylinder.

c) Ensure that the inside of the cylinder is dry after testing.

d) Do not modify the cylinder in any way.

e) After diving, rinse the outside of the cylinders in clean fresh water and let them dry thoroughly.

f) Where possible use a self-draining boot on a scuba cylinder. It should be removed regularly for cleaning and to check for rust and/or damage.

12.12 UNDERWATER EXPLOSION INJURIES

(see also pages 136-137).

If a diver has been exposed to an underwater explosion, no matter how trivial the injury may seem at first, it is essential that a medical opinion is obtained as soon as possible as well as making arrangements to transfer the casualty to hospital. This is because the very serious/lethal effects may not become apparent until some time has elapsed, sometimes days later. Oxygen should be administered if available. Fluids by mouth should be severely restricted but a sip of water can be given if coughing develops.

The body is affected by both direct and reflected pressure waves from the explosion which travel at the speed of sound. Factors that can influence the effect include the proximity of the diver to the explosion, and the distances of reflective surfaces (such as hard sea bed and thermal layers, etc) (see Fig. 1). The diver is least affected when at or near a rough water surface because the pressure wave is dispersed by multi-directional reflections off the surface waves.

Fig. 1 Pathways of pressure wave from an explosion

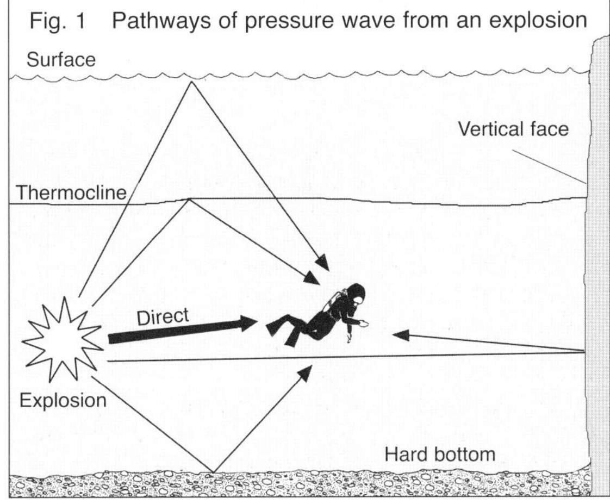
Surface
Vertical face
Thermocline
Direct
Explosion
Hard bottom

Injuries occur mainly in the gas-tissue interfaces within the body. Hence the lungs, air-filled intestines, sinus cavities and ears are principally affected. The pressure wave is usually transmitted directly through the skin and underlying tissues to the gas-tissue interfaces. The gas compartment is rapidly collapsed by the pressure wave and this causes the surrounding tissue to be torn apart.

The most vulnerable organs are the lungs and the intestines. In these areas massive bleeding and rupture may occur, causing varying symptoms depending on the force of the explosion and its proximity to the diver.

Signs and symptoms

1. Abdominal or chest pain.
2. Acute shortness of breath.
3. Coughing up or vomiting blood.
4. Passing black stools or bleeding from the rectum.
5. Headaches, unconsciousness and death.
6. Lesser effects include hearing loss and painful ears from burst ear drums, etc.

Treatment

All divers exposed to explosions should be admitted to hospital for observation and, if necessary, surgery. Often there are no external signs of injury despite widespread internal damage. It is quite common for infections to occur during recovery and it is important that they are properly treated. If the diver suffers respiratory distress he should be given 100% oxygen treatment and, if required, transfusions, etc.

12.13 KEEPING FIT

Physical fitness is necessary to maintain a state of good health for efficient operation and to help avoid and overcome dangers. A physically fit diver is able to withstand fatigue for longer periods, is better equipped to tolerate physical stress, is less likely to suffer from decompression sickness, is more resistant to hypoxia and has a stronger heart than the unfit.

How to estimate personal fitness

A simple way of estimating personal fitness is to step up and down onto a 50cm (20in) chair for 5 minutes at a rate of 30 times a minute. Lie down immediately afterwards. Take and note the pulse (for 30 sec) after 30 seconds, 2 minutes and 4 minutes of rest.

Physical fitness is calculated using the following formula:

$$\text{Physical fitness} = \frac{t \times 100}{p \times 2}$$

where t = time taken in seconds to complete the exercise. (For those who complete the entire exercise, t = 300 seconds, ie 5 minutes).

p = the sum of the three pulse counts

Score: less than 41 = unfit, 41-74 = average,
75-90 = good, over 90 = excellent.

To achieve a training affect on the cardio-respiratory system a threshold level of heart beats per minute has to be reached and maintained for a minimum of 15 minutes at least three times per week in order to improve fitness.

The following formula can be used to calculate the threshold level:

$$\text{Threshold level} = \frac{60 \times (220 - \text{age} - RP)}{10} + RP$$

where RP = resting pulse

EXAMPLE for a person aged 30 with a resting pulse rate of 70 beats per minute:

$$\text{Threshold level} = \frac{60 \times (220 - 30 - 70)}{10} + 70$$
$$= \frac{60 \times (120)}{10} + 70$$
$$= 72 + 70$$
$$= 142 \text{ beats per minute}$$

Any type of exercise routine involving total muscular activity which involves the threshold principle is acceptable. Running, swimming and circuit training are some ways. The exercise routine outlined in below provides a series of general body exercises which can be used in confined quarters to help you maintain your personal fitness. The importance of warming up before exercise cannot be over-stressed. A simple warm-up routine is given in Fig. 2a.

To help you achieve your goal, keep a record of your progress (see Fig. 1, Exercise Record Form).

EXERCISE ROUTINE

First training session

1. Warm up using the suggested routine in Fig. 2a.
2. Using Fig. 2b carry out, in order, as many repetitions as you can in 30 seconds of each exercise. Record the number of repetitions on your Exercise Record Form.
3. Take a 30-60 second rest between each exercise.
4. Warm down using the initial warm-up routine doing 10 repetitions of each exercise.

Next training session

5. Halve your recorded maximum for each exercise and note this on your Exercise Record Form.
6. Carry out three continuous circuits of the exercises using your new half-maximum repetition.
7. Write down the time this takes in the space at the top of the Exercise Record Form under 'Initial exercise circuit time' and insert the date.
8. Calculate two-thirds of that time.

EXAMPLE:

Maximum repeats in 30 seconds	= 20
Half maximum repeats	= 10
Time taken to complete 3 circuits	= 12 min.
Target time = $\frac{2}{3}$ x 12 min.	= 8 min.

This is now your new target time in which you must aim to complete the continuous three

Fig. 1 Exercise Record Form

EXERCISE RECORD FORM

Date: ________ Initial exercise circuit time: ________ Target time: ________

Exercise No.	Max. no of repeats of each exercise in 30 seconds	No. of exercises for the circuit
1		
2		
3		
4		
5		
6		
7		
8		
9		
10		
11		
12		

Progress:

Date:					
Time:					
Date:					
Time:					
Date:					
Time:					

Fig. 2a Warm -up exercises

(Repeat each exercise 10 times)

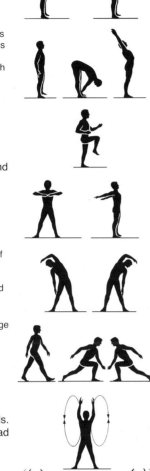

Swing arms forward; end elbows at full extent of the swing, hands reaching down behind the head.

Bend trunk forwards. Slide hands down front of legs as far as possible keeping legs straight. Do not overstrain. Return to standing and arch back, arms reaching out above head.

Alternately raise each knee raising opposite arm at same time.

With arms horizontal and bent at elbow, press arms backwards. Repeat with arms extended.

Alternate side bending. Slide hand down outside of leg with opposite arm reaching over head. Keep legs straight, feet apart and flat on the floor.

Standing stride. Take a large step forward bending front leg until knee is over the foot. Return to standing position. Repeat with opposite leg.

Circle arms alternately forwards and backwards. Keep arms close to head during inwards circle.

Circle whole trunk alternately left and right. Keep legs straight throughout. Arch back when passing through upright position.

Run on the spot raising thigh to horizontal position. 10 repeats for each leg.

The need for warming up before exercise cannot be over-stressed. Main muscle groups and joints should be taken through a full range of movement. All movements should be carried out ten times slowly and smoothly at first so that the muscles and joints have time to adapt to the new tensions placed on them. Finally repeat the exercises 10 times with more vigour but with movements remaining smooth and comfortable. Your body is now ready to take the extra stresses of an exercise routine.

Fig. 2b Exercise routine

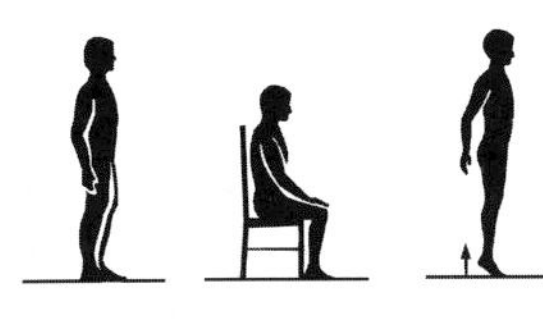

From standing position squat to chair. Return to standing position and rise up onto toes.

Lie on back. Sit up, reach forward towards toes keeping legs straight. Feet may be held/fixed if necessary.

From squat position, knees touching elbows, thrust legs back straight and jump back to start position.

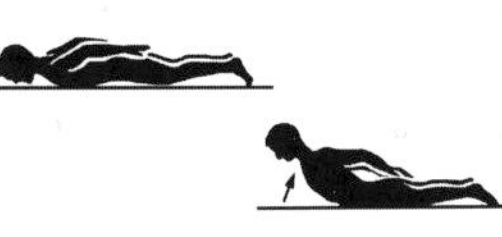

Lie face down on floor with hands clasped behind back. Raise head and chest from floor and lower.

Lie face down on floor with hands on floor at shoulder height. Keeping body straight push up till arms are fully extended. Lower till chest lightly touches floor.

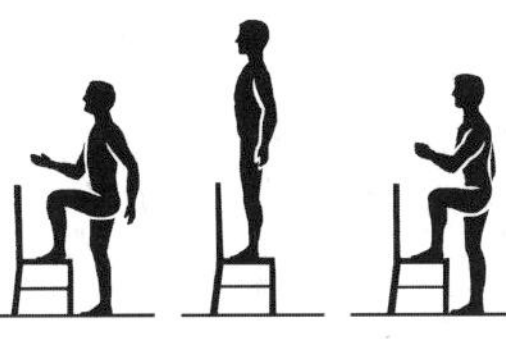

Step up onto chair with right leg. Stand upright on chair. Step down with right foot. Repeat with left foot. (30 seconds each leg).

Lie on back hands clasped behind head. Sit up twisting upper body so that elbow touches opposite rising knee. Alternate right and left.

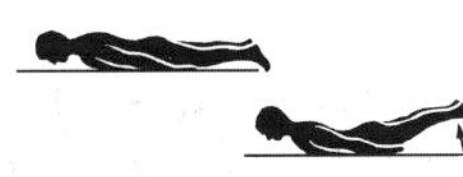

Lie face down. Raise and lower both legs.

As for exercise 3 but stand upright between each squat thrust.

Lie on back. Sit up raising one leg. Reach towards ankle of rising leg. Repeat raising other leg.

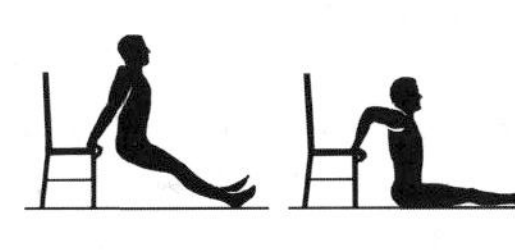

With back to chair place hands on edge of seat, legs straight out in front. Lower body until upper arm is parallel with floor. Raise until arms are fully extended. Keep body close to chair throughout.

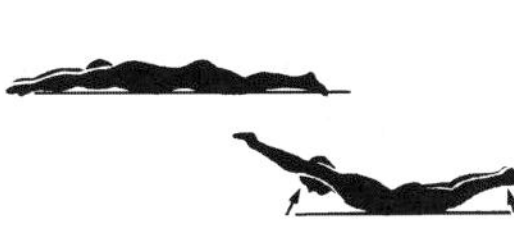

Lie face down arms extended above head. Raise arms chest and legs off the floor and lower. Keep arms and legs straight throughout.

circuits. Record this new time at the top right of the Exercise Record Sheet as 'Target time.'

9. Once you reach your target time, retest your 30-second maximum repetitions (as in item 2, above). It should have increased. Reset your new target time (see item 8, above).
10. The boxes at the base of the Exercise Record Form allow you to record your progress.

Subsequent training sessions
During the early stages of the training check your pulse after each circuit.
Are you reaching your threshold level? If not, you are not working hard enough.
Conversely, if your pulse is over your allowed maximum (ie, 220 minus your age) you are pushing yourself too hard.
Progress is achieved by gradually reaching your target time and resetting it once you reach it. However, once a good level of fitness is achieved you may find that you are unable to improve your 30-second maximum repetitions. Once this occurs you may want to increase your maximum repetition time by 10 seconds so that the maximum repetitions are recorded over 30 seconds, 40 seconds, 50 seconds and so on. This will further increase your work time over 3 exercise circuits and in so doing will increase the time that you are working above your threshold level.

EXERCISE DOs and DON'Ts

DO	Take medical advice before training if you have any concerns about your physical condition.
DO	Train regularly.
DO	Warm up before exercise.
DO	Wear suitable clothing (working up a sweat by wearing a tracksuit does not increase fitness).
DO	Give up smoking immediately.
DO	Diet if you are overweight (but only under medical supervision) while undergoing this training schedule.
DO	Limit excessive alcohol intake.
DON'T	Train until at least 1 hour after a meal, longer if the meal has been large.
DON'T	Train if you have a heavy cold or if you are feeling particularly off-colour.

SMOKING
In addition to reducing fitness, cigarette smoking also has the following effects:

1. It reduces breath-holding endurance.
2. It increases the risk of burst lung.
3. It reduces heart efficiency.
4. It reduces breathing efficiency.
5. It causes lung disease.
6. It causes heart disease.
7. It causes cancer.

Think about it.

DIET
Diet plays an important role in keeping fit because if more food is eaten than the body can consume it is stored as fat. Obesity should be avoided. (See recommended body weights in Fig. 3).
Overweight people are a liability in an emergency because they move more slowly than if they were their correct weight.
Offshore they are often an added handicap as they are unable to move swiftly in confined spaces and if they suffer an accident they are difficult to lift and manoeuvre. Divers should be particularly weight-conscious since fat people are more prone to decompression sickness.
To maintain a healthy diet:

- Avoid fried foods.
- Limit sugar and fat intake.
- Eat fruits, salads, fresh vegetables, bran cereals, wholemeal bread, lean meat and polyunsaturated fats in preference to fatty and sweetened foods.
- Don't over-eat to the point of feeling bloated.
- During decompression in chambers, avoid dehydration; drink plenty of liquid to increase resistance to decompression sickness.
- Alcohol is fattening and can cause both dehydration and increase blood pressure.

Fig. 3 Recommended height/weight/age statistics

Height without shoes		Correct weight unclothed		20% over correct weight	
m	ft	kg	lb	kg	lb
1.55	5' 1"	50.8	112	61.0	134
1.60	5' 3"	54.4	120	65.3	144
1.65	5' 5"	57.6	126	69.0	152
1.70	5' 7"	60.6	133	72.7	160
1.75	5' 9"	63.9	140	76.7	169
1.80	5' 11"	67.1	148	80.5	177
1.85	6' 1"	70.5	155	84.6	186

Age allowances:
18-29 years as above
30-39 years, add 2.3 kg (5 lb)
40-44 years, add 4.5 kg (10 lb)

Body type allowances:
No allowance has been made for variations in body type/build.

12.14 THE DIVING MEDICAL EXAMINATION

A diving medical is required so that a diver can safely and competently carry out his profession.
In the UK and many other countries only certain approved doctors can examine divers. A list of approved doctors can be obtained from the national government diving regulatory body. In the USA the medical examination can be carried out by any qualified doctor.
In the UK diving medical examination records are kept at a central registry so that it is possible not only to make a long-term evaluation of any individual diver's health but also to evaluate any adverse effects of diving on health.
The following information is intended as a guide to what a diving medical examination entails and what may disqualify a person from taking up or continuing a diving career.

In the United Kingdom

GENERAL
Any disease or condition which may require urgent treatment will disqualify a diver. Serious disturbances of the endocrine systems, such as diabetes, or other hormonal disturbances will exclude a person from diving as will a history of serious allergic disease. Any minor chronic recurring or temporary mental or physical illness which may distract the diver and cause him to ignore factors concerned with his own or others' safety must be given careful consideration.

AGE
The minimum age should be at least 18 years because of the need for physical and psychological maturity. There is no upper age limit providing all the medical standards can be met.

HEIGHT
There is no set limit but the person must be judged to have sufficient strength to work as a diver.

WEIGHT
Obesity may increase the chances of decompression sickness and implies a general lack of fitness. The diver should not exceed by more than 20% the standard weight for his age and height (see Fig. 3, Section 12.13, page 312).

SKIN
Some skin disorders will be aggravated by diving. Friction from dry suits, prolonged immersion, prolonged exposure to high humidity and elevated temperature environments encountered by saturation divers can all adversely affect skin conditions. They can give rise to social problems when sharing suits and can lead to psychological problems due to embarrassment.
Contagious (spread by touch) skin diseases such as scabies, warts on the feet and impetigo must be cured before diving is allowed. Other skin diseases of a more chronic nature must be assessed according to each individual case.

EARS, NOSE AND THROAT
The ear drums and sinuses are directly exposed to changes of pressure associated with diving. The ear drums should be healthy and the eustachian tubes functioning normally. A diver must be able to clear his ears to be able to dive.
Any infection of the middle or outer ear will disqualify a person from diving until it has cleared up. Chronic outer ear disease, perforations and scarring of the ear drum, history of chronic or repeated acute ear infection, deafness sufficient to affect hearing or normal speech, recurrent nose bleeds, chronic or recurrent sinusitis will all lead to disqualification, until resolved.

RESPIRATORY SYSTEM
It is essential that the respiratory system should be normal as it is directly exposed to changes in pressure associated with diving.
Any condition that might cause retention and trapping of expanding gas in any part of the lungs during decompression must disqualify.
In particular asthma (except childhood asthma of which there has been no recent evidence), chronic or recurrent bronchitis, bronchiectasis, pneumothorax, or tuberculosis, cysts, emphysema and bullae (blisters) will disqualify.
The diver's pulmonary function test must be normal.

TEETH
Teeth in an unsatisfactory state of conservation or unhealthy gums will disqualify.
Malformation of the gums resulting in the inability to retain an unmodified diving equipment mouthpiece after the removal of dentures, will also disqualify.

CARDIOVASCULAR SYSTEM
There must be no evidence of heart disease. Heart sounds should be normal. Any abnormality should be referred to a cardiological expert. Diseases of the blood or blood-forming organs will disqualify.
Performance of an exercise tolerance test should be satisfactory. An ECG (sometimes called EKG) is often given after the exercise tolerance test as exercise may reveal malfunctions of the heart.
A haemoglobin or haematocrit estimation should be normal.
Resting blood pressure should not exceed 140/90.
Severe varicose veins may disqualify until they are treated.

ABDOMEN
Peptic ulceration will disqualify unless there is evidence of healing and the candidate has been untroubled for 1 year.
Herniation (abnormal bulge, caused by weak abdominal muscles, in which gut may become trapped) should because for rejection, until satisfactory treatment has occurred.

Impaired kidney function, gall stones and kidney stones will disqualify as an attack underwater could prove fatal.

Venereal disease will disqualify, until treated.

Variocele (varicose veins of the testicles) or hydrocele (cysts of the testicles) will disqualify, until treated.

BONES AND JOINTS

A diver has to undertake a good deal of heavy work both in and out of the water as part of his job. Although the physical strain can be less when working under the water than doing the same job on land, there should be no gross limitation in functions of any major joints. A diver with 'recurrent back trouble' will need to be carefully assessed.

Bone necrosis is an occupational hazard of diving so all joints and long bones should be X-rayed periodically. Every case should be decided on its own merit, the diver's past history, age, general fitness and his future diving intentions.

Any disease or injury that could be potentially disabling will disqualify a person from diving.

CENTRAL NERVOUS SYSTEM

A full and careful examination is essential at the initial medical examination and any abnormalities should be documented.

Fits, black-outs, epilepsy or recurrent headaches will disqualify as these could prove fatal underwater.

Severe or repeated head injury resulting in prolonged unconsciousness or requiring surgery will disqualify.

Diseases or damage to the nervous system with abnormal function and disturbances of the blood supply to the brain will disqualify.

PSYCHOLOGICAL FITNESS

It is essential for a diver to have a stable personality, an equable temperament and no history of mental illness.

Any person taking psycho-therapeutic drugs is unsuitable. Alcoholics and drug addicts must be excluded.

EYES

Minor defects are not a bar to diving.

Colour vision will be tested at the initial examination and any abnormality detailed in the diver's log book and Certificate of Fitness.

Any reduction in the field of vision or uncorrected vision which is 15% worse than average will disqualify.

All divers must be examined annually. The diver's Certificate of Fitness will have to be renewed if he suffers an injury or illness which prevents him from diving for 7 days or more or if he suffers a Type II decompression sickness incident.

United States of America

Fig. 1 shows the tests for the diving medical examination required by OSHA (Occupational Health and Safety Administration).

Fig 1. US Diving medical examination requirements

Test	Initial exam	Annual re-examination
Chest X-ray	✓	
Visual acuity	✓	✓
Colour blindness	✓	
EKG: Standard 12L*		
Hearing test	✓	✓
Hematocrit or haemoglobin	✓	✓
Sickle cell index	✓	
White blood count	✓	✓
Urinalysis	✓	✓

*to be given to the employee once, at age 35 or over.

Unlike in the UK, there is no available list of disqualifying illnesses or diseases.

The decision on the employee's fitness to be exposed to hyperbaric conditions, including any recommended restrictions or limitations is down to the examining physician. However, a second and third opinion can be sought.

12.15 PROCEDURES FOLLOWING A FATAL ACCIDENT

In the tragic event of a fatality, it is the responsibility of a medical practitioner to certify the fact of death. This should be done as soon as possible. In the UK the body becomes the legal property of the Coroner from the time of death.

Procedures for dealing with a dead body

DECOMPRESSING A BODY

Standard decompression schedules are not applicable to a dead body. After death has been confirmed by a physician the body should be left at pressure for about one hour. Decompression at about 2m (6ft) per minute can then be carried out. This allows the release of free gas without causing excessive tissue damage. Too slow a decompression will cause greater tissue damage due to decomposition.

STORING A BODY

Ideally a body should be kept at a temperature between 0–4°C (32–39°F). On no account should it be frozen before an autopsy has been performed. When no refrigeration is available, the body should be enclosed in a polythene bag and surrounded by ice. Minimal interference should be maintained – do not remove or adjust the diving suit until the time of autopsy (see 'Procedures for dealing with the diver's personal equipment' for storage advice).

TRANSPORTING A BODY

Importing a body into the UK

The body should be transported to shore as soon as possible.

In the UK, arrangements should be made with the local Coroner's Officer to transport the body to a mortuary. Outside the UK, the services of an undertaker with experience in this field should be sought. In the absence of help the following procedural outline may be helpful:

1. A medical certificate giving cause or circumstances of death must be obtained from the appropriate authorities who will also give written authorisation for transport of the body.
2. Make several copies of all such documents.
3. For air transportation the body has to be embalmed before being sealed in a zinc-lined box. Embalming may have to be performed by a medical officer where local custom dictates.
4. On arrival in the UK the body passes into the custody of the Coroner into whose jurisdiction the body is delivered. The Coroner will decide whether or not an autopsy is required.
5. *Burial*: Certain documents are required where a burial is to take place. Foreign certificates are usually acceptable to the UK Registrar of Births, Marriages and Deaths of the district where the burial is to take place. A 'Certificate of No Liability to Register' is issued giving authorisation for burial.
6. *Cremation*: The procedure can be more complicated if cremation is required. The foreign certificate may not be acceptable to the medical referee of the crematorium who may then require an autopsy or refer the case to the Coroner requesting an autopsy.

Exporting a body from the UK

Embalming and sealing a body in a zinc-lined coffin is necessary before a body can be sent out of the UK. An 'Out of England Certificate' from the Coroner is required before authorisation can be obtained from the Home Office to allow the body to leave the country. A similar procedure applies in Scotland involving the Procurator Fiscal and the Scottish Home and Health Department. In addition, some countries require a certificate stating that no infectious or communicable disease was present at the time of death.

LEGAL CONSIDERATIONS AFFECTING A BODY

Once the fact of death is established there is usually a process of law to be followed. Around the world systems of investigation of sudden, violent or unexplained death fall into four main groups:

1. *Coroner system*
   A Coroner system operates in countries which have a 'Common Law' background (including England and many of its former colonies and dominions). In Scotland a similar system applies and is conducted through the Procurator Fiscal. In Britain, when the order for the autopsy is given by the Coroner or Procurator Fiscal the body passes into his custody. Only following the conclusion of the investigation is it released to the next of kin.
2. *Medical Examiner system*
   In the United States a medically-qualified executive officer is appointed.
3. *Continental system*
   In this system those deaths which have aroused the suspicions of the police are investigated.

   In the Netherlands, for example, the public prosecutor appoints the Lijkschouwer to investigate unexplained deaths or cases for cremation. In Denmark the Ligysynsmand has a similar duty but it is very rarely performed.
4. *Muslim countries*
   As a general principle autopsies are not allowed in Muslim countries.

Procedures for dealing with the diver's personal equipment

After recovery of the body, the victim's diving equipment should be collected and stored for further investigation. The equipment remains the property of the diving company but it will have to be presented to the local police, Coroner, or equivalent local legal authority. Handling and interference with the equipment must be kept to a minimum. Settings must not be adjusted. Only open valves may be closed. No attempt must be made to investigate or dismantle the equipment. Everything (except wet dive computers) will need to be sealed off and the equipment placed in polythene bags for later examination.

1. Record dive details including date, time, place, dive time, maximum depth, decompression schedules used and actual decompression procedures followed.
2. Recover all equipment. Make a note of any equipment lost, disconnected or damaged during recovery.
3. Do not disturb maximum depth recording on analogue depth gauges.
4. Do not disturb any dry suit automatic dump valve setting. Tape it in position. Do not alter the position of the inflation valve spigot. Do not adjust any settings on demand regulators – read and record all gauges and cylinder pressures.
5. *Cylinders*: In general, open valves should be turned off and the number of turns recorded. Seal with tape in the closed position. If necessary, mark their position with paint before sealing. If possible, get another cylinder charged from the same gas supply and keep it with the victim's diving apparatus.
   When gas cylinders are to be sent for laboratory analysis it should be noted that under current air transport freight regulations they cannot be transported by air while containing pressurised gas. It will probably be necessary, therefore, to have the gas tested on-site before transporting the equipment.
6. *Re-breathers* should be stored in an upright position. Close the mouthpiece and automatic pressure relief valve on the counter lung, noting the number of turns needed.
   Read and record any digital displays.
   Turn off any electronic dive controller handsets.
   If possible, keep a sample of any unused soda lime from the same batch that was used in the rebreather.
7. *Dive computers:* Displays on dive computers (or depth gauges) should be recorded as soon as possible after recovery. Do not disturb recordings. Turn off the dive computer (or allow it to go into standby mode).
   Do not put a wet computer into a sealed plastic bag as it may discharge the battery and consequently lose the stored data.
8. *Related records:* Ensure that all relevant voice recordings and/or video tapes and any recording dive computer(s) are acquired and made secure for later examination. Gather, copy or record details of all relevant documents, safety notices, etc at, or related to, the site of the accident.

Organisation of accident investigation

Following a fatal accident an investigation is essential for three reasons:

1. To establish the facts of the case.
2. To establish the cause of the accident.
3. To enable changes in procedure and equipment to be made to prevent a future recurrence.

It is usually mandatory that at some time the local legal authorities are involved. This may also be the case where injuries are non-fatal.

In the offshore situation most accidents require the expertise of medical, engineering and technical personnel to arrive at a satisfactory explanation. Team work with a central co-ordinator such as the Coroner or Procurator Fiscal is, therefore, very important.

Even where there is no authority such as a Coroner, such a team investigating on behalf of the employer or operator, will be most likely to arrive at factual, objective conclusions. Such a team may also be welcomed by local authorities who lack the technical expertise to conduct their own investigations in this specialised field.

ACCIDENT HISTORY

It is imperative that a proper and detailed history of the events leading up to the accident is obtained.

This may be a difficult and tedious procedure but if it is not properly performed it can prejudice the whole investigation.

In any accident situation witnesses accounts are often confused. They can be simplified by establishing a strict chronological plan.

All witnesses should be interviewed alone at the earliest possible time after the accident. More accurate descriptions are obtained if witnesses are questioned directly rather than if they are asked to submit statements.

If possible, the interviews should be tape-recorded and the recordings then written out.

TAKING STATEMENTS

When taking statements, include the following information:

1. *Witness details:*
   - Full name.
   - Date of birth.
   - Home address.
   - Contact telephone numbers, e-mail addresses.
2. *Incident details:*
   - Date and location of statement.
   - Reason for witness's presence at accident.
3. *The witness statement:*
   - Give a full account of the incident with as much detail as possible. Include:
     a) The chronology of all events leading up to, during, and following the accident.
     b) Provide names and positions of all relevant individuals.
     c) Times of events.
     d) Produce sketches as appropriate.

e) If possible, get the witness to check, sign, and date the written statement.
f) Provide the witness with a copy of his/her statement.

At every stage photography must be used to record the scene and equipment. Ideally shots should be taken from each quarter with a measurement scale appearing in each picture.
When a detailed report is being compiled all original notes must be kept for future reference in court.
Log books and tapes should be examined before commencing any interviews. No details should be omitted and facts such as subjective indications of trivial illness and the time of the last meal should be recorded. A check list can be used so that all aspects are covered.
Remember that accidents are more usually caused by passive negligence rather than active negligence.

Accident check list

In the event of a diving accident or incident the following details should be provided in order to ensure that a complete record of the incident is made.

1. MEDICAL HISTORY OF VICTIM
   - Pre-existing disease.
   - Recent illness.
   - Last physical examination.

2. PERSONAL HISTORY OF VICTIM
   - Diving experience and training.
   - Previous diving accidents/near-accidents.

3. ENVIRONMENT
   - Location.
   - Weather.
   - Sea state.
   - Visibility.
   - Wind.
   - Temperature (both at the surface and at working depth).
   - Hazards: including, for example: cables, rig legs, underwater obstructions, valves, pipes, propellers, tides, currents, visibility, water jets, any explosive demolition in the vicinity.

4. DIVE PROFILE
   - History of recent dives.
   - Depth and duration.
   - Current dive profile.
   - Dive of tender or buddy.
   - Ascent speed.
   - Stops and untoward incidents.
   - Pre-dive events.
   - Food and alcohol consumption.
   - Drugs administered.
   - Pre-dive behaviour.
   - Events in recovery, resuscitation, therapy, recompression.

5. DIVING EQUIPMENT
   - Suit.
   - Helmet/mask.
   - Buoyancy vest.
   - Gloves.
   - Weight belt.
   - Knife.
   - Depth gauge.
   - Valves.
   - Gas cylinders and contents.
   - Gas mixture and flow rates.
   - Purity of gas.
   - Safety line/umbilical.

6. TIMING
   - Establish precise chronological order of events.

7. DIVING TASK DETAILS

8. PERSONNEL
   - Names, with respective duties, of all personnel involved.

Rescue

13.1 OFFSHORE DIVING EMERGENCY PROCEDURES

The severity of an offshore incident must never be underestimated. Such situations can deteriorate rapidly and it is therefore essential that plans are in place to enable the swift and accurate dissemination of information to those organisations and individuals that will be responsible for enacting the emergency procedures. In many countries it is a legal requirement for offshore operators to have effective contingency plans in place for emergency situations. The management and co-ordination requirements of a major offshore diving accident will involve a heavy commitment by both the diving company and the client oil company. The level of capability of this effort will vary greatly in different parts of the world. In all cases, it must be emphasised that a co-ordinated effort with good communications and a clear channel of command is the key to success. The following example illustrates the arrangements that apply to the Continental Shelf of NW Europe.

North Sea Operators Co-operative Emergency Services (OCES)

The oil and gas companies operating in the NW European Continental Shelf have formed national associations to represent their interests and to co-operate in the event of an offshore emergency. Six countries are represented through their national offshore operators' associations: UK, Norway, Denmark, Netherlands, Germany and Ireland.

The North Sea has been divided into sectors (see Fig. 1), each of which can be conveniently co-ordinated by one of the principal oil operators. The major accidents which can be effectively handled include rig abandonment or lost bell situation where assistance from other diving support vessels might be required.

The system provides a weekly status of vessels (including diving and submersible support vessels) with emergency support capability in any sector. the same information is available from other sectors through the Operator Co-operative Emergency Services (OCES). This helps in the selecting the best available vessel to help in a diving emergency from the point of view of proximity, state of readiness, capability, etc.

The ultimate responsibility for any emergency lies with the oil operator, but primary safety responsibility for the divers remains with the diving contractor. The choice of the centralised co-ordination facilities site is extremely important and depending on the circumstances could be set up at the offices of either the oil operator or the diving contractor.

The actual arrangements are made as part of the contract negotiations and take into consideration the local capabilities.

The onshore plan will ensure good communications arrangements, the recall of key personnel and the establishment of the centre for operations. Liaison would be set up with the OCES, other vessels, diving contractors, coastguard, police, helicopter services, HSE, press, etc.

Offshore, an onboard procedure would include the general organisation, individual responsibilities and communications. In particular a very clear line of communication would be established between the vessel (Master and Diving Supervisor), installation/platform and shore.

TYPICAL EXAMPLE OF PROCEDURES

An example of the organisation needed to deal with a diving emergency might be as follows:

1. *Offshore field personnel*
   a) The Diving Supervisor handles emergency action as necessary, calling his duty personnel and informing the vessel's master, oil operator's representative and his own head office.
   b) The Oil Operator's Representative should call his duty engineer and/or onshore operations personnel as required. He alerts the Offshore Installation manager (OIM) of the nearest platform if appropriate. He sets up a communication link and undertakes liaison responsibilities between the Diving Supervisor, vessel, platform and shore, as required.
   c) The responsibility for diving action must remain with the diving contractor's offshore diving supervisor with advice from their own management as necessary and back-up from the oil operator if required.

Fig. 1 North Sea Sector Club organisation

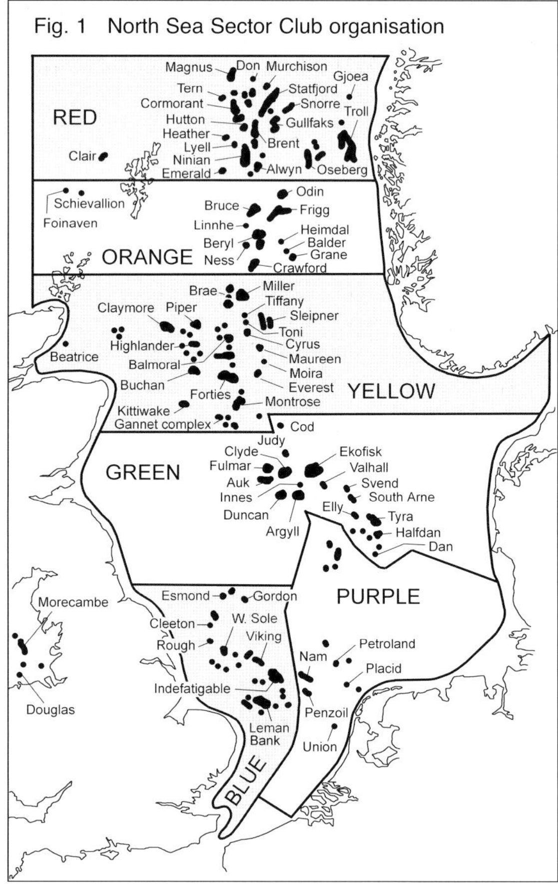

RED
ORANGE
YELLOW
GREEN
PURPLE
BLUE
Magnus
Don
Murchison
Gjoea
Tern
Statfjord
Cormorant
Snorre
Troll
Hutton
Gullfaks
Heather
Lyell
Brent
Clair
Ninian
Emerald
Alwyn
Oseberg
Schievallion
Foinaven
Odin
Bruce
Frigg
Linnhe
Heimdal
Beryl
Balder
Grane
Ness
Crawford
Brae
Miller
Tiffany
Claymore
Piper
Sleipner
Toni
Highlander
Cyrus
Beatrice
Maureen
Balmoral
Moira
Buchan
Everest
Forties
Montrose
Kittiwake
Gannet complex
Cod
Judy
Clyde
Ekofisk
Fulmar
Valhall
Auk
Svend
Innes
South Arne
Elly
Duncan
Tyra
Argyll
Halfdan
Dan
Morecambe
Esmond
Gordon
Cleeton
W. Sole
Viking
Rough
Petroland
Nam
Placid
Indefatigable
Douglas
Penzoil
Leman Bank
Union

Consultation should take place as soon as possible between the two supervisors but it is likely that the supervisor of the rescue vessel (who has responsibility for his own divers and diving equipment) will take charge of the rescue operation. If, due to poor or non-existent communications, it is not possible to obtain this endorsement then the Diving Supervisor of the rescue vessel should assume responsibility for the rescue if his own divers and equipment are going to be used.

2. *Oil company onshore representative*
   The Oil company's onshore representative immediately calls the diving contractor's contact staff and other emergency personnel as required. He clears the lines of communication from offshore and sets up an emergency room. He contacts the OCES.
   This should be all in accordance with an established procedure previously agreed with all departments and the contractors. Subsequent actions would be in accordance with developing requirements.

13.2 HYPERBARIC RESCUE

If a diver needs to be evacuated he should be transported to another system, ideally, without any change in his ambient pressure. Hyperbaric rescue is the process which enables this to take place.

Hyperbaric evacuation must be regarded as the very last resort in an emergency. This is because premature evacuation, or the evacuation itself, may introduce a greater risk to the divers than the initial emergency. This will depend greatly on the circumstances at the time.

A special procedure is provided for each evacuation system and this should take into account the possibility of the vessel listing, the loss of mains electricity and the possible loss of the use of a crane.

UK and Norway require special arrangements and procedures for the evacuation of divers under pressure. The need for evacuation could arise from any of the following situations:

1. The support vessel being in danger of capsizing or sinking.
2. The presence of an unacceptable fire or explosion risk or an occurrence such as a blow out.
3. A fire or other disaster within the diving system.
4. A medical problem with one or more of the divers that can be more safely treated elsewhere and does not incur unreasonable risk during transfer.
5. A lost bell.

Fig. 1 Hyperbaric lifeboat

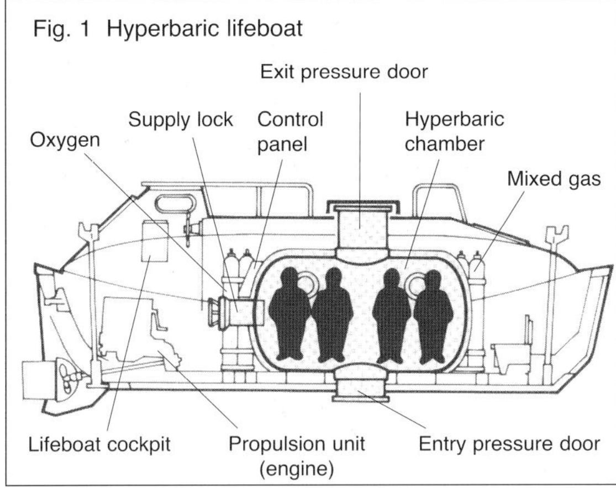
Exit pressure door
Supply lock
Control panel
Hyperbaric chamber
Oxygen
Mixed gas
Lifeboat cockpit
Propulsion unit (engine)
Entry pressure door

There are several options which can be used, depending on the circumstances and location. These include:

1. A hyperbaric lifeboat.
2. A bell-to-bell transfer.
3. A bell used as a rescue chamber.

1. Hyperbaric lifeboat

This is considered the primary evacuation option in the UK and Norway. The hyperbaric lifeboat consists of a compression chamber housed inside a lifeboat. It provides a means of evacuating an entire team of divers under pressure (see Fig. 1).

In order to carry this out the hyperbaric lifeboat's compression chamber is kept pressured up and mated with the deck chamber system via a trunking arrangement. When required, the divers transfer under pressure from the deck compression chamber (DCC) into the lifeboat and the trunking clamp is then released. The boat, with its crew and divers under pressure is then launched into the sea.

The lifeboat is self-powered and can travel to a place where it can be safely lifted out of the sea and mated with another system to complete decompression.

2. Bell-to-bell transfer

Bell-to-bell transfer may be carried out to rescue divers from a lost or entrapped bell or to evacuate a diving spread. Fig. 2 illustrates how bell-to-bell transfer may be carried out from a trapped bell.

In this procedure one or more divers swim(s) from the bell of their own diving spread to the bell of a second spread at the same depth. The two diving spreads may be on the same vessel or on two separate vessels.

In the case of a lost or entrapped bell a tapping code has been devised to assist in communicating with divers inside a stricken bell (see Fig. 3). A printed copy is normally kept inside the bell.

Emergency bell location arrangements are a legal requirement by the UK and Norwegian governments. These include the use of an acoustic transponder on the bell and a hand-held transponder (see Fig. 4) which operates on the International

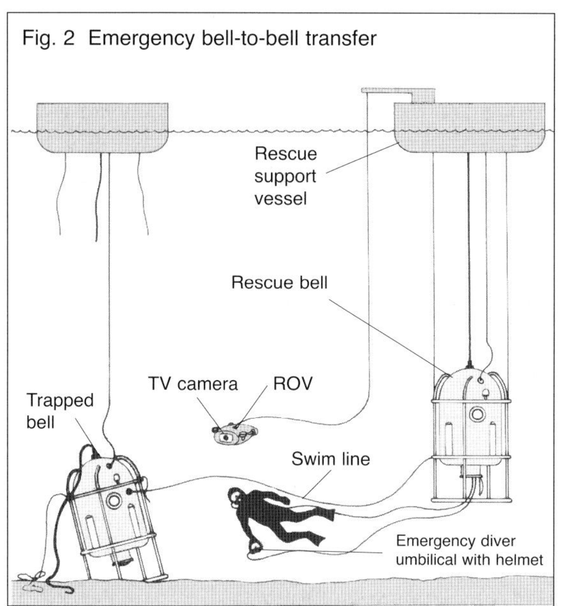
Rescue
support
vessel
Rescue bell
TV camera
ROV
Trapped
bell
Swim line
Emergency diver
umbilical with helmet
Fig. 2 Emergency bell-to-bell transfer

Maritime Organisation (IMO) Agreement's recognised frequency (37.5 kHz) and provides range and bearing data.

3. Bell used as a rescue chamber

In this case a diving bell is used as a rescue chamber. The bell needs to be prepared as well as possible for the transfer. Umbilicals, helmets, etc can be removed and additional facilities installed. These can include additional life-support capability, special ballast/buoyancy arrangements, restraining harnesses on seats and special launch and recovery facilities.

The number of divers that can be rescued using this method is limited. Ideally it should only be considered as viable when there is a second diving system within easy reach which has a compatible flange mating facility.

Fig. 3 Bell emergency communication code
for use between the crew of a lost craft and rescue divers

Tapping code	Situation
3.3.3	Communication opening procedure (inside and outside)
1	Yes, or affirmative, or agreed
3	No, or negative, or disagreed
2.2	Repeat phrase
2	Stop
5	Have you got a seal?
6	Stand by to be pulled up
1.2.1.2	Get ready for through-water transfer (Open your hatch)
2.3.2.3	You must NOT release your ballasts
4.4	Release your ballast in 30 minutes from now
1.2.3	Increase your pressure
3.3.3	Communication closing procedure (inside and outside)

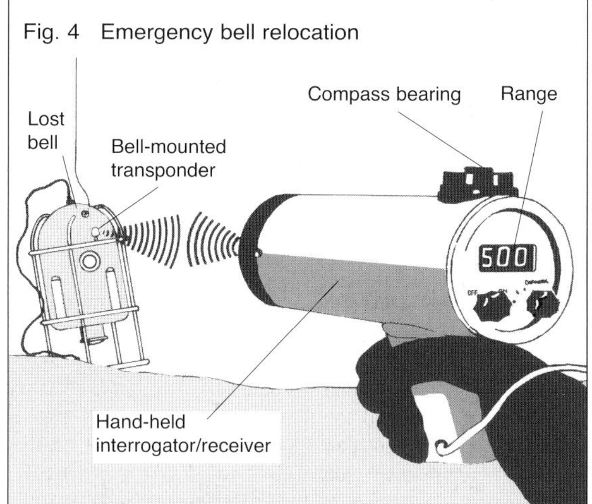
Lost
bell
Bell-mounted
transponder
Compass bearing
Range
500
Hand-held
interrogator/receiver
Fig. 4 Emergency bell relocation

13.3 COASTGUARD

The United Kingdom and United States Coastguard are responsible for co-ordinating search and rescue (SAR) operations in the waters under their jurisdiction (see Fig. 1). In this capacity, both Coastguards maintain and operate public rescue facilities co-ordinating the services of appropriate authorities such as the Navy, Air Force, Lifeboats, Police and a network of coastal radio stations.

United Kingdom

HM Coastguard (HMCG) is divided into three regions each of which are administered by two rescue-co-ordination centres and several sub-centres (see Fig. 2):

1. Scotland and Northern Ireland (Belfast, Clyde, Stornoway, Shetland, Aberdeen and Forth).

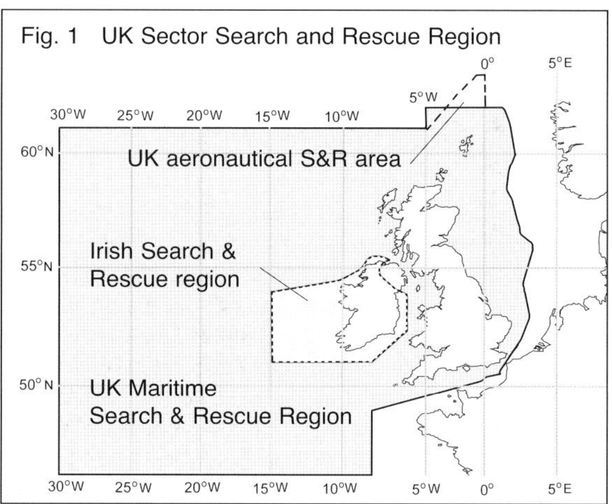
30°W
25°W
20°W
15°W
10°W
5°W
0°
5°E
60°N
55°N
50°N
UK aeronautical S&R area
Irish Search &
Rescue region
UK Maritime
Search & Rescue Region
Fig. 1 UK Sector Search and Rescue Region

Fig. 2 UK Coastguard Maritime Rescue Co-ordination Centres (MRCCs) and Sub-Centres (MRSCs)

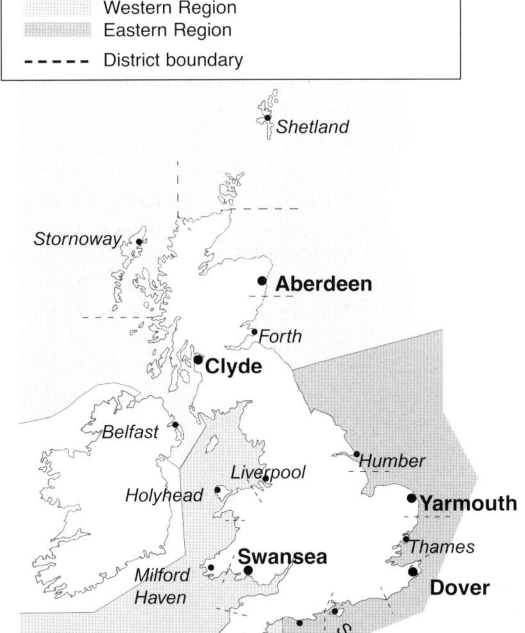
Key
Regions:
Scotland and Northern Ireland
Western Region
Eastern Region
District boundary
Shetland
Stornoway
Aberdeen
Forth
Clyde
Belfast
Humber
Liverpool
Holyhead
Yarmouth
Thames
Swansea
Milford Haven
Dover
Solent
Portland
Brixham
Falmouth

MRCCs:	Telephone	MRSCs:	Telephone
Aberdeen	01224 592 334	Belfast	028 9146 3933
Clyde	01475 729 988	Brixham	01803 882 704
Dover	01304 218 500	Forth	01333 450 666
Falmouth	01326 310 800	Holyhead	01407 762 051
Swansea	01792 366 534	Humber	01262 672 317
Yarmouth	01493 841 300	Liverpool	0151 931 3341
		Milford Haven	01646 699 600
		Portland	01305 760 439
		Shetland	01595 692 976
		Solent	023 9255 2100
		Stornoway	01851 702 013
		Thames	01255 675 518

Telephone numbers may change. Refer to website for confirmation.

www.mcga.gov.uk

2. Western region (Brixham. Falmouth, Swansea, Milford Haven, Holyhead and Liverpool).
3. Eastern region (Humber, Yarmouth, Thames, London, Dover, Solent and Portland).

All these centres, are equipped to enable the coastguard to make and maintain contact with any maritime distress call and to despatch appropriate rescue units. Each centre is manned and on watch for 24 hours each day throughout the year and it is from them, should a distress call be received, that the necessary rescue services will be mobilised.

As a general rule, because they are equipped for the task, offshore operators will manage and co-ordinate their own rescue services for their rigs and platforms. They will however, always keep the Coastguard informed of what rescue operations they are conducting and will call upon the Coastguard to supplement their requirements if necessary.

To avoid gas flares being mistaken for fires at sea all operating companies are requested to notify the MRCC or MRSC of any proposed well-testing operations involving the flaring of gas. Similarly any proposed detonation of explosives should be reported to the Coastguard.

When civil engineering divers are working from boats they should keep the Coastguard informed of their plans and movements.

In an emergency, the UK Coastguard can be contacted immediately by telephone by dialling 999 and asking for the Coastguard.

Check list of the information needed by the Coastguard in case of an emergency:

1. *Vessel/installation details*:
   - Type of vessel or installation.
   - Name of vessel/installation, how and where it is displayed.
   - Colours of hull and topside.
   - Special identification features.
   - Speed and endurance of vessel.
2. *Onboard personnel and related facilities*:
   - Number of persons on board.
   - Life-raft(s) and serial number(s).
   - Life boat type and colour.
   - Number and type of life-jackets carried.
3. *Communications details*:
   - Radio: HF/MF/transmitter/receivers
   - VHF channels and call sign.
   - Type of distress signal carried.
4. *Usual base, mooring, activity and sea areas.*
5. *Shore contact details*:
   - Name, address, telephone number of contact person onshore
   - Owner's name, address and telephone number.
6. *Date.*

United States

The US National SAR Plan divides the US area of SAR responsibility into internationally recognised inland and maritime SAR regions.

The US Coast Guard (USCG) is the Maritime SAR Co-ordinator and maintains SAR facilities on the east, west and Gulf coast, in Alaska, Hawaii, Guam and Puerto Rico.

Its maritime SAR region is divided into 2 main SAR Co-ordination areas: Pacific and Atlantic, each responsible for several Rescue Co-ordination

Fig. 3 US Coast Guard Rescue Co-ordination Centers (RCCs) and Sub-Centers (RSC)

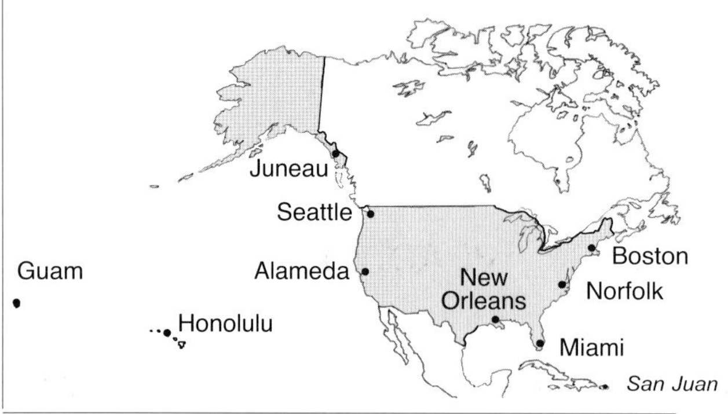
Juneau
Seattle
Guam
Alameda
Honolulu
New Orleans
Boston
Norfolk
Miami
San Juan

RCCs		*Telephone*
Atlantic Co-ordinator (Norfolk)		(757) 398 6231
includes:	Boston	(617) 223 8555
	Norfolk	(757) 398 6231
	Miami	(305) 415 6800
	New Orleans	(504) 589 6225
	Cleveland	(216) 902 6117
Pacific Co-ordinator (Alameda)		(510) 437 3700
includes:	Alameda	(510) 437 3700
	Seattle	(206) 220 7001
	Honolulu	(808) 541 2500
	Juneau	(907) 463 2000
MARSEC, Guam (with Honolulu)		(671) 399 2001

RSCs	*Telephone*
San Juan	(787) 289 2042

Telephone numbers may change.
Refer to website for confirmation.
www.uscg.mil

Centers (see Fig. 3). Guam co-ordinates SAR under Honolulu.

USCG resources include its own fleet of cutters, aircraft and numerous radio and communication stations. The USCG also administers commercial diving operations/equipment requirements and standards for construction and maintenance. It is also the investigating authority in the case of a fatal or serious accident.

Regulations

14.1 DIVING REGULATIONS AND CODES OF PRACTICE

Regulations are rules established by governments to control working procedures, usually with a heavy emphasis on safety. The regulations carry the full authority of the respective government and breaches of the regulations can lead to prosecution.
Many countries now have their own national regulations that control diving activities in their regional waters, both inland/inshore and offshore. The regulations apply at least out as far as each country's territorial limit (internationally recognised as 12 miles from the nearest land). In some cases, where the neighbouring countries have come to an agreement, the regulations can apply out as far as an agreed median line between the adjacent countries (for example as in the North Sea). Regulations can also apply to diving operations conducted from ships registered in the respective country. So for example, British-registered ships will be liable to UK regulations regardless of where they may be in the world.
Regulations place responsibilities on all personnel at work. In diving activities, these responsibilities can be considerable. It is very important that every person at work in a diving operation is fully conversant with the duties he/she has under the local regulations. New regulations are continuously introduced and existing regulations can be frequently amended so it is also important to keep up to date with the current situation.
In the UK, regulations are said to be 'target setting.' They are also designed to place a responsibility on the industry itself to self-regulate. The result is that the Regulations themselves can be general, rather than specific, in their requirements. In many cases, such as in diving matters, they refer to Approved Codes of Practice (ACOPs) which have been written in close cooperation with various sectors of the diving industry. ACOPs are detailed requirements and represent the government's interpretation of the regulations. ACOPs have the advantage of being relatively easy to update and they do not need to go through the lengthy process of sanction by Parliament (which regulations do).
In the UK, ACOPs that cover the diving industry include:

- Commercial diving projects offshore
- Commercial diving projects inland/inshore
- Media diving projects
- Recreational diving projects
- Scientific and archaeological diving projects

The ACOPs can refer to (and therefore give equivalent authority to) industry Codes of Practice. For example, the International Marine Contractors' Association (IMCA) provide a Code of Practice on the Initial and Periodic Examination, Testing and Certification of Diving Plant and Equipment.
These codes of practice effectively carry the same authority as the regulations so it is important to be aware of how they affect you in particular.
In parts of the world where there are no local governmental regulations covering diving activities, the local government can require diving contractors to comply with an internationally recognised code of practice. An example of this is the IMCA International Code of Practice for Offshore Diving.

14.2 DIVING EQUIPMENT TEST REQUIREMENTS

The International Marine Contractors' Association (IMCA) publishes a Code of Practice on the Initial and Periodic Examination, Testing and Certification of Diving Plant and Equipment. It is designed to reflect established good practice worldwide rather than the specific regulatory requirements of any one country. The ADC Consensus Standards are widely used by US-based diving contractors. Some countries have national regulations and these must always take precedence over guidelines.
Plant and equipment must be certified to show that it complies with the requirements of the country (or flag, if it is on a vessel) where it is being used.
If the equipment is built in accordance with a classification society's rules, the owner may request that it is assigned a class. To maintain classification it must comply with the statutory requirements of the national authority of the country/flag where it is installed.
There are five main international Classification Authorities: the American Bureau of Shipping, Bureau Veritas, Det Norske Veritas, Germanischer Lloyd, and Lloyd's Register. In addition, the US Coastguard (which enforces diving regulations in the USA) can issue/endorse certification which is at least equivalent to that of a classification society.
Certification can only be issued by a person competent to do so. The decisions made by the competent person have serious implications for the safety of anyone using the equipment. It is essential, therefore, that he is someone whose training, knowledge and/or experience of the plant being examined or tested enables him to competently detect and assess any defects or weaknesses.
IMCA identifies four categories of competent person which can be summarised as:

1. A diving or life support supervisor appointed by the diving contractor.
2. A technician, Class 1 Chief Engineer, or specialist in such work, who can act independently and professionally.
3. A Classification Society or Insurance Surveyor (or similar).

4. The manufacturer or supplier of the equipment, or specialist company with access to appropriate testing facilities.

The responsibility for ensuring that all plant and equipment is safe to use is divided between the diving contractor, the 'competent person' and the diving or life support supervisor.

- The diving contractor must ensure that all equipment (including standy equipment) has been certified and is available for use as necessary.
- It is the duty of the competent person to carry out the examination and testing diligently and thoroughly.
- The diving or life support supervisor must ensure that all the required in-date certificates are available and that the checks have been properly recorded in the diving operations logbook.

Record keeping

Most equipment needs to be regularly examined (every 6 months or less) with major re-examination occurring every 1–5 years according to the equipment concerned. For example, a decompression chamber needs to be visually inspected every 6 months and internally over-pressure tested every 5 years.

When modifications need to be made to a piece of equipment, it is left to the judgement of the appointed competent person to determine whether or not re-certification is required.

A list of the type of equipment that needs to be tested is shown in Fig. 1. Where the equipment being tested consists of several of the listed items, all the components must be certified in-date before the equipment can be put into service. For example, to certify a diver heating system all related electrical equipment, indicating gauges, diver heating system, pipework system, relief valves and welded pressure vessels must all be certified fit for use.

A planned maintenance system (PMS) helps to achieve a systematic and effective maintenance programme. It can be kept as 'hard copy' (such as a card index system or files), one for each major item of equipment; or it can be kept on computer (backed up on non-corruptible media).

Records should be kept for a minimum of 2–5 years depending on the equipment and its application.

A record should be kept for each major piece of equipment and should include the following information:

Fig. 1 List of diving equipment requiring certification

Note: All component parts also require testing and certification, eg, a hot water unit contains electrical equipment, gauges, diver heating systems, pipework systems, relief valves and welded pressure vessel all of which need to be periodically inspected, tested and certified.

A-frame (man-riding)
A-frame (non man-riding)
Air control panel
Air lift bags
Air reservoirs
Analysers
Bail out bottle
Basket (man-riding)
Basket (non man-riding)
Bell
Bell ballast release
Bell locator
Boosters
Breathing apparatus
Bursting discs
Caisson gauges
Cargo basket
Chamber
Communications
Compressor
Container
Control Panel
Control van
Crane
Cylinders
Decompression chamber
Depth gauge
Dive Basket
Dive control
Dive control van (structure)
Diver heating
Diving bell
Dropweights
Electrical equipment
Emergency location system
Emergency survival packs
Environmental control units
Excursion umbilicals
External regeneration units
Filter housings
Fire fighting systems
Flexible hose
Gas blenders/mixers
Gas control panel
Gas cylinders
Gas reclaim system
Gauges
Handling systems
Hot water units
Hydraulic power unit
Hyperbaric lifeboat (SOLAS type)
Hyperbaric lifeboat launch system
Hyperbaric rescue chamber (non SOLAS type)
Indicating gauges
Interlocks
Launch and recovery systems
Life support gauges
Lifting appliances
Oxygen systems
Parachute lift bags
Pipework
Pressure vessels
Quads (lifting points)
Regulators
Relief valves
Rigging equipment
Sanitary system
Shower tank
Surface chamber
Survival bags
Terminations
Umbilicals
Valves
Viewports
Welding habitat
Wet bell
Whips
Winch (man-riding)
Winch (non man-riding)
Wire rope and terminations

The IMCA Code of Practice provides 'Detail Sheets' for the required inspection of each of the above items including, 'Nature of examination/test', 'Validity period' and 'Category of competent person'.

a) A description of the equipment.
b) For new, first installed or moved equipment:
   - A certificate verifying that it is fit for the purpose it will be used for, according to the manufacturer's specifications.
   - Authorisation by a competent person (in most instances, this will be a competent person from category 3 or 4).
c) Once the equipment is in service:
   - Examination/test requirements.
   - Period for which the certificate is valid.
   - Authorisation by appropriate competent person.

14.3 CLASSIFICATION AND CERTIFICATION

It is the job of the Classification Societies and Certification Authorities to set standards of design, construction and maintenance of ships and structures and to carry out periodic checks to ensure that they are fit and safe for their intended services. The classification of vessels is long-established and many countries have their own Classification Societies (see Fig. 1). Certification, however, is a more recent development that applies largely to the offshore industry. Most countries with offshore installations have appointed organisations such as Classification Societies to act as Certification Authorities for offshore structures.

Fig. 1 Classification Societies

International

- International Association of Classification Societies
- International Naval Surveys Bureau
- American Bureau of Shipping (ABS)
- Bureau Veritas (BV)
- BVQi (Certification Division of BV)
- Det Norske Veritas (DNV)
- Lloyd's Register

The Americas

- American Bureau of Shipping, USA

Asia-Pacific

- China Classification Society, China
- Nippon Kaiji Kyokai, Japan
- Korean Register of Shipping, Korea
- Russian Maritime Register of Shipping

Europe

- Cyprus Bureau of Shipping Classification, Cyprus
- Bureau Veritas, France
- Germanischer Lloyd, Germany
- Hellenic Register of Shipping, Greece
- Hellenic Register of Shipping (Sweden), Sweden
- Registro Italiano Navale, Italy
- Det Norske Veritas, Norway
- Polski Rejestr Statków, Poland
- Russian Maritime Register of Shipping, Russia
- Turk Loydu, Turkey
- Lloyd's Register, United Kingdom

The fundamental difference between classification and certification is that in the case of classed equipment and systems, plan approval, surveys during construction and subsequent periodical surveys are all carried out in accordance with the Classification Society's own rules. Certification, however is carried out in accordance with the statutory requirements issued by the relevant government departments. In most cases certification of equipment is compulsory but it is up to the owner to decide whether or not he wishes his equipment to be classed.

In either case the procedures followed during construction are the same. The owner submits to the Classification Society or Certification Authority plans, data, design calculations, etc which are vetted and, if satisfactory, approved. The apparatus is then constructed under the supervision of the Societies' surveyors to ensure that the approved standards are complied with. On completion the apparatus will be given a final test and survey and, if up to standard, will be classed or certified.

In the UK the government requires all offshore installations to have an in-date Certificate of Fitness issued by an approved Certification Authority before they are allowed to operate. Such a certification assures that an installation is safe in every respect for its designed purpose and that the regulations are observed. Periodic checks must also be carried out during the time that the certificate is still valid.

Diver Tasks

Certification of an offshore structure usually requires special underwater inspection procedures using divers and ROVs to investigate wear and corrosion using a variety of techniques including photography, TV and NDT, etc. However, in the case of diving systems the certification procedure does not require diver involvement as inspection and pressure testing of equipment is carried out on shore or aboard a ship or platform.

Divers may be involved in the following aspects of the periodic survey programme for offshore structures:

1. Complete general visual survey of structures and risers.
2. Annual close visual inspection of approximately 10% of nodes, including critical nodes. Certification requirements may dictate that NDT be carried out depending on the structure. On older platforms NDT of selected critical node welds is specified.
3. Where a cathodic protection system is installed, a pattern of cathodic potential readings covering 10–20% of sacrificial anodes.
4. Preparation of a scour map (topographical survey of the seabed immediately surrounding the structure).
5. A visual survey of riser connections to jackets.

14.4 DIVING RECORDS AND QUALIFICATIONS

Diving Records

THE DIVING OPERATION RECORD

In the UK, the diving contractor must maintain a diving operation record. It is produced by the diving supervisor and should contain the information shown in Fig. 1. It must be retained by the diving contractor for a minimum of 2 years after the date of the last entry. Full details of requirements can be obtained from the Health and Safety Executive (*www.hse.gov.uk*).

US regulations also require the diving supervisor to maintain records including safe practice manuals, plant test and inspection records, depth-time profiles, dive records, decompression procedure assessment evaluations, records of hospitalizations and dive team medical records. With the exception of the safe practice manuals and equipment records (current documents required), all records must be kept for one year from date of last entry or five years if there has been an incident requiring hospitalisation. Full details of US diving regulations are available from the US Occupational Safety and Health Administration (OHSA) (*www.osha.gov*).

THE DIVER'S LOGBOOK (DAILY RECORD)

UK regulations require every diver to keep a personal record of dives. The logbook must contain the diver's name, signature and photograph. Every dive must be recorded and the diver should sign each entry and have it countersigned by the diving supervisor. The logbook must be retained for at least 2 years from date of last entry.

There are no US regulations regarding the diver's personal logbook.

Fig. 1 The Diving Operation Record UK requirements

1. **Name and address of the diving contractor**.
2. **Date** of diving operation.
3. **Name of the supervisor**(s). An entry must be completed daily by each supervisor for each diving operation.
4. **Location** of the diving operation (including name of any vessel or installation from which diving is taking place).
5. **Names** of those taking part in the diving operation – divers and other members of the dive team.
6. **Approved Code of Practice** that applies to the diving operation.
7. **Purpose** of the diving operation.
8. For each diver:
   - **Breathing apparatus** used.
   - **Breathing mixture** used.
   - **Start time** – when diver leaves atmospheric pressure.
   - **Bottom time**.
   - **Time of return** to atmospheric pressure.
   - **Maximum depth** reached.
   - **Decompression schedule** including details of **pressures (or depths) and duration** of time spent at those pressures (or depths) during decompression.
9. **Emergency arrangements**:
   - Details of **emergency support arrangements**.
   - Details of any **emergency or incident** of special note which occurred during the diving operation including details of decompression illness and treatment given.
10. **Plant/Equipment**:
    - Details of **pre-dive inspection of all plant used.**
    - Details of **any defect** found in any plant.
11. Relevant **environmental factors** during dive.
12. **Any other factors likely to affect the safety or health** of anyone engaged in the operation.
13. **Name and signature of supervisor** completing the record.
14. **Company stamp**, if appropriate

Fig. 2 The Diver's Daily Record UK requirements

1. **Name** (in block capitals) **and signature of the diver**.
2. **Name and address of the diving contractor** (in block capitals).
3. **Date** of the dive.
4. **Location** of the diving operation (including name of any vessel or installation from which diving is taking place).
5. For each dive:
   - **Start time** - when diver leaves surface.
   - **Bottom time**.
   - **Time of return** to surface.
   - If time spent in compression chamber: details of any **time spent outside chamber** at different pressure.
   - **Maximum depth** reached.
   - **Breathing apparatus** used.
   - **Breathing mixture** used .
   - Any **decompression schedule** followed.
6. - **Work done**.
   - **Plant and tools** used.
7. Incident details:
   - Any episode of **barotrauma, discomfort or injury** including details of any **decompression illness and treatment** given.
   - Any **emergency or incident** of special note which occurred during the dive.
   - Any **other factors likely to affect the diver's safety or health**
8. **Name** (in block capitals) **and signature of authorised representative of the diving contractor** (normally the diving supervisor) who confirms the details recorded.

Diving qualifications

Training requirements for divers vary from country to country. In the UK divers are required to hold an approved diving qualification suitable for the work they intend to do and it is advisable to have the original certificate with them at the dive site. In addition all divers must have a valid certificate of medical fitness to dive. A list of current approved qualifications can be obtained from the Health and Safety Executive (HSE) (*www.hse.gov.uk*). In addition to UK qualifications the list recognises qualifications from several countries including Australia, Canada, South Africa and many European countries. An approved diving qualification is not required by personnel providing emergency medical treatment in a chamber or by divers in training.

In the USA all dive team members are required to have experience or training necessary to safely perform the assigned task including experience or training in the use of tools, equipment and systems, the mode of diving, diving operations, emergency procedures, CPR and first aid (American Red Cross standard or equivalent). Personnel involved in hyperbaric diving also require training in diving-related physics and physiology. Any on-site training must be carried out under the direct supervision of an experienced dive team member. Diving supervisors must have experience and training in dive operations. Full details of US regulations are available from the Occupational Safety and Health Administration (*www.osha.gov*).

A summary of UK and US requirements is given in Fig. 3 below.

Applying for a diving job

There is often a great deal of competition for any one diving job. In order to secure the best chance of getting the job it is as important to present your application properly as it is to have the necessary qualifications and experience.

The following points should be regarded as essential when presenting yourself properly to a diving company:

1. *Interview.* Press for an interview with the Operations Manager rather than simply sending the details in the post.

   Take the following documents with you:
   - Personal résumé (CV).
   - Passport.
   - Diving record.
   - In-date diving medical certificate.
   - Trade certificates (welding, burning, inspection, NDT, explosives, first aid, etc). Take spare photocopies – it is helpful to be able to leave them with the company.
   - 10 spare photographs. If you are successful they may be required for visa applications.

2. *Visit.* Make an appointment and visit the diving companies at their operational bases.

3. *Personal résumé* [CV (curriculum vitae)]. You will need to leave one at every diving company visited. Contents and presentation are important. It should be typed, neat and clear. Include the following information:
   - Full name
   - Home address and phone numbers
   - Date of birth
   - Nationality
   - Marriage status
   - Professional and/or academic qualifications.
   - Membership of any relevant associations or institutes.
   - Passport number, date of issue, place of issue, details of any visas held.
   - Next of kin: name, address, phone numbers.
   - Summary of career to date.
     Be clear and brief. Use no more than one page. Use key words: job titles held, skills used, work procedures.
     Start with the most recent job and go backwards towards the first job held. Provide more detail with recent jobs; less with earliest work.
     Give dates of employment, name of company worked for, position held, location, tasks performed and any special experience gained.
   - Provide references. State name of referee and job title.
   - Keep it up-dated. Trim down details of earlier jobs to ensure that it doesn't turn into several pages of career details.

Fig. 3 Summary of qualification requirements for UK and USA

	UK	USA
Surface orientated diving < 50 m	A diving qualification approved by the by the Health and Safety Executive (HSE). See *www.hse.gov.uk* for full list of current approved qualifications.	Experience or training in: 1. tools, equipment and systems. 2. diving techniques. 3. diving operations and emergency procedures. First aid qualification.
Bell diving > 50 m	A diving qualification approved by the by the Health and Safety Executive (HSE). See *www.hse.gov.uk* for full list of current approved qualifications.	Training in diving-related physics and physiology. First aid qualification.

Arriving at a new job

The successful professional diver will own certain items of clothing and equipment in order to be able to perform his work and duties efficiently. The quantity and variety of these accessories will vary around the world. However, as a basic minimum, the following should be included (but add to this list as you see fit):

- Rig boots.
- Set of foul weather gear.
- Warm clothing.
- Blue and red overalls (so the diver can select the more suitable for a particular employer). Do not wear the overalls of a different company.
- Deck knife.
- Diving knife.
- Adjustable spanner (10-inch) for gas hose connections.
- Gas bottle key (for HP cylinders).
- Roll of PVC insulation tape (for sealing open hose ends).
- Paperwork including diving log book(s), certificates, medical certificate, CV, driving licence, etc.

Behaviour:

- Ask the Supervisor about the job, what equipment is being used, what is needed to be done. Discuss any concerns about safety.
- Ensure good time-keeping. Arrive on site in good time.
- Develop a reputation for reliability.
- Make yourself as useful as possible around the work site.
- Take every opportunity to gain further experience and knowledge.
- Learn surface skills such as cutting, welding, concreting. Consider night school.
- Get involved in mobilisations.
- Keep notes and record tips and good advice on jobs.
- Record contact details of members of the team and keep in touch. This can be useful in finding further work.
- Avoid acquiring a 'prima donna' reputation.

Useful information

15.1 TIME AND TRAVEL

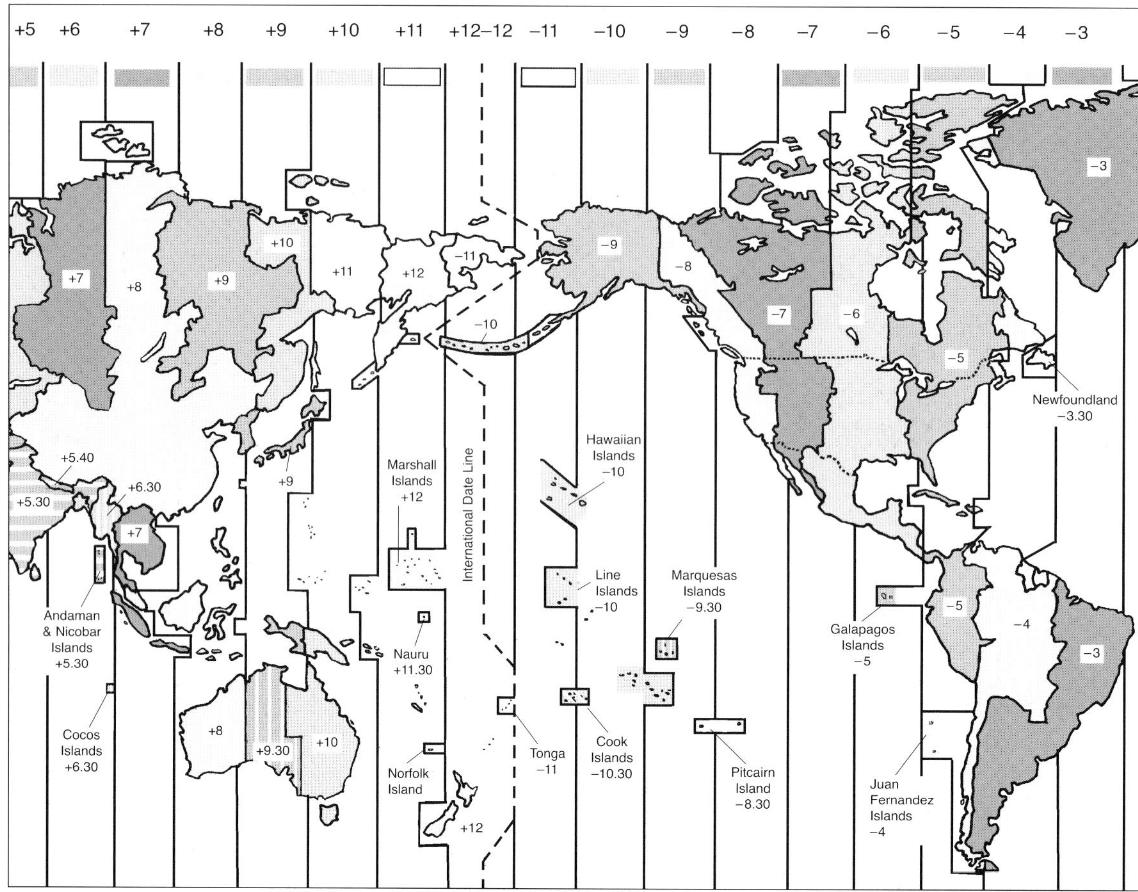
+5 +6 +7 +8 +9 +10 +11 +12–12 –11 –10 –9 –8 –7 –6 –5 –4 –3
+7
+8
+9
+10
+11
+12
–11
–10
–9
–8
–7
–6
–5
–3
Newfoundland
–3.30
+5.40
+5.30
+6.30
+7
+9
Marshall
Islands
+12
International Date Line
Hawaiian
Islands
–10
Line
Islands
–10
Marquesas
Islands
–9.30
Andaman
& Nicobar
Islands
+5.30
Nauru
+11.30
Galapagos
Islands
–5
–5
–4
–3
Cocos
Islands
+6.30
+8
+9.30
+10
Norfolk
Island
+12
Tonga
–11
Cook
Islands
–10.30
Pitcairn
Island
–8.30
Juan
Fernandez
Islands
–4
Fig. 1 World time zones in hours ahead or behind GMT (Greenwich Mean Time)

World Time Zones

When travelling or making overseas telephone calls it is useful to know the time differences between countries.

The world is divided into 24 time zones which were established in 1884. Each zone generally represents 15° of longitude or 1 hour of time. The world's time zones start at 0° longitude, the Prime (or Greenwich) Meridian which passes through Greenwich Observatory, in London, England. Countries to the east of the Prime Meridian are ahead of Greenwich Mean Time (GMT) and those to the west are behind. There are 12 zones to the east of the Prime Meridian and 12 to the west (Fig. 1). They meet half way around the world from Greenwich at an imaginary line called the International Date Line (IDL). Crossing the IDL from east to west would result in 'losing' a day while travelling from west to east means 'gaining' a day.

In some cases the time zones closely correlate to the longitudinal division between zones (eg northern Canada) but in most cases they follow state boundaries. While Canada has 6 time zones, China, which straddles 5 time zones observes no internal national time zones.

The Polar regions, where there are periods of constant daylight or night, do not use standard time zones.

Local inconsistencies may occur due to seasonal use of Summer Time (ST) or Daylight Saving Time (DST). ST is observed by many countries in Europe and occurs from the last Sunday in March until the end of October. In the USA, DST is used in all continental states except Arizona and parts of Indiana. It starts on the last Sunday in April and ends on the last Sunday in October. In both cases clocks are advanced by one hour in March/April and are turned back by one hour in October. In the southern hemisphere DST is practised between October and March.

In low latitudes (tropical and equatorial regions) where daylight hours are similar all year round DST is not used. In the high latitudes of Russia, all 11 time zones are 1 hour ahead of both standard time and DST all year round.

Visas and Work Permits

A visa is a stamp of approval placed on the page of a passport. It does not guarantee entry to the country and is usually valid for one entry or transit only. Multiple visas are obtainable at extra cost. Business visas normally require a letter from the company sponsoring the visit. Evidence of financial standing may also be required.

A visa and work permit are not the same thing.

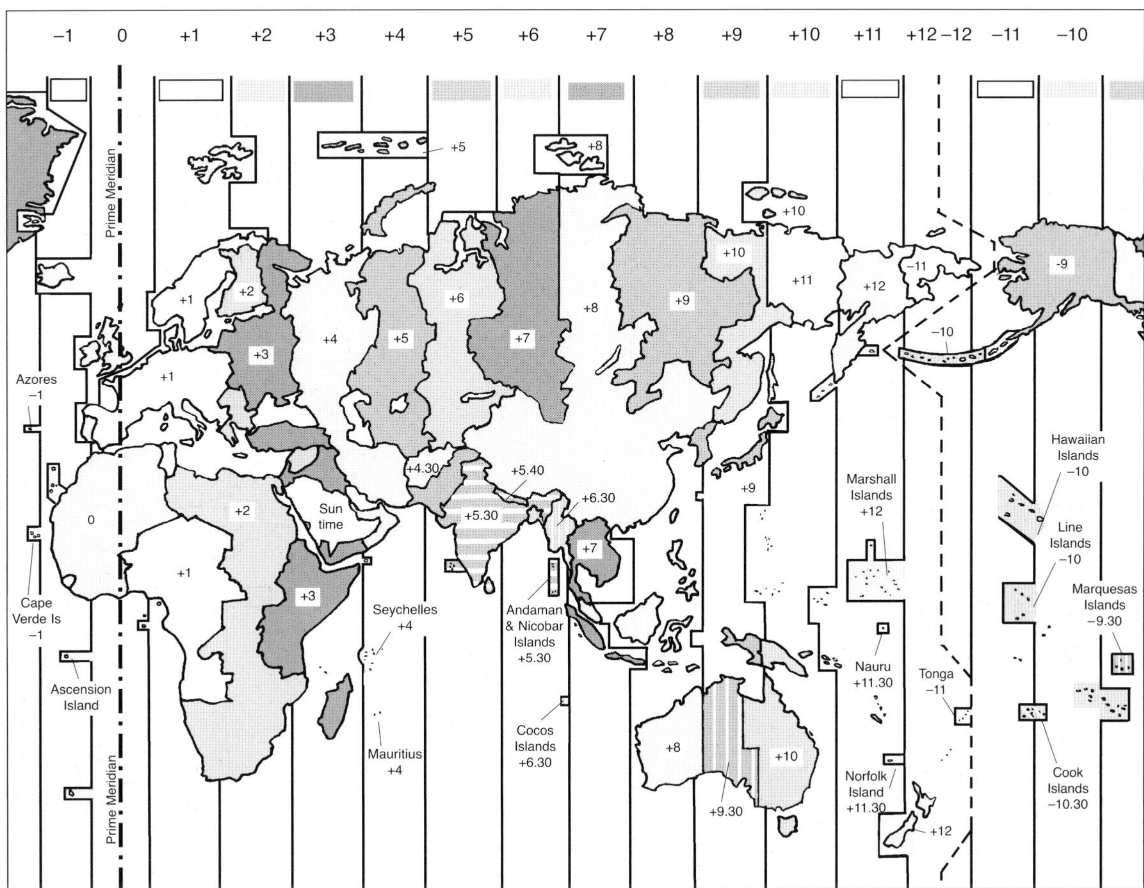

–1
0
+1
+2
+3
+4
+5
+6
+7
+8
+9
+10
+11
+12 –12
–11
–10
Prime Meridian
+5
+8
+10
+10
+11
+12
–11
-9
+2
+1
+6
+8
+9
+4
+5
+7
–10
+3
Azores
–1
+1
0
+2
Sun time
+4.30
+5.40
+6.30
+5.30
+9
Marshall Islands
+12
Hawaiian Islands
–10
Line Islands
–10
+7
+1
+3
Cape Verde Is
–1
Seychelles
+4
Andaman & Nicobar Islands
+5.30
Marquesas Islands
–9.30
Nauru
+11.30
Tonga
–11
Ascension Island
Mauritius
+4
Cocos Islands
+6.30
+8
+10
Norfolk Island
+11.30
Cook Islands
–10.30
+9.30
+12

Many countries do not require a visa but do require a work permit. Work permits are usually required prior to entering the country to be visited. Each country has its own restrictions so the appropriate Consulate or Embassy should be consulted.

Vaccination requirements

The World Health Organisation publishes comprehensive and up-to-date health advice for travellers in *International Travel and Health* and in three languages (English, French and Spanish) on the internet at *www.who.int* (Travellers Health section).

Destinations where accommodation, hygiene, sanitation, medical care and water quality are of a high standard pose few serious risks. However, if travelling to areas where these conditions do not apply stringent precautions should be taken.

Pre-travel precautions should include routine vaccinations (eg, Diptheria, Measles, Polio) for those who have neglected their booster doses. Other vaccines are advised according to the area of travel (see Figs. 2 and 3). Yellow fever

The following countries have no vaccination requirements: Canada, Denmark, France, Israel, Italy, Ireland, Japan, Jordan, Kuwait, Netherlands, New Zealand, Norway, Spain, Sweden, UK and USA.

Fig. 2 Vaccination requirements for selected countries

R = Required
A = Advised
a = Advised if visiting infected area
YF = Yellow fever

Country	Cholera	Yellow Fever	Malaria	**Comments**
Angola	**R**	**A**	**A**	
Australia	*a*	*a*	-	
Brazil	-	*a*	**A**	If visiting Belem area
Brunei	*a*	*a*	-	
Cambodia	-	-	*a*	
Cameroon	**A**	**R**	**A**	YF not required if staying less than 15 days
Ecuador	-	*a*	**A**	
Egypt	*a*	*a*	**A**	Malaria risk Jun-Oct in Nile Delta, El Faiyum, Upper Egypt
Gabon	-	*a*	**A**	YF required if staying longer than 2 weeks
India	**A**	*a*	**A**	Malaria risk March-Oct
Indonesia	**A**	*a*	**A**	
Iran	*a*	*a*	**A**	Malaria risk July-Nov
Iraq	-	*a*	**A**	Malaria risk in North, May-Nov
Ivory Coast	-	**R**	**A**	
Malaysia	-	*a*	**A**	
Mexico	-	*a*	**A**	
Myanmar	-	*a*	**A**	Malaria risk higher in Mar–Dec
Nigeria	-	**R**	**A**	Malaria risk higher in Jun–Nov
Oman	**R**	*a*	**A**	
Saudi Arabia	-	*a*	**A**	
Singapore	-	*a*	-	
South Africa	*a*	*a*	**A**	Malaria risk north, east, west Transvaal and Natal coast
UAE	*a*	-	-	
Venezuela	-	**A**	**A**	YF required for Amazon area
Vietnam	-	*a*	**A**	

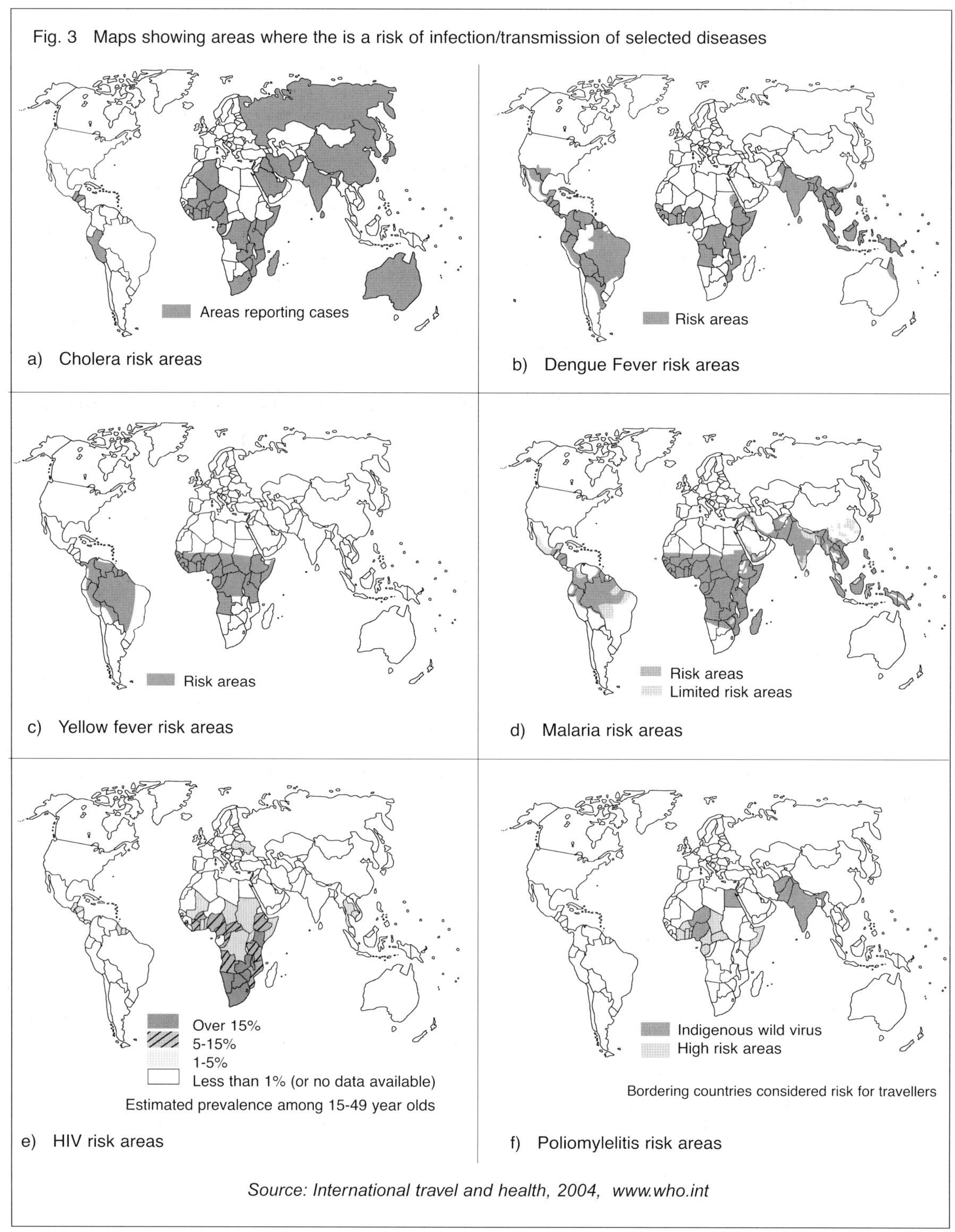
Fig. 3 Maps showing areas where the is a risk of infection/transmission of selected diseases
Areas reporting cases
a) Cholera risk areas
Risk areas
b) Dengue Fever risk areas
Risk areas
c) Yellow fever risk areas
Risk areas
Limited risk areas
d) Malaria risk areas
Over 15%
5-15%
1-5%
Less than 1% (or no data available)
Estimated prevalence among 15-49 year olds
e) HIV risk areas
Indigenous wild virus
High risk areas
Bordering countries considered risk for travellers
f) Poliomylelitis risk areas
Source: International travel and health, 2004, www.who.int

vaccination is mandatory if travelling to or through a yellow fever endemic area.

Travellers should seek advice 4–6 weeks before travelling in order to enable immunisation to be effective by the time of travel. Fig. 2 lists the vaccination requirements for three main diseases (cholera, yellow fever and malaria) for selected countries where offshore diving occurs. Different drug regimes are required for some parts of the world where resistance to certain vaccinations has built-up.

Always verify requirements for the country to be visited with a doctor, pharmacist, commercial travel clinic or WHO website before travelling.

15.2 METRICATION

The oil industry developed in the USA long before the metric system was established in Europe and elsewhere. Consequently, many units of measurement are unique to that industry and some were even invented specially for it such as the unit of force, the Kip, which equals 1000lb force and the unit of liquid volume, the barrel, which is a multiple of the US gallon.
The American Petroleum Institute (API) has rationalised standards for the measurement of length, mass, time and temperature.
In 1948 the International Committee of Weights and Measures began to study the establishment of a worldwide practical system of units of measurement. Le Système International d'Unités (SI) officially came into being in 1960 and has been adopted by nearly all countries although the application varies considerably.
However the API still has not adopted the metric system and the subsea industry has to work in many comparable units such as SI units, imperial units and API units. Conversion tables covering some of these systems are provided later in this section.

The metric system

The International System of Units (SI) is a modern version of the metric system in use throughout the scientific and industrial world. Its universal use avoids confusion in international trade and scientific work.

The SI is based on seven units:

1. The metre (m) is the unit of length.
2. The kilogram (kg) is the unit of weight.
3. The second (s) is the unit of time.
4. The ampere (A) is the unit of electrical current.
5. The kelvin (K) is the unit of thermodynamic temperature. *Note 'kelvin' is not used in conjunction with the word or symbol for degrees.*
6. The mole (mol) is the unit of the amount of substance equivalent to its molecular weight in grams.
7. The candela (cd) is the unit of luminous intensity.

DERIVED SI UNITS

Other SI units are called derived units and are formed by combining base units according to their corresponding physical properties (see Fig. 1).

Fig. 1 Selected derived SI Units and their symbols

Quantity	SI unit	Symbol
Area	square metre	m²
Volume	cubic metre	m³
Velocity, speed	metre per second	m/s or ms⁻¹
Acceleration	metre per second per second	m/s² or ms⁻²
Moment of force	newton metre	Nm
Mass per unit length	kilogram per metre	kg/m
Density	kilogram per cubic metre	kg/m³

Note: all symbols are correctly written in lower case, roman type without full points and without any plural form (for example, h (for hours) and not hs). The exception to this rule is that capital letters are used when the symbol is taken from a proper name, eg W for Watt.
When a unit for a physical quantity is divided by a unit for another physical quantity an oblique line (solidus) may be used, or the denominator may be expressed to the appropriate negative power. For example, metres per second can be expressed as m/s or ms^{-1}.
Some derived units have special names and symbols (see Fig. 2).

Fig. 2 Derived SI Units with special names and symbols

Quantity	Name	Symbol	Expressed in terms of	
			other SI units	SI base units
Activity (of a radio-active source)	Bequerel	Bq		s^{-1}
Quantity of electricity (electric charge)	Coulomb	C		As
Electrical capacitance	Farad	F	C/V	$s^4A^2(m^2kg)$
Inductance	Henry	H	Wb/A	$m^2kg/(s^2A^2)$
Frequency	Hertz	Hz		s^{-1}
Energy, work, quantity of heat	Joule	J	Nm	m^2kg/s^2
Luminous flux	lumen	lm		cd sr
Illuminance	lux	lx	lm/m²	cd sr/m²
Force	Newton	N		m kg/s²
Electrical resistance	Ohm	Ω	V/A	$m^2kg/(s^3A^2)$
Pressure	Pascal	Pa	N/m²	$kg/(ms^2)$
Electrical conductance	Siemens	S	A/V	$s^2A^2/(m^2kg)$
Magnetic flux density	Tesla	T	Wb/m²	$kg/(s^2A)$
Electrical potential difference	Volt	V	W/A	$m^2kg/(s^3A)$
Power	Watt	W	J/s	m^2kg/s^3
Magnetic flux	Weber	Wb	Vs	$m^2kg/(S^2A)$

There are other units, not themselves SI units, which are accepted for use with the international system and are often used in conjunction with SI units.

minute (of time)	min
minute (of angle)	'
second (of angle)	"
hour	h
day	d
degree (of angle or temperature)	°
litre	l
tonne	t
bar	b
atmosphere absolute	ata
nautical mile	no internationally-agreed symbols
knot	no internationally-agreed symbols

15.2 METRICATION

Usage

Some symbols might appear to be ambiguous. The symbol for litre, for example is 'l.' This is often confused with the numeral '1.' Similarly, the symbol for the metric tonne, 't,' is often wrongly used for imperial tons. In such instances it is recommended to use the whole word, litre or tonne.

PREFIXES

In SI there is only one unit for each physical quantity, eg the metre for length. If a unit seems too large or too small, a multiple, called a prefix, should be used (see Fig. 3). Only one prefix per unit should be used. 'Millimillimetre' for example is incorrect. It should be written as 'micrometre'.

Fig. 3 Some prefixes and their application

Prefix	Symbol	Factor by which unit is multiplied	
giga	G	1 000 000 000	$= 10^9$
mega	M	1 000 000	$= 10^6$
kilo	k	1 000	$= 10^3$
hecto	h	100	$= 10^2$
deca	da	10	$= 10^1$
centi	c	0.01	$= 10^{-2}$
milli	m	0.001	$= 10^{-3}$
micro	μ	0.000 001	$= 10^{-6}$
nano	n	0.000 000 001	$= 10^{-9}$

DECIMAL MARKERS

The decimal point may be either a full point or a comma written on the line.

To avoid confusion, the comma should never be used as a thousands marker. For example, three thousand five hundred should be written as 3500 and not 3,500).

For the same reason, the use of a hyphen is recommended when writing sums of money on cheques (eg £50-00 not £50,00).

15.3 CONVERSION TABLES

While most weights and measures are universally used, in some instances (notably gallons and tons) the UK and US versions differ. The US liquid gallon is smaller than the UK (or imperial) gallon. Both are equal to 8 pints but in the UK 1 pint = 20 fluid ounces while in the US 1 pint = 16 fluid ounces. Similarly, the UK (or long) ton = 2240 pounds; while the US (or short) ton = 2000 pounds. They are identified in the table below with the prefix 'UK' or 'US', as applicable.

The following table provides conversion factors enabling conversion of units by multiplying by the given factor. To do a conversion the other way, simply reverse the operation. For example, to convert feet into metres *multiply* by 0.3048; to convert metres to feet, *divide* by 0.3048.

To convert	Into	Multiply by
atmospheres	pounds/in^2 (psi)	14.696
	in of mercury (0°C)	29.92
	ft of water (4°C)	33.9
	fsw	33.072
	tons/ft^2	1.058
	cm of mercury	76.0
	kg/cm^2	1.0335
	kg/m^2	10332
	Pascals	101 325
bar	atmospheres	0.9869
	pounds/in^2 (psi)	14.5039
	pounds/ft^2	2089
	Pascals	100 000
	kg/cm^2	1.02
	kg/m^2	10200
barrels (oil)	gallons (UK)	39.9909
	gallons (US)	42
	cu feet (ft^3)	5.6146
	cu metres (m^3)	0.1590
	litres	158.9871
BTU (British thermal units)	Joules	0.000 9471

To convert	Into	Multiply by
calories	Joules	0.2388
calories/second	Watts	4.1868
centigrade/celsius	Fahrenheit	x 1.8, + 32
	Kelvin (absolute)	add 273.15
centilitres	litres	0.01
centimetres	inches	0.3937
	feet	0.0328
	yards	0.01094
centimetres of mercury	atmospheres	0.01316
	pounds/in^2 (psi)	0.1934
	pounds/ft^2	27.85
	ft of water (4°C)	0.4461
	kg/m^2	136
	Pascals	1333.22
centimetres/sec	feet/sec	0.03281
	feet/min	1.9685
	miles/min	0.0003728
	miles/hr (mph)	0.02237
	knots	0.01943
	metres/sec	0.01
	metres/min	0.6
	km/hr	0.036

To convert	Into	Multiply by
cubic centimetres	cu inches (in^3)	0.06102
	cu feet (ft^3)	0.00003531
	cu yards (yd^3)	0.000001308
cubic centimetres	ounces	0.03381
	gallons (US, liquid)	0.0002642
	litres	0.001
cu cm (carbon steel)	pounds	0.017
	kilograms	0.008
cubic feet	cu cm (cc)	28320
	cu metres (m^3)	0.02832
	cu inches (in^3)	1728
	cu yards (yd^3)	0.03704
cu ft (carbon steel)	pounds	489
	kilograms	221.8
cu feet of water	litres	28.32
	pounds	62.355
	gallons (US)	7.48052
	gallons (UK)	6.235
cubic feet/min	cu cm /sec (cc/sec)	472
	litres/sec	0.472
cubic feet/sec	US gallons/min	448.831
cubic inches	cu feet (ft^3)	0.0005787
	cu yards (yd^3)	0.00002143
	cu cm (cc)	16.38
	cu metres (m^3)	0.00001639
cu in (carbon steel)	pounds	0.283
	kilograms	0.128
cu inches of water	litres	0.01639
	pounds	0.03612
	gallons (US)	0.004329
	gallons (UK)	0.003607
cubic metres	cu inches (in^3)	61025
	cu feet (ft^3)	35.3156
	cu yards (yd^3)	1.308
cu m (carbon steel)	pounds	17300
	kilograms	7810
cu metres of water	gallons (US)	264.2
	gallons (UK)	220.1
	kilos	1000
	litres	1000
	tonnes	1 (approx)
cu millimetres	litres	0.000 001
cu yards	litres	764.555
dynes	Newtons	0.000 001
dyne/sq. cm	Pascals	0.1
ergs	Joules	0.000 0001
fahrenheit	centigrade/celsius	-32, x 0.56
	Kelvin (absolute)	add 460
fathoms	metres	1.8288
feet	millimetres (mm)	304.8
	centimetres (cm)	30.48
	metres (m)	0.3048
	miles (nautical)	0.0001645
	miles (statute)	0.0001894
feet of water (fsw)	atmospheres	0.0295
	bars	0.0299
	inches of mercury	0.8826
	pounds/in^2 (psi)	0.4335
	pounds/ft^2	62.43
	kg/cm^2	0.03048
	kg/m^2	304.8
	metres of water (msw)	0.3048
	Pascals	2989.067
feet/min	cm/sec	0.5080
	metres/min	0.3048
	km/hr	0.01829
	feet/sec	0.01667
	miles/hr (mph)	0.01136
feet/sec	cm/sec	30.48
	metres/min	18.29
	metres/sec	0.3048
	km/hr	1.097
	knots	0.5921
	miles/min	0.01136
	miles/hr (mph)	0.6818
foot pounds-force	Joules	1.355 817
foot poundals	Joules	0.042 140
gallons (UK)	barrels	0.0286
	gallons (US) (liquid	1.2009
	pounds of water	10.0122
	cu inches	277.274
	cu feet	0.1605
	cu metres (m^3)	0.0045
	kilograms of water	4.5420
	litres	4.546 09
gallons (US) (liquid)	barrels	0.0238
	cu inches (in^3)	231
	cu feet (ft^3)	0.1337
	cu yards (yd^3)	0.004951
	pounds of water	8.33
	gallons (UK)	0.8327
	cu cm (cc)	3785
	cu metres (m^3)	0.003785
	kilograms of water	3.7820
	litres	3.7854
grams	kilograms (kg)	0.001
grams/litre	kg/litre	0.001
gram-force cm	Newton metres (Nm)	0.0000980665
horsepower	watts	745.7
horsepower hours	Joules	2 685 520
hundredwt (UK)	kilograms (kg)	50.802
hundredwt (US)	kilograms (kg)	45.359
hundredwieght of water	gallons (UK)	11.2
	gallons (US)	9.326
	cu feet	1.795
inches	millimetres (mm)	25.4
	centimetres	2.54
	metres	0.0254
	feet	0.08333
	yards	0.02778
inches/sec	metres/sec	0.0254
inches of mercury	Pascals	3386.388
Joules/hour	Watts	0.000 278

To convert	Into	Multiply by
Joules/minute	Watts	0.1667
Joules/second	Watts	1
kilocalories	Joules	0.000 239
kilocalories/hour	Watts	1.163
kilograms	grams	1000
	pounds	2.2046
	tons (long)	0.0009842
	tons (short)	0.001102
kilograms/cu m	kg/litre	0.001
kilograms force	Newtons	9.80665
kg-force cm	Newton metres (Nm)	0.0980665
kg-force metres	Joules	9.80665
kilometres	feet	3281
	yards	1094
	miles	0.6214
	metres	1000
kilometres/hour	feet/sec	0.9113
	feet/min	54.68
	miles/hr (mph)	0.6214
	knots	0.5396
	cm/sec	27.78
	metres/min	16.67
	metres/sec	0.2778
	km/min	0.01667
	km/sec	0.0003
kilometres/sec	metres/sec	1000
kilonewtons (kN)	Newtons	1000
kilowatt hours	Joules	3 600 000
kips	Newtons	4448.222
kips	kilograms	453.592 37
kips/sq in	Pascals	6 894 760
knots	feet/sec	1.689
	feet/hr	6080.2
	yards/hr	2027
	statute miles/hr	1.1516
	metres/sec	0.5144
	kilometres/hr	1.8532
litres	cu centimetres (cc)	1000
	cu metres (m^3)	0.001
	cu inches (in^3)	61.02
	cu feet (ft^3)	0.03531
	cu yards (yd^3)	0.001308
	gallons (UK)	0.02201
	gallons (US) (liquid)	0.2642
metres	inches	39.37
	feet	3.281
	yards	1.094
	miles (nautical)	0.0005396
	miles (statute)	0.0006214
metres/min	cm/sec	1.667
	metres/sec	0.1667
metres/min	km/hr	0.06
	feet/sec	0.05468
	feet/min	3.281
	miles/hr (mph)	0.03728
	knots	0.03238
metres/sec	feet/sec	3.2808
	feet/min	196.8
	miles/min	0.03728
	miles/hr (mph)	2.2369
	km/min	0.06
	km/hr	3.6
metres of water	bars	0.0967
	feet of water	3,2808
	Pascals	9806.65
	kg/sq cm (cm^2)	0.1
microns	metres	0.000001
miles (nautical)	metres	1852
	kilometres	1.852
	feet	6080
	yards	2025.4
	miles (statute)	1.1516
miles (statute)	centimetres	160934
	metres	1609.344
	kilometres	1.609
	feet	5280
	yards	1760
	miles (nautical)	0.8684
miles/hr	cm/sec	44.7
	metres/sec	0.44704
	metres/min	26.8225
	km/min	0.02682
	km/hr	1.6094
	feet/sec	1.4667
	feet/min	88
	miles/min	0.1667
	miles/sec	0.0003
	knots	0.8684
milligrams/litre	kg/litre	0.000 001
millilitres (ml)	litres	0.001
millimetres (mm)	inches	0.03937
millimetres (mm)	feet	0.003281
	yards	0.001094
Newtons	pounds (lb)	0.225
	kilograms (kg)	0.102041
Newton cm	Newton metres (Nm)	0.01
Newton metres	Joules	1
ounces	pounds	0.0625
	cu inches (in^3)	1.805
	grams	28.35
	kilograms (kg)	0.02835
	litres	0.02957
ounces/in^2	pounds/in^2 (psi)	0.0625
ounces/in^3	kg/litre	1.73

To convert	Into	Multiply by
pints (UK)	litres	0.568
pints (US)	litres	0.473
poundals	Newtons	0.183255
poundals/sq ft	Pascals	1.448 16
poundal feet	Newton metres (Nm)	0.042140
pounds	kilograms	0.4536
	ounces	16
	Newtons	4.448
pounds of water	cu inches	27.632
	gallons (UK)	0.1
	gallons (US)	0.08
pounds/in	gm/cm	178.6
pounds/in^2 (psi)	atmospheres	0.06804
	bars	0.0689
	feet seawater (fsw)	2.250482
	pounds/ft^2	144
	kg/cm^2	0.07
	kg/m^2	703.1
	Pascals	6894.757
pounds/in^3	kg/litre	27.6799
	pounds/ft^3	1728
pounds/ft	kg/m	1.488
pounds/ft^2	pounds/in^2 (psi)	0.006944
	atmospheres	0.0004725
	kg/m^2	4.882
pounds/ft^3	kg/litre	0.016
	kg/m^3	16.02
pounds of water	cu inches	27.632
	gallons (UK)	0.1
	gallons (US)	0.12
pounds/gallon (UK)	kg/litre	0.9977
pounds/gallon (US)	kg/litre	0.1198
pounds-force	Newtons	4.448 222
pound-force feet	Newton metres (Nm)	1.355 818
pounds-force/sq ft	Pascals	47.880
pounds-force/sq in	Pascals	6894.757
square feet	sq mm (mm^2)	92900
	sq cm (cm^2)	929
	sq metres (m^2)	0.092 903 04
	sq inches (in^2)	144
square feet	sq yards (yd^2)	0.111
sq centimetres	sq metres (m^2)	0.0001
square inches	sq mm (mm^2)	645.16
	sq cm (cm^2)	6.4516
square inches	sq metres (m^2)	0.000 645 16
	sq feet (ft^2)	0.006 944

To convert	Into	Multiply by
square kilometres	sq metres (m^2)	1 000 000
	sq miles	0.3861
square metres	sq inches (in^2)	1550
	sq feet (ft^2)	10.76
	sq yards (yd^2)	1.196
square miles	sq metres (m^2)	2 589 988
	sq kilometres	2.590
square millimetres	sq metres (m^2)	0.000 001
	sq inches (in^2)	0.00155
square yards	sq metres (m^2)	0.8361
therms	Joules	105 575 00
tons (UK) of water	gallons (UK)	224
	gallons (US)	186.5
	cu metres	1 (approx)
	litres	1017 (approx)
tons (UK or long)	kilograms	1016
	tonnes	1.016
	pounds	2240
	tons (short)	1.12
tons (UK)/cu yard	kg/litre	1.329
tons (UK)-force	Newtons	9964.016
ton (UK)-force ft	Newton metres (Nm)	3037.032
tons (UK)-force/ft^2	Pascals	107251
tons (UK)-force/in^2	Pascals	15 444 256
tons (US or short)	kilograms	907.1848
	tonnes	0.9072
	ounces	32000
	pounds	2000
	tons (long)	0.89287
tons (US)/cu yard	kg/litre	1.1866
tons (US)-force	Newtons	8896.443
ton (US)-force ft	Newton metres (Nm)	2711.636
tons (US)-force)/ft^2	Pascals	95760
tons (US)-force/in	Pascals	13 789 500
tonnes	kilograms (kg)	1000
	long/UK tons	0.984
	short/US tons	1.102
tonnes-force	Newtons	9806.65
tonne-force metres	Newton metres (Nm)	9806.65
tonnes-force/cm^2	Pascals	98 066 500
tonnes-force/m^2	Pascals	9806.65
watt hours	Joules	3600
yards	centimetres	91.44
	metres	0.9144
yards/sec	metres/sec	0.9144

Feet to metres, Metres to feet
Ready reckoner

Central (bold) figure converts to feet (left) and to metres (right). Example, 5 lines down: 5 feet = 1.52 metres, and 5 metres = 16.40 feet.

Feet		Metres	Feet		Metres
3.28	**1**	0.30	167.33	**51**	15.54
6.56	**2**	0.61	170.61	**52**	15.85
9.84	**3**	0.91	173.89	**53**	16.15
13.12	**4**	1.22	177.17	**54**	16.46
16.40	**5**	1.52	180.46	**55**	16.76
19.69	**6**	1.83	183.74	**56**	17.07
22.97	**7**	2.13	187.02	**57**	17.37
26.25	**8**	2.44	190.30	**58**	17.68
29.53	**9**	2.74	193.58	**59**	17.98
32.81	**10**	3.05	196.86	**60**	18.29
36.09	**11**	3.55	200.14	**61**	18.59
39.37	**12**	3.66	203.42	**62**	18.90
42.65	**13**	3.96	206.70	**63**	19.20
45.93	**14**	4.27	209.98	**64**	19.51
49.21	**15**	4.57	213.26	**65**	19.81
52.49	**16**	4.88	216.55	**66**	20.12
55.77	**17**	5.18	219.83	**67**	20.42
59.06	**18**	5.49	223.11	**68**	20.73
62.34	**19**	5.79	226.39	**69**	21.03
65.62	**20**	6.10	229.67	**70**	21.34
68.90	**21**	6.40	232.95	**71**	21.64
72.18	**22**	6.71	236.23	**72**	21.95
75.46	**23**	7.01	239.51	**73**	23.16
78.74	**24**	7.32	242.79	**74**	22.55
82.02	**25**	7.62	246.08	**75**	22.86
85.30	**26**	7.92	249.36	**76**	23.16
88.58	**27**	8.23	252.64	**77**	23.47
91.86	**28**	8.53	255.92	**78**	23.77
95.14	**29**	8.84	259.20	**79**	24.08
98.43	**30**	9.14	262.48	**80**	24.38
101.71	**31**	9.45	265.76	**81**	24.69
104.99	**32**	9.75	269.04	**82**	24.99
108.27	**33**	10.06	272.32	**83**	25.30
111.55	**34**	10.36	275.60	**84**	25.60
114.83	**35**	10.67	278.89	**85**	25.91
118.11	**36**	10.97	282.17	**86**	26.21
121.39	**37**	11.28	285.45	**87**	26.52
124.67	**38**	11.58	288.73	**88**	26.82
127.95	**39**	11.89	292.01	**89**	27.13
131.23	**40**	12.19	295.29	**90**	27.43
134.51	**41**	12.50	298.57	**91**	27.74
137.80	**42**	12.80	301.85	**92**	28.04
141.08	**43**	13.11	305.13	**93**	28.35
144.36	**44**	13.41	308.41	**94**	28.65
147.64	**45**	13.72	311.69	**95**	28.96
150.92	**46**	14.02	314.98	**96**	29.26
154.20	**47**	14.33	318.26	**97**	29.56
157.48	**48**	14.63	321.54	**98**	29.87
160.76	**49**	14.94	324.82	**99**	30.17
164.04	**50**	15.24	328.10	**100**	30.48

Fraction - Decimal - Metric conversion table

Fraction	Decimal (of an inch)	Metric (mm)	Fraction	Decimal (of an inch)	Metric (mm)
1/64	.015625	0.3969	33/64	.515625	13.0969
1/32	.03125	0.7938	17/32	.53125	13.4938
3/64	.046875	1.1906	35/64	.546875	13.8906
1/16	.0625	1.5875	9/16	.5625	14.2875
5/64	.078125	1.9844	37/64	.578125	12.6844
3/32	.09375	2.3812	19/32	.59375	15.0812
7/64	.109375	2.7781	39/64	.609375	15.4781
1/8	.125	3.1750	5/8	.625	15.8750
9/64	.140625	3.5719	41/64	.640625	16.2719
5/32	.15625	3.9688	21/32	.65625	16.6688
11/64	.171875	4.3656	43/64	.671875	17.0656
3/16	.1875	4.7625	11/16	.6875	17.4625
13/64	.203125	5.1594	45/64	.703125	17.8594
7/32	.21875	5.5562	23/32	.71875	18.2562
15/64	.234375	5.9531	47/64	.734375	18.6531
1/4	.25	6.35	3/4	.75	19.05
17/64	.265625	6.7469	49/64	.765625	19.4469
9/32	.28125	7.1438	25/32	.78125	19.8438
19/64	.296875	7.5406	51/64	.796875	20.2406
5/16	.3125	7.9375	13/16	.8125	20.6375
21/64	.328125	8.3344	53/64	.828125	21.0344
11/32	.34375	8.7312	27/32	.84375	21.4312
23/64	.359375	9.1281	55/64	.859375	21.8281
3/8	.375	9.5250	7/8	.875	22.225
25/64	.390625	9.9219	57/64	.890625	22.6219
13/32	.40625	10.3188	29/32	.90625	23.0188
27/64	.421875	10.7156	59/64	.921875	23.4156
7/16	.4375	11.1125	15/16	.9375	23.8125
29/64	.453125	11.5094	61/64	.953125	24.2094
15/32	.46875	11.9062	31/32	.96875	24.6062
31/64	.484375	12.3031	63/64	.984375	25.0031
1/2	.5	12.700	1	1	25.4

Cylinder Pressure conversion table

lbf/in²	MN/m²	at	bar
1800	12.4	122	124
2000	13.8	136	138
2250	15.5	153	155
2500	17.2	170	172
2650	18.2	180	183
3000	20.7	204	207

Specific Gravity of Gases

Specific gravity is the ratio of the weight of a substance compared to another substance of equal volume. When comparing gases, air is used as the standard (1.0). Gases with a specific gravity greater than 1.0 are heavier than air; while those less than 1.0 are lighter than air.

Gas		Specific gravity ratio
Dry air	. . . .	1.000
Acetylene	C_2H_2	0.910
Ethane	C_2H_4	1.050
Methane	CH_4	0.554
Ammonia	NH_3	0.596
Carbon dioxide	CO_2	1.530
Carbon monoxide	CO	0.967
Butane	C_4H_{10}	2.067
Butene	C_4H_8	1.930
Chlorine	Cl_2	2.486
Helium	He	0.138
Hydrogen	H_2	0.0696
Nitrogen	N_2	0.9718
Oxygen	O_2	1.1053

1 cu ft of air at 15.6°C (60°F) and 29.92 inches of mercury actually weighs 0.3465 kg (0.7638 lb)

Cylinder Capacity conversion table

Capacity of cylinder			Mass of air	
cu feet	litres	cu metres	lb	kg
40	1133	1.133	3.1	1.39
45	1274	1.274	3.4	1.56
50	1416	1.416	3.8	1.74
55	1557	1.557	4.2	1.91
60	1699	1.699	4.6	2.08
65	1841	1.841	5.0	2.26
70	1982	1.982	5.4	2.43
75	2124	2.124	5.7	2.60
80	2265	2.265	6.2	2.78

Water Pressure conversion table
Ready reckoner

Central (bold) figure converts to feet head (left) and to psi (right). Example, 9 lines down: 9 feet head = 3.90 psi, and 9 psi = 20.78 feet head of pressure.

For feet head of pressure/psi at 15°C (62°F)

Feet head of pressure		(psi)	Feet head of pressure		(psi)
2.31	**1**	0.43	242.44	**105**	45.47
4.62	**2**	0.87	253.98	**110**	47.64
6.93	**3**	1.30	265.54	**115**	49.81
9.24	**4**	1.73	277.07	**120**	51.97
11.54	**5**	2.17	288.63	**125**	54.14
13.85	**6**	2.60	300.16	**130**	56.30
16.16	**7**	3.03	311.72	**135**	58.47
18.47	**8**	3.46	323.25	**140**	60.63
20.78	**9**	3.90	334.81	**145**	62.80
23.09	**10**	4.33	346.34	**150**	64.96
25.40	**11**	4.76	357.90	**155**	67.13
27.71	**12**	5.20	369.43	**160**	69.29
30.02	**13**	5.63	380.99	**165**	71.46
32.33	**14**	6.06	392.52	**170**	73.63
34.63	**15**	6.50	404.08	**175**	75.79
36.94	**16**	6.93	415.61	**180**	77.96
39.25	**17**	7.36	427.17	**185**	80.12
41.56	**18**	7.79	438.71	**190**	82.29
43.87	**19**	8.23	450.23	**195**	84.45
46.18	**20**	8.66	461.78	**200**	86.62
57.72	**25**	10.83	577.24	**250**	108.27
69.27	**30**	12.99	692.69	**300**	129.93
80.82	**35**	15.16	808.13	**350**	151.58
92.36	**40**	17.32	922.58	**400**	173.24
103.91	**45**	19.50	1039.01	**450**	194.89
115.45	**50**	21.65	1154.48	**500**	216.55
127.00	**55**	23.82	1269.90	**550**	238.20
138.54	**60**	25.99	1385.39	**600**	259.85
150.01	**65**	28.15	1500.79	**650**	281.51
161.63	**70**	30.32	1616.30	**700**	303.16
173.18	**75**	32.48	1731.68	**750**	324.82
184.72	**80**	34.65	1847.20	**800**	346.47
196.27	**85**	36.81	1962.57	**850**	368.13
207.81	**90**	38.98	2078.10	**900**	389.78
219.36	**95**	41.14	2193.46	**950**	411.44
230.90	**100**	43.31	2309.00	**1000**	433.00

Tonnage

DISPLACEMENT TONNAGE is the weight of water displaced by a ship and is equal to the weight of the ship and its contents. It therefore varies with the ship's draft.

DEADWEIGHT TONNAGE is the weight of the total *contents* of a fully-laden ship. It is the difference in displacement between a ship that is light or fully-laden.

GROSS TONNAGE is the official, registered tonnage. It is usually calculated from all the spaces within the ship (1 gross ton = 100 cu ft).

NET TONNAGE is similar to gross tonnage but with certain deductions, leaving only the cargo space.

Tonnage can be calculated using short (US) tons, long (UK) tons, or metric tonnes:

1 long ton = 2240 lb (1016.06 kg)
1 short ton = 2000 lb (907.2 kg)
1 tonne = 1000 kg (2204.6 lb)

A 'ready reckoner' conversion table is provided in the table below.

Tonnage conversion table - Long tons, short tons and metric tonnes

From Long tons			From Short tons			From Metric tonnes		
Long	Short	Metric	**Short**	Metric	Long	**Metric**	Long	Short
1	1.1	1.02	1	0.91	0.9	1	0.98	1.1
2	2.2	2.03	2	1.81	1.8	2	1.97	2.2
3	3.7	3.05	3	2.72	2.7	3	2.95	3.3
4	4.5	4.06	4	3.63	3.6	4	3.94	4.4
5	5.6	5.08	5	4.54	4.5	5	4.92	5.5
6	6.7	6.10	6	5.44	5.4	6	5.91	6.6
7	7.8	7.11	7	6.35	6.3	7	6.89	7.7
8	9.0	8.13	8	7.26	7.1	8	7.87	8.8
9	10.1	9.14	9	8.16	8.0	9	8.86	9.9
10	11.2	10.16	10	9.1	8.9	10	9.84	11.0
20	22.4	20.3	20	18.1	17.9	20	19.7	22.0
30	33.6	30.5	30	27.2	26.8	30	29.5	33.1
40	44.8	40.6	40	36.3	35.7	40	39.4	44.1
50	56.0	50.8	50	45.4	44.7	50	49.2	55.1
60	67.2	61.0	60	54.4	53.6	60	59.1	66.1
70	78.4	71.1	70	63.5	62.5	70	68.9	77.2
80	89.6	81.3	80	72.6	71.5	80	78.7	88.2
90	100.8	91.4	90	81.7	80.4	90	88.6	99.2
100	112.0	101.6	100	90.7	89.3	100	98.4	110.2
200	224.0	203.2	200	181.4	178.6	200	196.8	220.5
300	336.0	304.8	300	272.2	267.9	300	295.3	330.7
400	448.0	406.4	400	362.9	357.2	400	393.7	441.0
500	560.0	508.0	500	453.6	446.6	500	492.1	551.2
600	672.0	609.6	600	544.3	535.9	600	590.5	661.4
700	784.0	711.2	700	635.0	625.2	700	688.9	771.6
800	896.0	812.8	800	725.8	714.5	800	787.4	881.8
900	1008.0	914.4	900	816.5	803.8	900	885.8	992.1
1000	1120.0	1016.1	1000	907.2	893.1	1000	984.2	1102.3
2000	2240.0	2032.1	2000	1814.4	1786.2	2000	1968.4	2204.6
3000	3360.0	3048.1	3000	2721.6	2679.3	3000	2952.6	3306.9
4000	4480.0	4065.2	4000	3628.8	3572.4	4000	3936.8	4409.2
5000	5600.0	5080.2	5000	4536.0	4465.5	5000	4921.0	5511.5
6000	6720.0	6096.3	6000	5443.2	5358.6	6000	5905.2	6613.8
7000	7840.0	7112.3	7000	6350.4	6251.7	7000	6889.4	7716.1
8000	8960.0	8128.4	8000	7257.6	7144.8	8000	7873.6	8818.4
9000	10080.0	9144.4	9000	8164.8	8037.9	9000	8857.8	9920.7
10000	11200.0	10160.5	10000	9071.9	8931.0	10000	9842.0	11023.0

15.4 TYPES OF WOOD USED IN MARINE CONSTRUCTION

The following table is a summary of the characteristics of selected woods which may be used in underwater civil engineering operations.

Common Name	Latin Name	Origin	Heartwood colour	Density	Description	Application
Angelique batard, Basralocus, Berakaruballi	*Dicorynia guianensis*	Guyanas, Surinam	Reddish brown grey to reddish/ yellowish brown	0.65	Hard, shipworm-resistant, large lengths.	Hydraulic construction, lock gates, heavy construction, wharf decking.
Azobe, Ekki, Kaku West, Red iron-wood	*Lophira alata*	Tropical West Africa	Purplish brown, yellow veins	0.95 to 1.15	Heavy and hard, very strong, wide grain, heavy crossgrain, low cracking and warping, hard to process, ship-worm-resistant.	Sea defences, marine construction, bridges, wharves, sleepers.
Dahoma, Agboin	*Piptadeni-astrum africanum*	Tropical West Africa	Reddish to yellowish brown	0.56	Durable.	Heavy construction, wharves.
Douglas Fir, Oregon Pine, Yellow/Red Spruce	*Pseudotsuga menziesii*	Temperate latitudes North America	Light to golden brown.	1.00	Hard, dense, durable, strong.	Heavy duty marine structures, revetments, locks.
Greenheart	*Ocotea rodiaei*	Northern South America, Central and West Africa	Brownish green, grey spots.	0.75 to 0.87	Very dense, hard to process, shipworm-resistant.	Underwater construction, piling, docks, lock gates.
Kokoti	*Anopyxis klaineana*	Africa	Brownish yellow to white or grey	0.66 to 0.85	Strong and durable.	Heavy construction, marine work.
Limbali	*Gilbertio-dendron*	Tropical Africa	Brown to copper brown	0.63	Dense, durable.	Marine and heavy construction.
Manbarklak, Kakeralli	*Eschweilera*	Amazon basin, Trinidad, Costa Rica	Light brown, greyish/red-dish brown, brownish buff with black streaks.	0.85	Highly durable. Resistant to shipworm.	Marine and other heavy construction.
Mora, Nato, Pracuuba	*Mora gonggrijpii*	Guyanas and Surinam.	Yellowish red brown or dark red with paler veins.	0.76 to 0.84	Very durable. ship-worm resistant.	Heavy construction, ship-building.
Oak	*Quercus sp.*	Temperate northern latitudes.	Yellowish to reddish brown.	0.57 to 0.82	Hard, dense, strong, durable.	Ship construction.
Opepe, Kussia.	*Nauclea diderrichii*	West Africa	Orange/ golden brown.	0.63	Very durable.	Marine defence, sleepers.

Common Name	Latin Name	Origin	Heartwood colour	Density	Description	Application
Red Luoro, Determa	*Ocotea rubra*	Guyanas, Lower Amazon, Trinidad	Light reddish brown, golden sheen.	0.52 to 0.59	Durable to very durable.	Heavy marine construction.
Southern red/yellow pine, Pitchpine, Black Norway Pine.	*Pinus rigida*	Northern temperate latitudes	Reddish brown	0.5	Moderately durable.	Bridges, stringers in docks, bulkheads

15.5 GLOSSARY

The following glossary includes a selection of terms and definitions widely used in various aspects of professional diving. All legal definitions and regulations referred to in this glossary relate to UK Law.

ABS
American Bureau of Shipping. A major Classification Society responsible for setting standards and for inspecting design, construction and maintenance of ships and structures.

Absolute pressure
This is the total pressure at any point, including the contribution of atmospheric pressure.
(See also 'Gauge pressure'.)

ACFM
Actual cubic feet per minute. This refers to the actual volume of gas supplied to a diver, bell, etc at ambient pressure.

Actuator
A mechanism used to remotely or automatically open or close valves and stops.

ADC
Association of Diving Contractors.

Air lift
A suction pipe driven by a compressed air (usually a compressor) on the surface. It can be used to dig into the sea bed to make a trench or to uncover a buried object.

Air lift bag
Strongly-built, inflatable bags with attachment fittings. When filled with air (or any other gas) may be used to provide buoyancy and/or lift an item through the water. Some designs are open-bottomed whilst others are totally enclosed but fitted with relief valves. The bags may also be fitted with dump valves capable of being operated by a diver. Their operation can be hazardous and special procedures must be followed in their proper use.

Alveoli
Thin-walled sac in the lungs where the exchange of gases takes place between the blood and inspired gas.

Ambient pressure
The surrounding pressure at any point. The pressure that a diver, bell, etc is subjected to when at depth, whether actual or simulated within a hyperbaric chamber.

Approved Code of Practice (ACOP)
The Health and Safety Commission, by virtue of section 16(1) of the *Health and Safety at Work etc Act 1974*, can approve a code of practice and give it a special legal status. There are five Approved Codes of Practice which provide practical guidance with respect to the *Diving at Work regulations 1997* and came into force on 1 April 1998. These are:
- Commercial diving projects offshore
- Commercial diving projects inland/inshore
- Media diving projects
- Scientific and archaeological diving projects
- Recreational diving projects.

If a person is prosecuted for breach of health and safety law, and it is proved that they had not followed the advice of the relevant Approved Code, a court will find them at fault, unless they can show that they complied with the law in some other way. (Ref: *Diving at Work, Proposals for Regulations, Consultative Document, 1994*).

Approved Diving Doctor and
Approved Medical Examiner of Divers
An Approved Diving Doctor, in the context of professional diving, is a medical doctor who has received specialist, additional training in diving medicine and subsequently become approved by the HSE to conduct diving medical examinations of

professional divers with the view of certifying them either fit or unfit to dive. The HSE approval was given under the provisions of Regulation 11 of the *Diving Operations at Work Regulations 1981* and superseded by Regulation 15 (6) of the *Diving at Work Regulations 1997* which came into effect on 1st April 1998 when the term was changed to 'Approved Medical Examiner of Divers'.

Approved Dredged Depth (ADD)
The latest dredging depth approved for an area.

Approved Qualification
This is defined in *The Diving at Work Regulations 1997* as such qualification as is approved by the HSE under Regulation 14.

Arterial Gas Embolism (AGE)
This is a type of Decompression Illness. Arterial Gas Embolism is caused by gas escaping from a gas-containing cavity in the body (such as the lungs) into the arterial blood circulation such as can be a consequence of pulmonary barotrauma (burst lung). The symptoms can be similar to Decompression Sickness and the treatment is identical, primarily urgent recompression. It is a very serious medical condition.
(See also 'Burst Lung').

Artificial ventilation
Involves a first aider using expired breath to inflate the lungs and ventilate a non-breathing person. Sometimes known as mouth-to-mouth or mouth-to-nose ventilation, depending on the technique.

Attendant
A competent person on the surface who acts as a communications link between the diver and the diving supervisor and who continuously monitors the length of umbilical or lifeline paid out to the diver in the water and as far as possible, the diver's actions during the dive. He also monitors for surface hazardous activities which may endanger the diver or the dive site. He is sometimes called the Tender.

Attended diving
Diving with a lifeline or breast-rope (or air-pipe designed to serve as a lifeline) controlled by an attendant.

Automatic hyperbaric welding
Automated welding in a customised, watertight enclosure from which the water is evacuated in order to perform a dry weld. This method of welding is costly as the customised enclosures are designed for single use.

AUV (Autonomous underwater vehicle)
Untethered, self-propelled, underwater vehicle.

Bail out system
Reserve breathing gas supply carried by the diver.

Bell
Popular name for submersible compression chamber.

Bell man
Popular name for the diver remaining in the bell to act as tender to the diver locked out of the bell. He is also performs the duty of Standby Diver able to leave the bell and go to the assistance of a diver outside the bell.

Bell run times
The bell run which is timed from bell lock-off to final bell lock-on, must not exceed 8 hours. Lock out times must not exceed 6 hours. No diver should take part in a 6 hour lock-out or an 8 hour bell run more than once within a pre-planned 24 hour period. Diving Supervisors must ensure that the divers are offered a refreshment break of at least 15 minutes within 3 hours of the initial lock-out. If the diver agrees to forego such a break, then a timed entry should be made in the diving operations log book and subsequently signed by the diver and Diving Supervisor.

The Diving at Work Regulations 1997 ACoP for Commercial diving projects offshore states the following:

No. 96: Divers in saturation should be given at least 12 continuous hours of rest in each 24 hour period. To prevent 'ratcheting', divers should normally only take part in one bell run routine of no more than 8 hours in any 24-hour period.

No. 97: Bell runs should not exceed 8 hours from 'lock-off' to 'lock-on':

(a) *in a two-person bell each diver should spend no more than 4 hours out of the bell in the water;*

(b) *in a three-person bell two divers may 'lock-out' together. The third person will undertake the duties of bellman and should remain dry unless called upon to 'lock-out' in an emergency. Each diver may spend up to 6 hours out of the bell in the water so long as an adequate refreshment break is offered within 3 hours of start of the 'lock-out'.*

Bell umbilical
This is a bundle of gas pipes, electrical cables, a hot water hose and strength member leading from the diving bell up to the surface support vessel.
The umbilical provides life-support services to the bell including breathing gas mixtures, electrical power for carbon dioxide filters, lighting and instrumentation, video television from the bell and divers and voice communications and hot water for bell and diver heating.

Bends
The term used for some forms of decompression illness. (See 'Decompression sickness').

BCD
Buoyancy compensation device.

BIBS
Built-in breathing system. A breathing gas system built into compression chambers by which emergency breathing gas or a treatment gas can be supplied to a diver through an oral-nasal mask.

Blind flange
A flange on a pipe which effectively blanks off and/or terminates the pipe at that point.

Blowout preventer (BOP)
A ram or closing element designed to close the top of the wellbore and to provide a controlled release of wellbore fluids. The BOPs are arranged vertically in a BOP stack. Maximum working pressure for a BOP is 15,000 pounds per square inch (psi).

BOP stack
A vertical assembly of several rams or closing elements used to shut the well. The various closing elements can be connected with spools. The BOP stack typically weighs 20 to 25 tons (18–22.5 tonnes).

Bounce diving
A form of bell diving where the diver is exposed to pressure for an insufficient time for the dissolved gas in his body tissues to reach saturation.

Breathing mixtures
Air or any mixture of gases which are suitable for breathing at the ambient pressure.

Burst lung
The primary danger which is particularly relevant to this case is that of burst lung. This is a classic and well-known danger in diving activities.

The theory is that as the diver ascends through the water, the surrounding pressure falls. Any gas in the diver's body will thus expand in accordance with an elementary principle in physics referred to as Boyle's Law. The most dangerous compartment of gas in the diver's body in this respect is that inside his lungs. If the expanding gas in his lungs cannot escape freely through his mouth and/or nose (such as in the case of the breath being held or some obstruction being present within the lungs), his lung tissue may be forced to expand to a point where it is ruptured.

The consequences can include gas entering the blood stream (a condition known as arterial gas embolism) which is commonly fatal, and/or gas escaping into the void in the chest cavity causing collapse of the lungs (a condition known as pneumothorax), and/or gas escaping into the void surrounding the heart (a condition known as mediastinal emphysema). The consequences of these can include severe pains in the chest, violent coughing, difficulty in breathing, unconsciousness, embarrassment to the normal functioning of the heart and death.

The conditions require immediate recompression and specialised medical assistance.

BV
Bureau Veritas. A major Classification Society. Classification Societies set standards and carry out inspections of design, construction and maintenance of ships and structures.

Cardiac arrest
Inability of the heart to expel its contents and generate effective circulation. It is confirmed by the absence of the carotid pulse in an unconscious non-breathing person.

Cardio-pulmonary resuscitation (CPR)
Application of a combination of artificial ventilation and chest compressions to provide oxygenation and circulation to a pulseless person.

Carotid pulse
The pulse of the carotid arteries, found on each side of the neck.

Central nervous system (CNS) oxygen toxicity
Toxic effect on the brain caused by breathing oxygen concentrations usually greater than 1.6 bar absolute.

Cerebral embolism
Bubble(s) of gas in the arterial blood stream in the brain and interfering with brain function(s).

Certificate of Medical Fitness to Dive
This is defined in The Diving at Work Regulations 1997 as a certificate issued in accordance with regulation 15. It is normally issued on an annual basis following a medical examination by an Approved doctor/Approved medical examiner of divers.

Chart Datum (CD)
The datum for soundings shown on charts and tidal predictions. The level is defined such that the tide will not frequently fall below it, and is normally defined in the United Kingdom as approximately Lowest Astronomical Tide.

The value of Chart Datum to Ordnance Datum (Newlyn) can be found in Admiralty Tide Tables and should always be stated.

Chest compression
Technique applied to a pulseless person during which the lower sternum is rhythmically compressed to provide circulation.

'Chokes'
See Decompression Illness.

Christmas Tree
Surface completion equipment over a well that flows to the surface under its own pressure and is used to control the flow from the well.

Circulation
Blood flow through the heart and blood vessels to provide oxygen and nutrients to the body tissues.

'Clearing' the ears
Jargon used by divers to describe the act of equalising the pressure on both sides of their ear drums as they descend, to avoid and/or relieve pain in the ears. The equalisation process can be helped by sideways movements of the jaw, using muscles normally used when yawning or the 'valsalva manoeuvre.'

Client
The person, firm or company who contracts to use the diving (or other) services and for whom the services are carried out. Clients have a duty of care placed upon them by the *Health and Safety at Work etc Act 1994* and the *Diving at Work Regulations 1997* (Regulation 4).

Coding (of welders)
A welder requires to be trained and qualified. His skill is further advanced by the acquisition of work experience. This process takes time and costs money. Once a welder has reached this level he will require to be 'coded' for any particular weld he is then required to undertake. This is a trial to demonstrate that the welder (together with the materials, procedures and environment used, see Weld Procedure Specifications) can achieve a satisfactory weld. In the case of a hyperbaric weld, the coding procedure is carried out in a hyperbaric chamber which simulates the same pressure and environmental gas mixtures in which the working welds will be carried out. Should the Weld Procedure Specifications change, the welder must be re-coded.

Cyanosis
Blueness of the skin and lining of the mouth, generally caused by lack of oxygen in the blood.

Daily Record, Diver's
See 'Log Book'.

Deck compression chamber (DCC), also referred to as a 'surface compression chamber.'
A pressure vessel consisting of two or more compartments, not suitable for immersion in water, in which divers slowly return from the pressure of their dive to surface pressure, or in which they live at pressure during saturation diving operations. It may be connected to one or more additional compression chambers. One of these chambers may be designed to mate with a diving bell to allow divers to transfer under pressure (TUP). This chamber may be referred to as the 'TUP chamber' or 'wet chamber' in which divers normally change into and out of their diving suits.

Decompression
The controlled procedure by which ambient pressure is decreased to surface pressure.

Decompression Illness (DCI)
This is a collective term for several conditions caused by gas bubbles appearing in body tissue(s) as a result of a reduction in ambient pressure. It is broadly divided into two types of condition:

(a) Decompression Sickness (DCS) and

(b) Arterial Gas Embolism (AGE). Decompression Sickness is caused by gas(es) coming out of solution in body tissue(s) due to a too rapid reduction in ambient pressure (such as during a too rapid ascent through water).
Arterial Gas Embolism (AGE) is caused by gas escaping into the arterial blood system such as can be a consequence of pulmonary barotrauma (burst lung). The symptoms can be similar and the treatment is identical, primarily urgent recompression.

Decompression sickness (DCS)
A type of Decompression Illness.
Signs or symptoms are sometimes delayed in onset. They are directly attributable to a reduction in pressure sufficient to be associated with excessive formation of free gases from the dissolved gases in the body tissues.
The traditional classification of DCS describes two types, namely:

Type I: Musculoskeletal (pain), Skin, Lymphatic and Fatigue

Type II: Neurological, Cardiorespiratory ('Chokes'), Vestibular/Auditory and Shock. Type II is the most serious and requires very urgent recompression because it can be life-threatening or can leave the diver with permanent disabilities.

The consequences vary enormously between simple pains to choking and death.

Decompression schedules (or tables)
Predetermined steps or range of continuous 'bleed' decompression, by which a diver is brought back to surface pressure in order to avoid decompression sickness.

Derrick barge
A barge that has a heavy lifting capacity crane on the stern. A derrick barge is typically used to lift modules onto offshore platforms.

Demand system
A system that delivers a flow of gas when triggered by the inhalation of a spontaneously breathing person.

Diffuser
A device placed at the outlet of a discharge of a pipeline to reduce the velocity of outflow and to reduce turbulence.

Directional drilling
Intentionally drilling a well at an angle from vertical.

DIS
Diver intercommunication system.

Distance line
A line connected to the bottom of a shot line normally paid out by the diver primarily to give the diver the means of returning directly to the shot line. It can be used to control the distance from the shot and to carry out a circular sweep search.

The Diving at Work Regulations 1997
These are cited in *Statutory Instrument No 2776, 1997, Health and Safety*, ISBN 0-11-065170-7. They came into force on 1st April 1998 and were enabled by the *Health and Safety at Work etc. Act 1974 (a)*. These regulations supersede the following regulations which were revoked:

- *The Diving Operations at Work Regulations 1981(a);*
- *The Diving Operations at Work (Amendment) Regulations 1990(b) and*
  The Diving Operations at Work (Amendment) Regulations 1992(c).

Diver
This is defined in *The Diving at Work Regulations 1997* as a person at work who dives. It is any person who is engaged in underwater work and is required to breath a breathing mixture at greater than atmospheric pressure. His duties are covered in Regulation 12.

Diver grades
With effect from 1 November 1988 the Employers and the RMT have agreed that there will be two grades of diver for pay purposes, ie, 'Professional Diver' and 'Diver'. Before a diver can be advanced from 'Diver' to the 'Professional Diver' grade he must be in possession of either HSE Part I or II Certificate (or equivalent) and, since having held that certificate, have completed 300 days offshore as a member of a diving team and have completed 150 'approved' dives. The approved dives may use air or mixed gas as the breathing mixture; must be properly recorded in the diver's professional logbook; must be carried out offshore. Dives carried out as part of the HSE Part I or II (or equivalent) training or dry dives in chambers do not count as 'approved' dives.

Diver indicator lamp
A light, such as a strobe, attached to a diver for the purpose of indicating the position of the diver when he is on the surface of the water.

Diver, Offshore
A colloquial term for a commercial diver who worked in the offshore, oil and gas industry. He would be qualified either as an HSE Part I, Air Diver or an HSE Part II Mixed Gas Diver. His pay scales would be set by the RMT agreement (See 'Offshore Diving Industry Agreement').
Offshore divers tend to work for the period of an offshore project, on a two-weeks-on, and one or two-weeks-off, basis. The projects themselves vary greatly in length, so the number of offshore trips a diver may have on any one particular project can vary from one to six or even eight. While offshore, the divers often work a 24 hour shift arrangement with two shifts of 12 hours per day. Once again, the tasks have to be shared amongst the whole team. Usually, a diver has to take his turn as being a stand-by diver, diver tender, general surface support as well as actively diving. The supervisor is responsible for establishing the rota. Offshore diving work tends to be more weather-sensitive than onshore work largely due to the effects of high winds on sea conditions. Consequently, in temperate latitudes, there tends to be a definite season for offshore diving work, roughly between April and October with a high peak of activity around August.

Diver, Inland/Inshore (or 'civils' diver)
A colloquial term for a commercial air diver who works on inland diving sites, or in coastal waters, not associated with the oil and gas industry. He would normally be qualified to at least HSE Part III Air Diver standard. This type of diver is also referred to as a 'civils' diver because of his close association with civil engineering works at such sites as docks, harbours and canals etc. This term also tends to cover virtually all forms of diving other than the offshore work.
There are no industry-wide agreed pay scales for this type of diver. Inland/inshore divers have no industry-union agreements to establish normal rates of pay, as they do offshore. There is consequently great variation in the pay scales and terms of employment of divers onshore. These divers may work on a day rate, on a day-to-day or weekly basis, contracts for several months or in some cases may be salaried. While employed, they form part of a team. Each individual on the team would usually be eligible to dive with the exception of the supervisor. So the various non-diving tasks to be carried out by the team may fall on any of the divers in the team. These non-diving tasks can include being the stand-by diver, diving tender (tending the diver's umbilical), rigger, equipment maintenance and repair, storage, general handy-man, etc. The supervisor is responsible for deciding who would dive at any one time and he would have to take into account a wide range of factors in making the decision including any rota arrangement, fitness to dive, any special skills required underwater etc. Most onshore diving projects are run on a day-work principle approximating to an 8, 10 or 12-hour day. Divers generally return to local accommodation or even home

each night. Onshore work tends to be less seasonal than offshore work.

Diver worn equipment
That equipment required for the safety and well-being of the diver, worn or attached to the diver while underwater.

Diving bell
A manned pressure vessel used under water to support divers. Also known as a 'submersible compression chamber' or 'bell'. The bell normally has the facility to lock onto a deck compression chamber (DCC) to permit the divers to transfer under pressure (TUP) between the two.
The diving bell is defined in *The Offshore Installations (Safety Case) Regulations 1992* as *any compression chamber which is capable of being manned and is used or designed for use under the surface of water in supporting human life being a chamber in which any occupant is or may be subjected to a pressure of more than 300 millibars above atmospheric pressure during normal operation.*

Diving Contractor
This is any person, firm or company employed for the execution of diving work. It is defined in *The Diving at Work Regulations 1997* as follows:

5(1) No person at work shall dive in a diving project and no employer shall employ any person in such a project unless there is one person and one person only who is the diving contractor for that project.

(2) The diving contractor shall, subject to paragraph (3), be the person who:

(a) is the employer of the diver or divers engaged in the diving project: or

(b) dives in the diving project as a self-employed diver.

(3) Where there is more than one person falling within paragraph (2) those persons shall jointly appoint in writing before the commencement of the diving project one of themselves to act as diving contractor.

The diving contractor does not have to be an executive of the organisation.

Diving emergency medical doctor
A doctor trained to work with divers in all matters affecting their health and safety and, in particular, to cope with the medical aspects of every kind of diving emergency.

Diving Operation
This is defined in *The Diving at Work Regulations 1997* as a diving operation identified in the diving project plan pursuant to regulation 8(3) which states: T*he diving project plan shall identify each diving operation which makes up the diving project and the nature and size of any diving operation so identified shall be such that it can be safely supervised by one person.*

Diving Operation Record
This is defined in *The Diving at Work Regulations 1997* as the record required to be kept in accordance with regulation 6(3)(e) which states: *The diving contractor shall ensure that a record containing the required particulars is kept for each diving operation*

Diving Project
This is defined in *The Diving at Work Regulations 1997* as *any activity, made up of one or more diving operations, in which at least one person takes part or will take part as a diver and extends from the time when that person, or the first such person, commences to prepare to dive until that person, or the last such person, has left the water, chamber or other environment in which the dive, or any part of the dive, took place and has completed any requisite decompression procedures, including, where it may be reasonably anticipated that this will be needed, any therapeutic recompression.*

Diving Project Plan
This is a document prepared under regulation 6(2)(a) in accordance with regulation 8 of *The Diving at Work Regulations 1997*. A diving contractor must ensure that a diving project plan is prepared before a diving project starts. The diving contractor must first perform a risk assessment to identify site specific hazards and their risks. Based on this information the diving project plan must state how those hazards and risks are to be controlled.

Diving Rules
Rules issued by the diving contractor for regulating the conduct of his diving operations.

Diving Supervisor
This is a professional diver qualification and position. The Diving Supervisor is responsible for the safe conduct of the diving activities of a single diving team under his direct charge. The Diving Supervisor is appointed in writing by his employer to carry out these duties. He is an experienced person appointed in writing (in the UK) by the diving contractor to be in charge of a diving operation. A senior diving supervisor (or Diving Superintendent) may be responsible for a number of diving supervisors or for a major contract. Offshore Diving Supervisors must be qualified by examination by the IMCA/AODC Diving Supervisor Certification Scheme. *The Diving at Work Regulations 1997* define 'supervise' as 'the exercise of direct personal control.'
The Approved Code of Practice for 'Commercial diving projects offshore,' which came into effect with the *Diving at Work Regulations 1997*, require under Regulation 6 (3) (a):

94 A closed bell project normally requires ... a diving supervisor and a relief diving supervisor.

This effectively means that each shift requires two qualified Diving Supervisors on duty at the same time.

Diving Supervisor, Trainee
This is a diver who has satisfactorily completed a Company Diving Supervisor training programme (designed to comply with the AODC/IMCA scheme) and is gaining offshore experience prior to passing the theory examination and subsequent formal appointment as a Diving Supervisor.

Diving Superintendent (also Senior Diving Supervisor or Offshore Construction Manager)
The Diving Superintendent is a management position for the most senior member of the operating diving team at a diving site.
The Diving Supervisors are directly responsible to the Diving Superintendent.
The Diving Superintendent will normally report directly to, and liaise with, the on-site Client Representative and to the relevant, onshore Project Manager within his own company. He does not normally become directly involved in the running of a diving operation (which is delegated to his Diving Supervisors).
Diving Superintendents tend to be more permanent positions with a diving contractor. They tend to remain with one diving contractor throughout their career and tend not to move between diving contractors as much as Diving Supervisors may do. They are often full-time members of a diving contractor's staff.
The Diving Superintendent is the on-site representative directly responsible to the employing diving contractor for the cost-effective running of any contract. It is a very responsible position and critical to a successful diving operation.

In view of the unique importance of this position, Diving Superintendents are normally given substantial financial bonuses conditional on the completion of a project, either on time or ahead of time.

DMAC
The Diving Medical Advisory Committee of the Association of Diving Contractors (ADC)

DNV
Det Norske Vertias. A major Classification Society. Classification Socities are responsible for setting standards and for inspecting the design, construction and maintenance of ships and structures.

Down time
A commonly used term, which describes a period of time when planned underwater or other work cannot be carried out, due to circumstances outside the control of the contractor, for example bad weather.

Draught
The vertical distance from the waterline to the deepest point on the keel of a vessel.

Drive off
When a dynamically positioned vessel unintentionally moves off station under power due to a malfunction.

DUCS
Diver underwater communication system.

Dynamic positioning (DP)
A system enabling a vessel to hold station and heading automatically in a marine environment without the need for mooring with anchors or tying up to some fixed object(s).

EAD
When divers are diving on breathing mixtures other than air, the equivalent air depth (EAD) is required in order to calculate safe limits of partial pressure of oxygen and for dive decompression requirements.
For example, to calculate the EAD for decompression procedure when using nitrox mix: for a diver at a given depth, breathing a given nitrox mixture, his equivalent air depth will be that depth at which the diver would have to be whilst breathing air, in order to experience the same nitrogen partial pressure. This is his EAD.
Knowing the EAD enables the decompression procedure to take place using air decompression tables.

ECU
Environmental control unit.

EHS
Electrically-heated undersuit.

Embolism, gas
Bubble(s) of gas in the blood stream which may interfere with the normal circulation.

Embolism, fat
Small mass of fatty material in the blood stream which may interfere with the normal circulation.

Equinoctial springs
Greater than average spring tides occur near the equinoxes (March and September), at new and full moon.

Expired air resuscitation (EAR)
A form of respiratory resuscitation for a person who has stopped breathing, which involves repeatedly inflating the casualty's lungs by blowing air from one's own lungs. The air may be blown through the casualty's mouth or nose. This method is of special use when the casualty is in the water.

External cardiac compression (ECC)
Resusciation technique which stimulates the heart by applying rhythmic pressure to the chest.

Flexible marine-riser joint
The flexible connection between the lower riser package and the blow out preventer stack and the marine riser on a subsea wellhead. The flexible marine-riser joint compensates for the surface movement of the surface vessel and permits up to 10 degrees movement of the riser.

Flowline
Pipes and pipe fittings that carry fluids. Flowlines are used to collect produced fluids from wells and transport them to treating and storage facilities. Steel pipe is the most common, but fibreglass, cement-lined steel pipe and flexible plastic pipe are also used.

Flowline bundle
A cluster of flowlines with hydraulic hoses and electric cables on a subsea production system.

Frames
Transportable assemblies of gas cylinders which are interconnected by a manifold and held firmly together.

Freeflow
The diving band mask and helmet commonly used throughout the industry has a manually-turned valve which provides a freeflowing supply of air/gas.
The air/gas flows into a perforated tube positioned at the top of the faceplate and is directed down across the faceplate. This supply has several functions including demisting the faceplate, providing extra air/gas if the diver is becoming breathless and 'dewatering' the mask should it become flooded with water.

Gauge pressure
This is taken as the pressure above one atmosphere or one bar. Thus at the surface a pressure gauge indicates zero pressure even though the ambient pressure is one atmosphere absolute.
(See also 'Absolute pressure').

GPS
Global positioning system which interrogates GP satellites to provide accurate position-fixing data.

GR
Germanischer Lloyd. A major Classification Society. Classification Societies are responsible for setting standards and for inspecting the design, construction and maintenance of ships and structures.

Helicopter capsize simulator
This is a relatively crude structure which is intended to simulate the seating and cabin arrangements of a typical offshore helicopter and can accommodate a small group of trainees. It is rigged near a suitable water reservoir such as a swimming pool and has the facility to be lowered into the water and rotated 180 degrees (it is completely inverted). The trainees are expected to release themselves from their seat belts and escape from the structure through the doors and windows.
Close supervision is provided both in and under the water. At the conclusion of the exercise, the unit is then returned to its upright position and recovered to the surface. The purpose of the training is to prepare the trainees for the eventuality of their helicopter ditching at sea and subsequently capsizing.

Helium speech unscrambler
An electronic device fitted into the voice communications system of divers breathing a mixture of helium and oxygen (heliox) to remove the distortion which occurs when divers talk in such a gas mixture.

Helmet diving
Diving in which the diver wears a rigid helmet attached to a closed diving suit. The breathing mixture is normally supplied via a hose from the surface.

Hemiplegia
Paralysis of one side of the body.

High water
The highest level reached by the sea surface during any one cycle.

Highest Astronomical Tide (HAT) and Lowest Astronomical Tide (LAT)
The highest and lowest levels respectively which can be predicted to occur under average meteorological conditions and under any combination of astronomical conditions. These levels will not be reached every year. HAT and LAT are not the extreme levels that can be reached as storm surges may cause higher and lower levels to occur.

HPNS
High pressure nervous syndrome.

HSE (Health and Safety Executive)
UK government regulatory authority.

HPR
Hydroacoustic position reference system. This is a dynamic positioning system which uses GPS and an array of transponders placed on the seabed to keep the vessel in position.

Hyperbaric evacuation system
A system by which divers can transfer under pressure from a DCC under emergency conditions. It is based upon a pressure vessel which can be launched from an offshore installation from which the diving is being carried out.

Hypercapnoea/hypercapnia
This is defined as an elevation of carbon dioxide levels in the body.

Hyperoxic crisis (oxygen convulsions)
Seizure, resembling an epileptic fit, caused by breathing high partial pressure of oxygen

Hypoxaemia
Below normal oxygenation of the blood.

IALA
International Association of Lighthouse Authorities.

ICS
International Code of signals.

Immersion Suit
See 'Survival Suit'.

IMO
International Maritime Organisation.

Isocryme
Line connecting points on the earth's surface having the same mean temperature at the coldest month of the year.

Isothere
Line connecting points on the earth's surface having the same mean temperature at the warmest month of the year.

Laryngospasm (Laryngeal spasm)
Persisting spasm of the muscles of the larynx resulting in partial or complete blockage of the entrance of the trachea. Usually caused by irritation from a foreign body, mucus or vomit.

Larynx
A passageway connecting the pharynx and trachea (windpipe). It is composed of plates of firm cartilage which support the vocal cords.

Lazy shot line
A weighted line attached to a main shot line by a sliding shackle.

Lifeline
A safety line attached to a diver at one end and held by a diving attendant the other. It is intended as an emergency rescue facility, a means of sending signals to and from the diver and can provide the diver with an indication of direction in which he can return. It may consist of a rope, gas hose, communication cable, or any combination of these, that is strong enough and suitable for recovery and lifting a diver and his equipment from the water.

Life support system
Equipment installed to render a compression chamber or diving bell habitable. It includes breathing systems, temperature and humidity control equipment, waste disposal and toxic fume removal equipment and food and water supplies.

Life Support Technician (Saturation Technician)
The duties of this person are mainly concerned with the operation of the deck compression chambers and the maintenance of a safe environment within for the divers. This includes controlling the correct pressure(s), temperature and oxygen levels. They have to ensure that the contained gases are kept free of pollutants and waste products such as carbon dioxide. Other duties include provision of food and medicines as required and particularly to control the safe decompression of the divers. They would also be responsible for the administration of any therapeutic recompression treatments. They are responsible to the Diving Supervisor.

Live-boating
The practice of supporting a diver from a vessel which is underway.

Log Book (or Daily Record)
Under the UK legislation, *SI 399: 1981 The Diving Operations at Work Regulations* and the replacement SI 2776 The Diving Operations at Work Regulations and *SI 116: 1975 The Merchant Shipping (Diving Operations) Regulations,* every diver in UK waters or working from a UK registered vessel, must complete a daily log (referred to as a 'daily record' in the 1997 regulations) of every dive. The regulations specify the minimum details to be recorded which include the record of the annual diving medical examination and require that the log book is retained for a minimum of two years after the date of the last entry.

Low water
The lowest level reached by the sea surface during any one tidal cycle.

Lowest Astronomical Tide (LAT)
See 'Highest Astronomical Tide'.

LR
Lloyd's Register. A major Classification Society with responsibility for setting standards and for inspecting the design, construction and maintenance of ships and structures.

Manifold centre
The location at which flowlines from subsea wells come together and the oil is sent to the production station.

Manually triggered oxygen-powered resuscitator
A resuscitation device utilising a manual trigger or button to activate the flow of oxygen used to inflate the lungs of a non-breathing casualty.

Marine riser
A 16–20-inch diameter tube made of several joints that connects the cellar deck of a drillship or semi-submersible to the blowout preventer stack of a subsea well. The drillstring goes through the marine riser.

Marked diving
SCUBA diving using a lifeline secured to a surface float.

Mean High Water Springs (MHWS), and Mean Low Water Springs (MLWS)
The Height of MHWS is the average, throughout a year when the average maximum declination of the moon is 23.5°, of the heights of two successive high waters during those periods of 24 hours (approximately once a fortnight) when the range of the tide is the greatest. The height of MLWS is the average height obtained by the two successive low waters during the same periods.

Mean Sea Level
The average level of the sea surface over a long period, preferably 18.6 years, or the average level which would exist in the absence of tides.

Mediastinal emphysema
See 'Burst lung'.

Medical fitness to dive certificate
This certificate is issued by a medical examiner of divers (or from the Executive following an appeal) that the person issuing the certificate considers the person named in the certificate to be fit to dive. (Ref: Approved Code of Practice, Commercial diving projects inland/inshore, Diving at Work Regulations 1997).

Minibell Diving System
This is a hybrid arrangement, intermediate between a wet-bell and a closed bell.

The Minibell operates initially as a wet bell, open at the bottom as the divers are lowered into the sea and go to work. It operates in the air range, down to 50 metres maximum. At the end of their dive, the divers return to the bell and close the bottom door. The bell can then be raised and the divers transferred under Pressure (TUP) to a deck chamber where they complete their decompression.

As such, the procedure does not require a bellman to remain in the bell during the diving activities and two divers can operate outside the bell simultaneously.

Divers qualified in the use of the Minibell do not need to carry out the entire HSE Part II (or 'Closed Bell') training course if they wished to upgrade to that qualification. A Minibell Diver would have been classified as an 'HSE Part II (Restricted – Air Range only)' and that he would only require to carry out a saturation dive at a training centre to upgrade to the full HSE Part II Mixed Gas ('Closed Bell') Diver.

Mixed gas
A breathing gas mixture containing oxygen and suitable inert gas or gases (diluent). For dives deeper than 50 metres water depth, the divers cannot use air as the breathing mixture. The main reason is that the nitrogen in the air causes a serious drunkenness effect beyond this depth ('nitrogen narcosis'). A mixture of helium and oxygen ('heliox') is substituted for deeper dives.

Multiple Intermediary Decompressions
Multiple intermediary decompressions during a saturation dive is a questionable practice carried out with the intention to shorten the total duration of a saturation dive.

This procedure has been used when the requirement for the next bell run was uncertain.

The theory is that the divers can be quickly recompressed if the decompression has passed the depth of the required dive. The outcome is that the divers often undertake unnecessary decompressions with associated unnecessary risks of decompression illness.

AODC Safety Notice 1/95 states that *'In order to reduce the exposure of divers to the above hazards, the procedure of 'intermediary decompression' should be minimised'* and that *'It should be discontinued as a routine procedure during bad weather stand-by which affects only the ability of the divers to work but not the safety of the vessel or installation from which they are deployed.'*

Neap tides
Those tides of minimum range occurring about twice a month, at or near the first and last quarters of the moon.

Nitrox
A term in common use, referring to a synthetic breathing mixture of oxygen and nitrogen.

No-decompression diving
Diving which involves depths and bottom times shallow or short enough to permit an ascent without and decompression stops.

Oedema
A swelling of tissue with associated discharge of fluid.

OEL
Occupational exposure limit. Used in conjunction with specified hazardous materials to indicate maximum exposure limits in the work environment.

Offshore Diving Industry Agreement (UK)
This Agreement has been drawn up between a group of diving contractors variously called the AODC, IMCA or the Committee of Employer Signatories to the Agreement with the RMT now the International Marine Contractors Association (IMCA) and the National Union of Seamen (NUS) now the National Union of Rail, Maritime and

Transport Workers (RMT) to establish standard pay scales in the offshore diving industry. It was to generally apply from 1 November 1991 but with certain provisions from 1 November 1992 and others from 1 November 1993. The Agreement is currently renegotiated every two years, in advance.

OIM
Offshore installation manager.

Operations Manager
The Operations Manager is a permanent management position at the headquarters of a diving contractor company. He is responsible for the co-ordination and over-all administration of all the projects undertaken by the diving company. Depending on the size of the company, he may have two or more Project Managers responsible to him. The Operations Manager is normally directly responsible to the Managing Director (or equivalent) of the diving company.

OSHA (Occupational Safety and Health Administration)
US government (Department of Labor) regulatory authority.

Ordnance Datum (Newlyn)
The mean sea level as measured at Newlyn, Cornwall and is the datum generally used for all land surveys in UK. This may be found from Admiralty Tide Tables.

Oxygen provision
The provision of elevated inspired oxygen concentrations to an injured person.

Oxygen ventilation
Ventilating a non-breathing casualty using elevated oxygen concentrations.

Oxy-nitrogen
A synthetic breathing mixture of oxygen and nitrogen.

Paraplegia
Paralysis of the lower half of the body.

Part II diver (or **Mixed gas diver)**
A diver qualified to dive beyond 50 metres using heliox.

Partial pressure
The partial pressure of a gas in a gas mixture is that part of the total pressure of the mixture that is contributed by that gas.

Patent Foramen Ovale (PFO)
During pregnancy, the right and left sides of the baby's heart communicate directly through a hole in the dividing wall, short-circuiting the lungs, which are not in use. This is termed the Foramen Ovale. After birth, this hole normally closes to force the blood to travel through the lungs. However, in a proportion of the population (perhaps as many as 25%) this hole fails to close completely, resulting in a Patent Foramen Ovale (PFO). The consequence of this for divers is that it can increase the risk of decompression illness. The reason is that bubbles can leak across, through the hole, from the venous to the arterial circulation instead of going to the lungs where they are normally filtered out. Once in the arterial circuit, they can expand and obstruct important blood supply vessels. Serious cases of decompression illness can therefore occasionally occur, even when all proper decompression procedures have been followed.

Pathogen
A disease-carrying agent; also called a micro-organism or germ.

Permit-to-work system
A formal written system used to control certain types of work which are identified as involving risk.

Pharynx
The back of the mouth and upper throat.

Platelets
Particles normally circulating in the blood, smaller than corpuscles, which congregate at the site of bleeding forming a clot.

Pleural cavities
The space within both sides of the chest totally occupied by the lungs.

Pneumofathometer
A component of the diver's umbilical. It provides a simple, accurate method of constantly monitoring the diver's depth. It consists of a flexible but non-collapsible tube of about 6mm internal diameter. At the surface it is connected to a supply of compressed air and an accurate, calibrated pressure gauge which reads the depth. The other end terminates at the chest level of the diver and is open to the water. The depth is measured simply by noting the air pressure required to blow the water out of the end of the small tube at the diver's end.

Pneumothorax
Gas that has entered the pleural cavity such as a result of rupture of the lung. (See 'Burst lung').

Positive pressure ventilation
Inflating a non-breathing casualty's lungs by means of pressure generated by the expired breath of the rescuer or resuscitation equipment.

Predicted range of tide
The difference in height between successive high water and low water for one particular cycle.

Pressure drums
Defined in the HSE *Approved Requirements for Transportable Pressure Receptacles* as:
Pressure drums means welded transportable pressure receptacles of a capacity exceeding 150 litres and of not more than 1,000 litres, (eg cylindrical receptacles equipped with rolling hoops, receptacles on skids and receptacles in frames).

Pressure hull
The pressure restraining structure of a diving bell, deck compression chamber or submersible craft which is subject to differential pressures. It includes all sealing mechanisms, penetrations, doors etc.

Project Manager
The Project Manager is a full management position within the employing diving contractor's company. The position is normally held by a permanent member of the diving contractor's staff.
The Project Manager is normally the most senior management position within a diving contractor's company who is directly responsible for the planning, administration and operation of a single diving project or contract.
He is normally located onshore though he may be required to visit offshore work-sites as needs arise. He is the principal contact of the diving contractor for the client company.
On smaller operations, the position may be combined with that of Diving Superintendent.

Pulmonary barotrauma
Damage to the lung caused by difference in pressure.

Pulmonary oxygen toxicity
Toxic effect on the lungs caused by breathing oxygen concentrations greater than about 0.6 bar absolute for extended periods.

Quad
A colloquial term for a movable bank of upright gas cylinders. Defined in the HSE *Approved Requirements for Transportable Pressure Receptacles:*
Bundles of cylinders (also known as frames) means transportable assemblies of cylinders which are interconnected by a manifold and held firmly together.

Quadriplegia
Paralysis of all four limbs.

Ratcheting
A questionable procedure in saturation diving where a team of divers operates in work cycles of less than 24 hours in order to gain work time. The HSE disapprove of this procedure as stated in *Diving Safety Memorandum 2/1992*.

Regulations
As of 1 April 1998, the UK regulations have been *The Diving at Work Regulations 1997, SI No 2776* (DWR 1997). These regulations were accompanied by five Approved Codes of Practice to cover the various sections of commercial diving.
These are: Commercial diving projects offshore, Commercial diving projects inland/inshore, Media diving projects, Scientific and archaeological diving projects and Recreational diving projects.

Remotely operated vehicle (ROV)
A nearly-neutral buoyancy, unmanned, tethered, submersible craft mounted with equipment which allows inspection or other work to be carried out by remote control.
The vehicle can vary between simple TV video-carrying 'eyeball' ROVs (for observation work) to large, powerful ROVs fitted with manipulators and/or other specialised tool packages ('work-class' ROVs).

Respiratory minute volume
The amount of gas breathed in or out during one minute. It is the tidal volume multiplied by the respiratory rate.

Resuscitation
The preservation or restoration of life by the establishment and/or maintenance of the Airway, Breathing and Circulation (A, B, C) and related emergency care.

Risk assessment
A risk assessment is a systematic examination of potential hazards and their associated risks together with an evaluation of precautions that can be taken to prevent harm.

Roll-over bell handling system
This system is designed to minimise the size of a diving spread and the complexity of the diving bell. The diving bell is rotated through 90 degrees after recovery to bring the bottom hatch up to mate with the side of the transfer under pressure (TUP) chamber. The reverse procedure is effected to begin a dive. This procedure negates the requirement for a side-mating flange on the bell or the necessity to lift the bell on to the top of a deck compression chamber to carry out the TUP.
The rotation of the diving bell must be carried out very carefully to avoid injury to the divers inside and special provisions must be made inside the bell to secure loose items that might otherwise fall during the rotation.

Roustabout
This is common term in the oil industry describing a worker on an oil drilling rig or platform. It is a physically demanding and generally unskilled labouring job.

RT
Radio telephony.

Saturation bonus
This is an hourly rate of pay for a diver for the entire period he is kept under pressure within the surface compression chamber system throughout a saturation dive. It is timed from 'seal to seal' meaning from the moment the chamber doors establish a pressure seal at the start of compression to the moment the doors can be re-opened after the internal pressure has returned to atmospheric pressure.
The rate of pay is established in the UK by the National Union of Rail, Maritime and Transport Workers (RMT).

Saturation dive
A diver's body becomes saturated with the gases he is breathing at any particular depth or pressure after a period of about 12 hours' exposure. After this time, no more gas dissolves into his blood or other body tissues.
Once the diver is saturated, he may remain as long as he wishes at that pressure without incurring any additional decompression time penalty. Saturation dives may take as long as 28 days which would normally include the decompression time.
A group of diving chambers with one or two diving bells attached may remain under pressure for several months with divers commuting in and out for their periods under pressure.

Saturation exposure limits
The Diving Medical Advisory Committee (DMAC) of the Association of Diving Contractors (ADC) have recommended in their Notice , *DMAC 21 Rev. 1*, that under normal circumstances saturation duration should not exceed 28 days.
In exceptional circumstances it may be appropriate to consider a brief extension, but only with the written agreement of the diving contractor's medical adviser, the divers and the diving supervisors.
A diver's cumulative saturation exposure should not exceed 182 days in any 12 calendar months.
See also 'Surface Intervals.'

The Diving at Work Regulations 1997 ACOP No 82 states: *Because of the effects of long periods under pressure on the diver's health, safety and efficiency, divers should not be in saturation for a continuous period of more than 28 days under normal circumstances, including decompression.*

Scrubber (also 'CO_2 scrubber')
This is a loose term for a carbon dioxide removal unit. There will be such a unit inside a diving bell and there will be units associated with deck compression chambers, either inside or outside the chamber. The scrubbers are normally comprised of a chemical filter such as soda-lime (or 'Sodasorb') and a means of circulating the gas through it, such as an electrically-driven impeller fan.

SCM
Subsea control module.

Self-contained underwater breathing apparatus (SCUBA)
This is an alternative to surface-supplied diving, where the diver carries his principal air supply with him, on his back. The equipment may have a facility for a reserve supply to be held for emergency use or the diver may carry a small, separate, emergency cylinder with its own breathing regulator.

This procedure is generally avoided wherever possible as it is not considered as safe as surface-supplied diving.

Senior diving supervisor
An experienced individual who is responsible for a number of diving supervisors or for a major contract. He is sometimes called a Diving Superintendent or Offshore Construction Manager.

Shock
Shock occurs when the circulation is inadequate to meet the oxygen demands of the major body organs.

Shot line (Descending line)
A weighted line used to guide divers to and from the bottom. It also provides a means for the diver to control the speed of his descent and ascent.
(See also 'Distance Line' and 'Lazy Shot Line').

SHU
Surface heater unit.

Spring tides
Those tides of maximum range occurring about twice a month, at or near new or full moon.

Standby diver
A qualified diver ready-equipped and capable of rendering direct assistance to a diver at maximum depth to which dives are being performed. When diving from a bell, the standby diver is sometimes known as the bell-man. *The Diving at Work Regulations 1997 ACOP* for Commercial diving projects offshore states the following:
100 A standby diver should be in immediate readiness to provide any necessary assistance to the diver, whenever the diver is in the water. There should be one standby diver for every two divers in the water.

'Sticky ear'
Jargon used by divers to describe the cause of any difficulty they experience when attempting to 'clear' their ears as they descend.

Stinger
A guide or ramp mounted on the stern of a pipelay barge or vessel to support the pipe as it leaves the surface.

Stops
The planned periods during ascents, when the diver 'stops' at specific depths or pressures during the decompression schedule, to allow the safe elimination of excess inert gas absorbed by the body during the previous dive.

Storage depth (or living depth)
The depth-equivalent pressure at which divers are kept in the DCC during a saturation dive.

Subsea completion (SSC)
The equipment on a seafloor wellhead that regulates gas and/or oil production. An SSC is one where the well-bore terminates, or is 'completed', on the seabed, as opposed to a surface completion where tubing carrying full well pressure continues up to the deck of an offshore platform or equivalent. The subsea completion system includes the guide structures, wellhead housing, casing hangers, tree and flowline connector.

Subsea control pod
The manifold that is used to direct hydraulic fluid used to operate the blowout preventer stack on a subsea wellhead. Two subsea control pods are used for redundancy. The emergency system is controlled by an acoustic signal. Two types of subsea control pods are: all hydraulic; and electro-hydraulic. The subsea control pod is part of the lower marine riser.

Subsea manifold
A pipe system on a subsea template that directs production to the production riser(s).

Subsea satellite
A stand-alone subsea well connected to a host platform or other gathering system via a dedicated flowline and umbilical.

Subsea tree
A Christmas Tree, either wet or dry, depending on whether it is exposed to ocean water, on a flowing subsea well.

Subsea well template
A subsea frame that positions and anchors subsea wellheads, risers and guidance systems.

Surface Compression Chamber (SCC) or Deck Compression Chamber (DCC)
This a pressure chamber which can accommodate two or more divers. It may be used to recompress divers after surfacing to complete their normal decompression procedure or to carry out therapeutic treatment of decompression sickness.

Surface decompression
A decompression procedure in which a surface orientated diver is brought to the surface without completing decompression in the water. He is then recompressed in a deck compression chamber (DCC) prior to final decompression according to a specific decompression schedule.
(Surface decompression techniques are not permitted in certain countries.)

Surface Intervals
The Diving Medical Advisory Committee (DMAC) of the Association of Diving Contractors (ADC) have recommended in their Notice, *DMAC 21 Rev. 1*, that under normal circumstances saturation diving should be planned so that each period spent in saturation by a diver is followed by a surface interval of equal duration.
A diver may however be recommitted to saturation after a shorter surface interval subject to the following provisos:

(a) The surface interval should not be less than 50% of the duration of the preceding saturation dive or 10 days whichever is the lesser.

(b) Where a diver carries out two saturation dives separated by a shorter surface interval than the duration of the first dive, the surface interval subsequent to the two dives should be not less than the duration of the longer of the two saturations.

The Diving at Work Regulations 1997 ACOP No 83 states: *Saturation diving should be planned so that each period spent in saturation by the diver is followed by a surface interval of equal duration. Shorter periods at atmospheric pressure are possible, but only in consultation with the diving contractor's hyperbaric medical adviser.*

Surface-orientated diving
A diving technique where the diver enters the water from the surface and, after completion of the dive, returns to the surface without using a diving bell.

Surface-supplied diving
This is a diving procedure where the diver derives his principal air supply from the surface, along an umbilical hose between himself and the surface. The diver carries an emergency air supply in a 'bail-out' cylinder carried on his back.
The procedure is limited to the use of air and to a maximum depth of 50 metres.

Surges
Strong winds have three main effects on the sea:

a) a general raising or lowering of sea level.

b) oscillations of sea level.

c) generation of storm surges.

Survival Suit (or Immersion Suit)
This is the equivalent of a diver's dry suit. It is constructed of strong, water-proof material which

normally has little if any elasticity. It covers the whole body except the head and hands. A hood is attached (which may be fitted with a spray visor) that can be pulled over the head. Thin, flexible, rubber seals are provided at the neck and wrists to prevent the ingress of water. A waterproof zip-fastener in the garment allows relatively easy donning and doffing of the garment. The fastener is normally closed once the garment has been put on. The wearer's body is therefore kept dry even if he is immersed in water. Thermal insulation is normally provided by the air trapped in ordinary clothing worn under the survival suit.
All passengers flying in helicopters to and from work locations offshore UK are required to wear these suits throughout the flight.

SUTU
Subsea umbilical terminal unit.

Template
1. A metal plate with a design pattern with guides for equipment and structures. A template is part of a guide base on a subsea well. A template is used to align development wells as they are being drilled. Two types of templates are spacer and modular templates. An eight-slot template is common. The guide base has guidelines that extend up to the semi-submersible or drillship and are used to guide equipment, such as the marine riser and the blowout preventer stack, into position.
2. A large tubular structure used to conduct subsea equipment to the seabed, align the equipment and connect wells and flowlines to a manifold.

Tender
(See 'Attendant').

Therapeutic Schedule (or Table)
The procedure by which a diver who is suffering from decompression sickness is treated.
It involves recompression to a pressure to relieve the symptoms followed by decompression using a special decompression schedule.

Thruster Guards
Thruster guards are sometimes fitted to tunnel thrusters but they are not designed to prevent small items reaching the thruster.
The main problem is caused by car tyres which are commonly used as fenders on vessels and which have become detached. These can jam the blades and destroy the thrusters.
Azimuth thrusters do not normally have guards of any kind.
Some thrusters have cutters fitted inside the rope guard to cut ropes and umbilicals before they wind around the thruster and damage the seals of the propeller shaft.

Tidal diamond
Purple-coloured diamonds found on nautical charts which indicate areas where localised tidal streams have been calculated.

Tidal volume
The volume of gas that moves in or out of the lungs with each breath.

Tinnitus
Noises 'heard' in the ear as the result of injury. This is usually a continuous high pitched tone.

Toolpusher
This is the most senior position on the drilling floor of a drilling rig. The Toolpusher is the operational head of the team of men who operate the drilling plant and equipment.

Transfer under pressure (TUP) chamber
This is the deck compression chamber (DCC) to which the diving bell is normally mated.
When divers transfer into the bell to carry out a dive, they would normally get dressed into their diving suits in the TUP chamber and on their return, remove their suits in this chamber.
The TUP chamber is considered a 'wet' area and may also be relatively dirty if the diving suits become contaminated with mud, grease etc during a dive.
There are usually toilet and washing facilities inside a TUP chamber.

Tubes
Defined in the HSE *Approved Requirements for Transportable Pressure Receptacles: Tubes means seamless transportable pressure receptacles of a capacity exceeding 150 litres and of not more than 5,000 litres.*

Umbilical
1. A connecting link between the surface and the diver or between the surface and a diving bell or between a diver and the diving bell. It may contain elements for life support (eg, breathing gas, hot water), surveillance (eg, TV video), voice communication, power supply and a strength member.
2. A flexible cable that connects instruments. On a subsea well, the umbilical provides several functions:
   - acts as the conduit, transferring electrical power to the wellhead.
   - enables subsea pipeline valve and well control.
   - delivers injection chemicals such as corrosion, paraffin and shale inhibitors.

USCG
United States Coast Guard. It is responsible for administering commercial diving operations and

sets the standards for construction and maintenance of diving equipment. It is also the investigating authority in the case of a fatal or serious accident.

Valsalva manoeuvre
A method of 'clearing' the ears by assisting the Eustachian tube to open and thus allow equalisation of pressures either side of the tympanic membrane (ear drum). The manoeuvre involves pinching the nose and blowing to increase the pressure within the mouth cavity. Diving masks and helmets commonly have the facility for the diver to pinch or otherwise close his nostrils in order to be able to do this whenever required.

Ventilation
The movement of gas to the casualty's lungs by means of a first aider's expired air or the use of resuscitation equipment.

Vestibular
Concerning the vestibular system in the inner ear which is responsible for the sense of balance and movement.

Ventricular fibrillation
Unco-ordinated and irregular contraction of the heart muscles so that tremors occur and no effective circulation is generated.

Weil's disease (Leptospirosis)
Caused by direct contact with urine of an infected animal (such as a rat) or indirectly through water contaminated by that urine. It is prevented by using a dry diving suit including dry gloves and full face mask or dry helmet. Contact by any part of skin with polluted water should be avoided.
Signs and symptoms include (first phase, ten days after exposure) fever, headache, red eyes, aching muscles, extreme skin tenderness, jaundice, lip sores, second phase (three days after first phase) fever, headache, neck stiffness, light sensitivity.

Welder approval
This is a test carried out to demonstrate that the welder has the necessary skill to produce a satisfactory weld under the conditions used in production as detailed in the approved Welding Procedure Specification or Work Instruction.
As a general rule, this also approves the welder for all joints that are easier to weld.
Essential Variables are specified in the approval test such as material type, welding process, joint type, dimensions, welding position, barometric pressure, ambient gas mix, etc.

Welding bonus
This is an additional payment made to divers who are qualified to, and carry out, underwater welding operations. The bonus varies between diving contractors in the amount and in the way it is paid. It is not included in the Offshore Diving Industry Agreement. It may be a lump sum based on the size and nature of the task, a day rate for each day spent offshore on a welding contract or a day rate for each day the welding habitat is underwater.

Welding faceplate
A darkened glass/lens fitted in front of the diver's mask/helmet window to protect the diver's eyes from the glare of a welding arc. They normally come in three different densities (4, 6 & 8) intended for different water turbidity conditions.

Welding habitat
This is an enclosure, usually gas-filled, into which a hyperbaric welder-diver can enter to carry out a weld in 'dry' conditions.
The diver may transfer into the habitat from a diving bell in dry conditions (where the bell is connected directly to the habitat) or carry out a 'wet transfer' by swimming from the bell to the habitat.
Habitats are commonly used for connecting pipes, in which case they may have pipe-handling facilities for adjusting the position and aligning the pipe ends inside the habitat.
Alternatively, habitats can be custom-built to fit around a complex steel structure and permit a welder-diver to carry out a structural repair.

Welding Procedure Specification (WPS)
This details the welding variables to be used to ensure a welded joint will achieve the specified levels of weld quality and mechanical properties.
It is supported by a number of documents (such as, a record of how the weld was made, NDE, mechanical test results) which together comprise a welding procedure approval record termed the WPAR (EN288, Europe) or PQR (ASME, USA).

Wellhead
The portion of an oil well that is above ground.
The wellhead is the large, forged or cast steel hardware with machined surfaces, such as flange faces and ring grooves, that seals the top of the well onto the surface casing or conductor pipe.

Wet bell
An open-sided cage or platform for transporting divers to a work site in the air diving range (0–50m). It carries onboard emergency breathing supplies and has a canopy which traps a quantity of breathable air to provide a refuge for the divers' heads.

Workover
A general term for any remedial operation on a completed well that is designed to maintain, restore or improve production from a reservoir that is currently producing. Workover can include well stimulation but excludes routine repair and

maintenance that is generally covered under well servicing. Sand cleanout, removal of scale or paraffin build-up, acidising and fracing, deepening and plugging back are common workover procedures, and are done with a workover rig.

WT
Radio telegraphy.

Index

Numbers in italics indicate illustration on that page

INDEX

D

E

F

G

INDEX

INDEX

INDEX